CW01206678

A Handbook of Industrial Districts

A Handbook of Industrial Districts

Edited by

Giacomo Becattini

University of Florence, Italy

Marco Bellandi

University of Florence, Italy

Lisa De Propris

University of Birmingham, UK

Edward Elgar
Cheltenham, UK • Northampton, MA, USA

© Giacomo Becattini, Marco Bellandi and Lisa De Propris 2009

All rights reserved. No part of this publication may be reproduced, stored in a retrieval system or transmitted in any form or by any means, electronic, mechanical or photocopying, recording, or otherwise without the prior permission of the publisher.

Published by
Edward Elgar Publishing Limited
The Lypiatts
15 Lansdown Road
Cheltenham
Glos GL50 2JA
UK

Edward Elgar Publishing, Inc.
William Pratt House
9 Dewey Court
Northampton
Massachusetts 01060
USA

A catalogue record for this book
is available from the British Library

Library of Congress Control Number: 2009930430

ISBN 978 1 84720 267 3 (cased)

Printed and bound by MPG Books Group, UK

Contents

List of contributors	xi
Acknowledgements	xiv

Critical nodes and contemporary reflections on industrial districts:
An introduction xv
Giacomo Becattini, Marco Bellandi and Lisa De Propris

PART I   ORIGIN AND THEORIES OF INDUSTRIAL DISTRICTS

SECTION 1. EARLY INDUSTRIAL DISTRICTS 3
    Introduction by *Alberto Guenzi*

1. The genesis of a hybrid: Early industrial districts between craft culture and factory training 10
Carlo Marco Belfanti
2. Flexibility and adaptation in the formation of three Italian industrial districts 18
Corine Maitte
3. Apprenticeship and technical schools in the formation of industrial districts 32
Elisabetta Merlo
4. The emergence and development of industrial districts in industrialising England, 1750–1914 43
Andrew Popp and John F. Wilson
5. Industrial districts and large firms: The stubborn persistence of a 'weak' productive model 58
Andrea Colli

SECTION 2. FROM THE ENGLISH ROOTS TO THE ITALIAN REVIVAL 69
    Introduction by *Tiziano Raffaelli*

6. Forerunners of Marshall on the industrial districts 73
Peter Groenewegen
7. Industrial districts in Marshall's economics 78
Brian J. Loasby

8. External and internal economies 90
   Neil Hart
9. The Italian revival of industrial districts and the foundations of political economy 103
   Renzo Bianchi
10. The Italian revival of industrial districts and the foundations of industrial policy 111
    Anna Natali and Margherita Russo

SECTION 3. A MEETING GROUND FOR THE SOCIAL SCIENCES 123
   Introduction by *Carlo Trigilia*

11. The Marshallian industrial districts and current trends in economic theory 129
    Marco Dardi
12. The economics of context, location and trade: Another great transformation? 141
    Michael Storper
13. Flow-fund model, decomposability of the production process and the structure of an industrial district 158
    Piero Tani
14. Clusters and industrial districts: Common roots, different perspectives 172
    Michael Porter and Christian Ketels

PART II   THE NATURE OF INDUSTRIAL DISTRICTS

SECTION 4. SOCIO-CULTURAL AND INSTITUTIONAL ASPECTS 187
   Introduction by *Paolo Giovannini*

15. The industrial district as a local evolutionary phenomenon 193
    Maurizio Mistri
16. Semi-automatic and deliberate actions in the evolution of industrial districts 204
    Gabi Dei Ottati
17. The governance of industrial districts 216
    Arnaldo Bagnasco
18. The new Argonauts, global search and local institution building 229
    AnnaLee Saxenian and Charles Sabel
19. Web of rules in industrial districts' labour markets 243
    Jean Saglio

SECTION 5. KNOWLEDGE, LEARNING AND CREATIVITY 253
    Introduction by *Luciana Lazzeretti*

20. Conceptualizing the dynamics of industrial districts 259
    Michael J. Piore
21. Innovation processes and industrial districts 269
    Paul L. Robertson, David Jacobson and Richard N. Langlois
22. The creative capacity of culture and the new creative *milieu* 281
    Luciana Lazzeretti
23. Technology clusters, industrial districts and regional innovation systems 295
    Philip Cooke
24. Culture as a productive resource, international networks and local development 307
    Olivier Crevoisier and Leïla Kebir

PART III EMPIRICAL INVESTIGATIONS ON INDUSTRIAL DISTRICTS

SECTION 6. EMPIRICAL EVIDENCE 323
    Introduction by *Fabio Sforzi*

25. The empirical evidence of industrial districts in Italy 327
    Fabio Sforzi
26. The empirical evidence of industrial districts in Spain 343
    Rafael Boix
27. The empirical evidence of industrial districts in Great Britain 360
    Lisa De Propris
28. Measuring the district effect 381
    Guido de Blasio, Massimo Omiccioli and Luigi Federico Signorini
29. Measuring the internationalisation of industrial districts 394
    Stefano Menghinello

SECTION 7. THE ITALIAN EXPERIENCES 411
    Introduction by *Michael Dunford*

30. Sectors of excellence in the Italian industrial districts 417
    Marco Fortis and Monica Carminati
31. Regional peculiarities in Italian industrial districts 429
    Francesco Musotti
32. Medium-sized firms, groups and industrial districts: An Italian perspective 441
    Fulvio Coltorti

33. Knowledge dynamics in the evolution of Italian industrial
    districts 457
    Fiorenza Belussi
34. Banks' localism and industrial districts 471
    Pietro Alessandrini and Alberto Zazzaro

SECTION 8. THE EXPERIENCES IN OTHER INDUSTRIALISED COUNTRIES 483
    Introduction by *Gabi Dei Ottati*

35. Industrial districts in Europe 488
    Gioacchino Garofoli
36. Industrial districts and the governance of local economies:
    The French example 501
    Georges Benko and Bernard Pecqueur
37. Industrial districts in Spain 512
    Josep-Antoni Ybarra
38. Industrial districts in Scandinavia 521
    Bengt Johannisson
39. Industrial districts in Japan 535
    Yoshiyuki Okamoto
40. The university research-centric district in the United States 549
    Donald Patton and Martin Kenney

SECTION 9. THE EXPERIENCES IN EMERGING AND DEVELOPING COUNTRIES 565
    Introduction by *Werner Sengenberger*

41. The industrial district model: Relevance for developing
    countries in the context of globalisation 570
    Anne Caroline Posthuma
42. Industrial districts in Latin America: The role of local
    learning for endogenous development 585
    Mario Davide Parrilli and Renato Garcia
43. Trajectories and prospects of industrial districts in China 598
    Jici Wang and Lixia Mei
44. The complexity of upgrading industrial districts: Insights
    from the diesel engine industry of Ludhiana (India) 613
    Meenu Tewari
45. The scope of industrial districts in the Third World 630
    Werner Sengenberger

PART IV GLOBALISATION AND INDUSTRIAL DISTRICTS

SECTION 10. GLOBAL CHALLENGES — 643
    Introduction by *Enzo Rullani*

46. Massachusetts high tech: A 'manufactory of species' — 648
    Michael H. Best
47. Industrial districts, sectoral clusters and global competition in the precious jewellery industry — 666
    Frank Pyke
48. The internationalisation of production activities of Italian industrial districts — 682
    Giuseppe Tattara
49. Lessons from industrial districts for historically Fordist regions — 694
    Josh Whitford

SECTION 11. PUBLIC POLICIES AND INDUSTRIAL DEVELOPMENT STRATEGIES — 705
    Introduction by *Giovanni Solinas*

50. External economies, specific public goods and policies — 712
    Marco Bellandi
51. National industrial policies and the development of industrial districts: Reflections on the Spanish case — 726
    Joan Trullén
52. Public policies for industrial districts and clusters — 739
    Mikel Landabaso and Stuart Rosenfeld
53. The industrial district model in the development strategy of international organizations: The example of UNIDO — 754
    Giovanna Ceglie and Anna Stancher

Bibliography — 771
Index — 857

Contributors

Pietro Alessandrini, Università Politecnica delle Marche, Ancona, Italy
Arnaldo Bagnasco, University of Turin, Italy
Giacomo Becattini, University of Florence, Italy
Carlo Marco Belfanti, University of Brescia, Italy
Marco Bellandi, University of Florence, Italy
Fiorenza Belussi, University of Padua, Italy
Georges Benko, University of Sorbonne, Paris, France
Michael H. Best, University of Massachusetts-Lowell, USA and Judge Business School, University of Cambridge, UK
Renzo Bianchi, University of Venice, Italy
Rafael Boix, Barcelona Institute of Regional and Metropolitan Studies, University Autonoma of Barcelona, Spain
Monica Carminati, Fondazione Edison, Milan, Italy
Giovanna Ceglie, UNIDO, Vienna, Austria
Andrea Colli, Bocconi University, Milan, Italy
Fulvio Coltorti, Mediobanca Research Department and University of Florence, Italy
Philip Cooke, Centre for Advanced Studies, Cardiff University, UK
Olivier Crevoisier, University of Neuchatel, Switzerland
Marco Dardi, University of Florence, Italy
Guido de Blasio, Bank of Italy, Italy
Lisa De Propris, University of Birmingham, UK
Gabi Dei Ottati, University of Florence, Italy
Michael Dunford, University of Sussex, Brighton, UK
Marco Fortis, Università Cattolica, Milan, Italy
Renato Garcia, University of São Paulo, Brazil
Gioacchino Garofoli, University of Insubria, Italy
Paolo Giovannini, University of Florence, Italy
Peter Groenewegen, University of Sydney, Australia
Alberto Guenzi, University of Parma, Italy
Neil Hart, University of Western Sydney, Australia
David Jacobson, Dublin City University, Ireland
Bengt Johannisson, Växjö University, Sweden
Leïla Kebir, French National Institute of Agricultural Research, Paris, France and Swiss National Science Foundation, Bern, Switzerland

Martin Kenney, University of California, Davis, USA
Christian Ketels, Harvard Business School, USA
Mikel Landabaso, European Commission
Richard N. Langlois, University of Connecticut, USA
Luciana Lazzeretti, University of Florence, Italy
Brian J. Loasby, University of Stirling, UK
Corine Maitte, University of Paris X, France
Lixia Mei, Peking University, China
Stefano Menghinello, ISTAT, Italy
Elisabetta Merlo, Bocconi University, Milan, Italy
Maurizio Mistri, University of Padua, Italy
Francesco Musotti, University of Perugia, Italy
Anna Natali, Regione Emilia-Romagna, Bologna, Italy
Yoshiyuki Okamoto, Hosei University, Tokyo, Japan
Massimo Omiccioli, Banca of Italy, Italy
Mario Davide Parrilli, Basque Institute of Competitiveness, San Sebastian and University of Deusto, Bilbao, Spain
Donald Patton, University of California, Davis, USA
Bernard Pecqueur, University of Grenoble, France
Michael J. Piore, Massachusetts Institute of Technology, USA
Andrew Popp, University of Liverpool, UK
Michael Porter, Harvard Business School, USA
Anne Caroline Posthuma, International Labour Office (ILO), Geneva, Switzerland
Frank Pyke, International Consultant
Tiziano Raffaelli, University of Pisa, Italy
Paul L. Robertson, University of Tasmania, Australia
Stuart Rosenfeld, Regional Technology Strategy, USA
Enzo Rullani, Venice International University, Tedis, Italy
Margherita Russo, University of Modena and Reggio Emilia, Italy
Charles Sabel, Columbia Law School, New York, USA
Jean Saglio, University of Grenoble, France
AnnaLee Saxenian, University of California-Berkeley, USA
Werner Sengenberger, Former Official of the International Labour Office (ILO), Geneva, Switzerland
Fabio Sforzi, University of Parma, Italy
Luigi Federico Signorini, Bank of Italy, Italy
Giovanni Solinas, University of Modena and Reggio Emilia, Italy
Anna Stancher, UNIDO, Vienna, Austria
Michael Storper, University of California at Los Angeles, USA; Sciences Po, Paris, France, and London School of Economics, London, UK
Piero Tani, University of Florence, Italy

Giuseppe Tattara, University of Venice, Italy
Meenu Tewari, University of North Carolina at Chapel Hill, USA
Carlo Trigilia, University of Florence, Italy
Joan Trullén, Barcelona Institute of Regional and Metropolitan Studies, University Autonoma of Barcelona, Spain
Jici Wang, Peking University, China
Josh Whitford, Columbia University, USA
John F. Wilson, University of Liverpool, UK
Josep-Antoni Ybarra, University of Alicante, Spain
Alberto Zazzaro, Università Politecnica delle Marche, Ancona, Italy

Acknowledgements

The editors would like to thank the Section coordinators for providing valuable support throughout the project with advice and comments, as well as for helping reviewing the chapters.

We would like to thank especially Alessandra Pini for her sterling work in formatting the volume. Many thanks also to Marina Melotti (Introduction to Section 4) and Monica Borg (Chapters 16 and 17) for their translations.

We would like to extend our gratitude to Iva, Chiara and David for their constant support, encouragement and patience.

Critical nodes and contemporary reflections on industrial districts: An introduction

Giacomo Becattini, Marco Bellandi and Lisa De Propris

1. PROLOGUE

No matter how much has been written on industrial districts (IDs), they probably remain one of the most relevant socio-economic phenomena of the last decades, and they seem relevant now more than ever, as the disruptive forces of globalisation are uncovering the costs of the disparities between economy and society, and between economy and policy. This volume is meant to represent the main lines of a wide-ranging debate spreading over the last three decades on what IDs have represented in the past, what they are undergoing at the present time, and the challenges and opportunities they will face in a socio-economic context where global and local forces increasingly interact to shape the welfare of societies and the economic performance of firms and places.

Comprising articles written by distinguished international scholars and practitioners, the *Handbook* includes conceptual, critical and forward-looking contributions as well as case studies on Asia, Latin America, Europe and the US. The volume sits within the current revival of socio-economic studies, as it assumes at its core the view that IDs are a clear expression of local societies finding their way in the national and international division of labour through the constitution and elaboration of productive specialisations congenial to the attitudes and preferences of their people.

We start this introduction by recalling a few basic concepts and some of the most significant findings that have emerged from the recent debate on IDs, which in our view will make it easier to understand the overall structure of this *Handbook of Industrial Districts*. We then extract from its rich collection of empirical and theoretical contributions, themes that we think cut across the various sections, and that we see as coinciding with critical nodes on IDs and contemporary reflections on them. Finally, we present an overview of the volume.

2. A HISTORIC OVERVIEW OF BASIC CONCEPTS

The many contributions accumulated on IDs, and more generally on different types of local systems, over the last decades have generated a flourishing of concepts and definitions, which have tended to mirror the variety in the forms of local systems that one can observe. For this reason, we start by drawing the conceptual framework that encases this work, by recalling key concepts and well-accepted findings. The framework is aimed at providing a unified background to the diverse points of view and analyses that emerge in the various chapters of the *Handbook* where a variety of issues are explored more in depth.

A synopsis of the conceptual framework of the ID model is also a declaration of the general interpretative position upon which the editors have built the structure of the volume. We do not claim that each single contributor shares every aspect of this general position, as the reader will easily find out; however, many of them have contributed to its building, with various advancements on the theme, both intellectually challenging and novel.

The key aspects of the conceptual framework comprise three parts: the historical premises; the revival since the 1980s; and some reflections on the prospects for IDs in a fast changing environment.

2.1 Historical premises

Starting with some historical premises, the importance of local roots, and thereby the differences in the industrialisation processes of countries, has been commonly acknowledged in a wealth of historical and geographical accounts that have analysed the waves of industrialisation across Europe (see Sections 1 and 2 of the *Handbook*). However, at the same time, classical and neoclassical economic theories on market structures and capitalism tended to abstract from these variations and to seek the formulation of few 'presumed' general and objective laws (see Sections 2 and 3).

Among the great economists, Alfred Marshall assumed a complex position, summarised in the epigraph of his late *Industry and Trade*, that is 'the many in the one, and the one in the many'. In particular, it has been argued that Marshall's early studies on the IDs of his time profoundly, and persistently, shaped not only his views on industrial organisation, but more generally his conception of capitalism and market mechanisms. In particular, significant passages in his early writings, like the *Economics of Industry* and several fragments of essays included in his *Early Economic Writings* (edited by Whitaker 1975), show the importance of reflections on places characterised by the enduring presence of localised industries of specialised small firms. They were his preferred examples of what in his times were called 'industrial districts', and led him later to conceptualise the distinction between internal and external economies. The economies of the division of labour cannot always be explained in terms of the control of a large firm over the value chain, contrary to what was increasingly accepted already in his time, because they may be also realised by an appropriate integration of a set of complementary and specialised firms, none of them necessarily large in size (see Section 2 and Bellandi 1989). Here Marshall attained compelling confirmation of the importance of appropriate contexts for sharing social experiences, moral values, and productive knowledge.

Marshall recognised that IDs characterised by specialised firms were an ideal context for the emergence of entrepreneurial energies and for the increase of the social mobility that was argued to be able to blur the divide between employers and employees in a certain community. In this context, the distinction between external and internal economies went together with the formulation of other important concepts, like a firm's life cycle, the representative firm, and competition over particular markets preceding Chamberlin's monopolistic competition. However, this important conceptual connection was then played down by Marshall in many theoretical constructs of his *Principles of Economics* (Becattini 2003b; Raffaelli et al. 2006).

After Marshall's death, the attention increasingly shifted on mass production and mass marketing. At the time when the US and Europe were undergoing steady and fast growth, which spanned from the late 1940s to the 1960s, IDs, and more generally any clustering of specialised small firms, were pushed to the periphery of academic and political discourse.

2.2 The return of IDs in the second half of the 20th century: the Marshallian industrial district

In the 1970s, as the golden age of mass production was showing signs of weakness, the concept of the ID was resurrected by Becattini (1978 and 1979) to help understand 'unusual' regional paths of industrial takeoff in some Italian regions. His contribution was soon enriched by that of a multidisciplinary group of scholars, first within Italian academic circles then through widening international networks. The focus was on regional paths of industrial development characterised by bursts of local entrepreneurship and the proliferation of populations of specialised small to medium-sized enterprises (SMEs). Such a trend was first evident and studied in the central and north-eastern parts of Italy, largely coinciding with the so-called Third Italy (see Sections 1, 2 and 7).

The accumulation of refinements on the characteristics of IDs from empirical studies (see Section 6), and the recovery of both the Marshallian concept of external economies and industrial atmosphere (see Section 2), were the twin pillars supporting the construction of the ID model, building on, but going well beyond, what Marshall himself expressed. The so-called 'Marshallian industrial district' (MID), in the version developed within the Italian literature (see Section 2), is a model of a naturally and/or historically bounded place characterised by the presence and interpenetration of a community of people, and a production apparatus (Becattini 1990 and 2004a). The population of firms and the related market institutions are only one, though central, part of it.

The definition above goes together with a set of structural and evolutionary features for which the MID can be considered as an ideal-typical model of a local productive system, where a localised industry is embedded in a community of people. A local productive system has an economic and social identity shaped by an 'industrial atmosphere'; the latter coinciding with a set of shared cognitive, moral and behavioural attitudes drawing on locally-dense cultural interactions, and which orientate technical, human and relational investments towards forms consistent with local accumulation. The terms 'productive' or 'industrial' qualify a set of activities whose outcome is the production of a range of goods or services with markets progressively and largely external to the locality of industry, and based on the systematic and professional activity of competent producers helped by various forms of capital and relations.

The industrial structure of a MID is characterised by a certain degree of local economic dominance of an industry ('local specialisation'). This main industry includes a mix of horizontal (competitive), vertical (input–output), and diagonal (related services and instruments) specialised activities. Together with the main industry, other secondary industrial activities may be localised in the district, more or less related to the main one, as a result of various evolutionary adjustments and developments (for example, the nuclei of new industries, or the remains of old declining industries). Several specialised firms, generally small to medium-sized and independent, engage in similar or complementary activities, exchanging intermediate resources and outputs through local markets, as well as within formal or informal business teams supported by personal trust and knowledge ('production decentralisation'). A decisive (if not exclusive) role in private and public investments to technical, human and relational capital is played by locally-embedded centres of strategy and decision making ('endogeneity'). The effective functioning of this systemic organisation requires its incorporation into historically evolving conditions including technology, material needs, culture, policy and public administration, and characterised by a positive interaction of local forces with translocal and global forces. The integrated system propels the realisation of economies (reduction of costs, increase of revenues) which are 'external' to the firm but 'internal' to the district, which in part depend on the size of the resources organised within the single firms, but (more importantly) on the access of the firm (through local markets, team relations, specific public goods) to the pools of specialised resources integrated within the system (see, in particular, Sections 2 and 11).

Seen in evolutionary terms, the MID is a socio-territorial entity following an ideal-typical path of local development, included in a sheaf of alternatives consistent with its historically defined socio-economic structural features, and characterised by processes of reproduction, growth, and variation of the system itself (see in particular Section 4). Such processes of industrial and local development include:

(a) a continuous and fluid rearticulation of the local division of labour, that is the endogenous constitution and flexible reorganisation (integration by open teams, and so on) of the specialised tasks and functions making up the process of value creation; (b) the reproduction and renewal of contextual knowledge, merged with some transferable codified knowledge, and incorporated in specialised capacities for productive and creative purposes; (c) the preservation of common motivational tracts, such as a bent towards trust and cooperation in reciprocal exchanges, an attitude towards entrepreneurship and innovation, the open participation of workers on the job, and the engagement of citizens in community life; (d) finally, social and economic mobility and a thick fabric of social interactions which create an environment where entrepreneurship and innovation flourish, and one that is in several ways and degrees conducive to social cohesiveness as well as consistent with the preservation of a local identity and an industrial atmosphere.

The main localised industry and the industries which are complementary to the main one can be seen as corresponding to an ideal-type of local industrial cluster; more precisely, the cluster at the core of the industrial component of a MID is seen as featuring systemic properties coming from stable relations both between producers and between them and the local socio-cultural and institutional context. Industrial clusters outside district conditions may have a different nature, as we will recall in what follows.

Outside ideal-typical MID conditions, local development may be more generic (that is, based on a variety of unrelated businesses); more centralised (that is, dependent on the strategies of very few firms); less endogenous (that is, based on investments and capital controlled by extra-local decision makers, for example some multinational companies), or differently articulated (that is, with a poorly extended local division of labour); at the same time, district processes may be less robust and reproductive. Variety within local economic life is useful and even necessary in the face of unexpected changes and discontinuities in external market conditions, technology, institutional infrastructure and cultural contexts. However, beyond certain thresholds of sector dispersion across the agglomerated activities, of dependency of economic decision on external strategic control, and of business concentration, industrial clustering and economic development no longer mirror a MID. At the other extreme places become merely the stage for the variable location choices of more or less dis-anchored companies, as is the case with many industrial clusters.

2.3 Contemporary tendencies and prospects

Localities mirroring the MID model are prototypical examples of the vitality of local socio-cultural and institutional relations which find their way, within national and international contexts, by generating locally-based (but open) industrial clusters (where the cluster coincides with the core of the industrial activities of the district).

Historical IDs in the 19th-century first-moving industrialising countries (first wave of IDs) and IDs reemerging after the mass production golden age (second wave of IDs) were both largely characterised by manufacturing sector specialisation and competencies, and by locally-integrated production processes. In the current context of accelerated and overwhelming globalisation, the opportunities for the creation of new forms of clustering expand. However, such clusters do not necessarily combine with robust district processes, and sometimes the expansion of new clusters contributes to the decline of older IDs. On the other hand, with the fast pace of technological changes, the borders of traditional sectors become blurred, and the distinctions between manufacturing and tertiary sectors, not to speak of the one between low-tech and high-tech sectors, become less and less clear and meaningful. New or regenerated IDs may turn out to be characterised by an 'industrial' specialisation that has lost its traditional (like in the first and second waves) identity as a locally-integrated manufacturing *filière*. This exemplifies what has been already noted, that district systemic processes are being constantly combined with various internal and external factors, that determine opportunities, pose challenges and contribute to shape various types of local paths of development or decline (see Sections 5, 8 and 10).

Public policies and collective actions by private agencies are essential ingredients within specific paths of local development (see Sections 2 and 11). Currently IDs and district-like processes need the support of policy designs and tools, still related to local agencies and institutions, but more deliberate and aligned with an explicit reference to district models and local development approaches. Such interventions should be aimed at providing platforms to integrate highly-skilled and R&D-intensive competencies with traditional sources of local creativity, as well as to manage processes of market and process internationalisation, for instance, by means of new knowledge-intensive services firms. Furthermore, the local resources integrated by such platforms may be complemented through interactions at a regional level, for example among IDs, and between IDs and regional dynamic cities (see Sections 3, 5 and 10).

In the next section we will expand on some themes that we deem to be critical nodes in the current debate and cut across the various sections of the volume.

3. CRITICAL NODES

Within the wealth of contributions gathered in its chapters, in our view some common threads emerge as crucial for a deep understanding of the contemporary trend and conceptualisation of IDs. These are for us critical nodes and will be developed in this section. Drawing on basic concepts, they have to be seen as possible conceptual developments in the light of the advances accumulated with this *Handbook*.

One of our main concerns is the sources of the presence of ID forms and processes over time and across various regions; in other words, the conditions which explain a stronger or weaker presence of IDs, and their socio-economic role within regions and nations.

There are two key trends that, in our view, have a major impact on the capacity of IDs to contribute dynamically to the economic performance of the regions and countries where they are located, as well as to the welfare of their communities. These are, first, the expanding 'intrusion' of science-based knowledge in the world of production and, second, the nature, intensity and scale of the increasingly global networks that IDs have to engage with for knowledge, goods/services and labour exchanges. These issues underlie critical nodes in the evolution of IDs, as their capacity and capability to reproduce themselves according to endogenous mechanisms are threatened by conditions that alter their compass, and thereby their way of finding a desirable direction for their sustainable development. Related to the above points, key concerns become: (a) the governance of firms and of the capitalist process within IDs; (b) the centralisation and decentralisation of strategic decision making; (c) the changing patterns of industrial clustering; and (d) the translocal frames of ID policies and political processes.

3.1 Types of knowledge and worlds of production

We start by looking at how the worlds of production are being reshaped by the 'intrusion' of science-based knowledge and the impact that this is having on IDs. The dynamic factors driving the development of IDs are related to the generation, application and variation of practical and often tacit knowledge that coincides with specialised know-how and diffused creativity, intersecting with knowledge coming from a set of related trade and production activities. Various chapters of this *Handbook* illustrate how first- and second-wave IDs have combined, in various ways, such locally-rooted core knowledge with the ideas and innovations coming from external science-based knowledge (see Sections 1, 3, 7 and 8). The fact that knowledge within the worlds of production is increasing dominated by the latter is a challenge to many IDs. An extreme approach, which has been called 'neo-Fordist', posits a deterministic tendency towards a complete dominance of science-based knowledge in the conception, design, management and functioning of automated and flexible production processes throughout sets of integrated hardware and software just assisted by the ancillary services of labour according to predetermined routines. This model would seriously undermine the survival of IDs.

In reality, every new technology (for example, new machineries, software) is affected by points of discontinuity, interrupting its automatic working (for example, starting up, stopping, adaptation to changing external conditions, repairing the breakdowns seemingly related to working conditions, and so on). Here the importance of skilled labour cannot be denied, who have tacit, practical and first-hand knowledge of the technology and its functioning beyond strict predetermined routines. The acknowledgement of this relation changes the model of innovation that underpins technological progress.

A linear and determinist model of innovation is replaced by one where tacit and practical knowledge influences not only the adoption of science-based applications to production processes and systems, but also their success and development, especially in a volatile and uncertain environment.

The success of second-wave IDs was related to the responsiveness of a neo-artisan model of production to a new demand for differentiated products in the international markets, against the success in the 1950s and 1960s (the 'golden age') of large multi-divisional vertically-integrated firms with their substantial internal investments in R&D, mass production and mass marketing. At the end of the 1960s, a growing mass of customised goods started to be demanded in industrialised countries, where consumers had already saturated their basic needs and had purchasing power in excess. The volatility and diversity of demand's needs forced the end of a factory-based capitalist production, and the 'return' to a form of production that was disseminated across a number of laboratories or workshops within an economically active society. This took the form of artisanship and the customised production of goods and services, tied with historical and cultural sources of locally-embedded production activities. The tendency of economic activities to permeate the social life of a place in its totality (at the level of individuals and community) and their combination with the cultural and institutional specificity of the place is what has propelled this reemergence of ID processes.

Currently, increasing investment in science-based knowledge and its impact on production generate conditions which effectively diverge from the neo-Fordist vision. The possibility and importance of innovation processes where an open set of various and traditionally separate disciplines combine and interact have expanded. This multidisciplinary approach to innovation is consistent with knowledge becoming more complex and integrated across disciplinary fields. However, it is also a continuous source of queries and unexpected problems which necessarily require a combination of various types of codified and practical knowledge across a set of disciplines, as well as the interface of science and technology with communities of users and producers.

One of the more recent developments in the debate on the sources of value creation in a knowledge economy has been to consider the cultural, creative and also symbolic or artistic contribution to production. In this context, innovation is no longer dependent on hard inputs and is no longer science or technology bound; on the contrary, innovation is driven by soft and immaterial factors. A consideration of the importance of the creative and cultural content of innovation for products and processes implies innovation processes based on a form of knowledge that is tacit, cumulative and embedded in a locality, whilst being able to combine systemically manufacturing and more service functions. We would argue that, since IDs are familiar with such a form of knowledge creation and diffusion, they have the capacity and the capabilities to successfully undertake innovative processes of this sort. This systemic model of innovation fits with ID processes where tacit and practical knowledge interact with technological knowledge in a dynamic and evolutionary manner, as recalled and applied, in particular, in Sections 5 and 10 of the *Handbook*.

However, recently some contradictory forces are also in motion which should not be underestimated. Firstly, the local and systemic innovation process characterising the creation and diffusion of practical knowledge in IDs requires important adaptations as it faces stronger and more frequent influences from external information and parties. External influences are coming from relations with the national university system, with international networks of innovation-related actors, as well as international subcontractors or client firms. In fast-changing and globalised markets, these external forces challenge the established sets of well-absorbed knowledge and practices that steer and operate innovation and production processes in IDs. It is becoming crucially important that new channels and new actors are activated to enable the absorption, translation and combination of the incoming knowledge. Secondly, as investment in R&D is becoming increasingly important against a traditional innovation process based on incremental and learning-by-doing innovations, the need to appropriate the returns on such investment are reducing firms' willingness to cooperate and exchange ideas within IDs. This is altering not only the delicate balance between scientific and 'practical/tacit' knowledge, but also the delicate balance between cooperation and competition that drives IDs' vitality and dynamism. Finally, older and more traditional IDs need to adapt not only to a different industrial specialisation, but to quite different sets of organisational, social and institutional norms. Even if mature IDs have the opportunity to embark on new paths and jump technologic trajectories, the discontinuous and systemic nature of the transition may trap them in a condition of economic stagnation and social decline. The leadership and vision of public or private actors can therefore be necessary for the leap to take place.

This *Handbook* aims to address such challenges and opportunities with a variety of multifaceted contributions.

3.2 The changing patterns of socio-economic networks in an increasingly globalised world

Another powerful tendency, not unrelated to the neo-technological tendency referred to above, has impinged on the socio-territorial dimension of IDs more directly, especially since the 1990s. Globalisation has coincided with the ever increasing flows of goods, services, knowledge and people along what appear to be global networks that span across an increasing number of regions and countries.

According to the 'hyperglobalist' position, globalisation has created a borderless and 'global village', where socio-economic territorial models converge to a 'virtual' international community defined by a set of linkages among footloose and thereby locally un-embedded agents. According to another view, advocated and illustrated in some contributions of this *Handbook* (see Sections 3, 4 and 10 in particular), successful 'global' networks are made of linkages among agents who are embedded in different places. Their exposure and engagement in 'global' networking depend on both their experiences of local networking, and the attitude and capability of some local actors to combine locally embedded relationships with more open and risky external relationships.

In this view, success in global networking depends not only on the excellence of the agents' individuality, but also on their capacity to represent different contexts of local culture, and global networks may be seen, at least in part, as translocal or cross-cluster networks. In other words, only deeply rooted local systems can not only branch out, but more importantly stand firm in the strong winds of translocal mobility.

Some would argue that the world has always been interconnected through trade exchanges and migrations, and that globalisation is nothing new; however, what is true is that, although there was already a separation between places of production and places of consumption, the former represented the economic expression of a community of people. On the other hand, one of the main features of the modular, multi-plant and multinational organisation of production that has emerged with the global conglomerates is that places become the functional inputs of the economic design/expression of a third party/private interest. Scholte (2000) argues that globalisation is indeed a new and distinctive phenomenon to the extent that it has 'de-territorialised' production activities. Indeed the globalisation of production activities coincides with an organisation of production that mirrors a network of a mix of market and ownership relations that combines flexible specialisation throughout the value chain with Fordist-type productions for labour-intensive activities. What is crucial here is the geographical abstraction of such a network, whereby the location decisions of the various production or service facilities are motivated by the contribution that the different 'places' can make to the overall division of labour. This means reliance on low labour cost 'places' to carry out labour-intensive and large-scale tasks, and control over core high-value-added functions. Hymer (1972) observes that the multinational enterprise is the antithesis of the 'Marshallian entrepreneur', in that the head, the arms and the legs are not part of the same body, albeit the former control the latter with various forms of hierarchical power. Hymer (ibid.) also observes that as multinational enterprises sift through places for their location choices, they also consolidate patterns of uneven development.

The literature on global value chains (see the references in the chapters of Section 10 of the *Handbook*) that has flourished in the last few years has explored these issues in great detail, with particular attention to the impact of the operations and strategies of multinational enterprises on places and their development. It is in this context that firm clustering, both in developed and developing or emerging economies, has entered the debate on globalisation: the patterns of development of firm clustering within global value chains are mirroring the developing opportunities of localities.

Different forms of firm clustering respond differently to the challenges of globalisation (see Sections 3 and 10). Some forms of firm cluster that are often seen as successful in the international literature correspond to the dominance of both relatively large firms with local origins and local entities of external multinational corporations, showing an opportunity-seeking attitude to cooperation, and a high degree of openness through channels that accommodate the transfer of people, knowledge and technology, as well as of goods and services. Such clusters are in fact agglomerations of firms that benefit from colocation at various levels, but they are not in symbiosis with the space they occupy, and are able to seize the opportunities of globalisation by trans-nationalising their activities to their advantage.

Also IDs and the clusters embedded in district processes may benefit from globalisation, rather than be threatened by it, but they should proceed through different mechanisms from those of the types of clusters referred to above.

To some, the ID model might appear unfit to identify patterns of internationalisation that are compatible with its embedded nature, these including the outsourcing or relocating abroad of some production functions. These concerns arise from the fact that processes of innovation, learning and value creation in a district take place at all stages of production, making it difficult to split up 'the head from the arms'. The concept of global value chain is underpinned by the hypothesis that production stages can be separated and value creation is strictly controlled by the multinational parent company. In contrast, in a district, value creation infuses the entire circuits of knowledge and runs in parallel to the value chain.

Indeed, there is ample evidence that IDs, for instance in Italy, Spain or Portugal are shifting some functions abroad, or engaging in international joint ventures or hosting foreign capital (see Sections 7, 8 and 10), in search of efficiency, new knowledge or markets. What is interesting about this phenomenon is that it has been gradual and coinciding with a process of learning and adapting not of a single firm but of the system of firms.

If the 'know-how' was the key discriminating factor for competitive firms and places in the so-called knowledge economy, globalisation and the functioning of multinational enterprises have highlighted that more important than the 'know-how' is the 'know-where'. Knowing where to locate which functions has become one of the fundamental sources of competitiveness for globalised production organisations, like multinational enterprises as well as districts. This is not reduced to cost-saving location choices, but also includes knowledge sourcing and market positioning choices. Instead, what seems to drive the internationalisation strategies of IDs is actually the 'know-who' and 'know-with whom', whereby internationalisation is experienced as a collective process, which include a learning process, mechanisms of information and risk sharing (see Sections 3 and 4).

Some of the recent debate on the various forms of proximity (De Propris et al. 2008) can help understand that district firms will not choose to embark in footloose international operations, but instead they would prefer to develop and strengthen common patterns of behaviour, common practices and routines together with informal communications. Benefits from internationalisation would come from an ID being able to maintain a critical mass of its embedded know-how, together with 'bridging' actors (rather than gatekeepers) able to search, read, understand, translate and finally integrate external knowledge inside the framework of the local know-how.

At the time of writing, the high risks of globalisation borne by localities are becoming more and more real; like a castle of cards, global value chains have created a form of inter-connectivity between places that is not aimed at their mutual development. Some places are indeed at the top of a very unstable castle, and their fall will possibly lighten the weight borne by some localities at the base, while engendering high costs of transition and adaptation for all. The well-embedded firms in IDs are likely to be better able to weather the storm, thanks to their ability still to produce and innovate away from international value chains, and in some cases, also with the support of strong and committed international relationships.

Globalisation is also having an impact on the territorial scale of IDs' socio-economic context, thereby reshaping the limit of the proximity that underpins its socio-economic fabric. On the one side, the progress in metropolitan transport systems tends to enlarge the area of daily job and civic experiences; furthermore, the needs of international mobility and the facilities needed for research and knowledge services increase the strength of metropolitan economies. Small localities become parts of strongly interconnected metropolitan areas or regions, and this complex local architecture may be seen as the prevalent form of contemporary successful local systems as clots of business and social contexts. However, in this context, each small locality becomes more socially diverse and possibly less socially bounded; at the same time, larger areas do not have the same capacity to produce common experiences and shared values as the smaller ones when more self-contained in terms of daily social and labour exchanges. As diversity increases, the opportunities to generate novel ideas multiply, but the risk of undermining the reproduction of shared attitudes emerges as well. There are somewhat defined thresholds, in size and multiplicity, beyond which district processes of reproduction and change become weaker and weaker.

The fact that ID processes may be found, for instance, in quarters in large urban areas is not new, as some chapters of the *Handbook* referring to first-wave districts suggest (see Sections 1 and 5). However, first-wave IDs were generally found around large cities where capital accumulation drove growth, as well as spread around large industrial regions, such as the Black Country or Lancashire, as mentioned by Marshall. Second-wave IDs have typically developed outside large urban areas in some way as an alternative to large firms at the end of the Fordist age (see Section 6). At least those IDs that emerged or reemerged in regions of the Third Italy characterised by the overlapping of small towns with rich rural traditions, showed, as argued by Bagnasco (see Section 4), the possibility of an effective restoration or preservation of a correspondence between the organisation of production and the reproduction of related social resources. More recently, large urban systems characterised by a more fractious and conflicting dynamism have tried to recover from social and economic decline by means of strategic planning combined with leadership, participation and democratic legitimacy. Or, as in some American regions, solutions have been found by mobilising entrepreneurial, as well as local and sectoral resources. These are lessons which contemporary IDs need to learn, and the *Handbook* includes contributions along these lines of thought in particular in Sections 7, 8 and 11.

Finally, the considerations just presented may be extended to ID processes and forms in emerging and developing economies. Firstly, the rapid and often painful urbanisation processes in the industrialising regions of these countries coincided with a drastic break up from the rural economies and 'way of life' and with the emergence of an urban socio-economic context that is socially divided and economically separated from any endowed skill. Secondly, the opportunity and the trajectory of a transition from a 'low' road to a 'higher' road of local development are crucially supported by an endogenous mobilisation of science-based factors, integrating strictly economic and production activities with social services and infrastructure. Thirdly, the emergence of ID processes in these countries tends to be driven by their immediate participation in global nets of value creation which can be governed in different ways. As mentioned above, the hubs in the global value chains include industrial clusters, multinational corporations and forms of IDs in old or post-industrial countries. The high roads of local development for emerging and developing countries in this globalised context should be shaped also by equity, trust, and reciprocal empowerment in international translocal and cross-cluster relationships (see Sections 9 and 11 on this theme).

3.3 Capitalist relations within IDs

Increasing evidence is showing that both changes in the technological paradigm and the sweeping forces of globalisation influence the nature and mix of capitalist relations within IDs (see in particular Section 4). This occurs along two lines: one concerns the local embeddedness of entrepreneurial firms in the district *milieu*; and the other the possible role of a more concentrated ownership within IDs' decentralised industrial structure.

In relation to the nature of entrepreneurship in IDs, we would suggest that a newborn firm may originate from two very different geneses. A first type is the firm born out of the strategy of a capitalist entrepreneur for whom the new firm is an opportunity for a return on investment that is higher than the one coming from lending the same resources to a financial agent or to the State. The core existence of this first type of firm is to be a sort of particle of capital, which grows by assuming the form of one or more plants, that is, capital invested in fixed assets (for example, machinery) and paid labour. The production of goods, the management of employees, the effects on the environment and on the society, and so on, have here just an instrumental value, the final and essential aim being the financial returns which increase the size of the capital. If the expected financial returns turn out to be not enough against alternative uses, the capital is disinvested and the firm closes down. Those firms whose life is characterised by such a capitalist core are referred to here as 'particle firms'.

The second type of firm, often neglected, is one which is founded by members of a community who see themselves as owning human and relational capitals which may be used, with higher economic and social returns, in starting up their own enterprise rather than spending their economic life as employees. Their core being a project of life, they may be named as 'project firms'. The entrepreneurs invest in the firm not only personal savings and those eventually entrusted to them by the parental and friendship networks, but also and more importantly their reputation in terms of technical and managerial competence, leadership and energy on the job, trade acumen, and so on, that they have been able to build in the course of time within their community of life. This human and relational capital is much less transferable to different contexts than the financial capital at the core of the particle firm. Also the returns are measured not only in economic terms, but also in terms of the realisation of a life project, or of some revision of it. This adds to the local stickiness of such firms, even against conditions in which the pure financial calculus would suggest disinvestment and possible transfer of the financial capital to other contexts. Contexts characterised by project firms are more sustainable over time thanks to adjustments against crises which would instead bring about sudden delocalisation and deindustrialisation in contexts characterised by particle firms.

A lively ID, hosting a healthy interaction between district structures and processes, is an ideal context for project firms. This point may also be related to Marshall's idea of new entrepreneurship coming from the ranks of the working class, especially in industries characterised by small firms as in the case of many IDs. In the face of globalisation and neo-technological tendencies, this helps the preservation of local embeddedness, but too strong a loyalty to the place would hinder openness to change and translocal relations. At the same time, plurality in the nature of the firms nurturing IDs is essential. Along their life cycle, IDs will not only incubate project firms, but will also attract particle firms. At some stage, persistently successful project firms have the possibility to strengthen and absorb the life projects of a larger network of people. Indeed, the growth of an ID corresponds also to this expansion stage, which does not necessarily mean a growth in the size of firms. Here also particle firms are attracted to a district by the expectation of market growth and profits.

The combination of project and particle firms underpins business diversity and contributes to the vitality of an ID. Financial requirements for supporting successful business trajectories, and a combination of particle and project logic, may push in time some district firms to start a metamorphosis causing them to grow in size and become medium–large-sized particle firms, or a hybrid. Mature particles of hybrid district firms are expected to stay anchored to the original ID when they find that this still provides benefits in the form of ID external economies.

More recently, changes in the technological platforms and the international scale of demand and production have increased the opportunities for those paths of strengthening of business structures operating within IDs. This begs an important question which is discussed in various ways in the *Handbook*, particularly in Sections 7 and 8: how can an ID with its population of small project firms react to changes in the technological paradigm and to globalisation? What is the contribution of larger, medium-sized district firms in this respect? This is an intra-district variation on the old theme of the asymmetry principle of Joseph Steindl (1945).

Here we note that the fact that opportunities emerging from global value creation require resources which are more easily managed by larger medium-sized firms does not imply necessarily that the access to such opportunities needs the overall concentration of the ID industrial structure into a few large firms, with their ring of dependent smaller firms.

Indeed, beyond basic collective conditions, the core competencies of a portion of project firms are also crucial against contemporary challenges. Both medium-sized particle or hybrid firms and project firms contribute to determining the characters of the socio-economic interaction that shapes the functioning of cooperative behaviours in self-organised internal and external teams. Part of the answer comes from the role that social and labour mobility plays in enabling the realisation of life projects through entrepreneurial ventures that combine innovation, flexibility, creativity and quality. Indeed, a fabric of project firms contributes in specific ways to an extensive presence of workers' participation to entrepreneurial projects and self-determination. Firstly, such a fabric is a natural incubator of new projects of life coming from the experiences and energies of the ID working class, or at least of the more skilled and active part of it. Secondly, the prospect for employees to climb the economic ladder and become employers (and set up a project firm) is a strong motivation to learning and developing entrepreneurial attitudes on the job. Thirdly, the 'doing' in such 'learning-by-doing' is precisely active participation in the more engaging business projects of the employer. Finally, with their active participation as employees, and with some of them setting up project firms themselves, the entire IDs benefit from the most dynamic entrepreneurial energies which, in a world of capitalist relations and particle firms, would otherwise remain hidden and unfulfilled.

Medium-sized firms, and especially those grown out of particle firms, do not easily benefit from these advantages. But they need them, and if committed and significantly embedded in a district, they can gain some access to the same pools of energies, innovations and entrepreneurial dynamism. The diversity of firm forms in a dynamic ID is a crucial condition for its ability to adapt and adjust to external changes in ways that guarantee its reproducibility. In this context, medium-sized firms can become sensors of external changes and trends, as well as bridges connecting external actors with the more internal and ID locally-bound firms. They become therefore two-way channels of knowledge, goods and services exchanges for translocal cross-cluster activities. Actually, the collective exploitation of resources provided by sets of private firms is what is usually meant with the realisation of ID external economies (see in particular Sections 2 and 3). However, the trajectories by which medium-sized firms predate the resources and opportunities of small project firms are also possible, with the fabric of smaller firms becoming dependent on the local strategies of a few centres of capital, and the engine of ID external economies weakening irreversibly.

Finally, it is not to be excluded that in reality some IDs are endowed with medium-sized particle, hybrid and metamorphic firms, whilst other IDs present less firm diversity. This of course depends on regional and sectoral features, as various chapters of the *Handbook* illustrate. Even without medium-sized firms, sensor and bridging functions could be played by the more dynamic and open teams (formal and informal business groups) of small firms. This is not only possible but desirable, although the burden of such a strategy borne by such teams and the related public policy support increases with the coordination problems involved.

3.4 IDs, clusters and policies

We come to some considerations on the role and objectives of public policy for IDs as engines of local development. According to the localist and anti-statalist approaches, IDs are essentially the result of bottom-up and endogenous processes driven by the entrepreneurial spirit of small enterprises and by market exchanges. On the other side, the critics of IDs have repeatedly pointed to a key factor that explains, in their view, the fundamental weakness of IDs, that is the lack of access to the indivisible industrial, trade and research facilities needed to face the market and technological challenges of the time. However, IDs are also innervated by political processes necessarily emerging from their nature, as small-scale but complex human societies. Decision-making processes within IDs tend to produce, more or less deliberately, policies that combine the strategies of a set of public and private district stakeholders. They contribute to the systemic nature and to the infrastructure underpinning economies which are partly external to each individual organisation and firm, but internal to the networks of agents (for example, firms, policymakers, trade associations) more or less embedded within the same ID. The success of such strategies depends on the conditions in which they are implemented by agents who move tentatively within sets of reciprocal and evolutionary constraints and opportunities; with such sets being characterised by strong local roots coupled with a web of translocal (national and international) relations.

The crucial role that public policy for and within IDs has played in the academic debate and in the practice of policymaking explains why the *Handbook* devotes a whole section to it (Section 11), whilst touching on it also in most of the chapters of the other sections.

We defer to such a rich pool of contributions an assessment of the most cutting-edge themes in this respect (see Section 11 in the volume), and we wish here only to present a couple of considerations on the nature of the objectives of ID policies, and on the multi-level geography required for an effective design and implementation of such policies.

Policies are the results of political processes shaped by the underlying administrative structures which are almost always defined along sectoral lines. Quite naturally public policies for IDs fall under the remit of departments (at various levels of local, regional, State, and federal-union government) which have economic targets and competencies, and that are separate from those working on welfare, culture, environment, and so on. Furthermore within IDs, employers' associations and trade unions tend to be the most active private agencies able to contribute to the delivery of collective actions together with public policy initiatives. Finally, many among the consultants advising both public and actors in IDs are industrial or management economists. All this tends to influence the way IDs stop being considered a small-scale complex society, and start being looked at as a particular form of industrial organisation, that is an industrial cluster. The problem with the latter is that the ID is reduced to its production and economic features (the set of specialised producers and related institutional actors organising the realisation of the main products and services) neglecting the socio-cultural and institutional relations that crucially define it.

Furthermore, given the difficulties in understanding the variety of the nexus between industrial clusters and local societies in hugely different worlds, the focus on industrial clusters, and within them on selected networks of business and related institutional actors, has represented a practical solution for accumulating experiments and comparing results on the field. Cluster policies and initiatives are nowadays a large and expanding discipline, subsuming, in the view of many of its proponents and practitioners, policies and initiatives for IDs (see for example, Karlsson 2008). Concurrently IDs have come to be seen in those academic and practitioner quarters just as particular cases of clusters; that is, as in the Italian post Second World War experience, those made up of small specialised firms, in low–medium-tech sectors, and hosted in small–medium-sized towns and their surroundings. This point of view is illustrated in some important contributions within the *Handbook* in Sections 10 and 11.

In our view the diffused interest on cluster policies and initiatives may have beneficial effects also for the support to political processes innervating the local societies where industrial clusters are rooted, and for orientating the resulting application of public and collective resources towards specific systemic conditions helping industrial and human development. Still more, policy interest may avoid the trap of targeting only the formally recognised cases of IDs in a region/country/federation. Whatever method is adopted to identify IDs, their socio-economic complexity and their evolutionary forces always tend to make it hard for them to be formally identified. Instead, a looser definition of the object of policy initiative which coincides with the emergent production core of a firm clustering can be more easily recognised. This explains why clusters have been used as an umbrella term that in reality encompasses a broad range of firm clustering, all nevertheless having in common the colocation of sector specific activities. In the same way, the increasingly important relations between mature IDs and proto or infant IDs are more easily recognised in terms of possible cross-cluster relations.

This approach has, however, also some drawbacks which should not be ignored. The first and probably most relevant one is the strictly economic focus of policy intervention; the second one comes from a lack of appreciation of the distinction between clusters characterised by a good balance of project and particle firms, and clusters just dominated by particle firms. In the worlds of global financial and industrial oligopolies the second type of clusters is an important phenomenon related, as recalled previously, to the need of the big concentrations of capital to tap the local bases of human and natural resources. Policies supporting them may have the effect of both transferring public resources and helping the extraction of surplus from the original localities to the benefit of the capitalist centres.

A genuine ID approach to public policy would enable cluster policies to distinguish and define selective mechanisms targeting the embeddedness of business strategies in processes which contribute to human and industrial development in the localities. An appreciation of the importance of an ID approach to policymaking relies also on the identification of cases which are not simply industrial clusters, but present themselves as local societies with an embedded industrial (clustered) specialisation that expresses itself through an agglomeration of small firms.

We come finally, and shortly, to consider the importance of multi-level policymaking, especially when an ID approach to policy is considered. A local level of policy action is necessary for many reasons recalled in depth in Section 11. It is worth reminding us that local policy must not be driven by narrow localist interests, nor by strictly economic concerns. The sense of local belonging and identity may give to a small informal community of individuals – 'a nation within a nation' in Marshall's words –, or even to the disoriented individual consciences of the contemporary liquid modernity, a place to practise civic virtues and responsibility, contributing individually and collectively to a good out-of-the factory life and to the cohesive bases of participation on the job. Competition among localities may have the nature of civil emulation, being gauged in terms of indexes of standard of living or 'happiness' (Bruni and Porta 2007). IDs, when lively and vibrant, tend to reproduce such attitudes, but of course the success of such reproductive processes, and their extension to other localities, depend heavily on the broader regional and national conditions and policies. In particular, national governments should support and orientate their effort towards strengthening the most dynamic and open component of the local forces, against the dismantling social effects of global finance and capitalist accumulation. Instead, if national policies prefer a more *laissez-faire* approach, whereby forms of social and market competition prevail over forms of cooperation and participation, then the centres of global capitalist accumulation would dwarf local forces of economic development like IDs.

3.5 Capitalism with a human face

IDs following a high road of local development have been and are a laboratory for testing and reflecting on the conditions that determine the evolution of market economies and of capitalist forms of industrial societies.

The often overcrowded debate on the future of IDs should be understood in this type of scenario. Many IDs, as they appear to us today, are changing or will change and transform into something seemingly or effectively different as we write. However, what is crucial is that both the old IDs that succeed in preserving their vitality and the new generation ones continue to be living evidence of a form of capitalism that is different from the one purely dominated by selfish footloose capitalist calculus and oligopolistic predatory strategies, whereby the benefit of some coincides with the loss of others, or in any case where social inequalities are prone to grow.

ID processes exemplify the presence and action of competitive forces that Marshall would have called 'chivalrous', and that are not dominated only by opportunism, shirking or pure cut-throat rivalry, but rather are infused also with rules that reward fair, open and trustworthy behaviours and punish – often tacitly and informally, albeit effectively – cheating or breaching. In other words, beside the legal framework that encases more generally all economic and civil activities, those alternative competitive forces incorporate a reputational mechanism that is conducive to maintain the delicate, but crucial, balance with cooperation (see Sections 3 and 4 of the *Handbook*).

Furthermore, the combination of this reputational mechanism with the peculiar promotion of project firms (see above, 3.3) contributes to shaping a socio-economic dynamism whereby many have the opportunity to try to overcome social barriers through hard work and ingenuity. When this can be hoped for and tried by a relatively high number of members of the local working community, a diffused reproduction of entrepreneurial energy, plasticity and skills can be propelled from the bottom up.

Finally, the combination of social mobility with local policies oriented towards rewarding civic virtues and civil emulation gauged by personal and social happiness (see above, 3.4) may allow the preservation of a certain degree of social cohesion, collective participation and conversation, and local identity in a context still open to internal and external change (see above, 3.1, 3.2). A local life so characterised may be imagined as made of occasions of social interaction intersecting private business and public focal points. A metaphor of this could be an image taken from the history of Florence's renaissance when, at the peak of the city's artistic and economic life, citizens meet casually in the street looking at a newly completed statue or frescos, and stop for a moment from their daily businesses to discuss the merits and relative flaws of the latest great artist's work in comparison with the accomplishments of other artists.

No formal institution dedicated to economic education, business promotion, and welfare support would be able alone, in the world as it is now, to trigger such processes, which are rather sparked and cultivated by the intersection of individuals' ambitions with collective advances. This is why the social and economic system needs rich contexts whereby the realisation of peoples' capabilities and goals concur to a collective benefit, whilst rewarding the person not only in monetary terms but more importantly in terms of social recognition and ascent.

A social and economic system where such forces of social mobility and dynamic egalitarianism play a significant role is what has been referred to as a sort of 'capitalism with a human face': a capitalism where, in other words, the 'when', the 'how' and the 'with whom' of production and consumption activities are integral parts of the life of place (see Section 2 of the *Handbook*; Becattini 2004a and 2006). The pride of acknowledging personal and collective achievements with those whose life experiences, motivations and cognitions one shares, and the possibility of a decent work and life where the inequality in the distribution of material and immaterial (cultural) assets is not too large and crystallised, can be a powerful drive to human progress and with this to the prosperity of regions and countries. IDs do not always mirror forms of a capitalism with a human face; however, in our view, when working at their best they remain both a possible source of inspiration with respect to what path of socio-economic development would be desirable and a warning against other powerful capitalist forces that can lead to more destructive outcomes.

4. AN OVERVIEW OF THIS *HANDBOOK*

This *Handbook* comprises 53 chapters divided into four parts and 11 sections. Part I on the 'Origin and theories of industrial districts' includes three sections and looks at the historical context of the ID, both as a conceptualisation and as an empirical phenomenon. Section 1 on 'early industrial districts' provides an economic historical assessment of IDs: the genesis of the contemporary phenomena cases, ID processes and their relation with regional waves of industrialisation. Section 2 considers IDs 'from their British roots to the Italian revival', tracing an essential history of thought on IDs and touching upon key points in the past and contemporary debates. Section 3 comprises scholarly views on the IDs as 'a meeting ground for the social sciences', including disciplinary approaches, like economics, business science, economic geography and sociology.

Part II on 'The nature of industrial districts' is devoted to a more general discussion on the relations between the local forces of trust, entrepreneurship and cognitive proximity, and the district processes of industrial and local development. Section 4 looks at the 'socio-cultural and institutional aspects'; Section 5 explores the importance of 'knowledge, learning and creativity' in the current dynamism of IDs.

Part III on 'The empirical investigations on industrial districts' focuses on contemporary empirical investigations on IDs. Section 6, on mapping and measuring the 'empirical relevance', presents the methodology to map IDs by means of statistical data, and applications in three European countries. Section 7 concentrates on 'the Italian experiences' whilst Section 8 looks at the 'the experiences in other industrialised countries', including a survey on the European countries and specific analyses of France, Spain and Scandinavian countries, Japan and the US. The chapters not only provide evidence of the contemporary varieties of IDs and ID processes across developed countries, but also contribute with different interpretative approaches somehow mirroring the empirical differences. Section 9 explores IDs in 'the experiences in emerging and developing countries' and presents interesting experiences in countries undergoing a process industrial development and upgrading. This section includes Latin America, China, India and two contributions presenting more general trends and projections.

Part IV on 'Globalisation and industrial districts' concludes with contributions devoted to shedding light on the contemporary challenges faced by IDs and the role and dimensions of policy support. Section 10 discusses globalisation, technology, adaptability and institutional responsiveness as the key 'global challenges' that IDs have to face. Finally, Section 11 on 'public policies and industrial development strategies' addresses the key issue of what role is necessary for public policy to sustain IDs and related forms of local and industrial development.

PART I

Origin and theories of industrial districts

SECTION 1
Early industrial districts

Introduction

Alberto Guenzi

1. THE HISTORICAL PERSPECTIVE ON IDs

In the processes of formation and establishment of industrial districts (IDs), the historical perspective is of particular significance: not only should we look at what has happened within the system of enterprises but especially at what has happened in the location where the district is rooted. Attention should be focused not only on the economic performance but also on the quality of the functioning of the society in that particular place (institutions and organizations). However, the location is not simply a container that houses business systems intrinsically linked to society; it is a space that changes in time, due to the actions of enterprises, social bodies and institutions. The location of the district must not be perceived as a natural expression of the historical process, but as the artificial construction of the conditions of context suited to encouraging manufacturing as a factor of growth but also of general development. The theme of artificiality (that is, the presence of a conscious development project) deserves an emphasis that would permit, among other things, to take distance from the paradigm that mechanically connects the birth of the districts to endogenous or exogenous causes. In the various explanations of the formation of IDs – rural proto-industry, the creation of a large company, exploitation of a local resource, disintegration of *métayage* (sharecropping) – a question must be asked: why there and not elsewhere? In other words, there are many places that provide a favorable context to the birth of IDs, but in only some of these are IDs established and developed. This clearly relates to the issue of their historic role: it is not enough to explain how the development was achieved but it should be made clear why exactly it was achieved there.

A second argument concerns the organization of the manufacturing activity. While the birth and the diffusion of the large enterprise has a history that is consistent with the parallel consolidation of the capitalist production mode, IDs do not have such a considerable reference to a production mode (and consequently to a precise historical period). Depending on the point of view, they are either regarded as an unfinished form of capitalism or as an alternative form of mass production in order to ensure (with important economic results) the survival of typical productions. The chapters in this first section attempt to question this point of view and move towards the search of a reference model.

2. ORIGINAL PATHS OF HISTORIC RESEARCH ON THE DEVELOPMENT OF MANUFACTURING IN EUROPE

The lines of research are: (a) to take into account the origins of manufacturing in late medieval and modern Europe; (b) to put under analysis the organization forms of manufacturing; (c) to understand which of these forms have structural aspects that may represent the components of the model to which I referred earlier.[1] As is known, in the precapitalist era, different types of production organization appear in the secondary sector: I refer to the guild system, the putting-out system, the merchant entrepreneur and the concentrated manufacture (not mechanized).

These typologies are usually considered as alternative and sequential, as stages of a progressive approach to the 'promised land' of the industrial revolution. Questioning this interpretation opens the way to unexpected research developments. Though the three mentioned forms make their appearance in different times (with timelines that vary from country to country), nevertheless it is also true that they can be found together in the 150–200 years before the industrial revolution. Cases in which these production modes are phases of the same production process are frequent: production methods that often appear to be complementary rather than alternative. Some further and interesting consequences were derived from this integration: the town–countryside link and the leaning to produce for international markets (Berg, Hudson and Sonnenscher 1983; Butlin 1986; Pfister 1998).

It is well known that the emergence of an organized manufacturing sector is a purely urban phenomenon that took place in Italian cities (central and northern) and Flanders from the 13th and 14th centuries, to spread afterward to almost the whole continent. Guilds were the first that gave identity and language to manufacturing methods. Economic historiography blamed these bodies as being responsible for having created obstacles to the natural development of the market forces by conditioning the labor market, by prohibiting free access to the different production activities, and by undermining the growth of enterprises. By overtaking and/or attempting to evade the guild constraints, the other production modes (for example merchant-entrepreneur, rural proto-industry) were therefore perceived as forms that first determined the weakening, then yearned for the end of these restrictions, and consequently launched the free market season (Pirenne 1937; Thrupp 1942; C. Cipolla 1976; Farr 1997a; G. Richardson 2001).

This is a reassuring but superficial tale: scholars over the last 20–25 years have failed to correct this vision. Detailed investigations in many European countries have highlighted many cases in which the guild system opened itself to innovation and coordinated itself with other production modes. In short, guilds in the modern age certainly preserved their formal structure (the set of regulations in statutes) but profoundly renewed their behavior (Guenzi, Massa and Piola Caselli 1998; Nunez 1998; Wolek 1999). In particular, they showed willingness to accept product innovations, to organize production relying to the benefits of decentralization (in the city but also in the surrounding territory), to adapt to the requirements of production for export (standardization of products, coordination with the merchant-entrepreneur). A classic example is the withdrawing of guild control from the early and central stages of the production process, and the focusing on product finishing.

I would like to draw attention to a feature that, perhaps more than others, puts the ancient guild system in relation to the modern IDs. I refer to the central role of the formation of human capital, with particular reference to the creation and transmission of informal knowledge. It is a matter that affects the nature of the guild. Certainly the guild performed an economic function, which consisted in overseeing the production and the distribution of goods for the market; but its main aim was to convey and verify the technical skills. In its original frame, the economic function was a means to achieve a formative objective. The relevance of this formative function, during a historic phase where techniques did not have a language, cannot be underestimated.

The technical formation of human capital was a vital function without which skills and processes risked disappearing, and through which that same knowledge could renew itself. The workshop was the school in which the master was the teacher, apprentices were the pupils who were trained over the years with the aim of acquiring skills equal to those of the master. The ability to dominate the production process was a prerequisite in order to assume the role of teacher. In fact, the final examination (the masterpiece) certified the full grasp of production techniques that transformed the apprentice into a master. This point has, in my view, a particular importance. The physiology of the guild system resided precisely in the final aim of allowing workers to become entrepreneurs (head of the workshop) through a full, long and demanding training process. A clear similarity immediately springs out: among the forms of organization of manufacturing activity (present but also past) the ID is certainly the one which – despite not having a preconstituted design – allows greater upward mobility. In well-behaving IDs many employees have the opportunity to become entrepreneurs; instead in other production contexts such a path is perceived as a rare and fortunate case of personal success. As in guilds, the boundary between the entrepreneur and the employee is an obstacle that could be easily overcome. In IDs the limited presence of vertical integration of the phases of the production process is replaced by the vertical integration of human capital (S.R. Epstein 1998; Ogilvie 2004; De Munck 2006).

The rooting of systems (formal and informal) aiming at the formation of human capital for specialized production in a specific place represents an impalpable resource; yet, at the same time, it is a crucial element to determine the success of an ID. The predisposition of a local society to accept and together build the living conditions of IDs is generally considered one of the decisive resources of these production forms. However, this is comparable to a gas, an industrial atmosphere, which cannot be seen or touched even though unequivocal signs of its presence can be perceived (Allen 1983; Koepp 1986; Smail 1992; S.R. Epstein 2004; Van Zanden 2004).

3. THE FORMATION OF AN INDUSTRIAL ATMOSPHERE IN HISTORIC IDs

Three chapters of this section with different approaches, and addressing various aspects, deal with the issue of the formation of the industrial atmosphere. The authors develop long-term analyses that begin in the preindustrial age, a choice that clearly reveals an interpretative line: the rooting of the industrial atmosphere is a long-term process. For this reason, the historical dimension of IDs often presents a chronology that precedes and/or anticipates the birth of the enterprise system (Alto Bresciano and Lumezzane). It precedes the enterprise system, when the enterprises are established on a preexisting artisan network already oriented to the products of the future ID. It anticipates it, when the atmosphere of a place is formed on a product while the future ID will be characterized by the specialization in the production of another product (see Carpi from wood shavings to knitwear).

The ID has two dimensions: the material and tangible one of enterprises, of workers, of machines; the scarcely visible and impalpable one of informal knowledge, of techniques without language, of values assigned to typical production. This so-called 'soft' part represents a new field of investigation that can help to more fully define the district identity, separating it from concepts such as the cluster, the area system, the systems of small and medium-sized enterprises (SMEs). The brief considerations that I develop do not concern the 'state of the art' or even the abundant new knowledge that the section offers. I merely recall those aspects that provide a guideline on applicative and theoretical grounds. The first three chapters are linked by a common underlying vision and relate to the 'soft' part, following separate but parallel paths.

Carlo Marco Belfanti analyses the birth of IDs according to two paths that analyze and cover a period of several centuries. In the first place, he shows the importance of guilds as a context for learning and stresses that this model, strictly urban, is closely replicated by professional groups operating in the countryside and by other organizations established after the abolition ot the guilds. The guild model, therefore, is seen as an economic form that survives and inspires the behavior of manufacturers that needed to work together or had to negotiate with the other parties. A second, no less relevant, issue is the sedimentation of technical knowledge together with a fruitful dynamism that, for example, allowed the Morez nail producers to become producers of watches. This case provides an unexpected pattern: a guild model applied outside of the urban context, creating renewable and changeable skills and opening the way to the spreading of innovative processes. Belfanti's other fundamental indication is the role of the factory as an 'incubator' of skills that can be transformed into entrepreneurial experience. The factory sometimes generates the knowledge that leads to the development of small firms of the district; this is a process that often becomes even more rapid and intense when the factory closes down (Castelgoffredo). This phenomenon highlights how the large enterprises, historically considered, cannot be always and everywhere considered as an irreplaceable model. At times, their disappearance and the resulting birth of a district specializing in the same processing shows that the succession between forms of organization of manufacturing activity can take different trajectories. In its function as 'incubator' of technical skills, the factory recovers the function which (in my opinion) was the main one of the guild system.

The reflections of Corine Maitte integrate with Belfanti's by comparatively analyzing three IDs with ancient roots, giving particular attention to cultural, technical, social and institutional features. These are three textile districts corresponding to medium and small urban centers and their sorroundings. They undergo different growth and development models. The indications that this contribution provide are methodologically relevant: three extraordinarily similar cases regarding their starting conditions, sectors of specialization, and subsequent duration follow different models of development. The interpretative key of this work lies in the analysis of the relations that the enterprises together established with the community. In particular, Maitte explains that the persistence of these three century-old districts is the result of a continuous process of adjustment in the management of resources provided by local society (firstly, human capital), in the range of products, in the relationship with domestic and international markets, and in organizational forms allowing improvements in the quality of goods and the reduction of production costs. In sum, they were example of flexible systems which did not exclude concentration phenomena and which adapted themselves to the situation throughout processes of failure and birth of new firms. The flexibility and willingness to change is therefore a resource that in the long term determines persistence and growth. It is a valuable attitude that recalls the concept of spatial and institutional organization. The community–enterprise pairing has a central role in the three cases studied: it is an element that allows IDs to hold their identity in the presence of high-impact transformation processes (mechanization in the course of the 19th century for example). The possibility of breaking up and reshaping the organization of the territory in the function of its production and labor market shows a development model of unexpected change (and fundamentally explains the variety of historically determined models).

Elisabetta Merlo focuses on the transformation processes of three seemingly very different IDs by formation date, persistence of the original model and final outcome. She focuses on the processes of change considering the actions undertaken with regard to the formation of human capital, rather than the structure of the enterprises or the type of products. This very demanding approach is based on the concept of 'epistemic community'. Merlo confronts one of most important and delicate steps of European culture between the old regime and the 'industrial era', that is the need to give a language to technical knowledge in order to allow its transmission and dissemination, overcoming the learning model of the workshop. The process of codifying informal knowledge is, in general, a vital issue in the transformations of industrial society. The chapter analyzes different models. In Vigevano with it shoe industry, where advanced technology made use of not highly qualified human capital, the innovation movement generated the birth of an important sector specializing in the production of machinery for the shoe factories. In the silk industry of Como, the complex articulation of manufacturing based on family and domestic workshops did not stimulate a change of skills; rather, in the late 1800s the local Chamber of Commerce coordinated the resources of entrepreneurs destined to the foundation of the *Scuola di setificio* (School of silk industry). This was a positive experience to the extent that its formative content (focused not so much on the weaving of fabric as on the finishing operations, such as dyeing and printing) anticipated the transformations of the *setificio* in the following years and still does so today. In Lyon, the European silk capital, the issue of formation acquired dramatic importance after the French Revolution that disarticulated the previously existing system directed by guilds or associations of producers also inspired by the guild model. From the beginning of the 19th century, some formative and cultural institutions took the burden of organizing a system for the dissemination of technical knowledge and for promoting innovation. This choice achieved good results, contributing to the new takeoff of the Lyonnaise silk industry that held European primacy throughout the 19th century.

4. THE VARIETIES OF IDs ALONG INDUSTRIAL REVOLUTIONS

The contribution by Andrew Popp and John Wilson shows that in the UK, IDs played a decisive role in the industrialization process during the industrial revolution and afterwards, drastically correcting a historiographical interpretation that was dominant until a few years ago. A detailed analysis of the industrialization process shows how the concept of ID derived by Italian studies can be seen as unable to grasp all the variety and complexity of the English case in the 19th century as witnessed by Marshall. This is an important issue in itself, and it is absolutely relevant in this volume: according to these authors it is necessary to build a wider and more open theoretical model of ID to overcome the ideal type resulting from studies of Italian IDs. This is not the best place to assess the merits of this need; I am nevertheless obliged to point out that Becattini systematizes the concept of the Marshallian ID in relation to the value theory (Sforzi 2008). His theoretical apparatus therefore was not conceived to explain just atypical models of concentration of SMEs in parts of Italy (Tuscany, Emilia, Veneto and Marches). The issue is complex, and should be discussed beginning with the attention that Marshall dedicated to the concentration of specialized industries in particular localities. Becattini favors taking the community as a unit of analysis, where others focus on the local clustering of a production sector. Considering the contributions of this section, it seems to me that the community unit represents a standpoint well suited to studying local manufacturing development processes that are far apart in space and time.

In the last chapter of the section, Andrea Colli suggests an original interpretation of the role played by IDs over the last two centuries. The relations between large enterprises and IDs are analyzed in light of the transformations resulting from the three industrial revolutions. The chapter assigns a decisive role to IDs in the first phase of industrialization; it also explains the persistence of IDs after the second industrial revolution, shifting attention to the varied and segmented structure of demand that put up barriers to the spread of mass production. Colli also addresses the issue of the impact of the third industrial revolution on IDs, the effects of which are far from being measured and interpreted. Here the author's analysis focuses on what happens in the enterprise and between enterprises.

The works provided in this section drive the level of knowledge forward and offer some solid bases for an enrichment of the concept of the ID as developed by Becattini and others. Moreover, the cases which have been discussed give depth to the investigation. Historical analysis provides a feature that may also prove useful to scholars of other disciplines: the soft, intangible part of IDs has protected their identity in the long run. Certainly in the course of time, the material structures of industrial organization in IDs show elements of convergence with other production forms (I am thinking firstly of technology); nevertheless, the advantages of the soft part (human capital, informal knowledge, sales systems) appear to be the essential and distinctive component of growth and consolidation of IDs (Commons 1909; Markusen 1996; Chartres 2002). A requirement which seems to be taking shape from these investigations is to focus on the communitarian resources that determine the birth and change of an ID. This is not straightforward in historic research, since we must view and gauge how the local community helps to determine the creation and especially the following development of the ID. The local society is not a passive structure; basic resources must be activated in order to foster the establishment of manufacture. The community must 'act' by means of policies which necessarily have to be local; in fact the constraints to be removed in order to mobilize such resources belong to a local context.

NOTE

1. See Deakin (2006, p. 11): 'Certain aspects of guild production were carried over into emerging forms of industrial organization. A combination of competition and cooperation, and the preservation of solidaristic ties between independent producers, came to characterize the IDs of Italy and their equivalents in France, Germany and Japan, which economists rediscovered in the final decades of the twentieth century'. See also Althusser and Balibar (1971); Hickson and Hunter (1991); De Moor (2006).

1. The genesis of a hybrid: Early industrial districts between craft culture and factory training

Carlo Marco Belfanti

1. INTRODUCTION

The genesis of industrial districts (IDs) is a process marked by a multiplicity of evolutionary paths, in which according to the experience, diverse factors have played a decisive role. The element which seems common to the evolution of the majority of the IDs, if not to all, is the combination of the persistence of tradition and elements of modernity, with a social organisation permeated by consolidated values and an economic dynamic attentive to market challenges. All the scholars who have dealt with the question have underlined the coexistence of these apparently contrasting characteristics which have made of the ID an economic and social formation of an amphibian nature, still torn between fidelity to its own roots and the attraction exercised by modernity.

The ID as a hybrid is the main theme of this chapter which is divided into three sections. Section 2 takes into consideration those paths where significant sedimentation of tradition can been recognised as if it were in the district's DNA, which often matches an identity constructed around the craftsmanship of trade. On the other hand, Section 3 examines those dynamics which take their form from the experience of working in factories. Finally, Section 4 proposes a synthesising reflection.

2. THE LEGACY OF THE PAST

Sabel and Zeitlin (1985) were the first to focus on a model of industrial development alternative to that based on the factory and on mass production; a model instead based on the craftsman's workshop and on his flexible specialisation, capable of producing innovation and of competing on the international market. Thanks to these studies and to the many others which followed, European industrial geography began thus to appear not only as dots in correspondence with the cities where great factories tended to be concentrated, but also as clouds of small production units of the kind that Alfred Marshal (1919) had defined as 'industrial districts'.

Sabel and Zeitlin identified and analysed many of these formations, each of which was specialised in a particular production: Sheffield with its knife makers and Birmingham with its arms manufactures in England; the making of silk in Lyon, of trimmings in St Etienne and of wool cloth in Roubaix in France; and the production of cutlery in Solingen in Germany are only some of the examples taken into consideration, to which many others were later added as further research brought them to light.[1]

The character which defined and accompanied the district forms, making them competitive, was given by an institutional set-up constructed on three mainstays: a local –'municipal'– governance of the production system, a paternalistic vision of industrial development and a network of family-run businesses. Such a set-up ensured the stability of the productive system itself, guaranteeing its sustainability both in social and in economic terms by disbursing unemployment subsidies with the aim of avoiding dispersion of the human capital of the district, supervising prices and salaries with the intent of warding off damage due to excess competition, building or funding highly-indivisible resources available to the whole production community, safeguarding the brand that identified the typical products of the district, creating professional training schools, and activating a chain of bodies that could supply assistance (Sabel and Zeitlin 1985 and 1997b). These are practices that are anything but innovative, although renewed and revised in the light of changed contexts – as they seem to be direct descendants of that organisational culture that had grown up in urban Europe around the institutions which for centuries, albeit with alternating fortunes – had represented the prevalent form of regulation of craft activity: that is, the craft guild.[2] Policies aimed at regulating competition, safeguarding the know-how, promoting the identity of the craft, controlling the quality and supporting the training of apprentices were an integral part of the craft culture (Farr 1997b) elaborated within the corporative institutions and implemented in agreement and in collaboration with the city governments.[3]

In the case of Sheffield – one of those which inspired Marshall's intuition – the genesis of the ID appears as in continuity with the mediaeval guild of knife makers, the Cutler's Company (Binfield and Hey 1997), which was still regulating production in the 19th century, intervening on prices, on unemployment, on safeguarding the brand, on training (Berg 1993; Higgins and Tweedale 1995; White 1997). Also revolving around a network of workshops – mostly concentrated in the so-called 'gun quarter' – was the manufacture of small arms in Birmingham, where the production process was divided up into various phases, each of which came under the competence of a specialist craftsman. And even the 'masters', 'artisan-workmen' and apprentices in Birmingham in the 19th century shared a 'workshop culture', which was their common ground for debate on questions like 'fair price', the management of apprenticeships, hours and working time, comprising 'St Monday' (Behagg 1998). Manufacturing specialisation in Solingen was identified with an antique craft tradition, which had made the blades produced in this small city in the duchy of Berg famous since the 15th century (Boch 1997). The textile ID in Prato in Italy had established itself as a territory in which the working of wool had been successfully regulated by the guild – *L'Arte della Lana* – from the Middle Ages on; after its abolition the guild's functions were for the most part inherited by the municipal authority (Maitte 2001).

The organisational culture elaborated by the guild systems also spread outside the city walls, the usual territory of the guilds. A significant case in this context is that of the Lumezzane ID in the Brescia region. The manufacturing activity in the Lumezzane Valley, to the north of the city of Brescia, had been consolidated from the 16th century on, in connection with the concentration of firearms manufacture in a nearby village, Gardone Valtrompia. The Lumezzane blacksmiths created flintlocks, bayonets and other accessories for firearms destined to equip the armies of half Europe. Thus, in time, an articulated network of production had been created, based on a myriad of small forges, specialised in the making of firearm components, but able to convert to the production of goods for civilian use – such as nails, blades of all kinds, metal work and, above all, cutlery – when there was a lull in the demand for military products. During the 18th century, the need to create some form of coordination emerged, with the aim of reinforcing the negotiating power of the craftsmen with respect to the merchants who dealt with the subcontracting for the supplying of weapons, since the latter often imposed extremely low prices on the subcontractors and were able to exclude from the commissions anyone who opposed them. The form of association adopted by the Lumezzane blacksmiths to organise representation of their own interests was precisely that most widespread at the time: the guild. In 1758 the flintlock makers stipulated an agreement before a notary public as the founding act for the 'whole body of the workforce . . . on the regulations of the city brotherhoods in terms of craftsmen'. A couple of years later, under an identical procedure, the guild for craftsmen specialised in accessories for rifles was set up. The brief text drawn up by the notary public set out the rules for negotiating with the contracting merchants, the conditions of the orders and the criteria for an equitable sharing out of the work among those belonging to the guild. Driven by the need to equip themselves with a form of coordination of the small production units of the district, the Lumezzane craftsmen had opted for the organisational model which was prevalent at the period, precisely that of the guilds (Belfanti 1999).

It is not surprising that those practices were revised and remodelled in order to deal with the radically different scenario in the period following the abolition of the guilds.[4] In Italy, for example, the organisational culture established by the craft guilds was reaffirmed also as a model for other institutions, like the mutual aid societies that grew up in the course of the 19th century (Allio 1998; Trezzi 1998).

Outside Italy too the organisational models inspired by the guilds seemed effectively to offer, even if in some cases only partially, efficient solutions for the regulation of production systems based on craftsmanship. The Swiss watchmaking district was composed of a myriad of home-based workshops scattered throughout the Neuchâtel territory, a 'collective manufacture', as it has been defined, in which subjects with different profiles interacted: independent producers, subcontracting suppliers, specialist craftsmen, piece-workers, putters-out, and merchant-entrepreneurs (Veyrassat 1997). In this variegated production reality, in which there was no lack of advanced technical skills, the training of the young was carried out by forms of apprenticeship not too dissimiliar to those institutionalised by the guild systems (Fallet and Cortat 2001).

In Jura, on the French side of the same mountainous region, we may cite the history of the ID of Morez in the Franche-Comté region, recently reconstructed by Jean-Marc Olivier (2004). It is a case of great interest in that it deals with an ID which has been capable of renewing and reinventing itself in the course of time, remodelling its own production specialisation and converting from the manufacture of nails to the making of clocks, and from clockmaking to the production of spectacles. Emerging in the course of the 18th century, the loose configuration of nail-making workshops in Morez was integrated into the agricultural economy of the territory, to which many of the blacksmiths continued to dedicate part of their work in order to increment the income earned from metalworking. This integration between craftwork – and its income – and agricultural activity continued into the following period, when, between the 18th and 19th centuries, the making of nails was progressively substituted by the making of clocks, whose organisation continued to pivot around the 'putting-out system'. Although strongly rooted in the rural area of the mountains of the French Jura, intermediate quality clockmaking – for sitting rooms, for tables, wall clocks and pendulums – required specific competence: in short it was a typical craftsman's activity, whose exercise required adequate training, taught by the method of apprenticeship under a master and regulated by an apposite contract.[5]

However, numerous productive research carried out in Italy, stimulated by the fundamental studies by Giacomo Becattini (1987), has underlined how a large part of the Italian IDs developed on their own evolutionary paths in rural areas in which there is no trace of guild experience. These studies identified the social environment in certain rural areas in central Italy as a terrain which was particularly suitable for the setting up and consolidation of local production systems based on small businesses. In particular, some research carried out in Emilia, in Tuscany, and in the Marches assigns to the 'sharecropper' an important and decisive role in the genesis of the ID, albeit geographically differentiated. In the period after the Second World War, the experience acquired within the sharecropping family both in the organisation of the work of the family members and of the hired labour force, and in the management of the accounts of the farm, was an accumulation of managerial skills and entrepreneurial attitudes, which started to contribute in various ways to the proliferation of small manufacturing firms in nearby towns when the system of sharecropping began to disintegrate in the period after the war. The role played by people coming out of sharecropping families in the transformation of the social and economic structure, however, derives – almost mechanically – from the ubiquitous nature of sharecropping itself, which for centuries had underpinned the structure of the rural economy and society in many areas of central Italy.

A similar framework, to some extent, is suggested by the well-known model of 'proto-industrialisation': the rural genesis of the process of industrialisation is, in fact, central in this model (Mendels 1972). Of course, the outcome of the social and economic transformations caused by rural proto-industry was certainly not the consolidation of a class of small entrepreneurs, but rather the progressive proletarisation of a population of poor peasants. The evolution of the proto-industrial regions would therefore seem to be in net contrast with the rural areas transformed by the spread of small businesses. However, there are examples of IDs generated within 'proto-industrial areas', characterised by traditional manufacturing activity which was organised by merchants who employed on a large scale a country workforce which was underemployed in the fallow periods of field work.

One of the most-known cases is probably that of Carpi, near Modena in Italy, where the manufacture of hats (made by weaving extremely thin stripes of willow) had flourished from the 16th century and had been exported abroad in great quantities in successive ages. The process of plaiting the willow needed to make the hats was put out to cottage industry over a wide rural area and represented an important source of additional earnings for the peasant families.[6] When the demand for these hats began to decline in an irreversible manner, in the period between the two world wars, the production and commercial organisation was converted to a new function. The production of knitted goods, in fact, grew using the preexistent circuits that linked the ill-defined group of domestic workers to the qualified international commercial network. The business initiative that distinguished the development of the local economy in the period following the Second World War was directed by figures of different social origin; former merchant-entrepreneurs from the hat trade, intermediaries who had organised the putting out of the knitted goods, and the ex-workers in the cottage industry (Cicognetti and Pezzini 1994).

Therefore two evolutionary paths seem to be anticipated – of course parallel and not necessarily alternative – in the history of the ID: on the one hand, there are the numerous cases where the protagonists of the local production system come directly from activities of a craft nature, with their technical and organisational competence; on the other hand, the situations in which instead, the industrial progress of the territory is the product of entrepreneurial initiative on the part of individuals from the rural *milieu*. In other words, it is possible to imagine that the genesis of the IDs could be traced back to two possible starting points: one imbued with the craftsmen culture, the other permeated by the rural culture.[7] However, even in those districts where there were marked rural roots, the identity of the craft grew to be so relevant as to become a distinguishing element within the local community, within which the craftsmen came to represent a separate social group. This is what happened, for example, in the Gerenzone Valley in the Lecco area in Upper Lombardy, where the blacksmiths formed a craft community totally distinct from the surrounding rural world (Merzario 1989; Colli 1999). Even the so-called 'cottage industry' of the shoemakers in the Italian Marches was marked by a strong craft identity with which the craftsmen identified themselves, which consolidated their sense of belonging to kin links and association links: the location of the shoemakers' residences – prevalently centred in the villages and the semi-urban centres – itself emphasised how distant they were from the rural world around them (Sabbatucci Severini 1999).

In reality, the crucial point probably lies elsewhere, that is, not in the contraposition between the craft culture and the peasant culture, but in the different ways in which skill was acquired: namely, through apprenticeship in a workshop or through a workman's apprenticeship in a factory.

3. THE FACTORY EXPERIENCE

Artisans and pluriactive peasants – rather than proto-industrial peasants – were the actors who created forms of local development based on small businesses, but in many cases the presence of a factory, even though limited to a certain phase of the history of the territory, had a decisive role. The centralised industrial settlement played a fundamental role in the acquisition of technical competence and professional ability on the part of the local workforce: such an apprenticeship constituted a vital passage in the history of local development (Brusco 1989a).

The incubator for the small business activity that spread during the 1950s in Castel Goffredo, in the upper Mantuan territory, nowadays a centre of worldwide importance in the production of female hosiery, was a stocking factory which was set up in the last half of the 1920s, using German technology and labour. This hosiery factory was successful over a period of 20 years but after the Second World War progressively reduced its activity until it closed. The workforce laid off as a consequence of the plant closure put the experience gained in working with the cotton looms to good use, and set up a host of small or tiny businesses, at times little more than craft workshops which, at least initially, worked as subcontractors without having their own proper trademark. The competence and the technical ability acquired through the factory experience were fundamental in overcoming the challenge by means of innovation: the hosiers of the district, in synergy with the small mechanical-textile industry of the nearby Brescian territory, were able to perfect an extremely competitive production technology that allowed them to become continental market leaders. There is a similar case in the district of

Manerbio, on the Brescian plain. The wool factory, which had been created by local initiative combined with investments of foreign capital at the beginning of the present century, was taken over in 1928 by Marzotto, the leading company in the sector. The plant was considerably upgraded, and on the eve of the Second World War it employed more than 3000 workers. By the end of the 1960s, the business strategy of Marzotto was orientated towards downsizing the company, and the large Manerbio plant was restructured, which meant a contraction of its workforce. At that point, a local network of small businesses founded by the ex-workers began to form, to whom Marzotto offered support and commissions.

The relationship between small businesses and the large-scale factory was less linear and much more complex in the Lumezzane area, but no less interesting. The small workshops scattered throughout the valley right from the beginning of the 19th century became suppliers to the State-owned armaments factories situated in the area in the course of the century. Other factories for arms production opened in the area and also commissioned the Lumezzane blacksmiths to make some components. With the outbreak of the First World War a tidal wave of military commissions swamped the area's production apparatus and the few firms that had the size, organisation and the technology necessary to meet the demand of the army centralised the production, absorbing great numbers of workers. The general mobilisation of resources also involved those forges concerned with civil production and every effort was aimed at the production of weapons. The end of hostilities posed the question of the reconversion of the industrial apparatus which during peace times appeared overextended. Firms in the Lumezzane district embraced the challenge by returning to the manufacture they had to abandon at the outbreak of the war. The reabsorption of the excess workforce took place through the proliferation of small businesses set up by the ex-employees of the largest firms (Belfanti 1999; Belfanti and Onger 2002).

In the districts of Sheffield and Birmingham too (Berg 1993), in German Solingen (Boch 1997), in Italian Prato (Dei Ottati 1995) and even in the rural fortress of Morez in France (Olivier 2004) – to quote only a few examples[8] – the evolution of the ID, at least in some phase, crossed with, flanked, or lived with the factory, exploiting it as a source for the formation of skills that were then poured into the local production system. It is possible to imagine the factory as a factor able to generate positive output in terms of skills to the benefit of the ID. The alternative, therefore, was not so much between the craft culture on the one hand, and the country tradition on the other; but, rather, between the craft identity and the 'pride in the job' of the factory worker (Bigazzi 1978).

4. A SYNOPSIS

The craft culture elaborated by the European guilds provided the basic principles for the organisational 'know-how' that marked the beginning of the evolutionary process of the early IDs. Coordination among the protagonists, regulation of the competition, cooperation for purchases and sales, and, above all, the management of apprenticeships were the areas in which the IDs identified solutions which seemed different from the guild system. Although in limited or partial forms, they are recognisable not only in the urban districts, but also in those in rural areas where there had been no guild experience of any kind. The identity of the craft seems in fact to emerge as a distinctive element in the evolution of the majority of the IDs and was directly connected to skill. But there was another way to acquire skill, in places where the local conditions had not led to the formation of an artisan class: that is, in the factory. Apprenticeship within the factory represented for many districts a training opportunity that was often decisive, at least in particular phases of the life cycle of the district itself. The factory is, therefore, not to be considered as an alternative to the district or in contraposition to it, but rather as an experience which was, at least in part, complementary to it and also to the craft workshop, as Maxine Berg demonstrated some years ago (Berg 1993).

NOTES

1. The seam of research on the IDs has principally developed in Italy starting with the studies by Giacomo Becattini (1987), whose example has been followed by economists (Brusco 1989a; Bellandi and Russo 1994; Arrighetti and Seravalli 1999), sociologists (Bagnasco 1977) and economic historians (Guenzi 1997; Grandi 2007).
2. On the longevity of craftsmanship, see Crossick (1997).
3. For a discussion on the effectiveness of such policy, see Ogilvie (2007).
4. See for instance Sewell (1980).
5. 'The importance of apprentice is evidence of the strictly artisanal nature of such rural production in the 18th century' (Olivier 2004, p. 151).
6. However, even in the case of Carpi the guild had played a role: the hat makers of Carpi depended on the hat maker's guild in the city of Modena.
7. Olivier (2004) insists heavily on the 'rural' matrix of the Morez district.
8. For other Italian case studies, see Grandi (2007).

2. Flexibility and adaptation in the formation of three Italian industrial districts

Corine Maitte

1. INTRODUCTION

The need to examine industrial districts (IDs) over a long period, and not simply in the last 50 years of their history, is shared by an increasing number of researchers.[1] According to Alberto Guenzi's hypothesis (Guenzi 1997, p. 20) the 'industrial atmosphere' of a district is developed in the *longue durée* and 'the economic and social model of the current district is related to a production method that prevailed in the secondary sector during the precapitalist period'. This does not mean, however, that we should adopt a teleological attitude in establishing a necessary link between precapitalist structures and the current districts. We should nevertheless attempt to define favorable local conditions, 'capacities to evolve' towards forms of district organization that are based on cultural, technical, social and institutional knowledge as well as the experience developed over the years in the area. This chapter undertakes a comparative study of the *longue durée* of three textile cities: Prato in Tuscany, Biella in Piedmont and Schio in Veneto. I shall not simply compare the choice of products, but also the development of the production areas as well as the adjustment of the social fabric and local institutions in the *longue durée* of these manufacturing territories.[2]

These territories are fairly representative of the 18th-century Italian industrial expansion, and quite surprisingly they continue to be major textile centers today. They have shown ongoing capacities for adaptation, re-adjustment and reorganization that have enabled them to survive in the long term. They share a number of characteristics. First of all, they are relatively small centers. All three during the 18th century had a population of under 10 000 inhabitants, a relatively low figure on the Italian urban scale, even though they were located in the heart of densely populated areas.[3] They were representative of the vitality of small Italian towns, in an age characterized by the economic slowdown of nearby larger cities and the weakening of their dominating role. Biella had had to face Turin's rising power, Prato and

Schio especially had had to measure up to, and confront, the privilege and protection systems of Florence's and Vicenza and Venice's textile industries (Levi 1985; Malanima 1986; Panciera 1988; Ambrosoli 2000; Maitte 2003). In the 18th century the declining wool industry in these larger cities was been replaced by the silk industry (Malanima 1982; Panciera 1996; Fontana 1997). The development in the wool industry in Prato, Schio and Biella from the 1670s was not merely a shift in manufacturing activity from larger cities to smaller ones since there was no quantitative or qualitative similarity between Florence and Prato's production, nor between Schio's and Vicenza's or Venice's (Ciriacono 1983).

In spite of the similarities between Prato, Biella and Schio, local conditions shaped the industrialization process in a different way (Ramella 1997) and accounted for the disparities in orientation and organization of these industrial areas. A comparison of the differentiated means of adaptation of these centers between the 18th and 19th centuries, sheds light on local structures supporting the formation of the districts. A process of adjustment thus emerges, shaping paths of development which change depending on the ability to combine material and immaterial resources peculiar to the place and the society.

2. THE PATHS TO PRODUCTION EXPANSION IN THE 18TH CENTURY

The fiber that triggered Italian modernization – silk[4] – was, if not absent, at least of secondary importance in Schio as well as in Biella and Prato, where traditional textiles such as wool, linen and hemp represented a major part of production. The revival of these small centers did not come about *ex nihilo*. It was partly based on the mobilization of human and production resources present in the areas since the Middle Ages. Indeed Schio, Biella and Prato had been active textile centers from as early as the 13th century. Even if the phases of development between the medieval period and the end of the 17th century are far from well understood, what is certain is that their traditions, skills and experiences have been conveyed to modern times.

Working with the same fibers did not entail making the same production choices: in fact, these choices differed in each of the centers according to local and regional conditions of supply and demand, State incentives or prohibitions, opportunities and personal contacts.

To simplify, Schio mostly specialized in medium–high quality products, in imitation of what was being made abroad (Panciera 1988), while the other two centers were instead oriented to lower quality products linked to a mixture of fibers (wool, linen, hemp, some cotton). This is proof of the two basic qualitative orientations of the Italian textile industry at the end of the modern era: on the one hand, Italy had lost the primacy of innovation and imitation had become one of the ways to face competition from foreign textiles (Poni, in Panciera 1996, p. ix). On the other hand, the possibility to contain costs and prices became a principal issue.

The production choices of these three centers underwent radical transformations during the 18th century, showing their great capacity for adaptation. An example is the relatively rapid development of the production of Levantine-style caps (*chechia*) in Prato at the end of the 18th century[5] in the imitation of the *chechias* manufactured in Tunis. This successful imitation enabled Prato to open its sphere of activity to all the Mediterranean countries and, through Leghorn merchants, to resume former relations in international trade.

2.1 Sale markets and adaptation conditions

It was by taking advantage of the market possibilities offered at the local – or regional – level that these centers succeeded in developing their production. Several factors of dynamism were present in the regional markets: the population growth concurred with the development of peasants' taste for 'luxury' goods and the slow decline in self-consumption practices increased the demand for lower-quality textiles. In this sense, changes in demand were essential to the understanding of the revival of minor centers,[6] which were able to regain, at least partially, a domestic market that had become largely dominated by foreign fabrics, regularly prohibited, but still present through constant demand and smuggling.[7]

This insertion into regional production obviously did not exclude inroads beyond the borders: apart from the *chechias*, a third of Schio's and Prato's 'ordinary' textile production was intended for markets outside the region, linked to trade networks which did not necessarily pass through the larger cities (Malanima 1986; Verley 1997). These attempts at market diversification, both inside and outside the region, were based on the social diversification of the products: these centers attempted to turn to market segments corresponding to different social groups, explaining the diversity of their production. The types of fabric commissioned by traders held a central role and forced production to be readapted constantly to the market, as opposed to periodically as was the case for fairs. The mechanics of continuous adaptation to the volume and features of production through orders was particularly apparent in the manufacturing of Levantine caps in Prato (Maitte 2001 and 2004). It was the orders placed almost every week, if not every day, by the Leghorn merchants that determined the product's quality, quantity and features. This is a perfect example of flexible production, which relied, of course, on an extremely adaptable manufacturing system, capable of tailoring itself rapidly to these variations in demand.

2.2 The flexibility of production systems

The image conveyed by historiographers has long been that of very traditional modes of organization and technical processes becoming increasingly archaic, their modernization made impossible by the unwieldy guild regulations. The study of the production systems of these three centers, however, has led to different conclusions.

Production methods were indeed traditional and largely based on the accumulation of artisan skills and experience. However, they enabled Prato, Biella and Schio to gain recognition for their technical competence in the 18th century, and even earlier. The fulling mills of Prato finished more than 10 000 pieces per year coming from the Pisa and Florence areas (Malanima 1986). Likewise, Schio seemed to run cloth fulling for a part of the regional demand, while Biella dyed a good part of cloth manufactured in Piedmont.

On the other hand, the mastery of artisan skills also enabled the 'entrepreneurs' to adapt local techniques and lower production costs. They did not bring about any technical revolution of course but, contrary to the image of total stagnation in this field, they introduced certain innovations: for instance, the napping machines which allowed the acceleration of production and the cost reduction of finishing low-quality cloth, were introduced in Prato (Maitte 1996) – as in Schio (Panciera 1996, p. 20) – during the 17th and 18th centuries without any opposition from the guilds. Certain English and Dutch techniques were imported into Schio, where firms kept abreast of the latest trends in foreign textiles.[8] In Biella, the largest firms had employed workers from Holland or northern Europe since the end of the 17th century (Castronovo 1964). Focusing on the English technical revolution alone would make us wrongfully neglect these constant improvements brought to local technical processes and procedures.

The profiles of the innovators vary greatly. Most entrepreneurs interested in introducing technical innovations were distinctly local. In Prato, it was often the finishing artisans themselves who, during the course of the 18th century, covered the expenses of new equipment or improvements (Maitte 1996 and 2001). At the end of the century, the introduction of new technologies for the production of Levantine caps (cheaper pressing and lustering machines, calenders, fabrication of shearing scissors) was due to the initiatives of a small group of men – later known as 'mechanicians' – who could adapt their skills and experience to the most vital needs of the mill. They even acquired sufficient competence to supply other manufacturing centers with their imitations.[9] Similar processes were noticeable in Biella (Castronovo 1964) as well as in Schio (Panciera 1988 and 1996; Fontana 1990). Small groups of technicians capable of appropriating and adapting innovations useful to local production were established in these centers.

The entrepreneurs came mostly from old local families involved in cloth manufacture but also from the ranks of smaller firms dealing in artisan production, small-scale trade or the sale of raw materials (Castronovo 1966; Fontana 1990, 1997; Maitte 2001). In fact, in the 18th century, there was a constant renovation process from the bottom up due to the fact that prospects in the cloth industry and possibilities for upward mobility were still very good. In Prato, the finishing sector and the mixed textile field seemed to fulfill these hopes. In Biella, similar opportunities of upward mobility were offered to 'skilled workers, artisans having succeeded through hard work' (Castronovo 1966, p. 783), as well as to a number of weavers who had managed to rise above their traditional role and had become small manufacturers. Similarly, in Schio, a 'diffused class of entrepreneurs' (Fontana 1997, p. 51) was established. This was not exceptional: other regions offered similar opportunities at the time, opening new prospects even among the lower classes and the rural population, which did not seem to be the case in Prato, or in Schio or Biella.[10]

This, however, did not exclude the existence of parallel processes of increasing concentration of activities into a relatively small number of hands. A double phenomenon of broadening at the bottom of the industry and relative concentration of the production occurred in these entrepreneurial circles. This was accompanied by a rapid 'turnover' which was particularly noticeable in Prato and Schio (Panciera 1988; Maitte 2001). If hope was constantly present, failure was also frequent, especially during the recession years when the smaller producers that usually could only remain in production because of the credit granted them by larger entrepreneurs, sellers of raw materials or buyers, struggled to survive. Nevertheless, these crises did not result in the stagnation of the industry which, on the contrary, seemed to be able to quickly embark on another venture as soon as the economy recovered. This capacity for renewal within the entrepreneurial stratum is proof that industrial 'territories' were truly established.

2.3 Various territorial arrangements

These textile territories did not necessarily correspond to administrative boundaries which indeed evolved according to the needs and reorganization of production. This is why it is difficult to quantify the labor force. Estimates of the Napoleonic era should be considered very cautiously: according to these sources, Schio's manufacturers employed 30 000 workers – although other estimates indicate the more likely figure of 13 500 in 1794, whereas Prato's manufacturers employed 12 000 workers in 1811 and Biella's 8000 in 1797–98.[11]

Each of these towns maintained different relations with its territory and the secondary centers – villages, boroughs or other small towns – to which they were connected. Prato was a center in itself, separate from the other small regional centers with which it had competitive rather than complementary relations. The city organized the distribution of fibers, and activities aside from textile, on its own ground (Maitte 2001). The situation of Schio's territory, described as a proto-industrial 'nebula' (Ciriacono 1985, p. 317) was different. The main city integrated complementary relations with neighboring textile centers, for instance, Arzignano worked the wool waste discarded from Schio's manufacturers; Valdagno sold cloths pretending it came from Schio and Thiene. Other relatively nearby centers specialized in iron, wood and paper (Ciriacono 1985; Panciera 1988) productions. The situation in the Biella region was similar. The town was located in the middle of a region with multiple activities in which a process of production differentiation and specialization had begun between the various centers: Pettingo and Camaniona were especially active in the woolen undergarment sector; Sordevolo, Ochieppo and Biella in higher-quality products; Mosso, Trivero and Val Sessera in ordinary cloth and *mezzelane* (Sodano 1953).

In the context of these distinct territorial arrangements, the work distribution between men and women was different, particularly in weaving. In Prato, weaving was almost exclusively a woman's activity, keeping with a logic shared by the workers' families and manufacturers: a family logic since men could find better-paid or more socially rewarding occupations in crafts, small trade or agriculture; a manufacturers' logic since women's work – essentially urban – met their demands for cost reduction. In contrast, in Biella as in Schio, weaving remained a man's activity: the rural nature and the partially agricultural activities of most workers allowed labor costs to be reduced. In Biella, however, the interaction of credit and land and the persistence of the domestic system in the context of low-quality production enabled weavers to play an important social role in the communities and to remain relatively independent from the traders for a long time, as was shown by Ramella (1984). In Schio on the other hand, the relatively early establishment of the putting-out system and the concentration of part of the activities due to the need for quality control seemed to restrict the weavers' independence (Panciera 1988, p. 157).

In order to understand these territorial and human organizations, we must address their social structures and institutions. In the first place, the human resources of these three territories were very different. The Biella and Schio regions, located in mountainous Piedmont areas, were relatively poor agricultural areas, divided into small pieces of land, whilst in Prato, sharecropping (*métayage*) continued to intensify during the modern era. On the one hand, in Biella and Schio, there was a general need among the population to find complementary income for agriculture that ran at a loss and left a fair amount of idle time; on the other hand, in Prato, *métayage* arrangements that prevented the spreading of rural proto-industry and the scant control that the city wielded on the countryside, due to decisions taken by Florentine aristocracy, directed the development of manufacturing toward an urban model (Fasano Guarini 1986; Maitte 2001).

Secondly, the institutional organization of work was marked by a big difference: the existence of a corporation in Prato and its absence both in Biella and in Schio. The impact of the corporate factor in territorial organization certainly deserves to be revisited and investigated, avoiding the old *a priori* that made corporations a major element of ruralization of industrial activities in the modern era. To the contrary, in these three cases, a dichotomy can be noted between the urban territories of Prato, concentrated and controlled by the corporation, and the rural and scattered territories in the Biella and Schio region, where the corporation was absent.[12] Moreover, contrary to the old anti-corporate historiographical tradition, urban areas were not necessarily the place for productive underperformance. Incidentally, in Prato the *mezzelana* (mixed cloth of linen warp and woolen weft) weaved in the town was not in any way controlled by the corporation, whilst the weaving of the *pannilani* (woolen fabric putting-outers) progressed beyond the city walls with the blessing of the corporation. The corporation in this case issued favorable regulations to the manufacturers that governed it, instituting dialogue between the various entrepreneurs and arbitrating conflicts. There was nothing similar in Biella or Schio where the implied rules of the community played a fundamental role in elaborating regulations.

3. REORGANIZATION AND MULTIPLICITY DURING THE 19TH CENTURY

In the course of the 19th century Prato, Biella and Schio managed to survive, which was a great achievement in an era of radical changes. Actually, in Tuscany, Piedmont and Veneto, during the Restoration, a process of inexorable selection took place, which affected both the production centers and the enterprises. The dramatic changes brought in first by the French presence and then by the Restoration eliminated a large number of small woolen mill producers. The innovation capacity of entrepreneurs and the complex reorganization of the productive territory implemented in the previous century, guaranteed in some cases the survival of local production systems. This does not mean, however, that survival was easy for those systems, or that it did not impose radical transformations in the wake of new 'international labor divisions' through the introduction of new techniques. In the three centers, relations between mechanization, enterprise concentration processes and the reorganization of the territory in productive terms, presented themselves in complex and diversified forms.[13]

3.1 Mechanization, concentration and territorial reorganization

During the 19th century in Prato, Biella and Schio, and in general in all Italian industrial centers (Dewerpe 1985), small industry coexisted with large industry and with past production forms which in reality were not in danger of extinction; on the contrary, they contributed an indispensable element to the economic dynamism when considering that concentration and mechanization did not cover all stages of the production process, according to a model that has generated wide-ranging debate on the so-called 'delayed Italian industrialization'. The persistence of the old production model was longer lasting and more significant in Prato (Archivio del Comune di Prato – ACP, *Anagrafe*, 20, 1907).

To be more specific: the spinning mechanization process, already present in the French era, decidedly caught on in the three centers following the Restoration, as a result of imports of foreign machinery (in Biella and in Schio) or following their *in situ* construction using information acquired through industrial espionage (in Prato). This mechanization went through a powerful acceleration phase in the 1830s thanks to Pietro Sella in Biella, Alessandro Rossi in Schio and Alessandro Pacchiani in Prato. The three entrepreneurs reorganized their firms to create the first properly integrated and largely mechanized mills (Castronovo 1964, 1966; Fontana 1985; Maitte 1996). These figures, considered in their respective towns as the founders of modern industry, are representative of the leading group of local entrepreneurs: their families (of artisan or commercial origin) had their roots in the expansive phase of the 1700s. They asserted themselves in the business and local community in the Napoleonic era; then, following the Restoration undertook the adaptation of Italian textile production to essentially foreign, continental models (French or Belgian) that became known to them directly through their travels in those same years.

However, processes were more complicated and contradictory than they appear. In reality in Prato, as in Biella, 'the transition from proto-industry to industry did not cause the elimination of decentralized production, but its restructuring into new forms' (Ramella 1997, p. 927).

The choice to mechanize production can be understood by looking at the evolution of social relations in the territories and not only at the lowering of costs that they eventually consented. Economic and social changes, along with the need to reduce costs, foster the choice of mechanizing the production, with different paths being followed. In Biella, such a process (started in the late 1800s) follows a typical scheme: the introduction of mechanical weaving entails the expulsion of the male workforce and the employment of women. In Prato around 1820 a high number of female spinners moved from the wool industry to the more profitable straw work production. In this case, spinning mechanization was dictated by an alteration in the labor market. Technical innovation processes, thus tended to adjust to the changeable structure of employment, determining new shapes in the gender division of work.

In central Veneto the woolen mills went through a rapid concentration and mechanization process, experimented with especially in large companies. From the 1840s onwards, the Rossi mill represented a model factory to the whole country, with further innovations in 1848 thanks to the introduction of steam energy. Conversely, Biella introduced the mechanical loom much later (around 1880) and this process came several years after the workforce concentrations that occurred between 1853 and 1867. Ramella (1984) demonstrated that mechanization was introduced when the production needs of entrepreneurs could no longer be reconciled with the proto-industrial work organization. Proto-industrial workers were able to maintain a certain autonomy from industrial work through the persistence of a strong link with agricultural activity supporting credit movement within the community. Distrustful of the factory discipline that entrepreneurs demanded, weavers organized some more or less significant strikes (in the years 1845, 1854, 1863, 1867, 1870 and especially in 1877 and 1878). Even though in those circumstances strikers' demands were met, entrepreneurs nevertheless understood that the only way to impose a different labor organization on the community was to proceed with mechanization and at the same time replace male labor with female labor. In substance, the system of implicit rules that had dominated and inspired labor organization in the territory had to be broken up. From the 1880s, entrepreneurs imposed a production model on the communities who rejected it,[14] the territory was abundantly restructured through the diffusion of immigration, to date limited to certain areas, which revealed itself as being one of the main tools that allowed the contradictions in place to be overcome.[15]

However, the mechanization process did not mean inevitable and swift concentration, or the derangement of the equilibrium previously achieved, as occurred in Biella. In reality, in Prato, several new spinning enterprises were installed by entrepreneurs from outside the wool sector, often coming from the retail trade and establishing themselves into one of the phases of the production process. These operators worked for the *impannatori* who performed the coordination duties of the production phases. This model was resisted all over the 19th century. In 1864 there were only three mills in Prato. Thirty years later little had changed: the organization of manufacturing activity retained the traditional dualism marked by severe asymmetries. On one side, few full cycle businesses, and on the other many phase businesses, above all dedicated to spinning. This duality corresponded with the coexistence of hand-weaving with mechanized spinning under the coordination of *impannatori*.[16]

At the beginning of the 1900s, city administrators describe the functioning of the Prato system:

> The manufacturer, having purchased the necessary material, has it selected by the few workers he keeps employed: he mixes it according to the kind of fabric he wants to obtain, and after having carbonized and spun the resultant wool, works the yarn in-house and then gives it to individuals who own their own looms for weaving. Following weaving, he processes the fabric through all the dyeing, finishing plants etc. to then collect it, finished, measured and packed: the skill of these manufacturers is such that no damage is caused to the continued spread of big industry, so much so as to be able to live alongside them and visibly sustain competition. (Amministrazione Comunale di Prato, Anagrafe, 20, 1907)

Often the barriers between small trade and production were very permeable particularly given the growing importance of the rag trade in the city: significant volumes of mechanized wool raw materials were re-exported from Prato through foreign buyers' brokers who put small traders and entrepreneurs in contact with the whole world. Moreover, these operators were largely present in the straw sector and massively diffused in the Tuscan countryside, and especially in the Prato territory throughout the 19th century. A prototype of a decentralized manufacturing model, this rural industry strengthened the link between the city and the surrounding territory, contributing to the dissemination of diversified activities within the sharecropper family, and facilitating the decentralization of production.

In the same period, in Biella (as in Schio), the production activity was dominated by the large integrated company that established itself thanks to the profound changes following 1860. Around 70–80 companies at the end of the century constituted more than 60 per cent of the wool processing plants of the region, giving work to more than 80 per cent of employees in the sector.

However, it is, in our view, also important to consider secondary aspects of the three contexts analyzed. At the end of the century, the few large plants that were active in Prato introduced new social models that were weakly tied to the territory and its history. In Schio, not all followed the dominant model; some companies continued to produce traditional fabrics with local raw materials, using hand-weaving and still exploiting hydraulic energy to aliment the mechanized stages. Finally, Ramella demonstrated that 'artisan' activities represented an essential long-term element of the Biellese territorial equilibrium. Often the research, mindful of identifying the typical development models, tends to ignore the cases that are judged, on the surface, as secondary.

In any case, the territorial changes in turn promoted the new localization of activities and redrew the borders of the industrial areas: the industrial area in Prato tended to be concentrated compared to the previous area characterized by rural spinning, while the rationalization of hydraulic energy exploitation imposed by growing demand also imposed the creation of new plants (Guenzi 1997). In Biella too, the hydropower demand determined the displacement of the installations in mountainous areas to the plains and the urban center, although the industrial area remained vast. It actually seemed to expand further in the 1860s when textile production, present in 32 communities, reached its maximum territorial extension. Subsequently the production area was reduced and modified: some centers were deindustrialized (Mosso Santa Maria) whilst new settlements sprung up in the lower valleys of Mosso, Strona, Lessona, Cossato.

In Schio, new plants also moved out of the urban center as entrepreneurs counted on the competition between city and country workers to keep wages low. Only after 1860 did the population of the urban center grow drastically, from 6100 inhabitants in 1860 to 12 242 in 1885 (the year in which Rossi founded the

Alta Factory).[17] As a corollary to the series of change taking place in the city, a network of institutions was created, inspired by the paternalistic model, aimed at guaranteeing, at least until end of the century, the conservation of social peace.[18]

3.2 Industrial restructuring and territorial resources

In Schio, factories developed in accordance to a classic scheme. Small hill farmers, progressively pushed into the city by both the fragmentation of property and the dissemination of vineyards and mulberry growing, were recruited by the factory. For a long time in Biella, as mentioned, the land/loom binomial dominated, determined by a proto-industrial male labor supply that in time created, for entrepreneurs, unacceptable constraints that were overcome only with mechanization and the recruitment of female workers. Finally Prato registered a stable supply of female employment together with a cheap male workforce. It would be out of place to talk of a 'late proto-industry' because they were at the same time workers in the earliest factories and domicile hand-weavers, especially in the late 1800s. They generally came from the *pigionali* families who expanded considerably in the course of the century,[19] but there were also people who lived in the city. These new workers in the wool industry did not create in Prato the problems recorded in Biella. According to Alessandra Pescarolo:

> [T]he position of Prato hand-weavers, therefore, drew in a certain sense, greater force from a greater weakness. For a long time their position remained competitive. While in Biella, at the turn of the century, the hand-weavers were by then completely excluded from the production processes, in Prato the old nucleus was able to reproduce itself. (Pescarolo 1989, pp. 62–3)

More than simply reproducing itself as it was, the system was able to rebuild itself on new bases.

These changes should be interpreted in the light of the political choices on a local and national level: whilst in Piedmont, and with less intensity in Veneto, interventions continued in favor of manufacturing production, especially textiles, with particular attention to the birth of large industrial companies, the Tuscan economic policy in the early 1800s was oriented towards free trade in order to promote the interests of landowners showing hostility towards the industrial entrepreneurs and the large companies. The diversity of these industrial policies is a decisive element in understanding the different conditions for inclusion in the markets of Prato, Schio and Biella before 1860, as the role of the Piedmont monarchy in the process of unification of the country proved, without doubt, to be a key element for the different positioning of Prato and Biella.

Biella availed itself of a market that was in many ways protected, both before and after 1860. The Piedmontese State organized a tough system of customs protection. Biella'a entrepreneurs were therefore encouraged to imitate the range of textile products, including better quality products, which the previous government under the old regime had tried to prohibit. The high–medium quality product markets led entrepreneurs to raise the quality control, as happened also in Schio, where Rossi developed high-quality woven fabrics. Furthermore, the State commissioned the largest part of cloth in the region for the army: these safer markets ensured profitability of the fixed capital investment.

The situation was very different in Prato: following the Restoration, the government's free trade policy opened the regional market to foreign competition, in particular to the growing imports of low-quality English textile products. For entrepreneurs in Prato the risk of not being able to place their products on the market grew. For the whole first half of the 19th century, they chose to follow a productive model based on cost cutting, on a reliance on home labor and on production diversification. From 1860s onwards, following Italian unification, new markets opened up: Prato and Schio were the first ones in Italy to introduce wool regeneration techniques arising from a process developed in England at the beginning of the century. In Prato, the innovation of this process determined the birth of a new product made with this new fiber, the quality of which confirms a production choice towards low-cost woven fabrics. In the 1870s, one of the top products was an extremely low-priced regenerated wool shawl intended for the low end of the market. While in Schio, the introduction of regenerated wool reinforced a model of firm concentration, in Prato alongside the traditional model of several small and economically weak companies, operated also some more mechanized and therefore more vertically-integrated firms that internalized a number of different production phases under the same roof. These two production models justified themselves in the function of the outlet markets: the standardized low-cost goods produced in large quantities, for the domestic market first and then, in the late 1800s, for 'underdeveloped countries' (China, India, South Africa), whilst fabrics for women's garments required flexibility to adapt to changes in fashion, a broad product portfolio, and contained costs. Finally, at the end of the 19th century, Prato's production structure resembled an ID more closely than Biella's or Schio's.

4. CONCLUSIONS

As underlined by the ample historiography, there are different geneses of districts and it would be illusory to attempt to identify a model that is applicable in any context; on the other hand, instead of discussing districts from the Middle Ages up to today, it seems more interesting to investigate the wealth of resources that in time settled in particular territories. This process has helped these territories to keep their industrial vocation in the long term (with or without continuity in relation to products), encouraging in some cases the birth of new districts in the 20th century. The three cases presented clearly show how the propensity to consolidate industrial activities in time is based on a series of elements: the technical knowledge accumulated through the industrial events indicated – at least from the 1700s onwards – the continuous adaptation to turbulent markets; the predisposition to innovation and imitation; the interventions of adaptation of territorial resources for manufacturing activity; and the stable network of relations with external markets (regional and supra-regional); the system of intermediary institutions that on a local level were able to coordinate enterprises and, according to Belfanti's interpretation, facilitated access to credit. However, continuity does not automatically coincide with the absence of rifts. Two of the cases investigated had moments of deep schisms: in Schio, which Fontana defined as a 'proto-district', the way to large industry was accompanied in the 19th century by the 'apparent decline of the previous production nebula deeply rooted in the territory' (Fontana 1997, p. 52). In Biella too, in the second half of the 1800s, the human capital and the social relation models of that territory appeared incompatible with the industrial development processes pursued by manufacturers and were drastically changed. In Prato, things went a different way. The break-up of the relation between the industry and the territory never took place; on the contrary, the appearance of a single large firm (*Il Fabbricone*) introduced innovative elements in the complex territorial articulation without overturning it.

It has now become quite common to speak of IDs in relation to the early modern era, but to hold on to a concept originally created in order to understand certain forms of contemporary industrialization creates some problems. First of all, to speak of IDs in the case of Prato, Biella and Schio at the end of the 1700s implies the assumption, demonstrated well in these three cases, that IDs take very different shapes from spatial and institutional organizations. This is a point that certainly deserves further thought. But above all, we must acknowledge what the concept of IDs adds to our understanding of manufacturing organizations. Stressing the links between community and enterprise, between the industrial system and local institutions, on the conveyance of informal knowledge, as well as on the processes of collective innovation – and this list is by no means exhaustive – is of great significance. One could focus on the externalization of costs, highlighting the importance of independent workers and firms competing and cooperating at the same time in a flexible production system marked by the specialization of production stages. However, this latter approach would dangerously turn every preindustrial organized territory into an ID, thereby impoverishing this concept into a useless tool of analysis.

The process of adjustment to the background conditions, pointed out by the cases that have been provided, seems to confirm the existence of various paths of development. It is noteworthy that these differences emerge even when potentially unifying factors, like those deriving from the common specialization in wool cloth production, are at work. These diverging paths, that involve both the form and the time through which the development processes takes place, can be understood only by considering two features together. The first is related to the basic background resources; the second concerns those actions that are carried out by organized parts of the local society (entrepreneurs, associations, community banks, professional training schools and, more generally, local government bodies) to mobilize and reallocate these resources on the basis of a conscious strategy.

NOTES

1. As shown in a number of studies from Italian and Anglo-Saxon historiography, long-time pioneers in this field. For France, see Lescure (2006); Daumas, Lamard and Tissot (2007).
2. Maitte (2001); see also Becattini (1997); Fasano Guarini (1986); Mori (1989); Terrier (1997).
3. For example, the region of Biella had a density of more than 180 inhabitants per km^2 in the 18th century, see Quazza (1961).
4. There is a lot of research on this subject: see, for example, Dewerpe (1985); Cafagna (1989); and all the works of C. Poni.
5. On this product, see Valensi (1969) and Maitte (2004, pp. 1115–42).
6. See the study by Malanima (1990) based on the Tuscany situation.
7. It is in fact impossible to consider that the growth of production was due to the protection of the regional markets because smuggling was very important in the three States; Panciera (1996 p. 95) affirms that 'substantial freedom of trade' existed in the State of Venice and the same situation can be found in Tuscany and Piedmont (on this region, see Biblioteca Reale di Torino – BRT, *Storia Patria*, 851).
8. Panciera (1988). The English technician T. Bamford observed at the end of the 18th century that local 'entrepreneurs' had already introduced the necessary innovations.
9. Florence, but also Rome and Naples and certainly Venice.
10. Cento Bull (1989); see also Belfanti and Maccabelli (1997); it is impossible to consider the rural weavers of Biella as representative of the agricultural class.
11. Ciriacono (1985, p. 317); see also Quazza (1961); Maitte (2001). It is also important to remember that productions other than textiles existed in these territories.
12. This opposition can be found elsewhere, for example in the Eupen-Acquisgrana region: see Gayot (2003).
13. For international comparisons, see Terrier (1996 and 1998); Fontana (1997); Fontana and Gayot (2004); Lescure (2006); Daumas, Lamard and Tissot (2007).
14. A dynamic that recalls that described for northern France by Terrier (1996).
15. Although Fontaine (1996, pp. 739–56) rightly notes that the migratory phenomenon cannot be considered only as the result of misery and defeat.
16. The oldest use of the term that we know dates back to the beginning of the 1800s and is relatively derogatory.
17. This creation, however, was followed by a policy of 'territorial decentralization' adopted by Rossi himself: see Fontana (1990, p. xl).
18. For this transition, see Fontana (1985).
19. The *pigionali* rent their houses and differ from sharecroppers.

3. Apprenticeship and technical schools in the formation of industrial districts

Elisabetta Merlo

1. INTRODUCTION

Since industrial districts (IDs) have been discovered as units of analysis by economists and sociologists, economic historians have been increasingly requested to give their own contribution to the explanation of the emergence of concentrations of highly-specialised firms which benefit from skilled labour, suppliers, information, along with services provided by a large variety of associations and institutions, usually located within the district itself. This chapter focuses on some historical evidence on the role played by apprenticeship and technical schools in the formation of the Marshallian industrial atmosphere which helped the emergence of some IDs. Indeed, the rich literature devoted to the study of the organisation of the European urban economies in the preindustrial age depicts a social and institutional environment that paved the way for the subsequent achievements or failures in the development of the IDs.

Accordingly the importance of urban guilds and technical schools will be analysed in order to investigate if: (a) they really acted as the repository of a community's business, technological, legal and material culture that seems to be a distinctive feature of the IDs still today; and (b) if they were actively involved in building up cohesive and durable (or weak and transitory) epistemic communities (Håkanson 2005). This concept is borrowed by the economic literature and applicable to networks of knowledge in which membership is obtained – typically through some combination both of formal and on-the-job training and tacit as well as codified technical information – only after having achieved the complete mastery of the codes, theories and tools employed in a specific practice.

As far as the empirical analysis is concerned, some of the IDs which emerged in Europe during the 18th and 19th centuries will be compared as they provide interesting examples both of failure and success. Section 2 deals with the district of Vigevano, not far from Milan, which in the 1980s changed its specialisation from the footwear industry to the mechanical one. Section 3 focuses on the district of Como – an Italian town near Switzerland – which in the 18th century tried unsuccessfully to develop its silk industry and eventually in the 20th century specialised in dyeing silk and synthetic fabrics. Section 4 concerns the ID of Lyon which in the 18th century achieved an international standing as a producer of luxury silk fabrics. Section 5 concludes by attempting to suggest an interpretation of the role played by guilds and technical schools in fuelling districts' takeoff as well as in sustaining their economic growth.

2. VIGEVANO

The history of the shoemaking ID of Vigevano has apparently weak links with the guilds which were formerly active in this town. Indeed, documentary evidence referring to the presence of a group of footwear craftsmen in Vigevano dates back as far as the second half of the 16th century. Within this group there was a clear social and professional distinction between the shoe craftsman who produced new shoes in workshops and the cobblers who carried out shoe repairs and sold second-hand footwear. However, the craft of shoemaking remained for a long time a minority activity within the urban economy, where silk production was certainly more important, and the economy was mainly composed of products destined to a non-elite public. The processing of silk took over from the production of woollen cloth, which during the 16th century had been the main occupation among the manufacturing activities in Vigevano, and grew in the subsequent centuries, resulting in a continuous increase in the number of silk workers. By the end of the 19th century over half of the town's workforce was active in silk manufacturing (741 workers out of a total of 1385). During the same period the first manufacturing groups of the embryonic footwear district appeared in Vigevano. Their origins date back to the late 1860s when brothers Pietro and Luigi Bocca, who had worked for a time in a footwear workshop in Milan, moved to Vigevano and set up a business which in 1872 had 35 workers. In its early years this business was a school for enterprise and a model which inspired the first footwear factories, but it was only after 1887, thanks to the duty levied on imported shoes, that the footwear business flourished. One after another numerous shoe factories sprung up in Vigevano while capital, entrepreneurs and commercial representatives flocked there. American and German machinery started to be imported and firms producing spare parts were set up. According to the industrial census of 1911 – which in any case did not take into account the numerous independent craftsmen who worked from home in the various stages of footwear production or who made the single components – the shoe sector had by then become the most important industry in Vigevano in terms of both firms and workers.[1]

From its origins, the district of Vigevano specialised in the production of ladies' and children's shoes. Such a specialisation corresponded to a manufacturing process whereby the upper part was nailed to the sole, instead of being stitched. This method, which had been introduced in the US in 1778, was preferred to the machine stitching invented during the mid-19th century and promptly developed with a series of innovations that had resulted in superior quality and uniformity of production. The nailing technique, which spread throughout Europe during the first half of the 19th century, was initially used for the industrial production of coarse footwear, as it required using thicker soles than those that were normally stitched. Subsequent improvements of the nailing machines led to their use also in the manufacture of shoes for female customers – more sensitive to changes in fashion than males – and to the children's sector which, like the female, had little interest in a solid, long-lasting product. In fact, shoes which had been nailed were less sturdy than stitched ones, not only because of the different characteristics of the two techniques, but also due to the frequent use of poor quality material which was more suited to being nailed than stitched. The nailing technique – introduced by the Bocca brothers in Vigevano in 1873 – requested workers who – in an environment so dependent on the supply of machines from abroad – knew how the machines worked, and how to intervene on them in case of breakdown, and were able to introduce small changes in order to improve the machines' performance.

As a matter of fact, the shoemaking district of Vigevano was born basically under conditions of technological backwardness and specialisation in the production of low-quality footwear. Such conditions may be related to the dependence on Milan. Vigevano was a centre where manufacturing had been the prime occupation of the population since the 16th century but it could be said that, unlike the majority of little towns scattered in northern Italy, it had remained one of the economic suburbs of Milan throughout the centuries. In 1589 the Town Council members complained that Milan had a hypnotic influence on traders, entrepreneurs, workers and capital causing them to leave the small town attracted by the prospects of profit which could be offered only by a large urban economy, sitting at the crossroads of the most important commercial and cultural routes. The guilds, which participated with the Town Council in the government of the local economy, did not manage to come up with effective measures to stop the emigration of production, managerial and financial resources. At the end of the 1800s – when the first firms producing shoes began to appear, thanks to the initiative of two shoemakers who had been apprentices in Milan – the situation had probably not changed very much. According to a report by the Chamber of Commerce in 1892, the vicinity of Milan influenced all forms of commerce in general and in particular that of ladies' fashion articles, because it was thought that Milan produced more beautiful and better quality shoes. So all the district could do was to concentrate on producing shoes which were imitations of the elegant Milanese ones but without the same quality.

The First World War represented the occasion that confirmed the commercial strategies and the technological choices that had distinguished the district right from its origins. When hostilities began the shoe producers formed a consortium in order to enrol for the award by the State of rationed raw materials necessary for producing civilian shoes. Thanks to the exploitation of such a market opportunity, the footwear industry of Vigevano entered smoothly into the international scenario of the post-war years and at the beginning of the 1920s it began to export.

The problem of professional training was totally forgotten until 1935. In that year the *Istituto Roncalli* – which had started its activity in 1870 with training courses for blacksmiths, mechanics, carpenters, builders, stonecutters and decorators – set up a school for the footwear workers. Local producers equipped the school with the latest machinery for footwear manufacture. There were 146 students in the first year, but by 1941 this number was considerably lower: only 20 students were enrolled in the course for cutters of shoe uppers, while 64 students attended the evening course for stitchers of uppers. The school reproduced a factory environment with classes identical to workrooms, worktables instead of desks, and lessons focused on craft techniques. Finally, the war put a stop to this initiative that had never been a real alternative to on-the-job training. Such a failure in endowing the district with a technical school was a symptom of the crisis which exploded just a few years later. Following a post-war decade of ephemeral expansion achieved mainly thanks to the availability of a large unskilled labour force from the poorer parts of the country, during the 1960s the growth of Vigevano's footwear industry began to slow down. Between 1963 and 1965 the number of firms fell from 970 to 920 (they were 730 in 1954) and production dropped from 27.5 million to 22 million pairs of leather shoes per year. The national market absorbed only 5 million pairs compared with 17 million in 1955, while the share of exports fell from 14 per cent to 6 per cent of the national total. Not surprisingly, the skilled workers exited from shoe manufacturing during the restructuring of the 1970s, and migrated to the industry of shoe-production machinery contributing to the process of transformation of the district.

As far as apprenticeship is concerned, guilds are usually supposed to regulate it in order to guarantee high-quality output. However, in environments stressed by competition and market turbulence like those they all had to face, guilds tended to use apprenticeship primarily as a means to mobilize and allocate labour, knowledge and skills across time and space. In Vigevano – like elsewhere – such a role was part of an articulated involvement of guilds in the civic political action aimed to ensure for the local business community a stable presence within the surrounding economic region which was dominated by the supremacy of the major cities.

As a matter of fact, it is suggested that in order to understand how guilds contributed to shape the industrial atmosphere of Vigevano we have to think about apprenticeship as a means through which a business community actively reacts to changes in external conditions instead of seeing it just as a means to provide itself with intergenerational continuity.

The analysis of Como's silk district, that can be considered representative of IDs generated by proto-industrial activities, allows us to further deepen this topic.

3. COMO

The economy of Como, a town located in northern Italy close to the Swiss border, began to be dominated by the silk industry during the mid-18th century when the manufacture of the 'golden thread' started to sustain the demographic and economic recovery of the town, encouraged the re-forming of an artisan class which had disappeared during the Spanish rule, and boosted exports to Vienna and the main German fairs.[2] At the beginning of the 20th century, after over a century of continued crises and ephemeral recoveries, 82 per cent of all hand looms and 78 per cent of all power looms of the Italian silk industry were located in Como and its province.

The mechanisation of weaving dates back to the early 1770s when the Franco-Prussian war, having momentarily depressed foreign competition, offered new development prospects for Como's silk production. The spread of the power loom gave a strong boost to the process of centralisation of silk manufacture but did not completely undermine the methods of production which had been in use since the mid-1600s and which were based on three figures: the weaver, working at home or in the workshop of the head-weaver, who alternated his work between the loom and the fields; the head-weaver who supplied the technical knowledge, the means of production and the workroom where the production was carried out; the *fabbricatore*, a merchant who took care of the commercial aspects of the work – taking orders and distributing the product on the market – and who supplied the circulating capital. This division of work was the organisational reaction to the peculiarities that characterised the production and trading of silk cloth in general, but also reflected some features specific to the Como context. The joint participation of the head-weaver and the *fabbricatore* in the firm's financial outlays, and the clear distinction between the technical and the commercial responsibilities, suggest that the production and trading of silk were high-risk activities requiring specific skills. The silk cloth market was indeed extremely uncertain, being an international market continuously shaken by political turbulence. Furthermore, silk fabric as an article was at the mercy of fashion whims and, like all luxury goods, its consumption was extremely sensitive to variations in purchasing power.

The division of work between the *fabbricatore*, the head-weaver and the weaver was also based on the possibility of offloading the effects of alternating business trends onto the weavers, who were thrown out of work as soon as trends became unfavourable, only to return once the demand for silk began to increase again. As a result, the lack of qualified labour was a constant problem throughout the history of silk production in Como at the point that since its beginnings the international market associated the name of Como with poor quality silk, a thin cheap cloth even more vulnerable to the drop in excess income available for the purchase of luxuries than was the luxury damask fabric itself. Without suitable credit instruments and market stability, the contrast between the costs necessary to train workers and the immediate benefits deriving from the wide availability of cheap labour had dissuaded entrepreneurs and merchants from investing in apprenticeship, which was an investment with a long-term return. Instead of being a conveyor of technical knowledge, the head-weaver's workroom became just a container for occasional work. That does not mean that guilds had given up the training of their members. Rather, their focus moved from training craftsmen endowed with the complete mastery of the codes, theories and tools employed in manufacturing silk to training merchants endowed with skills in trading low quality silk in an extremely competitive market.

As a matter of fact, the new institutional actor which entered into the local scenario starting from the early 1800s – the Chamber of Commerce – was strongly influenced by the path of development outlined by its predecessors. The heir of the merchant guilds from which it descended, this institution soon recognised that a good weaver had to master weaving techniques as well as to speak at least one foreign language in order to cope with the tougher competitors, the export markets and the trendsetters who were the arbiters of European taste. Furthermore, as it was by then recognised that Como's silk could not face foreign competitors as far as weft and warp were concerned, the new frontier of knowledge moved towards research on design and colours. These were the ambitious training aims of the *Scuola di Setificio* (silk factory school) which was instituted in 1866 with the support of local entrepreneurs: from financing to teaching, from purchasing the fabrics produced by the students to the placing of orders for the research and execution of new designs and fabrics. The course of chemical dyeing was one of five specialist courses – the others were weaving, mechanics and machine design, textile technology, technical and artistic design – included in the three-year studies, in addition to lessons in basic subjects like Italian, accounting and foreign languages.

It only took a few years from the beginning of the 1900s, when over half of Como's silk production was still being sent abroad for dyeing, for extraordinary progress to be made, to the extent that in 1918 Como was dyeing 70 per cent of all the fabrics dyed in Italy. By mid-century the core of Como's textile industry was gravitating towards the finishing phases of fabric production – silk, but also artificial and synthetic ones – which still today distinguish the district. According to details supplied by the association of industrialists of the sector, whose offices were located in Como, the dyeing firms of the district were equipped with the latest machinery and were capable of performing every dyeing, printing and finishing operation on any type of yarn or fabric and of executing any type of decorative pattern proposed by the art designers and art studios located throughout the town working at the service of the silk industry.

It is not possible to describe the entire course which led to the birth of the silk factory school. However, its story mirrors the changes of the entrepreneurial, institutional and social context as it faced the growth opportunities and the destabilising effects related to technological innovation. The power loom created a gap between the older generation of entrepreneurs – who had remained firmly anchored to the hand-loom and to a decentralised production organisation – and the new owners of small firms which were equipped and organised in a modern way. It also separated the destiny of the old weavers from the young ones who saw the opportunity of new promising training paths. A new place to socialise – the factory – emerged alongside the traditional ones of the family home and the workroom. However, it was the idea of introducing an apprenticeship carried out in the chemical dyeing laboratory – not in addition, but as an alternative to the teaching of weaving techniques – that was a truly innovative step in the gestation of the silk factory school. Thanks to this intuition – which originated from imitating the experience of the French competitors, but also from an awareness of the transformations in the chemical industry, which in precisely those years was discovering artificial colourings – the silk factory school was able to give an autonomous contribution to the consolidation of Como's silk district, in particular to the transformation of its specialisation from the production of silk fabrics to the dyeing and finishing of silk fabrics – one of the most critical stages in terms of added value. Soon Como silk fabrics made a name for themselves on the international markets thanks to their unmistakeable striking colours, rather than the quality of the fabrics or the merit of the designs which were obtained through a special weaving of the yarn rather than being printed onto the fabric.

By comparing the continued crises suffered by preindustrial silk producers and merchants to the big spurt experienced after the emergence of school-based training, the snapshot of the history of Como's silk introduces us to a topic – to what extent guilded craftsmen were really skilled – largely debated by economic historians. Notwithstanding the deep clash dividing those who believe that guilds were neither necessary nor sufficient for ensuring craft skills, from those who are firmly convinced that guilds offered a superior organisational matrix for the acquisition and deployment of skills (Ogilvie 2004 and S.R. Epstein 1998 respectively), they all share the opinion that innovation depends on skills. Accordingly, what we can infer from the results obtained by the *Scuola di Setificio* is that attitudes and propensity to innovation are strongly sensitive to the skills embedded in human capital, whereas, as argued by the most recent literature on Italian IDs (Grandi 2007), the institutionalisation of school-based technical education can be considered a turning point in the process which makes school the main actor of long-term human capital accumulation, independently from the short-term fluctuation in labour demand.

However, guilds – and, later, technical schools – were not the sole providers of skills. Female employment in Lyonese silk industry allows looking at the role played by guilds in shaping IDs from the side of non-guilded apprenticeship.

4. LYON

After Paris, Lyon was the second largest city in 17th century France. In the economy of Lyon traditional activities coexisted with technologically advanced businesses. The city was crowded with merchants and craftsmen. Four times a year a fair, which attracted tradesman coming from across the continent, was held within its walls. At the end of the 17th century, when the European aristocracy began to look at the French royal court as the undisputed trendsetter in fashion, Lyon achieved an international standing as the main silk producer in Europe.[3]

At that time, five silk guilds existed in Lyon. Each one was specialised in a different phase of the silk pipeline, from loom makers to merchants passing through the thread dyers, the warp winders and the silk weavers. They formed the *Grande Fabrique* (The Big Factory) something like a large cooperative industry which counted more than 18 000 master silk weavers. However, because of the increasing importance acquired by the international market in influencing the strategies of the producers, during the 18th century the power of the master silk weavers weakened whereas merchants came to dominate within the *Fabrique*. Indeed, such a change in the professional hierarchy was fuelled by an innovative commercial practice introduced by the merchants of Lyon who were the first 'to use annual product differentiation as a strategic weapon to create barriers to entry, to capture important shares of the international market and to outmanoeuvre firms in competition with them' (Poni 1997, p. 41). As a matter of fact, the introduction of short-life products led manufacturers and merchants to go round – and even to infringe – the guilds' rules which prevented them from increasing their flexibility in order to adapt quickly to the fickle changes of fashion.

Available historical sources provide evidence that guilds managed apprenticeship in order to transmit and improve technical knowledge as well as to balance the labour demand and supply.[4] However, obligations concerning age, sex and social status which regulated the apprenticeship were among the rules more frequently disobeyed, at the point that the border between legal and illegal work became faded and slippery. Women, who were excluded from benefiting from the right to set up their own atelier, took advantage of the situation.

Normally, they had familiarised themselves with craft techniques in many ways besides apprenticeship, such as by attending sewing and spinning schools for poor girls, by serving as a maid in a family whose workshop was part of the household, by helping relatives involved in artisan activities. Being skilled in manufacturing silk and well introduced into the workshop, women set up their own ateliers in which they manufactured raw materials sometimes stolen from the master weavers who had trained them. Notwithstanding the official protests of guilds, in 18th-century Lyon

> the black market manufacturing sector created by women workers became a significant factor in the city's economy. Although it is impossible to document the number of individuals involved or the exact value of diverted production, this group of female artisans formed a system of illegal work that paralleled legitimate production. (Hafter 2001 p. 27).

In 1786 women won the right to become master weavers. Before then 'both theft of materials and illegal craft gave businesses needed flexibility, and unsupervised space in which to manoeuvre within the restrictions of the preindustrial economy' (ibid., p. 34). According to such historical evidence, one can reasonably assume that illegal business carried on by women in Lyon has been an essential complement of the regulated economy rather than a mere chance at disposal of a residual category of workers.

The French Revolution marked a turning point in the history of the European capital of the silk industry. Before then

> the Lyonese fabrique had been regulated by a series of old regime guilds and corporate institutions whose operation had been modified to permit greater innovation in products and production technologies. The revolutionaries' liberal program included the abolition of all such restraints on trade . . . The absence of a regulatory regime and the disruption of traditional market connections then paralyzed the silk trade. As they waited for trade conditions to stabilize, the Lyonese undertook a radical reconstruction of their old institutions. Their aim was to offset the power of the mercantile elite which had dominated the old-regime corporation by giving greater weight to representatives of the manufacturers and master weavers. (Sabel and Zeitlin 1997a, p. 26)

Indeed, apprenticeship remained a means to learn technical skills but diffusion of knowledge and innovations was also ensured by institutions and voluntary societies. In 1805 the *Ecole des Beaux-Arts* was established with the aim of training designers who provided the *Grande Fabrique* with constantly-renewed decorative patterns. The *Ecole* was strictly connected with the local *Musée des Beaux-Arts*, created in 1799 on the model of the *Conservatoire National des Arts et Métiers*. The *Musée* was managed by François Artaud – appointed head of the school in 1896 – and was run by the *Conseil du Conservatoire des arts*, that was in part comprised of silk manufacturers. These institutions did not restrict themselves to the diffusion of knowledge and innovations; they provided a place for debates between the leading inventors ..., launched research programs in the shape of public competitions ..., encouraged competition among loom-builders within the trade and brought public recognition for the respective contributions of each. (Cottereau 1997, p. 144)

Voluntary and official learned institutions born in Lyon at the beginning of the 19th century provide evidence that a new culture of technical supremacy was definitively moving forward, based on sharing knowledge protected by patenting innovations rather than by restricting access to it to a narrow circle of disciples. As a matter of fact, by building on the trend initiated at the beginning of the 18th century, silk remained France's leading export throughout the entire 19th century.

5. CONCLUSIONS

What can we infer from the districts of Vigevano, Como and Lyon about the role of guilds and technical schools in building up epistemic communities and how they can be considered typical? Indeed, the extreme heterogeneity – as far as performance, manufacturing organisation, and commercial strategies were concerned – described by the concise profiles outlined above makes it truly difficult to provide an unambiguous interpretation. Yet, the debate between historians who believe that guilds generated social capital that benefits the wider economy and historians convinced that they created monopoly rents for their members, can provide us with some useful suggestions, starting from the relevance of the context in which guilds were established and evolved.

Focusing on the phase of gestation of some IDs, one could well say that strenuous competition together with uncertainty and risk due to unpredictable changes in consumers' taste, are the main characteristics shared by the atmosphere in which the IDs of Vigevano, Como and Lyon were originated. They competed in order to gain market shares, to secure entrepreneurial resources, to attract knowledge and techniques, to adapt promptly to changes in consumers' taste and even to anticipate them. Comparison between Vigevano on one side, and Como and Lyon on the other, shows that those who introduced cost-saving innovations such as mechanical equipment and labour-saving techniques had a few chances to succeed in defeating competitors, compelling them to adjust or even change competitive strategies. On the contrary, the international standing eventually achieved by Como relies on high value-added innovations represented by the introduction of sophisticated methods of ennobling silk and synthetic fabrics. The same applies to the district of Lyon which emerged as the most important producer of silk in Europe thanks to the introduction of an innovative commercial practice – the annual product differentiation – along with an increasing juridical tolerance in applying the guilds' norms regulating the relationship between legitimated business and unlawful female work.

Comparison also shows that skills matter as far as attitudes, propensity and even the kind of innovation – cost saving or high value added – are concerned. Yet, as well demonstrated by female employment in Lyon, neither were craft guilds the sole providers of skills nor did apprenticeship have the sole aim of training human capital endowed with the mastery of the codes, theories and tools employed in a specific practice. Rather, apprenticeship – workshop or school-based – was a means to allocate labour across time and space in order to reduce unbalances between supply and demand. It was also a means to enforce quality standards and, therefore, to create a market for producers of lower-quality commodities.

In the end, institutions training workers as well as entrepreneurs can play a decisive role in shaping an epistemic community which, however, can be inclined either to produce a new source of competitive advantage, or to confirm traditional sources of weakness. The alternative depends on the attitude to assume the ambitious task 'to overcame the hurdles of technical transmission: how to teach skills, how to allocate costs to provide teachers and pupils with adequate incentives, and how to monitor the labour market to avoid major imbalances between supply and demand for skilled labour' (S.R. Epstein 1998). This is the task which allows institutions to succeed in providing districts with skilled labour, a source of innovations for the local knowledge network and an anti-cyclical instrument which could allow the effects of market fluctuations to be mitigated and even successfully opposed rather than passively suffered by firms. Institutions training workers as well as entrepreneurs can also play a decisive role in shaping epistemic communities sharing a distinctive and sophisticated understanding of competitors, markets, trends and tastes, besides the explicit and tacit elements of knowledge that inform a specific practice. This is a strategic resource for bridging the narrow economic region which usually hosts the emergence of high-specialised industrial clusters and the wider economic space which is decisive in feeding their subsequent development.

NOTES

1. This section is largely based on information and data extracted from Caizzi (1955); Sabbatucci Severini (1999); Merlo (1992); Bravo and Merlo (2002).
2. This section is largely based on information and data extracted from Caizzi (1957); Severin (1962); Guenzi (1986); Zaninelli (1987–2004); Cento Bull and Corner (1993); I. Cipolla (2001–02).
3. This section is largely based on information and data extracted from Garden (1969); Zemon Davis (1982); Cottereau (1997); Poni (1997); Hafter (2001).
4. See Garden (1969) who has collected and in-depth analysed a large amount of contracts between Lyonese silk masters and apprentices.

4. The emergence and development of industrial districts in industrialising England, 1750–1914

Andrew Popp and John F. Wilson

1. INTRODUCTION

In its industrial and business dimensions, the industrial revolution in England was a grass-roots, bottom-up and essentially undirected process in which the formation of industrial districts (IDs) played a fundamental and formative role. The formation and development of these districts reflected micro-processes taking place at the regional and subregional level. Thus, it can be argued that 18th-century England was the birthplace of the ID as a concrete form of industrial organisation and as a historically-located socio-economic phenomenon. Similarly, late 19th-century England was the birthplace of the ID concept, as witnessed in the pioneering work of Alfred Marshall (1919). Nonetheless, English IDs have been relatively neglected, both in the historiography of English industrialisation and in the wider theoretical and empirical literature on the ID concept. This chapter will trace and seek to explain the emergence and development of IDs in England in the period 1750–1914. In addition, the chapter will seek to assess the wider contribution to be made to the development of the ID concept through a study of the English districts.

The chapter will be structured in five sections. Section 1 is introductory and will state and justify claims for the centrality of IDs to the process and experience of industrialisation in England from the mid-18th century onwards. In so doing, we will explore the place of IDs in the historiography of English industrialisation and of the part they played in Marshall's initial formulation of the ID concept. Section 2 will survey the emergence, growth and development of IDs in England in the period from the mid-18th century to the outbreak of the First World War, paying particular attention to the sectors characterised by the formation of IDs, their structural and organisational characteristics, geographical locations and spatiality, and the timing of their emergence, growth, maturation and, in some cases, decline. It will be seen that English IDs do not fit a simple template in reference either to themselves of the 'Italianate' ideal. They were to be found across a range of very different sectors, displayed differing structural and organisational forms, differing socio-economic bases and did not conform to a single timeframe. Indeed, new IDs continued to emerge throughout the period studied, even as others declined.

Section 3 will nonetheless attempt to identify key generalities in terms of the forces that drove the emergence and development of IDs in England and will assess the impact of the specific historical and spatial context within which their development took place. In particular, it will be argued that English IDs are best understood as a central feature of England's status as an early industrialising nation, indeed as the world's 'first industrial nation' (Mathias 1969). This framework, it will be argued, is more pertinent than one based on the concept of proto-industrialisation. Thus, England's IDs did not represent merely a continuation and deepening of existing preindustrial concentrations (indeed, as is well known, several of the most significant proto-industrial regions in England failed to make the transition to full industrialisation). Instead, they were fundamentally new and radical formations and the industrial revolution in England was at its heart driven by and dependent on their creation. Significant features of the context into which these new districts emerged include England's status as not only a first mover in industrialisation but also the wider macroeconomic, political and social effects associated with her emerging hegemonic position in international trade and politics (particularly empire), the emergence of a distinctive political economy, her socio-cultural attributes, and her geography, natural resource endowments, infrastructure developments and experience of urbanisation. Thus, IDs emerged in England in the context of a nation that was not only undergoing an unprecedented process of industrialisation, but also one that was already highly urbanised and had experienced a commensurate 'consumer revolution'. All of these factors impacted on the character and developmental trajectories of English IDs.

Section 4 will explore the dynamics experienced by English IDs. Adopting a life-cycle perspective, particular attention will be paid to both the forces driving the growth and development of IDs in England and to the mechanism through which IDs accommodated themselves to these pressures for change. Networks, operating at a range of geographical scales, will be highlighted as particularly important mechanisms of accommodation – or governance. However, we will also highlight how the role played by networks was far from straightforward. In particular, we will see how networks could operate to frustrate pressure for change and adaptation, most especially during the saturation and maturity phases of the district life cycle.

The final section will, by way of conclusion, assess the place of English IDs in relation to a number of important debates in economic and business history, economic geography and area studies. These include the relationship between

IDs and the process of industrialisation and between IDs and economic and industrial decline in England. Relevant here is the Chandlerian thesis (Chandler 1990). Crucially, we will assess how the study of English IDs can contribute to the development of the ID concept itself. Here we will argue that the example provided by the English IDs calls for a 'thicker' and richer definition of the ID than has hitherto emerged from the study of IDs in other national contexts and timeframes, giving the English case a position of some importance in general analyses of the concept.

2. IDs AND INDUSTRIALISATION IN ENGLAND

Accounts of the first industrial revolution in England have conventionally focused on a few core industries, on changes in the methods, organisation, and technologies of production, on rates of economic growth in general and productivity in particular, and on resulting improvements in living standards, and have typically been undertaken at aggregate levels of analysis (Mathias 1969). The principal units of analysis have been the nation, the industry or sector, and, less commonly, the firm. In terms of sectoral biases, the focus has been on a few core, 'staple' industries; notably cotton, coal, iron and steel, heavy engineering trades such as shipbuilding, and, to a lesser extent perhaps, pottery. Excluded or relatively neglected have been a wide swathe of other sectors, non-production-oriented aspects of industrial and economic change, such as in marketing and distribution, and, most importantly for our purposes, regions. The result, it can be argued, is a skewed or incomplete understanding of the process of industrialisation. Two arguments are salient. The complex socio-economic changes involved in industrialisation occurred across a broader economic front than has in the past been allowed, and those processes unfolded or worked themselves out at a regional and subregional rather than national level.

Certainly the staple industries, and cotton especially, were central to Britain's increasingly dominant position in international trade. However, alongside the dramatic and highly-visible transformations taking place in sectors such as cotton, steel and iron, a whole host of other industries and trades were revolutionised in subtle but far-reaching ways across the long 18th-century: woollen textiles, lace and hosiery, pottery, jewellery, hardware, tools and cutlery, furniture, clothing and other forms of apparel (such as gloves), footwear, 'toys', trinkets and household ornaments, foodstuffs and brewing, watches and clocks, and light engineering. The transformation of these sectors occurred in step with and was supported by comparable revolutions in marketing, distribution and retailing, and by societal shifts in attitudes towards consumption and fashion (McKendrick, Brewer and Plumb 1982). It is these sectors, and the locations with which they became so intimately associated, from Birmingham, to Stoke-on-Trent, to Sheffield, that can rightly claim to have earned England the title of 'workshop of the world'. The latter phrase is both telling and accurate, for these were workshop- rather than factory-based trades. Few of them saw dramatic, 'revolutionary' changes in either technologies or scale of production, at least at the level of the individual business or production unit. Transformation was powered instead by shifts in organisation and by the proliferation of firms and production units. The underlying economic logic was one of generating and exploiting latent externalised economies of scale and scope. The results, over the course of the 18th and 19th centuries, were vast increases in production, in numbers employed, and a revolution in the conditions of life experienced by the majority of the population. At the same time, some of these industries, such as pottery, generated significant export trades and played their part, alongside the staple industries, in cementing Britain's international position. Their contribution to the English experience of industrialisation, in both quantitative and qualitative terms, is hard to overestimate.

As such, and as already indicated, these processes necessarily took on a powerful and distinctive spatial character in which concentrated 'hotspots' of economic and industrial activity took centre stage. Staple industries such as coal and iron were necessarily tied to particular locations through their reliance on natural resource endowments, but in those trades thriving in the shadow of the core trades quite different spatial forces and processes were at work. Crucially, this was as true of 'King Cotton', centred on Manchester, as it was of pottery in North Staffordshire, specialty steel, tools and cutlery in Sheffield, or hardware, tools, toys, and jewellery in Birmingham and the wider West Midlands (Tweedale 1995; Hopkins, 1998; Rose 2000).

In these and other centres small, flexible, specialised, partial process firms proliferated, drawing on deepening wellsprings of skilled labour, craft knowledge, potential entrepreneurs, localised sources of credit and finance and geographically-dense networks of interconnection rooted in family, religion and, above all else, locality. These dense local interconnections facilitated the transmission of information, goods and finance. Barriers to entry were progressively lowered and dynamic, centripetal forces set in train. Capabilities became focused on producing a dizzying and ever-changing array of goods destined for both consumer and producer goods markets at home and, in some cases, abroad. At the same time, many of these dynamic regions and sub-regions took on unique identities as industrial centres and so Stoke-on-Trent became 'The Potteries', Sheffield 'Steel City', and Manchester 'Cottonoplis'. These identities inculcated a sense of pride at the local level that acted to reinforce the dynamism that had been unleashed.

At the same time, it is important to note how these processes of deepening regional specialisation were accompanied by and driven on by equally powerful forces for integration at the intra-regional, national, and international level.

Dynamic districts, cumulatively enhancing their capacity on the basis of externalised economies of scale and scope, demanded an outlet and ever-expanding markets. This need was satisfied by an intense effort towards integration. Alongside manufacturing firms, merchants, factors and other species of trade intermediary proliferated in many new or transformed centres (Popp 2007). Correspondence and travellers flowed back and forth, creating increasingly densely-integrated national and even international markets where once there had existed high levels of geographical market fragmentation.

In the past, these dynamic districts have been relatively neglected by English economic and business historians focused either on aggregate national statistical and econometric analyses or on the core staple trades. Understanding the micro-processes at work at the level of districts requires quite different perspectives and methodologies. However, recent years have seen the beginnings of a reevaluation of the regional dimensions to English industrialisation and a recognition that spatial aspects of that experience need to be taken seriously, for both empirical and conceptual reasons. This reevaluation might be said to have been started by the publication in 1989 of *Regions and Industries*, edited by Pat Hudson. The introduction to *Regions and Industries* mounted a powerful critique of aggregate level analyses of industrialisation and in so doing also argued for serious consideration of the part played by regions in the industrial revolution. However, the book did not set out to provide a sustained exploration of the business structures and practices associated with England's historic IDs. Nor did it attempt to link in a consistent manner the insights to be derived from historical studies of past districts with those emerging at that time from other social sciences, notably economic geography, area studies, sociology and political science, that had been energised by the 'discovery' of the dynamic properties associated with the 'Third Italy' in the second half of the 20th century (Piore and Sabel 1984).

More recently a series of studies have emerged that do explicitly identify some of England's historic industrial regions as 'IDs' and at the same time attempt to ground their historical analyses of those districts in the relevant social science models and literatures. One important product of this new vein in English economic and business history was the publication in 2003 of the edited volume *Industrial Clusters and Regional Business Networks in England, 1750–1970* (Wilson and Popp 2003). That volume attempted both to make a valuable empirical contribution to the study of English districts and to engage constructively with the theoretical foundations of the ID concept. This chapter builds on that volume.

However, if, until recently, these developments have been relatively neglected by business and economic historians, they did not go unnoticed by the greatest English economist of the late 19th and early 20th centuries, Alfred Marshall (1919). We do not intend to rehearse in detail here Marshall's ground-breaking work on the ID concept; however, we do think it important to emphasise that Marshall derive his theoretical insights into IDs, including such core concepts as external economies and 'industrial atmosphere', from intense first-hand study of English districts conducted during several lengthy tours of the country's industrial regions during the later 19th century. The foundations of the ID concept are then empirical, inductive and English. At the same time, as his writings make very clear, Marshall was aware of and sensitive to the importance of both historical context and historically literate analyses. Thus, he was profoundly concerned not only with the economic logic (particularly external economies) that underpinned the ID concept but also with dynamic processes of change occurring over (historical) time. In particular, he was acutely alive to the possibility that districts might not only experience dynamic periods of growth but also episodes of decline and even extinction. As a set of preliminary conclusions then, we can say the formation and growth of IDs played a crucial if largely neglected role in the story of industrialisation in England and that those English districts were amongst the first in the modern world and provided the foundation for the initial formulation of the ID concept.

3. THE EMERGENCE, GROWTH AND CHARACTER OF IDs IN ENGLAND, 1750–1914

This section provides a review of the emergence, growth and, in some cases, decline of IDs in England in the period 1750–1914. The aim is to survey the sectors associated with the formation of IDs in England, the structural and organisational characteristics of those IDs, their geographical locations and spatiality (for example, size and span), and the timelines involved.

As already indicated the formation of IDs – often, in fact, a single ID nationally dominant in a given sector – was characteristic of a wide range of different trades. However, the vast majority of these IDs were devoted to the production of one form or another of consumer goods. Producer goods industries such as iron and steel also tended to display patterns of geographical concentration, but these patterns were often shaped by forces quite different from those that underpinned the formation of IDs, particularly by the distribution of natural resource endowments. Some classic consumer goods IDs, such as the Potteries in North Staffordshire or metalwares in the Black Country in the West Midlands, were initially influenced by natural resource endowments, especially with regard to coal, clays and ores, but these factors rapidly became much less important to their future development than the creation and augmentation of non-natural resources, such as human skills and knowledge, and powerful processes of social embedding.

As in other countries, English IDs were predominantly found in sectors and trades where potential for the decomposition of productive processes, often accompanied by difficulties in mechanisation and a continuing reliance on craft skills, met and combined with potential for the elaboration of wide arrays of products, styles and variations, leading to the creation, in Scranton's (1997) famously apt phrase, of a world of 'endless novelty'. Typically, specialty goods meant then specialisation, at a variety of different levels, both within and between firms. The characteristic organisational feature of the English ID (again, as elsewhere) was fragmentation. The most powerful example of this from English industrial history is the immense Manchester-Lancashire ID – in reality a complex of interlocking IDs – where firms not only specialised in either spinning or weaving (or, indeed, dyeing, printing and other aspects of the process of finishing cotton textiles, or in commercial functions), but also in various grades or qualities, from coarse to fine. Each of these dimensions of specialisation (process/quality) were mapped on to a highly specific spatial pattern of distribution across a wide area. Over time, in many IDs the trend in specialisation was towards ever finer distinctions, leading to a proliferation of firms. Some English IDs quickly came to be populated by many hundreds of firms; examples include cutlery in Sheffield, pottery in North Staffordshire and jewellery in Birmingham. Specialisation by firm, and their consequent proliferation, typically mandated that most firms remained small in size and that strategy remained focused on variety, differentiation, and quality rather than price.

However, we need to be careful to elaborate the very important structural differences that often existed between various IDs, for they by no means fitted a simple template. First, both across and within sectors, firms could vary very considerably in size. In the pottery industry, where for technical reasons decomposition of the production process was difficult, the smallest firms might employ only a handful of workers but the largest more than 1500. Cotton spinning and weaving firms could vary in size almost as much but firms typically showed far less size variation in industries such as cutlery, jewellery and metalwares. At the same time, some industries were characterised by considerable use of out-workers – examples include cutlery in Sheffield and gloving in Worcester – a feature virtually or entirely absent elsewhere, such as the Potteries (Coopey 2003). Similarly, firm numbers tended to display great variation. For example, the Widnes chemical cluster, though based in the decomposition of the production process for alkali, never contained more than 40–50 core firms (Popp 2003). All sectors and IDs did tend to display high to very high levels of turnover, with IDs growing through the entry and exit of new firms rather than the survival and growth of specific individual firms. Nonetheless, in some industries, some firms proved particularly long lived, across multiple decades or even centuries. Given these structural variations it follows that the articulation and organisation of IDs, the interconnections on which they were based, also varied. Some districts were highly hierarchical, centralised around core or lead firms, whereas others were more decentralised, with a wider dispersal of local industrial leadership. As might be expected, and as will be shown, these variations in the articulation of districts as systems, could and did impact on patterns of growth and development and could be particularly significant during periods of challenge and/or decline as they impacted the ability of an ID to respond to pressure for change.

However, English IDs showed far less variation in terms of norms of ownership or firm-level governance. Here, as is well known, personal capitalism predominated across all locations, all sectors and throughout the period covered. This is best conceived of as typical of English industrial capitalism (and, it must be stressed, that of other nations during the same period), rather than as specific to and characteristic of IDs. Nonetheless, it is also probably the case that the relatively small size of most firms in IDs, and their relatively low capital intensity given the reliance on handwork over mechanisation, permitted or even encouraged personalised forms of ownership beyond the early stages of industrialisation into that of maturity. Again, however, this is also seen in quite different national settings and should not be thought of as peculiar to English IDs.

Personal capitalism can be thought of as sole, family, or partnership-based forms of firm ownership and management – with, in particular, a marked lack of separation between ownership and control. Owners were managers and vice versa. As indicated, this norm held true across sectors and locations and very often also firm size. In the North Staffordshire Potteries, for example, the very largest (1500 or more employees) and most long-lived firms were as dependent on personal ownership and control as the tiny start-ups that, numerically, made up the bulk of the industry. Towards the end of our period of study, we do see some shifts in corporate governance in English IDs and, in particular, greater use of incorporation and limited liability status – the most famous examples perhaps being that offered by the so-called 'Oldham Limiteds' in the cotton textile industry. However, in most cases, this did not actually denote a significant shift in corporate governance norms. At 1914, most firms in most English IDs remained owned and controlled by families, partnerships or tightly interlocked cliques of directors.

Geographically, English IDs were widely distributed, being found not only across the expected areas – the Northeast, Northwest, and North, West and East Midlands – that formed the core of industrialising England, but also in the West Country (gloving, for example, in Worcestershire and Somerset). Furthermore, a very significant (but understudied) cluster of IDs was to be found within London, where micro-concentrations, often formed at the level of individual streets, were to be found in trades as discrete as furniture, clothing and printing. Thus, in contrast to the well-known example of the so-called 'Third Italy', IDs in England emerged from a wide variety of different geographical settings, spanning fully established metropoli, emerging urban agglomerations and the semi or even fully rural. This meant that English IDs also emerged from a range of different socio-economic contexts. In some respects, a few had their foundations in regions displaying elements of the classic mix associated with proto-industrialisation, principally a tradition of production amongst scattered rural outworkers organised by merchants; the cotton textile industry of Lancashire being one possible example. Other areas, less obviously proto-industrial in structure and organisation, could also draw on long traditions of craft skill in relevant trades, here cutlery and edge tools in Sheffield, pottery in North Staffordshire, and gloving in Worcester stand out. Conversely, some IDs emerged in the context of very rapidly expanding industrial and commercial centres that bore relatively fewer vestiges of past socio-economic structures and practices. Birmingham perhaps stands as the preeminent example of this class of location. Particularly significant about Birmingham (and much of the wider West Midlands) was the lack of guild, and other forms of corporate control over industrial developments. In contrast, London, where craft guilds were much more firmly entrenched and remained stronger, proved equally fertile for the generation of cluster effects and IDs. In a few instances, entirely new towns were in effect created through the process of ID formation. Widnes in Lancashire was to a very large degree a product of the implantation there of the alkali industry by John Hutchinson in 1848. It is difficult then to generalise too far about the socio-economic backgrounds to ID formation in England in the period under study.

Timelines for the emergence, growth and development of English IDs likewise show some important variations. Certainly, it is true that the core English IDs, perhaps best defined as cotton textiles in Lancashire, woollen textiles in Yorkshire, metal making and working in South Yorkshire and the West Midlands, and pottery in North Staffordshire, are strongly associated in their development with the 'classic' industrial revolution period, 1750–1846 (the repeal of the Corn Laws in the latter year representing the symbolic triumph of industrial and commercial interests over those of agriculture and land). By the end of this period, all of those named industries had attained national and, very often, international dominance and were firmly and fully established in their various locations. This period may then, with confidence, be associated with the critical mass, takeoff and cooperative competitiveness phases of the district life cycle for a range of core industries and IDs (we will deal in more detail with district life cycles shortly when we turn to conceptualising the English experience of IDs). This is not to say, however, that districts did not continue to emerge both during and after this period. The Widnes alkali industry, as we have seen, did not begin to emerge until 1848 and, in particular, the Southeast continued to generate new clusters throughout and beyond the longer period covered by this chapter (P. Scott 2007).

Experiences of maturity and decline across English IDs were rather more varied. Well established by the mid-19th century, many English IDs necessarily experienced periods of intense challenge from the third quarter of the century onwards. At the close of the period covered by this chapter, all remained nationally or even internationally dominant; but many were also showing unmistakable signs of stagnation or even decline. Most famously, the Lancashire cotton textile industry had entered on a downward spiral that was never arrested. Nonetheless, other industries and locations were more successful in resisting challenges and threats. The North Staffordshire pottery industry has, it can be argued, entered a terminal phase only in the last ten years whilst the Birmingham jewellery industry remains relatively vibrant today.

In concluding this section, we can see that English IDs displayed important levels of variation around some core themes – structure, organisation, location, and time spans. Nonetheless, in the next sections we wish to explore the extent to which it is possible to derive generalities from the English experience of IDs.

4. THE CONTEXT FOR ID FORMATION IN ENGLAND

Despite these important differences and variations, it is still important to try and search for those generalities concerning the growth and development of English IDs that might be derived from long-run, genuinely historical studies. That search will be the task of the next two sections. In this section we will explore the formative influence of a specific national context and in the next we will examine the dynamics of district formation, growth and development.

Here we wish to stress the particular context provided for the formation of IDs by England's status as an early industrialising nation. The concept of early industrialisation, we would argue, provides a more useful framework for analysis than that provided by the concept of proto-industrialisation – not least because, as is well known, several of England's most prominent proto-industrial regions failed to make the transition to full industrialisation and did not witness the formation of successful IDs.

Early industrialisation presented a quite different mix of both opportunities and constraints from that faced by developing regions in a late industrialiser such as Italy, the most famous home of IDs (Gershenkron 1962). In particular, England embarked on an incremental and diffused process of industrialisation as an increasingly secure, settled and powerful nation, a position cemented by gathering commercial and industrial might and eventual military dominance over continental European rivals post-1815. Nationhood increasingly stood then on the two interdependent pillars of international economic and political/military power. Within its borders, a coherent sense of nationhood was emerging that overlapped with but did not eclipse important sources of regional identity – identities that in some previously peripheral regions were actually being reinforced by strongly-localised experiences of industrialisation (Colley 1992). Important in forging the context for industrialisation at both national and regional levels was an increasingly numerous, prosperous, and confident middle class. Moreover, this middle class was increasingly located in a strengthening and deepening provincial urban system that was becoming ever more tightly interlinked by the growing sophistication of transport systems, a process enabled by the relatively compact geography of the country. At the same time, this urban system was also the principal site for the creation of a flourishing consumer revolution and consumer culture, in which the middle classes were the most enthusiastic participants (Stobart 2004). Importantly, many of the fastest growing urban centres, such as Birmingham or Manchester, had grown very rapidly and very recently from humble origins and were thus relatively free of control from guilds and other representatives of premodern vested interests. It is true that at the same time, the central State was gaining a legitimacy absent in many continental European countries at this time – but this was a State that over time became ever more wedded to a strongly *laissez-faire* ideology, particularly with regard to matters of economy and industry. The provincial middle classes, so important to both the consumer and industrial revolutions, acted as an advance guard for this ideology. What might be termed *ancien régime* vested interests were, of course, not defeated in the process but they were increasingly assimilated into the new socio-political settlement. It is also important to note how an early and ongoing 'agricultural revolution' had earlier begun a radical restructuring of rural socio-economic structures. English rural society in the early 19th century looked very different from that, for example, of mid-20th century Italy, with important implications for how industrialisation was experienced at both macro and micro-levels. Thus, the large peasant class central to many aspects of district formation in Italy did not exist in England.

What were the implications of this national context for district formation in England? First, this was an opportunity-rich environment for actors in newly industrialising regions. Geographical compactness, a robust middle class participating enthusiastically in a new consumer culture, and high and increasing levels of physical, social and cultural integration offered both the possibility of deepening and strengthening patterns of regional and subregional specialisation – the essence of the dynamic informing district formation and growth – and access to expansive and expanding national and international markets. At the same time, relative provincial autonomy and growing provincial confidence, in combination with the assimilation of older vested interests and a stable central State displaying a growing consensus around a *laissez-faire* political economy permitted or even necessitated a grass-roots or bottom-up approach to development. The State in England played very little positive part in the process of industrialisation – it had to start and be driven from micro-levels and from the regions in particular.

An inherent element of early industrialisation as a context was an inability to draw on lessons forged elsewhere. Industrialising regions and districts in England were forced by first mover status in to policies and practices of self-reliance. Localised resources, knowledge, know-how, information, technology and finance dominated, reinforcing processes of specialisation. Actors in England's industrialising regions and districts, relatively free from central control or direction, were able to attack the rich opportunities they faced equipped with deepening pools of localised resources and buoyed by a strengthening culture of self-reliance. What, then, were the dynamics associated with the formation, growth and development of IDs within this specific environment?

5. THE DYNAMICS OF ID GROWTH AND DEVELOPMENT IN ENGLAND

In turning to examine the dynamics associated with the formation, growth and development of IDs in England it is important immediately to note that long-run, historical studies of such districts provide strong support for the argument that districts are subject to powerful life-cycle effects (Wilson and Popp 2003). Such an observation can only be made, as is implied, through adopting a longitudinal approach or perspective.

The historical studies undertaken of districts in England suggest that IDs will move through a series of stages: from critical mass, through takeoff, cooperative competition, maturity, saturation and, potentially, decline or renaissance (Swann, Prevezer and Stout 1998; Wilson, Bracken and Kostova 2005). It is important to stress that this life-cycle model of district growth and development cannot be interpreted in a rigid or deterministic manner. The trajectory or progress of any given district through the full cycle is not inevitable. Districts may fail to develop genuine, sustainable competitive advantage and thus also to break out of the initial critical mass and takeoff phases. Similarly, some districts prove capable of escaping from the trap of decline, at least for very long periods. Others that suffer from decline have managed to achieve some form of renaissance, though often on the basis of the development of new forms and sources of competitive advantage.

The dynamics associated with the life cycle are derived from the intersection of number of different forces and, in particular, the interaction between a range of different drivers and the mechanisms for change and adjustment, structural and strategic, possessed by a district. Both drivers and adjustment mechanisms are too a large extent a product of the particular history and growth trajectory of any given district.

First, ID dynamics are closely associated with technological dynamics. Thus a major force shaping all English IDs was the progressive elaboration of their technological bases and capabilities. Technological dynamics are typically portrayed in a positive fashion, with deepening specialisation fuelling a virtuous process of innovation. But it is also true that specialisation and commitment could lead districts into technological cul de sacs and the possibility of being overtaken by fresh innovations made elsewhere – an observation to be found in Marshall's original work on districts. The most striking example of the latter effect is perhaps the Widnes alkali industry, which became deeply wedded to the Leblanc process and largely incapable of responding the challenge of the more efficient Solvay process, innovated and adopted elsewhere (Popp 2003). The Lancashire cotton textile industry displayed a similar commitment to increasingly obsolete technologies, and their associated working practices.

The key, then, for districts seeking to avoid technological or functional 'lock-in' of this nature was the ability to foster process (and product) diversity. A good example of the latter ability was to be found in a centre such as Coventry, which from the mid-19th century progressively built on a specialism in the manufacture of textile machinery and other precision engineering trades to move into a diverse series of industries, including bicycles, motorcars and motorbikes, and machine tools (Lloyd-Jones and Lewis 2003).

Process and product innovativeness necessarily also interacted with drivers originating in market forces, with both cyclical and secular movements being important. As an example of the latter, the Worcester gloving district was fatally undermined by wide-ranging changes in fashion that saw far fewer wearing leather gloves (Coopey 2003). However, IDs should not be seen as inert or powerless in the face of changes in markets and sources of competition. Many districts, as specialty producers of diverse consumer goods, were of course adept at creating, stimulating and selling new desires and products to expectant markets.

Aside from technological and market-based dynamics, many English IDs also displayed clear structural dynamics. Crucially, these structural dynamics were closely related to some of the core principals underpinning the economic logic of clustering: external economies of scale and scope, deepening product and process specialisation at the level of the firm, and the creation and elaboration of highly-specialised pools of resources at the local level. In particular, as pools of resources deepen and become more specialised at the local level they gradually shift the barriers to entry (and exit) to be found in specific locales. These shifts generally act in a positive fashion during the critical-mass, takeoff and cooperative competition phases of the district life cycle, with heightening competition at the local level spurring equally emulation and innovativeness. However, during the maturity and saturation phases, progressively lowered barriers to entry and the erosion of penalties for failure and exit, can turn negative, creating overcrowding and ruinous competition. These effects are to be seen particularly powerfully in the North Staffordshire Potteries during the last quarter of the 19th century (Popp 2001). Thus, structural dynamics may over time become a source of 'lock-in', frustrating responses to pressures for change.

The 'lock-in' concept is particularly important for understanding the mechanisms whereby English IDs attempted to accommodate themselves to challenge and crisis, not least because of the relationship between 'lock-in' and networks (Popp and Wilson 2007). Our studies of English IDs suggest that networks are central accommodation mechanisms. Networks may be thought of as governance systems for attempting to meet the challenge of coordinating decentralisation (Sabel and Zeitlin 1997a). However, whilst it is true that networks can be excellent means through which to mobilise resources, especially at the micro, local level and especially during the critical-mass and takeoff phases of district life cycles, it is also the case that historically they have frequently shown a tendency over the long run to become increasingly exclusive and inward looking, leading potentially to both political and cognitive 'lock-in' (Cookson 2003; Toms and Filatotchev

2003). Thus the functioning of networks as effective decentralised governance mechanisms shows a strong, though not inevitable, tendency to decline over time. In part, this decline may also be related to the changing spatiality of networks over time. Those networks least able to handle challenge in the long run, as in the Lancashire cotton textile industry, also tended to be those in which links to others beyond the district underwent a process of atrophy. Inward-looking networks were, it should be stressed, effective in the earliest phases of the life cycle, during which the mobilisation of local resources is crucial, particularly for early industrialisers undergoing, as argued above, a grass-roots or bottom-up process of industrialisation. However, as a district matures across both temporal and historical time, it becomes important that it is able to forge more and deeper extra-regional network linkages, enabling the mobilisation of the wider pool of resources of every description necessary to meet fresh, external challenges.

In addition, studies of networks in English IDs do not find the same role for strong social embeddedness that is common in the literature on Italian IDs. Certainly, it is of course vital that we investigate and fully understand the social context within IDs and, in particular, the relationship between that context and network formation and functioning. Such social contexts can and did have profound effects on the formation, growth and development of English IDs, as is demonstrated by Cookson's (2003) analysis of the role of Quakerism in the evolution of Darlington in Northeast England. Instead, the English cases provide little evidence to support the argument that districts emerge from or thrive best where there are strong, stable social structures enjoying high levels of legitimacy and consensus based upon, for example, a dominant and cohesive political, religious or ethnic platform. English IDs emerged and prospered where there were, in effect, no preexisting social structures, as in Widnes, or in situations where social structures showed important fracture lines, as in the North Staffordshire potteries or the Birmingham jewellery quarter. Such apparent barriers to effective district-wide coordination were most likely to be overcome in those districts where networks were marked by strong leadership. Thus, the example offered by English IDs would also suggest that the most effective networks were often those characterised by hierarchical as opposed to democratic structures.

6. CONCLUSIONS: LEARNING FROM THE HISTORIES OF ENGLISH IDs

These historical studies of IDs in England shed a valuable light on a number of debates across business, economic history and economic geography studies.

First, they suggest for economic and business historians, indeed for all interested in the process of industrialisation, the value to be derived from adopting a spatial perspective. Industrialisation in England was an intensely spatially-differentiated process at the very heart of which lay the formation, growth and development of a wide array of regional systems and, at the heart of those systems, IDs. The creation of those IDs was not incidental to or merely symptomatic of how England, as both an economy and a society, experienced industrialisation but instead played a causal role. In very simple terms, industrialisation processes were concentrated in particular locations for very real and powerful reasons; the underlying forces that promote clustering and regional dynamics. Over the long run too, the centrality of IDs to the English experience of industrialisation was to prove very significant. Spatial differentiation of economic and industrial activity, clustering or district formation, heavily conditioned why and how England experienced economic maturity, challenge and decline, particularly from the late 19th century onwards. Relevant here is the Chandlerian paradigm (Chandler 1990) that has dominated business history research for the last three decades. Studies of the often vital and highly dynamic networked, externalised business structures of English IDs are, in the first instance, a challenge to the Chandlerian emphasis on internalisation and hierarchy. They demonstrate that there are sources of economic dynamism and corporate and national competitive advantage other than those highlighted by Chandler. However, if it is possible to claim that the formation, growth and development of IDs provides, at least in part, an explanation for economic growth and development alternative to the Chandlerian paradigm then it must also be admitted that through various processes of lock-in (Popp and Wilson 2007) the economic geography of English industrialisation did contribute to declining corporate and national competitive advantage in the early to mid-20th century.

At the same time, however, as well as providing a fresh perspective on problems in English economic and business history, we believe that these studies have a valuable contribution to make to the development of district studies and theory. In particular, these studies, highlighting key differences between the English districts and 'ideal-typical' model derived from Italian studies, provide a powerful argument for a return to a thinner and more open model of districts that is able to accommodate a wide range of forms, practices, structures and outcomes. Linking the districts studied under such a thinner, more open model should be the underlying forces and dynamics that shape their emergence, growth and development. Here, because of the very long-run perspectives possible under historical approaches we again believe studies of English districts have made a valuable contribution through their emphasis on dynamics and district life cycles. English IDs tell then a fascinating tale of the powerful and multifaceted forces that drive regional development and of how these forces emerge with particular vigour in particular places and at particular times, with dramatic consequences for all involved. English IDs deserve a place at the heart of historical studies of the development of economy and society.

5. Industrial districts and large firms: The stubborn persistence of a 'weak' productive model

Andrea Colli

1. INTRODUCTION

This chapter looks at the evolution of the role of the industrial districts (henceforth IDs) over time in conjunction with other forms of production organization. The focus of the analysis is not – differently from other chapters in this section – on the organizational dynamics of IDs, nor on their governance mechanisms. Nor does it deal with a specific case study of an ID from which to draw more general perspectives. Instead, the aim of this contribution is to reflect on the changing relative efficiency of IDs in comparison with other forms of organizing the production process that have over time appeared in response to changes in technology and market dynamics. The reference to historical analyses enables a careful and detailed evaluation of the role played by specific organizational structures like those associated to IDs following the main technological shifts of the three industrial revolutions.

In general, literature (in several fields of research) more or less explicitly emphasizes the nature of the ID as an alternative organizational form to the scale-intensive, large corporation.[1] Large companies and self-organizing aggregations of small firms and 'dispersed factories' geographically concentrated, as in classical IDs, have been frequently considered two alternative ways of organizing the process of production in different sectors and industries.

From a macroeconomic perspective, the performance of a modern economy in terms of growth and development can be directly related to the presence of different organizational forms of the production process, suitable for different industries and technologies. Economic performances are, however, in many cases explained by a number of collaborative, though sometimes unequal and asymmetric, relationships among different organizational forms (IDs, medium-sized enterprises, large corporations). Another aim of this chapter is thus to assess the nature of these relationships. In particular I shall try to take into account, in a comparative and dynamic perspective, the role of technology in influencing the process of reorganization of both large firms and local production systems. The underlying idea is that IDs correspond to an enduring form of production organization also due to the capability to adapt their peculiar structure to shifts in dominant technological paradigms.

This chapter will be organized in three main sections, coinciding with the main technological and organizational divides of three industrial revolutions. Section 2 will briefly examine the role of IDs during the first stages of the industrialization process; Section 3 will be dedicated to the relationships between the 'alternative production models' and mass production during the second industrial revolution; and, finally, Section 4 will examine the role of IDs in more recent times, during a period which saw the transformation and restructuring of mass production.

2. THE ID AS THE 'PROPER' FORM OF ORGANIZING PRODUCTION BETWEEN THE PREINDUSTRIAL PERIOD AND FIRST INDUSTRIAL REVOLUTION

It is now a widely accepted idea that the ID, corresponding to particular forms of organizing the production process, is the result of a long and enduring historical process, in many cases dating back to the age before the first industrial revolution. An ID in this context is characterized by several factors: a high concentration of manufacturing activities, a certain degree of specialization in the production of a limited range of items, a number of different units of production, a social environment involving close informal relationships among economic actors, and cooperation mixed with competition. It is easy to single out several examples of such areas in preindustrial Europe. Economic historians have stressed the role played by guilds and trade associations in the creation of specialized and fragmented systems of production. Analogously, the diffusion of the putting-out system in textiles, shoemaking, and metalware production has often been connected to the rise of local productive specializations. Artisan traditions, present both in urban settings and in the countryside, have been seen in many cases as a kind of necessary premise, the seedbed for the emergence of a local production system (see other chapters in this section).

A relevant point which should also be stressed is that, in general, the role of such premises was not necessarily related to certain productive specializations, which may change in the long run, according to transformations in the structure of the market and/or of the dominant technology, or even in the availability of raw materials.[2]

The same premises were relevant also in terms of more intangible factors, like methods of knowledge transmission at the shop floor, human capital formation, the relatively free circulation of innovation and new techniques of production (as they were not yet subject to limitations of intellectual property), and the creation of wide networks of local producers. These individuals were linked together by relationships based on trust and mutual control, which were enforced by the strong correlations between the social and economic spheres. Locally specialized manufacturing systems and proto-IDs across Europe during the preindustrial period share (though not homogeneously) characteristics present also in subsequent time periods, most notably the presence of a strong collective action, aimed at the creation and maintenance of material and immaterial infrastructures. One interesting example is the process known as 'collective invention', whereby the majority of members in a local community, who share available knowledge and advancements in technology, select the most efficient productive technology. The concept of 'collective invention' is generally applied to explain the emergence of major and minor innovations from the first industrial revolution onwards.[3] However, it can also be easily applied to many local manufacturing systems well before the first revolution, as well as to the management of innovation which characterized craft guilds throughout Europe.

The more intangible factors recalled above have been a relevant part of the 'social capital' which is usually considered at the core of the IDs' competitive advantage. This 'social capital' demonstrated considerable resilience over time, especially in face of the impact of the new technologies of the first industrial revolution on the existent ways of organizing the production process.

The first industrial revolution is normally credited with the radical transformation of the logic and organization of the production unit,[4] bringing about the emergence of the factory and especially of the factory system as the basic building block of modern economies. With the first industrial revolution manufacturing impacted on the processes of economic growth and development, reducing the role of the primary sector, and transforming both the life of individuals and the entire societal structure. The 'great transformation', as the historian and anthropologist Karl Polanyi labeled the phenomenon, is, however, sometimes largely overemphasized. Generations of economic historians have shown that the overall impact of the revolution on the rate of economic growth both in Britain and in the continental followers was initially low on average, and limited to a small number of industries in which the factory system was more easily diffused (see, for example, Crafts 1985). It can be argued that the process was therefore far from being 'revolutionary' in macroeconomic terms, as the impact on the production cycle and on the organization of the production process was at the beginning concentrated in few industries, in particular in textiles. The first industrial revolution did not create the large vertically-integrated enterprise, though some phases of the production process were carried on a larger dimension, when technology allowed the exploitation of some economies of scale. However, most phases were performed sticking to the most common form of organization, based on craftsmanship and/ or a putting-out system (see, for example, Berg 1994). For instance, the diffusion of new technologies in spinning coexisted with large networks of peasants weaving at home. Some of the most important specialized production areas, both in Britain and in continental Europe in textiles, shoemaking, metalwares and mechanics production were, therefore, for a long period characterized by a creative mix of different production typologies, in which factories provided semi-finished goods to individuals working at home, performing the 'ennoblement' of the product and adding value to it. Already existent networks of producers were clearly the most hospitable environments to foster these transformations, although the process was not easy. Development was often hindered by local path dependencies and institutions giving privilege to traditional organizations of the production process based upon small shops or cottages instead of on the factory.[5] Obviously, the presence of these networks of competences in manufacturing was not a necessary and sufficient condition for the establishment of large factories. It is important to note, however, that when the new technologies of the first industrial revolution became diffused in already operating local manufacturing systems, they did not immediately (and frequently, never) alter the established organization of the production process. Some of the production phases, however, 'were' inevitably transformed by new technologies; factories emerged. The single small unit of production also underwent some transformations, for instance with the emergence of cheap small machine tools. But the basic characteristic of decentralized production did not change drastically, and the intangible factors discussed above remained fully active. Manufacturing and craft-scale production shared strong complementarities for a long period of time (Mokyr 2002, pp. 122ff.). The coexistence between craft and factory production is typical of all the cases of transition from the preindustrial to the industrial stage of economic development, shaping in this way local systems of production in which geographic concentration, flexibility, large numbers of different-sized producers with various specializations, and both formal and informal institutions regulating competition and cooperation continued to play a relevant role in shaping the competitiveness of the area itself.

Last but not least, a note concerning the management of labor, the labor market, and the supply of human capital inside these multiform local manufacturing systems and IDs is necessary. Given that one outcome of the factory was the creation of a new kind of 'unskilled' jobs, often taken up by female and child labor, it can also be inferred that, due to the existence of a craft-based production organization (a prerequisite for factory birth), skilled and trained human capital was freed up from old jobs in many cases to satisfy new requirements brought about by the same development of the factory system. In more technologically intensive production processes – metalware production, cutleries, leather, and mechanics as opposed to textiles – the factory system, when existent, was based largely on the presence of skilled laborers, coming largely from the world of small shops, and frequently ready to go back to it. Even the organization of the production process 'inside' the factory replicated, in many cases, some or even all the features of the traditional system. Before the 'scientific organization of work' (the introduction of which, as is known, never took place fully in Europe) teamwork and piece wages dominated inside the factory (see S. Pollard 1965, Chapter 5; Berg 1994, Chapter 8; Mokyr 2002, Chapter 4). Training of the human capital was generally on the shop floor. Above all, there was a continuous inward and outward flow of skilled labor linking the factory itself to the rest of the area.

3. THE IDs AND DEVIANT FORMS OF PRODUCTION ORGANIZATION IN THE SECOND INDUSTRIAL REVOLUTION

The previous section has recalled some of the features of the slow transformation from preindustrial local specialized manufacturing systems, based upon artisanal practices and techniques into IDs: characterized by an intense relationship between the social and economic sphere, and by territorial concentration of small and medium specialized independent (and technologically more sophisticated) units of production interconnected by market and non-market relationships.

The first industrial revolution only partially challenged the efficient persistence of decentralized local networks of independent producers, sometimes, on the contrary, adding technological dynamism to craft-based specialized manufacturing system characteristics.

However, this was not the case when the new technologies of the second industrial revolution are considered. Generally speaking, the new technologies radically transformed some industries, formerly characterized by fragmentation of the production process. The new technologies in fact put a great emphasis on continuous production processes, economies of scale and vertical integration.

If the greatest result of the first industrial revolution was the creation of the factory system and the Marshallian industrial district (MID), a marked outcome of the second was the rise of the giant, vertically-integrated enterprise. However, the small and medium size of the production units remained largely diffused. It is common to describe this as 'industrial dualism' and relate it to a distinction between 'capital'- and 'labor'-intensive industries. Each group is characterized by different organizational structures, different ways of organizing the process of production, different strategies, by different labor markets, and by a different nature of the working class itself. One significant body of literature (Chandler, Amatori and Hikino 1997) recognizes a direct relationship between the presence of large-scale, capital-intensive industries and the mechanisms of economic growth, implicitly (and sometimes explicitly) stressing the superior efficiency of these organizations over other forms. In this perspective, the small and medium enterprise still plays a role, but this is concentrated in labor-intensive, traditional industries, which are seen as giving a marginal contribution to economic growth. Suboptimal dependent survival of the small firm in the age of the large enterprise was normally explained both by the strategies of subcontracting undertaken by the large enterprises, and by the persistence of inefficiencies (for example, those linked to personal or family ownership) limiting the growth of the firms.

This point of view has been heavily criticized in the literature which refers to historical alternatives to mass production. Here it is pointed out that the large-scale enterprise was not *per se* efficient; it prevailed over medium and small sized industries also due to institutional and political support in certain geographical contexts. European business history is, in fact, an example of the existence of a 'world of possibilities' (Sabel and Zeitlin 1997a) of alternatives to mass production, present also in industries normally dominated by the large-scale enterprise.

The diffusion and stubborn persistence of IDs in Europe in the age of mass production is, in this perspective, a further confirmation of the existence of such historical alternatives, and a concrete example of organizational structures able to perform well in a particular context and under some conditions. A way to look at this phenomenon is through the relation of IDs with various types of markets, demand structures, and efficient technological alternatives to mass production, taking into account the shaping of the culture of consumption and of entrepreneurial opportunities. In other terms, given the presence of efficient technological alternatives, the nature of demand shapes the form of both the production process and the production unit.

The European experience shows quite well that in some industries – for example, metalware, iron and steel, mechanics, some branches of clothing and textiles, food and beverages – mass production can successfully coexist with specialized flexible production. The nature of consumption patterns in Europe and the cultural orientation towards differentiation rather than homogeneity in consumption, along with other social and political factors, explains to a large extent the slow penetration of the 'Americanization' wave that coincided with the golden age of the large corporation after the Second World War. The structure of the demand across Europe shaped entrepreneurial strategies, emphasizing flexibility and customization, differentiation and creativity. Moreover, if it is true that the new technologies of the second industrial revolution contributed to development of large-scale enterprises, it is also evident that some applications of these technologies were consistent with, and contributed to, a rise in the efficiency of the small unit of production. An example of this is the diffusion of electricity and its application to small domestic engines, which resulted in an increase of productivity for the small firms, while at the same time preserving their orientation towards flexibility and diversity.[6] This orientation – which even today is shown by the divergence in production and consumption patterns between Europe and the US – was also helped by the peculiar characteristics of the labor market and training policies in use in Europe, favoring skilled versus unskilled competencies.

The presence in many European countries of local manufacturing systems and IDs orientated towards differentiated production was therefore interrelated with specific patterns of consumption. So, technology and markets helped enhance the relative efficiency of these organizational forms in front of large integrated enterprises, at least in those industries – and countries – in which differentiation was preferred to standardization. IDs were thus able not only to deliver products according to the needs of the local or regional market, but also to activate, when necessary, a wide stream of export flows facilitated by the ongoing process of market integration in Europe. Thanks to their particular organizational structure IDs were also able to efficiently follow the steady rise in the quantity of goods required by the consumers. One example is provided by the sharp rise in demand during the so-called 'twenty glorious years' after the Second World War. In many European countries, the economic miracle resulted in better living standards for the population, and in a sharp and steady growth in consumption. This meant, obviously, the definitive affirmation of the large-scale enterprise, even multinational or State-owned, in staple products (steel, automotives, chemicals, pharmaceuticals, petroleum and refined goods, cement, household appliances) characterized by mass production and heavy price competition. However this same considerable market enlargement allowed the growth of specialized and differentiated demand for various products. Better living standards and growing urbanization meant, for instance, an increase in the demand of household goods, from furniture, to textiles, tiles, ceramics, and leather goods. The same effect occurred in industries related to personal goods as well: clothing, textiles, apparel, shoes, jewelry and related items. This considerable growth in the demand did not result directly in the establishment of large-scale enterprises, but in a further enlargement of the networks of specialized producers already present in the IDs, which proved to be particularly suitable in conjugating flexibility, differentiation and entrepreneurial creativity with increasing volumes of production at an aggregate level. This allowed IDs to enjoy a period of steady and autonomous growth (for a case-based comparative perspective, see Sabel and Zeitlin 1997a). It is also relevant to note that the enlargement in the volume of output and in the number of producers did not alter the role of the intangible factors formerly mentioned. On the contrary, the necessity to cope with a quickly growing demand fostered the evolution of local production systems that became increasingly characterized by the presence of entrepreneurial initiatives in services and in the production of instruments and machine tools. The peculiarity of the production process internal to the district, however, also shaped the strategies and the form of these 'diagonal' (Becattini and Bellandi 2006) activities. Producers of machine tools for instance, could only partially pursue strategies of standardization. More often than not, customization was the dominant strategy. In some cases, as in Italy for example, the wide diffusion of machine tools producers oriented towards customization strategies 'inside' the IDs contributed to the establishment of general features within the entire machine tools industry, and to the pattern of its competitive advantage on a world scale (see, for example, Capecchi 1997).

To conclude, in contrast to the outcomes of the first industrial revolution, the new technologies of the second introduced a divide between industries dominated by the large enterprise and oriented towards mass production, and others, in which small-scale production still proved to be efficient. This small-scale production was at that time probably even more efficient than that managed by the giant enterprise, and was also culturally and socially much more accepted and tolerated, at least in

Europe. In those 'light' industries, the enlargement of the market was easily managed through the already-existing decentralized structures of the IDs, which proved to be able to adapt quickly, increasing the scope of the networks of local producers. In other industries, the market was segmented comprising one part served by mass producers competing exclusively on costs, and a part where flexible specialization and differentiation were drivers of the entrepreneurs' competitive strategies.

Thus far, large firms, IDs and other complex forms of geographical aggregations of production units and producers have been considered as two separate worlds, each benefiting in a different way from the technological change and the sharp increase in consumption after the Second World War. A more complex research question to answer concerns the relationships between these two components of the modern economies, which have not been fully analyzed by current research (some approaches have been reviewed in Chapter 1 in this volume). An assessment of the nature of this relationship can provide further explanations of the issue of the 'stubborn' survival of IDs within modern economies.

4. THE THIRD INDUSTRIAL REVOLUTION AND ITS STRUCTURAL TRANSFORMATIONS IN THE 1960s–70s

Notwithstanding their sometimes very long histories, IDs began to show superior levels of performance (for example, in terms of international market shares) since the 1960s and 1970s, when the difficulties for the capital-intensive, large-scale enterprises became more intense. In some cases, and once again in Italy, it was because of well-performing local production systems that the whole national economy was able to maintain relatively high growth rates during a period characterized by the crisis and the restructuring of large firms. These good performances originated a large stream of research, first in the field of industrial economics and later in management studies, trying to clarify the nature, structure and competitive advantages of organizational forms other than the large, vertically-integrated enterprise (see the chapters in Part II of this volume).

Starting from the decades following the Second World War, the third, information and communication-based, industrial revolution brought into this scenario two new elements, which, although interconnected, had different impacts on these decentralized forms of production. The first element was new technologies for transport, communication and production. At first glance, these new technologies seemed to give further vitality to small-sized production units and to their systems. The effect was similar to the introduction of the small electric engine many decades before. In theory, new technologies based on the extensive use of computer-aided manufacturing and design could eliminate much of the advantages of scale intensity, allowing the production of small volumes at an extremely convenient cost and enhancing the flexibility of individual firms. In addition, these new technologies facilitated the sharing of information among the members of business networks, making the selection of partners simpler and more efficient. Furthermore, it could be expected that the steady decline in transportation costs, together with the ongoing process of globalization, should add further energy to the IDs that were already successfully competing in international markets.

What happened has however moved far less in this direction than expected. Apparently, the rate of adoption of new technologies by small firms in the IDs proved to be quite low, as did their impact on information and communication flows. Moreover, since the early 1990s, new technologies made it easy for competitors in less-developed countries to produce imitations of products realized in IDs, with far lower factor costs, and with a degree of flexibility and of qualitative standards gradually approximating the levels championed by the IDs.

The evolution of technologies and markets during the third industrial revolution had, as in the past, a relevant effect on the IDs, which once again were forced to adapt their structure to new challenges and opportunities. The process is still under way, and it is not easy to identify a unique pattern of evolution, as local manufacturing systems, IDs and networks show a historically unequal diffusion across Europe. Unfortunately, advances in comparative research (especially in a long-term perspective) are still relatively episodic in this field (see, for example, Garofoli 1992).

One concrete example of the impact of the process of globalization generated by the third industrial revolution is provided again by Italy, as it has been the country most affected by the transformations in the competitive scenario discussed above. At a general level, two effects can be identified.

The first was a selection process, which has eliminated low performers and marginal firms operating only on minimum-cost basis, while non-marginal firms and also newborn ones adopted strategies based upon high value added, positioning themselves at the top of the market, strengthening quality and design.

The second effect was a strengthening of the intermediate dimensional class, made up of medium-sized enterprises showing a considerable dynamism and above average performance. The globalization of markets has in fact enlarged the size of the niches in which specialized firms already dominated, on a national or possibly even continental scale. The result was the emergence of some global specialized suppliers who share a number of general features, including a strong tendency towards internationalization, where a considerable percentage of output is exported and in many cases where foreign direct investments have been set up. Another shared characteristic is the process of innovation, putting a strong emphasis on immaterial components of the product, co-engineering, customization, and services in general.

The 'pocket multinationals', as these medium-sized firms have been dubbed due to their relatively small dimension along with a high degree of internationalization, often maintained a very close relationship with local IDs; the IDs frequently enhanced the performance and competitiveness of the 'pocket multinationals' (for a discussion on this, see Chapter 32 in this volume).

More generally, the effects of the introduction and diffusion of the new technologies in transport and communication proper of the third industrial revolution on IDs are far from being obvious. As stressed recently by some scholars in industrial economics (see Langlois 2007 for the most recent update on this debate) the new technological opportunities – especially in the field of communication – have been essential in sustaining the Smithian process of specialization of the production units generated by the steady enlargement of markets characterizing the third industrial revolution. The process' main result was the progressive fragmentation of the large, vertically-integrated corporation, which will later be replaced by networks of specialized producers of different components combined through modular interfaces. In other words, pulled by new communication and transport technologies and modular production strategies, the market began replacing the hierarchy of the large corporation and the visible hand of management. As stressed above, from a theoretical point of view, the deverticalization of the production process and the emphasis on networks and modularity can be interpreted as a new 'world of possibilities' for IDs, which have been often nicknamed 'dispersed factories'.

The available evidence suggests, however, a more dubitative and prudent approach. Modularity and new technologies are in fact sophisticated devices to reduce transaction and information costs. Basically they can make the advantages deriving from the spatial and 'social' proximity of the local producers obsolete, while at the same time maintaining the possibility of high levels of flexibility and adaptation to market conditions. Efficient models of coordination of impersonal market relationships among different producers have thus been increasingly emerging in several industries, and not only in those more 'representative' of the third industrial revolution, such as for instance computer hardware and software production. The outcome has thus been the affirmation of peculiar and relatively successful new models of enterprise and of entrepreneurial capabilities, as in the case of Dell or Cisco, which, although characterized by a significantly less integrated organizational structure (the so-called N form), are closer to the structure of the large, complex corporation.

The effects of the third industrial revolution on the structural features of IDs can be detected from other perspectives as well. The decline in transportation and information costs introduced by the new technologies has surely been one of the main drivers of the process of delocalization of production networks outside the original boundaries of the district, thus weakening the relevance of proximity relationships (see the chapters in Part IV of this volume).

5. CONCLUDING REMARKS

This chapter has examined the issue of the enduring persistence of IDs and other non-integrated, or deverticalized forms of manufacturing production in the long run, from the preindustrial period to the present day, in Europe. In this analysis, changes and continuities in the nature of IDs have been discussed. Both 'e-technology', transforming the nature and structure of the production unit and 'demand' stimulating entrepreneurial initiatives, have altogether changed the features and the roles of IDs. Non-integrated forms of production, characterized by spatial concentration and by a close interaction between the social and the economic sphere, have evolved from being the only forms of manufacturing into a necessary complement of the factory system during the first industrial revolution. In the age of the giant enterprise, IDs provided flexible production in industries only partially affected by the technological transformations of the second industrial revolution, thanks to their peculiar structure and to the variability and volatility of consumption patterns, especially in Europe in the economic 'boom' of the post-war period. Finally, the threats that globalization has posed have been more relevant than the opportunities provided by the new technologies in electronics, computing and communication introduced by the third industrial revolution. European IDs thus started again a process of adjustment to increasing competition in international markets coming from new industrializing countries and international production networks led by multinational companies. The internal selection process led to the emergence of medium-sized global specialized producers, which for the moment, however, remained largely linked to the ID from which they originated. The combined effects of the new technologies of the third revolution and of the process of globalization on IDs are, however, still far from being clear. The impact of the new technologies has been in some cases positive, fostering the competitiveness of IDs in the enlarging international markets. From a different point of view, new technologies have accelerated the process of obsolescence of proximity advantages, once considered one of the IDs main assets.

From the point of view of institutional economics, this chapter has also emphasized that in the case of IDs, what has been historically crucial for their survival and performance has proved to be their ability to adapt their internal structure – in terms of both cohesion as well as entrepreneurial effervescence – to transformations of technology and markets.

NOTES

1. See Zeitlin (2007a), also for a review of the previous literature.
2. See, for example, Colli (1999) for the persistence and transformation of an ID in the long run.
3. For an application, see Nuvolari (2004).
4. A recent review of the debate is in Mokyr (2002, Chapter 4).
5. The obstacles to the diffusion of the factory system have been widely discussed in Mokyr (2002, esp. Chapter 4).
6. For a 'regional' historical example, see Colli (2002a, p. 7).

SECTION 2
From the English roots to the Italian revival

Introduction

Tiziano Raffaelli

1. A LINE OF DESCENT OF REFLECTIONS ON IDs

The line of descent connecting 19th century British reflections on industrial districts (IDs) to their recent Italian revival is here highlighted through four flashlight views that illuminate key episodes of the history, and more comprehensively reconstructed by Neil Hart's chapter, which spans the whole period from the early dismissal of Marshall's intuitions to their reappearance in contemporary economic geography and their fuller Italian recovery. The first two of the four flashlight chapters, by Peter Groenewegen and Brian Loasby, focus on the British origin of the concept, respectively on its forerunners and on Marshall's research programme, in which it easily fitted; the last two, by Renzo Bianchi, and Anna Natali and Margherita Russo, deal with its Italian rediscovery, respectively with Becattini and the Florence school, and Brusco and the Modena school. Not by chance, Florence and Modena are two of the main centres of the 'Third Italy', whose economies are characterised by thriving IDs unlike that of the 'industrial triangle' (Milan–Turin–Genoa), the homeland of big businesses. Hart's chapter helps to bridge the geographical and historical gap, calling attention to Becattini's Marshallian studies and the evolutionary interpretation of Marshall's work, which is here synthetically and clearly presented by one of its main exponents, Loasby. This interpretation is now widely accepted and finds expression in many a chapter of *The Elgar Companion to Alfred Marshall* (Raffaelli, Becattini and Dardi 2006).

2. THE 19TH-CENTURY BRITISH ORIGINS AND BEYOND

Starting from the British side of the story – which at first almost coincides with, and then expands into, world history – it is to be recalled that no theory of the ID could have been formulated without the concept of external economies that Marshall started to forge in the early 1870s. By that time, the term 'ID' was already in common usage and had gained the attention of social thinkers. Groenewegen provides an overview of this literature, in which Spencer stands out with his powerful philosophical framework of differentiation and integration, where the concept finds its roots. This development of Smith's division of labour fits neatly with and accompanies Marshall's later multi-level view of the organisation of industry, which is the object of Loasby's analysis.

In an ideal sequence to Loasby, Hart convincingly argues that the conceptual frame of static equilibrium analysis, which was the core of mainstream economics for decades, caused a complete misunderstanding of Marshall's problem situation and enervated the concept of external economies, reducing it to a device required only to allow for increasing returns to subsist within a perfectly competitive environment. The empty boxes and cost controversies of the 1920s played havoc with Marshall's economic thought: his ends were completely misconceived, his tools followed suit.

If the district was thus removed from theoretical economics, it fared little better in the field of empirical studies. Earlier work, which had shown the relevance and vitality of district organisation, appeared to have been superseded by the trend of economic progress. Chapman (1904) had indeed provided an elaborate historical description of the Lancashire textile ID, which relied on an elaborate theory of the relative advantages district localisation confers on manufacturing businesses. However, when *Industry and Trade* was published, 15 years later, Marshall himself, in a well-known passage fully reproduced by Hart, had to concede that financial and technological progress was causing a decline in the importance of localised external economies. By the end of the 1920s, and especially after the 'great depression', the future of capitalism appeared to be wholly entrusted to business giants. While general equilibrium theory set the pace of theoretical economics, Marxist and Schumpeterian economics set that of historical research, calling on it to investigate the relentless tendency to business concentration. In such a hostile intellectual climate, it is remarkable that some few dissenting voices did survive. Lavington (1927), in a comment on *Industry and Trade*, insisted on the advantages of vertical disintegration, revealing that Marshall's industrial analysis did not point to unidirectional outcomes. Another Cambridge-trained economist, Austin Robinson, kept calling attention to coordination costs as a countertendency to the growth of individual businesses. Out of Cambridge, apart from Young (1928), which would deserve a story of its own, Jones (1933) devoted a whole chapter to the localisation of industry.

These isolated attempts of the interwar period were no match against the rising tide. A recovery was later provided by two concurring trends in contemporary economics. The first is the surge of interest in strategic interrelations, learning processes and dynamic evolution, which called attention to industrial organisation, a research field almost neglected in the heyday of general equilibrium theory. The second trend originates from the recognition that small businesses are alive and well, against all expectations that they would quickly pass away. The new intellectual atmosphere is well exemplified by Langlois (2007), which compares these expectations to the poverty of historicism, denounced by Popper for its lack of imagination and unidirectional predictions, and insists on the viability of different organisational designs, whose success depends on contingent circumstances. If, in historical perspective, the issues raised by Lavington and Robertson seem to come to new life with Langlois, something similar can be said of Chapman's and Jones's reasoning on localisation, which is resurrected by Porter and Krugman and the new branches of economic research they have given rise to. It is no wonder that these contemporary tendencies of economic theory triggered and supported a thorough reevaluation of Marshall's work.

3. ITALIAN ANTECEDENTS AND REVIVALS

From this wide contemporary perspective let us now move backwards in time and confine ourselves to the Italian side of the story. In the early 19th century, in the wave of Sismondi's historical reconstruction that singled out Italy as the cradle of Europe's cultural, social and political primacy, the splendour of the small Italian republics of the Middle Ages became a motive for national pride. Soon afterwards, on these premises Cattaneo erected his original project of Italy's economic and social development: the peculiarities of the national tradition, he suggested, were no remnant of the past, but a favourable opportunity for Italy's comeback in the international arena.

This hints at a special relationship between Italian and English history, which helps reconnect the scattered pieces of this section. England too is characterised by the absence of centralised control. For Tocqueville this is a genetic trait that distinguishes England's multi-centred society from France, whose centralisation provides the clue to national history, so much so that it remained unaffected even by the turmoil and violence of the revolution. Reminiscent of Tocqueville, whom he greatly admired, Marshall judged 'the central administration of France ... inferior to England's enterprise in the power of adapting itself to new wants' (Marshall 1919, p. 741). Like these two giant social scientists, Cattaneo also considered decentralisation to be one of the main causes of England's strength, with her power to innovate through variation and experiment, whereas France, notwithstanding her culture and the gentle and flexible character of her people, paid tribute to 'the innermost weakness of the administrative principle which sacrifices any local and spontaneous movement to an artificial centralisation' (Cattaneo [1842] 1972, p. 227).

Besides this lack of *dirigisme*, Cattaneo thought that another typical trait of Italian history was the close interrelationship between town and country, welded together into wide territorial units. Weber would later charge the origin of the Italian towns for their backwardness. Heir to the ancient centres of landowners' residence, they were crippled by custom and habits, unlike the Hanseatic League towns, in which the pure mercantile and bourgeois spirit had free rein. From a reversed perspective, Cattaneo took this origin as their point of strength. While northern towns are like 'ships anchored to foreign shores', Italian towns, originally 'the seats of the families that owned the neighbourhood', form, with their surrounding territories, 'permanent and indissoluble' elementary State units that persist across historical vicissitudes (Cattaneo [1858] 1972,

p. 82). This view was further developed by an original mix of Vico's discovery of the 'native' element of cultural evolution and Romagnosi's stress on the variety of historical combinations caused by the grafting of new ideas into diverse native structures. This philosophical position upheld Cattaneo's federalist proposal to unite the country and integrate its different local cultures without impoverishing their genetic variety.

Becattini's insistence on the district as a territorial unit that persists through historical change and represents the nucleus of social analysis looks very much the heir to this national tradition. Both biographical and textual evidence suggest that this affinity is not merely fortuitous. During his economic apprenticeship, Becattini assisted his master, Alberto Bertolino, in the publication of Cattaneo's economic writings. They proved congenial to his way of thinking and exercised a deep and lasting influence on his approach to the study of economic phenomena, as witnessed by the title itself of Becattini (2002b), which discusses the ideas of leading Italian economists. Moreover, a certain family likeness between Cattaneo's and Marshall's thought may have acted as reciprocal reinforcement. That this likeness is not imaginary is confirmed by the fact that it was immediately noted by another neo-Marshallian, Loasby, on reading the English translation of Cattaneo ([1861] 2007), which makes economic development dependent on the acquisition and diffusion of knowledge, as Loasby's chapter shows Marshall does also.

It is suggestive to think that the concept of the ID was brought to new life by an unforeseeable encounter of two forgotten traditions in the fertile conjuncture of the economic boom of the 'Third Italy', once thought peripheral to economic development. With the revival inaugurated by Becattini in 1979 (see Becattini 2004a), an increasing number of other researchers started to be involved in taking on the challenge. One of the most important schools was established in Modena University, known for a long time as the seat of an attempt to restore the Marxian system on Sraffa's foundations. The Italian Marxist analytical and political tradition never lost contact with socio-economic reality and in the end Sraffa, who won the day, was the Cambridge sage who pressed young Italian economists to study the real economy. Natali and Russo highlight how the late Sebastiano Brusco came to interest himself in district studies and devote his research agenda to devise and promote policy measures apt to help districts thrive. Collective and political action, which calls together all the social actors to delineate the industrial policy of a district, is no mere follow-up to theoretical analysis, but an essential part of the process of social knowledge and discovery of which the district identity consists. The feeling of belonging to a community has its origin and explanation in the interconnection between economic, social, cultural and political life. Brusco's Sardinian origins induced him to consider how the district – the most specific model of economic development, since each district is unique, 'native', by definition – could be 'exported' to a new environment, through a delicate process of grafting, or better speciation, as the 'native' stock was not to be replaced. Nothing is more suitable to show the vitality of the philosophical outlook outlined above than this fusion of specificity and recombination, whose aim is to generate and preserve variety within an open environment that does not allow for any ossification.

6. Forerunners of Marshall on the industrial districts

Peter Groenewegen

1. INTRODUCTION

Marshall's discovery of the economic significance of industrial districts (IDs) probably came from two sources. His travels through industrial areas from the 1860s are one (Groenewegen 1995, pp. 187–9, 206–7, 208–13); the other is Marshall's reading. This chapter concentrates on several works whose contents probably assisted Marshall in reaching a specific stance on the notion of IDs. The first is W.E. Hearn's *Plutology* (1864) with its interesting chapter on 'industrial organization' (Pesciarelli 1999). The second is Herbert Spencer's *First Principles* and its detailed observations on industrial organization, including the geographical clustering of related firms. Thirdly, there are the writings of R.W.C. Taylor devoted to the factory system (Taylor 1842, 1886, 1891, 1894). Sargant (1857, pp. 108–9, 111) can also be briefly noted in this context. All these works were in Marshall's personal library (Marshall Library of Economics 1927, pp. 37, 73, 80, 83).

2. HEARN ON INDUSTRIAL ORGANIZATION

Hearn's chapter in Plutology on industrial organization (Hearn 1864, Chapter XVII) argued that when a large community of industry had been 'spontaneously' organized:

> a new phenomenon presents itself. The same separation which takes place between different occupations takes place also between different locations. The various branches of industry exhibit a strong tendency to fix themselves in, and confine themselves to, particular districts. Each district therefore acquires a distinctive character, and at the same time becomes dependent upon the other districts with which it deals. In England, this localization of industry is particularly marked. The manufacture of cotton, of wool, of stuff and of silk, the workers in hosiery and in lace, in coal and in iron, in cutlery and in earthenware, in straw-plait and in needles, and in a thousand other occupations have each their separate locality. In no place perhaps is it so conspicuous as in London. (Ibid., p. 305).

In this context, Hearn mentioned Kensington lawyers, Islington law clerks, tailors and shoemakers in St James, Marylebone and St Pancras, gardeners in Kensington and Wandsworth, the city for publishers and booksellers, musical instruments in St Pancras, watchmakers in Clerkenwell and St Luke's, leather-workers in Bermondsey, coopers near Shoreditch, rope and sailmakers in Stepney and Bethnall Green (Hearn 1864, pp. 305–6). Industrial clustering was not confined to England but manifested itself internationally. In Holland, various branches of trade selected their favourite locations: the wine trade in Middelburg, the shipbuilding industry in Saardam, the herring industry in Sluys (ibid., p. 306). In his *The Aryan Household* (Hearn 1879, pp. 240–41), a book Marshall seems not to have studied, these considerations are applied to Russian village economies. Hearn observed that some Russian villages made 'nothing but boots'; in others, the whole population were either smiths, or curriers, or manufacturers of chairs and tables, or earthenware. Hearn depicted the location of industry as a natural and efficient form of industrial organization based on the benefits of division of labour and the gains from specialization.

Hearn explicitly indicated that lowering the cost of production is the key explanation for specialized localization decisions by industry. First of all, raw materials are both more easily and more cheaply obtained under this form of industrial organization. Likewise power (whether in the form of coal or water power) as used in the production process is more easily or cheaply available but, most importantly, skilled labour suitable to the industry tends to be attracted to its concentrated location, benefiting manufacturers directly (in their own employment requirements) or indirectly (the presence of an adequate supply of skilled labour for repair and maintenance of their equipment and machinery). In addition, the specialization apparent in IDs is presented as an ongoing process of enhanced efficiency (Hearn 1864, pp. 308–9).

3. SPENCER AND THE FORMATION OF IDs

It is interesting to note that Hearn (1864, p. 303) cited Spencer's *Essays* on the organization of industry. Spencer treated this matter in considerable detail in his *First Principles* as part of his exposition of the law of evolution. The formation of IDs is there explicitly portrayed as a case of superior organization of the group. Interactions through industrial local organization are mentioned in this context and given some specific examples. These include 'the junction of Manchester with its calico-weaving suburbs'; York's cloth districts and the pottery manufactures of Staffordshire. Moreover, the concentration of particular occupations (corn merchants about Mark Lane, civil engineers in Great George street, bankers in the centre of a city) are taken by Spencer as clear cases of 'centres of connexion' (Spencer [1862] 1910, p. 255). Spencer then takes the argument into other aspects of organization such as language formation, the development of specific disciplines and the classification of zoological species. Mechanization in industry is also introduced as a form of the progress of interaction (ibid., p. 261).

The discussion of more complex social evolution processes as compound evolution (Spencer [1862] 1910, Chapter XV) is designed to illustrate processes generating the integration of components of a mass which simultaneously becomes more differentiated. From natural phenomenon (the solar system, the geological structure of the earth, climate dispersion on the earth, living bodies in plant and animal life), Spencer moved to the treatment of the process of integration and greater heterogeneity of man (ibid., pp. 274–5), first in its individual form, and then socially embodied as part of the process of civilization. 'In its first and lowest stage, society is a homogeneous assemblage of individuals [with] like powers and functions', the only differentiating factor being that of sex. Early in the course of social evolution, differentiation of powers and functions begins gradually, visible first in the generation of species of government and religion. These organizations in themselves evolve into complex divisions of functions, a process Spencer considered to coincide with a simultaneous evolution of complex industrial divisions of labour. In reporting this aspect of social evolution, Spencer introduced localized division of labour, thereby pointing to the formation of IDs as part of this evolutionary process. The following quotation illustrates this fully:

> Meanwhile there has been going on a differentiation of a more familiar kind; that namely, by which the mass of the community has been segregated into distinct classes and orders of workers. While the governing part has undergone the complex development [already indicated] the governed part has undergone a more complex development which has resulted in that minute division of labour characterizing advanced nations. It is needless to trace out this progress from its first stages, up through the caste-divisions of the East and the incorporated guilds of Europe, to the elaborate producing and distributing organization existing among ourselves. Political economists have long since described the industrial progress which, through increasing division of labour, ends with a civilized community whose members severally perform different actions for one another; and they have further pointed out the changes through which the solitary producer of any one commodity, is transformed into a combination of producers who, united under a master, take separate parts in the manufacture of such commodity. But there are yet other and higher phases of this advance from the homogeneous to the heterogeneous in the industrial organization of society. Long after considerable progress has been made in the division of labour among the different classes of workers, there is relatively little division of labour among the widely separated parts of the community; the nation continues comparatively homogeneous in the respect that in each district the same occupations are pursued. But when roads and other means of transit become numerous and good, the different districts begin to assume different functions and to become mutually dependent. The calico-manufacture locates itself in this county, the woolen-manufacture in that; silks are produced here, lace there; stockings in one place, shoes in another; pottery, hardware, cutlery, come to have their special towns; and ultimately every locality grows more or less distinguished from the rest by the leading occupation carried on in it. Nay, more, this subdivision of functions shows

itself not only among the different parts of the same nation, but among different nations. That exchange of commodities which free-trade promises so greatly to increase will ultimately have the effects of specializing in a greater or less degree, the industry of each people. So that beginning with a primitive tribe, almost if not quite homogeneous in the functions of its members, the progress has been and still is, towards an economic aggregation of the whole human race; growing ever more heterogeneous in respect of the separate functions assumed by separate nations, the separate functions assumed by the local sections of each nation, the separate functions assumed by the many kinds of producers in each place, and the separate functions assumed by the workers united in growing or making each commodity. And then, lastly, has to be named the vast organization of distributors, wholesale and retail, forming so conspicuous an element in our town-populations, which is becoming ever more specialized in its structure. (Ibid., pp. 278–9)

Note that Spencer here explicitly described the process as leading to a higher form of the division of labour. The development of transport and communications enables a geographical division of labour and, eventually, generates mutually dependent 'districts' in which specific industries concentrate 'in the one place'. Such differentiated localities continue to evolve and develop their own distinctive specializations.

Spencer's subsequent discussion of the 'instability of the homogeneous' returned to examples drawn from industrial organization. Settlements in larger areas generate local specializations associated with the resource base of these regions, and thereby develop industrial differentiations (Spencer [1862] 1910, pp. 343–4). 'Among the manufacturing classes', Spencer argued concisely, where production is not necessarily for the immediate local market, 'there is an aggregation of [manufactories] in special localities, and a consequent increase in the differentiation of industrial divisions' (ibid., p. 387). Thus the presence of coal, iron and a navigable river in close proximity gives Glasgow an advantage in building iron ships, 'leading to the aggregation' of associated industries 'around this place' (ibid., pp. 387–8). An earnest young student of Spencer's writings as Marshall was would have had no great difficulty in transforming these aspects of Spencer's views into a coherent framework of specialized industrial location or IDs as an instance of industrial organization clarified by the benefits of division of labour and specialization.

4. COOKE TAYLOR AND THE FACTORY SYSTEM

Richard Whateley Cooke Taylor wrote various works in which IDs were mentioned. The first of those known to Marshall dealt with Lancashire manufacturing districts (Taylor 1842), a term frequently used in this book (ibid., pp. 7, 9, 40, 46, 113). Its separate urban locations are identified, but Taylor's study only implied the specific nature of such districts and failed to analyze it. Most of the work is devoted to the consequences of the contemporary trade depression on Lancashire workers, and at best illustrates the interdependence of regional prosperity or hardship with national economic conditions and thereby the interdependence of markets and the living standards of social classes. As Taylor (ibid., p. 54) put it, 'manufacturing industry has not only raised the prosperity of all the places in which it was developed – it has extended its benefits to the surrounding neighbourhood'. Taylor (ibid., pp. 140–41) connected this development with the factory system and treated it as part of the 'social economy' of a cotton factory (ibid. 1842, Letter VII). Taylor's discussion, however, did little to clarify the interdependence of related industries in a cotton producing district such as Lancashire.

Taylor returned to the topic of IDs in three publications from the 1880s and 1890s, which analyzed the factory system and its locational implications (Taylor 1886, 1891, 1894). The first of these provided a general introduction to the 'factory system' beginning with developments in the textile industry in ancient times (Taylor 1886, pp. 79ff.), stressing locational factors such as proximity to the sea for ease of transport (ibid., pp. 211ff.) and the geographical clustering of factories (textiles in Flanders) and thereby the localization of specific industries in particular areas as a form of gaining the benefits of specialization, attracting local skills, and easy access to raw materials. It concluded on the mechanical innovations this development induced (ibid., pp. 384–6). Taylor (1891) analyzed the modern factory system as it had developed from the 18th century, noting its locational specialization, influenced by access to skilled labour, the necessary raw materials and ease of transportation. Examples were Birmingham and its metalworking, and cutlery in Sheffield. Taylor suggested that steam power and mechanization gave manufacturers greater freedom in making such locational choices. Taylor (1894) dwelled extensively on the contemporary factory system drawing largely on the work contained in the previous publications, without adding new material to the discussion. Marshall (1920 [1895, p. 807 n.; 1898, p. 370 n. 1]), it may be noted, cited Cooke-Taylor's work on the factory system only once in both the third and the fourth editions of his *Principles of Economics*.

5. CONCLUSION

Whether Taylor's first study, devoted to Lancashire cotton as an early illustration of an ID, was known as a source on the subject to Hearn or to Spencer, is difficult to say. It is easier to suggest from the evidence that British manufacturing experience in the 19th century included greater reliance on the development of IDs which thereby became more obvious to the thinking observer interested in studying the various aspects of industrial organization, including its locational features.

7. Industrial districts in Marshall's economics

Brian J. Loasby

1. INTRODUCTION

Marshall chose to allot a remarkable, and probably excessive, proportion of his time in the years preceding the publication of the *Principles* to the observation of productive activities in many areas of Britain, and also abroad (Groenewegen 1995, pp. 187–9, 206–13); visits to industrial districts (IDs) formed a natural part of this investigation. His analysis of IDs is correspondingly embedded in his elaborate discussion of the content and organisation of these productive activities in Book IV, which extends to 185 pages. Lionel Robbins (1932, pp. 69–71) subsequently judged Marshall's approach to be fundamentally misguided, substituting 'amateur technology' for 'a discussion which should be purely economic', founded on 'the governing factor of all productive organisation – the relationship between prices and cost . . . In the modern treatment, discussion of "production" is part of the Theory of Equilibrium'.

However, conforming to Robbins's prescription would have frustrated Marshall's purpose in choosing to specialise in economics, which was to contribute to improving the condition of the people – not an uncommon Victorian aspiration. A simple calculation demonstrated how little could be achieved by even the most drastic redistribution of income and wealth; the prime emphasis must be on increasing productivity, although this necessary condition was not sufficient to ensure the higher quality of life which was essential to Marshall's conception of progress – again like many of his contemporaries. That the means of increasing productivity might contribute to this ultimate objective was a recurrent theme of the *Principles*, illustrated by his marginal summary 'In a healthy state new activities pioneer the way for new wants' (Marshall 1920, p. 89); but what mattered was not so much the endogeneity of preferences as the moulding of character. As Whitaker (1975, vol. I, p. 112) noted, '[t]he role played in Marshall's book by ethical considerations deserves more careful consideration than it is usually given'; the moral dimension could not be excluded either from economic analysis or economic policy.

At the beginning of Book IV Marshall identifies the principal means of improving productivity:

> Knowledge is our most powerful engine of production; it enables us to subdue Nature and force her to satisfy our wants. Organization aids knowledge; it has many forms, for example that of a single business, that of various businesses in the same trade, that of various trades relatively to one another, and that of the State providing security for all and help for many. (Marshall 1920, pp. 138–9)

Indeed its significance is so great that 'it seems best sometimes to reckon Organization apart as a distinct agent of production' (ibid., p. 139), and this is what he does in Book IV, allotting it five chapters, of 74 pages, compared with two chapters, of 29 pages, for land, three chapters, of 47 pages, for labour, and a single chapter, of 20 pages, for capital.

That organisation might be included with land, labour and capital as the essential agents of production should be a clear indication that Marshall was not concerned, as were most subsequent theorists, with the efficient allocation of existing resources to known methods of producing a closed list of goods and services – without considering the costs of discovering and implementing such an allocation. Organisation is a continuing activity, because what has to be organised is a system which will deliver not only goods and services but continuing improvement based on increasing knowledge. However, it is only a hundred pages later, after discussing land, labour (where some of the subsequent analysis is anticipated) and wealth, that Marshall begins to explain precisely how organisation aids knowledge, and why to be most effective it needs to take many forms.

The explanation is derived from Adam Smith, who had introduced his *Inquiry into the Nature and Causes of the Wealth of Nations* by stating two principles: increasing wealth is primarily a consequence of increasing productivity, and increasing productivity is primarily a consequence of the division of labour (Smith [1776] 1976, pp. 10, 13) Having, as we have seen, adopted Smith's first principle, Marshall now adopts the second, and extends it by propounding

> a fundamental unity of action between the laws of nature in the physical and in the moral world. This central unity is set forth in the general rule, to which there are not many exceptions, that the development of the organism, whether social or physical, involves an increasing subdivision of functions between its separate parts on the one hand, and on the other a more intimate connection between them (Marshall 1920, p. 241).

These 'more intimate connections' are not only a necessary consequence of the interdependence which is a necessary counterpart of the benefits of specialisation, as Smith ([1776] 1976, pp. 23, 26) had pointed out; different kinds of connections, constituting different forms of organisation and many variations within each form, encourage different combinations of evolved specialist knowledge and skills and direct the development of particular kinds of new knowledge and skills.

IDs feature quite modestly in Marshall's work, but they are a distinctive element, both in their own right and because they mark a recognition, not common among economists, that economies have a spatial dimension (Martin 2006, p. 393). Moreover, because these districts combine three forms of organisation – single businesses, groups of similar businesses and groups of different kinds of business – they may serve as the equivalent in Marshall's scheme of the pin factory in Smith's, bringing into a single focus the essential theme of economic development, to which coordination is essential but subservient. They also provide a setting for comparing the advantages and limitations of small and large firms. Both characteristics will receive explicit attention later; but we shall proceed by examining Marshall's views of the three forms of organisation in turn.

However, it is important to conclude this introduction by drawing attention to Marshall's insistence that the *Principles* 'is concerned throughout with the forces that cause movement' because it studies 'human beings who are impelled, for good or evil, to change and progress' (Marshall 1920, pp. xiv, xv). 'The fundamental characteristic of modern industrial life is not competition, but self-reliance, independence, deliberate choice and forethought' (ibid., p. 5). What has to be organised, therefore, is a network of systems which can direct these motives towards the creation and application of knowledge. This network, Marshall notes, is both the result of and the framework for cooperation and competition; and it is both an economic and a social system. As already noted, it is also a moral system: 'Economic forces belong to the moral world in so far as they depend upon human habits and affections, upon man's knowledge and industrial skill' (Whitaker 1975, vol. II, p. 163). Therefore the ideals of individuals are part of the data, changes in these ideals are an important factor in socio-economic change, and economic activities have a pervasive influence on character. In Marshall's work, not only are goods, preferences and technology not natural givens (though they may be taken as data for some particular analysis); neither are the cognitive (which include moral) processes of the individual actors.

2. THE SINGLE FIRM

The individual business is a system for the creation and application of knowledge; and this is achieved by developing, and from time to time modifying, organisational arrangements which allow the coordination of a set of specialised activities. How this works, for each individual, is explained by Marshall in a passage which seems to recall his model of 'Ye machine' (Marshall 1994), especially in his illustration of learning to skate: with repeated practice individual operations which at first required conscious attention become automatic, and it then becomes possible to focus on other operations or new ways of combining now-familiar procedures (Marshall 1920, pp. 250–51). The transformation of novelty into routine releases cognitive resources for the imagination of further novelty, which, if successful, becomes embodied in further routines. Thus custom, though resisting change, serves the double function of testing new ideas and of establishing and diffusing those that pass the tests (Marshall 1919, p. 197). This mental and physiological conception of human cognition as a continuing dialectical process contrasts sharply with the monolithic notion of the rational agent now prevalent in economic theory. It is the basis of Marshall's theory of economic progress, later to be reinvented and developed by Edith Penrose (1959); and it requires various forms of organisation to realise its potential. It also clearly implies that the firms within an industry are not homogenous: perfect competition is not compatible with the continuing search for improvement.

What this implies for the businessman is set out in Marshall's chapter on business management:

> [T]he manufacturer who makes goods not to meet special orders but for the general market, must, in his first role as merchant and organizer of production, have a thorough knowledge of *things* in his own trade. He must have the power of forecasting the broad movements of production and consumption, of seeing where there is an opportunity for supplying a new commodity that will meet a real want or improving the plan of producing an old commodity. He must be able to judge cautiously and take risks boldly; and he must of course understand the materials and machinery used in his trade. (Marshall 1920, p. 297)

'Judicious, orderly and vigorous management of routine' therefore provides the springboard 'to invent or adopt new ideas; to put them into practice, bearing the risks of loss; to improve on them, and again to improve on them' (Marshall 1919, p. 645). Marshall's 'great principle of substitution', which appears several times in the *Principles*, is realised by the actions of businessmen who 'are constantly devising and experimenting with new arrangements which involve the use of different factors of production, and selecting those most profitable for themselves' (Marshall 1920, p. 662). This 'principle of substitution' would be excluded by making production simply part of equilibrium, where businessmen would merely select that factor combination from the production set which maximised profit at current factor prices.

The search for improvement is not to be undertaken by the business man alone; he is expected to both encourage and facilitate it in others.

> But secondly in this role of employer he must be a natural leader of men. He must have a power of first choosing his assistants rightly and then trusting them fully; of interesting them in the business and of getting them to trust him, so as to bring out whatever enterprise and power of origination there is in them; while he himself exercises a general control over everything, and preserves order and stability in the main plan of the business. (Marshall 1920, pp. 297–8)

Marshall did not think of the firm as a means of controlling opportunism, but as a means of encouraging the search for opportunities.

As well as not being homogeneous, the firms that Marshall wrote about were not anonymous; and both features were essential in explaining how the economy worked. Firms were principal agents of both improvement and coordination, and the internal coordination of each firm's activities had to be supplemented by the coordination of relationships with suppliers and customers. Transaction costs are an inevitable consequence of specialisation, and the costs of individual transactions can be reduced by investment in the creation of a set of institutions (Ménard 1995, p. 170). The incentive to undertake such investment is obviously greatest for those who expect to make many transactions; and that, as Marshall (1919, pp. 271–4) pointed out, is why the organizers of production are prominent contributors to market making, operating as suppliers in goods markets and customers in labour markets. Marshall (ibid., p. 270) suggests that for some firms the capital commitment necessary to build an external organis of appropriate size and complexity may exceed that required for the fixed plant; and the returns expected on this investment form 'a great part' of 'supplementary costs', which the business man will attempt to cover even in times of slack trade (Marshall 1920, p. 458).

It is a natural consequence of the role of firms in market making that

> nearly everyone has . . . some '*particular*' markets; that is, some people or groups of people with whom he is in somewhat close touch: mutual knowledge and trust lead him to approach them, and them to approach him, in preference to strangers . . . He does not generally expect to get better prices from his clients than from others. But he expects to sell easily to them because they know and trust him. (Marshall 1919, p. 182)

If, as Williamson has insisted, fear of opportunism increases transaction costs, it is not surprising that investment in trust-building reduces them. Thus, as Hayek (1948b, p. 97) observed, competition helps us to discover who can be relied on to serve us well. As Casson (1997, p. 94) noted, good service depends on both integrity and competence. However, this process takes time and effort, and is subject to mistakes (Marshall 1920, p. 377); and as in other evolutionary processes future potential may be destroyed by initial inefficiency (ibid., p. 597). (For a more extensive discussion, see Loasby 2000.)

It is a natural consequence that not only is marketing 'an integral process, and not a series of independent transactions' (Marshall 1919, p. 270), but '[p]roduction and marketing are part of a single process of adjustment of supply to demand' (Marshall 1919, p. 181); marketability may be crucially dependent on design and the quality of the productive process. This is especially true when the producer is 'creating new wants by showing people something which they had never thought of having before' (Marshall 1920, p. 280); that this was identified as 'a characteristic task of the modern manufacturer' by Wilhelm Roscher (1817–94) should give a sense of historical proportion.

3. VARIOUS BUSINESSES IN THE SAME TRADE

Because there can be no demonstrably best way of creating or using knowledge, Marshall believed that economic development required many such businessmen, even within a single industry, to act as the prime agents of variety. This variety is a natural consequence of the range and degree of 'abilities required to make an ideal employer' (Marshall 1920, p. 298), so that different 'combinations of advantages' will result in the trial of different procedures and products. Therefore 'even in the same place and the same trade no two persons pursuing the same aims will adopt exactly the same routes. The tendency to variation is a chief cause of progress; and the abler are the undertakers in any trade the greater will this tendency be' (ibid., p. 355). (Was he perhaps recalling the processes by which the mechanical brain of his early imagination developed associations according to its particular circumstances and, in part, according to the sequence of its trials, or his own observations during his industrial visits in developing this theme of the evolution of knowledge and skills within a population of firms?) As Hayek (1978) was later to argue, the principal significance of competition was its effectiveness as a discovery procedure; this was incompatible with the homogeneity required for models of perfect competition, but produced a continuing flow of enlargements to the opportunity set, and in the process, was not much less effective than perfect competition (as a model) in undermining the basis of monopolistic profits – which for Marshall were a special category of rather modest importance.

This evolution is accelerated by 'three closely allied conditions of vigour, namely hopefulness, freedom, and change' (Marshall 1920, p. 197). These conditions encourage travellers to entertain new ideas prompted by their contact with other practices, and which may often be more freely exercised through 'a shifting of places . . . It is chiefly for this reason that in almost every part of England a disproportionately large share of the best energy and enterprise is to be found among those who were born elsewhere' (ibid., pp. 197–8) – an association between mobility and enterprise which was a prominent feature of his report on his American tour of 1875 (Whitaker 1975, vol. II, pp. 355–77). The effects of this widely distributed experimentation is enhanced by the distinctive human propensity to observe and imitate what appear to be better practices (a propensity to which Adam Smith gave considerable emphasis, but which Marshall seems to have taken for granted) and by the developments in communication, notably in the coverage of trade journals, to which Marshall (1920, p. 210) drew attention as a major aid to the diffusion of knowledge – and thus to the creation of further knowledge.

Consequently the relationship between the various businesses in the same trade delivers external economies to each of them, in the form of improved products and falling costs. These economies become available over time, and require action – not merely alertness – by any firm that wishes to enjoy them. Since an expansion of the business offers a particularly convenient occasion for adopting improvements, a historical long-run cost curve for that business may show falling costs with increasing output, but this is not reversible. The principle that 'in economics every event causes permanent alterations in the conditions under which future events can occur' is stated in both 'The pure theory of foreign trade' and 'The pure theory of domestic values' (Whitaker 1975, vol. II, pp. 163, 201). For Marshall a firm's long-run cost curve does not constitute its production set, available for choice, but an expansion path. (This, of course, is entirely consistent with his view of what economics should be about.) Therefore, as Marshall observed, a subsequent reduction in output by that firm would not dissipate all the gains – and in any case the costs of any particular firm are not relevant to an explanation of price and output for the industry to which it contributes.

4. VARIOUS TRADES RELATIVE TO ONE ANOTHER

To achieve the benefits of an extensive division of labour, it is essential that those engaged in each specialised activity have access to goods and services produced by those engaged in a great many other specialised activities. In a fundamental sense, all these activities are complementary elements of an economic system, and the organisation of these complementary activities is the standard problem of allocative efficiency. However, what Marshall had particularly in mind was complementarity between the set of activities, sometimes very extensive, needed to produce a particular class of goods. This requires 'an increasing subdivision of functions' to be associated with 'a more intimate connection between them' (Marshall 1920, p. 241). This complementarity may be of two kinds, though the boundary between the two may be indistinct; and they call for different kinds of connection.

When one activity produces a standardised set of goods or services which may be used in a range of subsequent activities, the connections need not be very intimate – though they must still be provided. What is needed is confidence that goods of the particular pattern required will be available in appropriate quantities at an appropriate price; this may call for little in the way of direct negotiation between producer and purchaser. However, this can be true only if someone has already invested in the creation of a set of market institutions. Such investment had been very extensive by the time that Marshall produced the *Principles*: 'the intimacy and firmness of connections' is illustrated by 'the increase of security of commercial credit, and of the means and habits of communication by sea and road, by railway and telegraph, by post and printing-press' (Marshall 1920, p. 241).

The other kind of complementarity is created by activities that are intended to produce goods or services which are closely matched to specific requirements. This may call for close continuing relationships. Although on a superficial view one might assume that such relationships are best managed within a single business, George Richardson (1972) pointed out that activities which are closely complementary may require very different skills, resting on different cognitive bases, and therefore be difficult to combine within a single management system. (Even similar products designed with very different levels of technical specification within a single business may be best manufactured in separate premises.) Marshall's own presentation of business management as a dialectic between automaticity and novelty relies (like his 'machine') on domain-limited interpretative systems which are sharply differentiated, even if they then have to be selectively integrated. The most appropriate solution may then be an intimate collaboration for a specific purpose between selected members of formally independent organisations which each preserve their distinctive orientations.

As the scale of operations increases, so do the advantages of finer divisions of labour; and this is recognised in Marshall's (1920, p. 318) formulation of the law of increasing return: 'An increase of labour and capital leads generally to improved organization, which increases the efficiency of the work of labour and capital'. In formal language, increasing return is not a property of a known production set which exhibits economies of scale; instead the production set evolves as people respond to increased scale by imagining and exploring new possibilities. That, according to Marshall, this increasing return generally includes internal economies but always includes external economies suggests that this improved organisation often includes some adjustment of firm boundaries, as Allyn Young (1928) was to emphasise. A natural consequence is the increasing importance of external organisation, which is likely to be more complex when it connects firms in different trades than firms within a single trade, precisely because these connections must interpret systems of thought which embody differentiated assumptions and associations. These interpretations must be built and tested gradually, as has been repeatedly discovered. The costs of doing so, and the time required, are likely to be less if the different activities are carried out at no great distance, and also if the people responsible share the experience of a particular locality. Where many such connections are found within a modest compass, we have an ID.

5. INDUSTRIAL DISTRICTS

That Marshall's analysis of IDs is embedded in his general discussion of economic organisation is illustrated by his introduction to this analysis, which begins with a reference to early specialised trades in light and expensive commodities, leading to a brief survey of locations based on the concentration of particular natural resources or of favoured sites for particular kinds of natural products, the special demands of a court or the creation of immigrant communities, often under royal direction, leading to an emphasis on the importance of 'the character of the people, and . . . their social and political institutions' – and especially the development of 'free industry and enterprise' (Marshall 1920, p. 270). The implication is that these circumstances are most clearly illustrated when an industry has become concentrated in a small area.

There is a constant market for the skills on which the localised industry depends, providing reassurance for workers and employers alike; this is based on extensive formal and informal arrangements which constitute a major capital investment, to which many have contributed. These arrangements are likely to include some specialist educational provision as well as on-the-job training, the recipients of which may already have developed the relevant absorptive capacity as children. The potential danger inherent in such dense labour markets is their exposure to an industry-wide depression, but this can be mitigated in the larger IDs by the presence of other concentrated industries within the same geographical area. Even though firms are small they may have access to the services of many subsidiary trades, some of which may operate on a larger scale; Marshall cites the particular case of highly-specialised machinery, which may be operated efficiently by a firm which restricts itself to a particular stage of production but serves many customers.

The combination of three forms of organisation within an ID not only achieves efficiency through the exploitation of distributed knowledge which is already available; it is a means of increasing knowledge. The kinds of variation between businesses in the same trade, which are to be expected from the individual cognitive processes which were envisaged by Marshall, prompt modifications and combinations, encouraged by continual interactions between members of different firms based on common interests and the social relations that are encouraged by the coexistence of geographical and cognitive proximity, leading to the emergence of a dense network of epistemic communities and communities of practice. Thus an ID can exploit the external economies not only of the automatic operations which have already evolved in differentiated knowledge domains, but also the external economies of an evolutionary process of knowledge development which combines the advantages of specialisation and of variation and imitation within each specialism. Both kinds of economies are supported by shared membership of a social system, in which contact is easy, and knowledge of who to contact for what purpose is readily acquired. It is the product of much purposeful activity which creates a spontaneous order. That the ID appealed to Marshall as a system which encouraged personal development will be argued in the final section.

6. ECONOMIES OF LARGE SCALE

Marshall's chapter in the *Principles* on localised industries is immediately followed by an exposition of the advantages of production on a large scale. Though reverting from the interaction of three forms of organisation to focus on a particular category of a single form – the large firm – we shall use this sequence to focus on a particular aspect of Marshall's theory of industrial organisation which later provoked controversy. Of the economies attainable through increased size, more efficient use of material is quickly dismissed, precisely because of the network of arrangements open to small firms in a localised industry. Much more important is the continuing development of specialised and expensive machinery, despite the possibility of contracting out particular operations to which Marshall had already drawn attention, but now explicitly qualifies (Marshall 1920, p. 279). Furthermore the small manufacturer may lack up-to-date knowledge. What is particularly significant, in the evolutionary context of Book IV, is that in new or rapidly changing industries 'new machinery and new processes are for the greater part devised by manufacturers for their own use' (ibid., p. 280); the owner of a small business is hard put to find the time, money and thought to undertake the necessary experiments, or to bear the costs of failure, and may have difficulty in discovering what is going on in a large firm.

A large business is likely to have advantages in buying and selling, not least in being able to invest the large capital required to create the market institutions which will make access easy to a large number of customers (Marshall 1920, p. 282), and it can both establish a finer division of labour and a larger pool from which to select those of exceptional ability for particular activities or for promotion into the various grades of management (ibid., p. 283). This in turn will allow the head of the business to 'keep his mind fresh and clear for thinking out the most difficult and vital problems of his business' (ibid., p. 284). At the same time there is obvious merit in allowing those of exceptional ability scope to apply that ability in a large business.

However, large family businesses often had problems of succession (Marshall 1920, pp. 299–300), and conversion into a joint-stock company introduced problems of direction and management control which, though mitigated by 'the progress of trade morality, . . . a diminution of trade secrecy and by increased publicity in every form' (ibid., p. 303), could prevent the realisation of the potential advantages of scale, while inefficient expansion might be 'at the expense of small businesses with greater elasticity and power of origination' (Marshall 1919, pp. 321–2). Although Marshall was confident that the forces of competition were fairly effective in bringing the ability of businessmen into a closer relationship with the size of the businesses that they owned, he was concerned with the waste of potential, especially among the working classes:

'[E]very system, which allows the higher faculties of the lower grades of industry to go to waste, is open to grave suspicion' (Marshall 1920, p. 249).

This was one reason for his support of the cooperative movement (though he recognised its problems); it also underlay his sympathy for small firms, which from this perspective had two advantages: it was easier for a worker of skill and ambition to establish such a firm, and its employees would be much more conscious of its external relationships, from which they could learn a great deal, whereas many of the activities of a large firm, even among management, were internally oriented, and so provided relatively little experience of Marshall's second and third forms of organisation. IDs therefore had a dual role: they helped small firms to prosper by fostering external economies which matched (in varying degrees) the internal economies of large firms, and they provided valuable preparation for creating a business (as well as role models) for those workers who conceived the possibility. In doing so they enhanced the evolutionary process of knowledge creation on which Marshall's hopes depended.

7. MARSHALL'S PURPOSE

In the introduction to Book I of the *Principles*, Marshall declares his priorities in a passage which dates from the first edition:

> [Economics] is on the one side a study of wealth; and on the other, and more important side, a part of the study of man. For man's character has been moulded by his everyday work, and the material resources which he thereby procures, more than by any other influence unless it be that of his religious ideals. (Marshall 1920, p. 1).

It is worth remarking that 'the influence which the daily occupations of men exert on their character' is the theme of his essay on his American tour of 1875 (Whitaker 1975, vol. II, p. 357); Whitaker drew attention to the significance of this essay. Thus although the organisation of industry was of central importance in delivering the improvements in productivity which he believed were a precondition of a good life for all, it was of even more importance in ensuring that these possibilities were realised. Economics was the servant of ethics: it should not only enlarge people's freedom of choice, but also encourage what Marshall believed were better choices. Although Marshall 'developed a tendency to socialism' (Marshall 1919, p. vii) he was suspicious of 'socialist schemes', because they did not make 'adequate provision for the maintenance of high enterprise and individual strength of character' (ibid., p. viii), preferring cooperative societies (for both retailing and manufacturing) and, with some reservations, the influence of trade unions.

Although Marshall was impressed by the effectiveness of the evolutionary process which he sought to analyse in improving productivity, he was well aware that survival was an imperfect test of value; advantages were often accompanied by significant drawbacks (Marshall 1920, pp. 244–5). In particular, 'direct and immediate service at a lower price' would normally outweigh the potential for greater future benefits (ibid., p. 597). This was also a problem at the personal level; he had a recurrent concern for the failure of 'prospectiveness' (ibid., pp. 224–5, 233), which he regarded as a more important influence than the rate of interest – especially on parents' attitudes to the education of their children (ibid., p. 217), which contributed to the 'wasteful negligence' of so much potential (ibid., p. 212). In his report on his American tour, he identified two desirable ethical effects which might be produced by an appropriate organisation of industry: 'the peaceful moulding of character into harmony with the conditions by which it is surrounded' and 'the education of a firm will through the overcoming of difficulties' (Whitaker 1975, vol. II, p. 375). This apparently contrasting pair of attributes may perhaps be treated as a development of the dialectic between automaticity and novelty which guided the operation of his 'machine' and underpins his theory of economic evolution. In turn these effects foster the development of knowledge within a coherent but changing system and a good use of this knowledge in both production and consumption.

However, Marshall has no formula for success. A pervasive problem is that of large firms. Although 'great businesses alone are capable of some of the chief tasks of industry in the present age' (Marshall 1919, p. 577) – especially those requiring large-scale integration – they pose serious problems of management; and they often 'do little to educate high creative faculty' (ibid., p. 603), because they depend so much on routine and offer relatively little opportunity for many of their managers to interact with members of other firms and so encounter alternative ways of thinking and acting. This is particularly important when progress requires, not the experiments at the margin which are best distributed across a population of firms, but the creation of a new system of production or distribution. He therefore continued to be attracted by the notion of a localised knowledge community which could sustain the intimate cooperation which might provide an alternative means of developing new systems – and which offered far more openings for the development and application of ability. 'Even working men often have exceptional opportunities for starting and controlling cooperative, co-partnership, and ordinary joint-stock undertakings for work, with which they are familiar' (ibid., p. 319). Here was a continuing role for IDs, as social and economic systems which promoted economic and individual development. 'For after all man is the end of production' (ibid., p. 195): human character and the quality of life, not the 'maximisation of utility' or Pareto optimality, are the objectives that matter. These are the characteristics which Giacomo Becattini found so congenial in Marshall's account of IDs – and of industrial organisation in general.

8. External and internal economies

Neil Hart

1. INTRODUCTION

Much of the recent literature on industry location and industrial districts (IDs) has been premised on what has been termed a 'rediscovery' of Marshall's conceptualization of economies of scale, and external economies in particular. An examination of aspects of Marshall's analysis of economies of scale therefore represents a logical starting point in establishing the theoretical perspective from which these issues are currently being investigated. A consideration of the representation of economies of scale within mainstream economic theory subsequent to Marshall helps to explain why this 'rediscovery' of his contribution has been important in shaping the more recent investigations into forms of industrial organization such as the ID. A discussion of these themes also helps to delineate more clearly the forces that promote, sustain and threaten the viability of IDs as a variety of industrial organization.

Marshall's treatment of economies of scale must be placed in its intended setting if its inferences are to be fully appreciated. Despite the pivotal role accorded to Marshall among pioneering equilibrium economists, the approach Marshall brought to economics was, as described by Becattini (2003b, p. 24), 'mainly evolutionary', but also permitting 'considerable scope for idealities and human consciousness'. Marshall's representation of industrial organization and change combines aspects of Adam Smith's depiction of increasing returns based on the division of labour, extended to encompass more directly the growth of knowledge, with a blend of Spencerian and Darwinian notions of evolutionary change. In Book IV of Marshall's *Principles*, as well as in *Industry and Trade*, the discussion of industrial organization clearly depicts a continuous and irreversible process of change and reorganization, entailing the principles of 'selection', 'differentiation' and 'integration' that Marshall understood to be fundamental to an understanding of 'organic' processes. This is expressed in what Marshall (1920, p. 241) denoted as a 'general rule' that 'the development of the organism, whether social or physical, involves an increasing subdivision of functions between its separate parts on the one hand, and on the other a more intimate connection between them'. In this setting the interconnections between variation and selection were embodied in innovation realized though the establishment and replication of routines. Irrespective of its origins, economies of scale signifies increased complexity and differentiation in industrial organization, and reflects the transmission among firms of technical and organizational information. The origins of scale economies are not found within engineering blueprints contained in 'known' production functions.

2. SOURCES OF INTERNAL ECONOMIES AND EXTERNAL ECONOMIES IN MARSHALL

The now familiar internal–external economy distinction is clearly delineated in Marshall's *Principles*, having been developed from his earlier writings (see for example the passages from 'Pure theory of domestic values' in Whitaker 1975, vol. II, p. 198). External economies are defined as 'those dependent on the general development of the industry', while internal economies are 'dependent on the resources of the individual houses of business engaged in it, on their organisation and the efficiency of their management' (Marshall 1920, p. 266). Three major classes of internal economies are isolated: those generated through increased subdivision of labour, increased specialization of the managerial function and those arising as a result of creative innovations in the organizational and mechanical aspects of production. Internal economies are generally associated with the growth of large business enterprises and increasingly centralized modes of business organisation. In Marshall's treatment of internal economies, the efficiency gains and the ability to exploit new opportunities and to expand business size was largely a function of the 'vigour' and internal organization of the firm. The growth of business depended ultimately on an ability and preparedness to discover and incorporate new ideas and techniques, which in turn reflected the variable astuteness, enthusiasm and commitment of decision makers located within business organisations. In Marshall's view, there were limits to which these attributes could be realized within expanding business enterprises, even in the case of the large-scale joint-stock companies that had evolved during Marshall's time.

In relation to external economies, two general types can be discerned in Marshall's writings. Firstly there are economies arising from 'the use of specialised skill and machinery' depending on 'the aggregate volume of production in the neighbourhood'. The other involves 'those connected with the growth of knowledge and the progress of the arts' and which depend on the 'aggregate volume of production in the whole civilised world' (ibid., pp. 265–6). Most significantly, external economies can often be 'secured by the concentration of many small businesses of a similar character in particular localities' (ibid., p. 266).

This may then result in the 'localization of industry', occasionally referred to as IDs by Marshall, where 'numerous specialized branches of industry have been welded almost automatically into one organic whole' (Marshall 1919, p. 599).

As described by Marshall, each of the small firms within an industrial neighbourhood derives benefit from the external economies of scale associated with the locality as a whole. Firstly the local firms can derive benefit from access to a pool of 'special skilled labour', which is attracted to the locality because of the plentiful local demand for their skills. The use of expensive and specialized equipment may also be rendered more cost-effective among the local firms, and the localization of industries also encourages the growth of subsidiary trades which 'grow up in the neighbourhood, supplying it with implements and materials, organizing its traffic, and in many ways conducing to the economy of its material' (Marshall 1920, p. 271). Economies from reduced transportation and communication costs may also arise as a result of the regional proximity of the firms.

The most significant of the sources of external economies discussed by Marshall relates to the emergence of an 'industrial atmosphere' which promotes creativity and innovation and the transfer of knowledge among the geographically connected firms:

> When an industry has thus chosen a locality for itself, it is likely to stay there long: so great are the advantages which people following the same skilled trade get from near neighbourhood to one another. The mysteries of the trade become no mysteries; but are as it were in the air, and children learn many of them unconsciously. Good work is rightly appreciated, inventions and improvements in machinery, in processes and the general organization of the business have their merits promptly discussed: if one man starts a new idea, it is taken up by others and combined with suggestions of their own; and thus it becomes the source of further new ideas. (Ibid., p. 271)

3. MARSHALLIAN EXTERNAL ECONOMIES AND IDs

External economies therefore in Marshall's scheme are to a significant extent based on the transfer and sharing of knowledge facilitated by the ongoing interactions between people enhanced through the geographical proximity of firms. This emphasizes once again Marshall's theme that knowledge and creativity are embodied in the ideas of people, rather than in technologically determined input–output relationships. It is cooperation within the district, combined with competition, which provides the impetus for the self-perpetuation of the 'organic whole'. Marshall (ibid., p. 276) also alludes to instances where 'social forces cooperate with economic' in the realization of external economies in local regions. However, the significance of the 'social forces' dimension is often left implicit by Marshall in the *Principles*, with the local and social dimensions referred to more directly in his earlier writings.

As the following passage from *Industry and Trade* suggests, Marshall to some extent began to place less prominence on the external economies that sustained IDs as a mechanism through which the division of labour manifested itself:

> But with the growth of capital, the development of machinery, and the improvement of the means of communication, the importance of internal economies has increased steadily and fast, while some of the old external economies have declined in importance; and many of those which have risen in their place are national, or even cosmopolitan, rather than local. (Marshall 1919, p. 167)

This may, in part, shed some light on what Becattini (2003b, pp. 23–4) described as Marshall's inclination to 'jettison' the ID anomaly, to the point of not including it in the subject index of his books. It could also be concluded that Marshall's depiction of the localization of industry was primarily intended to illustrate the role of external economies in the essentially evolutionary process of industrial development, rather than to provide in a systematic manner the building blocks for a fully articulated theory of IDs (Martin 2006). Similarly, it could be argued that the treatment of external economies in the *Principles* may have been shaped to conform more directly to Marshall's partial equilibrium apparatus, where the analysis focuses attention on choices by firms within a given sector. No such restrictions are placed on the discussion of external economies in Marshall's earlier writings, where these economies can be seen to help nurture collections of interrelated producers that form a territorial system of communities each constituting an open subsystem of the economy as a whole. An attempt to confine these forces to a particular sector has the unfortunate affect of inviting the later Pigouvian construct of economies that are external to the firm, and yet at the same time, internal to a particular industry. If external economies are restricted to this type, then IDs would not form part of the economic landscape, and key aspects of Marshall's observations of industry would escape the analysis being undertaken.

A concluding observation on the context of IDs in Marshall's scheme is perhaps most aptly coined in the following interpretation offered by Loasby:

> For Marshall, [the] principle of differentiation combined with integration was the key to understanding the working of economic systems. Industrial districts were particularly clear manifestations of a universal economic phenomenon, and so it is important to respect Marshall's methodological principle of continuity and not exaggerate their distinctiveness as a form of industrial organization. (Loasby 1998, p. 70)

The essence of Marshall's approach to industrial organization survived in the teaching and published work of a group of his pupils and closest disciples, most notably Lavington, Chapman, Macgregor and Dennis Robertson. Some fragments of Marshall's approach were also discernible in the later work of Austin Robinson and Sargant Florence. While these writers contributed theoretical and empirical investigations that varied in terms of method, when viewed collectively Marshall's analysis of scale economies in terms of specialization, differentiation and integration can be observed to have been a common reference point. Importantly, the environment in which knowledge is shared and harnessed through innovation is emphasized, together with the problems associated with coordinating activities within large centralized productive units. Macgregor's (1906 and 1929) analysis of industry organization and progress stresses the role of differentiation and specialization through the subdivision of functions, together with 'invention'. The notion of conscious coordination and foresight is also central to Macgregor's account, where forms of ('inorganic') combination amongst firms can hasten the realization of the advantages of specialization otherwise attained through the mechanisms of natural selection and competition. The interconnections between internal and external economies and various forms of horizontal and vertical integration play an important role in Macgregor's analysis, with the role of 'giant' firms much more visible in his analysis in comparison to that of Chapman's (1904). Macgregor, for example, contended that large businesses in part evolved from the localized external economies that had been stressed by Chapman, and in turn contributed to the emergence and survival of IDs. Macgregor (1929, p. 28) distanced himself somewhat from the view that these external economies could be interpreted as being substantially internal to a particular location, instead arguing that a local body of people cannot have the full advantage of industrial progress 'unless they share it with a wider bodies of people'.

Similarly to Chapman and Macgregor, Robertson (1923, p. 26) recognizes localization as one of the 'forces which are strongly at work in modern industry'. Like Marshall, Robertson (ibid., p. 29) also highlighted what he termed the solid benefits conferred by the 'force of habit' within a locality, in that 'its problems become the common topic of conversation and saturate the atmosphere'. However, Robertson departed from Marshall's vision of IDs being comprised of collections of small interrelated firms, suggesting that, with some exceptions, the 'most evident effect of localization is an increase in the size of the individual firm' (ibid., p. 30). When comparing the writings of Chapman, Macgregor and Robertson, we observe that there is the absence of the emergence of a unique form of industrial organization best fitted to the evolving industrial landscape. As Raffaelli (2004, p. 214) suggests in his more detailed survey of the themes just outlined, the different and to some extent opposing perspectives revealed in the writings of Marshall's followers is paradigmatic of the open framework of Marshall's industrial analysis which shows 'the manifold trends of evolutionary processes'. The localization of industry and formation of IDs represents one possible pathway in which these evolutionary processes can lead. Clearly, the fitness of IDs to the industrial environment goes beyond considerations that can be defined in terms of the physical conditions of production. The most important of the external economies that nurture and sustain the ID anomaly are shown to depend on the distinctive patterns of cooperation and competition that evolve through time amongst the human beings that inhabit the districts themselves.

4. INTERNAL AND EXTERNAL ECONOMIES IN MAINSTREAM ECONOMICS

The 'Marshallian' analysis of industrial organization outlined above was largely ignored by the architects of the mainstream Marshallian theoretical apparatus that followed in the shadows of Marshall's *Principles*. A notable feature of mainstream economic theory subsequent to Marshall was a fundamental change in the treatment of economies of scale. Increasingly attention became focused on investigating ways in which economies of scale could be represented within static equilibrium models under 'competitive' conditions. In this setting, internal economies were acknowledged as being the 'adversary of competition', and instead the role of external economies was emphasized, although their form and role departed significantly from what Marshall had envisaged. Formal mathematical representations, in the Cunynghame–Edgeworth–Pigou tradition, constructed supply functions of individual firms that included aggregate output alongside the supply price of the individual firm as explanatory variables. It was also postulated that the output of each producer is small in comparison with the collective output of all competitors. Adopting this approach, Pigou (1920, p. 744) went on to claim to have resolved the 'apparent conflict between mathematical analysis and experience' when dealing with increasing returns by hypothesizing that each individual firm was operating under increasing costs, while the industry as a whole was operating under decreasing costs, therefore reflecting economies external to the firms in the industry.

The empirical irrelevance of the Cunynghame–Edgeworth–Pigou construction of external economies was emphasized by writers such as Young (1913) and Clapham (1922), while Pigou's (1922 and 1924) responses were based on a distinction said to exist between 'pure theory' and applied studies. However, the futility of the attempted theoretical depiction of economies of scale within the partial equilibrium framework analysis of competitive equilibrium was clearly demonstrated by the likes of Robertson (1924), Sraffa (1926), and Young (1928) in particular, leading to the Marshallian cost controversies of the late 1920s. A most unfortunate facet of the Marshallian cost controversies was the inference that Marshall assigned the key role to external economies in an attempt to reconcile increasing returns and 'competitive equilibrium'. It is also an interpretation which was further promoted by Stigler's (1941 and 1990) influential assessments of Marshall's contributions. This is a complete misinterpretation of the role of external economies in Marshall's writings, and had the effect of diverting attention away from the evolutionary account of industry organization that was central to Marshall's analysis in the *Principles* (Hart 1996).

The repercussions flowing from the Marshallian cost controversies did have a decisive role in shaping the analysis of scale economies in the years that have followed. In the partial equilibrium models, now based on notions of 'imperfect competition', internal economies were permitted to exist along the downward sloping portion of 'U-shaped' long-run average total cost curves. The precise source or evolution of the internal economies was largely irrelevant to the analysis. The cost functions themselves were based on input–output properties attributed to 'typical' or 'well-behaved' production functions. Unlike internal economies, external economies were seen as being compatible with competitive markets, and translated into positive externalities were treated essentially as instances of 'market failure'. When attention is shifted to the general equilibrium approaches, the role of economies of scale becomes more obscure. In many of its forms, general equilibrium analysis was to declare the absence of scale economies as one of its basic axioms. One of its chief architects, Debreu (1959, p. 41) had admitted that the assumption of convexity for each producer's production set (that is, constant returns to scale) was 'crucial' to the theorems derived from the Arrow–Debreu models, while Hahn (1984, p. 116) similarly conceded that the whole theory remains 'at risk' if there are increasing returns which are 'large relative to the size of the economy'. As Arrow (1985, p. 113) acknowledged, a theory of imperfect competition is 'badly needed in the presence of increasing returns on a scale large relative to the economy and is superfluous in their absence'.

The limitations in the treatment of economies of scale within the general equilibrium are often seen as complications arising from internal economies. However, the limited scope that can be granted to external economies in such a framework should not be overlooked. These limitations are perhaps most clearly observed through the distinction Scitovsky (1954) drew between technological and pecuniary external economies, a distinction not found in Marshall's earlier categorization. Technological external economies, which basically reflected non-market interdependencies between producers affecting production functions, were seen as being reconcilable with competitive markets. On the other hand, pecuniary external economies occur when the profits (that is, revenue and cost conditions) of one producer are affected by the actions of another producer. These economies include indirect interdependencies among producers that are revealed through market interaction between producers. In terms of Scitovsky's widely adopted distinction, pecuniary external economies are not amenable to the treatment of competitive markets within a general equilibrium framework. However, interdependence through the market mechanism is seen to be all pervading, so it is this type of external economy which is in fact most relevant for the analysis of issues relating to economic development (Chandra and Sandilands 2006).

The rather glaring divide that had developed between the equilibrium theoretic approaches and the more applied investigations of scale economies observed in the 'real economy' was often acknowledged (see for example the introduction to the volume on *Increasing Returns and Economic Analysis*, Arrow, Ng and Yang 1998). This divide may have gathered legitimacy from the distinction made by Knight (1921), for example, between the 'theoretical and the 'empirical' portion of economics; a methodological perspective that was divorced from that of Marshall who had rejected the notion of 'pure theory' being somehow divorced from economic realities (see for example Marshall's correspondence with John Neville Keynes, in Whitaker 1996, vol. I, p. 338). Within the divide that had been created between 'theory' and 'applied work', industrial organization became an area of investigation which was effectively isolated from the core of economic theory. Linkages with Marshall's representation of industrial organization and change were enthusiastically promoted in the work of P.W.S. Andrews (1951) and his followers; however, these approaches to industry economics had limited impact on the thinking of their contemporaries. Within the accounts of industrial organization that followed, economies of scale were included among elements of market structure from which economic efficiency implications could be drawn. There were only very isolated occurrences where attempts were made to establish backward linkages between the insights gained from the study of industrial organization and the core of the equilibrium-based mainstream economic theories of value, distribution and output determination.

5. FROM DEVELOPMENT ECONOMICS TO CONTEMPORARY APPROACHES TO THE NEW ECONOMIC GEOGRAPHY

Marshall's depiction of the role of internal and external economies is discernible in the 'high development theory' that emerged during the 1940s and 1950s. Here the likes of Clark (1940), Myrdal (1957), Hirschman (1958), Kaldor (1966) and Nurkse (1967) argued that the expansion of modern sectors of the manufacturing industry could only take place simultaneously with other interrelated sectors. The improved competitive position of enterprises in the expanding industries arose primarily as a result of the growth of the integrated sectors as a whole, and the increased investment opportunities that were associated with this growth. The associated economies often closely resembled causal factors emphasized in Marshall's treatment of external economies, particularly with the variety that Scitovsky had categorized as being pecuniary. Again these types of investigation struggled to find a legitimate role alongside the more accepted accounts of development economics where the fostering of market forces was seen as providing the key to overcoming barriers to development created by various forms of 'institutional rigidities' and 'market imperfections'.

The absence of a meaningful role for external economies within the equilibrium models that had come to dominate economic theory meant that anything resembling Marshall's ID was not part of the economic landscape being depicted. The geographical distribution of production instead was relegated to 'specialised' areas of study such as 'regional and urban economics' and 'economic geography'. However as Martin (2006, pp. 396–7) observed, initially at least economic geographers seem not to have been much influenced by Marshall's excursions into the economics of industrial locations, although more recently writers such as Markusen (1996) have investigated various forms of localized industrial space within the rather broad theme of the 'post-Fordist mode of specialized flexible production'. A.J. Scott's (2000) interesting account of the various 'paradigms' that have tended to define economic geography also emphasizes the recent resurgence of interest in what is referred to as the 'localities debate', and at the same emphasizes the multidisciplinary mode of thinking often observed amongst these contributions.

The work of Porter (1990a and 1998a) and his followers should also be noted. In Porter's (1998a, p. 90) analysis 'the enduring competitive advantage in a global economy are often heavily localized, arising from concentrations of highly specialized skills and knowledge, institutions, related businesses, and sophisticated customers'. Porter's geographical clustering of industries clearly resembled the environment in which Marshall's IDs had evolved, particularly in the context of the importance of the sharing of knowledge. Porter also emphasizes the importance of competition between producers within a cluster, and the multidisciplinary approach adopted emphasizes that the advantages associated with such geographical concentration does not simply result from easily found technologically-based input–output relationships. While widely acclaimed in many disciplines, Porter's work has often been categorized as belonging to 'business economics', where applied analysis of economic phenomena 'lacks' the rigor of formal economic techniques. However, as Martin (2006, p. 398) has argued, there is a clear intellectual path dependence between Marshall and Porter, and the inferences drawn from Porter's contributions could in many instances have been developed from Marshall's original analysis of the external economies that are associated with the localization of industrial production.

From around the 1980s and onwards, the emergence of what has been termed 'new growth theory', 'new trade theory' and 'new economic geography' has contributed to what is in fact a revival of the older Marshallian tradition of thinking about the effects of scale economies. Prior to the emergence of 'new growth theory', the dominant Solow–Swann neoclassical growth models had viewed economic growth as arising from the growth of (essentially homogeneous) capital and labour, together with 'technical progress'. However, technical progress was treated as an exogenous variable, and its source and rate were not explained within the theoretical model which permitted only those economies of scale that could coexist with competitive markets. Empirically, 'technical progress' was essentially treated as a 'residual', corresponding to economic growth that could not be accounted for by increases in capital and labour.

A defining characteristic of the 'new growth theory' approach is that economies of scale are treated as being endogenous, intimately associated with new knowledge. In this setting, technical progress is the product of economic activity, and the economies of scale associated with knowledge and technology are the key to broadening growth and development opportunities. Equilibrium growth in competitive markets is replaced with the likelihood of path dependency and locking-in effects. The origins transfer and application of knowledge takes centre stage, together with the nature of the institutional arrangements that evolve through time. The transfer of knowledge is not frictionless, and may well become entrenched in particular organizations or locations. This perspective on 'new growth theory' places the analysis of economies of scale in a setting that would not be unfamiliar to the reader of Marshall's *Principles*. These perspectives are also to be found in 'new trade theory', which emerged also during the 1980s as a challenge to the traditional analysis of international specialization based largely on neoclassical general equilibrium models. Briefly, 'new trade theory', recognizing the importance of intra-industry trade between countries, emphasizes trade between nations founded on specialization to take advantage of economies of scale, rather than national differences in factor endowments. Krugman's numerous contributions to this literature have at times stressed different sources of scale economies in explaining the 'advantages of large-scale production'. Most significantly, Krugman has increasingly tended to emphasize the role of external economies at a local or regional scale, rather than treating nations as economic units (Martin and Sunley 1996). This has led to what Krugman (1998) has himself referred to as the 'new economic geography', where the factors that influence the geographical distribution of production is the main topic for investigation.

In Krugman's own contributions, the ('centripetal') forces that promote geographical concentration are equated directly with what are termed the 'three classic Marshallian sources of external economies': market size effects, thick labour markets (especially for specialized skills) and pure external economies' (Krugman 1998, p. 3). These geographical concentration promotion forces are involved in a 'tug of war' with the ('centrifugal') forces that oppose localizations, such as immobility in factors of production, land rents and 'pure external diseconomies' (congestion being the example put forward). These forces that promote and oppose the spatial concentration of activities collectively come together to constitute a form of regional competitiveness that provides an economic rationale for the localization of industry. In his analysis of the market size effects (consisting of backward and forward linkages within the locality), Krugman tends to emphasize pecuniary (as opposed to technological) economies derived from both external and internal economies of scale. In cases where economies of scale are internal for firms, internal economies in the production of intermediate inputs can behave like external economies for the firms that purchase them. In this sense it can be seen that internal economies of scale may provide the incentive for the centralization of specific productive activities within a particular enterprise; however, at the same time, the backward and forward linkages encourage the regional agglomeration of integrated activities setting into motion the localised external economies emphasized by both Krugman and Marshall before him.

Krugman's 'pure external economy effects', potentially realised through the local concentration of economic activity, are equated with 'information spillovers', and linked directly with Marshall's original analysis through the expression, 'The mysteries of the trade become no mystery, but are, as it were, in the air' (Krugman 1998, p. 4). However, as is reflected in Krugman's (1991a) seminal contribution, the 'new' economic geography modelling tends to abstract from these 'pure external economies', instead focusing on the 'more tangible' market size and 'factor immobility' effects. Krugman (1998, p. 5) argues that the task of the economic geography would be 'ill defined' if the forces producing that geography are 'inside a black box labelled "external effect"'. In adopting this approach, the new economic geography departs company with the earlier 'Marshallian' treatment of external economies which were essentially knowledge based (that is, 'information spillovers') embedded in the 'industrial atmosphere' of the industrial neighbourhoods.

6. THE CONTEMPORARY REEMERGENCE OF IDs AND THE REDISCOVERY OF MARSHALLIAN EXTERNAL ECONOMIES

The analysis of what Krugman termed 'pure external effects' associated with the localization of industry is at the centre of an alternative approach to the investigation of IDs which has been inspired in the main by Becattini's (1986b, 1990, 2004a) examination of the ongoing role of IDs in the economic progress of the Italian economy. Rather than being developed within the new economic geography framework outlined above, Becattini's (2003b and 2006) contributions have been inspired by Marshall's original analysis of external economies. The role of what Krugman had termed 'pure external economies' invigorated by the 'industrial atmosphere' is at the centre of this analysis, and rather than being locked 'inside a black box' the forces shaping the vitality of the 'industrial atmosphere' are explored in detail. Becattini delineates the nature of these forces as follows:

Now, with the industrial district, the human community undergoes a transition from a passive entry into an actor, for what are the industrial atmosphere and the internal–external economies if not ways through which the local society affects the productivity of labour . . . The concept of a local society as an additional productive factor, together with accumulation and technical progress is understandable only within a dynamic conception of the learning process . . . and with a consideration of the economic function of a 'modern brotherhood' (i.e., a sense of belonging). These last two aspects are present only in Marshall, and in no other economist of his time. (Becattini 2003b, pp. 21–2)

Becattini clearly identifies the importance of social relationships in the productive systems of the IDs. Social and institutional features develop the industrial atmosphere nurture and sustain the economies associated with specialisation through the division of labour. The ID thus becomes a 'socio-economic notion', characterized by the embeddedness of the economic in the social systems. Becattini's extension of Marshall's external economies in the context of IDs has been adopted in the work of a number of writers such as Sforzi (1990, 2002), Asheim (2000) and Bellandi (2003c), along with many of the other contributors to this volume. From these contributions it can be concluded that Krugman's 'pure external economies' take on a socio-economic dimension, and the ID as a form of industrial organization cannot be properly conceptualized unless the scope of external economies is widened to incorporate the notion of social embeddedness.

If the recent literature on IDs is to be interpreted as in part a 'rediscovery' of Marshall's depiction of external economies, then some of the shortcomings in Marshall's analysis need to be recognized. As outlined earlier, Marshall clearly viewed economies of scale as part of an evolutionary process that shapes industrial organization and development. However, these insights tend to be clouded if not distorted in the equilibrium framework constructed in Book V of his *Principles*. Here the now 'familiar' demand and supply equilibrium framework is formulated so as to construct a theory of value which at the same time is intended not to jettison the evolutionary representation of scale economies that underpin supply conditions in the long period. The futility of attempting to reconcile equilibrium analysis with economies of scale of the variety considered by Marshall was identified emphatically in Young's (1928) insightful contributions to the Marshallian cost controversies.

In the process of developing this critique, Young (1928, p. 533) argued that economies of scale could only be understood in the context of a process of 'change that becomes progressive and propagates itself in a cumulative way'. In such a setting the distinction between internal and external economies had little or no operational meaning, and the extension of the division of labour among industries meant that 'the representative firm, like the industry it is a part, loses its identity' (ibid.). The significance of the argument to the analysis of IDs is clearly reflected in Becattini's (2006, p. 670) observation that the world of industry is not to be conceived as a network of technical interdependencies or interchanges between individual firms, but instead 'a kaleidoscope of local productive systems which compete and cooperate with each other'. This process of competition and cooperation is not detached from external economies of the variety emphasized by Marshall, Young and Becattini, and it is in this setting that IDs emerge as a potentially significant variant of industrial organization that helps to sustain economic development. As Marshall argued, a 'biological' approach to the analysis of such questions is required, a point that has been subsequently reemphasized in the contributions by writers such as Raffaelli (2003b), Tappi (2005) and Metcalfe (2007).

7. CONCLUSIONS

It can be seen that Marshall's distinction between internal and external economies has become central to the investigation of a wide range of issues within theoretical and applied economics. In the area of industrial organization and change, the distinction enables the depiction of IDs nurtured by external economies; an avenue through which the benefits of specialization may potentially be realized in addition to those related to the internal economies of larger productive units. However, these issues are not amenable to studies formulated within equilibrium models of the form which have dominated much of mainstream economics subsequent to Marshall's writings. The recent 'rediscovery' of Marshall's insights has been founded on an expansion of Marshall's depiction of external economies that is evolutionary in nature, whilst being connected with what Marshall had termed the 'industrial atmosphere' of a district. External economies in this setting take on very much a socio-economic dimension, and unless this is recognized IDs as a form of industrial organization and contributor to the pattern of economic development cannot be fully understood.

9. The Italian revival of industrial districts and the foundations of political economy

Renzo Bianchi

1. INTRODUCTION

Research carried out on industrial districts (IDs) by the Tuscan group of researchers headed by Giacomo Becattini has produced results that can be analysed from two complementary viewpoints. The first of these aims to highlight how the process, which stemmed from the urge to adequately interpret Tuscany's development in the late post-war period, led these scholars to rediscover, in Marshall's thought, the concept of the 'ID' in a context where the so-called standard approach to economic development was heading in a totally different direction. They also rendered this concept both more flexible and pertinent when attempting to understand the new efficient production units that were at the core of the industrial growth in Tuscany (and in other regions located in what came to be known as the 'Third Italy') at the time.

The second viewpoint aims at explaining what motivated Becattini and the other scholars collaborating with him to concentrate on the phenomenon of IDs and to conduct in-depth studies on this enlarging field.

With regard to the early studies on districts in Tuscany, there is a wealth of literature that refers to the research conducted initially by the Regional Institute for Economic Planning in Tuscany (*Istituto Regionale Programmazione Economica Toscana*, IRPET) and subsequently by a group of researchers coordinated by Braudel in his *Prato. Storia di una città* (Braudel 1986–97). In addition to this, there was a parallel and systematic study of Marshall's theories.[1]

The concept of ID had already been approached by IRPET in 1969 when Becattini was the director. But it was only in 1977 that Becattini, who was no longer at the head of IRPET, claimed that the ID was one of the pillar of Italy's development in the post-war period (Becattini 1978).[2] In 1979, Becattini gave a talk at a convention for industrial economists where he suggested that Marshall's concept of ID should be resuscitated, and reapplied as a means of analysis and method for interpreting the 'light' industrialization of Italy.[3] A crucial part of district studies comprises the attempt to define a general model for the district which would allow it to be identified within the territory. Without this model, research on the districts would have been limited to monographic studies, which although in-depth, would have not permitted a comparative approach. In 1985, Fabio Sforzi (Sforzi 1986) developed an algorithm which made it possible to elaborate statistical data at the level of municipalities to identify 'local labour market areas'; these became ideal geographical units of analysis for the statistical identification of IDs. This saw the birth of the 'econometric analysis of IDs'.

In the same years, a long and deep research on the Prato ID since the post-war period was underway. Gabi Dei Ottati (1987), collaborating with Becattini, pinpointed several traits of IDs in the post-war period in Italy and coined the expression of 'communitarian market'.

In the meantime common interests were shared with several research groups such as the one in Modena, led by Sebastiano Brusco, and to a lesser degree, with Sergio Vaccà in Milan to which Enzo Rullani greatly contributed, with Maria Teresa Costa Campi and Joan Trullén's group in Catalonia, and still others. Interaction between the Florentine scholars and the latter groups led to the establishment of a consolidated model of Italian district development.

During the 1990s the annual event *Incontri pratesi sullo sviluppo locale* (Prato's Meetings on Local Development), which took place in September at Artimino (nearby Prato), brought together experts from various fields related to Italy's development, and encouraged discussion on the subject. It was in this setting that the two main approaches concerning IDs were developed and confronted, that is the ones developed by Becattini's group in Florence and Brusco's group in Modena. The former developed particularly the effects of cultural and institutional factors, the latter favoured the analysis of relationships which stemmed from the technological and productive interdependence of the firms.

A key question is: what objectives has the study of IDs met for it to have remained such an important area of research for Giacomo Becattini and his group? The answer, which I wish to develop here, is that the energy behind this research comes in fact from a political vision, in the higher sense of the word, that is the desire to identify the various life styles and forms of evolution of communities of people who feel collectively responsible for their own destinies.

2. THE LOCAL COMMUNITY AS A SOURCE OF PRODUCTION SYSTEMS

Analysis into the development of Tuscany's production systems in the 1960s and 1970s – which conventional economic theory had not managed to understand – led Becattini to reject the fundamental preexisting argument that 'social sciences' could be split up into independent, autonomous sciences. Becattini wrote:

I view the current climate as a transition from the old, orderly, pre-explored world of economic patterns – and here I refer to work carried out by Kuzmets, Chenery and the early Fuà – to an orderly, yet all in all, different, more complex world of patterns which stem explicitly from the interdependence between socio-cultural and techno-economic data. Analyses and theories concerning socioeconomics should move towards, . . . and systematically override the pre-established canons and boundaries of the various disciplines which make up the field of social studies. (Becattini 2001b, p. 11)

The most mature outcome of these studies was the re-introduction of the 'territory' within the subject of economics and sociology thanks to studies carried out on 'places'. The subsequent result was that the economic development of Tuscany as well as Italy since the post-war period, was reinterpreted in an original way. A central concept in the interpretation of the economic development of Tuscany was its 'rural urbanisation', taking over from the sharecropping in rural areas and from the poly-centralised urban and artisan industry areas of central Tuscany (Becattini 1997, p. 508). This also included the 'thousands of small to medium sized urban settlements inherited from a past which was pervaded with separatist tendencies, local feuds and refined artistic handcraft' (ibid., p. 479), together with thousands of local communities in middle Italy, with its 'know-how and its productive expertise cumulated over centuries' (ibid., p. 473). (See also Becattini 1987, 2002b, Chapter VIII.) These studies and concepts led to a better understanding of how these communities – which benefited from a series of favourable domestic and international conditions – exploited the social assets accumulated over the centuries, thus allowing them to ride the wave of development and to supply the human, social, material resources on which to develop and mould the concept of an ID.

In 1989 Becattini wrote: 'I define the industrial district as a socio-territorial entity which is characterised by the active presence of both a community of people and a population of firms in one naturally and historically bounded area. In the district, community and firms tend to "inter-penetrate"' (Becattini 1989). It was on the inter-penetration of the community and the productive system that Becattini fixed his attention, in the belief that some of his ideals concerning social organisation could therein materialise. In fact, it is at this level that the mechanisms of direct democracy took shape (the summons to Prato of all the social classes in defence of 'our industry' undeniably recalls the life of the ancient municipality) and presented an important form of osmosis between the citizens and their representatives.

Regarding the model of the ID we can say that: (a) the economic relationships which produce a peculiar combination of competition and cooperation transcend the logic of the market; (b) the progressive segmentation of the production process allows even small firms to develop an appropriate scale of production; (c) competition between small producers specialised in the various phases of production helps keep costs down and creates a favourable climate for bottom-up innovations; (d) increased professional and social mobility makes it possible to best exploit both the current and future potential of the subjects involved; and (e) the presence of local authorities which control some aspects intrinsic to the accumulation process (such as the building regulations) determines an acceptable settlement of the conflict between capital and labour. In short, in a mature district we can find a model of capitalism which 'fits' the population as a whole, and which has what can be called a 'human face'.

Briefly, the ID can be described as a community whose identity is so deeply rooted, albeit in continuous change, that it develops as a collective entity, a small economic nation. Although this formula may appear to be vague, it is in fact adequate to fix the idea that the district on the whole offers a life style which satisfies both the moral and the material needs which have developed over a period of time and which have been perceived or assimilated by its 'citizens'. The needs which are satisfied concern not only a degree of certainty about the possibility of finding a job within the district (thanks to the specific organisation and integration of skills and jobs available), on the existence of a net of social protection during periods of recession, and on the fact that playing by the 'district rules' guarantees support to new enterprises and even opportunities to bounce back after the failure of an entrepreneurial project; but also, and above all, the district represents an environment where everyone has the opportunity to have different experiences and to share responsibilities.

Identity is based on the general belief, within a particular group of people,

> that they have been jointly responsible for developing their current conditions thanks to their ability to continuously adapt to the difficulties as and when they are presented by the world at large. That belief and the experience on which it rests constitute the 'active nucleus' of the history of a place, i.e. what is needed in order to cope with the succession of situations that the external world presents . . . Given that 'congruity' with the global dimension is essential if the local community is to survive, the industrial district tends to create a favourable environment 'by means of the constant re-adaptation of the skills and qualities of its citizens, and its local authorities to the needs presented by external competitiveness'. (Becattini 2002a, p. 143)

3. FROM THE ID TO LOCAL DEVELOPMENT AND BACK

An outcome of the conceptualisation of IDs just recalled coincided with theories of industrial development. The traditional ones, imposing a univocal path for each reality, characterised by basically standardised phases, came to be seen as inadequate against the rediscovery of the territorial dimension:

> In a world where the market expansion . . . keeps the economy, and its cultural roots, constantly on the move, the smaller unit of investigation is no longer the individual or the firm, but rather *a nucleus composed of relationships which are productive*, in particular which are closely linked to the territory and capable of reproducing themselves in the future. We can define this as 'place' (or local system). (Becattini 2001b, p. 18; italics added)

If a local system is to have an identity, it must have long-term stability. In other words, it must be able to reproduce the entire mix of congruent social, economic and institutional conditions that characterise it. However, this mix comprises elements with different characteristics whose relationship may have reached equilibrium by means of a different function and may evolve according to differing dynamics and time scales.

The time framework chosen by Becattini for his research is historically long term, during which a strong community can be established and the cultural identity of its inhabitants forged. This framework gives priority to the formation of a community over the emerging economic relations and the establishment of production activities:

> Rather than seeing the industrial district as a mass of firms, factories machinery or manufactured products . . . I suggest that it should be viewed as the process of building human groups whose principles differ from place to place. . . . Prato is not a human appendix to its textile industry but it is the latter which is the productive projection of the citizens of Prato (it is currently textiles but tomorrow, who knows?). (Becattini 2001d, p. 4)

Other 'places', other 'self-perpetuating' local systems can have different characteristics, which, based on different time scales, can be associated with 'ideal types' which are dissimilar from the district and could, nevertheless, have an important role in development processes.

More recently, and certainly since the research published in *Il caleidoscopio dello sviluppo locale* (Becattini et al. 2001), the methodological approach of the Florentine group revealed a significant shift from the structural concept of a district, to an evolutionary concept where a group of processes only occasionally converged on the district type (see also Becattini et al. 2003).

This shift allowed the recognition of the embryonic and subsequent phases of the 'self-productive local systems' and their coupling with policies supporting the diffusion of the ID and other possible models. These were issues which could only be hinted at in a vision locked into clear-cut concepts separating clearly IDs and non-IDs and leaving no space for possible variants. Economic history and theory were thus opened up to a huge range of dynamics which arose from social, economic and institutional conditions and which could give quite different results. Notwithstanding this, the Florentine group continued to compare all other models to the district model, which become a sort of point of reference. For the group, it was not only a question of recognizing the 'multiplicity of the stable forms of industrial development', but there also appeared to be the need for reaffirming the peculiarity of one of those forms, namely the ID.

The privileged position that the Florentine group continued to attribute to the concept of ID does not appear to stem from the fact that 'the industrial district reflects the self-reproductive model which is specific to Italy's economic reality' (Becattini 2002c, p. 149), but rather from the belief that of all the stable economic forms of industrial development, the district supplies ideally a well balanced mix of social, economic and institutional conditions. Other forms of local system tend to overlook one or the other among the essential dimensions of industrial development.

If we wish to follow more closely the complexities of reality – the multiple dynamics which lead to the construction and evolution of the self-reproductive local systems with their variety of development processes – then we are obliged to further extend our analysis by expanding our range of reference models. On the other hand, if we want to leave space for a social utopia, then we have to keep alive the indications dictated by a formula whereby the individual is able to live in a state of human well being and within a community which is democratically run; consequently the renewable events of the district must continue to remain at the core of our analysis.

4. A CAPITALISM WITH A HUMAN FACE

The opening up of new research channels lent multiple ways in which the model of the ID can integrate with other contemporary issues and frameworks of interpretation. For example, the contribution to productivity and innovation which stems from the firms in the district, and which is heavily influenced by the deep-rooted social culture of the area, inspired Sergio Vaccà to develop his theory of the 'illuminated transnational company' that would defend the local self-productive systems from the various local cultures it came into contact with (see Becattini and Sforzi 2002).

This has not prevented Becattini from continuing to privilege the concept of the IDs within the context of more or less self-reproductive local systems. The district becomes responsible for announcing and preempting a specific 'market utopia' which Becattini calls 'capitalism with a human face': 'In brief, the ID successfully epitomizes the fundamentals of a certain type of capitalism in such a way that the result is a perfectly acceptable compromise' (Becattini 2002c, p. 122). The basis for this line of research is the view that the evolution which has been historically predominant in contemporary capitalism and market economies, towards an increasing centrality of the financial dimension, is just one among those which are potentially feasible. A different and feasible evolution, endowed with general coherence and historical plausibility, is signalled by contemporary IDs:

> The industrial district is an authentic 'small-scale social market economy' and, contrary to what some believe, it is anything but the remains of pre-capitalism or a monstrosity of Italian capitalism, it is the paradigmatic, embryonic, symbolic

expression of a well-balanced capitalism which, I like to say, has 'a human face'. (Becattini 2004b, p. 244; apostrophes added)

It is within the context that it can be understood how the ID has become the underlying theme of a research path along which Giacomo Becattini has been travelling all his life:

> The debates on local development – which is what I deal with – . . . are embryonic thoughts concerning an ideal society, whose outcomes cannot simply be determined by theories alone, and which must present an alternative to the chaotic capitalism of our times. These thoughts are deeply rooted in the DNA of all political economists. (Ibid., p. 33)

As things stand at the moment, it is only fair to say that 'capitalism with a human face' has only been talked about. There are still no indications as to how this field should be organised, there are no established procedures, nor structural connections. It is particularly difficult to predict what a 'new world' might look like, and we all know how difficult it is to predict a recipe for what might be the cuisine of the future. Nonetheless, the specific role played by districts in evoking and predicting this possible form of market economy means that the functional and development analyses of the districts overlap with the reflections on how this 'utopia of the market' should actually function. Speaking more directly, it seems natural that the 'know-how' that has been acquired by analysing the IDs should, in turn, be used to pinpoint the individual piece making up the mosaic which still needs to be defined.

5. THE FIRM AS A PROJECT OF LIFE

Particularly important for highlighting probably one of the most salient elements of districts – also in relation to their future – is the experience gained from the entrepreneurial skills of the district (with its frequent overlap and exchange with employed labour). Indeed, Becattini stressed the importance of the 'entrepreneurs of the future', namely those 'who know how to explore and intuitively perceive latent needs'; those who are 'more leaders of men rather than financial speculators'; those who 'earn the trust of their collaborators at all levels, motivate them, give meaning to their contributions and win their support for new projects' (Becattini 2004b, p. 97). It is precisely the role of the entrepreneur that emerges from the society in which he/she is embedded thanks to a series of technical, economic and social mechanisms, who currently defines an ID.

The enterprise that the entrepreneur of the future will develop can be described as firms that mirror a life project; these represent a typology of productive unit common in districts.

An enterprise can begin ... as a life project. The catalyst here is not simply a molecule of private capital, which adjusts its financial position and aims to expand, but rather an individual who has an abundance of drive and initiatives at his fingertips. He decides to embark on a lifelong adventure in production which he well knows may have uncertain outcomes. ... He not only invests his own and his family's savings in the firm, together with any funds his friends are willing to lend him, but above all his reputation and technical competence, his commitment to his job and his correctness when dealing with others, all of which he has slowly built up within his community and which often represents his core asset ... In this type of enterprise results are not simply proportioned to income but rather to the extent to which the initial business plan, or modified part of it, has been satisfied. (Ibid., pp. 239–40)

In contemporary districts, even if not all companies set up by 'new' entrepreneurs necessarily share these characteristics, it can still be argued that a great part of them would fall in the 'project firm' category. That is to say, that they stand out from the model of the 'molecule of capital' firms, whose only objective is 'generic growth'. They should present themselves as the means by which, being active in the market economy, a life project is moulded and shared with those who join and collaborate with the entrepreneur.

In those districts which are already up and running, a continuous reproduction of 'life project firms' is essential if the local system is to keep on being known as a district. Similarly, the capitalism with a human face of which Becattini has outlined various traits needs such technical, economic and social conditions as to guarantee the continuous generation of project firms: in other words, to guarantee that the experience of living one's life in order to satisfy a goal, is systematically repeated in the community in which we live.

NOTES

1. The volume on contemporary Prato was coordinated by Becattini. The main collaborator of Becattini in this research was Gabi Dei Ottati.
2. In this phase Becattini's closest collaborator was Fabio Sforzi, who at the time was a researcher for IRPET.
3. Just after that speech Becattini gave a graduation thesis to Marco Bellandi on the ID. An article on the ID in Marshall was extracted from this thesis. In the same period, scholars of disparate disciplines started to contribute, in Florence, to a 'revival' of research into the ID. See Becattini (1987) which includes the republication of many of the early contributions of that period in Florence.

10. The Italian revival of industrial districts and the foundations of industrial policy

Anna Natali and Margherita Russo

1. INTRODUCTION

Problems of development were at the centre of the work of Sebastiano Brusco. Over a 30-year period at the end of the last century and in conjunction with a large team of collaborators, he made many fundamental contributions to the study of (mainly) Italian, industrial districts (IDs).[1]

Drawing particularly on the experience of Emilia Romagna in the 1970s, Brusco showed that a multiplicity of forms of industrial organisation could be efficient, if properly embedded in supporting social and institutional structures. He developed analytical and empirical tools on policies to help conceptualise a form of local development that was associated with the presence of IDs, and used these tools to rethink the effectiveness of policy instruments. This work was carried out in conjunction with a dialogue he had with trade unions in Italy in the 1970s on the one side and, on the other side, with an international scientific community that was then growing around the research on IDs and local development. Unfortunately, his premature death in 2002 has denied us his continued participation in a discussion that owes him much. But he has nonetheless left us a priceless legacy in his many and lucid writings, with their vivid demonstration that theoretical analyses and empirical studies can be fruitfully interwoven with research and didactic activity.[2]

Prior to launching on his studies of 'industry' and 'labour', to which he devoted his years at Cambridge (UK) in the early 1960s, Brusco found a cue for his research in theoretical, political and social experience in the Sardinia of the 1950s. He belonged to a group of intellectuals of the *Ichnusa* review, gathered around the jurist Antonio Pigliaru and sparking an intense discussion on themes of development. This context went on to shape Brusco's work in subsequent decades, and led him down a personal research path focused on the interpretation and analysis of IDs and local development.[3]

This chapter briefly reviews the problems and the analytical tools put forward by Brusco in his writing on local development (Section 2). We shall deal with

111

two fundamental concepts of industrial policy developed by Brusco (Sections 3 and 4): the role of real services to support district firms and the role of real services needed to transform groups of isolated firms into systems of firms; and the promotion of widespread changes at the level of knowledge, competences and social relations. These concepts emphasise both that industrial policies centred on real services can treat the ID *per se* as a key policy target and that local development policies should use the concept of IDs as a reference model to identify innovative approaches to policy design and intervention more generally. Thus, when policymaking used district planning contracts as a form of support for territorial policies in southern Italy, the IDs themselves became actors of policymaking on a national scale (Section 5).

2. THE DISCUSSION ON PRODUCTIVE DECENTRALISATION AND BRUSCO'S INTERPRETATION

In the 1960s, Italy's industrial policy viewed small firms as a marginal phenomenon of industrial development, and artisan firms as the residue of a past that would disappear with the modernisation process extending from the nuclei of industrial production in the northern area of the country. At the end of the 1960s, large firms (particularly in the automotive, mechanical, textiles and clothing sectors) started the widespread outsourcing of some production stages, especially the high pollution or health risk ones, and those with lower capital intensity. Productive decentralisation was used to confront variations in demand, so that the foundations were laid for a division of working conditions, contracts and wage bargaining, which trade unions found hard to control. This led to a period of severe conflict. Trade unions sought to define actions against the exploitation of workers in a large swathe of firms, heterogeneous in terms of sectors, but sharing the fact of being small in size and having poor working conditions.

Brusco's original contributions[4] were very critical of many of the regnant theoretical bases of that debate. His own approach, by contrast, was characterised by both intensive empirical investigations and the formulation of new research questions.[5] An example of this can be found in Brusco's (1982) study of working.

In the early 1970s, technology efficiency, working conditions and firm size became specific objects of research, attracting the attention of metal-engineering unions which were concerned, among other things, with the extent to which small firms were detached production units from the large ones (a concern rooted in the desire to protect workers from what they feared were more exploitative conditions in those small firms).[6] This concern led to research into the metal-engineering firms in Bergamo, which provided solid empirical evidence and increased our understanding of the systemic efficiency of local productive systems of small and medium firms.[7] At the theoretical level, references abounded (Brusco 1989a, pp. 491–2): in particular, following the teaching of Young and Stigler (and Smith), Brusco proposed to analyse the economies of scale at each stage into which the production process can be divided. This line of research subsequently broadened and showed that similar places in terms of productive specialisation could be efficient, even if they greatly differed in terms of firm size, technology, level of vertical integration, mechanisms of coordination and relations among the firms (Brusco 1995). Furthermore, it found that there were different types of small firms: the isolated ones, those working in a network of dependent subcontracting, and those operating in IDs (Brusco and Sabel 1981). The findings of the empirical studies highlighted the need to identify the most appropriate development and training policies for the various types of firm and for what started to be seen as different local production system. For example, if a productive structure is composed of micro-firms in which the entrepreneur is substantially one of the two or three production workers, it can hardly be thought that the problem of updating and requalification concerns the dependent workers alone, as would be appropriate in large companies. Indeed, as Brusco reminds us, in small firms the training of the entrepreneur is crucial, since only in this way is it possible to fuel the tension towards creating change that leads to development.

In order to analyse specific training requirements, the productive structure must be known: the role of the micro-firms, the minimum efficient size of the production and marketing stages, the local market characteristics, and those of the non-local and foreign markets; the variety of models of decentralisation and of relations between commissioners and suppliers, and the role of unwritten rules helping to regulate such relations. Hence, if the regions have different productive structures, then they must have different regional policies for training and different concern for industrial policy,[8] as we recall in the next section.

3. POLICY FOR REAL SERVICES

Brusco discussed policies for the IDs in much of his essays. Direct observation of the policymaking in Emilia-Romagna after the Second World War led him subsequently to consider the working mechanisms of certain fundamental institutions around which support for local policies targeted at systems of firms was constructed, such as the service centres (Brusco 1984; Brusco and Righi 1989) and the training centres (Brusco and Bigarelli 1995).

One theme that permeated the debate on policies was the consensus needed to make the design and implementation of policy actions effective (see Brusco and Righi 1989). The type of policymaker Brusco referred to was meant to dispose of a wide range of instruments for the actions to be understood and further developed (Brusco 1988; Brusco and Bigarelli 1995). In other words, policies were shaped through an interaction, with the subjects targeted by the interventions, in an open, creative dialogue that was able to interpret the needs of the productive apparatus and the society in question.

The first essay in which Brusco systematically presented the idea of real services for the ID was published in Brusco (1992a): the essay focuses on policies for IDs, drawing on the experiences in Emilia-Romagna, especially since the 1970s, in order to encourage the transformation of isolated small firms into systems of firms of the district type. To support such a transformation, policymakers must have a shared understanding of just what an ID is. Brusco thus proposed a working definition of district and, in particular, embodied certain 'controversial characteristics': namely, the coexistence of competition and cooperation and the absence of a dominating firm (Brusco 1992a).

For those systems of small firms that already coincide with an ID, *ad hoc* industrial policies for IDs are needed not because the district, by its very nature, is at a disadvantage with respect to the large firms for instance, but because, since it is a different socio-economic organisational form, it requires specific industrial policy measures.[9] These include, for example, financial interventions, measures for technical professional training or for training managerial capacities. Among these, Brusco highlighted especially industrial policy interventions that, in the Italian debate, go by the name of 'real services', by which firms are provided with the goods and services they need, 'instead of receiving the finance necessary for them to obtain those goods and services by themselves' (ibid., p. 224).

Brusco referred to real services as those coming from agencies in Emilia-Romagna from the 1980s[10] that provided, for instance, easy access to information on the technical standards for exports; firms' sharing of highly sophisticated software for design, production or input control; or the translation of tenders. The reasons for which the supply of these services requires public policy interventions is now well accepted, but it was then revolutionary and it was underpinned by the functioning of the ID. It is possible that the social fabric of the district lacks the competences needed for these services to be available; or, if and where such competences are present, there may be a scant understanding of their importance among small firms.

Crucial to Brusco's conceptualisation of real services is that what the district firms need is, substantially, information – which becomes, in some way, a public good and must therefore be produced at the expense of the community or of the State (ibid., p. 226). Brusco wrote:

> The idea is, basically, that while a large firm can directly gather useful information, keep it to itself and profit from it, small firms are unable to do this. The small scale on which they operate makes direct collection of information too costly and unrewarding. Yet the small firms cannot even purchase the information they need on the market, because the market for this information does not exist. (Ibid., p. 227)

This shortcoming occurs on the supply side, but above all on the demand side:

> There is need of information, but no awareness of this need. Selling information means, in reality, being involved in a process of increasing awareness, which, in many ways, can be likened to a process of technological transfer. This is essentially a training activity or, at least, every distinction between sale of information and training activity is blurred. (Ibid., p. 227)

Public intervention must therefore aim not only to produce the information, but also to diffuse it and to ensure its use.[11] Once it is 'shared by hundreds or thousands of persons, it may generate levels of creativity, imagination and knowledge that are important in both the design stage of the product and the design of the process' (ibid., p. 228).

It follows that real services should be provided to a set of firms, indeed no advantage would come from relying on actions aimed at supporting individual firms. A choice of this kind, Brusco reminded us, would basically imply that not a district system, but another model – with a leader firm in a network – is targeted (ibid., p. 229). Furthermore, there is the difficulty of acting with a single entrepreneur who may not be willing to provide the information needed, or may even be wary about finding his role threatened by the action of someone who apparently seeks to teach him his business.

In order to identify which services to provide, the productive fabric must be known: standard analyses of the productive *filière* and the inter-firm relations, and comparative analyses with other systems operating in the same final markets can lead to identifying the bottlenecks on which to intervene. While assessment of costs is not a problem, evaluation of the benefits that accrue is anything but easy. A further critical element is the fixing of the price for real services, and 'it must be borne in mind that a higher price will be seen by the entrepreneur as indicator of the usefulness of the service' (ibid., pp. 234–5).

In general, real services must supply tailor-made information appropriate to the set of firms targeted by the intervention: they must create the conditions for their acceptance

> without large shifts in the workforce or in the organisation of the work, without upheavals in the hierarchy or in the way the firms are organized – in other words, as painlessly as possible. In the awareness that once the new technique is understood and adopted, it will grow, will bear fruit, will be reinvented, will be modified, for better or worse, according to the changing requirements of the district and each person's creativity. (Ibid., p. 232)

Overall, real service policies must be able to graft the transformations necessary for the system of firms to embark on change. These policies are very difficult ('a matter of convincing rather than ordering'), but they are also not very expensive ('since the mechanism, once set in motion, works under its own steam') (ibid., p. 237). Here, in considering development as a process, one can see Hirschman's 'hiding hand' and the conceptualisation of policies that promote the perception of opportunities that are able to spark processes of transformation (Hirschman 1958 and 1967).

4. FROM INDUSTRIAL POLICY FOR IDs TO POLICY FOR LOCAL DEVELOPMENT

In the approach pursued by Brusco in the 1980s with reference to IDs, real service policies are only one of a range of possible initiatives: the zoning of sites of production, infrastructures, schools, welfare services, and much else. The demand comes from the needs of the firms and workers, but also, more generally, of families and local communities, whose organised civil fabric contributes to the vitality and reproducibility of the economic activities. Substantially, a suitable industrial policy has to do with everything the local industry needs in order to develop: at the level of production, services and local contexts. Special attention is paid to inter-firm relations, and to the relations between firms and local institutions.

For Brusco, in the 1990s, this conception of industrial policy supplied the basis for a rethinking of policies for all local systems – including those which are not districts or have little in common with districts, like the backward areas of southern Italy. At this level, his engagement in such study and proposals emerged clearly in conjunction with his participation in the 'Summer meetings of Artimino', which began in 1991. At these meetings, from the outset, Brusco discussed the possibility of transferring the lesson that had been learnt on the districts to the design of policies targeted at local productive systems (Brusco 1992a and 1992b). He drew on field work on the nexus between competences and production linkages in Sardinian industries (Brusco and Paba 1992) and on the development strategies of the natural parks (Natali 2005). His research was enhanced by the intense interface, ongoing year by year at Artimino, with Giacomo Becattini and his group, in which the districts had always figured out not as productive organisations but rather as fully-fledged local societies.[12] In that period, Brusco defined the local productive systems as

> a system composed of three main elements: the active firms, the territory on which these firms arise, and the people who live in this territory, with their values and their history... The distinguishing features in tracing the boundaries of the system... are the very close relations among the firms and the relative homogeneity of the social system. (Brusco 1993)

After identifying this distinctive intermesh of economy and society in space, one may investigate the possibility of viewing the local productive system as a unit when planning policy interventions; especially, considering two key aspects of IDs: knowledge and skills, and social relations.

The diffusion of knowledge serves to enable a very large number of operators in the district swiftly and correctly to perceive the opportunity for profit connected with a definite entrepreneurial project, and it is this general ability that constitutes the essential competitive advantage of the system. In backward areas, where a similar ability is absent, it needs to be actively sought and promoted with a strategy specifically dedicated to the development of knowledge. This strategy may assume two forms:

- Surveying the traditional knowledge rooted in the productive practices of the place, identifying those common to large segments of the population, and investing in the reinforcement and development of this widespread strain of knowledge, in such a way that, as it develops and becomes qualified, it acquires an economic potential for the local communities. The skills to be worked on are those of artisanal manufacturing and/or those linked with the old agricultural trades (wine making, stock-rearing, labouring): the important condition is that they be, indeed, widespread, statistically probable and, as such, employable for the development purposes.
- Instilling new knowledge from outside, and creating conditions for them to take root and develop in the local system. As new firms are set up in the district, or stable subcontracting relations are established, these effects of dissemination are reinforced and may be produced in fairly short times, even downstreaming from vertically-integrated factories (Brusco and Paba 1992).

Dealing with socially diffused knowledge leads towards a radical reformulation of the development project, since it becomes necessary to incorporate 'a strong dose of history' (Brusco 1992b). Prominent operations in that project are the search for well-established skills and the reconstruction of the presence and events of production that have deeply affected the life of the community. For that matter, the attempt to introduce new knowledge entails the planning of training paths, both by directly training entrepreneurs, technicians and workers, and by tutoring external firms.

Acting on the social relations represents the second most relevant plan of intervention. Discussion of the districts has shown that the success of a local system is fuelled by consensus, by concertation, by a regime of limited uncertainty, and by a sense of identity. In essence, it depends not merely on the rational operation of single firms and entrepreneurs, but also on the interaction between economic operators and institutions. These conclusions are valid not only for the districts but for all local systems (Brusco 2002, p. 280, from an opening lecture in 1998). The 'level of material life', which is relatively stable in every system, exerts a decisive influence on the processes by which the workforce is reproduced, on the saving and accumulation even in an advanced capitalist system. The family structure (patriarchal or mononuclear) influences the pension system and hence the cost of labour; the diffusion of the social services and the rate of activity and female employment affect wages; the family structures and the division of labour between genders strongly influence the birth rate of firms and social mobility. The 'long-term structures' (Braudel), on the one hand, govern the quality of the knowledge rooted in the social fabric, which crucially determine its competitive and innovative capacity; on the other hand, they determine the quality of trust or the style of behaviour on the markets, that heavily influence the transaction costs and the levels of cooperation between the firms (Brusco 1993).

The level of material life is not inaccessible or impracticable for policy (ibid., p. 48). Indeed, the emphasis on social relations entails practical implications and stimuli to action. Social relations must be held in consideration and studied with the aim of intervening on them.

5. THE DISTRICT FROM TARGET OF POLICIES TO ACTOR OF POLICIES

If in the 1990s, Italy witnessed an attempt at 'negotiated planning', this was partly due to the success of IDs, and to the fact that there was deeper awareness of their role as key mechanisms underpinning development processes. Negotiated planning was an approach to industrial policy that embodied a variety of instruments: 'area contracts' for industrial areas with employment crisis, 'planning contracts' to attract firms to the South, 'territorial pacts or agreements' to provide incentives for local agencies and institutions, as well as firms to come together as local coalitions for the production of collective goods.

The territorial pacts represented the most important experiment by virtue of the number of initiatives undertaken and the amount of investment made, especially in southern regions. They integrate incentive measures with public capital to offset the inherent disadvantages of the territory (DPS, various years). In Brusco's view, the model of agreement underlying all the above instruments, had to be justified by the awareness that local stakeholders must collaborate and produce goods of common interest. The underlying idea came from the study of IDs, where institutions and social forces collaborated to establish rules of coexistence, to set up service centres and welfare institutions (Brusco 2004a, pp. 66–7). At the same time, Brusco saw the weaknesses of this model, and in particular in the way in which the territorial pacts were implemented: across the country the local coalitions were very unequal with regard to quality and compactness; the administrative procedures were complicated and tortuous; the financial endowment publicly provided for each agreement was excessive. The resources supplied could have been far fewer. They could have been merely the amount needed for 'buying the time to convince them that they can do something'.[13] The incentive scheme of the territorial pacts was to reward only those who managed to agree (Brusco 2002, p. 279). However, as Brusco noted – referring no longer merely to local productive systems but also to local systems (societies) in general – this incentive scheme might have been applicable even when a local system had no particular vocation, either in terms of amount of the local technical knowledge, or of happy relations between entrepreneurs and employees. This would have justified an extension of the policy to 'all Italian local systems', from the most to the least organised: including IDs; local industrial systems which are not districts; the tourist systems, and so on (ibid., pp. 280–81).

At this point, the thinking on industrial policy and development crossed with the question on the institutional representation of districts and of local systems in general. Brusco suggested that every local system ought to set up a public–private organisation with public majority, to plan and implement the specific interventions most needed in the context (ibid., pp. 282–3). As well as canvassing for the idea of a systematic intervention in favour of all the local systems, Brusco advocated for an exogenous intervention in the development of the backward areas, by means of a new device of negotiated planning, the 'district planning contract'. This was meant to work by linking an ID in a developed area with a less developed area with a potential district; the tool had to include an agreement for the two to share an investment plan.[14] Brusco worked with others on the project, convinced that the district planning contract could have been potentially an important device in innovating policy for the South, and also for giving the districts a national role. With Giacomo Becattini he shared the view that 'in this case the emphasis is not on the capacity of the districts to set up a factory tailor-made for the demands of the area . . ., but on the process of accumulation of knowledge that may occur' (Brusco 2004b, p. 91): thanks to the stable relation with the district, the southern area would have moved from the simplest subcontracting tasks to increasingly more sophisticated ones, to the point where it would have actually competed with the northern district.

In Brusco's view, district planning contracts marked a turning point in the relation between IDs and policy: from being targets (for the most part ill identified), IDs turned into actors (even protagonists) in a national policy intervention. This also marked a break in the approach to development policy: for the first time, it signalled a clear-cut proposal for a path towards mobilising civil society in the stronger regions, as well as the State itself, in favour of the disadvantaged ones. Those involved are called upon to set up relations, not of a hierarchic type, nor of a purely contractual nature. They would tend, rather, towards a model of a stable network linked by the sharing of a medium-long-term project, within a framework of rules, principles and values.

The government failed to launch district planning contracts; nonetheless, the model they put forward continues to be of interest to identify horizontal cooperation among local systems as a key resource in development policy.

6. CONCLUSIONS

Brusco's contributions have paved the way for a different way of looking at and studying local development: the local dimension of phenomena of growth, the embeddedness of knowledge in the territory and the way socio-economic relations increasingly interweave with production, social and demographic phenomena underlie the network of relations across systems on a global scale. Pressures towards space mobility and to form relations at a distance are increasingly accompanied by pressures towards the permanence and sustainability of relations rooted in one place. The local dimension takes on increasing importance in reinforcing the potential of social relations.

The impact of Brusco's conceptualisation of the targets, design and instruments for policies for local development has been widespread as it introduced a new point of view from which to look at industrial development. The idea of designing policy tools targeting not individual firms by systems of firms is well accepted now, but was novel then. The concept of real services and service centres, which is accepted today in various forms, was also well a completely innovative way of solving the shortcoming of small size for firms by acknowledging their strength as parts of a system. Most of the policies currently labelled under the term 'cluster policy' have in their genes these fundamental principles as they accept the fundamental idea that policymaking for local development can be systemic and territorial.

NOTES

1. For a complete list of the works of Sebastiano Brusco, see Brusco (2008), also available on line www.biblioeco.unimore.it/sezioni/pag119.htm (at the bottom, go to *Bibliografia degli scritti di Sebastiano Brusco,* accessed 20 December 2008).
2. This topic is dealt with in Russo (2008).
3. This research path is described by Brusco himself: in 1993 in a letter to Rina and Francesco Pigliaru (published in Brusco 2008), and in the prefaces and afterwards in the essays published in the 1989 volume. In particular, these 1989 texts (now available on line at the web page previously cited) give a clear account of how Brusco's research questions were not fuelled by theoretical arguments inspired by Sraffa – though it did leave its mark on the interpretative tools of his research, in an original way. Brusco writes: 'I was curious to understand the things around me, and I wanted to work with the unions. To be sure, I was helped to further understanding by the idea that wages were connected with the conflict under way in Italy between unions and entrepreneurs, rather than with productivity and technological level. Somehow, I was freer and more disposed to let the facts speak for themselves. But my suggestions did not stem from Sraffa. Rather from Marx, from the Marx who went beyond the theory of value, from my reading, from my experience in Sardinia and Cambridge, from my wonder at the Emilian world – so different from the one in which I had lived up to age thirty; and, especially, from political and union debate' (Brusco 1989a, p. 490). With regard to Brusco's intellectual path, see the contributions by Becattini (2002d), the special issue of the journal *Economia e politica industriale* (2004), with contributions by Becattini, Cavazzuti, Ginzburg, Macciotta and Pigliaru; Natali and Russo (2006); Russo, Natali and Solinas in the introductions to the collection of essays by Brusco (2008); Vianello (2008). Vianello (2004)

presents Brusco's contribution in the Faculty of Economics, Modena. Russo (2008) discusses the use of survey in the study of industrial economics by Brusco. On the intermesh between Brusco's and Becattini's research paths, see Bellandi (2002).
4. The debate on productive decentralisation and trade unions' position on poor labour conditions in small firms is outlined in Brusco and Pezzini (1990) which provides an ample critical analysis of the stance of the Italian left concerning small firms.
5. Along with his economist, sociologist, jurist and historian colleagues with whom he was involved leading to the set up of the Faculty of Economics at the University of Modena, he shared a lively period of discussion and research (see Vianello 2004) that also led to a generation of former students of the faculty that contributed with a wealth of empirical research and theoretical analysis on a great many subjects intertwined with the study of development: on export credits (Simonazzi 1978 and 1985); on processes of international fragmentation of production (Bonifati 1982); on innovation in the IDs (Russo 1985); on the role of the peasant family in changing the agriculture structure (Forni 1987); on the conception of the small firm in the ideology of the Italian left (on which Brusco worked with Pezzini, see Brusco and Pezzini 1990); on paths of social mobility of workers and processes of training, growth and survival of small firms (Solinas 1996); on patterns of production and distribution in Europe (Ginzburg and Simonazzi 1995); on the analysis of local productive systems (among several studies we recall those of Bigarelli and Crestanello who worked with Brusco in investigations into the textile-clothing sector in Italy); on historical perspectives in the transformation of the local economy (Brusco and Rinaldi 1990); on the changes in the configuration of local development in Italy in the second half of the 1990s (Brusco and Paba 1992). The ranks of researchers who worked with Brusco in the 1980s and 1990s were swelled by others: with Cainelli, Forni, Franchi, Malusardi and Righetti (Brusco et al. 1996) on the changing social and economic structure supporting the Emilian model; with Paolo Bertossi and Alberto Cottica on local development and environmental policies (Brusco, Bertossi and Cottica 1996); with Anna Natali on non-district territories, for example the natural parks (see Natali 2005).
6. On the use of the survey as a research tool, see Russo (2008).
7. But, as Brusco (1989a, p. 64) reminds us, it revealed beyond all reasonable doubt how bad the workers' conditions could be in the small firms.
8. To a certain extent, a leading role is played by regional policymakers, since they are close to the local systems and able to design actions, taking into account the intra-regional differentiations. (Often it is not enough to act at a regional level: in the introduction to an unpublished work on regional policies, Brusco argues for the need to distinguish central Emilia from Romagna, from Ferrara, from Parma.)
9. For a comparative analysis of the units of analysis for the local development policies, see Russo (1996).
10. The Center of Information on Textiles of Emilia Romagna (CITER) represents an example of the service centres from which Brusco drew inspiration in formulating policies for real services. An exhaustive account of the experience of CITER can be found in Ligabue (1995).
11. Here Brusco recalls Hirschman (1967), and in particular the notion that bottlenecks – though real obstacles – can also be used strategically by policymakers to foster development processes.
12. The annual meetings on local development in Artimino (Florence) comprised discussions on contributions coming from various disciplines, such as industrial, agrarian and business economists, geographers and sociologists. See the collection of inaugural lectures in Becattini and Sforzi (2002).
13. See F. Barca, 'Intervento alla conferenza in onore di Sebastiano Brusco', 2003, www. economia.unimore.it/brusco_sebastiano/testimonanze, accessed 12 January 2009.
14. The district planning contract was included in the provision for reordering the negotiated planning in 1997. It envisaged that 'representative bodies of IDs' among the possible parties signing planning contracts subsidised by the State.

SECTION 3
A meeting ground for the social sciences

Introduction

Carlo Trigilia

1. POLITICAL ECONOMY AND IDs: A COMPLEX RELATION

Between the end of the 1970s and the beginning of the 1990s, the 'rediscovery of the district' has provided a meeting ground for different disciplines of the social sciences, with the investigations on Italian industrial districts (IDs) being the primary laboratory. Italy is the country where IDs first reemerged in that period, featuring massively in the industrial landscape of many of her regions, particularly the central and northern ones. Even if their local roots were deep in their historical past, IDs quickly appeared as a 'modern and vital' form of economic and social organisation, rather than a residual heritage of the past. Not surprisingly the research on IDs has been rich in Italian contributions from the beginning, but quite soon authors from other countries and with various disciplinary backgrounds started to contribute too, more or less directly, as this *Handbook* testifies.

The pioneering contributions came from two economists, Giacomo Becattini and Sebastiano Brusco. Following different but overlapping trajectories of research, they raised interest in the 'strange' development of Italian IDs, first in their country and then at the international level with the first English translations of their works. This international interest was then amplified and diffused in various academic and non-academic quarters by the well-known work of Michael Piore and Charles Sabel on the *Second Industrial Divide*, developed along institutionalist economic lines of analysis, and strongly influenced in its references to IDs by the collaboration of Sabel with Brusco.

The influence of such contributions on mainstream economics has been, by and large, modest, as is argued by Marco Dardi in this section. However, some contacts with the topic of the IDs, if not with the related contemporary literature, may be found within the 'new economic geography', and in particular by Paul Krugman. In this framework, the factors explaining the territorial concentration of economic activities are considered under a general economic theory perspective. Krugman refers to Marshall's external economies as 'information spillover', for clarifying the logic and the dynamic effects of such factors. This line of analysis is discussed among other related contributions by Michael Storper (see also the chapter by Hart in Section 2).

In his contribution, Piero Tani presents a formal if non-mainstream analysis, built upon an industrial economics model by Nicholas Georgescu-Roegen. The chapter focuses on a crucial point of the early economic interpretations on IDs, that is the possibility of giving an analytical foundation to the efficient realisation of industrial production processes by means of a division of labour among specialised productive plants, and not necessarily among large firms. It is an essential contribution to the contemporary reflection on district external economies, to which we return later.

Why has the economists' interest for IDs been limited to non-orthodox thinking and to some lines of industrial economics? The answer lies probably in the strong paradigm which dominated mainstream economics, and which was characterised by claims of highly theoretical generalisation, badly at odds with an understanding of IDs with their territorial, socio-cultural, and institutional variety. And even when the attention towards the effects of such variety grew, as it has been over the last years with concepts like trust and social networks entering the economics discourse and modelling, the two sets of literature do not seem to find points of convergence (see again Dardi in this section). The fact is that this new attention seems somewhat shadowed by a sort of 'economic imperialism', by which a strictly economic interpretation is extended to institutional aspects, as is clear for example with transaction costs economics; and an understanding of such aspects in conditions different from the assumed general principle of pure individual economic calculus are not acknowledged.

2. A MORE OPEN RECEPTION WITHIN OTHER SOCIAL DISCIPLINES

It is understandable therefore that an open interest towards IDs has been much more diffused within the business economics discipline. Here the lack of a strong paradigm, the bent towards case studies, and the natural sensitivity to an understanding of business contexts, have justified a diffused attention to IDs, even if usually read as a variant of business clusters. This point of view is finely illustrated by Michael Porter and Christian Ketels.

Another disciplinary approach which has contributed to the campaign of research stimulated by IDs, being influenced in its turn, is economic geography, such as for example with Allen Scott and Michael Storper. The chapter by Storper in this section shows clearly the interest of an important line of geographical thinking towards regional economies and the role of territorial contexts. In particular the investigations on IDs and the related conceptual frameworks seem to have had a not trivial influence on geographical studies about highly dynamic local systems in US, in sectors different from those of classical Italian IDs, like Silicon Valley, Hollywood, and Route 118 at Boston. It is worth recalling that in this interpretative framework, economic geography has met some institutional approaches to the economics of innovation, and has contributed to enlighten empirical and general aspects related to Marshallian external economies in the generation of new knowledge (see also Section 5 in this volume).

Last but not least, sociology also has had deep relations with reflections on and around IDs, articulating various sociological approaches to IDs, some of which are briefly evoked in what follows (see also Section 4 in this volume).

3. THE EXPERIENCE OF ECONOMIC SOCIOLOGY

The Italian experience has also been quite important in this respect. In the 1970s, the young Italian economic sociologic discipline, influenced by Marxist approaches, was trying to analyse the reorganisation of Italian capitalism triggered by tough and prolonged tensions in labour relations within large factories. At first the investigations focused on the dynamics of the labour market and on the so-called 'production decentralisation', whereby large companies were outsourcing more and more phases of production from smaller companies, in order to elude the constraints imposed by strong trade unions in large factories. The inadequacy of this key of interpretation emerged quite quickly, however, in the face of the dynamism of regions (particularly the northeastern and central ones) which had not been characterised by the centrality of large Fordist factories and related processes of industrialisation.

The research on the so-called Third Italy emerged under those circumstances, in the second half of the 1970s, focusing just on northeastern and central Italian regions and their sets of small firms. The research on Third Italy started with Arnaldo Bagnasco (see his chapter in Section 4), and other sociologists, like Massimo Paci, were involved and lured to contribute quite early on. The research aimed at understanding the socio-cultural and institutional conditions favouring the growth of local systems of small firms, specialised in the production of personal and household goods. The sociological studies met at this point with those of the heterodox economists who were working on defining an ID model[1] and the related models of 'light industrialisation' or of 'industrialisation without fractures'.[2]

Two specific contributions on such models came from the sociologists' studies. The first concerned an analysis of the conditions leading to the birth of IDs. Here a strong emphasis was placed on the support given by institutional factors to the formation of pools of entrepreneurs driven by a strong motivation and good competences, together with the formation of a local pool of labour characterised by flexibility and specialised skills. Institutional factors include, among others, the specific shapes of the historic relations between the cities and their rural surroundings, the role of the extended family in the organisation of small independent farms, the scaffolding of small and medium-sized urban centres rich in craft and trade traditions not eroded by the first wave of industrialisation, and the influence of local political traditions.

The second contribution of sociology was in relation to the working logic of IDs. It highlighted the role of territorial identities and community ties in supporting the collaborative propensities underpinning relations between entrepreneurs, between workers and entrepreneurs, and between collective actors such as business associations, trade unions and local policymakers. More recently all these relations have been reconciled in the concept of 'social capital'. These interpretative efforts have allowed a better comprehension of the role of socio-cultural and institutional conditions in the constitution and deployment of the intangible factors and the related mechanisms which underpin IDs' working and productivity. In particular, they may limit potentially high level transaction costs, strengthen the diffusion of information and the exchange of knowledge, and highlight important forms of external economies within the district.

The relations with IDs go beyond the Italian experience even in the case of economic sociology. Researches along sociological lines have been realised in various European countries, like Spain, France, and Germany; and a specific influence, in particular through the work of Piore and Sabel, has been exerted on the 'new economic sociology' elaborated in North America, for example on the critique to transaction costs economics developed by Mark Granovetter and others, on the work of Walter Powell on knowledge networks, and on various streams of reflection on the concept of 'social capital'. Finally, reflections on IDs, in particular those on their governance, have been assumed within the comparative political economy and the literature on the 'variety of capitalisms' for classifying the regionalised type of capitalism featuring the Italian case (David Soskice, Peter Hall and Marino Regini).

4. THE MEETING GROUND

How can this convergent interest of so many disciplinary perspectives be explained? And what have been the results of such convergence?

The first question has an easier answer. The ID model has become, quite naturally, a reference point for those who have been more interested in a deep understanding of contemporary processes of economic and social change, than in producing narrow disciplinary contributions. Since the 1970s those processes have been characterised by increasing difficulties in combining large Fordist firms with the welfare state management of labour relations in the industrialised world, together with transformations of demand in many markets (increasingly variable and fragmented) and of manufacturing and organisational technologies (increasingly flexible). We have already recalled that an important role in raising the international interest in IDs has been played by the relation with 'post-Fordism' and the types of socio-economic organisation which are seen as connected to it. The book by Piore and Sabel on the *Second Industrial Divide* emphasised looking at the IDs as a first example of such an organisation, perhaps even excessively, tying them too strictly to the so-called flexible specialisation.[3]

The second question leads to various possible answers. The more important result may have been the definition of an ideal-typical model, in the Weberian meaning of the term, where socio-cultural and institutional components are explicitly integrated with economic and technological components. Actually the ID model is a rare example of a meeting ground, where economists cannot consider institutions and technology as exogenous variables of a model, and where sociologists and geographers do the same with economic incentives and constraints. The integration is more comprehensive in the case of the model of the so-called 'Marshallian industrial district' (MID).

The integration is instead less clearly defined in the case of variations and soft definitions of the concept of ID, sometimes seen as a synonym of business cluster,[4] and extending to cases not necessarily characterised by small to medium-sized firms nor by a local manufacturing specialisation. It is quite clear that different forms of local system require a definition of specific conditions of integration, and the efforts in this direction have not yet reached satisfactory results, apart from important progresses in some cases, such as the high-tech districts or the local innovation systems (see Section 5, in particular the chapter by Cooke). In all cases, and even regarding strictly-defined IDs, the dynamic analysis aimed at understanding and anticipating paths of local change is not still well developed.

The various approaches to IDs and to models of local development share, despite their differences and even beyond the convergence on the specific issue of the ID, a common analytical thread represented by the reference to concepts and cases of external economies, recovered from the Marshallian tradition. This is the sign of an increasing awareness, in different disciplinary fields, of the importance of the territorial dimension of business strategies and performances in contemporary economies – both the advanced and the emerging ones. The socio-cultural and institutional factors related to the territory may support levels and growth of productivity and competitiveness not only through the reproduction of a local supply of skilled workers, specific infrastructures and specialised services, but also through the shaping of motivations and the sedimentation of tacit knowledge in ways which are crucial in periods of increasing speed of circulation of persons and codified knowledge. A further and not less significant influence of the same factors concerns the provision of dedicated collective goods on which the productivity of individual firms depends heavily too (see Section 11 in this volume).

This is perhaps the most important legacy of the meeting of the different disciplinary perspectives on and around ID studies. Such territorial awareness penetrates more or less deeply into the realms of the various disciplines, and from such outposts has been spilling over into the developmental policies of advanced and emerging economies. It has to be acknowledged, however, that on this last ground – in spite of proliferating experiments and initiatives in many countries and regions – the influence exerted by territorial awareness and the related instruments of analysis and evaluation is still small in face of the clout retained by mainstream economics.

NOTES

1. The 'pioneers' Becattini and Brusco were soon accompanied by a circle of other researchers.
2. Giorgio Fuà has to be recalled among the pioneers contributing on the model of industrialisation characterised by SMEs, together again with Becattini and Brusco.
3. Later on this relation has been relaxed, for example by Sabel.
4. We have already recalled this point, when referring to the contribution of Porter and to his chapter with Ketels in this section.

11. The Marshallian industrial districts and current trends in economic theory

Marco Dardi

1. INTRODUCTION

If the notion of industrial district (ID) is often associated with the name of Alfred Marshall, this is not only because of the sparse references to the small-firm agglomerations of Lancashire and Yorkshire to be found in his writings. As noted by Brian Loasby (1998, pp. 70–71), IDs represent an illustration of a broader concept introduced by Marshall, according to which geographic settlements, patterns of social relations, and forms of industrial organization coevolve all as different facets of the same process of organic development. This remained, however, a philosophical concept with no clear connection with the analytical apparatus that constituted the body of Marshall's economic theory. Thus, modern scholars studying IDs have found in Marshall's writings a powerful source of inspiration, but not a set of theoretical tools ready made for their field of study. They have had to make do with what mainstream research in general economic theory has been producing, to the dissatisfaction of those who felt that this research was uncongenial to the blending of social and economic considerations on which ID studies are based (Becattini 2004a, pp. 55–6).

The latter position may have been justified as long as the core of highbrow theoretical research was dominated by investigations on the properties of a socially faceless system in which prices were the only means of information diffusion, and the rule of social interaction. More recently, however, the impression that all this belongs to the past is widespread. In fact, the theoretical debate has changed in the direction of opening economics up to social and cultural factors seen as both the causes and effects of the ways an economy is organized and functions. Although Marshall is not much more popular now than he was when Walrasian equilibrium ruled the roost, it may be argued that features of his vision have finally found acceptance across several lines of research in the current post-Walrasian age. If any meaning is still attached to the label 'orthodox economic theory', it is as a minimalist set of very basic principles constituting a framework loose enough to accommodate a rich variety of models of social interaction.

Does this provide a sufficiently hospitable and inspiring theoretical environment for ID studies? That is up to ID specialists to judge. Not being one myself, in this chapter I shall venture to illustrate some trends in contemporary economic research that seem to be conducive to an intellectual framework in which ID studies may find an appropriate home. This does not purport to be a fully-fledged theory of the IDs. There may even be doubts as to whether such a theory is conceivable, at least as far as the dynamics of IDs is concerned. Possible lines of development in connection with present policy concerns will be discussed in the concluding section.

2. THE MID AND MAINSTREAM VIEWS

Let us start with Marshall's original ideas. As shown in recent research (see Raffaelli 2003a), the basic building block of Marshall's social philosophy is the notion of a fundamental opposition running through the whole hierarchy of phenomena that enter the scope of social theory. This is the opposition between mental automatisms and conscious control at the level of the individual's intellectual performance, between conformity to custom and individual freedom at the level of behaviour, and between permanence and change at the level of collective processes. Each term in each of the above pairs is in need of the other, while also being in conflict with it. In this philosophy, change comes to be associated with individual conscious responses to unprecedented situations that cannot be controlled by means of established routines alone. Repeated successful changes in analogous situations, however, tend to get fixed in new routines and thus transform the set of codified and tacit rules that, in their entirety, constitute the permanent structure, the 'form' of a social group.

The 'change within continuity' that characterizes Marshall's approach to economics is a story of the juxtaposition of fast and slow adaptations of this kind, with the former being linked to the exploitation of economic opportunities for profit and the latter to changes in institutions and customary ways of acting and thinking. Thus, a society adapts itself to the variability of the surrounding environment through economic changes in the short run, maintaining its form fairly intact at each episode of adaptation. As economic changes cumulate over time, however, its features evolve into something which, in the long run, will be perceived as a different form. In Marshall's view, the permanence of the social entity which is the subject of economic change or, rather, the embedding of economic phenomena within relatively more stable social structures, is what renders social evolution an orderly, hence intelligible, process.

The Marshallian industrial district (MID), an interpretation of the generic ID category that has been effectively advocated by Giacomo Becattini (see the essays collected in Becattini 2004a), is a particular instance of this universal principle of continuity. MID in Becattini's version is the concept of a local system in which the Marshallian embedding takes on an almost totalitarian character, in the sense that practically 'all' the social and economic features of the system fit each other so tightly as to leave no loose ends. This absorbing functional complementarity is underpinned by a culture that sees no separation between civic and economic institutions, with families merging into firms, communitarian bonds into business connections, socializing leisure activities into working activities. The kind of industrial structure typical of a MID – a single productive *filière* finely disintegrated into phases distributed over a clustering of independent small firms – is no accident, but is an essential component of this underlying cultural identity. Also the core business of the *filière* – usually manufacture of medium to low technology, with a balance between so-called 'tacit' and 'codified' knowledge tilting towards the former, and satisfying a volatile demand strongly influenced by novelties in design and style – is somehow necessary in order for the MID to attain the status of a long-run equilibrium organizational form. As amply illustrated in the specialized literature, the production and market conditions described above are such that the peculiarities of a MID are most likely to enhance economic efficiency and thus keep the district abreast with other forms of organization characterized by vertically-integrated *filières* and/or less dedicated social nestings.

In a nutshell, a MID can be said to be a synthesis – Becattini prefers to speak of 'interpenetration' – of cluster of firms and social embedding, with great emphasis on the latter. Clusters are quite familiar by now and here I will focus on the more unsettled issues on the 'social embedding' side. If it is true that MIDs pose a challenge for mainstream economics, as Becattini and others in his line of thought assert, then the trouble must lie here. Externalities and public goods are not a problem *per se*: it is the Marshallian key idea of continuity from which the MID emanates that may fly in the face of the ruling theoretical consensus. But in order to understand this point, a bit of historical perspective is necessary.

It is indeed true that, while making a good job of characterizing certain economic patterns as equilibria for 'given' social circumstances, the theory which has represented the consensus view since the mid-20th century made it a rule to keep institutional details to a minimum, and did not pay much attention to the question of whether the attendant social circumstances themselves are in equilibrium or not. In that view, the very idea that the equilibrium of a pattern of industrial organization is inconceivable without investigating at the same time whether the way of life of the community that embraces it and subsists on it is also in some sort of equilibrium, would have got short shrift.

Judging by the current output of the leading journals, however, and increasingly so over the last two decades, that view no longer represents the 'mainstream'. Social networks, social dynamics either equilibrium-bound or open-ended, psychological notions such as trust, altruism, reciprocity and the like, traditionally held to be outside the scope of economists, have all become the staple of much contemporary theoretically and empirically-oriented research. While this change of direction in the economists' interests was going on, however, very little revision of the theoretical core of the discipline was felt to be necessary. Here the distinction between 'mainstream' and 'orthodoxy' introduced by Colander, Holt and Rosser (2004) comes in handy: in recent years we have seen the former undergo substantial transformations without the latter being undermined to the extent one might have expected. It looks as if academia has begun to shed those blinkers that made it unaware of the full powers of its basic theoretical framework. As this may represent a decisive step towards integrating MID studies into the body of orthodox economics, let me state the point more in detail.

3. NEW WAYS OF USING AN OLD FRAMEWORK

An objection may be raised to the above reconstruction. The recent awakening of interest in the social embedding of economic phenomena would probably not have occurred without the substantial theoretical novelties introduced since the 1970s, due to the development of game theory and the partly related, partly imported developments in evolutionary game dynamics and in the application of methods of statistical mechanics and computational agent-based systems (known as agent-based computational economics, ACE) to economics. Game theory provided a formalized language in which direct interpersonal interaction can be modelled and the issue of the elusiveness of any notion of interactive rationality set into precise focus. Evolutionary dynamics, statistical mechanics and ACE provided techniques for exploring social interaction as a bottom-up process that, depending on the circumstances, may or may not lead to the emergence of unintentional collective regularities. Both contributed to opening our eyes to the vast variety of social contrivances by which the traditional production–distribution–consumption processes are regulated and of which the classical price mechanism is just one instance. But while all this has undoubtedly enriched both our theory and our understanding, it has not resulted in a rejection of any of the established principles of the orthodox economic theory. The question is, of course, where one draws the line that circumscribes the core of orthodoxy: to me, this must include the doctrine according to which the final 'agent' of economic theory is an individual human being whose actions can be understood in terms of 'beliefs' on how best to pursue his/her own interests, represented in the form of 'preference' judgements. This doctrine, which for short I shall call the agent–preference–beliefs (APB) framework, has not been substantially superseded by any of the above-mentioned developments of the theory: quite the opposite. On the whole, they have helped us understand it better and make better use of it in understanding social facts.

One has only to deviate from the standard textbook models of behaviour to discover the full range of possibilities provided by the APB framework. As remarked by Guiso, Sapienza and Zingales (2006), the agent's beliefs and preferences provide two natural channels by which practically all the relevant social and cultural factors can be made to influence economic motivations in a most natural way. From the perfectly rational egoist – once believed to represent the stronghold of economic theory – to the multiform boundedly-rational altruist, passing through snobbery, imitation, cognitive dissonance, menu effects and so on, a whole gamut of types of agents as well as psychological and sociological phenomena have been modelled just by imposing particular constraints either on preferences, or beliefs, or on both. Inversely, given a distribution of preferences and beliefs over a population of agents, a whole gamut of forms of social interactions among them has been replicated through dynamical systems that can be analyzed or at least numerically simulated. These have made it possible to investigate the evolution of preferences and learning processes seen as feedbacks of the outcomes of the interactions on the agents' individual characteristics. All these lines of research on the interaction between social and economic factors have taken the APB framework as their reference point. Building on it, therefore, does not *per se* qualify a piece of research as being committed to a stance of methodological individualism (see Hodgson 2007). Nor is the underlying idea that the real actors are always individuals an obstacle to acknowledging the role of collective notions such as 'community', 'family', 'team' and so on, in the explanation of social facts (Tuomela 1995).

One of the results of the many ways in which the APB framework has opened up to considering social factors has been the addition of 'thickness' to the analysis of decision making. The latter can be seen as a multi-stage process in which not only the final objects of choice, but also the evaluation and belief formation criteria, are subject to the agent's scrutiny and, sometimes at least, choice. This is where recent research trends allow us to recapture essential aspects of Marshall's conceptual framework concerning economic behaviour and the dynamics induced by it. Marshall did not elaborate a model of individual economic behaviour of his own, preferring to rely on Jevons' model of utility maximization when it came to the point, and to use informal arguments and discussions of representative cases when it did not. As recalled above, however, he had a concept of the internal structure of the deliberative process as engaging a mixture of heterogeneous faculties: those consisting of automatic (natural and acquired) not attention-consuming mental routines, and those requiring the application of conscious attention and creativity. The proportions of the above in the mixture depended on the degree of novelty in each situation of choice. Both the routines and the perception of novelty embody the cumulated experience that the agent absorbs from all the social bodies with which he/she enters in touch, especially (in Marshall's view) through the family and the workplace.

Thus, also for Marshall decision making is a 'thick' process, including, as it does, a personal and genuinely individual layer grafted on to an impersonal and collective one of which the decision maker may even be unaware. It is this thickness, together with the unavoidable dependence of the individual on the impersonal and often unconscious layer, which comes to be reappraised in some of the contemporary non-standard models of the APB framework, providing a possible theoretical underpinning for the Marshallian thesis of economic change within social continuity. An outline of how these ideas may coalesce into a logically consistent pattern is sketched out in the next section.

4. A LOOSE MODEL OF MID STABILITY

In a social environment characterized by constant reciprocal monitoring and non-anonymous transactions, such as the typical MID environment, even the most self-interested profit-maximizing agent will assess each alternative action not only on the basis of its direct profitability but also of the reputation or public image that it contributes to creating, as reputation affects his/her chances of future dealings. Consequently, he/she will constantly keep the socially established 'inference rules' in mind, and on the basis of these try to make his/her actions conform to recognizable patterns or 'practical rules'. The latter, revealed through repeated interactions and transmitted by word of mouth, become the premise of the collective inferential exercise by which his/her public image is defined.

To be a bit less vague, think of a practical rule as an observable behavioural regularity such as, for example, the habit of foregoing a best-reply whenever, by so doing, a Pareto-optimum becomes available, that is, the habit of 'cooperating'. Other practical rules may concern traditional ways of doing things, locally established business customs, most-favoured-partner status bestowed on insiders against outsiders, and the like. An inference rule is a function which maps a signal – the bundle of practical rules an agent has been observed to follow – into a bundle of personal characteristics or 'type': for example, 'this kind of person is trustworthy and ready to cooperate'. Thus, if r designs a bundle of practical rules and b is the socially-established inference rule, $b(r)$ is the type with which an agent who is known to conform to r is associated according to the public estimate. As r varies over the entire range of the possible bundles of practical rules (possibly including a 'no-rule' or systematically random line of behaviour), the images according to $b(r)$ describe a 'typology' T which also represents a stable feature of the local culture. For b to be an 'efficient predictor' of behaviour, the typology must separate classes of agents in accordance with their actual preferences, in the sense that for each r the type $b(r)$ should apply to all and only the individuals for whom r actually represents the best choice. If this is not the case, then $b(r)$ will end up including someone who belongs to a different type and/or excluding someone who actually belongs to it. Although not strictly necessary, the predictive efficiency of b is sufficient to guarantee that the relative frequency of the bundles of rules adopted by the population equals the frequency of the types in T.

In such an environment, each choice entails two distinct levels of decision making. At the *prima facie* level the choice concerns the set of alternative actions available, and relies on preferences and beliefs applicable to them according to the given situation. At a deeper level, the same choice is a chapter in a long story that concerns long-term regularities of behaviour through which public images may be slowly built or (less) slowly dismantled. Thus, preferences and beliefs concerning the latter are also applied, and to a certain extent influence the upper-level preferences used in evaluating the current alternatives. The argument is well known: one may prefer the least profitable action when it contributes to building up or maintaining the preferred long-term practical rule. The deeper level of decision making cannot, by its very nature, lead to the choice of a different rule every time that a contingent situation requires a choice between actions. The deeper-level choice should, therefore, be thought of as the choice of a 'commitment' which, as far as the agent manages to keep it, constrains upper-level preferences on actions. Indirectly, this is also a choice between upper-level preferences based on preferences of a deeper level.

Environmental factors are decisive in the formation of deeper-level preferences. The assessment of the benefits derived from adopting a given practical rule has two sides: one is intrinsic and related to its expected profitability, the other is extrinsic and related to the public image associated with the conformity to it. Both sides are linked to the characteristics of the surrounding environment: while the profitability of adopting a rule depends on the rules adopted by other agents, the public image rests on the socially-established inference rules. At this point we can also afford to flesh out this perhaps overly elementary story, justified solely in terms of economic motivations, by introducing other kinds of motivations. For example, one may be unable to rank practical rules with respect to expected profitability and yet have well-defined preferences based on considerations of ethics or civility in relation to the moral standards prevailing in the environment. Or, to take another case, people may care about their own public image not only because it affects their business connections, but also for the consequences it has on their socializing activities, or simply – if for no other reason – out of self-respect. Whatever the case may be, the choice of a practical rule presupposes preferences defined in a two-dimensional domain, made up of a set of pairs (r, t), where r indicates the adopted practical rule, and t is the public image or type to which the agent is attached. The evaluation of the first element of each pair depends on the distribution of practical rules established in the environment in which one operates. The choice between pairs is constrained by the socially-prevailing inference rule b, which binds the second element of each pair to the first through the condition $t = b(r)$. When b is an efficient predictor (see above), the agent who prefers $[r, b(r)]$ to all the other rules will always have all the characteristics specified by $b(r)$.

A socially-established inference rule b and a distribution of practical rules among the population represented by a relative frequency function f form an 'equilibrium' when b is an efficient predictor, so that $f(r)$ coincides with the frequency of the types $b(r)$ for all the possible r. Although a bit sketchy, this notion of equilibrium embodies the essential ingredients of a signalling equilibrium, along lines somewhat similar to those of Bernheim's (1994) theory of social conformity. An equilibrium is a situation which is both socially and economically stable, as no agent has any interest in changing his/her own practical rule or public image given that f represents the socially-established distribution of rules, and each one's public image faithfully reproduces his/her behavioural propensities.

This generic equilibrium comes closer to the description of a MID moving in a steady path if we add two further qualifications: (a) there is a locally prevailing bundle of practical rules r^* such that $f(r^*)$ is close to unity, and (b) the social assessment attached to it, $b(r^*)$, is unanimously considered to be the most favourable assessment one may ever receive. Type $b(r^*)$ is what everybody prefers to be believed to be, because $b(r^*)$ is the characterization of the ideal business partner and everybody would like to do business with such a type. At the same time, this equilibrium does not require r^* to be the most profitable rule given the circumstances, although this may help. The persistence of r^* as the prevailing rule simply requires that, for most of the actual types present in the MID, there exists no other rule r such that the pair $[r, b(r)]$ is preferred to $[r^*, b(r^*)]$, given that r^* represents the locally-established standard. But the $b(r^*)$ type is attached both to those who prefer (r^*, t) to (r, t) for any t, that is, types who consider r^* to be the best possible line of behaviour, and to those who prefer (r, t) to (r^*, t) for some $r \neq r^*$ (and given t), but are held back from choosing r by their dislike for the attendant characterization $b(r)$. The former may be said to be 'absolutely loyal' to r^*, while the latter are only 'conditionally loyal' to r^* and would switch to other practical rules were it not for the negative stigma attached to them. Logically, one may think of cases of locked-in MIDs, when all the individuals included in $b(r^*)$ are only conditionally loyal to r^*. This means that almost everybody thinks that the ruling standard of behaviour is non optimal; however, socially-entrenched preconceptions keep the community trapped in it.

We may summarize the argument so far by saying that a MID equilibrium can be seen as a kind of signalling equilibrium characterized by a considerable amount of homogeneity in the preferences on public images. These specific features in turn suggest the possibility of a sort of 'cultural drift' associated with a MID equilibrium. Suppose that the inference rule b includes default rules for newcomers (those who, because of either their young age or external provenance, have no publicly-known past record of behaviour) which discriminate between insiders and outsiders as follows: the former are assessed on the basis of their family background and receive the same evaluation as their parents or other nearest kin; the latter are submitted to formal (non-communal) procedures of inquiry and are evaluated accordingly. As in a MID equilibrium the frequency $f(r^*)$ equals nearly 1, the signal 'insider' turns out to be associated almost certainly with the characterization $b(r^*)$, while those who bear the signal 'outsider' and are new to the local environment receive all sorts of characterizations. Thus, $b(r^*)$ and the quality of being an insider become almost equivalent characterizations. At this point, the cultural shift towards merging $b(r^*)$ and the 'identity' of members of the district community becomes very likely, perhaps even inevitable if the equilibrium persists for a very long time. In the local culture, and gradually also outside it, the local identity comes to include all the qualities indicated by $b(r^*)$. Consequently, the preference for the public image $b(r^*)$ is confused with a fondness for one's own origins and a sense of belonging. Moreover, as argued in Akerlof and Kranton (2000), the practical rule r^* is gradually transformed into a 'norm', almost an unwritten constitution, sanctioned by the notion of identity built onto it.

If the equilibrium can support this kind of cultural mutation, the latter in turn can make equilibrium more robust to external shocks. In a frame of mind in which r^* is 'the' local identity-forging norm of behaviour rather than just 'a' bundle of practical rules, those whose preferences belong to the conditionally loyal type may be led towards adopting preferences of the absolutely loyal type. This move can be justified, if for no other reason, on the grounds that it minimizes the cost of having to evaluate the practical rule adopted at each change of situation: if r^* is 'how things are done here', and one wants to belong here, there is a good reason for preferring r^* without further questioning. As pointed out by J.M. Epstein (2001), the advantage of a convention (that is, a self-enforced norm, as r^* is in equilibrium) consists of obviating the need for a lot of thinking. As the absolutely loyal types become a strong majority in $b(r^*)$, the MID equilibrium becomes more resistant to changes in the external circumstances that determine the ranking of profitability of practical rules.

This analysis suggests that a MID with a strong sense of identity, let us say a 'self-conscious' MID, may be a very conservative social and economic organization. The drawback is, of course, that conservatism is more a hindrance than a help during periods of intense external variability. A counterbalance to this is provided by the amount of flexibility built into the prevailing rules r^*: the more these privilege the tendency to adapt and innovate, the higher the chances are of thriving on economic variability while, in Marshallian fashion, preserving the continuity of the social and cultural traits. This 'behavioural' flexibility may be a matter of survival for an inherently 'structurally'-rigid organization like a self-conscious MID: indeed, an evolutionary argument could lead to the conclusion that you cannot observe many non-flexible self-conscious MIDs because, in the long run, they are all extinct.

In general, the problem of the stability of a MID equilibrium in the face of external changes that are so far reaching as to unsettle the existing preferences on practical rules may be overwhelmingly complex. A model of social conformity like Bernheim (1994) provides interesting hints as to how signalling equilibria may react to changes in the distribution of preferences according to the extent of the 'pooling' of types into the socially-dominating one and to the weight of the public image in individual preferences (both very high in MID equilibria). However, these considerations are entirely based on comparative static arguments, with no dynamics (ibid., pp. 861–2). The reason for the inevitable complexity of a dynamic approach to the problem is the following: as external changes make the agents' preferences shift from absolute or conditional loyalty to r^* to other practical rules which become so much more profitable than r^* as to be worth the loss of the public image $b(r^*)$, the resulting movements in the distribution f feed back into the preferences themselves, generating potentially complicated loops. Moreover, as more and more agents with $b(r^*)$ characteristics begin to adopt rules different from r^*, receiving a social assessment different from the one they actually deserve, the inference rule b becomes less and less efficient as a predictor. It is difficult to say how long it takes for a community to change its entrenched standards of judgement, but it seems inevitable that sooner or later also *b* will give way. If the unravelling of the equilibrium gets this far, the whole process enters a stage in which anything can happen: with all their reference points shifting, the only way that agents have of coping with an apparently chaotic situation is to devise rules of thumb destined to last until a new order starts to emerge.

Any research programme aiming at a simple and general theory of the dynamics of MIDs seems, therefore, doomed. What one may look for is either a comparative statics substitute for the dynamics (in tune with Marshall's 'statical method'), or theoretical methods for dealing with artificially-isolated aspects of the dynamics through which MIDs evolve, and sometimes turn into other organizational forms (again, in tune with Marshall's 'partial' analysis). Dynamics has always been the weak spot of economic theory, and MID dynamics is no exception. As recalled in Section 3, however, ongoing research is elaborating methods that can deal with the bottom-up dynamic processes relevant for the study of this type of social changes. These include both the inductive methods of ACE simulations, and the deductive ones of evolutionary game theory and statistical mechanics (see, for example, Axelrod 1997; Young 1998; Durlauf and Young 2001, and many works in the spirit of the Santa Fe Program from 1988 to 2006). All these methods have the well-known drawback of being exceedingly sensitive to the way in which the law of motion of the system is specified, so as not to offer generalizable results. This seems to be inherent in the very nature of the problem, however, and the alternative of spinning conjectural stories on an entirely intuitive basis is no less case-specific and is possibly more prone to faulty or arbitrary conclusions.

5. IDENTITY, VARIETY AND ADAPTIVE CAPACITY

In whatever direction a theory of MIDs may develop, if it ever does, its Marshallian origin marks it under at least two important respects. First, it seems obvious that it cannot be a theory of MIDs full stop. Recall Loasby's remark cited at the beginning: for Marshall, the ID was just one possible form in which social and economic forces adapt to each other, the same theory that accounts for district-shaped equilibria in certain circumstances pointing to other organizational forms under different hypotheses. Indeed, we have only to remove qualifications (a) and (b) in the above definition of a MID equilibrium (see Section 4) to generate a variety of possible forms. Second, while based on the assumption of a fundamental coherence between the economy and the society in which it is nested, this theory should not give the impression that the relationship between the two is a balanced interaction between symmetrical forces. There is no doubt that Marshall had an asymmetrical view in which, typically, the economy is fast moving and pushy, in contrast with society, which is slow and adaptive. The former plays the role of the animating force while the latter serves as the 'permanent body' in which all impulses merge (see, among others, the neat passage in Marshall 1919, pp. 197–8).

His reputation as the founder of 'economic imperialism' was, after all, not ill deserved: while opening up economics to the contributions of the other branches of the social sciences, he turned the notion of social embedding into a doctrine of how economic forces, by striving to make the bed most comfortable for themselves, sooner or later mould the social structure to their will.

Thus, the guidelines of a theory of MIDs are defined by two key ideas: the structuring power of economic activities, and the wide variety of forms of territorial and social aggregation that emanate from them. According to the former, all productive activities tend to group producers into communities characterized by a distribution of practical rules highly concentrated on some particular bundle r^* which works as the informal constitution of the community. According to the latter, the specific content of these rules may differ greatly from one group to the other. By connecting the two ideas complex patterns emerge which no simple theory of trade among producers could possibly generate or explain. Consider the following: in the case of MIDs, r^* will typically include a 'rule of place' which states that local people must be preferred to non-locals whenever partnerships and employment relationships are in question. This accounts for the much-emphasized place-bound character of their industrial organization, business alliances, and pools of labour and expertise. As a consequence that the chief part of their external relationships will be represented by trade relations, a MID is an almost perfect example of a 'trading body'. But this is not so for other groups of producers, which may be identified by a bundle r^* that does not include a rule of place. These groups trade, make partnerships, plan the localization of productive units, and search for labour and specialized skills, with no commitment to any particular place. The obvious example here is the multinational corporation, a social body in its own right, with its own culture and customs, and also locations for its headquarters and branches, but possibly no territorial vocation. Besides being a trading body, a multinational is also a 'scheming' body that is always spinning its complex web of relationships of cooperation, coordination and control among bodies and places, with the final aim of influencing the flows of trade to its own advantage (see Amin 1994 for a similar view).

Marshall lived to see the rise of the multinational corporate power and culture in the world economy before the First World War, and to realize both its potential for social change and the impending conflict between this kind of organization and the traditional localized systems of which MIDs are an example. Nowadays, we are faced with similar processes but their hugely dilated scale and much speedier pace makes the conflict that Marshall had only glimpsed more evident and dramatic. With almost perfect worldwide capital mobility and the revolutionary facilities offered by the new ICTs, the fact of having a constitution unconstrained by rules of place may generate competitive advantages so powerful that they render the traditional resources of tacit knowledge and cooperativeness rooted in places and nurtured by the local 'industrial atmosphere' unable to compensate for them by their own force alone. Thus, in the big divide between place-bound and non-place-bound organizational forms, the former are inevitably cast in a passive role, as they are continuously engaged in defending their market niches against the mobile landscape of alliances, mergers, decentralizations, relocations and all the other kinds of strategic movements staged by footloose organizations. This is, I think, the core issue in the debates concerning IDs' policies in the present historical phase (see Bellandi 2007): namely, not merely to survive in some interstices of the global market, but rather to find ways in which to play a less subordinate and more prominent role.

The solution that some Italian IDs are putting into practice focuses directly on the main source of trouble, the rule of place, which they have tried to make less exacting by permitting a certain amount of external linkage and relocation of productive phases outside their territory. Tensions on this solution have not been lacking at the local level, for reasons that are easily understood within the framework of the previous sections. A constitution is not simply a list of rules: it must have internal consistency and make sense as a whole. If one rule is repealed or relaxed, this may remain a confined episode of adaptation with no further effects, or instead be the beginning of the unravelling of the preexisting equilibrium in the way sketched in Section 4. The falling out of favour of one rule jeopardizes other rules, setting in motion an avalanche that ultimately upsets the established practices and ways of thinking as represented, respectively, by f and b. In the case of the relaxing of the rule of place for MIDs it seems clear that the move is not likely to remain without consequences. The mix of productive functions performed locally changes as manufacturing phases are relocated outside, while management, finance, product design and marketing remain in place and probably require development. Predictably, tacit knowledge, mostly linked to manufacturing, will become relatively less important; and as many linkages become translocal, the related transactions will need levels of formalization and guarantees unheard of in the informal and fiduciary atmosphere of the MID. In the end, not only rule of place, but other old-established routines and aspects of the local way of life, will have to yield to the emerging new pattern of productive activities. These changes may be far reaching enough to bring about a transition from the MID form to some other kind of local, or translocal, system.

No wonder that, in the debate about the new trends in IDs, there has been resistance of a 'cultural' kind to the external relocation of productive phases, as though the subsequent restructuring and predictable disappearance of a number of characteristics of the MID entailed a loss of collective identity. As noted above, 'self-conscious' MIDs have an inborn conservatism. However, to end these notes in a Marshallian key, if we believe in evolution and continuity as Marshall did, we should not let ourselves be alarmed by the conservative argument. In fact, setting limits to the adaptive capacity can be a risky strategy. But more importantly, identities have many layers, and the deepest ones are so well guarded that economic changes are hardly cataclysmic enough to force a community to shed all of them at the same time.

12. The economics of context, location and trade: Another great transformation?

Michael Storper

1. CONTEXT AND THE GAINS FROM TRADE

The combined effects of the division of labor, specialization and gains from trade are widely agreed to be one of the two main forces behind world economic growth since its modern takeoff around 1820, the other being technological innovation (Mokyr 1990; North 2005). Contemporary debates about the geographical reshuffling of output and employment through outsourcing and offshoring ask whether we have crossed some kind of new threshold in the world division of labor. Is the scale and speed of geographical fragmentation fundamentally altering the process of economic development, replacing local and national levels of interaction with a new type of geographically-distributed system?

Even though there is no definitive answer to this question, trade theory is confident about the issue of potential welfare effects of a great transformation: there may be new kinds of adjustment costs from recomposition of local and national economies, but there will be gains to fragmentation and trade for the world economy as a whole, and in the long run for those local economies that successfully complete their 'churn' and absorb its costs. This holds even when a particular country or region has benefited from a strong cluster: according to trade theory, by definition the long-distance relations that replace a local cluster will be more efficient and hence generate welfare gains. Development economics has identified some highly-contested exceptions to this assumption that the overall level of geographical concentration and diffusion is optimal: economies of scale; timing of entry; sequencing and terms of trade; infant industry. Most of it shows, however, that there is 'not enough' diffusion or delocalization, not too much, that is, less developed countries have insufficient opportunities to get into the world economy. Moreover, some critiques of the ongoing transformation of localized into long-distance relations, that is, of the ongoing creation and destruction of local 'contexts' tend to be naïve, nostalgic or openly reactionary. These include various kinds of 'neo-localism', which are often traditionalist and communitarian, as well as expressing wistfulness about artisanal work versus large-scale divisions of labor.

An idea that has influenced much development policy consists in claiming that the more an activity has a local supply chain, the more developmental benefits for a locality can be captured over time through expansion of the activity. This idea expresses a fundamental bias against long-distance linkages and commodity chains that are highly fragmented over different territorial jurisdictions. In simple accounting terms, it has some empirical validity, in the short run, in that the more localized the value chain, the more of it will be captured locally for a given increment of output increase in the activity in question. In more dynamic terms, however, there are problems with this way of thinking (Puga and Venables 1999). One is that there is reciprocity: so if everyone adopts policies to capture these chains, it will negatively affect demand for our exports, with possibly negative overall consequences on our output. A second is that there are often political economy problems, that are signaling through such policies to local firms that they can be lazy about quality and innovation because they are protected. Thus, in the long run, such a notion addresses itself too simply to the static capture of output gains, and ignores the dynamic process of creating local advantage. In the latter, it is not necessarily how much of an input–output chain is concentrated locally that drives long-term growth, but rather whether certain local interactions are sufficient to recreate local comparative advantage, such that the ongoing recomposition of local output (sectoral and activity 'succession') increases local productivity levels enough to permit increasing local factor prices (and hence incomes). In other words, it is about local learning, innovation, and adjustment, not about mercantilist 'capture' of supply chains. This is why many of the most successful economies in the world (national or regional) have been successful over time, in spite of the ongoing loss of certain activities via recomposition of their economies.

But there are doubts about this scenario as well. An economy might appear to do very well by shedding parts of input–output chains and recomposing itself, and there might be aggregate gains to trade. Nothing in trade theory establishes that even this is a long-term welfare maximization, however. For example, if the sectors in question 'would' have developed, in the future, in different ways if they were geographically fragmented from how they do when they are more geographically localized, 'and' if there are strong irreversibilities and sunk costs once geographical fragmentation gets under way, then the current decision to fragment them geographically leads to future 'roads not taken'. This is a claim frequently made about lesser-developed economies as well as about some developed regions where, it is argued, a rich local feedback process within the supply chain encourages adaptive refinement of products and processes and generates 'staying power' (Bardhan 1971; Bruton 1998). In this case, retaining supply chains is a necessary precursor to learning and adaptation, which potentiate learning and adaptation later on. In trade theory, it is simply assumed that there cannot be 'foregone superior outcomes'.

This is the main problem addressed in this chapter. Both neo-localists and trade theorists have inadequate theory and evidence to deal with this issue.

This is because there is a *lacuna* in economics and economic geography about the question of what determines how productive activities trace out their developmental pathways. This *lacuna* is rooted in the idea that organizational and geographical features of such systems, because they are driven by appropriate decision-making processes, are the right outcomes. These assumptions are highly questionable. The effects of decisions to fragment and relocate production are not just measured in terms of outputs and productivity levels; they also involve the creation, loss and change of 'contexts', which affect 'future' development potential. Such change may or may not be optimal. Decisions about organization and geography of production may have unintended long-term welfare effects.

2. WHY WE NEED GEOGRAPHICAL FRAGMENTATION AND TRADE: THE GEOGRAPHICAL UNDERPINNINGS OF INCREASING RETURNS

Before we consider a possible counter-narrative to the case for geographical fragmentation and globalization of production systems, let us establish the strongest possible theory of why the economy must develop through a combination of organizational and geographical fragmentation of activity, and the ongoing recomposition of regional and national economies. The standard analysis of the welfare effects of geographical fragmentation concludes that there are almost always aggregate gains to trade. There is a dynamic extension of it in political economy: that the 'whip' of inter-place competition increases incentives to firms in different places to become more efficient over time (Wolf 2004).[1] Trade is thus seen as the outcome of cost-minimizing decisions to geographically fragment production and markets, and this may in addition have 'dynamic incentive effects' on economic actors in different places.

There is another way to see the positive effects of trade and fragmentation, however, which suggests an even more powerful set of beneficial effects. This comes from growth theory rather than location theory, and centers on the geography of positive externalities and increasing returns. The Romer growth theory establishes economy-wide increasing returns as the principal source of long-run economic growth under resource constraints (Romer 1990). Knowledge and technology are non-rival and generally only weakly excludable over time; hence they can be infinitely reused without loss and tend to spread their effects among communities of users (industries, for example) and geographical areas. The productivity of the R&D/innovation sector of the economy is not subject to diminishing returns, and becomes a source of long-run unconstrained growth. This point is reconciled with standard theory because even though the different specific activities to which innovations are applied are perfectly competitive in the long run, the economy as a whole is freed from diminishing returns (Romer 1986, 1990, 1994). The link between these two seemingly contradictory propositions is that monopoly rents to innovation are bid away through diffusion and entry into each sector, but at the economy-wide level the recombination and reuse of technology creates increasing returns.

Applied to the geography of economic growth, the Romer theory is frequently allied to earlier contributions from Marshall and Arrow, respectively about technology spillovers at the regional scale ('the secrets of industry are in the air') and 'learning-by-doing'. Both capture key mechanisms of increasing returns later formalized by Romer: those of reuse, spillover and improvement. Many such Marshall–Arrow (M–A) processes occur at definite territorial scales (local, regional, national innovation systems and spillovers). This leads many to claim that 'Marshall–Arrow–Romer (MAR) externalities' at the regional scale are the principal form of growth-enhancing increasing return in the economy as a whole.[2]

There is a key contradiction between this claim and a central point of the Romer theory, that is, that increasing returns can be reconciled with allocative efficiency through perfect competition. If the principal source of increasing returns were a set of restricted local relationships, then in effect they would merely generate localized technological or knowledge rents. We know that such rents exist when knowledge is sufficiently complex or uncodified that some kind of proximity (geographical, member of a network, often both) is necessary to gain access and know how to use it properly. That such rents allow regional wages and profits to rise above the economy-wide norm, at least for a time, and hence contributes to (at least temporary) successes in regional development is widely admitted among scholars of regional development and development economics.[3]

But if this were the end of the story, then there would be no way to account for long-term economic growth as a result of innovation: rather than increasing returns at the economy-wide level, there would simply be long-term accumulation of rents in certain lucky hands. Knowledge would be geographically excludable; one of the defining pillars of the Romer theory would be broken.

Moreover, though the spread of technology and knowledge are hardly similar to the fluid process imagined by standard theories, there is still ample evidence that much of the economic development process is driven by sharing and diffusion of technologies (Mokyr 1990). The reality is somewhere in-between durable monopolization of knowledge and rent-seeking, and easy, seamless sharing. There is sharing, but it is temporally and geographically-uneven, with rents accruing to some firms and places for some periods of time, and then slowly breaking down, as the 'potentially' non-rival and non-excludable character of technology progressively becomes real, allowing the economy-wide increasing return to become real in turn.[4] In other words, even though increasing returns are the key source of economic growth, they are only realized through the geographical, and organizational, process that leads from localization and monopoly rents to geographical (hence economic) diffusion of technology and the breakdown of those rents. This is a point that formed part of the intuition of early studies of the geography of innovation diffusion (Pred and Hagerstrand 1967) but those scholars did not have the benefit of theoretical advances in growth theory or the economics of agglomeration. We now can see just how important their intuition really was to understanding how growth can occur, but also why it is temporally and geographically not smooth. In the way we can formulate it today, there are no so-called 'MAR externalities'. Rather, there are M–A sources of 'local' technological externalities and possible local monopoly rents; but the true R-sources of 'economy-wide' increasing returns are not essentially local.

M–A and R are linked through: (a) the geography of where technologies and technological rents emerge; (b) sometimes, processes of localized learning and sharing, with both rent-capture and rent-destruction effects; (c) a process of codification, so that such innovations can be more widely used; leading to (d) a geography of the destruction of technological rents that creates increasing returns in the entire economy.

A reformulation of this sequence looks as follows. In t_1, innovations emerge in certain, specific places and organizational settings (firms). The geography of this innovation involves M–A effects of proximity and localized learning (Jaffe, Trajtenberg and Henderson 1993; Henderson 1999; Malmberg and Maskell 2006). There are monopoly rents to such innovations, for a certain amount of time. These monopoly rents last as long as there are barriers to imitation, which include both knowledge barriers and trade/communication costs associated with using the technology – it is effectively, if not juridically, excludable. The places where there are agglomeration economies for such technology production and use capture rents.

In t_2, these innovations can diffuse to a wider set of places, firms and uses. The knowledge is more amenable to imitation and copying because as it becomes more widely used, it tends to be codified, more people learn the codes for using it, and hence the trade costs associated with deploying it to other uses and places decrease. On the ground, there is geographical fragmentation of production and delocalization. The entry of other users will bid rents away. Schumpeterian competition is replaced by standard (or at least semi-standard) market structures. The locational dynamics of this are described by the product cycle, but the latter does not have an explicit growth theory dimension.

Simultaneously, the Romer process of economy-wide increasing returns comes into being. This is because geographical diffusion allows more and more non-exclusive application of the knowledge, so that its potentially non-rival aspects now can become reality. The knowledge goes into many different applications, and back into recombination into further rounds of innovation, the drivers of long-run growth in the Romer model.

The process repeats itself over an unlimited number of cycles. The precise parameters for technology creation, the trade costs and barriers to imitation, and Romer-like diffusion and reapplication of technology will determine such things as: the spatial hierarchy of incomes at any given moment; the amount of time it takes for a shift away from the rent-earning (first mover) part of the innovation cycle to economy-wide increasing returns; and the amount of increasing returns in the economy as a whole. Overlain on all this is the geography of innovation, where additional innovation processes get started and new rounds of monopoly rents are earned.

This account is a more powerful case for the gains to geographical fragmentation and trade than the standard Ricardian/Heckscher–Ohlin accounts of allocative efficiencies through cost-minimizing locations, because it adds to the latter static analysis a dynamic process.

3. WHAT IS CONTEXT?

In the account thus far, the local contexts of M–A processes need to give way to an economy-wide diffusion process if they are to generate long-run growth. Another way to state this is that local differences are good at certain moments in the economic process, but must ultimately be reduced at others (diffusion, end of monopoly rents), thus completing the development cycle from innovation-driven divergence to diffusion-led convergence and broad growth.

Anthropologists have long asked whether differences in economic organization between societies were simply reflections of great differences in resources (endowments), which then lead to different power structures or rules (incentives), or whether it is the actors from one place that have different processes of rationality, goal seeking, learning and cognition (Sahlins 1995). The anthropology of 'primitive' economies uses their relative isolation as an experimental control for this question ('weak contamination' of practices and resources through contact), but has not arrived at consensus about it.

Contemporary institutional economics sees such divergence as empirically important, but theoretically places itself in the first camp: such differences are an aggregation phenomenon, not due to systematic at the level of individual actors (Acemoglu, Johnson and Robinson 2004). Differences in endowments and initial conditions create different scarcities and collective action dilemmas, leading to the construction of different rules and market structures. From this, 'history matters', and can lead to durably different and lasting outcomes for economic organization and development. In spite of this, many analysts hold that the periods of relative institutional stability create particular 'local' environments of cognition, learning and incentives, thus differentiating economic contexts from one another.

A third perspective simply acknowledges institutional differences as a fact. Economies are such complex aggregates of microeconomic phenomena that in any given place, even with common overall rules and laws, important differences of practice and history will emerge. These will affect choices and perceptions, and reproduce themselves as 'varieties of capitalism' (Hall and Soskice 2001a) 'embedded firms and production systems', and 'regional worlds' (Storper and Salais 1993; Storper 1997). There can be ongoing differences in values and beliefs that influence political choices and hence institutional differences between places. In their different ways, all three of these perspectives insist that there are different 'contexts' for economic activity, and these differences have something important to do with performance, both positive and negative.

Arrayed against all of the above is the notion that such conditions for institutional divergence and hence diversity of contexts, no longer exist in a world of intricate divisions of labor, trade and interpenetrating markets. In this view, there is no longer enough separation of contexts to allow such differences to persist, except as residues of institutional rigidity (Friedman 2005). For some, this leads to worries about loss of diversity of behaviors and material cultures, whereas – as noted above – for the mainstream of economics it is a potential source of economic betterment as less efficient contexts are transformed through the 'whip' of global integration and competition. This is another reason why geographical fragmentation, integration and diffusion – the destruction and transformation of local contexts – might be a key source of long-term economic development.

3.1 Defining context

These different perspectives are nonetheless incomplete as inputs to a theoretical grasp of difference in economic environments. A step beyond them is to consider what psychologists who work on the economy call the 'situation' of the actor. They provide us powerful analytics that enable us to see difference neither as a simple aggregation phenomenon, nor as simply 'cultural'.

They start by challenging the notion that actors have universally powerful rational cognition and simple preferences (Ariely 2008). Experimental evidence confirms that action is very strongly 'localist' in the sense that choices are typically made with very imperfect information and on the basis of a set of limited criteria; hence, the 'normal' world of economic decision making is not one of ordered preferences, obtaining complete information and rationally weighing alternatives, but rather one of widespread and persistent cognitive errors and biases. The unifying theme in behavioral economics is, thus, 'situationalism' – the idea that decisions are always strongly conditioned by local influences, not perfect information and long-run optimization with it (Glaeser 2003, from Ross and Nisbet 1991), and that this may have strong evolutionary roots (Haselton, Nettle and Andrews 2005). There are five dimensions of the situation of the actor that can be drawn upon to define her context.

First, valuable specialized information is not uniformly available in this world. There are costs to obtaining it, and there are also barriers to access – one's social and economic position define whether and under what conditions, and sometimes at what cost, one can get such information. This point is relevant to all behavior, but we can consider it in relationship to productive activity. The information one needs, but also to which one has access, is strongly defined by one's place in the division of labor. Divisions of labor are dizzyingly complex in the 21st century, such that there is a great deal of opacity about what is going on outside of where we stand in a division of labor, or at the very least, outside of the 'neighborhood' of roles surrounding our place in it. Most people do not have an overall vision of the productive chain in which they work, not to mention the millions of other specialized systems that affect their lives as workers, consumers and citizens. This may be the beauty of the division of labor, that is, that we don't need to know these things in order to benefit from the productive power unleashed by such complex structures. But they also mean that what we know is partial. Hence, the situation that we define for ourselves is a 'local' – in the sense of partial – one.

This issue is ignored in welfare analysis because it is assumed that if it is worth getting information we currently lack, then we will search for it; this is the cognitive rationality assumption. But that assumption is challenged by prospect theory, which holds that people engage in very limited search behavior, and put enormous weight on limited reference points, even when these are quite arbitrary and ephemeral (Kahneman and Tversky 1979). This is the second dimension of the actor's situation.

A third dimension of situationalism is how actors form their goals. In the place of subjective preferences, on the one hand, or rationally-constructed ones on the other, an enormous body of evidence shows that goals are strongly influenced by comparison and emulation. Status comparison is a big element of this, and it affects virtually every dimension of preference formation. Since information is limited and prospecting is the norm, what we compare to and emulate is not some kind of exercise in global maximizing, but in many ways is highly dependent on where we are, socially, geographically, and in our position in the division of labor (Frank 2001; Fine 2006).

Fourth, most economic decisions are strongly present-oriented. Hyperbolic discounting, which places excessive weight on the present and not enough on even the medium-term future, is the norm, even in financial markets; and we use present-day cues, that stem mostly from ephemeral and situational forces, rather than information over a relevant spatial and temporal span, to form our choices (Laibson 1997). Though this may be tempered by structures of management, management studies show that it is far from having been eliminated.

Fifth, the information we do access is generally processed in a relatively narrow way. Mental accounting shows that people mostly make decisions by ignoring events and consequences outside of a particular narrow domain (Thaler 1985), and most decisions are made using rules of thumb that are far away from the processes that would be necessary to maximize.[5] Even such 'tricks' as 'reframing' a situation can induce big changes in choice behavior, as can the way that local stimuli trigger emotions (Romer 2000; Ariely 2008). People are inherently conservative in their decisions, as shown by the endowment effect that they want to keep what they have over almost any other goal (Thaler 1994). They are also averse to small-value risky gambles, and they are vengeful toward strangers (Fehr and Gachter 2000). None of this means that all decisions are merely the unleashing of emotions, because economic actors may be able to learn to manage, interpret and manipulate their own emotions (Gul and Pesendorfer 2001); but they cannot cut around them and construct a non-situational world for themselves. Intuitions are not inherently wrong, but they are strongly situational (Gilovich, Griffin and Kahneman 2002).

Theories of corporate bureaucracy vacillate between the idea that organizational structure can correct this inherent tendency to be situational, and another, that such bureaucracies are themselves situations (Simon 1986; Friedberg 1993). Theories of entrepreneurship do the same: from those that argue that the entrepreneur does rational arbitrage of unexploited opportunities to those that hold that he leaps into the void with courage and flair. In the end, it would seem that the very structures set up to control our worst situationalist errors end up creating new situations. The interaction of such structures and the inherent dilemmas of being situational is the reality for economic actors. Action is unavoidably contextual.

We can now propose a definition of 'context'. Its structural component is defined by the division of labor in which the actor finds himself, which has a decisive influence on the informational environment for the individual, hence his 'input' structure of cues and reference points. In turn, the individual actor engages in his search behavior (prospecting) and goal formation (emulation/aspirations), and does so with certain time horizons (cues and discounting), leading to choice/evaluation behaviors (rules of thumb and framing).

This is not to argue that this geographical architecture of interactions fully determines what actors then do, but rather that it influences what they do by defining the situation in which they find themselves. Following Piore (1995), we can say that the meaning actors make of their situation depends on a process of interpretation, itself in part dependent on the interactions that occur in the situation. Piore argues that time is a critical aspect of this – a string of interactions and interpretations, rather than a set of instantaneous and history-less discrete calculated choices. To that notion, we can add the importance of the geographical context of such interactions that lead to 'meaning making' and choices.

3.2 Different types of context

Though there are potentially innumerable forces that structure differences in context, two of them that have a particularly strong influence on the set of relationships between an economic actor and his wider environment: the division of labor and the geographical distance between activities. They influence the actor's relationships because they have strong effects on the five aspects of situation identified above. The economy's vast organizational and geographical complexity generates at least five dimensions that structure the actor's situation: the immediate environment of his task in the detailed division of labor; his environment in the work unit; the environment between closely-related work units, possibly inside an organization (for example, a firm); intended regular relationships to the environment (intra or inter-organizational or market); and unintended or unplanned relations to the external world. A key consequence of the geography of the division of labor is to define how an activity is placed in its wider environment. Thus, some resulting environments are more specialized and homogeneous, while other pieces of the division of labor are located in places with diverse, more heterogeneous local activity mixes. All these relationships are shaped by geographical location, which is in turn strongly related to productive organization, that is, the division of labor and the trade costs between parts of it.

A way to begin to see this is to extend the standard logic of scale and scope to the structure of the actor's situation. The more organizationally internalized the actor's relationships, combined with the effects of the internal division of labor in an organization, the more an actor's context is intra-organizational and, possibly, task-specialized. In turn, this will direct his communication within the organized chain and tend to simplify communications to the local, external environment. At the other extreme, shallow or artisanal divisions of labor, a great deal of externalization and narrow scope, less 'purified' task definitions, will generally lead to more diverse, irregular, and uncertain external communications. Locational economics suggests the latter will tend to be located in more 'diverse' and urban local economies, the former in more specialized and less urban ones, all other things being equal (Duranton and Puga 2002).

This is just a simplified vision of two ideal types at opposite ends of a spectrum. There is rarely a clean division between 'locationally-fragmented, highly-organized, specialized contexts' and 'highly-diverse, market-oriented, dense communication contexts', but rather some fascinating mixes of them. For example, in a local context such as a city, we can find firms involved in high levels of internal communication, using algorithms and rules, and highly-organized professional supply-chain relationships, as well as local, spontaneous, diverse interactions. The actor's context, in this case, is some mixture of the two, which is as yet rather poorly understood. Likewise, in the geographically-fragmented, highly-organized supply-chain environment, where information is strongly 'stovepiped' to actors,[6] there is still likely to be some leakage of unplanned information from the local or long-distance environment. The core issue is how the information and signals that are the key inputs into the actor's situation are defined and channelled, and then what actors do in different types of situations: how they learn, what choices they make, whom and what they emulate.

Let us now think about some examples of this phenomenon. The apparel industry has a high level of product differentiation, both because of functional and fashion diversity, and because of steep quality ladders. Market structures, organization, and geography are correspondingly diverse within this industry, which exhibits everything from geographically-fragmented chains of mass production within large firms to highly-localized, specialized clothing 'clusters' or districts. The processes of emulation, learning and innovation are very different in the many contexts defined by such a variety of organizational forms. Skills do not transfer readily between them. There is 'spillover' from one to another, in that mass production tries generally to knock off and copy what comes from fast fashion or high fashion, which in turn learns from an alternative circuit of cities, the arts, and the 'street'. So in this case, there is probably some kind of complementary relationship between two very different organizational and geographical contexts.

Another example comes from the literature on organizational diversity within capitalism (Sabel and Zeitlin 1985; Hall and Soskice 2001a). German, Japanese and American car makers have significant differences in the organization and geography of their core activities; so do Samsung and General Electric for consumer electronics. Unlike the clothing industry, the products here are roughly comparable, so we are confronted with alternative organizational and geographical arrangements for substitutable products (Krugman 1991b and 1991c). This might be due to the increasing market interpenetration of these industries and the international technology spillovers it facilitates and requires.

This might tempt some to conclude that context, in the way that we are defining it, is unimportant, since apparently it leads to the same ending point. But upon closer examination, these industries struggle with dynamic change in different ways and with varying degrees of success. No close observer would claim that Detroit, with its far-flung system of suppliers and arms-length relations, does as well as its German and Japanese counterparts in getting out new models with constant engineering improvements (Goldberg 1995). So, even in a world of enormous technology sharing and circulation, the actors in each system are keyed into at least some differences in information, and have different emulation dynamics, possibly discounting (time horizons), and choice behaviors. If not, universally-available information, world market structures, and international technological spillovers would push all three toward more organizational and geographical and performance convergence than in fact we observe. In this case, contexts are not simply complementary, around imperfectly substitutable products, but they are competitors, different ways of doing something. There are feedbacks from context to development and performance, a recursive relationship (Saxenian 1994; Essletzbichler and Rigby 2004).

A third example is the extreme case of winner-take-all systems in the world, such as the City of London, Silicon Valley, or Hollywood, or industrial districts built around a combination of distinctive products and locally-constructed techniques rooted in the local system as a whole (Becattini 1990). These highly-successful clusters serve the global market and are caught up in all sorts of long-distance, formal organizational procedures, professional and regulatory norms, and so on. Some kind of alchemy occurs in their core regions, extended through the local and worldwide informal and semi-formal networks at whose center they lie. As with any sector, they are subject to product cycle and quality ladder dynamics that can modify them organizationally and geographically. At the extreme, this might lead to the 'end' of their existing local contexts and their replacement by a different type of long-distance, organizationally-formal, big-firm oriented (plus suppliers and others) 'context'. We think of this as a natural and unproblematic dimension of economic development, with benefits for outlying regions in particular, and for the economy as a whole through technological maturity and Ricardian gains to trade. But in the case of such radical restructuring and change in context, how sure can we be about these presumed welfare effects? The Romer growth theory was offered earlier as the strong case for such positive welfare effects, through economy-wide increasing returns. But, viewed in the light of a theory of context as the basis for discernibly different economic behaviors, a different type of question is asked: how does the change in context alter the emulation, choice, and learning behavior of actors, and hence the dynamic development of the sector in question? If Hollywood were a global production network with no local core, would it be the same industry as with its present organization and geography? A producer of different, but better outputs? A producer of worse, less welfare-enhancing outputs? A fair guess is that the situations of its actors would have changed, and with them, the processes of emulation, cognition, learning and choice. It is not just a question of choosing alternative techniques, then, but that such a change in techniques has unplanned effects on the productive environment and hence on the industry's dynamics – what its people know, what they want to do, and what they ultimately do. The world movie industry would not just be a change in technique, but a change in what it produces (Jaffe, Trajtenberg and Henderson 1993; Boschma and Lambooy 1999; Martin and Sunley 2006).

3.3 Distributed context: a great transformation?

Finally, let us think about the contemporary process of globalization in the age of digital technology. Major changes are occurring in the feasibility and costs of managing long-distance relationships in the economy, and hence in the possibilities for fragmenting production, organizationally and geographically. Are we at the brink of a 'great transformation' in local versus long-distance relations (Polanyi 1944)? Such a transformation toward distributed contexts would be four-fold. First, previously-existing borders between using intra-organizational hierarchies and external markets to coordinate activity would be moved by the ways new technologies allow coordination and monitoring to occur. In production, the big vertically-integrated producers who were once necessary to coordinate complex transactions and eliminate bilateral hold-up risks in production, appear to be increasingly giving way to networked 'heterogeneous' production. The notion of a great transformation assumes the 'completion' of this process. Second, the role of geographical distance would be profoundly altered, with a lesser role for proximity, even for the most complex intra and inter-organizational relations. In the past, integration had very big distance costs. The same forces that reduce the need for integration also reduce the need for proximity: much more efficient communication technologies that permit complex monitoring and contracting at great distance (Baldwin 2006), and permit the fragmentation of production systems at the fine-grained level of tasks, rather than subsystems (Grossman and Rossi-Hansberg 2006).

Third, and underlying the first two, the boundary between formal and informal processes of coordination, contracting and monitoring would be modified in favor of new forms. It would be possible to 'quasi-formalize', thus combining ease of deal making with long distance and flexibility – the 'best of both worlds' – and greatly reducing the relevance of the current tradeoffs.

Fourth, information would be obtained via 'global pipelines' (Bathelt, Malmberg and Maskell 2004). Such distributed contexts would be more organizational than geographical, and the organizational basis would be radically different from the past, owing to the possibility of managing complex interactions via the radically increased intermediation of information technologies. The five dimensions of context would be radically altered for the actors in distributed contexts.

What we have just laid out is speculative. Much of the literature counters this vision, or at least parts of it, by asserting the ongoing (even heightened) complexity of deal making, increasing and more volatile output environments, thus requiring face-to-face contact, and social networks to carry out production (Storper and Venables 2004; Olson and Olson 2000). Communities of practice would remain central in this vision of things, and would become more important in the core 'nodes' of geographically-extended production systems in this alternative view. But at the very least, it is worth considering this stylized scenario of what a great transformation might look like.

4. SOME ECONOMIC ASPECTS OF CONTEXT

We argue above that contexts have strongly recursive relationships to individual action. This means that outcomes are contextual, especially the development of knowledge through different use of know-how, learning, experimentation and choice. If this is the case, then contexts create different pathways that can be achieved using an alternative organizational (hence contextual) form of production organization. It follows that the ongoing rearrangement of the organization and geography of production is much more than the interplay of trade costs and comparative advantage in seeking the most efficient organizational solution to a given production (allocation) problem. This is because, by changing the availability of contexts, it would also be rearranging the possibility set for 'future development' of the economy. Properly defined, the question of context cuts right to the heart of whether and under what circumstances processes of globalization (and economic development more generally) are truly welfare-maximizing or not.

4.1 Antecedents

There is considerable existing reflection on some of the dimensions of whether contexts are welfare-maximizing, though it uses different vocabularies from ours. For example, in economic geography, agglomerations are said to be sources of technological spillovers and to facilitate innovation, and in some cases to shape it 'locally'. In development economics, there is a notion that a country or region needs to develop an 'ecosystem', consisting of a complex geometry of parts of the division of labor and supporting activities (notably in R&D, training, and so on), if it wants to move up the hierarchy of functions in the world division of labor. Behind both of these currents is a debate about whether an economy does better being specialized (Marshall) or diversified (Jane Jacobs), that is, what kind of spillovers and interactions are maximized (Duranton and Puga 2002).

Another idea is that economies move up the developmental hierarchy when they are both able to absorb widely-available knowledge, often said to be 'codified' so that it travels well, as well as create their own innovations that cannot be easily copied (tacit knowledge). These notions are central to the geography of growth explored above in Section 2.

All of these contributions are of great interest, but notice that they are about specific places, and do not tackle wider questions about resource allocation and welfare effects of an increasingly interrelated global economic space, involving specialization and competition, and ongoing reorganization of productive activities between places. As noted, in mainstream trade theory, any such questions disappear axiomatically. Trade and monitoring/contracting costs change and permit new forms of fragmentation and patterns of location, then they will lead to long-term gains to trade.

But if context is more than just a residual effect of transportation and communication costs, then even an efficient process of fragmenting and redistributing a production chain does not exclude the possibility that there will be other changes in the way the production system performs, in the areas of emulation, cognition, learning and choice (Arthur 1994). Moreover, the resulting products, even in the present, can be imperfect substitutes, so that there is not just a change in production organization, but in the envelope of outputs in some cases. In other words, the decision to restructure a production chain involves not just discrete choice processes today, but 'roads not taken' (Arthur 1989, 1994; Dosi 1998; Hodgson 1998; Essletzbichler and Rigby 2004). We can compare the road taken to the existing road, but what we cannot measure is the possible qualities and quantities of future outputs of contexts that are being eliminated or restructured. Moreover, the creation or elimination of contexts is largely an unintended outcome of decisions made about the organization of production and location, with these dynamic effects not figured into the decision-making process. They are externalities.

4.2 Globalization and the diversity of contexts

Competition among contexts is viewed as the healthy basis of the contemporary globalization process. The digital revolution seems to be pushing this to new heights, as the possibilities for fragmentation and locational choice are vastly augmented by it. At the same time, new 'local' economies are able to use long-distance knowledge spillovers and inputs from far away to learn new production tasks and insert themselves in the global economy of competition among products, effectively introducing another layer to the competition among contexts.

Is this competition among contexts neutral to the supply of products, today and in the future? Hence, is it neutral to the developmental and learning dynamics of both organizational communities (in a technological area, let's say) and territorial economies? These are the questions that need to be tackled by economic geography and trade economics, but are currently out of their range, because context is not considered.

Consider an extension of our earlier speculation about a great transformation. The emergence of very large-scale distributed contexts might be 'reducing' certain dimensions of competition among territorially-anchored contexts, in that the major feature of the new context for economic action becomes the spatially-extended network. In this case, there might be enhanced 'within technique' competition among places, but within a world economy generating significant institutional convergence between production systems at a global level (single best practices), such competition is more about how places deliver up resources to the global network context, hence reducing the importance of local or national extra-organizational context in generating a variety of techniques and products (Gertler 2001). The information used by actors would be 'stovepiped' via the global division of labor. This information would increasingly take precedence over information coming from outside such a network (for example, from a local or national context of information exchange) in the key processes of emulation, cognition and learning. Certain formal models of trade with heterogeneous firms predict precisely this reduction in variety (Baldwin and Forslid 2006).

This brings us back to issues of long-term economic development. One key perspective on why the modern economic takeoff occurred in Western Europe argues that it was the combination of a balance between interrelationship – the dense trading and political relationships that emerged during the mercantile period – with separation and competition – the proliferation of different technological systems and their products – that promoted competition and overcame the possibility of progress-killing local monopolies (North 2005). Standard theories of globalization argue that a similar process is occurring today, at the global rather than continental scale. But if global distributed contexts are emerging and reducing such local and national environments to a subservient role of delivering up resources to global systems, with a strong degree of organizational convergence, then this assumption would be questionable.

If the process of globalization leads to the elimination of some contexts in favor of others, mainstream economics would say that such a loss of diversity leads to a better output of goods and services, and that it is therefore justified in welfare terms. But now we have seen that this conclusion may or may not be merited: though there are clearly many circumstances where eliminating or changing contexts is justified in efficiency terms, there is the problem of imperfectly substitutable products, on one hand, and dynamics on the other. Mainstream economic geography and international economics has had virtually nothing to say about these issues.

5. CONCLUSION

The argument of this contribution consists of four main points. First, the local or national differences in the ways production systems, labor markets, supply chains and relationships come together are just the entry point into their most interesting possible dimension, which is their dynamic properties – what people learn, develop, and innovate in them. This point is not new in the empirical sense: the vast literature on national and regional systems of innovation and on the role of geographical proximity in innovation suggests that certain kinds of innovations depend on proximity, while others can be carried out at long distances. We made a related, but different point: the 'qualities and types of product and innovations' fundamentally depend on their context. The question is not just about the line between local and non-local innovations, but about the contexts for all innovations.

A second point of this contribution has been to ask what we mean by 'context'. Most economists reject out of hand the possibility of significant differences in expectations and choices from one place to another, while geographers and sociologists tend to assume the importance of such differences without giving them precise analytical definition. Thus, most economists see local or national economies as outcomes of the forces that spatially distribute economic activity (trade costs plus comparative advantage): the residual effect is a local or national economic environment. Geographers and sociologists look for the 'bottom-up' sources of economic differentiation and dynamism, and sometimes consider how the local and the long distance interact, but this leads to a curious (again largely implicit) assumption that territorial economies are shaped by 'local' rationalities, and overlain on top of them are more abstract economic systems that are somehow 'not' contextual, expressing instead some kind of systemic rationality. Further, the ongoing process of fragmentation of production (divisions of labor) and reintegration through trade is one of replacing contextual economics with non-contextual economics, with the implicit assumption that the latter is better than the former. Situationalism, based on strong results from observation and experimental evidence, shows that 'all' economic actions are contextual. In some cases, the context is principally structured by formal, long-distance relationships, while at the other extreme, it reflects highly localized, informal and unplanned interactions (and then there is everything in-between). This leads us to the third point, which rejects the common opposition of 'local contexts' to globally-abstract systems of production; instead, we have applied the analytical concept of context both to local economies and to new forms of geographically-extended and fragmented production, and ask how each actor-environment shapes economic learning and development.

Finally, though much research questions how the process of globalization affects economies, there is virtually no inquiry into the question we have asked in this chapter, about whether the assumption that such organization and geographical changes may be presumed always to generate big gains is justified. Looked at from a situationalist and dynamic perspective, there may be reason to start asking such questions. In addition to this overall welfare issue, we may soon need to understand how radically geographically-distributed contexts function as economic systems, and as systems of context for economic actors and human creativity.

NOTES

1. There are some areas where temporary local costs of openness are argued to outweigh the benefits, having to do with existence of economies of scale, infant industries, and local dynamic externalities, but rarely are they considered to outweigh the long-term aggregate benefits of trade to all parties concerned.
2. The term 'MAR externalities' shows 221 000 listings in Google, accessed 25 January 2008.
3. One major debate between more neoclassical models of economic development and more heterodox ones is how long the rents can be enjoyed by the region or country before they are bid away due to rising costs, technological change or some other force, and how such 'short to medium-term' rents relate to longer-term economic development processes. Once again, strict neoclassical work emphasizes the return to equilibrium, whereas work based on an evolutionary or 'history matters' frame of reference emphasizes circular and cumulative construction of advantage.
4. What of the scenario of localized learning, sharing and reuse of technologies, creating localized increasing returns? This is a well-documented phenomenon. But the circle of beneficiaries of such processes would be limited if the use of such technologies remained localized, if for no other reason than that producers would be strongly tempted to extract monopoly rents for the knowledge involved. That they do so is a claim of much of the regional economics literature, as it is one potential explanation for why certain regions can support very high labor and land prices. At some point in the development process, however, the benefits of such technologies seem to leak out to the wider economy, and this is likely to involve codification of the knowledge, delocalization, and the bidding away of monopoly rents through entry and wider application. 'Both' of these processes deepen and widen the basis for Romer growth effects.
5. See www.rulesofthumb.com, accessed 2 February 2008.
6. Here I am adapting the idea of 'global pipelines' advanced by Bathelt, Malmberg and Maskell (2004).

13. Flow-fund model, decomposability of the production process and the structure of an industrial district

Piero Tani

1. INTRODUCTION

Among the main features of industrial districts (IDs) there are (a) the small size of firms, (b) a subdivision of the production process in a number of partial processes, (c) with the latter being implemented by different (small) firms, which (d) are localized in a specific place, (e) with unique social and cultural characteristics.[1]

In mainstream industrial economics, the small size of firms is argued to produce diseconomies of scale, thus making it difficult for firms to compete and survive. However, the literature on IDs has shown that the other features mentioned above provide a way to overcome such a constraint. This chapter presents an analytical framework which is apt to represent how this can be. This framework is based on Georgescu-Roegen's flow-fund model, which stresses the time dimension of production. This model has proved to be, at least in the opinion of some authors, more effective than the traditional production and cost theory based on production function.

Sections 2–5 introduce the flow-fund model and some connected concepts (flow, fund, stock, elementary process), with special attention on the properties of decomposability and divisibility of a process. Finally, the chapter demonstrates how the model can explain some of the features of IDs.

2. GEORGESCU-ROEGEN'S FLOW-FUND MODEL

In Georgescu-Roegen's flow-fund model,[2] the elements defining a production process are classified into three categories: funds, flows and stocks. Georgescu-Roegen defines 'funds' as the elements which, by their active presence, operate the transformation which constitutes the object of the process. Buildings, machinery, equipment, but also Ricardian land and workers, would belong to this category, as far as they act as inputs in a production process. In particular, these elements are not uniquely either a fund or a flow, rather, as 'inputs' of a process, buildings, machinery and equipment are funds and, at the same time, flows in the processes by which they are produced.

Funds act on the 'flows' of inputs – for instance, raw materials and semi-finished goods – possibly by means of other flows (energy, fuel and so on), in order to transform them into flows of output goods or services (which constitute the aim of the process) and waste.

Input and output flows may give rise to temporary stocks. The time dimension of both funds and stocks is such that their quantity must be measured at one point in time, while flows must be measured over a period of time. It is possible to consider the 'service' of a fund as measured by the length of time of its utilization within the process; this service has the same time dimension of flows. As an example, the contribution of workers to a given process may be represented both by the number of employees working at each 'point in time'; or by the number of workers' hours employed in the process over a 'time interval'. Nevertheless, a fundamental difference is maintained between funds and stocks: while the use of stocks is connected with their decumulation at a certain speed, funds produce one hour of their 'service' exactly in one hour. Therefore, while a stock of raw material of any dimension can theoretically be completely used in one day, an engine can produce only one hour of service per hour of active presence in the process. The total service that this engine can produce in one year (8760 hours) cannot be 'decumulated' in one day.

The existence of stocks testifies that there is a time lag between the instant output flows start being available and the instant they are introduced as inputs into some process, or sold to the final market (in the case of final goods and services). However, in principle, it is possible to conceive a perfect 'just-in-time' process in which there is no need for stocks. For this reason, in the following, we will not make reference to stocks.

A process is defined by its 'duration', a finite interval [0, T], and by the time profile of all flows and funds. For each flow, the time profile is represented by a function $F_h(t)$, $t \in [0, T]$, stating how much of that flow goes into the process (for inputs) or comes out (for outputs) in the interval [0, t], with $t \in [0, T]$ ($h = 1, 2, ..., H$). For each fund, the time profile is represented by a function $U_i(t)$, $t \in [0, T]$, stating how much of that fund is present (that is, is used) in the process at each instant t of the duration (see Figure 13.1); or by a function $S_i(t)$, $t \in [0, T]$, stating how much of the service of that fund has been used in the process over the period that goes from time 0 to time t ($i=1, 2, ..., I$). It results in:

$$S_i(t) = \int_0^t U_i(\tau)d\tau \qquad (13.1)$$

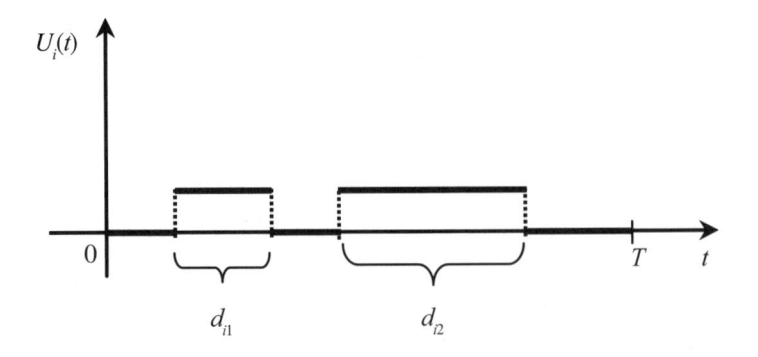

Figure 13.1   Time profile of a fund

3. ELEMENTARY PROCESS AND LINE PROCESS

Problems may arise with respect to the efficient utilization of funds from the fact that the service of a fund cannot be decumulated, and so utilized, at any speed. The concept of elementary process helps to clarify this problem and its possible solutions.

According to Georgescu-Roegen's definition (1976, Chapter 4 and p. 65), an 'elementary process' is 'the process by which every unit of the product – a single piece of furniture or a molecule of gasoline – is produced'. Clearly, for any specific good, many different elementary processes will exist. They may differ for technological aspects, but also for what Georgescu-Roegen calls the 'boundary', that is, the border which separates what is belonging to the process and what is not, and which may be variously defined. For instance, an elementary process resulting in a shirt may start from cotton yarn or by a roll of fabric. In the same way, an elementary process may also end with a roll of fabric, or with a shirt.

Apart from very special cases (the construction of a large ship, or of a motorway), an elementary process cannot be efficiently performed as such. It is only a technical recipe, to be arranged in various ways, first of all with respect to the dimension of the output per unit of time.

An elementary process can be defined by the same elements considered above for any process (duration, time profile of flows and funds). As to the funds, when in an elementary process, the function $U_i(t)$ can only assume value 0 (when at time t the fund is not used) or value 1 (when only one unit of the fund is used at time t). An alternative representation can be useful: it considers the durations of the intervals during which the fund is used: d_{is} designates the duration of the s-th interval in the use of the i-th fund in the process (see again Figure 13.1). In this representation the information concerning the duration of the intervals during which the fund would be idle is lost; but that is not important for the main results.

As far as input flows are concerned, there is no logical difficulty in assuming their perfect divisibility, and so – from this point of view – the perfect efficiency of the elementary process. The same is not true for funds, however. If a certain type of fund is needed within the process, it is possible that one indivisible unit of that fund might be used at the same time for more than one elementary process. In this case, efficiency can be reached performing simultaneously many elementary processes of the same type ('parallel' production); or activating several elementary processes which give rise to different products (joint production). That should make clear why it is necessary to distinguish between the flows and the services of funds.[3]

This is not the only efficiency problem concerning funds. In fact, a fund may be required only for certain intervals of the whole duration of the elementary process, whilst it remains idle in other intervals. The solution to this type of inefficiency may come either, again, by joint production or by an arrangement 'in line', by activating many elementary processes of the same type, one after another, with a suitable time lag.

Let us consider the time profile of a fund as it is presented in Figure 13.1. Assuming that this is the only fund of the process and that one unit of that fund can be used for two processes at the same time, a greater efficiency might be obtained by activating two elementary processes 'in parallel'. However, in this way, the inefficiency coming from slack times is not reduced, but it is in fact doubled.

In Figure 13.2, both types of inefficiency are eliminated by arranging the elementary process 'in line', with a suitable lag δ between the start of each elementary process and the following one. In fact, at each point in time after t_0, in the set of the simultaneously active elementary processes there are always six of them which require the presence of that fund. Since we assumed that each unit of the fund can serve two processes at the time, only three units are needed. On the other hand, there is no slack time and the whole capacity of the fund is utilized at each point in time.

The simplest way of utilizing these three units is to use each of them always for the same phase of the process (complete specialization). However, this is not a necessary condition: the arrangement in line may be consistent even with a situation in which each unit of a given fund performs different phases of the elementary process (Tani 1986, pp. 222–3).

An efficient utilization of the funds[4] requires the time lag δ which characterizes the line process to be a submultiple of all the durations d_{is} of the intervals of active presence of the funds. In order to be sure that such a common submultiple exists, we will assume the intervals to be commensurable; this assumption can be easily weakened without substantially changing the result (Tani 1986, p. 221).

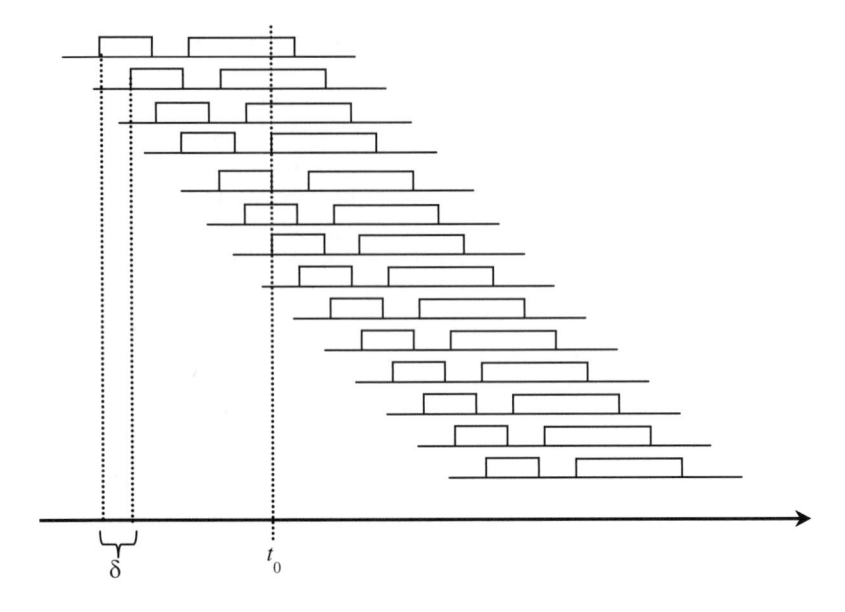

Figure 13.2 Reducing inefficiency by arrangement in line

On the other hand, the dimension of the line process (in terms of production per unit of time) will be larger the shorter is the time lag δ. Neglecting here for the sake of simplicity joint production, we may define the 'minimum (fully) efficient scale' (m.e.s.) as a minimum number of elementary processes which must start (and, therefore, end) per unit of time in order to have no excess capacity and no idle funds at any instant of time (Georgescu-Roegen 1971, p. 238).

Owing to what has been considered above, this m.e.s. process will be associated with the larger time lag δ^* which is a common submultiple of all the durations d_{is} of the intervals of active presence of the funds. Therefore, if c_i is the number of elementary processes which can be contemporarily served by one (indivisible) unit of fund i, we will have:

$$\delta^* = \frac{GCD(d_{11}, d_{12}, \ldots; d_{21}, d_{22}, \ldots; \ldots; d_{I1}, d_{I2}, \ldots)}{c_1, c_2, \ldots, c_I} \quad (13.2)$$

where GCD is the greatest common divisor of the d_{is}. The minimum fully efficient scale, that is, the minimum number of units of final output per unit of time if full efficiency is to be obtained, is measured by $1/\delta^*$. In the m.e.s. line process, the i-th fund will contribute to the process with k_i units of input, where:

$$k_i = \frac{\sum_s d_{is}}{\delta^* \cdot c_i} = \frac{1}{\delta^* \cdot c_i} \int_0^T U_i(t)dt = \frac{S_i(T)}{\delta^* \cdot c_i} \tag{13.3}$$

which, owing to the definition of δ^*, is a positive integer. It is interesting to observe that k_i measures also the total amount of the services of that fund per unit of time (for example, if ten 'workers' are constantly employed in a process, then the process uses ten 'hours of labour per' hour).

When the elementary process is arranged in line with time lag δ^*, all the funds will have a full utilization, with no excess capacity and no slack time. On the other hand, flows will enter the process, or come out of it, at an almost constant speed, and the same is true of the services of the funds. As Amendola and Gaffard (1988, p. 22) say, 'a synchronic representation of the process of production becomes possible . . . no trace is left, therefore, of the time articulation of the process of production'. However, it must be observed that, in order to treat the line process as an instantaneous one, the presence, within the process, of a new fund is needed, the one which Georgescu-Roegen (1971, p. 239) calls 'process-fund', substantially corresponding to the working capital.

From this result, it might seem possible to argue that the final output in question can be efficiently produced only in 'units of productions' whose dimension is given by the above minimum efficient scale. However this is not necessarily true, as we will see in the following sections.

4. DECOMPOSABILITY AND DIVISIBILITY OF A PROCESS. GRAPH OF A DECOMPOSABLE PROCESS

A feature of a production process which is relevant for the identification of an ID is decomposability,[5] also called fragmentability (Mir-Artigues and González-Calvet 2007, p. 35). This concept makes reference to the fact that different phases may be singled out within the process, and possibly performed in different production units.

More formally, a process will be said to be 'decomposable' if a set of production processes exists (which we will call 'components' or 'subprocesses') such that the output of each component either is the final output or is one of the input flows (a semi-finished good)[6] of other components; and if the arrangement of all these parts, possibly with suitable lags, reproduces the original process. Moreover, the definition requires that each of the subprocesses could be performed separately and its output could be kept in stocks or transferred into other processes as input.

The fact that an elementary process can be decomposed is connected to how the elementary process has been initially defined, in particular with reference to its boundary. If the analysis aims at the organization of production within one production unit, the elementary process will be defined – that is, the boundary will be drawn – so as to include all the phases which are under the control of that unit. If, on the contrary, the analysis aims at the organization of an industry or an ID, then the more encompassing concept of *filière*[7] will be effectively used.

It is useful to distinguish for a process between the property of 'decomposability' and the property of 'divisibility'.[8] Within the flow-fund model, a process will be said to be 'divisible' if there exists an integer $n > 1$ such that, dividing by n the time profiles[9] of all the elements of the process, one obtains again a process which can be implemented separately. Decomposability makes reference to the possibility that the total final output of a given production process could be obtained also by the functioning of many 'different' and separated processes; with divisibility the same result is obtained by the (simultaneous) running of many separated processes 'of the same type' (and so possibly in firms of a smaller scale).

Figure 13.3 below describes these concepts graphically. The subprocesses of a decomposable elementary process are the vertexes of the graph (the dots in the figure). Two vertexes are connected by an arc (an arrow in the figure) if the output of one component is an input of the other.

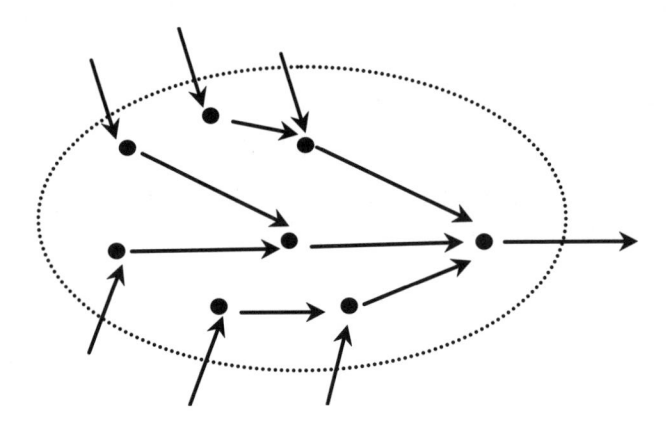

Figure 13.3   Graph of a decomposable process (or graph of an ID)

The graph can be interpreted also as a representation of a production system in which the decomposed process is implemented, in particular as a representation of the organization of production processes in an ID. In this case, each vertex represents a firm (or a group of homogeneous firms), performing one or more of the single components of the whole elementary process, thus producing semi-finished goods or the final good.

The arrows represent exchanges of goods from one component (or one firm) to another. Raw materials, energy and possibly some semi-finished goods will come from outside the district, and the final output, produced by some of the firms, will be sold to consumers. Therefore the graph of the district will be a part of a greater graph comprehensive of the relations of the district with the outside world (for this reason, in Figure 13.3 some of the arrows originate outside the oval that contain the process, or the district, and other arrows point to the outside).

From the definition of decomposability it comes that the graph must be such that any vertex is connected by a path to the vertex representing the final output. When the graph represents a productive system, this means that anything which is produced within the system is oriented towards the only final output of the system.[10] For the sake of simplicity, within this context we may assume the graph has no cycles.[11]

In order to represent the process as decomposable it is not necessary to include new types of funds with respect to the original process.[12] The same is not true for the flows: as any component is a specific process, we must add some new flows, one for each semi-finished good which is produced by one component and utilized by another. We assume here that the goods already considered in the vertically-integrated process come from outside the ID, while those of the second type are produced within the district.[13]

The production of a semi-finished good of the second type may occur either as an internal production of some firm of the district (showing a certain degree of vertical integration with respect to the maximum possible decomposability), or as the output of firms which sell it to other firms in the district. Let us make reference to the two possible interpretations of Figure 13.3. If the vertexes of the graph refer to the single components of the elementary process, independently of the fact that they may be activated inside or outside the firms which use the semi-finished good itself, then all the semi-finished goods of the second type will appear in the graph. On the contrary, if each vertex refers to a firm (or, better, to the group of all the firms with the same production process), then the graph will take into account only the semi-finished goods bought and sold by these firms.

The same ideas may be adapted in order to represent the flows of goods and services within an input–output framework (a framework largely used to study *filières*). In Figure 13.3, it would be possible to assign a number to each arrow, measuring the amount of the corresponding flow. Since the two vertexes of the arrow correspond to components, or to firms, or to groups of homogeneous firms, this number can be interpreted as an item of a table whose rows and whose columns are headed to the semi-finished goods.

The result will be an input–output matrix, such as the matrix A of Figure 13.4. The element a_{rs} of this matrix measures the amount of the flow of r-th good used as an input in the production of the s-th good. The r-th row refers to all the possible destinations of the r-th good as input in the production of other goods; the s-th column refers to all the semi-finished inputs of the s-th good.

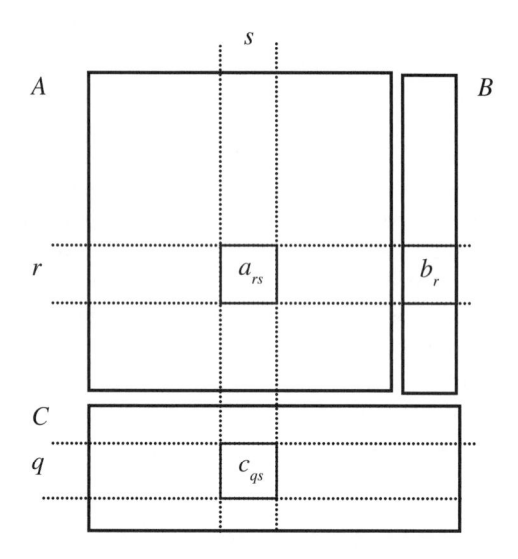

Figure 13.4 Input–output matrix of an ID

In the same figure, B is a vector whose generic element b_r measures the amount of semi-finished good r directly used in the production of the final output. The rows of matrix C are the input flows coming from outside the district; therefore, the element c_{qs} measures the flow of the q-th external input flow used in the production of the s-th semi-finished good or of the final output.

5. MINIMUM EFFICIENT SCALE OF A DECOMPOSABLE PROCESS AND THE DIMENSIONS OF THE FIRMS

This section illustrates the main results this representation can offer to the issue of the emergence of IDs. If an elementary process is decomposable, each of its components may be seen as an elementary process whose output is a semi-finished good (or, for one of the components, the final output of the original process). This process can be arranged in line and there will be a minimum efficient scale of that arrangement. Since the funds used in each component are also funds of the vertically-integrated elementary process, the set of the durations of the intervals for the use of the funds relative to each component is a subset of the corresponding set in the case of an integrated process (Tani 1976).[14]

Therefore, the minimum efficient scale of the arrangement in line of each component will be a submultiple of the minimum efficient scale of the line process of the integrated elementary process.[15] Except for very peculiar cases, it will be a 'proper' submultiple. Moreover, the ratio is expected to be so much larger, the larger the number of different funds involved is and the more such funds are specific to each component.

In other words, if an elementary process is decomposable, the same is true of the 'minimum efficient scale' line process. However, while this last process is, by definition, indivisible, the same may not be true of the single components of it; each one of them will have a minimum efficient scale, which is not greater, but possibly smaller, than the corresponding minimum scale in the integrated process.

We can summarise the above in Proposition A:

> The whole efficient total process may be performed either in one firm or in as many firms as are the components of the elementary process; moreover, it is likely that each component will be divisible and therefore could be carried out by different firms, each of them characterized by the same partial process.

The following Proposition B is more demanding:

> The two solutions (one vertically-integrated firm or many specialized firms) are economically equivalent.

For this to be true further assumptions are needed: (a) the cost of producing a semi-finished good is independent on the type of firm in which it is produced, provided the minimum efficient scale is reached; (b) there are no transaction costs; (c) no scale or scope effects; (d) no external effects. Other assumptions may lead to more attractive results and explain the prospects in terms of efficiency for district-type production organization. Some of these results are presented in what follows.

Let us consider how decisions are taken at the firm's level, by assuming, as a first approximation, that there is only one technology, that is, a unique elementary process for the whole production system carried out in a district.

Each of the already existing firms, defined only by the nature of their output, should decide how to produce it. Firms can only choose among how many of the components producing such output they will carry out. They may decide to specialize only in the last phase, buying from other firms the necessary semi-finished goods (or the corresponding services), or also to produce some of these intermediate goods. Although it will be not only a question of choosing between alternatives in order to minimize costs (for example, flexibility may be another aim, see next section on this point), costs are necessarily a key issue. Firms' decision will depend upon a comparison between the cost of buying the necessary semi-finished goods from another firm and the cost of producing such goods within the firm itself.

For both alternatives, costs tend to depend on many factors. For the buy-it option, firstly, costs will depend on the market price of the semi-finished good; secondly, costs are also connected with the use of the market (that is, information, transport or intermediation costs). There are many reasons and pieces of evidence to assume that in an ID these costs can be low, thereby making the buy-it alternative preferable to the produce-it one (Becattini 2004a, pp. 30–31; Signorini 2000, pp. xixff., 313ff.). As mentioned above, Proposition B is formally sustained by the assumption that such costs are zero.

On the other hand, as to the cost of producing intermediate goods, the proof of Proposition B rests upon the assumption that the cost of carrying out a given component of the elementary process is unrelated to the context within which production occurs, and in particular with the degree of the firm's vertical integration, provided that the scale is a multiple of the minimum efficient scale.

These conditions are likely not to be respected, and various factors may alter this cost, especially if technological alternatives are allowed. First, there might be 'scale effects', connected with the different minimum efficient scale of each single component when carried out by firms with different degrees of vertical integration. Scale effects are expected to be more important the larger the set of technological alternatives are. Another factor is associated with 'scope effects',[16] which may make it convenient to perform more than one component in the same firm. When these effects are considered, small firms specialized in single components might prove to be less efficient than a large firm carrying out the same components as a part of a vertically-integrated production process.

However, the research on IDs has shown that small firms may compete because of a surplus of efficiency coming from external economies associated with their belonging to this special system. Thus also 'district effects' should be considered as they correspond to cost reductions due to various types of external effects deriving from the peculiar organization of production IDs. Loasby, Bianchi, and Hart (in this volume) explicitly refer to these effects.

6. INDIVIDUAL DECISIONS AND THE STRUCTURE OF THE LOCAL SYSTEM

Let us now consider the use of this framework in order to state how the structure of an ID will appear as a consequence of different decisions, when a sufficiently decomposable technology prevails.

A necessary condition for firms to be able to choose the degree of their vertical integration is the actual availability of all the semi-finished goods on the market; which is not *a priori* ensured. In fact that depends upon other (one would say long-run) decisions concerning the convenience for other firms to enter the system in order to produce and sell those goods. When pondering on this decision, they must anticipate the choices of the potential buyers, confronting the cost of producing internally a semi-finished good and the price they are able to propose. This price is, in turn, related to the cost of producing the good separately; with free entry – such as is to be assumed dealing with IDs – this price will coincide with the full average cost.

Equilibrium can be reached when all the firms producing a semi-finished good for the market are able to sell it to other firms; moreover, for any semi-finished good not produced for the market, the minimum cost at which it might be produced separately is too high for any firm being induced to buy it instead of producing it internally.[17]

Such equilibrium, when it exists, may be not unique. In fact, the assumptions underlying Proposition B tend to generate multiple equilibria: any distribution of the components of the elementary process among firms is possible and equally efficient, from the greater decentralization up to the complete vertical integration.

Relaxing those strong conditions, a variety of possible equilibria does emerge, depending on the value assumed by the parameters which measure the different characteristics of the technology and of the system referred to above: economies of scale and scope, transaction costs, external (district) effects. Since the parameters may vary from time to time, the same will be for the equilibria. Moreover, even when parameters are given, many equilibria may exist and the one possibly reached may be strongly path dependent.

Some features of IDs help for what concerns the time and the conditions needed in order to reach an equilibrium, including a high degree of diffusion of information and of the ability of managing new firms with an efficient, and also innovative, technology.

This question is connected with the start-up and the structure of new firms, which are going to produce the final output, resulting from the joint effect of various elements. First of all, a sufficient demand must be expected. Secondly, the possibility of the specialization in the last phases of the integrated process may allow the 'birth' of a firm which is sufficiently small in terms of funds and, therefore, whose size is consistent with the available financial resources. Third, the fact that the cost has an acceptable level will foster this birth. Finally, an element that has proved to be of great importance in order to make the specialization in the last phases of the production attractive is flexibility. In fact, thanks to specialization, firms can rapidly change the features of the final output responding to demand changes. This flexibility is strongly increased by the fact that, when the firm producing the final output is part of a district, an easy access to the semi-finished goods is assured – in terms of proximity, information and control over upstream production – just owing to the specific characteristics of districts.

All these elements, and the last one in particular, may also be the origin of a change in the structure of an already-existing firm, which, starting from an integrated structure, may move towards a specialized one by expelling some of the phases of the integrated process and buying the corresponding semi-finished goods. On the other hand, again owing to these characteristics, the expectation of this choice on the part of the firm producing the final output affects the decision of start-up firms and defines the structure of firms producing semi-finished goods. The creation of new firms may be directly fostered by the same firm which is going to reduce its degree of vertical integration. Two mechanisms are at work here. The first one is outsourcing, which therefore creates markets for producers of semi-finished goods; the second one is the creation of a new firm by a former employee laid off as a result of the vertically-integrated firm downsizing.

7. CONCLUSION

This chapter has tried to show how the flow-fund model, with its representation of production as a process, can provide an interesting contribution to explain the emergence and the development of IDs.

For this result, decomposability proved to be of particular importance. However, considering its formal definition, one should say that almost any production process enjoys this property, and this fact might allow one to say that the emergence of an ID is less tied to the nature of the final output and much more to other aspects of the local environment and to its history.

On the other hand, no graduation of decomposability has been introduced here, while it is clear that the number of the components, their duration and the nature and dimensions of the funds involved in each of them are of great importance in order to make the emergence of a district possible. Also in this direction, even if the analysis of specific situations is to be preferred to a general taxonomy of processes, the general framework of the flow-fund model and the related properties considered here seem to offer a useful tool for the investigation.

NOTES

1. The entry on 'industrial districts' written by Giacomo Becattini and Marco Bellandi for the *International Encyclopedia of Economic Sociology* (Beckert and Zafirovski 2006), refers to 'industrial areas . . . consolidating around small and medium-sized firms, highly specialized and *embedded in a mainly local division of* labour' (italics added).
2. The model was first introduced in Georgescu-Roegen (1976, Chapter 5). It became the framework within which production is treated in *The Entropy Law and the Economic Process* (Georgescu-Roegen 1971, see mostly Chapter IX). The model obtained a contrasted *accueil*. Independently of the themes on which Georgescu-Roegen himself used the model – mainly entropy and bioeconomics – the model was appreciated and used especially in Italy and Spain for production models alternative or critical of the neoclassical one: see Tani (1986); Scazzieri (1993); Mir-Artigues and González-Calvet (2007). The model has provided a useful framework for many questions in applied economics: see, for instance, Landesmann (Landesmann and Scazzieri 1996, Chapter 9) for the study of production efficiency; Mariti (1980) for industrial

analysis of small firms; Morroni (1992) for problems of technological changes; and Romagnoli (1996a and 1996b) on applications to agricultural economics.
3. Winston (1982, p. 48), although stressing the importance of time in the analytical representation of production, finds this distinction inessential: the argument is that there will be markets for goods and markets for services of funds which establish prices able to adjust things. However, important aspects of the organization of production are lost when the treatment of funds is not separated from the treatment of flows.
4. Clearly, not all funds need a full utilization: a hammer is a fund, but possible idle time of it needs not be eliminated.
5. This concept, within a flow-fund framework and with reference to the problem of decentralization of production, was first introduced in Tani (1976). For the definition and a discussion of this concept within a flow-fund model, see also Morroni (1992, p. 7).
6. To be more precise, the input flow may also be a service; the fact the input flow can be either a semi-finished good or a service may depend upon the type of contract among the two firms. Here we will treat the problem in terms of semi-finished goods.
7. Morvan (1985, p. 7) defines the elements which characterize a *filière*: (a) a series of operations of transformation which can be separated and connected among themselves; (b) a set of commercial and financial relations among the different phases of the transformation; (c) a set of economic actions which succeed in valorising means of production.
8. See Tani (1986, pp. 211–12); Mir-Artigues and González-Calvet (2007, p. 33). It must be stressed that here we are concerned with the divisibility of a process and not with the divisibility of a good, although the two concepts are related. The undervaluation of this distinction has been the source of some misunderstandings and disputes, especially with respect to the problem of economies of scale. On how the flow-fund model can improve our understanding of this problem, see Morroni (1992, p. 145).
9. It must be remembered that the time profile of an element of a process (both a flow or a fund) is a function of time. If $f(t)$ is such a function, $t \in [0, T]$, then dividing the time profile by the integral n means considering the function $f(t)/n$. This applies both to functions of type $F_h(t)$, for flows, and to functions of type $U_j(t)$ or $S_j(t)$, for funds.
10. A possible generalization, not considered here, is the case in which a part of the semi-finished goods produced inside the district is sold to firms which do not belong to the district.
11. With reference to a district, Bellandi (1995, pp. 21–3) considers different types of decomposability. In case of joint production, Bellandi defines a horizontal decomposability referring to different outputs. Vertical decomposability refers to the case of a linear graph (a semi-finished good is produced in one firm and bought by another which performs the following stage of production). Bellandi also considers cases of mixed decomposability, when two firms exchange different goods with each other.
12. Nevertheless, the specialization which is usually connected with the arrangement in line (see Section 3 above) may be boosted by the decomposability, so that new funds might appear.
13. The assumption is a strong simplification: for example, delocalization of single components is a clear exception.
14. In Landesmann and Scazzieri (1996, pp. 219 ff.), an analytical framework based on the flow-fund model is used in order 'to contribute to the definition and characterization of a *production unit*', this definition being 'quite closely linked to the notion of a "network"'.
15. There is a clear connection between this result and the 'multiple principle' (Steindl 1945). This principle usually explains economies of scale and, thereby, the great difficulty that small firms have in surviving. Decomposability allows the matter to be seen from a different point of view.
16. Nothing prevents one from imagining that a firm may produce more than one good to be sold to the market. If, as we are assuming here, the choice of the firm is confined to a different degree of vertical integration, one may speak of 'vertical integration effect' instead of 'scope effect'.
17. For the possible special features of this equilibrium, and for the possible existence of non-efficient equilibria, see Tani (2004, pp. 102–4).

14. Clusters and industrial districts: Common roots, different perspectives

Michael Porter and Christian Ketels

1. INTRODUCTION

In 1990, two books appeared which addressed the role of locations in competitiveness and company performance. *Industrial Districts and Inter-Firm Co-operation in Italy* (Pyke, Becattini and Sengenberger 1990) discussed Giacomo Becattini's notion of industrial districts (IDs), 'socio-territorial entities characterized by the active presence of both a community of people and a population of firms in one naturally and historically bounded area [with] a dominant industrial activity'. *The Competitive Advantage of Nations* by Michael Porter (1990a) presented a comprehensive framework for understanding the competitiveness of countries and regions. It identified a prominent role for clusters, 'geographic agglomerations of companies, suppliers, service providers, and associated institutions in a particular field, linked by externalities and complementarities of various types'.

While agglomeration of firms enjoys a long and rich literature, these two publications have had a significant influence on the field. They also influenced related work including the new economic geography literature (Fujita, Krugman and Venables 1999), which consists of microeconomic models to systematically analyze conditions for regional concentration to emerge, the creative regions (Florida 2002) literature that analyzed the ability of regions to attract a specific kind of human capital seen as particularly critical for economic success, and the literature on regional or national innovation systems (Nelson and Rosenberg 1993; Cooke 2001a), particularly concerned with business-science relations in creating innovations.

Partly as a result of the two books, interest in the role of location has increased dramatically. Globalization, first believed to render location and distance unimportant (Cairncross 1997), turned out to raise the importance of understanding the specific conditions and cross-company interactions within and across locations. For companies, the need to choose the right location for specific activities in the value chain moved from an operational to a strategic issue. For countries, regions and other locations, global competition raised the stakes of understanding how to achieve productivity and attract firms in specific fields beyond providing low factor costs or subsidies. Numerous locations have launched competitiveness policies and cluster initiatives involving multiple constituencies (for example, governments, universities, companies, and others).[1]

Globalization has contributed to growth but heightened differences in performance across locations. Some countries and regions have improved standards of living much faster than had been thought possible. Others have been unable to meet the competitive challenge from new locations entering the global economy. The economic geography of clusters is also changing, with new clusters developing in some locations and some old clusters disappearing. Strong clusters are often getting stronger, as barriers protecting less productive locations have eased. Evidence is growing that cluster agglomeration is an important determinant of economic performance.

For the archetypical IDs in northern Italy, globalization has created intense pressure from competitors in Asia and Eastern Europe. Some activities are being outsourced from IDs to other locations, and there are serious concerns that this process will undermine the basis of the traditional ID model.[2]

This chapter explores the concepts of cluster and ID in order to better understand their theoretical relationship and to understand the seemingly different track records of these forms of agglomeration to globalization. Section 2 summarizes the cluster concept, focusing on the main elements of the theoretical framework and recent empirical findings. Section 3 then compares the cluster concept with the concept of IDs, identifying commonalities as well as differences.

2. THE CLUSTER CONCEPT

Clusters are defined as geographic agglomerations of companies, suppliers, service providers, and associated institutions in a particular field, linked by externalities and complementarities of various types (Porter 1998b). Clusters are a natural manifestation of the role of specialized knowledge, skills, infrastructure, and supporting industries in enhancing productivity. They are thus not defined by a specific channel that created interdependencies between activities in a given location. A combination of supplier relations, common labor markets, rivalry, knowledge spillovers, and learning effects drive clusters.

The definition of clusters builds on three key dimensions. First, clusters have a 'geographic dimension'. They arise due to externalities that depend on proximity, so clusters are often concentrated in particular regions within larger nations, and sometimes in a single town. Second, clusters have an 'activity dimension'. They encompass activities involving companies in different industries that are interconnected with each other in the provision of goods and services valued by customers. Third, clusters have a 'business environment dimension'. They are affected by cluster-specific conditions that are often the result of actions taken by companies, government agencies, universities, other 'public' institutions, and the private sector acting individually and collectively.

The externalities that give rise to clusters apply to virtually all parts of an economy, not only to knowledge-intensive industries such as life sciences and information technology as is sometimes assumed. In tourism, for example, the ability of a hotel to generate value for its customers is strongly dependent on the quality of local companies in many other related and supporting industries, from restaurants, to transportation, to travel agents, to shops, to financial services. Clusters incorporate both manufacturing and service dimensions, not one or the other. In chemicals, for example, transportation and logistics providers account for a significant amount of value-added, even though the core activity of the clusters is the production of chemical substances (EPCA Think Tank 2007; Ketels 2007a).

Clusters can take many different forms. Some have developed from networks of small and medium-sized companies. Others are linked to an anchor company that has given rise to a cluster by providing the launch pad for new companies or attracting suppliers. Yet other clusters have developed around universities, where spinoffs have arisen from the human capital and ideas of the academic institution. There is no one model for clusters, but a multitude of configurations reflecting the particular circumstances of a location and set of industries.

The nature of individual clusters evolves over time, a process sometimes described as a life cycle. Emerging clusters may have few separate companies and other entities, limiting the potential for cluster effects to set in. As the cluster increases in size and depth of different kinds of supporting services and related businesses, the potential for interaction grows exponentially and cluster size and performance can improve dramatically. Clusters may then start to attract companies, skilled individuals, and capital from other locations, further enhancing productivity and innovation. Mature clusters are sometimes exposed to rising factor costs and face the threat of becoming tied to a particular technology or operating model that can become obsolete through technological innovation or changes in market demand. While referred to as a life cycle, this process is far from automatic and only describes stages clusters might go through. At any stage, especially in the early stages of cluster development, there can be shocks that move the cluster to a new trajectory or which trigger dispersion of the existing economic activity to new locations.

2.1 Clusters and competitiveness

Clusters are one element of a broader framework of competitiveness (Porter 2000; Porter, Ketels and Delgado 2007). The prosperity of a location, and the opportunities for companies in that location to achieve high levels of productivity, depends on the general business environment that the location provides. Clusters are part of the business environment and a vehicle for leveraging the business environment to achieve higher economic performance. Cluster strength is not a substitute for the need for advantages in other dimensions of business environment. However, companies in strong clusters are often better placed to turn business environment advantages into competitive advantages. Clusters are also to some degree the 'result' of the general business environment: they are more likely to emerge and develop fully where the general business environment is favorable.

The nature and depth of clusters also depends on the state of development of the economy. In developing countries, clusters are less developed and firms perform relatively less advanced activities in the cluster. Clusters in these economies normally lack many supporting industries and institutions. Here, firms compete primarily based on cheap labor or local natural resources, and depend heavily on imported components, machinery, and technology. Specialized local infrastructure and institutions such as educational programs and industry associations are absent or inefficient. As economies get more advanced, some clusters usually deepen to include suppliers of specialized inputs, components, machinery, and services; specialized infrastructure emerges from public and private investment; and institutions arise that provide specialized training, education, information, research and technical support.

Clusters exist in metropolitan as well as rural regions.[3] In metropolitan regions, the higher density of economic activity benefits some types of clusters and cluster externalities. In urban areas, specialization often occurs simultaneously in a number of clusters. In rural regions, there tends to be greater economic dependence on a small number of clusters that are often linked to clusters in neighboring regions – often nearby metropolitan regions.

2.2 Clusters and economic performance

Location within a cluster enables companies to become more specialized, more productive, and more innovative. Clusters increase the value that companies can derive from business environment conditions. The presence of a cluster also tends to lower the barriers for entry into individual industries within a field, increasing the rate of new business formation and the intensity of local competition.

Economies tend to specialize in a subset of clusters, in which they develop a particularly favorable business environment. Such clusters often account for a disproportionate share of a nation's or region's traded output. This specialization of economies is even more evident in subnational regions than national economies.[4]

Clusters enable higher levels of 'productivity' through a variety of mechanisms. Companies in clusters gain more efficient access than isolated firms to specialized inputs, from suppliers to investors to employees, attracted by the accumulation of demand. Companies in clusters are also more exposed to best practices and other new knowledge that diffuses more quickly. More intense rivalry from local peers within clusters drives companies harder to explore opportunities for better productivity.

Clusters also enable higher levels of 'innovation'. Companies are in clusters exposed to an environment where concentrated needs and knowledge provide a fertile ground for new ideas to develop. Clusters then provide the specialized inputs and often also the lead customers needed to translate ideas into new products and services. Clusters also allow companies to quickly gauge whether a new offering is economically viable, a question critical for the efficiency of the R&D process.

Clusters also enable 'new business formation'. Clusters provide many opportunities for new, specialized companies to find lead customers for their products and services (Wennberg and Lindqvist 2008). Within clusters, entrepreneurs can more efficiently access the skills and resources of other companies that are much more critical for new than for established companies to operate. Inputs are more readily available, as are partners to reduce the cost of entry. Clusters can also mitigate the costs of failure, as entrepreneurs find alternative employment opportunities in their field for which the specific skills they have acquired in the start-up phase will be valued.

2.3 Cluster mapping

Cluster mapping, or the creation of systematic data on cluster presence across regions, has enabled statistical testing of the relationship between clusters and economic performance. The literature drawing on this data strongly supports the positive impact of cluster presence on prosperity (Porter 2003; Ketels and Sölvell 2006; Delgado, Porter and Stern 2007; Ketels et al. 2007). Conversely, the evidence reveals that lower levels of regional cluster specialization tend to be associated with lower levels of prosperity. In Europe, the history of barriers to trade and investment that encouraged breadth and limited cluster specialization appears to be one significant factor in explaining Europe's gap in prosperity and innovation with the US.[5]

Recent empirical research has also provided insights into a number of more specific impacts of clusters on economic performance (see Porter 2003; Delgado, Porter and Stern 2007). First, the overall level of cluster specialization matters – regions with a higher share of their employment in strong clusters, that is, whose national employment share is greater than the region's average share, register higher levels of prosperity. Second, the breadth of cluster industries matters – regions with significant positions in many of the industries that make up a cluster derive more benefits than regions where clusters have a narrow cluster footprint. Third, positions in related clusters matter – regions that have strong positions in clusters that overlap through common industries outperform regions with clusters that are unrelated. Fourth, the clusters of neighboring regions matter – regions with positions in clusters that are also present in neighboring regions derive additional performance benefits.

Interestingly, empirical analysis also indicates that presence in high-wage clusters are less important for prosperity than the strength of position in each cluster – on average, two-thirds of the gap between the regional wage and the national wage in the US is explained by a region's performance within each cluster, while only one-third is explained by the specific mix of clusters in which the region operates.

2.4 Clusters and organized collaboration

Many cluster benefits do not require active collaboration by companies within the cluster, and occur purely due to colocation. But collaboration in a variety of forms can enhance cluster productivity, through better exploiting complementary skills and joint action. Mechanisms for coordination can improve knowledge transmission between companies, universities, and other research institutions. Joint activities can reap economies unavailable to individual companies. Government policies can be better designed and more effective if cluster participants are organized to work with government.

Cluster collaboration often occurs through a class of organizations which we term Institutions for Collaboration (IFCs).[6] These organizations – trade associations, entrepreneurs' networks, standard setting agencies, quality centers, technology networks, and many others – are neither government agencies, educational institutions, nor private firms. They are surprisingly numerous, and especially prevalent in highly-advanced economies. However, IFCs also have crucial roles in developing countries where they often compensate for weaknesses or gaps in government. IFCs play an essential role in connecting the parts of the diamond and fostering efficient collective activities in both advanced and developing countries. For example, collective industry bodies, such as trade associations and chambers of commerce, have essential roles to play in improving infrastructure, organizing training and quality certification, and opening up export markets.

2.5 Clusters and economic policy

Clusters have become an increasing focus of economic policy, as their importance for competitiveness and economic performance in the modern economy is more widely recognized. The role of clusters in policy takes a number of forms.

Government agencies can organize policy implementation around clusters to improve policy effectiveness. Many foreign direct investment attraction agencies, for example, have reorganized around and focused their efforts by cluster (Ketels 2005). Special economic zones, industrial parks, and innovation zones have sometimes been organized around specific clusters. Workforce development programs aligned with clusters ensure that training matches skill needs and is concentrated in areas where jobs are available.[7]

By organizing policy implementation around clusters, policies benefit the competitiveness of multiple companies simultaneously. Instead of improving competitiveness company by company and running the risk of distorting competition, a cluster-based use of economic policy instruments, then, can be more efficient and more effective. In Austria, for example, the government has created economic development units with a particular cluster focus, tapping into all relevant regional, national, and EU programs for a specific cluster.

Government can also encourage public–private initiatives focused more directly on 'strengthening clusters' by improving weaknesses in the business environment and supporting private collaboration. A global survey of cluster initiatives launched in 2005 identified more than 1400 such efforts globally, and many more exist in practice.

Cluster initiatives can be seen as a particular form of IFCs[8] in which groups of companies, research and educational institutions, government agencies, and others come together to improve the competitiveness of a specific cluster. Cluster initiatives can be initiated by companies, universities, or government agencies. Survey research indicates that their success depends on the active involvement of all of these constituencies in setting and pursing an action agenda, not on who convened or initiated the effort.

One of the principal roles of cluster initiatives is strengthening linkages and spillovers within the cluster. Cluster initiatives achieve this objective by raising the awareness of common issues facing companies within the cluster, and creating more effective vehicles for interaction. For example, MassMEDIC, the cluster organization of the Massachusetts medical device cluster, was founded when it became apparent that the many companies in the region would benefit from active collaboration in areas of common concerns such as training, export development, and managing regulatory issues.

Cluster initiatives also enable better dialogue between the private and the public sector when making choices about how to improve the business environment. While many government choices on infrastructure, education, research institutions and regulation affect competitiveness, government often lacks the information about the specific needs of particular clusters. The Automotive Cluster Styria initiative in Austria, for example, has allowed government, universities and companies to identify skill upgrading in second-tier automotive suppliers as a crucial issue defining the competitiveness of the cluster, and enabled joint action to create a solution.

Cluster initiatives can lead to joint investments in research or testing facilities, better information on export markets, and the creation of other joint assets.

Individual companies, especially when they are small, often lack the resources to make such investments and are locked into competing on low costs. The coffee growers in Colombia have used such a joint investment approach to create a branded product with much higher margins as well as to improve production processes. Many tourism clusters, wine clusters, and flower clusters around the world have followed similar approaches.

Some countries and regions have attempted to create clusters from scratch, especially in the 1990s. Such policies were often based on the view that specific clusters, notably 'high-tech' clusters, were superior and would have greater impact on a region's economic success than other types of industries.

Efforts to create clusters without preexisting advantages almost invariably prove to be failures. The most visible examples are in life sciences, where billions have been invested but very few self-sustaining clusters have emerged. Those that are successful drew heavily on well-established universities and research organizations.

Clusters emerge naturally from the combination of beneficial endowments, purposeful action by government or companies, and sometimes chance events. Some clusters emerge from a specific geographic location with favorable access to markets, or proximity to clusters in neighboring regions. Sometimes the existence of a specific research or educational institution provides the knowledge base for a cluster to grow. An entrepreneur in a lead company sometimes becomes the anchor of an entire cluster. A related cluster may seed a new cluster through complementary skills and relationships. Recent research on cluster overlaps shows how new clusters can emerge out of existing clusters (Delgado, Porter and Stern 2007).

Efforts to create clusters fail when they attempt to artificially generate or attract companies without addressing the underlying drivers of cluster competitiveness. Policies that try to limit local rivalry to jump start a cluster only undermine the clustering process, reducing the likelihood of sustainable cluster growth.

In those clusters where strong government efforts have been important, such as the transportation and logistics cluster in Dubai, clusters have drawn on favorable locations, a critical mass or preexiting companies, and historical legacy. In such cases, government accelerated a process that would have happened naturally. Surveys suggest that cluster initiatives are more likely to succeed if they operate in a supportive business environment and can leverage an existing base of economic activity.

2.6 Clusters in a world of globalization

In a given field, it is rare that there is only a single cluster location in the world economy. Instead, there are an array of clusters in different locations with different levels of sophistication, specialization and depth. A small number of cluster locations in any field tend to be true innovation centers, such as Silicon Valley, Japan, and now South Korea in semiconductors. These innovation centers sometimes specialize in particular market segments: the Silicon Valley cluster, for example, is unusually strong in microprocessors, while Korea's strength is heavily in memory chips. Other cluster locations can play the role of manufacturing centers, while others become centers for regional assembly and customer support.

Firms based in the most advanced clusters seed or enhance clusters in other locations as they disperse some activities in the value chain to secure market access, reduce risk, access cheaper inputs, or better serve particular regional customers. Intel, for example, has moved much assembly and testing and some wafer fabrication to a number of non-US locations. Several of these sites have become regional electronics clusters in their own right. The same dynamic can be seen in other manufacturing and service fields, such as the offshoring by banks of call centers to the Philippines and the migration of auto assembly to Thailand, in both cases to tap lower labor costs. In dispersing less advanced activities, however, multinational corporations (MNCs) have a strong tendency to locate similar activities in a few locations, creating newly emerging clusters. A striking example is the textile cluster in Timisoara, Romania, where many subsidiaries are owned by Italian firms.[9]

This tendency of strong clusters to disperse some activities over time leads to a convergence effect for cluster employment. In high-employment cluster locations, there is a statistical tendency for employment to grow more slowly than in newly emerging locations (Delgado, Porter and Stern 2007). However, strong clusters continue to grow wages and innovation output more rapidly than weaker cluster locations even as employment is dispersed.

As international competition has become more open, companies have gained more freedom to choose the location of their activities based on economic efficiency, not just securing market access. This has 'increased' the importance of clusters by making their productivity advantages become more important. Truly competitive clusters are able to leverage their position and grow, while weak clusters that existed behind trade barriers are declining. At the same time, new clusters emerge in regions that provide particularly attractive business environment conditions. As the international division of labor grows, individual cluster locations become more specialized in particular segments, or in particular parts of the value chain. As competition moves to higher levels of sophistication and productivity, clusters shift to a higher level of specialization.

3. CLUSTERS AND IDs: SIMILARITIES AND DIFFERENCES

The concept of clusters and the concept of IDs share some essential characteristics. Most importantly, both ideas have brought the analysis of location into the mainstream of thinking about global competition. They both highlight the ways in which the agglomeration of related economic activities, and types of interaction among colocated activities, have a significant impact on economic performance. Both ideas combine theoretical work, case studies and cross-sectional empirical study.[10] Because of their basic alignment, the terms cluster and ID are sometimes used almost interchangeably.

Despite alignment at this basic level, however, the two concepts are not the same. It is important to understand the differences in the concepts in order to apply them appropriately. Lack of clarity about what differentiates the two approaches has sometimes created unnecessary confusion, especially among practitioners.

IDs are characterized by groups of colocated small and medium-sized companies operating in light manufacturing sectors of the economy (Goodman and Bamford 1989). In the ID model, there are not a few large companies within the region. Instead, the dense network gives the regional economy its character. The archetypal ID is akin to what was described by Marshall in *Principles of Economics*, which was a form of agglomeration more common during the period in which Marshall was writing. While some researchers use the term more broadly (for example, Markusen 1996; A.J. Scott 1992), the clear focus is on agglomerations of small companies operating in a specific range of light manufacturing industries.

Clusters are a much broader concept, encompassing many possible configurations of companies and institutions. Clusters encompass the configuration found in IDs, so that IDs are one type of a cluster. However, there are other configurations of clusters in which a few large companies coexist with small and medium-sized companies, where cluster participants are large firms, and many others.

IDs achieve economic efficiency primarily through local outsourcing and the flexibility of their production arrangements which owes much to the social fabric of the locations. Becattini, and researchers in his tradition, take the locality and its social structure as the starting point from which to analyze the role and dynamics of the local industrial cluster. IDs are more productive in certain types of activities than others. The ID literature concentrates on a specific type of cluster effect, and highlights social conditions rather than formal institutions. Researchers who have examined the role of IDs in innovation, for example, have found them more effective in incremental, reactive innovation rather than in achieving fundamental breakthroughs (for example, Corò and Micelli 2007; see also Asheim 2000).

Cluster research addresses a much broader range of external economies, encompassing many types of efficiencies, linkages, and spillovers that affect productivity as well as innovation. In cluster theory, some externalities occur naturally, while others can be facilitated through government, trade associations, universities, and other mechanisms.

The differences between the two concepts reflect their different intellectual traditions. The concept of IDs arose when researchers applied Marshall's original work on agglomeration to understanding the success of flexible (or 'neo-Fordist') production systems in the 1980s. Some of the leading researchers in the ID tradition have backgrounds in sociology or industrial relations, which provided them with unique insights into social and cultural factors as they analyzed the success of a number of specialized regions in northern Italy.[11] The ID approach highlights the types of social and cultural institutions that support close local interaction, and the role that different segments of the labor market, in particular part-time and migrant employees, play in achieving high levels of flexibility. IDs include an analysis of the social embeddedness into what that literature calls 'locality'.

Cluster theory also benefited from Marshall's work, but grew out of a broader framework for understanding the influence of locations on the competitiveness of companies. It drew heavily on industrial economics as well as research on the value chain, sources of competitive advantage, and company strategy. The cluster approach leads naturally to a concern with the way that companies compete across locations, and the locational choices of MNCs (Porter 1986; Ketels 2007b).

The increasing globalization of markets, value chains, and knowledge creates challenges for the ID configuration.[12] New opportunities haven arisen to combine local and global sourcing. New cluster structures often involve collaboration between large MNCs and small and medium-sized companies in particular locations.

Globalization has led to the restructuring of many clusters, and shifted the relative positions of clusters in different locations. In general, the form of cluster described by the traditional ID literature has faced particular challenges in sustaining competitive advantage. What is emerging is a mixed model in which a traditional ID relocates some activities to lower wage locations, sometimes establishing sister clusters in the process.[13]

4. IMPLICATIONS

Clusters and IDs trace back to similar theoretical roots, but have arisen to explain an overlapping but different set of phenomena and answer some different questions. IDs go deeper in examining the mechanisms that underpin a particular class of agglomeration economics. Clusters are by design a broader concept, and a more general one. The risk is that IDs are seen as the optimal form of agglomeration that firms and countries should aspire to, not one form that may not be optimal in all circumstances.

The debate about the recent performance of IDs in Italy highlights this issue. The cluster analysis using the diamond framework reveals a broad set of weaknesses in the Italian business environment that explain why the increasing global competition has been so challenging for Italy's IDs. The IDs approach would tend to highlight the deterioration of social linkages or disadvantages of small companies because these have been the crucial advantages identified in this literature.

Cluster literature can surely benefit from deeper insights about cultural and institutional factors that grow out of the ID tradition. However, the ID literature can also benefit from the more general analytical framework of clusters. The key to making the two research traditions complementary, rather than competing, is to see IDs as an important case of agglomeration which reveals important insights of general interest, rather than a general description of agglomeration itself.

NOTES

1. The Global Cluster Initiative Survey (Lindqvist, Sölvell and Ketels 2006) identified more than 800 cluster initiatives globally, almost certainly only the top of the iceberg.
2. For an example, see Rabelotti (2001). Corò and Micelli (2007) point out, however, that other parts of the Italian economy have suffered at least as much, suggesting that general weaknesses in the Italian business environment are another important influence.
3. See Porter et al. (2004) and the literature cited there.
4. See Porter (2003) and the Institute for Strategy and Competitiveness' Cluster Mapping Project data on US regions available at www.data.isc.hbs.edu/isc/index.jsp, accessed 20 March 2008. Using the Cluster Mapping Project data, Delgado, Porter and Stern (2007) separate the influence of convergence and agglomeration on the employment (and patenting) growth of industries, regional clusters, and regional economic areas. They find that after controlling for convergence forces, there is systematic evidence for cluster-driven agglomeration forces. See also Ketels and Sölvell (2006) for data on regions in the ten new EU member countries.
5. See findings reported by the European Cluster Observatory in 2007, www.clusterobservatory.eu, accessed 20 March 2008.
6. The notion of 'institutions for collaboration' has been developed further in joint work with Willis Emmons, Georgetown University. See Porter and Emmons (2003).
7. An example for such an approach is the WIRED program by the US Department of Labor, see www.doleta.gov/WIRED, accessed 20 March 2008.
8. For a survey of cluster initiatives, a specific type of IFC with the explicit purpose to mobilize and upgrade a cluster, see Lindqvist, Sölvell and Ketels (2003).
9. See reports by student teams at Harvard in 2003.
10. For clusters, see Porter (2003); Ketels and Sölvell (2006); Delgado, Porter and Stern (2007) and Ketels et al. (2007). Cluster databases have been created for, for example, the US, Canada, the EU, Russia, and Kazakhstan. For IDs, see Sforzi (1990) and Boix and Galletto (2009a); the focus has been largely at southern European countries.
11. Closely related is the literature on flexible production systems: see Piore and Sabel (1984).
12. On the discussion about challenges to IDs, see Whitford (2001).
13. Examples are given in a 2003 report by Harvard students Adrien Couton, Mattia Adani, Verena Kugi, and Marisa Joelson on the Romanian textile and apparel cluster and its linkages to Italy.

PART II

The nature of industrial districts

SECTION 4
Socio-cultural and institutional aspects

Introduction

Paolo Giovannini

1. THE EXTRA-ECONOMIC FACTORS IN THE LIFE OF IDs

From the very beginning, reflections and research works on industrial districts (IDs) have drawn categories and tools of analysis from other disciplines, first and foremost economics and sociology, with significant inputs also from history, anthropology, social psychology and political science. In the wake of Marshall and the interpretation proposed by Giacomo Becattini, explicatory elements of an extra-economic, institutional and socio-cultural nature were progressively introduced. Also, with the decisive help of many sociologists, a number of aspects related to IDs were highlighted and specified, in particular those social, cultural and institutional mechanisms operating in the process of the rise, transformation and decline of IDs.

This section, to which sociologists and economists alike offer significant contributions, focuses on the role played by different extra-economic factors in the various stages of the life course of an ID. Although all the analyses considered are largely based on the results of important research works (see in particular the chapters by Saglio, Saxenian and Sabel), the contributions presented try to outline some prudent empirical generalisations, with specific reference to the ideal-typical nature of IDs and the elements connected to the different stages of their life cycle. Theoretic and methodological instruments used in studying districts are sometimes freely applied also to explain more general processes of institutional and economic development, as proposed by Saxenian and Sabel, but also by others. The sequential order of the contributions in this section is meant to offer a basis from which to discuss some of the most relevant socio-cultural and institutional aspects today, both with reference to the past development of IDs, and especially to their present and future prospects.

2. LOCAL SOCIETY AND ITS INSTITUTIONS

First of all I would like to clarify some of the terminology used in this section. What is specifically meant by the expression 'socio-cultural aspects'? What are we referring to when we speak of 'institutions'? In my opinion both items mainly relate to the 'territorial' dimension, namely the particular area, place or locality where the ID is established. 'Territory' is not merely a geographical or administrative element but a social, cultural, experienceable feature shared by a great part of its population. The three adjectives mentioned above respectively refer to: (a) the local network of the mostly developed social relations, those attracting participation from most population; (b) the cultural and identity heritage specific to the area and consisting of the values, rules and expectations that the inhabitants historically feel as their own; and (c) the daily experience – not episodic and not precarious – of situational contexts that promote the adoption of relatively uniform life styles and behaviours that are spontaneously inspired to the principles of trust and reciprocity.

When these features exist, the territory qualifies itself as a 'local society', meaning a place where, because of its history and social geography, a 'society' (according to the definition given by Tönnies)[1] is 'locally' configured, thus physically allowing for the intertwinement of inevitable – and indispensable – societal elements with preexisting – and persisting – community elements such as a common way of feeling on the part of the population, sound relations of an organic and associational nature, and a widespread spirit of active solidarity among its members.[2]

To mediate between individuals and the local society are the 'institutions', first and foremost the 'family' that represents the pivotal element of social and cultural reproduction mechanisms in any given territory, ensures continuity and allows for controlled transformation from generation to generaton. The family is the interpreter and the main depository of local culture, its values, its ethical heritage, its tacit rules for coexistence and social intercourse. As a unit of survival,[3] the family transfers this cultural background in its economic action and its working activity and may evolve – under favourable conditions – into a family enterprise on which local productive processes become centred.

Next to the family, other institutional levels concur to define identities and vocations of a territory and to manage local regulatory processes. 'Schools' – particularly those schools with a strong local character[4] – support families in the process of cultural reproduction and promote the emergence of social circles of primary importance for the territory, which ripen in the friendly experience of school classes or, more broadly, in the elaborate social world of the higher school and the university (see Giovannini et al. 2001, pp. 123–9).

Family and school – as already noted by Marshall (see Giovannini 2006b) provide the basic and central core for the development of a complex institutional network within the territory, from local government to local banks, from political and religious organisations to trade unions and professional associations, service centres and applied research centres. Besides ensuring relations between individuals and families, enterprises and local society, these and other 'intermediate bodies' – as Durkheim would call them – combine, with modalities varying from place to place, to establish a certain formalised and stable level of local governance.

3. THE LIFE COURSE OF IDs: RISING AND CHANGES

Paradoxically (but not so much for someone who has participated in the debate on IDs for the last 20 years), the author of the first chapter of this section, which is about the genesis and reproduction of socio-cultural aspects and the role they play in an ID, is an economist and not a sociologist. Although in his interpretation, Maurizio Mistri may leave too much space to categories borrowed from other disciplines (biology in particular), he shows an in-depth and original understanding of the generative processes of an ID as well as of its functioning and reproduction. First of all, in the wake of Weber, he correctly refers to an ideal type of district; secondly he strongly underlines that it is the network of social relations that supports the network of economic relations (and not vice-versa, as economists often assert); finally he shows that, in ultimate analysis, an ID is founded on the positive interaction between social processes and productive processes. Material and moral proximity between families and enterprises alike, common values, the density and stability of social relations, reciprocal expectations of loyalty and trust are all 'immaterial factors' that ensure a system's connectivity and self-organisation while promoting the shared dissemination of what Mistri calls 'communicative competence', that is 'the capacity to read each other's messages, judge their real intentions, the meanings behind the words, and predict their behaviours'. Such competence promotes a spirit of cooperation, makes the recourse to opportunistic behaviours more rare, reduces transaction costs and makes the best use of the social capital locally available.

The chapter by Gabi Dei Ottati focuses on the assessment of the strengths and weaknesses of IDs *vis-à-vis* external but also (according to a recent essay by the same author)[5] internal threats. Dei Ottati offers a certainly interesting interpretation while discussing the different capacities of reaction of IDs to the changes that occur gradually (and that are usually tackled successfully) as opposed to radical ones that introduce strong discontinuity elements in the functioning mechanisms of IDs and to which the capacity for reaction may be extremely weak.

These are the changing scenarios that IDs must currently face, the alternative being their eventual decline or the complete disappearance of their productive profile. Dei Ottati correctly states that the traditional social and institutional mechanisms that promoted the establishment and early development of IDs and that for a number of decades allowed them to react promptly to the recurring external and internal threats (from the periodic economic and/or sector-related crises to the massive migratory processes from less developed areas of emigrant countries), are no more effective. Social and cultural instruments as well as institutional ones so well described by Mistri are no more capable – if left alone to operate according to a logic of a district's natural functioning only – to face new threats. In many cases, crisis can become irreversible and turn into real decline (Giovannini 2006a).

Renewed efforts are then necessary on several fronts: innovation and research, new mechanisms and modalities of coordination, vertical integration between enterprises, growth and development of collective resources such as renewed trust, stronger social cohesion, strengthened local identities, new institutional equilibrium. Yet, with respect to the stage of development and the level of threats, all this can be done provided that local institutions offer their total support and capacity of governance and decisively enter the game that can no more be simply left to the spontaneous action of traditional social and cultural actors.

4. DISTRICT REGULATION AND GOVERNANCE

Through very different approaches and with diversely founded arguments, Saglio and Bagnasco both contribute to identifying the main mechanisms of local regulation and institutional governance of an ID.

As highlighted in the title of his chapter, Jean Saglio focuses on the regulatory and governance processes needed for the efficient functioning of local labour markets. He does so starting from the results of an interesting empirical study on a French ID, the plastic ID of Oyannax. With great sociological subtlety Saglio reconstructs the social process and the 'network of rules' (most of them informal) that govern the functioning of the ID, suggesting that only through the understanding of the social and economic reasons that undermine such processes and networks can an institutional response be effective. However the author, who completely agrees with interpretations given by high-level sociologists who study IDs, does not dwell too long upon 'communitarian' explanations of local realities. Instead, with an acute awareness, he proposes a 'societal' reading of ongoing processes and difficulties characterising today's IDs and tries to identify possible explanations and remedies.

Just one thing to underline, among many important points Saglio highlights: although most of his chapter is devoted to clarifying the role and significance of 'integrative' social and cultural processes that have traditionally ensured good performances to local economic systems, however the author is not satisfied with the simple explanation that the productive mechanisms are lubricated essentially by a high degree of consensus plus a certain ideology and culture shared within the district. On the contrary, he warns those who believe that a 'consensus system' is at play whereas the reality shows that a 'system of conflicts resolution' is actually at work. Such a system – as many great thinkers of the past pointed out, from Marx to Dahrendorf – has an indispensable modernising function that cannot be suppressed or denied in the name of the 'community's interests'. Asserting exactly the contrary is both a possibility and a necessity. As the Oyannax district shows, local regulatory processes and governance actions shall not operate in the perspective of gaining an impossible consensus, but in the logic of intelligently managed internal conflicts, whose capacity of continuously developing and innovating the 'local society' shall be preserved and even encouraged.

The chapter written by Arnaldo Bagnasco further investigates the reciprocal influence between 'local society' and 'governance' in three specific directions: how local society can be strengthened through governance appropriate actions; what kind of resistance local society can put up against governance policies; and in which way the latter are an indispensable instrument to face changes imposed on the district by internal and external challenges.

As with Saglio's chapter, I will consider only a few of the many interesting reflections proposed by Bagnasco. For a number of problematic aspects connected to it, I will discuss in particular the complex and varied relation between governance processes and local social capital. Following a lasting discussion among sociologists (and not only among them), Bagnasco makes a first distinction between 'traditional social capital' (spontaneous and natural) and 'generated social capital' (generated by governance actions). He then elaborates on a proposal made by Trigilia (2005) and draws a distinction between generation of social capital by belongingness or experimentation. Admittedly, the stage of life of the district when the market acted as the main regulator of the combined use of local resources, including social, cultural and institutional ones is well over. Today, crisis and threats of rapid decline require solid, widespread and clever actions of governance that – at least in the perspective of this section – shall make the most of the remaining old local social capital and, if required, generate new social capital, maybe with weaker internal ties and with a less localised social texture. Whenever deemed necessary, governance actions must then be taken to destroy any social capital that hinders local development processes. Lack of action against hindering social capital has been observed in a number of places around the world where the attempt to generate new districts failed. This is a core issue and a very controversial one, dealt with by all the authors of this section. Some of them propose a more sceptical approach while others try to investigate how, through *ad hoc* modalities in new global scenarios, the rising of successful IDs is still possible.

5. THE SOCIO-CULTURAL AND INSTITUTIONAL BASES OF NEW DISTRICTS

We close this section by going to the beginning of the life course of an ID, with the chapter written by AnnaLee Saxenian and Charles Sabel who tackle the issue of the new generation of IDs. Although it is true that the two academics often divert their attention to explain the rise and success of high-tech medium-sized enterprises, which has more to do with the takeoff of the new economy than with the rise of new districts, their chapter focuses on the propulsive and self-propulsive mechanisms of development characterising emerging countries such as India, China, Taiwan or Israel. Saxenian and Sabel go through the process that allowed some areas of those countries (Bangalore in India or the industrial belt of Taipei in Taiwan for example) to become internationally competitive in technologically advanced sectors.

Allow me to synthesise the central point. In the 1960s and 1970s some thousands of students coming from what we then called the Third World moved to the US to study in American universities and there they remained to work in high-tech sectors and areas, such as Silicon Valley. After working in the US for a decade or more some of them returned to their native countries while others remained. However, over the years both groups had developed a well-established transcontinental network of relations that continued to prosper. The former in a direct way, while the latter in an indirect way, these two groups of pioneers (the 'new Argonauts') were the protagonists of a process of knowledge dissemination in their native areas. Such a process mainly occurred in the 1980s and 1990s but it is probably still underway. In brief, it consists of a complex activity of sedimentation of knowledge and transfer of technological and organisational know-how. It was pursued through skilfully exploiting real and virtual networks of high-level social relations developed and strengthened over the years by highly-educated emigrants, even when they returned to their native countries. These complex and diversified processes are analytically explained in the chapter by Saxenian and Sabel.

I would like to close this Introduction with a final remark. Although these research works did not intend to consider any territorial specificity in particular, in actual fact specific places and local societies play a crucial role, both in terms of socio-cultural and institutional aspects. Indeed, dissemination and transfer of knowledge is successful when 'institutional building' actions can be put in place, that is when economic, social, legal and political conditions exist and when there are interests and leaders able to activate them and, in doing so, trigger a new and solid process of local development.

NOTES

1. According to Tönnies, 'society' refers to groupings where rational types of relations prevail, based on forms of exchange and contract, which are more instrumental and conflict-oriented, in an impersonal and individualistic environment (1965, Book I, Chapter II).
2. For a discussion on these aspects, see Giovannini (2001).
3. This notion is borrowed, in a sociological key, from Elias (1987).
4. For example, the *Istituto Buzzi* in Prato, the *Setificio* in Como, the *Istituto Valeriani* for mechanics in Bologna, the *Escuela Industrial* in Barcelona, and so on. On this subject, see Saglio in this section.
5. See Dei Ottati (2009) where two kinds of internal 'threats' are considered with reference to the ID of Prato. The first one derives from a difficult generational transition, with entrepreneurs' sons and daughters refusing to succeed their fathers and taking up different careers (this is especially true in the case of small enterprises). The second and probably most serious one relates to massive immigration from China, with districts' indigenous community and local institutions being unable to integrate the Chinese community either economically or culturally, the result being the development of a sort of insulated and competitive Chinese, especially clothing, sub-district within the Prato ID.

15. The industrial district as a local evolutionary phenomenon

Maurizio Mistri

1. INTRODUCTION

The Marshallian industrial district (MID) has been much analyzed in recent times and significant contributions have been made especially in the light of Italian experiences (Bagnasco 1977; Bellandi 1982; Becattini 1987, 1989, 2004a; Brusco 1991). The industrial district (ID) stimulates some economic considerations that can have useful epistemological facets. In particular, the phenomenon of the ID seems to contradict the concept of a long-term entropic equilibrium of the market on which the neoclassical theoretical approach is founded.

This chapter refers to Becattini's definition of the MID in his seminal contribution of 1989 (Becattini 1989, 2004a). It is really the expression of a dynamic process of self-organization of the manufacturing activities that generates discontinuities in the territorial distribution of the economic activities. These discontinuities become manifest over a certain time span and generally become stable over a more or less lengthy period of time – which does not mean that a real ID is immune to processes of disintegration.

This chapter focuses on the forces that give life to the formation of a MID and the forces that ensure the stability of its structure over time. The analysis is mainly concerned with the role that institutional and cognitive processes can have in modeling the organizational shape of the ID.

In essence, we concentrate almost exclusively on the behavior of district enterprises in their interactions with one another, emphasizing the forces involved in the construction of the district's social capital.

In fact, the formation of a solid social capital at the district level is one of the factors contributing to the network of relations between enterprises within a district, based on a self-organizational logic, thereby reinforcing the competitive capacity of IDs.

2. THE EMERGENCE OF ORGANIZATIONAL AND SOCIAL STRUCTURES

The ID is the expression of a dynamic self-organization process, which generates an order capable of remaining stable at least for a certain period of time. Of course, the resulting order is entirely different from the one described in the theory of general economic equilibrium, which is strongly inspired by a Newtonian mechanicism (Lavoie 1989, p. 613). Nowadays the 'Newtonian approach' is no longer able to offer a satisfactory explanation for many phenomena of the physical or, worse still, of the biological world. The natural scientists are paying increasing attention to the self-organizational phenomena of dissipative type, that is, the phenomena characterizing equilibrium conditions that differ considerably from the long-term equilibria, with low levels of entropy. Dissipative and self-organizational phenomena come within the realms of the complexity approach that owes a great deal to contributions from Prigogine (1980), Nicolis and Prigogine (1989), Prigogine and Stengers (1999), and the Santa Fé school (Woldrop 1992).

The term 'dissipative processes' is used to indicate self-organization processes adopted by parts of the physical universe and living matter, guaranteed by energy exchanges between the said parts, or subsystems, and the outside environment. These subsystems can be seen as showing behavioral rules different from those of the systems to which they belong. The nature of a subsystem within its environment is determined by the relationships that keep the parts of the subsystem together, and by the relationships that keep each subsystem in contact with its environment. It is worth adding that a subsystem can be defined as such if it contains forces that keep its structure relatively independent from the structure of the surrounding system in the long term. Life sciences inform us on how subsystems are created and remain independent *vis-à-vis* the surrounding environment, though receiving from such an environment the resources they need to create and maintain their own structures. This is an idea that has given rise to the concept of autopoiesis developed by the biologists Maturana and Varela (1972).

In the economic sciences the interest in self-organizational phenomena has emerged after the development of dissipative models in the 'natural' sciences (Rosser 2004). A growing attention is paid to the self-organization of economic activities, in particular at the territorial level like the one illustrating the dynamics of the concentration, in a bounded territory, of a sectoral specialized productive system comprised by networks of small enterprises. As a practical economic phenomenon, the ID demonstrates that, not only sectoral, but also territorial differentiations count in a market. This poses a methodological problem, since a greater emphasis has to be placed on the forces of differentiation and self-organization into sectors and territories, in contrast with the view of the leveling action played by the market. The former can be called syntropic forces, while the latter can be considered as entropic forces.

Entropy is a concept that can be used to represent a competitive market, where enterprises can be seen as entities as small as you will, and where, by means of the movements of the productive factors, the marginal returns of these factors are leveled; in the meantime factors are uniformly distributed in the territory. The maximum entropy thus coincides with a condition of long-term competitive equilibrium, whereas the syntropy of a system expresses a condition of self-organization in which the equilibrium, far from the long-term one, is maintained due to the effect of dissipative processes. In economics there are numerous syntropic phenomena (Lavoie 1989) of which the MID is a practical example.

3. ID AND RELATIONAL NETWORKS

The concepts outlined above can prove useful in clarifying how IDs develop and reproduce. This chapter refers to a stylized, entirely abstract ID that draws inspiration both from the seminal work by Marshall (1920) and from the theoretical systematization conducted by Becattini (2004a). In this light, we can consider the district as a form of market organization with hybrid features; in some ways the ID resembles the competitive market (with some differences), and in others it has some features of the monopolistic competition market (again, without being the same). It comes close to the ideal type of perfect competition market given the large number of enterprises that operate in the same sector. On the other hand, it also comes close to the ideal type of monopolistic competition because, although the enterprises operate in the same sectors or in supporting ones, they tend to differentiate their products. This makes them compete on innovation processes, the quality and variety of products and on pricing.

Unlike in the extreme case of a perfectly competitive market where buyers and sellers are infinitely numerous, and have a very little chance (if at all) of reiterating business relationships, the market conditions in which district enterprises exchange goods are such that they are likely to meet more than once. As we shall see, this is a crucial aspect in the development of a behavior inspired by loyalty and trust. The density of the relations between enterprises in the same ID relies, upstream, on a technological condition, such that the production processes can be broken down and the single enterprises can consequently specialize in a part of the production chain.

This can be expressed in terms of the probability of a buyer choosing as a partner a supplier belonging to the same district rather than a supplier from outside the district. In formal terms we can use → to indicate a buyer/supplier relationship, $\{f_i\}$, where $I = 1, 2, ..., n$, indicates the set of buyers and $\{g_i\}$ the set of suppliers belonging to a given district, while $\{g_i^*\}$ stands for the set of suppliers from outside the district. Suppliers will be competing with one another to acquire contracts with the buyers; it is also important not to forget that some degree of competition also exists between buyers wanting to grab the best suppliers. These competitive relations are indicated by ↔. So $f_1 \rightarrow g_1$ indicates a relationship between a buyer 1, and a supplier 1, who both belong to the district considered, while $f_1 \leftrightarrow f_2$ indicates a competitive relationship between buyers (1 and 2), and $g_1 \leftrightarrow g_2$ indicate a competitive relationship between suppliers (1 and 2).

To understand why district enterprises tend to prefer to deal with other enterprises in the district, we need to focus on the nature of the network of social relations that provide the substrate of the network of economic relations in a MID. As already recalled, this is a system founded on the interaction, at local level, between social processes and production processes. They may be represented as networks of relations between enterprises, networks of relations between people and networks of relations between people and enterprises (J. Scott 1991).

It is the very fact that a production cycle can be broken down that allows for such a cycle to mirror networked processes. In fact, decomposing the production cycle means that enterprises produce material goods (and/or services) which are complementary and this consequently gives rise to buyer/supplier agreements. At the same time, there will be enterprises that produce the same, or very similar material goods (and/or services), who consequently compete with one another.

The relationship between the enterprises within the district develop and strengthen if these enterprises 'prefer' to do business with one another rather than with enterprises that do not belong to their district. We can express these preferences in terms of the probability of the commercial transactions happening, using $prob$ $(f_1 \rightarrow g_1)$ to indicate the likelihood of a buyer in the district choosing a supplier belonging to the same district. Moreover, we can use $prob$ $(f_1 \rightarrow g_1^*)$ to indicate the chances of a buyer in the district choosing a supplier from outside the district. If

$$prob\ (f_1 \rightarrow g_1) > prob\ (f_1 \rightarrow g_1^*) \tag{15.1}$$

a buyer belonging to the district is more likely to choose a supplier belonging to the district. Buyers may turn preferentially to suppliers in the same district not only because of their nearness in geographical terms, but also because they are more likely to share the same basic values and to be capable of knowing better each other's behavior. While complementary relations bind buyers to suppliers, competitive relations are established between enterprises producing the same (or similar) goods, be they buyers or suppliers. Given the above considerations on competition between enterprises within a district, we can focus now on the competition (relating to price and/or quality) between suppliers. The competition is likely to be stronger between two suppliers belonging to the same district (indicated as g_1 and g_2) than between one supplier that belongs to the district (g_1) and another supplier that does not (g_1^*). Thus

$$prob\ (g_1 \leftrightarrow g_2) > prob\ (g_1 \leftrightarrow g_1^*). \tag{15.2}$$

The competition in the district across individuals and enterprises serving the same function turns out to be a powerful force driving them to increase their commitment, both as individuals and as single enterprises.

4. SOCIAL NETWORKS AND COMMUNITY MARKET

As mentioned earlier, district enterprises, be they buyers or suppliers, all operate in the same area, so any behavior that is judged to be inadequate can rapidly make an enterprise lose its reputation. District enterprises are tied together not only by economic relationships, but also by individuals engaging in social and cultural relationships. As a result, people and enterprises have a shared heritage of values and know-how. These relationships often have their roots in the fact that the enterprises were originally family concerns, which have branched out also as a result of the ramification of the founding families of the original enterprises.

Sufficiently stable long-term social relations are generated in the same way: this stability also relies on the influence that well-established cultural and institutional models exert on the models of industrial organization. The role of the stability of the social structure was originally emphasized in the structuralist analyses of the anthropologists (Radcliffe-Brown 1935; Malinowski 1939; Bott 1957). In the case of ID, albeit in the stylized and abstract version considered here, the stability of the social structure relies on the particular role of the family in the organization of the work in the factories. The networks of economic and personal relations are very close-knit, a feature measurable by means of suitable 'connectivity' indexes. This approach is used in sociometry where attempts have been made to identify network subsets (subsystems) which have particularly dense internal relationships. These subsystems have been called 'cliques', where strong processes of social cohesion are associated with processes of economic integration. Without identifying these 'cliques', it would be difficult to explain the principle that lies behind the decision-making processes typical of the district enterprises, that is, the district enterprises' preference for doing business with other enterprises in the district.

As already suggested this preference lies on immaterial factors, such as the trust placed in the relations between agents, the sharing of communication protocols and a widespread, shared know-how. For what we have said so far, it is clear that the social relationships developing between members of district communities have an economic value. New small enterprises can spring up as a result of employees leaving the enterprises they worked for and securing the capital they need to get started from their families, and even from friends. In a sense, we can speak of the birth of new enterprises as the offspring of another enterprise and of social relations. This phenomenon is responsible, to some degree, for the territorial concentration of enterprises, because the 'new' entrepreneur tends to establish the 'new' enterprise in the area where he/she normally lives, where he/she has the support of the networks of family and friends.

Many of these people are, or have been engaged, in the particular sector featuring an ID, and that is why they possess the necessary professional expertise that enables them to judge the economic validity of a new project. The shared work experience, reinforced by social ties, promotes the sharing of cultural models. In fact, the stable grouping of operators in the same area usually means that the operators belong to the same cultural environment, that is, to an environment characterized by shared values, languages, meanings, and, above all, implicit rules of behavior (or customs) (Dei Ottati 1995, p. 23). In other words, these people share what we might call 'communicative competence' (Mistri 2006, p. 76), that is, the capacity to read each other's messages, judge their real intentions, the meanings behind the words, and predict their behaviors. This is a founding element of the shared, often tacit understanding distinctive of the relations between people who live and work in an ID and it also serves as a catalyst of non-opportunist behaviors. The vast majority of the literature on the topic emphasizes the competitive advantages ensuing when the economic behavior is inspired by loyalty and a cooperative spirit suitable for reducing the transaction costs (Coriat and Gennif 1998, p. 54).

By its very nature, the community market is strongly connected (in the sense used in graph theory) inward, and sufficiently (though not entirely) isolated outward. This relative closure is certainly the product of the people's aforementioned preference for dealing within the district rather than outside the district, and the outcome of the adoption of behavioral protocols that can be seen as social rules. The adoption of shared rules of conduct helps to reinforce the 'reputation' of the agents involved, reinforcing the stability of networks of economic relations. In practical terms, an agent's good reputation raises the expectations of third parties concerning the agent's fair behavior, that is, the agent's reputation is considered as the value added that he/she has acquired and that forms part of his/her individual human capital. But there is another aspect to consider too, that is that the growth and preservation of a reputation are an important justification for adopting a loyal behavior (Vanberg 1994, p. 53). In short, this set of behavior patterns provides the backbone of the 'social capital' that is a systemic element of the competitive force of the ID. Finally, it is worth noting that the current processes of globalization of the economy seem to have a weakening effect on the density of the social and economic relations within IDs, because they extend the relational branches to enterprises outside the districts, weakening the relative degree of social closure.

5. GENESIS OF COMMUNITY INSTITUTIONS

The social rules discussed above take on the nature of 'institutions'. In an institutionalist approach, institutions are defined by the uniformity of behavior of the members of a given group, and they are helped emerge when such members find themselves in recurrent situations (Schotter 1981, p. 11). The closure of such behavioral rules is expressed by the use of codes that become specific to a given community and that people from outside the community may not be able to interpret accurately (Lazaric and Lorenz 1998, p. 3). Moreover, the reiterated use of these codes increases the degree of mutual trust experienced among their users. These behavioral codes evolve with time according to a self-organizational logic, progressively becoming more and more stable. However, it is possible that, after a period of time, these norms collapse into new norms.

Institutionalist analysis points to the processes behind the formation of social norms. The emergence of an institution is thought to represent the outcome of evolutionary processes (Mistri 2003). In other words, the propensity to cooperate in economic activities is the outcome of an acquired propensity in the sphere of social relations that have been well established for some time. The end results of this scheme of things are not dissimilar from those deriving, in game theory, from the model of the prisoner's dilemma. In the prisoner's dilemma, however, we disregard any already-established behavioral models and imagine situations in which no well-defined behavioral norms exist at the outset. Taking the case of the IDs, the prisoner's dilemma approach would lead us to assume that enterprises existing in a given area and embarking on certain activities still have not 'chosen' what behavioral norms to adopt. For instance, they might have to choose between behaving in a cooperative or an opportunist manner. We know that the most suitable models for explaining the emergence of one or other set of behavioral norms lie in evolutionary game theory. These games are strongly inspired by conceptual schemes of a biological type, at the centre of which lies the idea of a 'stable evolutionary strategy'. This concept indicates the emergence of one strategy, from among the various available strategies, that prevails over all the others and that it is inconvenient for the agents adopting it to abandon.

On this issue, however, Larry Samuelson (1998, p. 37) made the point that it would be conceptually hazardous to transpose biological models to the field of economics without taking some preliminary steps. In fact, once an evolutionary process of biological type has developed, it tends to acquire a considerable long-term stability, while successful evolutionary strategies in the economic field do not have such a marked stability. It would be useful at this point to mention the need to distinguish time in the sense of biological eras from time in the sense of economic eras: we might say that a biological era is a time during which certain genetic codes remain stable; likewise, an economic era is a time during which certain economic institutions remain the same. An economic era is obviously shorter than a biological one. When referring to an ID, we might say that the duration of the system of norms supporting the district depends largely on changes made in the related production technology and also on the changes of the related consumption patterns and in the outside environment.

Be that as it may, over and above the more or less durable stability of the social norms, it seems important to study the evolution of new social rules in a community of people and enterprises. In the ID in particular, the norms inspired by an attitude of loyalty and trust, and that can briefly be defined as cooperative norms, appear to be important. As we know, the concept of cooperative behavior is found in game theory, and it derives from the rational choice made by agents involved in a strategy game who, as Nash (1950) puts it, define and make explicit the rules of the game *ab initio*. However, it should be added here that the concept of cooperative game in

Nash seems rather restrictive for the purposes of its application to the behavior of agents operating in an ID. We are more interested in games in which cooperation is determined implicitly, as part of a process of self-organized coordination. Such behavior develops within a network of economic relations that is influenced by the existence of networks of social and cultural relations. The behavioral norms of cooperative type are therefore an element that characterizes the organizational form of the ID (Sabel 1992). In a sense, we might say that the self-imposed social norms in an ID have a character of specificity in relation to the behavioral norms determined in other organizational contexts at territorial level.

It is important to emphasize that a cooperative behavior is an element of competitive advantage in the ID, but it is even more important to understand the processes by means of which these rules of cooperative behavior become so well established in an ID, to such a degree that we can now say that an ID cannot achieve self-determination, nor even come into being, unless it develops a cooperative behavior. As we know, in the usual prisoner's dilemma game, the decision to cooperate or to defect is a behavioral choice made by two agents with the same social role (being thieves) who may or may not enter into competition with one another. The theory has demonstrated that if there is only one move in the game or a finite sequence of moves, then Nash's equilibrium coincides with the defect/defect pair. On the other hand, Axelrod (1984, p. 11), among others, emphasized that cooperation can emerge when the agents play the game an infinite number of times, or when the game involves an indefinite number of interactions as well.

6. THE EMERGENCE OF COOPERATION

An ID is a highly complex entity, with a rather large number of agents and two fundamental types of interaction. As mentioned earlier, one is the relationship between buyer and supplier, which was indicated as →, while the other is the competitive relationship between suppliers, which was indicated as ↔. The competitive relationship between buyers is not discussed here because, in a sense, this can be assumed to formally resemble the competitive relationship between suppliers. Each of the two relational situations must naturally be treated using an *ad hoc* approach, emphasizing how the concepts of loyalty and disloyalty can be defined in different manners, depending on the role of each agent.

Referring to the buyer/supplier relationship, the interaction is represented by two correlated actions: one consists in the action of the buyer who places an order with a supplier, the other consists in the action of the supplier who accepts the order and undertakes the actions needed to fulfill it. In theory, such actions are set in accordance with a set of specifications agreed with the buyer. In reality, the level of the supplier's commitment to fulfilling the order can vary from a minimum to a maximum. We can arbitrarily assume that there is a line separating the levels of commitment that may be considered satisfactory, albeit to a variable degree, and the levels of commitment that may be considered unsatisfactory, again in variable measure. A commitment considered satisfactory is interpreted as cooperative or loyal (L), while the level of commitment deemed unsatisfactory is seen as disloyal (D).

Likewise, the buyer's commitment will be considered loyal (L) by the supplier if the buyer pays the agreed amount of money within the agreed length of time; if not, the buyer will be considered disloyal (D). To establish the payoffs to be obtained by the two agents, we consider not the output produced, but only the value added produced by the combined efforts of the supplier and the buyer, and how they distribute such value added between them. If the two agents are loyal, the value added is assumed (arbitrarily) to be 2π; if only one of the two agents is loyal, we can assume that the value added produced by such an agent alone will equate to π, from which he/she has to deduct the value of his/her efforts, c; he/she will share the value added with the other agent, who has sustained no effort. If both agents are disloyal, they will produce a zero value added, with a zero levels of efforts. In the game in Table 15.1 (which expresses the strategy game in its normal form), there are two possible equilibria: the pair (L, L) is a Nash equilibrium if the sum of the efforts is lower than the value added, that is, if $\pi > 2c$. Vice versa, if the sum of the efforts was higher than the value added, that is, if $\pi < 2c$, there would be no room for adopting a loyal behavior and the pair of disloyal strategies (D, D) becomes the Nash equilibrium instead.

Table 15.1   Buyer/supplier interactions

		Buyer Loyalty (L)	Buyer Disloyalty (D)
Supplier	Loyalty (L)	$\pi - c$; $\pi - c$	$(\pi/2) - c$; $\pi/2$
	Disloyalty (D)	$\pi/2$; $(\pi/2) - c$	0 ; 0

Generally speaking, a loyal behavior can develop if the agents find themselves in a situation in which their actions are reiterated. In fact, if the traditional prisoner's dilemma game is repeatedly played by two agents, a loyal strategy emerges as a result of the moves being repeated, because the agents are in a position to associate the gain from adopting strategy L or strategy D today to future gains (Dupuy and Torre 1998, p. 485). It should be said that a cooperative behavior cannot begin to develop if this cooperation becomes an option for agents who are unlikely to come repeatedly into contact with one another (Axelrod 1984, p. 21). A cooperative strategy can thus develop within groups of relatively limited size, consisting of agents who base their cooperative attitude on the trust and reciprocity and who have a good chance of interacting with one another over and over again. These considerations correlate directly with the previous comments on market forms. In a competitive market with a virtually infinite number of agents, the probability of reiterated meetings tends towards zero. As a corollary we can also assume that agents in a perfect competitive market will choose to adopt an opportunist behavior. They will be loyal only if the level of the effort involved is low relative to value added, and the information available to the agents is complete. The situation is more complex in the case of a monopoly: the monopolist will decide what level of effort to adopt and will also gain the majority of the value added.

In the case of the district type of market, on the other hand, we can assume that both the buyers and the suppliers are sufficiently numerous, but not so numerous to make it unlikely for them to meet repeatedly. In this case, the chances of the agents having multiple transactions with one another depend on certain aspects of the structural nature typical of the ID. One aspect concerns, as we already know, the way in which production is organized, which derives from the decomposability of the production sector. Another aspect stems from the relative closure of the district with respect to the 'wider' market.

Let us consider here only the behavior of suppliers, that can be expected to exhibit the maximum commitment because of the strong competition within the district and the fact that information on each supplier's behavior is bound to spread fast. The problem is to understand which type of behavior is more appropriate for the suppliers asked to provide a given product or service to a buyer. Table 15.2 illustrates the case of two suppliers, A and B, who have to decide how to behave in relation to potential buyers, assuming that the reward established by the buyers for the suppliers will amount to π. We assume that the transactions between buyers and suppliers are of two types, that is, either the one-shot transaction, or the recurrent transactions. Assuming that the buyers are always loyal, in the one-shot transaction, if the suppliers adopt an efficient behavior their payoffs will amount to $\pi - c$, where c represents, as we know, the level of the effort; if, on the other hand, they adopt a negligent behavior, their payoffs will be π (Table 15.2). The equilibrium is (N, N).

Table 15.2 Payoffs for suppliers in a one-shot transaction

		B Efficient (E)	B Negligent (N)
A	Efficient (E)	$\pi - c$; $\pi - c$	$\pi - c$; π
A	Negligent (N)	π ; $\pi - c$	π ; π

If we assume instead that the transactions are reiterated, and that supplier A adopts an efficient behavior at t_1, the initial period, while supplier B adopts a negligent one, at t_2 and thereafter, then the buyer will choose supplier A, rather than supplier B. The total payoff for A, Y_A, may be consequently larger than the total payoff for B, Y_B, so that $Y_A > Y_B$. In this case, the equilibrium would coincide with the pair (E, E), because it would be in both suppliers' interests to be efficient, since the negligent supplier would be expelled from the market. A similar case is also discussed in Kreps (1995), where it is shown that, in a series of transactions between enterprises on a multiple-period time horizon and with a certain number of customers, an enterprise will behave so as to maintain its good reputation because it attributes more value to its future earnings than to its present earnings.

7. CONCLUSION

In this brief analysis of the factors of competitive advantage of the 'ID' as an organizational form in its Marshallian sense, we have attempted to emphasize how this competitive advantage lies in the interaction of economic, technological, and social and cultural factors, in the light of Becattini's definition of an ID. The economic factors have to do with the evolution of international demand and the comparative advantages of the different areas taking part in the system of international trade. These comparative advantages are not just a matter of availability of material production factors, but also of availability of immaterial factors, such as the human and social capital. The human capital depends on the nature of the know-how incorporated in individual agents and on the nature of their behavior. The social capital depends on the strength of the social links between the agents and on how strongly they share given behavioral protocols. Such behavioral norms, or institutions, are reinforced by the particular way in which production is organized in an ID. The presence of a plurality of small enterprises within an area of limited extent drives the agents to maximize their commitment and to adopt a non-opportunist type of behavior. Of course the success of the ID is not grounded on everlasting factors, because environmental, technological, or social and cultural conditions may change. In short, the ID is a successful formula whose performance relies on the concomitant occurrence of several conditions, and this should prompt caution, especially to policymakers attempting to embark on a course of accelerated economic growth, in the belief that they can bring new IDs into being by administrative means. The effects of strategies relating to globalization might weaken the networks of relations between enterprises in an ID. This remains, for the time being, an open question.

16. Semi-automatic and deliberate actions in the evolution of industrial districts

Gabi Dei Ottati[*]

1. INTRODUCTION

When in the 1970s, the emergence of local systems of small and medium-sized firms captured the attention of social scientists, especially in Italy where these systems were and are particularly common, Giacomo Becattini was the first to note that this phenomenon coincided with the return of an organisational model that had already existed and had been analysed by Alfred Marshall (Becattini 1979). Since then the industrial district (ID) has become the focus for scholarly research and the notion has been further developed especially in Italy, where the emergence and consolidation of districts continues to this very day.[1] More recently, however, further research in the field has shown that, in response to the accelerating pace of globalisation, several IDs in developed countries are currently experiencing a deep crisis and are undergoing a phase of radical restructuring.

Taking the current state of the art in district theory as its starting point, this chapter will reexamine the typical modes of coordination of this peculiar form of social and economic organisation (Dei Ottati 1991) with the intent of highlighting its strengths when adjustments to gradual and conjunctural changes are required, but at the same time, its difficulty to cope with more radical and structural changes. This discussion will draw on relevant contributions on IDs, as well as on the work of Albert Hirschman (1982) in particular, on his idea that agents engaged in public action fuse striving and attaining. This occurs because public action is often prompted by a cognitive reversal which occurs similarly to a revelation; in that suddenly an agent realises that a step could be taken, together with others, in order to change a situation that is currently highly unsatisfactory. Moreover, public participation also involves a change in self-perception, often associated to self-realisation.

It would no doubt be extremely useful to avail of a general framework that would bring into sharper focus the ways districts respond to external changes – considering their typical features – especially at a time, as is currently the case, when this is causing a great deal of upheaval. Such a framework would lead to a better understanding of the transformations currently affecting districts and would contribute towards taking more conscious actions in order to reignite local development.

The chapter will proceed as follows. After having addressed the functional mechanisms of a district during its 'normal' evolutionary process (Section 2), it will proceed to examine the disruptive impact on the vitality of district processes that is triggered by radical external shocks (Section 3).[2] Section 4 will then look at the individual and collective strategies that can be taken in order to breathe life back into the district. The brief conclusion that follows will consider the recent empirical evidence on districts' transformations.

2. COOPERATION REINFORCING COMPETITION AND ID COMPETITIVENESS

As is well known, the production structure of an ID comprises many small and medium-sized firms specialising in the different activities of the production process of a localised industry and of the related sectors concentrated within a geographic area (Becattini 1989). Hence, the economic structure of an ID is characterised by an extensive division of labour among local firms. This means that every specialised activity will give rise to a form of local market within which firms will engage in similar activities, competing with one another, striving to deliver better quality and less costly products and services, and making sure they are capable of meeting stricter delivery deadlines than those offered by other district competitors first and, albeit indirectly, by external competitors. Generally speaking, firm competition within such district markets is vibrant because of the circulation of information and knowledge, as well as of the low entry barriers. Both contribute to generate new firms and to attract new workers that specialize in activities that are time after time in demand and where there is therefore scope to expand and for job opportunities. These typical features of the production structure of the ID make sure that the competitive urge is so active and widespread within it that all firms are forced to deal with its challenges, as they must constantly adapt their know-how, their tools, their products, their business relations and so on, either to make the most of opportunities to improve their economic and social situation, or, at least, to maintain the position that they had already reached. It can safely be argued, therefore, that competitive pressures in districts are much stronger than those in other production environments, because forces within it constantly stimulate learning, the entrepreneurial initiative and creativity (Bellandi 2003a, pp. 95–107).

At the same time, however, as underlined by scholarly work on the topic (Becattini 1989; Brusco 1995, 1999), this vitality also relies heavily on the mutual cooperation shared amongst agents who contribute towards the localised thickening of the economic and social relations that characterise this model. This cooperation can be argued to be mainly semi-automatic, in so far as it relies on the respect of shared customs (Dei Ottati 1991, p. 55) and implicit norms of behaviour of an institutionalised nature. These are rules that everybody tends to respect simply because everyone else does so, and, more importantly, because practice tells them that economic agents are rewarded – socially and economically – if they abide by them, whilst being sanctioned if they do not. Moreover, because it is institutionalised this behaviour will lead to establishing the identity and reputation of agents, in such a way that those who deviate from it will incur costly consequences also at an emotional level. This explains why in a district that is moving along a 'normal' process of evolution (that is, in a context where agents' expectations are met), economic change, even when this is continuous and widespread, is accompanied by the persistence of institutionalised behaviours which define the identity of the district (Becattini 1979).

As Brusco (1999) convincingly argued, in a district the implicit norms of behaviour find expression in a complex set of rules that regulate cooperative behaviours amongst firms and industrial relations inside firms themselves. Such rules dictate how to behave and what to avoid in order to promote an atmosphere that fosters trust and collaboration between all the agents in the district game. It is the district code that dictates the rules for each agent to abide by before, during, and after an economic interaction, prescribing precautionary measures (for example, by stating that exclusive subcontracting relations should be avoided if agents wish to minimize the damage caused by partners' uncooperative behaviours); interaction norms (that refer, for example, to the employer's responsibility to bind salary to productivity and to make sure that profits are reinvested as a condition for working participation), or social sanctions for those who do not abide by them (such as, for example, the loss of one's reputation which would cut all possible collaborations with other members of the district).

Semi-automatic cooperation is a key factor for the district's vitality and competitiveness, since it underpins the smooth functioning of the intra-district division of labour, as well as securing the circulation and sharing of knowledge crucial for diffused creativity and entrepreneurship. Moreover, this kind of cooperation promotes forms of conscious cooperation that lead to setting up infrastructures and other services useful to the whole district. In fact, the integration of the division of labour typical of IDs is accomplished mostly through the price mechanism within the local markets for specialised activities, and the mutual collaboration that results from agents abiding by the shared implicit rules. Thanks to this collaboration, opportunistic behaviour is reduced, and transactions are efficiently governed through a 'communitarian market' (Dei Ottati 1991, pp. 57–68), thus avoiding the costs of hierarchies. Moreover, semi-automatic cooperation facilitates the circulation of knowledge especially when this has not yet been codified. Semi-automatic cooperation also has the effect of reducing the risk of the fraudulent abuse of private information or innovative solutions, thus facilitating their dissemination and encouraging everyone to adopt and apply creatively any new idea, novelty or intuition. Semi-automatic cooperation also contributes towards the set up of voluntary organisations and formal institutions (such as industry associations or consortia) which can put in place deliberate forms of cooperation, that in turn enables small and medium-sized firms to overcome their limits, for instance, with respect to reaching the necessary scale to produce essential goods, including collective infrastructures, professional training and technology transfer.

A district, therefore, has a rather higher degree of cooperation and competition in its internal social and economic relations. What is being underlined here, however, is that the kind of vitality found in the organisational model of the district is generated by the positive interaction between the forces of competition and cooperation in such a way that the risk of both degenerating into mutually destructive forces is minimised. Thus, human progress in general is not jeopardised, as would happen, for instance, if competition were to mutate into a price war or unfair trading, or else if cooperation were to lead to collusive agreements, or restrictive practices.

However, in the absence of radical and permanent changes, the above-mentioned implicit rules and the diffused division of labour tend to generate constructive forms of cooperation and competition in the district that, feeding each other, trigger semi-automatic external economies, the main source of districts' competitiveness.[3] In fact, external economies of specialisation and flexible integration depend not only on the agglomeration of a large number of firms, but also on the dynamic positive interactions between competition and cooperation, mostly of the semi-automatic kind, that can be found within the district's local markets. Similarly, learning economies and innovation diffusion rely on the information that is exchanged across workers and specialised firms whose activities are partly similar and partly diverse, albeit related by being in the same industry or along the production *filière*. However, these external economies also rely on the fact that the mutual cooperation that permeates inter-firm interaction tends to shape competition towards constructive ends, like the unrelenting search for innovation, and products, processes and market upgrading. Finally, the prospect of building professional competence and benefitting from a good reputation within the local business community, together with low entry barriers typical of systems of small and medium-sized firms, provide district employees with the opportunity of developing their latent capabilities by setting up new firms, which in so doing, reproduce the competitive dynamism, as well as the implicit norms and values on which semi-automatic cooperation thrives.

In short, within the context of a 'normal' evolutionary process, the district constantly adapts its economic structure and, to some extent, also its internal institutional system to suit changing circumstances (for example, through the formation of *ad hoc* organisation to produce specific local public goods). However, it also gradually reproduces, with time and through the diverse relations that thrive within it, the positive interaction between competition and cooperation that is beneficial for economic development and social cohesion.

3. COMPETITION UNDERMINING COOPERATION AND ID COMPETITIVENESS

When cyclical – or partial – and rather gradual changes occur in the competitive environment outside the district, and especially worldwide, then the district's organisation shows that it is capable of responding very quickly to these changes. This happens thanks to the diffused creativity stemming from the industrial atmosphere and the flexibility that derives from the extensive division of labour and its integration through 'communitarian markets'. Indeed, by abiding by the rules of the 'district code', agents sustain the positive interaction between competition and cooperation, which in turns enables processes of continuous adaptation. In an ID moving along a 'normal' evolutionary path, therefore, a kind of institutional equilibrium emerges such that economic actors expect the implicit rules to be respected, as much as such expectations tend to be met. This equilibrium, however, might break under the strain of consistent and long-lasting changes that affect the demand and supply of the main goods produced by the district. This might happen, for instance, when new competitors emerge from low-cost countries, or when new technologies or more efficient forms of organisation become a serious threat; or, again, when consumers switch to products different from those the district is specialised on, therefore closing, in a very short period of time and in a definite way, the entry for many local producers to markets until then accessible. In all these cases, the excess of supply in the district can be so great as to make the short-term adaptation that would be required for firms to survive in the market virtually impossible. Feeling the pressure of external competition and of more immediate constraints (such as, for example, the urgent need for cash to pay for raw material, machinery and labour), entrepreneurs might be induced to start lowering the prices of their products and in turn to squeeze the costs paid to subcontractors, thus triggering a price war that will have a negative impact on the whole district. In fact, the race for undercutting prices would make profits plummet and hence lead to a reduction in the resources that would usually be reinvested in innovation; this at a time when such innovation would be crucial to regain a competitive advantage. Moreover, for the same reason, a price war may lead to many firms closing down, several of which are subcontractors; this will consequently lead to an impoverishment of the local competences and skills; as well as a thinning of the local relational economic networks. A protracted price war and the adoption of fierce competitive behaviours will also impact the institutional setting. As the trust in the 'district code' wanes,[4] also the motivation to learn and acquire skills, and in turn, to set up a new firm in one of the specialised activities of the local industry, will decline. Moreover, the chance of integrating the local division of labour through the district 'communitarian markets' decreases, because the implicit norms of 'bearing in mind the mutual need for survival' associated with reciprocity[5] is increasingly substituted by that of 'the survival of the fittest' in a competitive situation that is ruled by jungle short-sightedness and lawlessness. In other words, if the institutional balance is shattered, so also is the positive interaction between competition and cooperation that lies at the heart of the competitive advantage in the district model. When such a breaking point is reached, the synergy between the social and economic factors that constitutes the pillar in the district's vitality gives way. As trust in the implicit norms wanes, uncertainty sets in undermining investment and entrepreneurial initiatives; and at the same time, agents' behaviours and choices start being driven by narrow, self-interested and short-term pursuits. This happens essentially because the people involved have no more points of reference to formulate expectations, to interpret information, to make decisions and even to evaluate what is ethically acceptable and what is not. In such a situation, the district vital processes (of localised division of labour, of its flexible integration and of mutual learning) first start breaking down, then come to a halt. Consequently, the production of semi-automatic external economies (of specialisation, of flexible integration, of diffused learning), which result from the normal functioning of those processes, also dwindle.

Moreover, as the positive balance between the forces of competition and cooperation deteriorates, even cooperation runs the risk of becoming destructive, for example, by fostering the rise of coalitions of a number of local players with the end of accessing public resources that can benefit a few or by convening forms of resistance designed to maintain the *status quo*, rather than encouraging mechanisms of innovation that can help the local system to renew and adapt to the new context. When this happens, the effects can be doubly negative as they generate a trickle-down effect that can result in external diseconomies. So, a well-established district, that has benefitted for a long time from an industrial atmosphere dense of know-how, trust, initiatives and that has been capable of attracting resources from outside, might suddenly turn into a depressed environment lacking confidence, trust and open-mindedness, that shuts itself from the outside. When this happens the crisis can become irreversible, because in this case, the emergence and growth of energetic and skilful individuals will be highly unlikely, whilst the most entrepreneurial will have no choice but to leave in order to fulfil their ambitions elsewhere.

In brief, when external changes crowd out local production, then district entrepreneurs are likely to react by adopting fierce forms of competition. When the situation is long-lasting and persistent, the balance and positive interaction between competition and cooperation shifts with the former taking the upper hand and prevailing over the latter, and initiating therefore a process that leads to degenerative and destructive outcomes. Gradually, the trust and respect that agents have for the district' implicit norms start waning and, with this, the competitiveness and the adjustment capacity of the local system. Therefore, sheer inertia can be coupled with mechanism of accelerating decline due to the forms that competition and cooperation can take. At this stage decline becomes inevitable unless, having acquired insight and become fully aware of the situation, local actors decide to adopt individual and collective actions that are capable of triggering the economic and institutional changes necessary to produce new deliberate external economies and give birth to new development.[6]

4. SHIFTING INVOLVEMENTS AND MODES OF ECONOMIC AND POLITICAL GOVERNANCE TO COPE WITH DISCONTINUITIES

As mentioned above, when changes to the external context are so deep and long-lasting that the coping mechanisms incorporated in the 'routines' of the production system and in local society can no longer be relied upon to sustain economic adjustment, a process of deterioration sets in which can contaminate increasingly larger parts of the district and which – unless reversed through the deliberate introduction of substantial social and economic adjustments – can also lead to the district's decline. Conscious intervention – individual and above all collective – designed to arrest the degenerative process is not simple to achieve and in any case needs time, because the economic actors must first acquire knowledge and information that will enable them to identify and correctly evaluate the new challenges. Moreover, when faced with a number of lines of action potentially possible, they will have to know and choose those which are more likely to succeed, considering the resources available both internally and externally. In order to inject new energy and revive the district, measures must be taken to change not just one firm or two, but jointly all the relevant parts of the local economy and society as a whole, in order to create a critical mass 'of change' that is needed to modify expectations, and in turns behaviours, which thus can place the district on a new development trajectory.

In the economic sphere, new constructive forms of competition and cooperation will have to be introduced. In order to break the vicious circle of price and cost cutting, firms will have to start investing in innovation: new products and functions will have to be developed and new technologies adopted. In order to achieve this, first of all, new knowledge must be sought mostly from outside the district, which is therefore codified. Such new knowledge tends to be increasingly less embodied in equipment and machinery, but more and more it is intangible and needs to be absorbed and implemented autonomously in order to produce competitive advantages. Consequently, in order to introduce these innovations it will be necessary to establish new local relations (for example with university laboratories) and extra-local ones (for example with research centres and specialised national and international companies) and, hence, new forms of collaboration between firms, amongst firms and other organisations. Once a form of cooperation that relies on implicit rules becomes weak, other more explicit forms of cooperation must be adopted, in order to have a well-coordinated division of labour. In this context, even the coordination of transactions and economic patterns will change. The 'communitarian market' typical of a district that evolves 'normally', will be substituted by another more deliberate and conscious form of coordination whose functionality relies on different principles.[7] Thus, networks of local and extra-local firms will be set up, whose relations will be regulated by rules that have explicitly been set down in bilateral and multilateral contracts and, according to need, will include particular clauses or the exchange of 'hostages' (Williamson 1985).[8] Otherwise vertical integration (hierarchy) could emerge as a solution, although it could take various forms like the creation of groups or networks of firms where cooperation is based on contracts that give the entrepreneurs-managers the authority to direct resources (Coase 1937).

When a district experiences the breakdown of the positive synergy between the economic and the institutional spheres, then it is likely that it will witness a radical internal reorganisation that sees a growth in the size of those firms that are more innovative. These large and medium-sized firms have often better chances to regain competitiveness, by replacing the eroded district's external economies with economies they develop internally within the group or network, and that are related to their innovation capacity, their management competence, their marketing strategies and, more generally, to advantages derived from their internal growth. It is worth noting that the presence of medium-sized innovative firms is a key factor in the adjustment process. Not only can they encourage the inflow of new knowledge and new relations to the local socio-economic fabric from the outside, but through their success, they can become a role model for other firms to look up to. However, if the hierarchic reorganisation of local relations would so evolve as to concentrate a large portion of economic power and strategic functions in just one firm, then, even if small and medium-sized enterprises survive, the resulting type of local system would no longer look like a district, albeit a renewed one. This is because, inside it, the circulation of information and knowledge is constrained by the hierarchical character of its relations, which in turn will be thinned out leading to a reduction also in the incentives to entrepreneurship.

In other words, a real recovery for a district – understood as a local system whose dynamism relies heavily on its 'atmosphere', dense of knowledge and trust so as to generate diffused entrepreneurship and creativity – will be difficult to achieve if radical changes in the production apparatus fail to be accompanied by a collective action that mirrors a joint institutional and behavioural change. In this context, the most urgent adjustment would need to be in relation to the level of trust underpinning agents' behaviours. The sense of trust will have to be restored inside the local system by breaking the depressive spiral that fosters inertia or the search for rents positions that undermine any attempt to regain competitiveness. This is no easy target to reach, because it will have to rely on a form of collective action that is capable of leading to an understanding of the new context that is commonly shared and that will then form the basis for browsing the new opportunities surfacing in the new context. The latter scenario can emerge with great difficulties because, to the usual caveats associated with collective action (Olson 1965), one must add the urgency needed to overcome the sense of loss and apathy plaguing the local environment and pervaded by growing uncertainty. However, as underlined by Hirschman (1982), when situations become so desperate that no way out seems possible, it often happens that the belief spreads that 'something needs to be done' and that one needs 'to save one's living environment', in order for the decline to be arrested. If this happens and mobilisation is promoted under the leadership of a legitimate local player (usually an institutional actor) who is able to draw in a large portion of the local society, then a real cognitive mutation could take place which would lead the various subjects to see one's own resourcefulness and potential in a different light. In other words, a change of perception would occur that would entail a different overall understanding of oneself and the district.[9]

When the collective action – by and large political – is successful, it simultaneously generates new trust, new social cohesion and a new identity. All this usually paves the way for gathering the consensus, the resources and the institutional inventive necessary for the production of new deliberated external economies, thanks to the supply of local public goods (Bellandi 2006), being these tangibles or intangibles depending on the specific problems that need to be addressed in view of steering the district towards a new prospect of development. Examples of public goods, generated in this way, could entail training, R&D, as well as the establishment of contractual and quality standards. All this might, in the end, gradually lead to the formation of a new institutional equilibrium, although different from the old one, which will manage to reestablish the positive interaction between competition and cooperation, thus giving rise to the semi-automatic external economies.

5. CONCLUSION

If the conceptual framework presented above, which highlights the typical functioning mechanisms of a district when during the course of its evolution it is affected by exogenous either gradual and radical changes, is correct, then we would be in a better position to understand the difficulties and transformations currently affecting IDs in developed countries and more specifically in Italy. For quite some time now, and particularly with greater urgency since the beginnings of the third millennium, the international context has been experiencing profound changes. One just needs, for example, to think of the incorporation of the ex-Soviet Union States into the market economy, or the introduction of the single European currency, or more recently, the extraordinary growth of Asian countries, especially China. These extraordinary changes, combined with the spread of information technology and the drop in transportation costs, have led to the emergence of a new model of industrial organisation: the so-called 'global value chain' (Gereffi, Humphrey and Sturgeon 2005). Once Fordism was superseded by lean production (Womack, Jones and Roos 1990), now the latter model has increasingly been incorporated into the process of international fragmentation regarding production and, partly even innovation (Schmitz and Strambach 2008). The main, though not exclusive, aim of this reorganisation initiated by the multinational firms in developed countries is to take advantage of the lower labour costs in those countries hosting the new process of industrialisation.

No wonder, therefore, that under the strain of structural change of this importance (which in the case of Italian districts is aggravated by the rise of the euro with respect to the dollar, as well as by a drop in the demand for 'made-in-Italy' goods – personal and household goods – in comparison with other goods, such as, for example, electronic goods) several districts in Italy and in other developed countries are going through a phase marked by crisis. This can mainly be accounted for by the fact that the adjustment processes needed can no longer be incremental or rely on embedded knowledge, modes of behaviour, and coordination and innovation models received from the past.[10]

In order to recuperate competitiveness in the new context, entrepreneurs must learn new strategies that will allow them to enhance their existing experiences and competences with new knowledge that needs to be acquired from outside. In order to achieve this, a new division of labour will have to be deliberately introduced together with new forms necessary for its integration. This has been confirmed by empiric evidence gleaned through extensive research carried out both in Italian districts as well as in local systems of small and medium-sized firms in developed countries (Crouch et al. 2004; Guelpa and Micelli 2007; see also Coltorti in this volume). According to the findings of this research, the districts which are best equipped to meet the challenges of globalisation are those characterised by the presence of medium-sized and large firms, often referred to as 'leader' firms. These firms usually rely on relationships underlying subcontracting and supplying exchanges as well as co-partnership for goods and services (for example, ICT, design, R&D) usually located outside the district. This is because 'leader' firms often adopt strategies that differ from those of the past and that involve the shifting of manufacturing investment towards planning, design, marketing function and the setting up of one's own distribution network. This investment is usually large and specific, being targeted towards securing a market niche of one's own, so it is logical to expect coordination to assume not just more conscious forms, but also forms that are more reliant on hierarchy. Knowing this, it is hardly surprising that most of the competitive advantage of the new 'leader' firms does not come from the local external economies, but from the imagination and capabilities of entrepreneurs and their direct collaborators whose task is to spot and coordinate the resources necessary for innovation.[11] If this were the case, then there would be no need to believe that the 'leader' firms would be inclined to share such knowledge and those relations that have become crucial to their new competitiveness within the local system. Moreover, even if this were in part to be the case, if the number of 'leader' firms were limited, the effect achieved will probably not be sufficient to trigger the revitalisation of the whole of the local system.

According to the framework delineated above, when exogenous changes are so radical and fast as to upset the institutional equilibrium within the district, then, in order to enable the reproduction of the local development, changes in the economic as well as institutional spheres are required: these imply a shift of the economic coordination from being prevalently semi-automatic to being more deliberate. Moreover, since the production and innovative processes in the ID are diffused and collective – given that they rely on the input of a great number of independent but coordinated agents – it will not be enough for conscious action to involve just the transactions undertaken by one or two 'leader' firms, but must necessarily involve the local system as a whole. This can be achieved through collective action promoted and driven by a reliable 'institutional leader'; only through this action, in fact, is the collective learning process likely to be achieved, a process which first leads to sharing new prospects of development and then to the adoption of institutional and economic models that are likely to achieve success.

In conclusion, the opportunities of survival and of injecting renewed vitality in the development of districts when these are under the strain of exogenous shocks, will rely more on the power of the imagination and on the drive of the institutional and political leaders rather than on 'leader' firms – who nonetheless play an indispensable role.[12]

NOTES

* The author would like to thank Fulvio Coltorti, Marco Dardi and Paolo Giovannini for valuable comments. The author, however, is solely responsible for the ideas and opinions contained in this chapter.
1. For more detail, see Becattini and Coltorti (2006) and Becattini and Dei Ottati (2006).
2. This chapter deals with the consequences that radical exogenous changes can have on the reproduction of districts, while allowing that the district model can equally collapse as a result of internal changes; such as when the younger generations have values and attitudes that are very different from their parents', or in the case of a rip in the social fabric caused, for example, by the inability to assimilate immigrants with a different cultural background (Dei Ottati 2009).
3. External economies can be both semi-automatic and deliberate (Dei Ottati 2006). Nonetheless, in the normal evolution of the district, most of its external economies and its internal coordination rely on auto-organisational and semi-conscious mechanisms that rule the local markets and community (see Bagnasco in this volume).
4. For some empiric evidence, see Dei Ottati (2005).
5. According to Brusco (1999, p. 22), the basic rule governing cooperative interaction in IDs is the following: 'The agents who work together on a continuous basis will never fully take advantage of the market power that is available to them, owing to their reciprocal interdependence . . . Each of them will take into consideration the survival needs and the success opportunities of the other; both are tied to profit margins and to the ability to keep their respective technological standards high and to retain the best and most skilled workforce'.
6. For more information on the difference between crisis, deindustrialisation and industrial decline; and on the decisive role played by collective interpretation in order to shift from decline to governance of change, see Giovannini (2006a).
7. As noted by Raffaelli (2003a), the functioning model of the human brain suggested by Alfred Marshall is helpful in understanding his theory of industrial evolution and hence of the evolution of the ID. Marshall argues that the brain functions partly through automatic responses to known external stimuli and partly through deliberate choices made in response to new and unsatisfying situations. Only in the latter case does the highest part of the brain intervene, mobilising its ability to imagine the consequences caused by diverse possible lines of action, before finally settling for the one considered as being the most capable of resolving the new problem.
8. Even when the district evolves 'normally', repeated exchanges between firms specialised in complementary activities emerge and give rise to informal groups, or teams, that function in a similar manner to firm networks in a context unlike that of the district. In any case, whilst the coordination of the district team relies heavily on the implicit norms, such as a shared sense of belonging, other generic networks of firms tend to rely, for their interactions, on explicit norms, namely contracts that are not embedded in a common culture.
9. With regards to the cognitive changes that accompany collective actions, Hirschman states that 'large numbers of people grow up with the feeling that the existing social (economic) and political order is not subject to change or that, in any case, they are powerless to bring such change about. The sudden realisation that I can act to change society (economy) for the better and, moreover, that I can join other like-minded people to this end is in such conditions pleasurable, in fact intoxicating in itself' (Hirschman 1982, p. 89).
10. On the restructuring of the Italian IDs in response to the first wave of global pressure in the 1980s, see Cossentino, Pyke and Sengenberger (1996).
11. See, for example, Guelpa and Micelli's introduction to their book on IDs in the third millennium, where they argue that 'the thesis here suggested is that the district model, characterised by competitive advantages of a systemic kind, is rapidly gaining new contours which give increasing weight to the deliberate strategies undertaken by the actors and, particularly, by those undertaken by firms. The Marshallian district model, which relies on a complex balance between economic and social processes, and between competition and cooperation, leaves space for districts which are similar to local systems of innovation where competitiveness increasingly relies on the investments and strategies of leader firms operating worldwide' (Guelpa and Micelli 2007, p. 15).
12. On the role of politics in bringing together economy and the society in tracing a trajectory of shared development, as well as building a context of cooperative interaction amongst various actors, also see Bagnasco in this volume.

17. The governance of industrial districts

Arnaldo Bagnasco

1. GOVERNANCE: AN OLD TERM WITH NEW MEANINGS

The term 'governance' is a word of great currency in the English language and is used sometimes as a near synonym of government and sometimes to refer to more specific meanings. The term 'governance' is generally employed to refer to the process of governing, of decision making and implementation and this is one possible meaning covered by government (Kooiman 2000 and Hindess 2001). When used in this way government also incorporates a concern for agency and players, for resources and for the dynamics that are influential in forming concrete decision making in social groups (Le Galès 2003).

More recently, especially in the specialized language of social sciences, the two words tend to be carefully distinguished; this happens in particular in the study of complex action systems, such as international relations or city management. In such cases, if government involves acts of public authority and the exercise of functional institutions, then governance is a particularly appropriate term because it suggests that within the complex frameworks of contemporary societies even public policies are formulated through the direct participation of various public and private players who negotiate and reach agreements in order to ensure implementation. From this point of view, 'government', this time meaning public authority, becomes 'one' of the players involved in governance within contemporary social systems and assumes its own set of rules and resources. Thus, governance when used in this way also alludes to procedures that encompass new styles and modes of authority; it is precisely this aspect that is captured so aptly by the English term and that is responsible for its currency in languages such as Italian, whose vocabulary does not comprise a word having the same semantic scope to that of 'governance'.

Considering this and in view of the way the word is used in economic and social language, 'governance' can thus be seen as being strongly related to 'regulation'. Its emphasis on the way diverse mechanisms combine and its focus on the ways the economy is controlled by diverse regulatory regimes makes it part and parcel of that kind of interest that involves the study of complex action systems (Trigilia 2002) and, to a great extent the analytical tools applied to governance procedures are similar to those used in the study of the mechanisms and regulatory regimes. This happens particularly when local systems and issues regarding their management and development are addressed: and therefore, more specifically, in studies regarding industrial districts (IDs), the way they work, their dynamics over time; all topics which will constitute the subject of study in this chapter.

In brief, we could assume that the governance of complex systems, and therefore of the districts that constitute the topic of our interest, primarily regards the generation of normative rules, regulations and routines that allow players and social mechanisms to liaise in view of their elaboration and activation for collective ends.

One point must therefore be made clear at the outset: the study of governance or, in other words the study of the regulations that govern local systems, such as towns and IDs, overlaps with economics and society. In fact, it does not involve economic processes only, but economic and social processes that are intricately linked. Thus the output of governance involves not just economic efficiency, but also the broader processes that account for systemic integration (that is, between the various sections of society) and social integration (the ways in which bonds between one person and another are formed) (Lockwood 1964). From this point of view, we could argue, therefore, that the governance of a local system is a directive and regulatory process which recognizes, maintains and redefines any potential congruencies that exist between the economy and society. In this sense, governance must make sure – it has no choice – that it includes in its output a set of social assets that are relatively shared and that are compatible with the values, interests and resources of a local society. Any governance that is oriented towards development must be capable of spotting and capitalizing on existing opportunities by upgrading and maintaining any congruencies present. On the other hand, a local society might resist a kind of governance that is oriented towards development and it might do this for reasons that range from a lack of specific resources to value assets and interests that manage to lodge a successful objection. The study of local systems and, more specifically, ID governance is, therefore, a political economy that encompasses the interactions that take place between individuals, groups, organizations, classes and status groups; that generate choices and assets in an economy with given conditions; and that stabilize implicit and explicit rules which have to be followed. Every developmental process always modifies, at least in part, these conditions. Local-system governance, and in particular district governance, is capable of recognizing these modifications or responding to the conservation of assets that become inefficient or are no longer capable of gathering sufficient consensus. It is sometimes the case, and a rather frequent occurrence, that diverse potential alternatives emerge which offer the prospect of major economic efficiency and possibilities of social integration that are equally plausible or that are difficult to anticipate.

The problem of good governance, which might arise in cases such as these, raises political rather technical issues. The practice of good governance, therefore, emerges as a problem to which social analysts cannot apply a technical formula, or that can be presented as a useful tool for the resolution of each and every case. What analysts can do, however, is to reconstruct the governance of particular and typical local cases, and come to an understanding of their nature and the way they work, and evaluate how far this can be applied to cases that do not present the exact same conditions, or to cases that are completely different and so require specifically designed solutions. Later on I will deal with some aspects relevant to Italian district governance as it is today, and I will attempt to identify elements of good governance that could be applied, within specific limits, to the analysis of other cases.

2. DISTRICT GOVERNANCE: VIEWPOINTS AS SUGGESTED BY EXPERIENCE

To start with, it is useful to mention a few concepts and methods that are part and parcel of the points of view and a selection of analytical tools applied to the district studies.

A district, understood as a local socio-economic system, has its own 'organization'. The term organization refers broadly to the systemic coordination of people and resources with the aim of obtaining particular results. Some aspects of organizational theory might therefore be helpful in taking the subject of governance, discussed so far, a step forward and bringing it into sharper focus (Bagnasco 2003).

Two metaphors come to mind when thinking of organizations. These can be compared either to a biological organism or to a machine. Neither of these metaphors, however, manages to capture with precision a crucial aspect of action systems and this is the players' intentions. The former says too much and the latter too little when it comes to defining actors' intentions. The biological metaphor fails to capture the notion of 'intent', that voluntary component that triggers human action. The machine metaphor, on the other hand, places too much emphasis on the idea of planning and predictability, and hence does not fully apply or applies only partially to action systems. Within this particular context, men do not really function like the mechanisms in a machine in the sense that the final outcomes can never be fully worked out or always predicted. Sometimes, in fact, crucial outcomes are unanticipated consequences, and can only be fully understood by hindsight. In other words, social organization relies partly on unconscious drives and partly on rational planning. It involves processes that give directions and generate normative behavioral patterns; it recognizes and produces more or less explicit rules that have achieved relative stability with time and gone on to form 'equipped interaction fields' (Crozier and Friedberg 1977). We can therefore safely say that the term 'governance' captures that intentional, conscious aspect of organizational processes that also comprise its limitations.

Some forms of organization are more like machines than biological organisms (although the metaphor does not fully apply here either). Such is the case with large and small formal organizations based on organizational hierarchies, chains of command, standardized control procedures and set roles. It is within this context, as for example with reference to firms, that the term 'corporate governance' is used. We are therefore referring to forms of organization that are more artificial and rely on authoritative coordination. Even in this case general organizational problems, similar in scope and similar to those mentioned earlier, emerge; the question being how to resolve the cooperative issues when interdependent players do not completely share the same viewpoints or interests, and when they take lines of action that generate conflict, negotiations and exchanges.

IDs are, however, very complex and complicated systems. They certainly involve several organizations, such as firms, that are authoritatively coordinated. However, one thing must not be forgotten and that is the way these collective players interact and cooperate with each other triggering more or less predictable system effects.

Firms' action is essentially regulated by the 'market': the dynamics of their competition/collaboration are shaped by market relations. The market acts as a guarantor, albeit an imprecise one, for economic efficiency and continuously elicits a whole range of new entrepreneurial experimentation. Market regulations rely on automatic mechanisms: in their pristine form they produce systemic effects that none of the players is explicitly seeking. The market's invisible arm is diametrically opposed to the visible arm of formal organizations. Forms of coordination that are simply directed to the workings of the market must therefore be considered as a resource rather than a mode of 'governance'. However, this resource needs to be governed because if left to its own devices it could have a negative impact on the economy and the social fabric. The market is regulated by state laws or international agreements which legitimate practices and modalities; but we also know that public politics and development policies have a greater and broader impact on the workings and assets of the market and manage to reinforce or give direction to its outcomes.

We thus come across the intentional and explicit aspects of organizational processes; in general but more specifically in their application to districts. In districts, the workings of political institutions constitute a relevant aspect within the broader framework of regulations which, however, must be evaluated within the context of governance systems that comprise several public and private participants, who more or less consciously compete, from their diverse positions, to generate a series of anticipated system effects within a partially or wholly conceived plan. Contemporary economies are mixed economies in which market regulation and political regulations overlap and combine to varying degrees. The recipe for good governance in developmental processes is one that combines to varying degrees an amount of its constituent ingredients. We could analyze a particular case of experience in a district to see what it suggests. We must, however, keep in mind the fact that district governance sits on the border between economy and society and that it has to guarantee relatively shared social assets, and that it must be compatible with the shared values, interests, and the resources of the local society that must be reproduced. In other words, a governance that targets local development must recognize invested opportunities and value them by upgrading and reinforcing those elements that enable a sustainable link between economy and society. And in order to complete the picture, we must take into account one other aspect of social organization, that is, the 'equipped contexts' of social interaction. This aspect can be better understood through a close examination of direct interaction itself.

Those who have studied districts have taken care to emphasize the importance of the fact that they sink their roots in local communities in which people are cemented by a thick and complex web of relations. If we have recourse to the language of sociology we will get a better grasp of how this works because its definition of organizational processes does not only take into account formal organizations, or organizations of equipped interactive fields generated by politics, but also involves forms of so-called self-regulating social organizations that arise out of direct and iterated interaction, during which participants learn to combine strategy and behavior that does not jeopardize but indeed paves the way for collective results. From this perspective, protracted interaction appears as process that generates norms. When considering their rooting in local communities, however, there is one further element that must be addressed and clarified.

The nature of social relations in this context refers to norms and evaluation criteria that imply major commitments articulated in: non-specific roles, emotional investments and non-instrumental interactions dictated by principle. All this is evoked when the local context is referred to as 'community', a community based on direct acquaintances and one that is cemented by biographical anecdote, by family relations, by the colour of local history and local identities and the dictates of a range of modes of relating to others prompted by ease of familiarity and trust. From this perspective, direct interaction refers to the colours of a local culture that in the process of interaction multiply and adapt with time; interaction therefore generates a broad range of routines and rules that do not emerge out of a void, but that have been sown by an embedded culture that at once facilitates and limits its contours.

In current sociological language it is assumed that an actor/participant who can draw on a rich network of relational possibilities that is backed by an institutional context similar to the one described above, possesses 'social capital' that can act as a resource for him/her to fall back upon (Coleman 1990).

Social capital, however, also constitutes a sort of public good, that can be as a whole deposited in a group or in a society as a collective resource that facilitates cooperative interaction and that is available to people who can use it as an important resource in equipped interaction.

The governance of IDs relies heavily on the valuable resource of embedded social capital, some aspects of which will now be considered. We conclude by observing that self-regulation processes of society can be regarded as governance resources, and not as processes of governance, or to be more precise, they constitute only a part of this process. Hence the term 'spontaneity' is often used with reference to these processes. In other words, lack of awareness plays a role in the self-regulation processes of society; nonetheless from public debates and the cultural elaboration of colocation and sharing, a typical sense of awareness and rules of interaction might emerge. These can be considered aspects of the processes of governance that pertain to the whole system or to some parts of it. A case in point is the example given in the following section.

3. MARKET AND GOVERNANCE: AN EXAMPLE OF NORMS GENERATED IN INTERACTIVE PROCESSES

The market is a social institution which generates interaction within a fixed set of legally-established rules which, however, do not comprise all the known rules in force. Good economic governance needs good explicit rules in order to run its markets, but it can also count on forms of self-regulation or, in other words, on norms that are generated in the course of interactive processes. If governance means above all the setting up of rules, then we must assume that even those rules generated by the various social actors in the course of their interactive procedures are to be regarded as an aspect of governance. The selection of a set of norms meant to regulate market interaction is no doubt in many ways an emerging system effect; we must, however, also not forget that the participants make conscious evaluations drawing on their knowledge of the existing system of local market relations.

I will now examine an article written by the economist Sebastiano Brusco who has conducted a study and attempted to pin down the unspoken rules in force in a typical district of Emilia-Romagna (Brusco 1999). Brusco was aware that these economic systems, just like their implicit rules, are problematic in that they are not always strictly observed and that they are subject to change with the passing of time. Nonetheless, it is precisely these rules that were known and respected by all that explained the workings of the economy when this was at the peak of its success. These rules concern a couple of antonyms: the first lies in the conflict generated by the competitive and cooperative urge 'amongst' firms; and the second in the conflicts and participation 'within' firms; to cope with these antonyms is the way to the success in small-firm districts that host companies engaged in the production of light-industry goods and that bond with each other as a result of subcontracting relations. Brusco's article demonstrates that we are dealing here with institutionalized solutions. A close look at the details of this argument is very evocative in suggesting the range and complexity of the small-firm districts in question.

The firms in the districts are driven by a healthy competitive urge; the market is based on a high degree of transparency; information circulates with ease; and innovation is ongoing with imitation and incremental modification of the product or of the competitors' techniques. The rule set in place by the community to make sure that private knowledge is turned into a community-shared resource without violating legitimate mutual interest is the following:

> Final firms (i.e. firms assembling and selling the final good) are in competition with other final firms, taking advantage of any legitimate opportunities that might arise to pick up the clues that might have led to other peoples' success: trade-fairs, catwalks, exhibitions, shop windows . . . In the same way, sub-contracting firms ought to compete against each other. It would be unfair competition and therefore frowned upon, if a sub-contractor or an employee was bribed to access information about their firm. (Ibid., p. 368)

Once a relationship has been soundly established, then the fundamental rule is:

> When two agents are bound by continuous relations, they must not make full use of the market power by virtue of the economic situation, their size and other details. Each will respect the other's need to survive and to succeed, which determine profit margins, to the extent to which one is able to maintain a suitable technological profile, and to one's ability in securing the most highly-qualified labor force. (Ibid.)

Those who do not obey the rules for good interaction, for example those who do not respect delivery conditions/deadlines, will face more or less severe sanctions, the worst of which being the loss of one's reputation in the local *milieu*, a possibility made very likely by the dense network of relations within the local community.

The antinomy participation/conflict that is intricately linked to the conflicting interests of the cooperating agents within the firm is, on the other hand, governed by institutionalized rules and sanctions.

In this case we are again presented with cautionary rules expressed as follows:

> It is a good – and ideologically correct – thing to contribute as best as possible to the success of the company for which one works. However, prudence is both permitted and considered legitimate. If the employee requests adequate returns as guarantees for his commitment, this does not mean a lack of trust in the employer but rather the sign of respectable foresight. (Ibid.)

As for interaction a general and broad ranging rule is the following:

> One of the conditions for participation is that everyone must be aware that roles within a firm, regardless of whether you are an entrepreneur or employee, do not involve any cultural or political hierarchical subordination, and do not necessarily involve professional inferiority prejudice. So while hierarchy is necessary to the internal machinations of a company, as far as work is concerned, each one is allowed broad margins and initiatives and is expected to be responsible for the work done and to pay for the mistakes made. (Ibid.)

This interaction therefore involves relations between employer and employee that are diametrically opposed to paternalism and excludes 'deferential workers' as is usually the case with small firms. The conditions and relations within the firm are highly transparent, the workers know when no more can be obtained, on the other hand, however, if business thrives they claim their dues. Workers regard the requests made by an owner who is not active enough as a form of cheating. The corresponding rule is the following:

> The entrepreneur must be committed to the truth (which gives rise to salary dynamics rooted in merit and the success of the company) and to sobriety of life style which generates an appropriate level of investment in order to guarantee the best possible machinery in use in the factory. (Ibid.)

Within the restrictive context of the district, if an employer does not stick to the rules, it will be more and more difficult for him to find good workers, and if a worker does not respect the rules, this will have a negative impact on his mobility.

4. GOVERNANCE RESOURCES: SOCIAL CAPITAL AND OTHER THINGS

In some regions, successful IDs have constituted a post-Fordist surprise: no one, and least of all economists, had anticipated their emergence. When they were eventually spotted they were explained in terms of system: they were not seen as aggregations of individual small and medium-sized firms, but as economic systems that rose in reference to the resources and typical characteristics of the local society from which they sprung. It is doubtful whether the agents responsible for the birth of these districts were themselves completely conscious of those system effects that they had generated by their own behavior or indeed of the conditions that made these effects possible. It is likely, especially with regards to the former, that they were completely understood by hindsight. Whatever the case might be, these are often referred to as the 'spontaneous' workings of systems whose organization emerges as an effect of automatic mechanisms (such as the market) or of informal mechanisms (as is the case for the rules generated through interaction mentioned above). Some observers also came to the erroneous conclusion that districts could be explained as a free-market consequence and that only a minimum amount of governance was needed; indeed, they went on to suggest that the lack of explicit governance meant a higher chance of success in the districts.

More attentive studies brought to light a range of precious resources (to varying degrees in quality and quantity according to the case in question) that can be found in local communities such as: traditional craftsmanship, local banks that sustain growth, previously accumulated capital, good internal communication infrastructures and links to external networks, education programs that target professional formation and so on. These resources are usually not particularly rich but they are well spread and act as great assets in the development of districts of whole regions whenever overall conditions are ripe for growth.

Was it, therefore, just the market (to which the diverse sectors of society and various individual choices adapted with haste and ease) that acted as a regulating mechanism for the combined use of these resources? Was it just resources of this kind that were involved? The need to answer these questions shifted the focus to the quality of the social fabric and the nature of the local culture that are intricately linked to the emergence of districts in local communities. As I have stated above, the idea of social capital sprang from the need to explain a vital resource in the development of local communities.

This is, in fact, a key resource that must figure in our analysis. First of all, it must not be confused with those resources mentioned at the beginning of this section, sometimes also called social capital. The rapid success of Italian districts was also due to resources of this kind and we must not make the mistake of overestimating the importance of social capital (in the true sense of the word): this remains an important resource but it must be evaluated within the framework of local conditions and other resources.

My second point needs to be backed up by a theoretical clarification. There are in fact two kinds of social capital: (a) a more traditional, elementary, informal type of social capital that can be found in dense interactive networks. These networks are rooted in that strong sense of identity that is usually to be found in districts. They are responsible for facilitating combined economic action in areas, such as the reduction of transaction costs as a result of interpersonal trust; (b) a type of social capital generated in the process of planning new interactive contexts that, even when formalized through contractual or organizational schemes, show that they are capable of facilitate interaction through the preservation of loyalty and the iteration of interactive networking (see Trigilia 2005). The generation of norms addressed in the previous section is an excellent example of the latter. But even a formal organization whose plans explicitly allow for the conservation of basic social capital, interpersonal loyalty, responsibility for collective purposes and that manages to internally preserve relations that are not just instrumental, is an experimental generator of social capital. The quasi-organizations and the quasi-markets mentioned by economists are also organizational frameworks that often preserve and generate basic social capital within the overarching networks of companies: these organizational frameworks are unsurprisingly found in districts.

For some time now, in the wake of economic changes that have opened new possibilities for enlarged networks and more fluid relations, new forms of social capital have emerged that draw on much weaker bonds. In Granovetter's words the networks of this new economy do not draw on traditional social capital (such as that found in families) but develops a more appropriate kind of social capital. This is the case of the Silicon Valley in which professional communities have sprung on the basis of esteem and reputation. These communities are made up of highly-specialized people who know each other and who act according to a rigid set of norms and sanctions that pave the way for accepted professional behavior for those who belong to it. This is done in order to make sure that people remain loyal to the firms from which they are recruited while spreading innovation within the system (Saxenian 1994).

The above discussion and clarifications made about the diverse kinds of social capital shows that district analysis cannot be based on ideas of governance drawn on past experiences or inherited resources. Much as these might be important, especially in the initial stages of the set up of a district or in the case of emergent ethnic entrepreneurship, our attention must necessarily shift to the generation of 'new' social capital.

So far we have brought into sharper focus the issue regarding the kind of resources that governance can draw upon, but we have not yet answered the important question whether the market alone is capable of regulating and mobilizing these resources. The answer is obviously negative from the outset, because recognizing the social capital of belonging and experimenting social capital generation become evident useful resources for a more explicit and more general form of governance. Districts, in particular, show that both in their genesis and in the course of their development a more committed form of governance is at work. But in order to explore this issue, it needs first to be placed in its political context.

5. EXPERIMENTS AND PROBLEMS OF INSTITUTIONAL DESIGN

The organization of society is achieved through politics: this is done either through invasive intervention or by acknowledging the fact that civil society is both autonomous and capable of self-regulation. No district was instituted or governed by decree. This does not mean that politics have had no part in instigating growth within districts. Public policies have not always been the best of their kind; sometimes mistakes were made and sometimes obstacles of a political nature got in the way. What I will attempt to do now is draw the outlines of an ideal type of local governance, that is a model that will draw on types that exist in reality and that will capture the most typical and coherent characteristics of local systems geared towards development; considering that governance of local systems needs several elements, including non-political ones.

Districts will be better understood if they are not isolated from the broader regionalization processes that took place at the time of globalization. As a geographer has put it, the world is full of territorial, social and economic amalgams in search of political representation (A.J. Scott 2001). Local systems of various sizes, including anything from districts to metropolis, are sites of economic and social organization that can themselves be regarded, to some degree, as sole actors on the external stage. To get into shape these amalgams, that is to bring economy and society together, is the main function of politics as discussed above. This political action will promote and represent relatively coherent interests when they are applied to external action. In the fuller sense of the term, this action constitutes the 'governance' of a local system, which relies for its development on diverse local agents, and 'government' – that is, the set of public political authorities with their institutional functions – constitutes just one, albeit a crucial one, of these agents. Quite large local systems, IDs included, could involve – in opting for coordinate intervention – representatives from the local government, entrepreneurs, associations, banks, universities and foundations. Governance and the elaboration of emergent public policies are now based on this model, the same model I have dealt with and anticipated in the course of this discussion. Every agent remains independent and assumes responsibility for the decisions he takes; however a context sustained by institutionalized regulations to allow for cooperative decisions also makes it possible to coordinate and synchronize decisions on public and private investments.

The emergence of the interactive rule and cooperative frame of mind of the diverse players – just like the emergence of a relatively-shared image of the various possibilities that might occur in the course of the development of a local system – are, we must remember, developments that rely heavily on precise planning and political leadership that will demand new styles and new skills. A set of conditions must be created so that the various players – who could at any time break the rules of the local cooperative game (moving elsewhere), still find it would profit them to make congruent long-term investments. In this game, the local government will have to provide the appropriate infrastructures and will do so by respecting set deadlines; it will guarantee administrative efficiency but above all it contributes towards the formation of the collective subject; this is a feat of 'soft social engineering' which is responsible for the emergence of a developmental tendency that is shared by autonomous subjects who will contribute towards its creation setting up the building blocks of an architecture that will then form a local system.

This is the logic that drove the governance of district development even in the past. It regulated those districts operating on international markets by capitalizing on local system effects and by anticipating the drive towards regionalization at the time of globalization. As time went on, capital, people and resources were becoming increasingly mobile; agents, on the other hand, were finding it more and more difficult to find the resources needed within the same district. The game became complicated: market regulations, networking, social bonds are resources that belong to active governance, in conjunction, however, with the 'soft social engineering' mentioned earlier. The cooperative potential generated by this combination is 'appropriate' social capital that brings together mutual conveniences but also paves the way for a common vocabulary, mutual trust and acquaintances. Networks that are capable of coping with a given problem are also capable of coping with any other.

In the above discussion I have addressed an ideal type of local-system governance in a particular district; in other words, this is an analytical model borne out of a selection of observations drawn from concrete possibilities that capture the logic that governs a set of problems and possibilities that local agents have to deal with. In real life scenarios, conflicting views and interests give rise to conflicts that are followed by opportunistic behavior: the social capital generated and made available through governance can be more or less sufficient to deal with these problems; a social capital that comes equipped with the tools and institutional resources necessary to bring these conflicts to light and manage them is a fully-developed capital of governance.

A district cannot be taken out of its contextual framework. To start with there are certain problems that must be considered against a broader background (that of the infrastructures of transport and communications, for example): single district governance should be efficient in dealing with and prioritizing local necessities. More than one level of government participation is involved in local governance and each brings to local governance a baggage of particular competences. Mayors and local representatives are primarily responsible for local government, but so are the provinces, regions, national government and international unions. Any chaos that might result from laws that have not been well calibrated is a sign of bad governance. The governance of local systems might include more voluntaristic commitment, but many countries, including Italy, have experimented with laws designed to boost local development and create the conditions necessary to regulate and encourage coordination of diverse local agents. In Italy there is also an act that regulates IDs. Although these resources are open to misuse, they could also provide a framework for healthy local interactions (Consiglio italiano per le scienze sociali 2005).

6. AND TO CONCLUDE, ONE FINAL ISSUE

Can districts therefore be set up in places where they do not exist? No district – as already stated – has ever been set up by plan or decree. Indeed, the spontaneity of Italian districts seems to suggest that these can flourish only, when circumstances permit it, in the right time and the right place. But this is an excessive statement. Many places come already equipped with resources that can be drawn upon and with some traditional resources of social capital that acts as an asset in the development process.

The question regarding the possibility of setting up districts in places where they do not exist has already been addressed in Italy and scholars have come up with ambivalent results. Appropriate national and European schemes have been set up, the most notable of which is the 'territorial pacts' agreement that provides access to public funding in underdeveloped areas. The alleged aim of this scheme is to facilitate trust relations between public and private subjects with the double intent of designing and setting up projects for the development of infrastructures and improving services; and of triggering integrated entrepreneurial initiatives. It is evident in this case that an attempt was made to use the rationale of district development and some successful results were obtained in the production of public collective goods, cooperative networks between small firms, the elaboration of shared objectives, mutual trust and the simplification of administration governance processes.

Other cases, on the other hand, were not as successful as had been anticipated and this ended up by undermining the sense of trust in their potential. This happened when preexisting networks of local interests misused the opportunities offered, a particularized use of resources that were secured and redistributed but that were not invested in strategies that targeted development. We could argue that the social capital generated was not of the right kind, or that there was not enough of it for developmental governance. In cases such as these the district rationale fails to take off, or to generate districts. It is very likely that the initiative schemes on which they depended did not include measures to guarantee that the resources available were put to good use, or that their other shortcomings needed to be adjusted. The example of successful cases, even when these were difficult, show that the generation of social capital for developmental purposes is possible, and that the main obstacle lies in the social capital of those who have local interests at heart and who feel threatened by the drift towards modernization. An efficient local system designed to promote development is, in cases such as these, difficult because it calls for ruthless political intervention such as the eradication of existing social capital when this does not constitute a resource for development. Political action, however, must not fail to anticipate and aim for a kind of governance that draws on existing local resources. In a world that is increasingly drifting towards the redefinition of new regions, the creation of local systems, even in peripheral contexts, is a step that must be taken.

18. The new Argonauts, global search and local institution building

AnnaLee Saxenian and Charles Sabel

1. INTRODUCTION

The emergence of technology entrepreneurship and innovation outside, but closely connected to the advanced core of the world economy is one of the most striking features of contemporary capitalism. Israel and Taiwan, both small, peripheral agricultural economies in the post-war period, became home to dynamic clusters of entrepreneurial experimentation in the 1980s and 1990s. Today Taiwan's specialized producers define the state-of-the-art logistics and flexible manufacturing of low-cost, high-quality electronic systems. Israel, with a population of just over six million, is home to more than a hundred internet security and software-related technology companies listed on NASDAQ, more than any other country outside North America. In both countries venture capital systemically encourages the proliferation of companies that in effect co-design specialized components or subsystems for firms in the core economies.

The more recent emergence of clusters of, for example, software firms in mid-income developing economies like China and India is if anything more striking still. Vital urban hubs like Bangalore and Hangzhou are not only peripheral to the world economy, but are also located in large national economies that – (partial) liberalization of trade policy aside – lack most of the institutions economists view as preconditions for growth: the rule of law, secure property rights, good corporate governance, flexible labor markets, transparent capital markets, and so forth. If it is surprising that firms in the 'periphery' can co-design crucial components with firms in the core, then it is at least as surprising that institutions good enough to permit and sustain continuing growth can be built locally before such governance institutions are installed nationally, if at all.

This chapter looks at yet another surprising, but less understood, aspect of these cases that grows directly from the connection of the first two: the growing importance of global, or external, search networks that firms and other actors rely upon to locate collaborators who can either solve (part) of a problem they face, or require (part of) a solution they may be able to provide.[1] We focus here on the creation in emerging economies of publicly-supported institutions – venture capital in particular – organized to search systematically for, and foster the development of, firms and industries that can in turn collaborate in specialized co-design.

The emergence of venture capital in the periphery sheds light on current discussions in development economics of 'self discovery' – the search process by which an enterprise or entrepreneur determines what markets it can (come to be able to) serve (Hausmann and Rodrik 2002). The success of the new high-tech clusters strongly suggests that production is decomposable in ways that allow decentralized co-design of parts and their periodic re-integration into complex wholes. Enterprises in these clusters systematically look for collaborators who are already solving (parts of) the problems they face, rather than trying to elaborate comprehensive solutions on their own.[2] At the same time as production is becoming more collaborative, relying more and more on co-design, so too is the process of self-discovery. Firms and entrepreneurs seeking to enter a new market must demonstrate not just the ability to produce a certain component or product, but also the ability to improve its design or the process by which it is produced in cooperation with the potential customer and their suppliers (Sabel and Zeitlin 2004).

Producers in less developed economies face distinct challenges when seeking to enter these partnerships, and increasingly require bundles of inputs or services – standards, certification, *de facto* property rights, and specific regulations – that only public authorities can provide. This means that self-discovery also typically entails collaborative search with (parts of) government for institutional solutions that will facilitate certain kinds of transactions. Thus understood, self-discovery shades into open-ended industrial policy: a process by which firms and governments collaborate in the identification and pursuit of promising opportunities for development.[3]

This chapter examines the creation of venture capital in emerging economies as an illustration of the way that public and private actors, building on networks they 'find', can construct an institution that systematically creates further networks to foster and monitor the progress of new firms and industries. We focus on the case of Taiwan, where highly-skilled first-generation immigrant professionals in US technology industries collaborated with their home country counterparts to develop the context for entrepreneurial development. The chapter refers to the members of these networks as the new Argonauts, an allusion to Jason and the Argonauts who millennia ago sailed in search of the Golden Fleece, testing their mythic heroism while seeking earthly riches and glory. While most of the evidence here is drawn from Taiwan, relevant aspects of analogue developments in Israel, India and China are considered as well.

Our central argument is that new Argonauts are ideally positioned (as both insiders and outsiders at home and abroad) to search beyond prevailing routines to identify opportunities for complementary 'peripheral' participation in the global economy, and to work with public officials on the corresponding adaptation and redesign of relevant institutions and firms in their native countries. They are, in other words, exemplary protagonists of the process of self-discovery or open industrial policy – though surely there are in other contexts different institutional arrangements that are as exemplary as well. We argue further that in the cases considered here, the Argonauts' contributions to domestic institution building crystallized most clearly in the development of domestic venture capital, one of the, if not the most important, supports for technology entrepreneurship.

Venture capital is itself a powerful search network: it is an institution for identifying and combining pieces of companies – finance, technical expertise, marketing know-how, business model, standard-setting capacity and so on. Once integrated, these enterprises succeed by becoming nodes in the search networks for designing and building products in their domain. By supporting a diverse portfolio of ventures, and combining hands-on monitoring and mentoring with market selection, investors in developing countries are thus institutionalizing a process of continuous economic restructuring – and learning about how to improve restructuring itself – that transforms the domestic economy by linking it to the most demanding and capable actors in global markets.

The new Argonauts are therefore at once the product of search networks among the professionals and companies for whom they have worked and with which they associate, and – in collaboration with parts of government and other domestic public institutions – the co-architects of further networks that extend and adapt to home-country conditions the web of relations they already know.

Networks of overseas professionals are central to this story so we begin with the role of diasporas in development. Section 2 reviews the current debates to claim that the most enduring contributions of skilled professionals to their home countries are not direct transfers of technology or knowledge, but participation in the process of external search and domestic institutional reform. We argue that the focus on the high-skill diaspora as an asset has obscured processes of micro-level reform that, diffusing and cascading, can ultimately produce structural transformations.

Section 3 situates search networks with respect to current debates about the structuring principles of the new, global economy. We show that these networks are based on and transmit knowledge that is more formalized than that circulating in the local networks typical of clusters (where knowledge is, at the limit, purely tacit), but less complete than the knowledge said to flow in modular global production networks (where knowledge is assumed to be fully explicit). The following Section 4 illustrates this argument with the example of the creation of the venture-capital industry in Taiwan, which provided the context for entrepreneurial growth in high-tech clusters. The final coda draws early conclusions for our understandings of the process of institutional reform and economic development.

2. DIASPORAS AND DEVELOPMENT

In spite of the outpouring of research in the past decade, evidence that diaspora networks taken as various forms of intellectual capital or as 'knowledge networks' have a positive impact on economic development is limited. Diasporas are not new phenomena, nor is the interest of policymakers and scholars in their developmental potential.[4] What is new, or relatively so, is the focus of recent research and policy on the highly-educated (e)migrants who have long been viewed as a serious loss to poor economies (the brain drain). Low transportation and communications costs now allow those who go abroad for further training or in search of work to interact and collaborate with their home-country counterparts far more extensively than was feasible in earlier eras of emigration. A small but growing number of migrants have even become fully 'transnational' – with dual citizenship and residences in both their home and their adopted countries.

Early research on diaspora contributions investigated remittances or direct investments, which can provide a stable source of finance and alleviate poverty, but typically have limited long-term impact. The recent literature, by contrast, suggests that skilled migrants can alter the development trajectory of a poor country through the diffusion of knowledge and/or technology transfers – as for example in the shift from a brain drain of talent away from the home country to 'brain circulation' between it and the core economies (Saxenian, Motoyama and Quan 2002). Despite this attention to positive development impacts, much of the newer literature (and the public policies with which it is in dialog) continues to treat the diaspora as an asset, valuable insofar as it adds to the home country's stock of capital not through remittances but in intellectual property or reputational capital or related forms of wealth. There is, however, little evidence that diasporas have contributed substantially to development in this way.

The most direct mechanism for transferring intellectual capital to the home country would be for the highly-educated migrants to return to work. Yet in spite of the aggressive recruitment efforts of home-country policymakers, and some evidence of rising return rates (from a very low base) in places like India and China, there is no evidence that educated migrants to the US and other advanced economies are substantially more likely to return permanently to their home economies than they were a decade or two ago. Nor is there evidence that the brain drain has abated, except in small countries that have experienced rapid growth, such as Taiwan.[5]

Some researchers suggest that there is a diaspora effect in scientific collaboration by documenting how knowledge, as measured by patent citations and co-authorship, flows disproportionately among members of the same ethnic community, even over long distances (Agrawal, Kapur and McHale 2004; Jin et al. 2007; W. Kerr 2008). Yet efforts to demonstrate that diaspora scientific collaboration contributes to economic growth in the home country remain unconvincingly incomplete. Above all they have not identified a causal mechanism by which the findings of collaborative research are usefully transferred to firms and other domestic actors.

Research in related areas has yielded similarly promising but incomplete findings. Studies have found, for instance, that ethnic networks in the US increase trade with the home country, suggesting that a diaspora can help to reduce reputational and informational barriers to trade (Kapur 2001; Lucas 2005). Similarly case studies suggest that diaspora members can for the same reasons help direct corporate investments or contracts toward their home country. However the most significant findings from both the quantitative studies and the extensive case-study research come from a small number of Asian cases, particularly China and India (Lowell and Gerova 2004; Lucas 2005). As critics point out, there are many more cases of failed attempts to mobilize diaspora contributions to development, from Armenia to Argentina, which remain unexplained in current frameworks.

The rise of dynamic clusters in the periphery, and the experience of the new Argonauts generally, suggest that the debate on diasporas and development has been misdirected. The increased salience of diaspora networks to economic development does not lie in the direct contribution of assets, but rather in their role in the design and construction of new institutions in their home countries. While these contributions are often incremental, thus difficult to detect and even more difficult to quantify, over time they have the potential to create a context that supports self-sustaining growth.

In part because of the treatment of diasporas as assets, discussions focus on the macro-level: the relation of 'the' diaspora to 'its' home country. They overlook the internal heterogeneity of the diaspora, as well as the heterogeneity of the economy and the public sector in developing (as well as the developed) nations. The new Argonauts, for example, are only a subset of the diaspora, normally first-generation emigrants who work with ease in the institutions and environment of their home country, where they continue to have friends, family and colleagues. (Second- or third-generation immigrants, even if they speak the language of their country of origin, have greater difficulty doing business there because they lack both these personal connections and first-hand knowledge of local institutions and culture).

The spatial differentiation of economic activity typically linked to industrial specialization (another manifestation of heterogeneity) means that a focus on national indicators and institutions can obscure critical transformations occurring at a subnational level.[6] Likewise the State, in developing as well as in developed counterparts, is not a unified whole, but rather consists of multiple, differently organized units with varying political and economic resources, jurisdictions, and interests. Yet it is precisely this heterogeneity that permits innovation and growth within a generally hostile context (Kuznetsov and Sabel 2005).

The new Argonauts bring to their home countries expertise in specific industries that are located in a small number of urban areas or regions, and they collaborate only with a subset of domestic entrepreneurs and policymakers. This means that economic and institutional change begins in certain locations and/or domains, and advances through partial and incremental (micro-level) reforms that only with time aggregate into larger scale transformations. Only by disaggregating the diaspora and its interactions with (parts of) the equally differentiated public and private sectors it is possible to see whether and eventually how they are (re)building the institutions of economic development.

A small example from India illustrates how a micro-level reform can facilitate matching of collaborators, and how such reform can diffuse. In the early

1990s Indian products in general were suspect because of their reputation as low quality. Quality problems in software were an important obstacle to collaboration between local suppliers and customers in world markets. In software the problem was not particular to India: almost from the beginning of large software development projects, such as the operating system for the IBM 360 in the 1960s, it has been well known that quality problems can arise from the very partitioning of tasks which allows different groups to work on separate parts of programs simultaneously. Fixing performance specifications for each 'chunk' or module of the program introduces ambiguities which only come to light as defects when the parts are finally connected to each other (Brooks 1995). Anticipating this problem an Indian engineer from the Software Engineering Institute (SEI) at Carnegie-Mellon University traveled to Bangalore to speak at software firms about the institute's recently introduced 'capability maturity model' (CMM) for software engineering process improvement. The core of the CMM is a process of periodic peer review of development 'pieces' to ensure, by ongoing clarification of specifications, that the rate of error detection is higher than the rate of 'error injection'. Many firms immediately picked up the idea and sponsored conferences and consultations on the topic. By the end of the decade virtually all large Indian software companies had adopted the CMM. Today India is widely recognized for its high-quality software development processes; the country has more SEI-CMM Level V (the top level) certified companies than any other.

The development of a globally competitive software services and technology industry in Bangalore involved a multiplicity of similar micro-level reforms, both within the cluster and externally. In this case the best practice in software engineering processes was transferred to Indian firms as soon as they were being developed. Indeed the most extensive and practical guide to the use of the quality model today is a study of its application and development at Infosys, one of India's largest and most successful software firms, and published by the SEI (Jalotte 2000). Such changes occur incrementally, and there is no guarantee that they will continue. But, as we will see in detail in Section 4, when they accumulate, they have the potential to alter the institutional fabric of the economy.

3. GLOBAL SEARCH NETWORKS AND CROSS-REGIONAL COLLABORATION

The focus of the discussion so far on connections between the new Argonauts and Silicon Valley invites the objection that the construction of search networks is founded on, and therefore limited to the prior, 'natural' occurrence of tacit knowledge of technologies and persons associated with industrial clusters or professional and technical 'communities of practice' generally (Lave and Wenger 1991; Brown and Duguid 2000a). Indeed one pole in current discussion of links among firms in the emerging global economy sees that economy as a shift away from coordination by managerial hierarchies in vertically integrated firms towards informal coordination among networks of independent companies. These relations are said to be long term and grounded in 'informal restraints on self-interested behavior' (Lamoreaux, Raff and Temin 2003, p. 62). This view generalizes to the economy at large the stylized experiences of the industrial districts (IDs) or clusters, based on local cultures of trust, and the co-design relations among Japanese automobile firms and their subcontractor, based on an ethos of reciprocity, as these were understood in the 1990s. At the limit this view suggests the information needed to initiate, engage in and judge the performance of collaboration must be so deeply embedded in particular social relations that it is possible to foster collaboration institutionally only when social connections have become so dense and reliable that it is almost superfluous to do so.

However accurate this view may have been of the tacit or 'cultural' coordination of flexible networks of firms in past decades, it ignores the extent to which formalization of key aspects of collaboration is not only possible but necessary to sustain the co-design relations prevailing today. Recall the CMM method of software engineering process improvement and its use of peer review of development 'pieces' to reduce errors. The CMM is just one of a wide array of similar devices for creating information pooling regimes in which cooperating firms can teach each other to be better collaborators even as they monitor one another's capacities and intentions to do so.[7] Thus it is routine in contracts between, for instance, producers of computers or automobiles and suppliers of key components to specify not only acceptable quality levels but target rates of price reduction, procedures for jointly and regularly reviewing progress towards all these goals, agreeing on joint action when necessary to achieve them, and periodic consultation on emergent features of the next-generation components. Analogous regimes are common between firms co-developing new drugs or innovative computer hard or software.

These regimes do not of course eliminate the need for personal connections among buyers and sellers. But they do make a firm's capacities and disposition to cooperate much more accessible not only to current but also potential partners than the informal, tacit view of linkages suggests. Because the regimes make it easier for firms to scan the world, they make it easier for the firm to find partners itself; because in scanning successfully the firm becomes known for its ability to search, the regimes make it more attractive to potential partners (Gilson et al. 2008). Thus the new nature of inter-firm networks facilitates rather than obstructs the creation of higher order search networks and open industrial policy, formalizing the information exchange that give rise to the metrics on which venture capital and like institutions depend in the monitoring performance of firms with which they are engaged.

The prevalence of these collaborative, information-pooling regimes also casts substantial doubt on the modular view of inter-firm links at the opposite pole of current discussion of the global economy. In this view collaborative knowledge is not tacit and informal but rather fully explicit and formalized: new design and production tools allow development of technical standards and design rules that standardize the interfaces between organizationally-separate stages of production. This standardization so drastically reduces the volume of information required for inter-firm coordination that products can be decomposed into distinct and further decomposable modules, each produced in virtual isolation from the others (Sturgeon 2002; Langlois 2003, p. 374).

Some codification of this kind is obviously necessary to allow specialist producers to focus on their specializations. But too much codification just as obviously becomes a barrier to systematic innovation, locking component manufacturers and those who combine their products into more complex wholes into potentially obsolete product architectures (Sabel and Zeitlin 2004). Hence the prevalence, among all but the least sophisticated producers, of the information pooling regimes just noted, whose goal is the continuing elaboration of product and process specification, and the consideration of alternatives – not the clarification of fixed standards. So common are regimes of this type that 'their' organization – the way in which quality control information is to be collected and evaluated – has itself been standardized.

A more graphic demonstration of the limits of this view is the rapidly evolving relation between the economic core and periphery in general, and Silicon Valley and Taiwan and Israel in particular. The model of modular networks, with a relatively stable and hierarchical production chain dominated by global flagship producers, suggests that there is no potential for engineering improvements and innovation at any level of the supply chain but the top. In spatial terms there is no room in a fully modular world for indigenous entrepreneurship and innovation outside the core.

Development in Taiwan demonstrates the opportunities for innovation in the periphery, even at the lowest level of the supply chain. By the early 1990s Taiwan had become a highly efficient and flexible producer of low-cost integrated circuits, components, and motherboards – and left new product definition, high-end design, and equipment manufacturing to Silicon Valley. Producers in both regions benefited from distinctive capabilities that allowed them to deepen their specialized expertise, in part by recombining it with that of other specialists. A decade later Taiwan's firms had significantly upgraded their design and manufacturing capabilities; they were not only designing and making increasingly sophisticated and complex components such as LCD screens, microprocessors, and miniature optical components for cameras, but they were also responsible for the logistics and final integration of advanced products like laptop PCs and mobile devices. They simultaneously moved their high volume manufacturing to the Chinese mainland, where they could exploit economies of scale and lower cost inputs.

Open or external search networks, such as those that helped create venture capital in Taiwan, represent an intermediate form between the tacit networks of IDs and the fully explicit networks of modular production systems (Becattini and Rullani 1996a). Actors in these networks contribute, through intensive information exchange and comparisons, to the construction of shared, domain-specific understandings and languages (or interpretations) that allow them to search for new models of products and of organizing production, even in distant localities, and to collaborate in incorporating these new possibilities into existing practice. This process blurs the boundaries among firms, industries and regional economies – and, perhaps most fundamentally of all, between linkages and organizations that arise or are 'found', and those that can by reflection and design be made.

4. INSTITUTIONALIZING VENTURE CAPITAL: THE TAIWAN CASE

The collaboration of overseas Chinese professionals with government officials in Taiwan to create a venture-capital industry exemplifies the contribution of global search to domestic institution building. The institutionalization of venture capital was a critical turning point for Taiwan. It ensured that a few, isolated early entrepreneurial successes were followed by growing investment and collective learning in the electronics-related industries. Ultimately it supported the creation of a self-reinforcing cluster, or critical mass, of firms.

The creation of venture capital in Taiwan also shows how such institution building is enabled by, and helps encourage, new political alliances rooted in the incipient forms of cooperation that it fosters. The reform was initiated by an entrepreneurial ex-finance minister who leveraged both the search capabilities and the political influence of the diaspora to mobilize support for initiatives that were strongly opposed by older-line policymakers and traditional industries.

Last, but perhaps most importantly, the collaborative construction of venture capital in Taiwan shows how search networks can transform and give new meaning to the institutions they connect and to 'import'. Venture capital in Taiwan was as much a means of reorienting the country's emerging high-tech economy from competition to collaborative complementarity with Silicon Valley firms, and of redirecting investment by old-line industry and cautious commercial banks and family networks, as it was a tool for providing finance to start-ups that otherwise could not find it.

In the 1970s Taiwan was a poor, agricultural nation. Its economy was controlled by a combination of State-owned enterprises (in finance and strategic industrial sectors) and risk-averse family-owned and run businesses.[8] The 'high-tech' manufacturing sector consisted mainly of low-end, labor-intensive firms manufacturing calculators and electronic components almost exclusively for foreign customers. Intellectual property rights were notoriously disregarded, allowing in the early 1980s for the reverse engineering and production of 'clones' of the IBM PC and Apple's MAC. Few would have predicted that entrepreneurs in this peripheral economy would compete in the most technologically advanced sectors of the world economy. Yet by the end of the 1990s Taiwan was a leading center of technology entrepreneurship; today its specialized semiconductor and computer-related firms define the state-of-the-art logistics and manufacturing of low-cost, high-quality electronic systems.

Scholarly accounts of the growth of Taiwan's technology sector typically focus on a farsighted development strategy focused on industrial 'catch up', and particularly the transfer of leading-edge semiconductor technology through the creation of institutions like the Industrial Technology Research Institute (ITRI), a public–private research agency, and the Hsinchu Science-based Industrial Park (HSIP) (Mathews and Cho 1999; Amsden and Chu 2003). Yet they leave a puzzle. How did domestic policymakers manage to identify and supply precisely the institutional pieces required to support entrepreneurial growth in a highly-competitive global economy – particularly when many other nations, often far better endowed, tried and failed to develop venture capital and technology industries in the same period?

The answer to this puzzle is that the growth of the sector was only in part a planned or designed process; and the part that was designed was aimed less at moving Taiwan to a well-defined technology frontier than at creating institutions for identifying and pursuing appropriate economic opportunities – search networks. A plainly unplanned but crucial part was the decision by tens of thousands of Taiwan's most talented university students to pursue engineering graduate degrees in the US in the 1960s and 1970s. A majority took jobs in the US after graduation because the professional and economic opportunities in regions like Silicon Valley far exceeded anything then available in Taiwan. Policymakers complained bitterly about these losses and even sought to control them. None foresaw that the 'brain drain' might prove advantageous.

The initial adjustment of the job seekers to their new environment was also spontaneous. As outsiders in Silicon Valley the immigrants created technical associations and alumni networks that allowed them to find one another, as well as to stay in touch with their counterparts at home. Some participated in government-sponsored policy discussions or gave talks at universities and technical conferences in Taiwan but few considered returning home permanently.

The decision not to return home was as self-evident as the decision to go abroad in the first place: Taiwan's personal computer industry in the early 1980s was small and fragile, in spite of sizable public investments in higher education and technology research, and the efforts of the handful of entrepreneurs who did go back. The HSIP opened in 1980, but was unable to find tenants in spite of aggressive efforts to lure multinationals, including those run by Chinese.

The turning point, and the beginning of a deliberate policy – in the sense of a strategy for building institutions to fix and revise strategies – came in the early 1980s when Minister without a Portfolio, Kuo-Ting Li, formed an alliance with a group of foreign advisors, including members of the diaspora, to establish a venture-capital industry in Taiwan. Li, an engineer, headed both the Ministry of Economic Affairs (1965–69) and then Ministry of Finance (1969–76), and traveled regularly to Silicon Valley during the 1960s and 1970s to seek the advice of Chinese engineers and entrepreneurs on making Taiwanese industry more globally competitive. He was particularly impressed with the region's emerging venture-capital industry and the support it created for entrepreneurship.

By 1982, after mobilizing support from leading domestic entrepreneurs and policy leaders, Li convinced the ministry of finance to introduce legislation to create, develop and regulate venture capital in Taiwan, including comprehensive tax incentives and financial assistance. The concept of venture capital, uncontroversial today, was foreign to the Taiwanese of the day, where family members closely controlled all the financial affairs of a business. Leaders of traditional industries such as chemicals and textiles opposed Li's ideas. So did an influential consultant to the government, Dr Simon Ramo (a pioneer of systems engineering), who argued that Taiwan lacked the capabilities to develop a venture-capital industry.

Supporters of the project understood that venture capital would play a different role in Taiwan than in the US, and that the difference would help redirect the developing economy in a crucial way. They argued that rather than trying to replicate the high-level research and technological innovation of places like Silicon Valley, Taiwan should exploit its own strengths: a supply of relatively low-cost, high-skilled engineers. In this view, Taiwan would position itself to develop commercial applications derived from US innovations, and lower skill, mass production could be carried out elsewhere. Li envisioned the HSIP as the place for Taiwanese entrepreneurs to undertake this commercialization, collaborating with each other and with foreign companies. The availability of venture capital, and the networking and mentoring that it provides in addition to finance, would be key to this strategy.

Proponents of Li's vision recognized that the conservatism of Taiwan's established financial institutions was a major hindrance to the incubation of high-technology ventures. Most financial institutions at that time were commercial banks, which provided only mortgage or debt financing. The risk aversion of the government officials who managed the public 'Development Fund' and other financial-incentive programs limited the ability of these capital sources to spawn risky new technology enterprises. Only a publicly supported venture-capital industry would provide sufficient capital for such high-risk, high-return ventures.

In addition Taiwan's businesses were overwhelmingly (95 per cent) small and medium-sized enterprises and most, as we have noted, were family-run. Family-owned and managed enterprises of this type were typically oriented toward survival, rather than growth, and had little incentive to adopt modern management techniques. Policymakers believed that a venture-capital industry could help promote the introduction of modern financial and management skills by institutionalizing the separation of ownership and control. Finally, proponents understood that the introduction of venture capital would entail the development of a public capital market that provided an exit option for investments in start-ups.

Close scrutiny of the US experience had taught Li's group both that Taiwan could profit from domestic venture capital, but also that the country lacked the relevant institutional know-how to start a venture-capital industry and the incentives to draw local actors into the process. Policymakers therefore organized collaborations with large US financial institutions to facilitate the transfer of relevant financial and managerial expertise. For example, young Taiwanese were sent to the US to be trained venture-capital management. The ministry of finance created tax incentives to encourage domestic firms to enter the venture-capital industry; 20 per cent of the capital invested in strategic (technology-intensive) ventures by individual or corporate investors was tax-deductible for up to five years. The ministry also offered substantial matching funds through a 'Seed Fund' with NT$800 million from the Executive Yuan Development Fund. In addition regulation governing Security and Exchange was modified to support the development of a public capital market.

But even with these incentives, development was hesitant. When Acer founded Taiwan's first venture-capital firm in 1984 as a joint venture with the old-line Continental Engineering Group, there were no followers. K.T. Li then invited the overseas Chinese community to establish venture capital businesses in Taiwan. In response Ta-Lin Hsu, a former IBM executive based in Silicon Valley, set up Hambrecht & Quist Asia Pacific. Hsu reports that it was not easy to raise the initial $50 million fund: Li 'twisted lots of arms' to raise $26 million from leading Taiwanese industrial groups such as Far East Textile and President Enterprises. The balance came from the government.[9] A year later, in 1987, two other overseas Chinese engineers also responded to Li's invitation, establishing the Walden International Investment Group (WIIG), Taiwan's second US-style venture fund, as a branch of the San Francisco-based Walden Group. Both H&Q Asia Pacific and WIIG raised capital for the new funds with relative ease from the Silicon Valley's overseas Chinese who were already familiar with venture capital.

Taiwan's venture-capital industry took off only after these investments showed significant returns – after companies like Acer were publicly listed on the Taiwan stock exchange in the late 1980s. The 'Seed Fund' with matching grants for venture investments was depleted and the Executive Yuan committed a second fund of NT$1.6 billion that was also allocated quickly. Domestic IT firms such as UMC, D-Link, Mitac, and Winbond created their own venture funds to invest in new technology businesses, as did established corporations that had been reluctant earlier to get involved in the 'new economy'.

The emergence of Taiwan's venture-capital industry and the early successes of venture-backed start-ups attracted growing numbers of overseas Chinese to return from the US to start businesses. Miin Wu, a Stanford graduate who worked in Silicon Valley for over a decade before returning in 1988 to start Macronix International, one of Taiwan's first semiconductor companies, in HSIP with funding from H&Q Asia Pacific, is a well-known example. The availability of venture capital finally transformed HSIP into a fertile environment for the growth of indigenous technology firms. By 1996 over 2500 engineers and scientists had returned to work in the science park and 40 per cent of the 203 companies based in the park were started by returnees. The industry remained highly localized as it grew, with the personal computer industry in greater Taipei region and semiconductor and component firms in Hsinchu, creating a corridor roughly the same size as the Silicon Valley cluster.

The availability of venture capital in the 1980s also distinguished Taiwan from the rest of Asia: outside of Taiwan, capital was then available in the region only to large corporations with ties to governments or to wealthy families. One measure of the success of Taiwan's venture-capital industry is the performance of venture-funded firms in public capital markets. Ten of the 32 new ventures started in the HSIP in 1996 received funding from local venture funds. By 1998 over 130 venture-funded companies were listed on the Taiwan stock exchange and some forty were listed on NASDAQ.

The new Argonauts have influenced policy in other developing nations, using best practices and models from Silicon Valley to lever open and animate discussion of institutional reform in their home countries.[10] In Taiwan and elsewhere, policymakers and entrepreneurs clearly learned from the Silicon Valley model; some even believed that they were replicating that model. But in solving problems of domestic economic development by adapting venture capital to domestic contexts, they changed both the model and the contexts themselves. They also helped transform Silicon Valley, in ways that suggest the broad generalizability of these experiences to other industries and settings.

5. CONCLUSION

The experience of the new Argonauts in creating venture capital in peripheral locations such as Taiwan suggests that development today is a process of experimentation and learning in particular contexts. Economic decentralization creates possibilities for entrepreneurs almost anywhere in the world to identify promising opportunities at many points along supply chains. Diasporas, especially in the form of professional communities like the new Argonauts, can begin to connect suppliers and customers, producers and policymakers. But even in the presence of the social bonds and trust that grow from shared ethnic identities, the challenges of self-discovery – of identifying appropriate partners in a decentralized economy and of ensuring the public inputs needed to work with them – remain substantial. The crucial step in reducing the obstacles to faster, more sustained growth occurs when individuals, firms and policymakers jointly create institutions, or search networks, that extend the connections, not least by creating more nodes and links in currently-existing networks, and by connecting them to others.

Venture capital can serve as a powerful search network in developing economies when the investors have global as well as local connections. By supporting a diverse portfolio of ventures, and combining hands-on monitoring and mentoring with market selection, they are institutionalizing a process of continuous economic restructuring – and learning about how to improve the institutions of restructuring – that transforms the domestic economy by linking it to the most demanding and capable actors in global markets. In other contexts such search networks have taken the form of publicly-supported supply chain development and quality assurance programs.

Put another way, search networks can help link partners in micro-level innovations in public institutions and the organization of production. Over time these changes can cumulate into, or inform programs for larger scale transformations that 'endow' the economy with institutions that, on some views of development, it would have needed to grow in the first place. Learning more about how this contemporary form of economic development was possible in places where – improbable at first – it has already occurred can teach how it might be done in settings where it seems today unimaginable.

NOTES

1. See Sabel (2005a) which argues that search routines offer an alternative to the hierarchical decomposition of tasks as a solution to the problem of bounded rationality in organizations.
2. If this were not the case it would be impossible for high-tech clusters to emerge in developing economies by specializing in complex components or special-purpose software, and to grow by collaborating more and more closely with their customers in the elaboration of successive, more sophisticated generations and generalizations of the original specialties.
3. See Hausmann, Rodrik and Sabel (2008) and generally Rodrik (2007).
4. See, for example, Lowell and Gerova (2004); Kapur and McHale (2005); Lucas (2005); Brinkerhoff (2006); Kuznetsov (2006); Saxenian (2006).
5. Ironically there is now concern in policy circles in Taiwan that they have lost the 'bridge' to Silicon Valley as a result – at least implicitly recognizing the importance of the diaspora as a search network.
6. The literature on national institutions and development overlooks the evidence from India, China and many other cases suggesting that parts of economies grow rapidly and reliably even if the wholes to which they are connected do not have the institutions thought to be necessary for growth. The evidence suggests that the institutions of governance sufficiently 'good' to permit and encourage sustained growth can be built piecemeal, in particular sectors of the economy, and the regions in which they are located, in advance of comprehensive, national reform. No one looking only, say, at national legislation (or its absence) regarding property rights in China would have been able to predict the country's growth.
7. On such 'pragmatist' mechanisms such as benchmarking, simultaneous engineering, and 'root cause' error detection and correction, see Helper, MacDuffie, and Sabel (2000). All of these generate information for collaborative improvement or design innovation by triggering 'routine questioning of routines'.
8. Taiwan's per capita GNP in 1962 was US$170, on par with Zaire and the Congo.
9. Interview with Ta-Lin Hsu, San Francisco, CA, 1 June 1997.
10. Israel's venture-capital industry also grew out of the experimentation by a coalition of policymakers and overseas engineers and entrepreneurs. As in Taiwan, early initiatives faced considerable opposition, and success grew from improvements on failures (Avnimelech and Teubal 2004). For the cases of China and India, see Saxenian (2006).

19. Web of rules in industrial districts' labour markets

Jean Saglio

1. INTRODUCTION

Efficient labour markets are a major factor for the development of local firms in industrial districts (ID), since, like most small and medium-sized firms, ID firms do not internalize and control the regulation of labour and industrial relations. Most ID analysts would agree that such local labour markets (LLMs) are very active, especially in providing a pool and a supply of labour with the key skills needed within IDs; besides local entrepreneurs can also rely on a LLM where there is a high local labour mobility, and local customs rule earnings determination and labour relations. Paradoxically, whilst such a statement is quite well accepted, studies directly focused on exploring such aspect are quite rare (Daumas, Lamard and Tissot 2007, p. 31).

Marshall (1920) underlined this resource, which was later echoed by Kerr in his definition of labour markets:

> Employers are apt to resort to any place where they are likely to find a good choice of workers with the special skill which they require; while men seeking employment naturally go to places where there are many employers who need such skill as theirs and where therefore it is likely to find a good market. (C. Kerr 1954, p. 98)

Sebastiano Brusco, in his seminal 1982 essay, also focused on Emilia-Romagna's labour market considered by him as a basic resource for local economic performance. He described a segmented labour market, where, as usual in such analysis, large firms with strong trade unions were the primary sector, whereas employees in small firms and self-employed people in IDs were the secondary sectors. Some of the latter were craftsmen with very specialised skills and had pretty good working and wage conditions, but most employees in these secondary sectors endured bad employment and working conditions, low wages and employment uncertainty. However, such a system could adapt to economic variations of uncertain demand.

Such an analysis underlined the importance but foremost the difficulties in studying labour markets in IDs. Obviously, as a start, it is quite important to understand the social processes of manning, as well as skilling and manpower adaptation to economic variations. But, at the same time, the web of rules that regulates these labour markets is mainly informal and unstable, as Marshall observed with respect to local skills. Some important institutions for the LLMs, as universities in the new high-technology IDs, are regulated outside. Some collective strategies, notably those of employers lie on improbable returns and out-market resources (Saglio 1991). Social exchange (Blau 1964) is a useful concept to describe such relations: employment relations – and many other economic relations such as, for instance, subcontracting ones – are not fully embedded in formal contracts. Family circles, school networks and ethnic groups are also not only possible resources, but also institutions which give value to these economic behaviours. Local rules of games often mix competition and cooperation either in economic relations between the local firms or in labour markets (Brusco 1999).

Using our observations in the plastic moulding ID around the French town of Oyonnax (Raveyre and Saglio 1984; Saglio 1997) and results described in literature, I shall show that labour markets analysis may improve our understanding of economic dynamics in IDs. The first problem is to identify the various institutions involved in labour markets' local regulation. By focusing the analysis on the specialised part of the labour market, one can have a better understanding of the local process of firm foundation. Regulation does not coincide with consensus, and labour markets analysis will also shed some light in showing how local conflicts and crises are dealt with.

2. LABOUR MARKETS AS LOCAL INSTITUTIONS

Clark Kerr's classical definition of labour markets put the emphasis on the local history contingency of such markets' delimitation. Local markets are locations that employers use to seek employees and employees use to seek employment (C. Kerr 1954). Balkanised markets have few influences on each other. Conversely, in the 'segmentation' theory of labour markets (Berger and Piore 1980) there are linkages between the various segments, and the dynamics of the primary segments explain situations in secondary ones. Brusco first hypothesised using this segmentation interpretation (Brusco 1982), although he also noticed signs of relative autonomy in the regulation of IDs' labour markets, especially in wages determination. ID existence implies there is some strategic coordination, especially between the employers and local government. Collective actions for housing, schooling and training are quite common, being those areas where some autonomy for local actors is possible. Such collective actions, when existing, create a local 'common ideology' (Dunlop 1958): each actor knows the expected roles and strategies of others, and they share a common system of interpretations of actions inside the local system. Such an approach is similar to the approach where IDs are seen as 'epistemic communities' (Håkanson 2005), although it is focused mainly on labour market regulation.

Such a regulation (Reynaud 1989) is rather a system of conflicts resolution than a consensus. Carnevali (2004) underlined rightly that inside IDs, conflicts are frequent and survival rests more on the collective ability to provide conflict resolution than to avoid them. As usual in the history of industrial relations (Commons 1909) conflicts have been stages for ID modernisation (Cottereau 1997). As we tried to establish for the Oyonnax district (Raveyre and Saglio 1984), this autonomy hypothesis leads to a better understanding of internal dynamics and regulation.

Even without any formalisation and common formulation, customs and informal rules regulate the LLM. Employers know what they have to do in order to find skills they need; employees know what – wages and employment conditions – they may expect from employment. Everybody knows the institutions usually in charge of information, manpower training or conflicts arbitration. ID labour markets are then a form of 'internal labour markets' (Doeringer and Piore 1971) where most of the rules are only informal. These rules often regulate behaviours and manage various competition areas: for instance, the no-poaching rule is frequently informal (Billette and Carrier 1993) and conform firms' interactions when concerned with technical or trade competition, since it may be a way to limit, or support, technical spillover. When the firms' average size is small, the external regulations rule and apply to many economic actors – and notably labour relations – which would be internalised in larger organisations. When collective actions are necessary, and this is quite usual in the local dynamics, rules become complex and relate to various aspects, such as the collective management of jobs allocation, earnings determination, employees' careers and mobility, and formal or informal process of disputes resolution. Migration policy, schooling and housing programs, as well as mechanisms for knowledge spillovers, research and technological policies may also be linked with such regulations.

Many local institutions may be concerned with LLMs: education and training are the main areas of collective and public actions. In the early 20th century in Oyonnax, a local public school was created and devoted to clerks' training; while workers' technical training was mainly on the job and in the local union *Bourse du Travail*. After the Second World War, the same school opened a new training section for metallurgists and moulders for local industry; finally, after the mid-1970s crisis, a new school of plastic moulding engineers was further added to match the need of local skills. This experience helps understand the coevolution between the industrial base and the related jobs, and school training. In a similar way, high-technology clusters need highly-skilled labour and for this reason they tend to develop close to major universities with their innovation infrastructure. Nevertheless, on-the-job training and the benefits of mobility, even in new forms, can still be present in these new technology clusters (Trigilia 2001).

In old IDs, gender, ethnic and local origins are often linked with schooling in recognised skills and jobs allocation. During the early 1970s in Oyonnax, understanding jobs allocation rules was easy: unskilled workers and plastic moulders were men, non-European immigrants (Turkish and North Africans); foremen were European migrants men (Italian and Portuguese); skilled mould makers were French men; clerks were French women and non-European immigrant women were home workers, assemblers and stickers. The same findings were true for many large French firms before the Second World War: networks and migrations flux were the way of manning many large firms; in a situation where training is mainly on the job, social networks are the way to assure the success of social integration for the new employee. Employees' skills depended on their origin (Burdy 1989).

Local government may use a housing program to support an economic policy: after the mid-1970s local crisis, Oyonnax local government, led by a mayor who was a member of the French Communist Party, developed a program for housing that welcomed middle-class and technically-skilled workers and their families rather than only blue collar workers as before. This local government was also strongly involved in the creation of the local engineering school. Clearly, such political choices were driven by the belief that large-scale, mass production targeted at the low end of the markets was coming to a close for the local industry. The action taken to shape the LLM via a careful housing policy resulted in an economic strategy to strengthen the ID.

Which institutions are frequently involved in manpower production and jobs allocation? In usual internal labour markets, where leadership is assumed by large employment organisations, rules are explained in formal agreements and formal selection criteria are those legally in use inside bureaucratic organisations. Jobs allocation institutions, and mainly schools, are specialised for this purpose. Jobs allocation institutions in IDs are often more complex and difficult to identify and analyse. Watching the phenomenon of migration Fontaine (2005) draws a model which can be applied to most IDs: for many migrant people, after mobility, their strategies and behavioral patterns tend to be rooted in – and explained by – the societal customs of their origin rather than in those of the host location. Institutions involved in manpower production are not only functional ones such as schools and formal training institutions, but also families – and eventually tribes – as structures of the native society may be involved as labour market institutions. As usual in most of the labour markets, jobs distribution is gender ruled, and insists on the role of ethnic distribution in jobs allocation.

3. SETTING UP IN BUSINESS

The paradox of the small size of firms in IDs is often underlined. In fact, in spite of the global economic success of the local industry, the average firm size remains small. As often observed (Saxenian 1992; Maitte 1997, p. 1281; Boero, Castellani and Squazzoni 2004; Håkanson 2005, p. 450), district economic vitality relies on a high rate of new firm formation and rapid turnover of firms rather than on individual firm performance. Very dynamic IDs have both individual firm growth and numerous start-ups (Bresnahan, Gambardella and

Saxenian 2001, p. 836) but they always have a high rate of firm turnover. Thus, one specificity of IDs is the fact that starting a firm is often a mobility strategy for some specific social groups. IDs labour markets differ from large firms' ones, in that it is common for skilled workers to choose to start a new business and become entrepreneurs themselves; however, this does not happen for skilled workers in large firms (Bagnasco 1988).

Strictly defined, the concept of labour markets is associated with employees' job allocation, training, determination of wage rates and careers. Employers' situations and careers are not included in such markets because they are not the result of transactions between two independent actors – employer and employee – but follow individual decisions. However, one can use LLM analysis as a framework to describe the social stratification and the career patterns of the people working inside a locality. In this way, studies of the positions and the careers of self-employed workers and employers are possible. As observed also outside of ID debates, those who wish and try to start a new firm belong to precise social groups or networks. An analysis of firm registrations in Oyonnax by means of the *Registre des métiers*,[1] shows that the self-employed and creators of new firms are members of the same social groups rather than employees in similar occupations: namely, French men in the mould-making industry, European migrant men in the plastic moulding one, and some non-European women in assembly and sticking.

Empirical studies on IDs often find that the availability of financial capital is not an absolute prerequisite for self-employment and firm start-ups; indeed potential entrepreneurs are not necessarily characterised by capital ownership, although when necessary, they are found to be successful in raising financial resources locally. Oyonnax's local banker succeeded in providing local workers with capital in cases where other banks would never have provided support (Saglio 1997, pp. 453–6). Financial institutions supporting new firms – private banks, regional or local government funding organisations – are frequently active institutions in modern clusters. However, one must not overvalue the role of such financial institutions in supporting firm development: at the start, in high-tech clusters, entrepreneurs' financial support is found to be more relevant than in mature ones (Bresnahan, Gambardella and Saxenian 2001, p. 842). Lebeau (1955) found that the lack of resources was sometimes a rough incentive to industrial innovation and development. Conversely, it could be argued that economic growth in IDs relies on the presence of financial institutions devoted to encourage and drive the entrepreneurial spirit.

The individual propensity to self-employment or to firm start-up usually appears in situations where there is a strong proximity, and often a familiarity, with other self-employed or entrepreneurs (Feldman 2000). Entrepreneurs usually are imitators: they tend to target the same product markets and to use the same production technologies they did when working as employees. In other words, they tend to use procedures known by network proximity (Arocena et al. 1982). Compared with members of these networks, innovations in the new firms are often limited.

Networks of entrepreneurs are frequently rooted in peer groups, albeit some definition of peering may be useful. Having being educated in the same institutions is one of the key variables defining the common link across a group of local entrepreneurs. Entrepreneurs in Silicon Valley and Route 128, for instance, have been found to have gone to the same local universities (Saxenian 1994). In such cases, proximity has a quite direct economic sense: peers share the same professional project and starting a firm is a way of achieving it. In IDs of the 'old economy', peer groups of entrepreneurs tend to be employees who find themselves in the same situations, in that their initial professional project was not to start a new business, but once they realise that other members of the group have done it, the project becomes a real possibility.

Peer groups that share the experience of having started a new firm are not only defined by strictly professional criteria: for instance, in Oyonnax, when the local *maquis* liberated the town from the Germans in June 1944, one of the first bills they decreed was to restrict the right to set up a business to people who had been in the local resistance groups or prisoners in Nazi camps. This decision shaped a group of employers that was still active some decades after that. Here peer groups were rooted in political networks and legitimacy rather than in labour relations.

Families are often institutions within which the aspirations of entrepreneurs take shape. The function of *mezzadria* in many Italian IDs has long been questioned; as Stauffer (1998) observed in relation with the ceramics ID, there was no direct transfer of capital from farming to the start of new businesses. However, new entrepreneurs were found to have very specific positions in farmer families whose labour force was required only at certain peak times of the year, like in the case of Prato (Maitte 1997) and of Cluses (Judet 2001). Stauffer observed that many new firm entrepreneurs were members of local *mezzadria* family farmers, although they spent some time outside the village.

Capital owners seeking industrial opportunities, or innovators wishing to develop a new idea, would be the typical types of entrepreneurs; however, they do not necessarily apply within IDs. Firm start-ups are more likely to be driven by the aspirations of individuals due to their personal or family history, the structure of labour relations and employment careers, and in some cases by the district's political or social history. On the other hand, firm start-ups are often described as spinoff strategies: where the entrepreneur develops, often with his/her previous employer's agreement, a project s/he could not realize on the previous job. This means that there is a greater propensity to start a new firm among employees of small firms than among larger firms, especially in terms of the labour relations that characterise small firms allowing employees to share knowledge on the functioning of the business itself. Also, in a small firm, skilled workers and technicians are more likely to have good knowledge not only of their specific task, but also of the broader state of the firm's strategies, markets and customers. In IDs in particular, new entrepreneurs also have a network of peers who tried – successfully or not – to start a new business. Within this network, new entrepreneurs can benefit from the sharing of useful knowledge that is almost 'in the air'; indeed these can rely on the support of existing entrepreneurs as well as more specialised business support institutions – not only on financial issues. Such support is argued to be strictly inter-individual as it was in the classical craftsman patronage or in modern entrepreneur-mentors (Bresnahan, Gambardella and Saxenian 2001, p. 837).

In the French working class tradition, self-employed and craft workers were considered as working class members rather than employers; their employees were *compagnons* or apprentices. In the French more traditional IDs, self-employment or firm start-ups can be seen as individual strategies to gain job autonomy and independence from previous employers rather than strategies of capital accumulation. In the Oyonnax district before the 1953 strike, the collective agreement negotiated between local employers and the CGT union ruled both the employees' and the subcontractors' earnings. Union delegates were representatives of self-employed, craftsmen and even small employers. A lot of self-employed or employers were also employees, and if unsuccessful, they could find jobs again as employees according to their previous skill (Hakånson 2005, p. 435). Beatrice Veyrassat (1997, pp. 217–18) reported on a similar situation for Jura watchmakers.

Labour market analysis of the new firm start-ups in IDs would suggest placing more emphasis on status continuities rather than on business decisions. Entrepreneurship propensity is suggested to be related to the social status and the professional experience as well as to the business opportunities of the new entrepreneur. Individual career choices and family networks provide information resources to the new entrepreneur, since starting a firm does not break social linkages and social status positioning; peer groups remain and may be reinforced by such decisions. If unsuccessful, the new entrepreneur's risks are minimised, his/her social ties are still there and his/her social status is unchanged.

4. LOCAL REGULATION AND CONFLICTS

The conceptualisation of internal labour markets (Doeringer and Piore 1971) may be used as an analytical framework to understand employment systems in IDs, where employment and working conditions are regulated by a web of formal and informal rules. Indeed, IDs are not hierarchical organisations and they are less articulate organisations than firms or administrative bureaucracies. Unlike in classical bureaucratic structures, in IDs problem solving is not the function of a specialised department, instead it has a 'global' dimension, since problems are linked together: for instance, labour market rules are also useful to understand knowledge spillover or trade competition; employment, technology or trade strategies are intertwined and collectively managed; internal competition is working both within the employment and the trade markets. As observed in professions or as industrial branches in some industrial relations systems, ID employment regulation is applied in firms which compete in the product markets, either as direct competitors or as subcontractors in a production chain. Labour markets, technology and trade competition are ruled simultaneously by a web of mostly informal rules.

The definition of internal labour markets may be applied to IDs, but they are quite different from classical institutional markets or from firms' internal regulations (C. Kerr 1954). Unlike professional labour markets, where internal relations between members coincide with peers' relations, and which tend to be regulated by a unified hierarchy or by an external legal definition, internal labour markets in IDs deal with employment relations, and, notably, wages relations. Although career changes are possible, ID members do not share the same professions in labour markets, and access to self-employment and firm start-up is only limited by customs. So ID boundaries are not defined by strictly professional boundaries, but by historical circumstance.

Within internal labour markets, like in all social situations where employers and employees have to share the outcome of common activities, conflicts are possible and frequent, whereas consensus is limited and precarious (Carnevali 2004). Regulations, and collective rules do not eliminate conflicts, they only rule them (Commons 1934). The situation is similar in product market regulation, where competition is ruled by norms that are precarious and do not abolish competition and conflicts. Rules on wages relations are as precarious as product market ones, in that they are stable until they are disputed by someone (Reynaud 1989). Consensus is yet more improbable than in a formal organisation: in fact, beside classical conflicts where actors disagree on policy orientations, in IDs, conflicts can arise from contradictions between the various local rules.

As in most economic organisations, internal conflicts are also usual and frequently complex in IDs. The first reason for this is that norms are informal as well as customs; in this context, formal bargaining is not the way to solve internal conflicts: abiding to such informal norms depends on the fact that actors support them as an individual choice. Bargaining is a good way to build compromise whilst the emergence of a moral (and here economic) authority is the proper way to ensure compliance. Arbitration by a moral authority has proven necessary, for instance, in Oyonnax during the 1970s, the local banker was called on as such an authority in trade conflicts between local firms, especially on subcontracting; whereas, during the 1930s, such a role used to be played by the local mayor on arbitrations related to wages conflicts. The second reason is the complexity of the web of rules: usually, wage conflicts involve trade unions and employers, and at the same time, trade conflicts would involve employers – either competitors or buyers–suppliers. However, in IDs, the complex interaction among all actors results in complex strategies at different levels.

During the late 1970s, after the first oil crisis and the spread of new plastic moulding technologies, the Oyonnax district was in a deep crisis. Injection machine automation changed manpower needs; the increase in the price of raw materials and the emergence of new competitors all posed great challenges. At first, Oyonnax firms faced the crisis by increasing the working hours of male migrant workers employed as plastic moulders, whereas outside Oyonnax, the other French firms were employing women for the same jobs. As they could not increase working hours any more, they were obliged to buy new equipment to face competition. Competing firms tried to knock Oyonnax firms out of the market by negotiating a working-hour reduction collective agreement, which according to French labour law would apply to all firms in the same industry. Oyonnax firms' reaction was threefold: (a) they decided to specialise in B to B technical components; (b) they invested in new technologies; and (c) since they switched to high-tech functions, they attracted technicians and engineers rather than unskilled migrant workers. Local government, with a mayor member of French Communist Party, strongly supported this new strategic choice. This is evidence of how labour relations and employment strategies can be strongly linked with technological and business strategies, as well as housing.

The labour markets dualist model does not help describe such conflicts. Employers' collective strategy led to an economic change for Oyonnax firms' positions along the value chain. Rather than choosing to target the low end of the product market – low cost–low technology – they chose to invest in specialised technology at the subcontracting stages. The success of such a strategy depended on mobilising key actors (Pizzorno 1977). The local government was involved in the creation of an engineering school specialised in plastic moulding and in a housing programme for middle-class families, while local unions were involved in the negotiation for new collective agreements, especially on wage scales, skill and training policies. This example shows that strategic conflicts can be complex situations where many dimensions are linked together: employment, technology, business and finances are simultaneously of concern. The first strategic choice is problem 'labelisation'. Each actor has a complex strategy. Each of them can act within certain limits: for instance, unions' actions are limited to labour relations or subcontractors to prices competition. Within such complex collective actions, the local industry wins strategic autonomy and avoids the constraints of being subordinated to usual secondary segments firms.

Local regulation capacity to rule these internal conflicts is a key factor for development and survival. Difficulties in or the impossibility of solving them is frequently the cause of historical IDs collapsing. Internal conflicts do not work directly on the threat, but indirectly; they can seldom undermine the collectiveness of the strategic answer to the threat. When regulation is mainly informal, its power to work lies in the trust each actor grants to the others. Trust is necessary to build the collectiveness; but this trust is not generally but locally defined; 'actors did not distinguish as sharply between states of trust and mistrust as the conventional understanding would suggest. . . . There is a deontology of treachery, and a spy remains a peculiar sort of honourable person by complying with it' (Sabel and Zeitlin

1997a, p. 23). So, IDs' stability and development are the result of a collective ability to manage internal conflicts rather than impossible consensus, but, at the same time, the weakness of formal constraints requires actors to support regulation.

5. THE ID LOCAL REGULATION PARADOX

The regulation of labour markets and labour relations is paradoxical in IDs. It seems weak, because it is mostly local and informal; besides, informal rules can be used in court or changed by usual bargaining processes, with great difficulty. It seems weak because informal rules are not mandatory, but are explained only by local customs. On the other side, ID regulation is often extensive and complex: employment rules are strategically linked with other areas of regulation-like technology or trade. As mentioned by Marshall with respect to 'the mysteries of the trade': rules are 'in the air, and children learn many of them unconsciously' (Marshall 1920, IV.X.VII). Furthermore, one may apply to these rules a remark made by Anthony Giddens on the nature and the forms of such rules: that is, the stronger they are the more informal and difficult to express they can be (Giddens 1984).

When entering a unionised firm or organisation, employees are given the latest version of collective agreement spelling out employment and working conditions. In IDs, the rules of the local employment system are not written: they are 'in the air'; like superstitions, local people agree to speak of them seriously only with those known to share them (Favret-Saada 1977). Often they look more like tribal myths than juridical rules. As religious beliefs, the meaning of these rules may differ to different people. To new members, they are presented by the way of histories and anecdotes during informal meetings rather than formal knowledge. Sharing the same rules allows social exchanges inside the group (Saglio 1991). Gifts – in labour or information offered without payment – are an investment as much as evidence of commitment: one does not know what will be the counterpart, and even the identity of the group member who shall provide the counterpart is not specified. For instance, employment agreement success may be the creation of a rival firm, and the counterpart may be technical cooperation between both firms.

Labour market rules are only part of IDs' complex economic regulation, whose complexity and informality makes it more difficult for internal conflicts to be managed. Sahlins (1976) suggested considering the economy as a cultural category; in other words, considering local economic rules as part of the local culture makes it easier for IDs' economy to be understood.

NOTES

1. Craft Register: official register where every self-employed people has to register.

SECTION 5
Knowledge, learning and creativity

Introduction

Luciana Lazzeretti

1. RENEWING IDs

In the current scenario characterised by the profound transformations associated with the knowledge economy and new technologies, the missing dimensions of innovation (Lester and Piore 2004) are strongly emerging. The contributions of this session focus on the implications that may be generated by the many different paths of local development in general and of the industrial district (ID) in particular. The mechanisms inside district dynamics, innovation and creative processes are explored, emphasising problems of evolution, cluster mutation, new sector applications and relations with other forms of local development.

The red thread of our introduction winds through the idea of 'renewing' IDs. The contributions gathered are presented as a sort of open conversation in which reflections involving this idea are brought forward and fine tuned.

The conversation is articulated around different types of analysis (theoretic or applied), fields of application (including the culture and creative district, the ID, the innovative *milieu* and the regional innovation system, RIS), and theoretic frameworks (ranging from innovation economy to evolutionary economics and geography, to the organisation and management studies). The principal themes of the section are innovation, creativity and transformation.

2. AN OPEN DIALOGUE ON INNOVATION

An initial theme regards the affirmation of the 'open innovation model' and the growing role acknowledged to the 'social dimension of innovation', and the relation of these with the reconsideration of the district form as a 'socio-economic innovation community'.

Companies are increasingly rethinking the ways in which they generate ideas and bring them to the market – harnessing external ideas while leveraging their in-house R&D beyond their current operation (Chesbrough 2003a). Large firms and multinational firms increasingly look outwards to find ideas and innovations; the boundaries of firms become porous and smart people no longer interact only inside the firms, but between firms and outside firms. The importance of the context grows and the innovation strategies of large firms become ever more similar to those of innovation clusters. The new paradigm expands due to new technologies, from the movie industry to computer sciences, telecommunications, life sciences, and so on, sometimes modifying even the district innovation mechanisms.

The chapter by Paul Robertson, David Jacobson and Richard Langlois in this section is linked to the last aspects mentioned. They discuss some of the factors connected with the success of the districts in the 1970s and 1980s with particular reference to the impact of new technologies and communities of practice. They examine the operations of innovation processes within IDs by exploring the ways in which differentiation, specialisation and integration affect the generation, diffusion and use of new knowledge, including the various stages of product and process life cycles. The authors take into consideration numerous cases of the evolution, transformation and decline of IDs, particularly emphasising the 'negative effects of embeddedness'. Their analysis leads to a mixed evaluation of the advantages that IDs can provide. When circumstances are favourable, the high degrees of differentiation and specialisation in IDs, combined with the high degree of social embeddedness, can encourage knowledge creation in a Smithian sense.

As technology evolves in the wider environment, however, the advantages that IDs often offer for the generation and diffusion of knowledge may weaken. Furthermore, the new information and communications technologies (ICT) may make it possible for firms to draw more cheaply and effectively on diverse sources of knowledge and therefore to increase their access to innovative ideas. One of the negative aspects is the paradox of 'success myopia' which registers failures after a period of market leadership, due in great part to the effects of structural inertia. Problems of the 'right amount of distance' are also reported: too much and too little proximity are both detrimental to learning and innovation (Boschma 2005). This phenomenon may be referred not only to geographic proximity, but also to other forms of proximity, such as virtual or relational proximity, and may also be due to the proliferation of network relationships that may be cultivated outside the district.

A second aspect that should be taken into consideration is the rise of the 'social dimension of innovation', that Von Hippel (2005) successfully synthesizes in the idea of 'democratising innovation'. Innovations are increasingly 'disruptive', that is, able to substitute not only obsolete technologies, but also to deeply modify social behaviour (as in the case of the substitution of the fixed link telephone network by the mobile phone). In a scenario of this type, the district formula may once again be a winner. The centrality of innovation processes requires the transition from a 'manufacturer-centric innovation development system to a user-centered innovation process' and the end users, ever more aware of their necessities, become sources of innovation. The significance of an innovation resides in its 'use', and its legitimisation increasingly derives from the community to which it belongs. The IDs of the Third Italy and the open-source communities are two of the examples most often cited.

In relation to this, the chapter by Michael Piore demonstrates with great efficacy the renewed importance of the social dimension of innovation for the conservation of the mechanisms vital to the district formula and, considering the IDs as 'communities of action', entrusts a fundamental role to the method of conversation. The author recalls two fundamental characteristics that have guaranteed the vitality of the districts: first the apparently contradictory combination of competition and cooperation; second, the amoeba-like character of the technological changes. Both of these characteristics generate that 'ambiguity' that represents the necessary stimulus for conversation between different subjects. This is supported by an analysis and interpretation that are necessary to overcome the said ambiguity in the creation of shared and concrete goals. Such conversation must develop in a 'public space', often informal and far from the pressures of the market and competition. Studies on the districts of the Third Italy and more recently those on large firms by Lester and Piore (2004) share the recognition that a guiding role along innovation paths is held by the social dimension.

The public space is assigned such an important role because the community of action is seen as the real and permanent protagonist of the vitality of the district. As Arendt (1958) stresses in his studies on the *Human Condition* in Ancient Greece action can take place in the public space and is possible only in a particular social formation. Its formation involves a community of people who are equal in the sense of being alike. It is the community that acts, the strong subject that finds its creative energy in the double legitimisation, internal and external. Assuming another analogy, the districts work in the same way as athletic teams, they are winners not only due to the quality of the members, but of the team. Furthermore, when the community of fans supports them, the identity of the athletic team is legitimised and strengthened in the same way that happens with clients and suppliers of the district products.

3. THE ROLE OF CULTURE AND CREATIVITY IN LOCAL DEVELOPMENT AND CHANGE

A second theme in this section is the relationship between innovation and creativity. Districts have always been considered places where tacit and codified knowledge are combined to give rise to virtuous circuits of innovation and creativity amplified by knowledge spillover. However, the basis of this 'know-how' may be not only of a technological type, but also of an artistic and cultural type. This link is seen more clearly if referred to cultural and creative districts instead of IDs. The chapter by Olivier Crevoisier and Leïla Kebir, together with mine, specifically make reference to this different perspective and draw on concepts from cultural economics and creative economy.

In particular, my contribution develops along two distinct lines that endeavour to answer two basic questions: how does culture contribute to economic development and innovation? And which are the environments that promote and foster creativity and innovation? The two guide concepts are that of the 'creative capacity of the culture' (CCC) and that of the ID as the 'new creative *milieu*'(NCM). The chapter begins by arguing that the idea that the relationship between economy and culture represented by the economic enhancement of culture was seen as a flywheel for economic development (typical of the cultural district) has to give way to a new way of looking at it. One needs to start looking instead at 'cultural enhancement of economy', which considers culture a resource for innovation. Indeed, in the latter, the focus is switched from culture to creativity, and the CCC becomes the ability to rejuvenate places, sectors or professions, and to generate ideas and innovations. This involves researching new and different relationships, preferably unusual relatedness, which are at the basis of the innovation process. Urban and economic renewal, cross-fertilisation and serendipity are the principal creative pathways, which give rise to different types of innovation (rejuvenation, incremental and radical innovations) and involve several units of analysis (city, district, sector, products, professions). Here it is suggested that culture can enter and take part in the district innovation mechanisms thanks to creative thinking with lateral thinking (De Bono 1971), which, within the informal environment of the district, may facilitate the development of conversations that could lead to 'unusual relatedness' advanced by 'lateral proximity'. The conceptual elaboration of these premises touches upon the 'spatial dimension of creativity', the relationship between Marshallian industrial districts (MIDs) and Jacobian clusters, and leads to the introduction of the concepts of creative spillovers and creative absorptive capacity. This contribution shares some common ground with the chapter by Piore, who stresses the role of culture in the problem-finding process at the initial phase of the innovation process.

The chapter by Crevoiser and Kebir examines the articulation between economy and culture starting from the approach of the innovative *milieu*. Cultural resources constitute a relation between an object (cultural legacy, tradition, buildings, know-how, mineral, river and so on) and a production system (tourism, culture, industry). The cultural objects are the result of processes of creation (apprenticeship, collective experience, construction and so on) and destruction (oblivion, deterioration, wear and tear, destruction and so on). On the other hand, the actors of a production system identify certain objects as being a potential resource and use them in the production of goods and services. The authors develop the idea of a coevolution of these processes referring to Braudel, and suggesting an approach based upon three levels: the capitalism level, the market economy level and the self-production level. The concept of 'authenticity' emerges at the core of this analysis. If the culture is authentic it can revitalise territories, generate value and avert the risks of decontextualisation and 'Disneylandification'. The example is the watchmaking industry in the Swiss area of the Jura Mountains, which has undergone many transformations without losing its authenticity. That process is still in evolution. The local community is working towards 'regional and urban regeneration' by requesting that 'Watch Valley' be recognised in the list of the UNESCO World Cultural Heritage Sites, hence transforming it into a tourism cultural district.

A last main theme of this section regards the transformation of forms of local development. On this point Philip Cooke's chapter draws a scenario of 'cluster mutation' according to an evolutionary approach and widens the debate to the Jacobian clusters (Cooke 2009) and to the RIS with their more entrepreneurial (ERIS) or institutional (IRIS) versions. Scientific, technological and creative knowledge industries are found at the centre of such systems, included their variants as high tech, 'green' and creative clusters. The comparison between Marshall's IDs, the (neo)-MIDs, and technology cluster remains the central theme of the chapter, pointing out the different roles assigned to the structural characteristics of the district with respect to the network of socio-economic relationships. According to Cooke, MIDs and technology clusters are similarly embedded structurally more than relationally while neo-MIDs are relationally more than structurally embedded. It is a wide-ranging discussion that opens the way to the analysis of a multitude of situations and offers many occasions for thought on evolutionary paths.

4. VITALITY, IDENTITY, EVOLUTION

Finally, there are three key concepts recurring throughout the section. The first one is vitality. The district, in so far as it is a socio-economic community organisation, may still be considered an interesting organisational form that will be able to face the challenges of this century, thanks to the fact that it is coherent to the emerging paradigm of open innovation. It is again the socio-economic dimension of the district community, made up of people and firms, that takes on a strategic aspect. This is not necessarily connected, as recalled by Robertson, Jacobson and Langlois, with the structural characteristics of the district, with its success (success myopia), nor with the use of new technologies or the embeddedness of know-how. These factors are important, but they may have positive or negative aspects. The discriminating factor is instead to be found in its being a 'community of action', as recalled by Piore. IDs, with their apparent contradiction between cooperation and competition, with their boundaries spanning relations, are ambiguous and therefore vital. An open conversation should preferably take place in a 'public space', in an informal environment where 'lateral thinking' is more likely to develop. Ideas are in the air, in the contexts, and not all of the ideas are necessarily developed by those who originally had the idea. An idea representing problem finding for a production phase may be a problem-solving idea for another; open conversations serve to exchange ideas so that the right placement may be found. In this case the culture factor is strategic, because it helps to criss-cross boundaries (Hirschman 1981). Good conversations may occur inside the district facilitated by a common system of values, but fuelled by different cultures – that of craftsmanship, of engineering, of politics and so on – as recalled by Becattini (1991) in his initial reflections on MID as a creative *milieu*. However, it is just as possible to have good conversations in creative cities between actors belonging to different sectors. It is a question of the 'right distance' (physical proximity versus cognitive proximity). Creative ideas develop both by specialisation and by differentiation, in the MID and in the Jacobian cluster. Furthermore, the gap between types of language (Piore), between sectors (Lazzeretti), and between communities of practice (Robertson, Jacobson and Langlois) may be fruitfully bridged by an open conversation, by a route of analysis and interpretation.

The second concept is that of identity. The vitality of a community of action and the vital mechanisms of creativity and innovation are more easily maintained and developed in the presence of a strong, coherent identity that is recognised both inside and outside the community's boundaries. The example of the athletic team and its fans recalled by Piore is excellent and may usefully be applied also to the district case. The internal legitimisation of the district derives from the district populace and the external legitimisation from its public (stakeholders), first of all by clients and suppliers, and then by institutions and competitors, as well as the general public. There is a close relationship between identity and embeddedness that also occurs in the case of new technologies, as suggested also by Robertson, Jacobson and Langlois. Identity is also associated with authenticity, as discussed by Crevoisier and Kebir. The case of Watch Valley may be seen as a community of action that has witnessed the coevolution of the diverse populations involved, transforming its identity without losing its authenticity through processes of economic renewing and urban regeneration.

The third concept is that of evolution. Evolution may overwhelm the vitality of a district if the vital flow of exchange and conversation is interrupted, and it may also weaken its identity and authenticity. This is the case of some ethnic communities closed inside the districts, such as the Chinese community of Prato, a district inside a district (Dei Ottati 2009), where at the moment there seems to be no successful process of coevolution. However, the risk of identity loss may also exist with the new technologies. They may widen the space for relationships while weakening identity to the same degree. It is a question of balance, which is a goal to be reached in transformation. The central theme becomes that of the 'cluster mutation' knowingly sketched by Cooke, leading to transformations in specialisation sectors such as, for example, the transition from leather to plastic in the Montebelluna district or from mechanics to fashion, then to tourism as occurred in the Jura Mountains *milieu*. Yet another example is the ICT and biotechnology-producing 'platforms' of 'clean technology' in Silicon Valley or ICT, photovoltaics, agricultural and marine engineering evolving in wind turbine and solar thermal energy clusters in North Jutland, Denmark, along the new and important frontier of the 'green evolution'.

The theme of renewing is complex and open. We have endeavoured to provide here a hopefully useful contribution, although it is our aspiration that such conversation may continue further.

20. Conceptualizing the dynamics of industrial districts

Michael J. Piore

1. INTRODUCTION

The Italian industrial district (ID) first captured the attention of scholars in the 1970s. Since that time it has become a seductive model, attracting public policymakers and industrial development consultants across a wide spectrum. It has drawn the interests of developing countries seeking the survival and prosperity of their traditional industries in an increasingly open and global economy. But it has also become a model for local areas within advanced developed economies seeking to create high-tech clusters. The literature describing these districts has grown apace, and there is now an enormous body of case studies of such districts in virtually every part of the world. But analytically the districts remain something of a mystery. It is very hard to understand why they arise in some places and at certain times and not in others, or what determines whether or not, and for how long, they survive. Moreover, it has proven to be especially difficult to reproduce such districts through public policy.

This chapter is an attempt to draw together from several apparently disparate sources some elements of a conceptual framework through which IDs and related, dynamic and innovative organizational structures could be understood. It focuses on two characteristics of those districts, characteristics common to virtually all of the individual case studies: first, the apparently contradictory combination of competition and cooperation; second, the amoeba-like character of the technological changes which define their dynamism (the tendency for both production and product innovation to take place around the edges of existing products and processes rather than in discrete jumps). A much longer list is presented in a previous paper which developed a more limited version of the argument presented here; it strengthens the case for using these ideas, especially those of communities of action, but it makes the argument too cumbersome to be presented here (Piore 1992).

To understand these characteristics, the chapter draws primarily on two sets of ideas. One of these is a distinction between analysis and interpretation, which I developed with Richard Lester in a recent book, *Innovation: The Missing Dimension*

(Lester and Piore 2004), and which drew from a series of case studies on the organization of product design and development. The second is that of 'communities of action', a concept developed by Hannah Arendt based on a set of categories drawn from ancient Greece (Arendt 1958). The latter has certain parallels in the elements of the working-class subculture of a Boston community which Herbert Gans studied in the 1950s (Gans 1962). Both Arendt and Gans take on added significance in the light of the history of some of the Italian districts which Sabel and I encountered in the late 1970s and early 1980s (Piore and Sabel 1984). Both the product development cases and Arendt's communities of action point toward the centrality of what might be termed 'public space', but the meaning of this term is not necessarily the same, and they have somewhat different interpretations for public policy.

This chapter is divided into five sections as follows: Sections 2 and 3 summarize the ideas developed with Richard Lester and by Hannah Arendt respectively. Section 4 examines the parallels with Gans' *Urban Villagers*. Section 5 presents a schematic history of the districts which Charles Sabel and I visited in the late 1970s and early 1980s and draws parallels to Arendt and Gans. Section 6 concludes, drawing out some of the implications for the possibility of managing IDs through public policy.

2. INNOVATION: THE MISSING DIMENSION

The study of product design and development was conducted primarily in the 1990s through the Industrial Performance Center (IPC) of MIT. It was organized around three major case studies – cellular telephones, blue jeans and medical devices – with firms in each drawn from Europe, the US and Japan. In each company, we spent at least a full day, and often many more, interviewing managers and engineers. The study also involved extensive interviews with colleagues at MIT in engineering and management who taught courses or advised business clients on product development. What emerged from these interviews was a sharp dichotomy between theory and practice. Our academic respondents thought of design and development as an analytical exercise or, in other words, as problem solving. And the analytical vocabulary of academia dominated the interviews with operating managers and engineers. But the interviews with practitioners also revealed that there was another dimension to the development process; this dimension preceded and then accompanied analysis but was more difficult for the respondents to articulate.

Thus the analytical approach presupposed that a clear goal for the new product could be identified; designs were conceived in terms of this goal as means for obtaining it; and the design process was understood as one of arriving at an optimal design by working out the most efficient version of each design alternative and then comparing them in terms of cost and effectiveness. Particular emphasis was placed on breaking up the project into a series of separate, independent pieces for which this kind of analysis was feasible. But this approach begged the question of where the new product ideas and the various design alternatives came from in the first place.

In each of our case studies, it became apparent that the ideas actually emerged from something which was very different from analysis, something which appeared to be an open-ended discussion among the various participants in the design process. Those participants moreover came from very different backgrounds and engineering disciplines and the novelty and effectiveness of the innovations which emerged drew heavily upon the heterogeneous backgrounds. But the diversity of participants also made it difficult for them to understand each other and to interact in a constructive manner. This part of the innovation process involved overcoming these obstacles and the management of the interaction among the participants in a way which enabled them to move forward toward a set of design ideas.

We came to understand these interactions in terms of two metaphors. One metaphor was a cocktail party. The second was language. The interactions among the participants who in the early stages were basically strangers to each other were like a conversation at a cocktail party. The role of the manager is like that of the hostess at the party. His or her basic function is to invite the guests, introduce them to each other and get them to talk, prevent the kind of breakdowns which can occur in an argument or disagreement, on the one hand, and to introduce new topics or new participants when the conversation flags, on the other.

The conversation involved in generating new product innovation broke down into two distinct phases. The first phase involved developing a language in which the participants could actually talk and communicate with each other and with the customer to whom they expected to sell the product. The second phase involved using that language to work out and develop product ideas.

The nature of the process is easiest to illustrate in terms of the development of the cellular telephone. The cell phone is the marriage of radio and telephone technology. The initial idea was drawn from military walkie-talkies and car radios used by taxis, police and the fire service. Radio and telephone involved two totally different engineering cultures and business traditions. The telephone is by tradition a perfectly engineered instrument; you never lose a call. It is designed and produced in large, expert companies who sell to equally large and expert clients (historically often owned by the same firm). Radio engineers are by contrast cowboys; the engineering tradition is basically empirical; the signal fades in and out. The engineer fiddles with the instrument to recover it. Radios are produced by very large companies but the customers are small service organizations for whom the radio is incidental to their central mission. In the beginning, moreover, there was no market for the cell phone; possible uses had to be imagined. It was initially a large car-mounted instrument and the vision was of the car's interior as a living room. It evolved only gradually over time into a completely portable handheld instrument through a process in which the producers tried to 'read' the consumer and at once follow their lead and lead them through new designs in a direction they seemed to want to go. It is in this sense that one could say that the engineers had at first to learn a common language to communicate with each other while at the same time inventing a language through which they could speak to and with the consumer.

The initial phase of this process was particularly delicate because communication was so difficult and it was easily broken off through distrust and misunderstanding. Market pressures and the highly-competitive environment which the market generated, not only among companies but among different divisions and even individuals within the same company, heighted distrust and inhibited open-ended conversation. In all of the major companies we studied, the cellular business was initially developed in a unit sheltered from the competitive pressures of the market and among the other units of the company. It was only later, once the basic language had developed and the direction of evolution of the product had become clear, that the cellular division was reorganized along conventional business lines. The exact nature of these arrangements varied from company to company depending on its business tradition. But it was most dramatic (and is best illustrated) by AT&T, the American telephone monopoly subsequently broken up in the process of deregulating the industry. AT&T was an extremely bureaucratic company with its units managed in a very rigid style; but it contained within it Bell Labs which functioned in a much more informal, academic manner, and it was in Bell Labs that cellular technology was initially developed and brought to maturity.

The interpretative aspect of product development can be understood as suggested earlier in terms of a language community – first the development of such a community and then the use of the language associated with it to generate innovative ideas. The language metaphor suggests that we can turn to language theory for further insights into the process. Two insights in particular emerge in this way: the role of ambiguity and the way in which a language (and by extension a product) evolves through usage.

Language evolves from clarity to ambiguity. When strangers from different language communities first come into contact with each other, the first language which develops is a pidgin, what the dictionary defines as a trader's language, where meanings are clear and unambiguous. If intercourse between the two communities continues, however, a true language, or creole, emerges (usually only in the second generation) with a complete grammar. A creole is distinguished from a pidgin by the fact that meaning is ambiguous and it is continuously clarified through conversation. In the economy, it is in the space of ambiguity that opportunities for profit emerge; innovation can be seen as the product of ambiguity (note that this is a very different idea of profit from what comes out of theories of information and arbitrage). But the second point is that a language, once formed, evolves through usage. The determinants of its evolution include the kinds of people who use it and interact in the process, but also the topics around which that interaction revolves. Both sets of ideas point toward the centrality of what might be termed 'public space', that is, venues of open discussion and debate, sheltered from the competitive pressures of the market. But equally important to the openness of the discussion are the subjects upon which the discussion focuses and the character of the interaction which occurs within this space.

3. HANNAH ARENDT

A second set of ideas which are useful in understanding the underlying nature of IDs and which both complement and add nuance to those from the product development study are developed by Hannah Arendt in *The Human Condition*. Arendt's argument is built around a typology of human activity that she abstracts from classical Greek thought and then uses to trace the evolution of work (and the social value placed upon it) in Western thought. The typology first makes a fundamental distinction between *la vita active* and *la vita contemplativa*. The latter involves a withdrawal from interaction with the world (significantly both the social and the physical) and retreat toward introspection. This is a stance which Arendt herself rejects (and which is certainly irrelevant in an understanding of IDs given their preoccupation with production and community). Her focus is thus basically upon activity within the *vita active*. Here she distinguishes first between labor and work. The two words are now used interchangeably and both are associated with production in the conventional usage of that term. But Arendt argues that there is an important distinction between them that is residual in virtually every language.

Labor is the activity associated with the reproduction of life and nature. In ancient Greece, it was the activity of women and slaves, performed in the privacy of the household and separated from public life. It is cyclical and, in its cyclicality, is repetitive. Its products are ephemeral. It requires the individual to align him or herself with the rhythm of nature and to become part of it. Its original meaning survives in the use of the term 'labor' to refer to childbirth. In modern times, mass production, because it is repetitive, has taken on this character, although Arendt regards this as a distortion of the human capacities associated with labor.

Work, by contrast, is the activity of the artist or craftsman, signalled by the way we use the term when we speak of a 'work of art'. It is the production of an object which then exists separate from its creators and survives in the world (unlike labor) independently of the act of creation. It moves from the private realm of creation to the public realm of 'existence', where it is permanent and enduring, and in so doing gives the creator an immortality which labor, bound up in the perpetual cycle of birth and death, cannot confer.

But the privileged activity in ancient Greece was neither labor nor work, but 'action'. Action was the activity of political and military life and reserved for a limited class of citizens who were relieved of the necessity of labor by a private household staffed with slaves. Action took place in the public space. It was the small acts of rhetoric or battle spread out and accumulated over a lifetime. Arendt argued that together the sequence of such acts formed a story or narrative of a person's life. And if that story was great and unique, it would be recognized and told by one's friends and colleagues after death, and passed on from one generation to another, giving the person a kind of immortality. This was an immortality which labor could not confer and which in work, through the separation of the product from its creator, lost the intimate connection to the individual person. For Arendt, and for the Greeks, action was the greatest and most human of all activities. And it also seemed most relevant to an understanding of the Greek city-State.

But action was only possible in a particular social formation. That formation involves a community of people who are not only equal politically but who are equal in the sense of being alike. Only a community of people endowed with essentially the same material out of which to create their life can appreciate the uniqueness of what one of their colleagues has made with that material. Thus, the venue of action is like a theatre in which the audience and the players are one and the same, and the players play for each other.

The construction here is very much that of a team of professional athletes or an elite scholarly community. The athletes actually have a dual audience, the fans in the stands and their fellow players on the field. But the audience which matters is the one on the field. Like the Greek citizens in the forum, moreover, the reputation of a professional athlete is made not by one move in one game but by the long sequence of moves in many games over a player's career. Team sport is the canonical case of the marriage of competition and cooperation. The team members are competing against each other for fame and renown and yet they need their fellow players both to play the game and to validate their achievements.

Elite scholars within an academic discipline are similarly working for the recognition of their colleagues. And recognition (the Nobel Prize to the contrary) is accorded not for one major achievement but for the series of relatively small, but each particularly clever, contributions over a lifetime.

IDs embody exactly this construction: a community of people with essentially the same heritage producing a series of innovations, each small in itself, but together gaining the recognition of their colleagues. The focus in economic studies is always upon the district as a productive community, and the skills which they display are basically craft skills. But what makes these communities successful, and what is remarked in discussions with the members themselves, are not the skills but the innovations, and these are not particularly in the final product but can be in production technology, design or even business practice. In this sense, it is not the craft which is valued or 'work' in Arendt's sense of the term. But the activity there is not either labor in the sense of aligning oneself with nature; nor is it the production of objects. Rather, it is the production of small and particular innovations – in design, in production, even in sales or community leadership – that win the notice and admiration of those around them who are like them. Because what is involved are small innovations, the repertoire of the community evolves like an amoeba. Because the members of the community are working for each other's admiration but to distinguish themselves as individuals, they combine competition and cooperation in the same sense as an athletic team or a scholarly community.

But there is here a final parallel between a successful district and an athletic team which is not included in Arendt's characterization: The district and the team play for the insiders, but they survive only if the outsiders appreciate what they are doing. The team needs the fans to pay for the sport, and the ID needs the customers to buy their products. And in the latter case, it is not enough for one firm to succeed in the marketplace; the community only survives if the firms as a group succeed. In this sense, there is a strong tension in the orientation of these communities – but it is not the tension conventionally noted between competition and cooperation. It is a tension between the inside and the outside orientations.

In many ways, the most critical point in terms of understanding the implications of this is another point which Arendt herself does not make. Communities of action are like language communities. A language is defined by a set of grammatical rules and a vocabulary which all members of the community inherit as a basic resource. But, despite the well-defined nature each member of a language community speaks in a distinct way, recognizable to other members but not to outsiders, and the language evolves around the edges in an amoeba-like fashion in the process of use. It is this analogy to language that links Arendt's communities of action so closely to the process of innovation as it emerged in the studies at the IPC.

4. GANS' *URBAN VILLAGERS*

Arendt's communities of action appear in a totally different literature, far removed from Greek political life: a literature on working-class subculture. The parallels are particularly striking in the characterization in *Urban Villagers* where Herbert Gans summarizes the extensive sociological literature on class subculture and expands upon it through a study of a Boston neighborhood in the 1950s. Working class life as characterized by Gans is played out in terms of two distinct sociological structures which anchor individual (male) identity. One is the family and the series of roles which family life prescribes as one moves through the life cycle. The second structure is the peer group, composed of boys who grow up together in the neighborhood and spend their youth and adolescence hanging out and playing together. Gans characterizes this initial stage of peer group life (especially in adolescence) as 'adventure seeking', but he could well have used Arendt's term 'action'. The youth are engaged in a series of exploits in which each tries to show his daring and bravado, drinking bouts, trysts at local beaches and amusement parks, trespassing on the territory of forbidden gardens, orchards and other private property or in other neighborhoods, petty theft, spray painting and so on. Through these adventures the individual members of the peer group achieve particular identities signified by nicknames associated with particularly noteworthy exploits (adventures). For a more contemporary account with lots of specific examples, in this case an Irish working class neighborhood, see Hayes (2002).

When the youths mature, they marry and settle down; their roles in the family take priority, and these adventures come to an end. The peers continue to hang out together in their leisure time, mostly drinking and playing cards, again significantly in terms of Arendt's notion of action, reliving as narrative tales told to each other the adventures of their youth and reinforcing the individual identities anchored in these adventures.

The adventure-seeking peer group of Gans' depiction of working-class youth is actually a general feature of American life. It is reproduced in the youth of professional and managerial workers in their college fraternities. It also features prominently in studies of computer hackers, many of whom go on to seed the information technology IDs (Turkle 1984).

The other feature of Gans' characterization of some interest here is the way his working-class culture maps onto labor market roles. Adult working class men are engaged in regular industrial work, the kind of work which Arendt sees as the modern, 'artificial' labor of mass production. Indeed, Gans calls their life style 'routine seeking' in contrast to the adventure seeking of adolescence; the life style facilitates adjustment to industrial work. The adventure-seeking youth take temporary unskilled jobs which provide pin money for their peer group activities without distracting from them. But the ideal economic activity for the working class, according to Gans, is in the family firm, which is an extension of the household and takes place in what Arendt would call the private sphere. He does not describe these firms, but he suggests that they are largely engaged in petty commerce, although they could also be craft enterprises, which would complete the parallel with Arendt's typology.

Gans focused on the West End of Boston. At the time, it was a largely second-generation Italian immigrant community. Although he characterized it as working class and grounded his findings in the literature on class subculture, it could as well have been an Italian immigrant subculture that he was studying. It takes on added significance in the light of the history of the IDs that Sabel and I encountered in central Italy in the late 1970s and early 1980s (Piore and Sabel 1984).

5. ITALIAN DISTRICTS

The key factor in that story was the labor unrest associated with the hot autumn of 1969 and the rigidification of work rules in large manufacturing factories to which it led. That had three effects. First, the large firms laid off a number of their skilled workers, many of whom used the large severance packages mandated by Italian law to found their own small firms. Here they joined the ranks of small-scale producers which had already been seeded in this way by the purges of left-wing militants in the 1950s in reaction to previous waves of labor unrest. The firms operated with relatively little capital using family labor working out of the house and associated outbuildings. Second, companies sought to evade the restrictions in the large plants by subcontracting to these very small firms, and their erstwhile employers whom they knew well had an inside track to this work. The small firms took the contracts but sought out other customers whom they could work for in off hours and began to escape dependence on their erstwhile employers. Third, the rigidities led to a very large increase in youth unemployment, particularly in large organizations where jobs were reserved for senior and more experienced workers.

The key in the transition from subcontracting and evasion of labor rigidities to IDs were the children of the previous generation of skilled workers. These kids had grown up working summers and after school in their parents' shops, and in the process acquired a craftsman's on-the-job experience. But unlike their parents, they also had a better school education. In the face of youth unemployment, however, they were forced back into their parents' shops when they graduated. Thus, there emerged a new generation of craftsmen, with relatively good educations, exposure to the wider world of European trade fairs and technical periodicals, and a frustrated ambition for larger things. It was this generation which transformed the conglomeration of subcontracts into an ID of independent shops. Again and again, when we visited these shops, the younger generation was too busy managing the enterprise to take care of us and we were escorted around the shop by the proud but old and gnarled fathers (and once in a while, mothers). The story their parents told as they showed us their shops was how the kids had developed their own technologies and styles as they visited the trade fairs around Europe copying designs, studying catalogues, reengineering equipment, and picking up new ideas wherever they could. Finally, these kids began to specialize, some in production, some in equipment design, some in product design, working with their neighbors in other branches of the business.

6. CONCLUSIONS

It is conventional in an article of this kind to conclude by focusing on the implications for public policy. In this case, the implications of the ideas developed here are not formulaic; they do not suggest a list of specific policy measures. Rather, they suggest a way, or more exactly ways, to think about public policy. There are two implications which, broadly speaking, the two sets of ideas do share. First, they both point to a focus on the social, rather than the narrowly economic, nature of IDs. Second, they suggest a focus on process rather than on inputs and outputs. They imply a shift in emphasis from the provision of specific services (for example, capital, training, market research and so on) to the orchestration of the social interactions of the members of the community. But the two sets of ideas have somewhat different implications for the nature of the process one is trying to create and manage and for the likelihood of success.

Our *Innovation* book has more specific and more operational implications than Arendt's notion of communities of action. It suggests the need for sheltered spaces, protected from competitive pressures, in which an open conversation can occur and the management of that conversation so as to: (a) draw into it a set of actors with diverse backgrounds and experience; and (b) prevent it from getting stale by seeding it with new topics and new participants. How easy it might be to do this is an open question. The focus upon new products which actually found a market in the case studies upon which the book is based gives an optimistic cast to the prospects for success. But at least it does clearly suggest what to look for in order to improve these prospects.

Less optimistic on this score is Arendt's characterization of communities of action, especially as amplified by Gans' study of working-class peer groups and the early history of Italian districts. The critical social structures are deeply embedded, rooted in social experiences that are not easily created where they do not already exist. The language analogy, upon which the *Innovation* book draws so heavily, still seems relevant, but the application of this analogy to communities of action underscores the fact that the aspect of language at work here is not the way it operates as a vehicle for communication, and still less, as a vehicle for the exchange of information. Language is rather a marker of identity; the language community is the context in which identity is created and enacted. The act of speech which language permits is a process, in other words, of identity creation. Probably, such identity communities are latent in many social settings; maybe like language they are inherent in all human community, but they seem to be rooted in relationships which develop in youth and adolescence and not in the kind of adult interaction which the cocktail party metaphor implies. If they are universal aspects of humanity, economic production and exchange are not universally rooted in them. Perhaps public policy could nonetheless generate such communities or turn them toward economic ends. But it seems that to do so it would have to focus on something that happens in the schools rather than sponsoring forums in city halls as the cocktail party metaphor seems to imply. It is not the specific knowledge imparted in the classroom that is of concern but rather the way in which the students are encouraged to use the material of the classroom and the economy to express themselves and their relations to each other. It thus seems more likely that these insights will help us to preserve the communities of action that already exist (or are already focused on economic activity) rather than to create new ones.

21. Innovation processes and industrial districts

Paul L. Robertson, David Jacobson, and Richard N. Langlois*

1. INTRODUCTION

Innovation[1] is based on the generation, diffusion and use of new knowledge. While it is possible to conceive of a firm that is so hermetic in its use of knowledge that all stages of innovation, including the combination of old and new knowledge, rely exclusively on internal sources, in practice most innovations involving products or processes of even modest complexity entail combining knowledge that derives, directly or indirectly, from several sources. Knowledge generation, therefore, must be accompanied by effective mechanisms for knowledge diffusion and for 'indigenizing' knowledge originally developed in other contexts and for other purposes so that it meets a new need.

Because of their individual qualities, industrial districts (IDs) have special environmental characteristics for innovation. When accompanied by close social relationships, tight geographical proximity may affect innovation in ways that are less common in more highly dispersed environments. For example, an awareness of common problems can encourage several firms, or their suppliers and customers, to seek solutions, leading to multiple results that can be tested competitively in the market. These outcomes can then be relatively easily diffused among firms in the ID because of embeddedness in a common environment. The obverse of this commonality of inspiration and ease of transmission of knowledge, however, may be an inordinately inward focus that results in an ignorance of or disdain for innovation processes in other regions or in industries not represented in the ID. Furthermore, there may be a relationship between the degree of embeddedness[2] in the ID and innovation. It has been suggested that innovation increases as embeddedness increases, up to a point, and that beyond that point further embeddedness results in reduced innovation performance at the firm level (Uzzi 1997; Boschma 2005).[3] Thus, depending on circumstances, participation in an ID can either encourage or impede innovation.

In this chapter, we examine the operations of innovation processes within IDs by exploring the ways in which differentiation, specialization and integration affect the generation, diffusion, and use of new knowledge in IDs. We begin in Section 2 with an analysis of the importance of the division of labor in IDs and then investigate the effects of social embeddedness on innovation in the following section. The impact of ID forms of organization at various stages of product and process life cycles is discussed in Section 3, while the negative aspects of embeddedness for innovation are covered in Section 4. The possible consequences of new information and communications technologies on innovation in IDs are discussed in the conclusion.

2. SPECIALIZATION AND EMBEDDEDNESS IN IDs

2.1 Differentiation, specialization and integration

The traditional categories of differentiation, specialization and integration, which are among the most important aspects of the operation of innovation systems, are also defining characteristics of IDs. Firms in IDs form relatively compact networks that promote efficient trade along supply chains. Although technical and economic relationships are important, exchanges of knowledge are also vital to the efficient functioning of IDs (Albino, Garavelli and Schiuma 1999). Firms within an ID have different competences that are either the cause or the result of specialization, and that assist exchange and promote mutual prosperity. Many of the firms produce a narrow range of inputs used in final products or in other intermediate goods. Integration of the inputs then falls to other firms in the system. In an innovation system such as an ID, however, the technical characteristics of inputs and final products, and of production processes, are not necessarily fixed because the technical characteristics of both intermediate and final goods may change.[4] As adaptation usually takes time, a system that is optimized in the sense that there is near-perfect efficiency in the integration of inputs is probably not only stable but static and hence endangered if the surrounding environment is unstable (as is almost always the case). It is important, therefore, that an ID actively generates change in its internal relationships and in those with the outside world, and that it is flexible enough to absorb change without serious losses in efficiency. Inability to change either or both of the internal and external relationships contributed to the decline of such IDs as the textile and fashion district of Como (Alberti 2006) and the eyewear manufacturing district of Belluno (Camuffo 2003).[5]

2.2 Embeddedness and centralization

Many mechanisms are available for the generation, diffusion and use of innovative knowledge in open systems. These vary in their degrees of centralization.

The least centralized mechanism, and the benchmark against which the others are judged, is the traditional competitive market in which buyers and sellers act anonymously, transaction costs are close to zero, and something approaching perfect knowledge prevails. Frequently, even a good approximation of a competitive market is infeasible in practice because there are significant transaction and transport costs and because knowledge on prices and quality is not freely available. As a result, relationships tend to form among firms that, by grouping themselves together, are able to reduce search and other types of costs. The main feature that distinguishes IDs, sectoral systems of innovation (Malerba 2004) and similar groupings from systems that deal 'more directly' with wider markets is their high levels of social embeddedness that, by strengthening some relationships at the expense of others, lead to truncated search patterns. But even this does not exhaust the extent of the variety in centralization that may occur. IDs are more highly centralized than sectoral systems, for instance, because of the integrating roles of assemblers and other integrators.

Because of their structure, IDs offer important benefits in innovation processes. For one thing, the high levels of differentiation and specialization allow firms, in Smithian fashion, to focus on aspects of the supply chain in which they are especially competent. Secondly, since the time of Marshall (Whitaker 1975), commentators have recognized the importance of close social relationship among entrepreneurs and workers in IDs (Bellandi 2003a). The tight geographical proximity of competing firms within a district works to increase social ties within IDs and both the leaders of firms and their workers are embedded (Granovetter 1985) in networks outside their workplaces. Thus all three dimensions of embeddedness – territorial, social and network – are reinforced. The resulting meetings may be purely extramural (sharing drinks at a pub, attending the same church) but still promote discussion of common problems – and of new initiatives. Strong ties (Granovetter 1973) among workers, including managers, can increase the amount of information available to firms and the readiness of people to share what they know when relationships gain a dimension of friendship to counterbalance the competitiveness among firms.

Labor mobility further enhances the spread of knowledge within IDs. When there are many employers, workers can change jobs and roles, moving to other firms to become foremen as Whitaker (1975) suggests, or setting up in business themselves if capital requirements are low or financing is easily available.[6] New firms may fail, but talented people who have gone out on their own can then be reabsorbed as employees in other firms, especially where, as in Silicon Valley, entrepreneurship is rewarded but failure is not severely stigmatized (Saxenian 1994).

2.3 Communities of practice and knowledge diffusion

When embeddedness is strong, the creation of communities of practice (Wenger 1998; Brown and Duguid 2000a) generates competences that, although possessed by individuals, are collective in that they are based on a set of practices that is common to all members of a community. These competences (both tacit and codified) can transcend firm boundaries and become characteristics of an entire ID. As Marshall (Whitaker 1975, p. 197) wrote of 19th century Britain: 'To use a mode of speaking which workmen themselves use, the skill required for their work "is in the air, and children breathe it as they grow up"'. Even when a community of practice is not as all-embracing as Marshall suggests, novices become socialized to a community's mores and procedures as a result of continual association with colleagues. Communities of practice are also important as arenas of learning in which tacit knowledge is transmitted especially well (Lave and Wenger 1991; Wenger 1998), even though the range of ideas transmitted can be narrowed artificially by the stress placed on the local practices followed within the community. While in some cases the knowledge held by a community can be classed as shared routines, it often has dynamic aspects that help to direct attention to solving problems that are widespread within the community.

Relationships within IDs therefore lead to diffusion but also to the creation of new knowledge through shared preoccupations. Because many people or firms can work on a problem simultaneously, a number of different solutions may be found (Bellandi 2003b). The result is a larger and stronger 'gene pool' within the sector (Loasby 1990, p. 117), with the further advantage that solutions that are originally regarded as competing may turn out to be complementary and well suited to different niches within the district.

2.4 Differentiation and modularity

In addition to these casual relationships, close proximity within IDs can enhance the deliberate exchange of information. Managers who meet cheaply and frequently with suppliers, customers and competitors can gain a better appreciation of problems in a sector than when forced to communicate at a distance and through writing. The resulting changes to the system can then be integrated by lead firms that collect information along several segments of a supply chain. Lead firms can provide coordination not only of ideas and inputs, but also of people and of entire firms who might otherwise not be aware that they have complementary needs and knowledge. This integrating function can be performed by merchants who, as in the early modern putting-out system, are in touch with distant markets and are able to communicate information on what is popular to small localized firms, but it may also be a function of lead manufacturers that coordinate changes in the physical configuration of technology as well as in design. Rugman and D'Cruz (2000) call the lead firm the 'flagship firm' that 'pulls the network together and provides leadership for the strategic management of the network as a whole'. More recently, as in Silicon Valley, the integrating role has on occasion been undertaken by venture capitalists or lawyers who have a broad generalist knowledge of what is happening in a district and arrange packages of services and make other connections among small highly-specialized firms (Kenney and Florida 2000).

Some of these integrating activities can take place without spatial proximity (Jacobson, Heanue and Mottiar 2001; Heanue and Jacobson 2001–02). For example, networks of professionals like those in law or medicine are communities of practice that arguably constitute a geographically dispersed 'virtual' ID (Savage 1994). In this case, the virtual character of the network has to do in part with the dispersion of customers and the need to produce the product (provide the service) near the consumer. But it may also have to do in part with the knowledge-intensive character of the products involved. One might thus argue that manufacturing firms outsourcing knowledge-intensive business services are most likely to do so with suppliers elsewhere, because these services are not subject to transport costs and are amenable to provision over distances through information and communication technologies.[7] Evidence suggests, however, that manufacturing firms frequently outsource knowledge-intensive activities locally, with 'geographic proximity, knowledge spillovers and closer interaction among agents mak[ing] it easier for firms to manage complex transactions' (Antonietti and Cainelli 2007, p. 22). This result is supported by research that shows, among other things, that Italian manufacturing firms are more likely to outsource knowledge-intensive business services within IDs (ibid.).

Geographical proximity may also encourage implicit integration of firms. When common practices within an ID lead to high degrees of consistency of products and processes, the introduction of formal and informal modularity is easier. Formal modularity occurs when there are 'design rules' and specified interfaces between components that allow firms to change the components they produce while knowing that this will not require adjustments to other parts of an assembly (Baldwin and Clark 2000).[8] Codified design rules may be unnecessary in IDs, however, as informal modularity can arise when firms within a district have a common vision of what their business is and how they are expected to go about it. The self-image of such firms, as well as their public image, may involve distinctive designs or particular market niches (expensive or cheap products, for example), in this way providing guidance to firms along a supply chain on the kinds of innovations that are likely to succeed in the marketplace. On a technical level, familiarity with production processes within a district gives firms, including suppliers of capital goods, a good working knowledge of how their products relate to existing configurations of components. Thus differentiation and specialization within an ID can lead to implicit integration that is highly effective despite its informality because, as long as particular design and production paradigms do not change dramatically, they offer inexpensive guidance on the types of innovation that firms in an ID can expect to succeed.

3. LIFE-CYCLE CONSIDERATIONS

Inspired by Adam Smith's discussion of the benefits of the division of labor, a number of classic accounts of the life cycle have associated the development of decentralized production systems with an increase in the extent of the market (Young 1928; Stigler 1951). In Stigler's version, for example, firms start out vertically integrated because small markets do not permit specialization. An increased extent of the market permits the spinning off of those stages of production that benefit from increasing returns, thus generating the potential for an ID. As an industry ages in Stigler's account, declining demand for the industry's output would lead to an eventual reintegration. It is the central insight of transaction-cost economics since Coase (1937), however, that production costs alone cannot determine whether the division of labor will be coordinated through markets (as in an ID) or internally within vertically-integrated firms. Transaction costs also matter. And technological change is one important source of transaction costs.

When innovation is radical or systemic, dynamic transaction costs may oblige an innovative firm to produce many of its own inputs in the early stages of both product and process life cycles because the novelty of its activities makes it hard to communicate its requirements to potential external suppliers (Langlois and Robertson 1995). As in Stigler's account, dynamic transaction costs may initially militate against the appearance of an ID, with external suppliers appearing only after the product had established itself. But the reverse can also happen: an industry may develop quickly into an ID but transform into one of vertically-integrated firms when a systemic innovation raises dynamic transaction costs. Examples include automobiles in Detroit in the early 20th century (Langlois and Robertson 1989) and watches in Switzerland in the late 20th century (Langlois 1998).

Moreover, the relationship between innovation and the life cycle of an ID can be complex. Under appropriate circumstances, the organization of firms into IDs can have – and has had – important effects at all stages of product and process life cycles. Depending on the extent of economies of scale, networks of suppliers (multiple networks in the case of complex final goods) can develop to stimulate innovation for all of the reasons discussed in earlier sections, pushing products further along their innovation life cycles. As it takes time for knowledge to diffuse, the generation of clusters of suppliers located near lead firms is not surprising since the significance of new developments will occur first to those who have been closely exposed to them.

In the early stages of an ID, the increasing number of firms and accompanying increases in differentiation and specialization are similar to the network externalities that characterize patterns of adoption of high-technology consumer goods (Rohlfs 2001). Although Marshall (1920) based his argument primarily on pecuniary externalities derived from economies of scale, producers can also benefit substantially from membership in networks such as IDs. Assemblers and other integrators gain to the extent that, by being closely involved in a network of input suppliers, they are able to gain better services. While the latter may involve lower prices for inputs, improvement in the quality of the inputs (as measured by their suitability to perform designated functions) is another important benefit. Thus, an accelerated flow of innovations stemming from suppliers, or from the soundness of the relationship between the assemblers and their suppliers, can occur. Other things being equal, in comparison to geographically-isolated producers or members of more diffuse networks, integrators involved in a successful ID can reasonably be expected to benefit from the generation of a wide range of improvements offered up by their suppliers, just as users of a popular computer operating system can expect to have access to a wider range of software than would be available to users of a marginal operating system.

In addition to competing on cost, suppliers operating in an ID in the early stages of an innovation life cycle can offer new variations on their components, contributing performance improvements that can benefit assemblers in two ways. In some cases, all assemblers may adopt an innovative improvement that consumers perceive to be superior, but in other cases an innovative component that is not seen to be of general value will offer strategic advantages as some producers gravitate to particular market niches by (for a price) offering variations on a generic product for customers with special needs.

Because IDs do not comprise an entire market, their role in the generation of technical standards is complex. The relatively close levels of association between firms in an ID can ease the setting of standards within the district because much of the agreement may be achieved informally and the limited number of firms within an ID makes it easier to bring the interested firms together. Furthermore, when there are only a few integrators who are determining overall designs, less discussion may be needed to achieve commonly-accepted interfaces between components. The effects of concentration on overall industry standards are less clear cut and an industry may fragment into a number of groups dominated by local standards without agreement being reached on an overarching set of standards because there is sufficient volume of output within each ID to allow for self-sufficiency. As a result, while IDs may accelerate innovation along certain trajectories, they may also encourage myopic behavior in the gathering, generation and use of new knowledge.

The role of IDs in promoting innovation in mature industries may also be considerable. Although mature industries, especially those with high concentrations of small and medium-sized enterprises (SMEs), are sometimes portrayed as being technologically stagnant, this is far from the case (Hirsch-Kreinsen, Jacobson and Robertson 2006; Robertson and Patel 2007). The EU's Community innovation surveys and other studies show that the proportion of innovating SMEs in mature industries is at approximately the same level as for firms in general, a finding that applies to at least some mature IDs such as those in Emilia-Romagna where Cainelli and De Liso (2004) found significant levels of 'intentional innovation' among firms.

It is clear that more-or-less successful innovation can sometimes be undertaken in the traditional ID mode. In Prato, as processes have become more complicated and marketing arrangements have altered, the production of textiles has been accompanied by a reactive 'complexification' in which new clusters of specialist firms have been added within the district to deal with an increasingly complicated and differentiated environment. Although some of these new clusters within the Prato ID represent new techniques, in many cases new service firms have arisen to deal with areas such as marketing and sales (Lazzeretti and Storai 2003). In this case, at least, the traditional ID format has proved to be flexible enough to accommodate important organizational innovation.

4. NEGATIVE EFFECTS OF EMBEDDEDNESS

Much of the impetus behind innovation may nevertheless derive from events outside a district – as a result of innovations developed elsewhere and of shifts in consumer demand. The survival of firms, and of entire IDs, therefore depends largely on their ability to adjust to external developments. Indeed, Piore and Sabel's (1984) championing of IDs was based largely on their contention that small firms with generic equipment are more flexible in responding to shifts in demand than large, capital-intensive firms with substantial investments in dedicated equipment.

Nevertheless, the factors underlying successful innovation in some IDs may turn out to be weaknesses depending on the broader innovation environment within a trade or industry. Firms in an ID may simply be slow to notice changes arising outside their district because they do not have good external channels of communication. As Marshall recognized (Loasby 1990), close relationships among firms and their workers could reduce their access to knowledge developed outside the district and their willingness to consider ideas from unfamiliar or distant sources.

Paradoxically this failure of firms is possible after their IDs have had a period of market leadership. They become overconfident and suffer from what Alberti (2006) calls 'success myopia'. The result is that 'trends' in innovation (and not just innovation *per se*) in an ID tend to suffer from inertia[9] – that once tendencies develop, they are harder to stop or to reverse than might be the case if knowledge were generally collected far and wide and if new knowledge were not generated to accommodate implicitly standardized local interfaces. This can lead to severe, perhaps fatal, difficulties when the district is not at the leading edge or when consumer tastes have changed.

Boschma (2005, p. 62) argues that 'too much and too little proximity are both detrimental to learning and innovation'. That is, to function properly, proximity requires just the right amount of distance between actors or organizations. Geographic proximity, for example, may enhance inter-organizational learning and innovation, though in the absence of geographic proximity other forms of proximity may substitute for it. On the other hand, too intense proximity, geographic and otherwise, can result in lock-in. Proximity/embeddedness can evolve over time, too, from not enough, to just enough, to too much, suggesting a link between the issues of embeddedness and life-cycle considerations.

For instance, decentralized systems of innovation (including IDs) may be at a disadvantage in generating genuinely systemic innovations (Teece 1986), that is, innovations that require the development of new components as well as new ways of integrating components. In such a case, the location of much of the relevant knowledge within a tightly-coupled system is likely to facilitate innovation. This need not mean a single vertically-integrated firm, but it does mean that lead or coordinating firms – in modern terminology, systems integrators – must possess a wide range of knowledge or capabilities and must indeed 'know more than they do' (Brusoni, Prencipe and Pavitt 2001). They also need to be powerful enough to force other firms to follow their lead.

In addition, their reliance on local standards can impede efforts by firms in an ID to indigenize innovations from outside, again raising the costs of adjustment and the time required. Finally, firms within a mature ID that do develop innovations may not only find it difficult to generate interest within their ID but are poorly placed to market their innovations externally.

For example, the ability of firms in an ID to jump from one technological trajectory to another (Robertson and Langlois 1994) is often limited by the cumbersome decentralized organization of many districts. Because of high degrees of specialization and the large number of firms that participate in the production process, reeducation procedures are likely to be lengthy. Attributes that once were strengths, such as the presence of implicit standards, can turn into weaknesses that retard a transition from one technology to another. Thus, during periods of major change, the role of integrator firms with strong connections to the external environment is especially important since it is unlikely that smaller suppliers of inputs would have the resources to gather information from diverse sources quickly. The upshot could be major centralization of power and, perhaps, the destruction of many smaller firms as they consolidate or disappear. Nevertheless, there are exceptions, as in the ski boots and sports footwear district of Asolo and Montebelluna where, through concerted development efforts, the producers have coped successfully with a radical change from leather to plastic (Camuffo and Grandinetti 2006).

The problems in adjusting are illustrated by changes in the organization of two Italian IDs following the development of important export markets. Although innovative production processes in the *distretto murgiano*, which specializes in the production of leather sofas, were undertaken by small suppliers, the processes were introduced under the direction of a 'leader firm' (Natuzzi) that had penetrated international markets to become the world's leading producer (Albino, Garavelli and Schiuma 1999). Because of its special needs as a larger firm and of its knowledge of international best practice, Natuzzi was able to direct the upgrading of supplier technologies. In the process, however, the organizational model seems to have changed from the canonical ID to something approaching relationships in Japanese *keiretsu* in which the large firms routinely dictate innovation paths to their small suppliers (Miyashita and Russell 1994). A second example is the eyewear industry in the Belluno district in the Italian Dolomites. In this case, as a result of entering export markets and later of intensified competition in the domestic market by non-Italian firms, the organizational model fragmented as the larger firms, notably Luxottica (by far the world's leading producer of eyewear in 2001), first adopted a leader-firm model similar to that in the leather sofa industry, but eventually went all the way to vertical integration, eliminating dependence on external suppliers altogether. Ultimately four large integrated firms (including Luxottica) were established, but several hundred small firms have continued with diminishing success to operate in the traditional ID mode (Camuffo 2003).

The shift towards computer-aided manufacturing in the furniture industry in Ireland is also changing the nature of the relationships among firms in the region. Leading firms are emerging with the more sophisticated technology, with reduced linkages to the local region and closer ties with strategic allies – particularly but not exclusively upstream – in other countries (Heanue and Jacobson 2008).

In some cases, exogenous technological shifts can render obsolete virtually the entire set of competences of an ID. One such example is the venerable Swiss watch industry, which saw its advantage in mechanical watch movements destroyed by the development of the electronic movement in Japan (Langlois 1998). In such a case, no incremental or endogenous processes of innovation could have been expected to respond adequately to the challenge. In the event, the Swiss industry adapted with a centralized response that incorporated some existing competences (like design and marketing) but left the industry far more vertically integrated – far less an ID – than it had been.

Less positive results are also possible in the mature stage of the industry cycle. Alberti (2006), writing of the decline of the textile ID of Como, identifies a number of cyclical factors, including the 'erosion in top market segments' from new entrants. At the same time, there was a downturn in the global textile industry. In this case, rather than large firms emerging, as in Belluno, with vertical corporate integration providing solutions to low levels of inter-firm collaboration, production, exports, number of firms and employment all declined. The number of workers, for example, went from over 36 000 in 1991 to less than 1900 in 2003.

5. CONCLUSION: INNOVATION AND THE FUTURE OF IDs

Our survey leads to a mixed evaluation of the advantages that IDs hold for the generation, diffusion and use of innovative knowledge. When circumstances are favorable, the high degrees of differentiation and specialization in IDs, combined with high degree of social embeddedness, can encourage knowledge creation in a Smithian sense. As technology evolves in the wider environment, however, the advantages that IDs often offer for the generation and diffusion of knowledge may weaken.

As we have shown, much of the attractiveness of compact, highly-localized areas of production results from their ability to reduce search costs, but this is accompanied by the risk that the knowledge available in any given district may be substandard. But new information and communications technology (ICT), may make it possible for firms to draw more cheaply and effectively on diverse sources of knowledge and therefore to increase their access to innovative ideas (as well as their ability to market their own innovations if they wish) (Langlois 2003; Christensen 2006). This may not undermine all aspects of the operations of IDs because differentiation and specialization retain their importance, and proximity is useful in just-in-time and other lean ways of organizing production. For innovation, however, an ability to tap wider sources of knowledge quickly and cheaply can reasonably be expected to allow firms all along supply chains to consult more broadly than in the past. Improvements in ICT and new search techniques, many of them associated in one way or another with the internet, not only increase access to knowledge but may force innovation on firms that in the past could shelter in IDs. Because their customers can be better informed, firms in IDs need to keep up to date in order to maintain competitiveness.

This does not mean that all firms in IDs will need to become knowledge junkies in the sense of 'directly' searching their broader environments in detail. Commentators on IDs sometimes forget that many firms are embedded in several different networks albeit with different levels of strength and commitment. Firstly, as is generally recognized, even small and highly specialized firms in traditional IDs usually maintain indirect contact with the outside world through the sale of final products in external markets. In very traditional IDs, *impannatori* and distributors act as conduits for information, but even in more sophisticated markets such as eyewear, the manufacturers that develop marketing expertise are able to inform their suppliers on product and process innovations.

Secondly, IDs constitute only one type of industrial agglomeration and even in an ID some firms may belong to more than one type of cluster. In particular, in addition to regional or local systems of innovation, of which IDs may be considered to be one variant, many firms also belong to sectoral systems of innovation (Malerba 2004, 2005) that give them access to new knowledge from other regions or even globally.[10] When this is true, the close relationships in an

ID may be both devalued and enhanced because, although locally-developed innovations are no longer as well placed to capture attention within an ID as when isolation is greater, the close relationships among firms can still encourage a rapid and cheap diffusion of innovations, no matter their source. Because the benefits of cheaper global searches are unlikely to greatly affect many small suppliers, for whom the limited amount of time available to managers to consider non-routine activities remains the crucial bottleneck, the diffusion capabilities of IDs will remain important because they will allow one or two firms, or perhaps a cooperative association, to conduct efficient searches to the potential benefit of all firms in the district.

Therefore, while IDs will continue to offer advantages for knowledge diffusion, and also when considerations such as time and transport costs are important, it is probable that improved methods of communication will generate substantial changes in many cases as local exchanges of knowledge become less advantageous and systems integrators assume tighter control over their suppliers.

NOTES

* We gratefully acknowledge suggestions made by the editors and by Arnaldo Camuffo and Paola Cillo. Any errors, of course, remain our responsibility.
1. Defined here as the introduction of new products, processes and ways of organizing at the level of the individual firm.
2. Hess (2004) emphasizes three dimensions of embeddedness, social, network and territorial. All three dimensions are strong in traditional IDs.
3. This is discussed in more detail in Section 4.
4. For example, in contrast to Adam Smith's emphasis on learning-by-doing in a fixed technological regime, Kenneth Arrow has noted the importance of the introduction of new embodied technology in stimulating adaptive change (Cainelli and De Liso 2004).
5. Note that although we take most of our examples from among the Italian IDs, similar systems of production have emerged in many other regions of the world: see, for example, Pyke and Sengenberger (1992).
6. For a genealogical chart showing how people in the furniture ID in County Monaghan, Ireland, left firms to start their own businesses in the industry, see Mottiar and Jacobson (2002).
7. See Section 4 below. It should be noted that even where complex component manufacturing is outsourced, cost considerations can drive production to far distant locations. See Van Egeraat and Jacobson (2005).
8. One of the benefits of formal modularity is that it obviates the need for common ownership across stages of production. Because the use of design rules reduces transaction costs, it allows firms to communicate cheaply with little, if any, hierarchical coordination.
9. For an account of the decline of the Ruhr, see Grabher (1993b).
10. This may be called 'stretched' or 'distantiated' embeddedness: see Heanue and Jacobson (2008).

22. The creative capacity of culture and the new creative *milieu*

Luciana Lazzeretti[*]

1. INTRODUCTION

We are living in a second modernity, a period of great changes marked by the development of new technological, production and consumption paradigms, a time ruled by uncertainty and by the affirmation of globalisation and the knowledge economy. Old and new economies coexist in the same competitive scenario, and the effects of globalisation are progressively leading to an urbanised vision of the world. Economic and social scientists are asking themselves questions about the new waves of economic development, which are increasingly characterised by territorial competitiveness and by the 'rise and decline' not only of products, sectors and technologies, but also of places, cities, villages and other local systems. The new setting is under construction, and there is a great need for exploring fresh ideas, innovative actors, new combinations, different productive factors and original organisational models (Moulaert and Sekia 2003).

Culture becomes a strategic resource, a useful tool to face the challenge of uncertainty because of its tangible and intangible assets. Radical change cannot be led by rationality, instead it is necessary to develop techniques of creative thinking or lateral thinking,[1] as termed by the renowned Cambridge psychologist De Bono (1971) to foster an innovation capacity related not only to science and technology but also to culture and arts.

The lesson taught by cultural districts and clusters and cities of art is that culture can be a flywheel for economic development, capable of linking local networks with global networks. Viewed as high-culture local systems (Lazzeretti 2004), they may be considered as 'hub and spoke' (Markusen 1996) systems, namely the meeting points for artists or creative firms. They can set in motion innovative *filières* for particular events (Maskell, Barthelet and Malberg 2006) associating temporary clusters and embedded cultural institutions.

In this context, scholars of economic development exploring new paths of development between 'novelty' and 'renewal' can very well find in the cultural resources an opportunity for advantageously reconsidering the concept of the 'industrial district (ID) as a creative *milieu*' (Becattini 1991).

Drawing on the cultural districtualisation model in cities of art[2] (Lazzeretti 2003, 2008), in this contribution we would like to concentrate on the way culture can foster creativity and innovation. We define creativity as the 'creative capacity of culture' (CCC) and argue that it is important in relation with the emerging debate that focuses on the cultural enhancement of the economy. According to this perspective, culture is not only seen as a flywheel for economic development, but also as a source for innovation, because it has the power to revitalise cities, districts, sectors, professions, goods through the generation of new ideas, cross-fertilisation and serendipity.

The main research questions discussed here are the following: (a) how does CCC contribute to economic development and innovation; and (b) which environments promote and foster creativity and innovation?

Following the introduction, the chapter is divided into four parts. In Section 2 we have endeavoured to identify the evolution of the relationship between culture and economy, underscoring the transition between the phase of economic exploitation of culture (culture as a factor of production) and a new phase called the 'cultural enhancement of economy' (culture as a source of innovation). In Section 3 the CCC concept is discussed and four principal lines of development are singled out (urban regeneration, economic renewal, cross-fertilisation and serendipity). In Section 4 we define 'the spatial dimension of creativity' as our theoretical context. Then we propose a revised notion of the creative *milieu*, developed from a GREMI–Becattini–De Bono axis and completed with some contamination derived from culture/creative economics and the evolutionary approach. Section 5 consists of some conclusive remarks.

2. THE EVOLUTION OF THE CULTURE–ECONOMY RELATIONSHIP

Studies on the economic enhancement of culture have recently reached a turning point in the general understanding of the relationship between culture and economy, whereby creativity, rather than culture, is placed at the centre of the debate and economy-led models (for example, the creative city) have gained wider space compared to culture-led models (for example, the cultural cluster).

Within this new stage of the 'cultural enhancement of economy', culture becomes a source of innovation, and the focus shifts on human capital, innovation processes and firms viewed as innovative and creative actors. In the past, culture[3] was mainly seen as an asset first needing preservation and secondly enhancement; now the attention is shifting on its capacity to produce new knowledge and on the way its material and immaterial resources are able to generate 'novelty' and 'renewal'. This trend can be perceived in the latest studies of the creative economy, as well as in those pertaining to the economy of culture, all of which are in fact showing a tendency to converge to such common research ground.

2.1 The economic enhancement of culture

Within the economy of culture, a first important step was to move from the 'preservation to the economic enhancement of culture'. A variety of scholars contributed to this multidisciplinary debate: art historians, anthropologists, social scientists, and obviously economists of culture and art management (Towse 2003; Ginsburgh and Throsby 2006). Culture and economy were combined in a successful paradigm, which was first constructed in the US, later in Europe, and more recently also in transition and developing countries (Power and Scott 2004). The initial intent of this field of research was to show how culture could be considered as a production factor like any other, since it could play an important role in the traditional cultural industries (such as publishing) or in non-profit sectors. An exemplary non-profit case is that of museums, which clearly represent how an object of preservation can turn into the target of various kinds of economic enhancement. At the same time, the idiosyncratic value of resources (Marshall 1920 and Harris 1977) took up a strategic value, just like cultural districts and clusters in their different connotations, and became an emerging phenomenon emphasising the role of culture as a flywheel for economic development. Some American scholars define cultural districts as a 'well-recognised, labelled, mixed-use area of a city in which a high concentration of cultural facilities serves as the anchor of attraction' for other activities (Frost Kumpf 1998, p. 29); some authors worked out taxonomies meant to differentiate cultural districts from institutional, industrial, urban or museum districts (Santagata 2002); yet others drew attention to the role of cultural districts in territorial marketing, or pointed out the importance of their resources (Kebir and Crevoiser 2008).

Drawing on the literature on district dynamic processes (Becattini 2004a), 'cultural districtualisation processes' have been analysed with demographic and ecological methods (Lazzeretti 2006; De Propris and Lazzeretti 2009). In previous work, Lazzeretti (2003, 2008) developed and applied the cultural districtualisation model to cities of art, introducing a multidisciplinary methodology which combined the Becattinian–Marshallian approach with cluster theory (Porter 1998a),[4] the so-called 'cultural, artistic and environmental heritage' method. Under this perspective the cultural district is a complex and articulated model, but not the only one, in as much as it is possible to encounter more simplified forms that do not present all of the typical district processes to which the ID literature makes reference.

In the approach above two concepts play together: (a) the 'cultural, artistic and environmental heritage' that mirrors the set of resources necessary to define a 'high culture' (hereafter HC) place, and (b) the HC cluster, that is, the set of actors involved in the economic enhancement of the resources.

It is worth clarifying some key concepts. Artistic resources include strictly speaking the set of artistic assets and of art works (for example, monuments, architectural complexes, art works, buildings, archaeological sites); cultural resources refer to that set of activities, behaviours, habits and ways of life that makes one place different from any other (for example, universities and research centres, traditional arts and crafts, contextual knowledge, events and manifestations, or the neighbourhood 'atmosphere'); human resources comprise, for instance, artists, writers, scientists and artisans; and finally, environmental resources refer to typical elements of the urban, natural and environmental landscape (for example, urban morphology, ornamental gardens, parks, streets, squares, neighbourhoods, characteristic flora and fauna).

Both the concepts of Cultural, Artistic and Environmental Heritage and HC cluster flow into the synthetic definition of the HC local system.

> A High Culture Local System is characterised by the presence of a large endowment of artistic, natural and cultural resources which identify it as a High-Culture Place, and of a network of economic, non-economic and institutional actors who carry out activities concerning the conservation, enhancement, and economic management of these resources and which represent in their totality the High-Culture City Cluster (HC Cluster). (Lazzeretti 2003, p. 638)

Degrees and forms of cultural districtualisation are distinguished by the existence of at least three basic elements: (a) the presence of HC places (identified through idiosyncratic resources); (b) the economic enhancement of cultural resources (identified through the clusters of economic, non-economic, and institutional actors); and (c) the localisation of resources and actors (geographical proximity). The model has been so far tested in two cities (Florence and Seville) and two regions (Tuscany and Andalusia) in the sectors of art restoration, museums, music and cultural events.[5]

2.2 The 'cultural enhancement of economy'

A further step forward along this stream of studies was to start considering culture as a source of innovation capable of generating new ideas and improvements, of rejuvenating mature sectors or creating new ones. Analyses were especially concerned with the role of creativity, so much that the focus gradually shifted from cultural districts to creative districts (OECD 2005a) in the US, Europe and Asia – see for instance, A.J. Scott's (2005) work on the Hollywood film district which was replicated for the newborn Indian district of Bollywood (Lorenzen and Taeube 2007). Therefore, just as scholars previously studied the economy of culture by focusing on cultural heritage and performing arts, now those concerned with the creative economy are attracted to creative industries, knowledge economy and ICT. Moreover, while in the beginning a distinction was made between cultural and creative industries, now the two terms are more and more frequently used as equivalents (Caves 2000), and the creative industry as a whole represents today one of the emerging events in modern economy.[6]

In parallel to the rising concern with creative districts, there has been a renewed attention to the concept of the creative city, which is directly associated with those of the cultural city in the new millennium (Hubbard 2006) and the city of knowledge (Trullén and Boix 2008). The idea was immediately related to the creative industries (Hall 2000) and later to Florida's creative class (Florida 2002). Florida's contributions, in particular, gave rise to an intense debate (Glaeser 2005) on this matter and generated a huge quantity of empirical research. More recently, the attention has shifted to an entrepreneurial approach linking creativity, the formation of new firms and entrepreneurship (Lee, Florida and Acs 2004). Florida considers entrepreneurs as part of the creative class, while urban planners promote the entrepreneurial approach to urban regeneration (Hall and Hubbard 1998; OECD 2007a). Table 22.1 summarises the principle factors that characterise the transition between the two phases under examination.

Table 22.1   The evolution of the relationship between culture/creativity and economy

Economic enhancement of culture	Cultural enhancement of economy
Culture as asset	Culture/creativity as capacity
Culture as a factor of production and a flywheel of economic development	Culture/creativity as sources of innovation
Focus on artistic, cultural, environmental heritage	Focus on creative class, knowledge economy, ICT
Focus on local economic development	Focus on innovation process
Cultural district/cluster	Creative district/cluster
Cultural industries and non-profit sector	Creative industries
City of art	Creative cities

Source: Our elaboration.

3. THE CREATIVE CAPACITY OF CULTURE

As argued in the previous section, we are at the beginning of a new stage in the studies on the relationship between culture and economy. The attention is moving from the artistic, cultural and environmental heritage to the human capital; from the preservation and valorisation of cultural heritage to the production of culture. Culture and creativity are associated with innovation and local development, sometimes overflowing from the boundaries of the traditional cultural sectors. A concept helping to capture this shift is the CCC, which is the ability to rejuvenate places, sectors or professions, and to generate ideas and innovations through processes of cross-fertilisation and serendipity. CCC involves searching new and different relationships, preferably of unusual relatedness, which are at the basis of the innovation process. It originates from the manifold idea of proximity (Lorentzen 2005), not only of a geographical type, as explored in the cultural districtualisation model, but of a cognitive type (see Section 4.2; Boschma 2005). The concept of proximity evolves and is diversified, it is no longer applied only to conditions of exchange but above all to the conditions by which shared interests meet for constructing something together. Cognitive proximity can be found, for instance, in a situation where temporary artist networks come into play during the organisation of cultural events (that is, projects, exhibits and festivals) or at a virtual level in the epistemic communities like open-source software. The main objective becomes the search for 'relatedness', which constitutes the *incipit* of development paths for CCC.

3.1 The principal factors promoting creativity

Current literature suggests that creativity has a strong correlation with localisation. From Marshall onwards, study after study on economic development has discussed this relationship and explored the advantages produced by colocalisation of specialised firms in terms of agglomeration economies and knowledge spillovers. For example, Bellandi (1992) emphasised the importance of the 'decentralised industrial creativity' involved in the coexistence of different subindustries inside the ID *filière*. Some studies on cultural and creative industries instead underscore the tendency to form dense clusters within and around the cities (Maskell and Lorenzen 2004; Lazzeretti, Boix and Capone 2008), whether small or medium firms of the traditional sector (as in the case of art restoration workshops) or big firms of the technology-related sectors (as in the case of music and film industries). Clustering also affects creative class, in fact the artists usually tend to settle in the same neighbourhoods (O'Hagan and Kelly 2006).

However, diversity is the real motor of the creative process, the fuel for creativity that generates opportunities for development and contaminations. Culture economy studies stress the strategic role of 'cultural diversity' expressed in terms of people and talent (Florida 2002; UNESCO 2005), while urban economists and geographers emphasise the differences at the level of sectors and firms (Jacobs 1961). Nevertheless, beyond the various definitions the recurring fundamental principle is 'heterogeneity', of various natures, which ensures confrontation and exchange.[7]

Discussion has not taken into consideration an ideal size for creativity, nor a dominant type of organisation. Creativity is multifaceted and takes on a wide range of forms: from the creative neighbourhood to the large creative metropolis (in terms of territorial scale); from the multinationals of the multimedia to the firms of artistic artisans (in terms of industry scale).

Last of all, creativity is correlated to entrepreneurship. Innovative ideas need effective entrepreneurial action, able to find new and diverse combinations and to sufficiently develop their potentials and to transform them into innovations. Without entrepreneurial capability creativity could remain an opportunity only, without leading to actual innovations.

3.2 The principal paths of development for CCC

CCC is a fuzzy concept (Markusen et al. 2008) that may develop at various levels (territory, industry, business, profession) giving origin to different forms of innovation (rejuvenation, incremental innovation, radical innovation) that follow various paths of development. In the following we identify some of them:

1. 'Urban renewal'. This path was more extensively explored within the urban planning discipline and then applied through initiatives like place marketing. An OECD report (2007a) specifically devoted to this issue singled out three main urban-regeneration strategies, which are: (a) 'city branding', which endeavours to apply the same methodology employed in commercial product marketing to geographical locations and to create and nurture the narratives that give meaning to a place; (b) 'physical renovation' such as flagship city centre development was conceived to bring brand images to life by giving them material forms – like the Bilbao Guggenheim museum and the 'water front city promotion' (Baltimore model); and (c) 'culture-led strategies' regarding the organisation of exhibits and events like Olympic games and world expos.
2. 'Economic renewal'. This second path is not as well systematised, but nevertheless is no less important than the previous one. It pertains to the idea that culture can rejuvenate not only places, but also products, professions and sectors that are mature or declining. This can be achieved through: (a) 'industry regeneration' – that is, reliance on new cross-sector technology, or exploration of cross-sectional applications (design); (b) 'product rejuvenation' – for example, the case of the wine district in Piedmont's Langhe area, where the DOC denomination has rebranded the products (see Santagata 2002); and (c) 'profession rejuvenation' – consider, for example, the case of the high-tech artistic craft of the Florentine antique restorers who started to be considered as a creative class and as a source of urban regeneration.
3. 'Cross-fertilisation'. A third path is specifically associated with novelty rather than with regeneration. Jacobs (1961) stressed the importance of innovation in the cross-fertilisation of ideas between industries, as well as between economic actors and the broader community. The central points to be

considered are 'relatedness' and CCC, that is, the ability to seek and build new relationships. This ability can be affected basically by two factors: cognitive distance (Noteboom 2000) and cognitive proximity (Boschma 2005). Cross-fertilisation can take place in many ways: 'inside a cultural cluster/district' involving different professional abilities (specialisations) within a same productive *filière*; through 'related'[8] cultural clusters/sectors inside and outside the city, for example in fashion clusters, museum clusters and music clusters of art cities; through 'unrelated' clusters/sectors inside the city, as is the case of cross-fertilisation between the biomedical and health diagnostics sector and the cultural heritage sector; or 'over time', such as the rebirth of a 'creative district', like that of Birmingham jewellery, a classical Marshallian manufacturing district that has presently been revived as an urban cluster founded on design marketing and retailing (De Propris and Lazzeretti 2007).

4. 'Serendipity'. The last path is very different from the previous ones and is quite hard to trace. Usually, the term 'serendipity' is described as 'the capacity of discovering pleasing or valuable things by chance' (*Collins English Dictionary* 1998). In this case CCC has to do with the discovery of an unusual correlation that is the basis for an innovative idea, which may be connected with new uses for a product, diversification, or technological correlations. Coke, for example, was originally invented as a medicament and only later used as a soft drink; nonetheless, its formula is still a secret, just like that of many other medicaments. Diversity may also have a positive role in this sense, as suggested for example by Pasteur when he links his original idea of 'protection by inoculation with germs of weakened virulence' to his array of interests and his ability to make associations. Another case is that of laser cleaning technologies in art conservation discovered by chance while using them for a holographic archival recording of statues and monument (holograms for an archive of art works) (Asmus et al. 1973). Another typical example in the context of a creative district is that of the metal-detector technology applied to airports: it was conceived by an Arezzo jewellery firm and used for the selection process of metallic alloys to weight gold carats.[9]

4. THE NCM: MAIN THEORETICAL CONTRIBUTIONS AND A FIRST DEFINITION

Moving on to addressing another question initially posed – which environments promote and foster creativity and innovation – the concept of the ID as a creative *milieu* can be recovered and redefined under the perspective illustrated in the previous section, and finally linked to the concept of creativity as the CCC.

Following a creative *milieu* approach (GREMI–Becattini–De Bono) enriched by contaminations derived from culture and creative economics, a new definition of the creative *milieu* can be introduced that embraces the 'cultural enhancement of economy'. The new creative *milieu* (NCM) can be seen as 'an informal, collective open space, able to release the CCC within cultural clusters/districts or other environments, and characterised by processes of lateral thinking and problem finding'. The CCC, therefore, plays a strategic role in the innovation process, above all in the initial phase of ideas' generation, and, in the NCM, favoring the transformation of ideas into innovations, sometimes in sectors different from those where it was originally generated.

4.1 The theoretical context: the spatial dimension of creativity

In order to identify a theoretical context for NCM, we identify the spatial dimension of creativity with respect to two dimensions: local economic development and innovation processes. The 'Marshallian creative atmosphere' represents, moreover, the theoretical glue of different past approaches and the antecedent of the current relations between culture and creativity, and between local development and innovation.

The spatial dimension of innovation constitutes a common ground for studies on local economic development and on innovation economy; as well as a classical topic in terms of territorial competitiveness and endogenous development. In particular, the concept of *milieu innovateur* developed by the GREMI school is crucial, because it focuses on the relationship between local development and innovation, giving special attention to urban environments, which are considered of strategic importance for culture. We would like to recall how Camagni and Maillat (2006) underlined the role played by resources and institutions, and by the governance of innovation, which is capable of combining innovative networks between firms; theirs is a dynamic approach, fully open to the outside, capable of suggesting integrated solutions that link anchoring and embeddedness. Recently the GREMI approach, traditionally focused on high-tech and industrial sectors, has also taken into consideration cultural and natural resources (Camagni, Maillat and Matteaccioli 2004). In this case it constitutes an interesting antecedent for our reasoning.

A second important contribution comes from the studies of 'proximity', recalled in the definition of CCC, whereby the recent debate has moved towards a 'diversification' (Lorentzen 2005) of the concept. Boschma (2005) cleverly discerned this notion by classifying it into five categories: cognitive (based on knowledge gap); organisational (based on control); social (based on trust-social relations); institutional (based on trust-common institutions); geographical (based on spatial distance). Proximity has great relevance to the CCC, and the distance between sectors, clusters, professions or firms is not only physical or relational, but mainly cognitive. The creative city, viewed as a hub-and-spoke knot of local and global networks and a place of diversity, needs to reduce distances and to increase opportunities for exchange and confrontation in order to generate new ideas and innovations.

But how is it possible to go from the spatial dimension of innovation to the spatial dimension of creativity? To answer this question, we draw on Becattini (1991) and his notion of Marshallian industrial district (MID) as 'a creative *milieu*' developed by considering some reflections on lateral thinking by De Bono (1971). Becattini highlights the fact that creativity cannot be considered merely as a potentiality, since it is a real fact. He distinguishes a 'generic creativity', that is, the ability of an individual or a group to attempt making unusual connections, from a 'goal-oriented creativity', which expresses an efficient combinatorial ability. 'The Marshallian industrial district produces a constant synergic interaction between problem solving and problem finding' (Becattini 1991, p. 46), in other words, vertical thinking may be effectively used alongside lateral thinking.

In fact, lateral thinking is the ability to explore all the different ways of looking at something rather than accepting the most promising and proceeding from that. This ability may be enhanced by 'reasoned' use of chance[10] and may facilitate overflowing boundaries not only of sectors, but also of disciplinary paradigms (Hirschman 1981). This activity leads to unusual connections that may produce failures or achievements, which represent a tangible expression of creativity.[11]

'Connections' represent the strategic nexus that should be highlighted and trying to find them can be as good a practice as frequenting 'informal environments'.[12] Breit (1987) underlined the important role of convivial settings, and Becattini (2004a) showed that districts are life and working places likely to create many informal occasions for exchanges and confrontation not structured inside the organisation. Lester and Piore (2004) recently confirm this when they say that Italian districts, as well as universities and the emerging open-source communities, can constitute good examples of a 'public space' that facilitates conversations and not only problem solving.

Another related concept is that of creative economies, that is, those external agglomeration economies that can be explained in terms of both diversity and specialisation. Feldman and Audretsch (1999) link the latter with innovation, while Lorenzen and Frederiksen (2008) underline the coexistence of creative cities and knowledge. The analyses of the cultural districtualisation of cities of art place great emphasis on the advantages gained on the one hand by district specialisation and on the other by the diversity of cities (Lazzeretti 2008). Becattini himself (1991) reminds us that even in monosectorial districts, the coexistence of different competencies, and different approaches resulting from the division of labour, can lead to yet new combinations. Innovation has a diffusive capacity in districts and proceeds within various subsystems of the production processes and of the *filière* generating external economies of creativity (Bellandi 1992). According to Dei Ottati (2006), creative economies are semi-automatic economies characterised by continuous innovation; in other words, they are produced by the normal functioning of the district. The Marshallian creative atmosphere shaped by circulation of knowledge and mutual learning encourages industrial creativity, thanks not only to the great number of interacting subjects but also to the fact that competencies are various and interlinked.

How can this perspective be related to studies on creative economy and the evolutionary approach? We believe that the concept of creative 'habitat', developed by Florida in the context of the theory of human capital and based on the three Ts (Tolerance, Talent and Technology), can enrich the idea of creative *milieu* worked out by Becattini and De Bono. Florida (2002), starting from the observation of how competition is increasingly played at a global level, maintains that localities can create an economic and social microclimate capable of activating and mobilising the resources that are crucial to growth. He also underlines how the choice one makes of 'where to live' is as important as that of 'who to work for', and the city in this case may be considered a 'creative habitat'.

A last reference concerns some contributions of innovation economists that follow an approach of an evolutionary type. A crucial concept is that of absorptive capacity, coined by Cohen and Levinthal (1990), which emphasise how the ability of a firm to understand and 'absorb' external knowledge is dependent on its own 'knowledge base'. In this case, the unit of analysis is the firm with its path dependence and its ability to accumulate, although later on Giuliani (2005) extended it to the cluster, and evolutionary geographers linked it to the related variety approach (Frenken, van Oort and Verburg 2007), thus broadening this perspective to cities and regions. The latter approach is particularly relevant here because it allows the opportunity to seize the different typologies of relatedness within cross-fertilisation and because it considers the notion of related variety in terms of shared complementary competencies according to a cognitive base, which is a fundamental step in order to introduce the notion of lateral proximity.

Finally, a concept directly related to the absorptive capacity is that of knowledge spillover, which associates the local economic development approach with evolutionary economics. In this contribution, we consider the creative knowledge spillover connected with creative industries and creative class.[13] Further diffusive effects may occur in adjacent sectors also due to a 'creative use' of knowledge spillovers.

4.2 The NCM: towards a definition

There is no such thing as a creative place in itself, be it a city, a district or whatever else. What qualifies a creative *milieu* is not a potential creative environment (generic creativity), but a proactive environment able to generate innovation and knowledge transfer (goal-oriented creativity): this is the atmosphere in which the CCC can develop by cross-fertilisation and serendipity. The CCC is the ability to create 'relatedness' and it is advanced by lateral proximity, which is basically measurable in terms of cognitive distance. This kind of creativity promotes research and lateral thinking, and takes part in the development of creative economies where the strengths of cluster/district specialisations combine with the city's ability to diversify.

Five main elements of the NCM can be spelled out in relation to the 'spatial dimension of creativity':

1. 'Creative habitat'. It is a place likely to attract a creative class and be elected as a living and working place. Its attractive quality may be due not only to its human capital, but also to its creative firms. It is characterised by the existence of material and immaterial cultural resources, and by creative human and social capital. In this setting, social capital is an essential strategic resource for the creative class.
2. 'Creative spillover'. Creative spillovers are knowledge spillovers generated by lateral thinking, which is typical of artists as well as of creative industries and other creative actors. Ideas are 'in the air', shaping the atmosphere of creative habitats.
3. 'Lateral proximity'. Lateral proximity is based on lateral thinking and helps explore the different 'whys' of looking at something. It is basically a cognitive proximity favoured by informal *milieux*, such as convivial settings. Its effectiveness depends on 'cognitive distance', which is measurable in terms of related/unrelated knowledge and on the various typologies of links and nexuses which creative actors are liable to find (relatedness).[14]
4. 'Creative absorptive capacity'. This is the ability to transform generic creativity into goal-oriented creativity, so as to generate and even transfer ideas and innovations. Such a capacity depends on the tacit knowledge accumulated within a creative habitat and on the path dependence of creative actors. Its effectiveness can be measured in terms of individual or collective ideas and innovations, normally protected by intellectual property rights.
5. 'Creative economies'. These are external agglomeration economies achieved in creative *milieux*, that is, cross-fertilisation economies that can link the advantages of specialisation with those of diversification. Therefore, they are correlated with diversity, cross-fertilisation and serendipity.

5. CONCLUDING REMARKS AND RESEARCH OUTLOOKS

With this chapter we wish to contribute to the debate concerning the evolution prospects of IDs, in relation with our studies on cultural districts/clustering. We have explored the relationship between culture, creativity, local development and innovation, substantially to increase our understanding of how the CCC can contribute to economic development and innovation; and what environment can promote and foster creativity and innovation.

This chapter has illustrated the rise of a new phase in the relationship between culture and economy that we have named 'cultural enhancement of the economy', characterised by the transition of culture as a factor of production/asset to that of culture as a source of innovation/capacity. Culture and creative economy studies have broadened the traditional district perspective to include services and non-profit sectors, particularly artistic, cultural and environmental heritage. This perspective was further broadened with the diffusion of the ICT and knowledge economy. We witness the rise of creative industries and with them the attention is shifting to include not only more traditional IDs but also those relying on creativity. Creativity still remains a mainly urban phenomenon and studies of creative cities and urban clusters are still predominant, even if discussion has also begun in relation to rural creativity and other creative local systems.

A second contribution to the debate has been the introduction of the concept of CCC that endeavours to capture the connection between creative culture and innovation and contextualise the new phase identified (cultural enhancement of economy). Culture becomes creativity, in other words, the search for unusual 'relatedness'. Creativity is able to rejuvenate territories, sectors or products and also to generate ideas and innovations. Diversity is the engine of creativity and is fuelled by differences, whether in people or talent, industry or firms. CCC may also benefit from geographical proximity, but it only occurs in the presence of shared ideals and knowledge (cognitive proximity) and does not achieve fulfilment without effective entrepreneurial action. Urban and economic renewal, cross-fertilisation and serendipity are the principal creative pathways, which give rise to different types of innovation (rejuvenation, incremental and radical innovations) and involve several units of analysis (city, district, sector, products, professions).

The lines of research opened are many, but two in particular were considered: the analysis of creative districts – creative industries and creative class – and the study of CCC based rejuvenation processes for mature districts or districts in phase of crisis.

Concerning the environment which can support and foster innovation, two suggestions have been illustrated. The first is represented by the identification of a 'spatial dimension of creativity', which constitutes the theoretical premise necessary to begin the empirical study of creative environments. The second is the redefinition of the creative *milieu*: the NCM. The concept is not new to the district approach, but the route used to reach it is new, starting from the relationship between culture and economy. According to such perspective, creative environments are those where lateral thinking may reach its most free expression and where the CCC may develop its capacity to find unusual correlations. In this way attention is focused on the initial phase of the innovation process, represented by the generation of ideas (problem finding), where culture may play a decisive role. The definition of some characteristic elements of NCM constitutes a first theoretic effort to introduce a creative/evolutional dimension to the concept, which is not necessarily limited to the cultural district or cluster.

A noteworthy aspect that emerges from our studies is that the ID can be seen as a 'public space', and creativity is first of all a social factor. For this,

Marshallian districts can be ideal locations for sharing and exchanges, places to develop lateral thinking in the search for new ideas and innovations.

NOTES

* I wish to thank Francesco Capone, Tommaso Cinti, Rafael Boix, the participants of the RSA and ACEI conferences (2008) for their suggestions and comments. Any remaining errors are the responsibility of the author.
1. 'The lateral thinker tends to explore all the different ways of looking at something rather than accepting the most promising and proceeding from that . . . Vertical thinkers take the most reasonable view of a situation and then proceed logically and carefully to work it out' (De Bono 1971, p. 10). In this chapter we will use lateral thinking and creative thinking as synonyms.
2. The cultural districtualisation model for the sustainable economic development is based on the trinomial 'culture–economy–society' and based on the resources–actors–community axis that tends to enhance the artistic, cultural, human and environmental differences of localities.
3. We refer to a broader concept of culture, and the 'cultural, artistic and environmental heritage' method employed in the cultural districtualisation model, see Section 2.1.
4. In our approach, the analysis of the cluster constituted one of the fundamental components of the cultural districtualisation model, focusing on the actors that activate the processes of the economic enhancement of resources. However, in the district perspective, the place is a 'place of life', while from a managerial approach, place is principally a strategic resource, a key factor to be implemented for competition strategies (for example, territorial marketing).
5. A synthesis of the principal empirical researches carried out may be found in Lazzeretti (2008).
6. Creative industries include: Advertising, Architecture, The art and antiques market, Crafts, Design, Designer fashion, Film and video, Interactive leisure software, Music, The performing arts, Publishing, Software and computer services, Television and radio (DCMS 2001).
7. Some authors also consider diversity and variety (Lorenzen and Frederiksen 2008). In our studies concerning cities of art as HC local systems we have used the number of related and unrelated sectors present as a diversity index and the number of different firm categories as the variety index.
8. According to the evolutionary geography approach, sectors are related in terms of shared or complementary competencies (cognitive-based definition).
9. See Ceia, 'Patent n. AR2002A000029', 2002, www.Ceia.net, accessed 4 September 2008.
10. For De Bono (1971) creative thinking is not in itself undisciplined, but follows a logic which is ordered according to four fundamental principles: recognition of dominant polarising ideas; search for different ways of looking at things; relaxation of rigid control of vertical thinking; and use of chance.
11. The laser cleaning methodology used for the preservation of artwork is a case of serendipity, but for physics laser technology in restoration work is also a good example of problem finding. Nevertheless, it took almost 20 years for a successful innovation to develop from the discovery (Salimbeni, Pini and Siano 2002). Our current research hypothesis (Florence as a NCM) stresses that this innovation was put to practice in this city in particular and not, for example, in Venice where it was originally developed.
12. Some examples of convivial settings are the 'cafeteria effect' in the Parisian *milieux* pointed out by Camagni, or the High Table of Oxford and Cambridge economists evoked by Becattini, or Piore and Lester's cocktail manager, or – which I dare to include – the Staff House at BHM University.
13. An institutional creative spillover occurs in art schools and colleges which attract young artists, creating an artistic atmosphere and thus providing mutual inspiration and incentives for artists to stay on after their formal education has been completed (Bille and Schulze 2006).
14. In the district, this distance may be shortened because of the presence of collective goods and common knowledge, and by the common goals of the *filière*. In the city, it may be even shorter when it crisscrosses with other typologies of proximity, for example institutional or geographical. On the other hand, this distance can be wider even in the case of colocation, whenever the actors involved belong to different worlds and have conflicting values.

23. Technology clusters, industrial districts and regional innovation systems

Philip Cooke

1. INTRODUCTION: KNOWLEDGE ECONOMIES

In this chapter an effort is made to compare and contrast Marshallian industrial districts (MIDs), neo-MIDs, technology clusters and regional innovation systems (RISs). Key similarities and differences involving social and spatial issues will enable a clearer understanding of when and how each terminology is appropriate. Briefly, spatial scale is a crucial differentiating element in distinguishing districts, old and new, and clusters, technological and even 'creative', from RISs. In simple terms a RIS may embrace numerous clusters or districts because the latter tend to be subregional or even localised as 'quarters' as in creative or cultural quarters of cities but also other business quarters – for example, gun and jewellery quarters in Birmingham; see De Propris and Lazzeretti (2007). Technology clusters like Silicon Valley or Greater Boston can be city-regional in scale but still within at least their administrative region or State that often has resources and support instruments for regionalised technology policy. Indeed a RIS that encompasses a knowledge generation or exploration subsystem of well-networked research institutes and university or corporate centres of research excellence, juxtaposed with a functioning knowledge exploitation system of clustered (and unclustered) firms and intermediaries (for example, technology parks, incubators and risk capital) has legitimacy because it normally (not always) has democratically devolved innovation support powers.

Knowledge is now, as founding fathers from Marshall to Schumpeter and beyond proposed, clearly driving firm competitiveness and economic evolution. Scientific, technological and creative knowledge industries can be found included in such variants as high-tech, 'green' and creative clusters. Nowadays strict sectoral thinking about clusters is far less straightforward than it was in Marshallian times and even nowadays in Third Italy, for example, because of technological convergence, which elsewhere has been shown to involve 'cluster mutation' involving, for example, ICT and biotechnology, producing 'platforms' of 'clean technology' in Silicon Valley or ICT, photovoltaics, agricultural and marine engineering-evolving wind turbine and solar thermal energy clusters in North Jutland, Denmark. These 'Jacobian clusters' are a newly-identified and powerful driver of regional evolution (Jacobs 1969; Cooke 2008, 2009). Each type benefits also from RISs and national innovation policies. Such 'network regions' involve systematic communication and transaction linkages among nodes through networks of people and institutions intra-regionally and globally. National subsidies to cluster development may assist technology and creative clusters. Well-networked regions are said to develop more accomplishment economically and socially, enriching their inhabitants accordingly. The network imagery began to be applied in the 1980s, with prefigurative concepts like *milieu* being advanced from the Francophone community of economic geographers. Contemporaneously, the Italian interest in industrial districts (IDs) led subsequently and by others, to exploration of networks in new contexts, including high-tech regions. Later it was noticed that while IDs rely deeply on community, clusters rely more on the 'associational' advantages of shallower 'business networks'.

Subsequently, from an evolutionary economic geography viewpoint, these streams have folded into a master narrative of RISs. Here, a knowledge 'exploration' and generation subsystem, composed of research and learning units (including 'distant networks') interacts through a membrane of private and public intermediaries, with the knowledge 'exploitation' or commercialisation regional subsystem of firms. Such arrangements denote a well-functioning RIS. These can be more entrepreneurially (ERIS) or institutionally (IRIS) inflected. They are found in developed and developing countries, notably China, but they are by no means ubiquitous. The evolution of technology clusters can in exceptional cases be shown to follow the intrinsic form of 'species multiplication' rather as happened previously in the belts of IDs. But nowadays, national innovation policies and RIS linkages are important adjuncts. In this chapter, first, the relationships among IDs, technology clusters (including creative), and RISs are explored. Next the importance of systems integration of economic (and social) processes with policy interventions is noted, and as a clarification, the etymology of RISs is traced, showing varieties of Marshallian and Schumpeterian, but also 'general systems' theoretical influences, in the formation of the concept.

Finally, a novel analysis depicts certain important isomorphisms between Marshallian and modern technology districts that differentiate both from the more 'socialised' neo-Marshallian variant. However, on one key variable, innovation, Marshallian districts tended to be weak at continuous innovation, whereas that cannot be said of technology clusters. Indeed the latter show strong signs of evolutionary 'species multiplication' in innovative strongholds as different as California and Jutland, Denmark. Neo-Marshallian districts, possibly because of high 'sociability', change and survive, sometimes with innovation but also somewhat autopoetically (adaptive self-organization). It is concluded that RISs, too, are more 'associative' than 'communal', thus more 'structurally' than 'relationally' embedded (Becattini 1978; Granovetter 1992).

2. WHAT CONNECTS IDs AND TECHNOLOGY CLUSTERS TO RISs?

The concepts of IDs, technology clusters and RISs are all founded on the basic idea of 'networking'. The idea of a 'network paradigm' for regional economic development was first articulated in Cooke and Morgan (1993). However, the network concept had been bubbling up earlier than that, particularly in relation to innovation networks, but not especially 'regional' networks in the discussion by Camagni (1991). Nevertheless, given the latter's regional economic development credentials, credit is due in that quarter. However, it is clear that Camagni's colleagues in the Francophone 'Groupe de Recherche Europèen sur les Milieux Innovateurs' (European Research Group on Innovative *Milieux* – GREMI) were approaching a discourse of regional development in 'network' regions but without explicitly utilising that language (which in French is *réseaux*). This was because of a preference for the rather vaguer notion of *milieu* (Aydalot 1986; Aydalot and Keeble 1988). Curiously, in the last named, 'industrial' networks but not 'regional' networks are mentioned many times. What did *milieu* signify? It means medium or atmosphere, such as that which sustains us by enabling us to breathe, or water for fish, which performs an equivalent life-supporting function.

More economically geographical, it is not that far from Marshall's notion of the key to the secrets of industry, or in this context innovation, being 'in the air', again a vague but irritatingly fascinating term that continues to be cited at least a century after he first articulated it (Marshall 1920). Marshall, of course, wrote about, and in a way discovered, the secret of 19th-century capitalism, which is that its division of labour was highly selectively located in IDs that were, in modern parlance, suffused with informal network relations among managers and employees. In this way, knowledge, which Marshallians saw as the core issue of economics (ibid.), was in the air because it was the content of communication about technology, specialisation, labour processes, associated skills and their price in these constrained geographical spaces and industrial settings. Neo-Marshallian research had begun on highly-networked, localised 'IDs' even before these *milieu* dates (Becattini 1978; Brusco 1982; Piore and Sabel 1984). We shall differentiate Marshallian and neo-Marshallian characteristics of IDs towards the end of this chapter.

The other main lineament of network regions, though regions were secondary to networks and innovation, arose in a much-cited special issue of the journal *Research Policy* edited and contributed to by De Bresson and Amesse (1991). This also ultimately harked back to Marshall but more from a neo-Schumpeterian knowledge stream. 'Networks of innovators' were the objects of interest, and many economic geographers, such as Storper and Harrison (1991), Saxenian (1991), A.J. Scott (1991), Lawton Smith, Dickson and Smith (1991) and Glasmeier (1991) contributed. Perhaps only the second and fourth focused explicitly on regional networks as such. Freeman (1991) was more explicit, but less regional, in his review of 'networks of innovators', as were Bianchi and Bellini (1991) on policy support for such networks. Nevertheless, through these interventions and the collection edited by Grabher (1993a), such early awakenings to the notion of network interactions among innovators as a new understanding of the importance of geography to innovation, revealed economic geographers to be at the intellectual forefront of this burgeoning field.

Economic geographers like Grabher himself explored the neglected social dimension in economic networks conceived by neoclassical economists as 'asocial', while in Grabher's book, Ash Amin sought to show how globalisation was destroying regional networks, a peculiarly 'northern' perspective also later taken up by Coe and Townsend (1998) who stood on Amin's shoulders in seeking to 'debunk the myth of localised agglomeration', at least in London, something that now seems recklessly heroic. This is not least given, for example, Grabher's subsequent work on the modern advertising 'village' or quarter in Soho (Grabher 2002). Another author whose name would be much cited in the regional innovation and networks literature in subsequent years, Bengt-Åke Lundvall, also appeared in Grabher (1993a) writing about cooperation in innovation activities among firms. So this early-1990s era marks a break in the conceptual and real geography of innovation as smart entrepreneurial firms began running rings around large firms who, in turn, began outsourcing innovation to their supply chains. These, as Klaus Semlinger – yet another contributor to Grabher (ibid.) – noted, were often highly regionally networked, especially in his native Germany, but also elsewhere.

3. INTEGRATING REGIONAL NETWORKS AND REGIONAL INNOVATION POLICY

The enthusiasm for studying networks remained in a context of manifest decline in the coordinating capabilities of States and markets regarding leading edge research and innovation, which subsequent data (for example, Chesbrough 2003a) shows set in from approximately 1991. But if the central State had become as debilitated as many large private corporations were to become regarding the lack of productivity from their large budgetary allocations to R&D, the 'regional State' seemed from empirical reportage of the kind discussed above to be on the rise. A parallel strand of research had evolved, which focused on regional innovation policy (for example, Antonelli and Momigliano 1981; Cooke 1985). Thus the connecting concept of RISs evolved from this even earlier thinking about 'regional innovation policy', in relation to 'regional innovation networks' – an integration influenced by the 'systems view of planning' after McLoughlin (1969). RISs thinking, arguing for systems' integration of process and policy, emerged in two publications, the more widely-cited one being less theoretically and empirically rich than the almost totally uncited one. The difference between Cooke (1992) and (1993) lies in the absence of any bibliographical influence from the 'innovation systems' literature in the 1992 paper, which thus has purer lineaments to economic geography. Contrariwise, the 1993 paper shows this author had by then read Lundvall's (1988) contribution on 'innovation as an interactive process' to Dosi et al. (1988) but was probably more influenced by B. Johansson (1991) and Grabher (1991) in probably the first proper book on regional development from a 'network regions' perspective (Bergman, Maier and Tödtling 1991).

It seemed necessary to place these distinctive 'network and policy' concepts in relation to each other in a layered model. So, the innovation policy dimension evolved conceptually into the idea of a subsystem supporting with knowledge and resources the innovative firms in their networks. The latter formed a 'superstructural' subsystem dealing with actual innovation 'near market'. As we have seen, they had been spoken of as carrying out 'networking' with each other, not only laterally in alliances or partnerships and vertically in sometimes partly-localised supply chains but also with the innovation policy and knowledge generation (infrastructural) subsystem (Meyer-Krahmer 1990; Cooke, Alaez and Etxebarria 1991; Malecki 1991; Rothwell and Dodgson 1991). So these also had subsystem characteristics related to the governance of innovation support. Both subsystems were also seen to interact with global, national and other regional innovation actors, and even through technological or sectoral systems of innovation. Open systems ruled.

Over the years the RIS framework has been analysed in terms of many different 'varieties of innovation' relating to localised, networked and hierarchical innovation 'governance' systems. Third Italy, Baden-Wuerttemberg and French innovative regions exemplified each, respectively. Correspondingly, the 'exploitation' subsystem of firms, in the main, could be dominated by large firms or oligopolies – even foreign ones as with the Asian transplants to Wales in the 1980s and 1990s. Other regions, like Catalonia had a mix of large (SEAT) and SME 'district' type innovation relations, while other places might have innovation regimes in which only small, entrepreneurial firms predominated, as in places with observable 'IDs', not only Third Italy but also some newer technology 'clusters'. Later still, these more entrepreneurial SME systems, living by venture capital and exploitation of public research from universities, could be differentiated further as 'entrepreneurial' (ERIS), market-led systems, compared with those, especially in Europe, where they were more 'institutional' (IRIS) where state support was pronounced and 'entrepreneurship' was less advanced (Cooke 2004).

4. RISs: ORIGIN OF THE SPECIES

My memory of the ingredients here connects to KU Leuven (Catholic University of Louvain) in Flanders, Belgium. I was invited to give a lecture to the Geography

Department at KU Leuven in 1981, where I met a young student, Erik Swyngedouw, and his senior colleague Louis Albrechts. Not long after the publication of Cooke (1983) I received an invitation to be a visiting professor at ISRO, KU Leuven (City and Regional Development and Planning Institute), where Louis Albrechts was already head. The Cooke (1983) book was true to the systems approach because it advocated at great length treating spatial processes such as urbanisation and industrialisation analytically together with policies meant to intervene to produce better outcomes than mere market transactions might be expected to. To some extent, this integrated perspective was defeated by, amongst others, the neoconservative privileging of markets and downgrading of 'planning' in the 1980s. The resultant urban sprawl, suburbanisation of consumption, global warming and energy crisis faced by the West are one collective consequence of this unfortunate historical turn. Another is the competence-destroying rise of 'new public management' whereby civil servants and local government officers no longer practice their craft but manage contracts with consultants who sell dubious prospectuses around the world advocating 'clusters' and other difficult to realise business school 'buzz'. Institutional forgetting has thus occurred on a grand scale with the reification of markets.

During 1985–90 from Leuven, we often visited Jack Dyckman, the famous American planning theorist, and his deputy Frank Moulaert and colleagues, at the Johns Hopkins Regional Research Centre in nearby Lille, France. This involved my first focused, sentient visit to an ID *qua* ID, because Frank lived in Kortrijk (Courtrai) which was a traditional carpet cluster comparable to one I had once, as a studio training exercise, studied and replanned 1960s style at Kidderminster, west of Birmingham. I cannot recall Marshall writing about this classic ID and by the time I had begun researching what was even then still called the carpet district of Kidderminster (in 1967) it had evolved, like other 'dinosaur districts' I discussed at length in Cooke (2002), with the emergence of an oligopoly, although a still-successful one even 40 years later.

How had this occurred to the Kidderminster ID? It was similar to that other Midlands ID studied in Cooke (2002) at Stoke-on-Trent, Britain's principal, but not only, historic ceramics district, which came to prominence by the act of a single heroic entrepreneur, Josiah Wedgwood, also a close friend of Charles Darwin. At the later stages of the ID cycle – see also De Propris and Lazzeretti (2007) on the nearby Birmingham jewellery quarter – sometimes an originator firm is the only one left standing. In Kidderminster it was the Brinton dynasty who in 1785 founded the first 'modern' carpet industry utilising steam-powered factory production, which was subsequently imitated by many spin-out entrepreneurs who had knowledge of the appropriate routines (Klepper 2002). The equivalent in Stoke was, of course, Wedgwood. Brintons used the international trademark BMK (Brinton's Mills Kidderminster) for its carpets for the home. Nowadays, unlike Stoke, where there was, until the 1990s, a duopoly involving Royal Doulton, now also acquired by Wedgwood (itself earlier acquired by Ireland's Waterford Crystal glass manufacturer) and several smaller, newer designer ceramics companies, Kidderminster remains a duopoly of the founding firm alongside Victoria Carpets. This one is a 'complementer' rather than competitor to BMK's domestic carpeting focus. Victoria is involved in contract carpeting for commercial clients such as hotels, airports and large venues, the most notable of which is the Eiffel Tower.

In seeking some understanding of the evolution of MIDs into oligopolies, three key forces seem to have been at work in both these historic cases: first, vertical integration, as more successful competitors acquired their less competitive rivals, sometimes only for their intellectual property regarding, for example, process as well as product innovations. Second, technological change was a key factor, where facing the investment challenge and selecting the optimal technological system, including business organization, could prove a difficult challenge. Finally, early 20th century global competition from cheaper producers elsewhere meant those firms that were becoming uncompetitive became acquired, often after trying wage cuts and influencing municipalities to discourage new industries that would have bid up wages. In other words, innovation (usually by 'buy' from US rather than 'make' decisions) was at the forefront of the strategic minds of the winners, either in terms of technology or market selection.

5. GENERATING METHODOLOGIES

At Leuven a graduate-level intensive programme was based with EU ERASMUS funding, which from the late 1980s took the form of structured field research lasting two weeks each year with partners and programmes rotating among Leuven, Lille, Bilbao, Aveiro, Reggio Calabria and Cardiff. One amongst many important contributory factors to evolve from these interactions was the articulation of the concept and methodology for analysing RISs. An earlier research project (Cooke et al. 1989, 1992) with Basque partners had been the first European high-tech comparative one I had engaged in, and a test-bed for the numerous innovation projects and articles, monographs and books arising from our future innovation research which assisted the refinement of the original RISs framework.

Of considerable novelty to regional science was the elaboration of a RIS methodology, first tried out in Bilbao but refined later at Leuven and Lille, where graduate subgroups opted to pursue one of four projects. My group, usually in partnership with one of our Basque colleagues, focused on regional innovation networks and policies. Workshops, reading and literature review write-ups were followed by research design, methodology, drawing up of survey instruments, documentation and setting up interviews with firms, regional agencies, innovation intermediaries and research institutes. Then we all scattered to conduct interviews and gather further secondary material, notably from Lille's *Cité scientifique* 'Technopole'. The last stage was project write-up as a final project report and presentation at a final collective workshop. As noted, the first few of these in which I was involved took place in Leuven and Lille successively. The first one stays in the mind as an experiment that showed such a venture could be successful and enjoyable pedagogically for all concerned, but the second one was memorable for the detail and depth of the results we got on the Nord-Pas de Calais *système d'innovation régionale* as we called it. Whether because that is what we heard or because it was easier to say it like that in the interviews which were nearly all conducted in French, hence my presence, is uncertain. Probably the latter, but anyway that, as far as I remember, was where the concept first emerged. The Basque–Wales prototype had thus been successfully beta-tested in Nord-Pas de Calais.

The best recollection of the results of that, the first properly designed RIS study to my knowledge, was published in Cooke (1993) in a rather obscure, geographical series from Greece called *Topos*, recording the proceedings of an international workshop held in 1992 on the island of Spetses, in the school building where John Fowles taught before he became a celebrated novelist. This was one of a series organised biannually in Greece by our academic friends from mainly Athens and Thessaloniki, where in beautiful settings like Naxos, Lesvos, Samos and Lemnos, the Greek government, at the behest of organisers like Costis Hadjimichalis, Dina Vaiou, Grigoris Kafkalas and Panos Getimis, amongst many others too numerous to mention, would subsidise our 'international' regional science workshops as long as they were done within reasonable proximity to Turkey.

Stylistically, therefore, RIS thinking evolved conceptually from systems thinking. Its key elements in this regard are the following:

- it is based in systems theory, an epistemology it shares with much actual science, engineering and technology, but proximately with the tradition of 'systems theories of planning' (McLoughlin 1969; Chadwick 1971);
- it is interested in features of IDs, such as collaboration, trust, small-firm networking, local production systems and social capital (Becattini 1978);
- it populates its perspective on the object of interest with core systems concepts such as 'user–producer interactions' including feedback, iterative innovation and 'institutional learning' (Lundvall and Johnson 1994);
- it is consciously, in consequence, evolutionary, having pioneered the introduction of evolutionary economics thinking in regional innovation studies (Cooke, Uranga and Etxebarria 1997, 1998) and helped found the new and broader subfield of 'evolutionary economic geography', whose inaugural network meeting occurred in St Catharine's College, Cambridge in April 2006 (Boschma and Martin 2008);
- accordingly, it is open to small elements (increasing returns, asymmetric information, principal–agent relations, and possibly transaction costs) but not the whole conspectus of neoclassical economics or spatial econometrics. This is owing to its neo-Schumpeterian interest in variety, search, selection, routines,

trust, embeddedness, collaboration, innovation, learning, path dependence, institutional change, disequilibrium and knowledge intermediation practices of institutions and organisations, including firms. These 'bring life back into economic(s) geography' to paraphrase Hodgson (1993).

Of course, these latter research *focii* evolved over 15 years and could not be as clearly envisioned or stylised from the beginning as they can now, not least because very few regional scientists and economic geographers were writing 'evolutionary economic geography' as it has since come to be termed. But this is equally true of us (for example, Cooke et al. 1992) authors, labouring with operational difficulty in the vineyards of 'regulation school' modes of regulation and regimes of accumulation, yet another variant of systems theory. It was precisely the inoperability in practical research terms of that almighty edifice that led me to the evolutionary groves of RISs where, instead of regimes of accumulation and modes of regulation, more accessible 'knowledge exploitation' and 'knowledge generation' (later knowledge exploration) subsystems were more methodologically palatable. As we shall see, all of the foregoing meshed particularly well with a perspective I launched in my first 'proper' published article (Cooke and Rees 1977) and at great length in Cooke (1983). Briefly, once more these argued against the procedural or 'process' perspective on policy that, sadly, now dominates 'competitive tendering', the audit society and the 'new public management' – advocated in planning theory since the 1970s (for example, Faludi 1973). Contrariwise, I was in favour of an integrated theory which linked 'spatial development theory' and 'planning theory' in two interactive subsystems that would escape both the 'one size fits all' spatial policy of the practice world and the arid process obsession of the planning theory rising in academe in the 1970s. It was influenced by Gramsci's (1971) theorisation and intellectual transcendence (despite his 'pessimism of the intellect, optimism of the will') of the power of the ideological structures in his critique of 'Americanism and Fordism', a hegemony which now fully infects the EU, and against which many intellectuals continue to grapple in their writing, not least in relation to its effects on climate change in a context of 'peak oil' (Cooke 2007).

6. INDUSTRIAL DISTRICTS

Some authors, like Moulaert and Sekia (2003) wrongly equate *milieu* and 'ID' approaches. First it is a mistake because they are not equivalents, and second, the latter 'school' never cites the former, though the reverse may have occasionally applied. However there is no mention of 'IDs' in Aydalot and Keeble (1988), one of the GREMI 'bibles'. Nevertheless, the role of ID theory was influential upon RISs thinking. I did not confront the specific neo-MID literature until 1985 when I had a picnic with the 'California school' notably Allen Scott, on Venice Beach, Santa Monica, California. However, considerably earlier, and with my graduate student Artur da Rosa Pires, I had researched and by then already published a Portugal/Italy comparative analysis of what the literature called 'productive decentralisation' (*fabbrica diffusa*) at the time (Cooke and da Rosa Pires 1985). Of interest in this work was the discussion of network relations involving institutions like trust, reciprocity and cooperative 'social capital' as we would now call it, and distinctively, organisations like firms, banks, trade unions and special services they performed for members, like payroll and taxation, private intermediaries like *impannatori* and public ones like *servizi reali* (real services) and the role of regional governments in supplying them in cases of market failure so to do. This seemed and indeed was a plausible explanation of localised regional economic development. So, as a perspective, it informed theorisation on a number of elements that became RIS analysis, but it had little or nothing to say about 'innovation'. Thus it was its governance dimension of networking that contributed most. In this sense, the idea of the ID seemed more geographically interesting since it was the localised 'form' of *fabbrica diffusa*, at least as Scott explained it to me.

One reason for this *lacuna* (gap) was my formation at the time, which was effectively radical political economy of that peculiar Gramscian kind that evolved into an admiration for 'decentralist socialism'. Another was that the whole story about IDs belonged to my pre-university formation, where it was the basis in high school for the explanation of British industrial and historical geography. Indeed, Marshallian districts were still being researched in parts of Britain by the likes of Peter Hall, Michael Wise and Sargant Florence well into the 1960s, as something of a dying breed of industry organisation.

Theorisation of system weaknesses in heterarchic (networked), localised forms of economic coordination had also gone furthest in ID theory. Two key system weaknesses were identified in the canonical neo-Marshallian form of the ID. Writing from an evolutionary economics perspective, Varaldo and Ferrucci (1996) identified the following developmental blockages then visible in the district form of development. First, because of strategic cooperation between firms in districts there develops, of necessity, a common set of strategic expectations about behaviour amongst mutually dependent entrepreneurs. Institutional memory, rules, routines, ways in which mutual expectations are regulated, relationships ordered and rules governed, come to converge so that dissonance within the district becomes muted. This may explain the weak innovation aspect, and heighten the 'traditional' aspect of the form because the absence of dissenting voices reproduces district culture – in the commercial sense – but may delay 'strategic' creativity at critical points when a rapid response to the need for innovation is required. If we remember that innovation is defined as the 'commercialisation' of original knowledge, as distinct from invention, which is the original knowledge itself, then the need for rapid response becomes obvious.

Second, this is not a problem until the district system experiences an exogenous shock, such as a stabilisation, or even, as occurred in the global recession of the early 1990s, a contraction in demand. This can cause a number of panic responses: competition may become cut-throat and destructive; low prices make investment in restructuring impossible; reduced demand limits the high flexibility levels associated with district firms, revealing hidden costs as margins are cut and more standardised production is resorted to; firms seek cheaper offshore suppliers and even production locations; retail customers are more able to negotiate favourable contracts for themselves; new technologies may represent a threat where they are incongruent with the technical know-how of district entrepreneurs. All these reactions can be experienced in non-district settings too, and there is even limited evidence that in Italy, during the 1990s recession, district firms fared better than similar ones outside districts (Brusco et al. 1996).

7. MIDs, NEO-MIDs AND TECHNOLOGY CLUSTERS: SOME DIFFERENCES AND SIMILARITIES

What we see by observing some of the lineaments and problems of contemporary IDs is how much they rely on relational and structural embeddedness (Granovetter 1992). We might compare this with Putnam's (1993) distinction between 'bonding' and 'bridging' social capital respectively. The first is more informal, possibly communal, while the second is more institutional and, crucially, inter-institutional and inter-organizational. By relational embeddedness we mean that much of the ID's cohesiveness lies in integrated and familial social relationships. By structural embeddedness we mean the more formal organisations that underpin the district like governance, associativeness and services. Neo-MIDs seem to be, if anything, stronger relationally than structurally, added to which is the distinction between the Marshallian and neo-Marshallian ones described by Becattini and Dei Ottati (2006) for example, where there seems to be a moderately-pronounced degree of social egalitarianism between entrepreneurs and workers. However, as the hands-on experience I had of such original MIDs as Kidderminster, and through writing about senescent districts like Macclesfield, once the UK's leading silk district, and Stoke (Cooke 2002) this was never a strong feature of the first IDs. Employers kept separate domiciles from workers. In the main they were not related in familial terms, employers sought to impoverish workers by keeping wages down and frequently reducing them in hard times. Moreover they brought influence to bear on local government to disallow planning applications by inward investors in other, more modern industries for fear they would bid-up wages. Also they manifestly failed to innovate or change in any significant material ways. They suffered lock-in to a lethal degree. Hence they had higher structural than relational embeddedness.

Something of the same sentiment can be expressed about contemporary technology districts. They have 'councils' and representative bodies, they have sometimes quite formalised associations or networks – in Cambridge (UK) the Cambridge Network Ltd. is a formalised company, responsible for holding meetings, seminars and workshops for paying members who are local ICT or biotechnology (mainly the former) firm owners. The Cambridge Network has some 1300 members, involving a smaller basic needs business to business club for start-up companies with about 600 members. In our research on Cambridge published in Cooke et al. (2007, Chapter 7) we, for reasons of space, cut out the following quote from the head of the St John's incubator:

> Since we started in 1978, we have had to overcome the English problem in Cambridge of reticence, in other words, unless you have been introduced to somebody or have known them for 6 months, you won't talk to them, so what has been extremely important has been to encourage people to talk to other people and to try to share experience and gain business and this in a way has been formalised through the Cambridge Network Organisation run by Peter Hughkin. Now there is more collaboration and cross fertilization at business level. So the relationships between the local companies is good, they cooperate where it is sensible to cooperate but obviously sometimes IP is very important and people want to protect their IP, so that is fair enough but the total reticence to talk to anybody has been broken down.

This is suggestive, even today of a 'business networking' culture that has had to be introduced rather than the natural sociability of a community. A long way from Italy then. The 'Cambridge network model' was institutionally borrowed from San Diego's 'Connect' network which performed a similar function there. Ironically, to bring my personal intellectual biography full circle, it has since been successfully borrowed by KU Leuven, where it has helped create 20 000 new technology cluster jobs since 1998. So we conclude that MIDs and technology clusters are similarly structurally more than relationally embedded while neo-MIDs are relationally more than structurally embedded (on this see also Guenzi, Raffaeli, Giovannini and Trigilia in this volume). Could this simply be a macro-cultural difference between Britain (or Flanders and California) and Italy? To agree with that would be extremely culturally determinist since 'Italy' has no more of a homogeneous culture than 'Britain' as the absence of IDs in the Mezzogiorno testifies. So we probably have to look, from the economic perspective, at the apparently natural tendency towards forming an oligopoly in MIDs and the opposite tendency in neo-MIDs as a better, but still far from adequate, explanation.

24. Culture as a productive resource, international networks and local development

Olivier Crevoisier and Leïla Kebir*

1. CULTURES AND THE ECONOMY: A MUCH-DEBATED ARTICULATION

One feature shared by knowledge and culture today is the fact that they are widely thematised in economic literature and in discussion of regional development.[1] During the course of economic development over recent centuries, there have been numerous crisis and reconstitution phases. On each occasion they have raised the question of what basis, and from what 'objects' (deposits, soil, technologies and so on) can new innovative processes be triggered and subsequently, when they take place in line with the capitalist model, what new processes of accumulation will develop? Today, it would appear that knowledge, culture and art are all perceived as central 'objects' within economic development (Boltanski and Chiapello 2005). Aspects that bear witness to this are the rise of cultural industries, the dematerialisation of industrial assets – whose value increasingly lies in their symbolic and communication values – the development of new forms of tourism such as 'green' tourism and commercial leisure. They participate effectively and continuously towards constructing the economic value of regions and towards growth. Gaining an understanding of this phenomenon opens up rich possibilities for reflection on an academic level, where contributions linking 'economics' and 'culture' have multiplied over recent years (see, for example, James, Martin and Sunley 2007).

Culture can be distinguished from the other resources that are mobilised because of its intrinsic link to the societies and communities that produce it. If we acknowledge that economic relations do not exist independently of the social and cultural dimension, they do – on the one hand – 'emanate' from the social networks that constitute the basis thereof, and on the other hand 'dissolve' these networks by permitting other actors and markets to enter the arena with those that are purely at the forefront as a result of the tradition of exchange or because of proximity. Society and culture thus appear as 'substrates' of economic factors while at the same time they are subject to modification by the economy. In this context, culture produces the knowledge and practices that are necessary in order to establish social links, rules, codes of conduct and the forms of language needed in order for exchanges to take place. Culture generates shared history and visions at varying social levels. Moreover, it is a source of creative inspiration. More directly, culture is shown by means of 'objects' (cultural heritage, know-how, traditions, artistic practices and so on) which will be integrated within goods and services (industrial, tourism, leisure and so on) in the form of a resource.

Although political economics as a discipline tends to consider culture as simply a production factor like any other, various social sciences (sociology, ethnology or geography) are seeing the growing merchandisation of culture as leading to the development of specific tensions within societies. For Boltanski and Chiapello (2005), the Fordist period was characterised by a 'spirit of capitalism' opposing the economic sphere – perceived above all as functionalist and illustrated by the industrial model of mass production – and that of the world of culture, which stressed the necessity for humanity of emancipating and going beyond the satisfaction of basic needs. Within this analytical framework, culture and knowledge are in opposition to economic issues since their value resides precisely in the emancipation from utilitarianism and from social exploitation. In this perspective, culture and knowledge can develop to the extent that the State provides them with their own resources that are not subject to economic factors.

The movement from culture as a substrate to culture as a resource is at the centre of current concerns and debates. For some, this movement brings with it the alienation of the cultural objects mobilised in this way and eventually their loss of meaning and thus an impoverishment of the societies that produce these objects. For others, the moment can, in certain cases, make it possible to maintain and renew these objects: turning all or part of them into commercial goods provides the actors involved with the necessary means resources necessary to ensure that they live on. In this second perspective, economy and culture are not necessarily opposed, but are articulated in a more complex way, and can even reinforce one another.

As suggested by Hirschman (1986) economic exchange is always 'both' a social relationship and cultural communication. Seen from this perspective, 'culture' is no longer a homogenising factor. We shall therefore speak of cultures in the plural in order to place emphasis on the way in which these practices take place and the intra or inter-cultural interactions that are constitutive aspects of territory.

Without wishing to focus too exclusively on one or another of these approaches, this contribution proposes to examine the articulation between economy and culture by identifying the role of the *milieux* (Camagni, Maillat and Matteaccioli 2004) and of territorial production systems in the evolution of this articulation. A specific character of cultural resources, as we have seen above, is that they frequently stem from cultures that are attached to territories and constitutive aspects thereof. When reflecting on the economics of cultural resources, the question of 'authenticity' is one that rapidly arises. The commercial value of a cultural object – which is the result of an individual or collective form of expression – is ambiguous in that it implies a minimum of alignment in order for it to be communicated, understood, and thus evaluated within exchange. This aspect is enhanced in the case of cultural resources relating to cultural heritage. Even when their authenticity is not questioned, the relation between culture and economy remains considerable since the process of renewal/creation of these resources frequently remains linked to their territory of origin (for example, know-how, professions in the arts).

We will see that local *milieux* and territorial production systems are forms that favour the maintenance and renewal of cultural resources, being based on a proximity relation between the community producing the objects and the production system that exploits them in economic terms. *A priori*, the more this relation becomes distant, the greater the risks of the object becoming alienated (that is, the loss of the initial values). From another angle, any economic production that is successful on the market is led to expand its scope and thus to modify the social and territorial conditions of the production.

Thematising knowledge and culture would thus be part of a vast area of reflection on the relations between the economic sector (which periodically undergoes crisis and reconstitutes new possibilities for innovation and accumulation) and the rest of society. The current era appears to be marked by a tendency to 'enrich' economic exchange by providing it with an added cultural content that is also commercialised. In this context, today's resources appear as an opportunity for regions capable of constructing them and making use of them. This capacity, however, also leads to some risks on which careful reflection is needed.

2. FROM CULTURAL 'OBJECTS' TO CULTURAL 'RESOURCES'

In order to understand the relationship between the cultural objects/resources and the territory on a regional scale, we shall use the notion that resources constitute a relation between an object (cultural legacy, tradition, buildings, know-how, mineral, river and so on) and a production system[2] (tourism, culture, industry and so on) (Kebir 2004) (see Figure 24.1). From this perspective, cultural resources are all the objects of a cultural nature (knowledge, artefacts and so on) that can potentially serve a purpose, or be useful, within a production process. Within this approach, we again find types of know-how (skills, knowledge, historical traditions, history and so on) and artefacts (monuments, works of art and so on). The coordination methods (that is, legislation on the use of an item of cultural heritage, informal rules, conventions and so on) defining the modalities of using the resource are not considered to be a resource. They concern institutions that permit or prevent collective action intended to constitute cultural objects as economic resources.

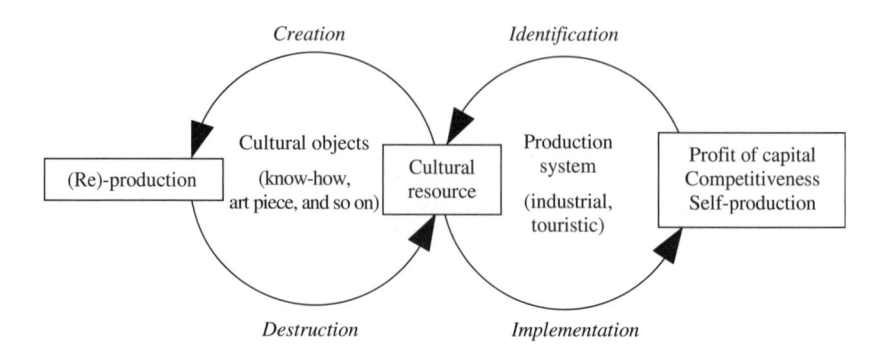

Source: Kebir and Crevoisier (2008).

Figure 24.1 Cultural resources as economic and extra-economic resources

   This relation between object and production system is marked by the co-evolution of two 'entities': on the one hand, the cultural objects constituted by the processes of 'creation' (apprenticeship, collective experience, construction) and of destruction (oblivion, deterioration, wear and tear, destruction), and on the other, the production system[3] in which the actors will 'identify' certain objects as being a potential resource and will 'implement' them in the production of goods and services. Depending on the way in which these processes coevolve, the resource in question will either develop or lose substance.
   The fact of using an object can lead to its destruction (such as mass visits to an archaeological site without it being protected). Implementing this resource can lead to apprenticeship-type effects (learning by doing), which in turn will renew the object. Technical development (development of the object) or market developments can render a resource obsolete and lead to a disjunction between the object and the production system. Know-how can disappear if the apprenticeship, transmission and renewal processes do not compensate the phenomena of oblivion and obsolescence. As an example, watchmaking know-how in the Arc of the Jura Mountains became considerably impoverished when quartz watches appeared on the market. The techniques used to manufacture mechanical watches became obsolete, the channels for training were abandoned, the machines destroyed and the practices partially forgotten. Nonetheless knowledge and skills were partially preserved due to museums in the region, watchmakers and other passionate individuals attached to their professions and to a certain idea of watches: they took care, outside the economic circuits, of some traces of the past (such as remarkable watches and machines). This heritage was

to constitute the driving force behind the renewal of watchmaking during the 1990s, with the triumphant return of the luxury mechanical watch. Without this territorial 'resistance' movement, which we shall term a 'community effort' (in the sense that it came from the community and not from the production system), the know-how would have disappeared.

The relation between object and production system is not established definitively. It evolves and constantly rearticulates according to the evolution of its components. This process is driven on the one hand by constraints regarding the reproduction of the object and the competitiveness of the production system, and on the other by the relations that each maintains with other systems (community, other production system and so on).

Cultural resources are particularly concerned by this last point, since they derive part of their value from their attachment to a community. It is in fact this 'extra-economic' attachment that constitutes the sign, the symbolic and communicational quality of the resource and that make it a source of economic value. The stronger the attachment, the more the articulation between the economic and non-economic values can be a source of tensions. So-called 'heritage' resources are a good illustration of this. As soon as a heritage dimension is attributed[4] to a cultural good, this becomes part of the common official heritage (common on a local, regional, national or worldwide level) and is given a value other than an economic one. The economic actors must then articulate the economic and non-economic values of the resource. For example, a building or an industrial site that is elevated to the rank of cultural heritage given its architectural or symbolic value in relation to a common history can no longer be used for economic purposes and transformed (the creation of a hotel, a cultural centre) except within the defined limits of an arbitration between conservation and operation (such as imposed norms regarding possible renovation work, need to respect the architectural style, impossibility of extending the building or constructing others nearby, restricted number of visitors).

The merchandisation of cultural objects raises the concern that they will become derailed, lose their authenticity, and consequently that their extra-economic value (in terms of identity and symbolism) will be destroyed. Underlying these fears, too, there is the risk of destroying the link between the producing community and the object thus mobilised. If communities no longer identify with an object, one could wonder what remains of the sign that was *a priori* so much admired. The more the link becomes distant, the more the object is derailed and deviates from its context, to become part of the 'global culture' that is constructed and diffused by the vast cultural industry via international networks. The phenomena of 'Disneyfication' or folklorisation are the direct expression of this simplification or rearrangement of cultural signs or messages.

Turning cultural goods into resources or their economic valorisation may, however, also produce beneficial effects on the resource, which is in fact frequently a necessary condition for maintaining or conserving it. For example, conserving or valorising by means of tourism can go hand in hand, even if the tensions are numerous.

Beyond this case, which is now a frequent one, there are other situations in which the relations between culture and the economy can not only permit a cultural object to be conserved but also to be developed.

3. CULTURAL RESOURCES AND TERRITORY

The constitution and implementation of cultural resources can be understood by referring to their territory. Relations between the community or society from which they originate and the production system(s) mobilising them characterise territorial dynamics, with varying degrees of local anchoring and with diffusion scales whose scope varies in terms of extent and distance. Thus, the evolution of the cultural resource, its renewal or its disappearance, depends on the form of this link.

We shall tackle these questions using the approach of Braudel (1981–84, 1985),[5] who identifies three interdependent levels for economic functioning and its insertion within society: self-production, guided by the 'use value', the market organised around the 'exchange value', and finally 'capitalism', where the accumulation of capital drives production (Figure 24.2).

As with Braudel, these three levels are seen here as coexisting simultaneously in economic structures, even if historically, capitalism was the last of them to develop. It is therefore not a sequential model like that of Marx who saw capitalism as the successor to serfdom, but a series of complementary levels that together characterise the economic system. Capitalism can only grow if the lower levels are dynamic and if capitalism models them for its benefit. There are thus ascending and descending movements.

3.1 Economic exchange and culture in self-production systems

On a level of self-production and self-consumption, it is the 'use value' that will orient economic activity in order to permit the reproduction and renewal of the community. Reciprocity is the main coordinating institution for the activity. The monetary institution does not mediatise social relations. On this level, the economic and cultural dimensions of the exchanges come into play jointly, and can hardly be dissociated. Giving and receiving generates mutual commitments which constitute the framework of the community via reciprocity. Economic exchange and the social link are the two sides of a same coin: that of the renewal of the community.

On this level, economic exchange and the vernacular culture develop at a local scale whose degree of isolation varies. In fact, reciprocity develops within the context of interpersonal relationships. The specialisation of activities is

Culture as a productive resource 313

CAPITALISM LEVEL
(economic exploitation and
maintenance of cultural specificities
of places from the top down)

MARKET ECONOMY LEVEL
(production and exploitation of
cultural specificity on the basis of
both the local use value and the
value of exchange with the
'elsewhere')

SELF-PRODUCTION LEVEL
(cultural production on the basis
of the local use value)

Multiscalar economic process

Multilocal economic process

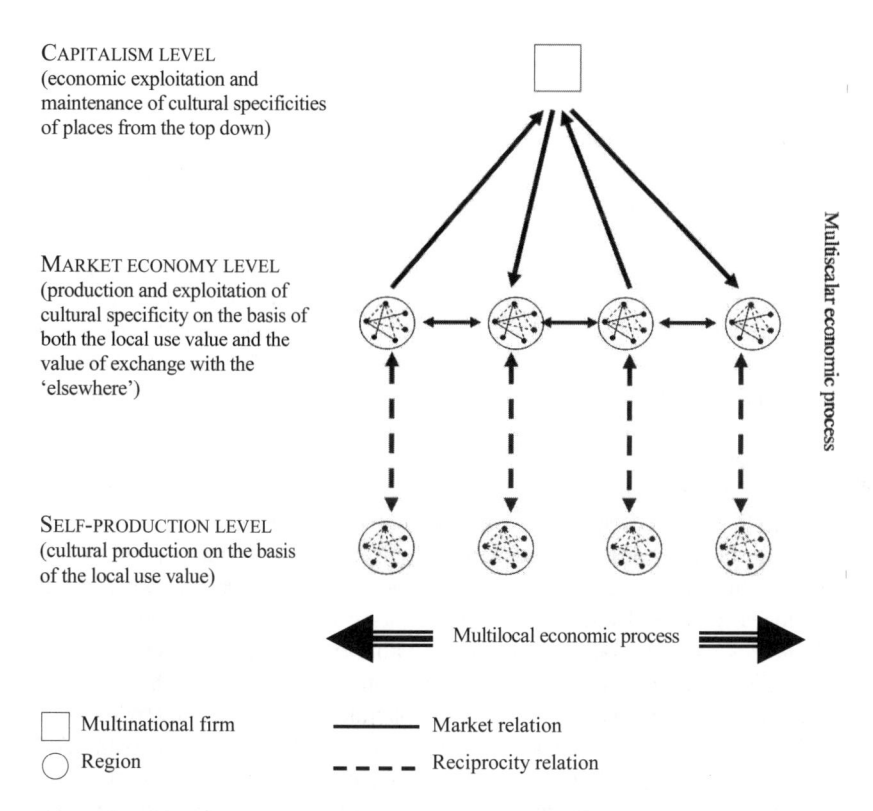

☐ Multinational firm ——— Market relation
○ Region – – – Reciprocity relation

Source: Our elaboration based on Braudel's theory of economic organisation (Braudel 1985).

Figure 24.2 Culture, economy and scales

highly limited since the sole purpose of the economic activity is to satisfy basic needs and assure the reproduction of the community.

In more complex societies, the production of 'cultural objects' (education, research, so-called cultural activities, land development and so on) which are more varied and more numerous are organised via State institutions. If the use value is in principle what directs these activities, they are, however, financed by monetary transfers and develop within the framework of the public authorities' territory, that is a proximity space, an action and decision space with a border as its demarcation.

3.2 Market exchange and cultural resources

On the market level, the 'exchange value' engages activities in a process of specialisation and diversification in relation to one another. Beyond that, we see the specification of resources, a differentiation in the territorial offer, and competition among spaces. 'Money' becomes the dominant institution, the standard for exchange, both linking the actors within production and consumption while permitting them to become engaged within a process of specialisation/specification. Monetary exchange is moreover characterised by certain balance, in the sense that service in kind and counter-service in money are equivalent in principle. There is thus no creation of 'debts', obligations, for one or the other to fulfil in future, as is the case with reciprocity.

The territories compete by means of differentiation, while together engaging in mercantile exchange. Here, the territory (the 'us and them', the 'here and elsewhere') is the basis that triggers the process of creating the difference: one that plays a decisive role in economic development. Here, economic exchange is also, and still, 'a matter of cultural and social communication'. Producing, selling and buying is also a question of re-forging one's position and identity.

The market level is expressed by forms of territorial organisation such as 'industrial districts' (IDs) or 'innovative *milieux*', and their production systems ('clusters'), which function internally on the basis of both mercantile and non-mercantile relationships whose principal characteristic is embedding the economic aspect within local society. Exchanges with the exterior, at greater distance, are all of a monetary nature. These *milieux* are operators that on the one hand mobilise local specificities and on the other valorise them within exchanges with other actors and other *milieux*. For such regions, local identity and the specificity of the dominant economic activity are closely linked: the economic activities are the producers of local culture, and local specificity makes economic specialisation possible and strengthens it. The question is that of knowing the extent to which, and according to which modalities, the economic activity contributes to the reproduction and enrichment of knowledge and local culture, or on the contrary weakens it. These local cultural resources can thus become stronger if the local *milieux* are able to mobilise part of the money necessary in order to preserve the resources. As we shall see below, these resources can be sullied and decline if their quality and more particularly their authenticity are no longer the subject of attention.

Regions whose cultural identity is marked by specific economic activities are highly diverse. Mining regions, districts with an industrial tradition, agricultural, rural, and tourism regions and so on are marked on a cultural level by their productive vocation. Metropolises are characterised by a certain diversity of their prominent activities. Thus Los Angeles is not just Hollywood alone, nor is Paris exclusively a fashion centre, even though specific activities produce 'cultural objects' linked to a territory and participate widely in the local production of identity and 'cultural objects' (knowledge, know-how, characteristic urban landscape).

From a spatial point of view, we see an emerging mosaic of territories that are all involved in monetarised economic exchange. These regions progressively reinforce their reciprocal economic specialisations thanks to exchanges. The result is a strengthening of the specificity of the local identity which in turn makes it possible to give more depth to the economic specialisation or to renew it.

It is thus a space of regions that engage in relations via economic exchange, existing in a network of continuity that creates differentiation.

Today, the specialisation of spaces is increasing more and more. The hypermobility of goods, individuals and knowledge is leading to a dispersal of production industries over numerous sites that can be at a considerable distance from one another. This affects the identification of a place with a product or a technology. In fact, as we shall see below, economic exchanges are today the fruit of recompositions that call into question – in a selective way – certain cultural resources with historical origins.

3.3 Capitalism and de-socialised culture

At the third level – that of capitalism – 'organisation' takes over from the market. Exchange is marked by the absence of transparency (because of compartmentalisation or distance) between the producer and the consumer and by asymmetry, since the producer always enjoys a certain power on markets and on the spaces that harbour the resources. The main driving force in the organisation of production is the profit in relation to the invested capital. This in principle applies to the large cultural industry, where multinational corporations are able to juggle between various territories while valorising their specificities.

The compartmentalisation makes it possible to escape from prices being fixed by the market. The mastery – as exclusive as possible – of 'distance' relations has historically been a favoured means of implementing such economic relations (Braudel 1981–84).

Related to the cultural resources, mastering multilocal and international relations makes it possible to operate the territories' cultural resources 'from the top down'. Multinational corporations will mobilise cultural resources from specific places and integrate them within production and distributive chains at a world scale.

Cultural and territorial specificities are 'instrumentalised' and 'decontextualised'. They are handled via their insertion within an accumulation process on a vast scale. The economic balance sheet of this interrelated space is no longer one that is produced at the scale of the region that has generated the resources (a scale that forces a certain balance between service and monetary flow). It is a balance established at a wider scale, permitting losses here or profits there. The essential difference between this and the level of mercantile exchange is that here, the flows of exchange in kind and/or of money among the various spaces are no longer necessarily balanced.

The capitalist level is thus characterised by the exploitation of a place's cultural resources but with the specificity that the actors within the operation either are not stakeholders in the local society or are part of it and 'at the same time' part of other places. Multinationals can exploit these resources without being located in the region. Of course, most of the time, they will hold some branch, or at least some activity there. Nevertheless, the direct presence of the multinational is rarely a question of survival for it. It can choose to close down that branch. Its location in such or such region is instrumental or, at least, is perceived as instrumental by other players. This results in a decoupling between the monetary flow and the cultural specificity. We should recall that at the market level, monetary exchange with other places was based on the cultural specificity and also 'strengthened it'. At the capitalism level, the identity between the economic exchange and the reproduction of cultural resources is no longer assured since one of the principal actors is either not part of local society or part of it, but with the suspicion of being there only for its own economic interests. Moreover, stripped of geographic context, the cultural expression becomes a 'shadow of the total experience' (Rifkin 2000, p. 253).

The mechanisms for producing knowledge and culture disappear. It is only the 'exploitation' of them that is essential, and for this reason their 'maintenance' is assured, notably by means of intellectual property law. The process of creating diversity and the process of exploiting diversity are thus dissociated. This raises the question of 'authenticity' since there is an absence of intersection between the processes: on the one hand, knowledge and culture as emanating from a local economic and social system inserted into the interplay of differentiating exchange, and on the other, reified knowledge and culture detached from the mechanisms of their production and enrichment.

During the 1960s and 1970s, the levelling of cultural differences among the various national markets was a condition for widening opportunities for standardised mass production. Fordism was characterised at the time by a 'deculturisation' of production, presented as being essentially functional.

Competition from low-cost production countries, but above all the necessity to innovate, led to a considerable rise in the 'cultural components' of production, and particularly within Western Europe, with a view to differentiating production and rendering it specific. Production was no longer functional and standard but also a form of social and cultural communication. Capitalism today has to a large extent integrated this order and, paradoxically, has succeeded extremely well in 'merchandising the difference' (Boltanski and Chiappello 2005). Local cultural resources will be mobilised and will participate in long-distance economic exchange.

This decontextualisation process will nevertheless transform the product and its accompanying cultural communication. Fashion, for instance, is not produced everywhere but above all in certain highly specific productive systems, generally metropolitan, where dynamics in this domain exist. Fashion sold by international chains in all European cities and elsewhere plays on cultural elements that are no longer attached to a place, or only partly, and in considerably stereotyped forms. World music or films produced by the major names in Hollywood are characterised by the use of cultural resources but which have been considerably re-formatted to permit their diffusion to wider markets.

This process of decontextualisation and re-formatting certainly brings with it certain suspicions regarding the authenticity of the cultural component of the products and services. In fact, the cultural component is only effective if it is a communication, that is a link with something or someone else: a person, a community or even the spirit of a place. The overriding issue for cultural industries is thus one of maintaining – usually by means of intellectual property tools (marks, designs, royalties, patents, various quality labels) – a certain degree of personalisation by the producers (whether designers, actors, artists or even brands): a personalisation that is, of course, to a large extent illusory.

3.4 The dynamic of cultural resources between local innovative *milieux* and international-level accumulation

Economic processes bring into play – simultaneously or on an alternating basis – these three phases within ascending or descending dynamics: certain regions are included at some point, then abandoned or ignored by the economic processes of exchange or accumulation.

During certain periods of history, capitalism reconfigures itself and seeks new products or services capable of reconstituting accumulation. These are relatively open periods during which the regional *milieux* can enter the scene in order to innovate and reposition themselves. During these periods formerly central regions are abandoned. Former industrial sites, the know-how, what they produced, all lose their economic value but not immediately their constitutive functions in the society and local culture.

As a result of this, the public authorities – usually together with various associative or private entities – proceed to operations intended to 'create cultural heritage' or more simply to 'rehabilitate' the regions.

We shall use one or two examples in order to gain a better understanding of how economic processes or those relating to local social dynamics may produce certain objects, and how ultimately the relation between those objects and the economic and cultural dynamics may change. More generally, the question is that of the forms of interaction between cultural and economic dynamics in society, and more particularly the interaction between the local scale and the international networks.

The case of the watchmaking industry in the Swiss area of the Jura Mountains is a typical example of the way in which a production system transformed itself and brought 'cultural objects' into play in a different way depending on the period. The Fordist period, because of standardisation and automation, led to a dequalification of the labour force. The end of that period moreover was one during which watchmaking museums were created, with their mission being to conserve know-how (restoration workshops, for example), documents and pieces from all periods. These 'objects' which had disappeared or were in the process of doing so were brought into a process of creation of cultural heritage. The end of the 1970s and the 1980s were marked by electronic watches and the importance of fashion. During this period, a few individuals with a passionate interest in watchmaking sought to bring the know-how and tradition of mechanical watches back to life. To do so, they sifted through documents, mobilised individuals who had been trained during the 1930s, and gradually succeeded in making a market segment for luxury mechanical watches emerge. On a small scale at the outset, this market has developed in an extraordinary manner, to the point that it today represents nearly 80 per cent of the value of watch exports.

What happened? Success led to the creation of new firms, then buyouts of firms and investments on the part of large groups. The groups were either indigenous or from the exterior, and in particular active in the luxury goods industry. From a marketing point of view, the considerable expansion of the outlets took place by coupling products not with fashion but with exclusivity, with the notion of being unique, and with tradition. Faced with a risk of becoming too commonplace, we have seen – over recent years – a new wave of innovation, concerning a coupling between the sale of the product and a visit to the local museum for clients, set up by the production companies and the manufacturing workshops. It should be noted that these changes were above all brought in by local companies rather than the large groups, either local or from elsewhere. On a regional scale, the tourist activities *milieu* has established the name of 'Watch Valley', and two towns particularly involved in the watchmaking industry are seeking to have it included in the UNESCO list of World Cultural Heritage Sites after having restored and 'recycled' some of the buildings and the urban environment related to the old watchmaking cluster.

This dynamic shows how, at certain periods, the economic system 'de-invests' regions, thus creating industrial wastelands and leaving workers who possess know-how unemployed. From an identity point of view, these objects still constitute a focal point within the local socio-cultural dynamic. In the present case, an innovative *milieu* emerged and focused on transforming the objects that had become part of the cultural heritage, or even forgotten, into new economic resources. This is a moment when economic exchange with the 'elsewhere' becomes the driving force behind cultural revitalisation, and vice versa. Then, once success is achieved, major groups enter the market, imitating, buying up and perfecting the new practices. The door is open to an instrumentalisation of the cultural objects incorporated in the watchmaking product. Magazines throughout the world abound with publicity for Swiss mechanical watches. The largest watchmaking group has registered over 50 000 designs, thus proving that the control of the market through intellectual property is becoming dominant in relation to what is created.

Finally, the development of the Watch Valley is a new movement whose point of departure is the local *milieux*. The content of the cultural communication and the economic exchange is reworked with a direct contact between the buyer and the producer, in the workshops, but also by visits to the region, to the architecture, the urban dynamics and the museums.

In such a configuration, the cultural resource 'progresses', since it has found a new use that makes it evolve. If the concern is to preserve the object, it nevertheless accommodates different ways of use and possible transformation: the former buildings are not simply restored but recycled and renovated, leading to a mixture of ancient and modern architecture. These projects go beyond the strict economic framework and have a scope that is cultural and specifically related to urban development. They are often driven by 'expanded innovative *milieux*' (Camagni, Maillat and Matteaccioli 2004; Peyrache-Gadeau 2007) that unite local actors (associations for the preservation of cultural heritage, real estate promoters, public actors) and articulate their expectations (safeguarding the building, financial interests, urban development, cultural activities). We are thus mainly situated at the first level of the economy, where the 'use value' takes precedence, where the aim is above all to respond to the collective needs for urban development, cultural activities and the enhancement of identity. The economic actors do not play a central role.

4. CONCLUSION

The case of watchmaking in the Jura region is exemplary, but it should not lead to a belief that ascendant dynamics are triggered automatically: this is far from being the case. It also reveals, however, how identity and symbolic dynamics make it possible to preserve objects from the first level: that of self-production and self-consumption. On a level of monetarised exchange with elsewhere, these objects can be mobilised and of course recycled, renovated and modernised in order to restore the cultural content of the economic production. This supposes the appearance of innovative *milieux*. Finally, the objects may be appropriated and widely instrumentalised by major corporations that do not usually participate, or do it only occasionally, in the dynamics of the local *milieux*.

Authenticity, that is the alignment between the cultural content of the product or service sold and the role of this same content in the identity of the local community, evolves according to periods and configurations of actors. Other examples would have shown us that at times authenticity disappears, as when cultural resources are overexploited and transformed into folklore, or when the local agents are not able to agree on how to preserve or renew them. Disneyfication is not exclusively the domain of large, hegemonic enterprises. A market economy that is not regulated by the local *milieux*, or that does not reach agreement around new projects, can be equally destructive.

NOTES

* The authors wish to thank Valérie Angeon for her comments.
1. Camagni, Maillat and Matteaccioli (2004). For a recent example, see Lazzerretti (2003, 2004); Cooke and Lazzeretti (2008).

2. This approach to resources is in line with notably the institutionalist perspectives developed by Ayres (1943); Zimmermann (1951); Hunker (1964); De Gregori (1987); and with Raffestin (1980) and Bathelt and Glückler (2005).
3. The production system refers to 'all of the actors involved in identifying and implementing the resource with a view to the production of a good or a service (companies, research and training centres, public institutions). It also designates all the relations that these actors maintain within and beyond the system' (Kebir 2004, p. 28).
4. We stress that we are speaking of 'attributing', since it is a qualification given collectively and officially to an object, often by means of clearly-defined processes. This qualification is one that evolves and that is situated in space. What constitutes heritage today will not necessarily do so tomorrow, just as heritage in one place will not constitute heritage in another.
5. It is interesting to note that Braudel coordinated a large project on the history of the city of Prato. Becattini, who in 1979 published his first famous paper on the ID drawing on Prato, was invited by Braudel to edit the volume on the recent history, corresponding to the constitution, development and change of Prato as a textile ID. From his long introduction to this volume Becattini extracted his seminal work in 2000 (English version in Becattini 2001a).

PART III

Empirical investigations on industrial districts

SECTION 6
Empirical evidence

Introduction

Fabio Sforzi

1. MAPPING AS A FOUNDING COMPONENT OF THE DISTRICT THESIS IN ITALY

This section of the *Handbook* deals with the mapping of industrial districts (IDs) in Italy, Spain and the UK (Sforzi, Boix and De Propris) and its impact on economic research, in particular with regard to the measurement of the 'district effect' (De Blasio, Omiccioli and Signorini) and the internationalisation of IDs (Menghinello).

Contrary to what one might think, the mapping of IDs is not an exercise in applied economics, that is to test hypotheses on IDs, but it is the completion of the research path that led Giacomo Becattini and the Florence school to formulate the ID thesis (Becattini 1987).

Of course, this applies to the initial mapping of Italian IDs based on data of the 1981 Census, and to the subsequent updates relying on the same analytical framework, albeit with some adjustments due to the experience gradually gained through the validation of results on the ground. This mapping methodology has been a founding component in the formulation of the ID thesis, and it has proved a valuable tool to identify IDs in countries other than Italy; see the chapters by Rafael Boix on Spain and Lisa De Propris on the UK.

A meaningful application of the mapping methodology to a country depends, in practice, on the possibility of identifying territorial units of analysis corresponding to its constituent local communities, like Italian local labour market areas (LLMAs). The robustness of results depends largely on the manner in which such territorial units are defined. Of course, the importance of the quality of socio-economic data to be used in the analysis should not be neglected.

The mapping of IDs for countries other than Italy has occurred only in recent years, although since the beginning of the 1990s 'industrial districts have captured the attention of a substantial body of researchers and policymakers across a wide range of countries and organisations' (Zeitlin 1992, p. 279).

2. THE MAPPING OF IDs IN SPAIN AND THE UK

The Spanish translation of the IILS seminal volume *Industrial Districts and Inter-Firm Co-operation in Italy* (Pyke, Becattini and Sengenberger 1990) in 1992 (published by the Spanish Ministry of Labour, and edited by Maria Teresa Costa Campi, Universitat de Barcelona) sparked a wealth of interest on IDs, with the first map of Spanish IDs being produced only in 2004. The cause of this delay lies in the lack of territorial units well-suited to significantly mirror local communities. Once data on daily journeys from home to work became available in 2001 and LLMAs were defined by applying ISTAT methodology (ISTAT 1997), the Spanish Government commissioned a research unit of the Universitat Autònoma de Barcelona coordinated by Boix to mapping IDs in Spain (Boix and Galletto 2004).

The mapping of IDs in the UK is a quite different story. Among the authors of the IILS book there were two British scholars (Ash Amin and Kevin Robins) who knew the theory and practice of IDs. One of them had already written on the same subject the year before in a British journal (Amin 1989a). Moreover, in the UK there was a well-established tradition in defining LLMAs. Labour market areas based upon home-to-work journeys have been available since 1974 (Smart 1974), and in the current form of 'computerised' TTWA from 1984 (Coombes, Green and Openshaw 1986). In short, there were all the operational conditions required to replicate the mapping of IDs in the UK. Nevertheless, the first application of the mapping methodology was only in 2005 (De Propris 2005).

Why has there been a general disinterest in the mapping of IDs? One possible explanation is that IDs were seen as 'the product of a singular and therefore unrepeatable history' (Zeitlin 1992, p. 279), namely, the process of Italian industrialisation. It is most likely the term 'Italianate industrial districts' (see for example, Bergman and Feser 1999) was later coined as an expression of this view.

However, the ID thesis was not tailored to fit the peculiarity of the Italian economic development (Sforzi 2008), nor did it follow from the scholastic application of Marshallian conceptual tools, such as the external economies, the industrial atmosphere, to Italian development – as Becattini reminded us recently (Becattini 2007).

It was the observation of the economic reality of Tuscany since the 1960s (Sforzi 2004, 2007b) that stimulated a theoretical thinking seeking to understand phenomena that could not be explained by mainstream economics: indeed, industries were not always located where the principles of industrial location theory would have suggested. The ID thesis sprang from here. The innovative re-reading of Marshall's economic thought made by Becattini (Becattini 1962b, 1975b) provided a conceptual framework to these studies.

The ID thesis proposed a 'reversal of perspective' in the approach to economic facts. While an industry concentrated in certain places was commonly interpreted as the result of choices of industrial location by firms within given sectors, studies on ID proposed an understanding of localised industries as the result of pathways of industrial specialisation (in terms of both organisation and goods produced) of certain local communities.

The failure to grasp the meaning of the ID thesis in the UK – an innovation of far-reaching consequences that went far beyond the 'Italian way' to industrialisation – was a sign of academic conservatism, which resulted from a bias against interdisciplinarity; the latter being a *sine qua non* for mapping IDs, because its implementation requires the confluence of different disciplinary theoretical and practical abilities inside a shared theoretical framework.

So, the delay in the application of the methodology in the UK should be explained more in terms of the prolonged domination of mainstream economics and economic geography and their dismissal of the ID thesis, rather than by the belief of the uniqueness of Italian IDs.

3. THE CONVERGENCE OF POLITICAL AND RESEARCH MOTIVATIONS IN MAPPING IDs AND THE MEASUREMENT OF THE DISTRICT EFFECT

The key role in promoting the mapping of IDs can be played either by political institutions or by the academic circles, as taught by the cases of Spain and the UK. Instead, the Italian case has seen a convergence of political and research motivations. From the 1960s some political and research institutions had started to cooperate, in order to improve the knowledge of the regional peculiarities of economic and social development and to design appropriate public policies in the framework of what was called regional economic planning. The regional institutes of research were the main operational instruments of such a cooperation. In Tuscany, the first was the Institute of Economic and Social Research (ITRES), followed by the Tuscany Research Institute (IRPET), founded in 1968 and directed by Giacomo Becattini. The ID thesis, including the mapping, is rooted in this experience (Sforzi 2007b).

The legal recognition of the ID – which was brought to completion in the years 1991–93 – was the outcome of this tradition of inter-institutional cooperation, which also involved the National Institute of Statistics (ISTAT) and the Ministry of Industry (see Sforzi in this section).

In Italy, the mapping of IDs paved the way to the econometric investigation. This strand of research was pioneered by Signorini who measured the 'district effect' finding positive and significant results (Signorini 1994a). Most of these econometric studies initially published in the Italian journal *Sviluppo locale* ('Local development') have been reviewed by Becattini and Musotti (2004). The chapter by Guido De Blasio, Massimo Omiccioli and Luigi Federico Signorini is specifically devoted to the subject.

Although the mapping of Spanish IDs is quite recent, further research has been carried out in relation to this, on the innovation performance of IDs in Spain (Boix and Galletto 2006–07). The continuity of this strand of research in Italy is exemplified by recent contributions on the financial constraints to innovation for firms belonging to IDs (Ughetto 2006–07). In most cases, econometric estimates confirm the advantages of being a district local community compared to non-district ones, in terms of both economic competitiveness and ability to innovate. The chapter by Stefano Menghinello belongs to this field of research, and it is focused on measuring the internationalisation of Italian IDs.

What matters, however, is that econometric analysis allows the testing of economic relationships producing comparable results and overcoming the limits of the more qualitative case studies analysis, and in particular, enabling more general comparisons to be meaningfully made to accumulate significant results across different IDs. It also allows us to measure, although sometimes only indirectly, a growing number of ID characteristics, to identify their determinants, so that the empirical findings raise new questions for theoretical thinking, nourishing new circuits of knowledge. All this, normally, has policy implications that foster the dialogue between the communities of academics and politicians.

The mapping of IDs now available in the above-mentioned European countries – along with the experience gained through econometric measurements – will enable in the near future the implementation of integrated research to develop cross-country analyses on levels of performance and national trajectories of change; an opportunity that researchers had never had before now.

25. The empirical evidence of industrial districts in Italy

Fabio Sforzi

1. INTRODUCTION

Interest in the industrial districts (IDs) and their role in the Italian economy has existed for over 30 years. But the book that popularised the ID concept in Italy was *Mercato e forze locali: il distretto industriale* edited by Giacomo Becattini in 1987 (Becattini 1987). The ID concept offered a new way to think about small firms which had had a remarkable increase over the previous decades.

The 'ID thesis' was formulated by Becattini at the end of a research path nourished through empirical research and theoretical thinking. Becattini had investigated the economic development of Tuscany through empirical research (Becattini 1966, 1969, 1975a), and had dug in Marshall's system of thought through the theoretical thinking (Becattini 1962a, 1975b). The result of continual 'coming and going' between theory and practice led Becattini to conceptualise the ID both as a way to classify the national economy (Becattini 1979) – that is, the ID as a 'unit of analysis' – and as a way to organise the production (Becattini 1989) – that is, the ID as a 'model of development'.

According to the theoretical framework dominant in those years, the economies of production (that is, the advantages of division of labour) could be obtained only in large factories. The small firms (when they were not craft firms producing for the local market) could act only as subcontractors employed by big companies, most often agglomerated in the vicinity, and benefitting from agglomeration economies.

On the contrary, the ID model stated that the advantages of division of labour could be achieved by small producers – specialised in one or a few stages of the same production process (that is, the same industry *lato sensu*, including subsidiary industries and business services) – embedded in a local community where social forces cooperate with economic ones. Small producers benefitted from local-external economies of production, resulting from the social division of labour within the local community.

This chapter is about the Italian experience of identifying IDs. After the Introduction, the remainder of the chapter is organised as follows. Section 2 summarises the political foundations of IDs. Section 3 briefly introduces the concept of ID for the purpose of its empirical definition. Section 4 discusses the methodological issues. Section 5 is devoted to the description of data and the algorithm used for mapping IDs, as well as a short comment on the results. Section 6 elucidates the quantitative importance of IDs in the Italian economy. The concluding section contains some final remarks.

2. THE POLITICAL FOUNDATIONS OF IDs

The preeminence of the book *Mercato e forze locali* on the previous writings – and its impact on politicians and academics in Italy – was due to the fact that in this book the ID thesis was exemplified through empirical evidence; that is to say, the mapping of IDs in Italy (Sforzi 1987). This empirical finding proved that the ID could be an 'instrument of analysis' to explain the Italian system of manufacturing, but also an 'instrument of policy' to support industrial development. This recognition had important policy implications.

In 1991 the Italian government enacted a law on small firms where the ID was constituted as a legal instrument to support industrial policy (Legge 5 ottobre 1991, n. 317). Two years later the Ministry of Industry established criteria to be applied by each regional government to identify IDs within its own territory (Ministero dell'Industria, del Commercio e dell'Artigianato 1993a). These criteria left each regional government free to define 'district industries', but tied them to use local labour market areas (LLMAs) as appropriate units of analysis to identify 'district areas'.

LLMAs had been introduced years before by the Italian National Institute of Statistics for the purpose of economic and social research (Sforzi 1986). LLMAs were defined on the basis of inter-municipal daily journey-to-work flows by using a quantitative approach. Although statistically an LLMA is geographically a proximate and interconnected group of municipalities – with the municipality being the smallest unit of observation – it mirrors a 'local community' of people that work and live within it.

It does not mean that the local population of each LLMA shares the same value system, or that it has matured a clear consciousness of its own social identity and relative economic autonomy. The term 'local community' is used to emphasise the fact that what actually constitutes an LLMA is the working and living community, rather than businesses or industries; although there are localised economic activities from which the local population earns a living. Thus, the LLMA is the most suitable unit of analysis to study to what extent this consciousness really exists. The importance of discovering that this consciousness exists or is maturing is evident if one believes that the social *milieu* can be a source of productivity and innovativity for the local industry.

Although an LLMA does not necessarily correspond to a district, and the intermingling, mutually sustaining and reinforcing, between the local economy and the local community may be found in other models of development, it is equally true that this relation is congenial to a district *milieu*, where the division of labour among many specialised firms is mediated by the common cultural imprint and a strong sense of belonging shared among both employers and employees, instead of by the hierarchical control, direct or indirect, of some big companies, like in the growth pole (Becattini and Rullani 1993).

The Law 317/1991 and subsequent Ministerial Decree of 21 April 1993 were the result of drafting and discussions between the central government and regional governments, which also involved national and subnational institutions (including chambers of commerce, regional institutes of research, associations of entrepreneurs and artisans, trade unions). The set of criteria that were established at the end for the identification, by the regions, of IDs was the operational translation – necessarily simplified – of the previous experience of identifying IDs carried out at the Tuscany Research Institute (IRPET) (Sforzi 1990).

Once IDs were recognised by law as appropriate entities for the design and implementation of industrial policy, they received an enormous amount of attention from the mass media, politicians and researchers.

The most important Italian economic newspaper, *Il Sole-24 Ore*, the organ of *Confindustria* (the Italian employers' confederation), launched an inquiry that lasted ten months mobilising 20 journalists who wrote 65 mini-monographs on districts, thus proposing its own map of IDs. The survey was published in the newspaper in episodes from July 1991 until 1992, then was collected in a volume (Moussanet and Paolazzi 1992).

In the preface to the volume, the director of the newspaper, Gianni Locatelli, wrote:

> Not only Fiat. But not only Mediobanca, too. Looked through the magnifying glass of industrial districts, the Italian reality appears quite different from that of monoculture industrial and financial governed by the two stars of Turin and Milan.
> ... Italy of industrial districts is, first of all, really a will to do that, beyond the problems which often obscure its image, gives this country a not subordinate role in the great arena of world development.
> ... The history of a district may be ancient ... or recent ... but in any case it has in the territory and product its identification. Size and organization, as production volumes and number of businesses may change, but another shared feature is the direct relationship employer–firm–society. Therefore, the district takes a clear cultural identity, where next to the defense of the local values lives the openness to international entrepreneurial competition. (Ibid., pp. xi–xii)

IDs of the *Il Sole-24 Ore* counted 52 000 firms, 450 000 employees, 30 000 billion of Italian lire of exports. As we read in the inside flap of the book, with these numbers IDs 'that do not gain the front page of newspapers, but highlight one of the Italian great competitive advantages: the flexibility of small business' contribute to national economic fortunes, while challenging a 'great competitive disadvantage, namely the absence of a country-system'. However, local communities which are IDs enjoy the support of 'a dense network of banks, public institutions and private associations'.

The involvement of regional governments in identifying IDs (after 1993) gave a further boost to the ID model, with the term becoming popular, albeit the concept not always well understood. For the first time, in the Italian formal institutional framework there was an orientation towards local industrial policy. Through the district, the first real test of the devolution of powers from central government to regional and local governments was realised.

Regional governments marked a frenetic activism – supported by the lobby of the historic districts which in 1994 had formed an association called the Club of Districts – justified by the fact that the law made them the protagonists of the mapping of IDs.

The possibility of 'discovering' IDs in the territories administered by regional governments meant the broadening of their power in the field of industry, and the possibility of receiving adequate financial resources to design and implement local industrial policies. In short, the mappings were handed over as a concrete opportunity to increase the autonomy of regional governments from the central State and to show that they were able to implement their own industrial policies, although restricted to IDs instead of expanded to the entire territory that fell under their administration.

For most industrialised regions, particularly those with the highest density of IDs – where the district model largely coincided with their model of regional development – this chance meant acquiring the political legitimacy to govern their own economy, even in contrast to central government policies.

The first assessment on the Italian experience of IDs was promoted in the late 1990s by the Ministry of Industry, through the Institute for Industrial Promotion (IPI). The IPI made a full screening of multiple experiences on IDs effected by regional governments in the decade (Ministero delle Attività Produttive and Istituto per la Promozione Industriale 2002). The assessment was not particularly satisfactory, especially since regional governments had devoted more time to map the districts – in an attempt to find as much as possible – than to design the contents of district policies. It was a clear sign of lack of familiarity with a place-based approach to economic facts that the ID thesis implied; but also with the design of local industrial policies, demonstrating the difficulty in reversing a firm-based analytical and policy approach.

Nevertheless, the Minister of Industry of the time, the economist Antonio Marzano, acknowledged that IDs opened – even for the central government – a new era of economic policies. His presentation of IPI (ibid.) began with the following words:

> Industrial districts represent a case of 'success' of the Italian economy. Success is measured also in the growing international interest in an experience that has been widely mentioned as a useful reference model for the promotion of local development.
> ... We must be grateful to the many scholars ... that with their passionate work identified in the Italian industrial system several local communities, firms and people able to compete and succeed in global markets. Without this work, the knowledge of the productive reality of the country would be poorer and therefore less opportunity for economic policies to accompany the processes of growth would be available. (Ibid., p. 7)

The words of Minister Marzano reflected an increasing international attention to the district model of industrial development that Italy had experienced.

The far-reaching consequences of the ID model – supported by theory (the Marshall view of economics recovered to the attention of the scientific community from Becattini) and facts (the Italian way to industrialisation focused on IDs) – was promptly seized by the International Institute for Labour Studies (IILS), a centre for advanced studies in the social and labour field at the International Labour Organisation (ILO).

In the late 1980s, the IILS was engaged in a comparative research on developments in the structure and organisation of small and medium-sized firms (SMEs) from the world's six largest industrialised market economy countries (France, Federal Republic of Germany, Italy, Japan, the UK and the US) as a part of a project launched in 1986 by the ILO within its 'New Industrial Organisation' Programme (Sengenberger, Loveman and Piore 1990).

The SMEs industrialisation of Italy – on the interpretation given by Becattini in the above-mentioned volume – suggested to the director of IILS, Werner Sengenberger, that experience of Italian IDs represented a benchmark for the purpose of the project.

Thus, that first book was followed by a second one entirely dedicated to Italy: *Industrial Districts and Inter-Firm Co-operation in Italy* (Pyke, Becattini and Sengenberger 1990), which would become the book on IDs most quoted in the world, and one year later (1991) it was translated into Italian.

For the ILO as an institution whose mission was focused on the concept and objective of 'decent work' – which is considered at the heart of the social progress – the interest in the district model can be summed up in one sentence: the ID was the model of success that honoured the dignity of work.

The role played by IILS was decisive in spreading the interest in IDs worldwide, including feedback on the Italian communities of researchers and practitioners.

Since the 1990s, IDs have often captured the front pages of newspapers, and have been subjected to periodic surveys in their economic supplements. Even the banking institutions (for example, Intesa-San Paolo of Turin, or Capitalia of Rome, now part of UniCredit Group) are interested in IDs, monitoring their economic performance (Guelpa and Micelli 2007) and comparing them with those in other countries (Barbato and Hongbo 2008). Then, there are the foundations, such as the Edison Foundation of Milan which has devoted several studies to IDs (for example, Fortis and Quadro Curzio 2006).

The pioneering role played by the Bank of Italy that dedicated significant research projects to IDs (Signorini 2000) and public initiatives supporting the debate on their importance for the Italian economy (Banca d'Italia 2004) should be recalled. This attention to IDs was directly encouraged by the Governor of the Bank of Italy, Antonio Fazio. Presenting the 1998 Annual Report, the Governor drew the attention of the political and economic world to IDs, to emphasise that IDs are not simple agglomerations of SMEs, but mainly local communities:

> The concentration of specialized industries in IDs stimulates the innovation of products and processing techniques, enhances the professionalism and social mobility of employees, promotes new business initiatives. The benefits of information management increase production capacity to respond to fluctuations in demand. (Banca d'Italia 1999, p. 29)

Of course, the ID both as theory and model of production does not have a unanimous consensus. Besides those who regret the loss of the industrial centrality of big businesses (Gallino 2003), over the years some views have emerged supporting a return to businesses being the basic unit of analysis for economic research and industrial policy. Now that in Italy most large companies have disappeared, the type of company to which the destiny of the Italian economy is entrusted is the medium-sized company. In this approach, the size of these firms would enable them to generate the economies of production they need, and to act with the necessary agility in the global economy. It is the thesis of the so-called 'fourth capitalism' – fourth in Italy, because it comes after the capitalism based on large private corporations, State-owned companies and IDs (Colli 2002b; Berta 2006; Coltorti 2008).

3. WHAT IS AN ID?

The ID is a global concept. It shares this feature with the cluster (Porter 1990a, 1998a; Ketels 2003) with which it is sometimes confused. In reality, it could be argued that metaphorically, the concepts of ID and cluster do not share the same DNA. It is true that both represent an overcoming of the sector as the unit of economic analysis, but while the district through this overcoming leads to the proposal of the 'local community' as the unit of analysis, the industry becoming its economic component, the cluster is a 'set of interrelated industries' (Porter 1990a) or, in the latest version, that geographically-based 'group of interconnected companies' (Porter 1998a).

The assimilation between ID and cluster stems from a misunderstanding, that is, from a mistaken interpretation of Marshall's thought about the meaning of 'the concentration of specialised industries in particular localities'. The interpretation that leads to include Marshall as the 'intellectual antecedent of cluster theory' is based on the belief that Marshall in those pages is talking about 'industrial location' (Porter 1998a), when, instead, he is addressing the issue of the industrial organisation of society.

This misunderstanding was possible because Porter, but also others like Krugman (1991a), approached the thought of Marshall, or rather, Book IV of *Principles of Economics* (Marshall 1920), from a 'sectoral' perspective (the firm and related industry), rather than from a 'territorial' one (the local community and related industry).

All this has a direct impact on the identification of the district. It is not a matter of bounding an agglomeration of firms (in the same industry or several industries, complementary or different), but a local community which mirrors an industrial specialisation and the way it (the community) is organising the production. When production is organised through small firms which tend to specialise in one or few stages of the same production process, then it is a district community.

The industry in which a local community specialises corresponds to the driving industry of the local economy, namely on which the life of the community mainly depends, because it is the industry that employs most of the local population. The growth or decline of this industry changes the life of the community.

A local community is defined as a working and living place that is shaped by the collective and individual behaviours of its people; by local economic and social institutions, and by the constant mutual exchanges with the outside world.

Therefore, the local community cannot match an urban quarter (Wise 1949) (which is the part of a whole), but the entire daily urban system, constituted by the city and its surroundings, where the local population lives, works and establishes most of its social relations. When the daily urban system is viewed from the perspective of workers who are gathered within its boundaries it takes the meaning of an LLMA.

Those who complains about the limits of the LLMA as the unit of analysis to identify IDs, because for instance it does not recognise industrial quarters within a city (De Blasio, Iuzzolino and Omiccioli 2008), are thinking of the ID not as a local community, but as the empirical outcome of an industrial location process; that is to say, an industrial agglomeration, which is the term used in literature to name the phenomenon of spatial clustering.

4. METHODOLOGICAL ISSUES

The mapping of IDs poses a number of methodological issues in relation to the way: (a) to define the unit of analysis, that is the smallest object of analysis able to bound the local community; (b) to define the district industry, that is the types of industry able to represent the industrial specialisation of the local community; and (c) to define the district firm, that is the size of firm able to approximate the organisation of production.

The first issue – concerning the appropriate unit of analysis – is solved by the availability in Italy of territorial units designed for the purpose of economic and social research. These are precisely LLMAs as established by ISTAT (1997, 2005). LLMAs are defined by daily journey-to-work flows between municipalities, which are the units of observation. Data on daily commuters are collected through the Census of Population, so the boundaries of LLMAs can be updated every ten years. From a statistical point of view LLMAs meet the principles of self-containment, internal contiguity and homogeneity (that is, to give small local communities located in the vicinity of large LLMAs a chance to maintain their relative autonomy). To satisfy this last principle, Italian LLMAs definition does not include a minimum size criterion concerning the local population or workers. LLMAs cut across administrative boundaries both of provinces and regions (respectively, NUTS 3 and 2 in the Eurostat classification). LLMAs have been available since 1981 and have been used to identify IDs since that date (Sforzi 1986, 1987).

From an economic point of view, LLMAs encompass economic activities that produce goods and supply services and workers who work and live there with their families. So LLMAs, boundaries are socio-economic instead of administrative, and they change over time as the local community reorganises itself under the influence of systems of social, economic and institutional interaction – both internal and external. This process of reshaping justifies the periodic review of the boundaries of the LLMAs.

The 2001-based LLMAs were reviewed in 2005 and the outcome was that 686 were identified (ISTAT 2005).

The second issue – concerning the district industry – depends on the pattern of industrial specialisation of the country under consideration, in this case Italy. The knowledge of the industrial model of specialisation can be gained in several ways: through literature, historical and economic, through field work, but mainly through the continued and careful scrutiny of statistics.

In Italy, the pattern of industrial specialisation is characterised by manufacturing industries that produce personal goods (textiles, clothing and leather products, jewellery, and so on), household goods (furniture, ceramic tiles, and so on), foodstuffs, mechanics (machinery, electrical and optical equipment), and metal products. The search for the district industries must consider these manufacturing industries, without excluding, nevertheless, others like transport equipment and chemicals.

Each district is characterised by an industry formed by an original combination of production activities that makes it different from any other. This implies to define a level of statistical classification of the types of industry (general enough) to allow the detection of these combinations of production activities within the variety of local economies (that is, LLMAs) constituting the national economy.

Ultimately, the definition of types of manufacturing to identify the district industry requires the use of common sense supported by 'an intimate and messy acquaintance with the facts' (J.M. Keynes) to which the classification has to be applied, finding a reasonable compromise between local peculiarities (that is, the multiplicity of LLMAs) and national generality (that is, Italy as a whole).

The types of manufacturing industry used for this study are ten: textile and clothing; leather and related products (tanning, leather goods and footwear); other personal goods (jewellery, musical instruments, and so on); household goods (wooden furniture, ceramic tiles, and so on); food, beverages and tobacco; mechanicals (machinery equipment, electrical and optical equipment, metal goods); basic metals; chemicals and related products (refined petroleum products, rubber and plastics products); transport equipment; paper, printing and publishing, as statistically classified in the 2001 Census of Industry and Services (ISTAT 2001).

The third issue – concerning the district firm – is perhaps the most controversial. In Italy there has never been a large-scale comprehensive government inquiry on the small firm and its role in the Italian economy like that promoted by the UK government through the Bolton Committee (Bolton Report 1971). Up to the early 1990s, researchers developed *ad hoc* definitions of small firms in manufacturing depending on the purpose of their studies, and varying what counted as 'small' according to the industrial sector and labour market areas in which firms were located.

On the other hand, scholars engaged in research and policymaking utilised an operative definition of a small firm: for Brusco (1990) it had fewer than 20 employees, and for others, a small–medium firm had less than 100 employees (see also Solinas and Baroni 2001). The Law 317/1991 established the size limit of a small firm to 200 employees.

In the end, the Commission of the European Communities adopted a Recommendation that defined a small firm as having 'less than 50 people', and a medium-sized as having 'less than 250' (European Commission 1992, 1996).

These size limits were more restrictive than those established by the Italian law, which had therefore to be adapted (Ministero dell'Industria, del Commercio e dell'Artigianato 1993b).

In this way, provisions of law contributed to set a standard for SMEs, until then based on discretionary decisions by researchers or defined by size limits associated with the employment-size class adopted in the industrial censuses. The impact on the identification of IDs was evident: 250 employees became the 'threshold point' to define the size of the district firm.

The definition adopted in this study sets the size of the district firm to 'fewer than 250 employees', since it meets our aim of coming as close as possible to the policy requirements.

5. MAPPING IDs

Mapping IDs requires decisions based on statistical data, local knowledge, and informed but subjective choices. Political considerations, including the possible adjustment of borders, come later, when the national map of IDs is used to implement a district-based policy.

Data consists of a cross-section of 686 LLMAs for the year 2001. All data is from the 2001 Census of Industry and Services conducted by ISTAT. The definition of the data is as follows.

'Economic activities' are expressed as number of employees engaged in: (a) agriculture; (b) mining; (c) construction; (d) manufacturing; (e) business services; (f) consumer services; (g) social services; and (h) traditional services (ISTAT 2006b, pp. 16–17).

'Types of manufacturing industry' are expressed as number of employees engaged in: (a) textile and clothing; (b) leather and related products (tanning, leather goods and footwear); (c) other personal goods (jewellery, musical instruments, and so on); (d) household goods (wooden furniture, ceramic tiles, and so on); (e) food, beverages and tobacco; (f) machinery and equipment (including metal goods); (g) basic metals; (h) chemicals and related products (including refined petroleum products, rubber and plastics products); (i) transport equipment; and (j) paper, printing and publishing (ibid., p. 18). The definition of these ten types of manufacturing industry is a reasonable combination between generality and detail, according to the specific pattern of specialisation of the Italian economy.

'Size of firm' is expressed as number of employees in small (up to 49 employees), medium (50–249) and large (250 or more) manufacturing firms (actually, local units) according to the definition recommended by the European Commission (2003).

Sforzi–ISTAT (Sforzi 2006) provided the basis to map IDs. The identification of IDs is a four-stage algorithm, which can be summarised as follows:

1. identification of the manufacturing LLMAs;
2. identification of the manufacturing LLMAs of SMEs;
3. identification of the main industry of the manufacturing LLMAs of SMEs;
4. identification of IDs.

Stage 1

The first stage is to identify 'manufacturing LLMAs'. This stage consists of two steps. The first step is to measure the manufacturing specialisation of each LLMA using a location quotient (LQ) based on employment. The equation used is as follows:

$$LQ_{LLMA} = (LLMA_{e(i)} / ITA_{e(i)}) / (LLMA_{e(t)} / ITA_{e(t)}) \qquad (25.1)$$

where:

$LLMA_{e(i)}$ employment in the economic activity (i) in an LLMA;
$ITA_{e(i)}$ employment in the economic activity (i) in Italy;
$LLMA_{e(t)}$ employment in all economic activities (t) in an LLMA;
$ITA_{e(t)}$ employment in all economic activities (t) in Italy.

LLMAs with an LQ greater than one in an economic activity are relatively specialised in that activity.

The next step is to compare for each LLMA the manufacturing, business or consumer services activities with an LQ higher than one to determine which of these economic activities has the largest weight of specialisation in terms of number of employees (E_{HN}). The equation used is as follows:

$$E_{HN} = [(LLMA_{e(i)}/ITA_{e(i)}) - (LLMA_{e(t)}/ITA_{e(t)})] * ITA_{e(i)} \quad (25.2)$$

LLMAs with the number of employees in manufacturing higher than in services are defined as 'manufacturing'.

Stage 2

The second stage is to identify manufacturing LLMAs of SMEs. Manufacturing LLMAs are examined to identify those in which there is a relative localisation of SMEs. The localisation of SMEs is measured according to the number of employees in small (up to 49 employees), medium (50–249) and large (250 or more) manufacturing firms. The equation used is as follows:

$$LQ_{LLMA} = (LLMA_{e(SML)}/ITA_{e(SML)}) / (LLMA_{e(t)}/ITA_{e(t)}) \quad (25.3)$$

where:

$LLMA_{e(SML)}$ employment in manufacturing firms by small, medium and large (SML) size in an LLMA;
$ITA_{e(SML)}$ employment in manufacturing firms by small, medium and large (SML) size in Italy;
$LLMA_{e(t)}$ employment in all manufacturing firms (t) in an LLMA;
$ITA_{e(t)}$ employment in all manufacturing firms (t) in Italy.

Manufacturing LLMAs with an LQ greater than one in small or medium-sized firms are defined as 'manufacturing LLMAs of SMEs'.

Stage 3

The third stage is to identify the 'main industry' of manufacturing LLMAs of SMEs. Manufacturing LLMAs of SMEs are examined to identify the main manufacturing industry. This stage consists of two steps.

The first step is to measure the specialisation of each manufacturing LLMA of SMEs in different types of manufacturing industry using an LQ based on employment. The equation used is as follows:

$$LQ_{LLMA} = (LLMA_{e(i)} / ITA_{e(i)}) / (LLMA_{e(t)} / ITA_{e(t)}) \quad (25.4)$$

where:
- $LLMA_{e(i)}$ employment in the type of manufacturing industry (i) in an LLMA;
- $ITA_{e(i)}$ employment in the type of manufacturing industry (i) in Italy;
- $LLMA_{e(t)}$ employment in all manufacturing industries (t) in an LLMA;
- $ITA_{e(t)}$ employment in all manufacturing industries (t) in Italy.

LLMAs with an LQ greater than one in a type of manufacturing industry are relatively specialised in that type of industry.

The next step is to compare for each LLMA the types of manufacturing industry with an LQ greater than one to determine which type has the highest number of employees (E_{HN}). The equation used is as follows:

$$E_{HN} = [(LLMA_{e(i)} / ITA_{e(i)}) - (LLMA_{e(t)} / ITA_{e(t)})] * ITA_{e(i)}. \quad (25.5)$$

The type of manufacturing industry with the highest number of employees is defined as 'main industry'.

Stage 4

The fourth stage leads to the identification of LLMAs as IDs.
To be identified as an ID an LLMA needs to meet the following two conditions:

1. The employment in SMEs of the main industry is more than half the employment of the main industry in firms of all sizes:

$$(LLMA_{e(SMEs)} / (LLMA_{e(t)}) > 50.0 \text{ per cent} \quad (25.6)$$

where:
- $LLMA_{e(SMEs)}$ employment in SMEs of the main industry in an LLMA;
- $LLMA_{e(t)}$ total employment (t) of the main industry in an LLMA.

2. The employment in small firms of the main industry is more than half of the employment of medium-sized firms, if there is only one medium-sized firm:

$$(LLMA_{e(s)} / LLMA_{e(m)}) > 50.0 \text{ per cent} \quad (25.7)$$

where:
- $LLMA_{e(s)}$ employment in small firms (s) of the main industry in an LLMA;

$LLMA_{e(m)}$ employment in the medium-sized firm (m) of the main industry in an LLMA.

This process of measurement led to the identification of 156 LLMAs as IDs (Figure 25.1).

Figure 25.1 evidences that northern and central Italy are the main location of IDs. This geographical pattern shows why the term 'Third Italy districts' is a

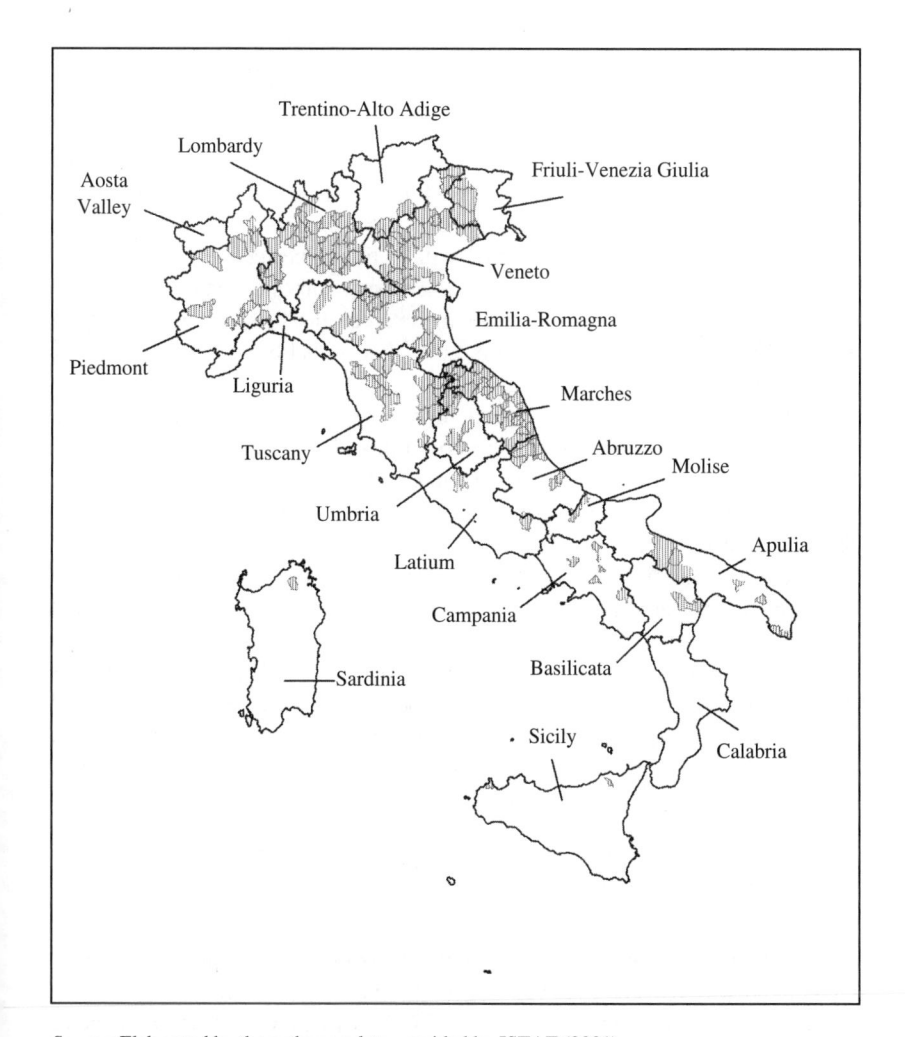

Source: Elaborated by the author on data provided by ISTAT (2001).

Figure 25.1 IDs in Italy, 2001

fallacy (Staber 1998). As a proportion of manufacturing LLMAs, the industrial regions with the highest density of IDs are: the Marches (in central Italy) with a value of 90 per cent (27 IDs), Veneto (in the Northeast) with 85 per cent (22 IDs) and Lombardy (in the Northwest) with 71 per cent (27 IDs).

Not even southern Italy is devoid of IDs. Although southern Italy is less industrialised than the north (11 versus 59 per cent of manufacturing LLMAs), however the share of IDs, as a proportion of manufacturing LLMAs, is only 9 points less than the north: 57 versus 66 per cent. This means that even the industrialisation of southern Italy is dominated by the ID model.

The 156 IDs are not all the same. Among them, there are historical IDs and IDs newly-shaped, as there are also 'potential' IDs identified by the algorithm that the researcher cannot arbitrarily reject.

The adjustment of ID boundaries, or the denial of an ID, is a task of politics, not research. The task of research is to state what are the criteria that the adjustment of borders must not disregard (for example, self-containment). Otherwise, policies applied on that ID will be likely ineffective.

Among the 156 districts there are some very small ones, that is where it is easy to guess that the division of labour between the firms is modest. There are IDs identified for the first time in 2001 that probably will not survive the verification of the 2011 Census.

In 1981, when IDs were mapped for the first time (Sforzi 1987), some researchers were sceptical about the possibility that some LLMAs could be IDs. Instead others, who believed in the possibility of industrial policy for local development, were not even shocked by IDs that might appear at first sight 'backward districts' (Brusco 1989a).

In a few cases, time has proved them right. But most of the IDs received a statistical and grounded validation. And on those LLMAs that seemed improbable IDs many researchers had to change idea, because those IDs held up to the evidence of the facts: the self-assessment of local communities, rather than statistical tests. This happened once the IDs' map started to circulate and policymakers of regional governments to use it in an intelligent manner to design a district-based economic development policy.

6. THE QUANTITATIVE IMPORTANCE OF IDs IN THE ITALIAN ECONOMY

Some figures on employment and export of manufactured goods will help to understand why IDs are important for the Italian economy and society.

In 2001 IDs made up 23 per cent of Italy's LLMAs and 65 per cent of the manufacturing ones. IDs specialised in textile and clothing were the most numerous (45), followed by those specialised in mechanicals (38), household goods (32), leather and related goods (20). There are others with a focus on food and beverages (7), jewellery and other personal goods (6), paper, printing and publishing (4) and chemicals (4).

In 2005 IDs were home to 22 per cent of the Italian population (13 million) and employed 27 per cent of people (4.5 million). They accounted for 39 per cent of Italy's manufacturing jobs, and 37 per cent of its manufacturing exports.

The main district industries produce personal goods (including textile and clothing, leather goods and footwear, jewellery) and household goods (including wooden furniture, ceramic tiles, glass items), followed by mechanicals. In 2005 personal goods' IDs were 59 per cent of the national employment (that is, textile and clothing 57 per cent of 491 935 employees; leather goods and footwear 61 per cent of 166 066; jewellery and other personal goods 67 per cent of 48 327), household goods 42 per cent of 628 872 of employees, and mechanicals 40 per cent of 1 724 533 employees.

Of course, the contribution of IDs to national exports of manufactured goods – here classified by divisions (Fazio and Pascucci 2006–07) – was particularly high in district industries: textile products (63 per cent), leather and related goods (60 per cent), wooden furniture (59 per cent), metal goods (53 per cent), clothing (46 per cent), machinery and equipment (43 per cent), electrical and optical equipment (40 per cent).

By definition, the dimensional structure of IDs is characterised by district firms of small and medium size. However, among these, firms with a size between 10 and 49 employees are the most typical (39 per cent); while the micro-firms (up to 9 employees) are the least present (25 per cent).

7. SOME FINAL REMARKS

Since their 'statistical discovery' (in 1987), IDs were considered 'the more' (in addition to large firms) and 'the different' (for their assumed Italian uniqueness) of the Italian economy compared to other industrialised countries.

Then, with the crises of large firms, IDs appeared to most as the 'new one best way' to industrialisation. Both academics and politicians questioned the replicability of the model to revitalise areas in industrial decline or to increase the competitiveness of areas poorly equipped with SMEs, especially to encourage the development of backward regions such as southern Italy.

Then, with the progress of globalisation seeping through all aspects of socio-economic life, the idea that production would be easily dis-embedded from places rose from the ranks. The expectation was that the process would have involved virtually all firms, not only the large ones, with the exception of small businesses which were to operate within local markets only. Consequently, IDs would have lost the agglomeration strength of their social *milieu* – namely, their true competitive advantage – and they would come to an inescapable decline.

Well, this was not the case in Italy. In the last two decades of the last century (ca 1981–2001), that marked the end of Fordism and saw the globalisation process reshaping the world economy, IDs 'statistically defined' suffered a moderate fall in manufacturing employment (8 per cent), that is half the national average (16 per cent) but four times less than manufacturing LLMAs polarised mainly by large firms (32 per cent); they had a growth in business services equal to 142 per cent, slightly less than that of metropolitan LLMAs (150 per cent) which supply services for the whole Italian economy. IDs and metropolian areas were the only two types of local economies where employment increased more than the national average (124 per cent).

The employment of manufacturing industries localised within IDs decreased less than those located outside (Sforzi 2007a): textile and clothing (–31 versus –42 per cent), leather and related goods (–24 versus –28 per cent), household goods (–17 versus –23 per cent), food and beverages (–2 versus –8.5 per cent), paper, printing and publishing (–3 versus –11 per cent); and, indeed, some increased rather than decreased: machinery (+16 versus –5 per cent), jewellery and other personal goods (+44 versus –39 per cent), chemicals and related products (+2 versus –25 per cent). Overall, while the district manufacturing employment was down by 8 per cent (as mentioned above), outside of IDs it was down by 20 per cent.

26. The empirical relevance of industrial districts in Spain

Rafael Boix

1. INTRODUCTION

During the period between 1996 and 2007, the economic development model of Spain was based on the expansion of a demand driven by the construction sector. This model generated rapid growth although was exclusively based on the use of cheap labour and nil or marginal contributions of capital and total factor productivity. After the general elections of March 2004, there was a change of party leadership in the Spanish government. Jointly with the maintenance of macroeconomic stability, one of the priorities of the new government was to induce a change in the development model of the Spanish economy, where productivity, competitiveness and innovation had to become the key variables. The manufacturing sector was perceived as central to these objectives. In contrast with the neoliberal approach to the industrial policy of the preceding government, the new government recovered the Ministry of Industry and assigned it the key role of leading such a change in the productive model.

Looking for new instruments for the industrial policy, the Ministry of Industry decided to consider the elaboration of the first map of Marshallian industrial districts (MID) in Spain (Boix and Galletto 2006), which was carried out using the Italian ISTAT (1997) methodology. For the first time, the map allowed MIDs to be quantified and showed that they were a widespread reality in Spain and that their quantitative importance was similar to that of Italy. In fact, this result was only to be expected since the two countries have similar territorial, social and productive structures. Furthermore, Spain and Italy (jointly with Portugal) are the only European countries where the average of large firms on total manufacturing firms is below 0.5 per cent, and their contribution to the total manufacturing employment is less than 30 per cent. Since manufacturing production continues to be successful in these countries (and not only in costs), models of production organisation alternative to large and integrated firms were largely expected. The MID proved to be one of the most important.

2. BACKGROUND

2.1 IDs in the academic debate

The social, cultural and urban characteristics of the Iberian territories and the historical evolution of the localised processes of industrialisation that took place in Spain during the 19th and 20th centuries, generated the conditions for the appearance of MIDs practically from the 1850s to the current day. Thus, industrial districts (IDs) are, by all means, not a new phenomenon but rather an important element in Spanish industrial history.[1]

The concept and theory of IDs entered the debate in Spain in 1986, when a further version of Becattini's seminal article (1979) appeared translated in the first issue of the *Revista Econòmica de Catalunya* ('Catalonian Economic Review') (Becattini 1986c). However, the permeability of this contribution into Spanish academic thinking has been slow until practically the year 2000 and, even now, the ID model is still viewed by many scholars as a minor interpretative model unable to explain the dynamics of the economic development. There are two reasons that explain this delay:

1. During the late 1970s and early 1980s, Spain was experiencing a transition phase from dictatorship to democracy and to a more open economy, both at the time of world crisis due to the effects of the oil shocks. At that time, the main concerns for Spanish scholars were related to macroeconomic conditions: unemployment, inflation and interest rates. Only a small number of academics were becoming aware of the deep changes in the international production model (Piore and Sabel 1984) and paid attention to local development and IDs a model of economic policy.
2. During the 20th century, the economic thought of Spanish scholars was not impervious to the main international economic thinking. Jointly with the importance of macroeconomics, mainstream economics was led by the industrial organisation paradigm dominated by large corporations. The 'place' had definitively slipped down in economic analysis and the importance of the historical analysis started to vanish. As in the Italian case explained by Becattini in *The Caterpillar and the Butterfly* (2001a), this paradigm was imported from the Anglo-Saxon context without any attention being paid to the different context whereby in some cases small firms were the dominant organisational form due to natural, historical and socio-economic reasons. On the contrary, the preeminence of small firms was thought to be a severe handicap and because of that industrial policy tended to rely on large firms as propulsive elements.

Despite this initial reluctance, research on IDs has developed in Spain since the end of the 1980s and has intensified in the last years. It has been characterised by three parameters:

1. The research has mainly been of an applied nature whereas the main theoretical developments have been imported from the Italian literature. The main lines have centred on the district accountancy (Ybarra 1991a; Boix and Galletto 2006), the proximity or distance of the Spanish districts from the canonical Italian model (Giner and Santa María 2002; Molina and Martínez 2004), the performance of the Spanish IDs (Hernández and Soler 2003), the characteristics of the innovation processes (Tomás Carpi et al. 1999; Boix and Galletto 2009a), and their utility as instruments for the industrial and development policy (Trullén 1990; Ybarra 2006).
2. It has mainly centred on specific districts and region-industry case studies, with only a few works having considered the entire country.
3. The research has relied on many industries (agro-food industry, textile, leather and footwear, furniture, toys and so on), several regions (Valencia, Catalonia, Madrid and so on) and several districts. However, the region of Valencia has been the most prolific in producing research on its IDs, which can be explained by the huge quantitative importance of the phenomenon in this region and the perception of its importance by the first regional governments in the early 1980s. If Prato is the canonical ID in Italy, in Spain this role corresponds to the districts in the middle of the Castellon Province. These districts, specialised in ceramic tiles and one of the main producers in the word, have been the most studied Spanish IDs.

2.2 IDs in the policy debate

There is an additional factor that explains the difficulty for the ID paradigm to permeate Spanish universities: the reluctance of policymakers. Ybarra (2006) suggest that, traditionally, both right- and left-wing Spanish parties have been reluctant to accept the economic implications coming from the ID paradigm. The right-wing party's view on industrial policy has been based on hierarchical and centralist approaches (contrary to the regional or local aspects), sectoral policy and support for large firms, and during the 1990s, it moved to the centre on the prevalence of finances as a driving force. On the other hand, the left-wing parties also have been dominated by Fordist and centralised approaches based on the economic-financial idea that the large firm is stronger than the small firm and on the political-ideological approach that relates the negotiating power of trade unions to the large vertically-organised firm. Finally, common to both thoughts has been a rigid industry-based conception of the industrial organisation. In this framework, IDs were perceived as a model based on traditional productions and therefore destined to extinction.

In this context, specific policies for IDs had been virtually nonexistent between 1980 and 2005. The only exception maybe was the policy developed by the regional government of Valencia in the late 1980s, that took into account the importance of small and medium-sized enterprises (SMEs) and created a network of technological centres although without a true comprehensive approach to the complexity of the ID. At the national level, there has not been any specific policy relying or drawing on IDs until 2005, when the Ministry of Industry developed its policy for Innovative Business Groupings (IDs, clusters and networks of firms) and other support measures for IDs.[2]

2.3 What is missing?

Despite the efforts made in recent years, it seems obvious that the analysis of IDs and the implementation of a district-based industrial policy in Spain were delayed in comparison with the Italian ones. One additional factor perceived to account for such a delay has been the lack of metrics of IDs for the country as a whole and their adoption by the policymakers. In Italy, this drawback was solved by Sforzi (1987, 1990) and ISTAT (1997, 2006a) although this methodology was not applied in Spain until the elaboration of the first map of MIDs (Boix and Galletto 2006) under the request of the Ministry of Industry. The metrics of IDs is a key point since it enables a better understanding of the importance of the phenomenon in the country as well as their localisation and dominant specialisations. This would also represent a necessary point of departure for further analysis, cross-country comparisons and for the formulation of some policy guidance for policymakers, for instance for the design of policies for districts or for development and competitiveness policies that use IDs as instruments for support.

3. THE APPROACH

Several studies have tried to identify IDs in Spain although they have mainly relied on regional level data and used municipalities or *comarcas* (counties) as units of analysis. It is worth mentioning the contributions on Valencia (Ybarra 1991a; Soler 2000; Giner and Santa María 2002); on Catalonia (Costa Campi 1988; Trullén 2002); on the Balearic Islands (Bibiloni and Pons 2001); on Murcia (De Luca and Soto 1995); and on Madrid (Celada 1999).

Research studies on IDs at the country level are scarce. Departing from a multi-variate methodology, Camisón (2004) obtains 35 IDs in around 60 municipalities. Boix and Galletto (2006) adapted the earlier Sforzi–ISTAT (ISTAT 1997) methodology, based on local labour market areas (LLMAs) as territorial units of analysis, to produce a map comparable to the Italian one. They identify 237 Spanish IDs, providing evidence that their importance was similar to that of Italy. The Sforzi–

ISTAT methodology changed in 2006, improving some aspects of the identification procedure. The next sections will explain this new methodology and its application to Spain.

3.1 The definition of ID

Becattini (1990, p. 38) defines an ID as 'a socio-territorial entity which is characterised by the active presence of both a community of people and a population of firms in one naturally and historically bounded area'. This community of people shares a system of values and common approaches which spread into the district through the customs and the institutional structure (markets, firms, professional schools, trade unions, employer's organisations and so on). The empirical translation of the concept requires the identification of a socio-economic unit of a territorial nature that can be used to apply measurable criteria able to identify IDs.

3.2 The problem of the unit of analysis

The ID is not an agglomeration of firms but the productive expression of a local society. Thus, the basic unit of analysis is not the 'sector' but the 'place' that expresses itself in the markets as an integrated productive unit.

In practice, the administrative boundaries of the region or the province are usually too vast to harbour the concept of 'community'. On the other hand, the district frequently extends across several municipalities so that the use of municipal units can also be misleading. Lastly, the district is a dynamic concept and its spatial boundaries change and renew so that it fits with difficulty into the administrative boundaries which, on the contrary, are steady.

The definition of an intermediate territorial unit between the single productive process and the economic system as a whole, not restricted by the administrative boundaries and able to change over time fits to the concept of 'local labour market areas' (Sforzi and Lorenzini 2002; ISTAT 2006a). LLMAs are constructed on travel-to-work data, and in so doing reflect areas where people live and work. Thus, this allows the condition that IDs can only be studied by relying on territorial units of analysis where there is an overlap between a community of people and firms to be satisfied.

3.3 What can and what cannot be measured?

Boix and Galletto (2009b) provide a detailed appraisal of the advantages and limitations of the Sforzi–ISTAT procedure regarding the identification of IDs. The main advantages are simplicity, transparency and control, reliability of the sources of data, the use of LLMAs as territorial units of analysis, and the simplicity to reproduce the procedure in other countries making international comparisons easier.

Among the main limitations of the procedure, the most important include: the potential inaccuracy of the LLMAs to capture the territorial distribution of some districts; the use of national instead of local input–output tables for the identification of supply chains; the existence of poly-specialised districts, the lack of local data on social capital and their performance; and finally, the general limitation that a quantitative method with imperfect information has when it tries to capture the socio-economic characteristics of the local community.[3]

As Sforzi and Lorenzini (2002) remark, in the absence of a more detailed and precise information, the maps of IDs are an element of a strategy in two phases. Firstly, the quantitative methodology is used to identify potential IDs and it provides valuable information on the significance of the phenomenon in a country, its territorial and sectoral distribution, and its dynamics. The findings of such data-based analysis could not be provided by a qualitative approach only. Secondly, a more precise and detailed qualitative approach can be used to assess which of those are really IDs, as well as to add other districts not identified in the first phase.

4. THE METHODOLOGY

4.1 The unit of analysis

The LLMA is the territorial basis for the ID. The delimitation of LLMAs is carried out using an algorithm in five steps which departs from the municipalities (8100 in Spain) and uses data on jobs, resident employees and travel-to-work flows collected as a part of the national censuses. The application of the algorithm to the year 2001 divides Spain into 806 LLMAs.[4]

4.2 The data

As in the Italian case, the identification of IDs is carried out using data on employment and jobs, taken from national censuses. However, Spanish censuses do not provide data about firms. To overcome this limitation, data from several sources are used. First, SABI[5] business database is used to build a database of employment in medium and large-sized manufacturing firms for the year 2001 (4958 medium and 719 large firms). This provides a good proxy for the number of employees (mainly for the large firms) in 4-digit industry detail. The main problem with SABI is that employment is recorded on a firm rather than establishment level.[6] For this reason, for each LLMA the number of large firms is compared with the number of establishments with more than 250 employees in the Spanish Central Directory of Enterprises (DIRCE).[7] If the number of DIRCE establishments in the LLMA is larger than SABI, this information is added considering firms with a minimum of 250 employees per establishment. Furthermore, we consulted annual industry reports from employers associations, trade unions and chambers of commerce to detail, whenever possible, the employment of the DIRCE establishments. Thus, after building the database for medium and large firms, the numbers in small firms was obtained as the difference between the employment by LLMA recorded in the census and the employment recorded in the database of medium and large firms.

4.3 Key variables

The objective of the procedure is to identify those LLMAs of SMEs specialised in manufacturing, and with a dominant manufacturing specialisation mainly composed of SMEs. It consists of four steps and considers potential IDs those LLMAs which include the four steps:[8]

1. Identification of LLMAs specialised in manufacturing. Departing from their ISIC/NACE codes, production activities are grouped in: agricultural activities; extractive industry; construction; manufacturing; business services; consumer services; social services; and traditional services.[9] For these groups we calculate a location quotient and a prevalence index for each LLMA. An LLMA is said to be specialised in manufacturing when it presents a location quotient greater than one (that is, above the national mean) for manufacturing activities, business services or consumer services, and the prevalence index for manufacturing is larger than those for business services or consumer services.
2. Identification of manufacturing LLMAs characterised by SMEs. Departing from the LLMAs specialised in manufacturing, a location quotient by firm size is computed using the three-size bands used by the UE (small firms up to 49 employees, medium firms between 50 and 249 employees, and large firms above 250 employees). An LLMA is characterised by SMEs when the maximum value of the location quotient corresponds to the small or medium enterprises.
3. Identification of the dominant industry. All the manufacturing activities are divided into 11 groups: textile and clothing products; leather and footwear; household goods (wooden furniture, tiles and other glass and ceramic items); jewellery, musical instruments and toys; food and beverages; machinery, electrical and optical equipment; manufacture of basic metals and fabricated metal products; chemicals and plastics; transport equipment; paper, publishing and printing; and 'other manufacturing' as a residual sector. Location and prevalence quotients are computed to each manufacturing group in each LLMA. The dominant industry corresponds to that industry with a location quotient above one and the largest value of the prevalence index.
4. Firm size of the dominant industry. The dominant industry is mainly comprised of SMEs when the employment in SMEs in the dominant industry is greater than 50 per cent of the employment of the industry in the LLMA. It

is considered as an exception to the criteria of the case of only one medium firm in the local dominant industry when this firm shares more employment than the rest of small firms.

The Spanish application faithfully follows the Italian procedure in all the steps. However, an additional filter was later introduced to remove those micro-LLMAs with characteristics of IDs but whose dimension was considered too small to be classified as an ID and does not add any important information to the analysis. This filter requires the dominant industry in an LLMA to have at least 250 employees, the same size as a large firm.[10]

5. THE MAP OF IDs IN SPAIN

5.1 Main findings

In the year 2001, Spain has 44 millions inhabitants distributed in 17 regions with a population density of 85 inhabitants/km^2. The manufacturing sector accounts for 18 per cent of total employment (2 750 000 employees over a total of 15.3 million). The identification's methodology shows the existence of 205 LLMAs with the characteristics of MIDs (25 per cent of the LLMAs) (Table 26.1).

Table 26.1   Main features of IDs in Spain, 2001

Mean features	Number of IDs	As percentage of manufacturing LLMAs	As percentage of all LLMAs
Districts (No.)	205	61.7	25.4
Establishments*			
Total	615 283	65.3	20.5
Manufacturing	82 782	72.9	31.5
Employment			
Total	3 105 401	64.0	20.3
Manufacturing	956 782	67.5	34.8
Population	8 252 988	63.5	20.2
Municipalities (No.)	2 099	57.0	25.4

Note: * Elaborated from DIRCE.

Source: Elaborated from 2001 Population Census (INE) and DIRCE (INE).

They account for 20 per cent of the country's population, employment and productive establishments (8 253 000 inhabitants, 3 105 000 employees and 615 000 establishments). Around 957 000 employees in the manufacturing sector are in IDs (accounting for 35 per cent of the total manufacturing employment in Spain); in particular 70 per cent are in small firms, 20 per cent in medium firms, and 10 per cent in large firms. Manufacturing employment adds up to 31 per cent of the total employment in IDs, whereas in the rest of manufacturing LLMAs it adds up to 29 per cent of employment and 18 per cent in non-manufacturing LLMAs.

IDs have the largest share of Spain's total employment in the sectors of leather and footwear (85.2 per cent), textile and clothing products (50.4 per cent), household goods (43.9 per cent), and jewellery, musical instruments and toys (42.3 per cent) (Table 26.2).

The dominant industry accounts for 402 500 employees in IDs (Table 26.3). Around 72 per cent of these employees are in small firms (292 000 employees), 21 per cent in medium firms (85 000 employees) and 7 per cent in large firms (26 000 employees). The dominant industry accounts for 42 per cent of the manufacturing employment in the IDs, 14.6 per cent of the total manufacturing employment in Spain, and 2.6 per cent of total employment in Spain.

The IDs appear in a defined pattern of territorial distribution. Most of the districts are concentrated on four axes (see Figure 26.1 below). The main axis follows the east coast of Spain from the north of Catalonia to the south of Murcia. The second axis starts in the south of Catalonia and goes as far as the Basque Country and the northeast of Castile and León. The third goes from the centre to the south of Spain. It starts just south of Madrid and extends to the Provinces of Toledo, Ciudad Real, Jaen and Córdoba. The fourth axis is scattered across the northwestern Provinces of Pontevedra and La Coruña. There are some districts outside of these four axes, but their number is very small.

5.2 Dominant industries

Dominant industries with the largest number of IDs are: household goods (62); textile and clothing products (46); food and beverages (37); and leather and footwear (23) (Table 26.2). These are followed by: machinery, electrical and optical equipment (14); chemistry and plastic products (9); and transport equipment (9). With a lower number of districts are: jewellery, musical instruments and toys (2); paper, publishing and printing (2); and manufacture of basic metals and fabricated metal products (1).

More than 80 per cent of the employment in the dominant industry is concentrated in only four industries (Table 26.3): household goods with 119 000 employees and 28 per cent of the national employment in the industry; textile and clothing products (85 000 employees and 31.4 per cent of the national employment in the industry); leather and footwear (73 000 employees and 74

Table 26.2 Employment of IDs in Spain by their dominant industry, 2001

Dominant industry	IDs Number	IDs Per cent	Dominant industry Number	Dominant industry Per cent	Manufacturing industries Number	Manufacturing industries Per cent
Household goods[a]	62	30.2	119 073	29.6	186 487	19.5
Textile and clothing	46	22.4	85 064	21.1	136 324	14.2
Leather, leather goods and footwear	23	11.2	72 786	18.1	83 808	8.8
Food and beverages	37	18.0	51 028	12.7	120 350	12.6
Mechanical engineering	14	6.8	34 665	8.6	213 775	22.3
Petrochemical, rubber and plastic products	9	4.4	22 510	5.6	81 065	8.5
Transport equipment	9	4.4	11 954	3.0	63 088	6.6
Jewellery, musical instruments and toys	2	1.0	3 632	0.9	7 603	0.8
Paper, printing and publishing	2	1.0	1 149	0.3	54 206	5.7
Metal goods	1	0.5	687	0.2	7 332	0.8
Total	205	100.0	402 548	100.0	956 7821[b]	100.0[b]

Notes:
[a] Household goods include wooden furniture, tiles and other glass and ceramic items.
[b] The total includes 2744 employees (0.3 per cent) in 'other manufacturing industries'.

Source: Elaborated from 2001 Population Census (INE).

Industrial districts in Spain 353

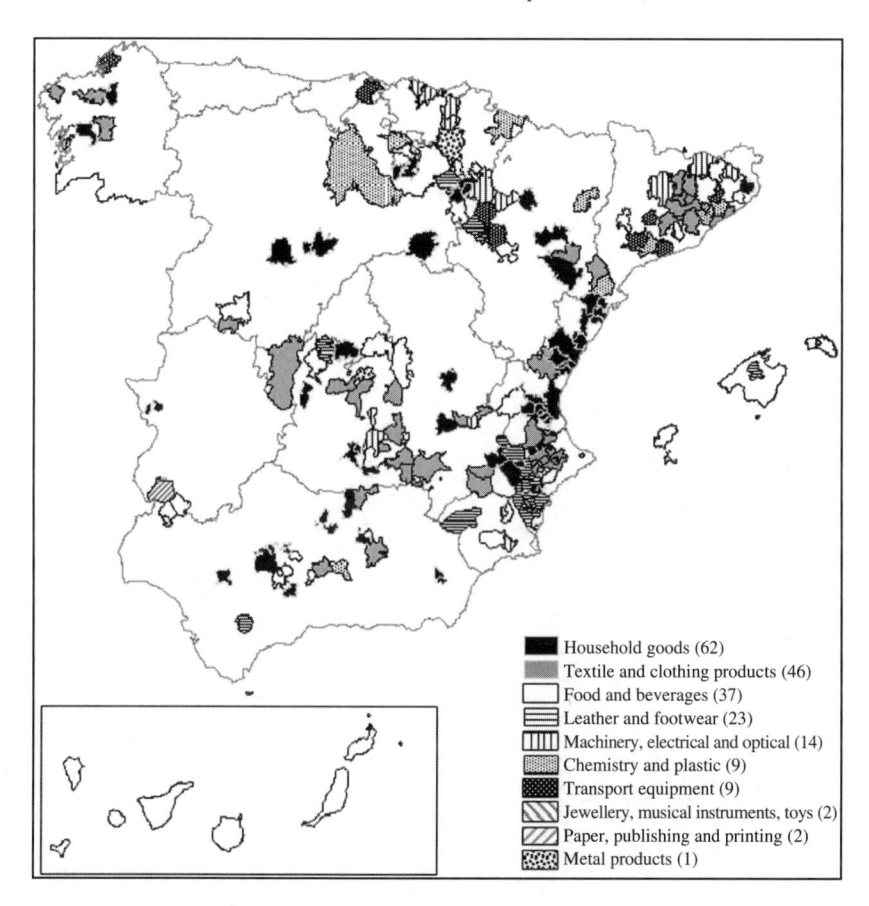

Source: Elaborated from 2001 Population Census (INE), SABI (Bureau van Dijk) and DIRCE (INE).

Figure 26.1   The map of IDs in Spain using the ISTAT (2006a) methodology, 2001

per cent of the national employment in the industry); and food and beverages (51 000 employees and 13.5 per cent of the of the national employment in the industry).

5.3   Regional specialisations

Focusing on the distribution of IDs by region, the highest number is found in Valencia (53 IDs and 25.9 per cent of the Spanish IDs); Catalonia (32 IDs and 15.6 per cent of the Spanish IDs); and Castile-La Mancha (32 IDs and 15.6 per cent of the Spanish IDs). IDs are also present in Andalusia (24); Aragon (11); Castile and León (9); La Rioja (9); Galicia (8); Murcia (7); Navarre (7);

Table 26.3 Quantitative importance of the employment of IDs in Spain by their dominant industry, 2001

Dominant industry	IDs (a)	LLMAs of Spain (b)	Percentage share of Spain (a/b)
Household goods[a]	119 073	424 960	28.0
Textile and clothing	85 064	270 519	31.4
Leather, leather goods and footwear	72 786	98 390	74.0
Food and beverages	51 028	378 990	13.5
Mechanical engineering	34 665	706 158	4.9
Petrochemical, rubber and plastic products	22 510	274 963	8.2
Transport equipment	11 954	280 835	4.3
Jewellery, musical instruments and toys	3 632	17 985	20.2
Paper, printing and publishing	1 149	231 494	0.5
Metal goods	687	56 963	1.2
Total	402 548	2 750 080[b]	14.6

Notes:
[a] Household goods include wooden furniture, tiles and other glass and ceramic items.
[b] The total includes 8823 employees in 'other manufacturing industries'.

Source: Elaborated from 2001 Population Census (INE).

Extremadura (4); the Basque Country (4); Balearic Islands (2); Cantabria (2); and Madrid (1). In Asturias, the Canary Islands, Ceuta and Melilla no ID was identified (Table 26.4 and Figure 26.1).

Considering employment in IDs, it is worth noting that 66 per cent of jobs in districts are concentrated in Valencia and Catalonia. In Valencia, IDs account for 1 169 000 employees (37.6 per cent of the Spanish employment in districts), whereas in Catalonia they account for 879 500 employees (28.3 per cent of the Spanish employment in districts (Table 26.5).

Another characteristic feature is that the specialisations tend to be very concentrated in few regions. In leather and footwear, Valencia concentrates 57 per cent of the Spanish IDs and 79 per cent of the employment in the dominant industry regarding the districts specialised on this sector. In household goods, 35 per cent of districts are located in Valencia although they have 68 per cent of the employment in the dominant industry. In machinery, the Basque Country concentrates 29 per cent of districts against 21 per cent being in Valencia and 21 per cent in Catalonia. However, the Basque Country accounts for 72 per cent of the employment in the dominant industry.

Other specialisations are shared across several regions. Districts specialised in textile and clothing products are mainly concentrated in Valencia (28 per cent), Castile-La Mancha (28 per cent), and Catalonia (26 per cent), although Catalonia has 56 per cent of the employment in the dominant industry. Food and beverages districts are maybe the most distributed, since 19 per cent of districts are in Andalusia, 16 per cent in Catalonia, 11 per cent in La Rioja and 11 per cent in Murcia. However, the main share of employment in the dominant industry belongs to districts in Catalonia (29 per cent), Murcia (17 per cent) and La Rioja (13 per cent), whereas Andalusia only has 8 per cent of the employment in the dominant industry.

6. THE QUANTITATIVE IMPORTANCE OF IDs IN THE NATIONAL ECONOMY

The results presented in the previous sections prove that the IDs are a widespread reality in Spain. Their main features are:

1. they have 20 per cent of the national population and employment as well as 35 per cent of the national manufacturing industry;[11]
2. IDs are present in 13 of the 17 Spanish regions, although the most relevant concentrations are located in Valencia and Catalonia, along the Mediterranean coast;
3. Spanish IDs are specialised in light manufacturing, especially in household goods, textile and clothing, food and beverages, and leather and footwear.

Table 26.4 Number of IDs in Spain by their dominant industry and by region, 2001

Regions[a]	Household goods[b]	Textile and clothing	Leather, leather goods and footwear	Food and beverages	Mechanical engineering	Petrochemical, rubber and plastic products	Transport equipment	Jewellery, musical instruments and toys	Paper, printing and publishing	Metal goods	Total
Valencia	22	13	13	3	–	–	–	2	–	–	53
Catalonia	3	12	–	6	3	4	4	–	–	–	32
Castile-La Mancha	10	13	2	3	3	–	–	–	1	–	32
Andalusia	11	3	2	7	–	1	–	–	–	–	24
Aragon	3	1	2	1	1	1	2	–	–	–	11
Castile and León	4	1	–	2	–	2	–	–	–	–	9
La Rioja	4	–	1	4	–	–	–	–	–	–	9
Galicia	2	3	–	2	–	–	1	–	–	–	8
Murcia	1	–	1	4	1	–	–	–	–	–	7
Navarre	1	–	–	2	2	1	–	–	1	–	7
Extremadura	1	–	–	2	–	–	–	–	–	1	4
The Basque Country	–	–	–	–	4	–	–	–	–	–	4
Balearic Islands	–	–	2	–	–	–	–	–	–	–	2
Cantabria	–	–	–	–	–	–	2	–	–	–	2
Madrid	–	–	–	1	–	–	–	–	–	–	1
Spain	62	46	23	37	14	9	9	2	2	1	205

Notes:
[a] Asturias, Canary Islands, Ceuta and Melilla do not have IDs.
[b] Household goods include wooden furniture, tiles and other glass and ceramic items.

Source: Elaborated from 2001 Population Census (INE).

The specialisations tend to be territorially concentrated forming in many cases bunches of districts.

Furthermore, they show four additional characteristics especially important for the Spanish economy:

1. their higher relative specialisation in manufacturing;
2. their ability to generate total and manufacturing employment is larger than the national average whereas manufacturing employment has fallen in the rest of the country (Boix 2009);
3. they produce almost 50 per cent of the Spanish exports (Trullén 2006);
4. their innovative performance regarding output indicators (patents and utility models, industrial designs) is almost 50 per cent above the national economy so that they are decisive for the innovative capacity of the country (Boix and Galletto 2009a).

7. SOME FINAL REMARKS

IDs are a widespread reality in Spain. They have 20 per cent of the total employment and 35 per cent of the manufacturing employment, they are specialised in light manufacturing (household goods, textile and clothing products, food and beverages, and leather and footwear), and spatially concentrated.

The definition of the map of IDs for the whole country using a solid and proven methodology has paved the way to the diffusion of the district theory as well as to the start of new lines of research on IDs at the national level. Because quite a few academic researchers are currently using the map, its real impact inside the country will be, necessarily, assessed over the next years.

The map of MIDs constitutes a tool for the analysis and implementation of policies aimed to support innovation and improve productivity, which are the most immediate challenges of the Spanish economy. A first version of the map of IDs served as a tool to guide part of the Spanish industrial policy which, on the basis of EU recommendations (COM 2005–121; COM 2005–488), are synthesised in a set of measures and laws centred on the so-called 'Innovative Business Groupings' (MITYC Order ITC/2691/2006 and Order ITC February 2007).

The extension of the methodology to other countries could provide additional comparisons by improving our knowledge of this phenomena and make things easy for the design of common policy strategies.

Table 26.5 Employment in IDs in Spain by their dominant industry and by region, 2001

Regions[a]	Household goods[b]	Textile and clothing	Leather, leather goods and footwear	Food and beverages	Mechanical engineering	Petrochemical, rubber and plastic products	Transport equipment	Jewellery, musical instruments and toys	Paper, printing and publishing	Metal goods	Total
Valencia	81 150	20 588	57 378	4 826	–	–	–	3 632	–	–	167 574
Catalonia	2 823	47 867	–	14 997	4 062	16 379	3 271	–	–	–	89 399
Castile-La Mancha	7 894	10 990	5 340	3 136	1 357	–	–	–	295	–	29 012
Andalusia	–	–	–	–	25 012	–	–	–	–	–	25 012
Aragon	11 518	1 842	3 125	4 249	–	591	–	–	–	–	21 325
Castile and León	6 580	–	843	8 667	462	–	–	–	–	–	16 552
La Rioja	1 371	2 831	–	3 004	–	–	5 855	–	–	–	13 061
Galicia	2 221	–	2 795	6 875	–	–	–	–	–	–	11 891
Murcia	2 746	641	–	2 345	–	4 394	–	–	–	–	10 126
Navarre	1 332	305	1 383	419	477	718	1 499	–	–	–	6 133
Extremadura	608	–	–	867	3 295	428	–	–	854	–	6 052
The Basque Country	830	–	–	597	–	–	–	–	–	687	2 114
Balearic Islands	–	–	1 922	–	–	–	–	–	–	–	1 922
Cantabria	–	–	–	–	–	–	1 329	–	–	–	1 329
Madrid	–	–	–	1 046	–	–	–	–	–	–	1 046
Spain	119 073	85 064	72 786	51 028	34 665	22 510	11 954	3 632	1 149	687	402 548

Notes:
[a] Asturias, Canary Islands, Ceuta and Melilla do not have IDs;
[b] Household goods include wooden furniture, tiles and other glass and ceramic items.

Source: Elaborated from 2001 Population Census (INE).

NOTES

1. The preconditions leading to the formation of the IDs can be found in the description of the process of industrialisation of Valencia performed by Ernest Lluch (2001).
2. For more details about this policy, see Trullén in this volume.
3. Despite these limitations, in Spain there is a remarkable correlation between the intensity of social capital by province (Pérez et al. 2005) and the location of IDs.
4. The same procedure is used for Spain and Italy. The complete algorithm can be described in ISTAT (1997, 2006a) and Boix and Galletto (2006).
5. SABI is the database for Spain and Portugal provided by Bureau van Dijk.
6. This problem is mitigated when working with LLMAs rather than municipalities since in many cases the establishments are located in the same LLMA.
7. The DIRCE database is provided by the Spanish National Statistical Institute. It includes the number of establishments by municipality and by 2-digit NACE classification. However, it does not directly provide the exact number of employees but classes of employees. Furthermore, DIRCE does not provide classes above 250 employees so that it is impossible to know whether an establishment contains 250 or 2500 employees.
8. Sforzi offers a detailed description of the procedure in this same volume.
9. Business services include: consulting, software, R&D services and advertising. Consumer services include: hotels, restaurants, real estate, and recreational activities. Social services include: insurance, education, health, and other social activities. Traditional services include: commerce, transport and public administration. See Sforzi in this volume for more details.
10. The application of the filter removes 49 micro-LLMAs with characteristics of IDs.
11. The quantitative importance of IDs in the Spanish economy is quite similar to that of Italy, where they have 22 per cent of the national population, 25 per cent of the national employment and 39 per cent of the manufacturing industry. See Sforzi in this volume.

27. The empirical evidence of industrial districts in Great Britain

Lisa De Propris

1. INTRODUCTION

This chapter will study the presence and nature of industrial districts (IDs) in Great Britain. In so doing, it will provide a comparative analysis with that contained in Chapters 25 and 26, whilst being also linked with the discussion in Chapter 4. After a brief survey of the recent contributions on the mapping of localised industries in the UK in Section 3, Section 4 presents the mapping methodology and describes what data is available in the UK. Section 5 analyses the main findings, and a discussion of how recent policymaking has related to the debate on localised industries is sketched in Section 6. Some concluding remarks are made in Section 7.

2. IDs IN THE BRITISH DEBATE

In the UK, the debate on 'localised industries' and forms of production clustering, including IDs, has been just as intense as in other European countries and the US over the 1990s and the early 2000s. However, it has been underpinned by very different premises and has produced a quite different contribution, as will be explored below.

One could be forgiven for thinking that the current debate on districts is simply the last episode of a flourishing debate stemming from Marshall's contribution in the *Principles* and in *Industry and Trade*. However, what became most popular out of Marshall's thought, especially up until the 1970s, was related to the economic theories of the firm and markets; this should not be too surprising given that such theories provided a crucial underpinning for explaining and justifying the large-scale capitalism pursued since the intra-war period by the British economy through industrial concentration and the creation of giant firms and conglomerates up to the 1980s (J.S. Pollard 2004). Evidence of this is the narration of the emergence of British capitalism in Chandler (1990). In this context, the role of smaller-sized firms was seen as somewhat marginal and 'place' as an exogenous variable.

Nevertheless, the premises of the debate of 'localised industries' certainly draw from the historical theoretical legacy left by Marshall's work through a thin trickle of nonetheless important contributions. These developed further the concept of external economies, in relation, however, to forms of firm agglomeration rather than strictly to 'places of production' and districts. Surprisingly in fact, Townroe and Roberts (1980) dedicated an entire volume on local external economies in British manufacturing industries, ignoring Marshall's work completely. In line with this, Brown (1972) expanded this argument underlining the links between manufacturing and service industries and face-to-face relationships as drivers of agglomeration economies.

More in line with Marshall's thought, however, one can trace a parallel, but nonetheless lively, discussion of the importance of 'the place' for the functioning of socio-economic activities. Clapham (1930) discussed British industrial organisation from 1820 to 1850 presenting an overview of the industrial specialisations of various places, from cutlery in Sheffield to distilleries in London and 'Marshall's flax mills in Leeds' (p. 192). Sargant Florence (1953) directly referred to the work of Marshall on external economies when discussing patterns of industrial location and went as far as using coefficients of location to measure industries' agglomeration from 'dispersed' to 'highly localised'. More precisely he described 'motor-cars, jewellery, plate, stoves, pins' as 'complex concatenations of linked industries localised in an area' (p. 88), to stress the importance of inter-sectoral linkages underpinning such localised industries. Again, from Sargant Florence's contributions (1948, 1953) there emerged an appreciation of the socio-economic drivers of places' industrial agglomeration in terms of external economies – namely, a specialised labour pool and inter-firm linked processes.

Loasby (2006) recalled that although Marshall thought that the firm was 'the most powerful engine of production' (Marshall 1920, pp. 138–9), it also embodied incomplete knowledge, so that firms benefited from setting up an 'external organisation' of connections or 'special markets' (ibid.), that in reality mirrors market organisational solutions that reduce transaction costs. Loasby (2006) argued that for this Marshall could be considered as the founder of 'dynamic transaction cost theory' (p. 374). Indeed firms' segmented capabilities explain why 'firms are not islands but are linked together in patterns of cooperation' (G.B. Richardson 1972, p. 895). Such arguments link back to Marshall's description of IDs where the boundaries of firms are so adjacent as to create a continuum of complementary knowledge bridges by 'external linkages', thereby anticipating some key debates within the Coaseian theory of the firms.

If mainstream economic theories have neglected Marshall's thoughts on localised industries, his theorisation of the organisation of production in IDs has not only inspired the theories of the firm; as Martin (2006) suggested, it also inspired economic geography until external economies and increasing returns were reclaimed to explain industrial concentrations within the so-called 'new economic geography'. Although underplaying the tie with Marshall's work, they did stress the importance of contextualising the organisation of production activities by re-emphasising a symbiosis between place and economy.

Directly or indirectly, this trickle of contributions has broadened out and streamed in the 1990s creating what is sometimes perceived of as a chaotic debate (Martin and Sunley 2003) on clusters, innovative regions, and innovative *milieux*. However, what these concepts have in common is an acknowledgment that there are systemic benefits emerging from firms' clustering in the same place with the related socio-economic–institutional strength of relationships.

More recently, Britain's scholarly debate on localised industries and industrial clustering can be argued to have stemmed from two fertile grounds. On the one hand, an emerging interest in regionalism and 'learning regions' associated with the then new-born concept of knowledge economy led to an increased awareness and recognition that regions can be engines of collective processes of learning and innovation (Storper 1995) and that small-sized firms have, in this context, a unique role to play. This framework consolidated itself around the 'new regionalism' (see Lovering 1999; Webb and Collis 2000; MacLeod 2001), and concepts like 'learning regions' (Morgan 1997) and 'regional innovation systems' (Cooke 2002). Discussions around these themes drove a shift away from sectors and a focus on the national scale, and helped position regions as key units of analysis in understanding processes of growth and innovation, as well as in shaping policymaking.[1]

In this context, localised industries became focal points for an understanding of the weakness and opportunities for growth for regions, but analysis thereof focused on the economic advantages that firm agglomerations can engender and nurture. This meant that the emphasis was placed on the benefits of colocation and production disintegration, namely: the external division of labour; external and agglomeration economies; specialisation; networking; and the mix of cooperation and competition.

In parallel to this, the post-Fordism debate from flexible production systems to Porter's competitive advantage provided a conceptual framework to unpack the monolithic concepts of firms and sectors, by breaking down the production process, leading to an understanding of systems of small, specialised and networked firms that incorporate such fragmented processes with gains in organisation and production flexibility. Seminal contributions on this came from across the Atlantic (see, for instance, Piore and Sabel 1984; A.J. Scott 1988; Storper 1995). At the same time, the shortcomings and constraints of the large 'trusts' also led the literature on the theories of the firm to reconsider the belief that high market transaction costs were necessarily leading to the emergence of vertical integration (Williamson 1985) and to suggest that quasi-market transactions could explain lower transaction costs in hybrid forms of governance. Finally, Porter (1990a) introduced into the discourse the concept of the 'cluster' and linked it to the concept of competitiveness, as a desirable outcome.

These contributions suggested that there was not a single optimal organisation of production, but that the latter depended on the conditions of demand and on technological progress which could vary across time and space. In other words, diversity in the forms of production organisation became accepted so much that small-sized firms, and in particular systems of production of small firms, emerged as valuable forms of production organisation.

Both streams, however, considered only the economic benefits derived from firm agglomerations and for this reason the concept of 'cluster' introduced by Porter (ibid.) satisfied both academic and policy constituencies. IDs are positioned in this debate as a special case of such firm agglomeration, and have been seen very much as an 'Italian phenomenon' simply because the roots of the literature were perceived as coming from Italian scholars, despite the fact that the seed of such roots was indeed Marshall's work.

It could be argued that the real reason behind Britain's adoption of the cluster approach is deeper. Firstly, similarly to the US and unlike continental Europe, in the UK one can witness a schism between economy and society, whereby economic activities, both in manufacturing and in services, have been influenced by the dominance of large-sized firms, greater openness to foreign capital and a well-developed venture-capital market. Foreign ownership has especially shifted decision making away from localities as key decisions have been taken in headquarters often thousands of miles away. This has meant that firms and industries in a place could not coevolve with local societies; on the contrary, the social impact of economic decisions was disregarded by foreign ownership which had no loyalty or interest in a locality or community beyond the strictly economic profit. One example of this is the automotive production system in the West Midlands (see Bailey 2007). The 'Wimbledonisation'[2] of economic activities has impacted on the dynamics of regional development, on the ability of places to shape their growth and on the capability of policymaking to support it.

This leads to the second reason as to why policymakers have embraced the concept of cluster because it suggests that clusters as drivers of competitiveness can be everywhere, and that under certain conditions and with the right mix of ingredients they can be set up from scratch. Socially abstracting localised industries appealed to policymakers who needed both a target and a tool for regional growth.

Last but not least, another reason for the British debate having neglected the social component of Marshall's thought was due to disciplinary fragmentation. Mainstream economics, geography, sociology and organisational studies have historically dealt with different themes and developed separately, preventing the study of such a multifaceted, complex and above all multidisciplinary concept as that of the ID.

It might be worth sketching quickly the key milestones that have shaped the UK economy since the 1960s; three elements are worth recalling. Firstly, in the 1960s and 1970s, in line with an emphasis on large-scale capitalism, industrial concentration rose dramatically with the 100 largest firms – in terms of output – jumping from 22 per cent of the total in 1948 to 40 per cent in 1970 (Zeitlin 1995), leaving small-scale firms isolated as old industrial localities were broken up through merger and acquisition, as well as closures. Secondly, there was a dramatic change in the composition of the UK economy between the 1970s and 1980s which resulted in employment falling in the manufacturing sectors, mostly spread in the North of England and the Midlands, and a rise in the service sector employment mostly in the southern regions (Martin 1993), causing a widening in the North–South divide. Thirdly, the change in the composition of the economy was particularly painful for those regions specialised in mature manufacturing sectors and undergoing restructuring, since a London-centred and free-market approach to policy meant that there was not a regional industrial policy willing to put in place mechanisms for socio-economic buffering. On the contrary, at the height of the Thatcher era, the government not only disengaged from localities, but its neoliberal outlook advocated for a withdrawal of government intervention in the economy, as evidenced by its large-scale privatisation programme, and the demise of any form of industrial policy (Pitelis 2006).

This changed only in 1997 when the Labour government set up Regional Development Agencies (RDAs) and delegated to these the formulation and implementation of regional development policy. Across the 12 UK regions, these agencies have over the last decade designed and implemented a broad range of policy initiatives that have not only paved the way for bottom-up regional policymaking, but have in so doing enabled localities and cities to regain control over their strategies and to be at the centre of new regional policies.

3. LOCALISED INDUSTRIES IN THE UK

3.1 Industrial clusters

Over the 1990s and 2000s, research on localised industries in the UK has progressed in two directions. On the one hand, there has been a flourishing of case studies looking at the features, dynamics and policy of a variety of industrial localities across the British Isles; on the other hand, there have been few rigorous studies that have aimed at describing, analysing and thereby improving our understanding of the phenomenon in its entirety by identifying business clusters.

The case studies have analysed specific manufacturing industries in specific locations: indeed what all these studies have in common is a conceptual framework close to Porter's cluster model and within the broader debate on new regionalism and regional development. For this reason, they share an understanding of firm clustering that mirrors an industrial agglomeration, namely an 'industrial cluster'. These would include, for instance, the study on the biotechnology cluster in Cambridge (Cooke 2001b) or on the biotechnology cluster in Scotland (Liebovitz 2004); others include the semiconductor industry in Scotland (Henderson 1987), the yatch cluster on the South Coast (Blundel and Thatcher 2005), the London ICT cluster (Sennett 2001) and whisky clustering in Scotland (Whittam and Danson 2001).

Since the early 2000s, rigorous mapping exercises in the UK have provided precious information to increase our understanding of the distribution, evolution, multiplicity and typology of production systems. In 2001, the then Department of Trade and Industry (DTI) published a report on *Business Clusters in the UK* which not only identified, for each of the 12 UK regions, the main manufacturing and service clusters, but also attempted to introduce a qualitative analysis aimed at ranking and classifying such clusters under four headings: the stage of development (embryonic, established and mature); depth (deep, shallow and unknown); employment dynamics between 1991–98 (growing, declining and stable); and significance (regionally, nationally and internationally). The DTI relied on regional and local authority data taken from various databases,[3] and integrated it with more qualitative information on such clusters gathered from local institutions and organisations. The objective of the analysis was to measure employment density via a basic location quotient[4] relying on data on industries' regional employment. A location quotient greater than one identified an industrial clustering. The report also highlighted 'high points' as those industries for which regional employment accounted for at least 0.2 per cent of the total regional workforce and for which the location quotient showed that the regional industry was 25 per cent more concentrated than at the national level.

In reality, the quantitative analysis of the DTI only measured industrial-territorial concentration as mirrored by employment density, and the corollary qualitative information was used to provide a better understanding of such phenomena. The great importance of this publication was not in its basic and approximate quantitative methodology, rather on the fact that it paved the way for an appreciation of nationwide quantitative studies on firm clustering in the UK, and the fact that it drew the attention of local policymakers to regional clustering as a tool to deliver economic growth.

3.2 Industrial local systems

At the same time, Crouch and Farrell (2001) applied a methodology that combined location quotients and indexes of units of production concentration and ratios relying on 1996 employment and units of production employment data by travel-to-work-areas (TTWAs) – namely self-contained local labour markets – and by 2 and 3-digit sectors. Their finding is interesting for two reasons. Firstly, they identified four types of localised industries: IDs, concentrated clusters, weak clusters and simple clusters. Secondly, by applying a different methodology from Sforzi (1990) and ISTAT (2006a), they identified 24 IDs mainly in food and drink; textiles, clothing and leather; chemicals; mineral products; metal goods and engineering.[5]

Applying the Sforzi (1990) methodology, De Propris (2005) identified for the year 1997, TTWAs that presented the characteristics of eight types of local production systems (LPSs) across England, Scotland and Wales, including 47 IDs especially in the Midlands and the North of England, in sectors like textiles and clothing, wood, chemicals, rubber and plastic, ceramics, fabricated metal and machinery, which together accounted for 21 per cent of the total British manufacturing employment. This first mapping exercise showed also that there was already a large portion of the economy dominated by services, with only one third of the TTWAs found to be manufacturing-intensive. Also, not surprisingly given the high degree of industrial concentration in the UK, just under 50 per cent of the TTWAs were found to be dominated by large firms.

By and large, the picture that emerged suggested that there were significant localised industries across British regions, including: mature systems of related auxiliary sectors – like the auto *filière* spreading across the West Midlands – in which some localised industries emerged as having a district form; local systems of large firms; and some historical localised industries of which IDs were a relevant portion (for a discussion on different types of local systems of production, see Bellandi 2003a). At the same time, British regions seem to be well under way in turning their economies away from manufacturing – especially around major urban centres – and from small-scale entrepreneurial capitalism.

4. MAPPING IDs: THE ANALYTICAL APPROACH

4.1 The unit of analysis

The geographical unit of analysis used to identify IDs in the UK are TTWAs.[6] TTWAs are approximations to self-contained labour markets based on commuting to work patterns; in the UK, 243 TTWAs were defined in 2007 using 2001 census information.[7]

The ABI Workplace Analysis has adopted the 2001 TTWA classification for data from 2003, although data is not available for the 11 TTWAs in Northern Ireland which remain therefore excluded from the present analysis. In this analysis only the 232 TTWAs in Great Britain will be considered.

4.2 The data

The data used to identify IDs in Britain was obtained from the UK Office for National Statistics (ONS) and the latest year available is 2006. Data is geographically broken down into 232 TTWAs for England, Wales and Scotland. IDs have traditionally characterised manufacturing sectors, so we here consider 23 2-digit sectors.[8] Employment data was also aggregated by firm size, with small firms having 0–99 employees, medium-sized firms 100–249 and large firms with more than 250 employees.

4.3 The methodology

The details of the methodology applied in this work are described in Chapter 25, so the key criteria will be only briefly summarised here. The methodology relies on employment data at the firm level by TTWAs and by sectors. Employment data are broken down also by firm size. The methodology comprises four sets of criteria which aim to identify key economic variables for each TTWA.

The first criterion looks at the overall economic make-up of each TTWA, by means of a location quotient and a prevalence index. They provide a clear indication as to which is the dominant industry, services or manufacturing.

Location quotient $$LQ1 = \frac{E_{TTWA, SECTOR}}{E_{SECTOR}} \bigg/ \frac{E_{TTWA}}{E_{GB}} \quad (27.1)$$

Prevalence index $$PI1 = \left[\left(\frac{E_{TTWA, SECTOR}}{E_{GB, SECTOR}}\right) - \left(\frac{E_{TTWA}}{E_{GB}}\right)\right] * E_{GB, SECTOR} \quad (27.2)$$

For IDs to be identified this first criterion must be such that the $LQ1$ is greater than one for the manufacturing sector, and the $PI1$ for the manufacturing sector is greater than those for business services (banking; finance and insurance; real estate; renting and business activities – Sections J and K) and consumer services (wholesale and retail trade; hotel and restaurant – Sections G and H).

The second criterion looks at the composition of firms in the TTWA in terms of size; in particular whether the TTWA is dominated by small, medium or large-sized firms. A location quotient for size is used to capture this information. In particular, for IDs $LQ2$ must be greater than one for small and/or medium-sized firms (firms with less than 300 employees),[9] namely the proportion of manufacturing employment in firms with less than 300 employees must be above the national threshold. This does not exclude the possibility that some large firms can be present, albeit not dominant, but a crucial feature of IDs is that they mostly comprise small and medium-sized enterprises (SMEs). It can be argued that the organisation of production, inter-firm dynamics and the governance of IDs relies on a community of firms of similar size (De Propris 2001).

$$LQ2 = \frac{E_{TTWA, MANUF, SME}}{E_{TTWA, MANUF}} \bigg/ \frac{E_{GB, MANUF, SME}}{E_{GB, MANUF}} > 1 \qquad (27.3)$$

The third criterion aims at identifying the TTWA's dominant manufacturing sector, by means of two indicators: a location quotient and a prevalence index. A TTWA is found to be specialised in one particular sector if for that sector $LQ3$ is greater than one and the $PI3$ is the highest across all manufacturing sectors. Industrial concentration mirrors therefore the accumulation of sector employment across all firms' size and identifies which sector a TTWA is specialised in.

$$LQ3 = \frac{E_{TTWA, SECTOR}}{E_{GB, SECTOR}} \bigg/ \frac{E_{TTWA, MANUF}}{E_{GB, MANUF}} > 1 \qquad (27.4)$$

$$PI3 = \left[\left(\frac{E_{TTWA, SECTOR}}{E_{GB, SECTOR}} \right) - \left(\frac{E_{TTWA, MANUF}}{E_{GB, MANUF}} \right) \right] * E_{GB, SECTOR} \qquad (27.5)$$

Finally, the fourth criterion brings together information about firms' size and industrial specialisation so as to clarify whether the sector in which a certain area is specialised is characterised by small, medium or large firms. This means looking at whether the proportion of employment in the dominant sector in SMEs accounts for 50 per cent of the TTWA employment. This last criterion enables us to flag up those agglomerations of specialised activities that mirror a concentration of small and/or medium-sized firms, which in turns reflects the industrial specialisation of the TTWA. These features are again associated with IDs.

$$\frac{E_{TTWA, SECTOR, SME}}{E_{TTWA, SECTOR}} > 0.5 \qquad (27.6)$$

This methodology presents two key advantages: on the one hand, it provides a rigorous procedure to identify local systems that can potentially be IDs by imposing some conditions though the four criteria above. On the other hand, it can also be a powerful and flexible tool in identifying a wide typology of local systems, including those dominated by service sectors. In addition to IDs, De Propris (2005), for instance, also found manufacturing LPSs in service-intensive TTWAs, as well as LPSs of large firms.

5. MAPPING IDs: FINDINGS

5.1 The geographical distribution

In applying this methodology, interesting findings emerge on the make-up of the British economy. Firstly, 97 out 232 TTWAs are found to be 'manufacturing-intensive', equal to around 40 per cent of the total number of TTWAs.[10] Considering the distribution of the 97 TTWAs across the 11 British regions, about two-thirds of the West Midlands' (13 out 17) and East Midlands' (11 out 16) and North West' (11 out 19) TTWAs are seen as manufacturing-intensive. Not surprising these regions show shares of manufacturing employment above the national average (Table 27.1).

Table 27.1 Distribution of manufacturing employment across British regions, 2006

Regions	Percentage
East	9.1
East Midlands	*10.1*
London	6.7
North East	4.5
North West	*13.2*
Scotland	7.8
South East	11.3
South West	8.8
Wales	5.5
West Midlands	*12.2*
Yorkshire/The Humber	10.8

Source: Our calculation from ABI-ONS data.

Secondly, in applying the second criteria, we find that 66 out of 97 manufacturing TTWAs are dominated by MS. It is worth noting that almost two-thirds of manufacturing TTWAs are characterised by small SMEs.

Table 27.2 IDs and their weight in the economy

	No. IDs	Employment in IDs	Total employment in sector	Percentage
15 Manufacturing of food and beverages	7	14 089	395 987	4
17 Manufacture of textiles	6	12 227	68 352	18
18 Manufacture of wearing apparel; dressing and dyeing of fur	1	3 185	29 838	11
19 Tanning and dressing of leather; manufacture of luggage, handbags, saddlery, harness and footwear	1	1 878	12 499	15
20 Manufacture of wood and products of wood and cork, except furniture; manufacture of articles of straw and plaiting materials	1	1 332	73 390	2
21 Manufacture of pulp, paper and paper products	2	4 321	67 677	6
22 Publishing, printing and reproduction of recorded media	1	5 614	301 229	2
24 Manufacture of chemicals and chemical products	2	8 175	188 710	4
25 Manufacture of rubber and plastic products	3	7 440	189 467	4
26 Manufacture of other non-metallic mineral products	1	922	100 434	1
27 Manufacture of basic metals	1	1 136	71 649	2
28 Manufacture of fabricated metal products, except machinery and equipment	5	39 845	305 082	13
29 Manufacture of machinery and equipment not elsewhere classified	3	6 509	263 828	2
32 Manufacture of radio, television and communication equipment and apparatus	2	3 116	58 621	5
34 Manufacture of motor vehicles, trailers and semi-trailers	2	5 456	161 059	3
36 Manufacture of furniture; manufacturing not elsewhere classified	2	4 646	152 612	3

Source: Our calculation from ONS data.

Finally, the imposition of the third and fourth criteria narrows down the number of TTWAs that present the characteristics of an ID from 66 to 40 overall.

The geographical distribution of IDs hubs around the Midlands and northern areas of England and spirals mainly along three axes towards the South East, the South West and Scotland, as shown in Figure 27.1. In fact, the presence of IDs is evident

Note: Data elaborated by author, map reproduced by kind permission of Ordnance Survey.

Figure 27.1   Map of IDs in Great Britain

mainly in regions around Manchester, Liverpool, Sheffield and Birmingham, which are historically the heart of the British industrial revolution and, therefore, dense in 'localised industries' (see Popp and Wilson in this volume).

The 40 districts account for just above 4 per cent of the total manufacturing employment, but in some sectors that can account for up to 30 per cent of employment such as with the combined textiles and wearing apparel sector, 15 per cent for the tanning and leather sector and 13 per cent for the fabricated metal products sector (Table 27.2). The 40 districts are spread across a wide range of manufacturing sectors. Although districts cannot be directly equated to sectors because they comprise a set of related sectors, in this quantitative analysis we flag up the dominant production specialisation for each district.

5.2 IDs and technology intensity

From this study it emerges that British IDs tend to specialise in medium- to low-technology industries. Indeed, on the basis of the EU technology intensity classification, we find that 31 districts are in medium–low to low-technology sectors, with only nine districts being in high to medium–high technology manufacturing sectors, including communications, machinery and equipment, motor vehicles and chemicals (see Table 27.3 below). This should not be seen as a weakness for two reasons. First, most of the IDs identified in this study have historical roots and are therefore in traditional sectors that tend to have lower technology content, although high in some new forms of soft innovation like design, artistic content and branding. Secondly, high-tech sectors tend to be characterised by a mix of manufacturing and service sectors, with the latter being linked with research and innovation activities. This is likely to skew the economy towards the tertiary sector.

In fact, in the UK high-tech activities tend to concentrate in the TTWAs around London, to Cambridge to the north, to Oxford to the east and to Crawley to the south. Here there are around 30 TTWAs specialised in computers and office machinery (NACE 30), electronics and communications (NACE 32), medical devices and scientific instruments (NACE 33) and transport equipment (NACE 35). This 'doughnut' of high-tech local systems around London has emerged over the last 40 years in a context characterised by the presence of the University of Cambridge and by a concentration of innovation/R&D-related facilities, as well as having benefited from its proximity with venture capital, and committed policy support. High-tech and dynamic industrial clusters are related to sectors like biotechnologies, ICT and mechanical engineering (Pinch and Henry 1999; Cooke 2001a; Pinch et al. 2003). These local systems are not flagged up in our analysis as IDs, because they tend to be associated with TTWAs which are not manufacturing-intensive. Indeed in the current literature they are referred to as 'clusters', since they present themselves as agglomerations of specialised activities, with a pool of specialised labour, varying degrees of inter-firm cooperation coupled with fierce competition. All in all these contribute to the well-known dynamic processes of learning and innovation (for example, Malmberg and Maskell 2006).

These findings flag up an important observation on localised industries in Great Britain: high-tech and innovation-intensive manufacturing activities tend to take place in areas with a mixed industry make-up where services dominate. This raises the question as to whether high-tech sectors by their nature tend to thrive in a context where there is a mix of economic activities (for instance, it is worth noticing that innovation and R&D activities are classified as a service industry). In relation to this study, what we find was not actually surprising, since IDs have historically been described as production systems soaked in a manufacturing context; only a few studies have recently explored district forms in sectors on the border between manufacturing and services (Lazzeretti 2004, 2008). It would be misleading, therefore, in our view to be overconcerned with the finding that British IDs are mostly in low-tech industries, in the same way as the classification itself of sectors' technology intensity is debatable.

Related to the point above, a more general observation refers to TTWAs associated with large cities. In the case of the UK, cities have historically hosted manufacturing activities and the divide between rural-agricultural and urban-industrial has persisted to present days. Therefore, manufacturing activities can still be found to be embedded in an urban context that is increasingly service oriented. Cities like Birmingham are excluded by the first criterion, because only 12 per cent of its employment is in manufacturing with 25 per cent in retailing and hospitality, however, a closer look will still find, for instance, the historical jewellery quarter (De Propris and Lazzeretti 2009). Clearly the concept of 'place of production' that underpins a district has a small scale, about the size of a 'quarter' within a large city. Furthermore, part of the jewellery system of production includes knowledge and competences that are 'intangible' – that is, non-manufacturing – like design. But if perhaps the small size of the jewellery quarter could justify its absence, the location quotient and the prevalence index confirm that Birmingham still embraces a historical concentration of manufacturing activities in the automotive sector (author's calculations from ABI-ONS data). Another example of this is the yachting cluster in Southampton, Portsmouth and the Isle of Wight (Blundel and Thatcher 2005).

Finally, we find there are localised industries not dominated by SMEs. Indeed, there are local systems where really economic life was and still is intertwined with the social one, like the ceramic industry in Stoke-on-Trent; here, however, recent cost-saving strategies have led to vertical integration and relocation, changing the nature of the system (Sacchetti and Tomlinson 2006).

5.3 Deepening the analysis of IDs

In this section we deepen our focus on some of the British IDs identified, in order to increase our understanding of the phenomena.

Table 27.3 IDs in Great Britain

	Sector	OECD	EU	Region
Chelmsford and Braintree	Radio, TV and communication equipment	H	H	East
Huntingdon	Rubber and plastic products	ML	ML	East
Chesterfield	Basic metals	ML	ML	East Midlands
Matlock	Non-metallic mineral products	ML	ML	East Midlands
Mansfield	Rubber and plastic products	ML	ML	East Midlands
Northampton and Wellingborough	Tanning-dressing of leather; luggage, handbags, saddlery, harness-footwear	L	L	East Midlands
Leicester	Wearing apparel; dressing-dyeing of fur	L	L	East Midlands
Bishop Auckland and Barnard Castle	Machinery and equipment	MH	MH	North East
Warrington and Wigan	Chemicals and chemical products	MH	MH	North West
Burnley, Nelson and Colne	Furniture; manufacturing not elsewhere classified	ML	ML	North West
Blackburn	Textiles	L	L	North West
Rochdale and Oldham	Textiles	L	L	North West
Falkirk	Chemicals and chemical products	MH	MH	Scotland
Invergordon	Food and beverages	L	L	Scotland
Lanarkshire	Food and beverages	L	L	Scotland
Moray	Food and beverages	L	L	Scotland
Peterhead	Food and beverages	L	L	Scotland
Kirkcaldy and Glenrothes	Pulp, paper and paper products	L	L	Scotland
Dunfermline	Radio, TV and communication equipment	H	H	Scotland
Forfar and Montrose	Textiles	L	L	Scotland
Hawick	Textiles	L	L	Scotland

	Sector	OECD	EU	Sector
Andover	Machinery and equipment	MH	MH	South East
Maidstone and North Kent	Pulp, paper and paper products	L	L	South East
Bridgwater	Food and beverages	L	L	South West
Launceston	Food and beverages	L	L	South West
Shaftesbury and Blandford Forum	Food and beverages	L	L	South West
Trowbridge and Warminster	Furniture; manufacturing not elsewhere classified	ML	ML	Wales
Monmouth and Cinderford	Fabricated metal products	ML	ML	Wales
Wrexham and Whitchurch	Motor vehicles, trailers and semi-trailers	MH	MH	West Midlands
Dudley and Sandwell	Fabricated metal products	ML	ML	West Midlands
Walsall and Cannock	Fabricated metal products	ML	ML	West Midlands
Wolverhampton	Fabricated metal products	ML	ML	West Midlands
Telford and Bridgnorth	Motor vehicles, trailers and semi-trailers	MH	MH	West Midlands
Hereford and Leominster	Rubber and plastic products	ML	ML	West Midlands
Kidderminster	Textiles	L	L	West Midlands
Oswestry	Wood, products of wood and cork, except furniture; manuf. articles of straw and plaiting materials	L	L	West Midlands
Sheffield and Rotherham	Fabricated metal products	ML	ML	Yorkshire-Humber
Calderdale	Machinery and equipment	MH	MH	Yorkshire-Humber
Bradford	Publishing, printing and reproduction of recorded media	L	L	Yorkshire-Humber
Huddersfield	Textiles	L	L	Yorkshire-Humber

Note: L = low; ML = medium–low; MH = medium–high; H = high (Eurostat 2008).

Source: Our calculation from ONS data.

In Scotland, the Moray ID in 'food and beverages' coincides with the well-known 'whisky valley' in Speyside that contains half of all whisky distilleries in Scotland; all distilleries and manufacturers of malt are small scale and have been embedded in the region for up to 200 years. Since the main ingredient for making whisky is the water of the rivers or springs that distilleries own, such production tends to be immobile and embedded, creating a district-like local system of production. However, the forces of globalisation have not spared it, and in fact most of the distilleries are now owned by foreign food and drink conglomerates; whether this has changed the nature of the district is open for further analysis (Whittam and Danson 2001). More broadly, the food districts in Scotland are in specialisations typical and historical to such localities, like fisheries (Peterhead), shortbread and whisky. Another district worth of mention is the cashmere district in Hawick; this is an historical place for woollen trade and more recently for high-quality wool and cashmere production. Currently, 70 per cent of employment is in the industry, evidence of a strong overlap between the agglomeration of firms and the local community.

In the South East, the district specialised in paper and paper products is part of the large publishing industry area that extends south from London (Todeva 2006). The food and drink districts in the South West are in dairy and cheese making; this is not a surprise given that the region is mostly agricultural and 30 per cent of UK dairy products come from this region.

In the West Midlands, the districts identified are, in fact, only the tip of the iceberg of a well-embedded localised set of related industries, including basic metals, metal processing and automotive sectors in Dudley and Sandwell, Walsall and Cannock, Wolverhampton, and Telford and Bridgnorth. Overall the *filière* accounted for some 53 000 jobs in 2007 (30 per cent of UK employment) (Bailey, Kobayashi and MacNeill 2008). Another historical localised industry that has emerged from the mapping exercise includes the carpet district in Kidderminster: this draws on a long established specialisation that has more recently shrunk its size whilst concentrating on high value-added and customised goods. For this, it is currently considered as an innovation and creativity-intensive interior and life-style sector.

Directly and indirectly linked to the automotive *filière* in the Midlands and Wales are the fabricated metal product district in Monmouth and Cindeford, and the motor vehicles district in Wrexham and Whitchurch. In the North West, the Rochdale and Blackburn textile district appears to be specialised in made-up-textiles and finishing textiles which include highly sophisticated and high-tech textiles for aerospace (Rose, Rubery and Penn 1994). Other surviving Marshallian districts are the cutlery district in Sheffield and clothing in Leicester (Simpson 2007).

This short 'close-up' on some of the IDs mapped leads to two considerations. On the one hand, some of these are the heritage of historical and well-embedded industries whose current small scale is the result of recent restructuring and downscaling, during which places have been reshaped and competences hollowed out. On the other hand, there are constellations of districts that reflect the multi-sectoral sprouting of very mature processes of 'districtualisation', whereby a series of districts are colocated and linked through the value chain. These latter are probably the most interesting to explore since at their latest stage they would also include service industries, bridging the manufacturing and service divide.

6. POLICY RELEVANCE

Awareness of LPSs being able to be engines of regional development and growth has not only been discussed in the academic debate, but it has also filtered down to inform and direct policymaking.

Until the setting up of RDAs in 1998, regional policy in the UK coincided with fiscal transfers from high-income to low-income regions, so-called 'assisted regions', whilst at the national level 'industrial policy' was mainly aimed at supporting national champions (Williamson 1985; Bailey and Sugden 1998; Pitelis 2006) and very much London-centred. The launch of RDAs by the incoming Labour government in 1998 was the result of a concurrence of two factors: both the commitment of 'new Labour' to some form of policy subsidiarity and the reform of EU Structural Funds which delegated to regions the design and implementation of regional policy. RDAs were set up as government funded umbrella organisations bringing together key public and private regional stakeholders (Webb and Collis 2000).

There is no doubt that the policy debate was ripe in the UK for a drastic change of approach which for the first time decentralised to new and inexperienced regional institutions the role of identifying the needs, instruments and processes of policy. In particular, the 2001 'Cluster document' published by the DTI endorsed a cluster approach to regional-level policy, without, however, assuming a coordinating or advisory role. The DTI delivered to RDAs a cluster map, and left them to find the most appropriate ways of using it. This 'induced' bottom-up approach focused the attention of RDAs which used the concept of the cluster to prioritise and shape regional policy. Indeed, regions' policies became a process of selecting and targeting strategic clusters, these being associated with localised industries in manufacturing and service sectors. Table 27.4 is evidence of the real and strategic interest of RDAs in targeting specific clusters in manufacturing and service industries within their regional economies.

Two comments are worth making. Firstly, although the policy arena has adopted the term 'cluster', this underlies a range of forms of local systems including IDs. Such terminological sloppiness cannot be overlooked, but it should not distract us from the fact that RDAs' cluster policies have coincided with the introduction of a dramatic new approach to regional development and growth in the UK, in

Table 27.4 RDAs' targeted clusters (2008)

Sector/cluster	EMDA East Midlands	LDA London	NWDA North West	ONE NE North East	SEEDA South East	SWERDA South West	Yorkshire Forward	Scottish Enterprise	Welsh Assembly	AWM West Midlands
Motorsports	✓									
Food	✓						✓			✓
Textile	✓									
Healthcare	✓		✓				✓			
Creative industries	✓	✓			✓	✓			✓	✓
Aerospace-defence	✓		✓		✓	✓			✓	✓
Production		✓								
Innovation		✓								
Life sciences		✓						✓		
Advanced engineering			✓	✓			✓			✓
Biomedical			✓	✓		✓	✓			✓
Professional services			✓			✓				✓
Energy and environmental					✓	✓	✓	✓		
Chemicals-pharmaceutical				✓		✓	✓		✓	
Multimedia/digital				✓	✓		✓			
Nanotechnology				✓	✓					
Tourism-culture					✓	✓		✓	✓	✓
Marine						✓				
Construction/built env									✓	✓
ICT								✓	✓	✓
Electronics								✓		
Financial services								✓	✓	
Automotive									✓	✓
Social care										
Rail										✓
High value-added goods										✓

378

particular by recognising the importance of regions' economic endowment (that is, existing clusters) and its weight in regions' employment and growth, and by understanding the link between the trends of industries and the consequent impact on the communities therein located. In other words, the details of regions' functioning and dynamics that were lost with nationwide policymaking, became of paramount importance within regions' focused and dedicated commitment to localities. (See Bailey 2003 for a discussion of the commitment of the West Midland RDA to the local auto cluster given the possibility of a Rover factory closure with an estimated 24 000 jobs at risk in the region.)

The other consideration is that the 'clusters' targeted range from traditional manufacturing sectors (such as textiles) to high-tech manufacturing sectors (such as aerospace) to service sectors (such as finance). These clustered industries reflect both existing industrial endowments and specialisations which regions aspire to develop either drawing on existing skills or diversifying the regional economy in high value-added, knowledge-intensive sectors. Given that the governance of regional-level policy is such that policy design and implementation is coordinated at the regional level, local industrial specialisation and embeddedness is edged with regional level sector diversification. This variegated approach and concern for supporting clustered industries is nevertheless framed within an appreciation that such phenomena can be drivers of sustainable regional competitiveness, coinciding with growth and employment.

Overall the awareness and understanding of the role of industrial clusters, IDs included, in the local economies of British regions, has realigned concerns that jointly affect the economic performance of places, namely the production regime and the socio-institutional community.

7. CONCLUSIONS

In Great Britain, the ID phenomenon appears to be necessarily more mature than in Italy or Spain and this is not surprising. In the British economy the tertiary sector is significantly larger, and historically British capitalism has favoured large size and foreign capital. This explains the small proportion of IDs, as against the overall presence of other forms of localised industries. Nevertheless, this study provides a valuable insight into the evolutionary trajectory of IDs as the broader economic context of economies change. Indeed, the district phenomenon in the UK captures only part of a range of increasingly diffused industrial clusters.

A dynamic, evolutionary approach to studying IDs in such local and global fast-changing times, provides an opportunity to extend and develop a model that has the unique and priceless quality of looking at places as socio-economic entities rather than commodities in a very competitive global market. Interesting contributions have already proposed evolutionary approaches to the study of

IDs and local development paths (see for instance, Belussi 1996; Lazerson and Lorenzoni 1999a; Bellandi and Sforzi 2003; Lazzeretti 2003; Sammarra and Belussi 2006), and it is in this context that a reevaluation of the methodology to map the forms that IDs can take in the knowledge economy could be of great interest. More research and experimentation on this is therefore needed.

NOTES

1. Note that the UK is divided into nine English regions, in addition to Scotland, Wales and Northern Ireland. These 12 regions have varying forms of local government and degrees of autonomy. For a discussion of British regionalism, see Bradbury and Mawson (2002).
2. This term has been coined in relation to the very famous Wimbledon tennis championship, where beautiful conditions are in place, however, it is foreign players who come and win. The term has been used metaphorically to describe situations where the openness of the British systems has led foreign players/actors to outnumber and outplay domestic ones.
3. The main data sources for the DTI cluster analysis are: the Inter-departmental Business Register, the Dun and Bradstreet database, the National Online Manpower Information System and Local Authority data.
4. The location quotient used in this report measured the relative concentration of industries across regions. It was defined as $LQ = (E_{ij}/E_j)/(E_{in}/E_n)$, where E is employment, i is industry, j is region, and n is the UK aggregate.
5. Given that a comparison and assessment of the different methodologies is outside the remit of this contribution, it will suffice to refer to their role in shaping the debate on mapping firm agglomeration in the UK.
6. See Sforzi in this volume for a discussion on the reason for using TTWAs to map IDs.
7. TTWAs are based on lower layer super output areas in England and Wales, data zones in Scotland, and super output areas in Northern Ireland. The basic criteria used in the exercise were: (a) at least 67 per cent of those who live in the area also work there; (b) at least 67 per cent of those who work in the area also live there; and (c) the working population as measured by the census should be at least 25 000. In areas of low population density these criteria were amended so that the minimum working population of the TTWA was 3500 and the self-containment criteria increased to at least 75 per cent (www.ons.gov.uk, accessed 20 December 2008).
8. Manufacture of food products and beverages; manufacture of tobacco products; manufacture of textiles; manufacture of apparel, dressing-dyeing fur, tanning-dressing of leather; manufacture of wood-products and cork; manufacture of pulp, paper and paper products; publishing, printing, repro recorded media; manufacture of coke, refined petroleum products; manufacture of chemicals and chemical products; manufacture of rubber and plastic goods; manufacture of other non-metallic products; manufacture of basic metals; manufacture of fabricated metal products; manufacture of machinery and equipment; manufacture of office machinery and computers; manufacture of electrical machinery/apparatus; manufacture of radio, TV-communications equipment; manufacture of medical, precision instruments; manufacture of motor vehicles, trailers; manufacture of other transport equipment; manufacture of furniture; recycling.
9. Firm size classes differ from those in Chapters 25 and 26 due to data constraints; nonetheless the differences are sufficiently small to enable an interesting comparative analysis.
10. Manufacturing employment has been contracting since the mid-1990s, from accounting for 16 per cent of Great Britain's employment in 1998 to 11 per cent in 2006. However, it must be said that such employment reduction has led to sustained productivity increases such that output has risen over the same period (www.berr.gov.uk, accessed 20 December 2008). It must be noted that value added per employee also measures the level of sophistication and innovation of manufacturing activities; this relates to the fact that across most manufacturing industries, value-added functions have been retained, whereas low value added and mass productions have been relocating to, or outsourced from, low-wage countries.

28. Measuring the district effect

Guido de Blasio, Massimo Omiccioli and Luigi Federico Signorini[*]

1. INTRODUCTION

As is shown in various chapters of this *Handbook*, the Italian economy provides an ideal setting to study industrial districts (IDs).[1]

Towards the middle of the 1970s a group of economists, initially small and isolated, noticed that in some Italian regions small enterprises and traditional branches of industry – considered until then to be the weaker sector of a 'dualistic' growth model – were surprisingly dynamic, a fact that did not fit with the ideas prevailing at the time with regard to stages of development. Their intuition was that the motor of this model of development consisted in the interaction between businesses and local community. They rediscovered the Marshallian notion of 'ID' and, on the basis of what they observed, began to theorise.

From the beginning, however, the relationship between the theory of IDs and the facts was unusual. Initially, the only facts that economists of the last 50 years have been in the habit of considering worthy of note – that is, quantitative statistical data that are reliable and abundant enough to permit technically robust econometric testing – were scarce. This is why the theory of IDs began, and for a long time remained, largely non-quantitative or, more exactly, non-econometric, a fact that contributed to the delay with which it was accepted by mainstream economists.

The first theoretical analyses of the IDs could be considered as an attempt to provide propositions of general validity based on the qualitative evidence of case studies. At the onset, the interplay between theory and quantitative empirics, the mainstay of modern economic discourse, was basically absent. On the one hand, the paucity of data for statistically and geographically meaningful local area made empirical investigation of ID theory exceedingly difficult. On the other hand, some of the factors that, according to ID theory, were at the core of the districts, such as trust among individuals or the quality of information flows, were (and are, despite the ingenuity of econometricians in finding proxies) inherently immeasurable. This explains why the economics of the IDs were mostly non-quantitative, which in turn helps to understand why mainstream economics sometimes found it difficult to relate with it.

The theory of IDs focuses primarily on social and institutional factors, while endogenous growth models and some recent core–periphery location models focus on the technological and economic factors. This difference in focus contributes to the difference in the methods of enquiry: while recent work on growth and location is invariably based on general and formal quantitative models, 'the ID school has based its analyses principally on case studies that are hard to generalise, ... many of the variables [considered] are latent and hence difficult to quantify' (Pellegrini 2000, p. 57). The measurement of some of them, and/or their effects, can therefore also be seen as a necessary step towards cross-fertilisation between theories. This undoubtedly explains part of the difficulty that the theory of IDs used to have in dialoguing with other strands of economic theory, especially growth theory and location theory, which have part of the subject matter in common.

As stated by Becattini and Musotti (2004), the lack of empirical underpinnings in this literature was a severe shortcoming for its development. Moreover, the difficulty in communicating with mainstream economics was a misfortune, as a few years later, mainstream economists started to devote a great deal of attention to agglomeration. On the theoretical side, the 'new economic geography' set the stage for the consideration of the location of the economic activity over the space. In the same vein, the various sources ('micro-foundations') of localisation economies, which, according to Marshall (1920), can be classified as labour market pooling, input sharing and knowledge spillovers, were carefully scrutinised (for a survey, see Duranton and Puga 2004).[2]

On the empirical side, there has been a growing empirical literature on the efficiency gains generated by agglomeration (see Rosenthal and Strange 2004, for a survey). For instance, Nakamura (1985) and Henderson (1986) find substantial evidence of productivity gains from localisation by estimating production functions for 2-digit manufacturing industries and using industry employment as a proxy for localisation. Henderson, Kuncoro and Turner (1995) confirm these findings by estimating employment growth for eight manufacturing industries. More recently, Rosenthal and Strange (2004) and Henderson (2003) find further empirical support for localisation economies, using, respectively, information on firm births and industrial plants. Empirical studies have also tried to shed some light on the relative merits of the various micro-foundations. In this respect, Diamond and Simon (1990) show that cluster wages capitalise labour market risk. Holmes (1999) supports the presence of input sharing. Jaffe, Trajtenberg and Henderson (1993) document that patent citations are highly spatially concentrated, so to suggest that knowledge spillovers do matter.

This chapter focuses on the studies on the existence of localisation economies in IDs and their sources. Most of it is based on research conducted at the Bank of Italy.[3] These studies aim at bringing the theoretical insights to quantitative data and, in doing so, facilitating the dialogue between district theory and mainstream economic research.

The chapter is structured as follows. We start in Section 2 by analysing some general methodological issues that arise when one wants to bring theoretical insights to data. Then, we turn in Section 3 to illustrate the empirical results reached so far, both for the ID productivity gains and their determinants. In Section 4 we focus on the ID credit market, of particular interest for the central bank. The final section presents the conclusions and suggestions for future research.

2. EMPIRICAL CHALLENGES

Suppose that locations for otherwise identical firms are chosen by throwing darts at a map. As a result, some firms will find themselves to be surrounded by others (that is, to be part of a district), while some other firms will find themselves to be isolated. Suppose also that apart from being or not being in a district, locations are indistinguishable. That is, the firm's discounted stream of future profits does not depend on location-specific characteristics. In these ideal circumstances, the district effect can be properly assessed by looking at some firms' outcomes and contrasting district firms to non-district ones. Unfortunately, the econometrician does not work under the above ideal circumstances. First, firms' locations are not chosen by throwing darts. Rather, firms self-select themselves into clusters of economic activity. Second, firms differently located are hardly ever identical. Third, location-specific attributes are relevant.

Nevertheless, the route taken by the empirical literature has tried to follow the ideal-circumstance case. The district effect is gauged by comparing district firms with non-district ones. This strategy is quite challenging, as it requires having a suitable map of districts, finding a sensible control group of non-districts units, and properly controlling for the confounding location-specific factors. Below we elaborate on some of the main empirical issues.

2.1 Mapping issues

IDs are defined by the ISTAT mapping algorithm (also known as the Sforzi algorithm), as the result of a two-step procedure, whose details are referred in Sforzi (in this volume).

In a first step, the Italian territory is divided into a number (686 in 2001) of local labour markets areas (LLMAs). LLMAs are 'functional regions', that is, aggregations of two or more neighbouring municipalities based on daily commuting flows from place of residence to place of work (see ISTAT 1997) as recorded in the Population Census. LLMAs are thus characterised by 'self-contained' labour markets, in the sense that both the share of resident LLMA employees in total LLMA employees and the share of resident LLMA employees in total LLMA residents must be at least 75 per cent. As emphasised in OECD (2002), labour mobility within LLMAs is by construction very high, while mobility from and to other LLMAs is low.

In a second step, the mapping algorithm identifies the IDs out of the LLMAs, according to the following four criteria: (a) the share of manufacturing employment in total (non-farm) employment must be higher than the corresponding share at the national level; (b) the share of small and medium-sized enterprises (SMEs) manufacturing employment in total enterprises manufacturing employment must be higher than the corresponding share at the national level; (c) the sector with a location quotient[4] greater than one and with the highest number of employees is identified as the 'dominant industry'; (d) for the dominant industry, the share of SMEs employment must exceed half; moreover, in case there is only one medium-sized enterprise, the share of small enterprises employment must exceed half of employment in the medium one. In 2001 the algorithm singled out 156 IDs.

Two features of the ISTAT algorithm are worth noting. Firstly, geography is defined on the basis of an economic concept – that is, the size of the LLMAs.[5] This contrasts with studies based on political boundaries – such as regions, provinces or municipalities – which have to assume that agents within a given administrative unit share the same economic environment only between themselves. It is worth noting, however, that in some special cases this may apply to the ISTAT algorithm as well: the ISTAT algorithm might fail to reveal relatively small infra-LLMA districts, since any district features would vanish when aggregated at the LLMA level (think, for instance, of a small ID specialised in apparel production located inside the service-specialised LLMA of Milan).[6] A related issue is that of spatial lags, which cannot be tackled when a spaceless economy is postulated. With the ISTAT algorithm, if one is willing to assume that the limited size of the local labour market captures the relevant geographic scope of localisation, spatial lags can be considered into the analysis. As shown by Rosenthal and Strange (2003), this seems to be a reasonable assumption, as agglomeration economies rapidly attenuate with distance.

Secondly, since the ISTAT algorithm defines 'local areas', it can in principle accommodate different views on the type of industrial activity to be included as part of the ID area. For instance, even though IDs are singled out on the basis of the prevalence of SMEs, there could be reason to distinguish the degree of polarisation among firms in the districts. Again, even if a degree of specialisation is required, nothing prevents taking in 'related' industries on the grounds of supply relations, the similarity of production and so on. This flexibility is a welcome trait of the algorithm, as the role of the industrial scope for localisation economies is one of the heavily debated issues in the literature, at least since Ellison and Glaeser (1997).

Although it provides an attractive classification of IDs, there is inevitably some arbitrariness in the ISTAT methodology. In particular, the algorithm is based on discretionary cut offs, so one might worry that minor changes in these parameters could deliver different results. In this regard, Iuzzolino (2000) shows that by including firms belonging to industry categories close cousins to that of specialisation, the share of cluster economic activities rises considerably. Cannari and Signorini (2000) provide two alternative measures, which are still based on the Sforzi–ISTAT methodology. A first measure identifies 'super-districts', that is a subsample of the ISTAT district-type LLMAs where the district characteristics are most pronounced, via a cluster analysis based on the four above-mentioned criteria. A second measure is the 'district continuous variable', that associates to each LLMA a value representing the degree of district-like features exhibited by the area. This is calculated with a logit model estimating the probability for each LLMA to be classified as an ID according to the ISTAT criteria, and thus represents a natural extension of this methodology to the continuum.

Having more than one possible definition of IDs is a helpful achievement. By adopting different definition of districts, the robustness of the empirical findings on the district effect can be checked.[7]

2.2 Control groups

Districts are not randomly located across a country, just as firms are not randomly localised in districts. To an extent, firms (and households) self-select into districts. Therefore, it is very likely that those belonging to a district are different from any control group, for reasons having to do with the way they self-selected.

Self-selection could arise for various reasons, even accidental ones. For example, as suggested by Frey (1975) and Varaldo (1979), some IDs were born out of an attempt from large firms established in the area to outsource stage production towards smaller entities in response to the tighter labour market regulation of the 1970s. Again, some IDs could have arisen by taking advantage of the tradition of agricultural self-employment in the area, which set the stage for extensive entrepreneurship (Bagnasco 1977; Fuà and Zacchia 1983; Musotti 2001).

It is important therefore to keep in mind that any 'district effect' that the econometric analysis may bring to light will inherently capture this selection bias. This is as it should be. The district effect, if any exists, is not manna from the sky, but results from the characteristics of firms as well as the quality of their interactions. However, this fact makes the selection of a control group a delicate choice. One must be careful to avoid both undercontrolling and overcontrolling for (observable) firm characteristics. The specific choice may depend on the issue under examination.

Of course the extent of controls partly depends on the limitations of available data. Many empirical studies are based, for instance, on company accounts. These provide only scant information on certain economic aspects that are relevant to district-type interactions. For example, company accounts usually do not provide information on the extent of subcontracting or the exact type of goods produced (the only information on the latter being given by a SIC code, which often does distinguish between intermediary or final goods).[8]

2.3 Econometric specification

In light of the mapping issues and the selection problem, the choice of the covariates to be included in the econometric specification is of crucial importance.

Undercontrolling occurs when a relevant control variable is omitted. For instance, suppose one wants to regress firm productivity on firm characteristics and a district dummy. Suppose further that districts benefit by better-than-average infrastructure, which in turn impacts on productivity. Clearly, omitting a measure of infrastructure in the regression might give rise to a spurious positive correlation between the district dummy and the dependent variable.

Overcontrolling occurs when a variable that is caused by, or otherwise inherently linked to, the variable of interest (district-ness) is also controlled for in the specification. Take again the case of productivity as dependent variable regressed on firm characteristics and the district dummy. Should the econometrician also control for firm size? There is no definite answer. To the extent that size impacts productivity, omitting to control for size will mean the district dummy picking up the effect of dimension on productivity. This is the undercontrolling problem. However, to the extent that a reduced firm size is also a key district feature (see Section 2.1), controlling for the dimension of the firm in the regression can lead to a bias in the coefficient for the district dummy, since part of the district effect is picked up by the size variable.

The issue of the proper list of covariates to include is an open one. As there is no ultimate solution, good empirical research should feature a clear discussion of the role of the covariates included for the results obtained.

3. EMPIRICAL RESULTS

Basically, the papers on measuring the district effects can be split into two categories. The first group of papers tries to estimate the existence and magnitude of localisation economies. These studies have little to say about the economic mechanisms which give rise to the competitive advantages of IDs (micro-foundations). As shown by Rosenthal and Strange (2004, p. 2146), 'agglomeration economies whose sources are knowledge spillovers, labour market pooling or input sharing all manifest themselves in a pretty much the same way'. Because of this observational equivalence, the results from this work should be seen as black-box results. The question of which mechanism is exactly behind the district productivity premium is left unanswered. The second group of papers has tried to shed some light on micro-foundations. In this regard, knowledge spillovers and the functioning of the labour and credit markets have been especially under scrutiny.

3.1 Performance

The simplest, yet useful way of looking into the district effect is to estimate the significance of a dummy variable for district membership in an equation designed to explain the variable of interest. This instrument was first used in Signorini (1994b). This contribution compares firms from two woollen textile districts,

Prato (Tuscany) and Biella (Piedmont), with non-district firms of comparable size in the same industry, in order to check the existence of productivity and profit differentials in favour of firms belonging to IDs. The core of the exercise is the estimation, using firm-level data, of a production function in which the district dummy appeared both in the overall productivity term and in interaction with the individual productive factors. The exercise confirmed that in this particular sector (which made no small contribution to the development of the theory itself, in light of the salience of Prato in any early discussion of the genesis and development of Italian IDs) district firms enjoyed a level of efficiency that was measurably and significantly above average.

The way was thus open to more general empirical studies which could reach more general conclusions. Fabiani et al. (2000) extended the method of Signorini (1994b) to the generality of Italian IDs, identified on the basis of the Sforzi–ISTAT methodology. By using balance sheet data from the 'company accounts database', this chapter shows that – after controlling for firm size and industry – the productivity and profitability (measured by ROI and ROE) of district firms is significantly higher than their non-district counterparts.

Building on the above general framework, the empirical analysis of the district effect can of course implement all the available theoretical and econometric tools in order to obtain richer and more robust results: estimation of production frontiers (as in Fabiani et al. 2000; and in Becchetti and Castelli 2005); non-parametric approaches (as in Hernández and Soler 2003); measures of total factor productivity (as in Cingano and Schivardi 2005).

Since there is a positive link between productivity and the propensity to sell abroad,[9] a different approach to inquire about the district benefits is to look at exports. On this respect, Bronzini (2000) shows that the degree to which a given area possesses the typical features of an ID ('district intensity') has a positive impact on local exports per employee. On the other hand, Gola and Mori (2000) carry out a panel exercise on data distributed over 84 sectors observed over a 13-year period and show that the district intensity of a manufacturing sector has a positive effect on Italian revealed comparative advantages (net sector exports). Finally, using firm-level data, the existence of a competitive advantage for district firms is found by Costa Campi and Viladecans-Marsal (1999), for Spain, and by Bagella, Becchetti and Sacchi (2000), Becchetti and Rossi (2000) and Bugamelli and Infante (2005), for Italy. Moreover, the empirical results on productivity and export performances of district firms appear to be robust to sample selection: they are confirmed even in very large samples, as in Becchetti, De Panizza and Oropallo (2007), where the entire population of Italian limited liability firms in the textile and machinery industries (more than 100 000 firms) is used.

Since more productive firms are also featured by a higher innovative activity, patent propensity and R&D expenditures could be used as an additional testing ground. In this respect, by using survey data from an Italian region (Emilia-Romagna) with a high density of district firms, Leoncini and Lotti (2004) show that ID firms have a higher likelihood to engage in patenting, even though the likelihood of having a positive R&D investment is less than their non-district counterparts. Moreover, Cainelli and De Liso (2004) show that district firms that introduce product innovations are characterised by better performances than non-district firms.

3.2 Micro-foundations

3.2.1 The labour market

In Marshall's 'three-pillar' doctrine, labour pooling is one of the main sources of localisation economies. Economies arise from the presence of a pooled market for specialised workers with industry-specific skills. While Marshall's idea was that labour pooling benefits not just firms but also workers, a long sociological (and political) tradition considers SMEs as the archetypal exploitative workplace. The debate goes on.

One approach is to study the compensation of labour and look for any differences between ID wages and those paid by similar firms not located in a district. A paper in this tradition is Casavola, Pellegrini and Romagnano (2000). This study uses administrative data from the Italian Social Security Institute and do not find any clear evidence of a district wage premium. Another example is given by de Blasio and Di Addario (2005b), who estimate Mincerian wage equations by using data taken from the Bank of Italy's 'Survey of household income and wealth'. Again, this paper finds no evidence of higher ID wages. These results should not surprise given the highly centralised Italian wage bargaining process. At least, they reject the idea that the competitive advantage of IDs rests on lower wages paid to district workers.

District theory goes beyond this, however. If ID firms are more productive, all factors for which entry is not entirely costless should share in the economic benefits of higher productivity (Roback 1982). This would seem to apply to specialised labour, one of the constituent elements of the district climate. Therefore the lack of evidence for a (positive) differential is potentially a problem.

The evidence on wages may be difficult to interpret. A tricky issue is given by non-monetary elements in factor compensation. The degree in which they are captured by wages depend on the presence of local attributes, like consumer amenities. For instance, if workers prefer IDs because of their superior quality of life, then *ceteris paribus* this will raise rents and reduce wages in IDs. If this effect is large enough, wages can fail to show up workers' benefits (Dalmazzo and de Blasio 2007).

Beyond wage differentials, there could be additional implications of labour market pooling. Some of them have been tested.

The structure of wages might provide useful hints. Agglomeration should favour labour specialisation, lowering the degree of mismatch between the skills demanded by the employers and those offered by the workers. If the improvement in match quality concerned primarily the more educated workers, as in Wheeler

(2001), agglomeration would produce higher returns to education. On related grounds, it is often argued (Solinas 1982) that districts are characterised by a wider role for firm-based training to junior workers and by higher returns for skilled senior workers. This would imply higher returns for seniority, as workers might be willing to accept reduced entry wages in exchange for on-the-job training, with the expectation of moving up the wage scale when they become senior workers.

Empirical investigations on the structure of wages have not lent support for these interpretations. De Blasio and Di Addario (2005a) estimate complete Mincerian wage equations, investigating whether returns to seniority and formal education (years of schooling) are a possible source of differentiation. They find that working in an industrial cluster 'reduces' the returns to education and does not affect the returns to seniority. On related grounds, in a study on the Provinces of Treviso and Vicenza, Cingano (2003) does not find evidence of a difference in the returns to seniority between IDs and non-IDs.

Lower returns from education in IDs can hardly be surprising. Several qualitative studies (see, for instance, Belussi, Gottardi and Rullani 2000; Becattini et al. 2003) highlight the fact that in IDs the relevant human capital is not acquired through formal education, but rather through experience and the 'informal transmission' of tacit knowledge and know-how. Additional insights come from Dalmazzo and de Blasio (2005). This paper estimates social returns from education for the Italian LLMAs and finds evidence of education spillovers, which however vanishes in the IDs.

Even though district workers do not seem to receive monetary extra rewards, additional benefits might materialise. First, the greater concentration of firms in a pooled labour market might increase workers' probability of having a job. Second, the likelihood of leaving the wage-and-salary group to start a business might be higher. As highlighted by Dei Ottati (1994a), ID entrepreneurs encourage their most active employees to start an activity of their own as subcontractors, so as to grant themselves an advantageous relationship with the subcontracting firm and increase flexibility. These predictions find some support in de Blasio and Di Addario (2005a).

Finally, worker mobility across jobs has also been investigated. This is a tricky point, as the theoretical link between agglomeration and mobility has not been clearly established. An implication of the labour market pooling hypothesis is that workers can readily change jobs and firms readily change employees. However, to the extent that workers are better matched in IDs, there could be a countervailing effect as better matches are less prone to termination (see Combes and Duranton 2006). Volpe (2001) examines labour flows in the Provinces of Treviso and Vicenza and does not find statistical differences in the frequency of hiring rates, job separations and worker turnover between the IDs and the non-ID subsamples.

3.2.2 Information spillovers and social capital
A fascinating line of research focuses on the role of knowledge spillovers. As recognised by Audretsch and Feldman (2004), for knowledge-based activities

the spatial dimension is of particular importance. As Glaeser et al. (1992, p. 1126) put it, 'intellectual breakthroughs must cross hallways and streets more easily than oceans and continents'. While the role of knowledge spillovers has been mentioned at least since Marshall (1920), it is only recently that it has been empirically investigated. The point is that information spillovers by their own nature leave no paper trails (see Jaffe, Trajtenberg and Henderson 1993) and therefore the econometrician faces many challenges in measuring them.

Guiso and Schivardi (2007) provide some indirect evidence on the relevance of information spillovers in IDs. By looking at firms' employment adjustment, they show that firms' decisions are affected by the behaviour of other firms producing similar goods and located in the same ID, while the action of the firms producing different goods or located outside the district have no impact.

Bugamelli and Infante (2005) show that sunk costs to export, which are mostly related to the need of gathering information on the functioning of foreign markets and their potential demand, are significantly lower for district firms. This suggests that this relevant piece of information flows more easily across district firms than across their non-districts counterparts.

Di Giacinto and Nuzzo (2005) perform an econometric test of the link between various aspects of social capital and economic development, in particular district development. With all the caveats required by the idiosyncratic element inherent in the connection between a local 'culture' and the operation of the economy, they conclude that there is clear evidence for the hypothesis that extended family institutions and social norms that discourage opportunism favour district-style development. Their results provide less support for the hypothesis of a significant role for business organisations and local government.

4. THE CREDIT MARKET

The literature on finance and growth (see Levine 1997) highlights that a sound and efficient credit market fosters development by channelling more resources to investments and providing a better selection of alternative investment projects. As IDs are populated by SMEs, which are typically considered those most likely to face financial constraints (since they have more opaque balance sheets and less collateral), the literature on the ID credit market has tried to check whether district firms are less subject to the financial constraints that applies to SMEs in general.

Some *prima facie* evidence seems not to lend support to the idea that financing relations in the IDs can be somewhat special. Farabullini and Gobbi (2000) report a larger presence of smaller and local banks in IDs (at least until 1994), but they show that the density of bank branches and bank loans are basically the same for IDs and non-ID areas. The evidence on the cost of borrowing and credit constraints is even more puzzling. Finaldi Russo and Rossi (2001) argue that both the interest rate charged by banks and the probability of rationing are lower for ID firms. This result, however, is not confirmed by other studies. For instance, Baffigi, Pagnini and Quintiliani (2000) show that cash-flow sensitivity is higher for district firms, rather than lower as it would be in case of less stringent rationing.[10] Pagnini (2000) shows that the gap between credit used and credit granted, which can be used as a proxy for credit constraints, is more frequent within districts.

Drawing from the banking literature, two additional mechanisms have been postulated as potentially relevant for the functioning of the ID credit market: relationship lending and soft-information lending. Relationship lending, which implies more effective screening and monitoring of borrowers, might be facilitated in IDs because firms belong to industries that are strictly interrelated; firms and (local) banks, moreover, share the same set of cultural values and relationships. This lowers industry-specific information costs (Pagano 2000) that a bank should bear to evaluate the profitability of alternative projects (as well as *ex post* monitoring costs). A related mechanism is based on the role of soft information in lending. Information about small businesses is thought to be 'soft', whereby hard information is defined as quantitative, easy to store and transmit in an impersonal way (Petersen and Rajan 1994; Berger and Udell 1995). Lending practices based on soft information require the lender to have personal contact with the borrower, and this can be guaranteed by the lender's local presence (moreover, since the information is soft and difficult to communicate, the decision to offer the credit has to be made very close to where the information is gathered). Candidates for being particularly effective in collecting and processing soft information are the local banks. As suggested by Becattini (1990), a local bank is heavily involved in the local business community. This type of financial intermediary, born in the same ID and very often spurred by local entrepreneurs, knows a lot about the true creditworthiness of the borrowers.

By testing these predictions with survey-based data, Cocozza (2000) shows that the main bank being local has no significant effect on the cost of credit and on the probability of being rationed for ID firms; the same is true for the share of the main bank on total bank credit to the firm. Moreover, Finaldi Russo and Rossi (2001), by using balance-sheet data matched with information from banking supervisory reports, find that bank–firm relationships are not significantly different in IDs as opposed to non-ID areas (the only difference being a larger presence of local banks, as in Farabullini and Gobbi 2000). By using more recent data, after the liberalisation of the Italian banking system, Gobbi (2005) shows that the relevance of local banks is now lower in IDs than in non-ID areas and the number of banking relations is higher. Gobbi points out that high industry concentration could represent the most important obstacle to a wider presence of local banks in IDs, while Beretta, Omiccioli and Torrini (2000) had already shown that a large presence of local banks amplifies local economic shocks.

Another distinctive mark of the ID credit market could be the use of trade credit. District firms are connected through a network of buyer–seller relationships. Exchange of goods often comes hand in hand with a supply of finance-credit relationships. As suggested by Dei Ottati, for those who want to set up their own firm, or ... want to buy new machinery, but who do not have sufficient financial means to do so, ... the simplest way of achieving this ends is through interlinking transactions of subcontracting and credit with entrepreneurs who know and trust them. (Dei Ottati 1994a, pp. 535–6)

In particular, the fact that the lender is also a customer allows the subcontractor-borrower to repay the loan by discounting it from the payment for the work ordered by the lender. Again, when confronted with data, this possibility loses most of its appeal. Cocozza (2000) shows that trade credit is unlikely to work as a substitute of bank credit: it does not contribute to finance investment; even more importantly, most of the times it happens that the subcontractor, rather than the buyer, acts as a lender.

Overall, the empirical evidence on the role of the credit market is quite inconclusive. Surely, these findings can be interpreted as an indication that the action is on the real-economy side. As Brusco (1989a) suggests, the district organisation of the production activities is itself a way of economising the need of external finance. This amounts to saying that districts will need a well-functioning credit market less than other areas. It could also be the case (Dei Ottati 1994a), however, that the role of the credit market was limited at the initial phase of development of the IDs (perhaps, by financing risky start-ups). In this case, as the econometric investigations refer to the last two decades, when the districts were in their adulthood, this might explain why the empirical evidence is so scanty.

5. CONCLUSIONS AND SUGGESTIONS FOR FUTURE RESEARCH

To summarise: (a) at the micro-level, district firms generally enjoy a measurable competitive advantage; (b) in some key markets (intermediate goods, productive factors) the peculiarities of district firms are sometimes clearly evident in the data, although in some crucial areas (labour, capital) they appear to rest largely on informal and even idiosyncratic features. In other words, while the competitive advantages of IDs are now well documented and established by the econometric literature, much work remains to be done as far as the sources of these advantages (micro-foundations) are concerned. Information spillovers represent the field where econometric research, though more difficult to perform, has yielded the most promising results. This may hint at where the very source of the competitive advantages lies.

Since the mapping of districts is the key to econometric research, a crude dichotomy leaves a number of problems unresolved. A first question is whether or not all the firms located in an area classified as a district are to be considered district firms, that is firms that enjoy the localisation economies characteristic of the district. A second question is whether we might not be able to attenuate our simple dichotomy by introducing elements of gradualism and/or multidimensionality.

Dissimilarities inside IDs can be strong and suggest an analytical approach that takes appropriate account of them. On the other hand, the same consideration applies to the areas defined as non-districts. Many papers try to evaluate the measure of a 'district effect' (in firms' performances or in the operation of some markets) by estimating equations with a simple district dummy. But if we agree that different typologies of LLMAs can account for very different sources (and intensities) of proximity advantages, then a simple dichotomy could be misleading. To overcome such a difficulty we need to introduce elements of gradualism in the measure of district phenomena, thus opening up new areas for possible future research.

However, absent a significant improvement in available statistical data, the benefits of further refinements of the selection criteria and/or of the estimation techniques will be limited (Commissione per la garanzia dell'informazione statistica 2005). In particular, a larger dataset on the flows of goods and services broken down by LLMAs and industries would make less arbitrary the identification of the vertical chains of production (*filière*), which forms the starting point for the definition and measurement of district phenomena. Likewise, information on worker commuting patterns by sector of economic activity would strengthen the power of LLMAs as a tool to identify IDs.

NOTES

* We thank Antonio Accetturo, Giovanni Iuzzolino and Fabio Sforzi for comments and suggestions. The views expressed herein are those of the authors and do not necessarily reflect those of the Bank of Italy.
1. Their importance cannot be overstated: in 2001, their share in total industrial employment was over 42 per cent and their contribution to total manufacturing exports was more than 46 per cent of the total (ISTAT 2006a).
2. Marshall (1920) micro-foundations do not exhaust the possible sources. There could be other causes, such as, for instance, home market effects.
3. Many of these studies have been collected in the volumes edited by Signorini (2000) and Banca d'Italia (2005).
4. The location quotient is the ratio between the share of sector employment in total manufacturing employment and the corresponding share at the national level.
5. Therefore, labour-market sources of agglomeration economies are at the centre of the stage. This is not the only possibility. For instance, it could be argued that knowledge spillovers across firms may be better captured by distance-based measures (see Duranton and Overman 2005; Iuzzolino 2005).
6. A related advantage of the ISTAT algorithm is that the countrywide coverage of the LLMAs minimises the selection problem that characterises studies confined to a smaller section of the national territory (Combes 2000).
7. This is the route followed, for instance, by Farabullini and Gobbi (2000); Bronzini (2005); de Blasio and Di Addario (2005b); Di Giacinto and Nuzzo (2005).
8. Field surveys (Omiccioli 2000) might help to tackle these issues, as comparison firms are chosen by selecting from the population of non-ID firms those who are more similar to ID firms.
9. The link is theoretically motivated by Melitz (2003) and empirically confirmed by Clerides, Lach and Tybout (1998); Delgado, Fariñas and Ruano (2002); Girma, Greenaway and Kneller (2004).
10. This approach to measuring credit rationing, pioneered by Fazzari, Hubbard and Petersen (1988), has been challenged, among others, by Kaplan and Zingales (1997).

29. Measuring the internationalisation of industrial districts

Stefano Menghinello

1. INTRODUCTION

Industrial districts (IDs) in advanced countries have experienced substantial structural changes in the past few decades. They have developed from export-oriented but locally self-contained production systems to globally interdependent production systems rooted in a local context. This metamorphosis has stimulated a rich theoretical debate on the evolution patterns of IDs (Becattini and Rullani 1993; De Propris, Menghinello and Sugden 2008). While Tattara (in this volume) focuses on the production internationalisation of IDs from an economic point of view, this chapter is devoted to the methodological and statistical issues underlying applied economic analysis on this topic.

As is now well understood, the increasing complexity of ID-based international linkages amplifies data shortage, traditionally plaguing empirical analysis on IDs. There are essentially three reasons for that. Firstly, the so-called 'globalisation statistics' are still at an early stage of development in most countries. Secondly, the measurement of firms' internationalisation with respect to a very detailed subnational scale raises additional problems in terms of data quality and availability. Thirdly and more interestingly, the shift from the enterprise or the industry to the ID as the reference unit of analysis calls for some substantial complications. For instance, which locally-based business activities and related local economic actors should be considered for the measurement of ID internationalisation?

This chapter aims to provide some basic guidelines to exploit the most from available data sources. In particular, it highlights how existing data sources can be combined to generate unique datasets finalised to ID internationalisation analysis. In addition, building upon various empirical works already carried out in Italy, it tries to define a common methodological framework to realise statistically sound and economically consistent analysis on ID internationalisation patterns, which can be profitably used in other countries.

The chapter is organised as follows. Section 2 brings together theoretical concepts that are relevant for the measurement of ID internationalisation. Section 3 illustrates the official and unofficial data sources that can be finalised to the measurement of internationalisation, while Section 4 focuses on the measurement problems of internationalisation from an ID perspective. Sections 5 and 6 report some examples of applied analysis on Italian IDs, focusing on the export performance and on the production internationalisation of Italian IDs through international subcontracting, respectively. These examples exploit unique datasets, and the methodology used in each example is consistent with the methodological approach pinpointed in Section 4. Finally, Section 7 draws some concluding remarks.

2. SOME CONCEPTUAL REMARKS ON THE DEFINITION AND MEASUREMENT OF ID NTERNATIONALISATION

An economically sound approach for the measurement of ID internationalisation combines different conceptual issues. Firstly, a clear-cut definition of firms' internationalisation must be distilled from the current debate on the definition and the measurement of globalisation (OECD 2005b and 2007b). Secondly, this definition, originally conceptualised from an industry or an enterprise perspective, has to be fine-tuned for the ID as the reference unit of analysis. Thirdly, the effects induced by local firms' internationalisation on ID basic characteristics should be carefully assessed.

An enterprise becomes internationalised when it establishes economically relevant linkages with foreign resident economic units. Two different typologies of firms' internationalisation are usually considered in this respect: trade internationalisation and production internationalisation. Trade internationalisation occurs when companies expand the geographical scope of their trading activities from domestic to foreign markets, either by selling final products and services abroad, or by buying inputs from the international markets. In contrast, production internationalisation takes place when an enterprise either expands or transfers abroad one or more phases of its production activities. In a broad sense, production internationalisation encompasses all economic activities directly run by the enterprise, such as core and secondary economic activities, as well as key business functions, like marketing, accounting, logistics and R&D.[1] This classification potentially reflects a theoretical conceptualisation. Following an evolutionary perspective, trade internationalisation is often seen as a preliminary stage to production internationalisation, which usually requires stronger managerial and coordination capabilities.

These two types of internationalisation have quite different implications in terms of measurement. While trade internationalisation can be easily inferred from firms' imports of inputs and exports of final goods, production internationalisation can assume different forms and be driven by different motivations. Production internationalisation can occur either through arms-length transactions or through hierarchical linkages (in effect by the company internalisation of economic activity realised abroad). The first mode refers to the purchase of intermediate inputs or business services from independent foreign resident companies (being international subcontracting the most usual way), while the second requires the acquisition of a foreign resident enterprise or the establishment of a production plant abroad. Motivations that drive production internationalisation can be related to the total or partial replacement of domestic activities with foreign ones (international sourcing) or to the expansion of company's activity abroad (development of new products, establishment of new production lines or access to new markets). The measurement issues related to production internationalisation will be discussed in Section 3.

The analysis of ID internationalisation requires moving from the firm or the industry to the ID as the reference unit of analysis. For the purpose of this analysis, an ID is considered as a (specific form of) spatial cluster of economic activities where these latter are carried out by a large number of locally-rooted and highly interdependent firms. It follows that ID internationalisation potentially occurs with respect to the entire set of production activities carried out within its geographical boundaries (Figure 29.1). Unfortunately, some business activities, such as those developed by footloose companies with plants located within an ID, may not be relevant for the ID itself.

All local business activities   Local production *filière*   ID-based cluster of economic activities

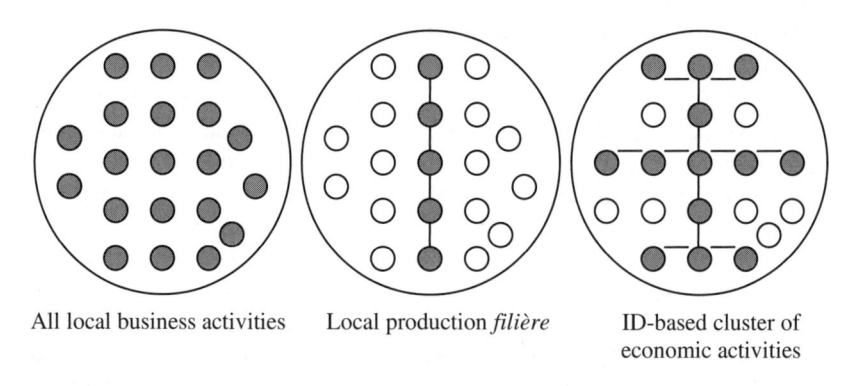

Figure 29.1   Classification of ID-based business activities

As a result, a more selective definition of ID-based production activities is needed. In particular, large companies cannot be excluded *a priori* from ID-based production activities, since a number of them may pursue a locally embedded behaviour and be fully integrated in the local network of production (Bellandi 2001).

From a production perspective, an ID may incorporate completely or partially an industry's production *filière*, including related business support functions. The stages of an industry's production *filière* that are located within the geographical boundaries of an ID constitute the local production *filière*.[2] Unfortunately, a local production *filière* might not correctly identify all ID-based activities being too narrowly defined with respect to the variety of productions that can be realised in an ID. Drawing on Becattini (1979, 1990), the set of activities that are relevant for an ID can be represented by a cluster of different but highly interdependent local productions, where the clustering is driven by the shared and locally embedded industrial culture.[3] This clustering of local activities is characterised not only by vertical linkages, mirroring the dominant production *filière*, but also by production to capital goods linkages (instrumental machines connected to production), as well as by horizontal linkages. In particular, horizontal linkages reflect not only production synergies buy also an increasing diversification of products driven by a more sophisticated final demand.[4] This approach, empirically tested by Becattini and Menghinello (1998), is included, as an example, in Section 5.

As Figure 29.2 shows, the internationalisation of an ID can affect its local production *filière* at different stages.

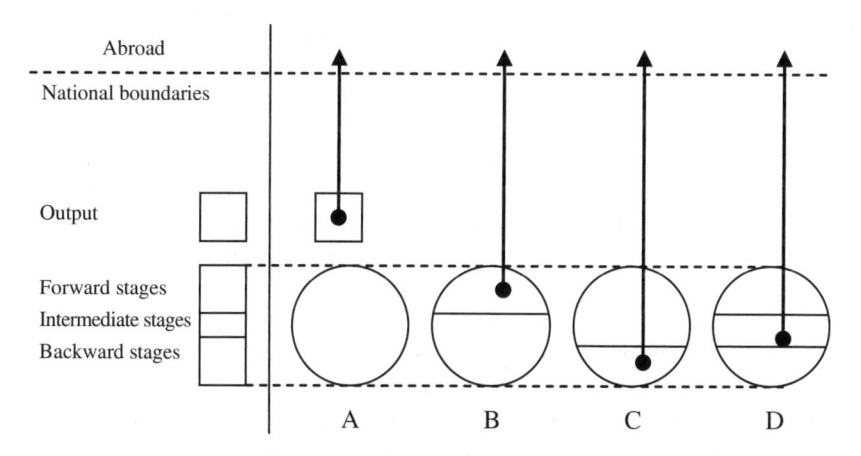

Figure 29.2 Patterns of ID internationalisation

If the products realised by the ID are exported abroad (A), this is in line with the definition of trade internationalisation. On the other hand, the production internationalisation of an ID may assume different forms, depending on the specific stages of the local production *filière* that are transferred or expanded abroad.[5] The forward stages of the local production *filière* are internationalised in case B, the backward stages of the local production *filière* are internationalised in case C, while the intermediate stages are shifted abroad in case D.

The production internationalisation of an ID may occur either through arms-length transactions (international subcontracting in most cases) or through ownership linkages (in effect multinational enterprise behaviour) (Figure 29.3).

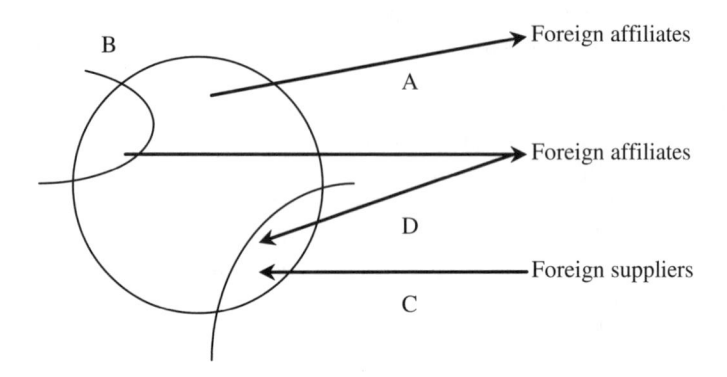

Note: A = production expansion abroad through foreign affiliates; B = shift of local production to foreign affiliates; C = imports of intermediate goods from foreign suppliers replacing local production; D = indirect effects on local production of foreign affiliates' activities.

Figure 29.3   Modes of ID production internationalisation

The scope of foreign suppliers is usually limited to international outsourcing,[6] in effect to the substitution of local production with the imports of intermediate goods and services (C). In contrast, companies under foreign control (hereafter, foreign affiliates) tend to have a multipurpose scope with respect to the local company's internationalisation behaviour. In effect, they can be used either to expand ID production abroad (A) or to replace it (B). In particular, the shift abroad of ID production can occur both directly or indirectly. In case B, foreign affiliates directly replace domestic (local) production, while in case D they act like foreign suppliers by generating import of intermediate goods and services. As it will be more clearly shown in the next sections, the complexity of ID internationalisation modes determines substantial problems for the quantitative assessment of their internationalisation patterns. In order to cover all possible forms of ID internationalisation, the entry of a foreign multinational enterprise in an ID should also be considered (De Propris, Driffield and Menghinello 2005).

From a broader perspective, production internationalisation may alter the structural characteristics of an ID, such as its geographical boundaries as well as its local production organisation. Furthermore, it leads to a reshaping at a global level of the value chain of the local industry (Gereffi 1994; Bair and Gereffi 2001; Dicken et al. 2001).

Measuring internationalisation 399

As Figure 29.4 shows, firms located in a heavily internationalised ID tend to combine local linkages with a selected pool of specialised firms and external linkages with foreign resident companies (Conti and Menghinello 1998). External linkages may include foreign affiliates and specialised foreign supplies engaged in an intensive trade of goods as well as knowledge transfer with ID-based firms, becoming in this case a crucial part of the global ID network.

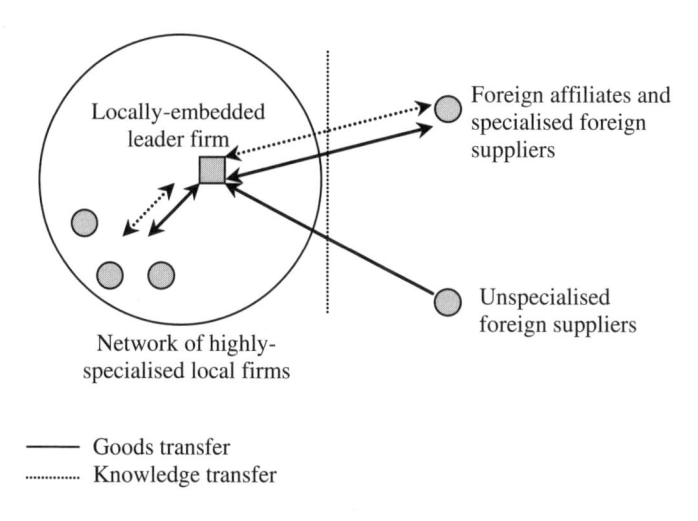

Figure 29.4   The global ID and its local and international linkages

The quantitative assessment of an ID global network represents the most complicated but also one of the most appealing goals for statisticians and applied economists.

The current empirical literature on ID internationalisation seems to suffer, in many cases, from the lack of a statistically consistent and economically comprehensive approach. Some scholars, to cope with data shortage, rely upon a territorial grid that represents a weak proxy of IDs' spatial distribution while others focus on a specific internationalisation mode. These oversimplified empirical approaches are very likely to provide a partial and potentially biased picture of ID internationalisation patterns. As an example, the use of outward foreign direct investment (FDI) flows to detect ID production internationalisation patterns provides an inadequate picture, since small and medium-sized enterprises, that represent the large majority of firms located in an ID, usually adopt flexible forms of internationalisation, such as an intensive use of international subcontracting (Helg and Tajoli 2005).

The most appropriate approach to measure ID internationalisation is critically discussed in the next two sections.

3. DATA SOURCES FOR THE ANALYSIS OF INTERNATIONALISATION

An economically sound approach to the analysis of internationalisation calls for the use of multiple data sources to cover all possible forms of internationalisation. Table 29.1 provides a general overview that links economic concepts illustrated in Section 2 with relevant data sources.

Table 29.1   Main data sources for the analysis of internationalisation

Data sources	Limits of the data source for an economic-oriented analysis of internationalisation
Trade internationalisation	
Trade in goods statistics (exports)	Part of the exports of semi-completed products may be related to production internationalisation (outward processing trade)
Trade in services statistics (exports)	Limited product and economic activity breakdown
Production internationalisation	
Trade in goods statistics (imports)	Because of data classification constraints, it is usually difficult to disentangle the imports of goods for production purposes from the imports of goods finalised to other economic destinations (household consumption)
Trade in services statistics (imports)	Limited product and economic activity breakdown, problems in correctly detecting internationalisation-oriented flows
Outward FDI statistics	These statistics have essentially a financial nature with limited information on classification and economic variables
Outward FATS statistics	These statistics are finalised to produce economic variables on foreign affiliates abroad
Commercial databases	They provide firm-level information on companies' economic accounts and ownership structure across a wide range of countries, but they are usually plagued by poor data quality

Trade in goods and services statistics represent an essential channel of information to detect both trade internationalisation from the exports side as well as production internationalisation through arms-length transactions from the imports side.[7] In contrast, FDI statistics and foreign affiliate trade statistics (FATS) embody the most relevant source of information to analyse production internationalisation by multinational behaviour.

Each source of information presents some data limits and constraints. For instance, it is not easy, in trade statistics, to disentangle the imports of goods incorporated in production processes from those oriented to domestic consumption. In this respect, the analysis of specific types of trade flows, such as intra-industry trade, inward and outward processing trade, as well as the classification of imported goods by economic destination, may mitigate but not completely solve this problem. The use of FDI statistics to analyse the strategies of multinational enteprises presents some problems given the essentially financial nature of these statistics. More recently, FATS have emerged, at least within the EU, as a new framework to collect information on multinational enterprises (MNEs). FATS statistics are explicitly oriented to measure MNEs' real activities in line with the production of other business statistics.[8] Nevertheless, both FDI and FATS statistics are not able to distinguish MNEs' investments abroad according to their economic purpose. As a result, production expansion abroad with no direct effect on domestic production and international sourcing[9] are mixed up in both outward FDI and outward FATS statistics.

Commercial databases including economic data (balance sheet and ownership information) at the firm level across a wide range of countries have recently emerged as a significant source of information to assess company performance and, potentially, internationalisation patterns. These data can be easily finalised to different analytical purposes, including regional or local mapping based on the company zip code as well as internationalisation analysis based on international ownership linkages. Nevertheless, the quality of these data and their consistency with respect to official statistics is often uncertain.[10]

4. MEASUREMENT OF ID INTERNATIONALISATION

Although the territorial breakdown for variables included in Table 29.1 may vary across countries, key internationalisation variables, such as trade and FDI statistics, are usually available with a limited territorial breakdown (region or macro-region) based on administrative territorial classifications. This causes substantial problems for the analysis on ID internationalisation, since administrative territorial classifications reflect political boundaries that are generally inconsistent with the spatial distribution of economic activities. As mentioned in other chapters of this section, an effective mapping of IDs extensively relies on functional territorial classifications, such as the local labour market (LLM) classification.

There are essentially two alternative approaches to cope with potential inconsistency between administrative territorial classifications and the effective spatial distribution of IDs. The first consists in an *ex post* quantitative evaluation of the extent to which administrative borders might represent a satisfactory proxy of IDs' geographical mapping. The second refers to the possibility of creating new datasets from either official or private sources that are *a priori* finalised to the analysis of IDs' internationalisation. These datasets are built using a territorial grid that mirrors an IDs' map.

A relatively simple way to test *ex post* the consistency of an administrative territorial classification with respect to the effective spatial distribution of IDs is based upon the following statistical indicator:

$$TCI_{jk} = \frac{\sum_{i=1}^{n} empl_{ijk}}{empl_{jk}} \qquad (29.1)$$

Where variable *empl* stands for the number of person employed in local units (plants), index *i* represents the number of IDs that are totally or partially located within the administrative territorial unit, and indexes *j* and *k* identify, respectively, the administrative territorial unit and the industry.

The computation of this indicator, hereafter called territorial consistency indicator (TCI), requires the availability of an auxiliary variable with a territorial breakdown that is consistent with both the administrative classification and the ID map. This means that the variable can be rearranged either by the ID map or by the administrative classification, including all possible combinations. Industrial or total employment variables derived from the most recent edition of the business census are usually the most appropriate variables for this goal.[11]

The TCI quantitatively assesses, for each combination of industry and region, the extent to which each regional industry represents a reasonably good proxy of the underlying IDs. This measure is reliable under the assumption that the key variables of interest, like exports or outward FDI, are significantly correlated with the auxiliary variable.

The empirical literature on the development of datasets directly finalised to the analysis of ID internationalisation is so far very limited. Some national statistical institutes have tried to build territorial estimates for key economic variables by adopting a functional territorial classification that is consistent with the ID mapping. The Italian National Statistical Institute (ISTAT) has developed in recent years a set of key economic variables broken down by LLMs by adopting 'small area' estimation techniques. These estimates include value added and number of employees as key variables. These data can be easily rearranged by IDs, the latter being a specific subset of LLMs. Unfortunately, these variables have a limited scope with respect to the analysis of ID internationalisation patterns.

An interesting experiment along this line of research was made by ISTAT a few years ago. Estimates of exports broken down jointly by LLMs and product groups were obtained by combining information on plants location from the economic census register with the satellite register on foreign exporters. More information on the methodological approach adopted to generate exports data by IDs are included in ISTAT (2002) and Menghinello (2004), while some of the analytical results are illustrated in the next section.

The availability of production internationalisation variables jointly broken down by industry and locality is usually very limited. Nevertheless, this data is important to carry out applied economic analysis on the internationalisation of local production *filières*. An example of that will be shown in Section 5 where trade and census data are combined to assess the production internationalisation of Italian IDs in the 1990s.

More generally, administrative data, and in particular commercial databases, can represent, in perspective, a valuable asset for the analysis of more complex forms of ID internationalisation patterns, as those highlighted in Figure 29.4. Despite their high informative potential, administrative data require a massive investment to improve their quality and to check their consistency against official sources. The location of multi-plants enterprises represents a major problem for these datasets, which usually provide information on the company legal location only.

Figure 29.5 summarises the basic ideas introduced in this section. In particular, a statistically sound approach to the analysis of ID internationalisation should include a comprehensive assessment of the following key issues:

- an analysis of the data available at the national level, including official statistics as well as private databases and covering all possible forms of firm internationalisation;
- an analysis of the territorial breakdown available for this data, including the possibility to carry out *ad hoc* calculations at the local level from national or regional data;

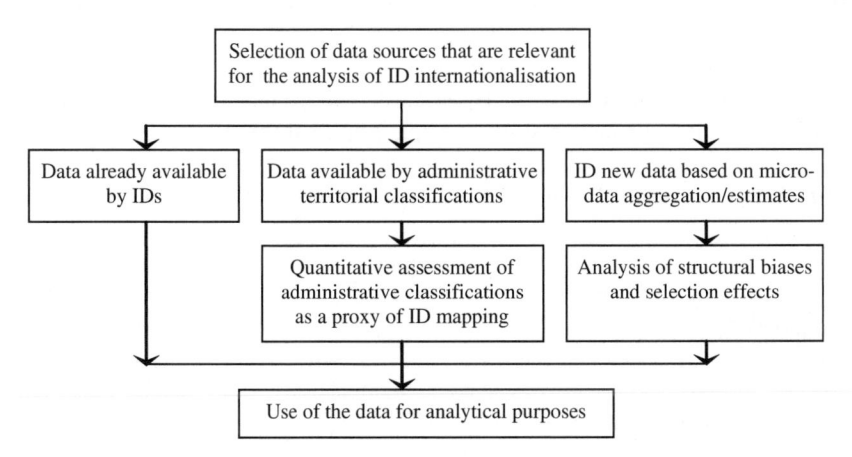

Figure 29.5 A general framework for the empirical analysis of ID internationalisation

- a consistency check-up of the territorial breakdown by which data is available with the effective spatial distribution of IDs;
- accessibility of territorial data with an industry breakdown in order to build and analyse local production *filières*.

It is clear from Figure 29.5 that a flexible approach, which combines different types of data available with dissimilar levels of territorial detail, is needed to exploit the most from information sources. Nevertheless, the optimisation of all available information should be constrained by a careful assessment of the extent to which territorial classifications are consistent with, or at least represent a reasonably good proxy of, the effective spatial distribution of IDs.

5. TRADE INTERNATIONALISATION OF ITALIAN IDs

Italian IDs are well known as highly competitive and strongly export-oriented local economies (Bagella, Becchetti and Sacchi 2000). Unfortunately, a quantitative assessment of their contribution to the Italian exports has been missing for a long time.

A first attempt to assess the quantitative contribution of Italian IDs to national exports based on exports data by province[12] was made by Becattini and Menghinello (1998). They used the list of 199 IDs identified by ISTAT and based on the LLM territorial grid as the reference territorial classification. In line with the methodological approach introduced above, Becattini and Menghinello (ibid.) first used the TCI to test the consistency of exports data by province with respect to the effective spatial distribution of IDs as mapped by ISTAT. As a result, only a limited subset of provincial industries were identified as ID-intensive, and used to produce the final estimates. In particular, the availability of a quite detailed industry breakdown (237 product groups) for exports data by province, permitted the identification of ID-based clusters of economic activities.[13] Table 29.2 summarises the main results from this empirical study.

Table 29.2   Italian IDs and national exports (provincial proxy approach)

	1985	1990	1995
Contribution (in percentage) of IDs to national exports	21.2	21.3	21.8

Source: Becattini and Menghinello (1998).

These results show that Italian IDs consistently account for one-fifth of national exports over the period 1985–95. Another interesting result from this study is the quite pervasive impact of ID exports across industries other that the dominant local industry due to the inter-industry effects induced by the ID-based cluster of economic activities. In particular, ID exports in core industries moderately decline over the period 1985–95, while the IDs' contribution in cluster-related industries, such as instrumental machinery, sharply increases.

This approach can be questioned in many respects. The definition of exclusion thresholds to identify 'ID-intensive' provincial industries as well as the classification of products to be included in the ID-based cluster of economic activities is probably plagued by subjective judgement. Nevertheless, this approach can be considered, given data constraints, as a first attempt to quantify the contribution of IDs to Italian exports based on reasonable statistical assumptions.

Table 29.3 *Exports of Italian IDs by main product groups, micro-data linkage methodology, 1996*

Total manufactured goods and key product groups (ranking of the top 20 product groups)	IDs' market shares in percentage of national exports
Manufactured goods, of which:	43.3
Sports goods	93.5
Leather products	84.2
Ceramic tiles and flags	82.0
Jewellery and related articles	74.6
Musical instruments	72.0
Agricultural and forestry machineries	71.5
Knitted and crocheted articles	71.1
Footwear	69.0
Textile weaving products	66.9
Furniture	65.8
Textile fibres	65.5
Tank reservoirs and containers of metal, radiators, etc.	65.4
Veneer sheets, plywood, laminated and chipboard	64.8
Knitted and crocheted articles	64.3
Leather clothes	61.8
Weapons and ammunitions	59.8
Cutlery, tools and general hardware	58.6
Basic iron, steel and iron alloys	57.0
Meat and meat products	56.2
Tubes	54.9

Source: Menghinello (2004).

A statistically-grounded approach to assess the contribution of Italian IDs to national exports based on micro-data linkage has been more recently developed by ISTAT (ISTAT 2002; Menghinello 2004). In this approach, information on enterprise location, including the location of production plants for multi-plant enterprises, is combined with exports data at the firm level broken down by 20 product groups. The results from this exercise are reported in Table 29.3 above.

These results significantly differ from the ones obtained by Becattini and Menghinello (1998). There are some methodological and economic reasons for that. The ISTAT approach is statistically more accurate, but it is also broader from an economic point of view, since it considers all the locally-based exported products, including those sold abroad by footloose large companies. In contrast, Becattini and Menghinello (ibid.) used a less sophisticated methodology, mainly because of micro-data accessibility constraints, but they were more selective from an economic point of view by considering ID-based cluster of economic activities only.

Some interesting results from ISTAT (2002) and Menghinello (2004) are included in Table 29.4. This table highlights the contribution of some notorious Italian IDs to national as well as worldwide exports with respect to some specific groups of products. In particular, the contribution of a specific Italian ID to the worldwide trade can be obtained, for the same group of products, by multiplying the ID share of national exports by the contribution of Italian exports to the worldwide trade.

Table 29.4   Export performance of some notorious Italian IDs (market shares in percentage), 1996

ID denomination and region of location	Product groups	National exports	World exports
Sassuolo (Emilia-Romagna)	Ceramic tiles and flags	51.3	28.1
S. Ambrogio di Valpolicella (Veneto)	Ornamental and building stones	25.6	8.9
Arzignano (Veneto)	Leather products	26.8	5.1
Santa Croce sull'Arno (Tuscany)	Leather products	21.5	4.1
Arezzo (Tuscany)	Jewellery and related articles	34.3	3.6
Prato (Tuscany)	Textile weaving products	24.6	3.5
Pietrasanta (Tuscany)	Ornamental and building stones	8.3	2.9
Vicenza (Veneto)	Jewellery and related articles	17.1	2.5
Lecco (Lombardy)	Cutlery, tools and general hardware	5.8	2.2
Udine (Friuli-Venezia Giulia)	Furniture	12.1	1.8

Source: Menghinello (2004).

In conclusion, the analysis of Italian IDs' exports seems to provide sound evidence on IDs' key contribution to the country's exports and thereby to the national competitiveness in international markets. More recent developments in the trade as well as in the production organisation of Italian IDs suggest an increasing transfer of local production functions abroad and then the direct export from IDs' foreign affiliates. This has prompted a critical reconsideration of some of the findings above.

6. PRODUCTION INTERNATIONALISATION OF ITALIAN IDs

As mentioned above, a comprehensive economic approach to the analysis of ID production internationalisation requires multiple data sources and a careful assessment of their reliability with respect to IDs as the reference unit of analysis. The empirical analysis described hereafter is quite partial in this respect, since it is exclusively based on trade data. In particular, it focuses on the substitution of local production with imported intermediate or quasi-finished goods. Nevertheless, international subcontracting seems to have been the dominant strategy adopted by Italian ID firms to shift local manufacturing activities abroad, at least in their early stages of production internationalisation.

Drawing on Cavalieri (1995), who focuses on the production internationalisation of IDs in Tuscany, Conti and Menghinello (1998) further expanded his analysis to consider the internationalisation patterns of all IDs in Italy from the mid-1980s until the mid-1990s. The methodology relies on the construction of local production *filières* and on the use of imports data by province. In line with the methodological approach proposed in Section 4, only provincial industries representing a reasonably good proxy of IDs wherein located were considered in this applied analysis. Local production *filières* were identified taking advantage of the relatively detailed level of economic breakdown available at the provincial level for both industry census data and trade statistics. More specifically, they build an indicator to assess the intensity of production internationalisation by each stage of an ID local production *filière*: the internationalisation intensity of the local production *filière* index (ILF). The ILF uses the imports per employee ratio as a proxy of the intensity in the use of foreign intermediate goods in each stage of the local production *filière*,[14] as described below:

$$ILF_{ijk} = \frac{import_{ijk}}{empl_{jk}} \qquad (29.2)$$

where index i represents a single stage of the local production *filière*, and j and k, which stand for the province and industry respectively, jointly identify the provincial industry.

The results from this empirical analysis show a significant acceleration in the production internationalisation of IDs specialised in traditional industries since the early 1990s.[15] More interestingly, Conti and Menghinello (ibid.) find a great deal of heterogeneity across IDs in the local patterns of production internationalisation (Table 29.5).

Table 29.5 Production internationalisation of Italian IDs in the textile industry (import values in thousands of national currency, per person employed), 1995

Stages of the local production *filière*	Italian 'ID-intensive' provinces			
	Cotton and other vegetable textile fibres			
	Como	Firenze	Varese	Vicenza
Inputs	3 837	226	3 241	6 774
Preliminary stages of textile production	567	251	894	1 172
Cotton yarn	6 635	12 078	11 296	3 557
Woven fabrics of cotton	15 563	25 277	36 980	15 539
	Wool			
	Como	Firenze	Vercelli	Vicenza
Inputs	3 710	342	16 618	342
Preliminary stages of textile production	5 327	27 119	18 883	20 941
Wool yarn	5 893	10 683	4 385	4 037
Woven fabrics of wool	9 097	2 977	652	2 053
	Man-made textile fibres			
	Como	Firenze	Varese	
Inputs	3 096	15 014	4 405	
Man-made yarn	19 340	25 671	39 044	
Man-made woven fabrics	16 134	7 873	17 361	

Source: Conti and Menghinello (1998).

These findings suggest that heterogeneity in local internationalisation patterns may reflect locally-specific characteristics, in effect local competitive advantages. In particular, the empirical evidence, combined with qualitative information provided by experts and scholars, show that IDs are generally adverse to re-allocate abroad the phases of their local production *filière* where the competitive advantages of the local industry are more intensively concentrated. Since the most competitive stages of the local production *filière* tend to be ID-specific, its pattern of production internationalisation also appears to be ID-specific.

The validity of these results can be deemed, however, limited in the very short run. In particular, the use of imports data as the exclusive channel to carry out production internationalisation from IDs reflects today a rather partial approach. This is because medium and large-sized companies embedded in IDs have already moved local production lines abroad through FDI, with limited impacts on inward trade flows. As a result, a more integrated approach, which combines different data sources, is recommended to fully assess the patterns of ID production internationalisation. Moreover, the use of micro-data, especially from large international databases, is suggested as a relatively promising way to explore more articulated forms of ID internationalisation (Chiarvesio, Di Maria and Micelli 2004).

7. CONCLUSIONS

The measurement of ID internationalisation represents a substantial challenge for both statisticians and applied economists. The complexity of tracking all ID-based international linkages dramatically amplifies data shortage, traditionally plaguing empirical research on IDs. In this context applied researchers might be tempted to adopt partial sources of information or to select weak territorial proxies to assess the ID internationalisation patterns.

This chapter has aimed to provide a conceptual and an operational framework to develop statistically sound analyses of ID internationalisation rooted into key economic concepts. Given that official sources provides little support in terms of standard data that are relevant for the analysis of ID internationalisation, a great deal of work should be done to set up new and original databases from both official and non-official sources.

In this context the increasing availability of commercial databases with firm-level information represents, in perspective, an enormous source of information to carry out applied economic analysis on IDs' economic performance and internationalisation patterns. In particular these databases are characterised by the pooling of firm-level information across different countries, including international ownership linkages. This is a unique source of information to explore the ID global network by using jointly location and ownership information.

NOTES

1. The sale of final products in foreign markets through a local wholesale company owned by the domestic resident enterprise is clearly a borderline example in this respect. Even if this is related to a purely trading activity, it can be considered a form of production internationalisation as long as it has determined the location abroad of one of the company's business functions.
2. The production *filière* of a given industry encompasses, no matter where the companies are located, all the stages of a production process, from early stages of input transformation to the

realisation of final products. In contrast, a local production *filière* includes only the stages of a production *filière* that are effectively carried out by firms localised within an ID.
3. This approach is also in line with recent streams of economic literature focusing on local knowledge spillovers.
4. In order to face an increasing competition from developing countries in labour-intensive industries, 'made-in-Italy' products realised by IDs have experienced a significant product quality and differentiation upgrading, being the Italian design and the brand appeal the most powerful drivers, quite independently from the nature and the characteristics of the products.
5. An ID usually does not represent a local and independent enclave within the national economy. Nevertheless, linkages between local firms and domestic companies located outside the ID are ignored, for simplicity's sake, in this chapter.
6. This is a simplification, for foreign suppliers may also be involved to expand ID production abroad. Nevertheless, the substitution of domestic production with foreign intermediate goods or services is usually considered the primary scope of international subcontracting.
7. Foreign trade statistics may also be used to take into account the indirect contribution of foreign affiliates to production internationalisation through the imports of intermediate goods (see Table 29.3). Intra-firm trade statistics are particularly suitable to meet this goal.
8. Unfortunately, these new statistics are still at an early stage of development in most EU countries.
9. The possibility to split international sourcing from production expansion abroad in MNEs investment data is limited, for the moment, to *ad hoc* surveys.
10. In particular, if some of the basic features of administrative data (threshold effects, exclusion of specific types of company by legal form) are correlated with the variables of interest in the empirical analysis, final results will be plagued by structural biases as well as selection effects.
11. As far as the Italian case is concerned, business census data on employment in local units jointly broken down by municipality and industry codes (NACE 3-digits) provides the most detailed set of territorial data. This database can be easily rearranged either by provinces or by LLMAs, where the latter functional classification is perfectly consistent with the classification of IDs in Italy published by ISTAT.
12. Up to 1994 there were 95 provinces in Italy corresponding to level 3 of the European nomenclature of territorial units for statistics (NUTS).
13. Merchandise groups, available for provincial data on exports and imports were available until 1999. This quite detailed product breakdown represents a unique asset to detect production *filières* as well as to define ID-based clusters of economic activities. In particular, they allow the main production stages for most traditional industries to be distinguished. They also permit the identification of instrumental machines related to a specific industry, such as textile machines for the textile industry. Unfortunately, this level of detail is not fully replicated by NACE 3-digits breakdown (about 100 product groups), which represent the standard level of product breakdown for the current dissemination of exports data by provinces in Italy.
14. The reliability of this indicator can be questioned in many respects. For instance, differences in the levels of this indicator may reflect heterogeneity in labour productivity and/or capital intensity across local industries with similar local production *filières*. Nevertheless, relevant methodological and data dissemination constraints prevent the use of more robust methodologies such as input–output tables, since these latter data are usually available only at the national or macro-regional level. In order to mitigate the bias related to the local consumption of imported goods by householders, the geographical origin of the import flow is restricted to emerging countries where most of the IDs foreign suppliers are traditionally located.
15. This evidence is consistent with the results provided by other studies, such as Graziani (2001), and Savona and Schiattarella (2004).

SECTION 7
The Italian experiences

Introduction

Michael Dunford

1. CONCEPTUAL PREMISES OF ITALIAN STUDIES ON IDs

The industrial district (ID) literature derives in part from general concepts developed originally by Marshall (1920) to explain the development of dense concentrations of interdependent small and medium-sized firms (SMEs) in a single sector and in auxiliary industries and services. According to Marshall, districts were driven economically by three mechanisms: (a) scale economies; (b) external economies; and (c) the availability of special skills and the pooling of the workforce. Marshall also argued, however, that districts are not simply an economic phenomenon: districts have an industrial atmosphere that itself involves the interaction of the economic and social system.

At the end of the 1970s and in the 1980s these ideas were extended to account for the evident dynamism of dense concentrations of specialised firms in traditional industries in Italian IDs. The first of Marshall's arguments was reflected in an initial wave of research on external economies and on vertical disintegration and productive decentralisation. Other research emphasised the role of economies of scope where costs are spread across a wide range of goods. A further dimension was added with the claim that districts are places in which local knowledge spillovers are important drivers of learning, innovation and creativity. More critical research emphasised limits to the model and its consequent restructuring. Four main issues were examined: (a) the rise of diseconomies; (b) ownership concentration, the emergence of groups of companies and the growing influence of lead firms; (c) the delocalisation via foreign direct investment–joint venture–strategic supplier–subcontract arrangements of wage-sensitive activities to adjacent low cost countries; and (d) the dependence of the model on social legislation that encouraged the growth of micro-enterprises, and on economic conditions that provided for relatively low wages and the depreciation of Italy's currency.

The second of Marshall's arguments was further developed by Becattini who argued that districts were communities of firms and people and their emergence required a change in the unit of analysis from the firm and the industry to the district. The first of these ideas opened the way to a large literature dealing with the social, cultural, political and institutional foundations of the district model. Becattini's second argument that districts should constitute the object of analysis was related to the first. The reason why was that its justification rested on the view that districts are systems whose structure and development depends on norms, values, institutions, modes of governance and social and cultural factors. As the influence of this argument grew, studies of industries and firms declined in importance.

This second set of arguments is consistent with the recognition that the economic sphere is not an independent realm. Instead it is underpinned by a set of collective beliefs which differ from one society to another, which are embodied in formal institutions that depend on the sovereign power of States and political institutions and which accordingly give rise to the diversity of actually existing capitalist societies.

2. IDs AND MADE IN ITALY

A merit of the chapter by Marco Fortis and Monica Carminati is that it takes as its starting point precisely the particular structure of the Italian production system and of one of the worlds of production that constitute Italian capitalism. The world they consider is the one characterised by districts and an exceptionally large number of SMEs mainly operating in so-called traditional sectors.

Fortis and Carminati identify four major sectors–areas of excellence in which Italy and Italy's IDs are specialised and which account for 66 per cent of manufacturing jobs. In addition a tourist sector underpinned by the quality of the natural environment, art, Italy's architectural heritage and hospitality sectors is identified as another pillar of the Italian economy and one of its sources of strength. These clusters and Italy's districts in which they are largely located help finally, they argue, to offset the relative weakness of the Italian economy in other industries (such as the automotive industries and electronics) in which large enterprises often dominate.

Fortis and Carminati present some significant evidence to support the claim that these sectors account for a large volume of exports (in 2001, 57 per cent of manufactured exports) and large trade surpluses. Some sectors have already lost ground to Chinese competition. Fortis and Carminati have a strong inclination to dismiss the Chinese challenge on the grounds that it rests on commercial aggressiveness and asymmetric competition including the artificial devaluation of the yuan, the holding of large foreign reserves and counterfeiting. The first two factors are, in fact, perfectly understandable responses to the consequences of the speculative attacks on East Asian currencies and the subsequent Asian crisis, while the consequent imbalances are a result of an asymmetric international order and the debt-fuelled growth of Anglo-America in particular. For their part the position of European producers was underpinned for a long period of time by a range of asymmetrical protectionist measures indicating the importance of seeing the context of district development as not merely a national one. As Fortis and Carminati indicate the challenge for Italian producers is to upgrade into higher value-added areas inside the traditional 'made-in-Italy' sectors, though it is also important to recognise that its new competitors will also seek to move into higher value-added areas.

This chapter is of course in part a reaction to some of the recent literature that has identified a decline in the economic performance of Italy's districts and that has criticised the dependence of the Italian economy on micro-enterprises and small firms that undertake little formal R&D and have difficulties in internationalising on the one hand and the weakness of Italy's presence in more research-intensive sectors on the other. Fortis and Carminati claim 'quite the opposite' and argue that 'a large number of SMEs, far from being a weakness in the country's economy, are in fact a source of great strength'. The suggestion, however, that the advocates of these arguments proposed an abandonment of these sectors is extremely questionable: most argued for a consolidation around medium-sized enterprises. And while this chapter provides evidence of the continuing importance of the 'made-in-Italy sectors' the evidence presented does not address some of the important issues raised by the deterioration in the relative performance of the Italian economy to which should be added the significant downturn in the relative position of many admittedly rich central and northern regional economies lest responsibility for national woes be laid at the door of the Mezzogiorno.

3. THE RISING INFLUENCE OF MEDIUM-SIZED DISTRICT FIRMS

Fulvio Coltorti's chapter addresses directly the question of the role of medium-sized enterprises. After drawing on some comparative international data demonstrating the relative importance of micro-enterprises and small firms in Italy and Spain, attention is concentrated on the changing size distribution of firms in Italy and on the role of medium-sized enterprises. As far as trends in the size distribution of firms is concerned Coltorti draws on Cave's claim that regression towards the mean is the norm. The reasons why are threefold: growth rates vary with size inversely; the mean growth rates of surviving firms tend to decline and decline with age; and entry and exit are more likely in smaller classes.

Coltorti then presents evidence to suggest that in IDs and in provinces characterised by the predominance of district organisation (district provinces) whose importance derives in part from the expansion of the geographical extent of districts the presence of medium-sized enterprises is significant and has increased in recent years.

The group Coltorti studies comprises stand-alone firms and industrial groups mainly assuming the form of family-owned holding companies. He shows for example that 59 out of 156 districts have medium and large local units accounting for 72 per cent of employment. In these districts there are many micro and small enterprises. In another 41 districts micro and small units account for 75 per cent of total employment but these enterprises account for just 13.6 per cent of total employment in all districts. In relation to district provinces he provides evidence of an increase in the relative importance of micro and small firms in 1971–91 and a decline in the importance of these size groups relative to medium-sized and large enterprises in 1991–2001. The former is not simply a result of the decline of Fordist enterprises: it reflects a shift in the sectoral composition of growth and it also reflects a shift in corporate governance including the adoption of economic value added as a performance indicator which itself drives in the direction of an increase in the variability of outlays and a concentration on core competences (Dunford 2009).

In the remaining sections attention is concentrated on the development of medium-sized enterprises and groups and on the development of affiliates of large enterprises in IDs and district provinces (sometimes as a result of the growth of district firms such as Benetton and Luxottica in eyewear which notably developed retail activities whose role warrants more attention). Of these developments the rise of affiliates of large enterprises in IDs raises potentially interesting issues of definition: while perceivable as 'a nonsense' if districts are seen as concentrations of small firms it is not if districts are seen as an instance of the agglomerations and clusters that are one of the foci of research in the new economic geography.

Coltorti in short confirms the presence of medium-sized enterprises in districts and the enlargement of district areas which itself, he argues, involves a change in the nature of district and district provinces and helps district enterprises to consolidate, enter new markets and confront new sources of competition. In spite of these changes, Coltorti expects local roots to remain strong.

4. THE TRANSFORMATION OF LOCAL BANKING

Pietro Alessandrini and Alberto Zazzaro raise some important issues concerning the nature of local roots. In their chapter they concentrate on the link between firms and banks in a situation in which these relationships are changing. Traditionally it was considered that districts involved small firm–small bank relationships. Alessandrini and Zazzaro identify two changes. One is the rise in the relative importance of medium-sized enterprises characterised by a higher degree of internationalisation, the coordination of small subsuppliers inside and outside districts and a stronger financial structure. The credit requirements of these enterprises (ordinary credit, commercial credit for network functions and development finance) are different from those of earlier generations of district firms. The second is the liberalisation, concentration and centralisation of the bank sector which has significantly reduced the number and role of local banks especially in less economically developed areas.

Alessandrini and Zazzaro argue that changes in (a) the spatial organisation of banks and credit allocation, (b) the size of banks, (c) functional distance (which generally increases especially in economically disadvantaged areas), (d) operational distance (which may decline due to the use of information technology) and (e) the territorial dimension of the short- and long-term, profit-driven credit strategies of banks, have mixed effects on support for customers and the stimulation of local growth. In Italy for example the decrease in the number of independent banks especially in the culturally-distinct South has significantly increased relative operational distance while diminishing it in the localities in the Centre-North more attractive to financial institutions with possible adverse effects on small firms in the Mezzogiorno.

These differing affects are captured in recommendations for a diversified (in terms of size, management and ownership) banking system capable of responding to the dual need for (a) attention to local context-dependent knowledge in making decisions and (b) the performance of global tasks such the provision of specialised financial competences and the allocation of financial resources to the strongest activities with the greatest opportunities for growth.

Alessandrini and Zazzaro finish by suggesting that greater commitment to the specific needs of local firms and local development will reduce the risks of devoting resources to standardised financial instruments of the kind that precipitated the recent financial crisis. Yet surely this crisis plus their advocacy of a diversified sector cannot be sustained if they really hold the view that the 'free market in property rights ... should not be impeded'.

5. EVOLUTIONARY PATHS AND REGIONAL MODELS

The chapter by Fiorenza Belussi is of value in that it deals with the origins, path-dependent evolutions and consequent heterogeneity of Italian IDs. To make some sense of this heterogeneity some 55 cases are classified in terms of their origin and their evolutions. As far as origins are concerned four triggering factors are identified: availability of craft skills and craft traditions; natural resource endowments; the existence of dynamic anchor firms; and the entry of a dynamic external enterprise. As for path dependent evolutions a variety of evolutionary growth factors are identified and used to classify the trajectories of the 55 districts. Four main factors are distinguished: innovation capabilities; local institutional support in the shape of training and support for technological innovation; firm product differentiation and diversification strategies; and internationalisation strategies. An alternative approach to the analysis of evolutionary strategies is to draw on current value chain approaches to upgrading where for example innovation relates to product and process while internationalisation is driven by a quest for cost advantages and markets. This approach is, however, more firm- rather than district-centred raising in important ways the question of the nature of the object of analysis in studies of local development.

Francesco Musotti's starting point is the socio-economic character of IDs and their non-reducibility to economic factors. He goes much further than Belussi in seeing the roots of differentiation in the late and incomplete integration of the Italian peninsula and more specifically in the establishment of three prerequisites. The first was the preservation of aspects of the late medieval communal civilisation of the Centre-North which saw city-centred artisanal manufacturing and commercial initiatives flourish. The survival of elements of this civilisation, he claims, lies in the activities of local banks, technical schools and communal self-government. The second was the creation of densely-populated rural areas and small rural centres with the development of family-centred sharecropping arrangements in central Italy and small tenancies in northern Italy with close inter-farm relationships. The third was a factor that brought them together and saw the rise of micro-enterprises and the urbanisation of the countryside: the stimulus provided by the demand for individual and household goods in the *Trente Glorieuses* that followed the Second World War. To these necessary yet differentiated preconditions was added the diversity of market opportunities on the one hand, and different political cultures and strategic choices of local administrations and trades unions on the other, to create a number of regional models: one in the centre of Italy (northern Abruzzo, Marche, Umbria and Toscana) and another in northern Italy with its distinctive white-Catholic political subcultures (with a larger presence of medium-sized firms, with a closer relation with central political power, where the federalist northern leagues took root and where spillover from the industrial triangle after the crisis of the early 1970s was marked). These ideas are close to the ideas at the origin of work on the so-called Third Italy and remain important, yet require more attention to evolutionary considerations and warrant closer integration with the economic factors considered in other chapters in this section.

30. Sectors of excellence in the Italian industrial districts

Marco Fortis and Monica Carminati

1. INTRODUCTION

The purpose of this chapter is to provide an organic picture of the Italian districts by highlighting the main features of the manufacturing sectors where they are operating. The large number of industrial districts (IDs) and an exceptional number of small and medium-sized enterprises (SMEs) are actually peculiarities of our manufacturing system, together with specialisation in the so-called traditional sectors (textiles, apparel, leather, footwear, wood and furniture) and light engineering.

Regarding the importance of IDs for Italy's economy there is substantial agreement in the literature on a few objective facts: (a) a strong contribution to employment through their own and allied-industry's workforce (not only in the manufacturing sector, but also in services); (b) the leading position of the IDs in international trade, both in major sectors and in dozens of niches. Despite this empirical evidence, there are still people who, rather superficially, keep blaming the district system for Italy's loss of competitiveness and modest presence in the most innovative sectors, which are less exposed to the emerging countries' competition. This fuels an often confused debate with those who, equally superficially, tend to magnify the IDs' role and believe that Italy can cope with the economic and technological challenges of the future by merely exploiting the traditional resources of its IDs. This sensitive subject will be taken up again with a couple of observations in the conclusions of this chapter.

The chapter starts with an analysis of the structural features of the Italian manufacturing system, followed by a description of the four macro-sectors of the 'made-in-Italy' business and by a synthetic analysis of the macro-sectors' performance in comparison with 16 major countries in the world. Some attention will be briefly devoted to the tourist districts, where Italy is an experienced player. The chapter will end with a few comments on the alleged decline of the Italian development model based on districts and SMEs and on the resulting debate.

2. STRUCTURAL FEATURES OF THE ITALIAN MANUFACTURING SYSTEM

The Italian manufacturing system has some peculiarities, in comparison with other advanced countries, which have developed over the last decades. The first outstanding aspect is the role of the manufacturing sector, whose GDP share is bigger than elsewhere, with a correspondingly smaller services share. Secondly, the Italian manufacturing industry covers a minor share of the high-tech sectors in comparison with countries such as the US, Germany, UK, France or Japan. Italy does actually hold important positions in some high-tech sectors, such as aerospace (with the Finmeccanica group and the Varese cluster that has been developing around it) and others ranging from cruising ships (Fincantieri) to yachts and luxury and sports cars, from cosmetics to some types of medical equipment. However, these are niches, whereas up to the 1960s Italy had a wider and more regular presence in high-tech sectors thanks to world-class groups in applied research (Montecatini and Olivetti) that later faced an irreversible decline. On the whole, therefore, Italy's manufacturing production (and exports) hinges on the traditional 'made-in-Italy' activities, with a resulting wide gap in R&D expenditure of the Italian industry in comparison to other advanced countries. Over the last 40 years manufacturing has been expanding in the sectors of textiles–apparel, leather–footwear, furniture and in medium to high-technology sectors of light-duty engineering (household goods, taps, heating equipment, industrial machines and so on) which, together with the food sector, now account for about two-thirds of Italy's total manufacturing workforce. In these sectors, Italy has gradually pushed the other main advanced economies to marginal roles thanks to systematic, often informal, process and product innovation that has not been recorded in the international R&D statistics (Fortis and Carminati 2004). The Italian manufacturing system has therefore slowly switched to patterns seemingly more similar to those of the emerging countries than to those of the advanced countries, with a remarkable emphasis on traditional sectors and medium to high-tech mechanical engineering. However, in these sectors Italy has achieved high specialisation and levels of excellence leading to top international positions and to a considerable trade surplus which proved essential to sustain the Italian economy. Without the trade surplus in these activities Italy would have been unable to offset the heavy deficit in the trade balance of energy products and in other manufacturing areas (especially automotive, electronics and chemistry), where the loss of a strong core of large firms has made Italy inevitably dependent on imports (Table 30.1).

The Italian manufacturing system is also characterised by a widespread and large number of SMEs; and by a small number of large business groups and large-sized enterprises. In particular, Italy has the largest number of manufacturing firms in EU-25 (about 550 000): many more than the total of Germany, France, Sweden and The Netherlands considered together. About 530 000 of them have fewer than 50 employees and account for 84 per cent of the manufacturing workforce. It is therefore thanks to this large number of SMEs that Italy retains a healthy manufacturing sector that ranks second in terms of employment (4.8 million) after Germany (7.3 million) across the EU-25. Moreover are such SMEs that have contributed to Italy's sustained high levels of income.

Table 30.1   Italian trade balances (€ billion), 2001–06

Balance	2000	2001	2002	2003	2004	2005	2006
Typical made-in-Italy sectors	82.9	88.0	84.8	81.4	85.8	86.2	91.9
Energy	−28.8	−28.2	−25.9	−27.1	−30.9	−42.8	−54.0
Other sectors	−52.2	−50.6	−51.1	−52.7	−56.1	−52.8	−59.3
Total	1.9	9.2	7.8	1.6	−1.2	−9.4	−21.4

Source: Fondazione Edison based on ISTAT figures.

According to the latest ISTAT update based on the 2001 census figures, the districts are officially 156, some very large in size. Forty-five of them are specialised in textiles and apparel, 38 in mechanical engineering, 32 in household articles, 20 in leather and footwear and 21 in other sectors, including the food industry. However, in some previous research Fortis (2006) identified 437 main cluster-type production specialisations, located in 153 local labour market areas (LLMAs) – out of the total 686 LLMAs identified by ISTAT – and covering 91 Ateco product categories corresponding to the various 'made-in-Italy' sectors.[1] About 178 clusters are operating in the personal goods sector, 124 in mechanical engineering, 91 in household articles, 45 in food and beverages and 35 in paper, rubber and plastics.

The original handicraft localised capacities, spread all over the country but mostly in north and central Italy, developed over the years, giving rise to many industrial businesses and resulting in local production areas which, though mainly consisting of SMEs, have reached top market share positions. As a matter of fact, IDs account for remarkable employment, production and export levels, thus somehow compensating the effects of the small number of large business firms and groups. In other words, it could be said that, though Italy has few 'national champions' (that is, large business groups and enterprises), it can rely on a large number of 'local champions', namely IDs. It is worth mentioning that, for example, Italy's top four textiles and apparel districts employ more personnel than BMW or Royal Shell and about the same as Pfizer; the ten top furniture districts employ more people than Coca Cola or L'Oreal, while the total workforce of the seven top metal and metal-products districts exceeds Bayer's or Shanghai Baosteel Group. And the list could go on.

3. THE 'FOUR MAJORS' OF THE ITALIAN MANUFACTURING INDUSTRY: A DESCRIPTIVE ANALYSIS

Italy ranks highly worldwide in particular in four manufacturing sectors: (a) apparel and fashion; (b) furniture and interior decoration; (c) automation and mechanical engineering; and (d) food and beverages. Besides these four macro-sectors, which can be referred to as Italy's 'four majors', there are a few high-tech niche sectors where the country shows market leadership, including luxury cars, helicopters and aerospace, cruising ships, chemical and pharmaceutical specialties, diagnostical instruments and biomedicals. In the service sector, Italy has a very strong tourism sector based on the valuable resources in four major areas: natural environment, art, architecture and hospitality – which will be briefly reviewed later on.

Table 30.2   Italian manufacturing industry, year 2001

Sectors	No. of firms	No. of workers	Share of national manuf. workers (%)	Exports (€ billion)	Share of national manuf. exports (%)	Trade balance (€ billion)
Apparel and fashion[a]	108 164	891 210	18.2	50.5	19.0	28.7
Furniture and int. decoration[b]	93 948	494 644	10.1	17.8	6.7	12.7
Automation and mechanical[c]	141 620	1 334 913	27.3	68.6	25.8	41.5
Food and beverages[d]	66 936	446 785	9.1	14.0	5.3	-3.0
Total, 'four majors' of Italian manufacturing excellence	410 668	3 167 552	64.7	150.9	56.8	79.9
Total, other manuf. sectors	132 208	1 727 244	35.3	114.6	43.2	-35.4
Total, manuf. industry	542 876	4 894 796	100	265.5	100	44.5

Notes:
[a] Textiles and apparel, leather and footwear, jewellery and handsmith's goods, glasses and frames, buttons, umbrellas and zips.
[b] Wood and wooden products, furniture, tiles and ceramics, ornamental stones, lamps and lighting fixtures.
[c] Metal products, equipment, machinery and electrical household appliances, bicycles, motorcycles, yachts and pleasure boats, sporting goods.
[d] Food and beverages (including low-processing products like fresh and frozen meat and fresh milk).

Source: Fondazione Edison based on ISTAT figures.

As can be seen from Table 30.2, in 2001[2] the above-mentioned four main manufacturing specialisations of 'made in Italy' employed a total of 3 167 000 people, corresponding to about 65 per cent of the overall domestic manufacturing workforce,[3] with over 410 000 firms – 76 per cent of the whole Italian manufacturing industry. These figures would be even higher if the contribution from the upstream farming system to the food industry[4] was added. Regarding foreign trade, in 2001 exports from these four 'made-in-Italy' macro-sectors accounted for 57 per cent of the national manufacturing exports (amounting to about €151 billion), with a foreign trade surplus of €80 billion, or €83 billion if the low-processing food products are excluded. The surplus rose to the new record of about €92 billion in 2006 (see Table 30.1). In the same year the exports from the 101 main Italian manufacturing districts included in the *Edison Index* reached the new all time record of €67 billion (see Table 30.3). As previously mentioned, this surplus was essential for Italy. The contribution of the 'four majors' manufacturing sectors has offset the country's foreign trade deficits in raw materials and in the other manufacturing sectors (amounting to a total of €59 billion in 2006).

It is worth reviewing each of these four macro-sectors in more detail.

Table 30.3 Exports from the 101 main clusters (Edison Index) (€ billion), 2001 and 2006

	2001	2006	Absolute variation 2006–2001	Percentage variation 2006–2001
Apparel & fashion index (31 clusters)	28.9	25.8	–3.1	–10.7
Furniture & int. decoration index (16 clusters)	9.7	9.2	–0.5	-5.2
Automation & mechanical + others (30 clusters)	16.5	20.8	4.3	26.1
Food & wines index (17 clusters)	3.8	4.9	1.1	28.9
High-tech index (7 clusters)	4.1	6.1	2	48.8
Edison general index (101 main clusters)	63	66.8	3.8	6.0

Source: Fondazione Edison based on ISTAT figures.

3.1 Apparel and fashion

The apparel and fashion system includes four big sectors: textiles and apparel, together with related accessories; leather goods and footwear; eyewear; jewellery and goldsmiths' wares.

Based on the 2001 census figures these four manufacturing areas employed 891 000 people – 18.2 per cent of the total manufacturing employment, with 108 000 firms. The occupational size of the apparel and fashion sector lost 244 000 jobs between 1991 and 2001 (of which 107 000 between 1996 and 2001) as a result of reorganisation, industry relocation or closures, especially in textiles and apparel, footwear and, to a lesser extent, leather. A better capacity to maintain their occupational levels, although with problems, was shown by eyewear, goldsmith's wares and jewellery and tanneries.

Highly-specialised locations[5] in the apparel and fashion sector are: the districts of Arzignano in leather tanning; Arezzo, Alessandria (with the Valenza Po area) and Vicenza in goldsmiths; Civitanova Marche in leather shoes and Castel Goffredo in women's stockings. But the largest workforce is employed in the four big textiles and apparel districts in Prato, Biella, Busto Arsizio and Como. Of remarkable importance in this sector is also Santa Croce sull'Arno, which is highly specialised in tanning and footwear.

As far as exports are concerned, in 2001, these highly-specialised locations accounted for around 19 per cent of the total national exports (a total amount of €50.5 billion including agricultural production), generating a foreign trade surplus of €28.7 billion. In international markets, Italy is still the world leader in many niches of the apparel and fashion production; however in the last few years China has been able to erode Italy's market shares worldwide to the point that both exports and thereby the foreign trade surplus dramatically contracted. By way of example, between 2001 and 2006 the exports from the 31 main apparel and fashion districts, selected from the *Edison exports index of the Italian industrial districts*,[6] fell by 10.5 per cent from €28.9 to €25.9 billion.

3.2 Furniture and interior decoration

The interior design sector consists mainly of four big components: wood and furniture, lamps and lighting fixtures, ceramic tiles and ornamental stones. Mechanical products such as household articles, taps, knobs and handles, heating and cooling equipment, instead, are included in the automation and mechanical engineering products. Other sectors where Italian companies appear to be in a leading position, though involving to a smaller extent exports, are those of glass and mosaics for furniture, as well as the building industry and related activities.

Based on the 2001 census figures, the four main furniture and interior design sectors accounted for 10.1 per cent of the total manufacturing workforce – corresponding to 94 000 firms and 494 600 employees. In particular, within the furniture and interior design sector, a large share of employment is in the wood and furniture component. Over the period 1991–2001, this sector recorded employment reductions too, although more moderate than in the apparel and fashion sector, for a total of around 19 000 jobs, later, however, substantially maintaining satisfactory occupational levels.

In the furniture and interior design sector, highly-specialised locations are: Sassuolo for ceramic tiles; Seregno (Brianza) and Pordenone (Alto Livenza) for wooden furniture; and Altamura, Matera and Gioia del Colle for sofas manufacturing. A very high specialisation coefficient was also found for ceramic sanitary ware in Civita Castellana, for the chair district in Manzano and San Giovanni al Natisone (Gorizia, Friuli region), and for ornamental stones in Verona and Pietrasanta-Carrara.

In 2001, exports from the furniture and interior design sector amounted to €17.8 billion, with a foreign trade surplus of €12.7 billion. As to its position on the international markets, this sector holds considerable exports records. However, again Chinese competition is a growing threat; for example, the exports from the 16 main furniture and interior design clusters, selected from the *Edison exports index of the Italian industrial districts*, fell by 5.6 per cent, from €9.7 to €9.2 billion between 2001 and 2006, though some recovery has been observed since 2005 when exports amounted to €8.9 billion.

3.3 Automation and mechanical engineering

The automation and mechanical engineering sector is another area of excellence in the Italian manufacturing industry. It includes metal products (except for the metallurgical industry), mechanical equipment, industrial machineries (for wood, footwear, packaging, plastic materials and the food industry), some segments of the transport sector (luxury cars, motorcycles and bicycles), taps and valves, houseware, electrical household appliances, farming machines, yachts, as well as some niche productions such as grape crushing, wine-pressing machines, automatic machines for product sales, bike saddles, metal casting machines, roundabouts and so on.

Italy is the exports leader in many of these sectors and competes with Germany, Japan and the US in some others. This is therefore an essential component of the 'made-in-Italy' business, with figures even above those for the apparel and fashion sector with respect to employment, number of firms, exports and foreign trade surplus. In 2001, this sectors (excluding luxury-sports cars and cruising ships) recorded more than 141 000 firms and 1 330 000 employees, equal to 27.3 per cent of the national manufacturing workforce. Contrary to the apparel–fashion and furniture–interior design sectors, between 1991 and 2001 automation and mechanical engineering increased its workforce by 146 000, of which 126 000 was in the 1996–2001 period, thus partially offsetting the unfavourable employment trends of the other two former sectors. The most significant employment increases were recorded mainly in the components of general-purpose machines and equipment, machine tools, taps and valves, metal moulding and treatment, and toll manufacturing in mechanical engineering. Based on the census figures, in 2001 the metal working sector involved about 696 000 jobs.[7]

Among the most highly-specialised locations, it is worth mentioning the Borgomanero and Borgosesia as well as the Lumezzane districts, both leaders in the taps and valves sector; Lumezzane is also strong in houseware and cutlery. Other important specialised locations are Bologna (which is not strictly an ID, but is hosting a strong industrial cluster) for packaging machines, Lecco for metal products, Parma for food processing machines, Vigevano for machines for the leather industry, Mirandola for medical equipment, Biella and Prato for textile machines, Omegna for metal houseware and Lucca for paper industry machines.

Mention should also be made of Viareggio and La Spezia in pleasure and sports boats, Reggio Emilia in farming machines and Recanati in musical instruments.

Regarding exports, which in 2001 reached €68.6 billion, with the remarkable foreign trade surplus of €41.5 billion, Italy is the top world exporter in many specific classes of products. In addition, Italy has the largest foreign trade surplus in the world in taps and valves, where it is the second-ranking exporter. A number of second and third positions, too, are held by Italy among exporters.

Unlike the apparel–fashion and the furniture–interior design sectors, automation and mechanical engineering has not been affected by the growing Asian, especially Chinese, competition. Over the 2001–06 period – which was rather critical for the household and the personal goods sectors – the mechanical products' exports kept growing; as a matter of fact, exports from the 30 main clusters in the sector and included in the *Edison exports index of the Italian industrial districts*,[8] rose by 25.8 per cent from €16.5 to €20.8 billion.

3.4 Food and beverages

The fourth 'major' of Italy's production excellence is the food and beverages sector: in 2001, it employed 447 000 people corresponding to 9.1 per cent of the Italian manufacturing workforce and counted 67 000 enterprises.

Among its most highly-specialised locations, top employment levels are recorded in Langhirano, Parma and Modena in meat-based products, and in Nocera Inferiore, Nola, Sarno and Torre del Greco (Campania) in industrial tomato processing, followed by Alba in wines and Gioia del Colle in cheese. It should be emphasised, however, that neither the agricultural districts, such as that of apples (Trent) and various fruits (in Emilia-Romagna), nor viticulture were considered here because they are not included in manufacturing.

As regards exports, in 2001 they amounted to €14 billion, with a €3 billion deficit because Italy is a big importer of meat, fish and dairy products. However, if low-processing products such as fresh and frozen meat and fresh milk are excluded, the industrial sector shows a small surplus: in 2003, for example, the trade surplus was about €2 billion. Products associated to the typical Mediterranean cuisine are the high points of the Italian agro-food industry. In particular, Italy is a leading world exporter of many types of such products; in 2003 exports for these products amounted to €9 billion, with a surplus of as much as €7 billion.

4. THE INTERNATIONAL PERFORMANCE OF THE 'FOUR MAJORS' OF THE ITALIAN MANUFACTURING INDUSTRY

Based on a Fondazione Edison analysis (2006b) comparing the 2005 foreign trade figures from authoritative statistics sources (UN Comtrade, WTO, OECD, Eurostat and ISTAT) concerning 16 major world countries[9] Italy is confirmed as the OECD area's trade surplus leader in the products from the 'four majors', followed by Germany and Japan, and ranks second after China in the world:[10] in 2005 the 'four majors' surplus amounted to US$100 billion, China's jumped to US$144 billion, while Germany and Japan recorded US$81 and US$52 billion, respectively.

Figures from the Fondazione Edison's research show that more than half of the Italian surplus in the four macro-sectors of the 'made in Italy' is concentrated in the automation and mechanical engineering sectors (US$53.2 billion); while apparel and fashion (US$27.1 billion) ranks at second place despite the growing competition from China and other emerging countries, followed by furniture and interior design (US$14.5 billion) and 'Mediterranean food' and wines (US$5.5 billion).

In particular, considering these four macro-sectors, in 2005 Italy recorded the second-best surplus in the apparel–fashion and furniture–interior design sectors (as seen above, with US$27.1 and US$14.5 billion) after China whose surplus figures were US$126 and US$19.3 billion, respectively. Italy was confirmed to have a leading position in the niche market of 'Mediterranean food' and wines (US$5.5 billion), before France and Spain (US$5.1 and US$2.5 billion, respectively) and to rank third in automation and mechanical engineering sector (US$53.2 billion) after Germany (US$99.5 billion) and Japan (US$88.7 billion).

The significant erosion of the Italian foreign trade surplus recorded in apparel and fashion between 2002 and 2005, and its more modest decline in the furniture and interior design sector were mainly the result of China's commercial aggressiveness, which is enhanced by asymmetric competition factors – among them the artificial devaluation of the yuan, which is still anchored to an increasingly weaker dollar even though Beijing's currency reserves have reached US$1000 billion and are among the largest in the world, and by the counterfeiting of 'made-in-Italy' brands and products. However, the good international performance of 'Mediterranean food' and wines and above all of the automation and mechanical engineering sector counterbalanced, to a large extent, the losses suffered by Italy in personal and household goods in the last few years, which remain nonetheless two essential pillars of Italy's foreign trade.

It is also important to stress that, within automation and mechanical engineering, the favourable trend of the machine and equipment surplus continued throughout 2006.

5. TOURISM, A VALUABLE RESOURCE

The presence of firm clustering is important not only in the manufacturing industry but also in other business activities like tourism. Tourism is actually a pillar of the Italian economy and it is an essential item in the trade balance of many local systems.

Although Law no. 135/2001 introduced the 'local tourist system', the maps of Italian tourist local systems developed so far are not as good as the maps on the IDs and clusters.

ISTAT identified 259 'tourist local systems' based on the latest Census (2001), that is over 37.8 per cent of the 686 LLMAs that partition the Italian territory. Their total population is 19.8 million, corresponding to 34.8 per cent of Italy's total population. However, these figures include some large metropolitan LLMAs which, in our opinion, give a somewhat distorted representation of the real size of the phenomenon. More selective maps of the local tourist systems (Capone 2004) are to be preferred in our opinion.

The Edison Foundation has identified 141 'specialised tourist local systems', still based on the ISTAT LLMAs' geography but following stricter criteria and excluding the LLMAs of the bigger municipalities. The 141 tourist local systems were selected as those LLMAs showing a combination of two parameters: (a) a minimum workforce in hotels, bars and similar services; (b) a minimum threshold of the location coefficients of the tourist services in the LLMAs.[11]

The 141 'specialised tourist LLMAs' selected by the Edison Foundation cover 6.7 million inhabitants, with a total employment in related business such as hotels and bars, of 207 800, corresponding to a quarter of the total sector's workforce in Italy.[12]

The importance of the tourist systems for a great number of local communities and for Italy in general is strategic, because of its major contribution both to employment and to the GDP. Italy's foreign trade surplus in this sector dropped by as much as €3.5 billion, from €12.9 to €9.4 billion between 2000 and 2003, with a sharp drop in foreign tourists in Italian hotels. Despite this reduction in 2003, Italy ranked third, after France and Spain, in terms of tourist arrivals and fourth in the world in terms of international arrivals and income from foreign visitors.

6. CONCLUSIONS

The peculiar structure of the Italian production system, characterised by districts and SMEs mainly operating in so-called traditional sectors, is frequently mentioned as a cause of Italy's alleged loss of competitiveness and, therefore, of its difficulties in the last few years. However, in this work we have tried to show quite the opposite. If, on the one hand, a slight increase in the average size of Italian firms could help and improve trading capabilities in the international markets, expand their presence in high-tech sectors and increase their R&D spending, it is also true that a large number of SMEs, far from being a weakness in the country's economy, are in fact a source of great strength. Italy has proportionally more entrepreneurs and less employees than elsewhere, with all the resulting advantages in terms of liveliness in the economic and social fabric, propensity to innovation (though often not formalised and therefore not recorded in statistics), and social welfare support.

Furthermore districts and clusters in Italy help to offset the relative weakness of this country in terms of the number and presence of large businesses and groups. Drawing on a Mediobanca-Unioncamere survey (2005), an important set of about 4000 medium sized enterprises[13] is gaining strength in Italy. Many of these enterprises are based in districts or other areas characterised by industrial clusters, and operate in the typical 'made-in-Italy' sectors.[14]

According to some commentators, the specialisation of the Italian manufacturing industry in the so-called traditional sectors could be a source of weakness now and in the future because of the relentless progress of China, whose overall foreign trade surplus is now larger than the Italian one in the four macro manufacturing sectors analysed above, coming to the overhasty conclusion that the Italian development model is superseded. Therefore, according to this way of thinking, Italy should urgently: (a) reduce its presence in manufacturing, withdrawing, if necessary, from 'mature' sectors such as textiles or footwear; (b) diversify its activity into new higher-tech industrial sectors; (c) expand quickly into the advanced service industry.

We agree on these recipes only to a very limited extent. In connection with the first point, figures such as those commented before show that Italy has not suffered a debacle in its foreign trade in the last years of China's roaring development, often based on dumping and asymmetric competition. In addition, it is possible that the China's offensive in the textiles–apparel and footwear sectors has reached its peak. As to India, in our opinion it is not likely to become a new China because it has a weaker manufacturing vocation and greater propensity to the service industry. There is therefore no reason why Italy, after overcoming the initial and more aggressive period of the Chinese trade boom with relatively modest losses, should now reduce or even give up manufacturing and seek other development areas. This is also because – moving to consider the second and third points above – Italy can hardly become a leader in the high value-added service industry, and at the same time, no high-tech sectors are in sight that could be expanded overnight, after abandoning chemistry and electronics in the past decades after the demise of Montedison and Olivetti.

The only realistic strategy for our enterprises is to switch to higher value-added areas inside the traditional 'made-in-Italy' sectors, which, far from facing an irreversible decline, will remain clear elements of strengths in the Italian economy now and in the future. To this purpose, however, a larger number of Italian enterprises should be able to expand in size; larger enterprises can invest more in R&D and, where necessary, can even relocate their production and commercial premises abroad with a view to entering new markets. They can promote stronger and internationally better known brands through adequate advertising and marketing investments to cope with the challenge of global competition, and they can expand more widely abroad (Fortis 2005).

In conclusion, under the present conditions, with Italian large enterprises becoming fewer and fewer and the State withdrawing from business activities, the districts are valuable 'incubators' of new enterprises able to compete effectively. This is witnessed by the fact that between 1991 and 2001 Italy recorded a net increase of 305 units in the number of medium to large-size manufacturing enterprises (50–499 workers), 281 of which emerged in a restricted sample of 20 districts. This shows that, if Italy has to hope for a new and larger breed of leading enterprises, efforts should be concentrated locally once again. The role of districts in Italy remains central in any scheme or project aimed at strengthening its competitive system.

NOTES

1. Note that the production specialisations identified in Fortis (2006) do not include all of the possible cluster specialisation cases, but only the major ones.
2. The last Italian Census of production by ISTAT was in 2001.
3. These figures do not include the car sector, though Italy is a big specialist in sport and luxury cars.
4. The links between agriculture and manufacturing are well visible in the sector of wine, spirits and vinegars, a real 'pillar' in the 'made-in-Italy' food industry. According to a study made by the Agricultural Science Faculty of Bologna University in collaboration with Federvini (association of wine producers) in 2001 this sector consisted of over 237 000 enterprises operating in viticulture and wine making, over 194 000 being wine grower and almost 43 000 wine growers and makers. Over 45 000 wine cellars and 800 producers of spirits, brandy and vinegars should be added. The vineyard workforce amounts to about 465 000 people, 94 000 being full-time workers, while about 86 000 people are employed full time in the distribution chain. On the whole, the wine, spirits and vinegar sector employs about 236 000 full-time workers and along the supply chain it reaches 700 000 people; its total sales revenue is estimated at over €20 billion; its allied consumption (energy, bottles, caps, labels and cardboard) exceeds €2 billion.
5. Highly-specialised locations/districts are those with a high specialisation coefficient, namely a location quotient above 5. See Sforzi (in this volume).
6. See Fondazione Edison (2006a) for the index construction.
7. Luxury cars are not included.
8. Four plastics processing and one paper districts were also included in this index.
9. Italy, Germany, France, UK, Spain, Sweden, Russia, US, Canada, Mexico, Brazil, China, Japan, South Korea and India.
10. Please note that in this study the furniture and interior design sector does not include lamps and lighting fixtures; in the same way, automation and the mechanical engineering sector does not include electrical, electronic and telecommunications equipment, precision instruments and means of transport (cars, planes, bicycles and motorcycles); the food and beverages sector includes here only processed products, namely: noodles, tomato products, olive oil, fruit juices, hams and other processed pork, and wines. In addition, though the products considered do not cover all the sectors of excellence of the Italian manufacturing industry, which extend beyond the 'four majors' (such as perfumes, glue and adhesives, other specialty chemicals, rubber and plastics articles, cruising ships and so on) they still represent fairly well the core of the more specialised 'made-in-Italy' sectors in the international trade.
11. The local tourist systems are LLMAs characterised by a high local concentration of workers in consumer services, and specifically by a tourist services localisation coefficient greater than the average national value (ISTAT 2005).
12. A few examples are Limone sul Garda, Badia, Ortisei, Moena, Castelrotto and Malcesine, where one family out of two–three has one component working in these sectors; one family out of four–five at Naturno, San Candido, Arzachena, Capri, Porto Azzurro, Cortina d'Ampezzo, Amalfi, Courmayeur, Meran and Bormio; one family out of six–seven at Brunico, Fiuggi, Pinzolo-Madonna di Campiglio, Montepulciano-Chianciano, Ischia, Portoferraio and so on.
13. Enterprises with 50–499 employees and sales between €13 and 260 million.
14. As mentioned in the Mediobanca-Unioncamere report, 'the main activity of medium-sized enterprises concerns the typical made-in-Italy sectors, which account for about two thirds of sales and 70 per cent of exports' (2006, p. xiv).

31. Regional peculiarities in Italian industrial districts

Francesco Musotti[*]

1. INTRODUCTION

An industrial district (ID) is a socio-economic entity which is much larger and more complex than its population of firms, and analysing the phenomena which affect it cannot generally be reduced, as for clusters *à la* Porter, to a study of inter-firm manufacturing systems.

First of all, each ID is a local society,[1] and thus an entity the formation of which was made possible by the history of not strictly economic prerequisites, but rather social, political, institutional and cultural. The mix between these prerequisites and the offer of particular public goods by institutional actors who operate in contact with firms, in relatively recent times and in favourable market conditions, have had the result of releasing the effects of the prerequisites, allowing stage specialisation (and the multiplication of the corresponding subpopulations of small productive units) in the most well-established industry in that territory, and gaining competitive advantages on international markets.

In the Italian experience in particular, these prerequisites have been so diffuse, extensive and pervasive that the proliferation of IDs profited by a kind of humus, equally propitious in regions formed by sometimes centuries-long, separate and very different histories.[2]

The political unification of Italy was tardy, 1861, and the later tendency to the persistence, more or less until the Second World War, of labour division between each city and its surroundings, led to considerable difficulties in creating markets and a truly national bourgeois class. These factors meant that the developmental patterns of IDs, from their very beginnings, were very clearly differentiated at the regional level. The variety of the economic opportunities and the strategies of extra-firm organisations which gave rise to these patterns, as well as the timescale of such opportunities and strategies, have both played a substantial part in defining the current Italian geography of IDs – a geography both fragmented and composite.

An exhaustive interpretation of these complex conditions would require in-depth analyses which are beyond the scope of this contribution. Nevertheless, we attempt here to summarise the prerequisites which have represented the approximately common background of Italian districts (Section 2), to recall the way in which they were combined with the different regional models, depending on the specific, and decisive, workings of economic, political and institutional circumstances (Sections 3 and 4), and to conclude with some personal reflections, directed towards favouring the lines along which path dependency runs.

2. PREREQUISITES

2.1 The urban manufacturing background: the civilisation of the *communes*

The Italian regions which afforded the most favourable socio-cultural environment to the birth and consolidation of IDs essentially share a geographic and historical trait: that of belonging to the mainland peninsula (Centre-North), that is, the part of Italy which lived through the so-called 'communal civilisation' (Fuà 1983). This was a time of social transformation which, ranging from the 13th century to the mid-17th century, included the end of the Middle Ages and the so-called 'civil humanism' (Garin 1994). Its flourishing civil economy (Gualerni 2001; Bruni and Zamagni 2004) was galvanised by manufacturing and crafts and by the entrepreneurial spirit of a network of cities of various sizes, enjoying extraordinary political liberty where, as Coluccio Salutati notes, the ideals of an active life were combined with an attitude towards 'contemplation' (Gualerni 2001).

In an environment of this kind, results were perceived as the reward, ethically founded, of the capacity to innovate both goods and commercial and financial techniques (Luzzatto 1978). This capacity in turn was supported by an equally fertile predisposition to create new institutions, which made the nature and functioning of markets increasingly more civil and transparent, to the extent of strengthening that basis of trust, on the part of producers and intermediaries, so essential to enhancing 'business affairs'.

Patronage was sustained by the wealth which, hand in hand with economic fervour, gradually accumulated, thanks to the demand for both mobile and immobile assets, and often reached levels of splendid formal refinement (for example, palaces and various kinds of residences, works of art, furnishings and decorations, ceramics, cutlery, fabrics, clothing), providing an enormous stimulus to artisan crafts. The world of 'artisan workshops', which were the basis for these trades, served as an eternally regenerative system of contextual and tacit knowledge which derived from the enhanced creativity of each buyer.

This (progressive) phase of the 'communal civilisation' only lasted a relatively short time, due to the conflicts between and among cities, the supremacy of local *seigneuries*, which harshly repressed political liberty, and the development as in the rest of Europe of new manufacturing systems, capable of producing qualitatively less precious but also far cheaper wares, and thus of imposing market expansion to their own advantage (C. Cipolla 1990).

However, the most characteristic elements of the Italian civil economy were not lost in the centuries to come (Zamagni 1990). Together with a production culture marked by the creativity, good taste and flexibility of artisan imprinting, even when it could be expressed in truly industrial forms, there are at least three types of modern organisations which reveal the relative continuity, if not precisely with that world, with what followed it: so-called local banks, technical schools (professional institutes, or true technical institutes) and the political organisations closest to civil society: the *communes*.

Today's local banks (including first of all independent savings banks and cooperative banks) support firms and savings rooted in the local environment. On the basis of relationships in which personal acquaintance plays a far greater role than for other types of banks (see Alessandrini in this volume), they share the principles that, at the peak of civil economy, inspired credit provision for the less well off through 'pawnbrokers'.

When closely related to a 'dominant' local industry, technical schools can act as essential links between the human capital requirements of firms and the socio-economic opportunities of families; they somehow inherit those training functions which were so typical of the artisan workshops, that is, they enable the dissemination of the codified knowledge which, together with local contextual (tacit) knowledge, forms the foundation of a place's production activity (see Section 1 in this volume).

For their part, the *communes* have always been the 'natural' space for the administration of local governance, since they have taken on the task of reconciling the stimuli to economic change, with the survival of the civic values and of the local sense of identity – for instance, through the redistribution of income, regulatory policies, supply of public goods, promotion of local interest to regional and national powers, and the creation of consensus with respect to paths of development.

2.2 The rural and agricultural economy: the emergence of small farms

In the Renaissance period, guilds opposed rural manufacturing (C. Cipolla 1990), which was quite extensive in other European countries, for example with the *Verlagssystem* and *Kaufsystem* (Kriedte, Medick and Schlumbohm 1984). During the declining phase of 'communal civilisation', the economy of central and northern Italian cities was concentrated on their immediate surroundings – essentially agriculture – in the form of small farms. In some regions, these were regulated by contracts of share tenancy; in others, they were in the hands of either small peasant owners or small tenant farmers.

The establishment of small farms coincided with the residential and productive expansion of the population, and thereby the dense territorial colonisation of the countryside, through more active agriculture and animal husbandry, and a great labour/output ratio. The size and characteristics of these farms were closely linked with the number and competence of the family members who worked on them. They were generally small in size, close to each other, and so dense as to form a sort of immense rural city, within which many smaller centres congregated, serving to support and coordinate the productive and reproductive activities of all.

An agricultural economy of this type was based on an abundance of labour which was coupled with land-improving investments, and minimised the need for working capital and mechanical equipment. This suited the hilly and uneven terrain of many Italian regions, whereas areas with more fertile land and on plains saw a form of proto-capitalist (and, from the 18th century onwards, capitalist) agriculture which heavily relied on fixed capital to maximise labour productivity.

The capacity to create and reproduce a socio-productive culture was intrinsic to both peasant and proto-capitalist systems. This was associated with the incorporation of codified knowledge coming from the most advanced agronomic sciences. In one case, it was the family – often a group of families in the case of shared tenancy – with its own structure and code of behaviour, which had an interest in passing on its knowledge so as to reproduce the system of agricultural production. The family autonomously organised very fragmented activities which were difficult to monitor (for instance, crop rotation), and managed labour and the distribution of task across the family members with a great level of flexibility, elasticity and adaptation to always uncertain environmental conditions. On the contrary, in the capitalist agricultural system, such management of agricultural activities was dictated by the 'entrepreneurial agronomists', who relied on principles of efficiency and technical discipline applied to a labour force paid for *ex ante* with respect to output production on the basis of parameters of efficiency derived from a specialised and standardised type of farming.

It is worth noting that, in the small farms, the social integration of 'neighbouring families', and the related emergence of shared civil values, was at same time entwined with a network of production activities that generated 'local external economies' (labour exchanges, phase markets, common purchases of farming services by third parties, public circulation of productive knowledge, and so on). Conversely, agricultural firms embracing the capitalist system tended towards technical self-sufficiency and maximised 'internal scale economies' instead.

By and large, according to Arrigo Serpieri (founder of the Italian economic and agrarian school), the term 'rurality' is associated with the agricultural economy of the small farming system (Serpieri 1946).

In farmed countryside, it is also worth distinguishing between areas occupied by small share tenants and those occupied by landowners. The former constituted a world in which families were frustrated by the impossibility of owning their own land, and succeeded nevertheless in organising production activities with a great sense of social achievement.

3. THE CREATION OF AN URBANISED COUNTRYSIDE AND THE 'COAGULATION' OF DISTRICTS

With the exception of the 'industrial triangle' between Milan, Turin and Genoa, many niches *à la* Von Thunen (that is, formed of relatively isolated towns and their surroundings) persisted in manufacturing activities unrelated to the production of mass-produced goods, and farms proliferated in the same territorial niches. Until the mid-20th century, they formed a socio-cultural block which was singularly opposed to Italy's taking the 'conventional' road of standard capitalist development of the English type. This same block, however, managed to activate its prerequisites for the emergence of IDs and a model of production that, in the surge of post-Second World War reconstruction, in the so-called 'Glorious thirty years' – and in any case supported by basic industry which had developed in the triangle – succeeded in leaving local niches and opening up to international markets.

Artisan knowledge, passed on from one generation to another in many sometimes small cities, was reactivated, thanks to the sudden new demand for goods for the person and for the home. From an increasing level of affluence, this demand was induced to reject mass-produced articles, and became fragmented according to tastes and fashions.

In this new scenario, artisans and small industrialists were obliged to counterbalance their own spirit of independence due to the generally limited availability of individual capital. It was impossible, in a reasonably short span of time, to shift from small- to large-scale firms. The only practicable solution was the division, and at the same time integration, of labour into local agglomerations of small, even tiny, firms, which: (a) allowed the threshold of necessary investment to be lowered, since each productive unit was specialised in a segment of a production process; (b) triggered a virtuous spiral of 'learning by doing' *à la* Smith; (c) benefitted by a constant flow of new entrepreneurial energy, essential if agglomerations were to satisfy volatile and increasingly demanding consumers.

Industrialisation became scattered among many small, independent factories, realising many local external economies (static, but above all dynamic) of many different kinds. Through 'communities' of producers with low transaction costs, industry managed to implement the breakdown of productive processes described by the fund-flow model (see Georgescu-Roegen 1976; Tani in this volume).

The countryside offered a labour force which was attracted more by the model of modern life than by higher wages, and which was ready to be involved in the industrial life of firms. In short, a labour force which was ready to make all the necessary sacrifices to learn new professional practices.

In a second phase, the successive generations who experienced leaving farm life at a young age found themselves no longer ready to be employed in factories but, instead, preferred to start up their own small businesses. The idea of an autonomous and entrepreneurial venture contributed towards the proliferation of small-scale firms in the local *filières*. This new generation of small entrepreneurs drew some of their skills from the family culture that had modelled for centuries the principles of labour organisation in the farming system, through reliance on acumen in buying and selling and an ambition to ascend socially.[3]

The territorial effects of this interpenetration between the urban-artisan world and the farming system in the countryside were considerable, and converged to create a true 'urbanised countryside' (Becattini 1975a, 2001c; Becattini, Bellandi and Falorni 1983). First, the rise of commuters who travelled from and to the rural localities led to the expansion of an urban sprawl of villages and towns where new houses were built nearer the new workplaces, yet not too far away from the old farms. A fabric of micro-firms then developed and flourished in these towns and their immediate surroundings, exploiting the professional competence which the commuters had acquired in the meantime (due to the 'spillover effect' of already launched industrial development or the propagation of other industries). These centres expanded to the point of being physically joined to each other. The manufacturing towns triggered the entire process of industrial development, and the intense activities of such dense, extended, urbanised countryside congregated into 'compact IDs' (Becattini, Bellandi and Falorni 1983).

4. FOUR REGIONAL DISTRICT MODELS

An understanding of the prerequisites of the districtualisation process must also include other strictly economic and political-institutional factors, arising in the post-Second World War period. In other words, the prerequisites sketched above must be understood as a necessary but not sufficient condition for a certain type of industrial development.

The diverse regional patterns of district development across Italy which we observe today derive not only from differences in the urban and rural background, but mainly from the different market opportunities, as well as from the nature and role of business and trade organisations which, in each region, supplied firms with indispensable support and local public goods.

4.1 IDs in central Italian regions (Tuscany, Umbria, Marches, northern Abruzzo)

The central Italian regions were undoubtedly the best equipped with the above-mentioned prerequisites leading to the emergence of IDs, from the urban-manufacturing case of Tuscany, to the colonisation of share tenancy in the Marches. This is confirmed by recent evidence which shows that these regions still host typical districts, especially in light industries, and have done so since the 1970s.

First, Tuscany's market specialisations mainly coincided with the fashion industries, and therefore with goods for the person, developed to create world class brands that are more generally referred to as 'made in Italy'. They were further enhanced by tourism, particularly in the highly-developed artistic centres around the formidable Pisa–Florence–Siena 'triangle' (Becattini 1986a).

Second, there was the role played by local policymakers, especially the Italian Communist Party with extraordinary pragmatism towards its ideological background, in mobilising all the instruments of the red political subculture towards a 'light' industrial model (that is, with a low capital/product ratio) (Trigilia 1986). These policymakers were able to match the very individualistic impulse to social revenge of the early share-tenant families with the maintenance of social cohesion. In our opinion, this match does much to explain the close links in the internal district markets (phase markets) between competitive mechanisms and cooperative attitudes. Although the two were generally incompatible, it was precisely in the districts that they found a precious synergy. The propensity to cooperate between producers, who nevertheless jealously wished to maintain their own independence, encouraged labour division, and the more this division was successful, the faster the barriers to entry to local industry (in terms of financial and technical capital, as well as relational capital) – in other words, the threshold of social ascent – fell.

This factor appears to explain why the average size of companies in the post share-tenancy regions tends even today to be smaller than in the north. On one hand, this may mean a finer breakdown of productive processes, and thus a greater capacity to generate local external economies; on the other, it may lead to a greater demand–supply of local public assets (Burroni 2001).

On the political and institutional plane again, equally important was the role of trade unions and of the model of industrial relations which they set up with the employers' organisations. This role was more pragmatic than that implemented within large-scale firms in the Northwest industrial triangle: moderate from the various viewpoints of possible claims (Brusco and Paba 1997), and inclined first of all to reinforce the basis for extending the productive base and the growth of good job opportunities.

Clearly, the combinations between these two sets of strategies, by local governments on one hand and by trade unions on the other, did produce some dynamic effects. The performance, for example, of an efficient, extensive, so-called 'municipal' system of welfare greatly contributed towards integrating salary levels, thus maintaining a delicate balance between efficiency and equity. With the help of trade unions, reduced labour costs (and thus the reproduction of firms' competitive advantages) were combined with the protection of widespread welfare and, thereby, of social cohesion.

Yet again, the high quality of life which derived from the virtuous spiral just described sharpened the already quick wits of IDs in competitively producing personal and household articles (ibid.).

4.2 IDs in the northern Italian regions (Piedmont, Lombardy, Veneto, Friuli)

The map of Italian IDs identified by the Italian Statistical Office (ISTAT) (IPI 2002) with the elaboration of 1991 census data overlaps with the territories of small rented property according the map of land properties prepared by INEA in the 1950s

(Medici 1956). This is evidence of the link between the distribution of districts in the northern regions of Italy and the agricultural jigsaw of small rented properties characterising those areas 35 years before. Indeed, small rented property appears to have taken over the role played elsewhere by share tenancy, in terms of both socio-economic 'settlements' and training for entrepreneurial ability.[4]

With respect to the share-tenancy regions, the prevalence of small rented property seems to have involved a social climate predisposed towards what has been called the 'white subculture' (Trigilia 1986), that is, the set of symbolic and material resources that were mobilised on a popular level by the Church and various Catholic organisations, including political, trade unions, social assistance, associations, related to it. In this system of values, the explicit aversion to binding and active forms of political regulation and, therefore, confidence in independence were of great importance; indeed, these attitudes involved entrepreneurs and single persons, and mobilised the autonomy of networks of civil cohesion as regards the redistribution of income.

In such a socio-cultural context, the development of IDs was characterised by greater recourse to market mechanisms, made reliable precisely by those networks of interpersonal relations and by activities which were not excessively penetrated by local government. Even at the present time, inside these IDs, all this enhances the dynamism of relatively large and more self-sufficient medium-sized firms, and involves a lower demand–supply of local public assets (Burroni 2001) and a greater propensity to set up production activities abroad.

The political dimension in these regions was not weaker than in the central ones. The ideological affinity between the white subculture (namely, Catholic) and the political party in power in the national government for almost 50 years after the Second World War, created a privileged link with central government (this was particularly so in the Veneto region). The two key contributions were the flows of public spending for supporting both large infrastructural networks and private investment, and the normative regimes permitting various kinds of relief and other facilities to artisan enterprises (Arrighetti and Seravalli 1997). Not by chance, the political movement called *Lega Nord* ('Northern League'), with its federalist connotations, has emerged recently in the Italian political scene from this very part of Italy, especially in those IDs which were more affected by the creation of the 'single market', the so-called 'Maastricht regime', which endangered that privileged link.

Another feature of the northern districts was their geographic location – within or nearby the industrial triangle and thus in the classic areas of large-scale capitalist development founded on capital accumulation and codified knowledge. It could be argued that the industrial triangle, with its spillover effect of technological and managerial competence and its generally mature industrial culture, enhanced the development of IDs in adjacent areas enabling the partial reconversion of these regions, particularly when extraordinary high wages seriously harmed the large firm sector. In that context IDs were able to absorb some labour and to trigger a process of regional reconversion that gave a role to firms of smaller size. In these regions such reconversion enhanced the socio-cultural energies which had existed before the development of large-scale enterprises and outlived them in several productive niches. This may explain, mainly in Lombardy, the distribution of IDs specialised in mechanical sectors.

4.3   IDs in Emilia-Romagna

Emilia-Romagna underwent a peculiar form of ID development, now visible in its two main market specialisations: the food, or rather, animal feed industry, and the mechanical industry.

In Emilia, share tenancy agriculture was not as strong as in the central regions. Large-scale reclamation works, like those near Ravenna, created socio-economic situations which destabilised the traditional family and favoured the establishment of firms with many employed workers. In many cases, Emilian share tenants managed to become emancipated and took on the role of the farmer-renters of very fertile land. The spread of an industrial crop such as hemp, destined for export, opened up the market considerably.

But other important aspects of the Emilian agricultural world, nowadays, should also be noted: the high incomes which owners managed to achieve were translated into robust demand and the strengthening of local artisan work (Zamagni 1997). And the rich agricultural production, *strictu sensu*, extended locally into industrial transformation. In addition to these, the same rich productions acted as a considerable stimulus to the development of the associated specialised mechanical industry. It is not by chance that, today, most of the Emilian IDs are concentrated in the food sector, animal feed products (an important example is the subregion in which the Parmesan Reggiano cheese *filière* developed) and the mechanical industry.

There are two main factors which have been incisive in more recent times. The first is the relation between large and small firms, generally in the mechanical sector (Brusco and Paba 1997), which shifted the technical expertise achieved in the former to the latter, and segmented the labour market into two 'layers', one defining the most advanced conditions of the so-called 'Emilian model', and the other, with fewer worker guarantees, capable of giving high elasticity to the manufacturing system with respect to the various conjunctures (Brusco 1983).

Mention must also be made of the very active, even super-hegemonic, role played by the Communist Party, through its control over local governments, trade unions and artisan organisations pertaining to it. The Communist Party has always taken on the task of making the flexibility of the strictly economic apparatus of industrialisation compatible with maintenance of social cohesion. Its influence was more pervasive than in the central regions in the sense that, in Emilia, it succeeded in bringing district development with it, while in the central regions it accompanied rather than supported the more spontaneous evolution of the productive fabric.

A very effective definition of the Emilian districts is 'productive disintegration and social integration', emphasising how and to what extent the pervasive political and social integration promoted by regional welfare operators, in all its local articulations, contributed towards creating the most suitable social environment for that disaggregation of productive processes so typical of the ID model. In this case, we could add that the division of labour among firms has been achieved very extensively, with a no less well-organised division of labour among other institutional actors to provide human resources. But perhaps this story could be reversed: the idea that the quality of civil life is an indispensable condition for economic development has been as pervasive as the local culture which the Communist administrators have concentrated in a practical direction, which has very little to do with the conventional 'prescriptions' of their ideological background.

4.4 IDs of the *Mezzogiorno* (southern Italy)

The situation of the southern regions, once part of the Kingdom of the Two Sicilies, is far removed from all of the above.

The establishment of the *communes*, key prerequisites to urbanisation, did not extend to Italian southern regions. This may be seen by just one example: at the time of the Italian unification, only four southern cities had more than 50 000 inhabitants: Palermo, Catania and Messina in Sicily, and Naples (Bevilacqua 2005).

Similarly, the rural-agricultural prerequisites did not apply, since southern regions were characterised by large land ownership, mirroring the still persistent feudal society. This greatly hindered and circumscribed the phenomenon of shared rented farming and therefore of embryonic agricultural entrepreneurship in the countryside. The unification of Italy, with the political compromise between the industrial bourgeoisie of the North and the landowners of the South (Gramsci 1975), did not give rise to the changes necessary to prevent inertial survival of such a social framework. The collapse of this framework was only to occur after the Second World War, with the imminent cold war, with the pledge of agrarian reform under a vigorous American impulse as a key moment in the construction of a new socio-economic arrangement of the entire country (Bernardi 2006).

With these premises, it is not clear why, in 1951, the presence of some forms of local IDs in the South (excluding Sicily and Sardinia) was widespread like in the rest of the country (Brusco and Paba 1997).

Although detailed historical research on this important aspect is lacking, we believe that there is a possible explanation based on two elements which, together, may have caused similar effects as the set of prerequisites in place in the central and northern regions – of course where large-scale organised crime did not extend its tentacles into local society (Arlacchi 1980).

The first element is the flight of labour from the countryside, thus creating some form of weak urbanisation with the proliferation of artisan centres, together with the rise of large towns. It should not be forgotten that the first industrial census of unified Italy, in the second half of the 19th century, counted a total number of people employed in manufacturing activities in the South higher than that of the rest of the country. Although these were very backward activities, shortly to become supplanted by competition from central-northern producers, they may have created sufficiently solid artisan or micro-industrial competences, at least in some areas.

The second element is represented by the land under peasant agriculture which, within the folds of the landlords' hegemony, was somehow able to impress on local society some features similar to those of the 'farming system' of the central and northern regions. A sociological study, carried out almost 20 years ago in the Calabria region (ibid.), supports this interpretation.

The fact that, in 1991, only 14 IDs (out of 199) were identified in the southern regions may be explained not so much by the lack of prerequisites to the emergence of IDs, but rather by the post-Second World War policy which envisaged a path of development for the South of Italy based on the creation of large-scale industrial poles, which in reality had the brutal effect of removing the preexisting manufacturing fabric (Becattini 2000b; Camagni 2000).[5] The fact that the number of southern IDs (26 out of 156) had almost doubled by 2001 may be explained by a drastic change in policy during the 1990s, with the promotion of a type of development based on small firms and entrepreneurship.

In summary, in the central-northern regions, political and institutional factors contributed towards creating the conditions for the prerequisites to ID development to emerge, whereas in the South the exact opposite occurred: this seems to be a hypothesis worthy of further examination (Becattini 2000b).

5. CONCLUSIONS

The geography of Italian IDs is quite complex and several regional models can be identified. In order to understand its variety, it has been argued that two sets of factors must be taken into account. First, the evolution of the urban and rural context concurred to determine the prerequisites for the development of a socio-economic system leading to the emergence of different forms of IDs. Second, political, institutional and strictly economic circumstances transformed these prerequisites, which have been studied over the last 30 years, into factors promoting real IDs in the period after the Second World War.

The main urban prerequisites consisted of civic traditions, with their customary institutions (local banks, technical training schools, self-government structures, various networks of social integration) and the manufacturing-artisan expertise which went back to the times of 'communal civilisation'. From the rural viewpoint, we have emphasised the importance of share-tenancy agriculture, stressing the role of the family in managing and organising productive processes in an autonomous way; in setting up stable relations with neighbours; in cultivating an albeit repressed propensity to social achievement; in giving a low value to non-primary needs; in the high propensity to saving; and in accepting harsh working conditions. On the other hand, small farms played an important role in creating contextual knowledge, external local economies, labour-intensive activities and mechanical equipment-saving techniques.

The different distribution of this double set of prerequisites in the Italian peninsula provides an initial explanation of the variety of regional and district models.

However, in giving rise to those models, the role of factors which operated in the post-Second World War period was particularly strong: strategies for regulating industrial relations, supply of public assets by local government, relations between the worlds of small and large firms, links of local subcultures with national government, the consequences of international tourism in many areas, and the nearness of the self-made entrepreneurs of 'made in Italy' to the needs of families and material working conditions.

NOTES

* The author would like to thank Alessandra Benni who has helped him to study the roots of Italian IDs for many years.
1. '"Strictly economic" factors do little to explain the success and decline of a district . . . The success of a district depends on the harmonic arrangement of several economic and social characteristics; it may be due to the conscious action of institutions, but also to the variable trend of markets and technologies and, to a non-negligible extent, also to the developmental pattern which summarises the history of the district itself' (Brusco and Paba 1997, p. 278).
2. In the early Renaissance, that is at the end of the 15th century, when the European national states which we know today began to coagulate, the Italian peninsula and its islands were divided into five large States (Duchy of Savoy, Duchy of Milan, Republic of Venice, State of the Holy Roman Church and Kingdom of Naples), together with several other minor States. These political entities, endlessly at odds with each other, if not actually at war, were further disaggregated into tiny, semi-autonomous components (Absalom 1995).
3. 'When ... modernisation processes lead to the collapse of share tenancy, a change occurs in the peasant family's strategy: the essential aim remains independence which, however, can no longer be achieved by buying a piece of land . . . entrepreneurial abilities and manufacturing competence acquired within the ambit of the family company, savings so parsimoniously accumulated . . . the habit of self-exploitation . . . group discipline maintained sometimes harshly by the head of the family: all this converges towards the new challenge which faces the members of the family, that of setting up on their own, giving rise to a small firm in the industrial sector' (Moroni 2008, pp. 196–7).
4. With respect to small owner-farmers, share tenants used qualitatively better land resources, whereas small renter-farmers, precisely because they paid rent, could integrate the property with others, since the original small-holdings were almost always too small. Both these circumstances, with respect to small owner-farmers, probably favoured a more highly-developed agrarian exploitation of the land, which served to create a better attitude towards farming.
5. 'In the case of locating a large steel works near Taranto, for example, a whole series of small artisan activities was ruined and its workers were obliged to abandon the city, due to the rise in the cost of living, rents, and salaries generated by the intrusion' (Camagni 2000, pp. 26–7).

32. Medium-sized firms, groups and industrial districts: An Italian perspective

Fulvio Coltorti[*]

1. INTRODUCTION

What is the most likely size of firms to be found when looking at the structure of an industry? In the largest European countries, based on Eurostat statistics firms falling in the size class from 0 to 49 employees (that is, small enterprises, SEs) accounted for a share of the total which in 2003 ranged from 90 per cent in Germany to 98 per cent in Italy; while in the US, based on figures from the most recent Census carried out in 2004, the share for this size class was 94 per cent if SEs are defined as firms with up to 99 employees. Enterprises with more than 499 employees (that is, large enterprises, LEs) accounted for just 1.4 per cent in the US and between 0.3 per cent (Italy) and 2.1 per cent (Germany) in Europe. A different picture emerges if we look at the distribution of employees: LEs account for 59 per cent of the total in the US and between 22–26 per cent (Italy and Spain) and 44–54 per cent (France, UK and Germany) in Europe; the share of SEs falls to 50–56 per cent in Italy and Spain, and to 22.5–31.0 per cent in France, the UK and Germany. Medium-sized enterprises (MSEs) account for 21–25 per cent in Europe and 17.5 per cent in the US (not including the 50–99 size class in the case of the latter, for which no details are available). In short, there is considerable diversity in the size of firms, with the smallest classes dominating in terms of number of entities, while employment tends to be distributed irregularly among firms of different sizes.

There are many reasons for these differences in size. They may arise as a result of social questions, statistical trends, specialization preferences and the search for efficiency in the production process. As for the social questions, we should look first at the differences in distribution of wealth among individuals. Firms may be viewed as a concentration of assets in the hands of their proprietors. The first economist to investigate the differences in size of wealth among individuals was Richard Cantillon. In 1755 he wrote his *Essai sur la nature du commerce en général*, where we read that even if the land (at that time a synonym for wealth) was initially distributed equally between all the inhabitants, it would ultimately end up being divided among a small number (Cantillon [1755] 1959, p. 5).[1] Concentration tends to increase when special progenitor rights are applied, and this is the case for most capitalistic economies.

Turning more specifically to the wealth concentrated within firms, that is, their assets, there is some evidence of the so-called 'law of proportionate effect' (Gibrat's law) which postulates that in fixed populations of firms, growth rates are independent of the firms' initial sizes, hence the trend is towards increasing concentration. Removing the condition of fixed population and introducing entry and exit movements, this original formulation has been altered, providing the following main conclusions: (a) the variability over time in firms' growth rates is not independent of their size but decreases with it; (b) mean growth rates of surviving firms are not independent of their size but tend to decline with it and also with the firm's age; (c) entry and exit are more likely to occur into and from smaller size classes (Caves 1998, pp. 1949–50). Caves concluded that regression toward the mean is in fact the norm. Hence, what must be expected regarding the populations of firms in motion is a greater or lesser degree of diversity in terms of size, because a state where firms have the same size is not a natural one.

When concentration of assets increases, a problem arises regarding how to manage them. Individuals may decide to hold their assets directly, but when their wealth is significant in size, several complexities emerge concerning how to administer it and the different options for transmitting this wealth to the holders' offspring to ensure stability of control. Having set up companies to hold their assets, individuals may easily pass control of these (industrial) assets to successors simply by transferring stakes in the capital of such companies to them, and so ensure stability in the management of the business. They may also select the son or daughter to be left in sole charge of managing these assets by giving him/her control of the company, without depriving the other offspring of their shares in the flows of revenues deriving from the wealth the founder accumulated during his working life. This is the case of ownership being separated from control of assets: a company which is governed by means of a family contract that gives power to one member of the controlling family.[2] Here we also find a first example of business groups emerging: a company holding the operating assets consisting of either material assets (for example, plant, machinery and so on) or investments in other operating companies (industrial affiliates). Let us call this the 'industrial group'. This ownership may in turn be concentrated into a corporate entity of a purely financial nature, holding the company operating the industrial business. The first is a sort of family safe, being a means for concentrating wealth (the 'family-holding company'), the latter heads up the industrial group that is a management device, which ensures the most productive way to operate specific assets (an 'industrial holding company'). Generally speaking, according to Granovetter (2005, p. 429) business groups are sets of legally separate firms bound together in persistent formal and/or informal ways. The industrial holding company allows entrepreneurs to choose the most efficient size for affiliated entities: hence one can hold an industrial group which is large or medium in size in its entirety by operating two or more entities each of which in turn is small or medium in size. I have outlined this general scheme in order to separate two distinct functions: the ownership and the management (control) of industrial operations; these will be useful in our analysis, although in reality the two may easily overlap in ways that can often be very confusing.[3]

Finally, specialization and efficiency come together in the Marshallian idea that entrepreneurs mainly produce goods to meet new needs or meet old ones in new ways (Marshall 1920); starting from this idea, Giacomo Becattini depicts them as tireless builders of their own 'niche markets', with the result that markets are not a mosaic of homogenous arenas populated by firms offering the same products, but a 'kaleidoscope of niche markets constantly changing inside it' (Becattini 2001a, pp. 13–15). Once again, we must not expect size to be a pure 'fact', whether technical or economical, but one of the means available to the entrepreneurs to build and defend their own markets. Firms tend to specialize horizontally, by market niches, and vertically or laterally by phases of production; in general, by doing so and being part of industrial districts (IDs), populations of firms which are not large in size can compete with large corporations organized by dividing manufacturing operations and industrial services internally (Becattini et al. 2003, Part II).

This chapter aims at providing some empirical evidence on these matters with a view in particular to two Italian phenomena that have emerged in the last decades: IDs and MSEs. The next sections will discuss in this respect: the distribution of firms within Italian IDs by size; then the emergence and diffusion of MSEs and business groups within IDs; and finally the diffusion of LEs' affiliates within IDs will be under examination in Section 4.

2. SIZE OF FIRMS IN ITALIAN IDs

One of the ways of dividing up the country into economically meaningful entities is that adopted by ISTAT (2006a). It starts by identifying local labour systems as proxies of communities of people, then selects manufacturing systems, and finally finds those systems mainly populated by small and medium-sized enterprises (SMEs). IDs are defined as those where a core business may be identified and that business is carried out mainly by SMEs. According to the ISTAT formula, the total number of persons employed in SMEs in the core industry must be more than half the total number of persons employed in that industry (ibid., pp. 18–22). SMEs are defined as those with no more than 249 employees. These conditions obviously lead to districts being populated by a prevalence of SMEs, but there are possibilities of polarization, with large businesses dominant in individual towns that are part of the district.[4] Important details of this methodology are as follows: (a) selection is based on local units, not firms, so firms which are large in terms of the aggregate employment of all their local units are not visible (this is not a problem for micro-firms, but could be for larger enterprises comprising small and medium-sized units); (b) the boundaries of the district are defined as those of the municipalities that fall within the local labor system. Firms that, being not too small, are able to profit from external economies linked to the industrial atmosphere of a district even if located at some distance from the centre, are therefore excluded. This applies in particular to MSEs; hence there is the possibility of underestimating the population of MSEs within a district area.

Territories are heterogeneous, so processes differ from one district to another (Becattini 2004a, p. 21). Table 32.1 provides some evidence. Here the ISTAT ID database for the year 2001 has been used (we may call this 'the ISTAT approach'), based on local units. We have divided the local units into four classes according to employment figures, assimilating them to size classes of firms and leaving aside for the moment the question of companies owning more than one local unit: the first class is that of micro-firms, that is, conventionally those with no more than nine employees; the second class includes SEs with 10–49 employees; then we have classes comprising medium-sized and large firms. Here I would rather define MSEs as those having 50–499 employees, following a broadly used definition (for instance small business administration in the US, German and French statisticians and so on). Unfortunately the ISTAT database provides no detailed evidence of firms with more than 249 employees,[5] so two different size classes have been constructed: one containing the first tranche of medium-sized local units, those with 50–249 employees, the other grouping the second tranche and all large local units.

There are different kinds of IDs according to the percentage of people employed in different-sized units. Obviously, where the share of MSEs is large, the importance of micro and small units is expected to be smaller; but it may be noted that 59 of the 156 districts are characterized by local units that are medium and large in size, which represent more than 42 per cent of total employment, and account for 52.6 per cent of all IDs' employment. Table 32.1 also permits us to note that the importance of IDs made up by a large prevalence of smaller firms is minimal: there are 41 IDs where micro and small units account for at least 75 per cent of the total employment, but they account just 13.6 per cent of the total for all districts. Finally, IDs with a high presence of medium and large local units are also populated by a large number of micro and small firms.

In Table 32.2 the unit of analysis is represented by the 33 Italian 'provinces' (territories corresponding to public authorities, dividing the territory of a region, and comprising many municipalities) where a district nature is prevalent (out of a total of 103 in 2001). This is defined on the basis of the most widespread

Table 32.1 *Italy: size of manufacturing local units in IDs (ISTAT approach), 2001*

Classes of percentage of employment in micro and small local units	No. of IDs	Percentage of all IDs' employment	Micro 0–9	Small 10–49	Medium-sized (first tranche): 50–249	Medium-sized (second tranche) and large 250+
			As percentage of total district employees			
IDs' local units:						
(Micro + small) > 74.9% of ID's total[a]	41	13.6	36.5	47.5	14.3	1.7
(Micro + small) between 62.5 and 74.9%[b]	56	33.8	26.8	40.1	24.7	8.4
(Micro + small) between 50 and 62.5%[c]	45	44.6	21.0	36.6	30.7	11.7
(Micro + small) < 50%[d]	14	8.0	16.9	31.1	35.9	16.1
All IDs	156	100.0	24.7	38.8	26.9	9.6
Total local units in Italian manufacturing industry			24.2	31.7	21.3	22.8

Notes:
[a] Includes Prato, Santa Croce sull'Arno and Arezzo.
[b] Includes Busto Arsizio, Seregno and Brescia.
[c] Includes Bergamo, Como and Lecco.
[d] Includes Biella.

Source: Based on ISTAT 2001 census figures.

organizational form observed in the industry of the province (for methodological issues, see Becattini and Coltorti 2006). A province may include one or more districts, but it is classified as a district area only if the districts have a particular weight; conventionally, when the ratio of aggregate employment in the province's IDs to its total employment is higher than the corresponding national average. So it may be the case that a province is populated by districts but manufacturing employment is mainly attributable to large firms; if this is so, that province will have an 'LE' rather than a 'district' nature. This methodology has some advantages: first of all national statistics often refer to provinces as the lowest territorial unit at which ISTAT data are released, which in particular enables greater detail to be gained on the size classes of firms; secondly, it allows broader areas of influence of different organizational forms (districts, MSE and LE systems) to be considered, such as when the district atmosphere extends to embrace firms located some miles outside a purely 'conventional' boundary of the district. This will henceforth be referred to as the industrial district province (IDP) approach.

Table 32.2   Italy: size of manufacturing firms in IDPs approach, 1971–2001

Firms by size (classes of employees per firm)	Total employees: all firms (percentage value)				Of which corporate enterprises (percentage of class)	
	1971	1981	1991	2001	1971	2001
Micro-firms (up to 9)	21.8	24.6	25.3	22.5	1.3	18.0
Small firms: 10–19	10.9	14.9	17.7	16.9	6.4	43.4
Small firms: 20–49	16.1	16.0	18.1	18.1	19.4	78.1
MSEs: 50–199	24.4	22.4	20.3	21.7	40.4	95.4
MSEs: 200–499	11.2	10.3	9.1	10.2	66.4	96.8
LEs: 500–999	6.8	5.4	4.1	4.8	83.2	96.5
LEs: 1000 or more	8.8	6.4	5.4	5.8	95.0	94.4
Total	100.0	100.0	100.0	100.0	35.4	66.2
District MSEs as percentage of total Italian MSEs	43.1	46.6	49.6	54.0	35.9	54.1

Note: IDPs of Alessandria, Arezzo, Ascoli Piceno, Bergamo, Biella, Brescia, Como, Cremona, Forlì-Cesena, Lecco, Lucca, Macerata, Mantua, Modena, Pavia, Pesaro-Urbino, Pisa, Pistoia, Pordenone, Prato, Ravenna, Reggio Emilia, Siena, Sondrio, Teramo, Treviso, Varese, Verbano-Cusio-Ossola, Vicenza, Viterbo; mixed LEPs–IDPs: Belluno, Vercelli, Verona.

Source: Based on ISTAT census figures. The definition refers to 2001. MSEs and mixed provinces included.

In 2001 IDPs were populated by 188 150 firms with 1.89 million employees, which represented 38.7 per cent of the total Italian manufacturing occupation. They account for the largest percentage, followed by large enterprise provinces (LEPs), which, together with the low industrialized ones (LILEPs), account for 25.6 per cent, with 3 per cent for mixed IDPs-LEPs and 5.3 per cent for medium-sized enterprise provinces (MSEPs); lastly, the residual provinces, with 27.4 per cent, most of which are in the Milanese area which has a prevalent tertiary nature. Within the IDP category, small firms are prevalent in terms of number of employees, accounting for 36 per cent of the total; large firms account for 9.7 per cent of the total: they are not enormous in size, averaging 1000 employees each. If we look at the changes in IDPs between 1971 and 2001 (Table 3.2), micro and small firms gained 8.7 points while MSEs and large firms lost 3.7 points and 5 points respectively. But there were opposite trends between 1971 and 1991 and between 1991 and 2001; in the first 20 years micro and small firms gained 12.3 points at the expense of all other categories of firms: medium-sized ones declined by 6.2 points, LEs by 6.1 points. The ten-year period from 1991 to 2001 saw a different story: micro and small firms lost ground in favour of MSEs (2.5 points) and to a lesser extent LEs (1.1 points).[6] In other words, IDPs, taken as an aggregate, appear to have changed their nature to some extent, tending towards a moderate increase in average sizes of unit.

A third method of dividing up Italian territories may also be used. The ISTAT classification of districts is based on local units. If a company owns more than one local unit, the real presence of SEs in districts could be overestimated. The ISTAT database does not allow the ownership of local units to be identified, and only includes information on firms whose head office is located in individual towns (municipalities). Considering the towns forming an ISTAT ID, we have three possibilities: firms which have both head office and local units within the ID; firms which have head office within the ID and local units in other territories too; and firms whose head office is outside the ID but run local units there. When a firm is small or medium-sized, there is a high probability that head office and local units are located in the same territory; indeed, on average in 2001 a small company owned 1.2 local units, a medium-sized one 1.9 local units, and a very large company with more than 1000 employees owned 11. In 2006 Unioncamere compiled a map of Italian provinces based on the actual size of firms crossed with information on local units' location and their ownership. This information was taken from the records of companies kept by all Italian public administrations (mainly chambers of commerce). Unioncamere did not define districts (Unioncamere 2007, pp. 58–70), but merely qualified provinces on the basis of prevalent size of firms owning local units; manufacturing firms and firms providing services to other enterprises were examined. This allows us to cross information on our 33 IDPs which were classified by Unioncamere in 2001 as follows: 14 mainly populated by units owned by SEs, 18 by MSEs and one by an LE. The other nine provinces had an MSE nature (one of which was an LE using an IDP approach). So the presence of MSEs in district areas is confirmed as significant.

The tendencies described above go hand in hand with three distinct phenomena: (a) a general decline in the presence and role of traditional Italian LEs, that is, those adopting a Fordist method of organization; (b) the ongoing expansion of areas characterized by a district nature; (c) the emergence of MSEs from IDs. The first was prevalent in 1981–91, when the decline derived from crises in major Italian groups (Coltorti 2006a); conversely, the years from 1991 to 2001 saw the emergence of new groups of district origin (the largest of which were Luxottica and Benetton), and even more, of MSEs which had evolved out of district firms. We may see also a transformation in terms of organization through the adoption of the legal status of corporate enterprise;[7] it is worth noting that nearly 40 per cent of SEs employing 10–19 persons have become corporate enterprises, and this percentage rises to 60 per cent in firms of the class size of 20–49 employees. MSEs have almost all been transformed into corporate enterprises, becoming very similar to LEs.

3. DIFFUSION OF MSEs AND BUSINESS GROUPS IN IDs

Baumol, Blinder and Wolff (2003, pp. 2–5) observed a clear pattern of decreasing size in the average US business from the early 1980s through the early 1990s, after increasing from about 1935 to about 1980. They restricted this pattern to manufacturing firms, mostly attributing it to technological reasons and observing that while large firms grew smaller, smaller firms grew larger; so the overall picture is one of movement toward the mean *à la* Caves. Something similar took place in Italy too, with areas of LEs in decline and emerging IDs. Here the drivers were a deep crisis in large firms, both in the public and private sector, as a result of both wrong industrial policies, and poor technological content in products whose competitiveness was mainly based on low labour costs. This contrasted with the flourishing of light industries carried out by small firms scattered among the peripheral Italian provinces (Becattini and Coltorti 2006).

From the mid-1990s MSEs displayed quite outstanding results in terms of growth and profitability. Evidence of this comes from Mediobanca-Unioncamere research on MSEs, which are defined as firms having a legal status of JSC, a size of 50–499 employees and annual sales of €13–290 million. Industrial groups are included as long as they meet the same size requirements, but companies affiliated to larger concerns are excluded. This research started in 1999 taking statistics on a census basis from 1996. The most recent data cover the 1996–2005 period. The most significant findings of this research to date are as follows: (a) there are 4000 MSEs accounting for approximately one-fifth of Italian manufacturing industry in terms of value added, including estimated contributions from allied industries; (b) MSEs achieved the most rapid growth in value added, 41.6 per cent from 1996 to 2005, compared with 11.3 per cent achieved by large Italian-controlled companies and 26.2 per cent by Italian affiliates of non-Italian multinationals; (c) return on capital invested by MSEs is considerably higher than that by large groups (between two and three percentage points in the years covered by the research); (d) MSEs' financial structure appears to be very strong, with shareholders' funds accounting for more than 45 per cent of financial resources and a negligible annual default rate (0.4 per cent, as opposed to 1.4 per cent averaged by all Italian JSCs).

The emergence and relevance in terms of profitability and competitiveness of a middle capitalism in Italian manufacturing industry appears to be closely linked to the decline of large industry. It was probably this decline, in conjunction with the strong consolidated base of IDs, which made it possible for this category of business to have resources (mainly specialized workers) and competences (mainly management capabilities) poured into it. We will come back to this issue in the Section 4.

According to our estimates based on ISTAT statistics of manufacturing corporations, MSEs are to be found mainly within IDPs and MSEPs: 56 per cent of firms in 2001, more than 18 percentage points higher than in 1971. Areas of LE account for around 20 per cent, while the Milan province alone (which now has a dominant tertiary nature) hosts 11.2 per cent. Milanese corporations are likely to control business groups with affiliates throughout other Italian provinces. Turning to the Mediobanca-Unioncamere census, ten of the first 15 geographical concentrations in terms of number of firms, that is, provinces where MSEs' head offices are located, have a district nature. Among the 4000 corporations that are medium in size emerging from the 2003 Mediobanca-Unioncamere census, we find 944 organized as industrial business groups (Table 32.3). Labour cost and value-added ratios as a percentage of turnover could be taken as a measure of vertical integration; in this case, based on these indicators, we see minimal differences between business groups and stand-alone corporations and between companies inside IDs as opposed to outside them. Regarding the degree of diversification a survey conducted by Mediobanca and Unioncamere at the beginning of 2006 (Gagliardi 2006) revealed the existence of a 'quasi-identification' between the firm and its lead product.[8] Hence an industrial group structure is not set up by MSEs to facilitate diversification. Obviously, this does not eliminate cases of diversification aimed at reducing the financial risk facing certain controlling families; but in these cases diversification is more likely to emerge at a higher level, that of family-holding companies, and forms of diversification may include investment in other manufacturing activities as well as in financial assets (baskets of shares, bonds and other publicly traded securities) or in real estate.

Table 32.3 MSEs: characteristics of industrial business groups and stand-alone companies, 2003

	Business groups			Stand-alone companies		
	IDs[a]	Other LPSs[b]	Other areas	IDs[a]	Other LPSs[b]	Other areas
Number of groups or companies	205	108	631	786	273	1884
As percentage of total	21.7	11.5	66.8	26.7	9.3	64.0
Average company size						
Total assets (million €)	57.2	55.2	61.7	25.0	24.6	25.9
Sales (million €)	54.2	49.9	56.6	27.8	26.9	28.0
Employees (No.)	235	244	231	123	118	119
As percentage of sales						
Value added	23.9	24.5	25.5	22.4	23.1	23.4
Labour cost	14.5	16.6	14.9	14.2	14.7	14.7
Exports	43.8	43.4	30.8	41.9	31.4	26.7

Notes:
[a] Industrial districts identified as such by the majority of Italian sources.
[b] Local production systems (quasi-district areas denominated as 'district' by Italian regional authorities but not identified as such by the majority of Italian sources).

Source: Based on Mediobanca-Unioncamere figures. IDs and LPSs are those selected by Mediobanca-Unioncamere (2006, pp. xxxvi–xli).

MSEs are distinguished by their low consumption of capital. This derives from their specialization in light industry. On the production side they are lean, whereas on the marketing side they have individual-brand networks with relatively low financing needs thanks to the use of franchising and similar methods (Coltorti 2006b, p. 397). So stand-alone companies are more common than business groups among MSEs.[9] Groups account for 25 per cent of the universe in terms of number of firms and for 38 per cent in terms of employment. When MSEs are not stand-alone, we see groups that are not enormous in size in terms of the number of affiliates. Firstly, 688 of the 944 groups are made up of a maximum of five companies. Groups located within IDs make up one-third of total and have fewer than 20 affiliates each (74 per cent no more than five, and 24 per cent no more than two). Their size in terms of capital does not differ significantly with respect to groups located outside IDs, but they are distinguished by a larger international volume of sales.

We selected a group of 100 firms from the MSEs' business groups universe; they were the largest in terms of employees and therefore those at which financial complexities must be expected to emerge. They included five companies listed on the Italian stock market and one company whose legal status was that of cooperative. In most cases these groups are controlled by families.

Out of these 100 MSE business groups, 34 were controlled by means or with the assistance of another company. We find three types of reasons for the presence of an intermediate participating entity: (a) provider of finance; (b) retention of control; (c) division of holding stakes between the members of the founding families. Our 34 companies mainly fell into the latter category, being devices for dividing up stakes between the expected successors of members of the founding families. The number of these expected successors could sometimes be large (more than ten in eight cases, with a maximum of 49).[10] Since we are dealing with private companies, a more centralized ownership may be the vehicle for centralizing control (Granovetter 2005, p. 433). Confirmation comes from a characteristic of most of them: expected successors often own merely the bare property of capital share, leaving the beneficial interest in the hands of the founder. Thus all of them seem to be adjusted so as not to pay inheritance tax at the precise moment of succession.[11] Summing up, we may say that the building of group structures by MSEs and district firms seems having nothing to do with their particular nature, but has to be considered as ordinary instruments for managing a business.

A wider look at the phenomenon can be gained from the Unioncamere database of all Italian business groups.[12] We selected 3094 groups whose controlling entity is a domestic company, classifying them as LE and MSE groups according to whether or not there was at least one large company (LE groups) or one medium-sized company (MSE groups), all others being SE groups. They include 6672 affiliates. The main issues are as follows: (a) LE groups comprise a large number of SMEs; there were 16 MSEs and 33 SEs every ten LEs; the same happens for MSE groups where there are 13 SEs every ten MSEs; (b) 43 per cent of groups have a head office inside an IDP; they account for 37.1 per cent of all MSEs and 37.7 per cent of all SEs; (c) once more there are no special characteristics for business groups within IDPs, except for a lower number of companies going to make up the group, especially those led by LEs (4.5 companies in every group located in IDPs, as opposed to 10.5 in those located in other areas).[13]

4. DIFFUSION OF LEs' AFFILIATES IN IDs

At first glance the presence of LEs within IDs could be seen as nonsense. Nonetheless they are found there and one has to ask why. At least four reasons may be suggested: (a) a matter of chance; (b) the advantages deriving from locating an LE within an ID; (c) a trend towards larger sizes among district companies; or (d) a residual phenomenon of the past nature of a territory. The first reason is easily related to the imperfect nature of the statistical identification of IDs. Second, we find cases where an LE locates some local units within a district with the aim of taking advantage of local competences (workforce above all). The third reason is more specific, as firms within a district may grow in size, both for technical reasons (for example, progress in terms of manufacturing by automatic machinery that cuts down phases of division of labour)[14] or social ones (for example, hereditary succession and sale of control to other entrepreneurs in the district). Finally, because most areas which now have a district nature were not such in the past, we inevitably encounter some LEs with a long history in that particular territory. We should not forget that the definitions of classes of size being conventions are always questionable. A last question is what kind of stability we should expect from the LE's presence that we now observe.

Table 32.4 shows firms with more than 499 employees (which we conventionally consider as large) whose head offices are located within IDPs. In 2001 we find 177 firms with 184 000 employees: these represent 10 per cent of total IDPs' employment. The main class of firms is that with between 500 to 999 employees (73.4 per cent of all LEs in IDPs and 47 per cent of employment). Firms with 1000 employees or more are rare; local units having 1000 employees or more accounted for 21 per cent of total LEs' employment in IDPs. We see some stability in these companies' presence, with two trends that appear to be contradictory: between 1981 and 1991 their number fell by 30 units (21 in the 500–999 class and nine in the 1000 or more class), but between 1991 and 2001 there was a reversal with 23 more units. In the 1980s, we witnessed the last episodes in the history of old great Fordist corporations, but more recently a new type of LE appears to emerge within a context dominated by light industries. Evidence of this is the decline in the number of local units with 1000 employees or more. Between 1981 and 1991, such large plants have halved in number causing consequently a huge fall in employment. These units are now very rare in Italy and especially within IDPs where their employees account for 17 per cent of total employment in the largest Italian class of local units. It is sufficient in this respect to note that Milan, the symbol of Italian large industry at the start of the last century, now hosts only three of these units and their employees represent no more than 4 per cent of total manufacturing employment in the city.[15]

It is instructive to see where these units are located. Based on the 2001 ISTAT Census, Italy had 33 such local units.[16] There are 14 units located within IDs and 19 units outside them but inside an IDP. Ten specialize in light industries including food, personal and household goods (textiles and clothing, eyewear, wiring accessories), mechanical engineering (braking systems, light weapons). Two local units in the Province of Belluno are part of a district (eyewear) where the introduction of new materials, technical progress in machinery and the search for full control over product quality resulted in the

Table 32.4 Italy: large manufacturing enterprises localized in IDPs, 1981–2001

Size of firms or local units (classes of employees)	1981	1991	2001	Change 1981–2001 Absolute values	Change 1981–2001 Percentage value
Firms whose head offices are located inside IDPs					
Number of firms					
500–999	134	113	130	–4	
1000 or more	50	41	47	–3	
Total	184	154	177	–7	
Number of employees (thousands)					
500–999	93	73	87	–6	–6.5
1000 or more	129	101	97	–32	–24.8
Total	222	174	184	–38	–17.1
LEs' local units located inside IDPs					
Number of local units					
500–999	151	98	100	–51	
1000 or more	61	33	23	–38	
Total	212	131	123	–89	
Number of employees (thousands)					
500–999	100	65	66	–34	–34.0
1000 or more	126	58	39	–87	–69.0
Total	226	123	105	–121	–53.5

Source: Based on ISTAT census figures. The definition of the provinces' borders is referred to 2001.

integration of different phases of manufacturing, pushing firms towards a larger scale;[17] this was a clear development of the original district. The other eight units, though large, operate in businesses that are core for IDs. Twenty-three units specialize in heavy industries, such as automotive industry (nine units), domestic appliances (six units) and steel operations (four units); these are all strong producers of either mechanical competences (which are very useful in aiding light mechanical organizations within districts) or intermediaries for those industries.

Here, two conclusions seem to emerge: (a) the presence of LEs in IDPs appears to be relatively homogeneous with the district light-industry core businesses; (b) we may expect flows of transfers of competences from LEs to district firms, either due to technical know-how or organization capabilities; (c) in the heavy industries the most impressive presence is in mechanical engineering and metal manufacturing; as both are very important businesses for IDs, this presence may appear to be a strong tool for transferring technological innovations to the territory.

5. CONCLUDING REMARKS

In conclusion MSEs' presence in district areas is very significant and has expanded in the most recent period. They include stand-alone companies and a certain number of industrial groups controlled by family holdings formed by a relatively small number of undertakings; but groups owned by family-holding companies appear to be a significant phenomenon, more so than pure industrial groups. The development in MSEs' presence within IDs probably derives from the new international scenario, where competition has become global and players come either from low industrialized countries' producers or from relocated multinationals' local units. The search for competitiveness has led to a difficult selection of goods to be produced, quality upgrading, a new division of labour with some phases moved outside the ID[18] and a more direct presence in non-Italian markets. So IDPs appear to have changed their nature to some extent by means of a greater percentage of firms that have increased in size. This does not mean, in our view, a change in the definition and function of IDs, but trends above appear to be leading to new local industrial configurations. The historical path we are looking at is that of a succession of stages in the post-war years which saw the decline of the Fordist firms; the emergence of IDs with systems of firms embedded in local societies and where the size of the business units was not a decisive question; and finally a new transformation caused by the need to face up to new competitors (see also Bellandi 2007, pp. 23–5). It is probable that in this context MSEs are able to perform two kinds of functions: more or less defined guidance of local producers into new markets outside Italy (which call for new competences in order to understand the habits and aptitudes of different customers in new countries) and a means for consolidating operations of small, troubled firms in industries under attack from low-cost countries.

MSEs are entities that either stay within the district (taking local resources and returning managing competences together with technological innovations) or outside it (building networks beyond the district boundaries). Their needs and strategies could not coincide with those of small district firms. Here the equilibrium size of companies is the crucial point: when it remains intermediate between the small entrepreneur and the large multinational, we may expect the local roots to remain sufficiently strong. This is consistent with high product differentiation and a niche market strategy, which is a result of competences originating from belonging to IDs. The adoption of a mass market view would put an end to such an equilibrium: we believe that this is not presently the case.

NOTES

* I am very grateful to the *Handbook* editors for their valuable comments and suggestions, and to David Gibbons who helped with the English revision.
1. Cantillon referred to inheritances, differences in abilities and skills of men, and so forth. Similar positions were expressed by Cesare Beccaria in 1769 in his *Elementi di economia pubblica* (1804).
2. Further developments include dispersion of ownership among a large number of shareholders. There are two stylized outcomes leading to two different models: the so-called continental or Rhenish model, where a few shareholders lock in control, and the neo-American model, where property is highly dispersed and control ends up into the hands of managers. See Albert (1991); Berle and Means (1997); Barca and Becht (2002).
3. Forms of groups around the world are highly differentiated. See Khanna and Yafeh (2007, pp. 331–2).
4. According to the ISTAT formula, the total number of persons employed in LEs may not be higher than 49 per cent of total.
5. This comes from a EU decision to define large companies as those with more than 249 employees. This limit has relevance for the banning of State aids to firms that are not small in size.
6. For the sake of consistency, changes in weight have been calculated assuming the status of province nature set in 2001 is fixed. For a dynamic approach see Becattini and Coltorti (2006).
7. As per the OECD's definition, by this term I mean corporations, joint-stock companies, cooperatives, limited liability partnerships and other non-financial enterprises which by virtue of legislation are recognized as business entities independent of their owners.
8. Details on products enable us to classify MSEs into three different categories: (a) producers of final consumer goods; (b) producers of capital goods; and (c) producers of intermediate goods and components. On average, the main product (to be viewed as product family) accounts for 93 per cent of the volume of business (Gagliardi 2006, pp. 416–17).
9. Differing views are expressed by Cainelli and Iacobucci (2007, p. 100); based on ISTAT data, they see that the group appears to be the normal way in firms exceeding 250 employees. Our contrasting statement is based on the evidence of MSEs only, and does not relate to individual companies linked to large groups. We believe that the most important cause of the difference is the presence of family-holding companies, which tend to be confused with industrial groups in the ISTAT dataset. It should be mentioned in this connection that in Mediobanca-Unioncamere research, groups are selected only if a consolidated statement is produced, thus omitting cases below the limit stated for exemption in the Italian civil code. But this limit

is very small; for turnover the grey area represents just 4 per cent of the range adopted for defining an MSE, and the cases ignored are to be assumed to be totally negligible.
10. It is not the same for large Italian companies quoted on the stock market. According to Mediobanca Research Department statistics, approximately half the capital of companies listed was blocked by controlling stakes, and in many of the most important capital concentrations in the private sector there was usually a pyramidal structure (see Pirelli-Telecom Group, IFI-Agnelli Group, De Benedetti Group and so on). Almeida and Wolfenzon (2006) explain why pyramids have both a payoff and a financing advantage over horizontal structures.
11. In Italy this tax was abolished by the Berlusconi government in 2001 and reintroduced in 2007 by the second Prodi government. In the past, ownership structures with a high presence of trust companies were motivated by the desire to conceal all properties from the tax authorities.
12. Unioncamere provided us with an anonymous database of all business groups including two or more manufacturing enterprises in 2002. Unioncamere identifies a business group as an entity where two or more companies are linked by means of controlling stakes.
13. Actually MSEs within districts and other local systems do not differ significantly from those located in other areas (Mediobanca-Unioncamere 2006, p. xxxii) by capitalization as well as by specialization in the light industries.
14. Doubtless the most famous instance of this was the pin maker that Adam Smith used as an example of the division of labour. In the 18th century, French pin makers, about whom Smith writes, were concentrated in the Laigle ID of Normandy. In the first half of the 19th century a new machine was invented by English entrepreneurs that eliminated all the 18 phases listed by Smith in Chapter I of his *The Wealth of Nations*; since then pin manufacturing became a purely automated operation usually performed by one individual large factory (see Peaucelle 2007, p. 222).
15. In fact Milan's size structure is very similar to that of IDs as shown in Table 32.1, but with a high density of MSEs which account for 37 per cent of manufacturing employment (micro and small firms combined make up an aggregate 53 per cent). Today the most important Italian city hosting large local units is Turin (a pole of the Italian automotive industry), with eight units and 25 000 employees; followed by Taranto in southern Italy (the major steel centre) with two units and 12 000 employees; then Pomigliano d'Arco near Naples (automotive and mechanical engineering), with three local units and 8600 employees.
16. Table 32.4 shows 23 units, which is consistent with the 33 units reported in 1991; the discrepancy is due to the different base used for the Census by ISTAT in 1991.
17. This was the case with Luxottica and other large firms such as Safilo and De Rigo.
18. A first restructuring process occurred during the 1980s coinciding with the emergence of groupings within IDs; for the Prato district, see Dei Ottati (1996a). The major difference with today is the nature of new competitors and the very low level of their production costs, as well as the global context of their competition.

33. Knowledge dynamics in the evolution of Italian industrial districts

Fiorenza Belussi

1. INTRODUCTION

The key questions discussed in this chapter are: firstly, what types of industrial districts (IDs) are there in Italy and where do they come from? And secondly, how have they been able to develop an original technological trajectory? In Section 2 the origin of the ID model is discussed, within a theoretical framework that stresses its heterogeneity. Section 3, based on an ample survey that uses information from previous studies published in academic journals and in the *Club dei distretti industriali* association, has collected detailed information for 55 cases and deals with the issue of the origin of Italian IDs. In particular, the impact of four triggering factors (ancient craft traditions, natural resource endowment, anchor firm and exogenous entry) is examined. Growth-evolutionary factors in the development of the Italian districts are, then, elaborated in Section 4. The main results in terms of district heterogeneity and multiple paths are examined in the conclusions in Section 5.

2. AT THE ORIGINS OF THE ITALIAN ID MODEL

While the expansion of the Italian districts historically dates back to the post-war period (Becattini 1990; Brusco and Paba 1997; Becattini and Coltorti 2006), the embryonic development of many of them dates back to the end of the 19th century. The Italian district model has enjoyed a long-term slow growth. Differently from the experience of others countries, Italy has not witnessed a sudden decline and dissolution of its IDs (like Britain prior to the Second World War) nor a rapid upsurge – such as in the case of the US high-tech districts of Silicon Valley during the 1970s (Saxenian 1994) or Boston during the 1980s (Powell, Koput and Smith-Doerr 1996).

In Italy very few districts are found in a 'pure' form, as has been the case of Prato which is a highly-industrialised textile area. In other words, very few local systems are characterised by just one dominant local industry to which almost the whole community is durably engaged (Dei Ottati 1996b; Becattini 2003a).

Many Italian districts specialised in light or medium high-tech sectors are smaller than Prato, and less spatially concentrated, as is the case, for instance, of several of them in Veneto, Emilia-Romagna and Tuscany (Cossentino, Pyke and Sengenberger 1996). Some industrial clusters that show districts' features are diluted in urban conurbations, so they do not clearly and distinctly 'emerge' from the statistical analyses, like the packaging machinery cluster in Bologna (Belussi 2003). More generally, behind the notion of a uniform Marshallian industrial district (MID) phenomenon there is a striking variety of forms of districts, which tend to vary according to the sectors' specialisation, age of formation, innovation capabilities, dynamics of internationalisation (either measured by export shares, FDI, and presence of international subcontracting chains), district structure (defined depending on firms' size, density and the possible emergence of large local coordinating local firms).

As is reported in the research of IPI (2002), considering the results of many classification grids and maps, Italy counts about 100–120 IDs. What characterizes the Italian experience is the fact that the IDs are typically characterised by clusters specialised in so-called low-tech sectors (textile, clothing, footwear, leather, mechanical items, home articles, furniture, tiles and jewellery) and they are formed by indigenous local entrepreneurs and labour force (Bagnasco and Trigilia 1984). Thus, the Italian case is quite opposite to the US one, where we observe mainly the presence of high-tech clusters formed around international leading universities where a significant contribution to local growth has been provided to a significant extent by foreign entrepreneurs and an immigrant labour force, as authoritatively described by Saxenian (1999) in the case of Silicon Valley. As case studies have showed, many Italian districts have followed a long-term evolutionary path from infancy to growth, followed then by maturity (and, subsequently, by stages of stagnation and decline or revitalisation). However, we are not in the presence of a predetermined, or standard, life cycle, as suggested by scholars interested in describing the pattern of growth of new industries (see Audretsch and Feldman 1996; Feldman and Audretsch 1999; Buenstorf and Klepper 2005), but we can observe a multiplicity of different paths, together with processes of differentiation, specialisation and integration, as suggested by Robertson, Jacobson and Langlois (in this volume). The key remark is that the evolution of the Italian IDs occurred without the collapse into a dominant oligopolistic local or national structure.

3. THE GENESIS OF THE ITALIAN IDs

In this section an ample survey on the existing Italian IDs will be proposed that applies a qualitative meta-analysis (Paterson et al. 2001). Instead of using some statistical data, textual reports developed in previous studies have been analysed, creating new interpretations from secondary sources. The rationale that informed the case-study selection strategy was twofold. On the one hand, we searched for IDs with different characteristics (for example, recent versus ancient IDs, high-tech versus low-tech IDs, small-sized versus large IDs) in order to include extreme situations and polar types in which the process under investigation is 'transparently observable' (Eisenhardt 1989). On the other hand, we selected IDs for which at least one published case study was available, containing information and description on the processes under investigation (for example historical roots, changes over time, process of internationalisation, technological dynamisms and so on).

This critical survey examines 55 Italian cases, using scientific publications which have appeared in academic journals and books[1] (see Table 33.1). The cases correspond to clusters characterising IDs or rooted in different types of locality but showing district-like features. The list is not meant to be a comprehensive survey of district cases in contemporary Italy; nor, given the method of collection and analysis employed here, it should be excluded that the accuracy of assessment of single cases can have an uneven level. However, the aggregate picture that emerges allows us to appreciate the presence of different types of evolutionary paths driving the ID phenomenon in Italy.

In the 1950s, the growth of Italian IDs was driven by the expansion of the small firm model: a growing number of local small and medium-sized firms (SMEs) populated the Italian districts. They were phase or component producers for the already existing firms or for new firms entering the market with novelties or slightly improved products in terms of the relation quality/cost. This was correlated with a parallel increase in local employment. Demand growth, in the post-war period, was captured not by the existing incumbents, but by new start-ups.

The expansion and numeric growth of IDs occurred in Italy in the post-war period, during the so-called 'Golden age' that stretched to a large extent over the 1970s, thanks to an expanding internal demand first, and to the creation of a European single market subsequently.

By the end of the 1980s, most of the districts had approached a phase of maturity, or a phase of no growth (either in the number of newly created firms and/or the level of the local employment in the firms that constituted the localised value chain).

We argue that there are mainly four triggering factors that can explain district genesis and evolution paths (see Table 33.1); these can be either endogenous or exogenous. The endogenous factors include: (a) the availability of craft skills; (b) the preexistence of certain natural endowments, like tannin from trees, used in the process of curing hides for leather products (see the case of Arzignano), or marble for the districts of Valpolicella and Carrara; (c) the presence of an important dynamic firm which develops unique capabilities – this is in line with the hypothesis of an anchor firm which generates new start-ups followed by a process of multiplication of firms.[2] The main exogenous factor seems to be related to: (d) the entry of an external dynamic firm (a multinational firm or a subsidiary), as for instance occurred in Catania in the Etna Valley, thanks to the relocation of the large Italian-French firm ST-Microelectronics.

For Italian IDs the most important triggering factor appears to be the preexistence of an 'ancient craft tradition', and this explains the fact that districts have emerged

Table 33.1 Triggering factors in the genesis of a selection of Italian IDs and clusters with IDs features by region

Nature	Key	Region	Sector and locality
Endogenous	Ancient craft traditions (with ubiquitous entry)	Veneto and Friuli	1. Sport system (Montebelluna) 2. Jewellery (Vicenza) 3. Cutlery (Maniago, Udine) 4. Furniture (Cerea, Verona) 5. Artistic ceramics (Bassano, Vicenza) 6. Chairs (Manzano, Udine) 7. Furniture (Livenza, Pordenone-Treviso) 8. Artistic glass (Murano, Venice)
		Emilia-Romagna	9. Footwear (Fusignsno and San Mauro Pascoli) 10. Wood processing machinery (Rimini) 11. Sofa (Forlì) 12. Clothing and knitting (Carpi) 13. Ceramic tiles (Sassuolo) 14. Agriculture machinery (Reggio Emilia)
		Lombardy	15. Furniture (Brianza) 16. Footwear, now footwear machinery (Vigevano) 17. Silk (Como) 18. Taps and fittings (Lumezzane, Brescia) 19. Nylon stockings (Castel Goffredo, Mantua)
		Piedmont	20. Jewellery (Valenza Pò) 21. Textile and wool (Biella)
		Tuscany	22. Textiles (Prato) 23. Furniture (Poggibonsi) 24. Tanning (Santa Croce sull'Arno, Pisa)
		Other regions and Mezzogiorno	25. Musical instruments, now electronics (Castefidardo) 26. Clothing (Urbania) 27. Sofa district (Matera-Altamura-Santeramo)

460

Endogenous	Natural resources endowment	Other regions and Mezzogiorno	28. Clothing (Val Vibrata)
29. Tanning (Solofra)
30. Ceramics (Caltagirone)
		Veneto and Trentino	31. Jewellery (Marcianise, Naple-Caserta)
32. Leather (Arzignano) (water and tannin)
33. Marble (Valpolicella, Verona)
34. Porphyry and stone material (Trento)
		Others	35. Leather (Solofra)
36. Paper (Fabriano)
37. Marble (Carrara)
	Anchor firm (with employee's learning and subsequent spinoffs)	Veneto	38. Vegetable preserving industries (tomatoes) (Agro Nocerino Sarnese)
39. Footwear (Riviera del Brenta – Voltan firm, 1898)
40. Eyewear (Agordo, Belluno – Luxottica firm, 1950)
41. Ornamental horticulture (Saonara in Padua – Sgaravatti firm, 1820)
42. Machine manufacturing (Schio Thiene, Vicenza)
		Emilia-Romagna	43. Biomedical (Mirandola – Dideco of Veronesi firm, 1960)
44. Packaging (Bologna – Ima and GD firms, the 1920s)
45. Agriculture machinery (Reggio Emilia and Modena)
46. Motorcycle (Bologna – Ducati)
47. Food processing (Parma – Parmalat)
		Others regions and Mezzogiorno	48. Ornamental horticulture (Pistoia – Bartolini firm, 1849)
49. Jewellery (Arezzo – Uno A Erre, 1926)
50. Ceramic (Sesto Fiorentino – Richard-Ginori, 1737)
51. Taps and fittings (Cusio)
52. Furniture (Pesaro – Scavolini firm)
53. Footwear district (Civitanova – Della Valle firm)
54. Footwear Barletta and Casarano district (Filanto firm)
Exogenous	Entry of MNCs	Sicily	55. Micro electronics (Etna Valley in Catania – ST-Microelectronics)

Source: Our elaborations based on Falzoni, Onida and Viesti (1992); Dei Ottati (1996b); Belussi and Pilotti (2002); Club dei distretti industriali (2003); Belussi, Sammarra and Sedita (2008).

461

in relatively low-tech product specialisations. As explained in Belussi and Gottardi (2000), the presence of demand-pull factors has allowed local entrepreneurs to explore some market opportunities, giving rise to a technological virtuous cycle of marginal product upgrading and the introduction of incremental technological innovations in product and processes. This has increased the competitiveness of the local firm within a process of 'decentralised creativity' (described by Bellandi 1992) and ubiquitous entry.

The presence of an 'anchor firm' hypothesis[3] covers a substantial number of Italian IDs and of industrial clusters with district features rooted in various types of localities (IDs, metropolitan areas and so on). The main idea is that many firm start-ups can be traced back to one firm alone: the so-called founder firm of the district. This was certainly the case of the Fairchild Semiconductor in Silicon Valley (Klepper 2001) whose most famous offspring have been Intel and Xerox in Paolo Alto, and whose technology was then developed by Apple and others (Chesbrough 2003b). Particularly innovative firms allow their workers to capitalise on the firm's existing specific knowledge, starting their own firm. Likewise, the Voltan firm, founded in 1989, was the founding firm of the footwear district of the Riviera del Brenta near Venice (Belussi and Gottardi 2000), or Luxottica, founded in 1950, the founding firm of the Agordo eyewear district near Belluno (Camuffo 2003); or again, the Ima and GD firms, established in the 1920s in Bologna, can considered as the founding firms of the local packaging cluster (Belussi 2003). This process can be divided in two subprocesses. In one, the new firms will use the same technology as their parent company, thereby producing identical products. In the other, spinoffs are generated to explore new ideas that employees wanted to explore independently; these new ideas led either to produce a differentiated product for a market niche that was neglected by the parent firm, or to launch a truly new innovation. For the latter, the new entrepreneurs either desired to develop such a venture autonomously driven by very ambitious strategies, or they had to leave the parent company where they could not develop such ideas due to the quite myopic and conservative strategy of the parent company (Belussi 2000).

Existing studies concerning Italian IDs reveal that spinoffs are generally sustained by the desire of senior engineers to become entrepreneurs (self-employed workers) and there is no evidence that many conflicts have occurred between the parent firms (Lipparini and Lorenzoni 2000) and the new initiative created. On the contrary, parent firms have often been supportive and helpful.

The 'natural resource endowment' driver concerns only few districts or clusters in our dataset, and seems a quite marginal explanatory factor.

The exogenous triggering factor, so important in explaining the takeoff of industrial clusters in developing countries (Markusen 1996; Ernst 2001; Guerrieri, Iammarino and Pietrobelli 2001; Giuliani, Rabellotti and van Dijk 2005), is practically absent in Italy. The only case is the electronic cluster which emerged from the location in Catania of the Franco-Italian multinational, ST-Microelectronics. This move was strongly pursued by the firm's former manager, Pasquale Pistorio, who desired both to support Sicily's lagging economy (his native land), whilst benefiting from Italian State subsidies available to firms investing in the Mezzogiorno.

Overall it is well know that Italian districts, as an organisational model, have more favourably emerged (but not in a exclusive manner) in the regions of the 'Third Italy' (Veneto, Emilia-Romagna, Tuscany and Marches), which have experienced in the past the development of small autonomous agricultural initiatives, small commercial activities, and cases of proto-industrialisation derived from the renaissance development (Bagnasco and Trigilia 1984; Garofoli 1989a). In other words, the existing entrepreneurial capabilities of the area have allowed a least traumatic shift towards some modern industrial initiatives.

The Mezzogiorno of Italy has few initiatives, among which the most interesting appear to be the sofa district of Matera-Altamura-Santeramo, where about 1000 firms and 20 000 employees (data refers to 2003) were involved in the production of leather upholstery exported worldwide especially in the US market (Belussi 1999a) and the above-mentioned Catania cluster.

Other clusters in the Mezzogiorno, like leather of Solofra, the vegetable preserving industries (tomatoes) of Agro Nocerino Sarnese, or the footwear of Barletta and Casarano, recently founded around the Filanto firm, are less dynamic and technologically more backward.

Besides their triggering factors, many Italian districts have old origins and are rooted mostly in a historical process of local knowledge accumulation. Some districts, for instance, can date their birth back to the end of 19th century, like Arzignano, Montebelluna, Riviera del Brenta, Brianza, Saonara, Vigevano, Pistoia, Lumezzane, Maniago, Solofra and Santa Croce sull'Arno. This means that even today, some districts still host very 'old' SMEs, which survived through many entrepreneurial generations for, in some cases, more than a hundred years. However, as noted above, a large number of districts emerged after the Second World War, at the end of the 1950s.

Table 33.1 also reports two district cases that emerged later, in the 1970s: the Agordo eyewear cluster near Belluno and the biomedical cluster of Mirandola, near Modena, in North Italy. The districts and clusters with district features of Mezzogiorno are also generally younger than the districts of northern Italy: they became well established in the 1990s (like the sofa district of Matera, or the high-tech Etna Valley of Catania). Districts emerging in the South during the 1990s could not count on the social capital existing in the civic traditions of the urban areas of the regions of North Italy.

4. GROWTH FACTORS IN ITALIAN IDs: KNOWLEDGE DYNAMICS AND STRATEGIC BEHAVIOURS

In this section, we look at the combinations of growth factors that can explain Italian districts' development paths, through an analysis of 55 Italian district cases (see Table 33.2 below).[4] From a critical scrutiny of the literature on such cases nine important factors have been selected and classified under four broad headings: (a) the innovation capabilities; (b) the positive role played by local institutions; (c) the firm strategy towards product differentiation and diversification; and (d) the strategy towards internationalisation.

Again, this analysis is not meant to give a comprehensive survey of cases related to the ID phenomenon in contemporary Italy. It results nonetheless in a robust assessment of the presence of a variety of growth-evolutionary factors, which helps understand how Italian IDs and district-like cases show nowadays differentiated dynamic capabilities.

The innovation capability factor has been divided in three subprocesses respectively related to: (a) the presence of diffused learning processes (with the absorption of external technical change and inter-firm district diffusion) – this deals with the classical Marshallian idea of 'decentralised innovation capabilities' and the introduction of marginal original incremental innovations; (b) the presence of Schumpeterian (radical) innovation with the creation of new knowledge embedded in technical innovation (either patented or protected by the existence of sticky knowledge localised within the district walls) in the district firms (indigenous innovations); (c) the adoption of process technologies deriving from sources external to the district. Firms' strategies related to products have been classically distinguished into product differentiation (including the introduction of new designs) and product diversification (with, for example the shift of the activity from product manufacturing to the manufacture of related machinery, or shifts towards the mere commercialisation).

The internationalisation strategies comprise two main segments. The first refers to the decision of districts' firms to delocalise production processes; to engage with or build international subcontracting chains; or to venture into outward foreign direct investments. The second segment regards a more passive strategy involving districts' internal restructuring as a response to pressures from more aggressive global competitors. Such strategy may imply mere district market decline or a shift towards more protected high-quality market niches.

An analysis of the growth paths of Italian IDs leads to quite striking findings (see Table 33.2). What emerges is not one direction of change, but multiple path-dependent mechanisms, influenced by the combinatorial variety of different evolutionary growth factors.

It has to be considered that these trajectories of evolution have in general been adopted by firms and districts typically positioned in low-tech sectors, where the existing technological opportunities were quite scarce.

The first consideration suggested by Table 33.2 is that the international competitiveness of Italian districts has been largely sustained by a flow of continuous incremental innovations in products and processes, namely factor 3 (Belussi and Gottardi 2000). It was the mechanism that Bellandi (1996a) called 'decentralised industrial creativity'. Within the ID model there is a decentralised model of absorption of new knowledge (market and technical knowledge), which in turn circulates as an involuntary output of localised agents' interactions. However, this is more the result of search strategies and random interactions rather than a planned and deliberate effort in which R&D activities are involved as described in the standard economic model (Gottardi 1996). Dynamic feedbacks and positive interactions are created along the production *filière* and the numerous networks existing in each district, where firms cooperate in the manufacturing of the various components and subcomponents. When the existing knowledge is recombined within firms, it generates new knowledge at least within the firm (which can be a pure imitation or a slightly modified form of the original innovation). Marginal modification occurs via numerous sources: design and engineering activity, learning processes coming from the production departments, interactions with clients and suppliers, reuse and reworking of existing external knowledge. This model envisages the innovative process as a circular process with feedback and information links between market needs, design, production and search processes. From time to time, the existing pool of knowledge is reused, and recombined with new knowledge, for contingent problem-solving goals, or for implementing new entrepreneurial ideas. While standard economics treats the creation of new knowledge as a 'one-shot' process, in IDs knowledge accumulation proceeds as a continuous process (Belussi 2000).

Often the accumulation of knowledge is addressed towards the constitution of localised firms that produce the machinery needed by district firms. Inter-firm linkages with the suppliers of machinery localised in the district intensify proximity-dependent interacting learning, and the generation of novel machinery or new technological products (factor 4). Factor 4 is related to so-called Schumpeterian innovations which in fact mirror new radical innovations (namely, innovations that are new to the market, and not just to the firm). These are not so frequent in the Italian district model, but once one firm in the district introduces them, they relatively quickly spread among all the other firms. In relation to Table 3.2, again only few districts appear to have given rise to a flow of Schumpeterian innovations: Montebelluna, Mirandola, Manzano, Arzignano, Sassuolo, Castel Goffredo, Reggio Emilia, Bologna (packaging and motorcycling), Parma, Belluno, Schio Thiene, Matera-Altamura-Santeramo and Catania. Districts with Schumpeterian innovations seem to be located more in the Northeast regions than in the Centre or in the South of Italy. It is important to note that the new technological innovations introduced were not conceptualised in the district embryonic phase of growth: they occurred more frequently during the development or maturity stage. Over time, Schumpeterian districts could lose their innovative capability. However, until now this has not been so for the Italian cases analysed here. For instance, Montebelluna (Belussi 2005), in which during the 1970s plastic ski boots were developed, introduced in the 1990s a new generation of casual shoes with new types of technical soles (Geox); another example is in Catania, where ST-Microelectronics, now a technological dynamic firm, has stretched beyond the localities with creative R&D centres in US and in Bangalore (Torrisi 2002).

Factor 6 (product differentiation) appears extremely diffused in our selected sample of Italian district cases. For instance, there were in such cases many highly

Table 33.2 Growth factors in the development for selected Italian IDs and clusters with ID features

Nature of the growth factor	Most important factors in development stage (ordered by relative importance)	Most important factors at maturity stage (ordered by relative importance)	Sector and ID
1. Local institutions	4-3-2-1	4-6-1-8	1. Sport system in Montebelluna
2. Demand growth	2-3-5-1	5-6-1-8	2. Jewellery in Vicenza
3. Diffused learning processes (absorption of external knowledge and local diffusion)	2-6-3-1	3-9-1	3. Cutlery in Maniago (Udine)
	2-3	9	4. Furniture in Cerea (Verona)
	2-1-6	9-1	5. Artistic ceramics in Bassano (Vicenza)
4. Creation of new knowledge embedded in technical innovations (indigenous innovations)	2-1-3-5-6-4	8-4	6. Chairs in Manzano (Udine)
	2-1-3-5-6	8-3	7. Furniture in Livenza (Pordenone-Treviso)
	2-3-6	9	8. Artistic glass in Murano (Venice)
	2-1-3	6-8	9. Footwear in Fusignano and San Mauro Pascoli
	3-5	3-5-9	10. Wood processing machinery in Rimini
5. Cost leaderships (only process innovations	3-6	9-7	11. Sofa in Forlì
	2-1-3-6	9-6	12. Clothing and knitting in Carpi
	2-1-3-4-5-6-7	1-3-4-5-6-7-8	13. Ceramic tiles in Sassuolo
deriving from external to the district sources)	2-1-3-4-5-6-7	1-3-4-5-6-7-8	14. Agriculture machinery in Reggio Emilia
6. Product innovation (new design) and differentiation	2-1-3-6	1-6-3	15. Furniture in Brianza
	2-1-3-6	5-9	16. Footwear, footwear machinery (Vigevano)
	2-1-3-6	6-9	17. Silk in Como
7. Diversification	2-1-3-5-6	6-9	18. Taps and fittings in Lumezzane (Brescia)
8. Internationalisations (building active strategy: international subcontracting chains and FDI)	2-1-3-4-5-6-7	4-6-9	19. Nylon stockings in Castel Goffredo (Mantua)
	2-1-6-3	6-9	20. Jewellery in Valenza Pò
	2-1-3-5-6	6-1-9	21. Textile and wool in Biella
	2-1-3-5-6	6-9	22. Textiles in Prato
	2-1-3-5-6	6-7-9	23. Furniture in Poggibonsi
	2-5-7	9	24. Tanning in Santa Croce sull'Arno (Pisa)

9. Reaction to global competition (more passive strategy involving internal restructuring)	2–1	9–7	25. Musical instruments, now electronics in Castelfidardo
	2	9	26. Clothing in Urbania
	2–1–3–4–5–6–7	4–8	27. Sofa in Matera-Altamura-Santeramo
	2	9	28. Clothing in Val Vibrata
	2–5	9	29. Tanning in Solofra
	2–1	9	30. Ceramics in Caltagirone
	2–1	1–4–6–8–9	31. Jewellery in Marcianise (Naple-Caserta)
	2–1–3–4–5–6	8	32. Leather in Arzignano
	2–1–3–5–6	9	33. Marble in Valpolicella (Verona)
	2–1	9	34. Porphyry and stone material in Trento
	2–1–3	9	35. Leather in Solofra
	2–3	9	36. Paper in Fabriano
	2–3	9	37. Marble in Carrara
	2–6	8–9	38. Vegetable preserving industries (tomatos) in Agro Nocerino Sarnese
	2–1–3	6–9–8–1	39. Footwear in Riviera del Brenta
	2–1–3–4–5–6	6–7–9	40. Eyewear in Belluno
	2–3–1	9	41. Ornamental horticulture district of Saonara in Padua
	2–3–6	8	42. Machine manufacturing in Schio Thiene in Vicenza
	2–1–3–4–5–6	7–6–8	43. Biomedical in Mirandola
	2–1–3–4–5–6	4–6–8	44. Packaging district in Bologna
	2–1–3–4–5–6	4–6–8	45. Agriculture machinery in Reggio Emilia and Modena
	2–3–4–6	4–8	46. Motorcycles in Bologna
	2–1–3–4–5–6–7	4–6–8	47. Food processing in Parma
	2–3	1–3–5–9	48. Ornamental horticulture in Pistoia
	2–3–6	7–3–9	49. Jewellery (Arezzo – Uno A Erre, 1849)
	2–3–6	9	50. Ceramic (Sesto Fiorentino – Richard-Ginori)
	2–3–4–6	4–9	51. Taps and fitting in Cusio
	2–1–3–6	3–6–8	52. Furniture district in Pesaro
	2–3–6	3–7–8	53. Footwear district in Civitanova
	2	9	54. Footwear in Barletta and Casarano
	2–1–3–4–6	4–7–9	55. Micro electronics in Etna Valley in Catania (ST-Microelectronics)

Source: See Table 33.1.

sophisticated and specialised suppliers, able to provide specific applications to demanding customers (final foreign firms, retailing chains, large multinationals, health institutions, mass-production-oriented producers) in a segment of the market characterised by high-quality performance.

In this group of firms, design capabilities, creativity, engineering skills, product know-how and understanding customers' requirements, are the major sources of incremental innovations and product customisation. The strength of the innovative performance of the Italian firms lies also in the firm's design capability, characteristics that are obviously strategic in the 'made-in-Italy' sectors, but which include the ability to integrate innovative parts and components into products.

Cost competitiveness depending on the fast adoption of process innovations (factor 5) is another diffused characteristic.

The transformation of Italian IDs has been guided also by various strategies of diversification. For instance, Vigevano has shifted its production from shoes to shoes machinery; likewise, Belluno had entered with Luxottica into the building of large international retail chains. Product diversification and differentiation, related to product upgrading strategy, appear the most common factors inducing change and giving rise to different district dynamics (Carabelli, Hirsh and Rabellotti 2006). Product diversification and differentiation are, on one side, the effect of strategies internal to the firm, but on the other side, they are the result of an enlarged inter-firm division of labour driven by greater scale economies and externalities connected to the mechanism of growth activated by the endogenous district dynamics.

In most of the cases, the proactive role of local institutions (factor 1) has been found to be very important in relation to the issue of technological upgrading and to the provision of real services to local small firms.[5] This has implied quite often the building of vocational training schools.[6] Local universities have not played much of a strategic role in the history of development of the Italian IDs. Local universities play a strategic role only in the case of high-tech districts, where they can strengthen the international ties of local actors with many global research institutions. Only in a few cases in Italy was the technological upgrading of the district supported by local universities or by national projects organised by them.

Outward processes of internationalisation (factor 8) and the internal reactions to the new global competition (factor 9) which emerged at the end of the 1990s (an exogenous market shock variable) are the final factors discussed. Since the 1990s, the entry of international competitors in the Italian or European market has constituted for many districts the most serious threat engendering an urgent response strategy. This has challenged district firms either to shift their production towards higher segments of the market (or to decline) and/or, alternatively, to develop international subcontracting chains and to invest abroad, in low-cost countries (FDI strategies).

In particular, adaptive passive strategies are associated with factor 9, while active forward-looking strategies are reflected in factor 8. Clearly within a single district both strategies can be found among firms, as in the case of the Riviera del Brenta. Relocating strategies have involved less strategic (labour-intensive) parts of the value chain in low-cost countries. This has been a diffused strategy adopted by nearly all districts specialised in the 'made-in-Italy' sectors, like footwear, furniture and clothing. The entry of foreign firms through globalisation has exerted a negative influence in many cases (factor 9) on, for instance, Carpi, Lumezzane, Verona, Barletta and Casarano, Val Vibrata, Riviera del Brenta, Belluno (only the smallest firms), Vicenza (jewellery) and Saonara. On the contrary, a more positive reaction (factor 8) can be seen in other Italian IDs where an interesting variety in firms' internationalisation trajectories has emerged. In some cases, the internationalisation process has been pushed by some leading firms in districts and small multinationals, which, thanks to superior technological capabilities, have been able to establish new plants or new commercial units in foreign markets. Such internationalisation processes have been driven by the fragmentation of the geographical distribution of the value chain by the relocation abroad of low value-added activities. This is, for instance, the case in Montebelluna (through the strategies of Geox and Stonefly), in Belluno (Luxottica), in Arzignano (Mastrotto), and in Matera-Altamura-Santeramo (Natuzzi) (Sammarra and Belussi 2006). In the case of the microelectronics cluster in Catania, the founding firm was a large multinational, ST-Microelectronics, which has pursued outwards processes of internationalisations linked to international expansion of the R&D networks (a form of knowledge offshoring) that has branched out its research capacity, particularly in California and in Bangalore.

Considering the inward investment processes, Schumpeterian districts have also been able to attract the entry of external multinational enterprise during their development (see the Montebelluna and the Mirandola cases).

5. CONCLUSIONS

This chapter has tried to address the following questions: where do IDs in Italy come from? Are they innovative? And how? Triggering factors of their genesis and subsequent growth in relation to a sample of the most representative ID cases in Italy have been analysed. They are responsible for the emergence of variation in IDs and for the retention, during time, of significant district heterogeneity. Clearly the meta-analysis adopted represents a methodology in which the success of the results very much depends on the interpretative capabilities of the researcher, and is not automatically embedded in statistical standard procedures, which benefit from the availability of large datasets. Clearly, the importance of the various factors considered depends on the qualitative evaluation of the researcher that, in turn, can be criticised because it is subject to data imperfection and scarcity.

All things considered, in this chapter a recursive sequence of cumulative growth-inducing mechanisms has been described, which has focused on the various stages of district growth.

IDs started with a small group of firms endowed with some artisan skills, or with access to specific natural resources, or from founding firms (see Table 33.1).

In one case only did the triggering mechanism come from outside, thanks to the entry of an external multinational company. At the genesis stage, within ID cases distinctive competences have been mobilised by the existing local productive forces (local entrepreneurial attitudes), and by a favourable external environment (demand growth and a positive role played by local institutions). What characterises Italian districts is that the governance of the local productive cycles has always been highly decentralised among several small entrepreneurs.

Advantages depending on cost competitiveness (and self-exploitation by self-employed small entrepreneurs) typically may be the principal attribute of the start-up phase.

Once the local system was able to capture a specific segment of the national or international demand, the growth mechanism kicked off (Table 33.2). It is not just the reaping of agglomeration economies that counted, but the ability to respond to fast-changing markets and technologies, and the existence of a social and institutional setting able to promote innovation. When demand growth increased, in a kind of Stigler-type effect, the existence of a larger market pushed ahead the returns related to a further division of labour among firms. Specialisation increased economies of scale and scope. In the course of their growth, some district firms generated new knowledge, introducing Schumpeterian innovations (radical innovations), which in turn made those districts even more competitive. This, it can be argued, set in motion a cumulative tendency that, once introduced, could keep the district at the forefront of the international frontier for decades. Other districts followed a different growth path characterised by a strategy of continuous learning, leading to a process of intense product differentiation.

Since the 1990s, the forces of globalisation have presented new and ruthless competitive challenges, testing the ability of districts to sustain their market advantage and pushing some districts over the edge; however, responses to adversity have prompted dynamic adjustments that take globalisation as an opportunity rather than a threat, through for instance the active internationalisation processes of the more vibrant districts and clusters.

NOTES

1. The main sources are reported in Belussi and Pilotti (2002); Club dei distretti industriali (2003); Belussi and Sammarra (2005).
2. As described by Lazerson and Lorenzoni (1999b) and Viesti (2000), and in the case of foreign high-tech districts by Klepper (2001), and Feldman (2004, 2005).
3. Tested in the American high-tech districts by Dyck (1997); Klepper (2001); Feldman (2004, 2005); Braunerhjelm and Feldman (2006).
4. For a reference on the methodology, see Belussi, Sammarra and Sedita (2008).
5. For an ample discussion of the Italian case, see also Belussi (1999b).
6. For instance, in the case of the packaging machinery district in Bologna and of the shoe district in Riviera del Brenta.

34. Banks' localism and industrial districts

Pietro Alessandrini and Alberto Zazzaro

1. INTRODUCTION

The aim of this chapter is to examine the link between firms and banks within industrial districts (IDs). At first glance the importance of the bank–firm relationship in IDs appears consolidated and easily identifiable on two grounds: first, since banks are the chief interlocutors of small and medium-sized enterprises (SMEs) both in ordinary credit relationships and in selecting investment projects, ID firms are largely bank-dependent; secondly, due to the distinctive characteristics of districts, known to be based on a close interweaving of relations among firms and with the local society, ID banks require in-depth knowledge of the local context and the local economy. The common conclusion is that banks are called upon to establish close relationships with firms, and that this role is usually played by local banks which have operated in small geographical ambits, with long-lasting relationships and in-depth cultural affinity with local firms. It is on the basis of such premises that the district stereotype of small firms–small banks has gained credence among scholars and observers.

A fresh view of the bank–firm relationships in IDs leads to a drastic revision of this stereotype, in line with the insights we have acquired by studying IDs with a systemic and dynamic approach to the analysis of local development. Such insights take on particular importance for economies which are characterised by the presence of many local systems of SMEs and marked territorial imbalances in levels of development. These features, found in several industrialised countries, are particularly important in the Italian economy, which represents a significant laboratory to which we shall chiefly refer in surveying the empirical evidence.

A systemic approach to local development takes account of the complexity of current development processes, in which many different actors interact and a variety of development engines are in motion. It takes seriously the matter of reconciling drives towards globalisation, which tends to level out and standardise, with the needs of localism, which recognizes diversity and promotes complementarity. In the presence of marked imbalances in the production structure of an economy, like that of Italy, the financial system has the hard task of making the specific needs of the various local production systems (LPSs) compatible with the diffusion of the standardised innovations of global financial markets. To succeed in this task, banks play a key role: they represent the most flexible link in the chain between local and global markets, between traditional and innovative finance, and between bilateral and multilateral relations.

The dynamic approach leads to adopting an interpretative picture that leaves room for the evolution of organisations and agents' behaviour and calls for flexibility in operative strategies and intervention proposals. From this point of view, the basic issue is whether the recent transformations which have affected firms and banks have changed credit relationships in general and, as far as we are concerned, in district systems in particular.

The first profound transformation concerns technological, production and organisational changes of SMEs, which are now called to withstand growing international competition, decide strategically the location of different production phases, and invest in improving the quality of products and production processes and consolidating size. When reported within the IDs these changes raise questions regarding their very distinctive features, which have to be reinterpreted dynamically, as maintained by Becattini (2000a). The signs of change in district areas are evident. According to the Mediobanca-Unioncamere survey (2005), a quarter of Italian medium-size enterprises is headquartered in districts and is distinguished by a greater degree of internationalisation and a better financial structure. We are dealing with firms, selected by international competition, which are large enough to coordinate groups of small subsuppliers not only within, but also outside the district. The increase in production size and market size, and the spread of the degree of internationalisation and innovation (Rabellotti, Carabelli and Hirsch 2009) contribute to diversifying the demand of district firms for credit and financial services, according to a more complex framework which includes ordinary credit, the internal network of commercial credit, and finance for development.

A second major change has affected banking systems over the 1990s and 2000s. The process of banking liberalisation that started early in the 1990s has opened for banks the possibility of making strategic choices in terms of mergers and acquisitions, of centralising decision-making structures, and expanding the network of branches, but at the same time it has constrained banks to assess and manage risk in relation to the value of capital. These changes have deeply transformed the structures of credit supply and financial services in and for local markets. Following many mergers and acquisitions the number of operating banks has declined and their average size has increased. However, the banks' presence in local systems has increased in terms of number of branches and innovative forms of contact. The very notion of bank localism has consequently expanded to include a heterogeneous group of banks, in size as well as in corporate and organisational structures: from small cooperative banks to inter-regional banks, from independent banks to banks belonging to financial conglomerates.

These changes have intensified the debate on the practicability of a competitive coexistence in local credit markets of banks locally headquartered and banks headquartered outside the region. Following successive waves of aggregations, the formation of large bank groups has led to the progressive centralisation of decisional power in a smaller number of headquarters and the vanishing of banks' strategic functions from almost all local peripheral systems and from many ID regions. This begs the first interesting question, as to whether local roots and 'environmental familiarity' still count in banks' territorial competition strategies. In relation to this, one has to wonder whether the information advantages acquired over time by the renewed local banks substitute or complement the advantages coming from the broader range of financial services the major bank conglomerates can supply; how to obtain the right mix of transaction and relationship banking, product standardisation and flexibility, centralisation and decentralisation of decision making. Broadly speaking, we need to understand whether the evolution of banking supply is matched by the changing finance needs of SMEs in district systems.

The discussion in this chapter will be organised around two strictly interrelated themes: (a) the spatial organisation of banks and credit allocation; and (b) the banks' territorial strategies. To conclude, we will formulate some thoughts on what could be called a 'desirable' local banking system.

2. SPATIAL ORGANISATION OF BANKS AND CREDIT ALLOCATION

There is now a broad consensus on the idea that local banking development facilitates access to credit for local firms, stimulates the propensity to innovate and boosts the growth of the local economy.[1] The 'development' of a local banking system has been measured in a great number of ways, including: the regulatory system, the competition/concentration of local credit markets, the observed or estimated credit availability to local firms, the presence of branches and their efficiency, and the type of bank branches working locally. The open yet crucial question is which indicator is most relevant to local banking development. The answer to this question is required in order to identify the spatial organisation of the banking system which is most suitable to promote the growth of areas with different levels of development.

The effects that the consolidation of banking structures has on credit availability at a local level and on conditions under which such credit is supplied are ambiguous. They depend on the effects of mergers and acquisitions upon the efficiency of the banks involved and on market competitivity. However, besides prices and quantities, the changes in the spatial organisation of banks also affect bank–firm relationships and credit allocation.

2.1 Large versus small local banks

A recurring theme in the banking literature is that large banks have a competitive disadvantage in small business lending and other soft information-based market segments, with respect to small local banks. Following this view, bank mergers and acquisitions (M&As) would risk penalising systems of SMEs especially if located in peripheral areas. The reasons for this competitive disadvantage have been ascribed to the presence of organisational diseconomies which make it relatively more costly to collect soft information on borrowers and transmit it within the higher layers of the bank organisation. However, are bank size and local rootedness the key variables affecting organisational diseconomies and the capacity to support dynamic small local firms?

At first sight, empirical evidence suggests a positive answer to this question: small firms are more dependent on bank credit than large firms, while large banks tend to allocate a smaller share of their assets to small business lending than small banks (Berger et al. 1998, 2005; Craig and Hardee 2007). On closer scrutiny, however, the reality is much more complex. First of all, the effects of bank consolidation on small business lending seem to depend significantly on the type of institutions involved. For example, evidence for Italy and the US shows that while consolidations occurring between medium–large banks have brought about a reduction in loans to small firms, mergers and acquisitions involving small banks have led to a bigger share of loans to small firms (Peek and Rosengren 1998; Strahan and Weston 1998; Sapienza 2002).

Second, to assess the effects of bank M&As on credit availability to small firms one cannot limit oneself to a static analysis, but should also take into account adjustment policies both of banks involved in aggregation processes and their competitors (Berger et al. 1998). Looking at the Italian experience, Focarelli, Panetta and Salleo (2002) found that M&As entail a significant and persistent reduction in the amount of credit supplied to small firms, especially in the case of acquired banks. By contrast, Bonaccorsi di Patti and Gobbi (2007) found that the reduction in credit available to small firms operating with banks involved in an M&A tends to disappear in the course of three years following the deal. Alessandrini, Calcagnini and Zazzaro (2008) found that acquisitions involving banks in the most developed area (central and northern Italy) were dominated by an asset-cleaning strategy according to which the bidder bank makes a clean sweep of all the negative net present value activities in the portfolio of the target bank without permanently changing the asset allocation of the target bank. Differently, in the case of acquisitions of banks in the less advanced area (generally in Italy in the southern regions) by banks of the Centre-North, the asset restructuring strategy followed by the acquiring bank led to a structural change in the portfolio of the acquired bank with a permanent reduction in loans to small firms and an increase in asset management activity.

Third, improvements in information technology and in credit scoring techniques have hugely facilitated the hardening of soft information. This has allowed a reduction in underwriting costs for small business loans and an enhancement in the failure prediction ability of banks, which has led to an increase in overall loans and easier credit access for marginal borrowers (Udell 2009).

If it is problematic to consider bank size a pure liability in small business lending, the idea that bank localism *per se* is able to ensure that credit is always allocated in a way which best suits local economic development does not appear fully convincing. Although the informational advantages of local banks, stemming from their historical roots and 'cultural affinities' with the local community, permit a sounder assessment of local firms, their same close ties with the area may further separate, through various channels, local banks from funding more dynamic firms. Exclusive knowledge of a given economic situation may, for example, reduce local banks' capacity to react to new ideas from the world of production. Alternatively, customer relations with local firms may drive local banks to limit the entry of new firms and the funding of strongly innovative activity which, if successful, could call into question the solvency of preexisting firms. Or yet again, to reduce liquidity costs, local banks might prefer to finance firms that are not open to the outside – which distribute income locally and allow an expansion in their own deposit multiplier – firms which, in peripheral areas, are often those that are less innovative and dynamic (Zazzaro 1997; Alessandrini and Zazzaro 1999).

The empirical evidence on Italy concerning the capacity of local banks to support local customers and stimulate the growth of local economies is somewhat ambiguous. Historically, local banks do not appear to have decisively performed the functions of a *Hausbank* for small firms. At the beginning of the last century, although local banks already had a strong presence in many areas in Italy, only rarely did bank–firm relations manage to evolve along the lines of the one-to-one bank–firm relationship model, as shown by the already widespread recourse to multiple lending (Conti 1997; Gigliobianco 1997; Chiapparino 2008). Moving on to the present day, available evidence is mixed. Several studies have shown that there is no significant relation between financial constraints and belonging to an ID (Guelpa and Tirri 2006) or even that district firms are financially more constrained (Baffigi, Pagnini and Quintiliani 2000; Pagnini 2000). By contrast, others have shown that for district firms the probability of being rationed by banks is significantly lower than for non-district firms (Finaldi Russo and Rossi 2001; Rotondi 2005; Ughetto 2006; Alessandrini, Presbitero and Zazzaro 2008a). Either way, such positive effects chiefly appear due to a 'district effect' rather than any privileged relations the firms establish with the local banks (Finaldi Russo and Rossi 1999).

2.2 Does distance matter?

While the root of the importance of bank spatial organisation for local development cannot be sought in the contrast of large banks versus small local banks, a more promising way to read the geography of a banking system can be found in the notion of distance. The combination of diffusion-centralisation, typical of bank globalisation processes, has resulted in two distance-contrasting effects. First, there has been a reduction in 'operational distance', that is the distance between banks and customers through the wide geographical spread of bank branches and the development of impersonal methods of communication – such as internet banking. Second, there has been a sharp increase in 'functional distance', that is the distance between bank decisional centres and local economies.[2] Functional distance condenses different physical and cultural elements. For example, it is reasonable to believe that the costs of monitoring loan officers per visit increase with physical distance from the bank's headquarters where loan reviewers are employed. Similarly, reliability of communication and trust between managers at the parent bank and local loan officers decrease with the physical distance between the bank head office and the local branch, but also with the socio-cultural distance between the geographical areas where the staff of the bank's decisional centre and operational peripheries work and live.

In Italy, the consolidation process which began in the 1990s has radically changed the geography of bank organisation and decision-making powers. The number of independent banks has greatly decreased, especially in the South where almost all local banks have been absorbed by banks from the Centre-North of Italy. Consequently, the increase in functional distance in the last 20 years has been much greater in the South than in the Centre-North. The same geographical evolution in functional distances can be obtained either if we measure it in physical (kilometres) or cultural (social capital) terms. If we look at the ID provinces,[3] bank proximity, whether operational or functional, is greater than elsewhere and such differences have increased in the past decade (Alessandrini, Presbitero and Zazzaro 2008a). This pattern suggests that district areas are more attractive for banks, that view proximity to IDs as a way to reduce information gaps and to obtain greater business opportunities than in other LSPs.

The effects of banks' operational proximity to borrowers on lending decisions and contracts are controversial, as we have to balance the benefits of greater availability of soft local information with the costs deriving from the banks' greater market power (Cerquiero, Degryse and Ongena 2009). On the contrary, functional distance between the bank headquarters and the local economy unambiguously make soft information-based loans more costly. Where information on credit valuation cannot be easily encoded and communicated within the bank, functional distance increases the cost of transmitting and processing 'soft information' and reduces the reliability of communication and trust between local loan officers and central managers (Stein 2002; Alessandrini, Croci and Zazzaro 2005). Economic, cultural and social disparities between centre and periphery broaden the liabilities of functional distance.

There is extensive evidence concerning different countries at different levels of financial and economic development that distance-related organisational frictions affect bank lending policies and credit allocation by local managers, limiting the amount of resources devoted to small business and relational lending.[4] As regards Italy, empirical evidence shows that small firms are more likely to be credit-rationed and are less inclined to introduce innovations if they are located in provinces where a greater percentage of branches belong to banks headquartered in physically distant provinces and in provinces with different social and economic environments (Alessandrini, Presbitero and Zazzaro 2008a, 2008b). Moreover, in Italian bank acquisitions, the greater the cultural distance between the provinces where the dealing partners are headquartered, the greater are the changes in acquired banks' asset allocation in favour of large borrowers and transaction-based financial activities, at the expense of small, opaque borrowers (Alessandrini, Calcagnini and Zazzaro 2008). Consistent with the hypothesis that functionally distant banks specialise in lending to more transparent and safer borrowers – but by using loan-level data – the results show that functionally distant banks tend to operate with safer borrowers who they can charge low interest rates (Casolaro and Mistrulli 2008). Finally, ID firms have a greater probability of establishing stable and exclusive relations with banks and less probability of being credit-rationed than non-district firms. However, this district effect tends to decline significantly for those firms that operate in provinces in which banks are functionally distant (Alessandrini, Presbitero and Zazzaro 2008a).

3. BANK TERRITORIAL STRATEGIES

Besides investigating the spatial distribution of bank 'thinking heads', it is also necessary to pose the question, 'What do they think?', that is, how much importance do they attach to the development of LSPs? To find this out we need to analyse banks' strategic objectives, their investments in organisational structures and their credit selection policies.

In terms of objectives, banking management has the difficult task of balancing two commitments: 'profit efficiency' and 'development efficiency' (Alessandrini, Papi and Zazzaro 2003). 'Profit efficiency' focuses attention on banks as profit-oriented firms, operating in competitive markets. Under this rationale, banking management should seek organisational solutions and operative choices that increase capital value and satisfy their shareholders. 'Development efficiency' focuses on credit allocation, in which banks select investment projects, promote innovations, assess the potential of local firms, and assert the principles of transparency, reliance and professional merit. Inescapably, banks contribute to selecting the ruling class of a production system. From this standpoint, banks assume a fundamental role as local development agents: a role that is institutionally important in the presence of local systems operating in regions with different levels of development.

Profit and development efficiency are interdependent. In the more developed regions it is easier to obtain a virtuous bank–firm interaction that allows banks to achieve both targets. In peripheral regions, this successful combination of efficiencies is more difficult to obtain in the short run. Therein, the development efficiency of banks often contrasts with the goal of maximising profit in the short run. The support given to the riskier, but creditworthy local firms could lead to an immediate decrease in profit. In this case, if local development efficiency has to assume priority, profit efficiency is a target to be postponed to the longer term.

Given the existence of regional disparities in development, the importance in bank strategies of being geographically rooted cannot be generalised and cannot be considered a bolstering factor for local development. Where it counts is in the forms of intermediation in which bank–customer operational proximity reduces information and transaction costs. It varies according to the level of socio-economic development of local contexts, according to risk factors, information and behavioural problems that assume particular importance in the case of IDs. In more advanced regions, bank branch density is greater, small firms are less penalised in credit conditions (rates, availability, collaterals) and the advantages of district agglomeration are enhanced. In peripheral regions, geographical rootedness can be more of a constraint than an opportunity, generating a local–local vicious circle which can be broken by opening up local banking markets to competition from out-of-market banks and the acquisition of local inefficient banks.

However, it is worth pointing out the importance of strategic proximity between the bank and the district firm, which maintains a high degree of information opacity due both to the small scale concerned and to the web of relations of cooperation and competition that need to be interpreted *in loco*. In addition to this, long-term bank–firm relations facilitate the acquisition of technological innovations and vertical re-specialisation from finished products to the production of equipment on the part of district firms, as reported by Ferri and Rotondi (2006).

Yet at the same time, we should not underestimate the risk of a systemic crisis which could have a negative chain effect among firms of a district suffering a competitive lag. Cases of insolvency could easily spread through the complex network of inter-firm relationships that characterize IDs, including the extended use of inter-firm trade credit (Dei Ottati 1994a). There is greater exposure to such risks among local banks, which have a higher geographical and sectoral concentration in their loan portfolios.

For district SMEs it is essential to have banks that know how to play their own role as local development agents. The fact that distance from decisional centres reduces the credit supplied especially to firms operating in districts may be seen as further confirmation of this hypothesis. It is therefore important that the banking system can satisfy the renewed demand for credit and financial services by maintaining functional proximity with the area.

These local development needs must be met not only by local independent banks but also by large banking groups. It is no longer a question of large or small size, but rather of strategic sensitivity. Local independent banks and community banks, selected by banking competition, can renew their role of maintaining an active presence in local systems provided that they invest in human capital and in strategic alliances to exploit their advantages of contextual knowledge of the local environment. To survive competitively their aim is to compensate for smaller size and a strictly local sphere of operations by pursuing several routes: (a) participating in joint agreements, exchange networks and circuits of shared services, which allow cost reductions; (b) extending the range of financial products; and (c) acquiring innovations and providing assistance to savers and firms that wish to link up with outside markets for more sophisticated operations. If this does not occur, local banks may become isolated and conservative, thus acting as a brake rather than a stimulus for development, as was seen above. In this case, the only practicable solution is to help them to be absorbed by larger banks or banking groups headquartered outside the area. This is the fastest route, albeit at the cost of increasing functional distances and at the risk of dispersing environmental knowledge and professional growth potential of local bank operators.

On the other hand, large bank groups may attenuate the adverse effects of greater functional distances with strategies of organisational decentralisation and flexible adaptation to the various environmental contexts. We must not forget that large banking conglomerates have a higher potential to diversify their area strategies. Operating in regions with different levels of development, they could use the higher profit efficiency in the more developed local markets to subsidise in the short run the profit inefficiency in peripheral local markets where development efficiency is overriding.

4. SOME CONCLUDING THOUGHTS: DESIRABLE LOCAL BANKING STRUCTURES

Our analysis in the previous sections leads to two major conclusions on appropriate bank structures for local banking systems, especially for IDs.

The first concerns the importance of promoting a competitive equilibrium between several banks, differing both in size and in their management and ownership structure (independent local, acquired local, independent outside banks). A diversified local banking structure tends to satisfy the combination of local and global tasks. The local task seeks to exploit the benefits of local knowledge supplied by geographical rootedness. The global task offers local operators the best solutions for allocating savings, financing investment and acquiring innovation. Resorting to several banking organisations is a sound practice: there is no single winning banking model *a priori* in achieving both objectives. Much depends on what one does, how one does it, with whom and where. Modern SME systems need a flexible approach with a mix of relationship activities, that offer bespoke products and services (specialised bank), and transactions activities, that offer standardised products and services (network bank).

As we saw in section 3, the problem must be tackled not in absolute terms, but in relation to the geographical area of reference. The needs of different local systems and the multitude of SMEs operating therein are complex and diverse: they range from size consolidation, technological and organisational innovations, to relocation investments and to problems of generational and professional turnover. Unlike in the past, such tasks can no longer be accomplished only by small local banks which grew in the same area where the firm operates. Relying only on their past local information advantages, may be a losing strategy for the local economy and for the same banks. At the same time, the variety of local development problems limits the contribution of efficiency made by large banking organisations which distribute standardised financial instruments.

In a local scenario of more banking competition, no operating bank, whether large or small, can afford to build up delays in acquiring innovations to deal with local development problems. Banks should grade financial innovations to the specific requirements of each system: the greater the development gaps to be filled and the endowment of small firms to assist, the more local-oriented such requirements should be. In this diversified field, the needs of local firms must be understood case by case, situation by situation. It is important to be able to exploit the advantages of relational and functional proximities. This holds not only for banks, but also for venture capital activities, which require an intensive long-term form of 'relationship financing'. Hence it is pointless in many firms and regions to have only transaction banks; what is needed are banks that can interpret bank–firm relationships in a modern viewpoint.

To support the competitive development of IDs, the local banking system must be able to select and assist more dynamic small firms, which express higher potential in terms of entrepreneurial and organisational capacity, absorption of technological innovations, efficiency and profitability, and penetration of markets both near and far. The qualitative consolidation of SMEs increases the demand for financial services at various levels: diversification and development investments, reorganisation of the ownership structure, partly in light of generational turnover, allocation of capital from institutional investors, as far as providing assistance for stock market quotation. With respect to such needs, the advantage of direct knowledge and cultural and environmental affinities is reduced for local banks. What is required are specific financial competences which may easily be provided by larger and, above all, specialised intermediaries, such as investment banks, venture-capital firms and investment trusts.

However, local banks are not *a priori* excluded from competition on innovative finance for development. Those that are more focused and far sighted may remain a point of reference for emerging local firms, acquiring the most appropriate information and contacts for the requirements of the entrepreneur wishing to develop his/her firm. Thus the bank–firm relationship can be enriched by the assistance that the home bank can provide the innovative local entrepreneur in filtering the choices and contacting intermediaries specialised in the more complex financial operations. Working together with the experienced and competent local banker, with whom a consolidated relationship of trust has been established, may help small entrepreneurs overcome their fears, mistrust and lack of a financial culture. These limits are often the main obstacle to making the necessary leaps forward in quality and size, as shown by experience in Italy.

The second conclusion on the desirable local banking structure concerns the strategic importance of being able to count at least on a strong banking competitor with its 'thinking head' in the region to which the district belongs. There are three good reasons to support this goal.

First, in addition to the positive effects on bank performance, functional proximity has important external effects. Specifically, it helps to maintain functional centrality, with important externalities for the accumulation of human, social and institutional capital. Usually, the most qualified and specialised human resources (managers, directors, professionals, financial analysts) reside in regions where banking decisional centres are located. Indeed, banks demand and produce their most qualified human capital in these regions. It is inevitable that, for example, local universities and other research and training centres strongly benefit from the presence of the headquarter of an independent bank in terms of job opportunities for students and research project financing. Externalities of this type affect entrepreneurship, as well as social and institutional capital. Indeed, the concentration of bank decisional centres through mergers and acquisitions leads to a change in the functional hierarchy between central and peripheral regions whose consequences need close scrutiny.

The second reason is that a significant presence of headquartered banks helps to maintain economic centrality in the region. In this case, outside banks have to consider the specific needs of the local area if they want to erode the advantages that headquartered banks have in terms of regional knowledge. This set of advantages is more relevant to less developed regions, as shown in the previous sections, where there is a stronger need to activate forces driving development not only from outside, but also from within the area. It is not a question of abandoning the selective process in the free market of property rights, which should not be impeded. What is instead desirable is also to promote the entrepreneurial and managerial skills of local banks, selected by competitive pressures, as a vital agent of economic and social development in IDs and, in general, in any LSPs.

Last but not least, the more IDs can benefit from local banking structures that give strategic priority to the specific needs of local firms and local development, the less they should be open to standardised financial instruments, transferred through globalised circuits and subject to international destabilising crises. In periods of greater worldwide financial instability, as experienced in the first decade of the new century, lower exposure to outside risks of financial contagion should not be undervalued in the picture of a desirable local banking structure.

NOTES

1. A review of this literature may be found in Alessandrini, Papi and Zazzaro (2003).
2. For the distinction between operational and functional distances see Alessandrini, Croci and Zazzaro (2005).
3. Becattini and Coltorti (2006) identify 28 district provinces.
4. For a survey see Alessandrini, Presbitero and Zazzaro (2008b).

SECTION 8
The experiences in other industrialised countries

Introduction

Gabi Dei Ottati

1. IDs IN VARIOUS DEVELOPED COUNTRIES

The chapters included in this section illustrate and reflect on the experiences of industrial districts (IDs) and, more in general, of patterns of local development in several industrialised countries.

The section starts with a general overview on European countries, by Gioacchino Garofoli, followed by specific contributions on France by Georges Benko and Bernard Pecqueur, on Spain by Josep-Antoni Ybarra, on Scandinavia by Bengt Johannisson; and outside Europe on Japan by Yoshiyuki Okamoto, and on the US by Donald Patton and Martin Kenney. Specific contributions on Italy are collected in a separate section.

These chapters differ from one another not merely because they refer to different national experiences, but also because they have somewhat different conceptual and interpretative frameworks. Although, the experiences described and the related policies that emerge from their reading are therefore multifaceted, there are important threads that link the different contributions and are worth stressing.

As Garofoli argues in his contribution, the discovery of IDs in Italy during the 1970s and the revitalisation of the concept of the ID (Becattini 1979), together with the crisis of the Fordist model (Piore and Sabel 1984), opened up a new area of study concerning, on the one hand, a variety of models of capitalist development and, on the other hand, research on IDs in countries other than Italy. In this way it was found that the Italian type of districts (that is, with localised industries characterised by small and medium-sized enterprises specialised in the manufacturing of goods for the person and home, and in light machinery) were more widespread in southern European countries, such as Spain and Portugal, than in, for instance, the Scandinavian countries. This is not only due to the different economic histories of those countries, and in particular to the wider distribution of the Fordist model of large-scale industry, and its effects upon society in North Europe, but also to the diversity of political and institutional action. This is made very evident, for example, by the fundamental role of local governments in the development of IDs in Spain (Ybarra) and, vice versa, by the influence of the central public administration in the constitution of science parks in Sweden (Johannisson). In Japan IDs appear to be present in a large number, however they have a modest weight in the national economy and their contribution has been much reduced over recent decades, most of all because of changes brought about by globalisation (Okamoto). A separate issue concerns the US where local development took place above all with the agglomeration of high-tech companies set up mainly as spinoffs of university research laboratories in the area. The best-known example is Silicon Valley, but of no lesser interest are the cases of Madison and Urbana-Champaign analysed in this section by Patton and Kenney.

2. IMPLICATIONS ON THE UNDERSTANDING OF DISTRICT PROCESSES

The chapters of this section provide therefore a rich overview of the weight and types of IDs characterising various developed countries. Besides, they contribute to our understanding of the forces that have driven the formation and normal evolution of IDs, together with insights in the current actions to revitalise them when and where under major challenges.

The case of Spain shows us that the formation of IDs requires considerable mobilisation of resources (in particular skills, initiative, creativity and reciprocal cooperation) within the local society.[1] It also confirms that this mobilisation is effective when it is promoted and coordinated by local political actors legitimated by a popular consensus built, for example, on a genuine commitment to provide a local community with a response to unemployment and economic crises. With regard to the evolution of the IDs and the continuous adaptation of their local industries to changing conditions of supply and demand, Johannisson maintains that the traditional dichotomy between 'functional rationale' – based on complex and codified competence, a global outlook and an urban life setting – and 'territorial rationale' – based on focalised and tacit competence, a local outlook and a rural life setting – must be superseded in order to pursue local development. He puts forward a proposal for the adoption of a new 'virtual' logic, which combines rural/urban, local/global and complex/focused conditions to create dynamism and change. All of this brings to mind a number of concepts developed in the study of IDs such as, for example, the concept of 'urbanised countryside' (Becattini 1975a), or that of the 'cognitive spiral' referring to the integration of contextual knowledge with codified knowledge (Becattini and Rullani 1993). The conceptual outline put forward by Johannisson, however, also brings to mind how fundamentally complementary competition and cooperation are in the ID model. It is the active coexistence of these two different forces which allows the regular functioning of district reproductive processes, in particular, comprising the process of localised division of labour among firms, the process of flexible integration of this division of labour through local markets, and the process of widespread learning and innovation (Becattini 2003a; Dei Ottati in this volume). More in general, development of the district-model type requires dynamic integration and mutual support between economic and social forces in such a way as to support the continuous adaptation of the productive apparatus and the renewal of knowledge, values and implicit norms. All this should allow the regeneration over time of an environment in which production knowledge circulates, entrepreneurship is stimulated and reciprocal cooperation is widespread.

As far as the reactions of districts in developed countries to current challenges related to globalisation are concerned, the reading of the chapters in this section allows us to make a number of considerations. Firstly, it appears evident from the experiences presented here that the pressure of global competition encourages firms' engagement in global relationships (delocalisation, international immigration, international finance), endorses a model of urban life (concentration in large metropolitan areas), and promotes complex and codified knowledge with digitalisation, and increasingly advanced technological innovation (see Johannisson). This leads to the undesirable situation where the reciprocal support between the economic sphere (functional rationale) and the social sphere (territorial rationale) breaks up. Competition can easily take over and become fierce, thereby destroying the social bases of local development (Ybarra).

The cases analysed show that the reactions of firms in districts to such challenges differ. There are those that delocalise production, those that invest in branding and distribution, and those that instead innovate products and markets, and adopt new technology. However, the experiences considered highlight the fact that some reactions do not lead to the reproduction of development. For example, the simple delocalisation in search of lower costs of production, if unaccompanied by strategies for the renewal of the local economic fabric, would most probably lead first to the downsizing of the productive apparatus and then to the dissolution of the 'industrial atmosphere' with the consequent decline of the district (Garofoli).

Finally, the experiences brought together in this section confirm that only strategies involving innovation and productive, technological and functional upgrading can allow a district to reproduce its competitiveness over time. Furthermore, since local development by means of IDs has a collective nature – in the sense that it requires mobilisation of resources, both manifest and potential, existing in the local environment – coherent public and collective actions are needed in order to reproduce this pattern of development (Garofoli, and Ybarra). In general, therefore, it is not sufficient, even if necessary, to have innovations being introduced by certain district-based firms; what is needed is that the local environment is able to constantly renew itself through new knowledge, a new business spirit and new forms of cooperation.

3. POLICY IMPLICATIONS

Finally, from these contributions, some policy implications for local development in the current context of globalisation can be derived. As already mentioned, IDs must continuously adapt and innovate in order to reproduce themselves as vital local systems; and in part this adaptation takes place in a semi-automatic way, thanks to the functioning of the internal socio-economic processes. When this adaptation is insufficient, collective action is required so that, by means of some form of conscious governance (for example, service centres, institutes for the transfer of technological knowledge, credit consortia), it is possible to produce those specific public goods needed in order to keep the district on an innovative path and therefore on the 'high road' of competitiveness (Garofoli, Ybarra, Okamoto, Benko and Pecqueur).

The experiences illustrated here also allow us to affirm that when changes are radical, such as those at the start of this millennium, the forms of conscious governance needed to reproduce local development are particularly complex. This is because they imply important innovations both in the economic and in the socio-institutional sphere: for instance, intermediate institutions which favoured adaptation in the past, can constitute an obstacle to changes needed in the present (Ybarra). Furthermore, all of this requires that there exist legitimate institutional entrepreneurs capable of vision and leadership, able to mobilise the combined commitment of both economic and social forces, in order to bring about an effective relaunching of local development.

Regional, national and supranational policies, consistent with what is advised from researches on districts, are also fundamentally important in view of supporting the revitalisation of IDs and the promotion of local development in industrialised countries. These are in fact the aims which, coherently with the regional policies of the EU, have inspired the recent national policy for innovation in Spain, which is aimed at driving firms to innovate by cooperation with other firms and by working with institutions and research centres (Ybarra; Trullén in another section of this volume). Other recent examples of national policies for local development are those of the 'competitiveness poles' in France (Benko and Pecqueur) and those of the science parks in Sweden (Johannisson).

Finally, the contribution by Patton and Kenney concerns districts that are driven and pivot around a university and a knowledge community, instead of the local community historically formed in a determined place. It provides us with an illuminating view of a future for districts along current tendencies. In this chapter (as well as partly in that by Johannisson), it is shown how universities and research centres can generate a social and professional environment with its own communicative and behavioural codes. At times, these also generate formal institutions, such as for example alumni associations, which facilitate connection between the world of research laboratories and that of local business, in such a way that information and people circulate between the two worlds and collaborative relationships are established.

The experience of districts centred on knowledge communities show also how, in post-industrialised countries and at times of increasing globalisation, forms of local development founded upon activities with a high knowledge and innovation content are possible. Here the social binding does not derive from a common place of birth, but from having lived through a common formative and professional experience. Moreover, the innovative capacity of these districts is nourished significantly also by the relationships that their firms and research laboratories have with other research centres and other universities specialised in similar and complementary disciplines in other parts of the world. Knowledge can be exchanged through such relationships thanks to the common scientific language. Thus, this new type of district, on the one hand, conserves some basic elements characterising classic IDs, but, on the other hand, it differs from them in the much greater presence of cross-cultural and translocal relations. Furthermore, the experience of research-centred districts suggests an interesting analogy between high-tech districts and cultural districts, with the latter being defined as territorial agglomerations of innovative activities of a broad artistic, aesthetic, symbolic and cultural sense (see Cooke and Lazzeretti 2008; Lazzeretti in another section of this volume). In fact, in the same way as knowledge communities around universities develop their own common language, the artistic and creative communities in places rich in art and cultural institutions develop a shared language, these being symbols and implicit behavioural norms, usually formed by talented artists who have a wide variety of origins and are in communication with other cultural concentrations in various parts of the world.

NOTE

1. As is also apparent from studies of some Italian IDs, for instance, in the case of the Prato ID (Dei Ottati 1994b; Becattini 2001a).

35. Industrial districts in Europe

Gioacchino Garofoli

1. THE PRESENCE OF IDs IN EUROPE

The emergence of industrial districts (IDs) in Italy in the second part of the 1970s and the rediscovery (Becattini 1979) of the alternative industrial organisation model introduced by Alfred Marshall in the late 19th century obliged scholars to reflect on the presence of this model of production organisations in other European countries.

Even in an historical perspective, IDs were important in the second part of the 19th century and the beginning of the 20th not only in Great Britain but even (if not especially) in the second comers (see the French and German cases).

The progressive disappearance of the ID model in northern European countries in the period between 1920–30 and 1950–60 was linked to the extension of the model of large Fordist firms (Sabel and Zeitlin 1982; Piore and Sabel 1984; Zeitlin 1985); whereas the presence of small-scale production survived in peripheral areas.

At the beginning of the publication of ID literature in the late 1970s and beginning of the 1980s, the enthusiasm which moved some Italian scholars in organising field research, visiting firms and discussing with social actors and local public bodies looking for information and evidences, analysing economic informal data and inter-firm links to understand the working mechanism of the industrial production model based on a high density of small firms and flourishing entrepreneurship was regarded as strange by northern European scholars.

At the same time Italian scholars looked ahead and outside Italy to understand if this model of production organisation was peculiar and specific to the Italian case or should be a more general alternative path to industrialisation and development.

The first mapping of IDs in Europe was produced in 1979 with a research report ordered by Prato ID[1] and presented at an international conference in Durham University in 1981[2] and with the first publication in an Italian journal – in a wider and more complete analysis – in 1983 (Garofoli 1983b). The international discussion on the Italian model started in 1984 with the publication of Piore and Sabel's book on *The Second Industrial Divide*.

2. THE REEMERGENCE OF IDs IN EUROPE DURING THE 1970s AND 1980s

2.1 The success stories of southern European IDs

In the middle of the 1970s a lot of Italian small firms showed they were able to work in an autonomous way in relation to large firms, working not only for local and regional outlet markets but even for national and international markets. Often they were highly concentrated in specific locations (often with more than 1000 firms; sometimes with 3000–5000 firms). The economic game was quite complex involving a set of different firms specialised in specific items or in specific phases of production along the production *filière*. Almost 100 IDs were recognised in Italy at the end of the 1970s, as was shown in the first mapping (Garofoli 1981).

The agglomeration of firms in IDs is supported by the realisation of external economies mainly linked to the historical localisation of skills and technical knowledge and capabilities to which local firms have access. The existence of a large variety of labour skills which are coherent with labour demand allows the working of a well-behaved local labour market: firms have free access to a wide and articulated labour supply with low transaction costs for recruitment. This also allows high labour mobility which fosters moreover the diffusion of technical and organisation knowledge among local firms.

The large amount of local firms and the increasing openness to international markets (especially to the European market) favour the division of labour among firms and increasing specialisation at the firm level. The variety and the high-quality levels of technical knowledge and capabilities support both the division of labour among firms and the reproduction of entrepreneurial capabilities, because the best part of the new entrepreneurs within IDs come from the ranks of technicians and highly-qualified workers.

The dynamics of the model and the capability of firms to enter new markets without competing on low labour costs showed the efficiency of small and medium-sized enterprises (SMEs) in IDs and the innovation capability embedded within this organisation model. This definitively broke the old paradigm which presumed small firms should represent the weak part of dualistic economies.

The success story of Italian IDs started to be diffused among international scholars thanks to international conferences and seminars[3] and thanks to organised visits to firms and districts for foreign scholars and practitioners; the idea of the existence of a new (or the rediscovery of an) alternative way of industrial organisation started to enter both the debate and local policymaking.

2.2 The possible explications of the different ID dynamics in northern and southern European countries

After the emergence of IDs in Italy, some scholars started to look at the presence of this model of production organisation around other European countries. In Spain and Portugal, besides Italy (Silva 1992; Costa Campi et al. 1993; Figueredo, Costa and Silva 1994) but also in the southern regions of France (Courlet and Judet 1986; Courlet and Pecqueur 1992; Courlet and Hsaini 1997) and other Mediterranean countries, it was possible to discover a high presence of local systems of SMEs (at least 25–30 areas in Spain, 10–15 areas in Portugal, and around 30 areas in France),[4] often corresponding to veritable IDs. In some cases they resulted from a progressive transformation of a diffuse handicraft productive culture (for example Ubrique in Spain, specialised in leather production, or Kastoria in Greece, specialised in fur production) or of a historical tradition of local raw materials processing (see Porriño in Spain, specialised in granite processing). In other cases they came directly from an ancient professional specialisation (for example the cutlery case of Thiers in France), from a long and consolidated experience on international markets (see Mazamet in France, specialised in the first phases of wool processing), or from the progressive accumulation of professional experience in mechanical engineering (see Cluses in France, specialised in the production of micro mechanical components).

Some regions are characterised by the enduring presence of important IDs, like the Valencia region (Spain), with the shoe district of Elche and Elda, the toy district of Ibi-Onil, the textile district of Alcoy, the tiles district of Castellón de la Plana; the Rhône-Alpes and Jura (France), with Cluses, Oyonnax (plastic materials), Roanne (textile), Morez (spectacle-frames), St Claude (wood products and transformation), Romans (shoes, until the 1980s); North Portugal with textile and clothing districts (Guimarães, S.to Tirso and Vila Nova de Famalicão in the Ave Valley; Feira and Agueda in Aveiro region), shoe districts (Felgueiras – north of Porto – S. João da Madeira, Feira and Oliveira de Azemeis in the Entre-Douro-e-Vouga region), furniture districts (Paredes and Pacos Ferreira in the region of Porto).[5]

On the contrary, in northern European regions there are few examples of IDs. In the UK, for instance, among the historical IDs existing in Marshall's time or even during the 1930s and 1950s few have preserved elements of a district organisation, like Nottingham with knitting, Northampton and Leicester with footwear, Sheffield with cutlery, Bradford and Halifax (Yorkshire) with the wool industry. Germany shows a similar condition: some district elements are still at work in Solingen (cutlery), Pforzheim, Göttingen and Tüttlingen, whereas historical districts such as Pirmasens have disappeared.[6]

At the same time, it seems important to mention the formation of new dynamic agglomerations, both in the UK and Germany,[7] based on high-tech professional skills and on research and creativity, with typical interactions among firms and organisations. The interactive learning, the existence of complementary and cooperation links, the formation of new professional skills and competences are indeed the specific features of these new agglomerations of firms.

The increasing importance of large firms in industrialised countries and regions in post-war period pushed many small firms to become subcontractors of the same large firms (Sabel and Zeitlin 1985; Zeitlin 1985). Furthermore, the increased weight of dependent workers and the changed role of SMEs decreased the capability to maintain specific resources and variety of production which, in the long term, reduced the entrepreneurial formation rate. The jobs opportunity in large firms, in fact, changed the expectations of the young generations progressively, reducing the space for autonomous jobs. The industrial policy followed by some central States added to this tendency, and favoured the expansion of large firms looking for scale economies. The role of industrial policies towards financial concentration in France and the role of financial incentives for the localisation of large firms in peripheral regions, following the 'growth pole' ideas of Perroux's theory, have been clearly clarified in several works (see Sabel and Zeitlin 1982; Zeitlin 1985; Courlet 2008). All this reduced the role of SMEs and created a negative environment for the reproduction and the survival of existing IDs in northern Europe, between the two world wars and, especially, during the 1950s and the 1960s. Finally, the delocalisation process of some large firms looking for cost reduction and unlimited labour supply in Mediterranean countries during the 1970s completed the destructuring process in the northern IDs, with the reduction of the linkages among firms at the local level and the opportunity to enlarge relationships among firms looking for specific competences.

2.3 The introduction of IDs in the economic debate in Europe and the different perception on the role of IDs

We will now briefly discuss the role both of scholars and policymakers in introducing the concept of IDs in different European countries.

In France, Claude Courlet and the research group working in Grenoble (Courlet and Judet 1986; Courlet and Pecqueur 1992), and the sociologist Bernard Ganne (1990, 1992) were promoting the awareness of the role of IDs; and the geographer Pierre Houssel wrote a paper on the ID of Prato and the Third Italy during the 1970s.

Maria Teresa Costa Campi (Costa Campi et al. 1993) and Joan Trullén in Barcelona, Josep-Antoni Ybarra (1991b) in Alicante, and Antonio Vazquez Barquero in Madrid were the first economists who introduced the concepts and the analysis on IDs in Spain; perhaps the first scholar who entered the subject was a geographer (Bernabé Maestre 1983).

In Portugal the scholars who introduced the debate on IDs were Mario Rui Silva (see Silva 1988, 1992; Figueredo, Costa and Silva 1994) and José Reis (1992), but also João Ferrão worked deeply on the new forms of regional development.

Regional policymakers in some countries understood very soon the role of IDs in their economies and the opportunity to intervene in their transformation processes. Spanish autonomous regions played a crucial role in regional development; and in particular the Valencia region intervened with several tools of industrial policy fostering solutions for SMEs' problems in IDs, through the introduction of service centres and technological centres often specialised for sectors and localised within the IDs.[8]

National policymakers entered these areas later: the Ministry of Industry in Spain financed research on IDs over all the country at the beginning of the 1990s (see Costa Campi et al. 1993) and the *Délégation à l'Aménagement du Territoire et à l'Action Régionale* (DATAR) – now *Délégation Interministerielle à l'Aménagement et à la Compétitivité des Territories* (DIACT) – demanded research on IDs and local production systems (LPSs) in France (Courlet and Hsaini 1997) and later on in Europe (Courlet et al. 2000).

DATAR and then DIACT accompanied IDs in their restructuring, favouring the orientation to innovation. State institutions at all levels were involved, making possible a balance between national planning and the 'bottom-up' approach.

During the 1990s in France, following the Italian experience, several meetings between scholars, practitioners and policymakers were organised to discuss problems and prospects of IDs and related policies.[9]

The participation of local actors, both public and private, in the governance process of IDs in France has been quite high. The perception of the relevance of the mobilisation of local actors but a the same time the needs of coordination of local instances through networks of territories were also clear enough. This explains the success story of the Club of industrial districts (CDIF), which was constituted in 1997, with the first presidency in Cluses.

In France the dynamics of IDs never obtained the high level of growth experienced in Italy, Spain or Portugal. Nevertheless they were able to orientate industrial and development policies. Since the end of the 1980s and the beginning of the 1990s, the opportunities to follow different paths of development and the existence of models alternative to the large firms' organisation had been clear to the majority of policymakers at both the national and regional level.

3. RISE AND DECLINE OF IDs IN EUROPE

3.1 The 'golden age' of IDs

The rising importance of IDs in Italy emerged between the end of the 1970s and the beginning of the 1980s. Their positive effects on employment, level of wages, share on international markets, rate of profits, industrial investments, and on the number of firms, increased the trust on this type of organisation. It was a 'golden age'.

The openness of European markets provided great opportunities, reinforcing the advantages of specialisation at the firm level and of the division of labour among firms. The enlarged market allowed cooperation among firms, avoiding strong competition among them, and increased the opportunity for followers to imitate the success stories of leader and innovative firms (which often played the role of 'flagship firms'). Also important, during this phase, was the role of buyers who helped SMEs access foreign markets. Many district firms progressively learned their strategic position within the new markets.

At the beginning the export capability of SMEs in IDs was linked with static competitive advantages (lower labour costs in comparison with northern European countries) and with the flexibility of firms in changing rapidly products and ways of working, following the proposals of buyers. Quite soon the SMEs' systems in Italian IDs started to upgrade to products characterised by higher levels of product quality, creativity and prices. Already at the beginning of the 1980s the average prices of Italian exports in footwear, textiles and furniture were higher than export prices in northern European countries (Modiano 1982). The Italian districts' competitive factors were becoming more and more linked with dynamic advantages (accumulation of knowledge and professional competences).

Spain and Portugal followed, in some circumstances, an analogous process of development after their entry into the European Community: the great expansion of production and employment in Spain occurred during the 1980s and the beginning of the 1990s, and a bit later in Portugal.

Spain and especially Portugal in those years were the countries with the cheapest wages in the European Community and the firms in IDs (thanks to agglomeration economies and the rapid learning process) were able to enter European markets especially where intermediate and final products of low to medium quality were intensive in labour costs.

The positive trend in employment and in numbers of firms in Portugal during the 1990s has been astonishing in comparison with the dynamics of IDs in other European countries (and especially in France, Italy and Spain) and the competition on costs at the European level has been a determinant. Of course, the competition of developing countries at the end of the 1990s and especially during the last decade, has modified dramatically the position of Portuguese IDs.

3.2 The present challenges of globalisation and the 'high road' to development

This last decade has showed the entry of new competitors (especially Asian competitors) in the sectors on which European IDs were specialised. This new phenomenon opens two main issues for possible development strategies to be followed in European IDs.

Firstly, the new industrialising countries also show strong agglomerations of firms, some of them with features similar to IDs. In India and China (but also in other countries, from Pakistan to the Philippines) there are a lot of clusters of specialised SMEs (for example Schmitz 2004; Gereffi, Humphrey and Sturgeon 2005). The division of labour and the cooperation among firms tend to be more limited than in the European experiences. In any case the export performances in these new countries are sometimes related to the advantages of IDs' organisation since the advantages of the new entrants are mainly linked with agglomeration economies.

Secondly, the effects of the international competition introduced by new competitors in the last ten years is quite clear: those among the European districts which are still based on low-quality production are collapsing. Static competitive factors alone cannot allow the survival of IDs in Europe.

3.3 Transformation versus crisis in the ID organisation

The ID model represents a dynamic model of production organisation and reproduction of knowledge, competences and human resources, innovation and change (Garofoli 1983a, 1983b, 1989b). Change is the veritable 'essence' of the model, making possible its resilience.

There are some significant examples of IDs in the 19th century and at the beginning of the 20th century (see for example the cases of the mechanical products system of St Etienne and the silk district of Lyon), based upon the form of social regulation and the intervention of local institutions favouring the introduction of innovation and the pursuit of specialised and diversified production and quality, in contrast to standardised mass production based upon low production costs (Zeitlin 1985; Garofoli 1989b). In St Etienne in particular, at the end of the 19th century, the city council – which controlled the electricity supply – cut off the supply to the companies after a certain time in the day, to prevent the companies from competing with each other, lengthening the working day and lowering the influence of the cost of labour. This forced the companies to take great care in the quality of their products and in the introduction of new ones, therefore preventing them from following strategies based upon low labour costs (Zeitlin 1985). After that, there have been strategies of progressive standardisation of production or of passive imitation of the organisational systems of large companies designed to stimulate, in many historical cases, the small firms' systems towards lowering their production costs and including them in the product cycle of the large external company, thus progressively moving away from innovative strategies based upon their own specific skills.

It is important nonetheless to underline some risk of breakdown of the model. In recent times there have been numerous cases of IDs that have undergone a process of progressive restructuring due to a shift of the core investments from the production side (and from the use of specific working skills and professional competences embedded in the area) to commercial control. This has driven the companies to introduce international decentralisation of production in search for lower costs of production. These strategies have progressively interrupted the interrelations and linkages between the local companies and the diffusion of knowledge, breaking the local productive cycle, wasting local specific resources, assets and competences and progressively stripping the area of its productive capacity.

The case of the footwear ID in Romans, the most famous and important existing footwear industry in France until the 1980s, is quite illuminating. The medium-to-large firms in Romans, between the end of the 1970s and the beginning of the 1980s, started to decentralise the simplest, more repetitive and more 'labour-intensive' production phases to the Italian firms which were already specialised in production phases within the production cycle. After the decentralisation of the leather cutting and sewing the uppers, the Romans' firms thought it would be convenient to decentralise even the assembly phases to the Italian firms (more and more efficient due to increasing investments). They believed they would be able to maintain the control of crucial phases in footwear production, that is engineering and trading.

After some years, this process caused the disappearance of, and then the lack of, a dense network among firms and of a critical mass of technicians and specialised professionals. This network is crucial for the creation and the achievement of new ideas, projects and technical solutions and makes possible the transformation of the designer's idea into a prototype and the final product. This means the creativity and engineering of Romans' firms was deeply reduced and the firms found it more and more convenient to use the large capability of Italian firms to introduce new products and new collections with a large variety of samples, buying their proposals and products directly and including them in their collections (with contracts of exclusive production).

Romans' firms still thought they would be able to control the trading function; but how is it possible to compete with the largest (and specialised) trading companies which historically were able to control national and international markets?

This story of the progressive destructuring of the footwear district in Romans represents a significant metaphor on the breaking up of this organisation model and it provides a good opportunity to look ahead to the possible trajectories for IDs and for the strategies and collective actions (and industrial policies) to foster ID's organisation in Europe.

The crisis (or the threat of crisis for those in existence) of the systems of small firms can in fact be attributed to the following reasons:

- the lack of capability to manage the process of technological and organisational innovation, that is the lack of local 'governance' of the transformation process;
- the incapacity to pursue a strategy of international positioning based on production hinged upon quality and on product diversification and innovation;
- the decentralisation of production to other areas (especially abroad) that 'breaks' the production cycle and the full use of the skills and specific resources existing in the local area;
- a lack of entrepreneurial reproduction (this has particularly serious results in the areas in which the major part of firms are run as traditional family concerns, without the division of entrepreneurial and managerial tasks);
- insufficient improvement in the employment structure, with regards to the labour supply change (especially in the youth section) and to the jobs' expectations for young generations.

3.4 Typologies of transformation in IDs

Looking at the transformation processes in several IDs in Europe during the 1990s and 2000s, it is possible to select the following typologies of transformation:

1. A progressive 'destructuring' of the district, due to the pursual of a cost reduction strategy looking for delocalisation of several phases of production or looking for new suppliers abroad in poor countries with an unlimited supply of labour. A process of international decentralisation determines the cutting out of phases of production, reduction of use of labour and progressive disappearance of specific skills and competences (see the case of Romans).
2. The 'formation of financial groups' due to the pursual of a strategy of scale economies on financial, commercial and organisational issues. This strategy is mainly followed by 'brand name' firms, and it is often combined with a strategy of increasing internationalisation. This produces a progressive increase in the size of leader firms within IDs. The likely consequence is often the introduction of a hierarchical organisation and internal restructuring, which cause the use of exclusive specialised suppliers (which operate, then, with only one client) located within IDs.
3. The pursual of a strategy of 'new markets penetration and new products introduction' just to escape from cost competitiveness. The strategy tends to reinforce 'external networks' (for the introduction of external knowledge) and 'strategic cooperation' among firms located in other areas (often in other IDs) which made possible productive diversification (for example the case of Lecco and, to some extent, Tüttlingen, Cholet and St Etienne).[10]
4. The historical creation of specific resources and competences within IDs. This could attract, sometimes, external firms looking for these specific resources (often crucial for creativity, engineering and the introduction of new products); when this process determines the localisation of external large and multinational firms there is the risk of the introduction of hierarchical relationships (see the cases of the sport system in Montebelluna and the shoe district in Strà and Riviera del Brenta).[11]
5. The last typology is characterised by the progressive *valorisation of external economies*, introducing continuously new competences and skills which foster creativity, quality of production and the introduction of innovation, increasing the value added per employee and escaping from cost pressure (see, mainly, the case of Biella). This trajectory is a veritable 'high road to development'.

It seems to me that the proposed typology may accommodate the restructuring process experienced by a lot of European IDs in the last 10–15 years, facing the challenges of international competitiveness. Very often, the IDs were obliged to react both to cost pressures (especially due to the entering of new competitors), and to the necessity to introduce new products to move ahead with their international position.

In the first case, when the process of international decentralisation of production and delocalisation becomes predominant, the 'low road to development' is a quite likely result, squeezing labour costs and increasing hierarchical ties in peripheral clusters. This produces, then, a 'strategic and technological divide' between the group of innovative (and often larger) firms in the advanced IDs and the group of labour-intensive and traditional firms (both in the IDs in advanced countries and, especially, in clusters of peripheral countries).

In the second case, the introduction of external knowledge (through 'strategic collaboration agreements' with firms located in different regions) into IDs could allow technological discontinuity, avoiding them being limited to incremental innovations (Garofoli 1993, 2003).

4. THE 'GOVERNANCE' OF TRANSFORMATION PROCESSES

4.1 Changing organisation and the role of intermediate institutions

In IDs the dynamic forces of development process intervene and produce interesting interplay among firms, creating multiplier effects through:
- imitation effects, which determine the diffusion of knowledge within the district;
- complementary effects, which favour the clustering among firms and the deepening of production *filières*.

This is based upon: the accumulation of knowledge and the progressive capability to solve technical problems; the reproduction of specific resources (especially human resources) not available elsewhere; collective efficiency (Garofoli 1983a, 1983b; Schmitz 1997); dynamic competitive advantages; and the introduction of informal regulations and norms, with the help of intermediate institutions.

The introduction of collective actions (which is a determinant feature of collective efficiency) is the main means to reproduce, on a voluntary basis, external economies and produce new specific resources (that is, new knowledge and competences) which could create veritable new public goods that will reinforce local dynamic competitive advantages.

The investments on external economies and on knowledge and high professional competences seem to be the main instrument to continue a process of development in which competition should be based on innovation, quality and the introduction of new products, with a large variety of products.

The challenge is to restructure without hierarchy,

> crucial to the restructuring process is the capacity of a district as a whole to permanently promote specialisation as technologies develop so that operations with a high minimum efficient scale of production can continue to be centralized and distinctive competences can continue to be developed in each phase of production. (Best 1990, p. 207)

The role of local actors in facing these challenges could be very crucial; when this happens collective entrepreneurship intervenes, creating new opportunities for the ID as a whole.

4.2 Collective actions for the reproduction of external economies: the experiences in European countries

Intermediate institutions can assume the following roles:

1. finding solutions to common problems among local firms within the district;
2. anticipating the needs of the market.

The first role is linked with the capability to cover the traditional weak points of SMEs, especially the access to strategic factors for development. The constitution of specific intermediate institutions represents the collective reaction to market failures, that is the limits to the access to specific factors or items and the lack of capability to find solutions through the market mechanisms. A lot of experiences show SMEs' consortia facilitate the access to credit and financial resources, service centres supply 'real' services to small firms, technological centres foster the transfer of new technologies to small firms and help them in funding new technical solutions.

The second role is very difficult but it is a crucial element for adapting the organisation of the district towards the 'high road to development', especially in this phase of increasing globalisation.

Concerning the first point, the intermediate institutions represent the reaction of the local community to the weaknesses of SMEs, covering the structural 'hiatus' of the small firm organisation with respect to the large one. The opportunity to cover a high number of implicit demands for services makes it possible to reach a threshold organisation, and to create specific capabilities and professional tasks necessary to solve problems common to small firms. The very large number of cases in service centres, in training and employment institutions and in SMEs' credit support consortia is quite telling. Even external scholars to IDs' experiences were able to recognise it, underlining the policy lessons for developing countries (see Schmitz and Musyck 1994).

The constitution of intermediate institutions is not a permanent 'panacea' against the weaknesses of a production system based on small firms; because the ID model is a dynamic one, this makes continuous transformation necessary even in the organisation of intermediate institutions which need to move on the 'frontier' of the changing implicit needs of local small firms, anticipating risks and new competitive factors. The service and technological centres must introduce new competences and skills not yet available in the market, solving new problems continuously.

It is interesting to note that the great ability in introducing collective actions in Italy during the 1970s and the 1980s was not accompanied by the introduction of laws and with the decentralisation of State competences to the region. Instead, it is possible to identify a coherent policy approach in France and in Spain in recent years towards IDs and, in general, towards the existing agglomerations of firms. In France, the industrial and innovation policies based on competitive poles (*pôles de competitivité*) and on LPSs (*systèmes productifs localisés*) seem clearly to have understood the main policy lessons of the research analysis on IDs during the last decades. The attention of the State on the interaction among local actors (and mainly between the research institutions and the industrial firms) and their role in enhancing investments for innovation and the opportunities to organise negotiation between the nation State and local communities are crucial elements for the *upgrading* of firms and the introduction of new skills among local firms and organisations (Benko and Pecqueur, in this volume).

A quite similar approach has been introduced in Spain, where industrial policy assumed a real territorial nature: the national State, through a tender mechanism, fostered the organisation of cooperative projects (with the presence of firms, training centres and research institutions) with the aim of enhancing collaborative links and networks to create knowledge, new competences and competitive advantages through the launching and the fulfilment of the joint project (Trullén, in this volume). The eligible areas for this public tender were all the areas based on agglomeration of firms and on an LPS (involving both IDs and development poles *à la* Perroux). The objectives of the State intervention have been, then, innovation and transformation as general conditions to favour the increase of national industrial competitiveness.

The governance of economic transformation in IDs has become more complex, involving other actors. In France, for instance, the industrial districts' French Club (CDIF) is supporting IDs and LPSs looking for strategies of development and restructuring, mainly fostering the introduction of innovation. The French Club is even able to negotiate with public administration, from the European level through the national one to the regional and local State.

Even the recent story of innovation policies in northern European regions (see Garofoli and Musyck 2003) shows how these regions learnt from the experience of IDs. Regional innovation policies in these countries, in fact, fostered not only the interaction among different organisations (not only among research institutions and firms, but especially among firms) but also the creation of spillover effects through the accumulation of new knowledge, collective learning and agglomerations of interactive and innovative firms.

The analysis of the productive organisation of IDs and of their social factors allows us to shed light on important new variables in the decision process (on localisation, investment, strategies) of economic actors. They condition the transformation processes of the local economy (and society) and consequently of the regional and national economy. These crucial variables include cooperative links among firms, relations between the production system and the socio-institutional system, the high level of workers' competences and the involvement of workers in the firms' productive organisation and, in the wider social model of the area, the role of specific local institutions for overcoming some 'failures' of the market. In other words, a social system of interrelations, of circulation of information, of production and reproduction of values, organizes itself to permeate and characterise the mode of production. This means that many crucial factors are historically embedded in the local society and are not easily transferable to other areas: the process of development acquires its definitive character of a 'social process' by refusing to appear only as a technical one.

NOTES

1. The research order came officially from the Prato local bank and was directed towards CENSIS (a leading Italian research centre on social issues) and subcontracted to a young (risk-taking) researcher and the results were presented in Artimino in 1981. This story is important because it underlines the links between innovative research (in this case inductive research analysis) and the knowledge needs of LPS to understand its international position.
2. The paper was submitted to an international journal but it was rejected because neither the referee reviewers nor the editor understood the significance of the proposed paper.
3. It is possible to mention the first two Aegean seminars on regional development in Naxos in 1983 and in Lesvos in 1985 where several scholars belonging to different schools, social sciences disciplines and countries were present; among them the future editors of *Regional Studies*, *European Urban and Regional Studies*, and *European Planning Studies*, that is some of the journals on which the theme of IDs have been often discussed in the last 10–15 years.
4. It is always difficult to have trustworthy estimations on the number of IDs in various countries due to the limited proper statistical information and to different methodologies followed by scholars.
5. The production and employment level in some of these IDs is quite significant. It is sufficient to remember that more than 2000 firms working in textile, clothing and footwear are localised (or at least were localised until the end of the 1990s) in the Ave Valley (in Portugal) involving around 100 000 employees. But even the size of Spanish districts is quite significant in the same years: the footwear district in Elche counts around 20 000 employees and the textile district in Alcoy shows an agglomeration of more than 600 firms with 10 000 employees.
6. Also in Scandinavian countries there are a few cases: Gnösjio is almost the only one in Sweden, whereas Jæren, Horten and Arendal are cases of some relevance in Norway.
7. The areas characterised by new technologies, such as Cambridge, but also on cinema and television services in Cardiff, are interesting cases. Some interesting cases in Germany are biosciences in Heidelberg-Mannheim, high-tech machinery in Aachen, medical electronic equipment in Freiburg and Tübingen, and multimedia technology in Köln.
8. Impiva, a public company created in 1984, played a crucial role, acting as a coordinator of a network of 11 technological centres in the region.
9. See the meetings in Cluses in 1992 (combined with an important international conference in Grenoble), in Mazamet in 1994 (with the presence of three parties' representatives belonging to 30 European areas based on small firms), and in Beziers in 1998.
10. The cases of Cholet and St Etienne are interesting because they were able to introduce new internal networks involving different sectors and competences among local firms, and transforming the economic structure of the areas. Cholet moved from the production of clothing and footwear for children into an integrated local system for children's products and services, involving sectors and competences outside manufacturing (like child care). St Etienne moved from textiles to the industry of health textile products and health and personal care instruments and equipment.
11. Montebelluna represents a quite extraordinary case because, on one side, it has attracted large multinational firms looking for competences of design and the engineering of new products, and, on the other side, Italian firms have been moving material production abroad.

36. Industrial districts and the governance of local economies: The French example

Georges Benko[†] and Bernard Pecqueur

1. INTRODUCTION

At the beginning of the 20th century, geography was taught in primary schools in France on the basis of *Le tour de la France par deux enfants* ('A journey round France by two children', Bruno 1877). André and Julien (the two children), going from town to town and region to region, encounter the range and varied nature of French industry. In the different places, they notice the concentration of hosts of small, specialist firms, and of accumulated skills focused around one sector of activity: silk making in Lyon, cutlery at Thiers, china in Limoges and clocks and watches in the Jura Mountains. France then appeared like a mosaic of local production systems (LPSs) related to historical traditions in a country that was not particularly industrialised. Only centres making iron and steel grew up around deposits of coal and iron, as did textile centres along river valleys (in particular the Rhone and the Loire).

In France in the post-war period, the so-called 'Glorious thirty years' (1945–75) because of the exceptionally high growth rate, the State encouraged large-scale public companies and destabilised the traditional sectors typically characterised by small and medium-sized enterprises (SMEs). The time was not ripe for an appreciation of industrial districts (IDs): in fact, for the practical involvement of the State in supporting SMEs, and *a fortiori* LPSs, one has to wait until the mid-1980s when the idea of local development starts to emerge in conjunction with the laws on decentralisation (1982–83). Specific policy initiatives have been targeting clusters of firms, or LPSs as they are officially called, since 1998; these are coordinated by a Commission in charge of national and regional planning (*Délégation à l'Aménagement du Territoire et à l'Action Régionale*, see DATAR 2004) comprising various relevant ministries. Until 2004, a hundred or so projects

Our dear friend Georges Benko left us during the elaboration of this Handbook; we are honoured to include here this last contribution.

were implemented, marking a clear policy change in favour of an approach that considers districts and regions as important phenomena in the French context.

Gradually, France moved on from a situation when it was dominated almost entirely by large-scale companies run by the State elites; with these shaping the country's industrial fabric, and contributing to dismantle what remained of local and regional economies by internalising and vertically organising the economic activities – with what success, everyone knows.

However, as times changed, so did the scales of organisation; whilst large firms went off to conquer the world, small firms, and regional and local economies, were rediscovered by local and regional governments.

In this context, this chapter aims to describe the regional and local dynamics behind the governance of local economies, by showing how, with varying degrees of success, different forms of spatial organisation of economic activity have taken turns to be dominant models for local growth, therefore influencing policymaking in contemporary France. We shall thus review chronologically the different forms of geographical and territorial organisation of production that have succeeded in France: namely, growth centres, localised production systems, and their most recent manifestation, poles of competitiveness.

2. GROWTH CENTRES AND THE UTOPIA OF LINEAR EXPANSION

In the immediate period after the Second World War, the urgency of satisfying major reconstruction (housing and infrastructure) needs formed the basis of a Keynesian macroeconomic growth driven by public expenditure. The efforts made in Western Europe appeared to bear fruit in so far as the decades that followed the war were times of strong and sustained growth (the 'Glorious thirty years'). It was in this context that the idea of growth poles developed.

It has been argued that development tends to be uneven (to use the term of François Perroux), 'it occurred around centres, focuses of activity which created a series of economic imbalances which had to be transformed into an ordered, induced development, through conscious planning of the context of propagation' (Lajugie, Delfaud and Lacour 1985). Location thus matters in the coordination of economic agents. This represents something new in relation to the orthodox theories on regional economics, which posited that space can be considered homogeneous and the distribution of activities could be reduced to transport costs differentials. An understanding of the importance of location is also linked to considerations on the critical mass effects, on one side, and on distance, on the other. The urban context becomes relevant in the sense that the effects of clustering can no longer be ignored and the issue of externalities as highlighted by Alfred Marshall reveals their effects more and more clearly.

The idea behind growth centres was that they were expected to generate propulsive effects both upstream and downstream. It is worth noting that they had already been experimented with by Soviet Russia – although mostly neglected – in the 1920s within an industrialisation model that gave priority to activities that were traditional (iron and steel making) and were likely to trigger the growth of downstream activities. Such induced growth effects along the production chain were considered to take place in an automatic way, simply as a function of the clustering of production activities and its nature.

In the first instance, the conditions for the concentration of activities and infrastructures in designated 'natural sectors' were determined by the presence of raw materials, and were supported by the related concentration of communications facilities, financial resources and all the required upstream industries. In Europe, the Ruhr region, the Po Valley and the Rhine-Rhone axis met these criteria. The notion broadened later with the inclusion of urban clusters whose size implied a greater portion of services for firms, which thereby promoted industrialisation.

The other decisive feature of these growth centres, when not in industries where there were natural advantages, was to be conceived to shape policies to be grafted on so-called 'propulsive industries'. Growth centres created from nothing constituted the grand developmental utopia of the 'Glorious thirty years' period. For example, the development model in Algeria in the first 20 years of its independence was characterised by the set-up of large-scale national companies designed to substitute imports. Oil revenues were not sufficient – as had been gold for the Spaniards in the 16th century – to buy goods made elsewhere, but instead policymakers were determined to create an indigenous industrial structure. In France, such utopian belief took the form of grand Gaullist or Pompidou-style projects, like the nuclear programme, investment in telecommunications, the Concord venture or, also, the iron and steel-making complexes in Fos-sur-Mer, or later the scientific park in Sophia Antipolis near Nice.

The achievements of these growth centres were mixed. Some evidence of success can be found, but at the same time, in some cases, it was difficult to integrate these centres within the fabric of the local economy; for this reason, such centres were often referred to as 'cathedrals in the desert'. They were, nevertheless, emblematic of a triumphant industrial model, which dominated all advanced economies in the post-war period, and whose characteristics reflected the dominant model of economic growth. It must be said that the utopian expectation that growth can result automatically from some triggering factors such as public investments, is not yet dead.

The main characteristics of the French growth centres can be summed up as follows:

1. Growth centres tended to work within a context of strong growth, rather than as forces driving growth. They may thus be deemed to be consequences of development dynamics rather than their stimulus.

2. In growth centres, development is based upon productivity improvements as the essential competitiveness factor, with the latter sought worldwide. In this respect, they are very different from the competitiveness poles that dominate the debate now, since the latter rely on specialisation and quality as competitive advantages.
3. Innovation is a process that takes place outside the centres, but influences them through technology transfer.
4. Finally, since intellectual and knowledge resources are not produced locally, they need to be imported, or transplanted as standardised knowledge from centres responsible for undertaking innovation activities.

These growth centres represent a scenario described by Vernon (1971) in his theory of the 'product cycle' according to which, as products with a high technological content move away from the original centre of activity, they become less technologically distinct as they supply wider markets. (See for example the case of the electronic calculator, which moved from being a product with a high technological content, when it was first launched in the US, to being a relatively standard and cheap product sold worldwide and produced in low-wage countries).

According to this approach, places are merely dots on the map, passive locations from where to launch a product with which the local inhabitants have no particular personal affinity; specific historical factors and hidden resources (in the sense of Hirschman 1958) in the region do not matter in this context.

Ultimately, growth centres represented a mechanism for growth that reflected a frankly utopian belief in linear development, prolonging curves and extrapolating long-term trends towards a deliberately positive future, which, however, started to be contradicted by the crisis of Fordism in the 1970s and 1980s.

3. FRENCH LPSs AND REGIONAL ECONOMIES

More recently, the utopian dream has collapsed, and the various contradictory processes of globalisation have not led to the elimination of growth differentials, or to a fluid world freed from all sorts of possible constraints. It is not a new beginning that prevails, a state of uniformity, but the 'telescoping and increasing interweaving of scales' (Veltz 2000). Some authors suggest that the strong winds of a pro-liberal globalisation are sweeping away the bases for local and regional economies, which may be destined to exist only on the fringes. Others, however, underline the fact that local and regional economies have at their disposal sufficient resources to adapt to the new constraints and to bring into play original combinations of resources which may lead to medium-term economic development, and also to original forms of local governance.

Analysis of the post-growth-centre era started with the works of Italian scholars which brought back to the fore Marshall's concept of IDs (Becattini 1992;

Becattini et al. 2003). However, there are some differences between the 'Italian-style' districts and the 'French-style' LPSs (Colletis, Courlet and Pecqueur 1990; Benko, Dunford and Lipietz 1996; Benko and Lipietz 2000; Courault 2000).

Together with the ID model, we would advance the hypothesis of diverse forms of local and regional economies in Europe in parallel with processes of decentralisation. Since nation states have lost, to some extent, the ability to control and shape their economies, it is not surprising to note that subnational agents, namely policymakers and entrepreneurs, attempt, with greater or less success, to promote more regionally-based forms of political, economic or social organisation.

The atmosphere in A. Marshall's districts can be described by a collection of goods and services placed at the disposal of small firms, and used by them; an organisation of production that resembles an alternative form of vertical integration.

In France, there are more than 20 000 SMEs (with between 20 and 499 employees) which represent 53 per cent of jobs in the manufacturing sector, 39 per cent of investments, and 26 per cent of exports; also, 80 per cent of them have fewer than 100 employees.

There is no determinism at work here; but this is rather a working hypothesis. Within LPSs, theory suggests that 'competitive collective local goods' are created to support firms. They result from cooperation between firms, from public policies and from strategies pursued by specialist organisations. The coordination of the production of these 'competitive collective local goods' and their use relates to questions of governance. An understanding of the role of these goods is one of the missing links in studies on local economies and proximity (*l'économie de proximités*).

As regards the geographic distribution of these LPSs, in France three quite distinct types can be identified.

1. A few specialist LPSs, rather like the Italian IDs. Differently from Italy, the French economy is under Parisian central control, and the competitive collective local goods are designed to favour national champions, with specialist LPSs remaining an exception. Studies in the 1980s and more recent overviews (Courlet 2001) have indeed highlighted the few atypical examples: on the one hand, Oyonnax, St Claude, the valley of the river Arve, in the textile industry, the Cholet region and Roanne (Courault and Trouvé 2000); and on the other side, the declining or smaller systems like the cutlery industry at Thiers. Finally, specialist areas are being set up, for example, in plastics in Chartres and Dreux. Most local systems of this type have disappeared, sometimes for a lack of support but often for the inability to adapt to changing market conditions. Since 1997, the government has given financial support to hundreds of specialist LPSs, defining them as 'groups of firms and institutions within the same geographical area which

collaborate on the same sector of activity'. We would argue that these systems present little resemblance with IDs, which have much more integrated and complex social systems.

2. The Paris region and the regional capitals, in particular Strasbourg, Toulouse, Grenoble, Montpellier, Nantes, Bordeaux and Rennes. This point is particularly important in the case of France: the most dynamic employment zones in industrial terms relate to cities which present three main characteristics: they are largely unspecialised, they bring together large-scale and small-scale companies, and they are rapidly growing in terms of population. The dynamic local economies in French cities are relatively unspecialised systems, at least in the narrow sense of the term. On the other hand, industrial sectors are relatively focused upon the large cities, like the aerospace industry in Toulouse, Bordeaux and Nantes, the chemical industry in the Lyons area, Michelin at Clermont-Ferrand or the production of semiconductors in Grenoble. It is in this kind of economic fabric that 'poles of competitiveness' are seen to emerge (see later).

3. Areas on the periphery of the Paris region. In Picardy, Normandy, Maine and the Loire, employment zones which are experiencing relatively high rates of growth are made up essentially of SMEs. Their fabric is fairly diversified, with the presence of the fundamental trades of industry (mechanics, boiler making, plastics processing, and so on). The same phenomenon occurs in the Lyons area and around the regional capitals. It is in these areas that one can find the basic conditions for existence of the typical ID, in the way in which the different agents integrate and cooperate (companies, universities, public authorities, and so on) over local developmental projects.

Regions, policies, societies and economies change fairly slowly, particularly in countries like France that are characterised by low rates of mobility. Change is not spectacular and, therefore, is difficult to appreciate.

French local economies, especially in manufacturing, are not governed by a single principle. An analysis in terms of governance and provision of competitive collective local goods can be used to ascertain the following hypothesis: at the heart of the French economy, which has lost its guiding principle in terms of governance (State regulation), large-scale companies (the hierarchy) have taken up the baton. However, a combination of the three following factors contributes to the appearance of a new means of coordination, of new modes of local governance which, however, are not organised into local specialist production systems: (a) the decline of the national industrial companies linked with the State; (b) the restructuring of SMEs; and (c) the mobilisation of local and regional public and private agents. In other words, the hierarchical model, dominated by large-scale companies, is increasingly combined with local forms of governance (Gilly and Pecqueur 1995).

Four models of governance of local economies can be identified on the basis of the ideal types of regulation highlighted above, together with the dominant agents and the degree of local horizontal integration.

An initial specific mode of governance exists on the fringes: that of the specialist LPSs, made up of SMEs, where the local production of competitive collective local goods is the result of a combination of community regulation and of associations of employers, in the context of market exchanges and a very limited State intervention. This model remains marginal in France. It has been maintained in areas that are rather isolated socially and culturally from the rest of the country: in Savoy, in the Jura, and in areas of Western France that are characterised by a cultural and political history of opposition to the State. As they are far enough away from Paris, these areas have maintained community resources which have been mobilised by entrepreneurs, for example in the Cholet area with the support of the local authorities. These systems are suffering today from changes in the scale of production and increased pressures from competition, which increasingly destroy some of their resources.

A second mode of local governance is clearly apparent in the case of France: that of networks of subcontractors under the control of a large company, for example in the motor industry or the chemical industry. In this case, competitive collective local goods are produced essentially by the large-scale firm within a hierarchical relationship. In fact, in this case, the large company plays a pivotal role in setting up the networks of cooperating and knowledge-sharing subcontractors. It thus organises and controls the local employment markets and the professional training strands. The public authorities are content to give to that production external recognition in the form of competitive collective local goods.

In several cases, a third model also appears, too, the one controlled by the market, weakly territorialised, within which neither political agents nor employers' associations play an important coordinating role. In this instance, there are few competitive collective local goods, the organisational externalities that could be contributed by the local agents. This is more or less the situation of Ile de France (even though the presence of large-scale companies' headquarters and a large share of essential of French research suggests caution). With firms of all sizes being so thick on the ground, this gives much greater importance to competition, to market regulation. This is undoubtedly the case too within smaller towns where there are rather isolated SMEs, no doubt more obviously in Southeastern France where employers' organisations, including the CCI (Chambers of Commerce and Industry) are particularly weak and the local authorities are more divided.

A fourth model can be highlighted, particularly – but not exclusively – in the towns where a local governance tends to emerge, with a combination of market competition, local government (more than State), large companies, plus a hint of community involvement and of employers' associations. This is marked by a still weak but growing level of horizontal integration between firms, reinforced in terms of economic development strategy and rationalisation by the provision of competitive collective local goods resulting from a rather political process. In other words, this is a relatively complex social situation where firms become more integrated in the social fabric and in the historical tradition of the area.

New agents emerge ('civil society', associations, users, and so on). This model results from the three factors identified earlier: (a) State support for SMEs and for networks of SMEs; (b) the drawing up of developmental local and regional economic policies; and (c) the fragmentation of the big business groups. Indeed the hypothesis could be further extended, to state that in this process the central figure of the employee (an anonymous and non-localizable employment unit, which is often used as a measure of local development) gradually makes way for a new emergent figure in the area set-up: the inhabitant (who is at one and the same time the user and consumer of the specific services linked to the place).

Of these four models of governance, only the first and the fourth emerge more or less obviously from the general model of IDs. The situation found in the second model and in the third is practically independent of considerations of place.

4. POLES OF COMPETITIVENESS AND THE SEARCH FOR ADAPTATION TO GLOBALISATION

The most recent manifestations of the form that the local organisation of production can take are the 'poles of competitiveness' that have been recently set up in France.

The vision of the Agency for the management and the competitiveness of territories (*Délégation Interministerielle à l'Aménagement et à la Compétitivité des Territories*, DIACT) is typical in the sense that it retains the objective of productivity while considering also the role of territorial factors. It means transforming production into what is commonly known as the 'cognitive economy', by showing that it incorporates a high degree of rather local-based knowledge, derived from local institutions that generate learning (including universities, public and private research facilities and start-ups). N. Jacquet and D. Darmon tell us in fact that

> our industrialised economies have embarked upon a new era: that of the economy of knowledge, where *increased productivity remains the principal vector of growth*, ... the arrival of the knowledge-based economy results from the switching of the production modes of a Taylorist system (which consisted in producing large scale for limited markets, which meant mainly national and protected) into a new system of differentiation and individualisation ultimately of products, with the aim of better meeting the heterogeneous needs of consumers (which means producing small scale for markets that have become world-wide and competitive). (Jacquet and Darmon 2005; italics added)

If the notion of this change and of the poles of competitiveness is to be understood rightly, it seems to us that the performance of poles of competitiveness should be evaluated not exclusively upon productivity (even if this remains largely important, see Colletis and Pecqueur 1995) but on the idea of specificity. The latter represents the ability of the places involved to make the most of their particular resources (Gumuchian and Pecqueur 2007) and therefore is fundamentally linked to the intellectual heritage of the same place. It is, then, the cultural and intellectual resources that form the essence of what makes the difference between a pole of competitiveness and a place that is not.

The forms that we have reviewed here reveal that the change is from a production realised by firms within an urban context to the production in a place where the agency is not restricted to the total of the firms at that place, but is extended to all those present who, mobilised by an appropriate governance, make the place a collective producer with manifold contributions (including generational, since the long term counts).

It is doubtless in their approach to knowledge and skills that the models differ most clearly. The 'technopoles' of the 1980s were kinds of growth centres. They aimed to concentrate skills in an area where the different agents could meet, exchange and produce public policy as a result of the synergy thus caused, a competitive advantage (what economists call an 'external factor') linked with the physical proximity of the agents. With the current clusters, there is an additional element in the territorial linkage. In fact, in the case of the poles of competitiveness, it is not enough to concentrate in one place activities which may well have come from elsewhere (as was the case with Sophia Antipolis near Nice); rather, the aim is to make use of the collective intellectual heritage which has been built up long term. Grossetti, Zuliani and Guillaume (2006) talk about 'a local system of skills' which most often has the benefit of being multi-sectoral, which allows 'freedom from dependence on one sector of activities', and reduces the uncertainties of economic activity.

5. WHAT CONSTITUTES A POLE OF COMPETITIVENESS?

The poles of competitiveness introduced in 2005, from the point of view of public policy, are the successors of the LPSs in the mid-1990s. This initiative was based upon the report by the parliamentarian Ch. Blanc (2004) who confirmed the link between industrial organisation, location and economic competitiveness, on the basis of a statement made about the industrial competitiveness of France in Europe and the world (see the report, ibid.). This old economists' notion thus finds its modern-day echo (albeit, tardily). The new stage launched in 2005 introduces the notions of networks, or clusters, as specific industrial subsystems at the very heart of French industrial policy and in part of European policy.

In the notion of poles of competitiveness the place is a good setting for an organisational interaction between industry and innovation, and the region is presented as the base for cooperation between companies, laboratories, and universities (production, R&D, knowledge transfer and training). The pole of competitiveness is thus defined by four central characteristics:

- The economic development strategy of the centre must be rooted in a dynamic local economic fabric, which is successful in the face of international competition. The coherence of the centre and of its strategy within the wider context formed by the region's economic development is an essential factor.
- The centre must represent a sufficiently visible international entity, on the industrial and/or technological level. The projects presented must be able to figure eventually in the ranks worldwide from the point of view of the activity.
- The form of partnership and the mode of governance adopted are important. The quality and efficiency of the R&D partnerships set up between the agents (industrialists, researchers, teachers) are indeed major criteria as regards the centre's title.
- The projects given the stamp of approval must give rise to synergies in relation to R&D, and thus be able to contribute to significant increases in added value and in the skills and knowledge of the human capital. The final aim is to improve the competitiveness of what the French State can offers to international markets.

Out of the 105 applications received, the 67 projects were approved by 2005 and among them six were designed as world-level projects and nine as projects with a world outlook. The total sum dedicated to financing the centres planned is more than €1.5 billion (see the site www.competitivite.gouv.fr, accessed 20 December 2008). Note that the centres approved as 'poles of competitiveness' are projects that are financed as such and are thus deliberate entities born 'top down' from public policy. However, only places which are innovation 'environments' and for which the society involved is in harmony with the economic development (particularly technological, but also cultural) can host projects which meet the selection criteria. The technological district is thus often hidden behind the administrative centre.

Earlier, we described the four characteristics of growth centres. Let us come back to them and apply them to the poles of competitiveness:

- A pole of competitiveness by its nature generates a kind of performance which (along with other contributions in the macroeconomic organisation) increases growth.
- Productivity is more a collective than an individual matter, since it is based on the use of a collective intellectual heritage which will define the area in relation to its competitors.
- In this sense, innovation becomes an essential element. It originates in the ability to seize information on a worldwide scale and integrate it into a productive system. It can be called a local partiality for technological mastery which allies globalised knowledge with on-the-spot culture.

- Finally the place becomes a central feature of coordination between agents seeking to solve novel production problems.

This new 'cluster model' represents a new horizon for industrial planning in France. Nevertheless, it is not a total panacea and has important question marks hanging over it (Martin and Sunley 2003).

A recent study of poles of competitiveness in France (Duranton et al. 2008) has systematically questioned the real effects of concentration within a locality: 'we find that the Local Production Systems have practically no effect on the productivity of the firms concerned, or indeed on the attractiveness of the locations concerned'. As regards the poles 'there are gains, but they are not miraculous'. On the basis of a very extensive statistical survey it is possible to quantify these gains: to increase the productivity of the firms concerned by about 5 per cent, you have to double the level of specialisation in an activity and a given place. These results do not rule out the advantages of concentration, but raise questions about its nature and its capacity.

6. CONCLUSION

The French example is not special as regards an overall view of situations in Europe, or no doubt elsewhere. The change from growth centres to the poles of competitiveness, via the LPSs, is completely representative of a general movement which seeks to test the limits of a purely Fordist model. Such a model was based on individual productivity within a context where the cultural impact of the place of production is of no consequence. Today the specific context is of importance.

It is possible to consider that local economies may be designed to a greater or lesser degree in their political and economic interactions. The different agents, the companies in particular, may be in relation with others within the same local context with long-term strategies, investing their resources in a coordinated manner, contributing to localised production of competitive collective local goods. In this instance, the resultant local economy is structured, modes of integration can be revealed and interactions stably established in time, as dynamics of the institutionalisation of the area. The potential or virtual resources of the area may be brought into play and this opens up new perspectives for public developmental policies.

We have tried to show how the new challenges of globalisation require new forms of governance on a regional and district level. State power, so dominant in the case of France, suffered from the emergence of large firms and the priorities imposed by globalisation; however, we are suggesting that the State ought to reshape its intervention at a more localised level. France is more recently adapting to globalisation through the imaginative powers of its regions who will, no doubt, leave a unique mark of a new age of globalisation, one dominated by competing territories rather than firms.

37. Industrial districts in Spain

Josep-Antoni Ybarra

1. INTRODUCTION

Industrial districts (IDs) in Spain are productive realities that have accompanied the transformation of the economy in general. They have been particularly important at times of profound change (economic crises, modifications of general Spanish policy, opening up of the economy, and so on); accordingly, it could be said that they are productive and social entities that are better able to overcome crises. Globalisation puts them once again in a situation where they have to face new challenges. A new industrial policy designed to meet the requirements and characteristics of Spanish IDs offers them a new opportunity.

2. THE BIRTH OF IDs IN SPAIN

The existence of IDs in Spain has accompanied the evolution of the Spanish economy over the course of time. Traditionally, there have always been towns specialised in certain aspects of production, where the physical resources of the environment or geostrategic conditioning factors have determined the way in which their economies have developed (as in the case of everyday consumer products such as textiles, footwear, ceramics, food, metal goods). This tradition has meant that, in some cases, the level of know-how and the sense of identity related to the activity in question have become firmly rooted at a local level, leading very often, in the case of Spain, to the subsequent development of IDs. However, in the beginning, their importance in the Spanish economy as a whole did not extend beyond the limits of their own communities or surrounding areas.

For the Spanish economy, the importance of specialised industrial concentrations would become clear when they had to compete within larger frameworks and on a wider scope (in regional, national and international markets), from the 1960s. In this new situation, two factors helped the strengthening of the first IDs in Spain: the opening up of the Spanish economy and, as a result, the new types of markets influencing both the types of products offered and the productive relations that would make these new products possible. These two factors took shape progressively in Spain. So it could be said that the transformation of Spanish districts took place in parallel with the opening up of the Spanish economy, which was definitively achieved when Spain joined the EU in 1986. It should be noted that two periods can be identified before this happened: an initial period when the basis for the Spanish proto-IDs were established, each one evolving out of its intrinsic character, history, circumstances, resources and so on, of greater or lesser local importance, but always restricted by the autarchic context in which the economy in general was developing. In this situation, protectionism was the factor that enabled the first Spanish proto-districts to take shape. The second period saw the consolidation of some of those production centres emerging from a diametrically opposite situation: the gradual opening up of the Spanish economy. This began, after the Spanish Civil War, with the implementation of the 'Plan for the stabilisation of the Spanish economy' in 1959, and later on it culminated in Spain's entry into the EU. In this new period, with the progressive opening up to external markets some proto-districts succumbed to the influx of foreign products; others became stronger, in the sense that they continued to strengthen until they became sufficiently competitive and acquired a reputation and prestige, not just in the Spanish market, but also at an international level. In parallel with the opening up of the Spanish economy, another significant event took place in the history of Spain, that is, the adoption of the new Constitution in 1978, bringing recognition of territorial diversity and acknowledgement of the different regions or Autonomous Communities as distinct territorial realities. This would serve to encourage industrial as well as political and administrative decentralisation. In particular, this new concept of industrial organisation and policy (which covers the problems relating to IDs) meant that it became possible in Spain to design different industrial policy initiatives to meet the diversity of the productive realities represented by the IDs.

In Spain in 2004, there are 237 industrial realities classified as 'local production systems' (LPS), including IDs (IDs) and other areas characterised by manufacturing industry and small to medium-sized firms, and they account for 46.8 per cent of the manufacturing industry (1 288 000 jobs) and 47 per cent of exports of manufactured goods (see Boix and Galletto 2005 and Boix in this volume). According to other sources, 40 per cent of Spanish industrial firms were located in these industrial concentrations in 2000 and in terms of jobs they employed 56 per cent of the Spanish working population (Santa María, Giner and Fuster 2004).

They have evolved in three ways: the traditional first generation light industry LPSs developed spontaneously in response to the historical characteristics of the place where they originated (textiles, footwear, toys, furniture, food processing) (Ybarra 1991b); the second-generation districts and LPSs emerged as a productive-spatial response to the dynamics of the changing character of

Spanish industry in the 1970s and 1980s;[1] and most recently the third generation LPSs are emerging around chemicals, electronics and optics (CES 2005, pp. 58–63).

It should be said that the variables that have played an essential role in shaping the Spanish IDs have been, firstly, the tradition and the social know-how focused on certain specialised areas; secondly, the opening up of the Spanish economy to the outside world that has forced these IDs to respond to the new requirements of foreign markets; and finally, the continuous rise in domestic income levels and the consequent increase in the level of demand – both domestic and foreign. All this shows that, in the Spanish case, the variable that structured the IDs was initially the market rather than policy. Later and more recently, policy – and in particular regional and local policy – has attempted to improve the situation of the IDs. In short, in Spain the market opened windows of opportunity for the takeoff and development of many IDs, but policy is regenerating them currently.

Actually in Spain, from an economic point of view, territory has always been acknowledged as an element of production but never as an important element of policy. The same is true for small and medium-sized enterprises (SMEs), which are essential for the development of the Spanish economy, but which have attracted few policy initiatives. The consequence of all this is the lack of a strategic vision for the territory and SMEs, both essential elements for undertaking any coherent action with regard to IDs.

3. THE LOCAL SITUATION AND THE ID: AN INEVITABLE CONVERGENCE

Changes in the political perception of territory and SMEs began in Spain when the Spanish Constitution was adopted in 1978. These changes were primarily driven by a number of town councils trying to give local answers to problems not tackled by the central government industrial policy, which was more concerned with general aspects of modernisation of the existing economic infrastructure. Many of the towns that had a long tradition of industry, now coupled with a new democracy, were confronting serious problems of growing industrial unemployment. It was a delicate time because of its political importance: the young Spanish democracy seemed unable to offer a satisfactory answer to society's demands for jobs and economic stability. In view of the gravity of the situation, a pragmatic solution was adopted: the main thing was to produce a local policy to deal with the industrial crisis. So, what should be done and how?

Since local councils lacked the administrative powers necessary to implement promotion policies and, furthermore, they lacked instruments that would have allowed them to take action to slow down the industrial crisis, they tried to use creatively the limited instruments at their disposal. Thus, local industrial regeneration policy was based on urban development policy and on fostering an atmosphere of local trust. Town-planning policies and the availability of industrial land with certain characteristics, for example rented industrial premises on small, well-equipped plots with good communications, meant that new entrepreneurs and older more experienced entrepreneurs with well-established industrial relationships were able to emerge from the industrial crisis and make a new start, providing jobs for some of the unemployed. Those local councils acted as industrial urban developers, at the same time fostering and revitalising the local economy. In addition the proliferation of meetings for dialogue and consensus, known as 'employment agreements', were creating a certain degree of trust in the capacity of local resources to foster employment. Where these capacities and potentialities included experience of trade, production know-how and knowledge, industrial relations and so on, as in the developing LPSs and/or IDs, they provided stimulus not only for local growth but also for the overall growth of the Spanish economy.

So, it can be said that the general basis of these local dynamics has been the internal resources liberated by the firm action taken by local leaders concerned with the existing situation of unemployment. Unemployment is the reason why local circumstances started to be seen as levels for opportunities and actions within the framework of the Spanish economic development (Vázquez Bàrquero 1987). Before that, industry was seen traditionally as independent of territorial capacities. At a later political stage the recognition of the districts – the union of the territorial and the industrial dimensions – and then the policies for them, eventually emerged.

The 1970s and 1980s were years of profound change for the Spanish economy, including: the tax reforms, the liberalisation of the movement of capital, the conversion of State-owned companies, the privatisation of the public utilities, the progressive deregulation of the labour market, and the increasing domestic and foreign competition. All these changes altered the methods of production and the industrial organisation. One of the consequences was that the majority of the centralised Fordist business structures began to be organised in a decentralised and dispersed way; the production chain became fragmented and distributed by stages across small specialised firms; structural unemployment gradually evaporated with the emergence of new entrepreneurs from the ruins of large factories, and the proliferation of the self-employed and new employees in small businesses – an entire social and industrial revolution in which small firms played a leading role.

The reform and strengthening of the LPSs and IDs were at the centre of this transformation as the most suitable response to the demands for flexibility, change and innovation confronting the Spanish industrial structure. Elements that were undervalued but played an essential economic role can be understood within this new framework, including: working women and family support for the business initiative, the accumulation of productive knowledge through learning in industrially-dispersed but territorially-concentrated entities, levels of trust and informal links between producers helping flexibility and creativity in a context of social relations embedded in the territory. This accumulation of elements was difficult to measure in monetary terms, but undoubtedly had a significant economic value. Could all these intangible elements that apparently operated independently be put in relation to one another? Did their combination correspond to a model? In addressing such questions, an interpretation of how growth was possible during a period of crisis emerged in Spain for the first time. The model of local development based on the 'ID'[2] was an interpretative paradigm that brought together all these aspects and formed a conceptual unit providing more comprehensible interpretive tools than those previously available. The existence and function of IDs as a productive response to industrial crisis started to be explicitly recognised in Spain by the academic community.

Despite the fact that the IDs and LPSs were the most receptive and dynamic places for meeting the demands for change imposed by the industrial recession, the Spanish national industrial policy was much slower in taking this situation into account. Spanish industrial policy continued in the 1970s and 1980s to neglect both SMEs and territories as possible drivers of change. Its proposals were both general and vertical (what is known as sectoral policy), without strategies and instruments for meeting the specific needs of SMEs, nor those of the various territories with their productive characteristics. The policy continued to ignore the SME as an industrial player and the territory as the physical and social repository of its needs.

4. REGIONAL POLICY: THE FIRST INSTRUMENTS FOR THE DISTRICT IN SPAIN

The national situation recalled above did not prevent some general initiatives being promoted to address the problems affecting SMEs and territories with greater propensity to change. It was the regions – the Autonomous Communities – that started to deal with the absence of a general frame supporting local industrial policy instruments. The 1980s were the years of regional support for setting up many of the Spanish regional development agencies, in particular the service centres and the technological institutes for the SMEs. These public, semi-public or private technological centres, always promoted by the different regional governments, served to compensate for the SMEs' internal deficiencies. Some centres were of a horizontal character – specialising for instance in training, quality control and support for exports – while others were more vertical or sectoral – focusing on industries such as textiles, footwear and furniture. However, in all cases they were offering SMEs 'real services' that were previously not available. That is, the regional governments provided or encouraged the creation of service centres and technological institutes with the idea of giving firms access to practical – not financial – services needed in their specific territory, since the vast majority of these enterprises – generally SMEs – could not afford them individually. These services were sometimes inaccessible to SMEs for financial or technical reasons, and other times firms did not know about them, despite the fact that they were necessary for helping firms to develop. Service centres and technological institutes became the great tool of regional industrial policy for the Spanish economy in the final decade of the 20th century and the early years of the 21st. They provided a wide range of practical services to SMEs, enabling firms to be more competitive and, in turn, enabled industrial policy to be more selective by attending to the specific needs of each territory. LPSs and IDs took great advantage of the creation and expansion of both service centres and technological institutes, encouraging many of their firms to improve the quality of products, standardise processes and find new products to sell or export (an important problem for many small enterprises). In this way, service centres became an essential element of Spanish IDs' productive infrastructure (Gracia and Segura 2003). In Spain service centres and technological institutes, directly promoted or indirectly encouraged by the regional governments, have been the agents of industrial modernisation, and this modernisation has been necessary to keep Spain a competitive country, at least in traditional industries.

In Spain the relative success of certain LPSs led to the general acceptance of the idea that any industrial concentration involving some degree of specialisation, in which there was a division of the production chain and in which government action was promoted to foster competitive activity, was *per se* a competitive area. This was the time when the concept of 'cluster' as an essential element for ensuring competitiveness and development in an international framework expanded. The idea that the existence of a cluster ensured the competitiveness of a certain activity in the international framework came to be generally accepted; the solution to the crisis then became a matter of creating or completing a cluster. Obviously this meant that the 'clusterisation' of the representation of Spanish economy broadened, that is, much of the industrial base appeared to have the capacity and the possibility to be characterised in terms of the 'cluster' concept. This situation has meant that many firms and also many business, financial and political associations started to pride themselves on being part of some cluster when presenting their competitive capacities, and when applying for public funding for various competitive strategies. Many activities and areas are susceptible to being presented as clusters or are on the way to achieving that status. Of course this is the case of industrial concentrations characterising the IDs and more generally the LPSs. What is more open to question is the reverse proposition, that all clusters characterise areas which are IDs. The existence, quality, availability and regeneration of the social capital is what differentiates the two concepts: in the case of clusters, the role of social capital is neutral, whereas in the case of IDs, the existence and characteristics of the social capital is essential for understanding how they work.

5. IDs IN SPAIN AND GLOBALISATION

How significant is the quantity and quality of the social capital of Spanish IDs? During the early stages of their development, informal relations between individuals and firms, and the efforts of local and regional institutions, form a fairly strong productive structure. The social capital that emerged at that time was characterised by aspects such as trust, security, identity, common language, shared knowledge, similar expectations or social mobility among individuals; an entire set of elements focused on the industry of the area – which in turn make IDs and LPSs more competitive than they could have been otherwise (Molina 2005). In these early stages the Spanish IDs' competitiveness was played mainly on price, and was favoured by the lower cost of labour relative to other European competitors. This competitive position was, however, destined to become vulnerable in an open environment such as the one that has been occurring recently with increasingly globalised economies.

Globalisation is calling into question the competitiveness of Spanish IDs. The adaptation to the new demands for change being made on the productive structure does not find adequate support in the existing social capital. This local social capital is not being regenerated either at the speed or with the intensity necessary to compete in the new context of globalisation. On the contrary, productive agents and institutions with obsolete strategies are blocking and preventing the growth of the ability to 'control the process of change' demanded by greater external competition.

Three important examples of inflexibility and obsolescence can be briefly mentioned: firstly, trade unions, concerned with the industrial crisis, are determined to keep vertical and sectoral representative structures rather than adopt territorial ones; secondly, employers' organisations, who face similar difficulties, are even more unwilling to change because of internal conflicts concerning their representation of local interests; and thirdly, one of the central instruments of ID policy so far, that is, the service centres and technological institutes, are losing their grip. Essentially it can be seen that they no longer fulfil one of the central functions originally entrusted to them, which was to provide the SMEs of a territory with services in anticipation of their needs. These technological institutes have been deliberately converted into quasi-private institutions at the service of the firms with a more prominent role in the local area; they are managed on the basis of financial profitability rather than on the original basis of social and local criteria (Asesoría Industrial Zabala 2006). This does not help IDs which today have such serious problems of governance revealed by globalisation.

Meanwhile, the response to globalisation being given by enterprises and economic agents in the various Spanish IDs is very uneven. Basically these responses can be grouped into three blocks. Firstly, there is a set of LPSs and IDs where considerable readjustments would need to take place, but where the structural reforms implemented simply eliminate the employment of the workers least suited to new activities (such as women, young people, older workers with experience in a very specialised activity); the failure to regenerate the industrial fabric is an obvious consequence. The second response, in complete opposition to the first one, is based on innovation. This is the case of firms in IDs in which major innovations are being incorporated into products, materials or their organisations; these changes can be seen in certain special areas of the textile, ceramic and plastics industries. However, while the first two are paradigmatic for observing the impact of globalisation on Spanish IDs, the third and probably most important and diffused set of responses is represented by the implementation of comprehensive or staged delocalisation.

The first opinions within the IDs concerning the possible transfer of flagship enterprises or some of their stages of production to countries and/or areas outside the ID expressed scepticism. The district's people, firms and institutions believed that the district possessed certain productive characteristics that would be difficult to reproduce artificially in other places outside the district in which they originated. However, things turned out to be otherwise: some of the large companies are using delocalisation as a mechanism to relocate certain stages of production in areas and countries outside the IDs where they emerged. In some cases, they even eliminate all the production from the original IDs and become mere commercial intermediaries for new factories that are now located outside the ID. Some of the enterprises that were emblematic of Spanish IDs have become itinerant logistics platforms, organisers of production chains that can be sited wherever they want. However, and even though such a response is worrying for the district, the fact is that some logistic, organisational and creative remnants have been able to remain in the places where they originated. Such a reaction could seem fairly logical from a financial and business strategy point of view. But how are these strategies affecting the Spanish IDs' prospects for adaptation and regeneration?

The network of inter-company, social, institutional and simple day-to-day relationships that exist in the district cannot be easily transferred into an international framework. However, certain strategic stages of production are being relocated in other places. The transfer and delocalisation of these strategic stages of production means that IDs are deprived of a central and substantial part of their fundamental technical reason for existing. This can be seen in ceramic IDs with frits, in plastics IDs with moulds and so on, stages that are very important for each of the IDs and that can lead to the transformation of the existing productive organisations.

It is against these challenges that a new national industrial policy has been designed in Spain (Trullén 2007 and Trullén in this volume). For the first time it has included a strategy with actions involving teams of innovative enterprises and has been implemented from 2006 onwards with some consistency.[3] Now both the territory and the economic peculiarities that can be developed in that territory are taken into account. Priority will be given to these 'groupings' so that they can instigate the dynamics of innovation, develop processes for change, and establish and disseminate these experiences in the surrounding territorial and productive areas as well.[4] With the implementation of these policies based on the innovative capacity of the IDs, somehow the history of IDs in Spain has come full circle, coming finally to give value to and focus on territories and small firms.

With this new policy approach, Spanish districts can gradually stop being mere passive receptacles of change brought about by crisis, and finally have the opportunity to become agents actively promoting innovation and driving national competitiveness.

NOTES

1. For the industrial concentrations of the 'Madrid corridor', the new Catalonian production centres, textile factories beside major centres of population or the territorial expansion of the metal goods and machinery industry, see Costa Campi et al. (1993).
2. Clear references can be found in Becattini (1979) and Brusco (1982).
3. Ministry of Industry, Tourism and Commerce (Official State Gazette No. 199, 21 August 2006); Ministerial Order regulating the bases, system of subsidies and management of measures of support for groupings of innovative enterprises. 'This programme aimed at Groupings of Innovative Enterprises, is a response to the needs of Small and Medium-sized Enterprises that are grouped in areas known as "Marshallian industrial districts", or clusters of interaction between different enterprises' (according to statements by the Secretary of State for Industry of the Ministry of Industry).
4. For the first time, the prestigious COTEC Foundation (2007) emphasises the opportunity of instigating the dynamics of technological innovation through clusters and IDs in Spain.

38. Industrial districts in Scandinavia

Bengt Johannisson*

1. SCANDINAVIA: A HISTORICAL AND SOCIO-CULTURAL BRIEFING

The Scandinavian countries, here including Sweden, Denmark and Norway, form the heartland of the Nordic countries – covering also Finland, Iceland, the Faroes and Greenland – and usually are presented as very homogenous, nationally as well as when compared with one another. A possible reason for this proposed homogeneity is that these countries, besides their geographical proximity, have colonised each other. Finland was part of Sweden until the beginning of the 19th century. After having lost Finland in a peace treaty with Russia in 1809, Sweden entered an alliance with Norway that lasted for about a hundred years. Before that Denmark had ruled in Norway, and in the Middle Ages also Sweden. Only in the 20th century did Iceland, the Faroes and Greenland become independent from Denmark, making its territory by far the smallest of the three Scandinavian countries. With its 44 000 km^2 it is smaller than one-tenth of the area of Sweden and slightly more than that portion of Norway. The differences in territorial size to a great extent explains why Norway and Sweden have more natural resources than Denmark and why the latter has an economy and embedding culture dominated by trading while the Norwegian and Swedish economies are technology- and production-oriented.

Not surprisingly Hofstede (1980), in his seminal international comparative study on work-related values, reports very similar findings from Sweden, Denmark and Norway on all the dimensions identified. As a matter of fact his research puts the Scandinavian culture quite close to the North American one although the Scandinavians rank higher as regards equality between the sexes. After the Second World War all Scandinavian countries have emerged into advanced welfare economies. A large public sector and, especially in Sweden, a number of large corporations have managed to create wealth and economic progress that lasted well into the 1980s. Because of these large-scale structures there was not much need of an active small business sector, nor of a proactive entrepreneurship policy. Such issues instead have been integrated into the regional policy, elaborate in Sweden and Norway because of the sparsely-populated territories they occupy. However, the regional implications of different sector policies have been even more important for regional development.

The political power in Sweden and Denmark, less so in Norway, for centuries has been centralised. A possible reason for this is that few wars have hit Scandinavia in modern times and the national boundaries for that reason have remained stable. The Scandinavian countries in the 20th century all developed corporatist regimes. That is, alliances including the State, the large corporations and the trade unions created highly-regulated societies that did not leave much space for individual initiative. A wage-earner culture has dominated the Scandinavian context since the 20th century, enforced by strong popular movements in all its member States. The small family business, mainly associated with the petite bourgeoisie, also encompasses localised clusters of small businesses adopting the features of industrial districts (IDs). Elsewhere we argue that the entrepreneurial energy these settings represent cannot be ascribed to individual firms as such, but it is produced by them as a collective factor (Johannisson 2003).

For a number of reasons the kind of agglomerations/clusters that adopt ID features have not to a great extent been researched in the Scandinavian setting. First, in the sparsely populated Sweden and Norway the basic structural conditions for that kind of small-firm agglomerations have not existed. Accordingly it should be no surprise that IDs have played a more significant role in the densely populated Denmark. Second, all three countries are highly institutionalised at the national level, which brings little need and space for the action of the local business community to partake in the creation of a local/regional infrastructure. Third, elaborate welfare policies have reduced the call for indigenous necessity entrepreneurship as a response to marginalisation. Nevertheless accessibility remains a key issue for many firms and localities in rural Norway and Sweden. Fourth, since industrial development in Scandinavia has been traditionally associated with technological competences, clustering and innovation systems caught the attention of Scandinavian practitioners and researchers, inspired not least by such visible phenomena as Silicon Valley. As small national economies these countries are generally very sensitive to external influences which often are absorbed into the existing institutional structure and/or even create their own institutions. Sweden, for example, has a special public board (Vinnova) which orchestrates much of the R&D programmes in the field of (regional) innovation systems. Fifth, while all countries have well-established and regionalised public support systems, programmes targeting agglomeration of firms and not individual firms were launched only in the 1990s. Before, public support focused on individual (small) firms and their growth.

Some recent and important changes and associated shifts in national characteristics are to be noted. First, the national settings have become ethnically less homogeneous. For example, today every fifth Swede is a first or second-generation immigrant. Second, natural endowments as well as institutional changes have forced the countries quite apart economically. Sweden, once the 'Big Brother' in the Scandinavian family, has lost its position as an exemplar welfare economy. Norway is prospering on its oil resources and Denmark on an internationalised and differentiated economy. Third, following Denmark, Sweden has only recently has become a member of the EU. Norway remains an outsider in the European context, probably because of a well-developed nationalism – and regionalism – in addition to the financial affluence of the country. Norway also stands out with respect to the degree of freedom granted to municipalities, for example as regards supporting individual businesses.

According to received knowledge these countries should produce a strong civic society, in turn benefiting new-business creation and entrepreneurship generally (Putnam 1993). Thus Section 2 reviews ways of conceiving economic development and entrepreneurship as a social phenomenon and the role of IDs in that context. In Section 3 some approaches to Scandinavian IDs are elaborated, focusing on the Gnosjö region in Sweden. Section 4 proposes a model that may bridge the present dominant views on regional economic development in the Scandinavian countries and the ID as a role model.

2. MODELLING (REGIONAL) FIRM COLLABORATION IN THE SCANDINAVIAN CONTEXT

Searching the roots of IDs in the Scandinavian countries, two cultural features come to the fore: individualism and high trust. Individualism originates most probably in a preindustrial agricultural society dominated by independent farmers, while the high level of trust presumably is an outcome of homogenous societies. Collaboration, whether functional – that is associated with, for example, industry or profession – or territorial – that is connected to place – is a feasible way of taking advantage of multidimensional proximity and trust while staying independent. For a number of reasons collaborations in the Scandinavian contexts have been more functionally than territorially (locally/regionally) oriented in practice as well as in research. First, strong farmers' associations have protected their members from external threats but certainly also from taking on extra-farming activities as a springboard to spatial clustering. Second, the small-sized Scandinavian economies have offered the overview needed to establish national innovation systems which provide them with the critical mass for international competitiveness. This development is enforced by the fact that the Scandinavian countries appeared early as 'knowledge economies' implying both a potential for high technology and, as we will see, intense learning. Third, the business community early on built alliances with the public sector, two strong actors with a shared interest in knowledge creation. Fourth, public support for collective business development until recently has mainly been geared towards the creation and enforcement of functional systems for business development.

This focus on functional systems in the Scandinavian countries when researching systems of firms in an institutional setting is, as indicated, well reflected in research. Scandinavian scientists have made several theoretical and/or methodological contributions associated with the elaboration of four analytical concepts/metaphors: development/competence blocks, (national) innovation systems, learning regions and localised collective entrepreneurship. The first three concepts will only be commented upon briefly since they are less applicable to IDs and also less concerned with methodological development. The understanding of the ID as materialisation of collective entrepreneurship will for obvious reasons be presented more in detail in the following section.

More than half a century ago the Swedish economist Erik Dahmén (1988), forestalling much of the present research and political interest in systemic approaches to economic development, coined the notion of the 'development (competence) block'. Also inspired by Schumpeter's work on creative destruction, Gunnar Eliasson has brought this model for systemic industrial development further and ascribes a 'competence bloc' of six features:

> 1. Competent and active *customers*; 2. *Innovators* who integrate technologies in new ways; 3. *Entrepreneurs* who identify profitable innovations; 4. *Competent venture capitalists* who recognize and finance the entrepreneurs; 5. *Exit markets* that facilitate ownership change; 6. *Industrialists* who take successful innovations to industrial scale production. (Eliasson and Eliasson 2006, p. 397; italics in original; see also D. Johansson 2001)

Although neither Dahmén nor Eliasson are explicitly concerned with the regional dimension, Eliasson by linking the competence-bloc framework to an image of the economy as experientially organised offers a bridge between entrepreneurially instigated high-tech agglomerations and low-tech IDs as emerging out of special production and living conditions. The boundaries between the functions that Eliasson's six key actors carry out are possibly more blurred in IDs due to their cultural and social embedding, a contextualisation that is disregarded in the competence-bloc framework with its national focus.

The development/competence-bloc framework has been translated into 'innovation systems' with Bengt-Åke Lundvall (1985, 1992). In the 1990s the innovation-system metaphor basically had replaced the previous decade's fascination with science parks. In this research the role of the individual entrepreneur is however basically disregarded. Furthermore the experiential, organic image of development processes is replaced with a strong focus on technology (Edquist 1997 and Carlsson 2003). Because of its reduction of socio-cultural influences to (formal) institutions and focus on technology this model for industrial development has had a strong influence not only on research on industrial and regional development in Scandinavia but also on the public policies in all three nations.

Parallel to the competence-bloc and innovation-system images a general concern for firm clustering has emerged, again out of a very close interaction between the research community and policymakers. The cluster metaphor is important because it recognises the role of individual members in addition to the system-level point of view. Due to these incompatibilities, in Sweden, for example, entrepreneurship and innovation are kept separate in both research and policymaking, and innovation systems and cluster issues are accordingly dealt with by different public institutions.

In a comparative Scandinavian research project (also including Finland and Iceland) Peter Maskell, Heikki Eskelinen, Ingjaldur Hannibalsson, Anders Malmberg and Eirik Vatne (Maskell et al. 1998), elaborate on the notion of localised capabilities and learning. They add a resource-based perspective to the original notion of ID as coined by Marshall (1920). The authors relate the competitive advantage of a region to its localised capabilities in turn related to 'the institutional endowments; the build structures; the natural resources; and, not the least, the knowledge and skills' (ibid., p. 10) of the region. By building unique competencies it is possible to create global competitiveness also in low-tech industries in developed countries, not least in settings characterised by high trust (as in the case of the Scandinavian countries, see above). This learning-region framework is promising in an emerging knowledge economy and would be even more so if linked to entrepreneurship theories and furnished with appropriate methodology. In a more recent study Andersen, Böllingtoft and Christensen (2006), also inspired by the original ID concept and its application in the Italian setting, review the international pressure on existing Danish regionalised clusters. The local dynamics are studied from the point of view of both the cluster at large and its individual member firms and its connections to the global market. These kinds of studies reveal the complexity associated with local cooperation and global competition.

3. RESEARCHING IDs IN SCANDINAVIA

Even adopting a quite broad definition of IDs, there are quite few in the Scandinavian setting. Most are located in Denmark, in the textile and furniture industries on the Jutland peninsula. Norway has only one ID, the Sunnmöre region where furniture and ship-building industries are colocated. After the decline of the textile-industry complex in the Borås region east of metropolitan Gothenburg only the Gnosjö region further to the east in southern Sweden, with its focus on light engineering and plastics, remains as an ID in Sweden.

The 'learning region' metaphor and its empirical applications on Danish IDs and other Scandinavian agglomerations of (small) firms emerged out of comparative Scandinavian research (also including Finland) (Maskell et al.

1998; Lorenzen 1998; see also Johannisson and Spilling 1986). This research has condensed some of its conceptual findings into attractive and moving metaphors such as the local organising logic as 'being in the air' (Marshall 1920) or localised networking as being carried by 'untraded interdependencies' (Storper 1995). The notion of 'local business climate' (Johannisson 1978, 1983) based on the concept of industrial atmosphere and of untraded interdependencies helps model the district as an organising context, complete with associated network modelling and measurement (see Johannisson et al. 1994; Johannisson 2000a; Johannisson, Ramírez-Pasillas and Karlsson 2002).

As indicated, much of the research into localised small-firm clustering in Scandinavia is biased towards high-tech, presumably innovative systems. The road to this current main focus however differs between Denmark, Norway and Sweden. In Denmark in-depth studies have been carried out aiming at both illustrating the ID phenomenon at large (for example, Illeris 1992) and elaborating upon it in a learning perspective (Lorenzen 1998; Maskell et al. 1998). In Norway little systematic research on IDs is reported and those involved in exploratory studies soon enough incorporated IDs as empirical phenomena in a locality's search for technological upgrading (Isaksen 1999; Spilling and Steinsli 2003).

A drawback of much of the Scandinavian research into IDs and other localised business activities is a lack of bridging between seductive metaphors such as learning regions and the reality as mapped and reported either by hard facts or stories told by those inhabiting the business communities and further local stakeholders. As indicated, Scandinavian researchers have contributed significantly with new concepts and perspectives on innovation systems and clusters. Further Scandinavian contributions to the ID research include qualitative approaches. Wigren (2003), for example, has made an ethnographic study of the Swedish Gnosjö ID, and Pettersson (2004), using discourse analysis, has critically reviewed the paternalistic values and behavioural norms dominating the same district.

The choice of unit of analysis and associated modelling becomes a crucial issue that depends upon the academic training of the researcher. Especially in Denmark much research on IDs is carried out by economists – or industrial economists – or geographers. The implication is that although localities are presented as settings where firms and institutions are tied together by multiple networks and thus producing different kinds of proximities, the empirical data as regards the core business community are reduced to firm and not relational data, empirically presenting the districts as aggregates of primarily economic activity. There has been a demand for ways of identifying the unique features of the ID as a holistic socio-economic setting for firms and further stakeholders.

The Gnosjö region, presumably the one and only Swedish ID, is located in rural southern Sweden. It consists of four municipalities (in addition to Gnosjö also Gislaved, Vaggeryd and Värnamo) and included at the turn of the millennium

80 000 inhabitants and 1500 manufacturing firms. The region's industrial traditions go back several centuries. Gnosjö as an entrepreneurial phenomenon relates to the community as a whole (Johannisson 2000a) and its business 'world' amalgamates with other 'worlds' expressed by the social, cultural and institutional fabric. Few local firms have a strong identity on the market that could create a potential for growth of the individual company, and such ambitions are anyway dampened by strong local social control. Nevertheless the small-business fabric has brought prosperity to the region for centuries. As late as in the 1990s the region, according to a number of conventional 'objective' criteria, thrived on substantial growth, whether in terms of economic wealth and high start-up frequencies in the dominant manufacturing industries (light engineering and plastics) or low unemployment. In addition, the region accommodates a high portion of immigrants in the labour force. At the turn of the millennium about 26 per cent of the people living in the municipality of Gnosjö were immigrants (Wigren 2003).

As early as the 1970s original network studies had been carried out (in the Gnosjö municipality) (for example, Johannisson 1978, 1983; Johannisson et al. 1994). Repeated investigations into this locality propose that there are limits to local networking in terms of what information and resources they provide. Comparative studies into different Swedish localities suggested early on that self-organising in a business community is conditioned by a minimum threshold in terms of number of business units and of density in networking. While these pioneering network studies lacked proper statistical tools to conduct complex network analysis, Johannisson et al. (1994) reports a more advanced network inquiry into a community of the Gnosjö region, namely Anderstorp. Similar graph-analytical studies have later been carried out in other Swedish contexts (Johannisson, Ramírez-Pasillas and Karlsson 2002). For a number of reasons these IDs/rural communities have, using network methodology, been compared with a science park (Ideon at Lund University in Sweden). First, at the time of the studies the science park was considered by both researchers and policymakers as a universal means for creating regional development. Second, as regards the social embedding, the Swedish science parks seem to have had the social community of the small-town ID in mind (in Swedish a science park was originally called a science 'village'). Third, the science-park programme was the first systematic attempt to enact the (naive) belief that networks between independent firms can be created from outside and above.

The empirical research clearly states that the local (organising) context is considerably more important to its member firms in the small town of Anderstorp in the Gnosjö ID than in the Ideon science park. The data, however, also show that the ID low-tech firms on average are as internationally oriented as the science park high-tech firms. As proposed the ID is much more densely networked than the science park and as expected local network (in-)activity does not vary according to firm performance. What is more, the findings indicate that in a Scandinavian setting there is no strong hierarchy in the social system of the

ID. This finding is in stark contrast to what came out in a comparative study with Argentina, which has, according to the Hofstede scheme, a national culture that is the opposite of the Swedish (Scandinavian) one (Johannisson et al. 2005).

Personal networking, more associated with spontaneous exchange than intentional choices made by firms and/or institutions, socially and emotionally integrates everyday (business) life in the ID. The myth concerning the business climate in this ID, known as the 'spirit' of Gnosjö, with its own entry in the National Swedish Encyclopaedia, also talks about continuous renewal by way of spinoffs from established (small) firms. Today a majority of the larger firms are externally controlled, by national and international owners, which suggests a potential threat to the local entrepreneurial spirit.

Considering the ID as a relational construct should however not only include (absolute) network density but an analysis of the (relative) composition of existing ties. Two important issues are brought up here. What are the effects of community/district size on networking and of planning and the intention of networking? To what extent does the ID stand out also with respect to the kind of network relations used in the business operations? For the sake of comparison Table 38.1 includes (dyadic) networking data concerning not only Anderstorp and Ideon but also a small community dominated by the furniture industry that was revitalised by local community entrepreneurs in the 1990s (Lammhult). (For details see Johannisson, Ramírez-Pasillas and Karlsson 2002.)

Table 38.1 Relative relevance of network ties in the ID and other territorial contexts (percentage)

Relation characteristic	ID (67 firms)	Revived community (29 firms)	Science park (42 firms)
Friendship	29.3	41.3	23.7
Commercial	49.0	32.3	37.3
Professional	38.8	38.4	52.7
Complex	13.7	13.6	13.6

Note: 'Friendship' means that the business leaders know each other and have talked during the last month; 'commercial' that the firms have had business exchanges in the last nine months; 'professional' that the staff of the other firm would be approached if a challenging problems turns up; and 'complex' that all the other strands coexist in the network tie.

Specialisation among firms is more common in the ID than in the other two settings, encouraging business exchange. Instead socialising via strong (friendship) ties is needed more in the revived community where new challenges and calls for creative organising continuously emerge. In the science park, where interactive knowledge creation is the very reason for its existence, professional networking has to be especially nurtured. However, in spite of these structural differences in relational contents, the portion of complex ties, combining specific features, is about the same in the three contexts being studied. This suggests that there has to be a minimum of strong, bonding relationships to create commitment to place.

EMBEDDEDNESS	FIRST ORDER Inter-firm networking	SECOND ORDER Firm/Institution networking	THIRD ORDER Holistic networking
Descriptions	Business to business	Firm to socio-economic institutions	Links between small firms through institutions
• Systemic (Economic)	• Commercial relations	• Business acquiring services, joint projects	• Indirect potential business exchange through interacting economic and social institutions
• Substantive (Social)	• Personal business relations	• Business leaders as association members	

Source: Johannisson, Ramírez-Pasillas and Karlsson (2002, Table 1, p. 301).

Figure 38.1 Alternative images of local, social and institutional embeddedness

In Figure 38.1 the generic image of social embeddedness of economic activity (Granovetter 1985), typically associated with the ID, is specified and presented as an analytical framework that goes beyond the business community and also includes the endowments included in the 'learning regions' framework (Maskell et al. 1998). It is important to differentiate between what is addressed here as 'systemic and substantive' embeddedness. Systemic embeddedness points to the structure of the social embeddedness of economic activity (Johannisson et al. 1994), while substantive embeddedness denotes the contents of the relationships that make the structure as illustrated in Figure 38.1. Systemic embeddedness thus refers to the overall system of relations that links economic and other agents in, for example, a local/regional cluster. It puts the individual actors in different positions, some more central, some more marginal, in the overall network. A favourable position usually means that many other network members are dependent on the focal actor as a bridge to become (or remain) connected. Following a rational logic agents systematically look for such positions (Burt 1992; Gulati and Gargiulo 1999). Substantive embeddedness instead underlines that the origin of and base for exchange are not just calculative but social aims as well.

With Halinen and Törnroos (1998) we recognise that besides business-to-business networks, linkages with economic institutions and social associations as providers of both resources and legitimacy become increasingly important. 'Institutional embeddedness' builds collective entrepreneurial capabilities by developing, producing and marketing goods, services and knowledge (Van de Ven

1993 and Johannisson 2000a). Interconnected ties indicate that firms may share meeting points with other actors in the networks created by economic and social associations. A unique feature of localised networks of firms is their embeddedness in a setting that accommodates economic as well as social institutions. This statement invites indirect networking, where such institutions may also bridge firms which otherwise may remain disconnected in the business system.

Summarising the argument, the framework identifies three layers of embeddedness: 'first-order' (firm to firm relations); 'second-order' (firm relations to social and economic institutions); and 'third-order' (firms indirectly related through social and economic institutions). The third kind of networking is called 'holistic' since it includes ties that can only be considered by studying the ID in its entirety, including both business–persons and economic–social institutions and taking into account not only direct but also indirect, that is mediated, relations. This model on one hand summarises the arguments for presenting the ID as a specific setting that invites (social) learning; and on the other hand condenses several crucial contributions by Scandinavian researchers to our understanding of localised business activities.

4. BRIDGING THE TERRITORIAL AND FUNCTIONAL RATIONALES

For reasons elaborated above practice and research concerning regional development have been more attracted by economic and technological factors than by social and cultural considerations. However, Scandinavian social-science research, as for example reported by scholars in organisation and entrepreneurship studies, points out that (ir-)rationalities of innovation and entrepreneurship as well as personal relations enforced by affection and commitment to place are significant contributions to the making of robust local communities in a globalising world. The former overly rational and under-socialised view reflects a 'functional rationale', while the latter is associated with a 'territorial rationale' which acknowledges the potential of spontaneous (inter-)action in creative organising and the need for improvisation in everyday business making (Johannisson and Lindholm Dahlstrand 2008).

In Figure 38.2 three pairs of contrasting/supplementing concepts are introduced as a means of mapping and reflecting upon contemporary public discourses on local and regional economic development. The three dimensions concern the dominant 'life setting' in the territory (place), the general 'outlook' of the people in the locality/region, and the critical 'competence' needed to materialise emerging ideas. The life-setting aspect juxtaposes the 'rural' and 'urban' ways of life. This dichotomy in our mind is closely associated with the Tönnies' distinction (1965) between *Gemeinshaft* and *Gesellshaft*. In the former case strong ties that originate in mechanistic solidarity create a sense of community including general and delayed reciprocity which connects people and produces strong informal institutions. Usually we associate this way of life with peripheral locations. Instead in the urban life setting ties are weak and asymmetric because people specialise. Informal institutions are replaced by formal structures that aim at keeping selfishness at bay.

A 'local' outlook means a great concern for established traditions implying that the search for ideas and ways to deal with challenges is centripetal. Identifying different spaces – physical, social and mental (Hernes 2003) – a local outlook also suggests, as indicated, that the three spaces, due to different proximities, overlap considerably. A 'global' outlook in contrast means that the mental and social spaces of the local communities, their members, individuals as well as collectives, are unbounded and therefore quite separate each from the other as well as from the physical space. People with a global outlook are to a great extent involved in distant networking and use values and norms that differ from those of the place where they live.

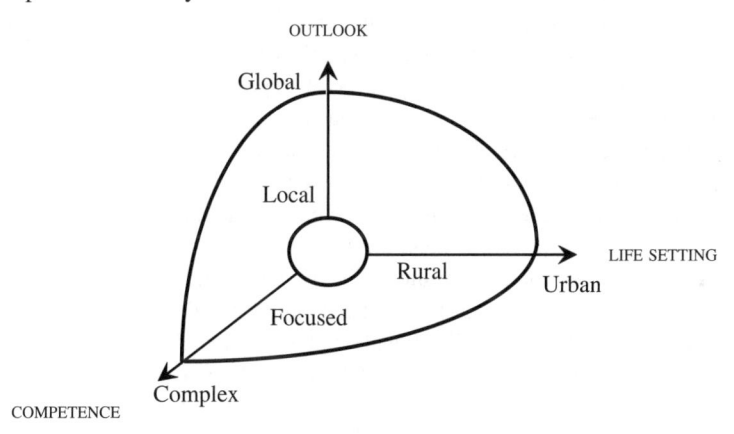

Source: Johannisson and Lindholm Dahlstrand (2008).

Figure 38.2 Contrasting images of territorial dynamics

The third aspect, that of 'competence', ranges from focused to complex. Focused competence here means approaching challenges with capabilities that the individual as a member of a community has gained from experience. Focused thus does not (have to) mean trivial and standardised behaviour but rather refers to insights carried by a reflective practitioner. When a focused competence is at its best it emerges into qualified craftsmanship that over time becomes embodied and intuitive, superior to formal knowing and analytical reasoning. Complex competence emerges out of an ability to combine insights from the frontiers of different knowledge fields, constantly reconsidering the knowledge base that is in use. Such complex competence is usually associated with advanced science-based findings but may also be found in art and in the humanities in general. Design is a field where aesthetics and science may combine into unique competence.

The outer circular profile presents the dominant recipe for growth and economic development in contemporary society. It is carefully nurtured by a majority of policymakers as well as by researchers studying spatial development. This rationale is associated with the global outlook of corporations, institutions and politicians that promote complex innovation systems within a worldwide frame of reference, systems which obviously only metropolitan areas can accommodate. The contrasting image, the inner profile, according to more unobtrusive public discourse produces a rural community with an outlook that is limited by local norms and networks and whose competences are tied to traditions that concentrate a hands-on knowledge base to a few areas. This view, though, not only accommodates disadvantaged communities in the periphery but also prosperous IDs.

It is important to point out that the outer and inner profiles according to Figure 38.2 are proposed as contrasting ideal images, feasible for the sake of analysis of subsequent empirical findings. However, suche profiles also mirror prejudice and wishful thinking originating in contrasting ideologies. The outer profile, constructed from the views of dominant coalitions in society, represents what we associate with a 'functional' rationale dominated by formal, preferably academic, knowledge and footloose financial capital. Since this logic thrives on centrifugal forces which deny any confinement, it articulates a threat to any specific place. The inner profile in contrast originates in the conviction that any sustainable initiative has to be taken from inside local encounters in order to create uniqueness and viability. Such a 'territorial' rationale unites centripetal forces, including the belief that concerted action calls for multidimensional proximity.

From both a generally rationalistic and from a logo-scientific point of view contemporary pressure in a globalising world is towards the functional, outer profile. Wishful thinking, however, does not always materialise. Typical discursive constructs such as the notion of 'triple helix' and 'innovation systems' seldom manage to reach the targeted coordination of the interest groups addressed. Already the divide between institutional and entrepreneurial regional innovation systems (IRIS and ERIS respectively, see Cooke and Leydesdorff 2004) signals an ambivalence within the functional rationale as regards its basic assumptions. The urban setting may provide a multitude of arenas where human encounters trigger creativity but segmentation, for example within the local academic community, often hinders the building of complex competence.

Domestic and international immigrants infuse localities with values and practices that from below may bridge the territorial and functional rationales. The proposed dichotomies and their interrelationships that construct each profile according to Figure 38.2 thus are constantly revised as an outcome of a dialogue, or rather 'polylogue', between their adherents, emphasising them as ideologies, that is, value-laden frameworks for action. Nevertheless to keep them apart appears an awkward solution, considering both their discursive and empirical manifestations. With the vocabulary proposed by the French philosopher Deleuze it is more productive to see each pair of dual concepts as a 'contrariety', that is, signifying two images that are different yet similar. The vitality of a region thus is constructed out of the awareness of keeping both (extreme) images alive, in ongoing discursive and embodied practices. Talking about 'rural', 'local' and 'focused' without (also) having the contrarieties 'urban', 'global' and 'complex' in mind does not make much sense. We thus propose the notion of a 'virtual' rationale for a mindset and a related (inter-)action repertoire that produces entrepreneurial energy out of the very tensions between the 'functional' and 'territorial' rationales and the associated centrifugal and centripetal forces. The notion of 'virtual' then refers to a potential to cross taken-for-granted borders, such as the illusion that peripherality and centrality are destined to reflect the rural/urban divide. The virtual rationale suggests that local practices constructively use the tensions between rural/urban, local/global and complex/focused competence to instigate and maintain change.

The (institutional and cultural) national context will define how the contrasting rationales interactively organise people's minds and actions. In the Scandinavian setting there are several reasons for nurturing the creative tensions on each dimension. Some arguments have already been provided. As regard the rural/urban divide, the fact that science parks in Sweden are labelled 'science villages' reveals that the Swedish culture has its origin in the rural way of life. On the other hand development programmes, financed by both the EU and national bodies that all carry urban values and vocabularies, have invaded many rural small-business settings. Thus in the Swedish ID of Gnosjö an industrial development centre was established in the 1990s as part of a national programme. Its functionalist rationale, for example proposing formal networking and clusters, challenged the local way of collective business development (Johannisson 2000b). However the tensions produced by these alien approaches to business development awakened the traditional ID and made it more aware of dominant worldviews in society. Today (2008) the industrial development centre has been closed down as an independent institution, while the business community has incorporated many of its competencies.

Constructive tensions also appear within the realm of competencies where techniques such as CAD qualify product development processes originating in hands-on experiences (Nonaka and Takeuchi 1995). As a matter of fact the Gnosjö ID early recognised the need for supplementing the experientially-gained knowledge with codified knowledge and collaborated with national institutes specialising in applied technology.

While the discourses on urban/rural and complex/focused competences have gathered momentum well ahead of the turn of the millennium, the local/

global dichotomy has gained special interest with the digital revolution. The Scandinavian countries as small economies have had to attend to developments on the global markets, and global market forces have also stimulated the call for national innovation systems with large companies as the main drivers. However, for a number of reasons there is also pressure towards alternative views on how to cope with the global challenge. First, with the new ICT the access to many markets has become easier in time and space. Second, although economies of scale may have survived, the shift from an industrial to a service economy calls for not just (industrial) customer adaptation but for sensitivity to individual consumer needs. Third, in an increasingly open world the sense of 'belonging' to a specific place becomes especially valued. Jointly, these and further pressures explain why the tensions between the local and the global and the energy thus released provide a foundation for appropriate business and local/regional strategies and tactics.

Scandinavian researchers contributed early in research on 'born globals' (see, for example, Madsen and Servais 1997; Madsen, Rasmussen and Servais 2000; Moen and Servais 2002; Andersson and Wictor 2003; as well as Andersen, Böllingtoft and Christensen 2006). From the point of view of the individual firm and the overall local business community, the ID and its member firms epitomise the 'glocal' strategy: gaining global competitiveness through local collaboration (Andersen, Böllingtoft and Christensen 2006). Scandinavian research demonstrates that that generic strategy is amplified by considering different kinds of proximity (Onsager et al. 2007) and further international marketing activities such as (firm) participation in international trade fairs (Ramírez-Pasillas 2007). There are reasons to believe that the emergent experience economy will encourage further glocal strategies, whether as original collective venturing or as an outcome of refurbished IDs originating in the manufacturing-industry era. Further pressures towards glocal strategies may be generated on the individual level when entrepreneurs take on glocal identities. Entrepreneurship is generally existentially driven and in a global world personal motives will become increasingly influenced by universal values while everyday activities keep the entrepreneurs local. The great concern for and public-policy focus on (regional) innovation systems as well as on clusters also would benefit from a glocal outlook. While innovation systems by definition aim at global competitiveness, in the Scandinavian current setting local clusters are often encouraged as universal means for development. However, only if taking their own initiative, and considering both local and global markets and factor markets, will such localised clusters produce robust communities.

NOTE

* I am indebted to Poul Rind Christensen, Sven Illeris, Mark Lorenzen and Arne Isaksen for suggesting appropriate research on IDs in Denmark and Norway.

39. Industrial districts in Japan

Yoshiyuki Okamoto

1. INTRODUCTION

In Japan, with local regional vitalization being a pressing political subject in recent years, industrial policy and regional policy at the national and local level have included a focus on industrial districts (IDs) and the creation and development of industrial clusters. This issue has attracted much attention from researchers in various fields, such as economics, sociology, management and geography. Various organizations related to small and medium-sized enterprises (SMEs), including government organizations, local governments, think tanks and consultants, have also carried out several related researches.

Many of these studies, however, merely give empirical illustrations of successful cases. There are few theoretical analyses or empirical studies beyond the level of case study. Unlike in Europe and the US, 'schools' developing original methodological points have not been formed in Japan. Moreover, research exchanges with overseas scholars are very limited, and foreign-cited articles are limited to those written in English. Also, most measures by the national and local governments for IDs or clusters do not have a theoretically-based ground.

This chapter reviews research conducted in Japan on IDs and related forms of industrial and local development (Section 2), describes the present situation of these forms (Section 3), and introduces some cases: Bishu, the place of woollen textiles; Tsubame, the place of metal goods; Hamamatsu, the place of textiles, musical instruments and motorcycles; and Ota-ku, the place of machine parts (Section 4). Section 5 describes how Japan has been coping with globalization in recent years.

2. THE DEBATE ON IDs IN JAPAN

In Japan, the concepts of ID and industrial cluster are relatively new. Other terms have been used traditionally for indicating related phenomena, such as the 'local industry' (*Jiba-sangyo*) and the 'place of production' (*Sanchi*). The definition of IDs has not been seriously discussed in the academic society.

In particular, in Japan, neither researchers nor policymakers fully recognize the function of the sociological factors of IDs which have been regarded as important by Italian researchers (see Becattini 1990).

Several types of IDs have been formed in Japan, as I will describe soon. Although IDs based on independent networks of SMEs like in many Italian cases exist, there are also some other types. For example, in such industries as car and electricity, many related companies, most of them SMEs, locate around and collaborate closely with establishments of large companies such as Toyota or Hitachi, forming what may be more properly called 'company towns'. In this chapter, I generally use the term 'ID' to refer to various types of industry districts, but also use the terms *Jiba-sangyo* and *Sanchi* if needed.

Many IDs were born and most of them grew rapidly after the Second World War up until the 1970s, which is the high-growth era of the Japanese economy. The support system for SMEs was at the centre of discussion on industrial policies, due to SMEs' important role in the regional economy as well as to some political reasons.[1] SMEs had been treated as dependent enterprises that must be supported and relieved, until the revision of Small and Medium Enterprise Basic Law in 2006. Regional economy, *Jiba-sangyo*, and *Sanchi* were discussed as issues related to SMEs. A neoclassical approach to regional economics was introduced. However, since it was highly theoretical, this approach did not give useful clues. Nor did economic geography offer a robust theoretical framework, even if it was the heyday of national land planning and community development by public sectors, and the concept of industrial location was discussed within these perspectives. Sociologists conducted various researches on local industries and farm villages, producing many reports on case studies, without explicit general implications.

With the oil crisis, the period of high growth of the Japanese economy ended. Regional differences in the degree of local development appeared more clearly. The substantial import restrictions (formally voluntary export restrictions by Japan) due to trade friction with the US and the increasing imports due to the economic development of East Asia began to affect *Jiba-sangyo* and *Sanchi* all over Japan. Government industrial policy started to consider *Jiba-sangyo* and *Sanchi* which were under threat due to the rise of imports from developing countries such as China. A revamping of local industries was required as argued in *Nihon no Jiba-Sango* ('Local industry of Japan') by Mitsuru Yamazaki (1977) and *Chiiki-shugi no Jidai* ('Time of regionalism') by Tadao Kiyonari (1978). Thus, development and support of local industries became an important issue. Researchers began to study *Jiba-sangyo* and *Sanchi*. There were also discussions about the attraction of investments by non-local enterprises and the problems of 'endogenous development' (*Naihatuteki-Hatten no Riron*, 'Theory of endogenous development', by Tsurumi and Kawata 1989), though it did not have any theoretical content.

The Second Industrial Divide by Piore and Sabel (1984) raised a new stream of contributions from Japanese researchers in the late 1980s. 'Flexible specialization', 'Third Italy', and post-Fordism were introduced and lent a theoretical foundation for studying IDs in Japan too. As mentioned before, in Japan the traditional view of SMEs saw them as either to be exploited by large companies or to characterize backward local industries. Stimulated by studies such as *Regional Advantage: Culture and Competition in Silicon Valley and Route 128* by Annalee Saxenian (1994), *Italia no chusho-kigyo Senryaku* ('The strategy of small and medium-sized enterprises in Italy') by Yoshiyuki Okamoto (1994), and *Enjeru nettowa-ku bencha- wo hagukumu amerika bunka* ('The American culture which cherishes an angel network of ventures') by Hiroyuki Kokado (1996), many researchers, public officers and consultants visited the places of Third Italy and Silicon Valley.

Although the IDs of Ota-ku, Tubame and Hamamatsu,[2] which had successfully coped with changes in their economic environment, had been studied already, *The Second Industrial Divide* provided a new perspective on ID research. Since then, the debate on IDs has continued to flourish, although many researchers did not present the results of their studies abroad.

Furthermore, following Michael Porter's industrial cluster even business scholars began to show interest in IDs, as illustrated in *Nihonngata Sangyo-shuseki no Mirai-zo* ('The future of the Japanese type of industrial districts') edited by Tadao Kiyonari and Toshiaki Hashimoto (1997), and *Sangyo-shuseki no Honshitsu-Jyu-nanna Bungyo · Shuseki no Jyoken* ('The essence of industrial districts. Conditions of flexible division of work and accumulation') edited by Hiroyuki Itami, Shigeru Matsushima and Takeo Kikkawa (1998). These studies indicate that it became important to discuss innovation not only at a firm level but also at an industry-district level considering both industrial and inter-firm connections in an area. The influence of the cluster approach is reflected in the Ministry of Economy, Trade and Industry (METI) advancing the formation of 'industrial clusters',[3] and the Ministry of Education, Culture, Sports, Science and Technology advancing the policy for formation of 'knowledge clusters'.

Researchers have begun to study the structure and mechanism of IDs in Japan, in an attempt to overcome the limits of a merely descriptive approach. However, this happens in a period in which most IDs in Japan are in decline and this does not help theoretical research.

3. OVERVIEW OF IDs IN JAPAN

There are various types of IDs in Japan, which have been typified differently by different researchers. We consider that the following typology enables us to classify the Japanese IDs effectively.[4]

1. Subcontract processing type, like Ota-ku or Higashi-Osaka: this is an ID that manufactures and processes parts, many of which are supplied to large companies outside the district.
2. *Sanchi* type: this is a traditional local industry or a place of production that produces finished goods, whether consumer goods or production goods. Although its form is similar to the Italian IDs, their organization may not be always the same. Examples include Bishu, specializing in woollen fabrics; Tsubame, specializing in houseware and tableware; and Okawa, specializing in furniture.
3. Company town type: this is an ID where various related industries are formed around a large company such as Toyota or Hitachi.
4. Industrial hybrid type: examples are Hamamatsu and Suwa. While the core is represented by a large company with various related industries, it also contains industrial clusters of SMEs with their own specialization.

Source: Author's elaboration.

Figure 39.1 Map of selected Japanese IDs

We can consider now an overview of IDs in Japan, using *The Survey on the General Situation of Place of Production* by the Small and Medium Enterprise Agency. In *The Survey*, *Sanchi* is defined as 'one of the existent forms of small and medium-sized enterprises whereby a local industry comprising many enterprises, under the same condition, manufacture products belonging to the same sector, and sell them all over Japan or overseas' (see Small and Medium Enterprise Agency 2007, p. 3). A lower threshold is defined, according to which the annual industrial production of a *Sanchi* should be '500 million yen or more' (ibid., p. 3). The *Sanchi* defined in *The Survey* is often expressed as a 'large area', indicating that the definition includes not only local systems, as in the Italian definition of IDs, but also cases of specialized industries spreading in a wider area. In any case they are formed only by SMEs. Although the IDs in *The Survey* almost correspond to the *Sanchi* type, they may also include a part of the subcontract processing type and the industrial hybrid type.

In the 2005 fiscal year, the total number of *Sanchi* in Japan was 486.[5] The 'miscellaneous goods and other sectors' had the largest number of *Sanchi*, 98 places. The 'textile' sector had 98, 'food' sector 83, 'woodwork and furniture' sector 67, 'pottery industry and soil-and-stone' sector 55, 'machine and metal' sector 52, and 'clothes and other textiles' sector 42. In terms of regional location, the places of production were unevenly distributed.[6] Fukui Prefecture had by far the largest number of places, 96. Saitama had 34 places, then Niigata 26 places, Shizuoka, Osaka and Wakayama 21 places, Nara 20 places, and Tokyo 19. Chiba and Tottori had only one place.

The number of companies located in the *Sanchi* was 41 656, corresponding to around 16 per cent of the whole small and medium-sized manufacturing enterprises in Japan. The number of employees was 381 521, about 8 per cent of the employees who worked for those companies. The annual production was 6 786 800 million yen, about 6 per cent of the annual production by the same companies.[7] (See Table 39.1 below.)

The number of the 'export type' places, that is, that exported 20 per cent or more of their products, was 22. This indicates that *Sanchi* are generally of a domestic demand type. The 'machine and metal' districts are the typical 'export type', and have been increasing their production in the last years. More that 40 per cent of their sales came from exports (see Small and Medium Enterprise Agency 2007, pp. 4–9).

These figures of production and export indicate that the *Sanchi* and the small and medium-sized manufacturing enterprises located there do not occupy a big part of Japanese economy. However, from the viewpoint of regional economy, they are important and their support is a crucial policy matter now.

On average, a *Sanchi* included around 87 companies in 2005. However, this figure varies according to the type of industry. The average numbers of companies of the *Sanchi* of 'textile', 'machine and metal', 'pottery industry and soil-and-stone' were around 128, 99 and 95, respectively. The *Sanchi* of 'food' had few companies.

Table 39.1 Number of districts, number of firms, total sales

Fiscal year	No. of districts	No. of firms	Sales (billion yen)
1966	188	49 020	1 284
1976	326	–	7 559
1981	436	112 309	13 584
1985	551	121 160	14 737
1990	543	102 913	15 854
1995	537	79 732	13 269
2000	553	60 183	11 002
2005	486	41 656	6 787

Source: Small and Medium Enterprise Agency (2007, pp. 115–16).

The average number of employees of a *Sanchi* was around 924. Among *Sanchi*, 'clothes and other textiles' *Sanchi* and 'machine and metal' *Sanchi* had a large number of employees, while 'woodwork and furniture' *Sanchi* and 'pottery industry and soil-and-stone' *Sanchi* had a small number of employees. The ratio of companies with five or less employees was high – 80 per cent in 'textile' *Sanchi* and in 'pottery industry and soil-and-stone' *Sanchi*. That ratio was high also in 'woodwork and furniture' *Sanchi* and 'miscellaneous goods and other sectors' *Sanchi*. These figures indicate that 'textile' *Sanchi* and 'pottery industry and soil-and-stone' *Sanchi* are formed by many small companies (ibid., pp. 76–86).

The period of *Sanchi* formation varies. The 40.9 per cent of *Sanchi* were formed during or before the Edo era (1604–1868).[8] Only 20.4 per cent of *Sanchi* have formed after the Second World War. In particular, about two-thirds of 'pottery industry and soil-and-stone' *Sanchi* and half of 'textile' *Sanchi* were formed during or before the Edo era. Many *Sanchi* were born also during the Meiji era (1868–1912), but not during the Taisho Era (1912–26) or in the following period before the Second World War.

In general, IDs show a local division of labour in the production process, although its extension depends on the type of industry. Independent makers and subcontractors correspond to 55 per cent and 32 per cent, respectively, of all companies in all places of production. The remaining 13 per cent of companies are manufacturer-and-wholesalers and wholesalers. Traditionally, manufacturer-and-wholesalers and wholesalers have played a key role in planning and organizing manufacturing within Japanese *Sanchi*.

In general, as the scale of the *Sanchi* reduces, the division of labour becomes weak, as exemplified in many small 'food' *Sanchi* and 'pottery industry and soil-and-stone' *Sanchi*, where the local division of labour is almost non-existent, and between 85 and 90 per cent of companies are independent manufacturers. In 'woodwork and furniture' *Sanchi*, 60 per cent of companies are independent manufacturers, and a little less than 20 per cent are subcontractors. On the other hand, in larger *Sanchi*, as generally are the 'clothes and other textiles' *Sanchi*, the 'textile' *Sanchi* and the 'machine and metal' *Sanchi*, the division of labour is strong. In 'textile' *Sanchi*, 40 per cent of the companies are independent manufacturers, nearly 57 per cent of companies are subcontractors. In 'clothes and other textiles' *Sanchi*, independent manufacturers and subcontractors correspond to 34.7 per cent and 36.7 per cent of all companies, respectively. The remaining 28.6 per cent are manufacturer-and-wholesalers and wholesalers. In 'machine and metal' *Sanchi*, 46 per cent are subcontractors and a little more than 43 per cent are independent manufacturers (ibid., pp. 76–86).

The distribution channels connecting *Sanchi* with marketplaces are critically important for the survival of *Sanchi*. Traditionally, the wholesale store system has played this important role. For consumer goods, trading companies and wholesale stores in *Sanchi* distribute goods to retail stores through wholesale stores and trading companies in consumer places.[9] This complicated system remains even now. The wholesale stores in *Sanchi* have played not only a role of distributor but also various critical roles such as planning and design, supplying working capital, and organizing production.

However, although situations vary according to the type of industry, traditional distribution channels are not functioning well any more. In particular, in recent years, it has become very difficult for the traditional system to deal with the diversification of consumer tastes, and the changing technologies. Manufacturers in *Sanchi* are facing the challenge of building a new distribution system. Streamlining distribution processes is required. Such efforts to shorten processes include manufacturers' own direct sales and private brands of large-scale retailers. Direct sales by district associations and individual companies are also increasing. At 'pottery industry and soil-and-stone' *Sanchi*, half of the associations and of the individual companies conduct direct sales. At 'food', 'clothes and other textiles' and 'woodwork and furniture' *Sanchi*, more than half companies are making investments for conducting direct sales, while at 'machine and metal' and 'textile' *Sanchi*, not many companies are planning to change to direct sales. Probably in these *Sanchi* direct sales do not fit with the characteristics of products that are intermediate products or parts.

4. TYPICAL IDs IN JAPAN

I will briefly describe here the outlooks of four cases in order to show the typical structure and feature of IDs in Japan.[10] All these IDs have been affected recently by the rising imports from China and Asian countries (Tables 39.2a and 39.2b), and are trying to cope with the changes of market situation and in technologies.

Table 39.2a   District, number of firms, fiscal year

	1985	1990	1995	2000	2005	2005–1985
Ota-ku	4996	4322	3483	3077	2391	47.9
Higashi-Osaka	5693	5653	4915	4366	3634	63.8
Hamamaysu	3389	3284	2831	2544	3004	88.6
Hitachi	848	803	674	599	508	59.9
Tsubame	985	957	828	702	577	58.6

Table 39.2b   District, total sales (million yen), fiscal year

	1985	1990	1995	2000	2005	2005–1985
Ota-ku	1 725 803	1 729 222	1 343 798	1 097 271	723 158	41.9
Higashi-Osaka	1 624 938	1 935 349	1 567 317	1 280 642	1 134 243	69.8
Hamamaysu*	1 696 101	1 938 531	1 965 927	2 016 425	2 753 302	162.3
Hitachi*	1 106 193	1 548 479	1 494 151	1 172 902	1 153 727	104.3
Tsubame	188 759	211 693	186 238	155 260	149 539	79.2

Source: Industrial statistics (1985–2005).

4.1 Ota-ku

Ota-ku is classified as a 'subcontract processing' type. Ota-ku is a part of Tokyo and was a key traffic point of Tokaido (the main road between Tokyo and Kyoto) while being a fishing village centring on dried seaweed in the Edo era. Companies that have grown large in the electricity, shipbuilding and steel industries, such as Toshiba, IHI, and JFE Engineering Corporation, were originally located in the vicinity of Ota-ku. In this area, many SMEs emerged and formed clusters that manufacture and process unique and rare components.

Ota-ku is still today an area of small businesses, where 80 per cent of companies have ten or fewer employees, centring on machinery, metal goods and so on, while large companies are located on the outskirts of Ota-ku. The features of SMEs in Ota-ku are as follows:

1. Each small company usually specializes in some part of a production process, such as press, cutting, and forge.
2. Companies usually engage in high-variety low-volume manufacturing, special order processing of trial products, or R&D. They are not mass producers.

3. Companies have multiple clients and are independent from large companies. They are not simple subcontractors of a large company.

The ID of Ota-ku is scaling down. The number of businesses in the district was 9000 in 1983, but it was 5040 in 2003. Although the number of manufacturers is decreasing at a national level, the decrease in Ota-ku is sharper than the national level and it is continuing. Needless to say, the reason for this decrease is shrinking demand. The clients may have moved overseas, for example to China, or started to procure from overseas suppliers, seeking cheaper prices. Craftsmen's techniques may have been substituted by machines due to technological progress. In some cases, small companies moved out of Ota-ku, even overseas, accompanying clients.

It is said that, due to the decreasing number of companies, the amount of orders received per company has begun to increase. However, fundamentally, companies in this ID depend on orders from large companies outside the area. Hence, in order to stabilize orders received, they need to carry out not only technological innovation but also new product planning and design. Actually, they are already trying to find a new direction by developing new products and demonstrating those products at exhibitions. Ota-ku will continue to provide the Japanese big manufacturing firms with essential parts.

4.2 Overview of Bishu *Sanchi*

Bishu *Sanchi* is the greatest *Sanchi* that produces woollen fabrics in Japan and represents well the *Sanchi* type. The area includes Ichinomiya City in Aichi Prefecture near Nagoya and its surrounding area (see Table 39.3). Besides the companies included within the woollen fabric industry the large-scale *Sanchi* includes wholesale stores, trading companies, related industries and various associations. Although Bishu was the second largest producer of cotton fabrics in 1884, it changed its core products from silk and cotton fabrics to woollen fabrics, after a big earthquake and the First World War.

Woollen fabric production requires a complicated production process that consists of many stages, such as spinning, twining, weaving and dyeing. Trading companies and wholesale stores in the *Sanchi* have taken the initiative in organizing such production. Conversion to the woollen fabric industry was not easy. At the beginning Bishu did not have the ability to complete the process of dyeing, arranging and finishing, and thus it had to rely on the factories in Nisijin[11] of Kyoto for the final process. However, Bishu was able to increase its production rapidly and eventually produced about 70 per cent of the national production. Many people adopted dresses more oriented to western styles, and as a result the demand for woollen fabrics increased rapidly in the period before the Second World War. When the production of woollen fabrics was resumed after the war, the manufacturers sold all that they made. In 1954, the district faced a crisis of overproduction and the installation of new looms was restricted. However, they expanded exports rapidly countervailing the saturation of the domestic market. Exports to the US increased from 1961, but in 1971 they almost stopped completely due to the voluntary export restraint of textiles to the US. At the same time, in 1980, imports from Italy and China began to increase, and the time came when the *Sanchi* had to do something to overcome the problems of increasing imports.

Table 39.3   The manufacturing structure in Ichinomiya

Industries	No. of businesses	No. of employees
Textile industries	2 044	12 272
Spinning	318	1 213
Warping and weaving	1 123	4 225
Dyeing and finishing	264	3 526
Wool yarn for knitwear	55	493
Others	524	2 813
Clothes and other textiles	337	1 810

Note: Ichinomiya City is a main part of Bishu.

Source: Industrial statistics.

During the period when demand was increasing and Bishu was developing as an ID, the division of labour progressed and various related industries emerged in the *Sanchi*. As a result of the competition from imported products, demand for *Sanchi*'s products has instead started to decrease, and some processes are on the verge of disappearance.

Companies that play a central role at a textile *Sanchi* are textile manufacturers, and they also carry out the function of a wholesale store or trading company. These companies have a planning function, bringing samples to apparel wholesale businesses located in consumer places, such as Tokyo, taking orders, and organizing production. In order to react to the competition with products imported from China and the shrinking market of pure woollen fabrics, the Bishu *Sanchi* has been making efforts to improve the design of products and utilize its brand name.

4.3   The Tsubame *Sanchi*

Tsubame is also a representative of the *Sanchi* type. It had to change its core products several times in order to adapt to changes in the market environment. Until modern times, farmers around Tsubame engaged in Japanese-type nail production as their side product. During the Edo era, demand for Japanese-type nails in Edo (Tokyo) grew, and production expanded to reach 'a thousand nail blacksmiths'. The manufacture of wire also started at the beginning of the 18th century. Moreover, the copper mine opened nearby and the production of copperware started. Furthermore, the production of Japanese-type tobacco pipes also started by adapting new technology.

After the Meiji Restoration (1868), various technologies and cultures were introduced from overseas. As a result Japanese-type nails were replaced with western nails, Japanese-type tobacco pipes with cigarettes, traditional pencils with fountain pens, copperware with aluminium. The industries of Tsubame declined.

During the First World War, western tableware such as spoons and forks were introduced from overseas, and Tsubame *Sanchi* succeeded in trying to produce them. After that, it expanded to manufacture western tableware by improving metal-working technology. In order to improve quality, new machines and, later, stainless steel were introduced. Export increased quickly.

After the Second World War, Tsubame *Sanchi* has produced western tableware and also houseware, taking advantage of stainless processing technology, and has exported them all over the world. However, recently, the export has been decreasing sharply, triggered by the strong yen, and the Tsubame *Sanchi* has faced a crisis again.

Currently, companies are acquiring the know-how of metalworking, such as metallic mould design, press processing, processing of plate metal, laser processing and surface-treatment processing. They are also dealing with various materials, such as titanium, aluminium and magnesium. Moreover, by means of high-variety–low-volume manufacturing, quick-delivery production, quality control, the correspondence to custom-made items, development of new metal goods and so on, companies are trying to regain competitive power.

4.4 Hamamatsu

Hamamatsu is a city located at around 250 km west of Tokyo, being a representative of the 'industrial hybrid' type. Its population is about 800 000. The three main industries are textiles, specializing in cotton goods; musical instruments, specializing in products such as pianos and organs; the automotive industry with products such as motorcycles, cars and outboard engines. In addition, more recently, optoelectronics, electronics and mechatronics industries have been growing. Representative companies include Honda, YAMAHA and Suzuki that are globally known as motorcycle makers. The pianos of YAMAHA or Kawai are also exported. A synthesizer maker, Roland, and woodworking machine makers located their headquarters in the Hamamatsu area. This area has about 4260 factories with 163 000 employees.

The shipment values of manufacturing industries are 6700 billion yen. The factories with 4–9 employees are about 60 per cent of the total, and factories with 100 or more employees only 4 per cent.

The Hamamatsu district seems to have developed endogenously. The industries in its early days were cotton fabrics and lumber. Around 1890, Hamamatsu was a place of production of cotton fabrics where Sakichi Toyota invented the automatic loom and established the Toyota Loom (Toyota Industries Corporation) which is the predecessor of Toyota Motor. The woodworking machine industry was born from the lumber industry. The musical instrument industry, such as organs and pianos, was also born endogenously. The motorcycle industry emerged when Soichiro Honda put engines on bicycles and sold them. At some point, 30 companies competed in the motorcycle market. The Japanese auto industry was also born there. Suzuki started its car business in this area. In recent years, companies based on optoelectronics such as Hamamatsu Photonics were endogenously born and have been growing rapidly.

The ID of Hamamatsu is one of a few examples that have endogenously produced new industries one after another. Some features of the Hamamatsu area are as follows: (a) flourishing entrepreneurship, (b) mutual support networks for material and mental support, (c) open atmosphere and climate, (d) contributions by the local government and the chamber of commerce, (e) contributions by the university (Shizuoka National University) and research institutions, and (f) competition among companies.

As existing industries decline, the Hamamatsu district has been promoting the transition to new industries by building Hamamatsu Technopolis and a network of cross-industrial associations.

5. CORRESPONDENCE TO GLOBALIZATION BY IDs

In a market economy, the economic environment surrounding IDs changes continuously. No place of production, be it an ID or some other form, can escape from global economic competition. Districts are characterized by the division of labour among various companies.

IDs such as Ota-ku, Bishu, Tsubame and Hamamatsu have evolved, coping with environmental changes. However, it has not been easy because of the maturity of the Japanese economy and globalization. In all these IDs the number of companies has fallen, especially since 1985.[12] There is no exception, and company towns have also been hit. If a large core company loses competitive power, surely the related industries in the area will decline. Once the performance of a big company like Hitachi and Nissan deteriorates, the subsidiaries are in a difficult situation.

Large companies and SMEs which once relocated factories to East Asia have begun more recently to return to invest domestically. The '*Sanchi* type' district, formed by SMEs, takes the following preponderant measures to meet the situation: (a) shift to high-value-added products, (b) new product development and expansion into new fields, (c) development of new channels, (d) high-variety–low-volume manufacturing, (e) information gathering for sales promotion, (f) development of skilled labour, (g) collaboration among enterprises, (h) technical and technological development, and (j) rationalization and labour-saving.

Now, many companies are striving to employ good designers and enhance product branding.

Like in other parts of the world, even in Japan there is an increasing attention to policies supporting the use of the intellectual property of universities and the transfer of technology to IDs. In particular, the METI specified 19 projects of the 'industrial cluster plan', and the Ministry of Education, Culture, Sports, Science and Technology specified 18 areas of the 'knowledge cluster creation enterprise', in order to strengthen the competitive power of IDs that try to utilize advanced technologies such as biotechnology or nanotechnology.

However the effects of top-down policies do not seem to be satisfactory. The policy of the government tends to be developed uniformly nationwide and cannot take local circumstances into consideration, while the local industrial promotion would need to focus on local peculiarities.

On the other hand, in Hamamatsu new industries have been endogenously born in sequence. The case of Hamamatsu may be an exception, supported by some characteristics which seem to relate to social factors.

6. CONCLUSION

From a static point of view, the promotion of information sharing, the construction of collaborative relationships, and cross-industrial associations were seen as policies carried out by the chambers of commerce and the local governments. It seems that these policies have not succeeded.

From a dynamic point of view, which means looking at the revitalization of IDs, measures that promote innovation and restructuring are required. It is necessary to transfer and acquire new technology and new information from outside of IDs. Therefore, the government has recently promoted a policy to strongly push forward cooperation with universities and SMEs and technology transfer. Creating new businesses, such as new ventures, is also important, so the government has also promoted the creation of new ventures from universities with the help of venture-funds. The 'industrial cluster plan' and the 'knowledge cluster creation enterprise' of the government have provided universities and/or firms with some incentives, but they do not always seem to succeed.

We think that it is essential to connect various information and resources to activate IDs. In Japan the government pushed forward this coordination from the technical side, but it did not work effectively enough. Coordination is necessary not only at the technology level, but also at the management and marketing levels. It is not easy to connect an ID and the outside, an ID and a university/research institute, or an ID and foreign countries, but talented people who take a role could be involved. The problem is the lack of human resources to assume the role of coordinating the connections and designing new businesses.

NOTES

1. See the White Paper on small and medium enterprises in Japan (Small and Medium Enterprises Agency 2007), and Braun et al. (2002).
2. These IDs will be illustrated later.
3. See www.cluster.gr.jp/en/index.html, accessed 20 December 2008.
4. In Japan, there are many categories of *Sanchi*. According to the Small and Medium Enterprise Agency, there are four types, namely the 'company town' type, the *Sanchi* type, the city-complex type, and the attraction-complex type.
5. Small and Medium Enterprise Agency (2007, p. 3). It collected the data from the association of the *Sanchi* (the METI or a local government has promoted and sponsored the establishment of the association). The figure of large-scale IDs such as the famous Ota-ku and Higashi-Osaka and the 'company town' industry districts of Toyota and Hitachi, are not included in the data.
6. In Japan there are 47 prefectures.
7. See note 5.
8. Ieyasu Tokugawa unified *Daimyo* (feudal lords) and established the government in 1603 as a Shogunate (general). The government collapsed under the Meiji Restoration in 1867. This period is called the Edo era. *Daimyo* were sealed off by the feudality all over Japan. The number of *Daimyo* was 276 at the end of the Edo period. Each *Daimyo* tried to promote local industry and many *Sanchi* were born.
9. Generally, the Japanese distribution channels are complex, and this has been the case especially for the textile industry. Indeed, wholesalers in the *Sanchi* and wholesale dealers in the marketplace have the possibility to liaise the *Sanchi* with final demand directly; at the same time, an outside wholesale dealer can deal with a *Sanchi* wholesalers, the latter therefore accessing demand both indirectly and directly.
10. For the four IDs, there are many references, though most of them are written in Japanese. The following illustrations are the result of direct research conducted by the author.
11. Nishijin is an area of Kyoto where the textile industry is concentrated. The Heian government promoted it in the Heian era (794–1192), but top quality goods were produced afterwards, dependent on the high culture.
12. According to Table 39.1, 1985–2000 changes are 49.7 per cent concerning the number of the companies, and 74.7 per cent with the total sales.

40. The university research-centric district in the United States

Donald Patton and Martin Kenney*

1. INTRODUCTION

The importance of new firms founded to exploit the technology developed by universities has grown significantly in the US as developing industries based on new technologies is seen as the essential means by which America competes in the global economy. This faith in the ability of universities to promote economic development, though, is by no means limited to the US. Indeed, Anne Miner (Miner et al. 2001) found in her survey of university officers in Canada, France, Germany, Japan, Singapore, Thailand, as well as the US, that an international consensus among policymakers has emerged that the university can be a basis for local and regional development.

In this chapter the characteristics and nature of a university research-based district in the US is described.[1] Although such districts exist in other countries, these districts first were noticed in the US in the post-war period and are most common in American settings. As Scott Shane (2004) observed in his extensive review of university start-ups, the Second World War and its aftermath transformed American research universities, particularly with respect to federal government funding of research. Throughout the last half of the 20th century and into the 21st, real university R&D expenditures increased significantly both absolutely and as a percentage of total US R&D. The Bayh–Dole Act of 1980 giving universities (and other federal contractors) the exclusive property rights to inventions certified and generalized a process of commercialization that had already been underway (Mowery et al. 2004). Since 1980 the number of patents filed by American universities has grown fivefold, and, according to an incomplete count generated by universities themselves, the number of university spinoffs increased from around 83 per year in the 1980s to 553 in the year 2006.[2]

This increase in entrepreneurial activity at US universities has been mirrored by an increased academic interest in the topic. A recent literature search of this topic (Rothaermel, Agung and Jiang 2007) indicated that 173 academic articles have been written on university entrepreneurship between 1981 and

2005, and that almost 75 per cent of these were published since 2000. What one finds in reviewing this literature is a very large number of articles investigating the relationship between the number and type of firms spun off from the university, and the attributes of the university from which these firms arose, including attributes of the university's technology transfer office. Relative to the level of interest, surprisingly little research has been done on the founding and performance of these firms with respect to the locality in which they find themselves. This focus on the university rather than the region is due, we think, to policy considerations such as: what should the university's technology transfer office do to promote new firm formation, or what is the appropriate relationship between the university and the private sector, or how much of the intellectual property produced by an invention belongs to the university and how much should be retained by the professors. A second reason for this focus on the university is that the data is more readily available. More comprehensive data on all of the high-technology firms in the region, and in particular those not directly related to the university, is much more difficult to collect because the university's interests are confined to firms directly related to the university.

Further, there is little research on the industrial setting of university spinoffs outside of large regions where universities have made a notable contribution such as the biotechnology clusters found in San Diego (Casper 2007) and Boston (Owen-Smith and Powell 2004), or the contributions of Stanford University and UC Berkeley to Silicon Valley (Kenney and Goe 2004). A notable exception comes from the UK, where the Oxford University and Cambridge University clusters have received considerable attention (Proudfoot 2004; Garnsey and Heffernan 2005; Lawton Smith and Ho 2006).

The literature on industrial districts (IDs), on the other hand, has little to say about the role of the university, due no doubt to the small role university spinoffs play in IDs in Italy and the more comprehensive understanding of universities as a public good drawn upon by many actors in the district. This does not mean, though, that the very extensive literature on IDs cannot inform a discussion of university research-based districts.[3] Quite the opposite. Because IDs have been so carefully studied in Italy and elsewhere, a large number of conceptual and theoretical observations have been derived that can be applied to regional production systems in general, including the university research-centric district (URCD).

2. UNIVERSITIES AND THE KNOWLEDGE-BASED THEORY OF THE CLUSTER

In our approach we are most influenced by Peter Maskell's (2001) concept of a knowledge-based explanation of geographical clusters. In particular, his discussion of the vertical and horizontal dimensions of a cluster applies to both the ideal form of a Marshallian ID, and the clustered ecologies of communities of practice Brown and Duguid (2000b) describe in their application of Marshall's insights to Silicon Valley.

Maskell argues that any satisfactory theory of a cluster must address the question of why the cluster exists, and what sustains it. That is, why is it better that N colocated firms of size S undertake related activities, rather than have a single firm of size $N \times S$ do the same bundle of activities? The most compelling explanations involve the benefits of colocation in the form of greater knowledge available about potential partners, and the greater ease in conducting business with them. Colocation makes it easier to monitor other firms' behavior in fulfilling contracts. Among firms along the same value chain colocation promotes adherence to agreements, voluntary exchange of information, and the sharing of tacit knowledge. Yet all of these benefits could be enjoyed by a single firm that vertically integrates these phases of the production process while eliminating most of the transaction costs associated with their coordination among independent firms. An additional reason why clusters exist, Maskell argues, can be found in the horizontal dimension of the cluster along with the vertical dimension discussed above.

The horizontal dimension refers to the similarity of activities between firms, while the vertical dimension refers to the complementary activities along the value chain. The advantages of multiple colocated firms pursuing the same activities arise from the knowledge obtained from running parallel projects. 'Co-localized firms undertaking similar activities find themselves in a situation where every difference in the solutions chosen, however small, can be observed and compared' (Maskell 2001, pp. 928–9). It is not just that the costs of input–output transactions among firms can be greatly reduced within a cluster, which Storper (1995, p. 201) refers to as the 'traded interdependencies' of a cluster. In addition there is a great advantage in having firms engaged in similar activities competing, and occasionally cooperating, with each other in the same location.

This ability to observe other firms pursuing the same activity in close proximity is the basis of Brown and Duguid's observation that there is both a high level of knowledge in firms in Silicon Valley, and a high level of knowledge about firms (2000b, pp. 20–23). This knowledge about firms is a function of proximity and shared practice, and explains Marshall's 'mysteries in the air' that is to be found in places like Silicon Valley. Shared practice is knowledge that is embedded in a social setting, a knowledge that comes from learning by being in the place where the knowledge is being used and having the opportunity to use it in that setting. Such a setting, where people working together produce a body of actionable, community-based knowledge, is a community of practice.

Because of its social and local origin, the concept of communities of practice seems very close to what Becattini and Rullani (1996b, pp. 58–60) describe as versatile integration. The knowledge that firms hold is not comprised solely of standardized code. 'On the contrary, it is a matter of complex, and often indefinite and "indescribable" skills which can be acquired only by direct experience, by repeated function practice, or by "seeing at work", both at single and collective level' (ibid., p. 59). The concept of communities of practice can assist us in understanding the role of universities in initiating new firms and sustaining existing firms in the URCD.

3. THE URCD

The university is a producer of knowledge, some of which is released into the economy in many ways including: students joining firms, professorial consulting, licensing to existing firms, and some of which is in the form of new, usually local, start-up enterprises. The existence of a permanent, externally supported, research university committed to the promotion of entrepreneurship is a distinguishing feature of the URCD. Because of the university's scientific and engineering research agenda, the knowledge it produces is often a new technological artifact or, in the process of producing the knowledge requires the creation of new artifacts be they gene sequences, new molecules, machines, process inputs or software programs. In certain cases, these artifacts may have potential economic value, despite the fact that the outcome of this research was independent of particular market considerations. In this sense, in most cases, the knowledge and artifacts generated by the university will enter the market as a technology push, rather than the pull of demand from the market.

Because the URCD is based on the research within the university, it is quite different from the ID in a number of ways. IDs, and other production agglomerations, achieve external economies by their specialization of product market. IDs are characterized by numerous competitors producing a certain good, resulting in deep horizontal and vertical relations, by which the ID reacts to market pull. URCDs, on the other hand, are characterized by the technology push that comes from a wide range of disciplines. As a result the new firms that spin out of the university may be as varied in their product as the research areas pursued by the university. It is important to recognize that certain departments may evolve particular micro-ecologies within which entrepreneurship will be particularly valued and thus may generate a greater number of start-ups in those research areas (Feldman and Bercovitz 2008).

This technology-push aspect of the URCD produces a quite different production district, at least in its ideal type, from the market-driven ID. In the ideal type of URCD, the university generates 'seeds' for high-technology firm formation, but unless the region in which these seeds are planted is a rich entrepreneurial environment, a well-functioning URCD may not emerge, though there may be some new firms formed.

The unique attributes of the ideal type of URCD explain its initial formation, how it is maintained, and how learning occurs within it. The URCD is initially formed by the start-ups based on university technology. Because most faculty entrepreneurs retain their position at the university, these start-ups will be established in close proximity of the university. Of course, the tacit, or contextual knowledge upon which the start-up is based will exert a strong centripetal force keeping the start-up close to the university as well.[4]

The contextual knowledge of the start-up is held in a research community of practice, originally located in a university laboratory.[5] In its early stages the start-up is basically an extrusion from the university laboratory, and the founders and original staff will most likely be drawn from this community. Initially a given start-up, and the URCD itself, is maintained by this interaction between the start-up and its university-based community of practice. Notice that a URCD is not necessarily characterized by an interaction between local firms, but rather by the interaction between university professors that are the source of the new firms, and the new firms themselves.

4. TWO EXAMPLES OF URCDs

The dynamics of these URCDs can be understood by examining case studies of two internationally ranked universities, the University of Wisconsin at Madison (UWM), and the University of Illinois at Urbana-Champaign (UIUC), both of which have experienced spinoffs and have conscious policies of encouraging URCD district formation.

UIUC is a large, very highly-rated comprehensive university with top-tier computer science and engineering departments. Technologies that can be traced to UIUC include the basis of Lotus Notes, the email program Eudora, and web browsers. In addition, technologies coming directly from UIUC include those that formed the basis of firms such as Netscape and Paypal. However, these two very important start-ups were not founded in Champaign, but rather were founded in Silicon Valley some two thousand miles away. The importance of regional considerations in the start-up process is captured in the following statement by Marc Andreessen, the founder of Netscape, on why he did not consider Champaign as the location for Netscape in the mid-1990s: 'There's no infrastructure at all in Illinois for a start up company. It is not there. No one does it. They just don't know how to react to it'.[6] In comparison Bill Linton, the founder of biotechnology firm Promega of Madison, said of the environment around UWM in 1976, 'A tradition of educational excellence has contributed to an environment of intellectual curiosity, exploring spirit, and intuitive visions – together they create a rich business development environment'.[7]

While these are only anecdotal observations, our research into the sources of firm foundings in these two university towns indicate that there has been and continues to be a difference between these two URCDs. UWM has a much longer history of promoting new firm formation, going back to 1925 with the establishment of a private non-profit entity, the Wisconsin Alumni Research Foundation (WARF) to patent inventions and license technologies emerging from UWM research. Several significant biotechnology firms have emerged in this URCD, including Promega, PanVera, and Tomo Therapy, all of which were founded in Madison and not outside the region. The most significant firms that have been founded on the basis of UIUC research have located in Silicon Valley. Our examination of firm founders in both Madison and Champaign showed that the university was by far the largest source of entrepreneurship. But unlike Champaign, Madison has developed a biotechnology cluster that supports spinoffs from existing firms. That is, the firms themselves seed new firms, not just the university, so new generations of firms emerge that are not directly related to the university. This pattern of firm founding was not observed in Champaign.

5. THE UNIVERSITY AS PLANTER OF SEEDS

5.1. The role of technology push

Because the university is the primary source of knowledge within URCD, and because this knowledge is the basis for many of the new firms founded within the district, we would expect that the new firm characteristics would reflect the relative disciplinary excellence of the university. In our study we recorded data on all of the high-technology start-ups in the two cities. (See Tables 40.1a and 40.1b.)[8]

In Tables 40.1a and 40.1b all start-ups founded by faculty, staff and students at UIUC and UWM respectively are tallied. To provide insight into the diversity of sectors of knowledge, all firms are grouped into five technological categories. The R&D expenditures are for the single year 2004 and the academic rankings of various American graduate programs are for 2006.

UIUC and UWM differ significantly in the types of firms that have spun off from the university. At UIUC, information technology (IT) and engineering start-ups account for almost two-thirds of the total. Over the years, only seven start-ups based on the life sciences had UIUC founders. At UWM, on the other hand, the life sciences account for over half of the total number of start-ups. Without reference to either the academic reputation of these universities, or the R&D expenditures by various programs, the differences in start-up technologies would be difficult to explain.

Table 40.1a Founded start-ups and R&D ranking at the University of Illinois at Urbana-Champaign

UICU Founded start-ups	Start-ups 1958–2006 (percentage)	R&D 2004 in $1000s (US rank)	2006 Program US rank
IT[a]	22 (36.7)	113 320 (1)	5
Engineering	17 (28.3)	120 032 (10)	4
Physical sciences[b]	14 (23.3)	50 152 (17)	
Biological sciences	6 (10.0)	61 911 (45)	24
Medical sciences	1 (1.7)	11 331 n.a.	No medical school
UIUC total	60		

Table 40.1b Founded start-ups and R&D ranking at the University of Wisconsin at Madison

UWM Founded start-ups	Start-ups 1957–2006 (percentage)	R&D 2004 in $1000s (US rank)	2006 Program US rank
Biological sciences	44 (39.3)	155,682 (6)	12
IT[a]	22 (19.6)	13,457 (23)	10
Medical sciences	19 (17.0)	272,640 (11)	26
Physical sciences[b]	15 (13.4)	51,853 (14)	
Engineering	12 (10.7)	94,860 (14)	15
UWM total	112		

Notes:
[a] Program rank and R&D expenditures on the basis of computer science.
[b] Physical sciences programs were not given a rank by US News and World Report.

Sources: University start-ups. Data collected by Martin Kenney and Donald Patton. R&D data: National Science Foundation, Division of Science Resources Statistics, *Academic Research and Development Expenditures: Fiscal Years 2004*. Academic ranks: US News and World Report, *America's Best Graduate Schools*, 2006 Edition.

The technology categories in both of these tables are listed in order of their contribution to the number of start-ups. In the case of UIUC we can see that this is an exact ordinal ranking match with the rank of these programs with R&D expenditures. UIUC's R&D expenditures on computer science (IT) were the highest in the US in 2004, and this was the most important category of start-ups. Its second highest program in R&D expenditure rank was engineering, and this corresponds to engineering being its second most important category of start-ups. This ordinal match proceeds through the other categories. Further, this roughly parallels the academic ranking of these programs as well.

UWM start-up technologies match up ordinally with R&D ranks and program ranks with the exception of information science which appears to have too low an R&D ranking, and engineering which appears to have too high a program ranking. Basically, though, the rankings are congruent for both universities suggesting that the types of start-ups within each URCD mirror the relative strength of the universities at their center. These results agree with empirical work on the characteristics of universities and their propensity to produce spinoffs (Di Gregorio and Shane 2003; O'Shea et al. 2005) and the finding by Feldman and Bercovitz (2008) that specific departments can have a 'micro-*ethos*'. In most studies the number of spinoffs per year are regressed on a variety of university level attributes. It is then found that the prestige of the university, measured by either the quality of faculty in science and engineering (O'Shea et al. 2005), or by overall graduate school ranking (Di Gregorio and Shane 2003), is positively and significantly related with the number of spinoffs per year based on university-licensed technology.

Because the spinoff data of these studies was based on the Association of University Technology Managers (AUTM) surveys, the individual identities of the start-ups was suppressed, thereby restricting the analysis to the university rather than department level. The results, though, clearly show that university prestige, and therefore the quality of the ideas emerging from them, is directly related to the number of firms founded upon those ideas.

5.2 The institutional role

The extent to which universities extrude their knowledge into the larger economy through start-ups depends not only on the quality of the technology and ideas of their departments. It is also shaped by the offices of the university to promote entrepreneurship, and the institutions and social relations in which faculty are embedded. Kenney and Goe (2004), in their comparison of the electronic engineering and computer science (EE&CS) departments of UC Berkeley and Stanford found that Stanford faculty were significantly more involved in entrepreneurship and corporate activity than UC Berkeley faculty, and that the primary explanation of this difference lies in the history of these universities. Stanford has a history of encouraging entrepreneurship, while UC Berkeley does not.

This explains why two departments of equal prestige, and roughly similar proximity to Silicon Valley, produce a differential number of spinoffs. The fact that Stanford produces many more EE&CS spinoffs than UC Berkeley lies in the institutional differences in these universities. Feldman and Desrochers (2004) argue that similar institutional factors are at work in explaining why Johns Hopkins University produces fewer start-ups than its reputation and size would predict.

Since the passage of the Bayh–Dole Act of 1980 which gave universities the property rights to federally funded inventions developed at their campuses, most universities have established technology licensing offices (TLOs) to expedite the licensing of university ideas and promote the founding of firms based on university technology. In addition, many universities have supplemented these efforts with university sponsored research parks and start-up incubators, as well as sponsored venture-capital firms and other types of institutions to provide support to university entrepreneurs.

For the University of Wisconsin, the Wisconsin Alumni Research Foundation (WARF) plays a unique and critical role in the UWM ecosystem as an intermediary in the commercialization of university research. Established in 1925 as a non-profit patent organization funded initially by UW alumni and managed by a board of trustees composed of alumni, it has always been independent of the university. As such, and as a result of a historical accident relating to the patenting of ultraviolet irradiation of food to increase Vitamin D, it is a unique institution unlike that of any other US university. Its independence allows it to operate in an entirely business-like fashion, separate from university politics and academic administration and concerns about the public role of the university in knowledge dissemination. WARF's primary purpose is to manage patents based on UWM research, and since 1928 it has provided more than $750 million to the university to support further research (Nelson, Patton and Kenney 2007).

The support, connections, experience and funds WARF provides help create an environment in which research and innovation are highly valued. This is especially important in the field of biotechnology, where the majority of advanced research is done at the university level, as opposed to private or industry labs. In addition, the University-Industry Research Program, established in 1963 and renamed the Office of Corporate Relations (OCR), is a critical institution providing links from the university to small and large business, as well as the office that manages campus invention disclosures. The OCR does not oversee programs related to business start-up and industry support, rather it behaves as an interpreter of and liaison between these programs and current businesses.

A recent addition to the support system for entrepreneurs is the Weinert Center for Entrepreneurship within the University of Wisconsin, Madison School of

Business, which interacts with the high-tech firms in a novel way through the Weinert Applied Ventures in Entrepreneurship (WAVE) Program founded in 1998. In this program business students are selected each year to work with a new local firm. The students get experience while creating comprehensive strategic, operating and financing plans for the firm. In return, the firm benefits from the student's knowledge, a set of skills very different from those of the professors who are developing the technology.

Madison has also experienced a proliferation of small business incubators. The UWM-sponsored incubator, University Research Park (URP), is a non-profit entity established in 1984 that develops land to lease to start-up companies (Sobocinski 1999, p. 306). The profits from this development are donated to UWM, and there are currently 110 tenants who have access to services provided by accountants, lawyers and venture capitalists.

The University of Illinois has similar institutions to UWM, but their experience is much more limited, having been established only recently. The university's agent for technology transfer, the UIUC Office of Technology Management, was only established in 1995, a full 70 years after the formation of WARF in Madison. Like UWM, UIUC has institutions to support entrepreneurs, but these too are of recent origin. The university-sponsored research park only began construction in 2000, and the university venture-capital fund, Illinois Ventures, was proposed as an entity in the same year. Another institution intended to provide mentoring to university entrepreneurs is the Technology Entrepreneur Center. Currently housed within the UIUC Research Park, it too was only established in 1999 (Carbahal 2007).

It is clear that UIUC is attempting to quickly develop university institutions to support technology transfer from laboratories through new firm formation. Yet such efforts take considerable time to obtain results as suggested by the history of UWM and other universities such as Stanford, MIT and UC Berkeley.

6. GOVERNANCE OF THE URCD

6.1 Governance inside the locality

Small and medium-sized firms achieve advantages by clustering geographically in areas where some types of goods and services are provided on an untraded basis to all firms within the locality. These goods and services comprise some of the external economies Marshall described in his discussion of IDs. These external economies assume a tangible form, such as the infrastructure and services discussed above, and an intangible form in the maintenance of conventions and specialized language within the locality. In discussions of the governance of high-technology districts, Trigilia (2004) observes that an essential feature of such a district is how the research infrastructure, which in the URCD would be the university, influences the informal ties and networks within the locality. 'This kind of relationship is important for the exchange of ideas and information, the development of tacit knowledge and local trust, the recruitment of qualified labour, the formation of new firms and support for their activities' (ibid., p. 322).

The role of the university in sustaining common codes of communication and networks among actors has been noted by several authors. Miner argues that universities can play a key role in industry formation because they provide a neutral territory in which scientists can form relationships outside of the world of competition (Miner et al. 2001, pp. 144–5). Paniccia (2006) observes that universities, together with alumni associations and others, act as social as well as professional institutions within science-based IDs. They may act as centers of socialization and as arenas for the exchange of ideas and reputation building. In this respect these types of districts can be distinguished from traditional IDs. 'Common codes of communication and work ethics do not develop among natives who absorb them from infancy; rather, they are absorbed and sustained by people with different social and national backgrounds, who join these "knowledge" communities after apprenticeship in undergraduate courses' (ibid., p. 107). Normally, in these university research-based start-ups it is not undergraduate courses that create the apprenticeship, but rather graduate courses where deep global-class knowledge in very narrow fields of study is developed. This socialization is also likely very narrow and discipline-based.

These observations lead to a conclusion that, in regards to entrepreneurial start-ups, the university may play a role in the maintenance of various networks of practice that exist between its departments, and the start-ups based on the knowledge developed in those departments. The history of Professor Hector DeLuca of the biochemistry department at UWM illustrates many of these points in the performance of the URCD in Madison.

Professor DeLuca came to UWM in 1951 and was the last graduate student to work under Harry Steenbock, the professor whose discoveries in Vitamin D research was directly responsible for the founding of WARF in 1925. DeLuca's subsequent work has resulted in both academic achievements and patent royalties of close to $100 million for UWM through WARF administration, as well as three university start-ups founded directly from his work: Lunar Corporation (1980), Bone Care International (1984) and Tetrionics (1990) (Sobocinski 1999, p. 294).

Over the years Professor DeLuca has established and maintained extensive networks of academics and entrepreneurs, effectively linking his laboratory to a set of firms within Madison and outside the region, as well as other university biochemistry departments. Such university entrepreneurs are not uncommon in Madison, and the richness of the networks and culture that have grown up are evident in the number of forums that have been established precisely for the purpose of networking in the area, such as the Wisconsin Technology network, the Wisconsin Angel Network, the Wisconsin Technology Council, and the Wisconsin Entrepreneurs' Network. These networks are embedded in both the business environment and the community of Madison.

6.2 The university as a pipeline outside the locality

In the knowledge-based theory of geographical clustering, innovation and knowledge creation are the result of an interaction process among actors with different types of knowledge and competencies. Typically, it has been believed that the more tacit and contextual the knowledge involved, the more important it is that interactions occur in close proximity. Bathelt, Malmberg and Maskell (2004) argue against a simplistic view that tacit knowledge is limited to localities while codified knowledge moves costlessly around the globe. This argument is based in part on Owen-Smith and Powell's (2004) findings that within the Boston biotechnology cluster tacit knowledge can be transmitted both by undirected 'local broadcasting' and by directed 'network pipelines'. Bathelt, Malmberg and Maskell claim that knowledge can be diffused among actors within a locality by local buzz, or by the fact that they are just there. Knowledge also travels from one firm to another firm outside the locality by pipelines, or directed channels of communication. In the framework we advance here, pipelines are a means that allow networks of practice to extend beyond the geographical confines of the locality. The pipelines that Bathelt, Malmberg and Maskell describe are focused on certain goals among clearly identifiable firms across local boundaries, unlike the undirected broadcasting, or buzz, of knowledge among firms within a locality.[9] We would suggest that in URCDs there may be no single technological buzz but rather many, and that these pipelines connect scientific disciplines across geographically-dispersed universities.

For firms to identify, evaluate and assimilate knowledge in distant localities they must possess absorptive capacity (Cohen and Levinthal 1990). The firms exchanging information must have employees whose knowledge base consists of shared language and symbols. That is, they must in some sense be part of the same network of practice. Although Bathelt, Malmberg and Maskell (2004) do not mention universities, disciplines of study share exactly the language and symbols that allow pipelines of knowledge to be established across universities in different localities. It is precisely through the function of paradigms in science that complex knowledge can be exchanged between universities and others who share the same paradigm. Given the role of the university in the URCD, it is clear that a wide variety of disciplinary pipelines transmit very detailed knowledge among localities.

6.3 The entrepreneurial environment of the URCD

In Tables 40.2a and 40.2b all high-technology start-ups of both representative URCDs is presented. The university-related start-ups are combined with other start-ups founded within Champaign-Urbana and Madison respectively. The middle column indicates the number of start-ups founded by university personnel, the left column gives the count of all start-ups, while the right column indicates the number of start-ups founded by one or more individuals coming from another local high-technology start-up. Several observations can be made from this data. First, in both localities around half of all start-ups were founded by university personnel. This holds across technology categories with IT having somewhat fewer university start-ups for both schools, with life sciences at UWM, and engineering and physical sciences at UIUC, having a greater proportion of university founders.

Second, the mix of technology of all start-ups parallels that of university start-ups. This is what one would expect if one believes that university-affiliated founders are only a portion of the channels of innovation within a locality. Third, the role of secondary foundings of firms is much greater in Madison than it is in Champaign-Urbana. Just two start-ups in Champaign-Urbana had founders who came from other high-technology start-ups in the area. What this indicates is that in Champaign-Urbana new firms come into existence but have thus far failed to produce any secondary offspring or create entrepreneurs not affiliated with the university.[10]

The situation is quite different in Madison where close to one in ten of all start-ups had founders from other, locally founded high-technology firms. This proportion rises to almost one in five in the biological sciences, the area in which Madison excels. What this indicates is that in biotechnology the Madison environment is encouraging the formation of secondary offspring. Although the university is the driver in Madison biotechnology, the resulting firms have spun off yet other firms, implying that they operate in a fertile entrepreneurial environment.

It is this generation of new firms, as measured by secondary spinoff activity that is the real indicator of a rich entrepreneurial environment in a URCD. Earlier we indicated that one of the best known spinoffs from UIUC, Netscape, was founded outside the region due in part to the shortcomings of the Champaign-Urbana environment. This was not an isolated case.

One in five of all start-ups founded by UIUC personnel were founded outside the Champaign-Urbana area.[11] Many of these were founded in Silicon Valley, but they are also found in other areas of the country suggesting that Champaign-Urbana is not retaining its entrepreneurs. In Madison all of the important start-ups were founded in the Madison area and have stayed in the Madison area. The question of whether this is a characteristic of the life sciences or the university is not entirely clear, but it should be noted that Madison retained start-ups in the physical sciences and IT as well though none of these matured into significant firms.[12]

Table 40.2a   University-related startups and other startups founded within Champaign-Urbana

High-technology start-ups Champaign-Urbana and UIUC founded combined	All start-ups 1958–2006 (percentage)	UIUC founded (proportion)	Other local founder (proportion)
IT	46 (39)	22 (0.48)	2 (0.04)
Engineering	28 (24)	17 (0.61)	0 (0.00)
Physical sciences	23 (20)	14 (0.61)	0 (0.00)
Biological sciences	11 (9)	6 (0.55)	0 (0.00)
Medical sciences	5 (4)	1 (0.20)	0 (0.00)
UIUC total	117	60 (0.51)	2 (0.02)

Table 40.2b   University-related startups and other startups founded within Madison

High-technology start-ups Madison and UWM founded combined	All start-ups 1957–2006 (percentage)	UWM founded (proportion)	Other local founder (proportion)
Biological sciences	65 (34)	44 (0.68)	12 (0.18)
IT	53 (28)	22 (0.42)	4 (0.08)
Physical sciences	27 (14)	15 (0.56)	0 (0.00)
Medical sciences	24 (13)	19 (0.79)	0 (0.00)
Engineering	22 (12)	12 (0.55)	2 (0.09)
UWM total	191	112 (0.59)	18 (0.09)

Source: Data collected and elaborated by Martin Kenney and Donald Patton.

7. CONCLUSION

We have shown that the URCD is a distinct form of economic agglomeration. At its heart is the research university, a permanent, externally supported institution that is mandated to teach and conduct research.

Because the URCD is based on the research of various disciplines within the university, it is quite different from the ID in a number of ways. IDs, and other production agglomerations, achieve external economies by their product market specialization. IDs are characterized by numerous competitors producing one type of good, resulting in deep horizontal and vertical relations, by which the ID reacts to market pull. URCDs, on the other hand, are characterized by a technology push that comes from a wide range of disciplines. As a result, the new firms that spin out of the university will be as varied in their product markets as the research areas pursued by the university.

This technology-push aspect of the URCD produces a very different production district, at least in its ideal type, from the market-driven ID. In the ideal type of URCD, the university generates 'seeds' for firm formation, but unless the region in which these seeds are planted is a rich entrepreneurial environment, a well-functioning URCD may not emerge. Indeed, one of the primary differences between the two examples of URCDs discussed in this chapter is the vitality of the entrepreneurial settings in which the universities of Wisconsin and Illinois are located.

Although there are no economic clusters in the US that share all the socio-economic attributes of IDs as they exist in Italy, there are sufficient parallels to allow for comparisons between these traditional IDs, and what we refer to as well-functioning URCDs. Well-functioning URCDs, such as Madison, Wisconsin, have several features defining them as being more than an economic agglomeration of firms. These features can best be appreciated by comparing the clusters found around UWM in Madison, and UIUC in Champaign, Illinois.

The economic cluster found around UIUC has only the structural core of a URCD, namely the presence of a large, highly ranked research university. UIUC satisfies the role of an institution which plants seeds for new firm formation. Yet a number of these seeds, such as Netscape and Paypal, took root in Silicon Valley rather than Champaign.

UWM has several features that UIUC lacks. First, the university is deeply involved in the governance of the URCD through such long-standing organizations as WARF and the Office of Corporate Relations, among others. The efforts made by UIUC in promoting entrepreneurship are much more recent, going back only to the 1990s, and are much more modest in size and scope.

Second, the ties of networks among entrepreneurs in the community, and their counterparts in university laboratories, are deep and long standing in Madison. These ties are promoted by university organizations and by private organizations that emerged from the entrepreneurial community in Madison. Such private organizations are almost completely absent in Champaign.

The distinguishing feature of IDs is the importance of community elements in the coordination of economic processes within the district (Dei Ottati 2003, p. 89). These community elements manifest themselves in the culture of the URCD by the shared attitudes, rules of behavior and sense of membership that supports entrepreneurship in the district. These community elements are certainly aspired to in a URCD, and in the case of Madison are to a significant extent realized.

NOTES

* The authors would like to thank the editors of this volume for their comments and criticisms, which have benefited our work considerably. In particular, we want to thank Gabi Dei Ottati for her very valuable comments and encouragement.
1. It is important to separate university research-based districts, such as Cambridge and Oxford in the UK or Cornell in Ithaca, New York, University of Wisconsin at Madison, from other 'district-like' agglomerations that emerged around universities in smaller towns, and that were based on servicing student needs, providing goods and services to the university and so on. These have been in existence for, in some cases, centuries.
2. See AUTM, 'FY 2006 US licensing survey activity survey summary', www.autm.net/about/dsp.Detail.cfm?pid=215, accessed 20 Dember 2008.
3. The articles that have informed our discussion are Becattini's discussion of the ID as a socio-economic concept (1990) and organization of production (2002e), Becattini and Rullani's (1996b) discussion of contextual and codified knowledge, Bellandi's (1989) review of Marshall and the ID, Amin's (1989b) model of the small Italian firm, Belussi's (2006) general discussion of clusters, Dei Ottati's (2002, 2003) discussion of the local governance of IDs and De Propris' (2001) comparison of IDs and monopsonistic clusters.
4. There is a large literature on the role of proximity in the transmission of tacit information, particularly in a university setting (see Audretsch and Stephan 1996; Zucker, Darby and Brewer 1998).
5. See Becattini's (2002e) discussion of contextual and codified knowledge and their relative impact upon the geography of production.
6. As quoted in Scott Shane's study of university spinoffs (2004, p. 99).
7. As quoted in Randall Willis' report on Madison's biotechnology cluster (2004, p. 41).
8. This data includes the year and location of the new firm, the firm's technology classification, as well as the founders of the firm and their previous employment.
9. Other researchers besides Owen-Smith and Powell have observed that not all knowledge linkages in biotechnology are the result of local buzz. See Zucker, Darby and Armstrong (1998) on the market exchange of knowledge within clusters, and Audretsch and Stephan (1996) on the importance of geographical proximity as the industry matures.
10. Admittedly since UIUC start-ups are more recent there may not have been sufficient time for further spinoffs.
11. Please note that 12 out of the 60 start-ups founded by UIUC personnel were established outside of Champaign-Urbana. These include four in IT, one in engineering, five in physical sciences, and two in biological sciences (data collected and elaborated by Martin Kenney and Donald Patton).
12. See Kenney and Patton (2005, pp. 223–5) for a discussion of the impact of the university on the geography of different high-technology start-ups.

SECTION 9
The experiences in emerging and developing countries

Introduction

Werner Sengenberger

1. NATURE AND INCIDENCE OF IDs IN THE DEVELOPING WORLD

A very large majority of the world's population, and also the bulk of the global labour force, lives in developing countries and emerging economies in Asia, Africa and Latin America and the Caribbean. The demographic shares of these regions continue to grow. Roughly speaking, the number of workers on our planet rises by 50 million annually, of which 97 per cent go to the developing world. In 2006, 78 per cent of the world's total labour force resided outside of the developed economies of Europe and North America and the Commonwealth of Independent States (ILO 2006, p. 4).

These statistical figures alone justify dedicating a full chapter in this *Handbook* to industrial districts (IDs) in developing countries and emerging economies. Yet, there are other good reasons for exploring and mapping the incidence, and the actual and potential role, of IDs in the developing world. IDs may be viewed as a particular approach and instrument of development. In particular, they can be looked upon as a vehicle for raising productivity and competitiveness in the countries of the South. They can help to create sustainable employment and income, combat poverty, and eventually narrow the income gap between the South and the North (see the final chapter in this section, by Sengenberger). Today, the developmental gaps between countries and world regions are enormous. For example, the average value added per worker in Sub-Saharan Africa is 13 times lower than that of a worker in the developed countries. The low starting level, as well as the slow and volatile growth rates of labour productivity, prevents an increase in income for many people in poor countries (ILO 2008a, p. 16).

This introduction provides an overview of the pertinent research on local industrial development in developing and emerging economies. Using the characteristics of the Marshallian industrial districts (MIDs) as a benchmark, few of the actual examples found in Third World countries satisfy the ideal-type criteria of IDs. The majority exhibit some features of the prototype ID but are void of others. Many are mere agglomerations of firms in a locality. Yet, an unspecified number of them show a potential for growing to a stature that approximates the configuration of the prototype district. The section we are introducing sets out to describe the state of research and policy prescriptions on IDs in developing countries; select a number of them for closer analysis; identify institutional factors that foster or hamper the emergence of districts; and finally, discuss the economic and social significance of districts for development.

2. IDs AND CLUSTERS

The term 'ID' has come to be associated with a peculiar type of socio-cultural productive system organized in a community of small firms in a particular economic sector and well anchored in a fairly narrowly-confined locality. The prototype ID that can be found in north and central Italy combines a number of characteristics such as common values among the producers, forms of collective organization, a mix of inter-firm cooperation and competition, implicit and explicit collaboration among local economic agents, and the provision of common technical and financial support services ('real services') for the benefit of the district as a whole.

These features make IDs distinct from 'industrial estates' or *zones industrielles*, which are merely agglomerations of enterprises in different sectors in a locality, and also 'clusters', defined as both geographical and sectoral concentrations of firms of different size. While IDs are also industrial and spatial agglomerations of firms, the crucial characteristic that differentiates them from estates and clusters relates to their embeddedness in a much more developed social fabric and permanent institutions. It was precisely the 'thickening of industrial and social interdependencies' (Becattini 1987, p. 5) that turned small firm industries in the Third Italy into proper IDs.

The institutional environment of IDs has implications for their functioning, economic performance, stability and resilience to economic shocks. Industrial estates can gain economies of scale, clusters can in addition draw competitive advantages from industrial specialization and a degree of input–output relations in the sector. The economic potential of IDs, though, goes much beyond. Their economic edge is derived not solely from external economies, but from collective efficiencies and the capacity for product and process innovation, facilitated by inter-firm cooperation, mutual trust, and strongly reduced opportunistic behaviour on the part of the individual firm due to a fair degree of social control exerted and facilitated by industrial associations and other collective organizations (for example, trade unions), or public regulation and public services. In other words, the economies generated in clusters are of a technical nature, whereas in the prototype ID, they are of social origin and embedded in strong social organization and cohesion of the producers.

In a dynamic perspective, however, clusters and IDs are not mutually exclusive. Industrial clusters can take up ID-like characteristics and be transformed into IDs, and conversely, the latter can degenerate into mere clusters of firms. For this reason, it is important to take an evolutionary view of district development. In the chapters below the concept of 'trajectory' is used to take account of the dynamics of districts.

3. THE INCIDENCE OF IDs

To date, we have no precise knowledge about the incidence of IDs and clusters in the various world regions. A few countries apart, no comprehensive surveys have ever been conducted. In fact, Italy may be the only country worldwide where systematic studies on the geographical and sectoral coverage of the economy by IDs have been undertaken. Among the emerging economies China stands out as being exceptional in mapping the large number of sectoral industrial agglomerations in the country. They are well documented in the chapter by Jici Wang and Lixia Mei. Generally speaking, the poorer the country the less is known about clusters and districts, or industrial organization in general, because statistical data on socio-economic indicators are missing, or outdated, or not very reliable. ID itself is not a statistical category in development studies, and proxies such as the size structure of enterprises, provide no more than very rough and incomplete estimation of the presence or absence IDs.

Our knowledge of the spread of IDs and clusters, their characteristics, their sectoral distribution, their contribution to GDP, the number of enterprises covered and the labour force employed by them, rests largely on subnational surveys and case studies. They suggest that clusters are fairly common in many developing countries and in a wide range of industries, whereas the incidence of IDs tends to be much more rare. The chapter by Anne Posthuma gives a succinct synopsis of the historical evolution of IDs and ID-like structures in both the developed and the developing world. Her survey starts in the 1970s, when the reemergence of small and medium-sized enterprises, the shift in the size structure of production units, and the shift in the paradigm of industrial organization away from what had been known as Taylorism and Fordism came into the focus of researchers and policymakers. She points to the importance of a profoundly changing economic environment for industrial production, notably the new macroeconomic policies and the unfolding process of trade liberalization, as key factors fashioning a new division of labour between large and small firms and between enterprises in advanced industrialized countries and emerging economies. These impacted on the formation and dynamics of IDs both in the North and the South, affecting in particular the geographic nature of districts through the outsourcing of production, the quality of labour and employment, and the institutional back-up of districts.

The chapter by Mario Davide Parrilli and Renato Garcia emphasizes the variety of IDs and clusters found in Latin America. The two authors use a typology initially developed by Markusen (1996) to characterise the configurations of clusters of local production systems (LPSs). They take the MID as a framework and a benchmark to show the development trajectories of selected clusters thereby identifying actual and potential prospects for upgrading from low-road to high-road organization, or vice versa. In their view, the crucial parameter for one or the other outcome is the capacity to initiate and sustain collective learning processes in the cluster. Unlike in Italy and other European countries where local collective organizations of small firms have been the drivers of such learning, in Latin America it has mostly been large companies or the State that have formed the main agents for growth and development of LPSs. Correspondingly, governance has been built on hierarchical relations among firms and external rather than internal control of operations. The survey of case studies of clusters in traditional manufacturing industries in the region indicates that so-called hub-and-spoke clusters and State-anchored clusters are relatively important among LPSs. Even more frequent are the so-called survival and craft clusters that show rather limited development capacities and low-quality employment relations in informal labour markets. Prospects for a transformation to inter-firm cooperation capable of promoting learning and technological innovation have been found in the former, but rarely in the latter type of structures.

Similarly to the chapter by Parrilli and Garcia, the study by Wang and Mei entertains the question whether or not the various industrial clusters found along the East Coast of China can be associated with the classical model of the Italian ID. The answer is not straightforward given the enormous variety of the local production in terms of origin, structures, ownership, governance and functioning. The conclusions reached by the authors point to both similarities and marked differences to the Italian model. The disparities with Europe originate in the cultural and institutional context of their formation and the actors involved in the operations. While in most of the Chinese cases local internal forces and external forces coexisted in forming the districts, on balance it was foreign influences, particularly by multinational enterprises, that played a significant, and in some instances, a dominant role for their development and functioning. Foreign direct investments, outsourcing of production to save labour costs, and the offshoring of jobs from developed countries in Europe and North America in the course of China's increasing opening of its commodity markets were key inputs to this process. In addition, the privatization of enterprises and the decentralization of production provided a major impetus to the creation of China's districts. Yet, while the origins and actors in China deviate substantially from the Italian model districts, the evolutionary path in Italy has to some degree paralleled that of China. This holds especially for an increased role of large companies, external capital formation, and the immersion of LPSs in global value chains. Beginning in the 1990s, IDs in the Third Italy successively resorted to outsourcing of production to low-cost countries in Eastern Europe and Asia. In China a similar process of relocation of production from the districts in the coastal areas to lower cost areas in inland provinces has begun. It tends to upset the local integrity of upstream and downstream linkages of firms, and beyond that the very notion of an internally organized and controlled LPS.

Finally, in her chapter, Meenu Tewari identifies key factors of economic growth and modernization of small firm industries. Her study draws from experience in the Ludhiana diesel engine industry in the northern Indian region of Punjab. From the 1980s, this industry has been ailing in the midst of other sectors of metalworking and light engineering in the same region that have been thriving. It has failed to reach technological upgrading and product innovation. By exploiting the differential performance of small firm sectors in her analysis, Tewari finds explanations for varying economic success in the wider structural and institutional context in which the industries operate. These include public industrial policies, the nature of linkages of end producers with raw materials suppliers and capital equipment manufacturers, and the ability to scrap outdated practices.

4. CONCLUSION

Pertinent research on industrial development suggests that few of the productive structures found in developing countries and emergent economies approximate the classical ID represented by the Italian model of IDs. Extensive cooperation among small firms in horizontally and vertically-integrated, locally confined industrial production systems, collective organizations of the entrepreneurs and the workforces, and a well-developed local infrastructure including comprehensive local services are rarely found. Much more common in the developing world are various forms of industrial clusters in the sense of sector-specific local agglomerations of manufacturing firms. Some of them exhibit some features of IDs but lack others. Analysis of the trajectories shows that clusters may gradually transform into structures that are characteristic of IDs, or conversely, lose such qualities. Their economic performance tends to vary accordingly.

41. The industrial district model: Relevance for developing countries in the context of globalisation

Anne Caroline Posthuma[*]

1. INTRODUCTION

Does the industrial districts (IDs) model propose an approach relevant to developing countries, in their pursuit of competitive industrial and small enterprise development, especially in the context of globalisation?

This chapter traces how the ID model, based originally upon the specific experience of the Third Italy, led to the development of a rich body of case studies that identified the existence of similar structures in other advanced industrialised countries. The ID model was taken up by some national governments and international agencies as a policy approach for the promotion of competitive small enterprise development. Subsequently, the ID model awakened interest among developing country researchers, small and medium-sized enterprise (SME) support agencies and policymakers, where important empirical studies and policy initiatives have been elaborated around this concept.

The chapter highlights three features that are central to the ID model: territoriality; the role of public and private institutions and relations; and a virtuous cycle between specialised firms requiring skilled labour and the supply of those skilled workers with the backing of active trade unions, thereby supporting the attainment of quality production with quality employment.

An important distinction exists between the definitions of clusters and IDs. While it is not the aim of this chapter to address such a distinction in detail, nevertheless, a short-hand description might characterise clusters as territorially-bound agglomerations of firms within the same sector. Meanwhile, IDs also include area-based sectoral concentrations of firms, but crucially involve a thickening of institutional structures and socio-economic and industrial interdependencies between members of the ID where associations, supporting agencies and the role of cooperative relationships based upon trust and joint action are all key elements (Becattini 1990). This distinction emphasises not only industrial and sectoral features, but also the role played by institutional structures, economic and less tangible social and cultural interdependencies in promoting dynamic and sustainable localities. Rather than seeing these as dichotomous, one may instead see the movement of firm agglomerations between more IDs or clustering models as part of an evolutionary trajectory (Sengenberger, in this volume), affected as much by external pressures as internal dynamics. Importantly, such an evolutionary perspective raises interesting considerations regarding the identification of policy approaches that promote more balanced economic and social development – of particular relevance for developing countries (where empirical studies often identify weaker institutional structures, and looser industrial and social interdependencies than have been described as being at the heart of the ID model).

Competitive pressures arising from globalisation, market liberalisation and more demanding production standards for goods and services compel firms in developing countries to adapt to new quality, price and delivery standards. Recent research points to differing outcomes among clusters in developing countries as they confront new competitive pressures and opportunities to participate in global value chains. Such changes are generating tensions that impact upon even the basic features of IDs, including their territoriality, the nature of public–private relationships and the role of skilled labour and representative trade unions in promoting greater alignment between quality production and quality employment. In some sector-based agglomerations of small firms, with weak institutional and socio-economic relations, firms may tend to engage more in rent-seeking behaviour and cost-cutting strategies that involve outsourcing and poor labour practices. Other cases suggest that the existence of some institutions and propensity for joint action may lead firms to work together and create the thicker web of institutions and relations more characteristic of the ID model. Current research on such questions raises significant research and policy implications that can inform decisions by governments, firms and workers in this rapidly-changing context of globalisation.

2. BACKGROUND

In the 1970s, a set of Italian scholars noted the outstanding dynamism of places dominated by SMEs in the northern regions of the country. These early studies of the 'Third Italy',[1] and the subsequent research and conceptual work they spawned, gave rise to the a wide literature on ID which presents an alternative production model that places SMEs as protagonists in attaining high growth rates, displaying innovative behaviour and competing successfully in domestic and international markets.

The ID model attracted the attention of scholars and policymakers, as the evidence suggested such production systems characterised by small firms were more resilient in periods of economic fluctuation than large firms and their non-clustered counterparts (Schmitz and Musyck 1994). This alternative model emerged at a time of changing production structures in Europe, which were shifting toward a growing number of SMEs during the 1980s, and the consequent search by policymakers for a framework that would support industrial development and job creation in this new context. The ID model opened new scope for SME policies – rather than considering SMEs as a marginal category, composed of mainly survivalist production units or representing a transition stage on the path to 'grow up' into large firms. The evidence in IDs showed that SMEs are an integral part of regional patterns of industrial development, and can play a potential role in incipient industrialisation (Schmitz 1989).

What distinguishes IDs from a merely casual agglomeration of business activities in the same territory? Indeed, not all agglomerations of small firms produce growth, stable employment and technical innovation, even in the Third Italy, indicating that such outcomes are not automatic and cannot be attributed solely to market factors. IDs are places characterised by clustering SMEs which demonstrated lively economic growth and high specialisation of production in small batches (versus mass production). Highly-skilled workers mastered their machinery to produce quality goods and could quickly change the tooling of their machines for the next small batch to be made according to client specifications. A division of labour among firms enabled them to capture economies of scale external to the individual firm but internal to the ID, while innovative activities and technical and design skills gave rise to economies of scope in product lines (Brusco 1982; Piore and Sabel 1984, Schmitz 1989). Other pioneers in this area drew attention to more subtle features that strengthened and supported competitiveness of these small firms by emphasising that clustered SMEs are embedded within formal and informal economic, social, cultural and political institutions and relations of the territory or area which define the community and its institutions of local governance within the ID (Pyke, Becattini and Sengenberger 1990; Locke 1995, p. 3; Criscuolo 2005; Bellandi and Caloffi 2009, p. 4). 'In the district, unlike in other environments, community and firms tend to merge [leading to a] thickening of industrial and social interdependencies' (Becattini 1990, p. 38). Finally, the coexistence of inter-firm cooperation together with competition generates a creative tension where entrepreneurs are willing to engage in joint action, leading to collective efficiencies arising from their interdependence (a deterrent to rent-seeking behaviour), while also following market signals to upgrade their products and win new clients.

3. COMPARATIVE CASE STUDIES OF IDs IN ADVANCED INDUSTRIALISED COUNTRIES

Influenced by the ID literature, research on the changing structure of industrial organisation in the industrialised countries explored how the ID model could be related to the decline of Taylorist production systems and Fordist capitalist organisation and proposed that this signalled the emergence of a different model of 'flexible specialisation' in the advanced industrialised countries (Piore and Sabel 1984). Similarly, renewed concern with local development and local industrial policy was also influenced by the ID literature as regards industrialised countries (Hansen 1996) and developing countries (Humphrey and Schmitz 1996).

These original ID studies from Italy inspired scholars in Europe and North America to explore whether the structure and competitive patterns of IDs could be found in SME manufacturing groups in other advanced industrialised countries. These case studies of IDs in countries outside the Third Italy helped to break a tendency in the early literature to build an 'ideal type' based upon the Italian experience. Subsequent studies reinforced this point by emphasising the heterogeneity among IDs (Amin and Robins 1990) and recognising the difficulty of replicating this model of development in other industrial settings (Piore 1990, pp. 225–7). Indeed, the acknowledgement of regional, sectoral and institutional variations within IDs in many ways facilitated cross-country comparisons, as well as sharing of lessons learned and policy experiences.

By the early 1990s, the ID literature generated interest among policy research institutions, and agencies of the United Nations system. Research based at the International Institute for Labour Studies (IILS) of the ILO explored, in its first phase, the ID phenomenon in Italy during the course of the 1980s (Pyke, Becattini and Sengenberger 1990; Sengenberger, Loveman and Piore 1990) and then moved to focus upon other configurations related to Italian IDs in (mainly European) regions and their policy implications (Pyke and Sengenberger 1992) and thereafter for small firm development in Latin America (Späth 1993). Other projects in international agencies were concerned with SME development, technological dynamism and innovative capabilities within clusters for the OECD and developing countries (United Nations 1994).

This burgeoning set of empirical case studies on IDs caught the attention of policymakers in the industrialised countries, leading to initiatives such as the OECD Cluster Focus Group, specialists' meetings on clustering and an OECD study of national policies to promote regional clusters (OECD 1999, 2007c), as well as the creation by the European Commission of a European Observatory of Clusters (see www.europe-innova.org/index.jsp, accessed 12 December 2008).

In the Introduction to Section 9, Sengenberger proposes an evolutionary view of district development that helpfully enables us to see how clusters in developing countries may foster the institutional and social features of IDs that permit them to transform from sector-specific agglomerations of firms into IDs, and similarly how a weakening of these features may cause them to slip away from ID characteristics. In a similar vein, Bellandi and Caloffi (2009) provide a useful typology that identifies different forms of SME clusters, the types of localities where they are based (with varying degrees of local social cohesion and local forces that boost trust and entrepreneurial attitudes) and the interplay between a cluster and a locality (ranging between clusters dependent upon footloose TNC investment, others with strong local ties and some overseas activities, and those where local firms are deeply embedded within the locality and local forces). Both approaches apply a dynamic view that bridges the two definitions of IDs and clusters and situates this within a development framework, where not only economic factors but also social, cultural and institutional structures and practices are seen as endogenous to a sustainable development process that yields both improved competitiveness and quality job creation.

4. CASE STUDIES ON CLUSTERING IN DEVELOPING COUNTRIES

Early researchers in the 1990s, concerned with the relevant insights that IDs and clusters[2] could provide for developing countries, framed a set of research and policy questions to guide future investigation (Schmitz and Musyck 1994). The productive structure in developing countries is characterised by a predominance of micro, small, medium and family-owned enterprises, frequently in territorial agglomerations, making IDs an appropriate model to consider as a guide in formulating SME support policies and even broader industrial development policies in such countries. A number of empirical studies in developing countries were conducted throughout the 1990s, bringing forth a rich body of literature and generating a critical mass of knowledge at the regional and national level, which also contributed toward cross-country comparisons. These empirical studies helped to explore key questions, including:

- Is there evidence of IDs in developing countries?
- If so, do they have a form that is similar or distinct from IDs in the industrialised countries? Which features are specific and endogenous to the Italian ID model and which features could be replicated in other settings?
- How do these socio-productive models operate and what are their primary challenges?
- What are the policy implications to support SME development in clusters in developing countries?

Some authors have taken an explicitly sceptical view toward attempts to characterise IDs in a developing country context (in this case, with reference to Argentina): 'There has been no form of industrial development (in Argentina) that fits the model of IDs, and one can only find in a few local settings some of the conditions and institutional social, territorial, economic-productive and organisational elements that constitute necessary prerequisites' (Boscherini and Poma 2000, p. 29).

Nevertheless, such authors do not exclude the possibility of building such elements in developing countries, but emphasise the need to promote aspects such as local institutional systems, stimulate forms of inter-firm collaborations and socio-productive organisation that can build collective efficiencies, strengthen public and private relations at local and national levels and stimulate entrepreneurial capacity and attitudes toward collective action.

Finding more scope for optimism, Schmitz (2000) argues that the processes of globalisation and economic liberalisation, which have intensified competitive pressure on product prices as well as quality, speed of delivery and flexibility of adjustment, have been a boost leading industries in developing countries to look for enhanced performance through clustering and cooperation. In a comparative review of firms in Guadalajara, Sinos Valley, Sialkot and Agra, Schmitz shows that external economies were gained through clustering of firms and that stricter requirements for price, quality and speed of production resulted in improved inter-firm cooperation (albeit at different degrees and very selectively in the four clusters). It is important to note, however, that this cooperation advanced mostly vertically within a supply chain concept (between manufacturers and suppliers-subcontractors) and less horizontally within an ID or clustering perspective (between producers at the same stage of the value-adding chain). Evidence was also found that engaging in more cooperation enabled improved economic performance and competitiveness. For example, thanks to inter-firm cooperation and collective organisation and action, greater economic dynamism was recorded in a jewellery cluster in Bangkok (A.J. Scott 1994) and the exchange of information, benchmarking and rejuvenated business associations enabled the ceramic tile cluster in Santa Catarina in Brazil (Meyer-Stamer 1999), the knitwear cluster of Ludhiana, North India (Tewari 1999) and the garment cluster of Dongdaemon, South Korea (Jun 2005) to overcome major economic crises and tap new export markets.

A number of empirical studies in the 1990s indicated that industrial clusters are common in a wide range of industrial sectors in the developing world (Nadvi and Schmitz 1994; Humphrey and Schmitz 1996). Important empirical research from this period include case studies on the cotton-knitwear industry in Tamil Nadu (Cawthorne 1995), the diamond industry of Surat in Gujarat (Kashyap 1992), the engineering and electronics cluster of Bangalore (Holmström 1998), the footwear clusters of Agra in Udar Pradesh (Knorringa 1996), the Sinos Valley in Brazil (Schmitz 1999a), León and Guadalajara in Mexico (Rabellotti 1999) and surgical instruments in Sialkot, Pakistan (Nadvi 1999). Other case studies of clusters in the metalworking, furniture, garment and other industries in Kenya, Zimbabwe and Tanzania, indicated that inter-firm division of labour and institutional support in these East African countries was less developed than in Asia and Latin America (Humphrey and Schmitz 1996, p. 1866). However, important evidence was found regarding employment and working conditions –

even in the more dynamic and successful clusters in Asia and Latin America, workers did not seem to enjoy the same improvement of labour standards and living conditions as was the case in the IDs in Europe (ibid.) raising the question of whether economic upgrading is being achieved without the development of institutions, the policies, the company-level practices and the representatives' organisations for workers that would promote upgrading of employment and working conditions in these clusters.

A study of industrial clusters in Africa examined how some industrial clusters can be a source of dynamic competition and economic development, by exploring how clusters can be transformed into local systems of innovation and be better connected to global producers (Oyelaran-Oyeyinka and McCormick 2007). Of importance is the emphasis upon the need for sustained policy support to transform clusters into genuine innovation systems. Furthermore, the study usefully unpacks the concept of joint action, to reveal that relationships between different sized firms within a cluster are not homogeneous and indeed involve confrontation, friction or domination by powerful actors over other firms. Differences in power relations between actors in a cluster can lead to outcomes such as deskilling and lost competitiveness where dominant actors force an unprofitable learning trajectory upon weaker firms. It is interesting that this observation regarding intra-cluster relations mirrors concerns normally raised regarding asymmetric power relations between clusters and global producers and impacts upon economic performance as well as labour conditions within weaker firms.

A collection of cluster studies conducted in Brazil and selected countries in Latin America, Europe, Africa and Asia emphasised the challenges posed by globalisation and the diffusion of information and communication technologies for SME clusters, as well as the tendency of public policies toward SMEs to ignore their dynamic potential and needs (Lastres, Cassiolato and Maciel 2003). Of interest, several studies in the collection observed the vulnerability of SME clusters in developing countries to take the role of low-wage, poor-quality employment provider in global production chains. Similarly, a case study of SME clusters in the Indonesian wood furniture industry found that engagement with global buyers helped raise quality and design standards and brought new export orders, but did not improve labour standards or reduce use of informal labour contracts, nor did global buyers act to ensure environmental standards that would prevent the rapid depletion of mahogany and teak forests providing raw material to these clusters (Posthuma 2008). Other studies cited in this article also note cases where firms in SME clusters fulfil the role of low-wage labour provider in global production chains, thereby requiring other support from institutional, policy and social actors to support their efforts to upgrade into higher road competition. Similarly, a study of ten manufacturing and artisan clusters in northern India conducted by the ILO confirmed that many clusters are increasingly contributing to rising exports, but most workers continue to be engaged in the informal economy where poor working conditions, the presence of child labour and low productivity are common features. In this context, globalisation poses a threat that these conditions will only be further deepened, unless improvements can be achieved in both the productive conditions in which these SMEs operate, as well as the terms and conditions of work for those labourers employed (Joshi et al. 2005).

The competitive pressures of globalisation have been a central feature in the development of Chinese clusters in light industries that have formed since the beginning of China's economic reform in the 1980s. According to one study of the textile and apparel industry, Chinese producers integrate in both directions – horizontally in local clusters and vertically in global value chains. With its abundance of cheap, unskilled labour, Chinese firms have specialised in labour-intensive operations, while more developed core countries have focused on design and marketing. However, this pattern is changing as production in China takes on more upstream activities or higher value-added processes such as apparel design or high-technology dyeing operations, software development and product R&D. Government policy is now giving high priority to escaping the danger of being locked into the 'low-road' labour-intensive and wage-squeezing approach and by seeking new and more effective governance strategies for improving the collective efficiency of local governments and firms (Wang and Mei 2008).

The Chinese case highlights the point that different policy options are being pursued by different countries, leading to divergent outcomes for SME clusters. Market-friendly policy prescriptions that promote rapid market liberalisation as an approach to economic integration can be contrasted with other policies being pursued, for example by many countries in the Asian region, that hinge upon limiting foreign ownership, promoting active industrial policies to develop domestic productive capacity and developing endogenous technological capability rather than relying upon imported technology. In the context of globalisation and market liberalisation, some countries have chosen to pursue development strategies founded upon strengthened domestic capacities and dynamic local production systems (LPSs). The implications for employment and labour market policies in this context also are great, as some pressure exists to implement more flexible labour policies and to lighten existing forms of social protection, on the grounds that this will reduce costs and help firms to become more competitive, although little evidence exists to substantiate the claim that such changes will, in fact, result in more productive economies.

The unfolding process of globalisation, with its opportunities and challenges, has opened the door for many developing country firms to engage as suppliers in global value chains. To understand the interaction of local and global relationships, scholars of IDs and clustering have joined territorial clustering approaches with value chain analysis, to examine how clustered developing country suppliers are linked to global buyers. Important findings were gathered through a project that explored the scope for local upgrading strategies of SME clusters in developing countries that are inserted in global value chains, where production specifications and parameters are set by global buyers who command the chain and standards are set by institutions external to the cluster in relation to labour, quality and environment (see Humphrey and Schmitz 2001, 2004; Schmitz 2004; www.ids.ac.uk/ids/global/projects/vw.html, accessed 12 December 2008).

Using a similar approach, a comprehensive review of the Latin American experience via 12 case studies of upgrading in clusters and value chains revealed that building collective efficiencies and pursuing upgrading opportunities may vary according to patterns of governance within the value chain and also within the economic sector under examination (Pietrobelli and Rabellotti 2004). Many case studies indicated that the requirements of competition within global value chains can weaken local cooperation. This is a troubling finding which raises concern that globalisation may create conditions where local clusters in developing countries may be undermined, rather than strengthened, especially if local institutional pillars are weak, if social relations of cooperation, trust and social capital are undermined and if economic opportunities offered by technology transfer, new skills and technical expertise are not bolstered by skills transfer, and the creation of stable and formal (not outsourced) employment. Crucial policy implications are suggested by these trends.

A number of research networks have been formed around issues of clustering and local or regional development strategies. For example, in China a network of clustering researchers around the country has been meeting regularly over the past decade to exchange empirical findings and discuss their implications. Similarly, an Iberian–Latin American network of researchers was formed in 1994 to examine the relationship between globalisation and territorial development (*Red iberoamericana de investigadores sobre globalización y territorio*).

Among the international agencies, UNIDO has taken a particularly active role toward the promotion of clusters in selected developing countries, including conducting in-depth case studies, policy documents and training materials (UNIDO 2001, 2004; see Ceglie and Stancher, in this volume). Some government policy initiatives have based their activities upon the application (and adaptation) of this model. In Latin America, the Brazilian government established a Working Group on Clusters that joins members across government ministries to focus upon elaboration of an integrated regional development strategy. The Brazilian agency for small enterprise development has also taken up proactive support to the development of clusters across the country, joining a sectoral and territorial approach (SEBRAE 2002 and www.sebrae.com.br, accessed 12 December 2008). Similarly, the Chilean government has focused upon regional development strategies with a sectoral approach, through such programmes as *Chile Emprende* and *El Sistema de*

Agencias Regionales de Desarrollo Productivo. The Inter-American Development Bank (IADB) has been a protagonist in this process of cluster promotion, supporting initiatives such as those mentioned above and many others throughout the region.

As seen above, the wealth of empirical case studies arising from developing countries reveals that the concept of ID – or the term 'clustering' as more widely used in developing countries – may be regaining value as, paradoxically, globalisation has emphasised the role of the territory, local endowments and LPSs. On the other hand, there is evidence that not only economic factors but also employment and labour conditions may be put under pressure by increased international competition. The following section considers some implications that globalisation may pose for the ID model, in both industrialised as well as developing countries.

5. WILL GLOBALISATION PLACE THE ID MODEL UNDER PRESSURE IN DEVELOPING COUNTRIES?

The unfolding process of globalisation and market liberalisation has brought new pressures that create tensions and possible challenges for IDs in developing countries. These considerations, mentioned briefly below, signal possible research issues to be explored in future studies of clustering in developing countries.

Recent studies show that due to the competitive pressures of globalisation and market liberalisation, even IDs in the Third Italy itself have evolved and adopted new strategies to retain competitiveness in terms of cost, quality and speed of delivery to domestic and export markets. Labour-intensive production has been outsourced from some IDs, in order to focus on higher value-added activities such as branding and design (Pyke, Nesporova and Ghellab 2002). The emergence of hub-and-spoke formations may alter the more horizontal relationships characterised in the IDs (Humphrey and Schmitz 2001). Another area of change involves the entry of foreign firms within some IDs, which may affect productive as well as social and cultural relations within the ID and thereby alter the role of joint action and collective efficiencies. One important question which arises in this regard concerns whether these adaptations will contribute to the continued competitive dynamism of IDs, or whether important elements are being lost in the process.

Important implications arise for workers within IDs in developing countries. While small firms are an important source of job creation in developing countries, they can also rely upon poor labour practices such as sweated labour and frequent use of informal employment relations. The ability of SMEs to upgrade by growing, generating profits for reinvestment and adopting new production practices and technologies all bear heavily upon the scale and quality of jobs created by these firms. The implications of job creation in clusters operating under labour surplus conditions, such as those found in developing countries, were already raised in early studies of IDs in the industrialised countries (Schmitz 1989; Locke 1995), cautioning that this could possibly lead to a 'low-road' path characterised by a strategy of reducing wage costs in order to maintain competitiveness. Now the rising pressures of globalisation to cut costs and outsource may encourage IDs to resort increasingly to the use of a peripheral labour force, using atypical and precarious contracts for workers. Earlier authors suggested that a middle path would emerge, where competition based upon production innovation, quality and price would coexist with labour surplus conditions (Nadvi 1994, p. 193) – it appears that this situation is being borne out in practice. This changing context for IDs raises important questions regarding what factors and policies could be put into place to encourage SME clusters to take a 'high road' strategy based upon product quality and sustained innovation.

A few further considerations are raised on three points of change, as related to the definition of three main characteristics of IDs.

5.1 Territoriality and links with new markets (as expressed by increased import and export markets and more extensive value chains rooted in the ID)

The analysis of IDs has been concerned primarily with horizontal and vertical productive relations between SME producers based in a common area or territory. Globalisation introduces and strengthens vertical production chains which extend beyond the limits of the territory, and may involve purchasing raw material inputs and selling to final consumer markets that are external to the ID. These production chains may either represent a competitive advantage, where the ID consolidates more value-added internally, or may represent a competitive threat where import barriers are lowered and new products enter the domestic market. In cases where production chains involve a trend toward fragmentation of the production process, this may force the IDs to spread themselves geographically. Such practices could potentially undermine the territorial nature of clustering and the institutions and informal relations related to its internal governance – at a minimum, these trends challenge our understanding of the role played by territoriality within IDs. Increased outsourcing and new relocation of parts of the production process (especially for cost reduction or new market access), raise an important question regarding the ID model that is based upon territorial embeddedness of economic, institutional and social relations: at what distance do the positive effects of local relations start to wane? Is there some inherent advantage to physical proximity and 'localness' or is it possible that improvements in transportation, communication technologies and the advent of global production networks have introduced changes that enable firms to retain their close inter-firm connections, trust and social cohesion characteristic of IDs while extending the geographical distance between firms from a few kilometres to span across regions, countries or even across continents? The ID literature emphasises that local proximity does make a difference, that frequent contact with other members of the ID in different institutional settings (at the local church, at political meetings, as members of trade unions) help to strengthen trust and social capital and thereby the ability to work together for common economic, productive and social goals.

Recent studies are examining the extent to which industrial communities must be located in specific and discretely bounded territories and how local sources of competitive advantages can be transposed to include global dimensions (Whitford and Potter 2007a), what some authors call 'translocal' development (Bellandi and Caloffi 2009). In the latter study of specialised manufacturing towns in Guangdong China and in Italian IDs, the authors consider the possible growth of international cluster-to-cluster relations. This is undoubtedly a crucial issue for further exploration, as the expansion of globalisation creates new pressures and opportunities for clusters in developing countries, in terms of their growth and their possibility for quality job creation which overall can boost competitiveness at the local level. The authors emphasise that public goods and collective private investments are needed in order to support translocal development, such as building high craft competencies, R&D and management skills to drive forward the internationalisation process. However, the emphasis upon the role of public goods may pose difficulties, given the recognised weakness of public institutions in developing countries, as well as the challenge to build sufficient trust among firms within the cluster to be willing to undertake collective investments, plus the predominant policy trend to reduce State interventions and leave market forces to function freely.

5.2 The virtuous cycle involving the demand for skilled workers, the supply of artisan skills and active representative labour organisations leads to quality terms and conditions of employment

The role of skilled workers, capable of handling specialised machinery and flexibly producing in small batches to match fluctuating order sizes and specific demands from different clients, has been identified as a key characteristic and strength of the ID model. Skilled workers were affiliated with representative organisations and trade unions that played a key role in forming a 'thick' institutional context in IDs and in defending the interests of these skilled workers, ensuring stable employment relations and good working conditions. This virtuous cycle between the demand for skilled workers by clustered firms and the good quality terms and conditions of work obtained by the action of representative work associations was a backbone to the unique productive capacity and competitiveness observed in IDs.

The discussion of translocal cluster development raises labour implications where the skills and innovative capabilities necessary to launch a path of quality and incremental innovation within a cluster may pose another challenge, as industrial 'district paths ask also for workers' participation to quality and innovation projects, and this goes together with good relations on the job and in the out-of-factory life' (Bellandi and Caloffi 2009). The demands for cost competitiveness and quick turn-around time experienced by developing country firms within global supply chains may be found to often create pressures which make it difficult for SMEs to provide good wages, formal employment contracts, good working conditions and hours and a basis of industrial relations that permits dialogue between workers and their employers. The strong role of workers' organisations in the ID experience in the Third Italy, which created the basis for better cooperation and for a balanced social and economic growth might not be replicated in similar ways within developing country clusters.[3]

The fragmentation of the production process and trend toward outsourcing raises important implications for labour and employment practices within IDs in industrialised and developing countries. The creation of a dual labour market, composed of core and peripheral labour, may undermine the basis for more generalised good working conditions, pay and industrial relations within IDs. If local or international outsourcing is used with the objective to cut labour costs, and if this escapes control under labour market institutions and regulation, then these practices may create conditions where the use of contract, casual and migrant labour at lower wage rates, without benefits or social protection, can proliferate in IDs even in industrialised countries (Baccaro and Qin 2005) and in their outsourced areas.

The coexistence of mixed labour practices may mark a significant rupture with the quality of employment which is seen to be at the core of the ID model, and poses challenges for the social actors, especially considering the important role of organised labour confederations and trade unions as cited in the ID literature. The growing presence of immigrant groups of workers, or in some cases as employers, who may not affiliate with organised workers' associations or employers' associations, both undermines the cultural unity which was seen as part of the ID model, as well as further fuelling the centrifugal forces that contribute to weakening of trade unions. The 'low road' of employment in global production is a potential outcome, or even 'dirt road' outcomes (Mehrotra and Biggeri 2007a) have been documented.

This discussion shows there is an important link between IDs and multi-national corporations that outsource to developing countries as a means to reduce production costs via low wages and unprotected labour. Future research is needed to identify what salient factors support upgrading of working conditions and employment, or which factors lead to precarious work and sweatshops.

More pessimistic scenarios may be countered by the economic and social strengths of the ID model making it an attractive policy option in developing countries. When conducted under supporting institutional, political and productive conditions, international outsourcing involving IDs can lead to technology transfer, upgrading and collaboration in ways that benefits all parties. Some examples have been recently described of translocal and cross-cluster international relationships between Chinese and Italian firms in IDs (Bellandi and Caloffi 2009). IDs could meet the trends of TNC buyers to consolidate their supply chain orders by selecting fewer, larger and more reliable suppliers. This discussion raises important new research considerations about how IDs could take greater importance for developing countries under globalisation, where thick institutional support, value-added factors such as skilled labour and design intensity and embedded endowments, traditions and labour in the local territory could be the best antidote to low-road competition in global markets.

5.3 The role of public and private/formal and informal institutions and relations

Are there pressures that may imply changes towards 'thicker' and 'better' institutions? Several factors can be identified that may either weaken existing institutions or bring in new actors with different economic, political, social and cultural practices and values which may start to alter what were seen as important endogenous features of the ID model as regards the three main actors – the State, business associations and trade unions.

First of all, structural reforms in the 1980s and 1990s, especially in developing countries, have reduced the role of the State, which runs counter to the strong role of the State and public sector actors in the ID model, with no other actor suitable to fill this space. Second, as regards the private sector, the operation of global production chains, and the presence of foreign companies at points along these chains, may open up new market opportunities, but may also change the character of IDs and their business associations, as foreign companies may introduce different cultural traditions and business practices which may be difficult to integrate into the productive tissue of the ID. This introduces a tension between 'global' and 'local' factors for ID entrepreneurs. Finally, as regards labour, outsourcing and dual labour market practices that involve the use of migrants and casual labour contracts may reduce the share of organised and formal sector workers in the ID and weaken the strength of the trade unions and representative workers' organisations.

6. CONCLUSION

The ID has spawned a vast body of empirical studies in both the advanced industrialised countries and developing countries that explores the underlying factors contributing to the dynamism and resilience of IDs. The relevance of the ID model for SME development has attracted the attention of policymakers and is particularly attractive for developing countries, given the predominance of small productive units and the desire to boost their competitiveness especially in the context of rising competition due to globalisation and trade openness.

Recent studies show that the Italian IDs themselves are changing in the face of globalisation and new competitive pressures. These changes suggest that the ID model itself may be evolving and taking new directions, although it is unclear how far this evolution would impact upon the core underlying features of IDs.

The pressures of globalisation and more demanding standards of price, quality and delivery of goods and services have dealt a hard blow to sectoral agglomerations of firms in developing countries and raise important implications for how clustered firms will respond. Increased competition may lead firms to engage in outsourcing beyond the ID, thereby benefitting the individual firms but undermining the capture of external economies of scale and greater cohesiveness among fellow firms within the ID. Similarly, companies may resort to rent-seeking behaviour or rely increasingly upon flexible labour practices among their regular workers and via contract and informal workers – this behaviour may be more likely where institutional and socio-economic relations are already weak and where labour market institutions and labour inspection do not operate effectively.

On the other hand, these pressures may encourage clustered firms to strengthen internal cooperation in ways that lead to a thickening of institutional and socio-economic relations and interdependencies, bringing them closer to the ID model. In such a context, IDs may gain renewed attention in developing countries as a model that involves a broader set of institutional, social and cultural factors – as well as more visible economic aspects – and thereby could foster more balanced social and economic development objectives.

NOTES

* The author is a senior researcher at the International Institute for Labour Studies (IILS) of the International Labour Office. The views expressed in this contribution do not necessarily reflect those of the ILO or of its constituents. The author is grateful for comments received from the volume's editors, as well as valuable discussion and suggestions from Werner Sengenberger.
1. A term coined by A. Bagnasco in the late 1970s (Bagnasco 1977), to challenge the dichotomy between the developed North and the less-developed South, and to indicate the existence of an alternative production model.
2. In developing countries, most empirical studies refer to clusters or sectoral agglomerations, rather than IDs, as reflected in the widespread use of the term 'cluster' in the literature. For this reason, this chapter also uses the term 'cluster' when referring to initiatives in developing countries.
3. Efforts at forging international framework agreements (IFAs) between Global Union Federations and TNCs have been aimed at enforcing compliance with labour standards in global supply chains (although difficulties in reaching lower tiers or subcontractors remain a challenge) (Papadakis 2008). This shows that the role of TNCs may be ambiguous, at times bringing technology transfer and opportunities to upgrade labour conditions, while other times failing to do so, stifling economic and social upgrading.

42. Industrial districts in Latin America: The role of local learning for endogenous development

Mario Davide Parrilli and Renato Garcia

1. INTRODUCTION

This chapter focuses on the potential development of Marshallian industrial districts (MIDs) in Latin America.

Since this concept refers to a place with a very specific cultural and social fabric and historic roots (Marshall 1920; Brusco 1982; Becattini 1990), we consider it appropriate to take into account a broader typology of local production systems (LPSs) that exceeds the traditional configuration of MIDs (Markusen 1996).

This approach allows us to frame the concept of MID in the magmatic environment of Latin America where this phenomenon is seldom available, but where the MID concept may represent a powerful benchmark for local economic development. Among the key relevant features associated to the MID model and trajectory, we focus here on the learning processes that can be activated in these production systems and that enable them to embark and remain on a high-road trajectory of growth (Pyke and Sengenberger 1992).

Starting with a conceptual section where the most common types of LPSs relevant for Latin America are presented, we will adopt a dynamic view on the analysis of LPS by focusing on the wider issue of development trajectories as a means to identify actual and potential development prospects.

A variety of districts are briefly referred to and positioned with respect to both their typology and their recent evolution. In this sense, this contribution aims at shedding some light on the development opportunity of industrial agglomerations in Latin America and, perhaps, in the wider context of developing economies.

2. A VARIETY OF LPSs

2.1 IDs versus clusters

The analysis of development models based on successful LPSs has promoted a passionate debate over the past 30 years. The limit of the Fordist paradigm and the emergence of the 'flexible specialisation' model paved the way for a different way to look at firm dynamics and localities. Italian scholars introduced the concept of MID (Brusco 1982; Becattini 1990) drawing on the previous seminal analyses of Marshall (1920). Shortly after, another relevant stream of contributions emerged, but this time referring to the concept of 'clusters' (Porter 1990b; Pedersen, van Dijk and Rasmussen 1994; Schmitz 1995). As a result, many scholars and practitioners have been using both concepts, almost interchangeably, as a means to analyse and promote LPSs via the clustering of a large numbers of firms able to develop joint actions and benefit from external economies.

To be precise, the 'cluster' can be defined as a generic agglomeration of firms of different sizes operating in the same sector within a specific locality (Schmitz 1995) or within a wider regional context (Porter 1990b), whereas the MID is a place where there is an industry specialisation (often circumscribed to one or a few close municipalities), and more importantly the social embeddedness of economic action, that is, social cohesion and self-realisation, that link together the local actors that participate in this special 'industrial atmosphere' (Becattini 1990; Parrilli 2004, 2009); this socio-economic environment promotes intense interactions and mutual and collective learning processes that, together with a significant 'institutional thickness' (Becattini 1990; Amin and Thrift 1994) help the LPS to specialise and coordinate labour, achieving significantly high levels of productivity and competitiveness (Becattini 1990; De Propris 2002; Bellandi 2005; Parrilli and Sacchetti 2008).[1]

Notwithstanding the fact that the debate has polarised around these two key concepts, very interesting taxonomies have provided useful elements for the analysis of both clusters and MIDs, in particular Markusen (1996). In addition to MID, Markusen identified three other forms of firm clusterings: (a) the 'hub-and-spoke cluster', that is centred around one (or a few) hub-firm, which plays a leading role within the locality and which orchestrates the evolution of the local industry through the creation of a number of linkages with suppliers and subcontractors (see also De Propris 2002); (b) the 'satellite platform'; and (c) the 'State-anchored district', which represent two variants of the former as the satellite platform implies a leadership located outside the locality, whereas the State-anchored form refers to a local economy that is controlled by a State enterprise or institution.

Two more typologies of clusters are relevant in the context of developing economies: the 'artisanal cluster' observed in the early years (1940s–50s) of development of Italian IDs (Brusco 1990; Parrilli 2004) and the 'survival clusters' (Altenburg and Meyer-Stamer 1999; Parrilli 2007). These latter are characterised by micro and small enterprises that adopt manual techniques of production and that do not benefit from an efficient division and specialisation of labour; as a result, their output is mainly of medium to low quality destined for local low-income consumers. It is clear that these types of firm agglomerations are quite different from MIDs; they often lack the industrial atmosphere that makes trustful and cooperative interactions prosper and that, in this way, promotes local learning processes that lead to the collective design of local development trajectories.

In this sense, our effort is to relate the forms of firm agglomerations in Latin America with the model and development trajectory of MIDs, with a view to improving our understanding of the collective learning processes as a basis for enhanced competitiveness.

2.2 The evolution of districts

From an analysis of the possible typologies of LPSs, the literature has recently moved on to analyse cluster and district trajectories, which implies placing an increased importance on a dynamic perspective of these systems, analysing their development over time, and promoting more effective development processes (Pyke and Sengenberger 1992). In the context of industrialised countries, these analyses have focused on the issue of innovation (Camagni 1991; Lundvall 1992; Maskell and Malmberg 1999; Boschma 2005) as a means to upgrade production from the low-road to the high-road of competition (Pyke and Sengenberger 1992).

In contrast to this literature, development socio-economists took a different analytical route, focusing on the formation of capabilities and joint actions that can promote productivity growth in LPSs. Humphrey (1995) argued that, in developing economies, it is more important to analyse 'development trajectories' than 'models' due to the wide gap observed in these contexts between 'models' and the reality of their production systems. Such a distance leads us to reason in terms of the most feasible steps ahead for these local systems rather than jumping across too many stages at once to achieve an unattainable model in the short term (Parrilli 2004, 2007).

In spite of the utmost appeal of the ID model linked to the dynamic and democratic socio-economic involvement of the local population that helps to better achieve the broader concept of competitiveness (OECD 1992), IDs are also, for instance in Italy, a dynamic phenomenon, with some of them more recently changing their structure and slowly transforming themselves into large firm-led agglomerations (Brioschi, Brioschi and Cainelli 2002; Guerrieri and Pietrobelli 2004). Studies in the Asian, African, Latin American and European contexts have highlighted the increasing importance of large firm-led clusters (Knorringa 2002; Guerrieri and Pietrobelli 2004; Pietrobelli and Rabellotti 2006). The few MIDs observed in developing economies (for example, Crisciuma in Brazil and Sialkot in Pakistan) also appear to be transforming into hub-and-spoke clusters controlled either from within or from outside the locality. This trend occurs for various reasons that include the need to exploit scale economies, and to easily access credit, R&D and distribution channels.

This type of evolution introduces significant doubts on the effective participation of local agents in strategic decision making and, even more, on the upgrading of their capabilities so crucial to promote endogenous development processes (Humphrey and Schmitz 2004; Parrilli and Sacchetti 2008). However, from the perspective of a development economist this prospect may not represent a prohibitive constraint since the main concern and target are to ignite endogenous processes that help create local skills and capabilities, which are useful for the growth trajectory of developing economies. In this sense, if committed to a locality through active public policies, the 'hubs' may help promote technology transfer, knowledge acquisition and capital formation.[2] This is in fact also part of the historic development of Italian MIDs that, in the 1950s–60s, went through a more hierarchical phase, as local large firms grew from within the system and helped transform production from craft to industrial standards (Parrilli 2004).

If these are the preliminary observations, what role can the MID model still play? Our preliminary answer focuses on the internal dynamics of traditional MIDs that promote cognitive and practical interactions, favour the spread of learning and capabilities, and create more opportunities to continuously reinvigorate the dynamic trajectory of the local systems of small and medium-sized enterprises (SMEs) (Bellandi 2005). We would argue that this is what all kinds of industrial agglomerations could 'learn' from the MID model and trajectory. In contrast, large firm-led local systems are always prone to the risk of poor knowledge transfer and technology; as well as to the threat of these 'hubs' leaving and setting up their operations elsewhere for cost or commercial convenience.

In this sense, a dynamic approach is needed in the context of developing economies; promoting a local system 'only when' it represents a MID portrays an awkward development approach as it excludes a wide range of local systems. The possibility of utilising more hierarchical clusters to favour the learning process of local agents and their endogenous development is not to be underestimated as a few cases in Latin America and worldwide show; for example, the software industry in Aguascalientes (Ruiz 2006) and in San Jose (Parrilli and Sacchetti 2008), the dairy products industry in Boaco and Chontales (Artola and Parrilli 2006), and the salmon industry in southern Chile (Maggi 2006).

3. DISTRICT DEVELOPMENT IN LATIN AMERICA

3.1 Latin American firm agglomerations

Here we focus on some LPSs in Latin America that present both differences and similarities with MIDs; in all of the cases discussed below, however, the benchmarking role of MIDs may be used to identify gaps and priorities; and to lead these SME systems along a feasible development trajectory (Humphrey 1995; Parrilli 2004, 2007). With no claims to be exhaustive, Table 42.1 captures a broad range of firm agglomerations, and in so doing it shows the richness and potentials for analysis and policymaking linked to these agglomerations in the region.

Most of these systems refer to traditional manufacturing sectors or natural resource-based sectors; only in the largest cities there is the start of involvement with high-tech manufacturing and services. The typology of systems described above is linked to the main leadership at play in the locality. These cases show the importance of large firms to promote the local capacity to serve the wider international market: for example, the footwear clusters in Brazil (Schmitz 1999a), the software industry in Mexico (Ruiz 2006), the salmon industry in Chile (Maggi 2006).

In these cases, large national or foreign firms have had the capacity to connect local producers to global buyers and to widen their market channels. In some cases, however (for example, Sinos Valley), the market power held by global buyers places severe constraints on the accumulation of higher skills and capabilities within local SMEs (Humphrey and Schmitz 2004; Suzigan, Garcia and Furtado 2008).

Other production systems exhibit some relevant economic aspects of MIDs as they do not include large firms and display a rather horizontal governance system; large numbers of SMEs work close to one another and benefit from agglomeration economies and joint actions; for example, the furniture industry in Votuporanga (Suzigan, Garcia and Furtado 2008), the dairy products industry in Boaco and Chontales (Artola and Parrilli 2006), the metalmechanic industry in Rafaela (Quintar et al. 1993), and the clothing industry in Gamarra (Visser 1997). In this typology a booming high-tech cluster can also be found, that is the San Jose software cluster (Parrilli and Sacchetti 2008).

A third group refers to the so-called 'survival clusters' (Altenburg and Meyer-Stamer 1999; Parrilli 2007) or 'dirt/low-road' ID (Pyke and Sengenberger 1992; Bellandi 2007) that represent a large number of production systems in Latin America; this is the case, for example, of the furniture industries in Sarchi (Parrilli 2007), Masaya (ibid.), and Ceara (Tendler and Amorim 1996).

Table 42.1 Typology of LPSs in Latin America (in the mid-2000s)

LPSs	Sector	MID	Hub-and-spoke/ State-anchored clusters	Satellite clusters	Survival and craft clusters	Growth tendency
Leon, MX	Shoes	×	×			=
Tonala, MX	Stone crafts	×			×	+
Olinala, MX	Wooden crafts				×	+
Guadalajara-Salto, MX	Software		×			+
Aguascalientes, MX	Software		×			+
Mexico DF	Software		×			+
Chipilo, MX	Furniture				×	+
San Pedro Zac., GUA	Furniture				×	=
San Pedro Sula, HN	Furniture		×	×		–
Masaya, NIC	Furniture				×	+
Esteli, NIC	Furniture				×	=
Masaya, NIC	Shoes				×	=
Boaco-Chontales, NIC	Dairy products	×		×		+
Leon, NIC	Leather				×	=
Matagalpa, NIC	Coffee		×			+
Esteli, NIC	Furniture				×	=
Leon, NIC	Furniture				×	=
Rivas, NIC	Furniture				×	=
Puerto Morazan, NIC	Prawns		×			+
Mosonte, NIC	Marble crafts				×	=
Sarchi, CR	Furniture				×	+
Naranjo, CR	Furniture				×	+
San Jose, CR	Software	×				+
Crisciuma, BR	Tiles	×				=
Sinos Valley, BR	Shoes		×			+
S. Jose d. Campos, BR	Aircraft		×			+
Franca, BR	Shoes		×			+
Ceara, BR	Furniture				×	+
Votuporanga, BR	Furniture	×				=
Gamarra, PE	Textiles			×	×	+
La Ligua, CHI	Knitwear	×				–
Maule, CHI	Wine			×		+
Araucania, CHI	Salmon		×			+
Rafaela, ARG	Metalmechanic	×	×			+

Source: Compiled on the bases of the sources mentioned in the case studies of Section 3.2.

3.2 Cluster trajectories in Latin America

There are many types of districts in Latin America; there may be hundreds of non-accounted LPSs that display similar characteristics to the above-mentioned typologies. None of them presents all of the characteristics of MIDs; in general, they have grown out of imitation, tacit knowledge flows and other external economies that made it easier to respond to fast-growing local demand. In many cases, at first, there were also ethnic ties to promote these clusters, but these often deteriorated when the entry of new global actors and the volume of transactions developed a market-oriented economy (Schmitz 1999a). Since these production systems are changing continuously, the MID model and trajectory represent an important benchmark for their evolution, whereby its key drivers (for example, social embeddedness, policy-inducement, dynamic local learning) may help the Latin American districts improve their internal coordination (Parrilli 2007, 2009).

In the case of the Sinos Valley footwear cluster in Brazil, the system evolved at an early stage from a rather homogeneous agglomeration into a hub-and-spoke cluster where a large number of national large firms have taken control of the cluster (Schmitz 1999a). The Brazilian ministry of labour shows that in Sinos Valley around 130 000 workers were employed in 2004 in 1500 firms, between tanneries, footwear and ancillary firms. Support institutions strengthen the competitiveness of this system. In the 1970s, global buyers started looking for new low-cost suppliers and, for this reason, connected to Sinos Valley; this helped local producers access international markets and increase significantly their production and exports (ibid.). In this process, local producers accumulated new capabilities related to producing higher-quality goods and to implementing just-in-time production, which represented the main local innovation processes. These capabilities focused on manufacturing, whereas few capabilities have been acquired in key areas such as product design and development, material technology and commercialisation. This limitation reinforced a skewed pattern of local governance as global buyers held control of both international market channels and the rate of knowledge transfer to local firms.

Despite these limitations, the growth of the industry has translated into local development and has brought about opportunity for further growth; in fact, local firms do not sell only to global buyers, but also to wholesalers in the Brazilian domestic market and in the close South American markets (MERCOSUR). In Latin American markets in particular, firms have been able to design and develop their own products, increase their capabilities and, in the case of the largest firms, control their own supply chains. Evidence of these increasing efforts is the growth in exports to a larger number of Latin American countries and the increasing average price of local products (Bazan and Navas-Aleman

2004). In this sense, Sinos Valley represents a very interesting case, where the LPS is able to undertake continuous upgrading and to nurture collective learning processes that help generate a dynamic local economy, albeit being a hierarchical cluster.

The furniture cluster of Votuporanga now comprises around 160 firms (from around 80 three years before) and employs 2800 workers within the town (from 2200 three years before) and many others in the surrounding area (Suzigan, Garcia and Furtado 2008). Firms sell mainly in the domestic market, whereas exports to South American countries are limited. Local producers have developed trusting relationships and tend to cooperate in joint actions. It is very common for local producers to share big orders with other firms thanks to a detailed division and specialisation of labour across firms. The formation of the Wood and Furniture Technological Center (CEMAD) in Votuporanga represents a mechanism of local coordination that does not only provide training programmes for firms and workers, but also promotes their access to design facilities, technologies for business management, and research and tests on new materials. The creation of CEMAD in 2001 led to the hiring of a professional figure that acted up until recently as broker of a series of collective initiatives; he also helped to shape a horizontal governance system, which stimulated collective learning processes and new cooperative actions aimed at increasimg the district competitiveness, although little by little. Behind these joint initiatives there was the strong local business association (AIRVO) that launched various projects together with the important (that is, for resources and operative capacity) federal development agency, SEBRAE (ibid.). In conclusion, it could be argued that the Votuporanga furniture system represents a proto-ID populated by SMEs that achieve significant levels of collective efficiency and that are improving their position within globalised markets.

The shoe cluster of Leon, in Guanajuato, represents the major Mexican location for production of men's shoes. Its 1700 firms succeeded in exploiting traditional factors of production, such as the density of local leather suppliers; significant agglomeration economies favoured by the large number of producers in town; and the traditional protection of the internal market that, however, weakened with the creation of the NAFTA (Rabellotti 1995, p. 33). Strong competition from China in the NAFTA market pushed local producers to search for new competitive solutions that focused on innovation in design, organisation and commercialisation as ways to drive the cluster to move to higher value-added phases. Over the years, this cluster seems to have become increasingly concentrated in the hands of six large local companies which have gained larger and larger export shares (Unger 2003). Smaller firms can still focus on export markets through *comercializadoras* (trading companies democratically controlled by member firms), although these tend to disappear due to organisational costs and inefficiencies. As local large companies are quite small in international terms, the concentration process is not changing the local industrial structure that remains based on SMEs that in some cases work for larger firms and in others exploit their own market channels. The governance system displays horizontal features as small firms continue to voice their needs and views to the main business association (CICEG).

Over the years, this industry has been maintaining a competitive position; exports rose to US$189 millions in 2006 with a steady increase over previous years (CICEG's webpage: www.ciceg.org, accessed 10 December 2007). This cluster is so successful because it is able to implement collective innovative strategies such as quality control and certification, as well commercialisation strategies based on upgrading fashion. In the industry, they have been able to transform the local annual shoe trade fair (SAPICA) in an international event visited by hundreds of thousands of customers and traders each year. Through CICEG the local producers have also been fighting against the illegal imports of hundreds of thousands of shoes (ibid.).

This case seems to point to a possible transformation of this cluster into a 'hub-and-spoke' cluster due to the increasing weight of local larger firms. In the short run, this might be good since it represents a way to retain local control within this industry, and to maintain jobs and skills. It is worth noticing that despite this trend, the local market structure has not changed; with its horizontal governance structure still conducive to promote cooperation networks that target the diffusion of skills and capabilities, in view of supporting a more competitive local economy. To conclude, the Leon shoe cluster shares with the MID trajectory a strong emphasis on the role of local policymakers and business associations at key stages in the development of the system and as catalysts for initiatives and support.

The craft cluster of Gamarra, Lima, grew in the early 1990s on the basis of informal production including production of knitwear, trade and services taking place in about 6800 micro SMEs (Visser 1997). These firms represented an informal economy aimed at generating subsistence income for their family. The cluster was in a condition to generate significant external economies that were displayed for example in the higher average income with respect to similar firms located outside the cluster (US$1148 per worker versus US$380); this additional income was driven by higher productivity, longer working hours and a better product (ibid., pp. 72–3). However, subcontracting was not quite developed as 80 per cent of the firms were outsourcing only none, one or a maximum two phases of production (ibid., p. 75); horizontal cooperation was also weak and so was also membership to formal institutions representing the interests of the artisans (ibid., pp. 77–9); all this showed a limited division of labour and a poor coordination among local economic agents.

Despite these significant limitations, this cluster has been growing on a significant scale in the past 15 years. It has activated 14 000 micro and small-sized firms that employ around 75 000 workers; last year alone production increased by 35 per cent and exports to the US by 40 per cent (Marin-Arana 2007). This was also due to more intense cooperation and a deeper division and specialisation of labour within the cluster, which was catalysed by informal and formal agreements between small groups of producers (often less than ten firms). Nine small business associations have also been recently formed, such as the Federation of Small Business of Peru (FEDEGA) (Proexpansion 2003, pp. 79–82), suggesting an increasing value attributed to institutional representation.

Overall, this cluster seems to be in a trajectory from craft agglomeration into a MID as the increasing recognition of common values and mutual reputation leads to the formation of a number of joint formal and informal actions that, in turn, build up a 'thicker institutionality' (Marin-Arana 2007). In this cluster, learning processes that display the importance of cooperation reflect the growing awareness that collective efficiency is not based on involuntary external economies alone, but also on joint actions and that associating is worthwhile for both individual firms and the system.

Rafaela, Argentina, is a quasi-district devoted to the production of metal-mechanics and auto-parts that developed in the 1960s in the Santa Fe region (Quintar et al. 1993). Fifteen years ago around 100 SMEs were operating without much division and specialisation of labour as more than 70 per cent of them were not subcontracting anything or less than 10 per cent of their production (ibid., pp. 24–7); they produced mainly for the national market. Over the past ten years this cluster has withstood the big national financial crisis of the 1990s, and has grown significantly comprising today about 432 firms. In 2006, 44 firms have exported for US$200 millions, much more than in the 1990s (Fernandez 2007). The success of this cluster seems to be linked to the development of 'institutional thickness', which is visible in the efficient working of the public administration and the active involvement of business associations that together spur a higher division and specialisation of labour. Institutional thickness seems to be supported by a growing social cohesion based also on cultural compactness (Costamagna 2000). Simultaneously, public policy has been active with the creation of two dynamic industrial parks: a technology institute that trains workers and an IADB-FOMIN financed project for upgrading local competitiveness (Fernandez 2007).

This expansion created a change in the structure of this cluster as 3 per cent of the firms are now large; similarly to Leon, Rafaela's large firms do not appear to control hierarchically the local strategic development as they represent former SMEs that grew over the past decade and that keep themselves open to sharing and debating on local needs and priorities. The long-run transformation makes one hypothesize that in a MID developed from a former craft agglomeration a more open exchange of knowledge and of other factors of production is currently taking place, which enhances the local learning processes (Costamagna 2000; Fernandez 2007). This evolution makes the MID benchmark relevant for Rafaela and other forms of firm clustering that do not need to transform into 'hub-and-spoke' or 'satellite' clusters; in this way, they may be retaining the control over their strategic decision making as well as over their long-run development process.

Sarchi (Costa Rica) and Masaya (Nicaragua) represent two 'survival clusters' that operate in furniture production. Our analysis emphasizes that they have also been able to build-up skills and capabilities, and a general upgrading trajectory, although at a limited speed and extent. For 20 years they represented survival clusters oriented to respond to the demand of low-income local consumers through the production of low-quality goods made completely in-house. However, recent surveys show the dynamic patterns of firm creation and growth within these localities (more than 120 micro and small firms have grown in these clusters from the 1980s); together with their efforts to innovate their products with new designs and materials (using for example melanine boards, certified plantation wood), and their organisation (production in bigger series through increased division of labour); and, finally, to explore all sorts of market channels in order to capture demands on more competitive terms (Parrilli 2007). This is done for instance by setting up shops for Sarchi or connecting directly with international buyers for Masaya. These indications highlight new accumulation patterns that permit some of the firms, and the two 'survival clusters' more generally, to grow in size and to constantly upgrade their production standards.

A number of constraints limit the speed with which survival clusters upgrade from craft production to industrialisation. In this case, local (in Sarchi) and national policymakers (for Masaya) are not as supportive as they have been in other more competitive contexts. Social embeddedness seems to be quite dense and developed in the case of Sarchi, where the push to self-realisation (through entrepreneurship) and to trusting and cooperative relationships promote the development of a dynamic and cohesive environment; whereas in Masaya limits to reciprocal trust are due to the long civil conflicts that plagued Nicaragua in the 1970s–80s, undermining people's attitude towards trust. The lack of business associations in both contexts sharply reduces the possibility of collective efficiencies (ibid.).

In these two clusters the distance between the MID model and the reality is huge and the objective cannot be to replicate anything similar; however, the benchmark of the MID trajectory may be relevant to show local producers and policymakers what drivers are likely to promote and support their success, in particular in relation to the processes of interaction, mutual and collective learning, and institutions formation that constitute ingredients of the socio-institutional embeddedness. The future opportunities and trajectory of growth may take these survival clusters towards different typologies; however, the benchmark of MIDs may still be relevant to stress the key role that mutual trust, cooperation and collective learning have on competitiveness and endogenous development processes.

4. CONCLUSIONS: THE VALUE OF LEARNING IN LATIN AMERICAN DISTRICTS

Firm clustering is very common in Latin America; very few of them, however, display the full characteristics of the MID model. Indeed, most of them represent hub-and-spoke, satellite and survival clusters; in some cases the social embeddedness is not as cohesive as to promote trustful relationships that enhance collective efficiencies and lower transaction costs; this is what happens, for example, in Gamarra and Masaya, In other cases the support institutions are not sufficiently locally rooted and effective (Sarchi); and elsewhere the growth of large firms may skew the governance system toward the interests of a few leading firms like in Sinos Valley, and possibly in the near future in Leon and Rafaela.

Notwithstanding these clear limitations, these successful experiences prove that firm agglomeration represents a real opportunity, especially when a prospect is taken to transform it into a more horizontal and cooperative environment that, in turn, promotes learning and the formation of endogenous capabilities as it occurs in traditional MIDs (Bellandi 2005). The agglomerations of firms, their interaction and collective actions are key drivers in the creation and diffusion of knowledge and capabilities.

Over time, these clusters undergo structural changes (that is, market structure evolving towards hierarchical patterns), which imply a departure from the MID trajectory; however those capabilities may remain a key aspect as these set up the basis for renovating the competitiveness of the LPS *vis-à-vis* global competitors. In this context, the benchmarking role of MID model and trajectory may be highlighted for many LPSs in Latin America. The MID trajectory illustrates the great dynamism that individuals and firms acquire from the local culture that promotes the creation of new firms and makes these competitive by means of hard work and the wise coordination across agents due to a very detailed division and specialisation of labour (Brusco 1982; Becattini 1990; Parrilli 2004, 2009). Many interesting experiences are arising in Latin America, in both advanced (for example, the software sector in Aguascalientes, the aircraft sector in Sao Joao do Campos) and traditional sectors (for example, the metalmechanic district of Rafaela, the textile cluster of Gamarra). In spite of extant 'market hierarchies', some local systems show that SMEs have undertaken a process of learning and upgrading that is helping them to increase their competitiveness and independence from large hub(s); in prospect this process implies the capacity to set up a new basis for igniting endogenous development processes within localities. In the context of Italian MIDs this learning process is activated by the sharing of secrets (and of technical protocols), the existence of an accumulation of competences (based on technical-scientific education), and the ever changing and adapting social division of labour that allows customised goods and services to be produced and, on these bases, enhances the opportunity for interaction and exchange of knowledge and for mutual and collective learning across the district's actors (Bellandi 2005). This learning process may even involve periods of transformation of the LPS into a more hierarchical trajectory, which is what happened to Italian IDs in the 1950s that helped to create new technological knowledge and entrepreneurial skills that were later exploited in the booming phase of MIDs (Parrilli 2004, 2009). Activating such dynamic learning processes is a key also in 'hub-and-spoke' and 'satellite' clusters, as this process may favour the creation of capabilities across local SMEs that would spur endogenous development processes.

These could hardly take place without industrial development policy, which targets feasible steps within specific timeframes, focusing more on trajectories and on the elements that provide and direct such dynamism. As argued in this contribution, models, and in particular the MID model, are important because they represent a benchmark for policymakers, development operators, academics, producers and their business associations. In the Latin American context, the MID model provides a relevant framework for analysing the development of various forms of firm clustering, rather than a rigid blueprint of what to do; a flexible approach to the identification of feasible steps and trajectories is complementarily necessary as a methodological basis to ensure that the development process of these countries is feasible and sustainable in the long run.

NOTES

1. The typologies elaborated by Bellandi (2007) portray an interplay between local cohesion and local forces; the local input–output relations and the related cognitive endowments of these districts and clusters. The different combinations of these elements can lead to identifying proto-IDs (the traditional ID) and prototypical IDs (an evolution of the traditional mode) as well as foreign-based districts (satellite clusters) and dirt-road agglomerations (that may represent satellite, hub-and-spoke and survival clusters) (Mehrotra and Biggeri 2007b).
2. We refrain here from a thorough discussion on the importance, risks and negative effects that FDI produces within developing economies as a number of contrasting views should be analysed and this is beyond the remit of this work. For a review see Dunning (1988), and Cowling and Sugden (1994).

43. Trajectories and prospects of industrial districts in China

Jici Wang and Lixia Mei

1. INTRODUCTION

The concept of industrial district (ID) was revised to describe the thriving local development witnessed in the Third Italy (Becattini 1978, 1990). It is defined as essentially a territorial system characterized by a clustering of small and medium-sized enterprises (SMEs) with spatially concentrated networks, often using flexible production technology and extensive local inter-firm linkages (Harrison 1992; Asheim 1994). Rich literature in the 1990s concerning IDs has focused on their local embeddedness in the context of changes in technological-institutional systems in the post-Fordist era (Piore and Sabel 1984; Storper and Scott 1992; Staber 2001). It is noted in particular that not all spatial agglomerations of small firms in the same or related sectors necessarily correspond to IDs. In a local context where there are extensive local inter-firm linkages, untraded-interdependence, as well as a flourishing of tacit knowledge and local buzz, processes of learning and innovation emerge (Piore and Sabel 1984; Harrison 1992; Asheim 1994; Storper 1995; Gertler 2003). Here this key area is considered from the angle of Chinese experiences.

Drawing on its vast population and mix of free-market and central-command economic policy, China has seen the development of a large number of industrial clusters, some of them embedded in territories which can be assimilated to IDs.[1] These cases, in particular, have become new sources of growth for non-metropolitan areas,[2] enabling them to attract both foreign and domestic investments and resources that would otherwise be concentrated in major cities. The localities characterized by industrial agglomerations of small firms used to be labeled 'lump economies' (*Kuai Zhuang Jingji*) in Zhejiang Province (Huang 1999), and 'specialized towns' in Guangdong Province (Bellandi and Di Tommaso 2005). Both of them include cases corresponding to what can be seen as China's classical IDs, founded by rural entrepreneurs and local private investments. The sectors which are associated to many such cases include, in particular, apparel, footwear, furniture, TV sets, home electrical appliances, toys, motorcycles, and the like. They create the real background of China's 'weapons of mass production'.

'Increasingly, the places that best accommodate orders are China's giant new specialty cities . . . where clusters or networks of businesses feed off each other, building technologies and enjoying the benefits of concentrated support centres' (Barboza 2004). The extreme diversity among China's disparate regions adds a geographic dimension to the process of capability building (Rawski 2005). It is worth examining the differences between the IDs in the developed world and those in China, not only in their characteristics, but also in their development conditions, processes, opportunities and sustainability.

The next section identifies, as a significant development context for China's IDs, the global/local tension at three levels: global, national and local. Section 3 puts China's IDs and their evolutionary trajectories in a broadly global context, but focusing on the local spirit of China's IDs, including the characteristics of local firms, local labor markets, local specialized markets, and local industrial linkages. In Section 4, we shift to the impacts of globalization, particularly the power and different influences of multinational companies (MNCs) and global buyers on China's local producers within IDs. Section 5 puts forward the comparisons between Chinese and Italian IDs, and Section 6 will conclude the chapter with our thinking about the prospects of China's IDs and policy implications.

2. A MULTI-SCALAR VIEW OF THE ID FORMATION IN CHINA

It is well known that particularly important for Italy are the production processes intimately bound up in the local territorial context, and with communities usually richly endowed with contextual knowledge (Becattini 2002e). What is more, successful localized industrial clustering is most likely to enhance territorially-bound learning processes (Malmberg and Maskell 2006). Many of China's IDs are similar to Italian IDs in their dependence on the local context; however, there are important differences in relation to China's increasing openness to the global world and its domestic changing market situations and political institutions. In this chapter, we will focus on the locally-based, locally-rooted and embedded IDs in China, and try to draw a comparison between them and the Italian IDs.

Have these Chinese IDs been formed by internal forces or external forces or by the interaction between the two? The effect of international outsourcing by MNCs co-exists with the local effects of external economies. In a context of increasing integration with global networks, the origins of the districts in China differ from case to case, reflecting the complex transitional institutions. These districts serve both domestic and foreign markets (J. Wang 2001). They are associated not only with sector-specific activities in the same area, but also with institutional and social features that support their creation, survival and growth. To understand the unique context and formation mechanisms of China's IDs, we have to analyze them from three different but interrelated scales: global, national and local perspectives.

2.1 Global perspective

It is important to pay more attention to the 'concentrated dispersion' (Guerrieri and Pietrobelli 2004) caused by offshore outsourcing after the 1980s. The Chinese economy has been subjected to the fragmentation of production associated with the 'global factory' concept related to the global shift of international manufacturing (Dicken 2003), as well as the offshoring of global jobs from advanced nations to low-cost nations (Bair and Gereffi 2003; Gereffi 2006).

The emerging IDs in China have been increasingly involved in the international fragmentation of production, involving both huge flows of foreign direct investments (FDI) and increasing foreign trade. China has successfully attracted tremendous FDI, stimulating China's IDs to grow quickly in the domestic and global markets. In 2006, China's dependence on foreign trade has risen to 65 per cent, which means that exports and imports together account for two-thirds of the nation's GDP; while at the same time, the foreign trade dependence rates in the US and Japan were both around 20 per cent, a much lower level. However, the fragmentation of production and knowledge actually brings opportunities of earning and upgrading to local firms (Schmitz 2006). Given the rich components of any single ID, it may either concern a single segment (for example, manufacturing of parts and components in a particular industry) or cover multiple segments (such as R&D, marketing and other higher value-added activities).

2.2 National perspective

Thanks to China's rural reform toward market regulation and more liberal attitudes towards entrepreneurship, township and village enterprises (TVEs) in the rural area of China boomed in the late 1970s and became 'one wing' ready to take off. Since the 1980s urban and industrial reforms have been in full swing, along with the proliferation of private enterprises set up by professional personnel – the 'second wing' to take off. At the same time, the household contracted responsibility system[3] reform in rural China has created a great deal of surplus labor forces, which deluged into cities after the mid-1990s and became the primary sources of cheap labor. Up to 150 million rural migrant workers in recent years have provided a globally competitive cheap labor cost advantage for China's high-speed economic growth. Over 40 per cent of migrant workers are normally involved in industrial manufacturing.

A large number of SMEs have also rapidly developed pulled by the growth of China's domestic markets. The scale of these markets ballooned over a very short period, but demand is still largely absorbing standard and cheap goods. In fact, even though the average per capita GDP in China has increased dramatically during the last ten years, a large portion of the Chinese society has still relatively low income. Generally speaking, there are very few powerful private companies or social intermediate organizations that are able to organize production or distribution within such a huge area. Under these market conditions, as common sense dictates, intense price competition is more diffuse than competition characterized by quality control, brand management, or R&D (Ding 2007). Lacking robust distribution channels, SMEs rely heavily on local commodity exchange markets to collect product and market information and to trade with their customers. For this reason, localized commodity exchange markets are one of the triggers which help the constitution of IDs, reducing the transaction costs of searching for products or price information for wholesalers and promoting the regional reputation of local manufacturers.

2.3 Local perspective

The tension between localization and globalization is shown in each ID's development. Capital investments originating from Hong Kong and Taiwan account for nearly two-thirds of FDI in China and were the initial impetus to the formation of IDs in Guangdong Province and Fujian Province; however, many districts in Zhejiang Province originated from the economic strength of local peasant-entrepreneurs and have developed by consanguinity, affinity and geographic ties (Wei and Wang 2007).

Just one example is a label-and-badge manufacturing district in Cangnan County, southwest of Zhejiang Province. Here local producers are involved in more than a dozen production stages including designing, aluminum melting, engraving, drilling, plating, pin making, assembling and packing and so on. Each process is done by independent and specialized enterprises, and every semi-finished product is traded through the commodity exchange market in the district, which coordinates all activities in the production process.

Local governments usually play pivotal roles in favor of China's ID formation and growth, in terms of deregulation, facilitating infrastructures, public sources for innovation and assistance in financing. Also local governments in different places tend to launch policies that are specific to local IDs' development.

The different attitudes shown by local governments explain, to a certain extent, the different ways in which Chinese IDs were formed and their different trajectories. For example, in an area of Zhejiang Province where there are several IDs, the local government adopted a rather tolerant and *laissez-faire* policy, labeled 'Three let it go', which means 'let the local market economy go, let the multiple ownership system go, and let the local comparative advantages go'.[4] This was of significant importance to local entrepreneurs in the early 1990s, in terms of deregulating the centrally planned economy system, and in freeing people's entrepreneurship at the beginning of China's economic reform. Conversely, the provincial government of Guangdong seemed to play a very active role in stimulating local development, by setting up 108 'technological innovation platforms'[5] within 229 'specialized towns' to assist their clusters in improving innovation capabilities.

3. LOCAL SPECIALIZATION AND DIVERSIFICATION

3.1 Distribution, specialization and diversification

In China, nearly 70 per cent of GDP and over 40 per cent of SMEs' employment are concentrated in 15 selected provinces: Guangdong, Shandong, Jiangsu, Zhejiang, Hebei, Sichuan, Fujian, Jiangxi, Henan, Liaoning, Hubei, Hunan, Heilongjiang, Anhui and Shaanxi. The top four provinces – Guangdong, Shandong, Jiangsu, Zhejiang – account for 33 per cent of China's total GDP, 55 per cent of SMEs, and 61 per cent of the total numbers of China's IDs in 2006 (see Table 43.1 and Figure 43.1).

Table 43.1   China's IDs in 15 selected provinces (2006)

Selected provinces	GDP ($ billion)	Per cent of China's GDP	No. of IDs	No. of SMEs	Employment in SMEs
Guangdong	286.39	10.55	73	230 474	6 376 904
Shandong	237.09	8.74	53	177 407	5 001 380
Jiangsu	234.39	8.64	70	270 669	6 563 781
Zhejiang	172.06	6.34	136	241 220	5 705 517
Hebei	130.55	4.81	37	87 605	2 696 972
Sichuan	94.56	3.48	15	75 330	2 138 436
Fujian	84.11	3.10	45	77 230	2 151 462
Jiangxi	51.95	1.91	9	43 605	1 424 390
Henan	135.56	3.78	25	110 182	3 566 630
Liaoning	102.55	3.08	7	110 081	2 323 698
Hubei	83.48	3.08	24	51 682	1 621 358
Hunan	83.37	3.07	25	57 720	2 004 921
Heilongjiang	70.56	2.60	6	40 790	1 027 397
Anhui	68.82	2.54	7	59 902	1 758 246
Shaanxi	47.07	1.73	4	45 906	1 173 463
15 provinces in total	1882.51	69.38	536	1 679 803	45 534 555[*]
China as a whole	2713.48	100.00	n.a.	n.a.	110 000 000

Notes:
[*] About 41.4 per cent of the total SMEs employment in China.
a) Data about China's IDs and SMEs come from authors' datasets.
b) A majority of the above 536 IDs belong to the type of Marshallian industrial districts (MIDs), including labor-intensive manufacturing IDs based primarily on SMEs, such as many export-orientated 'specialized towns' and 'lump economies'; but not including the increasing high-tech and research-based innovative industrial clusters in China.

Source: GDP data from the *China Statistical Yearbook* (2006 and 2007).

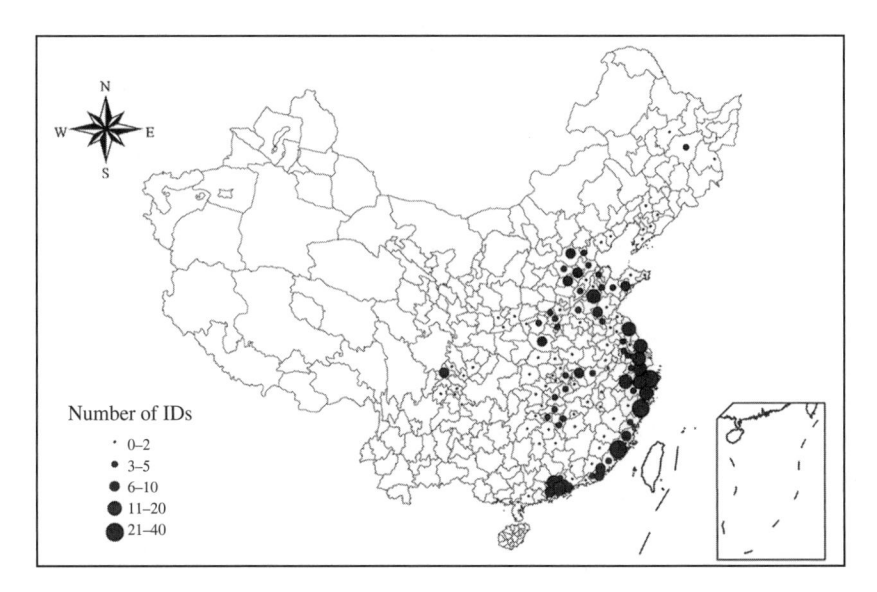

Figure 43.1 Geographical distribution of IDs in China

Harvard economist Rodrik agrees that specialization patterns are not pinned down by factor endowments, however, he insists that economic development requires diversification, not specialization (Rodrik 2006). Some empirical studies about the efficiency of China's industrialization in different areas also prove that local diversification beyond certain extents of specialization will be better for local development.

Our study shows that most of China's IDs specialized in the production and distribution of textile and apparel, footwear, furniture, TV sets, home electrical appliances, toys, motorcycles, and the like, are basically all labor-intensive manufacturing sectors, which always stand at the bottom of global value chains. However, after 30 years of learning by exporting, these IDs have begun to diversify into multiple products and activities, nevertheless, still in a very narrow sense, as can be seen from Table 43.2.

China's rise as a primary manufacturing producer relates not only to the global manufacturing shift from developed economies to emerging and developing economies, but also to the growth of China's domestic demand and to the dramatic improvement in its people's living conditions. However, this growth can be fragile in the face of intensified international competition, in that these industries are fundamentally labor-intensive and cost-sensitive, which are very easy to be imitated and substituted. The invested capital is never soundly embedded, but constantly looking for lowest costs and maximum profit.

Table 43.2   Specialization and diversification of IDs in Zhejiang Province

City/County	Sectors of specialization and diversification in the IDs	Related NAICS codes (5-digit or 6-digit)
Wenzhou City	Footwear making, textiles and garments, eyeglasses, cigarette lighters, locks, food machinery, men's shavers, pumps and valves, pens, etc.	31621, 31521, 31529, 339115, 423460, 312221, 332211, 332919, 339941
Ningbo City	Apparel, household electronic appliances, kitchen utensils, moulds and plastics, chemical fibers and weaving	31521, 31529, 33712, 333511, 313312, 313320
Shaoxing County	Textiles and materials, chemical fibers and weaving, knitting, kitchen utensils, electric fans, etc.	31331, 31324, 31521, 332214, 333412
Taizhou City	Auto-parts and components, eyeglasses, furniture, garment machinery, plastic moulds, pumps and valves, rubber products, etc.	336211, 339115, 337121, 337122, 337124, 337125, 333511, 332919, 325212
Shengzhou City	Neckties, silk products, socks, etc.	31511, 315993, 314129
Yongkang City	Small hardware, scooters and skates, stainless steel products, commercial gifts, etc.	332722, 339993, 423710, 441210, 532120, 332214, 339912
Jinxiang Town	Badges, packaging, printings, etc.	327112, 322221, 323110, 333315, 326112
Haining City	Leather, apparel, shoes, etc.	31511, 31521, 31522, 31523, 31529, 31599, 31621
Datang Town	Socks and stockings, neckties, etc.	31511, 314129
Liushi Town	Low-tension electrical machinery, electronic products, large sets of electronic facilities and machineries, etc.	33331, 33351, 334513, 335314
Yongjia County	Fasteners and slide fasteners, pumps and valves	332722. 339993, 332919
Yiwu City	Commercial gifts, specialized small commodities markets, etc.	337112, 315999, 453220, 333999

Sources: The industrial sectors information comes from authors' own collections. For the NAICS codes see www.census.gov/eos/www/naics, accessed 20 December 2008.

3.2 Local roots

Why do certain IDs emerge in some places rather than others? If the resource endowment does not explain the differences in their economies, then differences in quality and quantity of local human resources must matter. Major emphasis should be laid on that elusive factor of production called 'entrepreneurship' rooted in local places (J. Wang 2007).

With regard to the dominant roles played by key actors, we categorize China's localized IDs into three major types: IDs where (a) firms are mainly founded by rural entrepreneurs; (b) firms are mainly spinoffs from universities and public research institutes; and (c) firms come from State-owned Enterprises (SoEs) reforms. The three types of IDs differ from each other in regard to the key actors; however they share the same context of China's economic transition from planned economy to market economy, and from local production system (LPS) to global value chains.

3.2.1 IDs founded by rural entrepreneurs

Since 1978 when China's economy began to open and reform, a group of rural entrepreneurs in small and medium-sized towns and villages of several provinces such as Zhejiang, Hebei, Jiangsu, Fujian and Guangdong, 'washed up their feet and went to industry from agriculture' (*Xi Jiao Shang Tian*),[6] and started up local private businesses and family enterprises, which were later recognized by China's central government as TVEs (*Xiangzhen Qiye*) and 'Private Economy' (*Minying Jingji*). These pioneer rural entrepreneurs succeeded in penetrating many light industrial sectors, within which niche markets existed extensively because of the commodity shortages under the previous central-command economy. These local private businesses were gradually integrated into supporting public policies and were directly involved in China's transition to a market economy (Wang et al. 2001).

In Zhejiang Province, hundreds of villages, towns and counties emerged specializing in the manufacturing of certain kind of products, such as footwear, garments, cigarette lighters, men's shavers, food, pens.This phenomenon of spatial agglomeration and industrial specialization used to be labeled 'lump economy' (*Kuai Zhuang Jingji*) by Chinese scholars (Huang 1999). In Guangdong Province, this phenomenon of industrial agglomeration was designated the title of 'specialized towns' (Bellandi and Di Tommaso 2005). Both the Zhejiang 'lump economies' and the Guangdong 'specialized towns' include many classical China's local IDs founded by rural entrepreneurs and local private investors. Their evolutionary trajectories follow a 'bottom-up' strategy. They started in spite of the fact that China's market systems were not that perfect.

3.2.2 IDs and clusters related to spinoffs from universities and public research institutes

The emergence of *Zhong'guancun* (ZGC) new-tech agglomeration in Beijing tells a story about the possibility and difficulty of a different trajectory of formation of IDs in China (Wang and Wang 1998). The Beijing' ZGC progressed initially as an embryonic ID, which appeared to contain all three elements of entrepreneurship in its early development: small firms, new firm formation and innovativeness.

However, it has eventually evolved into a unique combination of weaknesses. These include strong hierarchical restraints from the State-owned institutions or firms on the local networking, and direct global linkages with the multinationals, which expose local economies to volatile world competition.

From the shadow of the planned economic system which governed the country before 1978, China has been approaching a more market-oriented society. Under such enormous changes, there are many basic problems faced by all the firms in China concerning property rights, commercial and financial laws, share-holding and so on. What is special to the firms in the new-tech complex ZGC in Beijing is the lack of these regulations and market laws. The inconsistent and unclear policy from the government has somehow hampered fostering local networking among firms in the region for the sustainable innovation *milieu*.

3.2.3 IDs and SoEs transformation

Increased industrial disintegration around the world has provided technical possibilities for expanding labor division within a particular industry in developing countries (Pei 2004). China launched its economic reform and open-door policy toward a market-oriented economy in the late 1970s; and in the mid-1990s, the reform of SoEs was accelerating under the administration of former Prime Minister Zhu Rongji. During this decade, a large number of SoEs were transformed into equity share or privately-owned enterprises, and parts of them were transforming into diversified SMEs, with which a kind of new IDs were coming into being.

We found a few successful cases of SME-based IDs spun off from SoEs (Mei and Wang 2008). For example, over a thousand private bicycle SMEs have emerged in Tianjin City, after the transformation and privatization of the local two big SoEs, Tianjin Bicycle Factory and Tianjin Flying Pigeon Factory. And most of these private bicycle producers are spinoffs from the big two SoEs, in terms of the technicians who used to be workers in the SoEs but later became managers and engineers of those private bicycle SMEs. They formed a local bicycle ID, and they managed to increase their bicycle production and market share dramatically, after nearly ten years of struggling in the era of China's transition.

There are many other cases of IDs evolving from SoEs transformation in China. These IDs are different and specific to local contexts, but they are similar in the sense of local roots. What we can conclude from the process of transformation from SoEs to SME-based IDs is the diversification and complication of China's IDs.

3.3 Specialized markets and industrial linkages

3.3.1 Specialized markets as local linkages

The colocation of specialized markets and up–downstream industrial linkages, as kinds of visible and invisible complementary assets within China's IDs, is also a sign of strong local forces.

Specialized markets, defined as 'wholesale markets located in industrial clusters, and dealing with the related commodities of the local industry' (Ding 2007), can be found in almost every ID of China, especially in Zhejiang and Guangdong Provinces. Examples are the footwear machine and leather markets near the Wenzhou footwear ID, the fabric and dying markets around the Ningbo Men's apparel ID, and the Shunde wooden material market for local furniture ID. The specialized markets usually provide raw materials for local specialized production, as well as certain producer service to local producers. By doing so, specialized markets create important market transaction conditions and information conditions, and can be regarded as visible complementary assets for local specialized producers. Specialized markets are effective proofs of the great extent of division of labor in China's IDs.

Furthermore up–downstream industrial linkages mean that as a specialized producer in the IDs, you can find anything before and after your production activities. Take the case of Dongguan Personal Computer (PC) ID (Tong and Wang 2001): 95 per cent of components and parts for PC manufacturing, as well as all kinds of producer services such as accounting, financing, distribution and logistics, can be found locally. These local up–downstream industrial linkages attract more and more SMEs and foreign capital to the IDs, and makes them difficult to relocate to other places, which in Markusen's word, is the power of being in a 'sticky place in slippery space' (Markusen 1996).

3.3.2 Industrial relocation and changing linkages

Local roots are important to the formation and growth of IDs, but this does not mean the 'sticky place' will thrive forever, nor does it mean the local linkages will never be changed. Enterprises in these IDs are now beginning to create their own-brand products, based on the local collective brands, but these strategies are not yet widespread enough. Recent price rises in almost every raw material and the increase in China's general labor wages, Chinese currency appreciation, and Chinese central government's strategic adjustment to lower subsidiary rebate taxes to exporting firms in the past few years, have together caused serious difficulties to many of the still predominant base of manufacturing firms devoted to specific original equipment manufacturing (OEM) or low-cost production. In the face of such problems, some lead firms within IDs began to expand and relocate to China's inland provinces, even to nearby East Asian countries, where they can find an even cheaper labor force and land to maintain their business. But whether they can survive with such strategies is not clear.

The provincial government of Guangdong put forward the policy to push the industry relocation within Guangdong Province from the developed Pearl River Delta to the developing North. It promotes the collaboration of twin cities, one economically advanced and the other lagging behind, in order to build so-called 'relocation parks'. It plans to build more than 20 such parks in Guangdong. If China's interior provinces can provide a hospitable investment climate to complement massive new investments in infrastructure, firms compelled by rising wages and land costs may depart from eastern and southern coastal locations and find new homes in central and western China rather than moving overseas. A good example is the famous apparel company of Ningbo, Younger Group, which located its branch plant in the largest western city, Chongqing. Since then, firms specialized in the productions of wool textiles and many accessories are setting up around it, so that a new apparel district is in the making.

4. GLOBALIZED PRODUCTION NETWORKS AND CHINA'S IDS

4.1 Why insertion into global production network?

As discussed above, China's IDs have strong local roots, in the sense of local firms, local labor markets, local specialized markets and local up–downstream industrial linkages; however, these IDs are increasingly moving into global value chains (Gereffi 1999; Gereffi, Humphrey and Sturgeon 2005), particularly after China's access into WTO in 2001 (Liu 2003).

Many scholars deem that insertion into global value chains, or global production networks, provides access to global powers such as the world number one retailer, Wal-mart, and hence a good opportunity to learn and upgrade under global value chains (Schmitz and Knorringa 2000; Ernst and Kim 2002). Many others believe that knowledge can spillover from MNCs and FDIs, which can help local producers in emerging and developing countries and improve their innovation capability, without investing much in R&D. This was labeled 'later-comer advantages' (Mathews 2002).

What is more, MNCs are inclined to relocate close to existing industrial agglomeration, say, industrial clusters within IDs or other territories, in emerging and developing countries, so as to access local markets easily. As pointed out by the *World Investment Report* 2001 (UNCTAD 2001):

> [Industrial clusters] are playing an increasing role in economic activities . . . Clusters comprise demanding buyers, specialized suppliers, sophisticated human resources, finance and well-developed support institutions, such concentrations of resources and capabilities can attract 'efficiency-seeking' FDI (and more and more FDI is of this type). It also helps to attract 'asset-seeking' FDI to the more advanced host countries. . . . Investors – domestic and foreign alike – seek to take advantages of dynamic clusters. In joining a cluster, they often add to its strength and dynamism. This, in turn, turns to attract new skills and capital, adding further to the dynamism of the location. Where agglomeration economies are significant, the rest of the country might be of little relevance to the locational decisions of firms. Hence, attracting FDI in these activities depends increasingly on the ability to provide efficient clusters. (Ibid., pp. 13–14)

It seems that local IDs and local dynamism from emerging and developing countries can be very attractive and significant to MNCs; vice versa, MNCs may sometimes be very important cooperative partners for learning objectives along global value chains.

4.2 Two cases of interaction between local IDs and global MNCs

In China, we have observed a few cases of MNCs or FDIs colocating with local SMEs in certain IDs. For example, the global leading brand company, Colgate Palmolive, entered Chinese toothbrush market by purchasing a big local producer, Sanxiao Group, in 1999, to access local production capability as well as local markets. Sanxiao Group was located within a locally-born ID of toothbrushes in Hangji, Yangzhou City, where there are over a thousand SMEs producing toothbrushes, accounting for more than 80 per cent of China's toothbrush market share. In a joint venture with the Sanxiao Group, Colgate Palmolive easily gained access to China's domestic toothbrush market. In 2003, the Colgate-Sanxiao joint venture company became a wholly foreign-owned enterprise and thus the world toothbrush production base for Colgate Palmolive.

Another case is the strategic cooperation between US General Electric Company and Zhengtai Group, a local leading electric power equipment producer in Yueqing County, Zhejiang Province, in 2002. Yueqing is a primary ID for low-voltage electric power equipments production in China, with over 1200 small firms locally agglomerated.

However, this is only one side of the coin, and maybe an overestimated one for emerging and developing countries. International scholars like John Humphrey and Hubert Schmitz have already found that insertion into global value chains by local small firms can help the latter to obtain product and process upgrading, but functional upgrading is much more difficult to be reached in this way (Schmitz 2004). Functional upgrading relates to higher value-added activities such as design, R&D, brand and marketing, and so on. An empirical study by He and Pan (2006) tested the 'spillover' effect versus the 'crowding out' effect of FDIs on the manufacturing industry in Beijing. The latter was found to be larger than the former, which means that sometimes FDIs can be harmful to LPSs. Therefore, the structure and relationship of international division of labor between IDs and global leading powers are actually decided by the different positions of foreign firms and local systems in the global value chains.

This is also manifested by Cantwell and Iammarino's (2000) research about MNCs' innovation location, in which they found 'the pattern of MNC networks for innovation conforms to a hierarchy of regional centers, and that the pattern of technological specialization of foreign-owned affiliates in different regional locations depends upon the position of the region in the locational hierarchy'. A practical story to verify this theory is the case of the entry of US Carlyle Group into the Xuzhou Construction Machine Group in 2006. The former is one of the largest 'private equity companies' in the US, and the latter is the number one Chinese national giant company for construction machines.[7] For the powerful global brander

Carlyle Group, the entry into the Xuzhou construction ID is the best way to gain access to China's domestic construction market. But for the LPS, this case may result in a destructive shock if the giant global buyer operates a 'hostile merging'.

Export-orientated economic growth strategies turned China into the 'world factory'. China's local SMEs within IDs interact in different ways with MNCs or global buyers. Some firms earn and learn, while some lose and fail, having to close their factories or leave the place. The development trends of China's IDs prove that the global/local tension can be an opportunity for less developed regions; but it can also generate enormous challenges and pressures, even turn into a severe crisis that may radically change local IDs' fates. It cannot be denied that there are sets of firms in those IDs that managed to survive and succeed in the changing global economy, with improved technological innovation capability, upgrading to more innovative and higher valued-added regions; but on the other hand, more and more local small firms may have to confront the intensified global competition and finally quit the production world, just as the US small firms and labor-intensive industries experienced in the 1970s, and later, Japan in the 1980s.

5. COMPARISON BETWEEN CHINESE AND ITALIAN IDs

As discussed above, China's IDs based on rural industrialization are primarily evolved from rural private enterprises, with some possible and minor cases evolved from universities and research institutes, and some spinoff firms from SoEs, in the transition process of China from a central command economy to a market exporting-orientated economy. Many of China's IDs are based on local linkages, whilst being also part of and dependent on global value chains. This specific formation context of global/local tensions makes China's IDs different from Italian IDs in many aspects (see Table 43.3).

Most of China's IDs stand at a lower position on the global value chains compared with Italian IDs. However, the global value chains are not constant, and latecomers can learn and upgrade from lower value-added activities to higher stages. Concerning the fierce competition between Chinese and Italian products in the international markets, it could be said that it is not the Italian IDs that are 'downgrading' or declining, but rather that Chinese IDs are upgrading and rising, at a much faster speed than others.

6. CONCLUSION AND PROSPECTS

In this chapter, we discussed the theoretical and practical context of global/local tension as a driving force for the development of China's massive labor-intensive IDs.

Table 43.3 Comparisons between Chinese and Italian IDs

Historical tradition for business and commerce	China's IDs (weak)	Italian IDs (strong)
Primary places of IDs	South and east coastal areas of China, such as Zhejiang, Guangdong, Jiangsu Provinces.	North-central and northeast areas of Italy, the so-called 'Third Italy'
Primary products from IDs	Textiles and apparel, footwear, stockings, neckties, furniture, toys, ceramics, electronic products, bicycles, commercial gifts, etc.	Footwear, fashion apparel, glasses, ceramics, furniture, pearl and jewelry, handbags, traveling products, mechanical goods and instruments, etc.
Dependence on exporting to other countries	High	High
Openness to the foreign investment	High	Low
Main forms of firms in IDs	Private SMEs	Family firms and private SMEs
Entrepreneurs	Rural entrepreneurs, and some science and technical entrepreneurs	Businessmen
Workers	Mainly rural migrant workers	Mainly local workers, technicians and engineers
Comparative advantages	Low cost	Product differentiation
		Fashion design
		Incremental innovation in technologies
Competitive advantages	Low-cost, middle quality and quick delivery	High quality and brands
Technological content	Low and middle	Middle and high
Value added	Low	High
Innovation capability	Low, but increasing	High
Employment characteristics	Labor-intensive	Crafts and skill-intensive
	Low wage	Middle and high wage
Significance of industrial association	Not that important	Very important
Role of governments	Strong	Weak at the national level, sometimes strong at the regional and local levels
Training and education for workers	Little	Great
Producer service	Shortage	Advanced

Source: Authors' collected.

From the three different but interrelated perspectives of global, national and local, we can conclude that most of China's IDs have the support of rather strong local forces, in the sense of locally-born, locally-rooted and locally-embedded small firms, with their production and innovation capabilities rooted in a network of local social–cultural relations.

The formation process and evolutionary trajectories of China's IDs can be classified into three types with regard to the key players: from local rural entrepreneurs, from universities or public research institutes, and from SoEs in transformation. Different processes, as well as different places, explain different types of specialization and of diversification dynamism across these IDs. They nevertheless share the same transitional process from a centrally-planned economy to a market-orientated economy. Hence China's IDs share the same characteristics in terms of the combination of local forces and openness to the global world.

Export-orientated economic growth strategies turned China's IDs into the 'world factory', which makes China's IDs more open to the globalized production world than those in Italy. China's local SMEs within IDs interact in different ways with MNCs or global buyers. Insertion into global value chains will bring opportunities of learning and upgrading to local small firms in those IDs; however the global power of MNCs may also impede LPS from innovating and upgrading functionally by all means. Therefore, an insistent problem for the prospects of China's IDs will be the upgrading from production capacity to innovation capability for the local small firms so as to compete and win in the global markets. The time they need to accumulate such an innovation capability might turn out to be of crucial importance.

NOTES

1. In a debate on the Italian model of IDs, Markusen (1996) rejected the dominance of the MIDs in regional development. She identified three additional types of IDs, that is, the hub-and-spoke ID; the satellite platform; and the state-anchored district. The IDs in China in this chapter refer mainly to the MIDs or the Italian model of IDs, that is classical IDs.
2. Probably we could call them the 'second' tier cities (Markusen, Lee and Digiovanna 1999).
3. Household contracted responsibility system (HRS), is a major institutional reform in rural China since 1978, when individual households replaced the production team system as the unit of production and accounting in rural areas of China (see Lin 1987).
4. See Chinese economist Du Runsheng's interview, 'Understanding Wenzhou economic pattern', *Jiedu wenzhou Jingji Moshi*, 2002, www.people.com.cn/GB/shizheng/252/9387/9388/20021105/858885.html, accessed 20 December 2008.
5. Guangdong Province technological innovation web for specialized towns: www.zhyz.gov.cn, accessed 20 December 2008.
6. 'Wash up their feet' (*Xi Jiao Shang Tian*), was used to describe the phenomenon of China's rural entrepreneurs leaving the farms, and starting up their own businesses in the 1980s.
7. See 'Carlyle holds 45 per cent stake in Chinese construction machine giant', www.news.jongo.com/articles/07/0319/9517/OTUxNwwPv1faHp.html, accessed 20 December 2008.

44. The complexity of upgrading industrial districts: Insights from the diesel engine industry of Ludhiana (India)

Meenu Tewari*

1. INTRODUCTION

This chapter is motivated by the puzzle of differential performance among small firms in related sectors located in the same institutional setting and geographical region. Why do some sectors in seemingly vibrant industrial districts (IDs) appear to perform poorly even as other related industries in the same region do well? Firms in IDs are assumed to derive their resilience from an ability to draw on common resources, tacit knowledge and specialized services generated by competition and cooperation among interlinked firms in spatially concentrated and closely-related local industries (Sabel 1994, 2005b). Why then do some colocated and linked industries prosper while others lag? This contribution draws on evidence from the diesel engine sector of Punjab (India) to address this question. Since the 1980s the diesel engine industry in Punjab has been languishing relative to other light engineering and metal-based industries in the region, such as bicycles, sewing machines, machine tools and auto-components that have consistently done well in terms of output, employment and exports. Why are related industries in a well-performing ID not able to share equally in its dynamism? What are the blocks that inhibit and limit adaptation and resilience in the lagging industries?

The chapter draws on field work I conducted in the diesel engine industry in the North Indian industrial belt of Ludhiana-Phagwara districts in the State of Punjab (along with comparative material from earlier field work I had conducted in the other metal-based industries in Ludhiana, such as sewing machines, bicycles and basic machinery), in 1997–98 and in 2001 and 2005.[1] The issue was a curious lack of dynamism in Ludhiana's diesel engine industry, despite being located in a region well known for its robust, dynamic and innovative metalworking and light engineering industries.

The chapter argues that the differential performance of related industries in the same region can be explained in part by the unseen and hidden factors that inhibit technological upgrading among small finished goods producers if their ability to upgrade depends on prior technical upgrading by other key intermediary firms in the production chain, notably input and machinery suppliers. Using Punjab's diesel engine industry, and its district context, as an illustrative case I argue that under some circumstances, the underlying production structure and the 'strong ties' that bind small firms in spatially-agglomerated production networks – the very ties that provide the production network with its key strengths – can also present powerful constraints to widespread technical upgrading.[2] This is because cascading, structural connections across the production chain call for upgrading across different nodes of the chain in the region – for example, the input and upsteam machinery industries in addition to the final goods segments of the sector. This 'demand-pull' upgrading and its region-wide spillovers are desirable, but in the short run they pose challenges to policy because typically modernization programs focus on finished goods sectors (diesel engines or bicycles or sewing machines), rather than on upstream intermediate goods producers that are linked to these firms, but in distinct subsectors. In these circumstances, the state has a distinctive and specific role to play in helping firms get past this bottleneck.

The chapter is organized as follows. After a brief description of Ludhiana's ID and the trends of growth and stagnation in Punjab's diesel engine industry, I elaborate three themes to explain why this sector now lags behind others even while being embedded in an otherwise robust industrial landscape. I examine, as explanatory variables: (a) the industry's origin, modularity and the structure of government policies that supported its early growth, but which inadvertently tethered the industry to low-end models; (b) the cross-regional pattern of the sector's geography that led some innovation-intensive portions of the value chain to become localized outside Punjab; and (c) the paradox of the sector's strong inter-firm ties that promote cost-effectiveness in the industry, but also limit the sector's technical upgrading.

2. PUNJAB'S DIESEL ENGINE INDUSTRY: STAGNATION AMIDST STEADY GROWTH

Ludhiana,[3] the leading industrial city of Punjab State[4] in North India is documented in the literature as being a vibrant ID and the site of some of the most dynamic woolen hosiery and light engineering industries in the country, such as bicycles, sewing machines and machinery (Wall 1973; Dasgupta 1989; Singh 1990; Taub and Taub 1994; Tewari 1996, 1998). Over 60 per cent of the nation's output of bicycles and parts comes from this region, as do about 85 per cent of the country's sewing machines and parts; and a large proportion of the country's output of general purpose lathes, hand tools and related metalworking machinery is produced here. Ludhiana is the country's largest producer and exporter of woolen knitwear and hosiery, accounting for over 90 per cent of the nation's woolen knitwear output, and the bulk of India's exports of woolen knitwear. Much of the region's industrial strength comes from its innovative skill base, its strong inter-firm networks in the metalworking and hosiery industries, a thick network of active producers' associations, and the presence of an adaptable and diversified intermediate goods manufacturing base (Taub and Taub 1994; Tewari 1996). These institutions, along with strong and active local business associations and an engaged industrial bureaucracy, have enabled Punjab's industrial sector to cope resiliently with numerous external crises.

For example, throughout the 1980s and early 1990s, when Punjab was rocked by political adversity and separatist violence, local firms grew at average annual growth rates that were consistently higher than the national average throughout this period (Tewari 1996, 1998). Most recently the region's woolen knitwear industry overcame relatively quickly and successfully the collapse in 1991 of its primary overseas market, the former Soviet Union. It did so by relying upon the strength of local institutions and networks of firms that were inserted in different market segments and had the knowledge that some firms were able to draw upon to enter more demanding markets at home and abroad with relative success (Tewari 1999). Against this background of industrial success, the poor performance of the diesel engine industry seemed surprising.

From the start, Punjab's diesel engine industry has been dominated by small producers. The region has over 1500 firms, and employs over 40 000 workers directly and indirectly (Gulati 1997) with only around 50 being medium-sized firms; and even fewer exporting directly. Most others produce either for the domestic market or export indirectly, via merchant exporters. Discussions with firms, and public reports on the diesel engine sector in this region, seem to suggest that although once important, Ludhiana's diesel engine industry is now a small and declining sector plagued with quite stagnant domestic demand, low prices and depressed profits. During field work it was clear that most firms had not upgraded their production processes in a long time, and many continued to produce old – in some cases over 50 years old – models. Internationally, the diesel industry has moved toward lightweight, highly fuel-efficient engines made of aluminum alloys, sophisticated fuel-consumption mechanisms and low-pollution technologies. But the bulk of small firms in India's diesel engine sector continue to produce old Lister-Petter type engines that were first introduced in the late 1940s. This combination of obsolete models, low prices and shrinking demand has kept firms tied to low-margin products for low end markets which has further prevented modernization. One industry official noted that unless Ludhiana's (and India's) small-scale diesel engine sector upgrades itself – by improving product quality, introducing better designs, newer models and adopting lighter materials – 'in less than ten years, our engines will fail'.

On closer examination, however, it turned out that the situation was not monolithically poor. Some firms had made significant improvements, and a key distinction emerged: exporters were doing much better than firms producing solely for the domestic market, as were component producers relative to final good assemblers. Indeed, nearly 51 per cent of the country's total exports of diesel engines originated in the Ludhiana region and in the neighboring city of Phagwara.[5] Similarly, component producers were also doing well – they had more orders than they could currently meet and were expanding production. This good export performance and healthy component production was surprising given the general picture of slow growth and technical stagnation in the industry painted by local officials and the firms themselves. For example, most of the firms interviewed reported that the majority of the technically-sophisticated components in the diesel engines that they assembled came from outside the State. They were not produced locally but were 'imported' from a district hundreds of miles away,[6] Rajkot in Gujarat State.

A second surprise and mismatch between the overall image of the sector and what firms were actually doing had to do with the paradoxical relationship of the industry to technical standards. One would expect that small firms producing outdated, low-end models would have little to do with following standards. But to the contrary, Ludhiana's diesel engine producers simultaneously emphasized the key role that the Indian Standards Institute (ISI)[7] had played since the 1980s in setting new product standards for the engines in an effort to upgrade the industry and obtain greater product safety. Although the models the firms produced were old, and had initially been copied and introduced through reverse engineering; firms had to obtain full certification from the ISI on the quality of the engines they produced. Almost all exporters and the vast majority of small domestic suppliers have since produced ISI certified machines.[8] One interviewer repeatedly emphasized how, through this move towards modularity 'ISI had changed the shape of the industry' by insisting on standards and showing small firms what good quality diesel engines should look like (Alamgir interview). This might seem odd, given that such standards referred to old models, however, as producers themselves noted, even this preliminary step of standardizing existing models has helped educate local firms on the importance of national norms and how to meet them. Most importantly, standardization, and the modularity that has resulted from this standardization has deepened subcontracting ties between small and medium firms.

Clearly this concern with ISI standards has not been enough to make the small-scale sector competitive. Most firms continue to produce outdated models, and the industry lags far behind its global competitors. The international market is dominated by light weight and fuel-efficient Japanese and Chinese diesel engine producers: two Japanese diesel engine models (Kobota and Yanmar) control nearly 70 per cent of the world market, while two Chinese models control another 20 per cent.

Three issues stand out from this picture of the diesel engine sector's overall lack of competitiveness mixed with instances of good performance and growth. First, odd as it may seem, the ISI set standards that legitimized outdated models holding back the introduction of new product design. At the same time, standards contributed to improve small firms' productivity by upgrading what they already produced and exposed small firms to better production techniques which has been 'key to the survival' of even the smallest firms (interview, Ludhiana, 1997). The certification served as an important, and incremental, first step to raising the awareness of a sector dominated by myriad small producers to the importance of following product design guidelines. This exposure has had the most visible results among small exporters, many of whom are now building upon this awareness about quality to respond to increasingly stringent quality demands made by their overseas buyers (mainly in the Middle East) (interview, Ludhiana, 1997).

Secondly, the piecemeal improvement of product design and production technology among a handful of leading firms, exporters and component producers is not enough to turn around an ailing sector. Much more broad-based technological and organizational upgrading by the Punjab's diesel engine sector as a whole is critically important to improving the sector's performance.

The importance of broadening individual efforts at upgrading raises the third key issue. Why is Ludhiana's diesel engine industry doing so poorly when other localized industries in the region are doing well, especially bicycles and auto-components? Why are all industries (or at least all metal-based industries) in the same region not able to share equally in the region's overall economic growth? During the field work, this difference was stark. While diesel engine factories seemed resigned to being players in a declining sector with bleak future prospects, firms in the bicycle industry were growth-oriented, virtual beehives of activity and focused on innovation and expansion. Many firms had actively initiated modernization programs and although led by medium and large firms,[9] the momentum of change had impacted on the entire industry including small firms. (Over 90 per cent of the firms in Ludhiana's bicycle industry are small in scale, and most are performing very well.)

Why are these diesel engine producers stagnating? Why are they unable to tap into local networks of skill, expertise and specialized services available in Ludhiana to initiate innovations or make improvements? In light of the view in the district literature that secondary institutions are important to providing skill, information, advice and services that lend dynamism to a local industry precisely because they are adaptable, jointly constituted by local firms, and easily accessible given their local base, why were Ludhiana's diesel engine firms unable to benefit from the same institutions that have made the region's bicycle and sewing machine industries so competitive? Why does the advantage of dynamic clustering, namely skill formation and upgrading, intermediate goods production, and other manufacturing services, appear to remain product specific?

I would argue that three factors have complicated the successful modernization of Punjab's diesel engine sector: (a) on the demand side, the structure of the government's 'agricultural' policy and energy subsidies and how it has shaped the structure of the domestic market for small diesel engines in India; (b) the spatial distribution of the diesel engine industry in India has led to cross-regional specializations at the expense of the Ludhiana-Phagwara district; and finally (c) on the supply side, the nature of the diesel engine assemblers' backward linkages to local input suppliers and to suppliers of base machinery that circumscribed the possibilities of technical upgrading in the sector. These issues will be expanded below.

2.1 The 'derivative' nature of the sector's origin and the role of the government's agricultural and energy policies in shaping demand

Many analysts and policymakers like to point out that India's diesel engine sector owes its existence to the failure, or at least inadequacy, of India's infrastructure and energy policies. The industry practically originated in response to chronic power shortages, inadequate canal-based irrigation, and growing demand from agriculture for irrigation in the post-war period (Gulati 1997). From the time when the industry first took root in Punjab in the 1940s, the region's diesel engine industry has been dominated by small firms and structured around a low-end product – the low-speed, low-horsepower (3–25 hp) stationary diesel engine used primarily for agricultural purposes, such as operating farm equipment including irrigation pumpsets, threshers, de-watering equipment and electric generators (Government of Punjab 1970). The most popular early models in the industry were the British Lister and Peter engines, and variations of these engines are still used today.[10]

Three government policies have directly and indirectly influenced the growth of the diesel engine sector and are, in part, responsible for this long holdover of old models in the industry: (a) the government's policy of reserving the production of certain items (such as low-speed diesel engines) exclusively within the small firm sector; (b) its past policy of fiscal support for agrarian users by tying subsidies to specific low-cost models of diesel engines; and (c) its energy policies in the 1970s that sought to deal with rising global oil prices.

Since 1967, the Indian government has reserved the production of low-speed diesel engines of up to 15 hp, with fuel consumption less than 180 bhp exclusively for the small firm sector.[11] But, even within this low-end category, engines with fuel efficiency better than 180 bhp per hour can be produced by firms of all sizes. This means that small firms wishing to take advantage of the exemptions from excise and sales tax that the reservation policy provides them, face an implicit disincentive to improve fuel efficiency beyond 180 BHP per hour. Producing improved engines not only opens them up to competition from better endowed larger firms, but also eliminates the tax advantages they would otherwise enjoy. Clearly, the reservation policy, in specifying a threshold of fuel efficiency below which only small firms could participate, and above which firms of all sizes are allowed to compete, has perversely locked the smallest firms into the least efficient segment of the small diesel engine market.[12]

A second set of policies that has dampened innovation in this sector is linked to subsides given to farmers to buy diesel engines for agricultural equipment and generators. Since the mid-1960s, when irrigation and farm mechanization became important ingredients of the green-revolution package being diffused across the country, State governments have provided subsidies of up to 25 per cent, as well as soft loans to farmers for the purchase of agricultural equipment.[13] Diesel-powered pumpsets, generators and threshers fall within this category of subsidized equipment. Purchase subsidies are a key source of demand for locally-made diesel engines, pumpsets and generators. The odd twist is that these subsidies have been restricted to only two types of models – the Lister and Petter type of models, both of which are over 40 years old (Gulati 1997). This perverse linkage of policy support for specific brands that are now outdated has kept small producers from introducing new more fuel-efficient, less polluting and less noisy models because their main buyers – farmers – can get government subsidies only for the older models. The main motivation for this criterion in the allocation of subsidies was driven by the government's desire to keep costs low for small farmers – and were ironically intertwined with the government's efforts to 'improve' fuel efficiency in the wake of the global oil crisis in the 1970s.

Starting with the energy crisis of the early 1970s and late 1970s, a consortium of government and industry groups led by the ISI, as noted earlier, launched an effort to standardize (and rationalize) the key diesel engine models that were available in the Indian market at that time in order to improve fuel efficiency. Once the standardization of the key models was complete, the government sought to encourage consumers to buy the 'improved' models (and for firms to produce them) by attaching subsidies to the new models for agricultural and industrial users. While in the short run this led to the elimination of poor performing knock-offs, and improved demand for the more fuel-efficient engines, the long-run consequence was that it locked the industry (at the low cost, low horsepower ends) into the production of models that soon became outdated. But because of powerful political economy dynamics that are associated with agricultural subsidies, the government found it difficult to remove the product subsidies until recently.

The government's subsidy and the lack of demand from farmers for the more expensive, upgraded products, resulted in a stifling of incentives for diesel engine firms to introduce new and improved models and upgrade their production processes, and segmented the market between a few modernized large firms and a vast number of small, noncompetitive firms. Indeed, recent efforts by some large domestic firms to produce (or import) new versions of lighter, more efficient diesel engines that are popular in the world market have received little policy support from the government. Competing against cheap and subsidized engines produced by small local firms, the innovative firms that have introduced new models have fared badly. For example, the SriRam group recently introduced a small, lightweight 3.1 hp engine with a built-in pumpset using alternative fuel and state of the art materials (at 27 kg, the SriRam-Honda aluminum-alloy engine is over six times lighter than the 180 kg Petter engines). But in their effort to reach agrarian buyers, they have not done well on the market, mainly because their engines 'cost twice as much as a regular 5 hp stationary diesel engine' (Gulati 1997, p. 116). Other firms producing high-technology, low-weight engines in collaboration with Lombardini (Italy) and Hertz (Germany) are struggling to find buyers because of their higher unit prices.

Thus, the first general reason for the surprisingly slow technical modernization of the small-scale diesel engine sector in India, and of the Ludhiana district in particular, is the price-sensitive nature of the primarily agrarian consumers of small diesel engines, and perverse effects on product upgrading and innovation of the government's reservation policy and fiscal support for outdated and less efficient models.

2.2 Cross-regional specialization in the diesel engine industry

A second reason why Ludhiana's diesel engine industry, specifically, is doing poorly and appears less successful than other sectors in that region, I would argue, is that the heart of the diesel engine manufacturing process – precision machining – lies elsewhere. This relates directly to the geography of the diesel engine industry in India. India's diesel engine industry (in the small-scale sector) has three main production centers: Ludhiana-Phagwara in Punjab State, Rajkot in Gujarat State[14] and Agra in UP State. Although these clusters compete with each other, the spatial structure of the industry presents 'cross-regional' specializations. That is, even though assembly occurs in all locations, a rough division of labor has evolved in these regions, and different bundles of activities and different phases of the production process have become localized in different regions. Most of the casting and forging work is done in Ludhiana and Agra, while the more sophisticated and skill-intensive activities that are critical to defining product quality, such as precision machining, are carried out in Rajkot, Gujarat. Some of the most critical components of the diesel engine (piston, piston rings, fuel pumps) are sourced from large firms, some of whom are also based in the Gujarat region. Of the three locations, Gujarat's Rajkot district is the best performing diesel engine center in the small and medium-scale sector.

The cross-spatial structure of the diesel engine industry contrasts with the localization of all key production phases of an industry in one region that is usually emphasized in the ID literature. In the ID literature the benefits to firms from colocation come from close ties that develop among firms across all key phases of a subsector that are geographically concentrated in one region (Piore and Sabel 1984; Nadvi and Schmitz 1994; Clara et al. 2000). The segmentation of specializations across space in the diesel engine industry described here, led to the development of quite different circles of skill formation and productive capabilities in each region. Because key processes such as machining, which make strong demands on worker skills, were localized in Rajkot (Gujarat), such skill-based spillovers have atrophied in Ludhiana's diesel engine sector. The ability to innovate and change designs or product quality is closely associated with having control over the production of components that are responsible for the inner working of the engine. These components are manufactured mostly in Rajkot.

Of the over 300 components of various sizes and of varying importance that go into a diesel engine, Punjab specializes in the manufacture of sheet-metal parts, cast and forged parts (including the casting and forging of some of the core components that are then machined in Rajkot), and in general components that require foundry work, as well as certain types of machining. These components include the body block, crankcase, flywheel, balancing weights, oil pump, gears, crankshaft, camshaft, fuel tank and so on. Only about a half dozen firms in Punjab produce the more sophisticated machined components such as crankshafts, camshafts and pistons. Indeed, firms in both Agra and Rajkot procure a significant proportion of cast and forged components from Punjab, and reciprocally, Punjab's assemblers are dependent on Rajkot for the more critical components. The casting and forging functions that dominate in Ludhiana-Phagwara and in Agra are the initial, basic manufacturing stages; some of these parts are machined in Punjab, but most of the output is sold by Ludhiana's foundries to machinists in Rajkot. Ludhiana's assemblers then buy back the machined parts from Rajkot for assembly into the finished engines they put together. Firms in Rajkot also assemble and produce the whole engine, but Punjab specializes in selling finished engines in the form of knock-down kits. Thus, a large proportion of Punjab's diesel engine firms are either component producers, casting and forging units, or final assemblers of full machine kits.

A second kind of division of labor emerges in the distribution of activities across the three industrial clusters in relation to the size of components firms produce. Rajkot's firms produce nearly all of the 'larger' structural components of the engine (cranks, piston, cylinder head); while nearly 80 per cent of the smaller, often non-structural components that go into the engine are manufactured in the Ludhiana-Phagwara district. These smaller parts are cast (or forged where necessary), machined and finished in Ludhiana.

On the face of it, this local specialization in components by size appears puzzling. The growth of the diesel engine industry in Punjab has historically been nurtured by key spillovers from the forging and machining industries associated with the region's bicycle, sewing machine and auto-components sectors. Thus it is curious why the casting and forging industries that have served the other metal-based industries in the district so well have not been able to accommodate the needs of the diesel engine sector by expanding to produce the components that the sector currently imports from Rajkot which is hundreds of miles away. Why, in turn, have Ludhiana's diesel engine producers not been able to make demands on the skilled networks and machinists already present in the district to make such localization possible? Part of the reason behind this, firms reported, lies in the economies of scale and engineering efficiencies that Rajkot has developed over time for the production of the core diesel engine components (cranks, pistons) that are generally much larger in size and heavier than the parts used in bicycles, sewing machines, and the kinds of auto-components produced in Ludhiana. Apart from forging and casting, the tools, dies, and machinery needed for machining the larger parts of the diesel engine with precision are different from those used in the bicycle and sewing machine industry and would need to be specially manufactured and installed. Ludhiana's forging and machining firms repeatedly said there simply was not enough demand in the diesel engine sector to localize these parts in Punjab and that there was no point in competing with Rajkot when the firms there had organized production in a way that had brought down costs 'as low as they can go'.[15] Thus, while the productive infrastructure – good quality machining equipment and sophisticated workers – available in Ludhiana can handle 'smaller' and 'finer' parts, small firms in Rajkot have developed a capability for handling larger parts more efficiently.

This cross-regional specialization is an aspect of the industry's geography and history that is likely to complicate the process of modernizing the diesel industry in any one production site because the existing structure of the industry cannot sensibly be regarded as comprising self-contained regional clusters that can be dealt with separately. In order to intervene meaningfully in one region (such as Ludhiana-Phagwara, Rajkot or Agra), the industry's linkages with the other sites and the cross-regional nature of the industry as a whole will need to be taken into account. For example, as we saw, the lack of core machining functions in Ludhiana is an important reason why technological modernization has been slow and piecemeal in that region compared to more dynamic centers such as Rajkot. Certain key skills, capabilities, and productive infrastructure related to specific, quality-determining segments of the diesel engine industry never developed in Punjab.

Policy implications of the industry's cross-regional nature and current circumstances are that any such localization of sophisticated machining, forging or casting will need to be accompanied by substantial new growth in demand in the sector as a whole. Without an infusion of new demand, or change in consumer preferences for the low-cost but outdated models linked to government subsidies as mentioned above, to lighter weight, innovative and efficient, albeit costlier, products, the industry would likely maintain the existing division of labor between firms in Ludhiana, Agra and Rajkot and perpetuate the *status quo*. This does not mean that upgrading necessarily must occur in all sites simultaneously to succeed. The point, rather, is that an awareness of the nature of the industry's cross-regional ties provides clues about the conditions under which upgrading can occur in the various sites. The sequence of steps needed for modernization of the Ludhiana cluster may differ from the strategy in Rajkot.[16] A policy that focuses on localizing the core, precision-intensive parts of the production chain currently missing from Ludhiana's diesel engine sector in isolation from demand-enhancing policies, is likely to fail. A policy sequence that focuses first on increasing the overall demand for the diesel engine sector may create the very conditions for large volumes and hence economies of scale, triggering the localization of the more sophisticated operations to occur in Ludhiana-Phagwara.

Initially at least, it may work well for any such a modernization program to target the export sector, where international competition has already forced Indian firms to upgrade and innovate and where prices are accordingly set higher than domestically. The most plausible connection may be to help improve the quality of component producers whom both exporting firms and domestic assemblers can jointly tap. Another way to revitalize the diesel engine industry in Ludhiana would be to identify other high-growth-related sectors that would increase its demand threshold; this would mean, for instance, shifting to the production of diesel-based components for the fast growing two, three and four-wheeler automotive sector.

2.3 Lack of raw materials of good quality?

The issue over which there was perhaps the greatest consensus in the field among firms, consultants and government officials was that a key impediment to technological upgrading in the diesel engine sector is the chronic lack of availability of good quality raw material at affordable prices. In this view, adopting new technologies and introducing new models require the use of sophisticated raw materials, such as high-quality steel alloys or modern aluminum alloys.

Raw material inputs such as these are neither easily available to small firms nor affordable. Most small firms in the diesel engine sector throughout India and in Ludhiana therefore use low-grade steel, such as mild steel or pig iron, for many components. Even the small firms that do use alloy steel use lighter, or less dense alloy steel in place of the higher-quality standards that are the industry norm. For example, one Ludhiana-based firm that in recent years has made the most headway in upgrading its engine design said that even after upgrading, the best it could afford was EN18 alloy steel for the same components that larger firms use EN52 for. The quality, weight and density of these two kinds of alloy are completely different, as are their final prices.

Small firms and the agencies serving them complain that they are ignored by specialized input providers, including government parastatals such as the Steel Authority of India and importers. The reason is that they lack the scale economies that large producers enjoy, and hence place smaller orders which result in higher per unit costs for the smaller firms. Importing raw materials directly is also cumbersome and costly for small firms for the same reasons of low demand and small orders – and few have attempted to do so. In addition to this cost differential, many small firms pointed out that even if they were able to procure the appropriate raw materials, they would still be penalized due to the brand-name recognition that the larger firms enjoy: small firms noted that they would 'never get the rates' that larger firms are able to command for their engines and components to economically justify the upgrading.

One obvious way to approach this dilemma would be to try and eliminate the cost gap that small and large firms face for every ton of steel by pooling input demand across small firms to lower unit costs. The empirical literature on IDs has repeatedly shown that under certain circumstances the pooling of input demand across small firms via input and marketing consortia helps lower procurement costs as well as marketing by allowing small firms to jointly exploit the economies of scale in these activities (Schmitz and Musyck 1994; Nadvi and Schmitz 1994; Tendler 1997).

In regions like Ludhiana, where there is a history of collaboration, this may be a feasible option. However, field work showed that if 'broad-based' technological upgrading among small diesel engine producers in the Ludhiana district is the goal, it is unlikely to follow automatically from the pooling of input demand or improving small firm access to good quality raw materials. Upgrading is not just a matter of making better quality alloy steel available to small firms at reasonable rates, but it is a process that would involve a chain of changes throughout the production process before small firms could adopt and use the new materials. These cascading structural changes will need to occur not only among small diesel engine producers, but also across firms that service them, test their products, repair the final product, and provide them with locally-made tools and machinery. In other words, for upgrading to really take place it will need to extend far beyond the circle of diesel engine producers, all the way down to component suppliers and the producers of base machinery.

For example, if Punjab's small diesel component producers use alloy steel of the appropriate integrity (for example, EN52 instead of EN18), they will have to alter their entire casting and forging processes. Specifically, service-providing firms will have to shift away from their current practice of pattern casting toward the more standard practice of die casting – a far more accurate process, but also a far more expensive operation, currently used mainly by larger firms. Pattern casting cannot be done with alloy steel which is much harder and denser than the lower-quality mild steel that firms currently use, and requires much higher temperatures to be cast or moulded than does ordinary steel. A shift away from pattern casting would therefore mean that most of the current furnaces used by small diesel component producers would have to be scrapped and replaced entirely.

Similarly, local firms would have to restructure their entire system of testing, machining, and finishing. Currently most small firms use softer steel such as mild steel to make some components, and they are able to conduct a number of boring, punching and grinding operations on the components with specialized tools, jigs and fixtures that can be mounted on simple lathes or milling machines. These specialized tools, jigs and fixtures are made locally by firms in Ludhiana's well-established and quite innovative machine tool industry. The latter not only supplies small firms with tools and machinery cheaply, the presence of skilled craftsmen means that they can custom-build tools for use on general purpose machines lowering costs by eliminating the need for complicated special purpose machines.

For example, diesel engine firms often use these locally-made tools and fixtures to cut gears one by one, instead of using costly special-purpose gear-hobbing machines. All of these tool-based operations are carried out on the steel or sheet-metal component before it is hardened to the requisite degree; however, if high-strength alloy steel is used, this sequence of steps would have to change. Alloy steels are already hard. The locally-made tools, jigs and fixtures that small firms use to bore and grind and do machining simply would not work on alloy steel. The components cut out of alloy steel would first have to be heated to a high-enough degree to be softened adequately, and then worked upon by a whole different class of tools, dies and fixtures – which themselves would have to be made of hardened, superior materials.[17] Such tools – as opposed to the improvised, and often innovative tools currently used by firms to achieve complex operations on simple general purpose machines – would cost a lot more and would require quite different kinds of skills to manufacture locally. Indeed, the base machinery that firms currently use – lathes, milling machines, planers and so forth – would themselves have to be upgraded, in terms of being made of higher-strength materials themselves. Several of the locally-made machines currently used by small diesel engine firms cannot take the temperatures required to handle alloy steel and still yield adequate accuracy. The same is true for the oils, fuels and solvents used to operate (and maintain) these machines.

Upgrading raw material quality is not such a straightforward proposition after all. Apart from the changes needed in the diesel engine sector, the ancillary machinery sector in Punjab would have to upgrade its own production processes and material used to manufacture machinery and tools that can work on harder alloys. Radical changes would be needed along the entire production chain surrounding small diesel engine producers to fully implement the upgrading. Small suppliers and machinery producers in an industry suffering from stagnant demand and low end-product prices are unlikely to initiate these broad-based changes, unless there is large enough future demand to justify the restructuring. A consensus among firms and local officials that poor raw materials and outdated technology are the culprits behind the diesel engine industry's lack of dynamism does not necessarily lead to one unique solution. The barrier to improving quality, then, is not only the lack of availability of cheap alloy steel, but an institutional process that involves the local social and knowledge system in Ludhiana. A set of simultaneous policy reforms would have to aim at providing public and private funds and technical support to allow the substantial swath of interlinked firms that provide machinery, services and components to the diesel industry to also upgrade. In the long run, in order to upgrade the final product, the entire production chain and the set of skills and technologies underpinning it has to be upgraded as well. The simple bottom line is that those seeking to intervene need to be prepared to handle the larger ripples of change that will emerge from underneath this issue. From the perspective of the region's competitiveness this would be a desirable outcome.

3. CONCLUSION

This chapter started with a puzzle. In a region noted for its industrial resilience, why are some industries doing poorly while other, linked sectors are performing well? This contribution used the case of Ludhiana's diesel engine industry to reflect on why some localized industries perform poorly even though they are anchored in institutional environments where other, related sectors, are doing well. I argue that there are three key reasons behind this lag in the sector's modernization. First, the origin of the industry and the structure of government policy kept firms locked into the production of old models. Government subsidies were tied to particular models rather than to diesel engines *per se*. Second, local firms remain locked into existing networks that are cross-regional. The dynamic portion of the production process was located in another State, and therefore there are fewer pressures and incentives for local firms in Ludhiana to initiate innovative changes. The larger point here relates to how, and under what conditions, inter-industry spillovers occur or do not occur within clusters. Third, in the context of low demand and a spatially-dispersed location of the industry's core operations, the very features that are a source of institutional strength for the cluster's other metal-based sectors, namely the local production of low-cost tools, dies, jigs, fixtures, machinery and components, became an impediment to modernization in the case of diesel engines.

Grabher (1990) characterizes the 'weakness of strong ties' as arising when tightly-linked networks of producers miss signals for change and transformation coming from the outside environment because local networks reinforce old practices that were once useful, but are no longer viable. Punjab's diesel engine industry is similarly locked into a vicious cycle of this 'obsolete reinforcement' of outdated practices due to a variety of factors related to both national government policies and rigidities in the local production chain.

This has two implications for thinking about policies and programs that support small firm upgrading. First, it is critical to place the design of modernization programs within the wider context of the structure of the industry, its production chain and its geography; and second, in cases such as those described here, it is important to combine technical upgrading with demand-enhancing policies. As the evidence from the diesel industry suggests, a narrow focus on technical upgrading *per se* is unlikely to be effective unless embedded within efforts to link local firms with 'demand pull' from growing sectors or broader markets. Local firms in the diesel industry and government officials, for example, said that access to raw materials is a key constraint on upgrading: new models need new materials, that are expensive and not easily available. But I found that the problem of upgrading is not merely a problem of procuring good quality materials at low rates. It is rather institutional: given the interlinked nature of the industry, the circle of upgrading would need to extend far beyond just the diesel engine firms themselves, down to the machinery-producing firms and the casting and forging industries for product and process upgrading among final producers to work. The more general point here is that when thinking about technological upgrading and, in particular, designing modernization programs we often narrowly target the end-user industry of interest – diesel engines, electronics and so on – often overlooking the underlying production structures and the system of knowledge and technology formation into which the specific industry is anchored.

The pockets of success within Punjab's own diesel engine case illustrate this point. Despite the sector's overall decline, some component producers who produce spares for the local and export market, and exporters who export finished diesel engines and 'knock-down kits' to low and middle-income overseas markets are doing very well. These firms have been able to tie into growing, albeit more competitive, markets, and have had better unit value realization and greater incentives to upgrade and modernize. Building upon the Indian Standards Bureau's efforts at standardization, local exporters have been working hard in recent years with their overseas buyers to meet newer and increasingly demanding quality standards. In most cases this has involved successful product and process upgrading. These successes point to the important role of demand linkages in helping revitalize the sector.

Modernization programs can explicitly look at this case study on the Ludhiana diesel engine industry to understand how greater exposure to dynamic end markets, and strategic assistance by agencies that set technical and performance standards can trigger upgrading and firms' innovation capacity. At the same time, the case also illustrates how the same mix of collective behaviors and government policies that can engender innovation at one point in time can also keep segments of the production chain stagnant and tied to obsolete technology and demand if they become too engrained and backward looking. Government policies and inter-firm linkages need to be upgraded and adapted just as much as production processes and technologies do.

NOTES

* Funding for field-research reported in this chapter was provided by the Small and Medium Enterprises Branch, UNIDO, Vienna, as part of a larger project, and is gratefully acknowledged. I am grateful to Ray Burby for extensive feedback on an earlier draft. A modified earlier version was published as a chapter in P.M. Mathew (ed.), *Beyond Old Equations: Small Enterprise Experience and Perspectives in India*, New Delhi: Kanishka Press, 2003.
1. Field work involved factory visits, interviews with manufacturers, assemblers, exporters, component producers, government officials and trade associations in both regions. I also attended two full day meetings between government officials, local business associations and visiting overseas buyer delegations, including a meeting in Ludhiana between a visiting delegation from Egypt of public and private sector buyers of diesel engines, and members of the Ludhiana-Phagwara Diesel Engine Exporters Association.
2. See Grabher (1990) for a similar argument.
3. Ludhiana is Punjab's richest district. With a total population of three million, of which 1.7 million are urban, Ludhiana has 43 467 firms of which 99.6 per cent are small and medium in scale. These firms, noted for their productivity, export a third of their output and control a substantial national market share in their leading sectors. These are, in order of importance, woolen hosiery and mills, bicycle and bicycle components, auto-components, sewing machines, hand-tools and cutting machinery and a variety of agricultural implements, including diesel engines.
4. Punjab, a primarily agrarian State was at the heart of India's green revolution and has the third highest per capita income in the country.
5. The total exports of diesel engines in India amount to roughly Rs. 3600 million. Of this Ludhiana-Phagwara accounts for about 10 per cent of direct exports (Rs. 350 million) and about 41 per cent via indirect exports (Rs. 1500 million). (Data from Mukesh Gulati's discussions with secretary of the Phagwara Diesel Engine Exporters Association.)
6. Six hundred seventy miles to be precise.
7. Now called the Indian Standards Bureau.
8. ISI or the Indian Statistical Institute formulates national standards for all final goods produced in the country and getting an ISI mark implies that a firm's product meets the national standard.
9. For example, a medium-sized firm had developed its own cold-forging technology (for Rs. 0.4–0.5 million as against the import price of Rs. 10 million). Another large firm, the Hero group, had paid Rs. 30 million to McKinsey for a study of the modernization strategy of the group. Many small bicycle producers were similarly focused on modernization and

making improvements, such as using cold instead of hot forging technologies, and turning to aluminum alloys instead of steel components.
10. In the 1960s a large firm, Kirloskar, located outside Punjab in Pune in Western India improved on these original models and established the 'Kirloskar' engine, which became the new industry standard and was widely copied across the country.
11. Only a few large firms (such as Kirloskar) that were already in place prior to the enforcement of the reservation policy are allowed to produce low-speed engines.
12. Another contributor to cost is operating expense. The Lister-type diesel engine can run on cheaper fuel – for example, 50 per cent crude oil. More recent models (including the middling 'Kirloskar' model) need purer fuel (refined oil) to operate. From the demand side, then, given the bottlenecks in procuring purer oil, and its higher cost, farmers are arguably reluctant to switch to machines that are not only costlier but lock them into higher recurring cost of using pumpsets because of expensive fuel oils, whose easy supply is far from assured (interview, Ludhiana 1996).
13. Some States with chronic power shortages, low levels of canal irrigation and lagging agriculture that continue to provide these subsidies are UP, Rajasthan, Madhya Pradesh, Bihar and parts of West Bengal.
14. Along with Indore and Pune in the Center-West.
15. Indeed, the Lister-type model which was the diesel engine produced by small firms throughout India in the 1960s and 1970s, was first introduced in Phagwara in Punjab and almost simultaneously in Rajkot (Gujarat). While Punjab's machinists were already heavily geared toward producing parts for bicycles and sewing machines, the producers of diesel engines in Rajkot soon developed an extensive division of labor and equipment base to produce large-sized, machined pumpset and diesel engine components with great precision and economy.
16. For example, between 2003 and 2005 a number of agencies such as UNIDO, the Entrepreneurship Development Institute of Gujarat and local industrial development banks intervened in the Rajkot cluster to make it more competitive in the face of challenges from lighter weight diesel engines from China that were then flooding the market. Because Rajkot already controlled the main engineering segments of the sector the focus was on benchmarking, technical upgrading and the formation of an informal 'entrepreneurship' circle of a subset of engineering firms to introduce new products. The cluster's productivity rose by 20 per cent by 2007, rejections fell from 12 to 5 per cent and a new indigenously upgraded model was to be launched by 2008 (Foundation for MSME Clusters 2007 – MSME stands for micro, small and medium enterprises). These institutions did not intervene in Ludhiana's diesel cluster, in part because of the sector's smaller size there and because several segments in the value chain were missing.
17. In interviews, local firms said repeatedly that using raw materials such as steel of lower strength, instead of alloys, does not necessarily compromise the accuracy of the machines themselves; but it lowers the machine's economic life, and prevents materials that require high levels of tempering to be used on these machines. That in effect is the 'cascading' quality effect of the kind of base machinery a firm uses. If the base machinery is of lower order materials, the quality of raw materials it can handle will also be circumscribed.

45. The scope of industrial districts in the Third World

Werner Sengenberger

1. FOREWORD

Industrial districts (IDs) may be viewed as instruments of economic and social development. They may help to reduce widespread poverty and income gaps within and between nations. This chapter aims at exploring the chances for the emergence, growth and viability of IDs in developing countries. Particular attention is paid to the economic, social and institutional environment prevailing in various parts of the developing world and the impact of economic globalisation.

2. SCOPE FOR IDs IN THE THIRD WORLD

In taking a broader perspective on the chances for the emergence and viability of IDs in developing countries, both favourable and adverse predicaments can be identified. First of all, it helps if a country has a setting conducive to manufacturing industries. Manufacturing is important for development because it is the most stable source of higher incomes and jobs in a locality due to its large potential to improve productivity. Virtually all cases of IDs studied in Italy and elsewhere in the industrialised countries, but also all instances of IDs or clusters in the developing world, relate to the manufacturing sector. Most of the districts that have become known produce durable consumer goods, but there are also IDs operating in the investment goods sector.

Starting from this observation we may expect that IDs are more likely to be found in countries with a comparatively large industry or manufacturing sector. While in almost all advanced industrialised countries the share of employment in industry is more than 20 per cent, and in some even more than 30 per cent, it is on average lower in countries of medium-level development, and even less in the least-developed countries (LDCs). In Africa, the proportion of employment in industry can be as low as 3 per cent, whereas agriculture still employs as much as 90 per cent of the working population. But there are exceptions to this pattern. Newly industrialised countries, including Mexico, Ecuador, Morocco, Mauritius, Iran, Republic of Korea and Taiwan have reached similar, or even higher, proportions of industrial employment than the older industrialised countries (see ILO 2008b).

A small manufacturing sector within the national economy does not rule out a potential for future development of IDs. For example, there is a huge scope in many poor countries for the development of an agro-industry by way of processing agricultural products (for example, to food, textiles and garments) in rural areas. In fact, rural industrialisation has emerged in some areas of the South during the last decades and has become highly important for employment generation for the rural masses.

Significant scope exists for the development of knowledge-based 'creative industries' including traditional crafts, books, visual and performing arts, music and film industries, new media and design. Today, these are among the most dynamic sectors in developed countries, and increasingly in developing countries. According to UNCTAD, they are a feasible strategic option for diversifying the economies of developing countries, including LDCs, offering new venues for those countries to leapfrog into value added high-growth sectors. They can help to foster income generation, job creation and export earnings while preserving and promoting social inclusion and cultural heritage and cultural diversity. China is leading this process. In Shanghai, for example, creative industries accounted for 6.5 per cent of GDP in 2006. The city has 75 creative industrial parks or clusters, with a focus in areas such as design in architecture and fashion, new media, and publishing and audiovisuals (UNCTAD 2008a).

Second, macroeconomic policies are a critical factor for business development in general, and that of small and medium-sized enterprises (SMEs) in particular. Monetary and fiscal policies have to be sufficiently expansionary to generate a level of aggregate demand that will enable the economy to grow and create jobs. The macroeconomic environment has to also provide economic stability to reduce risks for enterprises and for developing business linkages in the internal and external markets. Small firms that operate in export markets are particularly vulnerable to exchange rate fluctuations. With few exceptions, macroeconomic volatility occurs much more frequently in developing countries than industrialised countries, and it has much higher welfare costs for poor countries than for rich ones. The appreciation of a national currency can render firms uncompetitive, especially those unable to use forward purchasing. Vulnerability and shocks loom where countries have piled up huge deficits in their current accounts. Sooner or later, they are likely to suffer from currency depreciation triggering financial crisis.

Third, public regulation of SMEs may be propitious or adverse for the development of IDs, and especially for small enterprises in districts. There are countries where certain economic activities are reserved for small firms. A notable example is the ancillary industries in India where as many as 850 product items, largely consumer products, were designated by the government for manufacturing in small enterprises. As a result, large enterprises started to decentralize to qualify for operation in the designated product fields. Of course, small-sized production units alone do not engender IDs or clusters, but they may be considered as a favourable prerequisite.

Fourth, viable small business communities depend on a favourable residential structure. High population density and the resulting spatial concentration of supply and demand appear to be conducive for the 'thickening' of industrial activities and the clustering of business. A critical mass of firms within a given space has proven to be necessary for the development of successful business linkages (UNCTAD 2006). The known cases of performing IDs in Italy and elsewhere are mainly located in or around highly-populated urban centres. The same seems to be true for IDs in developing countries. he growth of China's industrial clusters and its extremely rapid urbanisation appear be closely interrelated. An estimated 155 million people have migrated from rural areas to cities during the last twenty years. Between now and the year 2025, another 200–250 million Chinese will migrate to urban centres (World Bank 2008).

Fifth, the composition and professional qualification of the labour force is an important determinant of the chance for ID-type industrial organisations to emerge and prosper. Among the critical factors are a sufficient supply of vocational and technical skills and entrepreneurial and managerial competence. In the absence of qualified human resources it is likely that survival clusters and low-road development occur.

Sixth, one of the outstanding features of developing countries is a large proportion of self-employed and contributing family members in the labour force, whereas the share of dependently employed workers is typically small. In many developing economies, the share of the self-employed labour force is more than 20 per cent, and in some LDCs it reaches more than 50 per cent. One may assume that sizeable proportions of self-employed would constitute a good precondition for small-firm districts. It is not clear, however, how the causation runs: whether self-employment is a prerequisite for the spread of IDs, or conversely, whether it is the result of the formation of IDs. In this connection it is interesting to see that among the industrialised countries Italy, that is known for its high density of ID structures, has a comparatively large proportion of self-employed (23.1 per cent in 2003), compared to less than 10 per cent in countries like Sweden, France and the US (for statistical data see ILO 2008b, pp. 138ff.).

Seventh, another conspicuous feature of many developing countries is the high level and the continuing growth of 'informal economic activities'. Often, these cover nearly all sectors of the national economy. (For this reason, the earlier term 'informal sector' has been replaced by the term 'informal economy'.) Reliable data on the size of the informal economy are available for

47 countries. In 17 of them the share of informal employment is in excess of 50 per cent. It runs as high as 64 per cent in Pakistan, 65 per cent in Nepal, 67 per cent in Tanzania, and 90 per cent in India. The share has increased in all developing regions except East Asia (ILO 2002). In Latin America the urban informal economy was the primary job generator during the 1990s. Informal employment increased by 3.9 per cent per annum in that decade, while formal economy employment grew by only 2.1 per cent. On average, 60 per cent of new jobs were created by micro-enterprises, own account workers and domestic services (ILO 2005, p. 106). The rise of the informal economy runs counter to the earlier expectation that it would successively be absorbed by the formal economy. The reasons for the growth include the conversion of formal enterprises to informal ones in order to save taxes and to escape protective labour laws; and the tolerance for such practices by public authorities that believe that the attractiveness of the country for foreign investors would rise.

Eighth, the literature on IDs directs attention to the importance of social, cultural and institutional conditions. For example, Becattini points to the significance of a homogeneous system of values and views (Becattini 1990, p. 39), and he and almost any other analyst of IDs emphasize the role of social institutions, such as families, churches, technical schools, professional associations, local authorities, political parties and trade unions. Piore (1992, p. 54) alerted us to the frequent ethnic roots of IDs, such as immigrant groups in the US, and the ethno-industrialisation in North Africa. The presence of trust stands out as an extremely important precondition for sustainable and successful business communities. Trust may be defined as 'the mutual confidence that no party to an economic exchange will exploit the other's vulnerability' (Sabel 1992, p. 215). The presence or absence of the formation of 'social capital', and especially trust and accountability, may explain why IDs prosper in some countries but not in others. For Italy it was found that trustful relations that are partly favoured by the inherited institutional context and partly through conscious action of individuals and collective organisations were crucial for the formation and reproduction of the competitive advantage of district firms (Dei Ottati 2004, p. 9). By contrast, in the former communist countries of central and eastern Europe, we find no or only weakly developed IDs, particularly those that resemble the prototype district. In the command economies, active participation of workers and the citizenry at large in economic and social life was discouraged by the centralist decision-making processes. Trade unions had a peculiar unorthodox role in the communist system, employers' organisations were absent, and communities played a minor role in development. In brief, civil society was underdeveloped. According to the Polish sociologist Sztompka there had been a shortage of trust as a requisite resource in transition countries, largely because the moral norms necessary for a market economy eroded under communism when it was a virtue 'to beat the system, to outwit authorities, and to evade rules and regulations' (Sztompka 1995).

Ninth, 'public support and local funds' form are an important contextual parameter. While developed countries usually have the budgetary capacity to provide massive public support to the private sector, for example to high-tech firms, R&D, access to venture capital, upgrading of infrastructure and promotion and protection of intellectual property, the lack of public funding in many developing countries leads to inadequate infrastructure and public services for small enterprise development. The cutting of import tariffs imposed as conditionality for loans on developing countries by the international financial institutions (notably the World Bank) under the so-called Structural Adjustment Programmes (SAPs) has deprived the poor countries of one of the few options left for securing public revenues. Overseas Development Aid (ODA) from rich countries has strongly declined during the last 15 years, and donors in rich countries have not lived up to promises made at various development conferences. Moreover, corporate tax competition among countries and communities, and the establishment of tax havens in order to lure investors have tended to reduce public revenues and the scope for public investment.

Finally, 'lacking or weak local credit facilities' hamper the emergence of small firm development. In response to that, micro-credit systems have emerged. They are capable of remedying the shortage of capital to some extent. Probably the best known example of a micro-credit system is the Grameen initiative in Bangladesh. The Grameen Bank not only provides financial services to small producers but also promotes an active social agenda. It brings both information technology and education to the poor. One outcome of this enterprise is that today there are 40 000 'telephone ladies' selling mobile telephone services in half of the villages of Bangladesh. Other examples of local support systems, including the provision of micro-credit, include the Self-employed Women's Association (SEWA) in India, and its replication as the Self-employed Women's Union (SEWU) in South Africa.

3. ECONOMIC AND SOCIAL SIGNIFICANCE OF IDs IN DEVELOPING COUNTRIES

The role of IDs for development, and in particular the contribution of performing prototype districts, may be gauged against two overriding conditions that we witness in the world economy today. One concerns the persistence of extreme poverty and deprivation in large parts of the developing world; the second relates to the increasing divergence in the average income and other welfare indicators, both within and between nations. The two interconnected trends pose utterly serious challenges to the global community.

'Extreme poverty' remains the number one global problem. The political will to redress this ill is reflected in the Millenium Goals of the United

Nations, the most important of which is to cut by one-half between 1990 and 2015 the number of people living in absolute poverty and suffering from hunger. According to the most recent World Bank estimates (Ravallion and Chen 2008), the share of the world's population struck by extreme poverty has been declining during the past quarter century, but the remaining poverty level is much higher than previously thought. Under the new figures, the Bank estimates the global number of extreme poor (with an income of less than US$1.25 per day) to be 1.4 billion people in 2005 (one in four of the world's population), as compared to 930 million using the former calculation. China's rate of extreme poverty was established at 16 per cent, and India's rate at 42 per cent. In Sub-Saharan Africa, despite recent average GDP growth, more than half of the population is living in extreme poverty, which means no shrinkage from the rate in 1981. Almost all of the recent decline in global poverty can be attributed to the diminution of poor people in China. Excluding this country from the calculation, the world is 'off track' from achieving Millenium Goal number one. There can hardly be any doubt that China's success in reducing its poverty is closely related to its industrialisation – a good part of it in industrial clusters – in the recent decades.

To be sure, next to economic performance and a highly-skewed income distribution, there are various other causes of poverty, including natural disasters, armed conflict, HIV/AIDS and other epidemics, shortage of clean water and a generally poor state of health of the population. But the predominant reason for persistent poverty in developing countries does lie in the economic organisation of the countries. Most of the poverty there arises from the unproductive nature of economic activities, especially in the informal economy. Hence, improving the productivity of the sectors that affect the working poor is a promising route to poverty reduction. On average, both labour productivity per capita and multi-factor productivity are low in many poor countries even though very large proportions of the working population work very long hours. There is empirical evidence of the link between labour productivity, low wages and poverty (ILO 2005, pp. 95ff.). Other sources of economic plight in developing countries are economic vulnerability and strong dependency on foreign countries or organisations. Bilateral trade agreements between developing countries and the most developed economies with subsidised production and export facilities have exacerbated the disadvantaged position of the poor countries in international trade. They have led to distorted, unfair trade. Many poor countries lack a viable manufacturing sector which is important as a source of income and employment. Often, their economies depend excessively on raw materials.

The other mega trend of our time relates to increased inequality of income, wealth and economic well being. The size of the income and welfare gaps between North and South have become grotesque. Between 1960 and 2002, the average GDP per capita (in constant 1995 US$) of the 20 poorest countries on earth increased from $212 to $267, while in the 20 richest countries, they increased from $11,417 to $32,339, marking a gigantic divergence in the average income level. In 24 African countries, GDP per capita is less today than in 1975 and in 12 countries it is even below its 1960 level (World Commission on the Social Dimension of Globalization 2004, p. 37). Globalisation has been cited as a major reason for this trend, but there are other reasons rooted in domestic policies and institutions. The liberalisation of capital markets has opened up the possibility of large-scale cross-national financial transfers. Contrary to what mainstream economists expect, net capital flows are not in the direction of developing countries, but instead to the rich, developed countries. This trend has been hardly counteracted and reversed by increased income due to higher prices for oil, gas and other raw materials simply because the revenues are largely appropriated by a small minority of the population. There is no doubt that this engenders continuing large global imbalances and grossly inequitable distributions of global resources. There are various economic, social and political implications of the divergence, all of them negative and worrisome. Among them are increased migration pressure and threats to peace and social cohesion. There is every reason to look for ways and means of reversing the trends.

Even where FDI flows from the North helped to engender industrial growth and employment in developing countries, this did not necessarily lead to a narrowing of the income and developing gap. The reason is that within the cross-national division of labour the poor countries often ended up at the low-value-adding end of production, for example, assembly operations, while high-value-adding activities, such as R&D, design, finance and marketing remain in the high-income countries. As a result, income levels between the poor and the rich countries do not converge as predicted by the standard economic theory. Instead they diverge. This does not hold for the East Asian countries that have increasingly taken higher value-added upstream activities and also medium and high-tech production. In fact, almost the entire increase of manufacturing value added from 1980 was recorded in East Asia, and industrialised countries still account for more than 70 per cent of manufacturing value added world wide (UNDP 2004, p. 117). The divergence pattern applies to other developing regions. Thus, Latin America has lost its manufacturing value-added share relative to Asia. Even Mexico, the region's most dynamic exporter, has been losing market share to East Asia, especially to China (ibid., p. 118). Mexico is a low-value-added producer of high-value-added, high-tech products. Much of its export growth has been built on simple assembly and re-export of imported products manufactured in maquiladora plants, with limited technological upgrading. The Mexican model of high export growth and low value added is characteristic of a larger group of countries, including garment producers in countries like Bangladesh, Honduras and Nicaragua.

Where the Mexican model prevails it works against the emergence and vitality of vertically-integrated IDs. While it does not preclude horizontal cooperation at the same stage of production (for example, assembly), it provides very limited chances for cooperation across production stages in the value chain. Worse, the production plants that are typically foreign-owned and -controlled are susceptive to relocation to other places as soon as opportunities for cheaper production open up.

In addition, there is the issue of the impact of international trade and investment on the quality of employment and work, and their link to local, national and international labour standards. There is a severe risk that globalisation depresses labour conditions and there is a development-retarding 'race to the bottom' of terms of employment and work. In a study of the furniture district of Cuidad Hidalgo in Mexico, Piore (2000) showed that pressure from the international market forced the shops in the district to violate not only international labour standards (such as the prohibition of child labour), but also their own standards existing prior to market opening. One option to avoid the depressive effect on employment quality would be to move up-market into the production of customised items for specialty niche markets, thus following the strategy of the Italian IDs and the earlier Marshallian districts in England.

Endogenous development based on local production systems, and small firm IDs in particular, could provide at least a partial answer to stem the two mega trends. Provided that current net capital flows could be redirected to poor countries, domestic investment scaled up and capacities and enabling environments in these countries upgraded, IDs have the capacity to combat poverty and rising inequality. They show a potential to generate the efficiency necessary to reduce economic plight and deprivation and satisfy consumer needs. They can help to strengthen the domestic economy in the context of advancing economic globalisation, thereby creating local growth, employment and income. They can widen the policy space for local actors, much of which has been lost during several decades of market liberalisation. The potential benefits of IDs and performing industrial clustering as competitive and productive social organisations explain the interest that the international donor community and aid agencies have shown in this type of organisation (see Posthuma in this section).

Domestic demand-led growth is a promising alternative to export-led growth which has increasingly dominated the international development strategy under the so-called Washington consensus. Export-led growth is beset with many problems, especially for the LDCs. These often lack the consumption power to allow people to buy their own products. Domestic growth depends critically on the rise of domestic markets and rising wages and consumption power, and these will not come about without sustained productivity enhancement. To create a virtuous circle of wage improvement, domestic market development and productivity improvement, IDs with large efficiency and innovation potentials can play an important role.

A further relevant dimension is product quality. IDs in the Third Italy and elsewhere in Europe have amply demonstrated that they are capable of delivering high product and service quality, and that this facility has much contributed to their competitive power in world markets. As Piore (2000) has shown, the problem with traditional industries in the developing world has been that that they cannot meet industrial standards of quality and reliability. They are forced therefore to compensate for their defects by reducing prices. One may add that lowering prices, in turn, entails low rates of investment and low wages which aggravate further the chances to compete on quality instead of price, and to succeed in the markets of developed countries which put increasing emphasis on high qualitative and technical standards. IDs might point the way to escape this vicious circle.

In this regard, it is worth looking at the case of China. Western observers have been telling us that the country owes much of its competitive performance to product and brand pirating, wage dumping (due to the suppression of free trade unions), and currency dumping (due to keeping the external value of its currency artificially low). It is questionable whether such policies and practices can be maintained for long and whether the steep growth path of China's industry is sustainable. The country already encounters social tensions because it develops highly unevenly, in terms of sectors, regions and urban and rural areas. Even greater conflicts may come from the heavy burden that the present growth pattern produces for coming generations due to fast degradation of the natural environment. Its symptoms are the shortage of clean water, heavy air pollution and health problems. On the other hand, recent research suggests that the competitive regime may be changing. In a study focused on the textile and clothing industry, Wang found that Chinese producers no longer rely just on the abundance of cheap labour in labour-intensive, low-value-added operations. China now takes over from developed countries more upstream activities or higher value-added processes such as clothing design or high-technology dyeing operations, software development and product R&D. Furthermore, the government made it a high priority to escape the danger of being locked in the 'low-road' labour-intensive and wage-squeezing approach and develop new and more effective governance strategies for improving the collective efficiency of local governments and firms (J. Wang 2006). Wang and Mei (in this section) confirm that in confronting the intensified global competition an unspecified number of firms in Chinese IDs have managed to upgrade their technological innovation capacity while others seem to be unable to do so, either continuing on the low-road regime or quitting production altogether. Upgrading may mean that the Chinese firms emancipate themselves from the control by western multinational companies that are interested in preserving their benefits derived from the received division of labour and low local production costs. In large part, the local effects depends on the competitive strategies of the transnational corporations (TNCs): whether they create footloose industries that migrate whenever cheaper locations are found, or whether they stabilize local production and commit themselves to stable local development.

4. RISING ECONOMIES IN THE CONTEXT OF GLOBALISATION

There remains a compelling case for public policy intervention to foster economic development in the global South. The emerging economy countries with the highest rates of GDP growth from the 1990s to the present, including China, the Republic of Korea, Vietnam, Malaysia and India, have been far from strictly following the free trade doctrine. They have used the opportunities provided by the international market, but they have retained import controls, regulations and subsidies. China still has not liberalised its capital accounts. Also, the East Asian economies went beyond relying on 'comparative advantages', starting to develop their endogenous industry potential. Activities of foreign TNCs were controlled in accordance with national policy goals, and directed to the transfer and upgrading of technology and the setting of local content rules, in order to maximize technological and economic spillover to the domestic enterprises. The US, the EU countries, Japan and other advanced countries had themselves gained their prosperity through mixed, extensively regulated economies. For their industrialisation, they have consistently deployed industrial policy, performance requirements, soft intellectual property regimes, subsidies and government procurement. They have been selective, slow and cautious in opening their economies. They protected their infant, and sometimes even their mature, industries. They restricted the entry of foreign investment. Why should the same be denied to the developing countries? What legitimizes the imposition of the Northern WTO agenda on trade and investment on countries of the South that was characterised by two observers (Chang and Green 2003) as 'Do as we say, not as we did'?

China has been able to escape the adverse effects of intensified global competition as it joined the multilateral trading system from a position of strength: spectacular success in export expansion; a sound balance-of-payments position; and abundant international reserves. Unlike China, however, most developing countries have a weaker economic, political and technological structure, and they do not have the same policy space to set propitious conditions for nourishing competitive enterprises and technological upgrading. Not only are they unable to achieve the required export surplus, they are also restrained from turning towards their internal markets due to the restrictive fiscal and monetary policies of their governments (Bhaduri 2005). Many have opened their capital accounts prematurely. Thus, they are placed at a particular disadvantage. Competition among the countries in the South has become fiercer than the competition between the North and the South, and most Southern countries have less financial capacity for counteracting the negative effects of this competition. The deadlock confronting the global trade talks in the present Doha Round of the WTO has resulted not only from disputes among the rich nations, and the rich and the poor countries, but also from disagreements between the top tier of the emerging market economies (including China, India and Brazil), a second tier of developing countries (including Mexico and Thailand) complaining that they are shut out by the rapid developers, and a third tier of the poorest countries in Africa that complain that their needs are being ignored (*New York Times*, 21 July 2007).

5. CONCLUSION

With few exceptions, the structural, institutional and socio-economic setting in the developing world is less favourable for the emergence and stability of prototype IDs than in developed countries. An adverse macroeconomic environment of financial plight, vulnerability to economic shocks and currency volatility, distorted trade regimes, widespread informality of economic activities and correspondingly poor labour standards, and a lack of public support for small enterprise development, hampers the evolution of viable districts. However, in some regions, notably in a number of countries in Latin America and in East Asia, there have been much more propitious preconditions for performing clusters.

The chances of district-type industrial organisation to set foot and prosper in developing countries are of great significance for overall global development. Small-firm districts in a confined locality present an alternative to global value chains organised and controlled by the increasing number of TNCs operating under liberalised trade regimes. Yet, TNCs can also contribute to dynamic local industrial development in poor countries if instead of simply exploiting cheap labour they help to upgrade local production by transferring capital, knowledge and technology. If efficient and dynamic, districts could be created on a larger scale in the South. This could be instrumental for redressing poverty and reversing the increasing gap between rich and poor countries. Without doubt, the spread of performing industrial clusters in China has done much to reduce the number of poor people in that country.

PART IV

Globalisation and industrial districts

SECTION 10
Global challenges

Introduction

Enzo Rullani

1. WILL IDs SURVIVE?

Will industrial districts (IDs) survive – in practice and in theory – the spread of globalization which is blurring the boundaries between local and global areas of production?

The global village brings together, day by day, a mass of local differences, and in so doing it becomes the natural place for 'hybridizing' local cultures and models. IDs are, as other forms of localized production systems, part of this creative and multipurpose 'melting pot'. If IDs, as Charles Sabel said, are 'on the move', this happens because they are trying to extract from their history those features and qualities that can remain valuable in this new perspective.

The resources of a typical local system (specialization, proximity) are challenged by the pressure of global economy, that force IDs and other localized productive chains to evolve towards more general codes and meanings, as sources and markets enter an extended world network. It is possible that this path can, in the future, destroy local differences and identities, making our world more 'flat'. But it is also possible that, in other cases, the same trend could increase the value of native differences. In a global chain, each single difference could, in fact, have a greater market and a greater value.

2. FROM DISTRICT EXPERIENCE AND THEORY: THREE MAIN FACTORS

Each district, nowadays, is looking at its history and at its specificity with some disquietude. The concerns that emerge can be summarized in some key questions: in what ways do local people and firms need to change their local identity, putting aside old, non-valuable features and acquiring new, more valuable ones, to be used in worldwide markets? Are IDs rich or poor in resources which allow this type of translation from local tradition to future possibilities?

The answer to these questions is that we do not know, and that we can only guess something on a hypothetical basis.

In the past, both the conceptualization and function of IDs were strictly linked to local knowledge, trust, links and institutions. However, local roots do not imply the absence of ideas and solutions of general validity and usability. So, we can extract from the district empirical experience some critical factors and translate them, to some extent, to other and more general situations.

Districts have relied, for their development, on three critical factors:

1. the 'social collaboration' between the relevant actors in the local economy and society;
2. 'shared platforms' for diffused knowledge access and use;
3. the 'evolving specialization' of local competences in the recent reconfiguration of the global value chain.

3. THE ID AS A LABORATORY FOR THE STUDY OF MODERN CAPITALISM

ID theory contains all the three factors mentioned above. They became visible and meaningful in the empirical experience of many local production systems in the past and this has helped their inclusion in the theoretical literature. More recently, social collaborations, shared platforms and evolving specializations have acquired a more 'general' meaning, with the increasing globalization of markets and the dematerialization of value creation. Nowadays the shift in these three factors is redefining the business models for all kinds of firms, in IDs and outside.

As Giacomo Becattini stated, the ID is an 'ideal laboratory' to study the real complexity of modern capitalism and its process of value generation. In effect, some of the key factors that economists and sociologists observed being driving forces in the IDs' history can also be successfully used and work in 'other contexts'. Some of these contexts can be very far from the classical form of a district but, as this section of the *Handbook* shows, social collaboration, shared platforms and evolving specialization work, all the same.

The 'hybridization' among different models and experiences is not a theoretical imperfection, but a source of variety. And variety, as we know, is a precious evolutionary resource that can be used to explore new visions and possibilities.

4. SOCIAL COLLABORATION

The advantages of social collaboration in value production – the first step along this evolutionary path – is analyzed by Josh Whitford, who depicts the transition path of the State of Wisconsin, a region of Fordist and declining economy. Social collaboration helped the local economy to advance towards new organization forms.

Initially, in this area, the growing fragmentation of productive system, due to the crisis of previous centralized and rigid structures, prevented local firms from improving the quality of competences and products, because competitive fragmentation created dispersions and conflicts. This weak performance was corrected when local policymakers – following the lesson of ID experience – began to promote social collaboration between capital and work, suppliers and customers, large and small firms, and public and private initiatives.

Local institutions, social forces and business enterprises were gradually involved in a process of growing linkage, in order to increase work competences, to share knowledge in some critical functions and to make this investment rentable.

5. SHARED COGNITIVE PLATFORMS

Shared cognitive platforms identify the second point. This theoretical tool is used by Michael Best to examine the evolution of a high-tech region (Massachusetts), that changed its industrial organization. Its path was based on mixing different sectors of production and on creating a continuous space for new technological entrepreneurship. The frame that allowed this fluid 're-construction' and 're-construction' of the past industrial order is due to two localized connective resources:

- a 'shared technological platform', that enables an efficient and capillary specialization, in critical fields;
- a 'shared managerial and professional platform', that allows continuous innovation and entrepreneurial birth.

The local system of Massachusetts succeeded in maintaining its cohesive force in the global evolution of firms and production forms because it transformed local proximity links into new source of connections, through shared ideas and languages.

6. EVOLVING SPECIALIZATION

Evolving specialization of firms and territories is the third item, and is considered by the other two authors of this chapter: Frank Pyke, and Giuseppe Tattara.

Pyke's analysis studies the effects of low-cost global competition on jewellery clusters, with special reference to the evolution of Italian firms. Chinese competition forced the leading companies of the jewellery industry to change their functions in the global value chain, focusing on flexibility and creativity, and – consequently – on new labor skills. Political strategies and learning processes are changing the role and composition of old industrial districts in this field.

Giuseppe Tattara considers the evolution of competitive advantages and organizational forms of some Italian districts, examining the effects of internationalization strategies of the more dynamic firms (generally medium-sized firms). The general tendency is towards a reengineering of past productive processes and clusters: more outsourcing, more delocalization of manufacturing phases and reduced links with local artisan subcontracting. On the other hand, many leading firms continue to have roots in their territories, even if a growing part of their activities is distributed at distance and committed to external suppliers. This changing role requires, locally, new service competences and skills, that are often missing or scarce. Hence, it is not easy to calculate the final expected result of this trend towards more light structure and involvement in local production. There is the possibility, according to Tattara's conclusions, that the leading firms change their value chain for profit reasons, thereby weakening the district economy.

7. THE FUTURE: NETWORKED ECONOMY IN NETWORKED SOCIETY

By and large, this Section discusses key issues in relation to the resources and obstacles that local production systems (LPSs) have as they face the deep and structural transformation of their external environment.

Some ideas about the evolutionary path of local and industrial change are exposed and applied to a variety of situations, among which the ID is only a special case. As a matter of fact, the uniqueness of IDs is now less neat and recognizable than in the past. As complexity of forms grows, singularities can be found everywhere and classification criteria weaken.

In this context, one may wonder: what is the most important feature that IDs can preserve and reproduce as they embark on a path along which the contours of their previous identity tend to be redefined? Our idea is that the core of the ID model is – and needs to remain – the 'strict connection' between society and economy.

This connection works in two ways. First of all, the district society acts as a 'localized productive force'. Consequently, in regions, local life and communities are shaped by value-seeking 'behaviors' and ideas. Secondly, the district economy is deeply rooted into a lot of 'social and interpersonal networks'. Hence, in theoretical representations, such a type of economy cannot be reduced to the usual set of markets and hierarchies. On the contrary, it is a complex grid of connected men and women, that imagine, dream, communicate and interact with each other. All these men and women are creative social actors, and cannot be conceived as (simple) productive tools.

When one glances into the future, one must avoid thinking that firms (the economy) will become global, whereas, people (society) will remain local. Life, intelligence and experience are now globally-networked flows that have localized anchors, without necessarily mooring within confined harbors. Both economy and society are becoming local and global at the same time.

In 'old' IDs economy and society were connected locally. Now, we can imagine the 'new' districts as underpinned by a networked economy and a networked society, both spreading their connections all over the world and in each of the places with which they share the realization of production processes and value.

Physical proximity will not be the main glue of this socio-economic construction. We can guess that the networked economy will be aligned to networked society through another type of glue: shared ideas and languages. Strong ideas and powerful languages express the life style of many in the next, multi-desired, collective world.

Slow Food, in Italy, is an example of this economic-social construction that bases a flow of new and old entrepreneurial initiatives on a strong idea of production, consumption and living experience. But many IDs and many LPSs in the so-called 'made-in-Italy' sectors could be organized in the same way: fashionable lifestyles support many products and districts (textiles, clothing, shoes, eyeglasses and so on). Other ideas could be, for example, the 'good home living', the concept of health and well being, the entertainment, the global service to final customers or to intermediate producers, just to mention a few. Many and many links between districts, and many and many links between local and global can be identified.

So, IDs will survive, even if they have to accept and actively organize a major change. Their core resource, physical proximity, has to be translated into a semantic and creative glue, to be used in local/global networking. A very ambitious result, that is not suitable for all.

46. Massachusetts high tech: A 'manufactory of species'

Michael H. Best

1. INTRODUCTION: FROM MANUFACTURING TO HIGH TECH

At mid-20th century the economic outlook for Massachusetts was bleak. The president's Council of Economic Advisors described New England as an archaic economy beset by aggressive, low-cost competitors (Browne and Sass 2000, p. 202). The region's per capita income dropped by roughly 20 per cent relative to the national average in the 1940s.[1] Textiles and the shoe industry still employed 25 per cent of the region's manufacturing workers in 1948 and both industries were in rapid decline. Textile employment fell to 180 000 by 1954, a loss of 100 000 between 1948 and 1954.

The forces of structural decline were deeply entrenched. This is an old story in economic history. Once-thriving regions get locked into mature industries and lose competitive advantage to lower cost competitors. Few were willing to bet on the economic future of Massachusetts. Nevertheless, the expectations of industrial gloom turned out to be wrong.

By the end of the century, Massachusetts income per head was 20 per cent above the US average. The engine of growth was not manufacturing. The immediate post-war defense industry and the minicomputer industry had fostered a growth rebound. But the end of the cold war and the collapse of the minicomputer industry drove an abrupt loss of one-third of the State's manufacturing jobs in six years between 1986 and 1992; they dropped another third in the first years of the present century to less than 10 per cent of the labor force.[2]

Thus while the Massachusetts economy was hemorrhaging manufacturing jobs it was generating a per capita income level that few if any regions could match. If not manufacturing, what were the wealth creating powers of the State's economy given its history of losing major industries and the collapse of manufacturing in the State?

The answer has two parts: one straightforward and the other complex. The straightforward answer is that industry is still the major source of wealth generation in Massachusetts but that it depends upon inter-regional specialization in new ways. In fact, many leading Massachusetts high-tech companies generate both manufacturing and white collar jobs, but they are performed in out-of-State and offshore affiliates. The four Fortune 500 manufacturing companies headquartered in Massachusetts employ only a small proportion of the global labor force in Massachusetts. Raytheon, the defense giant, employs 11 500 in Massachusetts and 87 000 globally. EMC, the data storage industry leader, employs 9000 in Massachusetts and 28 000 globally. Thermo Fisher Scientific, maker of lab equipment and scientific instruments, employs 1100 in Massachusetts and 33 000 around the world. Boston Scientific, medical devices giant, employs 2400 in Massachusetts and 28 000 worldwide (*Boston Globe*, 'Top 100', 2007).[3]

The second part of the answer is more complex and is the subject of this chapter. The first clue can be found in the region's capacity to create and grow new 'high-tech' sectors. In fact, the region is a virtual 'manufactory of species' to use Darwin's expression but applied to sectors. The State's ratio of gross R&D expenditure as a percentage of State GDP of over five is a second clue. This is the highest in the US and considerably higher than leading countries such as Finland with 3.4 per cent, or in fast-growing, technology-following countries like Ireland with 1.2 per cent (MTC 2007).

Useful as these clues are, they do not tell us why manufacturing jobs have declined sharply or the reasons for the links between R&D and the emergence of new sectors. For this we need to explore the 'business model' that both drives the region's 'manufactory of sectors' and operates with ever fewer manufacturing jobs. The simple answer is the growth in services but as we shall see this hides the region's distinctive capabilities.

How does one explain a region's capacity to foster new high-tech sectors? If research-intensive universities were the drivers then Baltimore, Maryland and Champaign-Urbana would, like greater Boston, be cities with rapidly growing, high-tech companies (Patton and Kenney in this volume). Important as science-led basic research is to the knowledge-intensive industries, these examples suggest something else is involved in accounting for the serial emergence and territorial concentration of new high-tech sectors in Massachusetts.

Brian Loasby's (in this volume) evolutionary account of Marshall's industrial district (ID) offers a conceptual framework. For Marshall, economic progress is explained in terms of knowledge and organization or, more precisely, increases in the complexity of organization and in sources or creation of new knowledge. Marshall drew on Adam Smith's postulate that advances in productivity are a consequence of increasing specialization of labor combined with more 'intimate connections' integrating the increasingly differentiated activities (Marshall 1920, p. 241). Darwin (1859), it can be argued, applied the same principles, but with respect to the evolution of species.[4]

Industrial organization, for Marshall, was key to understanding progress and the relationship was suffused by knowledge creation. The complex whole comprises, in the words of Loasby, 'different kinds of connections, constituting different forms of organization and many variations within each form, [which] encourage different combinations of evolved specialist knowledge and skills and direct the development of particular kinds of new knowledge and skills' (Loasby, Chapter 7 in this volume, pp. 79–80). The specific forms of organizational sources of productivity improvement identified by Marshall are three: inside the firm, amongst various businesses in the same 'trade' or sector, and various trades relative to one another (Marshall 1920, pp. 138–9).[5] Instead of Marshall's trades, and Darwin's species, I will refer to industrial sectors. In this contribution, I apply Marshall's organization and knowledge-creation framework to examine the emergence of new, fast-growing sectors within a population of some 3000 high-tech companies in the greater Boston area. To a lesser extent, connections to complementary capabilities with affiliate business units in mutually growing regions elsewhere in the global economy are brought into the story.

2. THE HIGH-TECH FIRM

The firm, to paraphrase Edith Penrose (1959), is a system for the production of goods and new knowledge-based resources. For Loasby, Penrose independently originated a dialectical process of resource creation internal to the firm that was invented by Marshall: 'The transformation of novelty into routine releases cognitive resources for the imagination of further novelty, which, if successful, becomes embodied in further routines' (Loasby, Chapter 7 in this volume, p. 81). This knowledge-increasing dialectic, in Loasby's interpretation, is the basis of Marshall's theory of economic progress; but it 'requires various forms of organization to realize its potential'.

Penrose, I believe, extended Marshall in important ways. Her theory of the growth of the firm locates the novelty/routine dialectic within a second, encompassing dialectic between a company's 'core competence' or unique capability and market opportunity. Refinements in a firm's distinctive capabilities enhance its capacity to imagine, identify and seize emerging market opportunities and, in the process, offer insights for a new round of capability refinement.

Furthermore, capabilities for Penrose are about collective cognition,[6] they can not be reduced to expertise attributes of individuals. Teams of people working together can create and act on knowledge that is beyond the capacities of individuals working alone.

The high-tech firm is a more pure expression of the Penrosian distinctive capability development and market opportunity growth dialectic.[7] High-tech companies compete on the basis of distinctive technological capabilities that have been established by collective action. Success depends upon leadership in technological innovation. Each company's goal is to establish a core competence based on a unique technology platform which, in turn, can be leveraged to generate a new product pipeline. Ever increasing technological differentiation is the result.

Growth is critical to high-tech companies because growth empowers them to attract resources to fund R&D, make acquisitions, and otherwise protect and advance their intellectual property portfolio. In this the resource-increasing internal dialectic is complemented by the attraction of external resources.

The term 'high tech' was first used in the late 1960s to describe 'science-based' companies and government sponsored labs along Boston's Route 128. One contemporary observer estimated some 690 such entities fit the description (Lieberman 1968).[8] In the 1970s and 1980s, the population of high-tech business units in Massachusetts had increased to more than 3000.[9] This number represents all business units that engage in R&D and seek to establish a novel technology platform.[10]

A useful exaggeration is to think of the high-tech business enterprise as centered around two teams: a technology integration team and a business development team. A technology integration team is the organizational or institutional means to combine the expertise of a range of scientific and engineering disciplines all of which are required to develop and support distinctive technology platforms. The challenge is that every discipline has its own language, concepts, and perspectives and communication across disciplines is both problematic and critical to success.

Initially, a business development team has the challenge of transforming a fledgling company with a novel technological idea and facing several years of zero sales revenues into a fully developed, growing entrepreneurial enterprise under the pressure of time. First-mover advantages can be critical to success particularly in competition over technology platforms and industry standards in an emerging sector. This necessitates attracting successive rounds of finance to fund both technology and business development teams and to build, acquire and defend the company's intellectual property rights and to do so ahead of the competition.

Early success in technology, product and market development will mean organizational transitions that accompany rapid growth from a company that employs, say, 10–20, to a mid-size company with say, 50–75 employees, to a larger company in the hundreds of employees and, in exceptional cases to thousands of employees. Building teams, acquiring resources, researching markets are all specialized activities that must be undertaken, sequenced, and coordinated alongside and in sync with technology platform development.

Many large and rapidly growing Massachusetts high-tech companies concentrate technology and business development activities in-State and outsource or locate non-core including production activities in foreign-based affiliates. Their offshore units share a common requirement and characteristic: remote management of non-core activities. The affiliate's function is to leverage the parent's technology platform by specializing in localization, production, marketing, distribution and sales in nearby markets, all functions for which Massachusetts does not offer a comparative advantage.

Countries, such as Ireland, offer extremely attractive incentives for foreign direct investment (FDI) which facilitate rapid ramp-up of production. The foreign affiliates of high-tech companies do not participate in technology platform development. This does not preclude engagement in R&D activities for extending the parent company's technology portfolio. But even here, the parent company will soon pull into the home region any activities that are valuable enough to require oversight by the company's chief technology officer.

The flow of FDI has been two-way. More than 8 per cent of the 3000 plus high-tech business units in Massachusetts are foreign headquartered. In some sectors it is much more such as photonics (16 per cent), instruments and equipment (15 per cent) and pharmaceutical (14 per cent) (Best, Paquin and Xie 2004, Chart 2A). Most are attracted to Massachusetts because of the consolidation of technological capabilities and the establishment of a high-tech ID in which the whole range of specialist service activities required to grow fast are readily available.

3. NEW HIGH-TECH SECTORS

To paraphrase Darwin, Massachusetts' industrial history can be interpreted as a manufactory of sectors. The State has constructed a comparative advantage in the creation and growth of new sectors. This has not changed with high tech. In fact, the manufactory of sectors' regional capability has become more organized with greater ramp-up speeds of new sectors than in previous periods.

What is it about the industrial organization of Massachusetts that generates new sectors? While Marshall did not address this question directly, he originated the concept of ID and associated externalities to explain the localization or territorial concentration of industry. While much research has been conducted on the benefits from a concentration of 'various businesses in the same trade' less has been focused on 'that of various trades relatively to one another'.

Marshall's concept of ID did not preclude the idea of the colocation of various sectors and mutual interactions contributing to the progress of each. In fact, he saw at least one important advantage: 'A district which is dependent chiefly on one industry is liable to extreme depression [This evil] is in a great measure avoided by those large towns or large industrial districts in which several distinct industries are strongly developed' (Marshall 1920, p. 227 nd).

The idea of large or of a 'composite' ID fits the population of high-tech companies in the greater Boston area. At the broadest level, three categories of Massachusetts high-tech companies can be identified: complex product systems, software, and life sciences. Software and life science have emerged and become specialized in the State in the high-tech period, complex product systems as a production capability category has a long history in Massachusetts.

But the advantages of a composite ID with multiple sectors extend beyond offsetting depression. Variety or diversity contributes to economic progress: 'The advantages of variety of employment are combined with those of localized industries in some of our manufacturing towns, and this is a chief cause of their continued growth' (ibid., p. 226).

The task of characterizing sectors boundaries is not easy. Official classification systems were created long before the industries that have driven the post-war Massachusetts economy and were not designed to cope with increasing sectoral differentiation or companies with product applications in multiple markets. Characterizing an emerging sector is particularly difficult, the boundaries are not clear, and overlap is common.

All is not lost. Somehow sectors, if overlapping, do eventually get a name, a collective identity, and government recognition with the establishment of an industry council formed by self-organizing companies cooperating around shared interests. In this chapter I rely primarily upon growth estimates of the numbers of companies and employment from published reports of the high-tech industry councils in Massachusetts, from articles by the business staff at the *Boston Globe*, and a longitudinal dataset developed to study high-tech companies in Massachusetts and the rest of the US. The dataset is organized using a technology taxonomy based on engineering expertise.[11]

3.1 Complex product systems

The story of the building of the world's first reliable digital electronic computer at MIT's Lincoln Labs in 1953, followed by the founding and growth of Digital Equipment Corporation, and its growth to the world's second largest computer company employing 124 000 at its peak in the early 1980s is oft told. So too, is the establishment of the minicomputer industry in Massachusetts.[12]

The minicomputer is the archetypal, but not the only example. It followed microwave technology which likewise was funded by defense-related budgets and developed in non-profit research laboratories administered by MIT before becoming the basis for the rapid growth of a leading company, in this case Raytheon, and the emergence of a new industry. Guidance systems were developed at MIT's Instrumentation Lab and packet switches, a key internet technology was developed (not invented) at Bolt Beranek and Newman (BB&N), a private research company founded by three MIT professors.

The scientific knowledge, technological expertise and business capabilities created in these industries have been, in turn, leveraged by yet new, emerging sectors in Massachusetts. A prime example is the emergence of a rapidly growing data storage system industry, the 'file cabinets of the electronics age'. EMC, founded in 1979, became the second largest industrial employer in Massachusetts. It began as a supplier of add-on memory boards for the minicomputer market, moved into mainframe storage a decade later, and 'added software to help manage its boxes as it made the switch to open systems in the middle of this decade' (Degman 1998, p. 1).

EMC employed 9000 in Massachusetts and 28 000 globally in 2007. Equally important, EMC 'spawned a new generation of software and service companies providing ways for corporations to monitor and manage data, back up and protect it, find and fix disk-storage bottlenecks, and warn desktop computer users to clean out their hard drives before they run out of space' (R. Rosenberg 1999).

The story of communication equipment manufacturing is similar to that of data storage equipment. Cascade Communications, founded in 1990, was eventually acquired but at least 11 technologically differentiated start-ups followed in rapid sequence, all located north of the Massachusetts Turnpike on Interstate 495. The earliest entrants combined networking and optical technologies (a core regional technological capability present in many industries) to direct streams of data flowing along telephone lines.

The emergence of the minicomputer, microwave, data storage and network switching equipment industries are leading cases in the category of complex production systems, as noted a recurring theme in Massachusetts' industrial history. Jet engine design and development is another. Other smaller subsectors that emerged in the high-tech period include: semiconductor equipment manufacturers (Eaton Semiconductor, Varion Ion Implant, Micrion); electronic test equipment suppliers (Teradyne); digital signal processing semiconductors (Analog Devices, Mercury Computer Systems, Alpha, BKC Semiconductor, C.P. Clare); and industrial automation (Brooks Automation, Foxboro Instruments, Groupe Schneider's Amicon Division).

All of these sectors contribute to the region's distinctive production capabilities in industrial rather than consumer products. Massachusetts, unlike the American Midwest or Silicon Valley, has never had mass production capabilities let alone world-class manufacturing associated with the just-in-time production system established in Japan and widely imitated in the fast-growing technology followers. But while the industrial focus of manufacturing in Massachusetts may be often overlooked, it is not because it is insignificant. Industrial and commercial machinery (including computers), and electronic and electrical equipment (including telecommunication exchanges and switches, electricity transformers, chip making machines, air traffic control systems, electro-medical devices) accounted for close to half of the region's exports at least until the early 1990s. The share went up to 75 per cent by adding in instruments, engineering chemicals and transportation equipment (primarily aircraft engines and parts) (Little 1993, p. 9; Best 2001).

3.2 Software

Software emerged as a distinctive industry in the 1970s, developed in the 1980s, and grew rapidly in the 1990s. Between 1989 and 1996 Massachusetts' software companies, output and employment nearly tripled: companies increased from 800 to 2200 (many are not strictly high tech), revenues from $3 billion to $7.8 billion, and employment from 46 000 to 130 000.

As with computers, early software development stemmed from MIT and Harvard defense-related work. Individuals played key roles at pivotal moments.

Grace Hopper wrote the programs that enabled Harvard's vast Mark I computer to make ballistic calculations. She later headed the development of COBOL, the first standardized language for business calculations (Browne and Sass 2000, p. 221). Lotus, a software tools company, was founded in 1992 and acquired by IBM in 1995 for $3.2 billion (Gerstner 2002, p. 144); it grew out of Visicalc, an electronics spreadsheet developed by software engineer Dan Bricklin. These were early days in the development of the software tools industry, a large, growing and highly regionally-concentrated industry in the greater Boston area.

A burst of growth in telecommunication equipment companies in the 1990s was part of a single process of growth in telecommunication software tools companies (Best, Paquin and Xie 2004). While software tool companies with product and service applications in biotechnology are a small proportion of the total sector, 'bioinformatics' is a rapidly growing new industrial subsector and another industrial 'speciation' example.

However, the number of companies and direct employment seriously underestimates the role software engineering plays in high tech and in industrial change. Software engineering is integral to technology platform design, product development and enterprise differentiation in all high-tech sectors as well as most other sectors. In this software tools companies are a high-tech counterpart to the region's historical specialization in machine tool companies.

3.3 Medical devices

Before 1980, medical device companies were primarily small instrument companies that built custom devices to the specifications of physicians. The market did not yet exist, except mainly as a bespoke industry.[13] That was before. Between 1980 and 2005 the national industry expanded by ten times from $10 billion to nearly $100 billion.[14] In 1990, the first year of the *Boston Globe*'s annual report of the State's 'Top 100' companies, there were no medical device companies in Massachusetts; in 2005 there were 12. Today Massachusetts has the highest medical device enterprise location quotient in the country[15] and the Massachusetts Medical Device Industry Council, established in 1996, has over 300 members.

Three groups of companies were pivotal to the emergence and rapid ramp-up of medical device companies and output in Massachusetts: rapidly growing large and medium-sized companies; established companies repositioning into medical devices; and global leaders acquiring product design and development business units within Massachusetts. Nearly 10 per cent of the 300 medical device companies in Massachusetts are units of foreign headquartered companies.

A single company, however, stands out as the sector-defining enterprise. The sales of Boston Scientific grew from $2 million in 1965 to $5.6 billion in 2004 and it employed more than 17 000 people worldwide. Boston Scientific's vision became the defining idea of the region's medical device industry: minimally invasive therapy. Instead of, for example, open heart surgery the new concept involved channeling a small device to the heart using the body's coronary arteries. But Boston Scientific's major contribution was to set in train a dynamic iterative process of market creation and business organization development which extended from itself to propel the emergence of a localized industry in medical devices.

Market creation for Boston Scientific involved the lateral integration of a wide range of expertise, communities and institutional activities inside and outside the company: physicians, the healthcare gatekeepers, had to be convinced of the benefits of minimally invasive therapy and educated in the new procedures; the medical scientific community had to be convinced of the superiority of the new techniques; device engineers had to be responsive to the physicians' knowledge and use their feedback in the product design process; production staff had to manufacture to the quality standards required for a device that was to be inserted in the body; and parts suppliers had to be linked into the new product development and production processes.

On the technology platform side, Boston Scientific's drug-eluting coronary stent represented drug-device combination products that countered implant-related complications. Design and development interdisciplinary teams anchored in physics, including fiber optics, polymeric chemistry and biologics. In this, Boston Scientific was a pioneer in the technological convergence of instrument making and drug development that is redrawing the rapidly shifting industry boundaries of medical devices and biotechnology.

Boston Scientific did not create the medical device industry of Massachusetts alone. Many other entrepreneurial companies were involved. Four other medical device companies grew rapidly over the same period to employ over 1000, two of these were founded in the 19th century. Another, Analogic Corporation's Medical Imaging Division, founded in 1969, expresses Massachusetts' distinctive capability in both optics and complex product systems but applied to computed tomography (CT) systems and magnetic resonance imaging.

A much larger group of 18 mid-size (between 200 and 1000 employees) medical device operating units grew rapidly over the period, five of which were acquired by out-of-State companies. The acquirers represent two of the biggest and most successful specialist medical device-making companies in the US, Medtronic and Stryker, and two global giant healthcare companies, Abbott Laboratories and Johnson & Johnson.

Another 13 companies not generally classified as medical device companies either design and make medical device products or have repositioned into the industry. Not surprisingly, many of the non-medical device companies with medical device products are in the life sciences or healthcare technologies. In some cases, bio-pharmaceutical companies, such as Genzyme, are extending into medical devices as a means of drug delivery.

Two major, long-established instrument and tool-making companies have morphed into medical device companies. Thermo Electron merged with Fisher Scientific to form Thermo Fisher Scientific and become the region's second largest medical device company and the fifth largest of the 2007 *Boston Globe*'s 'Top 100' companies measured in market value, one behind Boston Scientific. Perkin-Elmer, which began as EG&G in 1947, restructured away from defense to become the State's third largest medical devices company and 29th largest in the *Boston Globe*'s 'Top 100'.[16]

The third major group behind the rapid growth of the medical devices industry in Massachusetts are investments, usually by acquisition, by foreign headquartered, medical device companies. The behemoth here is Philips Medical Systems with 6650 employees, an estimated 2000 of whom are in Massachusetts. Philips joins a strong group of local and foreign headquartered companies in imaging, optic and laser technologies.[17] In fact, of the 21 foreign-headquartered medical device companies with operating units in Massachusetts more than half are in imaging and/or optics.

Medical devices is the largest employer within a rapidly-developing and differentiating life science-based group of sectors in Massachusetts which includes biotech, pharmaceuticals and genomics. According to a recent report, New England has the highest concentration of biotechnology companies in the US with 456 bioscience companies employing 26 000 people.[18] Thus the region employs roughly one in six biotechnology employees in the country, nearly ten times its population ratio. While the scientific revolution in the discovery of DNA triggered the emergence of biotech, many companies in the Massachusetts biotech industry preceded the DNA sequencing research breakthroughs of Boyer and Cohen in the early 1970s. Here, as in medical devices, regional 'tool' companies recognized new market opportunities, redesigned their technology platforms and repositioned into the growing sector (Best 2003).

4. INFRASTRUCTURAL NETWORKS: MARSHALL'S 'COLLECTIVE PROPERTY'

The emerging sectors illustrated above fit a common pattern. A rapidly growing entrepreneurial firm set in motion an iterative dynamic between the development of a unique technology platform and incipient market opportunities and initiated the proliferation of a technologically differentiated group of rapidly growing companies into a growing sector.

What enabled not only the leading company but a whole group of companies to grow rapidly and achieve global market success? While a single firm could be expected to grow rapidly without depleting scarce productive resources within a region, the emergence of a new sector on the scale of medical devices would seemingly be confronted by technical expertise and other resource constraints. And why did rapid growth occur in the cited sectors and not others? The answers, in part, point to causes that 'lie deep down in resources and faculties that are not wholly individual' which Marshall termed 'collective property of a nation as a whole' and more specifically the 'collective organization of the district as a whole' (Marshall 1920, p. xii).

The collective property of the Massachusetts high-tech economy can be conceptualized in terms of 'infrastructural' networks that individual companies can build and draw upon to meet challenges.[19] Four infrastructures that take the form of Marshallian 'collective property' are suggested below. These infrastructures are not separate from the region's firms. Instead they are a way to think of the 3000 high-tech enterprises and associated institutions as a system of actual and potential inter-firm connections and networks, formal and informal. The sheer density of potential connections constitutes a regionally unique resource for addressing technological and business development challenges by any firm embedded within the system.

4.1 Science and technology infrastructure

The greater Boston area has up to 3000 technology integration teams combining individuals with various scientific and engineering backgrounds conducting experiments and trying to be a leader in the next technology generation. Many seek to establish a technology platform that will enable their company to grow and become a major player if not the standard setter in a potentially rapidly growing, global market.

Each member of the technology integration team is connected, actively or passively, to a scientific or technical community and collectively the team has connections to many such knowledge communities. The challenge of each team is not simply to use the enormous number of potential connections to transfer knowledge from outside to inside the company.

The central challenge is one of collective cognition: to create new knowledge by the peculiarly human capacity to define, address and solve problems. While many challenges can be addressed by individuals acting alone, others can not and this is the reason technology teams and high-tech companies exist. But they do not exist or create new knowledge in isolation. Each technology platform development team is like a 'brainstorming' node linked, potentially, by tens of thousands of 'intimate connections' crisscrossing the region's population of technology development teams in other companies, universities and government labs. Converting potential into actual connections and actual into critically important connections is an ongoing process central to the activities of the technology integration team. In many cases proximity can, serendipitously, enhance the number and quality, or degree of intimacy, of the connections.

For Massachusetts, the term 'high-tech ID' suggests an intangible collective property in the form of the quality and density of the system of nodes and intimate connections that collectively enhance the innovative or knowledge creation potential of each of the nodes. Together, the company technology platform development teams are interconnected by invisible social networks of skills and technical expertise and knowledge. A successful technological experiment in one lab or company resonates with echos of varying intensity through many of the others as if part of a single resonance machine with hundreds of reverberating nodes.

The conventional usage of the term 'science and technology (S&T) infrastructure' implicitly assumes a technology transfer mechanism, and conceives of innovation in terms of connections between companies doing developmental research and universities doing basic research. While technology transfer is important to understanding greater Boston's high-tech economy, it ignores the critical 'intimate connection' dimensions hinted at by Marshall's concept of 'collective property' or 'collective organization of the district as a whole'.

4.2 Business development infrastructure

In Schumpeter's words, 'The money market is . . . the headquarters of the capitalist system' (Schumpeter 1911 [1934, p. 122]). It is in the money market that economic projects are compared, that development is financed, and the 'system of future values first appears' (ibid., p. 125). 'Future values' represent the creation of new technologies, products, processes and organizations by strategic investment decisions and investment.

Industry innovation, unlike production, is not financed by current revenues. Equally important, high-tech company creation, and rapid company growth are not funded by current sales. Instead, building a high-tech business enterprise is a long-term, investment-intensive process often with a several year gap between the original entrepreneurial idea and a sales or license-generated revenue stream.

Consequently, before sales revenues are generated, a high-tech company will go through a sequence of intermediate stages requiring a wide range of expertise, such as applications for patent, proof of concept, early-stage technology development, product development, establishing or engaging production systems, supplier networks, marketing relationships and sales channels. If basic research activities are included, the business development time span is even longer.

Not surprisingly, the growth of the high-tech industry in Massachusetts to over 3000 companies, most with large early investment requirements, has been accompanied by the evolution of a specialist, differentiated, counterpart financial system matching the phases of technology development. Venture capital has been critical.[20] California has the nation's largest venture-capital industry, but Massachusetts has the second and a long history of both financial investment in industry and financial innovation.

The venture-capital industry mediates between the technology development projects of high-tech companies and its 'limited partners' – wealthy families, State pension funds, university endowments – to 'pick winners' for investments of up to a decade. The fortunes of emerging high-tech companies can depend critically upon gaining credibility with the venture-capital industry.

The mediation role between internal technology projects and external funding sources involves the creation of a board of directors and advisors with extensive and deep connections in the financial, technical and business communities. The venture-capital industry performs, to an imperfect degree, the Schumpeterian function of the headquarters of the capitalist system but it does so by informally linking the members of the boards of some 3000 high-tech companies. Each company strives to develop boards in which the members are linked via social and technical networks to enhance its attractiveness to venture capitalists.

Important as it is, venture capital targets mainly the intermediate stages of high-tech company development. In the early stages of company formation the federal government has often been pivotal. The basic research, proof-of-concept, and early-stage technology-development phases are more often met by a range of federal government instruments that are disproportionately accessed by Massachusetts companies.[21] These include funding from Small Business Innovation Researches (SBIRs),[22] the National Institutes of Health (NIH)[23] and the National Science Foundation.

Many other regions have high rates of new company formation and high-tech clusters but few have the capability to grow rapidly a large group of companies. This second form of Marshallian 'collective property' can be described as a business services infrastructure to grow and transform companies into global leaders. A vast array of specialist service activities are required to successfully engineer the building of successful, innovative enterprises. Here, again, the regional resources that can be drawn upon include not only specialist, knowledge-intensive service activities that can be found in the marketplace, but the accumulated expertise and skills that permeate the management teams of the region's high-tech enterprises. Here, too, innovations in a business development activity in one application can reverberate to or send waves across the regional pool of business development experts to other applications where the effects may be even larger.

4.3 Tooling, instruments and equipment infrastructure

High-tech business units located in Massachusetts draw from, and contribute to, yet a third 'infrastructure' in their pursuit of distinctive technology platforms. Massachusetts has a long industrial history going back to the early 1800s specializing in instruments, tools, equipment, and complex product systems (Best 1990, 2001). The region has never had a competitive advantage in volume manufacturing or world-class manufacturing capabilities. The legacy of production and technology capabilities unique to Massachusetts' industrial history has, in many cases, reasserted itself in high-tech forms.

Perhaps the most critical legacy, and continuity, from two centuries of Massachusetts' industrial evolution is the deep and wide base of tool and instrument-making production capabilities. It began with the application of the principle of 'interchangeable parts' to arms making at the Springfield Armory in the early 1800s (Marshall 1920, p. 257). The application of product engineering was a stimulus to the emergence of extraordinary machine tool and instrument-making IDs first along the Connecticut River Valley and then along the Blackstone River Valley. The labor pool of deep craft machinist skills was critical to the emergence of a rolling sequence of new sectors some of which became large including: arms, clockmaking, sewing machines and bicycles, sometimes supplied by the same machine shops. This capacity for the tool and instrument-making population of companies to reposition from industrial customers in declining sectors into emerging high-growth sectors has been a signal characteristic of the greater region. In some cases the instrument-making companies themselves became major player in emerging sectors.

The core competence of these companies is not in volume manufacturing or even manufacturing but more in systems integration and technology management. In this they share a deeply anchored, regional production capability in complex product systems which is at the heart of the region's success in related subsectors of jet engine design and development and telecommunication network switching gear equipment. These are low volume production processes that are highly engineering intensive and which tap the region's basic research infrastructure. Not surprisingly, these same capabilities have been successfully leveraged to seize market opportunities created by the growth in demand for medical instruments and equipment.

The instruments and equipment sector has always had an additional role: it provides the instruments, tools and equipment to the S&T infrastructure within the universities, research hospitals and laboratories that later feed back via scientific and technological advances (N. Rosenberg 1994, Chapter 13). In this way, amongst others, the population of high-tech companies in Massachusetts interacts with the region's renowned S&T infrastructure.

4.4 Education R&D infrastructure

Government-funded, research-intensive universities and the emergence of knowledge-intensive sectors go together. Massachusetts' education institutions, particularly MIT, have a long history of close, interactive relations between the creation and advance of knowledge-intensive sectors not only in high tech but in early 20th-century electrical and chemical engineering industries. Exemplified by Raytheon and DEC, the emergence and development of high-tech leading companies and growth sectors in Massachusetts involved long-term defense-related government investments much of which was channeled through universities and their affiliated labs.

The extraordinary cluster of university hospitals and medical research institutes in Boston are pivotal to the State's disproportionate share of NIH funding. Today's small, fast-growing companies in sectors such as advanced materials, nanotech and genomics benefit not only from federal funding of R&D but also from technology-based economic development initiatives by the State government.[24]

Marshall would not have been surprised about the role of the State in the early stages of the development of modern industries particularly in defense and health-related sectors. The full quote excised above in the introduction is as follows: 'Organization aids knowledge; it has many forms, for example that of a single business, that of various businesses in the same trade, that of various trades relatively to one another, and that of the State providing security for all and help for many' (Marshall 1920, p. 138–9).

5. IMPLICATIONS AND CONCLUSIONS

The Massachusetts economy has been transformed over the last decades nearly as much as the fast-growing, low-cost manufacturing-based economies. While the State has long lost its comparative advantage in manufacturing, it has developed infrastructures that foster sectoral transitions and enjoyed the high value added that accrues to the early developers of next generation technologies and rapidly growing new industrial sectors.

While the rapid growth success stories of the technology-following nations involve a proactive role of political leadership and industrial strategies (Evans 1995), the story in Massachusetts is different. It is more like a self-organizing system that has reacted quickly and effectively to market creation opportunities by stimulating the development and growth of entrepreneurial, technology-driven enterprises and thereby converted these impulses into engines of business investment and sector growth. Nevertheless, the role of the federal government in the basic research and 'proof of concept', pre-venture capital stages of new high-tech companies in emerging sectors has been critical to success.

The idea pursued in this contribution is that business organization is critical to understanding innovation and here, too, evolution has been at work. The argument is that the Massachusetts economy, in effect, seized the opportunities of globalization by establishing a large composite high-tech ID in which business enterprises, individually and collectively, are organized to pursue strategic advantages based on global leadership in new technologies and technology platforms. In the process the sources of wealth generation in Massachusetts have been transformed: the greater Boston area has an organizational comparative advantage in the creation and rapid growth of new technology-intensive subsectors. Or, to paraphrase Darwin, Massachusetts is a virtual 'manufactory of species' in which species are new industrial subsectors.

The high-tech ID of Massachusetts has itself been created in an interdetermined process of localization and globalization. When the minicomputer companies were being built in Massachusetts, the prevailing business model was one of vertical integration and integral product architecture. The opportunities for globalization shifted the pressures in favor of a focus and network business model and, not surprisingly, advanced the region's specialization in technology platform development.

Globalization meant that large investments in high tech could generate returns by leveraging technology platforms with offshore production, marketing and sales facilities. In many cases, such as Boston Scientific, much of the enterprise growth in employment is out of State and offshore, but not outsourced. Nevertheless, the crown jewels of the company, its technology platform, design and development, as well as early stage manufacturing, remained firmly rooted in Massachusetts. This is not simply for control or governance purposes, important as they are, but because of the region's comparative advantage in technology platform and business development. Technology platform and new product development virtually always involve technology integration, new technology combinations, and often occur at the intersect of preexisting clusters.

Albert Hirschman suggested the expression 'multidimensional conspiracy' to capture the development implications of a sector filling a particular niche in the international division of labor (Hirschman 1977, p. 96).[25] Schumpeter wrote of economic evolution as 'the changes in the economic process brought about by innovation, together with all their effects and the responses to them by the economic system' (Schumpeter 1939). Darwin's 'manufactory of species' metaphor is equally suggestive; furthermore, his research methodology of focusing on mutual adjustment processes within populations suggests an analogy which likely influenced Marshall's elaboration of the concepts of ID and 'collective property' as tools to understand wealth-creation processes in economics. I would guess that none of these intellectual giants would have been surprised by the emergence of a self-organizing, high-tech ID with extraordinary industrial innovation capabilities.

NOTES

1. New England's relative per capita income dropped from 126 to 107 per cent of the national average in the 1940s (Browne and Sass 2000, p. 202).
2. Manufacturing employment plummeted from 675 000 to 450 000 between 1986 and 1992, and another third to 300 000 by 2007.
3. The 25 largest Massachusetts-based employers in the *Boston Globe*'s 2007 ranking of top companies includes estimates of another ten 'manufacturing' companies' worldwide employment. Mass High Tech's database of high-tech companies (version 1.7.10) provides numbers on Massachusetts' employment for seven of these companies (Iron Mountain, Analog Devices, Genzyme, Perkin Elmer, Charles River Laboratories, Millipore and Waters). The *Boston Globe*

worldwide employment totals are 68 700 employees; the Mass High Tech's local employment total for the same seven companies is 8435. Allowing for substantial errors, different years and so on, and the conclusion would not likely change: Massachusetts-based large high-tech companies employ, on average, somewhere between 10 and 20 per cent of their global labor force in Massachusetts.

4. Marshall, influenced by Darwin, propounded a 'general rule . . . that the development of the organism, whether social or physical, involves an increasing subdivision of functions between its separate parts on the one hand, and on the other a more intimate connection between them' (Marshall 1920, p. 241).
5. The quote in full brings out a fourth factor which will become important in the story below, that is the role of the State.
6. A 2002 Santa Fe Institute 'collective cognition' workshop characterized the idea as follows: 'Many forms of individual cognition are enhanced by communication and collaboration with other intelligent agents. We propose to call this "collective cognition", by analogy with the well known concept of "collective action". People (and other intelligent agents) often "think better" in groups and sometimes think in ways which would be simply impossible for isolated individuals. Perhaps the most spectacular and important instance of collective cognition is modern science. An array of formal organizations and informal social institutions also can be considered means of collective cognition. For instance, Hayek (1948a) famously argued that competitive markets effectively calculate an adaptive allocation of resources that "could not" be calculated by any individual market-participant'. www.santafe.edu/~dynlearn/colcog, accessed 15 July 2008.
7. The eligibility criteria of the Deloitte Technology Fast 500 program (www.deloitte.com/dtt, accessed 20 December 2008) offer a useful initial definition of a high-tech company: 'Owns proprietary technology or proprietary intellectual property that contributes to a significant portion of the company's operating revenues or devotes a significant proportion of operating revenues to research and development of technology. Using other companies technology or intellectual property in a unique way does not qualify'.
8. 'It is not clear whether the name [high tech] derives from the high technologies flourishing in the glass rectangles along the route or from the Midas touch their entrepreneurs have shown in starting new companies. Maybe both' (Lieberman 1968).
9. The number 3000 is a conservative estimate. Rosegrant and Lampe write that in 1965 there were 574 companies along Route 128; by 1973 the number was 1212 and by the mid-1980s nearly 3000 high-tech companies existed in Massachusetts (Rosegrant and Lampe 1992, pp. 130–32). CorpTech's directory contains in excess of 3000 throughout the 1990s. Mass High Tech Directory has over 5700 listings but they include many that do not develop as distinct from use high-tech products and services.
10. According to CorpTech data for 2003, Massachusetts had 3736 high-tech business units broken down as follows: private-independent companies 2578 (69 per cent); units of private-independent companies 253 (7 per cent); public-independent companies 237 (6 per cent); units of public-independent companies 318 (8.5 per cent); units of non-US headquartered companies 283 (8 per cent); independent partnerships 22 (0.5 per cent) and non-profit independents 45 (1 per cent).
11. The database is vTHREAD (techno-historical regional economic analysis database and the letter v for making visible) which was created at the Center for Industrial Competitiveness at University of Massachusetts Lowell. Descriptions and applications can be found in Best, Paquin and Xie (2004) and Best (2006).
12. The category of complex systems connotes engineering, the integration of software and hardware, process controls and precision instruments, computer and communication technologies. See Best (2001, pp. 140–43) for a fuller treatment and Prencipe (2003).
13. This section in particular, and the chapter in general, draw from a longer study of the medical device industry which includes a description of the database of high-tech companies (Best 2006).
14. For these and related statistics and their sources on the size and growth of the US medical devices industry go to www.devicelink.com, the website for the trade publication Medical Device and Diagnostics Industry, and www.AdvaMed.org, the website for the Medical Technology Association, accessed 20 December 2008.
15. By US Department of Commerce data, Massachusetts is ranked within the top five medical device States in value of shipments, employment, payroll and value added by both per capita

and absolute size (Clayton-Mathews and Loveland 2004). The enterprise location quotient data is from vTHREAD (Best 2006).
16. EG&G is one of the earliest and most illustrious of the region's high-tech companies. Formally incorporated as Edgerton, Germeshausen and Grier, Inc. in 1947, the partnership of MIT graduates began with a firm established by the first two in 1931 to develop of stroboscopic photography; Grier joined in 1933 (Roberts 1991, p. 4).
17. The acquisition of Agilent Technologies' Healthcare Solutions Group added cardiovascular ultrasound imaging, patient monitoring, electrocardiography, resuscitation products and e-care business to Philips' portfolio. This reflects the region's technological capability in both cardiovascular and imaging technologies.
18. Ernst & Young (2000) reported that more than 1200 biotechnology US companies employed 153 000 up 42 per cent from 108 000 in 1997. For the Massachusetts biotech and pharmaceutical sectors, see Owen-Smith and Powell (2006) and Lazonick, March and Tulum (2007).
19. The adjective 'infrastructural' is used to signal a different form of networks from vertical, supplier, horizontal and other networks that imply links, closed or open, along a supply chain or amongst firms within a sector. Here the focus is on connections by which enterprises can draw upon expertise, capabilities and knowledge that have been cumulatively and collectively shaped by the region's enterprises over many product, technology and sector generations.
20. Venture capital, however, is not the only source of investment funding for high-tech companies in Massachusetts. For example, of 268 medical device business units in CorpTech's Massachusetts' dataset for 2005, 46 have been or are venture-capital backed, 52 are listed companies, 33 are units of listed companies, 23 received 'outside' corporate venture investments, and 94 are 'private investment' backed.
21. Government contracts have been crucial to Massachusetts' high tech from the beginning. Lieberman referred to research by Edward Roberts attributing the success to two factors: 'the "uniqueness" of the average company's technology – which makes it relatively immune to competition – and the availability of Government contracts during its crucial early years' (Lieberman 1968).
22. The federal Small Business Innovation Research (SBIR) Program provides competitive grants to entrepreneurs seeking to conduct 'Phase I' proof-of-concept research on technical merit and idea feasibility and 'Phase II' prototype development building on Phase I findings. The SBIR Program has been a preeminent seed capital fund for the development of new technologies and often provides the initial source of financing for many high-tech companies. Recipients of SBIR funding use the credibility and experimental data gained to attract strategic partners and next stage capital investments. The dollar value of SBIR awards per capita to Massachusetts companies is 3.5 times greater than to California and 2.5 times greater than to Virgina, the other leading State (MTC 2006, p. 42).
23. The NIH is the principle source of funds for health-related research in the US and a critical driver of the biotech, medical devices and health services sectors of the Massachusetts economy. The per capita health and human services R&D expenditures in Massachusetts were over four times the national average and over three times those of any other State in 2003 (MTC 2006, p. 48).
24. See MTC (2007) and previous years of the *Innovation Index*.
25. To paraphrase Peter Evans, Hirschman's 'multidimensional conspiracy' involved an assemblage of entrepreneurial energies, positive spillovers into other sectors of the economy, an alignment of government ministry policies with business capability development, and a molding of political interest groups into a development coalition (Evans 1995, p. 7).

47. Industrial districts, sectoral clusters and global competition in the precious jewellery industry

Frank Pyke

1. INTRODUCTION

Recent years have witnessed a growth in public policies focused on local economic development, involving the engagement of actors in promoting industry and employment at the micro-level. Geographically-concentrated sectoral clusters are popular targets of action. Such actions generally seek to help local firms be better fitted to meet the competitive challenges pertaining to their sector, and so must be sensitive to the latest industrial trends occurring inside and outside the cluster. These could, for example, include trends in consumer preferences, buyers' sourcing strategies, regulatory developments, fashion changes, technological possibilities, and so forth.

The importance for competitiveness of being tuned into changing global economic trends has been a long-standing feature of discussions of clusters. In fact, part of the reason why the Italian industrial districts (IDs) and their networks of clustered enterprises came to public attention in the 1980s and 1990s was because these local economic systems were perceived as being especially well suited to the major global trends of the time, in particular the movement away from Fordist mass production towards the break-up of markets and the organisation of industry on a basis of flexible specialisation (see, for example, Pyke, Becattini and Sengenberger 1990).

Today, for district and cluster competitiveness, effective response to industrial trends occurring both upstream and downstream in the value chain is no less crucial. This is the case for the subject of this chapter: the precious jewellery[1] sector, a truly global industry undergoing rapid change and where manufacturing clusters located along the international jewellery value chain is being challenged to respond to emerging trends. This chapter examines the global pressures on places characterised by jewellery clusters, and asks what kinds of public policies might be appropriate for competitive success, especially in the context of an emerging knowledge and creative economy.

2. THE GLOBAL PRECIOUS JEWELLERY INDUSTRY AND ITS MANUFACTURING CLUSTERS

2.1 The global value chain

In the precious jewellery industry, manufacturing clusters are integrated into an international value chain spreading across dozens of countries, with different places tending to specialise in particular activities. The main stages of the value chain are the following.

2.1.1 Raw material production
At the upstream end of the chain, some countries are proficient in the production of raw materials, such as gold, silver and platinum, and gemstones such as diamonds, emeralds and sapphires. For example, diamond mining is especially significant in Botswana, Russia, South Africa, Angola, Canada, Democratic Republic of Congo and Australia.[2] Much gold comes from South Africa, US, Australia, China, Peru, Russia and Indonesia.[3] Platinum largely comes from South Africa and, to a lesser extent, Russia.[4]

2.1.2 Refining and processing
Further downstream, there is metal refining and gemstone processing – mainly cutting and polishing – which also has its geographical centres or nodes. India is the major global centre for stones processing, especially diamonds and emeralds. Russia, China and Israel are also significant diamond processing centres, the latter specialising in bigger higher value items. Thailand is another important gems processing country.

2.1.3 Manufacturing
Further down the chain, and often in other parts of the world, are the manufacturing centres. Numerous countries have jewellery manufacturing traditions, such as the UK, US, Germany, and especially Italy, but in recent years of particular significance has been the emergence onto global export markets of new jewellery manufacturing supplier countries, namely China, India and, to a lesser extent, Thailand and Turkey. These four countries have progressively and rapidly challenged the erstwhile global leader, Italy, for global export market share.

It is at the processing and manufacturing stages that the industry is often geographically concentrated in sectoral clusters. For example, in India, in the State of Gujarat the town of Surat is the location for 10 000 diamond processing enterprises, while Rajkot hosts around 5000 gold jewellery enterprises and another 10 000 making silver jewellery and related wares (Sethi 2005).[5] Thailand has gemstone processing clustered in Chantaburi, and a purpose built manufacturing and trading cluster at Gemopolis, near Bangkok. In Turkey, thousands of jewellery workshops, retail establishments and other businesses are clustered around

Grand Bazaar in Istanbul (Korolu, Ozelci and Uurlar 2007), and the city also hosts a new purpose-built jewellery cluster at Kuyumcukent (Jewellers' city) where over 2000 production workshops, wholesalers and retailers are located. In China and Italy jewellery manufacturing is also clustered (see later).[6]

2.1.4 Trading and consuming

Finally in the value chain are the main jewellery consuming and trading countries, and the (often major) retailers, brand holders and distributors which inhabit them. The biggest consumption market is easily the US, followed by countries that include in particular India, Italy, Japan, China and some Middle Eastern countries. Some countries – not necessarily the biggest consumers – are high importers and so are particularly important for the international flow of jewellery goods, and thereby the globalisation of the jewellery industry. The biggest jewellery importer country in the world is by far the US, followed at some distance by the UK, the United Arab Emirates and Switzerland. These four leading importers are also significant jewellery exporters, reflecting their trading 'import–export' roles.

3. EMERGING GLOBAL JEWELLERY TRENDS

The global jewellery industry is characterised by huge turbulence as protagonists at many points along the value chain take action to further their interests, and the frequently clustered processing and manufacturing centres located in the middle of the chain are being impacted by trends emanating from both upstream and downstream in the industry. These clusters and the public policies to promote them are in strong international competition with one another.

Price pressure has been an important trend driven by the arrival on the world scene of the low labour cost manufacturing supply countries, such as China and India.[7] However, there have also emerged other important competitive variables which may very well become increasingly significant. In particular, findings from research carried out in the UK in 2006 (Pyke 2007) – the second biggest precious jewellery import market in the world – point to the growth of 'product competition', and also competition on the basis of 'supply-chain processes'.

In respect of product competition, fashion and design have risen in importance for all levels of the market. This means that manufacturers able to make well-designed, in-fashion products have a significant competitive advantage. For example, recent years have seen a significant broad fashion shift from plain gold jewellery (typical of products traditionally made in Italy) to 'white' products (silver, platinum and white gold) and to gem-set jewellery, that is metal (gold, silver or platinum) pieces set with precious gemstones such as diamonds, emeralds or rubies. This has been to the advantage of those countries such as China, India and Thailand which have the appropriate product traditions and competences.

Further, in response partly to consumer tastes, but also to strategies by retailers and others to differentiate their offers, product ranges are broadening, and life cycles are shortening, especially, it seems, in the volume market.[8] Thus suppliers in touch with market needs and with a capability to design and produce products quickly are likely to do well.

Branding of products also has grown in importance as a market differentiator and as a means of capturing more value, and many retailers, distributors and manufacturers have been keen to sell jewellery under their own brands. Thus manufacturers who can act as 'original equipment manufacturers' (OEM) and 'original design manufacturers' (ODM), helping buyers develop their own exclusive designs and brands, are likely to be in demand.

Also significant could be a trend towards ethical sourcing as consumers in countries such as the UK demand products made according to acceptable levels of labour and environmental conditions. Thus 'ethically made products' is another source of differentiation.

Further, product markets appear to be segmenting, with not only significant variations in tastes between countries but also even within countries, according to age, region or other attributes. In the UK, for example, there is a particularly strong demand for items made of 9 carat gold, whereas other countries prefer other degrees of fineness. The US, for example, has a preference for 14 carat gold. Consequently, suppliers with a capability to serve segmented, rapidly changing markets are likely to have a competitive advantage.

Finally, also important have been changes in distribution channels and supply-chain processes. In the UK, major jewellery retailers and distributors are increasingly buying direct from manufacturers wherever they are, and new sales outlets such as supermarkets, television and internet selling are spreading. There has also been a trend towards greater supply-chain cooperation on matters such as design and inventory control, and customers have wanted manufacturers to become more flexible, change their product runs more often, produce in more varied quantities, and provide a quick response.[9] Further, actors in the supply chain have been offering their customers, or are being requested to provide, an increased range of services, such as packaging, repair services, stock replenishment, customisation and special order services, and more.

The upshot is that the emerging trends have produced a strong element of product and process (supply chain) competition, which seems likely to continue, and possibly intensify. If so, we can expect brand promotion to grow and become an important battleground. Also, design will continue to be paramount as will sensitivity to fashions, and variations in such – including differences between national markets and within national markets. We can also expect a strengthening trend towards innovation, in the use of new technologies, new materials, and attempts to create new products or product combinations. Supply chain innovations are also likely to continue, involving, for example, developments in international supply-chain organisation, relations between actors, distribution networks and links to consumers, supply flexibility in product variation and quantities, and services along the supply chain.

All the above set the stage for a new level of international competition between jewellery processing and manufacturing industries, many of which are clustered. Such product and supply-chain process competition will require a capability for creativity, innovation and flexibility, and an ability to manage continual change.

4. THE CHINESE COMPETITIVE CHALLENGE TO ITALIAN JEWELLERY IDs

In China and Italy jewellery manufacturing is mainly geographically clustered, and a comparison of how their industries are faring, and the implications for public policy, illustrates elements of an emerging international battle that encompasses a range of countries.

4.1 Italy

In Italy, jewellery is geographically clustered in five places. These include agglomerations in the three principal jewellery IDs of Vicenza in Veneto, Arezzo in Tuscany and Valenza Po in Piedmont,[10] and the areas around Milan in the North and Torre del Greco in Campania, in the South.

In general, Italy is renowned for its plain gold jewellery, including gold chain products produced in Arezzo and Vicenza, although Valenza Po is more oriented to gemstone jewellery. These three IDs are dominated by small and medium-sized enterprises (SMEs) and typically contain an array of supporting institutions, such as design schools, fairs, chambers of commerce and employers' and workers' organisations.

For the Italian jewellery industry, the export market is important. Italian jewellery exports are reported to account for 50 per cent of sales, and of those exports the three IDs of Vicenza, Arezzo and Valenza Po account for 81 per cent. The Milan area accounts for another 11 per cent (Sethi 2005).

The three main Italian jewellery districts, together with Milan, have been responsible for many years for making Italy easily the biggest precious jewellery exporter in the world. However, since the late 1990s, the Italian export dominance has been severely challenged by the arrival onto world markets of products from the new supplying countries of China and India, and, to a lesser extent, Thailand and Turkey.

4.2 The challenge of China

The challenge of China can be illustrated by presenting a comparison of Italian and Chinese precious jewellery exports over ten years between 1997 and 2006.

As can be seen from Table 47.1[11] and Figure 47.1, China has rapidly caught up with Italy.[12]

Table 47.1 Precious jewellery exports, by value, Italy and China, 1997–2006 (US$ millions)

	1997	1998	1999	2000	2001	2002	2003	2004	2005	2006	% increase 1997–2006
Italy	4539	4471	4773	5089	4649	4577	4261	4702	4714	5211	+15
China	1339	1306	1608	1916	1928	2334	2813	3383	4021	4506	+236

Source: COMTRADE, Code 7113, own elaboration, not including internal 'exports' between Mainland China and China Hong Kong.

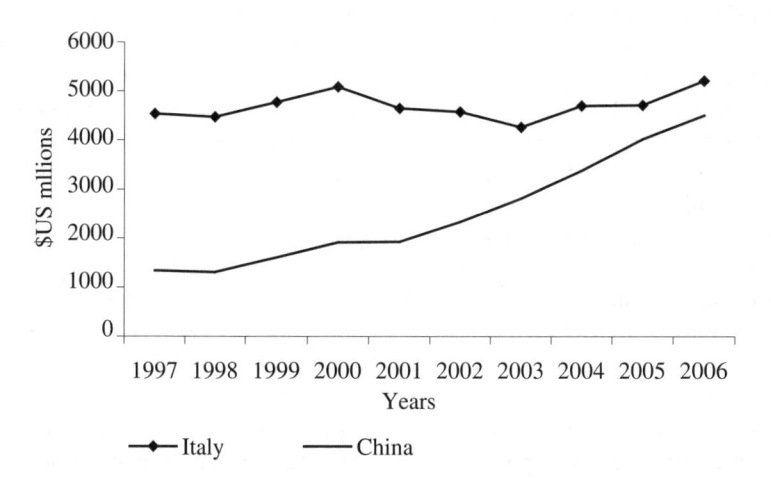

Source: COMTRADE, Code 7113, own elaboration, not including internal 'exports' between Mainland China and China Hong Kong.

Figure 47.1 Global precious jewellery exports, Italy and China, 1997–2006

The Chinese precious jewellery industry is located mostly in the south and forms clusters in Hong Kong, Shenzhen, Huadu and Panyu, the three latter locations all being in Guandong Province.[13]

Of these, the very export-oriented jewellery cluster in the city of Panyu has developed in less than 20 years, much of it thanks to outsourcing from Hong Kong. Panyu could be particularly significant in the growth of Chinese export share. In 2005, this jewellery cluster was reported by Chinese sources to account for 30 per cent of all diamond jewellery exported from Guandong Province to Hong Kong, US, Europe and elsewhere (Singapore-China Economic and Trade Cooperation 2006). By 2006, it was exporting $US1.16 billion worth of jewellery (Life of Guangzhou 2007), and substantial proportions of that which went to Hong Kong was then being sent on to other countries. Thus Panyu's products, whether by direct exports or via Hong Kong, have established a significant presence on global markets.

The growth of the Panyu jewellery cluster has been very rapid, such that by 2005, it included around 250 jewellery enterprises, employing about 50 000 workers, carrying out various upstream and downstream value chain activities, including diamond processing, jewellery machinery manufacture and finished jewellery manufacture (ICE 2005). Since then, the cluster has continued to expand, with sources now indicating up to 400 jewellery related enterprises employing up to 70 000 workers (Gem News 2007; Diamond Administration of China 2008; Diamond World 2008).[14]

Detailed research on the reasons for the growth of the jewellery cluster in Panyu is lacking. However, there is suggestive circumstantial evidence. For example, descriptions of prominent Hong Kong/Panyu companies, as described on web sites and in the Hong Kong Jewellery Manufacturers Association Directory, indicate a prevalence of, often large, enterprises[15] carrying out OEM and ODM[16] work, and frequently specialising in the manufacture of jewellery set with gemstones, especially diamonds. Also, UK research in 2006 compared large jewellery retailer and distributor buyers' perceptions of how China and Italy (and other countries) compared on various supply attributes. China in general scored significantly well on price and various supply chain competences associated with service, a readiness to cooperate with customers, and flexibility – such as fast response and a flexibility to respond to changes in orders (Pyke 2007).

It seems likely that Panyu's growth and competitive success, especially on export markets, has resulted from the cluster's effective adaptation to the requirements of global jewellery trends. This may very well include: price competitiveness due to low-cost labour; some product competitiveness due to a competence in manufacturing gemstone products, which have become increasingly fashionable; and competitiveness in supply chain processes, responding to a trend for major retailers, brand owners and distributors to be sourcing directly from manufacturers capable of carrying out OEM and/or ODM work; and, possibly, an ability to supply flexibly in varying quantities including small and large volumes.

4.3 New directions for public policy

However, successful as Panyu's jewellery cluster has hitherto been, its current competencies may not in themselves be enough to satisfy emerging trends, including, especially, the heightened importance of design, branding, differentiation and fashion sensitivity, and product innovations in materials, technologies and jewellery applications. These may require new public policies.

In fact, there are indications that the Chinese authorities are aware of current limitations and are now trying to employ policies to encourage their jewellery clusters to move onto a new level of knowledge-driven and product and innovation-led, and higher value adding, competition which sets the scene for further challenges to the Italian counterparts, as well as to other places in the world where jewellery is manufactured, including, for example, India, Thailand and Turkey.

In China, as elsewhere, leveraging knowledge is becoming an important aim and one policy has been the encouragement of the sharing of ideas and expertise between jewellery clusters. The Hong Kong and Panyu industries have agreed to cooperate by jointly establishing an R&D centre for the jewellery industry in Panyu, organising training on jewellery design and production, and promoting the adoption of innovative technologies and management systems aimed at enhancing productivity (Hong Kong Productivity Council 2005).[17] Also, it has recently been reported that Panyu has entered into an agreement with the United Arab Emirates, a very important jewellery trading hub and a developing manufacturing centre, in order to cooperate over the exchange of knowledge in jewellery design, and educational and training initiatives, as well as promote business opportunities (JCK 2008).[18]

There are also efforts to develop Chinese brands. A 'famous brand strategy' has been advocated by the government, and an intention to promote large enterprises that have established their own brands, and to promote brands at the levels of regions, are featured in the Guandong Province 11th Five Year Plan (Li and Fung Research Centre 2006). Already, gold and jewellery enterprises in Shenzhen are actively working to develop brands (Shenzhen Government Online 2007, www.sz.gov.cn, accessed 30 August 2008), and in Panyu there is an intention to help the jewellery industry develop its own brands (Life of Guangzhou 2007).

Such policy efforts are occurring in the context of an enhanced awareness in China of the importance of design and creativity and active efforts to promote creative industries.

4.4 The end of Italy's jewellery industry?

There is no doubt that the Chinese jewellery clusters are posing a formidable challenge to their Italian rivals, as well as to other manufacturing clusters in the global value chain. However, as of 2006 Italy remains the number one global precious jewellery exporter and it is by no means certain that China's rapid progress will continue.

In respect of a capability to compete on a basis of creativity and product differentiation, it is notable that the UK 2006 research found that Italy may already have an advantage because it is perceived by jewellery buyers for retailers and distributors as strong in quality and the clear leader when it comes to design capabilities and strength of brands. Further, other places where jewellery is

> **Box 47.1 Promoting precious jewellery clusters in India, Thailand and Turkey**
>
> India, Thailand and Turkey are engaging in active public policies to promote their precious jewellery processing and manufacturing industries, which are often clustered. For example, in India, design training schools have been established in Surat, Jaipur and Delhi; national jewellery design competitions have been inaugurated; and initiatives have been taken to increase Indian designers' exposure to international trends, such as, for example, by helping them attend international fairs and exhibitions. In Turkey, the Kuyumcukent jewellery complex ('Jeweller's city') in Istanbul is being purpose built with the aim of making the Turkish jewellery industry 'the world leader'. Facilities in the process of being built include over a thousand small and medium-sized workshops, and many more offices, wholesale and retail establishments, infrastructural and telecommunication facilities, a hotel, a chemical waste processing plant, and educational institutions to train Turkish jewellery designers as well as other jewellery workers. In Thailand, Gemopolis, located near Bangkok, is another purposely created cluster. It includes a full range of activities in the value chain, including gems trading, processing, machine manufacture, jewellery manufacture, jewellery wholesale and retail, and various service functions. The cluster also includes a training facility, incubator space and support, an exhibition centre, hotels and living accommodation for workers. In 2008, the cluster is reported to include over 80 jewellery related export oriented manufacturers, as well as service providers and wholesalers and retailers. Over 10 000 workers work in the cluster.
>
> *Sources*: Kuyumcukent (www.kuyumcukent.com.tr, accessed 30 August 2008); Gemopolis (www.gemopolis.com, accessed 30 August 2008).

manufactured, often in the form of clusters, in countries such as India, Thailand and Turkey are not standing still (see Box 47.1).

Moreover, there could be other centres of production developing elsewhere, such as in Russia and the United Arab Emirates, which can only add to the competition and uncertainty of outcomes.

Much may depend on how public and private policies carried out by competing jewellery locations meet the challenge of emerging trends described in Section 3, especially in respect of the rise to prominence of a need to be able to compete on 'products' and 'supply chain processes'.

5. THE ROLE OF PUBLIC POLICIES IN THE ERA OF THE KNOWLEDGE AND CREATIVE ECONOMY

The global jewellery industry is going through tremendous change with important implications for those places where the industry is clustered. It is clear that there is a range of product and supply-chain process-related influences at work – such as design and fashion requirements, brand identification, ethical sourcing and flexible supply. Added to these is the dynamic of change as product cycles shorten, markets segment, and the demand for variation increases, and the development and implementation of new ideas – new products, new services, new ways of producing and selling – takes on added importance. Such jewellery trends are mirrored in other sectors and are associated with a new stage in competition associated with the rise of the knowledge economy, and the growth in importance of creativity and the creative industries. Such industries are characterised by the use of knowledge and intellectual capital as inputs, and are reported to be outperforming more traditional manufacturing and commodity sectors (UNCTAD 2008b).[19]

Awareness of a need to respond to the requirements of the creative economy has grown in policy circles, and governments such as those for New Zealand, Australia, China, Singapore and the UK are developing appropriate national and regional strategies (DCMS 2008). Policy ideas in various countries include the development of 'creative cities' and 'creative clusters'.

In the jewellery sector, authorities promoting manufacturing clusters in IDs, towns and cities of Italy, China, India, Turkey, Thailand and elsewhere will also need to develop policies to improve capabilities for competition on a basis of knowledge, creativity and innovation. In some sectors actions have already been taken, and it is noticeable that already these five countries are currently amongst the top 20 world exporters of creative goods. China and Italy occupy the first and second positions respectively (UNCTAD 2008b).

This begs the question of what kinds of policies and conditions are likely to promote the required competitiveness. Some key aspects will be touched upon below. These are likely to be the battlegrounds on which international competition will be fought.

5.1 Knowledge generation and dissemination

A major focus for policymakers must be on the creation of the conditions for optimal generation and dissemination of knowledge through developing clusters' capacities as 'learning organisations' (Steiner and Hartmann 2006) that can promote new innovations in designs, materials, technologies, productivity and products, supply-chain processes and cluster flexibility *vis-à-vis* quantities, product ranges and timing. To such ends, the establishment of collective institutions such as design schools, art centres, fashion forecasting agencies, market research centres, international fairs and technology training schools may promote the generation and dissemination of information and new ideas and innovations.

Government or private sector programmes can promote learning and product innovation networks, where there is cooperation between enterprises and between enterprises and institutions, such as productivity centres, design schools, innovation agencies and universities. For example, in the UK, the Technology Strategy Board

(TSB) aims to launch a 'knowledge transfer network' for the creative industries (including jewellery) that bring together a range of industry players in order to help industry access the knowledge and information that will improve innovation. The TSB will also facilitate 'knowledge transfer partnerships' which partner individual companies with an appropriate higher educational institution, for the purpose of sponsoring graduates to help companies on particular projects (DCMS 2008)

Such collaboration and networking can occur within places where clusters are located, but also possibly there could be useful opportunities for collaboration 'between' places – such as, in China, between Panyu, Shenzhen, Huadu and Hong Kong, or, in Italy, between the IDs of Arezzo, Vicenza and Valenza Po. There could even be international collaboration along the value chain (see, for example, Bellandi and Caloffi 2009). There may also be collaboration between enterprises and institutions in jewellery clusters and those in other sectors such as clothing, footwear, fashion accessories (such as handbags) or ceramics, in order to innovate and create new products, or new applications for jewellery and/ or develop common marketing and branding strategies.

Knowledge can be generated locally and internally to a cluster, and at the same time, be transferred 'horizontally' between enterprises, and also 'vertically' from external sources, such as between the branch plants of incoming investors and local enterprises. Inward investment policies could target, for example, leading enterprises in design innovation to encourage them to import their competences. Programmes can be designed to induce vertical supply-chain cooperation between branch plants and local enterprises, and/or between branch plants and R&D agencies or universities, which can act as intermediary knowledge distributors.

5.2 Addressing market and supply chain requirements

Another battleground relates to marketing, product promotion, the creation of adequate distribution networks, and the development of effective supply-chain processes.

In respect of product promotion, the establishment of strong reputations for quality and design competence are likely to be major foci of competition, and countries hosting major jewellery manufacturing industries may seek to develop images of general superiority in these areas by promoting national brand labels such as 'made in China' or 'made in Italy' or 'made in Turkey'. A country's reputation for quality could be boosted by the setting up of testing and hallmarking centres which guarantee precious metal content. More broadly, promoting a country's quality and design reputation might be of a general scope rather than just for jewellery.

However, not only must clustered jewellery industries be capable of quality, creativity and design, they must also be able to make products demanded by the market. The segmentation of market demand, coupled with an accelerating turnover of fashion and products, makes the acquisition of knowledge about consumer and buyer trends increasingly important. For this, large enterprises might be able to afford their own market research departments. Small enterprises could benefit from collective institutions such as cluster-based market research and fashion forecasting centres.

International fairs help manufacturers keep up with trends by enabling them to see the offer of others and through interaction with competitors and, especially, buyers. Closer supply-chain collaboration with retailers, distributors or brand holders could be a further way of maintaining links to changing market trends – with customers providing regular feedback on popular selling lines. Manufacturers could also acquire consumer information by integrating downstream through the establishment of own distribution networks, or own retail and internet selling outlets.

Another challenge is the establishment of flexibility of supply in terms of quantity and breadth of products. Large enterprises may be able to go it alone. Clusters of small enterprises might benefit from the presence of intermediaries or network integrators, which can, upstream, control quality and procurement and generally collect the products of the cluster, and, downstream, interface with buyers over design, promotion, ordering and delivery, and various producer and marketing services. In such a system, a lead company, or cooperating group of companies, or agency, is able to offer buyers a complete service while acting as a coordinator of subcontractors. By such means, clusters are able to innovate in supply chain processes that offer possibilities to cater for a fast-changing differentiated market.

5.3 Labour and social conditions as inputs to competitiveness

A third crucial terrain of competition between clusters is likely to focus on the mobilisation of labour and social assets at the local level. This derives particularly from the fact that the coming to the foreground of competition on a basis of knowledge, creativity and innovation implies an enhanced role for labour as a crucial input to competitiveness, at both the levels of the individual firm and that of broader clusters and communities.

Consequently, we see that in recognition of the need to address local specificities, while at the same time responding to accelerating changes in skill needs, governments are increasingly decentralising labour market policy formulation and implementation to the local level. Further, the trend is to ensure better skills relevance by integrating labour market policies and actions, including training, with those of other spheres, such as economic development strategy, including on a sectoral or cluster basis. The provision of a high-quality flexible labour supply as inputs to established enterprises, or as creators of new enterprises, has become a major aim.

Inside the enterprise, a speeding up of innovation in products and processes – involving new technologies or new ways of doing things – has produced a derived need for a greater involvement by workers in workplace learning. Indeed, research at the International Labour Organisation has shown that the utilisation of workplace learning is already generally high, while specific research in Mauritius reported a perception by entrepreneurs that its use was accelerating, derived from a need for enterprises to keep up with changing trends, such as a need for higher quality, or flexibility, or new technologies.

Thus the role of labour in enabling enterprises to keep up with changing demands is crucial for the jewellery clusters. For this, it is known that high-performance adaptive workplaces require a satisfaction with working conditions and an atmosphere of trust and collaboration inducing thereby a desire by workers to continuously learn and apply lessons for the benefit of the enterprise.

Not only do labour and social conditions in the workplace matter. In local economic development settings economic and social spheres in general often overlap. In developing countries, in particular, some people may in fact work from home and housing and living conditions and costs (such as lighting, heating and rental costs), and the opportunities and constraints imposed by household roles, have a direct impact on competitiveness. Moreover, even where living and work places are separate, as Brusco (1996) pointed out in respect of the IDs of Emilia-Romagna, bringing the right attitudes to work and being prepared to 'give of one's best' is influenced by a general satisfaction with conditions outside the workplace. Social cohesion in the community is likely to be reflected in greater cooperation in the workplace. Further, good housing, schooling, transportation, environmental and cultural conditions significantly influence entrepreneurs' behaviour when it comes to locating new businesses, and workers' behaviour when changing jobs.

Other community and social conditions also matter. Particularly significant could be access by entrepreneurs and workers to social protection schemes which provide insurance against contingencies such as accidents, illnesses, unemployment and death of family members. In labour-intensive industries such as jewellery manufacture, poor social protection undermines efforts by entrepreneurs and workers to contribute to the development of sustainable enterprises. Moreover, there is a growing awareness that the ensuring of an adaptive flexible labour supply for an innovative economy requires the presence of adequate social security provision that can facilitate change both within enterprises and on an area or cluster basis. In Europe, the strategy of combining enterprise flexibility with worker protection and security has been given the name of 'flexicurity' (Cazes and Nesporova 2007).

Enterprises and communities have another good reason to ensure acceptable working and living conditions. An important trend in recent years has been the rise to prominence of ethical sourcing whereby consumers are selecting products according to perceptions of adherence to adequate labour, social and environmental standards in the enterprises where products are made and in the communities they inhabit. In response, leading retailers and distributors and other jewellery actors, in the UK, US and elsewhere, have formed an ethical sourcing initiative under the auspices of the Council for Responsible Jewellery Practices which aims to control standards all along the chain. Such pressure coming down international value chains is of great significance for industries such as jewellery which are substantially oriented towards exporting. It is likely that in the future, demonstration of adherence to adequate standards will become another element in the establishment of competitive advantage as enterprises, and maybe even whole clusters and their communities, seek to establish their ethical credentials and differentiate themselves from competitors. In the future, place of origin branding might very well commonly include a labour, social or environmental element.

It is clear that the creation of conditions for high-performance adaptive and creative jewellery enterprises and clusters has broader socio-economic connotations than simply the narrow 'economic' sphere. The upshot is a requirement to integrate key labour and social aspects into jewellery (or other) cluster competitiveness raising strategies. Such integration will require the development of appropriate cluster and community – wide governance structures that can ensure coordination and coherence in economic and social policies, involving actors from a range of training, community, employers' and workers' representative organisations, and other institutions, brought together in the form of public–private partnerships. Such partnerships can act locally, and also, possibly, cooperate with similar institutional organisations located at other places along the precious jewellery value chain, at both the national and international levels.

6. SUMMARY AND CONCLUSION

In the global jewellery industry, forms of processing and manufacturing clusters are common. In recent years, a number of low labour cost manufacturing countries, namely China and India, and, to a lesser extent, Thailand and Turkey, have rapidly expanded their exports and threatened established industries elsewhere. Italy's jewellery industry, mostly represented by three leading IDs, has, in particular, as a consequence experienced a significant decline in global market share.

No doubt price competitiveness has played a significant part, as it has in other sectors, but it is clear that product aspects such as design, branding and fashion sensitivity, and supply chain processes have also risen to the fore. Such features have been associated with the rise of the knowledge economy and the heightened importance of a capacity for creativity and innovation. All the indications are that this will form a crucial terrain for what is increasingly looking like a global battle between locations hosting jewellery clusters.

It is clear that such locations and their clusters are not homogenous. For example, while Italian IDs are composed predominantly of small enterprises and have a history of entrepreneurial endogenous development 'from within', the Chinese Panyu cluster is characterised by the presence of larger enterprises and appears to have been driven by a reliance on inward investment of capital, and technological and marketing expertise, especially from Hong Kong. No doubt other clusters in Thailand, India, Turkey and elsewhere also vary in their characteristics. Some could very well be developing on a basis of a mixture of both small enterprise endogenous growth and large firm inward investment.

It is by no means clear which jewellery manufacturing locations will win out. There is tremendous turbulence all along the global value chain with buyers, manufacturers, processors and raw material producers all taking proactive actions to further their interests, which only serve to further complicate the competitive environment for others. Those manufacturing clusters which will do best might be the ones which are most able to adapt to changing trends. An important factor could very well be a capacity to develop an enabling mix of policies that promote creativity, and new knowledge, and provide an innovative *milieu*. In this endeavour, the awareness of the role of labour and social conditions as inputs to competitiveness, and the characterisation of districts and their communities as 'socio-economic' phenomena will be important.

NOTES

1. 'Precious jewellery' refers to jewellery articles made from gold, silver or platinum with or without precious gemstones, such as diamonds, emeralds and rubies.
2. These seven countries account for 96 per cent of diamond production in volume terms in 2005 (GJEPC-KPMG 2006).
3. These seven countries account for 63 per cent of gold mined in volume terms in 2005 (ibid.).
4. South Africa accounts for 78 per cent of the world's production. Russia supplies 13 per cent (ibid.).
5. Also in India, Jaipur in Rajastan is the location of a cluster of thousands of enterprises engaged in processing emeralds and other gemstones and manufacturing jewellery (Sethi 2005). Other significant Indian jewellery centres include Ahmedabad in Gujarat, which makes gold products, and Mumbai, an important trading centre.
6. In other countries also there are examples of clustered jewellery manufacturing centres. For example, in the UK, jewellery has traditionally been made in districts of Birmingham and London. In France manufacture has been concentrated in Lyon and Paris, and in Germany, Pforzheim, known as 'Gold Town', is a traditional manufacturing centre. See CBI (The Centre for the Promotion of Imports from Developing Countries), 'EU Market Survey: 2004, Jewellery', www.cbi.nl, accessed 10 October 2008.
7. Mention should also be made of the part played by the use of discriminatory import duties, especially by the biggest importer in the world, the US; and the effect of exchange rates, such as the high value of the euro against the US dollar. Also soaring gold prices have added to price pressures.
8. As early as 2001, the Hong Kong Trade Development Council (HKTDC) was advising manufacturers there that the market trends generally were for precious jewellery products with reduced life cycles, and that for exporters there was 'an increasing need to handle orders of smaller quantities but wider varieties, along with shorter lead times, especially for mass market items' (TDC 2001). A 2006 review of global jewellery trends (GJEPC-KPMG 2006) also highlighted the occurrence of highly volatile design and fashion trends and accelerating product cycles.
9. See also GJEPC-KPMG (2006) which points out that changing consumer preferences and the increasing influence of fashion in jewellery is resulting in retailers putting pressure on manufacturers to produce orders more quickly. The implications for manufacturers are that in order to meet the requirements of short-term demands and accelerating product cycles, it is necessary 'to develop more efficient design, production, distribution and inventory control processes'. Adopting the latest technologies, it is pointed out, would provide manufacturers with 'the flexibility to quickly churn out designs in smaller batches to keep up with highly volatile design trends'.
10. These three IDs have jewellery manufacturing clusters composed of SMEs. Valenza Po is reported to have 1300 enterprises (including 900 production units) employing 7000 workers,

Vicenza 1000 enterprises with 11 000 workers, and Arezzo 1100 enterprises employing 10 000 workers (Sethi 2005).
11. Note that the reference is to exports by value. Over recent years there have been strong rises in gold prices which have increased the value of exports without necessarily increasing the volume of articles sold. In fact, for Italy the volume sales of exports have declined in recent years, even if values (thanks mainly to rising gold prices) have increased.
12. Note that the other new supplier countries, especially India, have also caught up with Italy. Between 1997 and 2006, Italian exports increased from $US4.5 billion to $US5.2 billion (+15 per cent) (see Table 47.1); Turkish exports increased from $US163 million to $US1.1 billion (+575 per cent); and Indian exports increased from $US624 million to $US4.7 billion (+653 per cent). Thai exports increased from $US837 million in 1999 to $US1.7 billion in 2006 (+103 per cent) (COMTRADE, code 7113).
13. Hong Kong is (in 2005) the location for 453 mainly small or medium-sized precious jewellery manufacturing companies, employing 4132 people (TDC Trade 2007). The large metropolitan area of Shenzhen contains a cluster of over 1100 gold and jewellery enterprises, employing 110 000 people (Shenzhen Government Online 2007, www.sz.gov.cn, accessed 30 August 2008). Shenzhen's gold jewellery output is concentrated in the Shatoujiao Bonded Area (C. Wang 2004). Huadu is an urban district hosting a rapidly developing jewellery manufacturing cluster. Currently the Huadu Jewellery Industrial Park houses more than 60 enterprises, and another major international park covering an area of 5000 acres is being created. Eventually, the new park should host 300 jewellery enterprises (Life of Guangzhou 2007; Invest Huadu, www.investhuadu.gov.cn/topic.php?channelID=14&topicID=132, accessed 30 August 2008; www.gjepc.org/SOLITAIRE/magazines/Oct05_Nov05, accessed 30 August 2008).
14. The cluster is supported by a range of institutions such as an industry association, a technology training institute, and the Worldmart Jewellery and Gem Emporium Centre which promotes trading in raw materials and finished products, and provides a range of promotional and logistics services.
15. For example, there are at least ten plants in Panyu employing 800 or more, and five of these employ between 1400 and 4000. Those ten plants in total employ around 16 000 people, not far below the 17 000 employed by all the 2400 enterprises of Valenza Po and Arezzo combined.
16. OEM refers to the making of a jewellery product to another company's specifications which may be sold under the customer's brand. ODM refers to situations where the local manufacturer carries out some or all of the product design, often in line with general ideas provided by the customer.
17. In 2005 the Hong Kong Productivity Council signed a collaboration agreement with the people's government of Panyu district of Guangzhou to foster the development of the jewellery industry in the two clusters. Actors are also actively promoting other Chinese jewellery clusters. In Shenzhen, a gold and jewellery quarter is being developed which is supported by an international trade centre and an international fair, and there are plans to establish an R&D centre, a production examination centre, a training institute and a quality control centre (Invest Shenzhen, www.szinvest.gov.cn/info/park/5.htm, accessed 30 August 2008). In Huadu, the intention is to support a new jewellery park with institutions that include: an exhibition centre, a gold and silver examination centre, and a jewellery school (Huadu International, www.huadu.gov, accessed 30 August 2008.).
18. In April 2008 the Dubai Multi Commodities Centre signed a memorandum of understanding with the people's government of Panyu district for increased cooperation in jewellery.
19. UNCTAD includes within the definition of the creative industries: performing arts, audiovisual activities, new media products, publishing and printed material, creative services, visual arts, cultural heritage activities and products, and design rich products such as furniture and jewellery. The creative industries are among the most dynamic sectors in world trade, and UNCTAD estimates that international trade of creative goods and services reached $445.2 billion in 2005, with an annual growth rate of 8.7 per cent from 2000 to 2005 (UNCTAD 2008b).

48. The internationalisation of production activities of Italian industrial districts

Giuseppe Tattara*

1. INTRODUCTION

Industrial districts (IDs), since the 1970s, have been the engines of Italian industrial growth and of the rapid increase in Italian manufacturing exports. They have developed in particular in the 'made-in-Italy'[1] and mechanical engineering sectors (Becattini 1995–96; Becattini and Menghinello 1998). Since the Italian economy has always been poor in raw materials, manufacturing activity has developed as an industrial process that transformed imported goods. Consequently, Italian districts tend to be importers of raw materials and exporters of finished goods, that is, they are connected abroad through large flows of imports and exports (Piore and Sabel 1984; Becattini, 1995–96; Brusco and Paba 1997; Foresti and Trenti 2006). Few districts, if any, are dependent on domestic demand.

Globalisation has brought about a sharp increase in the real and financial integration of the worldwide economy and the structure of the Italian districts has evolved in parallel. Italian districts are no longer self-contained systems of small firms where firms' competitiveness is the result of physical proximity, connected to foreign markets at the initial and the final stage of the production and distribution activity. In the new context, firms often expand or transfer abroad one or more phases of their production activities. Thus production abroad has become the focus of industrial strategies followed by district firms seeking to reduce costs and/or to exploit potential new markets.

Globalisation has reshaped the form of the district. Most district firms are now organising their value chains by coupling district knowledge and competencies (Becattini and Rullani 1992) with opportunities offered by the globalisation processes. It is often the complementarity between the location-bound 'strengths' of domestic components and the non-location-bound knowledge of the foreign components that leads to valuable new resource combinations. For example, foreign multinational enterprises setting up production in a district may provide access to assets, skills and routines that may usefully complement the location-bound knowledge of domestic firms. At the same time, foreign firms have access to important knowledge relations. The rise of integration at the international level has contributed to the transformation of IDs and in some cases has proved to be the real driver of a district firm's competitiveness in recent years (Di Maria and Micelli 2007).

The shift of manufacturing towards low labour costs countries began, according to some scholars, at the beginning of the 1970s,[2] and at first involved countries with high labour costs such as the US, Germany, Sweden, Denmark and the UK (Ádám 1971; Finger 1976, 1977). Italy and Spain entered the process much later in the early 1990s, in response to the increased competition from firms that had already outsourced to low-cost countries, and in the context of a more liberal international setting. Italian firms were induced to outsource by the opening up of the central-east European countries, while the decision by Italy to join the euro zone has prevented a familiar recourse to currency devaluations, a policy that previously periodically readjusted the competitive power of Italian exporters.

Additionally, the participation of East European countries, including Russia, as well as India and China, in the international consumption market, with their high rates of growth in a world developing at low speed, has provided a further incentive to transfer manufacturing production abroad and to locate close to growing final markets.

Although many economists associate internationalisation (especially exporting and foreign direct investment, FDI) with size, the district firm is typically small. In fact, the relation between size and the various forms of internationalisation is rather uncertain in a production context where network relations prevail. The firm's size, traditionally measured by the number of employees, is an ambiguous measure of its level of activity. District firms tend, in many cases, not to grow in size, but to follow alternative strategies, such as relying externally on specialised production phases, or being part of formal and informal collaborative groups – unfortunately, these phenomena are not adequately accounted for in the available statistics. Final production and exports from districts emerge from informal networks that remain invisible to the usual statistical measures. At the same time, the fragmented production structure of the district can be an advantage when firms are sourcing from abroad as, in many circumstances, such sourcing means in fact simply transferring production phases that already exist in the local territory. This process can develop through FDI, but in most cases it takes place through simple subcontracting; frequently this implies either transferring functions abroad to firms that for instance use the same technology previously employed in the district, or pushing former subcontractors to establish their plants abroad in order to reduce costs – a common practice for the Italian clothing and footwear district firms internationalising in Eastern Europe.

The way district networks are organised affects their degree of internationalisation. Lazerson and Lorenzoni (1999b) and Tattara (2001) suggest an important role for lead firms in developing districts, and according to Lazerson and Lorenzoni (1999b) the districts with a strong presence of lead firms are the most inclined to international success. Lead firms, generally firms of medium size, tend to organise key activities in the district, including the development of technologies, the generation-diffusion of skills and knowledge, the search for new markets, and the management and organisation of efficient value chains at the international level through FDI and subcontracting.[3]

Porter emphasises the importance of domestic rivalry as a prerequisite for successful internationalisation (Porter 1990a, 1998a; Sakakibara and Porter 2001). According to Porter, domestic rivalry pressurises firms to innovate and upgrade while fostering positive externalities in the local business environment, such as supplier availability, easier access to technology, market information, and specialised human resource development. Excessive horizontal and vertical concentration reduces domestic rivalry, generates inefficiencies and local subcontractors are transformed into passive agents of a static player, rather than being actors able to face successfully the international competitive market.

The scenario for most of the Italian districts is one of a presence of several medium-sized lead firms, operating in closely-related niche markets, linked by elements of collaboration and rivalry that create strong competitive incentives together with greater pressure to upgrade production, an idea that goes back to Schumpeter (1911) who saw competition as a dynamic process of creating new products and processes. Dynamic competition spurs innovation and production improvement and in turn international competitiveness.

2. PRODUCTION INTERNATIONALISATION

District firms establish relations with actors in foreign countries through a multiplicity of channels: through import and export trade flows; through direct investments abroad and the attraction of inward investment; through subcontracting; and through commercial, technological and other kinds of formal and informal agreements.

A significant part of firms' overseas activities involves the use of intermediary forms of internationalisation in the shape of trade agreements and subcontracting, both of which are particularly important in the case of Italian small and medium-sized enterprises (SMEs) (Bigarelli and Ginzburg 2005; Capitalia 2005). These 'light' forms involve less capital flows compared to FDI, but greater commodity flows, as commodities are sent abroad to be processed and, subsequently, reimported for the finishing stages. Such commodity flows are not, however, separately recorded from the general transit of goods passing through customs, and can be therefore identified with difficulty. More because of this statistical constraint than for such light forms of internationalisation being judged unimportant, international trade experts have not being able to rigorously analyse them (Bugamelli, Cipollone and Infante 2000; Mariotti, Micucci and Montanaro 2004). Although empirical evidence shows that internationalisation in the form of direct investment involves a limited number of businesses, it is well known that a significant number of firms have engaged in intermediary forms, such as technical collaboration agreements with overseas companies.

In Italy, the little analysis available seems to indicate that the traditional sectors, and those sectors characterised by economies of scale, are less present in foreign markets and account for a smaller portion of FDI than the high-tech sectors. This finding is nonetheless controversial: anecdotal evidence indicates that in Italy the delocalisation of firms in the textiles, clothing and footwear sectors is highly significant (Rossetti and Schiattarella 2003; CEPS-WIIW 2005; Constantin, De Giusti and Tattara 2008), and occurs in the light forms mentioned earlier. For example, within traditional sectors there has been a steady and substantial increase in the number of firms that have established trade agreements with foreign partners (Bugamelli, Cipollone and Infante 2000). Also, a large study on Italian manufacturing sectors with firms with more than ten employees, for the period 2000–03, confirmed, as already well known, that the large majority of Italian firms are exporters (70 per cent of the total), and has also revealed that a large number of firms were increasing, maintaining, or starting up, trade operations and foreign trade agreements with foreign correspondents (Capitalia 2005).

2.1 Trade flows

Trade is the most well-known form of internationalisation. Studies on the export performance of Italian districts have aimed to provide empirical evidence that district firms have a better export performance than non-district firms. A first difficulty encountered in the analysis has been to reconcile trade statistics with the spatial scale of districts.[4] Trade statistics are often available only at the provincial, regional and national level. The empirical analysis in Bronzini (2007) showed a solution: relying on 'local labour systems' relevant statistical data on districts' foreign trade were collected. From this, it was possible to define an index of district intensity for each province[5] so that the export performance of Italian provinces could be related to their district intensity. Bronzini (ibid.) found that Italian districts presented a stronger export performance compared with the national average, and some of the most dynamic export areas were typically districts.

Menghinello (2004) and De Propris, Menghinello and Sugden (2008) have more recently found that IDs are among the most competitive local industrial systems in Italy, and that the districts account for a remarkable share of national exports across different sectors, thus disproving the traditional view of a sector-specific effect on the Italian economy.

The positive relation between districts and exports has several possible explanations. The positive role of the Marshallian district economies on exports is specifically tested by Bronzini (2007) and looks significant, even when controlling for sectors, size and infrastructures. Interestingly, the author shows that the positive impact that size has on exports for firms located outside districts, is 'equal to' the positive effect that territorial agglomeration has for smaller sized district firms; economies of scale in the provision of export services and informal face-to-face exchanges of information about export markets can explain the export performance of small district firms.

Becchetti, De Panizza and Oropallo (2007) tackle the problem of the relation between districts and exports with the help of a more sophisticated database. They study the export, and value-added, performances of IDs by integrating information on the population of Italian firms (from the ASIA database of the Italian Statistical Institute) with balance sheet data for all limited liability companies in selected manufacturing industries. Their findings show that firms located in IDs export more, and have higher value added, than firms located elsewhere, net of the impact of appropriate control variables.

De Arcangelis and Ferri (2005) provide a new insight into the export dynamics of Italian districts. They advance the idea that the specialisation of the Italian IDs has gradually changed since the 1990s, and many districts are now specialising in the production of capital goods directly linked to districts' traditional areas of specialisation, mainly exemplified by 'made-in-Italy' consumption goods. The same line of argument is advanced by Russo (2006) who argues that the tile district of Sassuolo is slowly shifting towards the production of tile processing machines; and also by De Giusti (2006) who points out that there has been an increase in the exports of machines for clothing and shoemaking towards those countries where the Veneto district firms have relocated their outsourcing. These studies reopen the question posed long ago by Becattini (1979), about the usefulness of defining district specialisation with reference to the entire vertically-integrated manufacturing process (*filière*). They also draw attention to the ambiguity of measuring districts' export propensity only in terms of the final product without considering capital goods.

A *filière* approach would require a definition that embeds the manufacturing of capital goods into a district specialisation. But the link is not a straightforward one. In many cases machine manufacturers inhabit a territory that stretches beyond district borders and so the scale of proximity might need to be reconsidered. In particular, machine manufacturers are less prone to agglomerate or to locate close to downstream firms, they are limited in number and serve customers located in a wide area (N. Rosenberg 1963, p. 219). For this reason, the concept of *filière* is not necessarily associated with territorial proximity.

2.2 Foreign direct investment

FDI is an important strategy for the production internationalisation of medium and large-sized firms. It is well known that the main drivers of both inward and outward FDI are resource seeking – for example, to access cheap resources – market seeking or knowledge seeking. The large direct investments of the past by the UK and later on by the US were mainly directed at exploiting natural resources, while today integration at the international level has stressed the capacity of low-cost countries to perform significant phases of manufacturing production. In this context, district firms have been outsourcing specific production phases abroad in search for low-cost labour; whilst, at the same time, their high level of performance has attracted foreign investors who want to 'breathe' the district air.[6]

A study by De Propris, Driffield and Menghinello (2005) employs an inward investment database stratified by industry and province to show that the specific properties of territorial agglomeration are an important explanatory variable of inward investment flows. IDs are particularly attractive to foreign investments which enter the locality and become part of the local networks; foreign firms look to gaining access to a district's specialised know-how and seek to embed in its governance structure. Harrison (1994), in a more descriptive and less systematic way, provides anecdotal analysis of inward investments into the Italian region of Emilia-Romagna, mainly brown-field, by foreign firms wishing to enter the more successful Italian districts.

More generally, multinationals have entered Italian districts in order to augment their knowledge base in specific and highly competitive localised knowledge clusterings, via the acquisition of key district firms: for instance, the acquisition of Canstar by Nike in the Montebelluna district (subsequently sold, the direct investment being substituted by a permanent subcontracting relation); the acquisition of Calzaturificio Monique, a leader in the lady's footwear district Riviera del Brenta, by Louis Vuitton; the purchase of Marelli Motori and Lowara, two of the most important producers of the electric motor district of Vicenza, by FKI energy technology and by ITT respectively; and many others. The number of inward FDIs in Italy has recently rapidly increased and if globalisation has diminished many of the traditional roles of location, districts seem to be able to exert a growing importance as attractors in an increasingly complex, knowledge-based and dynamic economy.

Much more debated by Italian researchers is the issue of outward investments. Using data from *Ufficio Italiano dei Cambi*, Federico (2006) analyses for the period 1997–2001 the distribution of FDI outflows by sector and local area of origin and investigates which industrial locations had the largest propensity to invest abroad. Controlling for a set of variables, the author finds no evidence of the presence of districts having a positive impact on FDIs, contrary to what happens for exports. Foreign investment outflows are mainly generated from firms in the two metropolitan centres of Milan and Turin where larger size firms are located. Additionally, FDIs tend to be associated with firms producing in capital-intensive goods sectors, which are not typical of district production.

The explanation for the weak role played by IDs in outward FDIs can be found by the author in the sunk costs connected with the decision to invest abroad, which penalises smaller firms. This also explains why the latter prefer light forms of internationalisation, mainly subcontracting and informal agreements. Therefore for district firms – and smaller firms more generally – the amount of FDI does not capture the extent of production internationalisation actually undertaken, as such firms as well as international brands and retailers that lead consumer-driven value chains (providing designs, supervising quality and the delivery of products from abroad) make recourse to subcontracting and informal agreements (Gereffi 1994; Gereffi, Humphrey and Sturgeon 2005).

Although Italian districts do not account for a large share of FDIs, when it happens, it has an impact on the structure of the domestic value chain. Maggi, Mariotti and Boscacci (2007) studied the effect of FDI from district firms in the northeastern regions (34 districts in 'made-in-Italy' and electro-mechanical sectors) on the local value chain and found that the internationalisation of some production phases tend to lead to a more expensive and complex logistics system, and to require more supervision, coordination and control over geographically-dispersed activities.

2.3 Subcontracting

SMEs extend their supply chain abroad through international strategic alliances that can take various forms (Dunning 2001). The most common form of outsourcing is a non-equity agreement between a firm and one or more of its suppliers to act as subcontractors, supplying, producing or distributing the firm's products. Subcontracting does not involve separate venture or equity investments and is less formal than equity relations.

The incentive to rely on subcontractors is either to reduce costs or to mitigate project risks. Through such means, the contractor receives the same or a better service than the one he/she would have provided by him/herself, at lower overall risk since one of the main aims of subcontracting is an increased flexibility along the supply chain. Many subcontractors work regularly for the same customers, allowing them thereby to develop specialised competences.

Sourcing from abroad through subcontracting is one of the most common ways of opening up the value chain beyond the ID. If in the past it was mainly the case that goods and services were domestically accessible maybe from another Italian region, more recently district firms have started to look abroad to outsource production phases in countries with low labour costs. In those IDs where a decomposition of production phases is common practice, sourcing from abroad has been relatively straightforward, and small firms, having limited finances, have made recourse to subcontracting. For example, many firms in the clothing districts have developed growing subcontracting relations with firms located in Southeast Asia, in Central-East Europe and in North Africa, while numerous firms in footwear districts have looked mainly to Central-East Europe and East Asia.

Italian districts also contain clusters of firms which are part of international chains whose head offices are located abroad and which source significant phases of production from within the districts. Rather well-known examples include: the plastic moulds cluster (Montebelluna-Oderzo) that supplies the international automotive industry; the Livenza furniture cluster which is, in Europe, a large supplier of Ikea; the jewellery cluster in Vicenza that supplies watch cases to large international watchmakers; and the lady's footwear cluster of Riviera del Brenta that supplies high-fashion international brands such as Vuitton, Dior, Jimmy Choo and others.

Due to low transport costs and the use of information technology, subcontracting is profitable even when production lots are small (say hundreds of pieces of clothing, not thousands) and products vary considerably in kind. Subcontracting is accompanied by a process of standardisation and codifiability, although face-to-face relations prove still to be very important, particularly for complex products. FDIs are prevalent when production quantities are large, where a hierarchical organisation is more suitable and where fiscal conditions in the country of investment are favourable.

In some cases, successful subcontracting can benefit from governments' support for instance through specific tariff provisions. The Outward Processing Trade provision of the EU and the preferential tariff treatment envisaged by the Trade and Development Act for the US in respect to the Caribbean are examples. Those transactions which make recourse to the Outward Processing Trade provision are largely concentrated in labour-intensive sectors, such as textiles and clothing, footwear, some categories of machinery and mechanical appliances, other industrial goods, vehicles, processed food and leather products.

Recent subcontracting outwards trends show that a lot of outsourcing involves SMEs in the host countries as much as SMEs in the home Italian districts. The trade flows of merchandise related to outsourcing are very unstable due to the absence of sunk costs (which is in fact a characteristic of the FDI process), although changing partners is costly – due to the need to build up commitment and trust – and spot relationships do not guarantee quality and time to market.

When Portugal joined the EU in 1986, and during the transition period to membership, Portugal attracted a lot of outward processing trade. When the low labour cost attraction weakened or disappeared, the EU's outward processing operations shifted to North Africa, Turkey and Yugoslavia, and later to Eastern Europe. By the early 1990s employment and output were falling in Portugal, particularly because German retailers switched orders to Eastern Europe. Exports from Portugal to Germany fell sharply and clothing employment in Portugal declined by almost 25 per cent between 1991 and 1995 (Thiel, Pires and Dudleston 2000). The same happened subsequently with Poland and there are signs that the same process is now affecting Romania.

International subcontracting can take different forms. In one form, known as industrial subcontracting, only some production phases, frequently the most highly labour-intensive ones, are transferred abroad. The product is then reimported at some stage in order to perform final assembly and finishing. In the case of 'made-in-Italy' goods, this process can guarantee a legitimate use of the made-in-Italy label.

The way relations with foreign suppliers is organised reflects numerous elements, including transport costs, product codifications, the confidentiality of customer–supplier relations, and the levels of technology in the supplying country. In Eastern Europe and North Africa, raw materials of high quality are seldom available, so it is necessary for the outsourcing firm to send them for processing. The technological infrastructure is often discontinuous and some production phases are unavailable. Modern production requires complex phase processing in all sectors from traditional to more technology-intensive ones. For example, Italian clothing, footwear and furniture firms sourcing in Romania have faced bottlenecks in fabric printing and dying, sole ignition, and trivalent chrome plating respectively. In order to complete the production phases abroad the customer firm in the district had either to invest directly to guarantee a certain level of competence or encourage the outsourcing firms to make the appropriate investment (Constantin, De Giusti and Tattara 2008). Sourcing is profitable only if the production process abroad is smooth and effective;[7] in fact, and in many cases both subcontracting and direct investments are used to remove costly bottlenecks along the production chain.

Another form of international subcontracting is full package sourcing, where suppliers take on the responsibility of delivering a complete product, which is practised in countries with raw material availability and a strong experience in manufacturing, as it is the case, for example, of South Asian countries (Gereffi 2002). Full package subcontracting is often accompanied by the establishment abroad of distribution and commercialisation outposts, and is referred to also as horizontal subcontracting.

Both vertical and horizontal subcontracting relations are difficult to measure from available statistics. Ideally, what is required is a measure of intra-industry flows. As things stand, intra-industry trade can refer both to subcontracting and FDIs, and it comprises imports and exports of both intermediate and final products. Again full package subcontracting and FDIs generate trade flows that are indistinguishable from the exports and imports of finished products, so again it is very difficult to disentangle the components of the complex inward and outward trade flows and estimate the extent of foreign sourcing.[8]

3. THE EFFECTS OF SOURCING ABROAD ON ENTERPRISE PERFORMANCE AND EMPLOYMENT

An important aspect of studies on the production internationalisation of Italian IDs is the impact that this has on the home economy and on firms in particular. Several studies have looked at the effects of outsourcing on firm performance and employment. Assuming (majority) equity investment as a proxy for production outsourcing blurs the analysis, since FDI is only part of a larger set of decisions: sometimes direct investment acts to complement and sometimes to substitute for other forms of sourcing, and cannot be meaningfully analysed in isolation.

Rossetti and Schiattarella (2003) examined the sourcing from abroad in the typical 'made-in-Italy' sectors looking at trade flows, following the approach pioneered by Yeats (1998) and Kaminsky and Ng (2000). The quantitative measure of intermediate trade flows for different regions, carefully scrutinised at the commodity level, was related to an estimate of new employment abroad and to an estimate of job creation at home. The encouraging result is that while sourcing from abroad in the 1990s grew rapidly in some regions, employment and income per employees also rose in the very same regions.

Gianelle and Tattara (2009) analysed the impact of outsourcing on district firms' performance, taking into account various forms of sourcing from abroad, relying on data coming from a survey of 70 final producers operating in the clothing and footwear districts of Veneto, who in the 1990s began to manage production on a global scale. In the study, direct investments, subcontracting and partnerships that result in increased production abroad were jointly considered. The research was based on an *ad hoc* database that put together the findings from the abovementioned survey on production manufactured abroad in relation to turnover, data on employment at the firm level and data on firms' balance sheets during the years 1990–2003. The study found that sourcing from abroad has a net positive impact on profits and turnover for the firms in the home districts. However, the positive effect is one-off since it does not trigger a sustained rate of growth over time; in fact, it disappears when the movement towards foreign production is completed. The rationale for this conclusion is that outsourcing, in the majority of cases, occurs with the transfer abroad of phases and processes previously carried out in Italy, encouraged by increased price competition at the international level, while the machinery and the production techniques remain substantially unchanged. The positive impact on the home firms tend to stretch if there is continuous effort to introduce governance innovations (such as the introduction of product modularisation, or further transfer of knowledge) in order to constantly increase productivity and encourage the adoption of new technologies.

Working in an increasingly complex international setting encourages final producers to improve managerial and organisational efficiency and increases domestic demand for skilled high value-added services.[9] Nonetheless, the choice to delocalise abroad has an immediate strong negative impact on employment of small artisan workshops and on the connected skill base, particularly in a region where the number of people employed in manufacturing is as high as in Veneto in clothing and footwear, and where local sourcing was common practice in the 1980s, just before the onset of foreign sourcing (ibid.). The negative consequences of both the substitution of local sourcing with foreign sourcing, and of the crisis of some big brands not able to manage their value chain internationally, are evident.

The impact of outward FDI on domestic employment is negative in the case of vertical investment undertaken – especially by smaller firms – in less developed countries, and positive for horizontal and market-seeking investments in advanced countries (Barba Navaretti, Castellani and Disdier 2006). The first kind of investment points to a substitution, while the second points to an expansion of firms' activities towards new markets and a positive overall effect on the domestic employment, basically due to the extension of the functions provided by the lead company and outsourced in the local economy in order to manage more complex networks. In many circumstances both motives are present, and the end result is uncertain. This is often the case for sourcing from East Asia, with a view to access markets in China and India, and also from Central-East Europe, considered a gateway to the rapidly growing Russian market.

Sourcing from abroad makes the management of the value chain more complex and for this a positive correlation between internationalisation and employment growth in the logistics sector is expected.[10] There is a limited evidence, in the case of the Montebelluna district (Maggi, Mariotti and Boscacci 2007), that logistics are mainly sourced locally by the final producers. In fact, the logistics could alternatively be supplied by third party providers located outside the districts, or even located in host market where the foreign investment has been made. The aggregated evidence that Italian firms are buying abroad more logistics services than they sell, the Italian balance of payment in logistics services being heavily negative, is significant but not conclusive.

4. CONCLUSIONS

Falling transport costs, a more liberal environment and the intensification of trade has allowed firms to extend their competitive advantages beyond the district borders. At the local level, production internationalisation has triggered both centrifugal forces as firms have looked for and grabbed the new opportunities that were emerging in a growing international market, and centripetal forces as inward foreign investors have entered Italian IDs attracted by their competitive advantages often embedded in a tight socio-economic local community (Leamer and Storper 2001).

A large and rapid outsourcing of production activities from districts can lead to an impoverishment of their production base, in terms not only of employment but also of knowledge and skills. The innovations that have been at the root of the 'made-in-Italy' success have nearly always developed out of very close contacts between people who design and people who make. In the district, product and process innovations are intertwined in a production context and come out of the daily familiar use of machines and production materials: in other words, production integrates tacit and codified knowledge (see Robertson, Jacobson and Langlois in this volume). A key question is whether IDs will run the risk of losing their competitive advantage in designing once they lose their production competences. Can a favourable scenario reasonably be assumed where Italy maintains within its districts the high value-added stages, such as marketing, design and logistics, while realising in other countries the more labour-intensive and less skill-intensive functions? These issues are fundamentally important. Some entrepreneurs are already appearing to have increasing difficulties in finding workers in Italy with the necessary skills and knowledge, and this is a clear indication that the local pool of competences, from which enterprises have drawn in the past, is today increasingly depleted and thinning. On the other hand, firms embarking on the internationalisation venture are in need of highly-qualified people with a new set of competences to assist and manage the delocalisation process abroad.

Production internationalisation can also affect the basic social principles that underpin the nature and the fabric of the Italian IDs, including their capacity to regenerate in locally coherent forms the work, culture, social relations, and material and immaterial infrastructures that make up the district identity (Becattini and Rullani 1992). In the district, a large part of the process of knowledge transmission has been historically based on the interconnections between the economic-production conditions and socio-cultural conditions of the social system. Moreover, in districts a mutual solidarity has connected entrepreneurs, territory and society towards the attainment of a mutual progress: the destiny of the firm has often been considered in symbiosis with that of the community of people.

Over the last decade, firms of the Italian 'made-in-Italy' districts are leading their way along a different trend. Profit realisation is now further and further away from the places where companies that lead the production chains are located. Therefore, a positive profit by the final producers no longer directly leads to a positive effect on the district economy, for instance in terms of employment. This inevitably corrodes some of the constituent characters of the IDs.

NOTES

* I would like to thank Renzo Bianchi and Frank Pyke for their helpful comments.
1. The 'made-in-Italy' sectors include clothing–footwear–fashion, furnishing–house, food and wine.
2. For brevity we do not take into account the numerous historical experiences of delocalisation. For an account, see Findlay and O'Rourke (2003).
3. Rugman and Verbeke (2005) speculate that asymmetric clusters, that is clusters with the presence of leading firms, are more oriented to success in the international market. See also Rabellotti(2006).
4. This point is carefully analysed by Menghinello, in this volume.
5. See Meghinello, in this volume, for an exposition.
6. The creation of the FDI database in Italy is the result of careful work directed by Cominotti and Mariotti (1994) at the Polytechnic of Milan. Their database reports detailed information on foreign ownership for all manufacturing firms located in Italy, and foreign-owned manufacturing firms located abroad and owned by Italian entrepreneurs with a turnover superior to €2.5 million. On the recent statistics provided by the Italian Central Statistical Office, see Menghinello, in this volume.
7. According to Dahmén (1988), economic success in certain processes may require the realisation of one or more specific complementary processes or stages and such complementarities appear in many different forms as important elements of the process dynamics. Part of a process can be completed by a single entrepreneur or a group of entrepreneurs: 'the aim is making products and services saleable by initiatives to find new technical solutions, and to invest, or make others invest, in other sectors of the economy' (p. 113).
8. A large part of the increments registered in trade values at the world level in most recent years is due to trade in intermediate products (Yeats 1998; Kaminski and Ng 2000) and this has been related to the practice of external sourcing, but, of course, not all intermediate flows are intra-industry flows. The stages of production and countries involved must be carefully considered in order to avoid misleading conclusions. The problem of disentangling the horizontal and vertical elements of intra-industry trade is the object of several studies. See, among others, Al-Mawali (2005) and Fontagné, Freudenberg and Gaulier (2005). An attempt to connect the problem of vertical intra-industry trade with district specialisation is in Corò and Volpe (2006).
9. Gereffi (1999) stresses that being part of a value chain at an international level helps enterprises acquire knowledge and therefore provides a significant opportunity for production upgrading.
10. On the causal relation between FDIs and services, see Nefussi and Schwellnus (2007).

49. Lessons from industrial districts for historically Fordist regions

Josh Whitford

1. INTRODUCTON

This chapter is not so much about industrial districts (IDs) *per se* as it is about lessons the model might offer to regions that are decidedly 'not' IDs. Much of the literature on IDs has used them to show that there is more than one way to organize a regional political economy, that it is thus problematic to speak of a 'one best way', and therefore to fight Chandlerians and their ilk. But what does this mean for regions that are already on a particular path? In this chapter, I use a case study of the metalworking sector in the American Upper Midwest to show that changes in the organization of those industries have made analyses of IDs relevant even to some of those historically Fordist manufacturing regions that have long represented, at least rhetorically, the antithesis of the ID. The chapter's role in this *Handbook* is to underscore in yet another way that studies of IDs are not merely curiosities, and that insights drawn from their study should thus be of interest to readers across a broad array of academic and policy fields.

2. THE DECENTRALIZATION OF AMERICAN MANUFACTURING

The very development that first thrust IDs into the international limelight – the fragmentation of once-predictable mass markets – thrust them into that limelight precisely because it so fundamentally rocked the Fordist order. The 1970s inaugurated an era of dramatic corporate restructuring the effects of which are still felt today. Large firms that sell products on the final market in end-user industries like automobiles transportation equipment, industrial, farm and construction machinery, and electrical appliances had years of relative stability in core technologies (steel and mechanical engineering) shaken by the entry of new competitors in the developing world, and by the incorporation into their production processes of technologies developed in other sectors, such as new materials and electronics.

In the US, the effects are almost hard to overstate. 'Downsizing' became a part of the national lexicon and American manufacturing – then a much larger portion of that economy than it is today – shed millions of jobs. Those who survived did so in many cases by retrenching to their so-called core competencies in design, marketing and assembly, and by subcontracting ('outsourcing') other activities to a series of smaller, often non-union, supplier firms located in rural and semi-rural areas (Luria 2000). Indeed, it is not atypical for a manufacturer today to purchase between 60 and 80 per cent of the 'value added' from supplier firms.

In so doing, they were seeking in many cases to draw lessons from the flexible manufacturing practices and technologies that had allowed the economies 'in vogue' in the wake of the crises of the 1970s – especially Japan, but also Germany and IDs in central and northeastern Italy – to continuously maintain strong manufacturing sectors premised on innovation and quality production (Kenney and Florida 1993; Appelbaum et al. 2000; DiMaggio 2001). That is, they had often radically reconfigured their internal operations, incorporating team production and other means of fomenting worker participation; and they were developing teams of specialized suppliers upon whom they relied not simply for parts but also for aid in design.

However, patterns of restructuring have also been deeply marked by particularities of the American historical-institutional context. These have affected relations both internal and external to American manufactures. Internally, manufacturers hoping to compete in the higher value-added markets that privilege innovation generally require broadly skilled workforces. Yet, as Parker and Rogers (1999) have observed, there are a series of barriers that leave the US labor market to 'approximate a "low wage, low-skill" equilibrium' in manufacturing industries.[1] An initial skill mismatch and the ability to pay low wages gives firms an incentive to choose a work organization and product strategy that requires few worker skills. Moreover, there is an important cooperation problem that undercuts private investment in training: either firms train workers in such a narrow way that the new skills have little general valence on the labor market – meaning almost by definition relatively inflexible skills – or they risk having their trained workers 'poached' by other employers.

In terms of external relations, it is important to recall that outsourcing – the decentralization of production – can reflect very different underlying logics. In the words of Walter Powell (1990, p. 302), subcontracting may reflect efforts to obtain parts almost purely on the basis of price, in a 'campaign to slash labor costs, [to] reduce employment levels, and [to] limit the power of unions', or it may reflect an effort to build long-term collaborative relationships with suppliers, focused on security and quality production from skilled and innovative suppliers. The latter model bespeaks 'functional' flexibility. But it is the former – which reflects instead 'numerical' flexibility (Streeck 1987; Kalleberg 2001) – which tends to dominate in an American context historically dominated by arms-length relationships and capacity subcontracting. Put simply, when customer firms push their suppliers to invest in higher-level competencies, those suppliers are reluctant to do so for fears that their customers are themselves habituated to arms-length relationships likely to 'hold them up' if they do.

Of course, these are but variants of classic coordination problems that potentially bedevil any political economy. Supply must meet demand and vice versa. But they are particularly vexing in the US 'liberal market economy' (Hall and Soskice 2001a). American secondary associations – particularly of employers, but increasingly also of workers – are notoriously weak and in any case not well integrated with the public sector in the governance of the economy. This leaves few mechanisms to permit the monitoring and sanctioning of those firms that undermine collective efforts to push firms toward high-skill strategies. The upshot is that low-skill strategies are often 'in fact' relatively desirable.

Although such strategies do expose firms to competition from lower-wage areas and thus perhaps not feasible in the longer term, firms must also survive in the short term. Those who attempt strategies requiring significant training may see their investments go to naught as their workers are poached by others who have similarly invested. Similarly, reorienting purchasing strategy towards higher-cost suppliers who promise to acquire in new competencies is only a good idea if those suppliers in fact have the wherewithal to do so.

Since so many jobs are now in supplier firms, a sustainable and generalized high-wage, high-productivity manufacturing economy requires that small supplier firms take on high value-adding operations, develop new products, and train their workers. It is thus no surprise that American public authorities at various territorial levels have experimented with policies intended to ease the transition to a more decentralized production regime, often under the rhetoric of 'cluster' development popularized by Michael Porter (see especially Porter 1998a and 2000). However, beyond just a policy focus on sectors that already have 'critical mass', there is wide variation in what this actually means on the ground (Martin and Sunley 2003). In most cases, policy efforts differ little from traditional American industrial policy, captured in what Hall and Soskice (2001b) call 'blunt' policy instruments, by which they mean deregulation and market incentive policies that 'do not put extensive demands on firms to form relational contracts with others'.

But need it be this way? The experience of IDs suggests it need not. By this, I do not mean that restructuring, outsourcing, and the end of vertically-integrated Fordist production could reasonably have led to the formation or renewal of fullfledged IDs in the American industrial heartland.[2] At a national level, the US likely does lack the necessary associations and institutions to mediate interests either among workers or employers (Hall and Soskice 2001a). But at the same time, it is too easily forgotten that the US, particularly for industrial and training policy, is quite heterogeneous and considerable powers are delegated to the State and local level (Lowi 1985; Eberts and Erickcek 2002). As production is decentralized it increasingly makes sense for such regions to draw upon elements of the conceptual and theoretical apparatus that has been used to analyze IDs.

3. THE ID AS A UNIT OF INITIATIVE

The claim that studies of historically Fordist manufacturing regions can and should learn from IDs is a controversial one. IDs have – since their rediscovery – at times been dismissed in academic and policy debates as interesting but anomalous, ultimately too dependent for their functioning on local particularities to usefully instruct those unblessed with the right history (see, for example, Amin and Thrift 1992; and Harrison 1994 for notable examples). However, such dismissals have been based on a misunderstanding of the underlying thrust of at least the best studies of IDs. One of the key figures in the rediscovery of the concept, Sebastiano Brusco (cited in Natali 2007), remarked for example in his 'American lectures' that he 'hated people who think that Italians are easy-going people who like working together'. His point was that IDs are particular regional economies, but in fact 'all' regional economies have particularities. This trick is to recognize that IDs can and should be analyzed in general terms.

The key issue is one of organizational learning (Malmberg and Maskell 2006). The rediscovery of IDs simply made clear that organizational learning takes place in a context. That context, moreover, goes beyond the single firm or even the network of firms to include actors outside that network in training institutions, associations, and, more generally, the 'territory'. Misreadings to the contrary, this never implied that particular systems were (or could have been) self-sufficient in terms of knowledge (ibid.), and it was recognized early on that IDs' vibrancy depended very much on firms' simultaneous embedding in both local and global economies and knowledge networks (Brusco 1994). Certainly, standardized inputs could – and often did – come from elsewhere, but the resurgence of regional economies did, at the least in the boom years of IDs, show that the territory can represent a functional response to a fundamentally 'organizational' fragmentation of production, as the need continuously to adjust and recombine the production process has been favored when many of the relevant productive players can jointly be embedded in a localized 'network within networks' (see Dicken and Malmberg 2001).[3]

The lesson for historically Fordist regions was not so much that they needed to find ways to embed their producers in the global. That was in fact their relative strength. Their problem was embedding producers in the local. The experience of IDs suggests that in a world that privileges producers able to capture niches, successful regions are places that find ways to balance cooperation, conflict and competition both within and between firms. The more rapid introduction of new technologies and shortened product life cycles has driven a reintegration of conception and execution at the point of production, which in turn privileges worker participation in the improvement of products and processes; at the same time, absent the possibility of conflict and resistance workers are unlikely fully to participate. And because production has so radically been decentralized, no single firm has the competencies necessary to compete at the cutting edge of world markets. Innovation thus requires cooperation; but without competition and copying, ideas would not diffuse as rapidly across regional producers.[4]

If the economic performance of regions is usefully to be understood in terms of the balance of cooperation, conflict and competition in relations within and between firms, what regulates these balances? Here the literature on IDs is again too vast and variegated to be easily summarized (fortunately, this volume gives it some order). I thus rely on the relatively authoritative and consistent conceptualization put forth by Sebastiano Brusco.[5]

Brusco argued that the answers cannot simply be imputed from the incentives and interests of actors, as these are not independent of what he called the 'rules of the game'. These rules go far beyond the usual attention given to laws, property rights and so on. They include as well 'unwritten norms' of commerce, understood and enforced by the community, that dictate such things as when a contracting party can ask for guarantees without undermining trust, with whom one can and cannot share information, when third parties are expected to sanction 'malfeasance', and so on. This both improves economic actors' ability to find other parties with complementary skills with whom to transact, and makes them better able to coordinate strategy with those partners once found.

In short, successful IDs are those in which relations are governed by rules that somehow underpin a relatively felicitous mix of cooperation, conflict, and competition in relations between and within firms. But whence come these rules? Here, studies of the Italian IDs are instructive. There is enough variation in their structure and performance to demonstrate that while every regional economy has its own rules, these rules are neither independent from their embedding in the larger global system, nor are they simply 'written' by history. Rather, they are the fruit of at times conscious, at times incidental, action by firms, associations and institutions that interpret and mediate local systems' insertion into the global economy.

The variability of these rules, and their importance in the coordination of the economic activity within an ID, underpin what is perhaps Brusco's (1992a, p. 195) most important policy insight: the concept of the ID, he wrote, should be seen 'not only as a unit of analysis but also as a unit of initiative: as a fully-fledged and organically unified organization, whose development is slowed down or impeded by bottlenecks that public action must turn into opportunities' to resolve problems the private sector would be unable to solve alone. Such policymaking aims not so much to direct the economy, as it does to incite local actors to revisit and adjust the formal and informal rules they use to coordinate their productive activities, to act 'as a system', not merely 'in a system'.

4. SOME LESSONS DRAWN

The question in historically Fordist regions in general, and in the US in particular, is whether such policies are feasible. As I have already noted, few would accuse machinery producing regions in the American Upper Midwest of being institutionally ripe for the emergence of fullfledged IDs, the waves of outsourcing and the vertical disintegration of production that took place in the 1980s and early 1990s notwithstanding.

Still, the region is extremely rich in competencies and although there has certainly been some relative shift of manufacturing industries to the American Southeast, the 'great lakes' States have long been – and are at time of writing – disproportionately represented in the distribution of American manufacturing employment (Whitford 2005). The problem is that the 'rules of the game' are not those of a well-functioning ID. They do not balance cooperation, participation and competition. In fact, they have tended to privilege only the last. The results, of course, are the aforementioned difficulties in promoting skill upgrading among the frontline workforce, and unwillingness to develop the sorts of collaborative relationships between firms that might allow firms to compete in more profitable quality-sensitive market segments.

So what to do? There have been some notable and innovative initiatives to stimulate associational initiatives to support firms trying to flexibly produce high-quality goods using a skilled workforce. Two of these initiatives, both in the heavily industrialized American State of Wisconsin, are exemplary of the possibilities of learning from IDs even in the American rust belt.

4.1 Sectoral training

The Wisconsin Regional Training Partnership (WRTP) was born of the manufacturing crisis of the 1980s and the ensuing conviction of many in the State that some sort of re-vamping of the regional training system was necessary if the manufacturing-dependent greater Milwaukee area was to retain a substantial core of high-paying manufacturing jobs. In light of this, and armed with strong ties to organized labor and the support of some elements of business, academics at a research center at the University of Wisconsin proposed and organized the formation of a jointly governed consortium of employers and unions. Their goal was to get a critical mass of firms to agree upon some common standards and to commit to a baseline training expenditures.

The consortium they put together did not so much fight the poaching of trained workers as it sought to ensure that enough firms committed to training, thus ensuring an adequate pool of skilled labor, thus allowing firms that have been raided to expect to 'cross-raid' someone else (and thus to be willing to train). The organization focused initially on metal manufacturing industries. It was founded in 1992 with around a dozen large union shops and their unions, covering around 10 000 workers, and at its peak included more than 100 employers (mostly, though not exclusively, unionized) with some 65 000 workers. Bernhardt, Dresser and Rogers (2001–02, p. 116) of the Center on Wisconsin Strategy (which continued to provide logistical support to the WRTP) explain that at the core of the WRTP is employer agreement on a sort of 'code of industrial conduct' (though not a formalized one) in which employers commit to train frontline workers, to share curricula, and to benchmark against each other; to commit to modernizing operations and to preparing the future workforce; to permit workers a say in firm governance, especially in areas of training and human capital investment; and to support workers seeking career advancement with training support and to pay rewards for skill advancement.

But of course, ensuring the commitment of multiple firms is only a part of the story. The WRTP also offered logistical support through partnerships that coordinate the delivery of training and modernization services using a series of working groups in which employer and union representatives try to identify common problems and best practices, to develop pilot projects, and to implement them. In each of the areas in which the WRTP has been particularly active – pushing modernization and new investment, the training of incumbent workers, and the finding and training of new workers – the organization's strategy is not so much to provide direct services, but rather to serve as an intermediary, working to coordinate the many agencies and service providers that do exist in the US but that too rarely work effectively as a single system.

To play this role, the WRTP has built on its access to a regionally-focused organized labor presence, something that is decreasingly available in the US, but that proved extremely useful in the Wisconsin case. Organized labor has a very strong vested interest in employers undertaking strategies that require the capital investment and the worker skills that can in turn support high wages. It also brings knowledge of what works and does not in the day-to-day productive reality.

In short, it is perhaps difficult, but it is possible in the US to stimulate the integration of employers, unions, elements of the State training and modernization infrastructure, and community groups to improve labor market coordination. Rather than simply training workers under the assumption that a job will be forthcoming – the usual 'uncoordinated' approach in the US – the WRTP tries to query employers as what jobs 'could' exist were there skilled workers to fill them, pushes employers to invest to create such jobs, and then ensures that skills are produced to fill them. This, as Bernhardt, Dresser and Rogers (ibid.) write, is a 'level of coordination that does not happen on its own' but that requires an 'organization, such as the WRTP, with strong ties' to all the relevant communities.

The WRTP is generally recognized as a success story but it should be emphasized that it is an organization whose creation was very much a conscious political struggle. It has had its share of difficulties in the wake of the recession that hit American manufacturing in the early years of the 21st century. We are, as Dresser and Rogers (2003, pp. 284–5) write, talking here about the very 'resistible' rise of a workforce intermediary built against an 'infrastructure supporting, informing, and extending these local efforts [that] is fairly weak'. Nevertheless, workforce intermediaries like the WRTP and other examples from around the US 'can' form the basis for systemic change – a 'new sort of "American model" in training'.

4.2 Coordinating decentralized production

The second exemplar begins in 1998 with a manager at a large Wisconsin manufacturer who was frustrated by the reluctance of many of his suppliers to undertake investments in lean manufacturing and new services associated with the new logic of organizing. He sought out the State Manufacturing Extension Partnership (MEP) and like-minded managers at five other large State manufacturers and at key State agencies to undertake collectively to resolve this problem. These managers believed that the roots of this reluctance were to be found in suppliers' rational mistrust of their customers. Relations between these large companies and their suppliers had historically been quite difficult, and were exacerbated by pressures on personnel in those large companies to extract price reductions by threatening exit. But they also knew that their own efforts to institutionalize collaborative logics of relational action would founder absent reciprocal commitment from the supply base. They included the MEP because they realized it would be difficult to encourage that commitment without help from a third party.[6]

The MEP Program is an important, albeit perpetually embattled, piece of the American industrial policy apparatus.[7] Established in the 1950s but greatly expanded during the Clinton administration, it is a network of territorial centers founded to deliver services to small and medium-sized manufacturing firms. Funded partially by the federal government, partially by States, and partially by selling those services, these centers have considerable autonomy. However, as Robert Turner's (1999, p. 10) dissertation on the program has shown, they have for the most part operated by selling off-the-shelf technologies at subsidized rates on a first-come–first-served basis, with a 'persistent theme' being a 'difficulty in promoting increased cooperation among businesses and public sector programs'.

In Wisconsin, the director of the MEP was willing to experiment and, along with these large firms, solicited a small amount of financial aid from the State to form a consortium to deliver training and services to their small and medium-sized Wisconsin suppliers. There is not space in this venue fully to describe the functioning, governance and subsequent development of this consortium. Its effects upon supplier performance have been documented elsewhere,[8] so I emphasize here only that this consortium was founded to provide suppliers with a problem-centered training program to improve firm performance in lead and cycle time reduction, delivery, product quality and cost.

In and of itself, this is not remarkable. What is remarkable is the way in which it was done. The consortium aimed to deliver these services by leveraging and enhancing partial collaboration between large firms and their suppliers in order to align the organizational models of the firms involved (that is, to spur investment in co-specific assets). And it had some success. The point was well made by the manager of a supplier firm who had received training and development services from the consortium:

> The idea that two of my major customers would form a consortium with other people to help train their supply base ... I saw that as, 'We're in a whole different world now'. This is no longer, 'We do three quotes and send it to the lowest bidder and every year we go out and rebid it ... and if things slow up at all, we cancel everybody's orders and we make it in our own shop'. That was the paradigm in 1990 [but it is changed today].

In short, the consortium gave this manager, and others like him, confidence that he could expect the 'collaborationists' at his customers to win in struggles over strategy. The original consortium was since supplanted for a period by a smaller but more intense subset of the original members with broadly similar goals, with more resources and commitment required now of both customer and supplier participants. More recently, elements of the approach have formed the backbone for a proposal to expand a similar public–private model of supplier development in ways that allow for the delivery of services across multiple States and in ways that take greater advantage of the national MEP network. Indeed, far more has happened since 1998 – some good, some bad – than can be recounted here. But the point remains: by taking the regional economy as a unit of initiative, a mix of policymakers and business actors undertook to reorient the rules of engagement by means of a collective solution based on credible commitments, the exchange of information, and some form of monitoring in order to better balance competition and cooperation in inter-firm relations.

4.3 What it means, and where things seem to be going

This chapter has focused on coordination problems associated with the organizational fragmentation production, including particularly those associated with the balance of competition, cooperation and participation across a decentralized productive structure. Insofar as historically Fordist regions have seen a decentralization of production – and most have – policymakers in those regions can usefully draw lessons from IDs. The exemplars described in the chapter have not fundamentally changed the character of manufacturing industries in the State of Wisconsin. They are but two institutions in a larger political economy. They are also far from perfect; a fuller recounting of their development and functioning would be much more attentive to their limitations and ensuing evolution. But their very founding and functioning does underscore that – even in apparently unfertile ground – some of the most fundamental lessons to be drawn from analyses of IDs have valence.

There are ways to alter the rules that govern the mix of cooperation, conflict and competition in relations between and within firms even in historically Fordist regions. Many such regions have at least some of the bits and pieces of existing associational and relational structures that so often underpin processes of institutional change (Crouch 2005). When this is coupled with administrative decentralization, policymakers can and should try to identity those elements of their regional economy that are as much units of initiative as they are units of analysis.

Recognizing this is today more important than ever. The reader will surely note that this chapter has focused on parallels and lessons learned through the 1990s, which was the period in which historically Fordist regions reorganized to meet the challenges of an 'organizational' fragmentation of production. I have focused on this period in part because the lessons to be drawn are by now reasonably well established and can thus be used more clearly to show that there are in fact useful parallels to be drawn.

Today, it is more difficult to draw lessons from IDs. Manufacturing industries now face emergent governance challenges that, at time of writing, remain unanswered but provocative. As Herrigel (2009, p. 2) observes, there is new reason to question whether industrial communities must be 'located in specific and discretely bounded territories'. Do social and territorial proximity necessarily overlap? This seems less clear than it once did. What had been a relatively territorially circumscribed, and thus fundamentally 'organizational', fragmentation of production has acquired a more pronounced 'spatial' dimension in recent years as even complex processes have been spread across ever more geographically disparate locales.

The examples discussed above show that studies of IDs can serve – and have served – to illuminate strategies for managing the organizational issues associated with outsourcing. But will studies of IDs, with their attention to territorial solutions to organizational problems, again instruct the world when it comes to the issues associated with the spatial fragmentation of production? It is too soon to tell, but, as Charles Sabel has written, it is worth noting that IDs are 'on the move'. There is a relative consensus that particularly in Italy such systems are no longer well understood, again in Sabel's (2004) terms, as the 'world in a bottle'. They are instead 'windows on the world' or 'open networks' (Chiarvesio, De Maria and Micelli 2006) whose prospects and functioning depend ever more on the interplay between – and variation in – modalities of local and global action. This has in turn led studies of IDs to begin to look beyond the perspective of a single specialized cluster to incorporate inter-sectoral and inter-cluster linkages and to show that the multiplication of external relations up and down the value chain has engendered new constraints and opened new possibilities that firms and academics are only beginning to identify.

NOTES

1. Skill production in technical and scientific occupations that depend on general credentialing, on the other hand, are found by many to be favored by the American institutional infrastructure (Hall and Soskice 2001a).
2. To be clear, in American 'history', one certainly does find regional economies that are IDs by any definition. See for example Scranton (1991).
3. There is reason to think that some IDs today have increasingly to manage the dispersion of complex value chains across territories in a 'spatial' fragmentation of production. I return briefly to this theme at the end of the chapter. See also Whitford and Potter (2007b).
4. The references for this description could number easily into the hundreds. See Whitford (2001) for a review of the literature. Or read the other chapters in this volume.
5. For a recent and excellent overview of Brusco's thought, see especially the volume edited by Natali, Russo and Solinas (2007).
6. For a full description of this consortium, see especially Whitford and Zeitlin (2004); Whitford, Zeitlin and Rogers (2000); Whitford (2005).
7. All 50 States are currently served. For the centers that have consistently been shown to improve the productivity of the firms they serve, see Shapira (1998) and Bartik (2003).
8. See especially Rickert et al. (2000) and Whitford, Zeitlin and Rogers (2000).

SECTION 11
Public policies and industrial development strategies

Introduction

Giovanni Solinas

1. ALTERNATIVE APPROACHES TO IDs AND LOCAL DEVELOPMENT

This *Handbook* hosts two ways of seeing industrial districts (IDs) and local development. The first revolves around the various kinds of interconnections and interdependencies – in technologies, markets, competencies – developing among the local producers. In this view, competitiveness relies upon the specific nature of such interconnections and interdependencies: the analysis of the interconnections developing within a local production system (LPS) provides a complete understanding of the specialisation and the division of labor among the firms, and of the attractiveness for traders and buyers. The understanding of these interconnections explains the realisation of positive externalities and of Marshallian external economies. In other words, the denseness of this ideal map (in terms of quantity and quality) is what determines the growth of the local system. The second interpretation includes something more, which cannot be fully explained by any map of interconnections and interdependencies. It includes a cooperative factor that helps the network of industrial interdependencies with institutional and regulative support, and is rooted in the social relations of the local actors. The relative wealth (both potential and actual) of the ID also relies on this cooperative element, and not merely on the technological and productive relations. The two interpretations constitute the underlying theme of the introduction to this section on the policies to promote IDs and local development in industrialized, emerging and developing countries.

2. LEVELS OF POLICIES FOR IDs AND CLUSTERS IN EUROPE AND US

The chapter by Mikel Landabaso and Stuart Rosenfeld provides an analysis of the EU policies supporting IDs and LPSs, comparing them with similar strategies adopted in the US. After identifying some of the main differences between the local development policies implemented within the two areas (and their different theoretical background), the central part of the chapter analyses the most relevant directions pursued by industrialized countries, and by the EU in particular, through the European Regional Development Fund.

More specifically, the authors identify four main policy axes that define the development of IDs and clusters. The first policy axis concerns the building and strengthening of the relationships among enterprises; and it includes the promotion of networks across local enterprises and of other forms of collaboration focusing on a nucleus of common needs (on services, information, markets and so on). Particular attention is also devoted to the promotion of linkages between local and extra-local enterprises or other economic actors. The second policy axis concerns the reinforcement and the expansion of the local base of knowledge and competencies through the strengthening of the local organisations providing education, training and services for the diffusion of technological information and innovation. In this context, given that skills and competencies are related and transmitted also through interpersonal relationships, particular attention should be paid to the mechanisms regulating both job recruitment within the local networks of firms and career advancement for talented people. The third policy axis considers the processes to promote innovation. The authors refer to policies aimed at favouring the development of R&D activities, innovation in design and in product differentiation, and innovation in the enterprises' processes and organisations. They argue that such policies should fruitfully promote the development of organisational forms supporting the creation of linkages between technical colleges, public and private research centres and technology transfer centres, universities and innovative enterprises. The last policy axis concerns the promotion of entrepreneurship. This may include support for enterprises to enter the market, the creation of specialized incubators, enterprise tutoring activities (for example through the channelling of young enterprises into networks of more experienced entrepreneurs), and training initiatives supporting the growth of the managerial skills most suited to a specific ID. The four axes thus define a very broad area of experimentation with some pivotal elements: targeting specific local characteristics and competencies, promoting local leadership, identifying local needs and aggregating potential demand.

Joan Trullén presents and discusses how, in an economic context of low productivity growth, the Spanish government has designed and implemented a set of national policies to promote R&D activities and to guide the national economy towards more technologically-intensive sectors and more innovative activities. The most original aspect of these policies is the national dimension of the programme against the local dimension of its implementation. Since 2006, using the EU Structural Funds and the Regional Cohesion Funds, the national government has established a general framework for the funding of specific local innovative projects, somehow anticipating the guidelines provided by the EU for the 2007–13 programming period. The programme includes two stages. The first stage is aimed at identifying and selecting both local networks of enterprises and individual enterprises that can play a leading role within industrial poles. They are required to act as legal entities and to submit a project proposal that includes collaborations with innovation centres and technology transfer centres, business associations and universities. In this sense, the first impulse is local. The projects are then screened at the national level (second stage) and – following refinement of their strategic goals – they are declared eligible for funding. This stage sees the direct involvement (though with different roles) of the Ministry of Industry and the Ministry of Education.

A number of interesting aspects may be identified: the substantial amount of public funds, the attempt to involve a large number of local enterprises, the identification of local leadership and the specific targeting of the interventions. One of the main targets of the program is the promotion of relations between universities and industrial firms. During recent years, in some European countries, major changes in these relations have taken place. On one the hand, a small but not negligible part of the manufacturing firms have developed new links with universities, collaborating on process/product innovation activities, on processes of organisational change and so on. On the other hand, universities are increasingly oriented towards new forms of partnerships with enterprises, and not solely to obtain short-term funding. However, a note of caution is in order. There are traditional problems marking the relationships between universities and firms (small firms in particular) that have yet to find easy solutions. Major differences persist in the objectives pursued, communication levels, and time horizons, that are primarily induced by the different institutional missions of the two actors.

In several European countries, universities have not been able to foster growth processes such as those realized in the US, in the UK or in few other European countries. The full deployment of these processes appears to be hampered both by the scale of the university system and by the traditional manufacturing specialisations of the LPSs. As is the case in several European IDs, when the product requires relatively low levels of codified knowledge, the main source of the innovative processes (and that of the diversification of the productive system) continues to lie in the network of relations created by the local firms, linking both local and non-local producers. Not infrequently, when innovation is not radical, the technicians employed by the local firms may very well be more knowledgeable than universities' researchers. Thus programmes of this sort, experimented with on a regional scale, have transferred funds to the universities, the public and private innovation centres, and the enterprises directly involved in these programmes, while the effects on growth often remain uncertain.

3. LEVELS OF POLICIES FOR IDs AND CLUSTERS IN EMERGING COUNTRIES

Thus far we have discussed processes of 'maintenance' and refocusing, involving LPSs (be they in IDs or not) in industrialized countries. The picture changes radically when developing countries are considered: in such cases the creation *ex novo* of relations, organisations, institutions and competencies supporting local development plays a crucial role.

The chapter by Giovanna Ceglie and Anna Stancher deals with this issue from the viewpoint of the local development policies implemented by the United Nations and Industrial Development Organisation (UNIDO). The specific processes of capacity building and governance building, which characterise the UNIDO approach, are discussed at length. Capacity building involves two main aspects: (a) activities aimed at creating and strengthening the ability of organisations to provide efficient and effective services which can satisfy local needs; and (b) contextual activities aimed at building networks of relations and competencies within the system. These networks are often created *ex novo* and they link local producers among themselves and with local and extra-local buyers. This sphere is connected with the skill upgrading activities provided by local training centres and with the creation/strengthening of the local service centres. The governance building process basically relates to the creation of the institutional LPS network. It is aimed at promoting organisations and normative systems favouring coordination on a local scale and supporting local collective action. More specifically, this process is based on institutional action aimed at creating organisations that can operate as nodes of the local network of relations and competencies. These nodes can participate in the (re)construction of the local rules, in the definition of contracts, quality standards, and norms regulating the local interactions, in the modelling or (when necessary) (re) focusing of local customs and traditions on entrepreneurship and market activities. Both capacity building and governance building are learning processes. They are complementary and intertwined processes, where 'learning how to learn from the others' is often the first prerequisite for triggering endogenous development.

An additional element of the UNIDO approach is the pro-poor orientation of the policies. Social and cultural proximity and the diffusion of mutual assistance practices make the district a relatively favourable environment for the redistribution of development benefits, for social inclusion and for poverty reduction. However, these outcomes are not certain. The peculiarity of the UNIDO approach is that of combining the capacity and governance building interventions with the containment of economic, social and cultural deprivation. In this sense, 'what' to produce (goods at affordable prices also for the low income groups) and 'how' to produce it (labour-intensive technologies raising the employment level) are as important as intervention on the different dimensions of poverty, favouring the inclusion of both minorities and the more vulnerable social groups, as well as the development of individual capabilities, in the sense defined by Sen and Nussbaum.

Accordingly, economic development policies are strongly intertwined with social policies aimed at reducing marginalisation and favouring social integration. The resulting picture is complex: starting from adverse conditions (a small number of producers, often isolated from the markets, having a small set of competencies and weak relations), policies may act on several interconnected levels with the aim of creating and strengthening the local production and the institutional framework, and, at the same time, of supporting local demand. At the same time, policies may attempt to preserve and promote some degree of local cohesion. Yet, projects and programmes should be simple, comprehensible and capable of being assimilated by a vast number of subjects, while also being compatible with a not fully developed productive and institutional structure. In this tension between the complexity of the design and the simplicity of the implementation tools, development policies are tested that can help growth and well being without jeopardising the competitiveness of the local system. The recipe is never definitive, and it needs to be constantly (re) discovered and (re)invented.

4. INSTITUTIONAL ARCHITECTURE, SOCIAL RELATIONS AND POLICIES

In his contribution, Marco Bellandi offers an approach that conceptualises some of the policies discussed previously. The approach builds on the notion of specific public goods (SPGs). The entire 'institutional architecture' of the LPS (and specifically that of the ID) is connected to these SPGs. They may be public goods in a strict sense, but also quasi-public or club goods, from which local enterprises benefit (or could benefit). Examples of such goods include services (such as education and training and 'real services'), the common use of intangible goods (for example trademarks, patents, R&D activities), local standards and technical jargons, or specific collective agreements adopted locally. These SPGs are supplied by dedicated organisations and a system of norms, both of which can modify the behaviour of the economic agents since they constitute a framework of non-market coordination of the individual actions. This dedicated institutional architecture requires specific organisational forms, but it is the result neither of market exchange, nor of hierarchical decisions imposed by a large enterprise or an enlightened planner. SPGs are the result of a collective action emerging from a specific need. They form and become effective in relation to high-level normative systems – the law – and in relation to the rules grounded in the local set of values, culture and customs. In particular, as stressed by Bellandi, the local rules or 'informal institutions' are 'a joint product of economic and social encounter in a context where individual agents share common experiences, experiments and factual problems, that is, a common nexus'. These local rules are a constitutive element – an 'organic' element, according to Bellandi – of the ID 'which emerges evolutionary from social relations'. The institutional architecture is embedded in the local factor, namely in the cooperative nexus that characterises the ID. This common trait represents fertile ground for nurturing district competitiveness (that is, its productivity, the quality and the innovative content of its products) and for favouring the realisation of the district external economies. It also distinguishes the district from a generic agglomeration of enterprises, and favours effective integration among the enterprises and full deployment of the local entrepreneurial capabilities, appealing to a common cognitive and behavioural background. The institutional architecture does not fully coincide with the cooperative nexus. The former is in constant evolution, being progressively shaped by collective action, while the latter responds to the (slow) evolution of the social relations. However, there cannot be separation between the two: the evolution of the institutional architecture progressively modifies both local rules and local behaviours and even the same basic elements of the cooperative nexus, with feedback mechanisms that also act upon social relations.

Public policies concerned with the 'maintenance' and the refocusing of clusters and IDs such as those described by Mikel Landabaso and Stuart Rosenfeld, and Joan Trullén may be traced back to this analytical structure. The same holds true for the capacity and governance building processes discussed by Giovanna Ceglie and Anna Stancher. Both sets of public policies are underpinned by collective actions that, in different contexts and at different levels, lead to modifications of the institutional architecture of a district.

5. OPEN QUESTIONS

Two main questions remain unanswered. The first one concerns the variety of outcomes that the previously discussed strategies and policies may achieve, since both may result (and usually do) in different actual programmes and interventions. Even when the public policy aims and objectives are the same, the local specificities may lead the very content of such policies as well as their effectiveness to be modified. Aspects of local specificity would include production specialisation, the industrial structure and the division of labour among the local enterprises, the specific character of the local industrial and political leadership and that of the actors implementing the programmes, as well as the characters of the institutional set-up. This can happen both in developed and in developing areas. Even the identification and an understanding of the basic elements of what is often referred to as 'good practices' require a remarkable degree of caution regarding the translation of policy guidelines for local development. The modes of implementation are not the only aspects involved. The processes of the radical transformation affecting LPSs operating in open and integrated markets, the uncertainty characterising the innovative processes, and the continuous evolution of the institutional architectures, all contribute to making local development policies a sphere of constant experimentation.

These observations point to an unavoidable need to define *ex ante* and intermediate policy objectives and to recognise the importance of implementing ongoing policy evaluation in order to assess the network of the relations and competencies involved, and to adopt suitable *ex post* evaluation tools capable of capturing unexpected outcomes. The evaluation of policy outcomes aimed at promoting local development constitutes a necessary complement to the theoretical analysis of local development and to policy implementation. Rigorous evaluation ensures against the risk of proliferation of self-referential public or private organisations that are highly skilled in acquiring and defending rents, but unable to stimulate development dynamics.

The second issue has more general, but also deeper implications. Two different perspectives on the LPS and the ID have been briefly outlined at the beginning of this introduction. The first one focuses on 'interconnections', while the second considers a 'plus' connected to the nature of the social relations. At this point, the implications of these two views are quite clear. In the first case, collective action and public policies are aimed at providing the district and the local system of 'firms' with what is missing, what is lacking and what is poorly developed in terms of technological linkages, competencies and interactions with the markets. Institutional action is therefore focused on the interdependencies and interconnections linking local firms; at most, it may include some non-market coordination and regulatory mechanisms. In the second perspective, collective action and public policies have a broader scope. They explicitly include social policies aimed at strengthening the cooperative nexus discussed by Bellandi. Collective action (and the related institutional architecture) must necessarily also be concerned with working conditions and the local welfare system.

The efficiency of the local system and of the ID relies on conditions in the workplace and on the quality of what Sebastiano Brusco referred to as 'life outside the factory'. Thus, the previously mentioned pro-poor policies in developing countries (and in emerging economies) have the same fundamental role as policies promoting good child care or good care for the elderly and the disabled, or acceptable levels of education, housing and perhaps even a reasonable degree of personal safety in industrialized and developed regions. The wealth of a local system and of an ID also lies in this same set of conditions, which concern the relation between capital and labour both within and outside the factory and which make it possible to achieve and preserve a reasonable degree of social cohesion. The willingness to consider these aspects as the foundations of the mechanism that underpins an ID, and, therefore, the motivation for organically incorporating them into a theoretical framework, are perhaps the most decisive factors separating those who see the ID merely as a system of productive and technological linkages and those who see the ID as 'something more than that'.

50. External economies, specific public goods and policies

Marco Bellandi

1. INTRODUCTION

Industrial districts (IDs) are localities characterised by the economic and social prominence of a cluster of small to medium-sized enterprises (SMEs) embedded within the social relations of the area (Becattini 2004a). Steady paths of development in IDs, as those associated to the model of the so-called Marshallian industrial district (MID), are characterised by a virtuous link between the SME cluster and the locality. In these cases the social core of the cluster is a set of independent producers sharing: (a) a bent towards trust in reciprocal exchanges; (b) a diffuse attitude towards value producing (against rent-seeking) entrepreneurship, proactivity of workers on the job and joint action on shared interests; and (c) cognitive proximity, that is similarity of some basic know-how among the producers.

Producers are 'embedded' locally in the sense that, living and working in the district, they develop qualities that allow access to, and give contribution to such common subjective tracts (a 'cooperative nexus'). They better understand when one of them can be trusted; they look for the acknowledgement of their economic success and innovation within the group; and the sharing of familial, civic and school experiences makes it easier to understand and compare the 'mysteries' of the industry, as noted by Marshall. This systemic foundation of the district helps economic agents to realise productivity gains specifically in the form of 'district external economies', and pulls them to reinvest largely in locally-centred productive plans. This accumulation is consistent with an enlarged reproduction of an ID's socio-economic configuration. At the aggregate level, the plans combine and result in processes that can generate new local division of labour, peculiar human capital formation, and creative variation of knowledge. Even in localities not strictly corresponding to IDs, such as some large cities or some rural or tourist areas, both in old industrialised regions and in newly industrialising ones, it is possible to find clusters showing similar processes of accumulation related to fruitful local relations. What distinguishes a cluster in all such cases, from agglomerations of business activities lying on simple spatial advantages, is that it is kept together by, and evolves with, some sort of 'local cooperative nexus'. The presence of a shared systemic basis is more directly expressed by referring to such clusters as 'local production systems' (LPSs).[1] In the sociological wing of the ID literature the cooperative nexus has been explicitly discussed under the name of (local) social capital.

In Sections 2 and 3, I will illustrate a general framework featuring the concept of specific public goods (SPGs), where the systemic basis to district external economies is given an expanded definition, beyond the core represented by the cooperative nexus. Section 4 necessarily touches upon the problem of how the enlarged basis is more or less effectively constituted and regulated through mixes of emergent informal institutions and deliberate actions of governance. Sections 5 and 6 will explain by means of some examples the relations between district external economies, SPGs, and the subtleties of their governance. The framework should help to disentangle the various and variable conditions of collective productivity in IDs, showing how generally they depend also on appropriate combinations of private and public strategies, though enacted by reasonable (not hyper-rational) agents who move tentatively within sets of reciprocal and evolutionary constraints and opportunities; such sets being featured by strong local roots coupled with a web of translocal and extra-local relations.

2. THE SYSTEMIC SUPPORT TO ID EXTERNAL ECONOMIES

As originally suggested by Marshall, what characterizes economic performance within the IDs' steady paths of development is a not casual realisation of economies whose sources are partly external to the single firms but internal to the district. These economies are productivity (not only in quantity, but possibly in quality and innovation terms) advantages gained by independent producers thanks to their inclusion within a set of connected activities and business fields. The set aggregates a relatively large pool of complementary and substitute human and technical resources, and is related with evolving external markets in a stable and open manner. Organisation is needed for integrating the specialised contributions, but such organisation is the outcome neither of planning by a predominant centre of strategic decision making, nor of 'simple' market exchange.

This last proposition has a double nature. On one side, it recalls a well-known defining feature of IDs: the main clusters of an ID comprise SMEs which are, at least in part, specialised, whilst being integrated with the other firms through locally specific market and non-market mechanisms. On the other side, it identifies, in organisational terms, the breadth of the competitive advantage of IDs. This means that IDs have to find their way where an extended and changing division of labour with high productivity potentials in a set of related business fields is not easily integrated by means of pure hierarchical command (internal to large companies possibly extended to their satellite networks), nor by simple market relations. When hierarchical command prevails the area takes the nature of a company town centred on a monopsonistic cluster (De Propris 2001); when simple market relations prevail the area is a sort of generic town or of urbanised countryside hosting various types of weakly-related activities exploiting generic localisation advantages.

The core of organisational solutions specific to IDs is to be found precisely in the cooperative nexus. Such intuition has been elaborated with reference to well-known models of IDs. In a model combining interpretations of Marshall's thinking with the experience of some Italian IDs in the second half of the 20th century (in particular the Prato textile district), the integration of the division of labour is realised through 'communitarian local markets' (Dei Ottati in this volume), that is market exchanges between specialised local SMEs supported by trust, entrepreneurial attitudes and cognitive proximity. Another model could be named as an oligopolistic ID, perhaps closer to many historical cases of IDs in Britain at the time of Marshall (Cooke in this volume; Popp and Wilson in this volume), where the cooperative nexus countervails the local power of the larger companies, and makes room for both their enduring embeddedness and for opportunities of high valued contributions from local SMEs, within the oligopolies' networks and/ or within secondary but partly related industries as well. An intermediate type combines monopolistic competition between networks of SMEs running non-routine projects on the typical products of the district (teams), and communitarian phase markets on more routine local intermediate products (Becattini 2004a).

All these models and types point more or less explicitly to the fact that the cooperative nexus brings about a systemic support for the integration of the local division of labour. This helps explaining why even in cases of oligopolistic IDs there is a fundamental role for economies whose sources are partly external to the firms but internal to the district; and why even in communitarian market cases, the local external economies do not leak easily outside the ID, for instance through extra-local market relations.

Fascinating as they are, representations of the systemic support to district external economies based on the cooperative nexus alone are partial. In the literature, the concern for appropriate public policies and collective strategies on various types of collective and public goods have appeared from the beginning, as exemplified in Goodman and Bamford (1989), where some of the early Italian contributions on IDs first appeared in English. In particular Becattini (1979, p. 133), Brusco (1989b), and Trigilia (1989) make explicit reference to basic concerns related to policies for IDs, for instance including their support for steady paths of local development, as well as against drastic challenges to traditional paths; types of services and infrastructures on which, or through which policies operate; alternatives in provision of such services and infrastructures between public and private associations, markets, or some combinations of them, consideration also being given to the interplay among different territorial levels of public or collective agency; and strengths and weaknesses of different types of policies and agencies.

In the 1990s, the relation between the competitiveness of not strictly centralised LPSs, as in IDs, and the provision of public goods became the object of deeper investigations. For example, Zeitlin (1989) relates the decline of UK IDs to the decay of the local 'industrial public sphere'; Bellandi (1996b) makes reference to the relations between collective goods such as market rules and indivisible specific infrastructures, and the realisation of external economies in decentralised production systems; Porter (1998a) relates clusters' competitive advantages not only to private strategies and rivalry, but also to the provision of a list of collective goods; Schmitz (1999b) illustrates the possibility of collective local efficiency coming from joint action in developing regions, and distinguishes this source from externalities or 'involuntary external economies'; Goglio (1999) refers the concept of local public goods to local development and to cycles of local political leadership; Crouch et al. (2001) define the governance of different types of local competition goods as necessary to the success of LPSs; Lane (2002) relates the control of ontological uncertainty in processes generating systemic innovation with the presence of scaffolding structures which align interaction, in physical, cognitive and motivational terms, between a variety of agents.

It was explicitly stated that collective goods essential to the working of decentralised production systems may be partly the result of, or may be influenced by, strategies having roots at the local level. It was also suggested that roles and difficulties in the governance of local development can be related precisely to the collective or public nature of such essential goods. These reflections have grounded more and more firmly the idea that the realisation of district external economies needs systemic conditions with a collective and public nature. Their provision comes not only from organic social relations (viz the cooperative nexus), but also from 'constructive actions'[2] seen as the manifestation of political and strategic capabilities which are not a simple prolongation of the same social relations.

In several chapters of this *Handbook* references are made to and examples are presented on local governance, and collective and public goods. In what follows in this chapter, a unified conceptual framework based on the concept of 'specific' public goods is illustrated, with some applications to the questions referred above.

3. SPECIFIC PUBLIC GOODS

The key idea here illustrated is that an intermediate[3] 'architecture of systemic conditions' to external economies lies upon and above the cooperative nexus; and it is made of public goods whose net benefits are specific to the system itself. For example, teams of firms share intangible goods, such as patented or private knowledge on innovative products and processes, private access to common financial or market channels, and quality certifications; and/or tangible goods, such as means of production with indivisible capacities specifically adapted to certain productions or product development. At the cluster and locality levels, there are, for example, rules for setting prices and drawing contracts within local markets, technical standards and jargons, codes on permitted imitation and bankruptcy, vocational and professional schools, and production services needing both an adaptation to specific district demands and a provision facilitated by technical and human resources with large indivisible capacities.

In general, pure 'specific' public goods are defined not only by no rivalry in consumption and no exclusion rights, but also by the relevance of a third property, that is an uneven but not casual distribution of net benefits (before funding) for accessing the good (or its services) among a population which has a general right to access. In particular, the individuals of a subset of the total population have higher net benefits, because they share a nexus of subjective tracts, possibly connected to common experiences and factual problems, which explains both specific interests and focused collective demand.[4] The variations on pure SPGs include club goods, where the right to access may be effectively limited to entitled agents only; quasi-public goods, where the benefits of free access may be limited by congestion (that is, when demand exceeds a given carrying capacity); and combinations of the conditions above. Within the general set of SPGs, the composition of intra-team club goods, inter-team club goods, cluster and district public and quasi-public goods, and translocal club and public goods is argued to change over time and according to the characteristics of the clusters and the localities themselves.

The mechanisms of constitution, provision and distribution of SPGs, and their relative importance, vary as well. Rules, standards, routines and shared knowledge, that is, intangible SPGs, may be embedded in customs, conventions, or in private or public archives and regulations, the last ones coming from deliberate leading private action, joint action, focused public action, or distant public action. Tangible SPGs usually require deliberate joint or public action. SPGs may not imply a local economic domain. However, public goods specific to clusters embedded in localities of industry do, even if a distinction is usefully kept between the industrial space of the cluster and the territorial space of the locality. Furthermore, the local economic domain does not correspond necessarily to a single local jurisdiction. For example, the territory of Italian IDs usually covers several contiguous municipalities. For these and other reasons, SPGs may be provided by (or with the support of) upper level jurisdictions and non-local agencies. However, the awareness and a certain degree of consensus among cluster producers and local people are needed for an effective provision, since specific local details are not well understood and cared for from a distance (Sandler 1998). The focused collective demand supports the constitution of public goods whose characters are shaped in ways consistent with increasing gross benefits, lowering access costs, and potentially allowing a positive surplus even against self-financing of the good by the subset itself. Figure 50.1 provides a synthetic representation of such relations.

Inside the district, informal institutions, as customs and conventions, are a joint product of economic and social encounters in a context where individual agents share common experiences, experiments and factual problems, that is a common nexus. In a way, informal institutions are the more operative expression

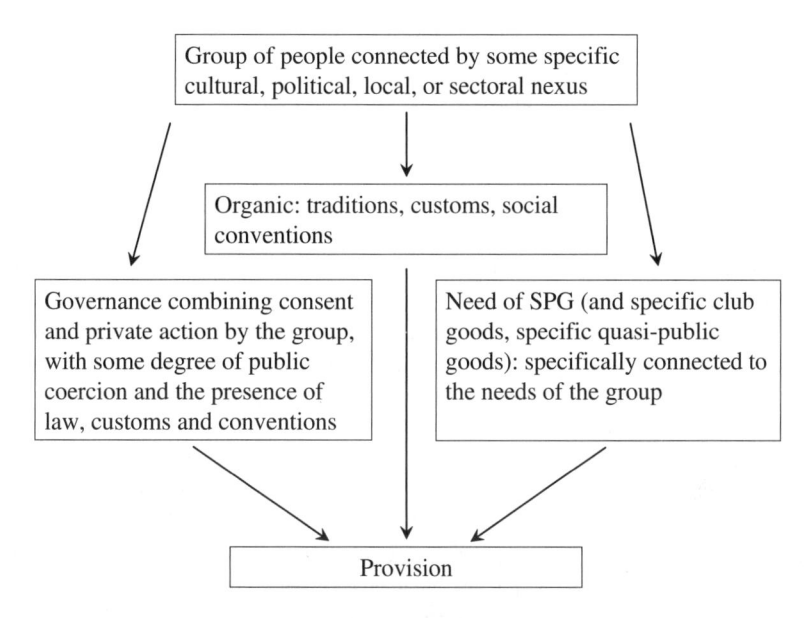

```
                ┌─────────────────────────────────────────┐
                │ Group of people connected by some specific│
                │ cultural, political, local, or sectoral nexus│
                └─────────────────────────────────────────┘
                 ╱              │               ╲
                ╱               ▼                ╲
               ╱   ┌──────────────────────────┐   ╲
              ╱    │ Organic: traditions, customs, social│   ╲
             ╱     │ conventions              │    ╲
            ╱      └──────────────────────────┘     ╲
           ▼                  │                      ▼
┌──────────────────────┐      │      ┌──────────────────────────┐
│ Governance combining consent│      │ Need of SPG (and specific club│
│ and private action by the group,│   │ goods, specific quasi-public│
│ with some degree of public│         │ goods): specifically connected to│
│ coercion and the presence of│       │ the needs of the group│
│ law, customs and conventions│       └──────────────────────────┘
└──────────────────────┘                          
              ╲               │                ╱
               ╲              ▼               ╱
                        ┌───────────┐
                        │ Provision │
                        └───────────┘
```

Figure 50.1   The provision of SPGs

of the 'organic' foundation of district systemic conditions; 'organic' indicating here something which emerges evolutionarily from social relations. It is plausible that a fruitful correspondence between the informal institutions and the district collective specific needs be facilitated by a cooperative conformation of the nexus itself. But customs and conventions, as noted also by Marshall, change and adapt slowly and coarsely. So, IDs and district enterprises moving in a complex and rapidly changing competitive global environment should not entrust the satisfaction of their specific collective needs only to the organic foundation. Actually such a basis is complemented more or less broadly and effectively by the results of various types of strategic deliberate actions recalled above, that is with both individual business strategies and a locally-based governance of public goods specific to the locality and its clusters and enterprises. Weaknesses on this side damage the prospects of ID prosperity.

4. THE COOPERATIVE NEXUS AND A LOCALLY-BASED GOVERNANCE OF PUBLIC GOODS SPECIFIC TO IDs

The cooperative nexus could be seen as a quintessential pool of SPGs, a 'local factor' both giving social motivation and orientation to producers (as suggested in the introduction), and favouring the constitution of the intermediate architecture of SPGs. What justifies a distinction between the nexus and the other SPGs is the view that the first is deeply rooted within the social relations of the district, which cannot be effectively the object of deliberate choices, changing evolutionarily in the long run, if not subverted randomly by epochal discontinuities (Dardi in this volume). Being outside the sphere of deliberateness, the effects of a cooperative nexus would be true examples of externalities.[5]

It is to be noted that even within such a view, district external economies are not to be identified with externalities. The external effects of the organic basis contribute instead as inputs, together with the effects of other more deliberately supported SPGs, and with appropriate internal (to the firm) resources and strategies, to the exploitation of sources of productivity tied to the division of labour within the district (Loasby in this volume). The district external economies contribute to district firms' 'differential' performance against firms competing in the same or related markets, but not able to access a similar combination of factors. The under-production of positive external effects (a classical problem of welfare economics) may be seen from two angles. Firstly, a fruitful organic basis (with its core cooperative nexus) benefits only a limited number of localities owning effective or potential ID characteristics, and just a limited number of enterprises whose internal teams share and contribute to the subjective attributes of the corresponding local nexuses. This helps to explain the not easily transferable advantages (Storper in this volume). Secondly, an obsolete organic basis may be difficult to revamp against local or extra-local challenges, and in that case under-production turns against a previously gifted locality (Grabher 1993b).

The obsolescence question takes us to a more comprehensive view of the evolution of the cooperative nexus, which is implicit in traditional thinking on public deliberate actions for IDs and local development. It is well known that such actions may and should extend to 'political interventions on life in the out-factory sphere'.[6] It is aimed at promoting and supporting mobility and equity in local society, the participation and involvement of workers on the job, the resolution of conflicts within bilateral economic relations and so on. It tends to integrate actions and relations evolving within the productive space and those pertaining to other social spaces. Its true final target, though generally not explicitly enunciated as such, is a positive influence on the cooperative nexus. Usually, in the district literature, a large uncertainty of results of such interventions is acknowledged as the necessary caveat due to the complexity of social relations within 'small nations within nations', in the words of Marshall, as dynamic IDs and cities are. The belief that the uncertainties of action on deep social relations are not only great, but more properly radical, justifies the restricted view recalled above, with its strict distinction between collective goods (here the intermediate architecture of SPGs) which can be effectively influenced by deliberate action, and the cooperative nexus which cannot.

Within the more comprehensive view such a distinction is a bit too simplistic, because the various levels of systemic effects are necessarily interrelated, and a 'holistic' vision of the local society (Johannisson in this volume) should constitute the background of any experiment of cautious action for local development and change.[7] From this perspective, the concept of externality is to be related not to factors that can be defined statically, but to the emergence of opportunities of contribution to reciprocal advantages (net benefits) within a cluster, or more generally at the level of a district, that: (a) if realised are perceived as dependent on peculiar, not governed historical conditions; (b) if not realised are seen as only potentially feasible due to the lack of local deliberating power on collective solutions which could be adopted within the district and which are suggested by the governance of similar problems in different local and business settings (Dardi 2003). Inadequacy of deliberating power on the architecture of SPGs may be not felt as such during periods of steady development, however, it emerges dramatically during transitional periods with a multiplying of externalities related to SPGs which are not reproduced, destroyed or reconstituted appropriately.

The presence of institutional frames, meta-management skills, and political attitudes consistent with an appropriate locally-based governance of systemic conditions, against and out of local lock-in conditions, can be thought of as a 'strategic' factor, which is related to the cooperative nexus in contradictory ways: for example, shared trust attitudes favour consent on collective action, but may direct it towards a dodgy conservation of obsolete traditions. Other conditions play a role too, such as types of policy cultures and methods, cycles of political leadership at the local level, and chance. For example concerning political methods, the public policy at the core of local governance may be seen as an industrial policy with a rich local dimension, balancing autonomy and embeddedness with respect to the interests and views of local economic agents (Bellandi and Di Tommaso 2006). According to Rodrick (2004, p. 17) autonomy is not separation, but the capacity to stay out of the pockets of business interests, and to run the process with a certain degree of democratic accountability and public legitimacy. Strategic capacities and leadership coexist with cognitive and motivational failures within and between agencies tackling governance problems. Solutions ask for effective sequences of action and discovery, whereby public and private agents invest and learn about the costs and opportunities of collaboration, and engage in experimental processes of strategic coordination (Trigilia 2005). In general, as Rodrick (2004, pp. 17–18) aptly points out, in order to understand the possibilities of good results in industrial policy it is not enough to identify requisites and outcomes, but it is also necessary to understand the processes of governance and how they evolve together with market actions and processes.

Therefore the architecture of SPGs supporting district external economies ought to be the object of deliberate but 'experimental' strategies. The experimental nature of the architecture of SPGs, together with its linkages to a local cooperative nexus on one side and to a specific pool of specialised human and technical resources with associated sunk costs on the other side, is an integral part of the support to competitive advantages which, once in place, do not have an ephemeral and fortuitous lease of life. In particular, the intermediate part of such an architecture supplies an adaptable and articulated organisation to the complementary specialised contributions of a set of independent producers, helping a substantial realisation of economies of division of labour in complex and evolving (not strictly hierarchical) production systems, and their distribution in the form of external economies. In the next two sections some examples of relations between external economies in IDs and SPGs are illustrated in some detail.

5. CLASSICAL ID EXTERNAL ECONOMIES

A typology of external economies in IDs suggested by Marshall's writings includes: (a) 'specialisation economies' – advantages stemming from the efficient use of production capacities already in place, within a given framework of specialised activities, for the production of a given set of goods; (b) 'economies in the development of competencies' – by means of diffused learning (by doing, using and interacting) in a given framework of specialised activities; and (c) 'economies of decentralised industrial creativity' – variety and novelty in the framework of activities and products emerging from the interplay between exchanges of products and exchanges of ideas, in a population of competent specialised producers.

With respect to Marshall, the contemporary debate has gone deeper into the analysis of the local micro-foundations, as well as of the general market and technological tendencies which define spaces of opportunity to ID external economies. These analyses have provided a better understanding of the needs and the conditions of provision of various types of SPGs in relation to particular types of external economies. In what follows in this section a classical example is considered and illustrated in general conceptual terms.[8]

According to a well-known classification (Robinson 1958), specialisation economies include: economies of the balances of processes, of massed reserves, of large machines and large transactions. Let us just consider the economy of massed reserves which is particularly important in front of the 'state of permanent flux ... in which real world economies find themselves' (G.B. Richardson 2002, p. 8) in general, and the competition in markets characterised by highly variable and differentiated demand in particular. Stocks of raw materials, intermediate goods and finished goods, or reserves of productive capacity can be held in order to reduce the risk of unexpected excess in demand or shortage in supply. If a type of reserve is required for different uses, and the unexpected necessity in each use is largely unrelated to what happens in the other uses, then the total amount of reserves (given the risk) is lower if they can be pooled for assisting the different uses jointly, than if each use is assisted by a separate reserve. Seen from the other side, a given stock of a specialised good or a given reserve of specialised productive capacity runs a lower risk of (long) idleness or unemployment if it is pooled with similar stocks supplying a set of uses with a largely unrelated variability (in the time in which each use manifests its demand).

Well-known methods for managing massed reserves are applied within large business organisations and their networks of dependent suppliers, like 'just-in-time'. The market solution is the specialised supply of general purpose intermediate goods.[9] Here we consider instead an ID configuration, in particular an LPS characterised by a set of teams of independent SMEs, each team being engaged in the design and management of the *filière*, the direct realisation of some strategic parts of the production, and marketing (on national and international markets) of competing differentiated goods. Local phase markets provide the teams with various intermediate products and services of more standardised but still specific character (in terms of technical details, timing, quality control and so on). It is the monopolistic competition model recalled in Section 2 above.

Within a single SME's team, those stocks of specialised resources or reserves of capacity of each member which are potentially substitutable, that is applicable to similar uses by other members, may be easily adapted in ways consistent with effective exchange or sharing if needed. Such advantages are limited by both the fact that within a single team uses (that is activities) tend to be complementary more than similar, and the fact that, as regards similar uses, their variability among different members tends to be correlated. The risk of excesses in the demand or supply of specialised capacity and resources within the single team may be managed by means of exchanges among different teams and with recourse to local phase markets. However, the possibility of pooling among teams is not automatically granted by their coexistence within the same district. The features of specialised resources and capacities could be designed and destined to specifically-defined needs within the single teams, and the costs (time lost included) of change to a similar use in a different team could be correspondingly too high. Alternatively, apart from those at the core of the distinctive competence and competitive capacity of each team, resources may be designed in ways consistent with exchanges among the ID teams, that is with capacities or features which may be adapted quite easily to the uses in different teams. The common adoption of designs consistent with inter-team pooling is a technical standard which can be specified so as to grant a good compromise with the needs of differentiation and specialisation of the teams involved. It is a public good (pure or club) specific to the teams involved. An example is the contribution by teams' leaders to a common definition of local educational curricula for upgrading important skills among specialised producers. Of course sharing favours the distribution of the fixed costs of the educational activities. But it also makes easier, in prospect, temporary transfers of the upgraded capacities across teams.[10]

More standardised intermediate resources are pooled through more anonymous market relations. Standards may be imposed by external firms and markets. In this case local phase markets are operative only when the standards are public and there are some generic location advantages to a local supply. Even if public, such standards are not specific to the district and its enterprises. Alternatively, within an ID standards may be adapted in line with local production peculiarities and are often adopted and built in locally as customs or conventions. Local phase markets are filled both by team members with temporary excesses in input demand or supply, non-networked suppliers, and even occasional producers willing to enter and exit the local markets according to the prospects. The adjustment of demand and supply is favoured by price signals. Price volatility may be increased by the exploitation of temporary positions of market power. This tends to spoil local trust relations. The damage is contained when local business associations, perhaps pulled together by public agencies, are able to define and impose collective prices and fees for products and services exchanged in the local phase markets. These and similar collective contractual standards are public goods specific to the district. They do not abolish volatility, but lend focal points reducing it and supporting trust relations (Dei Ottati in this volume; Mistri in this volume).

It would be possible to expand our discussion further around this set of SPGs. For instance, one might consider the specialised trade infrastructures aimed at facilitating the transmission of information and the distribution of excess demand and supply within an ID, both in inter-team relations and on phase markets; but which also bring about monopolistic private positions or public rents. Or it would be possible to think about pools of redundant general purpose but specialised resources going into new uses, so helping the growth of local productive novelties (Bellandi 1996b), and even the 'manufactory of sectors' (Best in this volume).

6. PUBLIC GOODS SPECIFIC TO CROSS-CLUSTER AND TRANSLOCAL COLLABORATIVE RELATIONS

A second, less classical, example of external economies related to IDs takes us to cross-cluster and translocal relations. The current phase of globalisation poses big challenges to traditional IDs in older industrialised countries, whilst offering opportunities for growing new industries in old and new localities of industry, some of them in new industrialising countries.[11] Among the traditional IDs, some show a capacity to respond to the main challenges, with actions that include: (a) international subcontracting set up by district entrepreneurs who are used to managing links external to their firm; (b) direct or indirect assistance, provided by district entrepreneurs who have chosen to live abroad, to the management of relations of district firms with foreign suppliers; (c) active foreign direct investments (FDIs) taking a district form in the host economy as when a leading district firm induces other district firms to invest in the same foreign area; and (d) some district firms taking part in the governance of international value chains such as when they produce an intermediate product locally that is sent to a foreign country to be transformed into a final good sold from the same foreign country.

Some authors (see note 11) question the capacity of an ID soaked in international fluxes to preserve an effective local identity (that is, its cooperative nexus). The question is not tackled here in its complexity. We just propose a possible enlargement of the SPGs framework. The point is that the architecture of SPGs can be articulated and expanded so as to lend bridges supporting cross-cluster and translocal collaborative relations, at a regional and international level. These bridges help the limited internal resources of district-specialised firms to apply to and invest in international processes in a coordinated way: (a) expanding inter-firm exchanges based on trust and personal knowledge, while limiting lonely trader or predatory multinational strategies which spoil local relations (De Propris 2009); and (b) increasing positive expectations against local lock-ins (Grabher 1993b). Table 50.1 gives a summary.

Included are both those SPGs which help to increase local productivity (in technological, quality and innovation terms) within a supportive and integrated regional context (see Zeitlin 2007b; Cooke in this volume); and those more directly related to international translocal relations (see Rullani in this volume). Without revamped sources of inner productivity, international investments and relations do not lend solutions to ID problems, more probably they make them worse. Without international strategies, the value produced by inner productivity may be predated by multinational agents, or spill over too easily to global markets.

It is quite clear nonetheless that the very concept of public goods specific to cross-cluster and translocal relations, especially at an international scale, is problematic. SPGs are based on a common motivational and cognitive nexus in a set of people with overlapping life experiences and problems. The twinning of distant communities is necessarily partial and variable. However, the bridges support the transfer not only of production projects and investments, but also of people who have learnt to feel at home in different localities, and learnt how to communicate with those who, on the different sides, have just one homeland. In a sense part of the bridges are these same 'Argonauts', in the words of Saxenian and Sabel (in this volume). This recalls the discussion in Section 3, on the various levels of locally comprehensive governance,

Table 50.1   A typology of public translocal SPGs

HOMELAND LEVERS

- Enhanced systemic conditions for the ID productivity, at the local level and in relation with nearby regional cities and other developed districts in the same country.

INTERNATIONAL CROSS-CLUSTER AND TRANSLOCAL LEVERS

- Help from the ID in strengthening local SPGs in localities with district potentialities in developing/backward regions and countries.
- Shared competencies that make it easier to learn about and adopt systems for managing business relations to a translocal scale.
- Educational/training structures, business incentives, and life facilities which support the formation and circulation of people able to liaise among the localities and among the clusters.

Source: Adapted from Bellandi and Caloffi (2009).

touching cautiously upon the organic basis of an ID. The experimental methods of governance in such cases should be enhanced to include guidelines and trials for matching clusters in different localities, according to lists of complementary and similarity requirements (Bellandi and Caloffi 2009).

External economies supported by cross-cluster and translocal collaborative relations span specialisation, learning and creativity. They are not strictly internal to a single ID, in this sense they are not classical ID external economies; but they are still partly dependent on local resources, and represent returns which in part come back to such resources. Perhaps, against strong challenges from globalisation, they are the expression of one of the main ways to keep feeding local accumulation and economic and human development.

7. CONCLUSIONS

In the second edition of the *Principles of Economics* (1891) Marshall introduced more diffusedly the concept of external economies, together with a decoupling of them from the narrow association with the localisation of industries and the concentration of many small businesses, which characterised the first edition and his earlier writings. The district economies are still seen as 'very important', and Chapter X is still devoted to them. But other types are given an appropriate consideration too, in particular 'those connected with the growth of knowledge and the progress of the arts' which 'depend chiefly on the aggregate volume of production in the whole civilised world' (Marshall 1920, p. 266). The decoupling may be seen both as application of the principle of continuity, and as acknowledgement of the progress of some important market and technical tendencies.[12] It is suggested that the role of 'place' could be extended from a single locality of industry to different interlinked territorial levels, much as 'time' in Marshall has different interlinked scales. However Marshall, contrary to what he did with time scales, did not dare make explicit a definition of a multi-territorial framework, even if in *Industry and Trade* many illustrations confirm that Marshall had a vision of it.

Whatever that may be, the articulation of a set of SPGs provided or supported by deliberate private collective and public action, upon and beyond the organic basis at the core of lively IDs, provides a clue to a better understanding of the various and changing scales of external economies which are accessed by and fed back from ID producers.

On the other hand, such architecture intermingles in various (complementary, contradictory, subsidiary) and changing ways with less specific (that is, generic or universal) public goods which are the objects of standard extra-local upper level policies. This has been touched upon only casually in the chapter. We refer finally to the other chapters of this section of the *Handbook*, for cases and concepts which contribute the essential material for an assessment of the point.

NOTES

1. Just to add something to the terminological intricacies, it may be recalled that in the Italian debates and laws on IDs, the localities of industry referred to above in the text are sometimes referred to as local 'productive' systems. They are localities characterised by one or a few local 'production' systems. See Becattini et al. (2003).
2. Quite recently some serious references to 'constructive action' at the local level have been recovered from Alfred Marshall's *Industry and Trade* in a chapter devoted to 'aggregation, federation, and cooperation in British industry and trade' and starting with external economies, IDs, and British textile industries. On the notion of conscious coordination and foresight applied to studies of UK industry by disciples and followers of Marshall see Hart (in this volume). Schmitz (1999b) maintained instead that the external economies discussed by Marshall and the early contemporary district literature have an involuntary source, that is they are (positive) externalities.
3. 'Intermediate' represents between the cooperative nexus and the market strategies of the district producers.
4. For a more analytic definition I would refer to Bellandi (2006).
5. Externalities are effects of choices taken by someone on the utility or productivity of some other without a regulation incorporating a deliberate if not perfect acknowledgment of reciprocal costs and benefits.
6. Brusco (1996) suggested that in a vital ID many employees are required to have a proactive mentality about the job, in order to give an effective contribution to teams engaged in quality and innovation projects; and that the strength and continuity of such contributions are favoured not only by good working conditions, but also by life outside the factory. That is employees have to enjoy their life when not at work, or at least to be not upset by ugly social conditions and prospects. On a general framework subsequently envisaged by Sebastiano Brusco on the management of district rules see Bagnasco (in this volume), Russo and Natali (in this volume), Saglio (in this volume). An industrial policy with a rich local dimension necessarily combines actions on productive processes with other types of policy, such as those aimed at the reproduction and the improvement of systemic conditions supporting: (a) learning and creativity within old and new industrial clusters (labour, educational, innovation policies); (b) an open and dynamic rooting of industrial clusters within the life of localities of industry (labour, educational, social welfare, environment policies). For more on new industrial policies see Vázquez Barquero (2002) and Bianchi and Labory (2006).
7. See Bagnasco (in this volume), Ceglie and Stancher (in this volume), and Whitford (in this volume) on developed and less developed localities. Not surprisingly historical IDs, or similar and proto-forms, suggest compelling examples: see Section 1 of this volume.
8. In this *Handbook*, see Tani on specialisation external economies in the IDs; Saglio on development of competencies, and Robertson, Jacobson and Langlois and Patton and Kenney (in this volume) on innovation.
9. 'Such goods, when released by a reduction in the output of one commodity are, by their nature, suitable for the production of a number of others . . . In buying general purpose intermediate products, a firm does not merely pass on a risk from itself to its suppliers. As these suppliers, having a number of customers, can benefit from the pooling of risks, the total exposure of users and suppliers combined is thereby reduced' (G.B. Richardson 2002, pp. 8–9).
10. Traditional Williamsonian transactional problems are involved too. See Dei Ottati (in this volume).
11. See among others: Coltorti (in this volume); Menghinello (in this volume); Pyke (in this volume); Tattara (in this volume); Wang and Mei (in this volume).
12. See Hart (in this volume, Section 2). More in Raffaelli, Becattini and Dardi (2006).

51. National industrial policies and the development of industrial districts: Reflections on the Spanish case

Joan Trullén

1. INTRODUCTION

The concept of the Marshallian industrial district (MID) expounded by Giacomo Becattini in his article of 1979[1] has raised great interest both in the field of economic analysis and in the field of economic policy. His proposal to replace the 'sector' with the 'district' as a unit of analysis for research led to a major advance in the understanding of a significant part of current industrial processes. The identification of industrial processes with increasing outputs in small and medium-sized enterprises' (SMEs) environments opened the door to proposing a 'new development model' as an alternative to the one based on big companies. Since then there have been major advances in the theoretical, empirical and historical analysis of MIDs (see Becattini et al. 2003). Nevertheless, the progress made by industrial policies based on districts has been uneven: very considerable in the case of local and regional development policies; more limited in terms of national industrial policies.

In effect, from the standpoint of public policies, the Marshallian–Becattinian approach has focused from the outset more on the local and regional level rather than on the national one.[2] The unit of analysis itself focused on the local context, as well as on the nature of the external economies involved in the dynamics of the district; this has led to a systematic use of the concept of industrial district (ID) within policies for local and regional development. At the same time, in countries where SMEs dominate, with sector specialisations favour the phenomena of spatial concentration, with highly flexible industrial processes and with very high degrees of openness to the outside, the importance of MID-type industrialisation and the need to promote new industrial policies based on the Lisbon Strategy, open up new possibilities for operating the idea of the ID on a national and not only a regional or local scale.

The new Spanish industrial policy implemented since 2004 by the first government headed by José Luis Rodriguez Zapatero has, since 2006, incorporated specific content based on the notion of the MIDs, as part of a new economic policy programme of support for a process of industrial transition aimed at strengthening the competitive base of the Spanish economy. This chapter examines the nascent Spanish experience based on the concept of MID, within the framework of the new national strategy for strengthening productivity – with the readoption of industrial policy as a specific economic policy – and support for SMEs, particularly in the European context of the relaunch of the Lisbon Strategy.[3]

The notion of MID has proven useful both in guiding a significant part of the new industrial strategy being implemented by the new General Office of Industry, and in defining specific elements of its industrial policy. The programme known as 'Innovative Business Groupings' (IBGs) instigated by the General Policy Office for Small and Medium-sized Companies (*Dirección General de Política de la Pequeña y Mediana Empresa,* DGPYME) and the programme for financing technological development in cooperation projects for IBGs and clusters (the Technological Research and Development Fund), has been run via a State agency called the Centre for Industrial Technological Development (CITD).

The Spanish experience of industrial policy on a national level based on MIDs focuses on the support to innovative processes that require cooperation between companies and other parties involved in R&D, such as technology centres and universities. It does not envisage dealing with all the sources of external economies but only with those directly related to technological R&D. It is aimed at financing technological development projects in IDs or innovation clusters. It is a centrally-run policy that is 'bottom up' in nature: that is, the initial impulse must come from the agents located within the territory, with the collaboration of the autonomous government authorities or local authorities.

It is a two-stage policy. The first stage is devoted to the identification, selection and financing of initiatives within the IDs or clusters covered by the policy, the IBGs. An initial impulse is required by the companies themselves and the representative agents located in the territory, which need to be constituted as legal entities. The IBG will have the immediate task of drafting strategic plans. In a second stage, joint projects for technological development, involving a limited number of companies, technological centres and universities have to emerge from these strategic plans.

This second phase is aimed less at financing research projects than industrial technology development projects with innovative potential, that are close to the market; projects that are assessable (technologically and financially) in 'open' calls for projects, within the framework of the community policies for promoting R&D activities, and co-financed by the government of Spain and the European Regional Development Fund.

The idea is to harness the potential synergy of the MID in order to channel the central administration's public resources devoted to financing research and technological development. Cooperation projects among IBGs will be given priority.

2. THE NEW SPANISH INDUSTRIAL POLICY AND THE APPROACH BASED ON MIDs

The recent Spanish experience on industrial policy designed to encourage innovation in SMEs, while still in its early stages of implementation, offers a case that can be studied from the standpoint of MID. It should be categorised within a broad range of European experiences based on clusters, poles or districts such as France's 'competitiveness poles' proposals,[4] the Italian 'technological districts'[5] or the cluster policies of various European countries such as the Czech Republic, Slovenia and Sweden.[6]

The European Commission refers to the various European initiatives generically as 'clusters'. The European Cluster Memorandum defines 'clusters' as 'regional concentrations of specialised companies and institutions linked through multiple linkages and spillovers', and understands them as being instruments aimed at promoting innovation. 'ID' and 'cluster' are very close concepts, despite originating in different paradigms. The first assigns a fundamental role to the community of companies and families, emphasises local development and has been developed from the studies carried out by Becattini; the second focuses on competitiveness, and has been developed from the studies carried out by Porter.

For EU policy purposes, the use of the term 'cluster' covers both the ID and competitiveness poles and similar formulas. The Council of Ministers of Competitiveness and the vice president of the European Commission, at the informal Council of Competitiveness in the Netherlands in July 2004, and especially in the light of the momentum provided by the new Commission, have highlighted the need to use 'clusters' as instruments for promoting innovation by encompassing the different experiences. The Councils of Competitiveness of the most recent presidencies, particularly that of Austria, Portugal, Slovenia and France have dealt systematically in the various 'informal Councils' with the need to promote industrial policies for innovation on the basis of clusters, poles or IDs alike.

The case of Spain is an example of a national economic policy geared towards industrial development based on SMEs. The emphasis is on the existence of a system of technological cooperation between companies: these are the IBGs mentioned above. In particular, IBGs are made up of companies, technology centres and universities, and are aimed at receiving priority funds on shared technological development projects.

This section begins by examining the main characteristics of the growth model of the Spanish economy at which the new industrial strategy based on MIDs is aimed. The main concepts that define the policy are then identified. Subsection 2.3 defines the new approach based on MIDs, contrasting it with other models such as that of François Perroux.

2.1 The Spanish economy and the problem of productivity: the mainstay of the new industrial policy

To understand the direction of the new industrial policy in Spain, and the place that MIDs occupy in it, we first need to appreciate the economic context in which it emerged.

Between 1996 and 2007 Spain underwent an extraordinary process of economic growth, with a very high level of investment.[7] Over these 12 years the rate of investment exceeded the OECD average, reaching very high levels of up to 31 per cent of GDP. Even though the construction sector grew very substantially, contributing two-thirds of the aggregate investment growth, growth in investment was widespread throughout the manufacturing sectors as a whole.

The volume of employment rose from 12.5 million to more than 20 million, with production growth rates of 3.35 per cent per annum cumulative, 1.02 per cent higher than the average for the EU (15).

However, the growth in aggregate productivity over these 12 years was close to zero. The available capital grew, as did employment, yet there was no growth in productivity. This point is essential in understanding the new Spanish industrial strategy, and why it was necessary to improve the channelling of the resources available for investment towards activities with an innovative potential. The Spanish economy was exploiting its advantage in labour costs but with a relatively low presence of human capital, and incorporating less technical progress than most advanced countries. The industrial policy needed to be geared to promoting innovation.

Together with the macroeconomic developments, we must stress a fundamental structural point: the Spanish economy has a high number of IDs showing MID features. The economies of Catalonia and Valencia have around two-thirds of industrial employment concentrated into IDs which in many cases come from a long history.[8] In the period 1996–2007 the Spanish IDs increased their production and employment significantly, in contrast with the majority of European experiences. It should be noted that Spanish IDs contain a high level of innovation, meaning that they hold a high proportion of patents, utility models and industrial designs (Boix and Galletto 2009a).

There are other structural characteristics of the Spanish economy that areworth mentioning because they are relevant to this analysis. Firstly, production specialisation is high in sectors which, in the terminology of the OECD, have medium–low or low levels of knowledge intensity. The Spanish economy has two-thirds of its industrial employment in activities with low or medium–low knowledge intensity, compared to 55 per cent in the core countries of the EU. The second structural point refers to the average size of firms, which in Spain is lower than the Community average.[9] Also, large Spanish companies and the production branches of foreign multinationals in Spain (with a dominant presence in leading sectors such as the automobile, chemical or steel industry) tend to be smaller in size than similar companies in other European countries. Finally, another structural character is the low expenditure in R&D in Spain, and the private sector in particular. The historical effort in private R&D is extraordinarily low, close to 0.5 per cent of GDP, although the existence of sectors with process or product innovations based on other means such as design or marketing may partly compensate for this shortcoming.

Accordingly, if the aim is to strengthen productivity growth, it is not enough to adhere to the traditional Schumpeterian-type approach and sustain industrial policies that support the innovative process based on big companies. The development of innovative processes in IDs that are of such great importance to the Spanish economy should also occupy a central role.

2.2 The question of productivity: two routes to growing outputs

In fact, the approach based on MIDs has had an important influence in defining the new Spanish industrial policy. The analysis of the production situation in the advanced economies during the last quarter of the 20th century carried out by Giacomo Becattini[10] identifies a far-reaching process of productive transition, in which the expansion of the markets and the increasing flexibility of production are accompanied by the existence of increasing returns in various economic activities. Not only large companies participate to this process, but also SMEs, which in particular can benefit from globalisation if certain conditions of location and environment are met. These are the conditions facing precisely a significant part of the Spanish industries.

The role of industrial policy is to help and coordinate changes in the organisation of industries and production. In tune with the approaches of the European Commission, the new Spanish economic policy is based on the idea that strengthening manufacturing industry is essential for achieving sustained economic growth.[11] In addition, in the case of the Spanish economy, the existence of a very high and persistent trade deficit meant that there was a need to improve the country's competitiveness worldwide, taking into account that trade in industrial goods contributes more than three-quarters of foreign trade. However, production adjustments can be made by adopting three different approaches: by intensifying the capital available (K), by improving the quality of the work (L), and/or by increasing multi-factor productivity (MFP). The efforts of the Spanish new industrial policy are precisely aimed at supporting improvements along this third direction: strengthening that part of productivity growth linked to a better use of labour and capital.

How is the approach based on MIDs to be incorporated into the diagnosis of the Spanish industrial economy? The Becattinian approach to the problem of productivity constitutes a fundamental point of reference, since, as we have seen in the previous section, it responds to a significant part of the Spanish industrial situation.[12]

The new industrial strategy draws heavily upon it. If the aim is to increase aggregate productivity by means of a greater and better use of labour and capital, there are two basic ways to achieve this. One is by strengthening the advantages deriving from the traditional Schumpeterian-type scale: generating increasing returns associated with firm size or forcing specialisation in areas with a long technological tradition. The alternative route lies precisely in the possibility of strengthening the advantages deriving from cooperation and spatial concentration of SMEs with a great capacity for innovation.

In both cases, it is crucial to take advantage of the opportunities provided by the process of globalisation, although taking different routes and adopting procedures that are also differentiated. Traditionally industrial policy is aimed primarily at the main Schumpeterian objective, that is, at the big industrial companies. The Becattinian analysis has illuminated what until now has been seen as a 'black box' process. Drawing upon Marshallian doctrine, Becattini stresses that it is also possible to find increasing returns associated with the concentration of SMEs in fragmented production processes.

2.3 The new Spanish industrial strategy and the new approach based on MIDs

The new Spanish industrial strategy put in place over the last few years has not been a one-way process, but rather a multidirectional one, even if it has had a single overriding objective: increasing aggregate productivity by strengthening the innovation processes at the firm level by focusing on processes of R&D. However, a single instrument cannot be associated to more than a single goal, as sustained by the traditional economic policy doctrine. The complexity of the innovative process and the existence of very different conditions in which firms' innovative capacity is generated suggested the need to address industrial policy using various instruments and with different analytical approaches, the MID among them.

In fact, within this policy framework four main paths towards industrial innovation were put in place:

1. support to large-scale 'industrial research' within large companies (*à la* Schumpeter), with an ambitious programme financing strategic national consortia for technological research (*Consorcios Estratégicos Nacionales de Investigación Tecnológica,* CENIT);
2. support to 'technological development' based on 'propulsive companies' (*à la* Perroux), the idea being to finance industrial development projects driven by large companies, which however had the specific capacity to trigger knock-on effects towards SMEs (the PROFIT Programme);
3. support to 'permanent innovation'; this refers to the innovation machine put forward by Baumol (2002), aimed at improving the propensity to innovate of companies more generally regardless of their sector or size, through initiatives that impact on firms' investment decisions on R&D (for example tax breaks);
4. and, last but not least, a support to the innovation capacity of IDs, in particular those of the MID-type according to a Becattinian approach, based on the setting up of innovative business groups and the drafting of strategic plans (the General Office of Small and Medium-sized Companies' IBG Programme), and the

financing of technological development projects (the CITD agency's financial support programme for IBGs).

As a whole, public funding for R&D were meant to double between 2004 and 2007, making it a priority element of the government's financial policy.[13] This priority remains also for the period from 2008 to 2011, with the government committing itself to spending 16 per cent per annum cumulative on R&D, thereby doubling the importance placed on R&D compared to 2004.

A two-way strategy to support R&D was developed. The Ministry of Industry will support R&D at the company level: the needs of business innovation demanded technological developments which in turn required industrial research, however the leading role and final direction of the process was in the hands of companies and technology centres. In contrast, the Ministry of Education will support policies promoting research carried out by universities and science parks; in this case the aim was to boost scientific research to generate technological developments which could eventually lead to new processes or new products.

The new National Plan for Scientific Research, Technological Development and Innovation was aimed at sealing these sections, with a leading role acknowledged to industry in R&D policies. This two-way approach to R&D contrasts with the traditional, more one-way approach to public policies.

In fact, the traditional views on the dynamics of the innovative process (both in Schumpeter and in Perroux) were concerned more with supply than with demand aspects. Basic research would open up new opportunities for technological development that eventually generated new processes or new products for the market. Public policies were then aimed at channelling scientific research towards the needs of the market.

In contrast, with the new approach, demand plays a leading role in channelling the process of R&D towards innovation: the idea here is to bring the company to the university and to the technology centres, and not the other way round.

Yet there are also important differences between the approach *à la* Becattini ('Marshallian-type' ID) and the approach *à la* Perroux ('growth pole' type), from both the theoretical standpoint and the applied or public policy standpoint. These differences will also illustrate the originality of the new 'Marshallian' approach in the field of economic policy, as applied in the Spanish experience.

In fact, in the case of the growth pole, external economies respond to Zoran Scitowsky's analysis (1954) and would be of two kinds: pecuniary and technological. This notion of an external economy in the pole, expounded by François Perroux ([1961–69] 1991), leads inexorably to the notion of there being a 'driving industry'; this is a key part of the traditional French-style industrial-territorial strategy. In the pole, there is a driving industry that plays a key role and, unlike for Schumpeter, it does so with the support of public authorities which guide the development of the poles mainly due to the location of the large companies. The dominant type of market in the pole is monopolist competition with a very limited number of propulsive companies (ibid., p. 184).

In the Becattinian approach, the ID is based on a much broader Marshallian notion of external economies.[14] The spillovers are not only technological, but also affect the community of people and producers: Marshall's industrial atmosphere. The existence of a broad range of SMEs that compete among themselves and also cooperate is crucial. Although the public powers can support the development of the district, there is no room for a public strategy aimed at 'replicating districts'. The dominant type of market in the district would also be that of monopolistic competition, but with a much larger number of companies in a much larger number of phases into which production is subdivided. Increasing returns appear, coexisting with forms of competitive market, due to the existence of cooperation and the fact that a number of different positive external economies are operating.

From this there also arises the need to manage the industrial policy in ID terms. As a result, the MID approach has come to play a prominent role in defining the Spanish government's new industrial strategy, channelling its content to promoting industrial productivity for SMEs by financing cooperative research projects and developing innovation.

In the following sections, we shall see how this new district-based policy is implemented by central government, from general reform programmes sponsored by the European Commission to the defining of specific financing instruments.

3. INDUSTRIAL POLICY INSTRUMENTS AND THOSE PROVIDING SUPPORT FOR SMEs BASED ON MIDs: THE IBGs

In Spain, the programmes provided by central government to support MIDs or innovation clusters emerged in the framework of the new industrial policy designed in 2004. Its first realisation was within the context of the 2005 National Programme of Reforms (NPR) approved in the framework of the revision of the Lisbon objectives (Trullén 2006, 2007). The seven key aspects of the reform strategy include a Business Promotion Plan (BPP), which was adopted in January 2006, and which contains five guidelines, including that for increasing the capacity for innovation in companies. This guideline led in 2006 to the 'Innovative Business Clusters' Programme where the Ministry set out the rules, the aid scheme and the management of the support measures for IBGs.

It is worth stressing that this is a bottom-up policy approach that requires the prior existence of a group of companies, generally linked to a territory or district, with the ability and willingness to carry out joint action in specific areas, generally aimed at increasing their innovative potential. The aim is to achieve a close collaboration between the central administration, the autonomous communities and local entities in the process of identifying, assessing and monitoring the IBGs that are recognised.

Economic policy must support collaboration initiatives that emerge from this group of companies, which need not be made up of all the players existing in a cluster or district, but rather of a representative subset.

The programme defines an IBG as 'the combination in a geographical space or specific industrial sector of companies, training centres and research units, whether public or private, involved in the process of collaborative exchange, intended to obtain advantages and/or benefits arising from the implementation of joint projects of an innovative nature'

In addition, the 'IBG thus structured must reach a critical mass that ensures competitiveness and international visibility'. As a result, it is expected that the group of participants (companies, technology centres, research units) will have a minimum of 30 members, of which about 90 per cent will be companies. The IBGs will consist preferably of SMEs, although the programme allows for the possibility that a big company that is well established in a particular area and is interested in strengthening the value chain would be able to head an IBG as a propulsive company if it has generated a significant number of SMEs in its area with which it collaborates on a regular basis.

The projects and actions that are expected to be financed are the following: the drafting of strategic plans; the structures for coordinating and managing IBGs; specific projects designed to strengthen the innovative potential and the competitiveness of the companies in the group; and lastly, consortium projects aimed at promoting joint ventures between different IBGs. Within this set of actions, special importance is attached to ensuring that IBGs are treated as a priority within the set of companies for research, development and innovation (R&D&I) support programmes, by giving a higher rating in the selection process to projects submitted by IBGs and their associated companies or organisations.

IBGs that generate strategic plans rated as excellent will form part of a special registry located in the Ministry of Industry. The autonomous communities will also participate in their selection.

The typology of IBGs is broad, and they can be classified into four groups: those which are related to IDs in traditional industrial sectors (textiles, ceramics, shoes and so on); industrial activities with the presence of big propulsive companies that promote SMEs in their area of influence (automotive, aerospace); knowledge-intensive activities in which companies market product innovations deriving from scientific and technological R&D projects (pharmaceutical industry); and lastly, ICT-intensive activities that are highly innovative and that provide products and services (such as media content industries).

IBGs are also a fundamental element in the new National Plan for Scientific Research, Development and Technological Innovation (2008–11). This plan envisages a more efficient integration between reseach, development and innovation. Line 6 of the plan emphasises the need to strengthen the critical mass of the players involved in R&D&I financing programmes. Together with the technological platforms, it stipulates that IBGs are specific cases which should be given priority in promotion.

Lastly, we should emphasise that the IBG Programme is part of the European strategy for supporting competitiveness and innovation in SMEs, as set out in the EU's 7th Framework Programme (2007–13) for Competitiveness and

Innovation, as well as in the rules of the Structural Funds, which include specific references to support for innovative clusters.

4. FINANCIAL INSTRUMENTS FOR SUPPORTING TECHNOLOGICAL DEVELOPMENT BASED ON IBGs

The bulk of the funding of the IBG initiatives is to be found in the programmes for financing scientific research, development and technological innovation activities. Recognising the IBGs as specific agents in such programmes is a fundamental requirement for their funding. As we have seen, the approval of an IBG is a necessary condition for benefiting from preferential treatment in the process of allocating funds aimed at company R&D&I. The bulk of the financing is to be found precisely in these funds, which in the case of Spain are expected to reach around 0.5 per cent of GDP in total by 2011.

One of the specific new financing instruments is related to the Research and Technological Development Fund. This fund was negotiated by the Spanish government with the European Commission for the period 2007–13, and is intended to compensate Spain for the negative consequences stemming from the process of enlarging the EU. The technological fund is worth €2 billion and represents an addition to the amount of European Regional Development Funds (ERDFs). It operates under a community/national co-financing system, with different levels of aid depending on the region in which the project operates: regions of convergence, phasing in, phasing out and competitiveness.

The CITD channels finance for IBG operations that are experimental technological development projects, executed by the IBGs, aimed at using innovative technologies to solve common problems in a particular area or economic activity, and involving implementation, validation or demonstration technologies in several or all of the participating companies. The aim is to promote the strengthening of regional IBGs by providing financing for R&D, via the implementing of cooperation projects designed to increase the scientific and technological capacity of the companies and research groups present in the region. The aim is also to extend and optimise the joint use by companies, technology centres and universities of the public and private research infrastructure existing in the autonomous community.

The idea here is to extend the culture of cooperation in R&D activities by mobilising SMEs' partnership projects of a certain size.

Beside the financial instruments implemented by CDTI, we must point the set of instruments included in the VI National Plan for Scientific Research, Development and Technological Innovation (2008–11) that consider IBGs specifically as targets of policies. The IGBs are included in six of the 13 national programmes: Applied Research Projects, Experimental Development Projects, Innovation Projects, Networks, Public–Private Cooperation and Internationalisation of the R&D. The National Programme of Networks is very important because it supports the

Technological Platforms, the Centres on Network and IBGs, as they try to provide incentives for inter-firm cooperation with the objective of increasing competitiveness. The programme promotes technological research between different agents of the National System of Science and Technology encouraging the constitution of public and private groups for the discussion and design on strategic actions.

The VI National Plan comprises also important financial provisions specifically targeted at IBGs, in particular through three key programmes: the Programme of Applied Research, the Programme of Technological Development and the Programme of Innovation. These programmes finance almost a half of the public financing of R&D in Spain, with the second one specifically tailored to IBGs.

In short, it is not a case of financing the IDs and clusters in an abstract way. The idea is to finance technological development projects in cooperation, selected on the basis of strategic plans that have been previously validated, and that concern IBGs that have been previously selected; a bottom-up process, which implies the assigning of public resources to the simple but effective funding of specific projects emerging in IDs. In any case, Spain has developed a two-step strategy: firstly, IBGs are identified and their strategic plans set out specific R&D&I projects; secondly, these projects are financed according to their characteristics by different programmes.

5. THE MAP OF IBGs IN SPAIN

Despite the fact that the IBG Programme is very recent and has not yet been deployed completely, we already have the first results from the first call for projects.[15] This is the process of identifying IBGs from a selection of the more than 171 proposals received from all over Spain to finance strategic plans.

In this first stage 60 IBGs have been selected, including 3124 companies and 148 research associated bodies (technology centres, university departments and training institutions). The average IBG includes 50 companies (see Trullén and Callejón 2008).

Among the IBGs selected, those operating in IDs with activities in traditional sectors make up 35 per cent of the whole. The IBGs pertaining to activities that operate with propulsive companies make up 25 per cent, while IBGs based on the development of knowledge provide 27 per cent, and those based on ICT represent 13 per cent.

The territorial distribution of the IBGs selected covers all the autonomous communities of Spain.

We must insist that the programme is bottom up in nature, and that the selection process has not been based on previous delimitation of districts or clusters using statistical procedures. The studies on the delimitation of ID were carried out in order to demonstrate the importance of the phenomenon and the need to pursue policies of this kind in Spain; however their results have not determined the selection process.

Despite this, the distribution by region or by autonomous communities that emerges from this first call for projects responds fairly accurately to the importance that the industrial activities and IDs have in them, as can be seen clearly in Figure 51.1. Thus the two communities with the highest number of IBGs are Catalonia and Valencia – the two communities with the top industrial weight and with the highest number of IDs respectively (see Boix in this volume) – followed by Madrid and Andalusia.

6. CONCLUSIONS

The MID approach is appropriate for designing new national policies for SMEs, aimed at encouraging productivity growth in industry. The idea is to support the innovation process in SMEs by strengthening cooperation between businesses, universities and technology centres in a very specific situation: research and technological development activities. In particular, the aim is to obtain increasing returns associated with the cooperative technological development of sets of companies and other players operating in the context of innovative clusters and IDs.

The Spanish experience of industrial policy based on MIDs is in line with the European context of strengthening R&D as part of the Lisbon Strategy, and is 'bottom up' in nature. It is aimed very specifically at central government funding

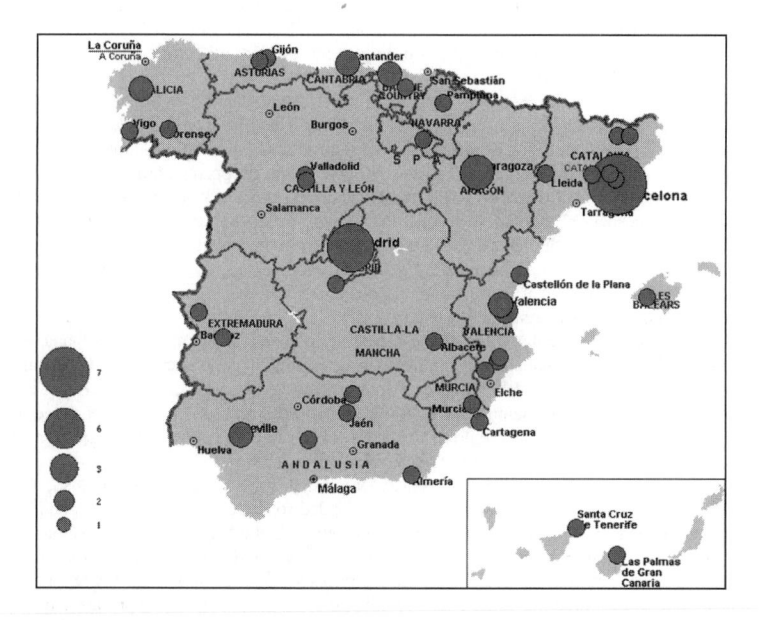

Source: Ministerio de Industria, Turismo y Comercio.

Figure 51.1   The map of IBGs in Spain, localisation of IBGs which have presented strategic plans, 2007

of technological development projects, arising within the framework of innovative clusters or IDs. The approach involves a two-stage strategy. In the first stage IBGs registered in IDs or clusters are identified, selected and financed, so that they can draw up strategic plans to identify key R&D projects to be developed. In the second stage, specific technological development projects arising from these strategic plans and submitted by companies belonging to the IBGs are selected and financed. The IBGs' priority within financial support instruments for research and business development at a national level is also established.

In conclusion, the priority of the national industrial policy is not so much to finance IDs generically, but rather to provide case-by-case finance for technological development projects submitted cooperatively by groupings of their companies.

NOTES

1. See Becattini (2004a) for some remarks on the conceptual foundations of industrial economics.
2. Signorini (2000) argues that the industrial policies in favour of IDs have operated at a local or regional rather than a national scale, and that they have been implemented not so much as a specific regulatory intervention but rather as a set of actions that catered for several areas of local government activity such as infrastructure, services, training and land planning.
3. A synthesis of the new Spanish industrial strategy can be found in Trullén (2006).
4. On the notion of competitiveness pole, see Ministère de l'économie, des finances et de l'industrie (2006).
5. On the notion of 'technological district' in Italy, see www.distretti-tecnologici.it/centro_miur.htm, accessed 12 November 2008.
6. The creation of the High Level Advisory Group on Clusters, chaired by Senator Pierre Laffitte is an important landmark. This group has promoted *The European Cluster Memorandum*, coordinated by the Centre for Strategy and Competitiveness, Stockholm School of Economics and performed under the Europe INNOVA initiative of the European Commission and Center for Strategy and Competitiveness (2008), presented in the framework of the European presidency conference *Innovation and Clusters* which took place in Stockholm on 22–23 January 2008. From the company standpoint see also the document from the Enterprise Policy Group (2007).
7. The rate of investment has in different years exceeded 30 per cent of GDP, which gives an idea of the economic transformation, especially since the launch of the third phase of monetary union and the creation of the euro.
8. See the Chapter by Boix in this volume. The Catalan and Valencia economies present characteristics of the location of SMEs that are very similar to those existing in what is known as Third Italy.
9. In the Spanish economy 99.5 per cent of manufacturing firms are SMEs, 73.8 per cent of the persons employed in manufacturing working in SMEs and 58.1 per cent of value-added industrial manufacturing has occurred in SMEs. These figures contrast with the average for the EU: 99.1, 57.7 and 45.5 per cent (see Trullén 2006, p. 98).
10. When Becattini (1979, 2004a) was translated for the first time in Catalan and Spanish, it raised great interest in Spain, probably because it responded to the existing economic condition in production areas like Catalonia and the Valencia country at the beginning of the 1980s.
11. This point is crucial to understanding the Lisbon Strategy, and the insistence of the European Commission on strengthening the innovative process via public support for R&D, in order to reach the target of three per cent of GDP, with two-third generated by the private sector.
12. A study on the new Spanish industrial policy and IDs can be found in COTEC (2007).
13. In fact, it exceeded the goals with increasing central government's spending on R&D by more than 125 per cent in the period from 2004 to 2007.
14. On external economies in IDs, see Bellandi in this volume.
15. This work is limited to the policy defined and implemented up to April 2008.

52. Public policies for industrial districts and clusters

Mikel Landabaso and Stuart Rosenfeld*

1. INTRODUCTION: IDs AND CLUSTERS POLICY IN A HISTORICAL PERSPECTIVE

Industrial districts (IDs) and clusters have been central concepts in regional economic development literature for more than two decades, moving into the forefront of the public policy debate in about the mid-1990s. But public authorities responsible for economic development first began to take notice of the advantages of 'clustering' and 'networking' as early as the 1980s and began to design policies to support and encourage them. At first, networks and clusters were treated as parallel strategies, but by the mid-1990s policymakers understood their connections. Clusters were geographically bounded and specialized economic environments that gave birth to the networks of companies that gave clusters their synergies. IDs, in turn, referred to richer and more complex notions than clusters for policymaking, in which planners had to deal with particular forms of local systems of production, including essential territorial features such as social capital, business culture, governance and institutional issues.

The seminal work by Michael Porter in 1990 provided the theoretical framework for 'clusters' and legitimized them in economic development policy (Porter 1990a). By the end of 1992, both Arizona and Oregon had adopted cluster strategies, and since then cluster policies (Rosenfeld 1995, 2001, 2002; EDA 1997, pp. 1–4)[1] have become widely recognized in the US as an efficient organizing framework for economic development (NGA 2007).

In Europe, where clusters originated as IDs, there has been a flourishing literature on the impacts of IDs and networks on regional competitiveness and innovation for nearly three decades. In 1979, Giacomo Becattini introduced a new concept that was going to go far in economic literature and would get to our days as a central issue in the debate around regional policy and territorial development. Today many of us have forgotten this contribution to economic thinking and it has been largely substituted by the notion of clusters. Both concepts share some common characteristics but they do not actually refer to exactly the same notion.

Nevertheless both share a common root: Alfred Marshall, who already at the end of the 19th century had established that the advantages of large-scale production can also be achieved by regrouping in a single district a large number of interconnected specialized small producers which share the same 'industrial atmosphere'.

ID and cluster-related policy as such – with the possible exception of regional policies in a few central-northern Italian regions – is a fairly recent policy approach. This is evident, for example, in the little use made of the EU Commission's Structural Funds aid for clusters and business networking during the planning period 1994–99. A substantial increase, however, took place in the period 2000–06, largely thanks to EU Commission initiatives such as the Regional Innovation Strategies (Landabaso and Reid 1999, pp. 19–39) and the EU innovative actions, so that cluster-based actions became a key part of regional policy, in particular in advanced regions.

Many regional and national governments in Europe now have turned their attention to Porter's 'diamond' when looking for ways to promote their industrial/regional competitiveness rather than drawing from the wealth of knowledge from the European regional 'schools' of thought referred to above. Other than Italian regions pioneering the ID approach (for example, Emilia-Romagna and Tuscany), the Basque Country was one of the first to apply Porter's cluster policy approach by 1990, which was soon followed by other regions and countries throughout the 1990s.

Porter's 'diamond' is easily translated into a replicable clear-cut methodology widely used by economic consultants internationally although it 'has generally proven to be more helpful in understanding clustering than in actually formulating policy' (Rosenfeld 1995, p. 57). But it also enjoyed an echo in the business and academic communities, and clusters become a more politically correct form of 'industrial policy'. They offered an acceptable way of presenting interventions in the economy and contributed to a broad consensus about regional development policies.

European[2] and the US cluster approaches have both deviated from the original IDs but in different ways. The US has stayed more with regional production systems, although with a heavier emphasis on innovation and with larger geographic regions. European approaches have evolved into regional innovation systems (RISs) and 'learning regions', which are broader in scope than clusters and are more in line with the ID approach. They focus attention on relationships among a wider set of actors in the regional economy. Regional innovation and learning systems promote networking adapted to the conditions of a given territory and consider institutional factors and governance issues much more into the analysis. They focus in particular on the way in which universities, educational and R&D institutions, technology centres, the public sector, and firms interact with each other in order to generate, diffuse and economically exploit knowledge in a given territory.

The other European progeny of clusters, knowledge or learning regions, are geographically-concentrated socio-economic environments in which intense knowledge exchange occurs as a result of personal contacts, economic/technological transactions, and workers' mobility. Flexible and multidirectional networking among different agents (for example, finance, technology centres, universities, firms, public agencies, business consultants and higher education) fosters innovation and regional development. Public policies for learning regions focus on helping create the appropriate 'climate condition' for these 'economic ecologies' to expand and flourish by 'irrigating knowledge' throughout, attracting talent, diminishing business entry barriers by encouraging risk taking, and fostering entrepreneurship.

IDs and clusters in Europe are, of course, quite diverse in nature because they are embedded in the cultural and institutional framework of each of the European regions in a Union with 27 different countries and nearly 300 regions, with different languages and radically different governance systems, from a large regional autonomy found in federal or quasi-federal States to very centralized countries.

In different ways local development actions inspired to clusters and districts have surged in Europe. One may be talking about centres of expertise in Finland, competence centres in Sweden and Austria, clusters in the UK, networks of competence in Germany, or regional technological networks in Spain, but all share a number of key characteristics and objectives:

- promoting economic development through enhancing the regional innovation capacity;
- using regional business cooperation and networking in a given territory as a basis for linking business to knowledge and increasing learning capacity among SMEs;
- seeking critical mass and try to understand and respond to innovation demand by adapting the local or regional research, technological development and innovation (R&TDI) supply;
- looking for ways to brand the place, the locality or the cluster;
- emphasizing the use of new information and communication technology (ICT) tool to enhance (virtual) networking;
- addressing global markets;
- emphasizing needs for better knowledge management in firms and improved knowledge-related services;
- focusing on particular types of firms;

They also deal with broader issues such as improving the innovation management and entrepreneurial culture, technology forecasting and benchmarking, and synergies between the different parts of the existing R&D system to accelerate the flow of tacit and codified knowledge.

Cluster strategies explicitly include a role for the public sector, which has been more substantial in Europe than in the US. The major emphasis of US cluster policies has been encouraging, sometimes with modest incentives, associations, networks, and other forms of collaboration or targeted investments in education and training, and R&D.

In Europe, in contrast, there is an explicit recognition and a rather active view of the public sector role in developing clusters (European Commission 2001, p. 6). In this sense the establishment of a network structure that may lead to a new 'cluster' and contribute to jobs and economic development in a region is considered to be a collective good. It is assumed that since cluster generation does not immediately benefit enterprises, they tend to underinvest or not invest in it, especially in less favoured regions. In these regions, small and often family-run firms tend to compete in local markets and therefore see other local firms more as competitors than eventual partners for penetrating new markets, producing new products, sharing information, R&D and training costs, or lobbying public authorities for new innovation-development policies – forms of cooperation which may eventually result from clustering.

This is one of the main reasons why, in the early stages, it is thought that the necessary coordination and network structures must be sponsored by a third party representing the collective public interest and further ensured and maintained by a 'neutral' partner which can: (a) ensure a continuous flow of information and communication; (b) achieve a balance of interests and conflict settlement among participants; (c) create mutual trust between network partners; (d) prepare decision making; and (e) build on and strengthen common interest.

Recent important development in cluster policy includes the support of business networks and clusters under the new European Regional Development Fund Regulation (ERDF) for the programming period 2007–13. This means that all European regions are invited to use part of the European aid under cohesion policy (€308 billion) to support business networks and clusters as one of the priority investment fields, as established in arts 4 and 5 of the new ERDF Regulation.[3]

Moreover, 'Community Strategy Guidelines on Economic, Social and Territorial Cohesion 2007–13' published in 2006[4] clearly establish the 'need to focus aid on the provision of collective business and technology services to groups of firms, in order to help them improve the innovative activity'. In the field of R&TDI, these action guidelines identify as a priority 'strengthening cooperation among businesses and between businesses and public research/ tertiary education institutions, for example, by supporting the creation of regional and transregional clusters of excellence'. This includes support to European technology platforms promoted under the European Research and Development Framework Programme in cooperation with leading edge private firm consortia, and to high-technology poles of excellence comprising SMEs clustered around research and technological institutions, or around large companies.

For the first time European competition law officially establishes a legal framework specifically to aid innovation clusters under the new 'Community Framework for State Aid for Research and Development and Innovation' published in December 2006.[5] Under this framework market failures in the efficient use of R&D and innovation are used to justify State aid 'first to support investment in open and shared infrastructures for innovation clusters, and second to support cluster animation, so that collaboration, networking and learning is enhanced'. This legal framework allows investments 'for the setting up, expansion and animation of innovation clusters exclusively to the legal entity operating the innovation cluster'.[6]

At the time of writing of this book, *The European Cluster Memorandum*[7] to promote European innovation through clusters is under public consultation and acknowledges that the strategic importance of clusters for European innovation and global competitiveness 'is only now becoming recognized'.

2. WHY ARE IDs AND CLUSTERS INTERESTING FROM A PUBLIC POLICY PERSPECTIVE?

IDs and clusters concepts offer regional planners a framework to better understand their regional economies, target and prioratize actions, and engage the private sector. This implies that to succeed, any public policy in this field requires an understanding, cooperation and consensus with the private sector within a broad public–private partnership, not a directed top-down approach or recipe from public authorities, but a collaborative approach designed for a particular region's economic specialization and business culture. Firm clustering improves governments' understanding of regional economies, increases the formal and informal transfer of knowledge, and accelerates innovation and public sector efficiencies by aggregating demand.

- 'Knowledge spillovers'. Within new growth theory, the main explanation for increasing returns to production factors, which is key to explaining cumulative processes of economic growth, is knowledge spillovers resulting from the 'tacit' and 'sticky' nature of certain types of knowledge and know-how and its territorial nature. Within this framework, 'intra-regional knowledge spillovers are considered to arise when universities, the business sector and the government sector tie close links leading to fertilizations and feedback relations' (Greunz 2004). Public–private cooperation, business networks and university–enterprise connections are of utmost importance in generating spillovers and, therefore, in increasing the knowledge generation, diffusion and absorption capacities in regions. Thus in this view clusters and IDs can be seen as innovative systems.
- 'Understanding regional economies'. Identifying clusters and/or IDs are efficient means to mapping regional economies and their potentialities. From

the ISTAT methodology for identifying IDs based on 'local labour systems' (see Section 6 of this volume), to the sectoral location coefficient utilised by the British Department of Trade and Industry (DTI 2001) and the method utilised in the European Cluster Observatory[8] (259 regions) or other methods using a variety of statistical techniques (for example, the 'Cluster Mapping Project' of Harvard University (2003).
- 'Innovation'. A recent study (Parvan 2007) shows that less than half of the sources of information for innovation for nearly half of the innovative enterprises of the EU come from internal sources, that is the enterprise or enterprise group, while most of the highly important sources come from suppliers, clients or competitors. Cooperation with other enterprises, in particular, is a strategic capability for innovative enterprises to become competitive in the global scene. Numerous studies show that cooperation based on trust, shared norms and reciprocity facilitates the exchange of tacit knowledge and promotes innovation among SMEs within clusters and IDs (Arzeni and Ionescu 2007).
- 'Aggregating demand'. Clusters also offer policymakers the possibility of addressing business demand collectively, thus avoiding automatic public policy schemes based on individual business demands and ensuring a cost-efficient way to address a critical mass of recipients with a substantial policy impact. In the US, skills alliances, export consortia and entrepreneurial networks are common means of addressing needs of groups of businesses.

In general, cluster building is seen by regional governments as an opportunity to promote regional development through innovation, networking and higher value-added economic activities. But they view clusters not as an end in themselves, but rather as a means to identify pilot projects in the innovation field which can be further financially supported by the regional development schemes existing in the region, a way of aggregating (SMEs) innovation demand and as a source of information for the design of better adapted regional policy measures in the field.

3. PUBLIC POLICIES FOR IDs AND CLUSTERS DEVELOPMENT

3.1 Strategies to grow clusters

How can a deeper understanding of how their economies work be converted by governments into effective interventions and successful outcomes? The rubber meets the road in formulating and launching 'cluster initiatives', the term typically used for projects, resources and investments that benefit a cluster. Most take one of the four forms shown in Table 52.1.

Table 52.1 Forms of cluster actions

Form	Purpose
Convening	Organizing and networking businesses to aggregate needs, create scale economies and build recognition
Specializing	Aligning expertise, programmes, services and resources with special needs of clusters to add relevance and value
Innovating	Supporting research, development, design and creativity infrastructure and capabilities to generate new innovations
Connecting	Facilitating networks and pipelines to markets, ideas, designs, partners, and underserved places and people to create opportunities

The following section presents a variety of cluster initiatives that have been used in one form or another that are organized around five general categories of cluster needs:

- building relationships;
- increasing skills and talent;
- opening global pipelines;
- igniting innovation;
- accelerating entrepreneurship.

3.2 Building relationships

The most common and popular cluster initiatives are those that move tacit knowledge and innovation, whilst encouraging and supporting collective activities. The real strength of clusters lies in their ability to network to achieve economies of scale and in the intangible knowledge that resides within the experiences of employees and routines of companies. Even in a web-connected world, 'local buzz' keeps ideas flowing and companies innovating often in exchanges that take place in cafes, coffee shops, meetings and conference hallways.

3.2.1 Promote networks

Most industrialized nations invested in a strategy to promote networks. An early example is that which was designed in Denmark in 1989. These networks, originally noticed in Italy's IDs, are more common within the confines of districts, or clusters. In the survey of clusters performed conducted for the Competitiveness Institute, respondents named 'networks' and 'networking' as the two most useful activities of clusters.

3.2.2 Form associations

Almost every cluster programme begins with some form of 'mobilization strategy' involving membership organizations typically called councils, associations, or alliances. These organizations become collective voices for their members, mechanisms for engaging industry and aggregating needs and demands, pipelines for information to members and to government, platforms for networking and learning, and, in some cases, pathways of public monies into the cluster. The most successful associations provide a menu of needed services, useful information, and networking venues. They are quite easy to start and generate considerable early excitement, but have proven difficult to sustain without long-term support.

Membership rosters, however, do 'not' define a cluster. Non-members miss out on the access to services provided by and relationships developed within the associations, but can still benefit as 'free riders' from specialized public and private services, labour pools and local knowledge. The experiences of cluster organizations over almost two decades have produced useful lessons for what to do and not to do in building cluster organizations (Table 52.2).

Table 52.2   Dos and don'ts of successful cluster organizations

Elements of successful organizations	Elements of unsuccessful organizations
Strong industry leadership	Club-like exclusivity
Staff to organize and manage activities	Compete with existing industry associations
Provide needed services	Measure success in terms of funding
Support for collective projects	Dominance by public sector
Facilitate networking	Too broad a set of industries

3.2.3 Ensure inclusivity

Although clusters and districts are open systems, social and educational barriers leave some individuals and places by the wayside. Cluster initiatives ought to include ways to extend the existing systemic relationships to include people, places and firms that have been on the periphery of the economic mainstream.

3.2.4 Extend relationships outside cluster boundaries

To be competitive and innovative, clusters and districts have to be globally aware and engaged. Exposure to different operating environments and different cultures is a powerful stimulant for innovation. Successful clusters establish linkages to foreign suppliers and customers and build relationships with similar clusters in other countries to monitor trends and get different perspectives. Maintaining connections with counterpart clusters in other parts of the world, including networks, and exchanges of faculty or employees, can prevent clusters from being too locked-in to their internal strengths.

3.3 Deepening know-how and talent

Companies need talented managers and researchers; mid-level technical, clerical and support staff; and entry-level workers. The pool of employees is more regionally bound and less importable or exportable than almost any other production factor. Companies depend on an uninterrupted flow of workers with the necessary skills and knowledge of the industry and the ability to apply them to both routine and unanticipated situations.

3.3.1 Create cluster hubs at technical colleges or R&D, or technology centrs
The cluster hub is a new breed of industry-driven technology centre that concentrates on the distinctive nature of work in a set of related industries (Rosenfeld, Liston and Jacobs 2003; Rosenfeld and Liston 2006). Specialization allows technical and community colleges to achieve excellence, be relevant to their regional economies and use resources more efficiently. It provides students with access to better and deeper programmes (know what), better employment information and more rungs on career ladders (know who), deeper understanding of industry context (know why), and more informal learning opportunities (know how). It gives businesses access to a more specialized labour pool and a greater array of programmes and courses, and more opportunities for training networks.

North Carolina's BioNetwork includes five colleges specializing in different aspects of biotech (bio-processing, pharma, bio-ag, short-term training and business support service), a mobile lab, grants available to all college for equipment and innovation, and a joint training centre at North Carolina State University. The regional development agency of Yorkshire and the Humber has developed the Centres of Industrial Collaboration (CIC) scheme, with each centre being hosted in a regional university, and covering all the seven Yorkshire priority industrial clusters.[9]

3.3.2 Form training networks
Offering company training to consortia rather than one company at a time makes programmes more affordable to small firms and encourages them to invest more in training. In the US, some States have offered grants to networks of three or more companies. Connecticut introduced a full-blown Business Training Programme in 1999 that by 2002 had funded 11 cluster-based networks, including a metal-working training network in Bridgeport that became the core of the State's metals cluster.

3.3.3 Find and recruit talent
Many cities and towns are looking to their art districts and creative quarters as magnets for young talent, an idea originating in Europe. Small and mid-sized

cities also are competing for young talent by recreating themselves as creative and entrepreneurial places (Cortright 2006).

Educational credentials are not the only measure of creativity – and in some cases not the best. Creative talent exists in unexpected places, including among many considered failures of the educational systems. These talents, if nurtured, could fit many of the emerging clusters that thrive on unconventional ideas, for example media arts, design and entertainment.

3.3.4 Promote career advancement paths

Career pathways are a way to connect education and training programmes with support services to help individuals – especially those who are most disconnected and disadvantaged – gain employment and/or advance within an occupational or industry sector (Jenkins and Spence 2006). Cluster-based career paths pay significant attention to the industry know-how acquired along the way and to informal grapevines among students to identify opportunities.

3.4 Igniting innovation, freeing creativity

Behind every strong cluster is a set of innovative companies that are never satisfied with the *status quo*, companies that are continually looking for improved products or practices or searching for the next new big breakthrough. Clusters need creative and innovative people as well as implementers and users to create commercial value, and they need imitators to keep innovations flowing (OECD 2001a). There are basically three major sources of innovation: R&D that is commercialized; process and product improvements that come from inside or outside a firm; and innovation from the aesthetics and creativity that distinguish, package or market a product.

Table 52.3   Innovation sources

Form of innovation	Examples of institutional sources
R&D	University research
	Private and federal research labs
Product and process improvements	Technical colleges
	University extension services
	Small business centres
Design and differentiation	Colleges of arts and design
	Private design companies

Innovation, however, is difficult to quantify. Patents produced by research labs are only the tip of the iceberg in terms of value to a cluster. Common measures such as investments in R&D, concentrations of high-tech companies, IPOs, and numbers of patents per capita miss most of the innovation that occurs in companies lacking internal R&D departments or dedicated expenditures – which includes nearly all SMEs. Innovations such as creatively retrofitting a machine to a new use, reducing waste, or suggesting a better office management system are rarely counted.

3.4.1 Invest in cluster-based innovation centres
A cluster-based innovation centre is a bottom-up institution driven by members' interests. R&D centres located at the University of Alabama, University of Michigan and Clemson University are all linked to their respective regional automotive clusters. Each centre has close ties to the industry, sending a stream of students to intern and graduates to work. In Europe, the Stuttgart region has established twelve Competence and Innovation centres, each employing a professional cluster manager, whose role is to organize joint activities and provide supporting services including the search for complementary partners or independent technological consulting. On a smaller scale, in the West Midland region (UK) financial support is provided for groups of firms actively engaged in jointly developing innovative products, processes or services.

3.4.2 Target R&D funds to clusters
The tendency at universities is to conduct basic research that reflects the interests and expertise of faculty members and/or agencies providing funds. Local demand is not typically the driving force; universities serve larger regions and global customers. There are, of course, many exceptions, and a certain proportion of the research has local relevance because farsighted leaders have invested wisely.

3.4.3 Encourage R&D networks
Since innovation is a consequence of iterative and interactive processes across disciplines, and rarely the solitary inventor in the proverbial garage, cooperation enhances the process. About 20 hosiery companies in North Carolina invested in developing an automated boarding machine that would make the entire cluster more competitive against low-cost competitors. Cooperation, of course, must be balanced by the need for confidentiality since partners may be competing for financial rewards. Large corporations are able to build research networks within their organizational structure and they have the international connections to readily find partners to complement their in-house competencies. Small and medium-sized firms are more isolated and need assistance to find partner companies, nearby and abroad.

3.4.4 Emphasize design as an innovation strategy
Government economic development programmes have paid little attention to the aspect of design that adds new value to products and induces customers to pay

for appearance or style. Yet markets for high fashion and high experience goods are growing, and States have an opportunity to strengthen design capabilities in their educational systems, design sectors and companies. Designers themselves cluster and represent a growth industry, but most are in large cities – New York, Boston, Seattle and Portland in the US; Milan, London and Copenhagen, and Singapore abroad. The EU is in the forefront of public support for interdisciplinary research, funding programmes at universities and research centres across Europe that require teams of artists, scientists and engineers.

3.5 Accelerate entrepreneurship

Clusters are carefully weaved into a complex tapestry by cadres of enterprising entrepreneurs and innovators who see and seize opportunities to add value to an existing set of regional competencies. The addition might be a new element of an existing value chain, a way to be more competitive in existing markets or supply chains, a new compatible niche product, or a new application of some cluster technology. Many regions pin their hopes for growth and target their venture capital on the 'gazelles', the high-tech companies considered capable of rapid growth. But focusing only on high-growth companies misses many emerging creative and alternative clusters dominated by self-employment and micro-enterprises.

3.5.1 Support entrepreneurial networks
Entrepreneurs thrive on networking. They may have a great idea but have only some of the knowledge necessary to convert it into a business. Networks give entrepreneurs opportunities to meet other entrepreneurs with complementary knowledge, different connections, and common concerns. If the entrepreneurs are in somewhat similar or complementary businesses, the knowledge and contacts that develop are bound to be more relevant.

3.5.2 Create specialized incubator space
Many incubators have a particular focus, generally on areas such as high tech or manufacturing, and most look for businesses that bring new wealth into the community. Incubators that target companies in specific clusters have the added advantage of being able to offer even more highly-specialized services and expertise and create more opportunities for networking and learning. Some of the most successful cluster-based incubators target biotechnology or food processing, which require special equipment that can be shared, and software or the arts, both of which thrive on creative environments.

3.5.3 Educate for entrepreneurship
Although many skills apply to any types of business, there are skills that are specific to a certain kind of industry. Knowledge of cluster-specific skills, relationships,

and language can make the difference between success and failure. Policies that adapt initiatives to specific clusters have the potential be more effective. Starting a technology-based company with products and clearly defined market is very different from starting a film company that is project-oriented and dependent on networks and personal reputation. Linking entrepreneurial education to clusters suggests three possible cluster-specific approaches:

- recognize enterprise distinctiveness and include skills that are specific to the particular cluster;
- integrate entrepreneurial competencies into existing workforce curricula by, for example, posing problems that require an understanding of the cluster and by framing discussions in business cluster contexts;
- establish real or fictitious cluster enterprises operated by student teams as a context for learning technical and business skills.

4. VALUE ADDED AND LESSONS LEARNED

After more than a decade of starts, stops and course adjustments for cluster initiatives and of efforts to start, organize, sustain and rescue clusters, these remain useful and cost-efficient targets for public policy. Cluster initiatives provide advantages and opportunities that can often make the difference between the success or failure, growth or stagnation, of a regional economy. Public sector initiatives have proven effective in improving clusters' ability to compete and, in selected instances, have influenced growth patterns (Wolfe, Holbrook and Lucas 2005; Wolfe and Gertler 2006) (see Table 52.4).

But conditions have changed since the early and somewhat experimental period of cluster initiatives. Easier and quicker access to global markets for supplies, services and expertise extended the boundaries of value chains and outsourcing, not only of components and parts but also of routine R&D, and specialized services have become commonplace.

Further, clusters that remain competitive in advanced districts and regions increasingly depend on innovation and talent. They need an environment that supports a creative and entrepreneurial culture and attracts creative and entrepreneurial talent. Having a critical mass of cultural amenities and tolerant attitudes boosts clusters' chances to attract young talent, for example, entertainment venues, coffee shops, restaurants, boutiques, green space and bike paths. Cities everywhere are searching for that set of conditions and opportunities for artistic expression that attract young professionals. Cluster strategies must pay attention to quality of place as part of the cluster support structure.

Clusters, like any popular and heavily marketed concept, if misapplied or over-promoted become empty promises. Many investments in clusters have not paid off where a proper foundation was missing. But many more public sector investments have been used very effectively to stabilize, spur growth and increase the competitiveness of clusters. The numerous 'cluster initiatives' have increased levels of activity and rates of growth within existing clusters. At their best, clusters are a means for better understanding an economy in order to formulate effective and cost-efficient public sector interventions that serve the public good. At their worst, clusters justify poorly conceived public sector interventions.

Table 52.4   Helpful hints for successful cluster-based interventions

1	Dare to be different: cluster success is often linked to differentiating or branding a region
2	Promote innovation: from all sources everywhere, including universities, employees, customers and competing clusters
3	Cultivate culture: local amenities and attitudes are closely associated with success of clusters that rely on attracting and retaining talented workers
4	Be creative: use design and novelty to secure competitive advantages in clusters that are shifting toward design niches and mass customization
5	Look outward: clusters need global pipelines as much as local networks for benchmarks, ideas, talent and markets
6	Support entrepreneurs: both gazelles in high-tech clusters and creative micro-enterprises in content-based clusters
7	Target education and training: workforce matters most and context counts
8	Support relationships among clusters: seek areas of convergence and overlap that may lead to new market opportunities

Only a few European regions are planning to develop 'clusters' in a strict sense.[10] They are mostly concerned about strengthening their RIS through the development of the missing parts and broader considerations about networking; linking SMEs to the knowledge base, deepening public–private partnerships and promoting SMEs' interaction in particular. That is, planners are thinking more along the lines of what the ID literature points at.

It is clear that be it IDs, clusters or RISs, public authorities are more and more concerned with how regions, less favoured in particular, participate in shaping the globalized knowledge economy (Isaksen and Hauge 2002). In this sense, it is important that we understand better the life cycles of clusters and therefore explore further how policies might affect them, in order to identify the best 'timing' and form for such policies. Moreover, we also need to understand better how globalization is altering cluster formation (for example, can there be efficient clusters with delocalized production sites?), including the way in which virtual interactions through improved ICTs can affect the nature of interactions within clusters and they way they can expand worldwide into related communities of practice.

In conclusion, new policy tools largely inspired by cluster and ID concepts, based on increased and more efficient public–private partnership and business networking are being designed in many regions. This is why it is so important to have room for policy experimentation and facilitate the exchange of good practice and hard-learnt lessons among planners and regional/State governments.

NOTES

* The responsibility for the accuracy of the analysis and for the judgments expressed lies with the authors alone. This document does not constitute the policy positions of the EU Commission.
1. For a detailed description of 17 US case studies lessons learnt-recommendation for 'cluster' building, see EDA (1997).
2. For a good empirical analysis of clusters in Europe see Isaksen and Hauge (2002) and Sölvell, Lindqvist and Ketels (2003, Chapter 6, pp. 59–69). See also Rosenfeld (2002).
3. Reg. (EC)1080/2006 of 5 July 2006, arts 4.1 and 5.1.
4. Council decision 2006/702/EC, *Official Journal of the European Union*, L/291/11.
5. *Official Journal of the European Union*, 2006/C/323/01.
6. Such aid may be granted for the following facilities: facilities for training and research centres; open access research infrastructures, including laboratory and testing facilities; broadband and networking infrastructures.
7. www.proinno-europe.eu/index.cfm?fuseaction=nwev.NewsReader&news=1908, accessed 20 August 2008.
8. The European Cluster Observatory, www.clusterobservatory.eu, accessed 20 August 2008.
9. www.yorkshire-forward.com, accessed 20 August 2008.
10. CLOE (Clusters Linked Over Europe) is a European network on clusters which was created in 2004. It was initiated by the Karlsruhe City Economic Development Department and co-financed by the European Commission through INTERREG IIIC West with an initial total budget of €1.8 million. Ten partners from eight regions participated – Nottingham (GB), Lyon (FR), Linz (AT), Timisoara (RO), Kaliningrad (RU), Wermland (SE), Tartu (EE) and Karlsruhe (DE). Partners developed a 'Cluster Management Guide. Guidelines for the development and management of cluster initiatives'. This document describes in detail the steps to take when establishing a cluster. Eight new partners have joined the consortium to take part in the experimentation. They come from Bulgaria, the Czech Republic, Hungary, Lithuania, the Slovak Republic and Slovenia, and include an innovation centre, as well as regional development agencies and city and regional authorities. There are now 18 partners from 14 regions (including Russia).

53. The industrial district model in the development strategy of international organizations: The example of UNIDO

Giovanna Ceglie and Anna Stancher[*]

1. INTRODUCTION

The cluster concept has gained increasing prominence on the agenda of international development organizations over the last decade. Starting in the 1980s, analysis of successful clusters in industrialized countries provided evidence that agglomerations of collaborative firms could turn into drivers of economic growth and become hubs of innovation. More recently, a body of research[1] has shown that clusters are a widespread phenomenon also in developing economies and can display levels of dynamisms and innovation similar to those registered in developed countries. The high-tech industry of Bangalore, India, the Chilean wine clusters and the Sialkot surgical instruments clusters, Pakistan, are but a handful of many successful cases. These dynamic clusters have achieved high levels of growth, gained a stable foothold in the international market and generated wealth and prosperity at the local level.

Yet, this is only one part of the story. A considerable number of clusters in developing countries are lagging behind and are trapped in a vicious circle of cutthroat competition, which contributes to local stagnation and poverty. Although they represent substantial pockets of entrepreneurial activities and provide means of living to numbers of workers, they are unable to break out of poverty and refocus their local communities on innovation and growth.

An approach to cluster development that tackles the root causes of their underperformance, identifies opportunities for growth and fosters joint action, can become a powerful policy instrument for helping these clusters out of the poverty circle and bringing about local economic and social development.

The United Nations Industrial Development Organization (UNIDO) has been actively assisting clusters in developing countries since the mid-1990s.

The engagement of UNIDO in cluster development was triggered by the observation of the accomplishments achieved by successful industrial districts

(IDs) in Europe, particularly in the so-called Third Italy, and abundantly reflected in the literature. Reviewing the experience of industrialized economies allowed UNIDO to identify the defining features of vibrant districts and set benchmarks for the clusters to be promoted as ways to social and economic development of mainly poor localities.[2]

The present chapter builds on the experience of UNIDO in its worldwide project activities to show how cluster development can be used to achieve a number of pro-poor outcomes.

2. WHY AND HOW A FOCUS ON CLUSTERS

The private sector is the main contributor to economic growth and employment generation in both developed and developing countries (see OECD 2007d). A thriving and dynamic private sector enhances the ability of the poor, men and women, to participate in and benefit from growth. Therefore international development organizations have identified private sector development as a main strategy towards the promotion of pro-poor growth and the achievement of the Millennium Development Goals (MDGs) that call for halving poverty by 2015.[3]

In the framework of private sector development initiatives, cluster-based interventions have gained momentum. Two main arguments can be advanced to explain the focus on clusters as targets of development assistance:

1. collective efficiency gains and district effect; and
2. pro-poor impact potential.

2.1 Collective efficiency gains and district effects

Clustered enterprises can achieve levels of competitiveness that reach beyond the potential of individual enterprises. While the growth of individual small-scale firms is constrained by limited access to resources and inability to achieve scale and scope economies, firms within clusters benefit from collective efficiency gains, that is, 'the combined advantage firms experience as a result of external economies and gains from joint action' (Albu 1997). External economies include the availability of a specialized labor force, machinery and input suppliers, the attraction of traders and buyers as well as an industrial atmosphere where information and knowledge are easily shared. Joint actions range from collaborative relations between individual firms to the establishment of multilateral institutions such as associations, cooperatives or political lobbies.

Therefore, cluster enterprises are able to achieve higher and sustained growth rates for synergies and collaborative linkages allow them to specialize in complementary stages of the production process. They pool resources and efforts together for the achievement of shared economic goals and are supported by a responsive institutional and policy infrastructure. An example of collective efficiency gains is offered by the analysis that Nadvi (1997) makes of the Sialkot surgical instruments cluster.

Box 53.1

The surgical instrument cluster of Sialkot (Pakistan) encompasses about 300 SMEs located in the Punjab Province of Pakistan. Sialkot producers have gained Pakistan the position of second major exporter of surgical instruments in the world, since 90 per cent of their output is exported, which accounts for 20 per cent of global trade in this sector. Moreover, a large share of their production is absorbed by the European and North-American markets, confirming that Sialkot is supplying the world market with high-quality products. Nadvi reports that the growth of this cluster rests on the benefits deriving from the presence of specialized suppliers that ensures ready availability and quick delivery of inputs at competitive prices. Thus the flexibility of producers is increased, since they can respond rapidly to new orders. The presence of global couriers accounts for stable linkages to existing and potential buyers. A widespread network of subcontractors allows for the achievement of scale and scope economies through division of labor and specialization. The concentration of skilled labor ensures reasonably low wages and availability of employees, whose credentials are easily proved. Formal and informal meetings account for the spread of market/export/technical information among producers. Finally, inter-firm cooperation and a good understanding with subcontractors and inputs suppliers allows the cluster to satisfy large orders and achieve steady improvements in the production process.

Source: Nadvi (1997).

Leveraging collective efficiency gains lays at the core of the UNIDO approach to local development through cluster. Assistance is thus aimed at groups of enterprises instead of individual firms as well as at improving the portfolio of service providers and assisting policymakers to establish an enabling business environment, which will benefit the localities and the region at large well beyond direct beneficiaries and project life span.

Although enterprise networking, especially in a globalized environment, has no geographic boundaries, it has been observed that the achievement of collective efficiency gains is facilitated by socio-cultural proximity between economic actors, including attitudes and traditions such as work ethos, values and common cultural background. Proximity generates reputation effects and moderates the moral hazard associated with the performance of economic transactions. On the one hand, risk is decreased when cluster firms know their partners and can easily gather information on their reliability. On the other hand, firms have fewer incentives to engage in opportunistic behaviours since this will affect their future ability to acquire economic partners as well as attract social stigma. More generally, proximity may facilitate the development of trust-based relations that lower transaction costs and support collaborative interactions.

Moreover, because of the spatial proximity between enterprises, 'crowding in' or 'spontaneous replication' effects result in a higher number of stakeholders than those directly assisted, which benefits cluster development. Indeed, the extensive web of relationships shared by cluster stakeholders facilitates the dissemination of information, knowledge or commercial gains from the assisted enterprises and institutions to the cluster at large, thus producing a 'district effect'.

A final point worth mentioning is that cluster initiatives can help regions or localities regain or maintain a competitive edge also in those sectors wherein national/sectorial analysis identifies little competitive potential. Collective efficiency and district effects facilitate, namely, the development of specialized human and physical capital as well as support services and policies that increase the resilience of the economic system and its ability to cope with changes in technology and market trends.

When a specific territorial advantage is identified, which can be enhanced through a cluster approach, a region can manage to successfully anchor productive activities and attract investments also in (mature) sectors whose performance is affected by globalization, and heighten international competition (for example, garment or footwear production).

2.2 Pro-poor impact potential

Under the impetus of the MDGs, international organizations have faced the challenge of identifying approaches that maximize the pro-poor impact of development assistance. This concern has its origin in the growing awareness shared by academia and the international community that economic growth *per se* does not necessarily benefit the poor. Growth may follow a pattern that is skewed against the poor, and, even when it benefits the poor, some paths of growth have greater impact on poverty than others (OECD 2001b; UNDP 2004).

The experience of UNIDO shows that a cluster approach, if adequately focused, can be a valuable tool to tackle poverty and generate a process of inclusive growth. This is partly due to the fact that clusters are also socio-economic systems where the population of firms overlaps with the community of people and their families, living and working in a delimited territory, as shown originally in European IDs. Not only do entrepreneurs and workers share a similar social, cultural and political background, but also norms of reciprocity and collective practices of self-help are common among employers and employees. Overall, this accounts for a distribution of the benefits of growth that is likely to be more inclusive than in other economic systems.

The pro-poor growth potential of cluster development can be enhanced when assistance is provided along two self-reinforcing lines oriented, respectively, at: (a) generating economic opportunities for the poor; and (b) tackling the other (non-economic) dimensions of poverty.

The first element (a) reckons that thriving clusters have the potential to generate substantial economic benefits for the local communities. Employment and income opportunities can be created for entrepreneurs and workers as well as for unemployed individuals whose skills match the needs of local firms. Cluster development can spur greater demand for locally supplied inputs and equipment thus benefiting suppliers, including farmers, machinery and spare parts producers. Also it may result in greater quality and availability of affordable goods and services for local consumers.

Cluster economic gains, however, do not automatically accrue to the poor. A cluster development initiative that aims to maximize poverty reduction effects will thus need to take an explicit pro-poor focus. This means, for instance, opting for labor-intensive choices rather than capital-intensive ones, investing on upgrading the skills and employability prospects of marginalized segments (such as women, migrants, minorities), encourage the production of goods and services demanded by the poor.

In a nutshell, within a poverty reduction framework, the collective efficiency gains of the cluster approach can be purposefully geared towards the poor, so that they can increase the productivity of their assets and deploy them to respond to emerging demands and market opportunities. The challenge is to tackle poverty reduction without losing sight of cluster competitiveness.

The second component of this two-fold strategy (b) acknowledges that poverty cannot be equated to the lack of material assets. Taking the view of Amartya Sen (1999) it recognizes that poverty is a multidimensional concept encompassing economic deprivation but also lack of political, socio-cultural, human and protective capabilities. The poor may be unable to take advantage of emerging economic opportunities, if additional constraints are not removed. A few examples follow (ODI 2008):

- the lack of voice mechanisms reduces the capacity of the poor to advocate the provision of services, infrastructure or assistance necessary to enter the market for labor and products–services;
- the lack of human capital, that is, low levels of basic education and high incidence of illnesses, hampers the capacity of the poor to deploy their assets in the most productive way or to access better paid jobs;

- exclusion or discrimination on the basis of race, ethnicity, language, religion, caste or gender restrict access to assets, income-generating activities and basic services; and
- a high degree of vulnerability (for instance to natural disasters) increases the risk of investing, innovating or specializing.

In order to strengthen the capacity of the poor to participate in economic activities, UNIDO relies on a range of practices designed to maximize the pro-poor impact of cluster development.

First, the adoption of a participatory approach, openly oriented at empowering the poor fringes of the society (for example, disabled, women, minorities) contributes to reduce their marginalization and encourages their active participation in the economic life of the cluster by improving their self-confidence and social status.

Box 53.2

In the handloom cluster of Barpalli, India, women were confined to their houses and had no control over household income despite their substantial participation in pre-loom activities. In order to promote the participation of women into the economic life of the cluster and help them gain recognition *vis-à-vis* their male partners, the UNIDO project promoted the establishment of a Federation of women. As a first step in building their self-confidence and overcoming the reluctance of men to allow women to step out of their houses, UNIDO promoted the organization of social activities such as sanitation and literacy camps. Once their confidence increased, UNIDO facilitated their engagement into economic activities. On the one hand, the members of the Federation have started saving and inter-lending activities to help members in financial distress and prevent borrowing from informal moneylenders. Additionally, the Federation oriented efforts on the provision of capacity building to its members especially in the areas of self-management, leadership development and financial management. At a later stage, the women started to jointly undertake weaving activities while the Federation provided them with support services such as joint training in design, market exposure and assistance for new product development.

Source: UNIDO (2008a).

A further factor is represented by investments in capacity-building activities aimed at improving the human capital of the poor, which allows them to better manage their business, plan investments and utilize their limited assets in the most productive way.

Capacity building in poverty-related contexts, needs to be multifaceted and therefore UNIDO seeks the partnership of specialized agencies that have a mandate to address education- social- or health-related issues.

> **Box 53.3**
>
> In the handloom cluster of Chanderi, India, poor health affected the capacity of women to participate in income-generating activities. UNIDO identified the necessity to introduce awareness raising initiatives related to health issues as a first crucial step towards poverty reduction. In collaboration with the Madhya Pradesh Voluntary Health Association (MPVHA) and UNICEF Bhopal a health awareness package including Community, Reproductive, Adolescent, Mother and Child Health Care was set up. At the end of the project, a survey found that this had increased women's awareness of health issues and access to local health services. As a result, women's self-esteem, mobility and capabilities have increased with a positive impact on their participation in the weaving industry and overall the industry's productivity.
>
> *Source*: UNIDO (2007a).

Besides the above, a cluster approach can contribute to improving the access of the poor to utility supply, basic services or social provisioning. A direct intervention in this area falls beyond the mandate of UNIDO. However, by virtue of the district effects, significant spillover can follow from the joint actions undertaken for economic purposes. In other words, although animated by an economic rationale (for example, improving roads to facilitate market access), investments in services and infrastructure produce effects that reverberate on the entire local community, particularly the poor who would otherwise lack resources to access private services (for example, clean water, electricity or energy) or the political weight to lobby for their provision.

> **Box 53.4**
>
> In the framework of the UNIDO project for the development of the dairy products cluster of Chontales, Nicaragua, cluster entrepreneurs identified the lack of energy supply as one of the main factors affecting their capacity to store and process milk. In order to overcome this obstacle, a committee representative of the cluster brought the issue to the attention of the National Energy Commission, with the support of UNIDO. The intense lobbying by the cluster was met by a government-sponsored initiative to build 337 km of new energy lines, which would ensure steady energy supply to the cluster producers. In the framework of the infrastructural improvements, the energy supply was extended to the local communities and, within them, to schools, located along the cooperatives' supply network.
>
> *Source*: UNIDO (2008b).

3. UNIDO'S APPROACH AND SERVICES FOR CLUSTER DEVELOPMENT

The competitive advantage produced by collective efficiency is often out of reach for developing countries' clusters, where firms operate in isolation and institutions are not receptive to their needs.

In spite of the potential benefits of clustering illustrated in the previous sections, the propensity of enterprises and of supporting institutions to work together in a locality is constrained by a number of obstacles. First, sealing contracts and ensuring against losses due, for instance, to opportunism are difficult and expensive. These costs increase in certain contexts, such as in developing countries, where institutions are weak and unable to exercise control and enforce sanctions that reduce the risk of default and opportunistic behavior between the partners of a contractual agreement. Low levels of trust also hamper interaction between cluster firms and their support institutions, reduce their propensity to information exchange and hinder the development of business partnerships.

In developing countries, business associations, in which firms should find a forum for dialog and coordination, are often dominated by a few large enterprises, or are weak or politicized. Business Development Service (BDS) providers are unable to deliver services that are customized to the needs of small-scale firms and business regulations may be skewed against SMEs. In many cases the entrepreneurial population is constituted by a few large-scale enterprises (often foreign-owned) and a large number of micro local enterprises with few medium-size actors. This determines a large imbalance of power and a wide technological gap among these two types of enterprises that makes the integration of the industrial fabric difficult to achieve.

Considering these elements, UNIDO's approach to support clusters in localities of developing countries focuses on two main areas:

1. trust and governance building in order to remove obstacles to and reduce the costs of collective actions; and
2. capacity-building activities aimed at improving the institutional environment in which the entrepreneurial and productive capacities of the cluster develop.

3.1 Trust and governance

Trust is a precondition for the development of collective activities in that it decreases the risk associated with the achievement of common business goals, it enhances information exchange thus facilitating learning and the absorption of new techniques, and it encourages private–public sector cooperation for the establishment of appropriate services and infrastructure. Trust-based relations can also compensate for institutional weakness, for example by supporting a reputation mechanism instead of contractual control, when the legal basis for the latter is insufficient. However, it is not only the propensity of cluster actors to work together that matters, but also how interactions are coordinated by formal and informal institutions, which is captured by the concept of cluster governance. Governance can be understood as the capacity of the cluster to start and sustain joint actions in a systematic and strategic fashion. A sound governance system allows the cluster actors to identify shared objectives, agree on a common strategy for their achievement, articulate collective actions and solve related problems, monitor outcomes and ensure their sustainability over time.

When left to the market, investments in trust and governance are unlikely to be performed due to their strong public goods features. This means that no private actor can take exclusive possession of the benefits deriving from an investment in these goods, even if he/she has invested in it far more time and resources than anyone else. Nor can other actors be prevented from free riding on their benefits. It follows that the willingness of cluster actors to pay for their provision is limited.

Evidence from thriving IDs shows that trust and governance-building functions are most often performed by public sector agencies or institutions, such as the local government, a local development bank, a public-sector SME support agency, a regional development agency and so on. Given their non-profit orientation these or such like organizations have a mandate to invest in public goods. In developing countries, however, a shortage of skills and suitable operational and financial means limit the effectiveness of such institutions. This is where international development organizations, such as UNIDO, can come to help with the promotion of business linkages and public–private partnerships, the establishment of cluster-wide coordination bodies and platforms of interactions, assistance in the diagnostic of cluster needs and planning of strategic activities, and launching pilot projects to showcase the benefits of collective action.

To carry out these functions UNIDO trains and employs Cluster Development Agents (CDAs), who are in charge of facilitating the development of collective activities. On the one hand, the CDA encourages local actors to engage in activities that, while generating economic gains, showcase the benefits of collaboration and division of labor, such as joint input purchase, joint participation in trade fairs or joint use of shared facilities. On the other hand, the CDA focuses on the creation or strengthening of a governance system that will be able to autonomously promote collective activities.

Governance rests within the institutional arrangements underpinning the activity of the cluster. These include organizations, norms and values. Therefore, the CDA spends considerable efforts in strengthening the management capacity of organizations or networks thereof and their degree of representation of all categories of cluster actors. Similarly, the CDA promotes the adoption of norms that regulate interaction and transactions between the economic actors (for example, contracts and standards but also statutes and collaborative agreements) and fosters a business ethics based on compliance to commitments and collaboration.

3.2. Capacity building

Within the second broad area of activities, capacity building, UNIDO mainly targets policymakers, BDS providers, business associations and the training system. Capacity-building activities pursue a two-fold objective: on the one hand, they aim at increasing the responsiveness of the institutional infrastructure to the clusters needs by building dialog mechanisms between entrepreneurs and institutional actors. On the other hand, activities seek to strengthen the capacity of institutions to provide efficient and effective services.

In what follows examples of capacity-building activities are reviewed.

3.2.1 Development of enterprise networks and business linkages

This is a crucial feature of cluster development, since networks and linkages act as a catalyzing spark for the emergence of trust-based relations among the cluster stakeholders, and they showcase the benefits of collective efficiency. Horizontal networks are groups of enterprises engaged in the same or similar stages of the production process that seek to achieve shared commercial goals. They allow producers to reap the benefits of economies of scale and of a larger and more diversified product offer. Vertical linkages refer to relationships

---

Box 53.5

In the Merkato cluster of Addis Ababa, Ethiopia, approximately 1000 producers are engaged in footwear production. When UNIDO started assisting the cluster, inter-firm competition was high and eroding the profit margins of producers. Indeed, despite the existence of cooperatives, a culture of 'do it alone' prevailed. The UNIDO thus focused on strengthening the cooperatives and helping members identify areas for collaboration. As a result, the cooperatives have engaged in a range of joint activities. Bulk purchase of raw material allowed them to achieve a 15 per cent reduction in price while more stable market linkages could be established through joint retail practices. A pressing issue related to the lack of appropriate work premises and the limited access to utilities (electricity), which was affecting cluster productivity. To tackle this, the members of a cooperative have pooled resources to build common working premises. These ensure the producers have access to utilities and a safer working environment, while the proximity between the newly-built workshops enhances information exchange and collaboration.

Overall, the cluster initiative has resulted in an average 20 per cent increase in the daily income of the cooperative members, while the price of footwear has risen between 20 and 50 per cent.

Source: UNIDO (2008c).

between enterprises located at different levels of a production chain. They can be forged backward and forward, and include subcontracting agreements, supplier development initiatives as well as the establishment of linkages between producers and buyers, both domestic and international. Initiatives aimed at improving communication between actors located at different levels of the production chain are likely to increase the quality of the produced goods or services as well as improve producers' performance in terms of timely delivery and reliability (see Boxes 53.5 and 53.6).

Box 53.6

The livestock cluster of Chontales, Nicaragua, encompasses about 7000 farmers and a handful of slaughterhouses processing the meat and selling to supermarkets and end consumers. Despite its high production capacity, the cluster was unable to cater the market with quality products, mainly due to the lack of coordination between its actors. The farmers were unaware of the requirement of the meat industry, which led to the irregular supply and low quality. On the other hand, the slaughterhouses felt little commitment towards their suppliers who lamented a non-transparent pricing policy and delays in payment. In order to increase the coordination capacity between producers and processors, UNIDO facilitated the drafting of a supply agreement between farmers' cooperatives and a leading processing industry, and sensitized the farmers on its time and quality requirements. As a result, the farmers' cooperatives have defined a supply calendar to ensure regular delivery of cattle to the industry. The slaughterhouse, on its side, has devised a clear payment system. Overall, this has led to regular payments to the livestock producers and an increased and steadier processing capacity for the slaughterhouse *vis-à-vis* competing industries.

Source: UNIDO (2008b).

3.2.2 Skills upgrading

Skill deficits are common to underperforming clusters and range from the scarce technical competences and low level of education of the workforce, through poor business management capacities, to weak capabilities of the staff of local institutions. These hamper the capacity of the cluster to learn, absorb new technology and upgrade. Skills shortages also reflect the inability of the local training system to supply the cluster with the qualifications required by an innovative private sector. Therefore, UNIDO works with local training providers to improve the skill base of the clusters, facilitates contact building with external sources of expertise and knowledge, and helps skills providers to reorient their training offer towards the provision of skills that match the needs of the cluster (see Box 53.7).

> Box 53.7
>
> The competitiveness of the hosiery cluster of Ludhiana, India, was severely affected by the insufficiency of the trained labor force. Several technical support institutions existed in the cluster but had no interaction with the industry and could not match the skill needs of the cluster. With UNIDO's support, a network of exporters created a committee that documented the various mistakes workers made which led to productivity loss or rejection. Based on these inputs, five training modules were identified. These included industrial stitching and tailoring, linking, cutting and pattern making, designing and merchandizing and overall supervisory skills.
>
> The Government Polytechnic for Women (GPW), an existing technical institution, was entrusted with the provision of this demand-based training and formulated a training course that became progressively tuned to the needs of the industry. APPEAL and GPW thus obtained support from the All India Council for Technical Education (AICTE) to create a skill development center in the GPW premises.
>
> The better match between skill demand and training is illustrated by the increase in the number of GPW students now working in the industry. Finally, the program's success laid the groundwork for establishing a fullfledged design center within GPW.
>
> *Source*: UNIDO (2007b).

3.2.3 Strengthening support institutions

BDS providers (technical institutions, industry associations and non-governmental organizations among others) are the main recipients of UNIDO's assistance since they play a crucial role in improving the access of cluster enterprises to financial and non-financial services. They can do so directly by developing or updating their service portfolio, or indirectly by providing information to cluster firms on service availability and facilitating access to them. The services that can be offered or facilitated include counseling, information dissemination, training, business plans development for credit access, advice on equipment purchase, establishment of shared facilities and so on. Overall, the focus of UNIDO is on the development of a competitive BDS market. On the one hand, this implies increasing the outreach of existing services as well as developing new ones to meet the demand of cluster firms. On the other hand, it fosters the demand for BDS, making firms aware of their needs and of availability of support services.

Local governments and municipalities are also extensively involved in the initiatives since they play a crucial role in sustaining the momentum of collective activities. They are thus sensitized on the relevance of cluster dynamics for economic development and exposed to international good practices on cluster promotion (see Box 53.8).

> *Box 53.8*
>
> The garment cluster of Atuntaqui, Ecuador, had based its competitiveness on low-cost production. However, with the adoption of the dollar as regular currency, prices increased to the extent that producers lost access to their traditional export market in Colombia. In order to overcome the crisis, the cluster needed to regain competitiveness via quality and productivity improvement and several institutional capacity-building activities were initiated. One of the initiatives was the establishment of a CAD centre and a library of accessories within the local Chamber of Commerce which are run as cost recovery centers, selling services to local enterprises. Another initiative looked at the technical skills and identified a striking mismatch between the demands of the private sector and the training offered by local educational and vocational institutes. By strengthening the articulation between these institutes and the enterprises, the project has contributed to improving the skill base of the cluster through the establishment of an apprenticeship scheme, the updating of curricula and the training of teachers.
>
> A third activity focused on helping the municipal government with the launch of a strategy of territorial marketing to promote all the main economic activities performed locally (that is, garment-making, tourism, agro-industry and handicraft). One of the instruments of this strategy has been an annual fair of the city that has attracted an average of 100 000 visitors in each of its four editions and has greatly strengthened the image of Atuntaqui as a centre for garment making and local tourism.
>
> *Source*: Piedad Velasco (2007).

Institutional strengthening can also extend into financial service provision. In Senegal, in order to facilitate access to finance by local SMEs, UNIDO partnered with local banks and credit associations and a new scheme providing mutual guarantee funds for SME networks was developed. This scheme is managed by a Senegalese bank in collaboration with the local system of Mutual Guarantee Cooperatives, and provides loans at suitable conditions for projects in the manufacturing sector.

4. CONCLUSIONS AND LESSONS LEARNED

The experience of UNIDO in the delivery of cluster-based technical assistance to developing countries offers a number of lessons that can be useful for other organizations dealing with clusters and local development.

To start with, the sustainability of a cluster initiative is highly dependent on the full involvement of the private sector. Empowering private sector actors and shifting responsibilities to them for the accomplishment of cluster development activities will increase their commitment to the initiative and prevent the emergence of dependency or over-reliance on external support. An important step in this direction is represented by the introduction of cost-sharing practices and the payment of fees to access the services provided by the project from its very onset. The support agency can certainly co-finance activities that are beyond the reach of the individual cluster actors (for instance those with public good content) or accept in-kind contributions (for example time, facilities, equipment). However a progressive shift towards the mobilization of local resources is desirable. Linked to this is the importance of promoting the participation of private sector organizations, for example business associations, which represent a large share of the cluster actors and offer them a platform of interaction and a legitimate channel to voice their needs. Strengthening their ability to perform cluster development functions and to provide related services will thus expand the outreach of a cluster development initiative to a number of entrepreneurs that may not benefit from direct assistance during the project's life. Overall, a basic rule for cluster development initiatives is not to substitute for functions and services that can be provided by the private sector, but rather to improve the capacity of the latter to supply services to clustered firms.

Emphasizing private sector leadership should not detract from recognizing the role of the public sector. The very fact that cluster development hinges upon the provision of public goods calls for a strong involvement by public sector institutions. These are crucial to the performance of trust and governance-building functions as well as to the continuation of cluster development initiatives, once the support agency withdraws. Widespread institutional weaknesses, however, call for considerable efforts to be spent on strengthening institutional capacities at the local, regional or national level, which makes public sector institutions the main targets of assistance.

The involvement of public sector institutions becomes particularly important when scaling-up project activities are concerned. Upscaling refers to transferring lessons and good practices learned from a pilot project to a broader level. In the context of cluster initiatives it requires translating field-level experience into meaningful policy recommendations, tailored on the institutional and economic structure of the country at stake.

In spite of the challenges this poses in terms of rethinking the scale and scope of the project (among others), the formulation of a strategy for upscaling is key, when development assistance aims to maximize its impact and outreach on the beneficiary country. The buy-in and commitment of the central government is crucial in this direction (see Box 53.9).

The UNIDO methodology of cluster development, resonating IDs' experiences and lessons, is based on the creation and strengthening of trust and governance. These cannot be accomplished overnight nor imposed on the cluster and its locality and institutions in a top-down fashion by bringing in rules and patterns of interaction that are not shared by the cluster and local

> **Box 53.9**
>
> In the State of Orissa, India, clusters are a widespread phenomenon and employ a considerable share of the population, particularly among the poor. In a pro-poor growth framework, UNIDO implemented a cluster development initiative based on a two-pronged strategy. On the one hand, it provided direct assistance to four clusters in the State in the sectors of handlooms, non-timber forest products and handicraft. On the other hand, it assisted the government of Orissa, particularly the Departments of Handicrafts and Cottage Industries, Handlooms and Industry, to replicate cluster development projects across the State. The government departments were exposed to the achievements recorded within UNIDO-assisted clusters, received training in the UNIDO methodology and were supported in the implementation of the approach in other clusters under their jurisdiction. At the same time, UNIDO facilitated the revision of other SME policy schemes to harmonize them with cluster development principles. New tools and procedures were also formulated and a dedicated budget created for cluster development activities within each government department. Finally, knowledge resources were transferred to a business school, based in the capital city, and its personnel trained, in order to establish a focal point for the dissemination of the concepts and methodologies of cluster development. As a result, an increasing number of clusters, 150 by 2008, have received assistance by the government of Orissa based on the UNIDO methodology, wherein the adoption of an explicit focus on poverty is expected to trigger a process of equitable and inclusive economic growth.
>
> *Source*: UNIDO (2008a).

community. Conversely, trust and governance building will benefit from the adoption of a participatory approach and the ability to leverage local values and nurture local social capital. This has important implications in that a cluster initiative is likely to be a time-consuming process, which requires a long-term commitment to produce endogenous change and therefore sustainable payoffs. At the same time, it is clear that the motivation of the entrepreneurs can only be safeguarded if they see tangible benefits in the short term. This is why a cluster initiative needs to move quickly into action to maintain momentum by generating early, visible benefits. Progressively, as the strategic priorities of the cluster are identified and trust levels increase at the local level, the initiative can move into longer-term, higher-risk activities. Also at this stage some key but complex issues may need to be broken down into small-sized tasks and milestones that can be more easily achieved by the cluster.

The role of CDAs, facilitators or brokers, cannot be overemphasized. Providing them with training, operational support, incentives and motivation as well as promoting knowledge-sharing and exposure to best practices are major determinants of the success of a cluster initiative.

Finally, cluster and local development entails commitment to an open and dynamic development vision. Clusters can exceed administrative boundaries and regional borders should not be taken as limits to exploring joint action and collective efficiency options. Sectoral specialization should also be looked at in a dynamic and visionary way, since like in many experiences of IDs in developed countries, it can change over time and new clusters can emerge from the traditional ones: a seafood cluster can evolve into a yachting center and a furniture-making cluster into an ecological housing hub.

To conclude, cluster development should not be exclusively inward looking: the performance of a cluster also depends on the wider business environment in which it operates. Cluster initiatives that lose sight of the broader national and international context are certainly doomed to produce a limited impact. Also, clusters initiatives often need to be complemented with other private sector support policies (for skill development, business regulation, entrepreneurship development and so on) and should not be considered as all-inclusive solutions for private sector growth. Rather, the capacity to look beyond the cluster boundaries both in the sense of business opportunities and policy complementarities, also suggested by IDs' experiences in developed countries, is a key ingredient in the success of a cluster approach to development.

NOTES

* The authors would like to thank Mr Michele Clara, UNIDO Industrial Development Officer, who has contributed through many discussions and exchanges of ideas to the content of this chapter. The views expressed herein are those of the authors and do not necessarily reflect the views of the UNIDO.
1. See McCormick (1998), Schmitz (1998); Ceglie and Dini (1999); Knorringa (1999); Schmitz and Nadvi (1999); Tewari (1999); Weijland (1999); Giuliani and Bell (2005); Oyelaran-Oyeyinka and McCormick (2007); among others.
2. The terms cluster and ID refer to related phenomena, as is amply illustrated in this *Handbook*. UNIDO generally employs the term 'cluster' for referring broadly to agglomerations in which linkages and organization may be incipient or non-existent such as often in developing countries.
3. The MDGs are eight international development goals agreed by international community and development institutions. See www.un.org/millenniumgoals, accessed 20 December 2008.

Bibliography

Absalom, R. (1995), *Italy since 1800*, London and New York: Longman.

Acemoglu, D., S. Johnson and J. Robinson (2004), 'Institutions as the fundamental cause of long-run growth', *NBER Working Paper*, no. 10481, Cambridge, MA.

Ádám, G. (1971), 'New trends in international business: worldwide sourcing and domiciling', *Acta Oeconomica*, **7** (3–4), 349–67.

Agrawal, A., D. Kapur and J. McHale (2004), 'Defying distance: examining the influence of the diaspora on scientific knowledge flows', Working paper.

Akerlof, G.A. and R.E. Kranton (2000), 'Economics and identity', *Quarterly Journal of Economics*, 115, 715–53.

Albert, M. (1991), *Capitalisme contre capitalisme*, Paris: Seuil.

Alberti, F.G. (2006), 'The decline of the industrial district of Como: recession, relocation or reconversion?', *Entrepreneurship and Regional Development*, 18, 73–501.

Albino, V., A.C. Garavelli and G. Schiuma (1999), 'Knowledge transfer and inter-firm relationships in industrial districts: the role of the leader firm', *Technovation*, 19, 53–63.

Albu, M. (1997), 'Technological learning and innovation in industrial clusters in the South', *SPRU Electronic Working Paper*, no. 7, Brighton.

Alessandrini, P. and A. Zazzaro (1999), 'A "possibilist" approach to local financial systems and regional development: the Italian experience', in R. Martin (ed.), *Money and the Space Economy*, New York: John Wiley and Sons, pp. 71–92.

Alessandrini, P., G. Calcagnini and A. Zazzaro (2008), 'Asset restructuring strategies in bank acquisitions: does distance between dealing partners matter?', *Journal of Banking and Finance*, **32** (5), 699–713.

Alessandrini, P., M. Croci and A. Zazzaro (2005), 'The geography of banking power: the role of functional distance', *Banca Nazionale del Lavoro Quarterly Review*, 235, 129–67.

Alessandrini, P., L. Papi and A. Zazzaro (2003), 'Banks, regions, and development', *Banca Nazionale del Lavoro Quarterly Review*, 224, 23–55.

Alessandrini, P., A. Presbitero and A. Zazzaro (2008a), 'Banche e imprese nei distretti industriali', in A. Zazzaro (ed.), *I vincoli finanziari alla crescita delle imprese*, Roma: Carocci, pp. 244–66.

Alessandrini, P., A. Presbitero and A. Zazzaro (2008b), 'Banks, distances and financing constraints for firms', *Review of Finance*, published online, 24 April.

Allen, R.C. (1983), 'Collective invention', *Journal of Economics, Behavior and Organization*, **4** (1), 1–24.

Allio, R. (1998), 'Welfare and social security in Piedmont: trade guilds compared with mutual aid societies', in Guenzi, Massa and Piola Caselli (1998).

Al-Mawali, N. (2005), 'Disentangling total intra-industry trade into horizontal and vertical elements', *Atlantic Economic Journal*, **33** (4), 491–2.

Almeida, H.V. and D. Wolfenzon (2006), 'A theory of pyramidal ownership and family business groups', *Journal of Finance*, **61** (6), 2637–80.

Altenburg, T. and J. Meyer-Stamer (1999), 'How to promote clusters: policy experiences from Latin America', *World Development*, **27** (9), 1693–713.

Althusser, L. and E. Baribar (1971), *Reading Capital*, New York: Pantheon Books.

Ambrosoli, M. (2000), 'The market for textile industry in eighteenth century Piedmont: quality control and economic policy', *Rivista di Storia Economica*, **16** (3), 343–63.

Amendola, M. and J.-L. Gaffard (1988), *The Innovative Choice. An Economic Analysis of the Dynamics of Technology*, Oxford: Basil Blackwell.

Amin, A. (1989a), 'Flexible specialisation and small firms in Italy: myths and realities', *Antipode. A Radical Journal of Geography*, **21** (1), 13–34.

Amin, A. (1989b), 'A model of the small firm in Italy', in Goodman and Bamford (1989), pp. 111–20.

Amin, A. (1994), 'Case study III: Santa Croce in context or how industrial districts respond to the restructuring of world markets', in R. Leonardi and R.Y. Nanetti (eds), *Regional Development in a Modern European Economy: The Case of Tuscany*, London and New York: Pinter, pp. 170–86.

Amin, A. and K. Robins (1990), 'Industrial district and regional development: limits and possibilities', in Pyke, Becattini and Sengenberger (1990), pp. 185–219.

Amin, A. and N. Thrift (1992), 'Neo-Marshallian nodes in global networks', *International Journal of Urban and Regional Research*, **16** (4), 571–87.

Amin, A. and N. Thrift (1994), 'Living in the global', in A. Amin and N. Thrift, *Globalisation, Institutions and Regional Development in Europe*, Oxford: Oxford University Press, pp. 1–22.

Amsden, A. and W. Chu (2003), *Beyond Late Development: Taiwan's Upgrading Policies*, Cambridge, MA: MIT Press.

Andersen, P.H, A. Böllingtoft and P.R. Christensen (2006), *Ehrvervsklynger under pres. Globaliseringens indflydelse på dynamikken i udvalgte danske ehrvervsklynger*, Institut fo Ledelse, Århus: Handelshöjskolen.

Andersson, S. and I. Wictor (2003), 'Innovative internationalization in new firms: born globals. The Swedish case', *Journal of International Entrepreneurship*, 1, 249–76.

Andrews, P.W.S. (1951), 'Industrial analysis in economics. With especial reference to Marshallian doctrine', in T. Wilson and P.W.S. Andrews (eds), *Oxford Studies in the Price Mechanism*, Oxford: Oxford University Press, pp. 139–72.

Antonelli, C. and F. Momigliano (1981), 'Problems and experiences of regional innovation policy in Italy', *Micros*, 2, 45–58.
Antonietti, R. and G. Cainelli (2007), 'Spatial agglomeration, technology and outsourcing of knowledge intensive business services: empirical insights from Italy', *Nota di Lavoro*, no. 79, Fondazione Eni Enrico Mattei.
Appelbaum, E., T. Bailey, P. Berg and A. Kalleberg (2000), *Manufacturing Advantage: Why High-performance Work Systems Pay Off*, Ithaca: Cornell University Press.
Arendt, H. (1958), *The Human Condition*, Chicago: University of Chicago Press.
Ariely, D. (2008), *Predictably Irrational: The Hidden Forces that Shape our Decisions*, New York: Harper.
Arlacchi, P. (1980), *Mafia contadini e latifondo nella Calabria tradizionale*, Bologna: Il Mulino.
Arocena, J. et al. (1982), *La création d'entreprise, une affaire de réseaux?*, Paris: La Documentation Française.
Arrighetti, A. and G. Seravalli (1997), 'Istituzioni e dualismo dell'industria italiana', in F. Barca (ed.), *Storia del capitalismo italiano. Dal dopoguerra a oggi*, Roma: Donzelli, pp. 335–88.
Arrighetti, A. and G. Seravalli (eds) (1999), *Istituzioni intermedie e sviluppo locale*, Roma: Donzelli.
Arrow, K.J. (1985), 'The potentials and limits of the market in resource allocation', in G.R. Feiwel (ed.), *Issues in Contemporary Microeconomics and Welfare*, London: Macmillan, pp. 107–24.
Arrow, K.J., Y.K. Ng and X. Yang (1998), *Increasing Returns and Economic Analysis*, London: Macmillan.
Arthur, W.B. (1989), 'Competing technologies, increasing returns and lock-in by historical events', *Economic Journal*, 99, 116–31.
Arthur, W.B. (ed.) (1994), *Increasing Returns and Path Dependence in the Economy*, Ann Arbor, MI: University of Michigan Press.
Artola, N. and M.D. Parrilli (2006), 'The development of the dairy cluster in Boaco and Chontales, Nicaragua', in Pietrobelli and Rabellotti (2006), pp. 43–70.
Arzeni, S. and D. Ionescu (2007), 'Social capital and clusters of enterprises: some essential questions', in M. Landabaso, A. Kuklinsky and C. Roman (eds), *Reflections on Social Capital, Innovation and Regional Development: The Ostuni Consensus*, Novi Sacz: National-Louis University, pp. 183–92.
Asesoría Industrial Zabala (2006), *Estudio a nivel nacional para estimular la cooperación entre pymes y centros tecnológicos*, Madrid: General Directorate of SME Policy, Ministry of Industry, Tourism and Commerce.
Asheim, B.T. (1994) 'Industrial districts, inter-firm co-operation and endogenous technological development: the experience of developed countries', in United Nations (1994), pp. 91–142.

Asheim, B.T. (2000), 'Industrial districts: the contributions of Marshall and beyond', in G.L. Clark, M.P. Feldman, and M.S. Gertler (eds), *The Oxford Handbook of Economic Geography*, Oxford: Oxford University Press, pp. 413–30.

Asmus, J.F., G. Guattari, L. Lazzarini, G. Musumeci and R.F. Wuerker (1973), 'Holography in the conservation of statuary', *Studies in Conservation*, 18, 49–63.

Audretsch, D.B. and M.P. Feldman (1996), 'Innovative clusters and the industry life cycle', *Review of Industrial Organization*, 11, 253–73.

Audretsch, D.B. and M.P. Feldman (2004), 'Knowledge spillovers and the geography of innovation', in J.V. Henderson and J.-F. Thisse (eds), *Handbook of Regional and Urban Economics*, vol. 4, *Cities and Geography*, Amsterdam: Elsevier, pp. 2713–39.

Audretsch, D.B. and P.E. Stephan (1996), 'Company–scientist locational links: the case of biotechnology', *The American Economic Review*, **86** (3), 641–52.

Avnimelech, G. and M. Teubal (2004), 'Venture capital–start-up co-evolution and the emergence and development of Israeli new high tech cluster', *Economics of Innovation and New Technology*, **13** (1), 33–60.

Axelrod, R. (1984), *The Evolution of Cooperation*, New York: Basic Books.

Axelrod, R. (1997), *The Complexity of Cooperation. Agent-based Models of Competition and Collaboration*, Princeton, NJ: Princeton University Press.

Aydalot, P. (ed.) (1986), *Milieux innovateurs en Europe*, Paris: GREMI.

Aydalot, P. and D. Keeble (eds) (1988), *High Technology Industry and Innovative Environments: The European Experience*, London: Routledge.

Ayres, C.E. (1943), *The Theory of Economic Progress*, Chapel Hill, NC: University of North Carolina Press.

Baccaro, L. and F. Qin (2005), 'Twenty-five thousand Chinese immigrants in Prato', internal note from an exploratory research trip, October.

Baffigi, A., M. Pagnini and F. Quintiliani (2000), 'Localismo bancario e distretti industriali: assetto dei mercati del credito e finanziamenti degli investimenti', in Signorini (2000), pp. 237–56.

Bagella, M., L. Becchetti and S. Sacchi (2000), 'The positive link between geographical agglomeration and export intensity: the engine of Italian endogenous growth', in M. Bagella and L. Becchetti (eds), *The Competitive Advantage of Industrial Districts: Theoretical and Empirical Analysis*, Heidelberg: Physica-Verlag, pp. 95–126.

Bagnasco, A. (1977), *Tre Italie. La problematica territoriale dello sviluppo italiano*, Bologna: Il Mulino.

Bagnasco, A. (1988), *La costruzione sociale del mercato*, Bologna: Il Mulino.

Bagnasco, A. (2003), *Società fuori squadra. Come cambia l'organizzazione sociale*, Bologna: Il Mulino.

Bagnasco, A. and C. Trigilia (eds) (1984), *Società e politica nelle aree di piccola impresa*, Venezia: Arsenale.

Bailey, D. (2003), 'Globalisation, regions and cluster policies: the case of the Rover task force', *Policy Studies*, 2–3, 67–85.

Bailey, D. (2007), 'Globalization and restructuring in the auto industry: the impact on the West Midlands automobile cluster', *Strategic Change*, 16, 137–44.

Bailey, D. and R. Sugden (1998), 'Current British economic policy: the continued absence of strategic intervention', *The Shogaku Ronshu. The Business Review of Kansai University*, **43** (1).

Bailey, D., S. Kobayashi and S. MacNeill (2008), 'Rover and out? Globalisation, the West Midlands auto cluster, and the end of MG Rover', *Policy Studies*, **29** (3), 267–79.

Bair, J. and G. Gereffi (2001), 'Local clusters in global chains: the causes and consequences of export dynamism in Torreon's blue jeans industry', *World Development*, **29** (2), 1185–93.

Bair, J. and G. Gereffi (2003), 'Upgrading, uneven development, and jobs in the North American apparel industry', *Global Networks*, **3** (2), 143–69.

Baldwin, G.Y. and K.B. Clark (2000), *Design Rules: The Power of Modularity*, Cambridge, MA: MIT Press.

Baldwin, R.E. (2006), 'Globalization: the great unbundling(s)', Helsinki: Economic Council of Finland, www.hei.unige.ch/~baldwin/PapersBooks/Unbundling_Baldwin_06-09-20.pdf, accessed 10 October 2008.

Baldwin, R.E. and R. Forslid (2006), 'Trade liberalization with heterogeneous firms', *NBER Working Paper*, no. 12192, Cambridge, MA.

Banca d'Italia (1999), *Considerazioni finali*, Assemblea generale ordinaria dei partecipanti, centocinquesimo esercizio, Roma, 31 May 1998, Roma: Banca d'Italia.

Banca d'Italia (2004), *Economie locali, modelli di agglomerazione e apertura internazionale. Nuove ricerche della Banca d'Italia sullo sviluppo territoriale*, Roma: Banca d'Italia.

Banca d'Italia (2005), 'Local economies and internationalization in Italy', Roma: Banca d'Italia, www.bancaditalia.it/studiricerche/convegni/atti/econ_loc), accessed 10 October 2008; published in Italian in L.F. Signorini and M. Omiccioli (eds) (2005), *Economie locali e competizione globale: il localismo industriale italiano di fronte a nuove sfide*, Bologna: Il Mulino.

Barba Navaretti, G., D. Castellani and A.-C. Disdier (2006), 'How does investing in cheap labour countries affect performance at home? France and Italy', *Development Studies Working Papers*, no. 215, Centro Studi Luca d'Agliano.

Barbato, M. and L. Hongbo (eds) (2008), *Industrial Districts and Economic Globalization. Italy and China Compared*, Roma: Institute of European Studies CASS and Unicredit Group.

Barboza, D. (2004), 'In roaring China, sweaters are west of sock city', *New York Times*, 24 December.

Barca, F. and M. Becht (eds) (2002), *The Control of Corporate Europe*, New York: Oxford University Press.

Bardhan, P. (1971), 'On optimum subsidy to a learning industry: an aspect of the theory of infant industry protection', *International Economic Review*, **12** (1), 54–70.

Bartik, T. (2003), *Thoughts on American Manufacturing Decline and Revitalization*, Kalamazoo, MI: WE Upjohn Institute for Employment Research.

Bathelt, H. and J. Glückler (2005), 'Resources in economic geography: from substantive concepts towards a relational perspective', *Environment and Planning A*, **37** (9), 1545–63.

Bathelt, H., A. Malmberg and P. Maskell (2004), 'Clusters and knowledge: local buzz, global pipelines and the process of knowledge creation', *Progress in Human Geography*, **28** (1), 31–56.

Baumol, W.J. (2002), *The Free-Market Innovation Machine: Analyzing the Growth Miracle of Capitalism*, Princeton, NJ: Princeton University Press.

Baumol, W.J., A.S. Blinder and E.N. Wolff (2003), *Downsizing in America. Reality, Causes, and Consequences*, New York: Russell Sage Foundation.

Bazan, L. and L. Navas-Aleman (2004), 'The underground revolution in Sinos Valley', in Schmitz (2004), pp. 110–38.

Becattini, G. (1962a), *Il concetto di industria e la teoria del valore*, Torino: Boringhieri.

Becattini, G. (1962b), 'Il sistema marshalliano', in Becattini (1962a), pp. 88–125.

Becattini, G. (ed.) (1966), *Aspetti dell'economia industriale lucchese*, Lucca: ITRES-Amministrazione Provinciale Lucchese.

Becattini, G. (ed.) (1969), 'Lo sviluppo economico della Toscana: un'ipotesi di lavoro', *Il Ponte*, **25** (11–12), 4–32.

Becattini, G. (ed.) (1975a), *Lo sviluppo economico della Toscana, con particolare riguardo all'industrializzazione leggera*, Firenze: IRPET-Guaraldi.

Becattini, G. (1975b), 'Introduzione. Invito a una rilettura di Marshall', in A. Marshall and M. Paley Marshall, *Economia delle produzione*, edited by G. Becattini, Milano: ISEDI, pp. ix–cxiv.

Becattini, G. (1978), 'The development of light industry in Tuscany', *Economic Notes*, **18** (2–3), 107–23.

Becattini, G. (1979), 'Dal settore industriale al distretto industriale. Alcune considerazioni sull'unità di indagine dell'economia industriale', *Rivista di economia e politica industriale*, **5** (1), 7–21; reprint in Becattini (1987); published in English in Becattini (2004a).

Becattini, G. (1986a), 'Riflessioni sullo sviluppo socio-economico della Toscana in questo dopoguerra', in G. Mori (ed.), *Storia d'Italia. Le regioni dall'unità ad oggi, La Toscana*, Torino: Einaudi, pp. 901–24.

Becattini, G. (1986b), 'Small firms and industrial districts: the experience of Italy', *Economia Internazionale*, **39** (2–3–4), 98–103.

Becattini, G. (1986c), 'Del "sector" industrial al "districte" industrial. Algunes consideracions sobre la unitat de recerca de l'economia industrial', *Revista Econòmica de Catalunya*, 1, 4–11.

Becattini, G. (ed.) (1987), *Mercato e forze locali: il distretto industriale*, Bologna: Il Mulino.

Becattini, G. (1989), 'Riflessioni sul distretto industriale marshalliano come concetto socio-economico', *Stato e Mercato*, **25** (April), 111–28; published in English in Becattini (2004).

Becattini, G. (1990), 'The Marshallian industrial district as a socio-economic notion', in Pyke, Becattini and Sengenberger (1990), pp. 37–51.

Becattini, G. (1991), 'The industrial district as a creative *milieu*', in G. Benko and M. Dunford (eds), *Industrial Change and Regional Development*, London: Belhaven Press, pp. 102–16.

Becattini, G. (1992), 'Le district marshallien: une notion socio-économique', in G. Benko and A. Lipietz (eds), *Les régions qui gagnent. Districts et réseaux: les nouveaux paradigmes de la géographie économique*, Paris: PUF, pp. 35–55.

Becattini, G. (1995–96), 'I sistemi locali nello sviluppo economico italiano e nella sua interpretazione', *Sviluppo locale*, 2–3, 5–25.

Becattini, G. (ed.) (1997), *Prato, storia di una città*, vol. 4, *Il distretto industriale, 1943–1993*, Firenze: Comune di Prato-Le Monnier.

Becattini, G. (2000a), *Il distretto industriale*, Torino: Rosenberg & Sellier.

Becattini, G. (2000b), 'Dal "miracolo economico" al "made in Italy"', *Economia Marche*, **19** (1), 7–30.

Becattini, G. (2001a), *The Caterpillar and the Butterfly. An Exemplary Case of Development in the Italy of the Industrial Districts*, Firenze: Felice Le Monnier.

Becattini, G. (2001b), 'Metafore e vecchi strumenti. Ovvero della difficoltà d'introdurre "il territorio" nell'analisi socio-economica', in Becattini et al. (2001).

Becattini, G. (2001c), 'Alle origini della campagna urbanizzata', *Economia Marche*, **20** (2), 105–20.

Becattini, G. (2001d), 'Cittadinanza onoraria di Prato', Note preparatorie al discorso tenuto in occasione dell'ottenimento della cittadinanza onoraria di Prato, unpublished.

Becattini, G. (2002a), *Miti e paradossi del mondo contemporaneo*, Roma: Donzelli.

Becattini, G. (2002b), *I nipoti di Cattaneo*, Roma: Donzelli.

Becattini, G. (2002c), 'Il caleidoscopio dello sviluppo locale. Contributo ad un dibattito napoletano', in Various Authors, *Il caleidoscopio dello sviluppo locale. Un dibattito*, Napoli: Istituto Banco di Napoli-Fondazione.

Becattini, G. (2002d), 'Il contributo di Sebastiano Brusco alla Libera scuola di Artimino', *Stato e Mercato*, 70, 121–41.

Becattini, G. (2002e), 'Industrial sectors and industrial districts: tools for industrial analysis', *European Planning Studies*, **10** (4), 483–93.

Becattini, G. (2003a), 'From the industrial district to the districtualisation of production activity: some considerations', in F. Belussi, G. Gottardi and E. Rullani (eds), *The Technological Evolution of Industrial Districts*, Boston and Dordrecht: Kluwer Academic Publishers, pp. 3–17.

Becattini, G. (2003b), 'The return of the "white elephant"', in R. Arena and M. Queré (eds), *The Economics of Alfred Marshall. Revisiting Marshall's Legacy*, New York: Palgrave Macmillan.

Becattini, G. (2004a), *Industrial Districts. A New Approach to Industrial Change*, Cheltenham, UK and Northampton, MA, USA: Edward Elgar.

Becattini, G. (2004b), *Per un capitalismo dal volto umano. Critica dell'economia apolitica*, Torino: Bollati Boringhieri.

Becattini, G. (2006), 'The industrial district and development economics', in Raffaelli, Becattini and Dardi (2006), pp. 664–71.

Becattini, G. (2007), 'Industria e territorio: riflessioni su un tema marshalliano', in G. Becattini, *Scritti sulla Toscana*, vol. I, *La ricerca sul campo e la 'Libera Scuola' di Artimino (1969–2007)*, edited by F. Sforzi, Firenze: Le Monnier, pp. 113–18.

Becattini, G. and M. Bellandi (2006), 'Industrial districts', in Beckert and Zafirovsky (2006), pp. 342–4.

Becattini, G. and F. Coltorti (2006), 'Areas of large enterprise and industrial districts in the development of post-war Italy: a preliminary survey', *European Planning Studies*, **14** (8), 1105–38; published in Italian as 'Aree di grande impresa ed aree distrettuali nello sviluppo post-bellico dell'Italia: un'esplorazione preliminare', *Rivista italiana degli economisti*, 1, 61–101.

Becattini, G. and G. Dei Ottati (2006), 'The performance of Italian industrial districts and large enterprise areas in the 1990s', *European Planning Studies*, **14** (8), 1139–62.

Becattini, G. and S. Menghinello (1998), 'Contributo e ruolo del made in Italy distrettuale nelle esportazioni nazionali di manufatti', *Sviluppo locale*, **5** (9), 5–41.

Becattini, G. and F. Musotti (2004), 'Measuring the "district effect": reflections on the literature', in Becattini (2004a), pp. 88–111.

Becattini, G. and E. Rullani (1992), 'Global systems and local systems', in Pyke and Sengenberger (1992).

Becattini, G. and E. Rullani (1993), 'Sistema locale e mercato globale', *Economia e Politica Industriale*, **20** (80), 25–48.

Becattini, G. and E. Rullani (1996a), 'Local systems and global connections: the role of knowledge', in Cossentino, Pyke and Sengenberger (1996), pp. 159–74.

Becattini, G. and E. Rullani (1996b), 'Local systems and global market', in Becattini (2004a), pp. 48–66.

Becattini, G. and F. Sforzi (eds) (2002), *Lezioni sullo sviluppo locale*, Torino: Rosenberg & Sellier.

Becattini, G., M. Bellandi and A. Falorni (1983), 'L'industrializzazione diffusa in Toscana: aspetti economici', in Fuà and Zacchia (1983), pp. 47–66,

Becattini, G., M. Bellandi, G. Dei Ottati and F. Sforzi (eds) (2001), *Il caleidoscopio dello sviluppo locale. Trasformazioni economiche nell'Italia contemporanea*, Torino: Rosenberg&Sellier.

Becattini, G., M. Bellandi, G. Dei Ottati and F. Sforzi (2003), *From Industrial Districts to Local Development: An Itinerary of Research*, Cheltenham, UK and Northampton, MA, USA: Edward Elgar.

Beccaria, C. (1804), *Elementi di economia pubblica*, Milano: Destefanis.

Becchetti, L. and A. Castelli (2005), 'Inside the blackbox: economic performance and technology adoption when space and product relationships matter', *Rivista di Politica Economica*, **95** (1–2), 137–75.

Becchetti, L. and S.P.S. Rossi (2000), 'The positive effect of industrial district on the export performance of Italian firms', *Review of Industrial Organization*, **16** (1), 53–68.

Becchetti, L, A. De Panizza and F. Oropallo (2007), 'Role of industrial districts externalities in export and value-added performance: evidence from the population of Italian firms', *Regional Studies*, **41** (5), 601–21.

Beckert, J. and M. Zafirovski (eds) (2006), *International Encyclopedia of Economic Sociology*, London: Routledge.

Behagg, C. (1998), 'Mass production without the factory: craft producers, guns and small firm innovation, 1790–1815', *Business History*, **40** (3), 1–15.

Belfanti, C.M. (1999), 'Istituzioni intermedie e sviluppo locale in prospettiva storica', in Arrighetti and Seravalli (1999), pp. 124–44.

Belfanti, C.M. and T. Maccabelli (1997), *Un paradigma per i distretti industriali. Radici storiche, attualità, sfide future*, Brescia: Grafo.

Belfanti, C.M. and S. Onger (2002), 'Mercato e istituzioni nella storia dei distretti industriali', in G. Provasi (ed.), *Le istituzioni dello sviluppo. I distretti industriali tra storia, sociologia ed economia*, Roma: Donzelli.

Bellandi, M. (1982),'Il distretto industriale in Alfred Marshall', *L'Industria, Rivista di economia e politica industriale*, 3, 355–75.

Bellandi, M. (1989), 'The industrial district in Marshall', in Goodman and Bamford (1989), pp.136–52.

Bellandi, M. (1992), 'The incentives to decentralized industrial creativity in local systems of small firms', *Revue d'économie industrielle*, 59, 99–110.

Bellandi, M. (1995), *Economie di scala e organizzazione industriale*, Milano: Franco Angeli.

Bellandi, M. (1996a), 'Innovation and change in the Marshallian industrial district', *European Planning Studies*, **3** (4), 357–66.

Bellandi, M. (1996b), 'On entrepreneurship, region, and the constitution of scale and scope economies', *European Planning Studies*, **4** (4), 421–38.

Bellandi, M. (2001), 'Local development and embedded large firms', *Entrepreneurship and Regional Development*, **13** (3), 189–210

Bellandi, M. (2002), 'Modelli di analisi distrettuale e azione collettiva per lo sviluppo locale: alcuni spunti di riflessione', *Economia Marche*, 1, 89–98.

Bellandi, M. (2003a), 'The incentives to decentralized industrial creativity in local systems of small firms', in Becattini et al. (2003), pp. 95–107.

Bellandi, M. (2003b), 'Paths of local learning and change in vital industrial districts', in F. Belussi, G. Gottardi and E. Rullani (eds), *The Technological Evolution of Industrial Districts*, Boston and Dordrecht: Kluwer Academic Publishers, pp. 195–204.

Bellandi, M. (2003c), 'Some remarks on Marshallian external economies and industrial tendencies', in R. Arena and M. Queré (eds), *The Economics of Alfred Marshall. Revisiting Marshall's Legacy*, New York: Palgrave Macmillan, pp. 240–53.

Bellandi, M. (2005), 'Pequenas empresas y distritos industriales', in M.D. Parrilli, P. Bianchi and R. Sugden, *Alta tecnologia, productividad y redes*, Mexico: Coltlax Press, pp. 351–77.

Bellandi, M. (2006), 'A perspective on clusters, localities and specific public goods', in C. Pitelis, R. Sugden and J.R Wilson (eds), *Clusters and Globalisation: The Development of Economies*, Cheltenham, UK and Northampton, MA, USA: Edward Elgar, pp. 96–113.

Bellandi, M. (2007), 'Industrial districts and waves of industrialization: a rich and contested terrain', *Scienze Regionali. Italian Journal of Regional Science*, **6** (2), 7–33.

Bellandi, M. and A. Caloffi (2009), 'District internationalization and trans-local development', *Entrepreneurship and Regional Development*, forthcoming.

Bellandi, M. and M.R. Di Tommaso (2005), 'The case of specialized towns in Guangdong, China', *European Planning Studies*, **13** (5), 707–23.

Bellandi, M. and M.R. Di Tommaso (2006), 'The local dimensions of industrial policy', in Bianchi and Labory (2006), pp. 342–61.

Bellandi, M. and M. Russo (eds) (1994), *Distretti industriali e cambiamento economico locale*, Torino: Rosenberg & Sellier.

Bellandi, M. and F. Sforzi (2003), 'The multiple paths of local development', in Becattini et al. (2003), pp. 210–26.

Belussi, F. (1996), 'Local systems, industrial districts and institutional networks: towards a new evolutionary paradigm of industrial economics?', *European Planning Studies*, **4** (1), 5–26.

Belussi, F. (1999a) 'Path-dependency vs. industrial dynamics: the analysis of two heterogeneous Italian districts specialised in leather upholstery', *Human System Management*, 18, 161–74.

Belussi, F. (1999b), 'Policies for the development of knowledge-intensive local production systems', *Cambridge Journal of Economics*, **23** (6), 729–47.

Belussi, F. (2000), 'Accumulation of tacit knowledge and division of cognitive labour in the industrial district/local production system', *Papers on Economic and Evolution*, no. 0012, Max-Planck Institute, Jena, 1–19.

Belussi, F. (2003), 'The generation of contextual knowledge through communication processes. The case of the packaging machinery industry in the Bologna district', in F. Belussi, G. Gottardi and E. Rullani (eds), *The Technological Evolution of Industrial Districts*, Boston and Dordrecht: Kluwer Academic Publishers.

Belussi, F. (2005), 'The evolution of a western consolidated industrial district through the mechanism of knowledge creation, ICT adoption, and the tapping into the international commercial nets: the case of Montebelluna sportwear district', in Belussi and Sammarra (2005).

Belussi, F. (2006), 'In search of a useful theory of spatial clustering: agglomeration versus active clustering', in B. Asheim, P. Cooke and R. Martin (eds), *Clusters and Regional Development: Critical Reflections and Explorations*, London: Routledge, pp. 69–89.

Belussi, F. and G. Gottardi (eds) (2000), 'Models of localised technological change', in F. Belussi, and G. Gottardi (eds), *Evolutionary Patterns of Local Industrial Systems: Towards a Cognitive Approach to the Industrial District*, Aldershot: Ashgate, pp. 13–47.

Belussi, F. and L. Pilotti (2002), 'Knowledge creation, learning and innovation in Italian industrial districts', *Geografiska Annaler*, 84, 19–33.

Belussi, F. and A. Sammarra (eds) (2005), *Industrial Districts, Relocation, and the Governance of the Global Value Chain*, Padova: Cleup.

Belussi, F., G. Gottardi and E. Rullani (2000), 'Il futuro dei distretti', *Piccola impresa*, 2, 3–22.

Belussi, F., A. Sammarra and S. Sedita (2008), 'Industrial districts evolutionary trajectories: localized learning, diversity and external growth', paper submitted to *EURAM*, 14–17 May, Ljubljana.

Benko, G. (2001), 'Développement durable et système productifs locaux', in P. Pommier (ed.), *Réseaux d'entreprises et territoires. Regards sur les systèmes productifs locaux*, Paris: La Documentation Française, pp. 117–33.

Benko, G. and A. Lipietz (eds) (2000), *La richesse des régions. La nouvelle géographie socio-économique*, Paris: PUF.

Benko, G., M. Dunford and A. Lipietz (1996), 'Les districts industriels revisités', in B. Pecqueur (ed.), *Dynamiques territoriales et mutations économiques*, Paris: L'Harmattan, pp. 119–34.

Beretta, E., M. Omiccioli and R. Torrini (2000), 'Banche locali e amplificazione degli shocks economici', in Signorini (2000), pp. 271–85.

Berg, M. (1993), 'Small producer capitalism in eighteenth-century England', *Business History*, **35** (1), 17–39.

Berg, M. (1994), *The Age of Manufactures 1700–1820. Industry, Innovation and Work in Britain*, London: Routledge.

Berg, M., P. Hudson and M. Sonnenscher (eds) (1983), *Manufacture in Town and Country Before the Factory*, Cambridge: Cambridge University Press.

Berger, A.N. and G.F. Udell (1995), 'Relationship lending and lines of credit in small firm finance', *The Journal of Business*, **68** (3), 351–81.

Berger, A.N., A. Saunders, J.M. Scalise and G.F. Udell (1998), 'The effects of bank mergers and acquisitions on small business lending', *Journal of Financial Economics*, **50** (2), 187–229.

Berger, A.N., N.H. Miller, M.A. Petersen, R.G. Rajan and J.C. Stein (2005), 'Does function follow organizational form? Evidence from the lending practices of large and small banks', *Journal of Financial Economics*, **76** (2), 237–69.

Berger, S. and M.J. Piore (1980), *Dualism and Discontinuity in Industrial Societies*, Cambridge: Cambridge University Press.

Bergman, E.M. and E.J. Feser (1999), 'Industrial and regional clusters: concepts and comparative applications', in S. Loveridge (ed.), *The Web Book of Regional Science*, Morgantown, WV: Regional Research Institute, West Virginia University, www.rri.wvu.edu/regscweb.htm, accessed 17 December 2008.

Bergman, E., G. Maier and F. Tödtling (eds) (1991), *Regions Reconsidered: Economic Networks, Innovation and Local Development in Industrialized Countries*, London: Mansell.

Berle, A.A. and G.C. Means (1997), *The Modern Corporation and Private Property*, New Brunswick, US and London: Transaction Publishers.

Bernabé Maestre, J.M. (1983), 'Industrialización difusa en la provincia de Alicante', mimeo, Facultad de Geografía, Universidad de Valencia.

Bernardi, E. (2006), *La riforma agraria in Italia e gli Stati Uniti*, Bologna: Il Mulino.

Bernhardt, A., L. Dresser and J. Rogers (2001–02), 'Taking the high road in Milwaukee: the Wisconsin regional training partnership', *Working USA*, **5** (3), 109–30.

Bernheim, B.D. (1994), 'A theory of conformity', *Journal of Political Economy*, 102, 841–77.

Berta, G. (2006), *L'Italia delle fabbriche. Ascesa e tramonto dell'industrialismo nel Novecento*, Bologna: Il Mulino.

Best, M. (1990), *The New Competition*, Cambridge: Harvard University Press.

Best, M. (2001), *The New Competitive Advantage*, Oxford: Oxford University Press.

Best, M. (2003), 'The geography of systems integration', in A. Prencipe, A. Davies and M. Hobday (eds), *The Business of Systems Integration*, Oxford: Oxford University Press, pp. 201–28.

Best, M. (2006), 'Massachusetts medical devices: leveraging the region's capabilities', *MassBenchmarks*, **8** (1), 14–25, www.massbenchmarks.org/publications/issues/vol8i1/06v8i1.htm, accessed 20 July 2008.

Best, M., A. Paquin and H. Xie (2004), 'Discovering regional competitive advantage: Massachusetts high tech', The Business History Association, www.thebhc.org/publications/BEHonline/2004/beh2004.html, accessed 20 July 2008.

Bevilacqua, P. (2005), *Breve storia dell'Italia meridionale. Dall'Ottocento a oggi*, Roma: Donzelli Editore.

Bhaduri, A. (2005), 'Macro-economic policies for higher employment in the era of globalisation', *Employment Strategy Papers*, no. 11, Geneva: ILO.

Bianchi, P. and N. Bellini (1991), 'Public policies for local networks of innovators', *Research Policy*, 20, 487–98.

Bianchi, P. and S. Labory (eds) (2006), *International Handbook of Industrial Policy*, Cheltenham, UK and Northampton, MA, USA: Edward Elgar.

Bibiloni, A. and J. Pons (2001), 'El lento cambio organizativo en la industria del calzado mallorquina (1900–1960)', in F. Arenas and J. Pons (eds) *Trabajo y relaciones laborales en la España contemporánea*, Sevilla: Mergablum, pp. 355–69.

Bigarelli, D. and A. Ginzburg (2005), 'Gruppi di impresa e processi di internazionalizzazione nelle PMI in provincia di Reggio Emilia', *Economia e società regionale*, **92** (4), 5–29.

Bigazzi, D. (1978), 'Fierezza del mestiere e organizzazione di classe: gli operai meccanici milanesi, 1880–1900', *Società e Storia*, **1** (1).

Bille, T. and G. Schulze (2006), 'Culture in urban and regional development', in V.A. Ginsburh and D. Throsby (eds), *Handbook of the Economics of Art and Culture*, Amsterdam: Elsevier, pp. 1051–93.

Billette, A. and M. Carrier (1993), 'Régulation socio-identitaire des activités économiques beauceronnes', *Recherches Sociographiques*, **34** (2), 261–77.

Binfield, C. and D. Hey (1997), *From Mesters to Masters. A History of the Company of Cutlers in Hallamshire*, Oxford: Oxford University Press.

Blanc, Ch. (2004), *Pour un éco système de la croissance*, rapport au premier ministre, Assemblée nationale.

Blau, P.M. (1964), *Exchange and Power in Social Life*, New York: John Wiley and Sons.

Blundel, R. and M. Thatcher (2005), 'Contrasting local responses to globalization: the case of volume yacht manufacturing in Europe', *Entrepreneurship and Regional Development*, **17** (6), 405–29.

Boch, R. (1997), 'The rise and decline of flexible production: the cutlery industry of Solingen since the eighteenth century', in Sabel and Zeitlin (1997a).

Boero, R., M. Castellani and F. Squazzoni. (2004) 'Labor market, entrepreneurship and human capital in industrial districts. An agent-based prototype', in R. Leombruni and M. Richiardi (eds), *Industry and Labor Dynamics: The Agent-based Computational Approach*, Singapore: World Scientic, pp. 332–49.

Boix, R. (2009), 'Los distritos industriales en la Europa Mediterránea: los mapas de Italia y España', *Mediterraneo Economico*, forthcoming.

Boix, R. and V. Galletto (2004), *Identificación de sistemas local de trabajo y distritos industriales en España*, Madrid: MITYC, Secretaria General de Industria, Dirección General de Política para la Pequeña y Mediana Empresa.

Boix, R. and V. Galletto (2005), *Identificación de sistemas locales de trabajo y distritos industriales en españa*, Barcelona: Universidad Autónoma de Barcelona.

Boix, R. and V. Galletto (2006), 'El mapa de los distritos industriales de España', *Economía Industrial*, 359, 95–112.

Boix, R. and V. Galletto (2006–07), 'Innovazione e distretti industriali: misura e determinanti dell'effetto distretto', *Sviluppo locale*, **12** (28), 3–31.

Boix, R. and V. Galletto (2009a), 'Innovation and industrial districts: a first approach to the measurement and determinants of the I-district effect', *Regional Studies*, forthcoming.

Boix, R. and V. Galletto (2009b), 'Marshallian industrial districts in Spain', *Scienze Regionali. Italian Journal of Regional Science*, forthcoming.

Boltanski, L. and E. Chiapello (2005), *The New Spirit of Capitalism*, London and New York: Verso.

Bolton Report (The) (1971), *Small Firms: Report of the Committee of Inquiry on Small Firms*, London: HMSO, cmnd 4811.

Bonaccorsi di Patti, E. and G. Gobbi (2007), 'Winners or losers? The effects of banking consolidation on corporate borrowers', *Journal of Finance*, 62, 669–95.

Bonifati, G. (1982), 'Chi produce dove. Paesi e imprese nell'evoluzione dell'industria mondiale dei trattori', *Studi e ricerche dell'Istituto Economico*, no. 9, Modena: Stem Mucchi.

Boscherini, F. and L. Poma (2000), 'Más allá de los distritos industriales: el nuevo concepto de territorio en el marco de la economía global', in F. Boscherini and L. Poma (eds), *Territorio, conocimiento y competitividad de las empresas*, Buenos Aires: Miño y Dávila Editores.

Boschma, R.A. (2005), 'Proximity and innovation: a critical assessment', *Regional Studies*, **39** (1), 61–74.

Boschma, R.A. and J. Lambooy (1999), 'Evolutionary economics and economic geography', *Journal of Evolutionary Economics*, 9, 411–29.

Boschma, R.A. and R. Martin (eds) (2008), *The Handbook of Evolutionary Economic Geography*, Cheltenham, UK and Northampton, MA, USA: Edward Elgar.

Bott, E. (1957), *Family and Social Networks*, London: Tavistock.

Bradbury, J.B. and J. Mawson (2002), *British Regionalism and Devolution: The Challenges of State Reform and European Integration*, London: Routledge.

Braudel, F. (1981–84), *Civilization and Capitalism, 15th–18th Century*, 3 vols, New York: Harper and Row; original edition in French 1979.

Braudel, F. (1985), *La dynamique du capitalisme*, Paris: Flammarion.

Braudel, F. (ed.) (1986–97), *Prato. Storia di una città*, 4 vols, Firenze: Le Monnier.

Braun, B., W. Gaebe, R. Grotz, Y. Okamoto and K. Yamamoto (2002), 'Regional networking of small and medium-sized enterprises in Japan and Germany: evidence from a comparative study', *Environment and Planning*, 34, 81–99.

Braunerhjelm, P. and M. Feldman (2006), *Cluster Genesis. Technology-Based Industrial Development*, Oxford: Oxford University Press.

Bravo, G. and E. Merlo (2002), 'Sviluppo e crisi del distretto di Vigevano', in G. Provasi (ed.), *Le istituzioni dello sviluppo: i distretti industriali tra storia, sociologia ed economia*, Roma: Donzelli.

Breit, W. (1987), 'Creating the Virginia school: Charlottes Ville as an academic environment in the 1960s', *Economic Inquiry*, **25** (4), 645–57.

Bresnahan, T., A. Gambardella and A.L. Saxenian (2001), '"Old economy" inputs for "new economy" outcomes: cluster formation in the new Silicon Valleys', *Industrial and Corporate Change*, **10** (4), 835–60.

Brinkerhoff, J.M. (2006), 'Diasporas, skills transfer, and remittances: evolving perceptions and potential', in C. Wescott and J. Brinkerhoff (eds) (2006), *Converting Migration Drains into Gains. Harnessing the Resources of Overseas Professionals*, Asian Development Bank.

Brioschi, F., M.S. Brioschi and G. Cainelli (2002), 'From the industrial district to the district group', *Regional Studies*, **36** (9), 1037–52.

Bronzini, R. (2000), 'Sistemi produttivi locali e commercio estero: un'analisi territoriale delle esportazioni italiane', in Signorini (2000), pp. 101–22.

Bronzini, R. (2005), 'Industrial districts, agglomeration, and FDI in Italy', in Banca d'Italia, *Local Economies and Internationalization in Italy*, Roma: Banca d'Italia, pp. 281–312; published in Italian as 'Distretti industriali, economie di agglomerazione e investimenti diretti in Italia', in L.F. Signorini and M. Omiccioli (eds) (2005), *Economie locali e competizione globale: il localismo industriale italiano di fronte a nuove sfide*, Bologna: Il Mulino, pp. 263–81.

Bronzini, R. (2007), 'FDI inflows, agglomeration and host country firms' size: evidence from Italy', *Regional Studies*, **41** (7), 963–78.

Brooks, F.P. Jr (1995), *The Mythical Man-month: Essays on Software Engineering*, anniversary edition, Reading, MA: Addison-Wesley Pub. Co.

Brown, A.J. (1972), *The Framework of Regional Economics in the United Kingdom*, Cambridge: Cambridge University Press.

Brown, J.S. and P. Duguid (2000a), *The Social Life of Information*, Boston: Harvard Business School Press.

Brown, J.S. and P. Duguid (2000b), 'Mysteries of the region: knowledge dynamics in Silicon Valley', in C.-M. Lee, W.F. Miller, M.G. Hancock and H.S. Rowen (eds), *The Silicon Valley Edge: A Habitat for Innovation and Entrepreneurship*, Stanford, CA: Stanford University Press, pp. 16–39.

Browne, L. and S. Sass (2000), 'The transition from a mill-based to a knowledge-based economy: New England, 1940–2000', in P. Temin (ed.), *Engines of Enterprise: An Economic History of New England*, Cambridge MA: Harvard University Press.

Bruni, L. and P.L. Porta (eds) (2007), *Handbook on the Economics of Happiness*, Cheltenham, UK and Northampton, MA, USA: Edward Elgar.

Bruni, L. and S. Zamagni (2004), *Economia civile. Efficienza, equità, felicità pubblica*, Bologna: Il Mulino.

Bruno, G. (1877), *Le tour de la France par deux enfants*, reprint Paris: Belin, 2000.

Brusco, S. (1982), 'The Emilian model: productive decentralisation and social integration', *Cambridge Journal of Economics*, **6** (2) 167–84.

Brusco, S. (1983), 'Flessibilità e solidità del sistema: l'esperienza emiliana', in Fuà and Zacchia (1983), pp. 103–24.
Brusco, S. (1984), 'Quale politica industriale per i distretti industriali?', *Politica ed economia*, 6, 68–72.
Brusco, S. (1988), 'Industrial districts and real services (Preliminary note)', speech given in the US, www.economia.unimore.it/userfile/27/Brusco_StatiUniti1988_rev.pdf, accessed 12 January 2009.
Brusco, S. (1989a), *Piccole imprese e distretti industriali: una raccolta di saggi*, Torino: Rosenberg & Sellier.
Brusco, S. (1989b), 'A policy for industrial districts', in Goodman and Bamford (1989), pp. 259–69.
Brusco, S. (1990), 'The idea of the industrial district: its genesis', in Pyke, Becattini and Sengenberger (1990).
Brusco, S. (1991), 'La genesi dell'idea di distretto industriale', in F. Pyke, G. Becattini and W. Sengenberger (eds), *Distretti industriali e cooperazione fra imprese in Italia*, Firenze: Banca Toscana, pp. 25–34.
Brusco, S. (1992a), 'Small firms and the provision of real services', in Pyke and Sengenberger (1992), pp. 177–96.
Brusco, S. (1992b), 'Quali politiche industriali per lo sviluppo locale?' relazione agli 'Incontri pratesi sullo sviluppo locale', Artimino, September, www.economia.unimore.it/sezioni/pag337.aspx?id=759&liv=3&numpag=337, accessed 12 January 2009.
Brusco, S. (1993), 'Il modello emiliano rivisita il distretto. Regione e industria', *Politica ed economia*, **24** (1), 47–55.
Brusco, S. (1994), 'Sistemi globali e sistemi locali', *Economia e Politica Industriale*, **84** (2), 63–76.
Brusco, S. (1995), 'Local productive systems and new industrial policy in Italy', in A. Bagnasco and Ch.F. Sabel (eds), *Small and Medium-size Enterprises*, London: Pinter, pp. 51–68.
Brusco, S. (1996), 'Global systems and local systems', in Cossentino, Pyke and Sengenberger (1996), pp. 145–58.
Brusco, S. (1999), 'The rules of game in industrial districts', in A. Grandori (ed.), *Interfirm Networks: Organization and Industrial Competitiveness*, London and New York: Routledge, pp. 17–40.
Brusco, S. (2002), 'Politiche e strumenti per lo sviluppo locale', in Becattini and Sforzi (2002), pp. 271–88.
Brusco, S. (2004a), 'Autonomie, la riforma bicefala', in S. Brusco, *Industriamoci. Capacità di progetto e sviluppo locale*, Roma: Donzelli, pp. 63–7; 1st edition 1997.
Brusco, S. (2004b), 'Mezzogiorno. L'ideologia non fa posti', in S. Brusco, *Industriamoci, Capacità di progetto e sviluppo locale*, Roma: Donzelli, pp. 87–95; 1st edition 1998.

Brusco, S. (2008), *I distretti industriali: lezioni per lo sviluppo. Una lettera e nove saggi (1990–2002)*, Bologna: Il Mulino.
Brusco, S. and D. Bigarelli (1995), 'Struttura industriale e fabbisogni formativi nei settori della maglieria e delle confezioni in Italia. Un'analisi per regione, 1993', *Rivista italiana di Economia*, 0, 7–47; published in English as 'Regional productive systems in the knitwear and clothing sectors in Italy: industrial structure and training needs', *Working Paper Series*, no. 51, ESRC Centre for Business Research, University of Cambridge, 1997.
Brusco, S. and S. Paba (1992), 'Connessioni, competenze e capacità concorrenziale dell'industria in Sardegna', in M. D'Antonio (ed.), *Il Mezzogiorno. Sviluppo o stagnazione?*, Bologna: Il Mulino, pp. 229–75.
Brusco, S. and S. Paba (1997), 'Per una storia dei distretti industriali italiani dal secondo dopoguerra agli anni novanta', in F. Barca (ed.), *Storia del capitalismo italiano. Dal dopoguerra a oggi*, Roma: Donzelli, pp. 265–333.
Brusco, S. and M. Pezzini (1990), 'Small scale enterprise in the ideology of the Italian left', in Pyke, Becattini and Sengenberger (1990), pp. 142–59.
Brusco, S. and E. Righi (1989), 'Local government, industrial policy and social consensus: the case of Modena (Italy)', *Economy and society*, 4, 405–24; published in Italian as 'Enti locali, politica per l'industria e consenso sociale', OECD, Italy Seminar *Opportunities for Urban Economic Development*, Venezia, 25–27 June, in Brusco (1989a), pp. 433–60.
Brusco, S. and A. Rinaldi (1990) 'Gli anni della democrazia: vicende e protagonisti dell'economia', in P. Golinelli and G. Muzzioli (eds), *Storia illustrata di Modena*, vol. 3, *Dall'unità nazionale ad oggi*, Milano: Nuova editoriale AIEP, Part I, pp. 1021–40, Part II, pp. 1041–60.
Brusco, S. and Ch.F. Sabel (1981), 'Artisan production and economic growth', in F. Wilkinson (ed.), *The Dynamics of Labour Market Segmentation*, London: Academic Press; published in Italian in Brusco (1989), pp. 293–316.
Brusco, S., P. Bertossi and A. Cottica (1996), 'Playing on two chessboards: the European waste management industry. Strategic behaviour in the market and in the policy debate', in F. Lévêque (ed.), *Environmental Policy in Europe: Industry, Competition and the Policy Process*, Cheltenham, UK and Brookfield, US: Edward Elgar, pp. 113–42.
Brusoni, S., A. Prencipe and K. Pavitt (2001), 'Knowledge specialization, organizational coupling and the boundaries of the firm: why do firms know more than they make?', *Administrative Science Quarterly*, 46, 597–621.
Brusco, S., G. Cainelli, F. Forni, M. Franchi, A. Malusardi and R. Righetti (1996), 'The evolution of industrial districts in Emilia-Romagna', in Cossentino, Pyke and Sengenberger (1996), pp. 17–36.
Bruton, H.J. (1998), 'A reconsideration of import substitution', *Journal of Economic Literature*, **36** (2), 903–36.

Buenstorf, G. and S. Klepper (2005), 'Heritage and agglomeration: the akron tire cluster revisited', *Papers on Economics and Evolution*, no. 8, Max Planck Institute of Economics, Evolutionary Economics Group.

Bugamelli, M. and L. Infante (2005), 'Sunk costs of exports: a role for industrial districts?', in Banca d'Italia, *Local Economies and Internationalization in Italy*, Roma: Banca d'Italia, pp. 343–72; published in Italian in L.F. Signorini and M. Omiccioli M. (eds) (2005), *Economie locali e competizione globale: il localismo industriale italiano di fronte a nuove sfide*, Bologna: Il Mulino, pp. 211–29.

Bugamelli, M., P. Cipollone and L. Infante (2000), 'L'internazionalizzazione delle imprese italiane negli anni novanta', *Rivista italiana degli economisti*, 3, 349–86.

Burdy, J.-P. (1989), *Le Soleil Noir, un quartier de Saint-Etienne 1840–1940*, Lyon: Presses Universitaires de Lyon.

Burroni, L. (2001), *Allontanarsi crescendo. Politica e sviluppo locale in Veneto e Toscana*, Torino: Rosenbeg & Sellier.

Burt, R.S. (1992), 'The social structure of competition', in N. Nohria and R.G. Eccles (eds), *Networks and Organization*, Boston, MA: Harvard Business School, pp. 57–91.

Butlin, R.A. (1986), 'Early industrialization in Europe: concepts and problems', *The Geographical Journal*, **152** (1), 1–8.

Cafagna, L. (1989), *Dualismo e sviluppo nella storia d'Italia*, Venezia: Marsilio.

Cainelli, G. and N. De Liso (2004), 'Can a Marshallian industrial district be innovative? The case of Italy', in G. Cainelli and R. Zoboli (eds), *The Evolution of Industrial Districts: Changing Governance, Innovation and Internationalisation of Local Capitalism in Italy*, Heidelberg and New York: Physica-Verlag, pp. 243–56.

Cainelli, G. and D. Iacobucci (2007), *Agglomeration, Technology and Business Groups*, Cheltenham, UK and Northampton, MA, USA: Edward Elgar.

Cairncross, F. (1997), *The Death of Distance*, New York: McGraw-Hill.

Caizzi, B. (1955), 'Economia e finanza a Vigevano nel Cinque e nel Seicento', *Nuova rivista storica*, **34** (3).

Caizzi, B. (1957), *Storia del setificio comasco*, vol. 1, *Economia*, Como: Centro lariano per gli studi economici.

Camagni, R. (ed.) (1991), *Innovation Networks: Spatial Perspectives*, London: Belhaven.

Camagni, R. (2000), *La teoria dello sviluppo regionale*, Padova: Cusl Nuova Vita.

Camagni, R. and D. Maillat (2006), *Milieux innovateurs. Théorie et politiques*, Paris: Economica Anthropos.

Camagni, R., D. Maillat and A. Matteaccioli (eds) (2004), *Ressources naturelles et culturelles, milieux et développement local*, Neuchatel: EDES.

Camisón, C. (2004), 'Shared, competitive, and comparative advantages: a competence-based view of industrial-district competitiveness', *Environment and Planning A*, **36** (12), 2227–56.

Camuffo, A. (2003), 'Transforming industrial districts: large firms and small business networks in the Italian eyewear industry', *Industry and Innovation*, **10** (4), 377–401.
Camuffo, A. and R. Grandinetti (2006), 'The nature of industrial districts: a knowledge-based perspective', paper presented at the British Academy of Management Conference, Belfast, September.
Cannari, L. and L.F. Signorini (2000), 'Nuovi strumenti per la classificazione dei sistemi locali', in Signorini (2000), pp. 123–51.
Cantillon, R. (1755), *Essai sur la nature du commerce en général*, edited with an English translation by H. Higgs (1959), London: Frank Cass.
Cantwell, J. and S. Iammarino (2000), 'Multinational corporations and the location of technological innovation in the UK regions', *Regional Studies*, **34** (4), 317–32.
Capecchi, V. (1997), 'In search of flexibility: the Bologna metalworking industry', in Sabel and Zeitlin (1997a), pp. 381–418.
Capitalia (2005), *Indagine sulle imprese italiane. Rapporto sul sistema produttivo e la politica industriale*, Osservatorio sulle piccole imprese, ottobre.
Capone, F. (2004), *I sistemi locali turistici in Italia. Identificazione, misurazione ed analisi delle fonti di competitività*, Firenze: Firenze University Press.
Carabelli, A., G. Hirsh and R. Rabellotti (2006), 'Italian SMEs and industrial districts on the move: where are they going?', *Quaderno SEMeQ*, no. 13, Università degli Studi del Piemonte Orientale.
Carbahal, L. (2007), 'The University of Illinois at Urbana-Champaign: technology firm generation in a research university context', unpublished manuscript, Community and Regional Development, Davis: University of California.
Carlsson, B. (2003), 'Internationalization of innovation systems: a survey of the literature', paper presented at the conference in honour of Keith Pavitt, *SPRU Electronic Working Paper*, Brighton, November.
Carnevali, F. (2004), 'Crooks, thieves, and receivers: transaction costs in nineteenth-century industrial Birmingham', *Economic History Review*, **3** (57), 533–50.
Casavola, P., G. Pellegrini and E. Romagnano (2000), 'Imprese e mercato del lavoro nei distretti industriali', in Signorini (2000), pp. 51–66.
Casolaro, L. and P.E. Mistrulli (2008), *Distance, Lending Technologies and Interest Rates*, Roma: Bank of Italy.
Casper, S. (2007), 'How do technology clusters emerge and become sustainable? Social network formation and inter-firm mobility within the San Diego biotechnology cluster', *Research Policy*, 36, 438–55.
Casson, M. (1997), *Information and Organization*, Oxford: Clarendon Press.
Castronovo, V. (1964), *L'industria laniera piemontese nel secolo XIX*, Torino: UTET.
Castronovo, V. (1966), 'Formazione e sviluppo del ceto imprenditoriale laniero e cotoniero piemontese', *Rivista Storica Italiana*, **78** (4),773–849.

Cattaneo, C. (1842), 'Di alcuni Stati moderni', reprinted in D. Castelnuovo Frigessi (ed.) (1972), *Milano e l'Europa. Scritti 1839–46*, Torino: Einaudi.
Cattaneo, C. (1858), 'La città considerata come principio ideale delle istorie italiane', reprinted in D. Castelnuovo Frigessi (ed.) (1972), *Storia universale e ideologia delle genti. Scritti 1852–64*, Torino: Einaudi.
Cattaneo, C. (1861), *Del Pensiero come principio dell'economia pubblica*, English translation in M. Vitale (ed.) (2007), *Intelligence as a Principle of Public Economy*, Lanham, MD: Lexington Books.
Cavalieri, A. (1995), *L'internazionalizzazione del processo produttivo nei sistemi locali di piccola impresa in Toscana*, Milano: IRPET-Franco Angeli.
Caves, R. (1998), 'Industrial organization and new findings on the turnover and mobility of firms', *Journal of Economic Literature*, **36** (4), 1947–82.
Caves, R. (2000), *Creative Industries: Contracts between Art and Commerce*, Cambridge, MA: Harvard University Press.
Cawthorne, P. (1995), 'Of networks and markets: the rise and rise of a South Indian town and the example of Tiruppur's cotton knitwear industry', *World Development*, **23** (1), 43–56.
Cazes, S. and A. Nesporova (2007), *Flexicurity: A Relevant Approach in Central and Eastern Europe*, Geneva: ILO.
Ceglie, G. and M. Dini (1999), 'SME Cluster and Network Development in Developing. Countries: The Experience of UNIDO', Private Sector Development Branch, Vienna.
Celada, F. (1999), 'Los distritos industriales en la comunidad de Madrid', *Papeles de Economía Española*, 18, 200–211.
Cento Bull, A. (1989), 'Proto-industrialization, small capital accumulation and diffused entrepreneurship. The case of Brianza in Lombardy (1860–1950)', *Social History*, 14, 177–200.
Cento Bull, A. and P. Corner (1993), *From Peasant to Entrepreneur: The Survival of the Family Economy in Italy*, Oxford: Berg.
CEPS (Centre for European Olicy Studies)-WIIW (Winer Institut für Internazionale Wirschaftgeshichte) (2005), 'Final report, Part 1: The textile and clothing industries in an enlarged community and the outlook in the candidate States', www.europa.eu.int/comm/enterprise/textile/documents/tc_study_jan2005_new_ms_bg_ro.pdf, accessed 27 July 2008.
Cerqueiro, G.M., H.A. Degryse and S. Ongena (2009), 'Distance, bank organizational structure and lending decisions', in P. Alessandrini, M. Fratianni and A. Zazzaro (eds), *The Changing Geography of Banking and Finance*, Berlin: Springer Verlag, forthcoming.
CES (2005), *El proceso de creación de empresas y el dinamismo empresarial*, Madrid: Regional Department of Economy and Welfare.
Chadwick, G. (1971), *A Systems View of Planning*, Oxford: Pergamon.
Chandler, A.D. (1990), *Scale and Scope. The Dynamics of Industrial Capitalism*, Cambridge, MA: Harvard University Press.

Chandler, A., F. Amatori and T. Hikino (eds) (1997), *Big Business and the Wealth of Nations*, Cambridge: Cambridge University Press.
Chandra, R. and R. Sandilands (2006), 'The role of pecuniary external economies and economies of scale in the theory of increasing returns', *Review of Political Economy*, **18** (2), 193–208.
Chang, H.-J. and D. Green (2003), 'The Northern WTO agenda on investment: do as we say, not as we do', Geneva: The South Centre.
Chapman, S. (1904), *The Lancashire Cotton Industry. A Study in Economic Development*, Manchester: The University Press.
Chartres, J.A. (2002), 'Clustering in the British textile industry between the mid-seventeenth and the mid-nineteenth centuries', paper for Diebold Institute of Entrepreneurship and Public Policy, New York.
Chesbrough, H.W. (2003a), *Open Innovation: The New Imperative for Creating and Profiting from Technology*, Boston: Harvard Business School Press.
Chesbrough, H.W. (2003b), 'Creating and capturing value from technology: the case of Xerox spin-off companies', mimeo, Harvard Business School.
Chiapparino, F. (2008), *Credito, comunità e sviluppo*, Affinità elettive, Ancona.
Chiarvesio, M., E. Di Maria and S. Micelli (2004), 'From local network of SME to virtual districts? Evidence from recent trends in Italy', *Research Policy*, **33** (10), 1509–28.
Chiarvesio, M., E. De Maria and S. Micelli (2006), 'Global value chains and open networks: the case of Italian industrial districts', Society for the Advancement of Socio-economics, Trier.
Christensen, J.F. (2006), 'Wither core competency for the large corporation in an open innovation world?', in H. Chesbrough, W. Vanhaverbeke and J. West (eds), *Open Innovation: Researching a New Paradigm*, Oxford: Oxford University Press, pp. 35–61.
Cicognetti, L. and M. Pezzini (1994), 'Dalla lavorazione delle paglie all'industria delle maglie: la nascita del distretto industriale di Carpi', in Bellandi and Russo (1994), pp. 107–26.
Cingano, F. (2003), 'Returns to specific skills in industrial districts', *Labour Economics*, **10** (2), 149–64.
Cingano, F. and F. Schivardi (2005), 'Identifying the sources of local productivity growth', in Banca d'Italia, *Local Economies and Internationalization in Italy*, Roma: Banca d'Italia, pp. 89–121; published in Italian as 'Struttura produttiva locale e crescita', in L.F. Signorini and M. Omiccioli (eds) (2005), *Economie locali e competizione globale: il localismo industriale italiano di fronte a nuove sfide*, Bologna: Il Mulino, pp. 65–82.
Cipolla, C. (1976), *Before the Industrial Revolution. European Society and Economy: 1000–1700*, New York: Norton.
Cipolla, C. (1990), *Storia economica dell'Europa pre-industriale*, Bologna: Il Mulino.

Cipolla, I. (2001–02), 'L'Università della seta: la Regia Scuola di setificio a Como', degree thesis, Milano: Bocconi University.
Ciriacono, S. (1983), 'Protoindustria, lavoro a domicilio e sviluppo economico nelle campagne venete in epoca moderna', *Quaderni Storici*, **17** (52), 57–80.
Ciriacono, S. (1985), 'Echecs et réussites de la proto-industrialisation dans la Vénétie: le cas du Haut-Vicentin (XVIIe-XIXe siècles)', *Revue d'histoire moderne et contemporaine*, 311–23.
Clapham, J.H. (1922), 'Of empty economic boxes', *Economic Journal*, 32, 305–14.
Clapham, J.H. (1930), *An Economic History of Modern Britain, 1820–50*, vol. 1, Cambridge: Cambridge University Press.
Clara, M. et al. (2000), 'Business services for small enterprises in Asia: developing markets and measuring performance', paper presented at Hanoi, Vietnam.
Clark, C. (1940), *The Conditions of Economic Progress*, London: Macmillan.
Clayton-Mathews, A. and R. Loveland (2004), 'Medical devices: supporting the Massachusetts economy', University of Massachusetts Donahue Institute, www.massbenchmarks.org, accessed 20 July 2008.
Clerides, S., S. Lach and J.R. Tybout (1998), 'Is learning by exporting important? Micro-dynamic evidence from Colombia, Mexico, and Morocco', *The Quarterly Journal of Economics*, **113** (3), 903–47.
Club dei distretti industriali (2003), *Guide to the Italian Industrial districts*, Fondazione del Museo dello scarpone, Montebelluna, Treviso.
Coase, R.H. (1937), 'The nature of the firm', *Economica*, 4, 386–405.
Cocozza, E. (2000), 'Le relazioni finanziarie nei distretti industriali', in Signorini (2000), pp. 359–83.
Coe, N. and A. Townsend (1998), 'Debunking the myth of localised agglomeration', *Transactions of the Institute of British Geographers*, 23, 1–20.
Cohen, W.M. and D.A. Levinthal (1990), 'Absorptive capacity: a new perspective on learning and innovation', *Administrative Science Quarterly*, **35** (1), 128–52.
Colander, D., R.P.F. Holt and J.B. Jr Rosser (2004), 'The changing face of mainstream economics', *Review of Political Economy*, **16** (4), 485–99.
Coleman, J. (1990), *Foundations of Social Theory*, Cambridge, MA: Harvard University Press.
Colletis, G. and B. Pecqueur (1995), 'Politiques technologiques locales et création des ressources spécifiques', in A. Rallet and A. Torre (eds), *Economie industrielle et économie spatiale*, Paris: Economica, pp. 445–63.
Colletis, G., C. Courlet and B. Pecqueur (1990), *Les systèmes industriels localisés en Europe*, Grenoble: IREPD.
Colley, L. (1992), *Britons: Forging the Nation, 1707–1837*, New Haven, CT: Yale University Press.
Colli, A. (1999), *Legami di ferro. Storia del distretto metallurgico e meccanico lecchese tra Otto e Novecento*, Roma: Meridiana Libri-Donzelli.
Colli, A. (2002a), *I volti di Proteo. Storia della piccola impresa in Italia nel Novecento*, Torino: Boringhieri.

Colli, A. (2002b), *Il quarto capitalismo. Un profilo italiano*, Venezia: Marsilio.
Collins English Dictionary (1998), Glasgow: Harper Collins.
Coltorti, F. (2006a), 'Dal NEC di Fuà al nuovo ruolo delle medie imprese', *La Questione Agraria*, 4, 39–54.
Coltorti, F. (2006b), 'Medium-sized manufacturing firms in the years of zero growth', *Review of Economic Conditions in Italy*, 3, 389–411.
Coltorti, F. (2008), 'Le medie imprese industriali italiane: aspetti strutturali e dinamici', in A. Arrighetti and A. Ninni (eds), *Dimensioni e crescita nell'industria manifatturiera italiana. Il ruolo delle medie imprese*, Milano: Franco Angeli, pp. 43–69.
Combes, P.-P. (2000), 'Economic structure and local growth: France, 1984–1993', *Journal of Urban Economics*, **47** (3), 329–55.
Combes, P.-P. and G. Duranton (2006), 'Labour pooling, labour poaching, and spatial clustering', *Regional Science and Urban Economics*, **36** (1), 1–28.
Cominotti, R. and S. Mariotti (eds) (1994), *Italia multinazionale 1994. Le nuove frontiere dell'internazionalizzazione produttiva*, Milano: Etas Libri.
Commissione per la garanzia dell'informazione statistica (2005), *Le metodologie di misurazione dei distretti industriali: rapporto di ricerca*, www.palazzochigi.it/Presidenza/statistica/rapporti_indagine.html.
Commons, J.R. (1909), 'American shoemakers, 1648–1895: a sketch of industrial evolution', *Quarterly Journal of Economics*, **24** (1), 39–84.
Commons, J.R. (1934), *Institutional Economics, its Place in Political Economy*, New York: Macmillan.
Consiglio italiano per le scienze sociali (2005), *Tendenze e politiche dello sviluppo locale in Italia*, Venezia: Marsilio.
Constantin, F., G. De Giusti and G. Tattara (2008), 'Processi di internazionalizzazione nei distretti del Nord-Est', *Working paper DSE*, University of Venice.
Conti, G. (1997), 'Banche e imprese medie e piccole nella periferia economica italiana (1990–1939)', in F. Cesarini, G. Ferri and M. Giardino (eds), *Credito e sviluppo*, Bologna: Il Mulino.
Conti, G. and S. Menghinello (1998), 'Modelli di impresa e di industria nei contesti di competizione globale: l'internazionalizzazione produttiva dei sistemi locali del made in Italy', *L'Industria, Rivista di economia e politica industriale*, **19** (2).
Cooke, Ph. (1983), *Theories of Planning and Spatial Development*, London: Hutchinson.
Cooke, Ph. (1985), 'Regional innovation policy: problems and strategies in Britain and France', *Environment and Planning C: Government and Policy*, 3, 253–67.
Cooke, Ph. (1992), 'Regional innovation systems: competitive regulation in the new Europe', *Geoforum*, 23, 365–82.
Cooke, Ph. (1993), 'Regional innovation systems: an evaluation of six European cases', in P. Getimis and G. Kafkalas (eds), *Urban and Regional Development in the New Europe*, Athens, Topos New Series.

Cooke, Ph. (2001a), 'Regional innovation systems, clusters, and the knowledge economy', *Industrial and Corporate Change*, **10** (4), 945–74.
Cooke, Ph. (2001b), 'Clusters as key determinants of economic growth: the example of biotechnology', in Å. Mariussen (ed.), *Cluster Policies. Cluster Development?* Nordregio Report no. 2, Stockholm.
Cooke, Ph. (2002), *Knowledge Economics: Clusters, Learning and Cooperative Advantage*, London: Routledge.
Cooke, Ph. (2004), 'Introduction: regional innovation systems. An evolutionary approach', in P. Cooke, M. Heidenreich and H. Braczyk (eds), *Regional Innovation Systems*, London: Routledge.
Cooke, Ph. (2007), *Growth Cultures: the Global Bioeconomy and its Bioregions*, London: Routledge.
Cooke, Ph. (2008), 'Knowledgeable regions, Jacobian clusters and green innovation', in S. Sacchetti and R. Sugden (eds), *Knowledge in the Development of Economies: Institutional Choices under Globalisation*, Cheltenham, UK and Northampton, MA, USA: Edward Elgar.
Cooke, Ph. (2009), 'Green clusters, green innovation and Jacobian cluster mutation', *The Cambridge Journal of Regions, Economy and Society*, 1, forthcoming.
Cooke, Ph. and A. da Rosa Pires (1985), 'Productive decentralisation in three European regions', *Environment and Planning A*, 17, 527–54.
Cooke, Ph. and L. Lazzeretti (eds) (2008), *Creative Cities, Cultural Clusters and Local Economic Development*, Cheltenham, UK and Northampton, MA, USA: Edward Elgar.
Cooke, Ph. and L. Leydesdorff (2004), 'Regional development in the knowledge-based economy: the construction of advantage', *Journal of Technology Transfer*, 31, 5–15.
Cooke, Ph. and K. Morgan (1993), 'The network paradigm: new departures in corporate and regional development', *Environment and Planning D: Society and Space*, 11, 543–64.
Cooke, Ph. and G. Rees (1977), 'Faludi's *Sociology in Planning Education*: a critical comment', *Urban Studies*, 11, 312–20.
Cooke, Ph., R. Alaez and G. Etxebarria (1991), 'Regional technological centres in the Basque country: an evaluation of policies, providers and user perceptions', *Regional Industrial Research Report*, no. 9, Cardiff University.
Cooke, Ph., M. Uranga and G. Etxebarria (1997), 'Regional innovation systems: institutional and organisational dimensions', *Research Policy*, 26, 475–91.
Cooke, Ph., M. Uranga and G. Etxebarria (1998), 'Regional systems of innovation: an evolutionary perspective', *Environment and Planning A*, 30, 1563–84.
Cooke, Ph., C. De Laurentis, F. Tödtling and M. Trippl (2007), *Regional Knowledge Economies*, Cheltenham, UK and Northampton, MA, USA: Edward Elgar.

Cooke, Ph., G. Etxebarria, J. Morris and A. Rodriguez (1989), 'Flexibility in the periphery', *Regional industrial Research Report*, no. 3, Cardiff University.
Cooke, Ph., F. Moulaert, E. Swyngedouw, O. Weinstein and P. Wells (1992), *Towards Global Localization*, London: UCL Press.
Cookson, G. (2003), 'Quaker networks and the industrial development of Darlington, 1780–1870', in Wilson and Popp (2003), pp. 155–73.
Coombes, M.G., A.E. Green and S. Openshaw (1986), 'An efficient algorithm to generate official statistical reporting areas: the case of the 1984 Travel-to-Work Areas revision in Britain', *Journal of the Operational Research Society*, 37, 943–53.
Coopey, R. (2003), 'The British glove industry, 1750–1970: the advantages and vulnerability of a regional industry', in Wilson and Popp (2003), pp. 174–91.
Coriat, B. and S. Gennif (1998), 'Self-interest and institutions', in N. Lazaric and E. Lorenz (eds), *Trust and Economic Learning*, Cheltenham, UK and Northampton, MA, USA: Edward Elgar, pp. 48–63.
Corò, G. and S. Micelli (2007), 'Industrial districts as local system of innovation', Working Paper, Department of Economics, University of Venice.
Corò, G. and M. Volpe (2006), 'Apertura internazionale della produzione nei distretti italiani', in G. Tattara, G. Corò and M. Volpe (2006), *Andarsene per continuare a crescere. La delocalizzazione internazionale come strategia competitiva*, Roma: Carocci.
Cortright, J. (2006), *Making Sense of Clusters: Regional Competitiveness and Economic Development*, Washington, DC: The Brookings Institution.
Cossentino, F., F. Pyke and W. Sengenberger (eds) (1996), *Local and Regional Response to Global Pressure: The Case of Italy and its Industrial Districts*, Geneva: ILO.
Costa Campi, M.T. (1988), 'Descentramiento productivo y difusión industrial. El modelo de especialización flexible', *Papeles de Economía Española*, 35, 251–76.
Costa Campi, M.T et al. (1993), *EXCEL, Cooperación entre empresas y sistemas productivos locales*, Madrid: IMPI.
Costa Campi, M.T. and E. Viladecans-Marsal (1999), 'The district effect and the competitiveness of manufacturing companies in local productive systems', *Urban Studies*, **36** (12), 2085–98.
Costamagna, P. (2000), 'La articulación y la interaccion entre las instituciones: la iniciativa de desarrollo local de Rafaela, Argentina', LC/R.2011/E, Santiago: CEPAL.
COTEC (2007), *Informe COTEC 2006 sobre tecnología e innovación en España*, Madrid: Fundación COTEC para la innovación tecnológica.
Cottereau, A. (1997), 'The fate of collective manufacturers in the industrial world: the silk industries of Lyons and London, 1800–1850', in Sabel and Zeitlin (1997a), pp. 75–152.

Courault, B. (2000), 'Districts italiens et PME-systèmes français, comparaison n'est pas raison', *La lettre du CEE*, no. 61, Paris: Centre d'Etudes et d'Emploi.

Courault, B. and P. Trouvé (eds) (2000), *Les dynamiques de PME. Approches internationales*, Paris: PUF.

Courlet, C. (2001), *Territoires et régions, les grands oubliés du développement économique*, Paris: L'Harmattan.

Courlet, C. (2008), *L'économie territoriale*, Grenoble: Presses universitaires de Grenoble.

Courlet, C. and A. Hsaini (1997), *Les systèmes productifs localisés et leur identification en France*, Grenoble: IREPD-DATAR.

Courlet, C. and P. Judet (1986), 'Nouveaux espaces de production en France et en Italie', *Les Annales de la recherche urbaine*, 29, 95–103.

Courlet, C. and B. Pecqueur (1992), 'Les sistèmes industriels localisés en France: un nouvel model de développement', in G. Benko and A. Lipietz (eds), *Les régions qui gagnent. Districts et réseaux: les nouveaux paradigmes de la géographie économique*, Paris: PUF, pp. 81–102.

Courlet, C., G. Garofoli, A. Hsaini and P. Faillenet (2000), *Premières reflections pour l'élaboration d'un Livre Blanc des districts industriels et des SPL européens*, Beziers-Cluses: Almatec-Sidemva.

Cowling, K. and R. Sugden (1994), *Beyond Capitalism*, London: Pinter.

Crafts, N.F.R. (1985), *British Economic Growth During the Industrial Revolution*, Oxford: Oxford University Press.

Craig, S.G. and P. Hardee (2007), 'The impact of bank consolidation on small business credit availability', *Journal of Banking and Finance*, 31, 1237–63.

Criscuolo, A. (2005), 'Considerations for upgrading clusters of local enterprises in the global economy: the experience of the Third Italy', unpublished *LED Working Paper*, Geneva: ILO.

Crossick, G. (1997), 'Past masters: in search of the artisans in European History', in G. Crossick (ed.), *The Artisan and the European Town, 1500–1900*, Aldershot: Scolar Press.

Crouch, C. (2005), *Capitalist Diversity and Change: Recombinant Governance and Institutional Entrepreneurs*, Oxford: Oxford University Press.

Crouch, C. and H. Farrell (2001), 'Great Britain: falling through the holes in the network concept', in Crouch et al. (2001), pp. 154–211.

Crouch, C., P. Le Galès, C. Trigilia and H. Voelzkow (eds) (2001), *Local Production Systems in Europe: Rise or Demise?*, Oxford: Oxford University Press.

Crouch, C., P. Le Gales, C. Trigilia and H. Voelzkow (2004), *Changing Governance of Local Economies: Responses of European Local Production Systems*, Oxford: Oxford University Press.

Crozier, M. and E. Friedberg (1977), *L'acteur et le système. Les contraintes de l'action collective*, Paris: Seuil.

Dahmén, E. (1988), 'Development blocks in industrial economics', *Scandinavian Economic History Review & Economy and History*, **36** (1), 3–14; also published in B. Carlsson (ed.) (1989), *Industrial Dynamics*, Boston, MA: Kluwer, pp. 109–21.

Dalmazzo, A. and G. de Blasio (2005), 'Social returns to education: evidence from Italian local labour market areas', in Banca d'Italia, *Local Economies and Internationalization in Italy*, Roma: Banca d'Italia, pp. 251–80; published in Italian as 'I rendimenti sociali dell'istruzione in Italia', in L.F. Signorini and M. Omiccioli (eds) (2005), *Economie locali e competizione globale: il localismo industriale italiano di fronte a nuove sfide*, Bologna: Il Mulino, pp. 163–86.

Dalmazzo, A. and G. de Blasio (2007), 'Production and consumption externalities of human capital: an empirical study for Italy', *Journal of Population Economics*, **20** (2), 359–82.

Dardi, M. (2003), 'Alfred Marshall's partial equilibrium: dynamics in disguise', in R. Arena and M. Queré (eds), *The Economics of Alfred Marshall. Revisiting Marshall's Legacy*, New York: Palgrave Macmillan.

Darwin, Ch. (1859), *The Origin of Species*, reprinted 1979, New York: Random House.

Dasgupta, S. (1989), 'The spirit of success', *India Today*, 31 October.

DATAR (2004), *La France, puissance industrielle. Une nouvelle politique industrielle par les territoires: réseaux d'entreprises, vallées technologiques, pôles de compétitivité*, rapport, Paris: DATAR.

Daumas, J.-C., P. Lamard and L. Tissot (eds) (2007), *Les territoires de l'industrie en Europe (1750–2000). Entreprises, régulations et trajectoires*, Besançon: Presses Universitaires de Franche-Comté.

DCMS (Department of Media, Culture and Sport) (2001), *The Creative Industries Mapping Document*, London: HMSO.

DCMS (Department for Culture, Media and Sport) (2008), *Staying Ahead: The Economic Performance of the UK's Creative Industries*, London.

De Arcangelis, G. and G. Ferri (2005), 'La specializzazione dei distretti: dai beni finali ai macchinari del made in Italy?', in L.F. Signorini and M. Omiccioli (eds) (2005), *Economie locali e competizione globale*: *il localismo industriale italiano di fronte a nuove sfide*, Bologna: Il Mulino, pp. 283–97.

De Blasio, G. and S. Di Addario (2005a), 'Do workers benefit from industrial agglomeration?', *Journal of Regional Science*, **45** (4), 797–827.

De Blasio, G. and S. Di Addario (2005b), 'Labour market pooling: evidence from Italian industrial districts', in Banca d'Italia, *Local Economies and Internationalization in Italy*, Roma: Banca d'Italia, pp. 213–50; published in Italian as 'Salari, imprenditorialità e mobilità nei distretti industriali', in L.F. Signorini and M. Omiccioli (eds) (2005), *Economie locali e competizione globale: il localismo industriale italiano di fronte a nuove sfide*, Bologna: Il Mulino, pp. 187–208.

De Blasio, G., G. Iuzzolino and M. Omiccioli (2008), 'Medición del "efecto distrito": una approximación no paramétrica', *Mediterráneo Económico*, 13: 97–113.

De Bono, E. (1971), *The Use of Lateral Thinking*, Middlesex, UK: Penguin Books Harmondsworth; 1st edition 1967.

De Bresson, C. and F. Amesse (1991), 'Networks of innovators: a review and introduction to the issue', *Research Policy*, 20, 363–80.

De Giusti, G. (2006), 'Processi di internazionalizzazione nel distretto liventino del mobile moderno. Alcuni casi di studio', degree thesis, Venezia: Università Ca' Foscari.

De Gregori, T. (1987), 'Resources are not; they become. An institutional theory', *Journal of Economic Issues*, **21** (3), 1241–63.

De Luca, J.A. and G.M. Soto (1995), *Los distritos industriales como estrategia de desarrollo regional*, Murcia: Caja Murcia.

De Moor, M. (2006), 'The silent revolution. The emergence of commons, guilds and other forms of corporate collective action in Western Europe from a new perspective', paper for the Conference *The Return of the Guilds*, Utrecht, Utrecht University, 5–7 October, pp. 1–39, www.iisg.nl/hpw/papers/guilds-demoor.pdf, accessed 20 December 2008.

De Munck, B. (2006), 'How did guilds define human capital? Social capital in the crestion of human capital in Antwerp guilds, 15th and 16th centuries', paper for the Conference *The Return of the Guilds*, Utrecht, Utrecht University, 5–7 October, pp. 1–20, www.iisg.nl/hpw/papers/guilds-demunck.pdf, accessed 20 December 2008.

De Propris, L. (2001), 'Systemic flexibility, production fragmentation and cluster governance', *European Planning Studies*, **9** (6), 739–53.

De Propris, L. (2002), 'Types of innovation and inter-firm cooperation', *Entrepreneurship and Regional Development*, **14** (4), 337–53.

De Propris, L. (2005), 'Mapping local production systems in the UK: methodology and application', *Regional Studies*, **39** (2), 197–211.

De Propris, L. (2009), 'Trust and social capital in glo-cal networks', in P. Bianchi, M.D. Parrilli and R. Sugden (eds), *High Technology, Productivity and Networks: A Systemic Approach to SME Development*, Basingstoke: Palgrave Macmillan, forthcoming.

De Propris, L. and L. Lazzeretti (2007), 'The Birmingham jewellery quarter: a Marshallian industrial district', *European Planning Studies*, **15** (10), 1295–325.

De Propris, L. and L. Lazzeretti (2009), 'Measuring the decline of a Marshallian Industrial district: the Birmingham Jewellery Quarter', *Regional Studies*, forthcoming.

De Propris, L., N. Driffield and S. Menghinello (2005), 'Local industrial systems and the location of FDI in Italy', *International Journal of the Economics and Business*, **12** (1), 105–21.

De Propris, L., S. Menghinello and R. Sugden (2008), 'The internationalisation of local production systems: embeddedness, openness and governance', *Entrepreneurship and Regional Development*, **20** (6), 493–516.

Deakin, S. (2006), 'The return of the guild? Network relations in historical perspective', WP, no. 322, Centre for Business Research, University of Cambridge, March, www.cbr.cam.ac.uk/pdf/WP322.pdf, accessed 20 December 2008.

Debreu, G. (1959), *Theory of Value*, New York: John Wiley and Sons.
Degman, C. (1998), 'EMC breaks a billion', *Mass High Tech*, Nov., 9–15.
Dei Ottati, G. (1987), 'Il mercato comunitario', in Becattini (1987), pp. 117–41.
Dei Ottati, G. (1991), 'The economic bases of diffuse industrialization', *International Studies of Management & Organization*, **21** (1), 53–74.
Dei Ottati, G. (1994a), 'Trust, interlinking transactions and credit in the industrial district', *Cambridge Journal of Economics*, **18** (6), 529–46.
Dei Ottati, G. (1994b), 'Prato and its evolution in a European context', in R. Leonardi and R.Y. Nanetti (eds), *Regional Development in a Modern European Economy: the Case of Tuscany*, London: Pinter, pp. 116–44.
Dei Ottati, G. (1995), *Tra mercato e comunità: aspetti concettuali e ricerche empiriche sul distretto industriale*, Milano: Franco Angeli.
Dei Ottati, G. (1996a), 'Economic changes in the district of Prato in the 1980s: towards a more conscious and organized industrial district', *European Planning Studies*, **4** (1), 35–52.
Dei Ottati, G. (1996b), 'The remarkable resilience of the industrial districts of Tuscany', in Cossentino, Pyke and Sengenberger (1996), pp. 37–66.
Dei Ottati, G. (2002), 'Social concertation and local development: the case of industrial districts', *European Planning Studies*, **10** (4), 449–66.
Dei Ottati, G. (2003), 'The governance of transactions in the industrial district: the community market', in Becattini et al. (2003), pp. 73–94.
Dei Ottati, G. (2004), 'Trust and economic development in Italy: the case of the industrial district of Prato', in H.-H. Höhnemann and F. Welter (eds), *Entrepreneurial Strategies and Trust, Arbeitspapiere und Materialien*, no. 56, Forschungsstelle Osteuropa Bremen, January.
Dei Ottati, G. (2005), 'Global competition and entrepreneurial behaviour in industrial districts: trust relations in an Italian industrial district', in H.H. Höhnemann and F. Welter (eds), *Trust and Entrepreneurship. A West-East Perspective*, Cheltenham, UK and Northampton, MA, USA: Edward Elgar, pp. 255–71.
Dei Ottati, G. (2006), 'El efecto distrito. Algunos aspectos conceptuales de sus ventajas competttivas', *Economia Industrial*, 359, 73–9.
Dei Ottati, G. (2009), 'Italian industrial districts and the dual Chinese challenge', in G. Johanson, R. Smyth and R. French (eds), *Living Outside the Walls: The Chinese in Prato*, Cambridge: Cambridge Scholars Publishing, pp. 26–41.
Delgado, M.A., J.C. Fariñas and S. Ruano (2002), 'Firm productivity and export markets: a non-parametric approach', *Journal of International Economics*, **57** (2), 397–422.
Delgado, M., M.E. Porter and S. Stern (2007), 'When do clusters matter for regional economic performance', mimeo, Harvard Business School.
Dewerpe, A. (1985), *L'industrie aux champs. Essai sur la proto-industrialisation en Italie du nord (1800–80)*, Roma: Ecole française de Rome.
Di Giacinto, V. and G. Nuzzo (2005), 'The role of institutional factors in fostering the development of industrial districts in Italy', in Banca d'Italia, *Local*

Economies and Internationalization in Italy, Roma: Banca d'Italia, pp. 187–212; published in Italian as 'Il ruolo dei fattori istituzionali nello sviluppo dei distretti industriali in Italia', in L.F. Signorini and M. Omiccioli M. (eds) (2005), *Economie locali e competizione globale: il localismo industriale italiano di fronte a nuove sfide*, Bologna: Il Mulino, pp. 145–62.

Di Gregorio, D. and S. Shane (2003), 'Why do some universities generate more start-ups than others?', *Research Policy*, 32, 209–27.

Di Maria, E. and S. Micelli (2007), 'District leaders as open networks: emerging business strategies in Italian industrial districts', *Working Papers*, no. 0038, Dipartimento di Scienze Economiche 'Marco Fanno'.

Diamond Administration of China (DAC) (2008), 'ICA to hold 2009 congress in Panyu, China', www.dac.gov.cn, accessed 30 August 2008.

Diamond World (2008), '2009 ICS congress scheduled for Panyu', www.diamondworld.net/contentview.aspx?item=24, accessed 30 August 2008.

Diamond, Ch.A. and C.J. Simon (1990), 'Industrial specialization and the returns to labor', *Journal of Labor Economics*, **8** (2), 175–201.

Dicken, P. (2003), *Global Shift: Reshaping the Global Economic Map in the 21st Century*, London: Sage.

Dicken, P. and A. Malmberg (2001), 'Firms in territories: a relational perspective', *Economic Geography*, **77** (4), 345–63.

Dicken, P., P.F. Kelly, K. Olds and H.W. Yeung (2001), 'Chains and networks, territories and scales: toward a relational framework for analysing the global economy', *Global Networks*, **1** (2), 89–112.

DiMaggio, P. (ed.) (2001), *The Twenty-first-century Firm: Changing Economic Organization in International Perspective*, Princeton: Princeton University Press.

Ding, K. (2007), *Domestic Market-based Industrial Cluster Development in Modern China*, Tokyo: Institute of Developing Economies.

Doeringer, P. and M.J. Piore (1971), *Internal Labor Markets and Manpower Analysis*, Lexington: Heath.

Dosi, G. (1998), 'Sources, procedures and microeconomic effects of innovation', *Journal of Economic Literature*, **26** (3), 1120–71.

Dosi, G., C. Freeman, R. Nelson, G. Silverberg and L. Soete (eds) (1988), *Technical Change and Economic Theory*, London and New York: Pinter.

DPS (Dipartimento Politiche per lo Sviluppo, Italia) (various years), 'Rapporto annuale sugli interventi nelle aree sottoutilizzate', www.dps.tesoro.it, accessed 12 December 2008.

Dresser, L. and J. Rogers (2003), 'Part of the solution: emerging workforce intermediaries in the United States', in J. Zeitlin and D. Trubek (eds), *Governing Work and Welfare in a New Economy*, New York: Oxford University Press.

DTI (Department of Trade and Industry, UK) (2001), *Business Clusters in the UK. A First Assessment*, 3 vols, prepared by Trends Business Research, February, London.

Dunford, M. (2009), 'Globalization failures in a neo-liberal world: the case of FIAT Auto in the 1990s', *Geoforum*, forthcoming.

Dunlop, J.T. (1958), *Industrial Relations Systems*, New York: Holt, Rinehart and Winston.

Dunning, J.H. (1988), *Explaining International Production*, London: Unwin Hyman.

Dunning, J.H. (2001), 'The eclectic (OLI) paradigm of international production', *International Journal of Economic and Business*, **8** (2), 173–90.

Dupuy, C. and A. Torre (1998), 'Cooperazione e fiducia nelle imprese spazialmente raggruppate', *L'Industria, Rivista di economia e politica industriale*, 3, 479–500.

Duranton, G. and D. Puga (2002), 'Diversity and specialization in cities: why, where and when does it matter?', in Ph. McCann (ed.), *Industrial Location Economics*, Cheltenham, UK and Northampton, MA, USA: Edward Elgar, pp. 151–86.

Duranton, G. and D. Puga (2004), 'Micro-foundations of urban agglomeration economies', in J.V. Henderson and J.-F. Thisse (eds), *Handbook of Regional and Urban Economics*, vol. 4, *Cities and Geography*, Amsterdam: Elsevier, pp. 2063–117.

Duranton, G. and H.G. Overman (2005), 'Testing for localization using micro-geographic data', *Review of Economic Studies*, **72** (4), 1077–106.

Duranton, G. et al. (2008), *Les pôles de compétitivité, que peut-on en attendre?*, CEPREMAP, éditions de l'ENS.

Durlauf, S.N. and H.P. Young (eds) (2001), *Social Dynamics*, Washington, DC: The Brookings Institution.

Dyck, B. (1997), 'Exploring organisational family trees', *Journal of Management Enquiry*, 6, 222–33.

Eberts, R. and G. Erickcek (2002), 'The role of partnerships in economic development and labor markets in the United States', *Working Paper*, no. 02–75, Kalamazoo MI: Upjohn Institute Staff.

EDA (Economic Development Administration) (1997), 'Cluster-based economic development: a key to regional competitiveness', prepared by Information Design Associates (IDeA) with ICF Kaiser International, US Department of Commerce, October.

Edquist, C. (ed.) (1997), *Systems of Innovation: Technologies, Institutions and Organisations*, London: Pinter.

Eisenhardt, K.M. (1989), 'Building theories from case study research', *Academy of Management Review*, **14** (4), 532–50.

Elias, N. (1987), *Die Gesellschaft der Individuen*, Frankfurt: Suhrkamp.

Eliasson, G. and U. Eliasson (2006), 'The Pharmacia story of entrepreneurship and as a creative technical university. An experimentation in innovation, organizational break up and industrial renaissance', *Entrepreneurship and Regional Development*, **18** (5), 293–420.

Ellison, G. and E.L. Glaeser (1997), 'Geographic concentration in US manufacturing industries: a dartboard approach', *Journal of Political Economy*, **105** (5), 889–927.

Enterprise Policy Group (2007), 'Innovation clusters in Europe: a statistical analysis and overview of current policy support', *Europe Innova/PRO INNO Europe paper*, no. 5, Brussels.

EPCA Think Tank (2007), *A Paradigm Shift: Supply Chain Collaboration and Competition in and Between Europe's Chemical Clusters*, Brussels: EPCA.

Epstein, J.M. (2001), 'Learning to be thoughtless: social norms and individual computation', *Computational Economics*, 18, 9–24.

Epstein, S.R. (1998), 'Craft guilds, apprenticeship, and technical change in preindustrial Europe', *Journal of Economic History*, **58** (3), 684–713.

Epstein, S.R. (2004), 'Property rights to technical knowledge in pre-modern Europe 1300–1800', *The American Economic Review*, **94** (2), 382–7.

Ernst & Young (2000), 'Convergence: biotechnology industry report, Millennium Edition', 13th Annual Report, October. www.ey.com/global/gcr.nsf/International/Knowledge-Center, accessed 20 July 2008.

Ernst, D. (2001), 'Global production networks and the changing geography of innovation systems: implication for developing countries', *Economics of Innovation and New Technology*, **11** (6), 497–523.

Ernst, D. and L. Kim (2002), 'Global production networks, knowledge diffusion, and local capability formation', *Research Policy*, **31** (8–9), 1417–29.

Essletzbichler, J. and D. Rigby (2004), 'Competition, variety and the geography of technology evolution', *Tijdschrift voor Economische en Sociale Geografie*, 96, 48–62.

European Commission (1992), *Commission Report to the Council on the Definition of SMEs*, SEC (92) 351 final of 29 April 1992, Brussels.

European Commission (1996), 'Recommendation of 3 April 1996 concerning the definition of small and medium-sized enterprises', *Official Journal of the European Union*, L Series 107, Brussels.

European Commission (2001), 'Methodology for Regional and Transnational Technology Clusters: Learning with European Best Practices', Brussels, March, www.forum.europa.eu.int/irc/sme/euroinformation/info/data/sme/en/library/studies.html, accessed 12 October 2008.

European Commission (2003), 'Recommendation of 6 May 2003 concerning the definition of micro, small and medium-sized enterprises', *Official Journal of the European Union*, L Series 124, Brussels.

European Commission and Center for Strategy and Competitiveness (2008), *The European Cluster Memorandum. Promoting European Innovation through Clusters: An Agenda for Policy Action*, The High Level Advisory Group on Clusters.

Eurostat (2008), 'Technology and knowledge-intensive sectors', *Statistics in Focus*, no. 18, February.

Evans, P. (1995), *Embedded Autonomy: States and Industrial Transformation*, Princeton: Princeton University Press.

Fabiani, S., G. Pellegrini, E. Romagnano and L.F. Signorini (2000), 'Efficiency and localisation: the case of Italian districts', in M. Bagella and L. Becchetti (eds), *The Competitive Advantage of Industrial Districts: Theoretical and Empirical Analysis*, Heidelberg: Physica-Verlag, pp. 45–69; published in Italian in Signorini (2000), pp. 21–49.

Fallet, E. and A. Cortat (2001), *Apprendre l'horlogerie dans les montagnes neuchâteloises, 1740–1810*, La-Chaux-de-Fonds: Institut L'homme et le temps.

Faludi, A. (ed.) (1973), *A Reader in Planning Theory*, Oxford: Pergamon.

Falzoni A., F. Onida and G. Viesti (eds) (1992), *I distretti industriali: crisi o evoluzione?*, Milano: Egea.

Farabullini, F. and G. Gobbi (2000), 'Le banche nei sistemi locali di produzione', in Signorini (2000), pp. 167–201.

Farr, J.R. (1997a), 'On the shop floor: guilds, artisan and the European market economy 1350–1750', *Journal of Early Modern History: Contacts, Contrasts and Comparisons*, **1** (1), 24–54.

Farr, J.R. (1997b), 'Cultural analysis and early modern artisans', in G. Crossick (ed.), *The Artisan and the European Town, 1500–1900*, Aldershot: Scolar Press.

Fasano Guarini, E. (1986), *Prato storia di una città*, vol. 2, *Un microcosmo in movimento (1494–1815)*, Firenze: Comune di Prato-Le Monnier.

Favret-Saada, J. (1977), *Les mots, la mort, les sorts. La sorcellerie dans le Bocage*, Paris: Gallimard.

Fazio, N.R. and C. Pascucci (2006–07), 'Le esportazioni dei sistemi locali nel 2005, con particolare riguardo ai distretti industriali', *Sviluppo locale*, **12** (29–30), 3–35.

Fazzari, S.M., R.G. Hubbard and B.C. Petersen (1988), 'Financing constraints and coirporate investment', *Brookings Papers on Economic Activity*, no. 1, 141–206.

Federico, S. (2006), 'L'internazionalizzazione produttiva italiana e i distretti industriali: un'analisi degli investimenti diretti all'estero', *Temi di discussione*, no. 592, Servizio studi, Banca d'Italia.

Fehr, E. and S. Gachter (2000), 'Fairness and retaliation: the economics of reciprocity', *Journal of Economic Perspectives*, **14** (3), 159–81.

Feldman, M.P. (2000), 'Where science comes to life: university bioscience, commercial spin-offs, and regional economic development', *Journal of Comparative Policy Analysis: Research and Practice*, 2, 345–61.

Feldman, M.P. (2004), 'Knowledge externalities and the anchor hypothesis: the locational dynamics of the US biotech industry', paper presented at the Annual Meeting of the Association of American Geographers, Philadelphia, 14–17 March.

Feldman, M.P. (2005), 'The locational dynamic of the US biotech industry: knowledge externalities and the anchor hypothesis', in A. Quadrio Curzio and M. Fortis (eds), *Research and Technological Innovation*, Berlin: Springer Verlag.

Feldman, M.P. and D.B. Audretsch (1999), 'Innovation in cities: science-based diversity, specialization, and localized competition', *European Economic Review*, 43, 409–29.

Feldman, M.P. and J. Bercovitz (2008), 'Academic entrepreneurs: change at the individual level', *Organization Science*, **19** (1), 69–89.

Feldman, M.P. and P. Desrochers (2004), 'Truth for its own sake: academic culture and technology transfer at the Johns Hopkins University', *Minerva*, 24, 105–26.

Fernandez, N. (2007), 'Porque sigue creciendo mas el interior del pais', www.clarin.com, El Clarín, accessed 2 February.

Ferri, G. and Z. Rotondi (2006), 'Does finance matter in the re-specialization of Italy's industrial districts?', in G. Bracchi and D. Masciandaro (eds), *Banche e geografia, XI Rapporto sul sistema finanziario italiano*, Fondazione Rosselli, Roma: Edibank, pp. 397–433.

Figueredo, A., J.S. Costa and M.R. Silva (1994), 'Estratégia para a competitividade da Indústria do Norte', *A Indústria do Norte*, 1.

Finaldi Russo, P. and P. Rossi (1999), 'Costo e disponibilità del credito per le imprese nei distretti industriali', *Temi di discussione*, no. 360, Servizio studi, Banca d'Italia.

Finaldi Russo, P. and P. Rossi (2001), 'Credit constraints in Italian industrial districts', *Applied Economics*, **33** (11), 1469–77; published in Italian as 'Costo e disponibilità del credito per le imprese nei distretti industriali', in Signorini (2000), pp. 203–35.

Findlay, R. and K.H. O'Rourke (2003), 'Commodity market integration, 1500–2000. Globalization in historical perspective', in *NBER Conference Report series*, Chicago and London: University of Chicago Press, pp. 13–62.

Fine, C. (2006), *A Mind of its Own: How your Brain Distorts and Deceives*, Cambridge, UK: Icon Books.

Finger, J.M. (1976), 'Trade and domestic effects of offshore assembly provision in the US tariff', *The American Economic Review*, **66** (4), 598–611.

Finger, J.M. (1977), 'Offshore assembly provision in the West German and Netherlands tariffs: trade and domestic effects', *Weltwirtschaftliches Archiv*, **113** (2), 237–49.

Florida, R. (2002), *The Rise of Creative Class*, New York: Basic Books.

Focarelli, D., F. Panetta and C. Salleo (2002), 'Why do banks merge?', *Journal of Money, Credit and Banking*, 34, 1047–66.

Fondazione Edison (2006a), 'Indice Edison dell'export dei distretti industriali italiani', Approfondimenti statistici, *Quaderno*, no. 2, February.

Fondazione Edison (2006b), 'L'Italia ai vertici mondiali nelle "4A"', Approfondimenti statistici, *Quaderno*, no. 7, December.

Fontagné, L., M. Freudenberg and G. Gaulier (2005), 'Disentangling horizontal and vertical intra-industry trade', *WP Cepii*, no. 10.

Fontaine, L. (1996), 'Gli studi sulla mobilità in Europa nell'età moderna: problemi e prospettive di ricerca', *Quaderni Storici*, Dec., 739–56.

Fontaine, L. (2005), 'Montagnes et migrations de travail. Un essai de comparaison globale (XVe–XXe siècles)', *Revue d'histoire moderne et contemporaine*, **52** (2), 26–48.

Fontana, G.L. (ed.) (1985), *Schio e Alessandro Rossi. Imprenditorialità, politica, cultura e paesaggi sociali del secondo Ottocento*, Roma.

Fontana, G.L. (1990), *Mercanti, pionieri e capitani d'industria. Imprenditori e imprese nel vicentino tra '700 e '900*, Vicenza: Neri Pozza editore.

Fontana, G.L. (ed.) (1997), *Le vie dell'industrializzazione europea: modelli a confronto*, Bologna: Il Mulino.

Fontana, G.L. and G. Gayot (eds) (2004), *Wool, Products and Markets*, Padova: Cleup.

Foresti, G. and S. Trenti (2006), 'Apertura delle filiere produttive: la nuova collocazione dell'industria italiana nello scenario internazionale', in G. Tattara, G. Corò and M. Volpe (2006), *Andarsene per continuare a crescere. La delocalizzazione internazionale come strategia competitiva*, Roma: Carocci, pp. 87–112.

Forni, M. (1987), *Storie di famiglia e storie di proprietà. La scomparsa della mezzadria in Italia*, Torino: Rosenberg & Sellier.

Fortis, M. (2005), *Le due sfide del made in Italy: globalizzazione e innovazione, Profili di analisi della Seconda Conferenza nazionale sul commercio con l'estero*, Bologna: Il Mulino.

Fortis, M. (2006), 'I distretti produttivi e la loro rilevanza nell'economia italiana: alcuni profili di analisi', in Fortis and Quadrio Curzio (2006), pp. 109–288.

Fortis, M. and M. Carminati (2004), 'Le azioni a sostegno della ricerca science based', *Economia italiana*, Quarterly review published by Capitalia, **1** (Jan.-Apr.), 117–47.

Fortis, M. and A. Quadrio Curzio (eds) (2006), *Industria e distretti. Un paradigma di perdurante competitività italiana*, Bologna: Il Mulino.

Foundation for MSME Clusters (2007), *Policy and Status Paper on Cluster Development in India*, New Delhi.

Frank, R. (2001), *Luxury Fever*, New York: The Free Press.

Freeman, C. (1991), 'Networks of innovators: a synthesis of research issues', *Research Policy*, 20, 499–554.

Frenken, K., F.G. van Oort and T. Verburg (2007), 'Related variety, unrelated variety and regional economic growth', *Regional Studies*, **41** (5), 685–97.

Frey, L. (1975), *Lavoro a domicilio e decentramento dell'attività produttiva nei settori tessili e dell'abbigliamento in Italia*, Milano: Franco Angeli.

Friedberg, E. (1993), *Le pouvoir et la règle: dynamiques de l'action organisée*, Paris: Seuil.

Friedman, T. (2005), *The World is Flat*, New York: Farrar, Straus, Giroux.

Frost Kumpf, H.A. (1998), *Cultural District: The Arts as a Strategy for Revitalizing our Cities*, Washington, DC: Institute for Community Development and the Arts, Americans for the Arts.

Fuà, G. (1983), 'L'industrializzazione nel Nord Est e nel Centro', in Fuà and Zacchia (1983), pp. 7–46.

Fuà, G. and C. Zacchia (1983), *Industrializzazione senza fratture*, Bologna: Il Mulino.

Fujita, M., P. Krugman and A. Venables (1999), *The Spatial Economy: Cities, Regions, and International Trade*, Cambridge, MA: MIT Press.

Gagliardi, C. (2006), 'Supply-chain strategies and local roots of Italy's medium-sized industrial firms', *Review of Economic Conditions in Italy*, 3, 413–42.

Gallino, L. (2003), *La scomparsa dell'Italia industriale*, Torino: Einaudi.

Ganne, B. (1990), *Industrialisation diffuse et systèmes industriels localizes: essai de bibliographie critique du cas français*, Geneva: Institut international d'études sociales-BIT.

Ganne, B. (ed.) (1992), *Développement local et ensemble de PME*, Lyon: GLYSI.

Gans, H.J. (1962), *The Urban Villagers: Group and Class in the Life of Italian-Americans*, New York: The Free Press.

Garden, M. (1969), *Lyon et les lyonnais au XVIIIe siècle*, Paris: Flammarion.

Garin, E. (1994), *L'umanesimo italiano*, Roma-Bari: Laterza.

Garnsey, E. and P. Heffernan (2005), 'Clustering as multi-levelled activity: the Cambridge case', presented at the *4th European Meeting on Applied Evolutionary Economics*, 19–21 May, De Uithof, Utrecht, The Netherlands.

Garofoli, G. (1981), 'Lo sviluppo delle aree periferiche nell'economia italiana degli anni settanta', *L'Industria, Rivista di economia e politica industriale*, **2** (3).

Garofoli, G. (1983a), *Industrializzazione diffusa in Lombardia*, Milano: IReR-Franco Angeli.

Garofoli, G. (1983b), 'Aree di specializzazione produttiva e piccole imprese in Europa', *Economia Marche*, **2** (1), 3–46.

Garofoli, G. (1989a), 'Modelli locali di sviluppo: i sistemi di piccola impresa', in G. Becattini (ed.), *Modelli locali di sviluppo*, Bologna: Il Mulino, pp. 75–90.

Garofoli, G. (1989b), 'Industrial districts: structure and transformation', *Economic Notes*, **19** (1), 37–54.

Garofoli, G. (ed.) (1992), *Endogenous Development and Southern Europe*, Aldershot: Avebury.

Garofoli, G. (1993), 'Economic development, organisation of production and territory', *Revue d'économie industrielle*, 64, II term.

Garofoli, G. (ed.) (2003), *Impresa e territorio*, Bologna: Il Mulino.

Garofoli, G. and B. Musyck (2003), 'Innovation policies for SME: an overview of policy instruments', in B.T. Asheim, A. Isaksen, C. Nauwelaers and F. Tödtling (eds), *Regional Innovation Policy for Small–Medium Enterprises*, Cheltenham, UK and Northampton, MA, USA: Edward Elgar.

Gayot, G. (2003), 'Frontières, barrières douanières et métamorphoses des territoires industriels entre Meuse et Elbe (1750–1815)', *Revue du Nord*, 352, 781–808.

Gem News (2007), 'ICA signs MOU with the CCPIT Panyu branch to promote colored gemstones in China', 29 September 2007, www.gemstone.org/gemnews/icanews_panyubranch.html, accessed 30 August 2008.

Georgescu-Roegen, N. (1971), *The Entropy Law and the Economic Process*, Cambridge, MA: Harvard University Press.

Georgescu-Roegen, N. (1976), *Energy and Economic Myths*, New York: Pergamon Press; published in Italian as N. Georgescu-Roegen (1982), *Energia e miti economici*, Torino: Boringhieri.

Gereffi, G. (1994), 'The organisation of buyer–driver global commodity chains: how US retailers shave overseas production networks', in G. Gereffi and M. Korzeniewicz (eds), *Commodity Chains and Global Capitalism*, Westport, CT: Greenwood Press, pp. 95–122.

Gereffi, G. (1999), 'International trade and industrial upgrading in the apparel commodity chain', *Journal of International Economics*, **48** (1), 37–70.

Gereffi, G. (2002), 'The international competitiveness of Asian economies in the apparel commodity chain', *ERD Working Paper*, no. 5.

Gereffi, G. (2006), *The New Offshoring of Jobs and Global Development*, ILO Social Policy Lectures, Geneva: ILO.

Gereffi, G., J. Humphrey and T. Sturgeon (2005), 'The governance of global value chains', *Review of International Political Economy*, **12** (1), 78–104.

Gerschenkron, A. (1962), *Economic Backwardness in Historical Perspective: A Book of Essays*, Boston, MA: Belknap Press.

Gerstner, L. Jr (2002), *Who Says Elephants Can't Dance?*, New York: Harper Collins.

Gertler, M.S. (2001), 'Best practice? Geography, learning and the institutional limits to strong convergence', *Journal of Economic Geography*, 1, 5–26.

Gertler, M.S. (2003), 'Tacit knowledge and the economic geography of context, or The undefinable tacitness of being (there)', *Journal of Economic Geography*, **3** (1), 75–99.

Gianelle, C. and G. Tattara (2009), 'Manufacturing abroad while making profits at home: Veneto footwear and clothing industry', in M. Morroni (ed.), *Corporate Governance, Organization and the Firm: Co-operation and Outsourcing in a Globalised Market*, Cheltenham, UK and Northampton, MA, USA: Edward Elgar.

Giddens, A. (1984), *Constitution of Society, Outline of the Theory of Structuration*, Cambridge: Polity Press.

Gigliobianco, A. (1997), 'Banche locali negli anni Cinquanta', in F. Cesarini, G. Ferri and M. Giardino (eds), *Credito e sviluppo*, Bologna: Il Mulino.

Gilly, J.-P. and B. Pecqueur (1995), 'La dimension locale de la régulation', in R. Boyer and Y. Saillard (eds), *Théorie de la régulation: l'état des savoirs*, Paris: La Découverte, pp. 304–12.

Gilovich, T., D. Griffin and D. Kahneman (eds) (2002), *Heuristics and Biases: The Psychology of Intuitive Judgment*, Cambridge: Cambridge University Press.

Gilson, R., V. Goldberg, Ch.F. Sabel and R. Scott (2008), 'Contracting for innovation', draft, Columbia Law School.

Giner, J.M. and M.J. Santa María (2002), 'Territorial systems of small firms in Spain: an analysis of productive and organizational characteristics in industrial districts', *Entrepreneurship and Regional Development*, **14** (3), 211–28.

Ginsburgh, V. and D. Throsby (eds) (2006), *Handbook on the Economics of Art and Culture*, Amsterdam: Elsevier.

Ginzburg, A. (2004), 'Sebastiano Brusco e la facoltà di Economia di Modena', *Economia e Politica Industriale*, 121, 99–106.

Ginzburg, A. and A. Simonazzi (1995), 'Patterns of production and distribution in Europe: the case of the textile and clothing sector', in R. Schiattarella (ed.), *New Challenges for European and International Business*, Roma: Litografia Ranieri, pp. 261–83.

Giovannini, P. (2001), 'Società locali in trasformazione', *Sviluppo locale*, **8** (17), 5–15.

Giovannini, P. (2006a), 'Declino o trasformazione?', in P. Giovannini (ed.), *La sfida del declino industriale. Un decennio di cambiamenti*, Roma: Carocci, pp. 23–41.

Giovannini, P. (2006b), 'Economics and sociology', in Raffaelli, Becattini and Dardi (2006), pp. 162–71.

Giovannini, P. et al. (2001), 'Il distretto e la città: pratiche di disuguaglianza', in L. Bianco (ed.), *L'Italia delle disuguaglianze*, Roma: Carocci, pp. 117–68.

Girma, S., D. Greenaway and R. Kneller (2004), 'Does exporting increase productivity? A microeconometric analysis of matched firms', *Review of International Economics*, **12** (5), 855–66.

Giuliani, E. (2005), 'Cluster absorptive capacity', *European Urban and Regional Studies*, **12** (3), 269–88.

Giuliani, E. and M. Bell (2005), 'The micro-determinants of meso-level learning and innovation: evidence from a Chilean wine cluster', *Research Policy*, 34, 47–68.

Giuliani, E., R. Rabellotti and M.P. van Dijk (eds) (2005), *Cluster Facing Competition: the Importance of External Linkages*, Aldershot: Ashgate.

GJEPC-KPMG (2006), *The Global Gems and Jewellery Industry: Vision 2015: Transforming for Growth*, Mumbai, India: The Gem and Jewellery Export Promotion Council of India.

Glaeser, E.L. (2003), 'Psychology and the market', *Discussion paper*, no. 2023, Cambridge, MA: Harvard Institute of Economic Research.

Glaeser, E.L. (2005), 'Review of Richard Florida's *The Rise of the Creative Class*', *Regional Sciences and Urban Economics*, 35, pp. 593–6.

Glaeser, E.L., H.D. Kallal, J.A. Scheinkman and A. Shleifer (1992), 'Growth in cities', *Journal of Political Economy*, **100** (6), 1126–52.

Glasmeier, A. (1991), 'Technological discontinuities and flexible production networks: the case of Switzerland and the world watch industry', *Research Policy*, 20, 469–86.

Gobbi, G. (2005), 'Il ruolo della banca locale nel finanziamento delle reti di imprese: il caso dei distretti industriali', in F. Cafaggi and D. Galletti (eds), *La crisi dell'impresa nelle reti e nei gruppi*, Padova: Cedam, pp. 115–36.

Goglio, S. (1999), 'Local public goods: productive and redistributive aspects', *Economic Analysis*, 1, 5–21.

Gola, C. and A. Mori (2000), 'Concentrazione spaziale della produzione e specializzazione internazionale dell'industria italiana', in Signorini (2000), pp. 67–100.

Goldberg, P.K. (1995), 'Product differentiation and oligopoly in international markets: the case of the US auto industry', *Econometrica*, **63** (4), 891–951.

Goodman, E. and J. Bamford (eds) (1989), *Small Firms and Industrial Districts in Italy*, London: Routledge.

Gottardi, G. (1996), 'Technology strategies, innovation without R&D and the creation of knowledge within industrial districts', *Industry and Innovation*, **3** (2), 119–34.

Government of Punjab (1970), *Ludhiana District Gazetteer*, Ludhiana: Government of India Publications.

Grabher, G. (1990), 'On the weakness of strong ties. The ambivalent role of inter-firm relations in the decline and reorganization of the Ruhr', *Discussion Paper*, FS I 90–4, Berlin: Labour Market and Employment Research, WZB.

Grabher, G. (1991), 'Building cathedrals in the desert: new patterns of cooperation between large and small firms in the coal, iron and steel complex of the German Ruhr area', in Bergman, Maier and Tödtling (1991).

Grabher, G. (ed.) (1993a), *The Embedded Firm: On the Socioeconomics of Industrial Networks*, London: Routledge.

Grabher, G. (1993b), 'The weakness of strong ties: the lock-in of regional development in the Ruhr area', in Grabher (1993), pp. 255–77.

Grabher, G. (2002), 'Production in projects: economic geographies of temporary collaboration', *Regional Studies*, **36** (3), 229–45.

Gracia, R. and I. Segura (2003), 'Los centros tecnológicos y su compromiso con la competitividad, una oportunidad para el sistema español de innovación', *Economía Industrial*, 354, 71–84.

Gramsci, A. (1971), *Selections from Prison Notebooks*, London: Lawrence and Wishart.

Gramsci, A. (1975), *Sul Risorgimento*, Roma: Editori Riuniti.

Grandi, A. (2007), *Tessuti compatti. Distretti e istituzioni intermedie nello sviluppo italiano*, Torino: Rosenberg & Sellier.

Granovetter, M. (1973), 'The strength of weak ties', *American Journal of Sociology*, 78, 1360–80.

Granovetter, M. (1985), 'Economic action and social structure: the problem of embeddedness', *American Journal of Sociology*, 91, 481–510.

Granovetter, M. (1992), 'Problems of explanation in economic sociology', in N. Nohria and R.G. Eccles (eds), *Networks and Organizations: Structure, Form and Action*, Boston: Harvard Business School Press, pp. 1–22.

Granovetter, M. (2005), 'Business groups and social organization', in N.J. Smelser and R. Swedberg (eds), *The Handbook of Economic Sociology*, Princeton, US: Princeton University Press, pp. 429–50.

Graziani, G. (2001), 'International subcontracting in the textile and clothing industry', in S.W. Arndt and H. Kierzkowsky (eds), *Fragmentation. New Production Patterns in the World Economy*, Oxford: Oxford University Press, pp. 209–30.

Greunz, L. (2004), 'Knowledge spillovers, innovation and catching up of regions', doctoral thesis, Université Libre de Bruxelles, Dulbea, CERT: Faculté des Sciences Sociales, Politiques et Economiques, Section des Sciences Economiques.

Groenewegen, P. (1995), *A Soaring Eagle: Alfred Marshall 1842–1924*, Aldershot, UK and Brookfield, US: Edward Elgar.

Grossetti, M., J.M. Zuliani and R. Guillaume (2006), 'La spécialisation cognitive. Les systèmes locaux de compétences en Midi-Pyrénées', *Les Annales de la recherche urbaine*, **101** (November), 23–31.

Grossman, G.M. and E. Rossi-Hansberg (2006), 'Trading tasks: a simple theory of offshoring', *NBER Working Paper*, no. 12171, Cambridge, MA, www.nber.org, accessed 20 December 2008.

Gualerni, G. (2001), *L'altra economia e l'interpretazione di Adam Smith*, Milano: Vita e Pensiero.

Guelpa, F. and S. Micelli (eds) (2007), *I distretti industriali del terzo millennio. Dalle economie di agglomerazione alle strategie di impresa*, Bologna: Il Mulino.

Guelpa, F. and V. Tirri (2006), 'The effect of market structure and relationship lending on credit tightening', mimeo, Banca Intesa.

Guenzi, A. (1986), 'La tessitura domestica a Como tra Sette e Ottocento', in *Archivio Storico Lombardo*, 112, 233–52.

Guenzi, A. (1997), 'La storia economica e i distretti industriali marshalliani: qualche considerazione su approcci e risultati', in Belfanti and Maccabelli (1997), pp. 19–29.

Guenzi, A., P. Massa and F. Piola Caselli (eds) (1998), *Guilds, Markets and Work Regulation in Italy, 16th–19th Centuries*, Aldershot: Ashgate.

Guerrieri, P. and C. Pietrobelli (2004), 'Industrial districts' evolution and technological regimes: Italy and Taiwan', *Technovation*, **24** (11), 899–914.

Guerrieri, P., S. Iammarino and C. Pietrobelli (2001), *The Global Challenge to Industrial Districts: Small and Medium-sized Enterprises in Italy and Taiwan*, Cheltenham, UK and Northampton, MA, USA: Edward Elgar.

Guiso, L. and F. Schivardi (2007), 'Spillovers in industrial districts', *Economic Journal*, **117** (516), 68–93.

Guiso, L., P. Sapienza and L. Zingales (2006), 'Does culture affect economic outcomes?', *Journal of Economic Perspectives*, 20, 23–48.

Gul, F. and W. Pesendorfer (2001), 'Temptation and self-control', *Econometrica*, **69** (6), 1403–35.

Gulati, M. (1997), *Restructuring and Modernization of Small and Medium Enterprise Clusters in India*, report, New Delhi: UNIDO.

Gulati, R. and M. Gargiulo (1999), 'Where do interorganisational networks come from?', *American Journal of Sociology*, 104, 1439–93.

Gumuchian, H. and B. Pecqueur (2007), *La ressource territoriale*, Paris: Economica-Anthropos.

Hafter, D.M. (2001), 'Women in the underground business of eighteenth-century Lyon', *Enterprise & Society*, 2, March, 11–40.

Hahn, F.H. (1984), *Equilibrium and Macroeconomics*, Oxford: Basil Blackwell.

Håkanson, L. (2005), 'Epistemic communities and cluster dynamics: on the role of knowledge in industrial districts', *Industry and Innovation*, **12** (4), 433–63.

Halinen, A. and J. Törnroos (1998), 'The role of the embeddedness in the evolution of business networks', *Scandinavian Journal of Management*, 14, 187–205.

Hall, P. (2000), 'Creative cities and economic development', *Urban Studies*, **37** (4), 639–49.

Hall, P. and D. Soskice (eds) (2001a), *Varieties of Capitalism: The Institutional Foundations of Comparative Advantage*, Oxford: Oxford University Press.

Hall, P. and D. Soskice (2001b), 'Introduction', in Hall and Soskice (2001a), pp. 1–68.

Hall, P. and P. Hubbard (1998), *The Entrepreneurial City*, Chichester: John Wiley.

Hansen, G. (1996), *A Guide to Entrepreneurial Initiatives for Local Economic Development*, ILO-UNDO LED Programme, Geneva: ILO.

Harris, M. (1977), *Cannibal and King. The Origin of Culture*, New York: Random House.

Harrison, B. (1992), 'Industrial districts: old wine in new bottles?', *Regional Studies*, **26** (5), 469–83.

Harrison, B. (1994), *Lean and Mean: Why Large Corporations will Continue to Dominate the Global Economy*, New York: Basic Books.

Hart, N. (1996), 'Marshall's theory of value: the role of external economies', *Cambridge Journal of Economics*, **20** (3), 353–69.

Harvard University (2003), 'Cluster Mapping Project', Institute for Strategy and Competitiveness, Harvard Business School, www.hbswk.hbs.edu/item/3245.html, accessed 20 December 2008.

Haselton, M.G., D. Nettle and P.W. Andrews (2005), 'The evolution of cognitive bias', in D.M. Buss (ed.), *The Handbook of Evolutionary Psychology*, Hoboken, NJ: John Wiley and Sons, pp. 724–46.

Hausmann, R. and D. Rodrik (2002), 'Economic development as self-discovery', *NBER Working Paper*, no. 8952, Cambridge, MA.
Hausmann, R., D. Rodrik and Ch.F. Sabel (2008), 'Reconfiguring industrial policy: a framework with an application to South Africa', *HKS Working Paper*, no. RWP08–031, August.
Hayek, F.A. (1948a), *Individualism and Economic Order*, Chicago: University of Chicago Press.
Hayek, F.A. (1948b), 'The meaning of competition', in Hayek (1948a), pp. 92–106.
Hayek, F.A. (1978), 'Competition as a discovery procedure', in F.A. Hayek, *New Studies in Philosophy, Politics, Economics and the History of Ideas*, Chicago: University of Chicago Press, pp. 179–90.
Hayes, J.G. (2002), *This Thing Called Courage: South Boston Stories*, New York: Harrington Park Press.
He, C. and F. Pan (2006), 'Spillover effects or crowding out effects. An empirical study on FDI in the manufacturing Industry in Beijing', *China Soft Science*, 7, 96–104.
Heanue, K. and D. Jacobson (2001–02), 'Organizational proximity and institutional learning: the evolution of a spatially-dispersed network in the Irish furniture industry', *International Studies of Management and Organization*, special issue on *Clustering, Capabilities and Coordination*, 31, 56–72.
Heanue, K. and D. Jacobson (2008), 'Embeddedness and innovation in low and medium tech rural enterprises', *Irish Geography*, **41** (1), 113–37.
Hearn, W.E. (1864), *Plutology*, London: Macmillan and Co. and Melbourne: George Robertson.
Hearn, W.E. (1879), *The Aryan Household*, London: Longmans and Co.
Helg, R. and L. Tajoli (2005), 'Patterns of international fragmentation of production and the relative demand for labour', *The Northern American Journal of Economics and Finance*, **16** (2), 233–54.
Helper, S., J.P. MacDuffie and Ch.F. Sabel (2000), 'Pragmatic collaborations: advancing knowledge while controlling opportunism', *Industrial and Corporate Change*, **9** (3), 443–88.
Henderson, J.V. (1986), 'Efficiency of resource usage and city size', *Journal of Urban Economics*, **19** (1), 47–70.
Henderson, J. (1987), 'Semiconductors, Scotland and the international division of labour', *Urban Studies*, **24** (5), 389–408.
Henderson, J.V. (1999), 'Marshall's economies', *NBER Working Paper*, no. 7358, Cambridge, MA, www.nber.org, accessed 20 December 2008.
Henderson, J.V. (2003), 'The urbanization process and economic growth: the so-what question', *Journal of Economic Growth*, **8** (1), 47–71.
Henderson, J.V., A. Kuncoro and M. Turner (1995), 'Industrial development in cities', *Journal of Political Economy*, **103** (5), 1067–85.
Hernández, F. and V. Soler (2003), 'Cuantificación del "efecto distrito" a través de medidas no radiales de eficiencia técnica', *Investigaciones regionales*, 3, 25–40.

Hernes, T. (2003), 'Organization as evolution of space', in G. Czarniawska and G. Sevón (eds), *Northern Light. Organization Theory in Scandinavia*, Liber, Malmö, pp. 267–89.

Herrigel, G. (2009), 'Flexibility and formalization: rethinking space and governance in corporations and manufacturing regions', in K. Bluhm and R. Schmidt (eds), *Small and Medium-sized Enterprises and New European Capitalism: Persistence and Change*, forthcoming.

Hess, M. (2004), '"Spatial" relationships? Towards a reconceptualization of embeddedness', *Progress in Human Geography*, 28, 165–86.

Hickson, P. and E. Hunter (1991), 'A new theory of guilds and European economic development', *Explorations in Economic History*, **28** (2), 127–68.

Higgins, D. and G. Tweedale (1995), 'Asset or liability? Trade marks in the Sheffield cutlery and tool trades', *Business History*, **37** (3), 1–27.

Hindess, B. (2001), 'Power, government, politics', in K. Nash and A. Scott (eds), *The Blackwell Companion to Political Sociology*, Malden, MA: Blackwell, pp. 40–48.

Hirsch-Kreinsen, H., D. Jacobson and P.L. Robertson (2006), '"Low-tech" industries: innovativeness and development perspectives. A summary of a European research project', *Prometheus*, 24, 4–21.

Hirschman, A.O. (1958), *The Strategy of Economic Development*, New Haven, CT: Yale University Press.

Hirschman, A.O. (1967), *Development Projects Observed*, Washington, DC: The Brookings Institution.

Hirschman, A. (1977), 'A generalized linkage approach to development, with special reference to staples', *Economic Development and Cultural Change*, **25** (supplement), 67–98.

Hirschman, A.O. (1981), *Essays in Trespassing: Economics to Politics and Beyond*, Cambridge, MA: Cambridge University Press.

Hirschman, A.O. (1982), *Shifting Involvements. Private Interest and Public Action*, Oxford: Martin Robertson.

Hirschman, A.O. (1986), *Vers une économie politique élargi*, Paris: Seuil.

Hodgson, G.M. (1993), *Economics and Evolution: Bringing Life Back into Economics*, Cambridge: Polity Press.

Hodgson, G.M. (1998), 'The approach of institutional economics', *Journal of Economic Literature*, **36** (1), 166–92.

Hodgson, G.M. (2007), 'Meanings of methodological individualism', *Journal of Economic Methodology*, 14, 211–26.

Hofstede, G. (1980), *Culture's Consequences: International Differences in Work-related Values*, Beverly Hills, CA: Sage.

Holmes, T.J. (1999), 'Localization of industry and vertical disintegration', *Review of Economics and Statistics*, **81** (2), 314–25.

Holmström, M. (1998), 'Bangalore as an industrial district: flexible specialization in a labour-surplus economy?', in P. Cadene and M. Holmstrom (eds),

Decentralized Production in India: Industrial Districts, Flexible Specialization and Employment, New Delhi: Sage, pp. 169–229.

Hong Kong Productivity Council (2005), 'Hong Kong productivity council collaborates with Panyu government to support the development of the jewellery industry', Press Release, Hong Kong, China.

Hopkins, E. (1998), *The Rise of the Manufacturing Town. Birmingham and the Industrial Revolution*, London: Sutton.

Huang, Y. (1999), 'An analysis of the Zhejiang "Lump Economy"', *China Industrial Economy* (in Chinese), 5, 58–60.

Hubbard, P. (2006), *City*, London: Routledge.

Hudson, P. (1989), *Regions and Industries: Perspectives on the Industrial Revolution*, Cambridge: Cambridge University Press.

Humphrey, J. (1995), 'Industrial reorganization in developing countries: from models to trajectories', **23** (1), 149–62.

Humphrey, J. and H. Schmitz (1996), 'The triple "C" approach to local industrial policy', *World Development*, **24** (12), 1859–77.

Humphrey, J. and H. Schmitz (2001), 'Governance in global value chains', *IDS Bulletin*, **32** (3), 19–23.

Humphrey, J. and H. Schmitz (2004), 'Governance and upgrading', in Schmitz (2004), pp. 1–19.

Hunker, H.L. (ed.) (1964), *Erich W. Zimmermann's Introduction to World Resources*, New York and London: Evanston.

Hymer, S. (1972), 'The multinational corporation and the law of uneven development', in J.N. Bhagwati (ed.), *Economics and World Order. From the 1970s to the 1990s*, London: Macmillan, pp. 113–40.

ICE (Italian Institute for Foreign Trade) (2005), 'Research Report on the Jewellery Sector in Hong Kong', Hong Kong.

Illeris, S. (1992), 'The Herning-Ikast textile industry: an industrial district in West Jutland', *Entrepreneurship and Regional Development*, **4** (1), 73–84.

ILO (2002), 'Decent work in the informal economy', *Report VI to the International Labour Conference*, 90th session, Geneva.

ILO (2005), *World Employment Report 2004–05: Employment, Productivity and Poverty Reduction*, Geneva.

ILO (2006), *Global Employment Trends*, Geneva.

ILO (2008a), *Global Employment trends*, Geneva.

ILO (2008b), *Key Indicators of the Labour Market*, 5th edition, Geneva: ILO.

IPI (Istituto per la promozione industriale) (2002), *L'esperienza italiana dei distretti industriali*, Roma: Ministero delle Attività Produttive.

Isaksen, A. (ed.) (1999), *Regionala innovasjonssystemer. Innovasjon og laering i 10 regionale naeringsmiljöer*, STEP R–02. Oslo: STEP.

Isaksen, A. and E. Hauge (2002), 'Regional clusters in Europe', *Thematic Report*, no. 3, European Observatory for SMEs, European Commission, September.

ISTAT (1997), *I sistemi locali del lavoro 1991*, edited by F. Sforzi, Roma: ISTAT.
ISTAT (2001), *8° Censimento generale dell'industria e dei servizi. 22 ottobre 2001*, Roma: ISTAT.
ISTAT (2002), *Le esportazioni dai sistemi locali del lavoro*, edited by S. Menghinello, Collana Argomenti, no. 22, Roma: ISTAT.
ISTAT (2005), *I sistemi locali del lavoro. 2001*, research report prepared by A. Orasi and F. Sforzi, www.dawinci.istat.it/daWinci/jsp/MD/download/sll_comunicato.pdf, accessed 21 July 2008.
ISTAT (2006a), *Distretti industriali e sistemi locali del lavoro 2001*, edited by F. Sforzi, Collana Censimenti, Roma: ISTAT.
ISTAT (2006b), *Distretti industriali e sistemi locali del lavoro*, edited by F. Lorenzini, 8° Censimento generale dell'industria e dei servizi, 22 ottobre 2001, Roma: ISTAT.
Itami, H., S. Matsushima and T. Kikkawa (eds) (1998), *Sangyo-shuseki no Honshitsu: Jyu-nanna Bungyo· Shuseki no Jyoken* ('The essence of industrial districts. Conditions of flexible division of work and accumulation'), Tokyo: Yuhikaku.
Iuzzolino, G. (2000), 'I distretti industriali nel censimento intermedio del 1996: dimensioni e caratteristiche strutturali', in Signorini (2000), pp. 3–20.
Iuzzolino, G. (2005), 'Identifying the geographical agglomerations of manufacturing industries' in Banca d'Italia, *Local Economies and Internationalization in Italy*, Roma: Banca d'Italia, pp. 27–51; published in Italian as 'Le agglomerazioni territoriali di imprese nell'industria italiana', in L.F. Signorini and M. Omiccioli M. (eds) (2005), *Economie locali e competizione globale: il localismo industriale italiano di fronte a nuove sfide*, Bologna: Il Mulino, pp. 41–64.
Jacobs, J. (1961), *The Death and the Life of American Cities*, New York: Random House.
Jacobs, J. (1969), *The Economy of Cities*, New York: Vintage.
Jacobson, D., K. Heanue and Z. Mottiar (2001), 'Industrial districts and networks: different modes of development of the furniture industry in Ireland?', in D. Felsenstein, R. McQuaid, Ph. McCann and D. Shefer (eds), *Public Investment and Regional Economic Development*, Cheltenham, UK and Northampton, MA, USA: Edward Elgar.
Jacquet, N. and D. Darmon (2005), *Les pôles de compétitivité: le modèle français*, Paris: La Documentation Française.
Jaffe, A.B., M. Trajtenberg and R. Henderson (1993), 'Geographic localization of knowledge spillovers as evidenced by patent citations', *Quarterly Journal of Economics*, **108** (3), 577–98.
Jalotte, P. (2000), 'CMM in practice: processes for executing software projects at Infosys', Addison-Wesley: Software Engineering Institute.
James, A., R. Martin and P. Sunley (2007), 'The rise of cultural economic geography', in R. Martin and P. Sunley, *Critical Concepts in Economic Geography*, vol. IV, *Cultural Economy*, London: Routledge.

JCK (Jewellers Circular Keystone) (2008), 'DMCC, Panyu, China to promote jewellery trade', 25 April, www.jckindia.com, accessed 30 August 2008.

Jenkins, D. and Ch. Spence (2006), *The Career Pathways How-To Guide*, New York: Workforce Strategy Center.

Jin, B., R. Rousseau, R.P. Suttmeier and C. Cao (2007), 'The role of ethnic ties in international collaboration: the overseas Chinese phenomenon', IN Proceedings of the *ISSI* 2007, Madrid: CISC, pp. 427–36.

Johannisson, B. (1978), *Företag och närsamhälle. En studie i organisation*, Växjö: Högskolan i Växjö.

Johannisson, B. (1983), 'Swedish evidence for the potential of local entrepreneurship in regional development', *European Small Business Journal*, **1** (2), 11–24.

Johannisson, B. (2000a), 'Networking and entrepreneurial growth', in D. Sexton and H. Landström (eds), *The Blackwell Handbook of Entrepreneurship*, Oxford: Blackwell Publishers, pp. 368–86.

Johannisson, B. (2000b), 'Modernising the industrial district: rejuvenation or managerial colonisation?', in E. Vatne and M. Taylor (eds), *The Networked Firm in a Global World: Small Firms in New Environments*, Aldershot: Ashgate, pp. 283–308.

Johannisson, B. (2003), 'Entrepreneurship as a collective phenomenon', in E. Genescà, D. Urbano, J. Capelleras, C. Guallarte and J. Vergès (eds), *Creación de empresas, entrepreneurship*, Barcelona: Servei de Publicacions de la Universitat Autònoma de Barcelona, pp. 87–109.

Johannisson, B. and Å. Lindholm Dahlstrand (eds) (2008), *Bridging the Functional and Territorial Rationales in Regional Entrepreneurship and Development*, Örebro: FSF.

Johannisson, B. and O.R. Spilling (1986), *Lokal naeringsutveckling*, Oslo: Universitetsforlaget.

Johannisson, B., M. Ramírez-Pasillas and G. Karlsson (2002), 'The institutional embeddedness of local inter-firm networks: a leverage for business creation', *Entrepreneurship and Regional Development*, **14** (4), 297–315.

Johannisson, B., O. Alexanderson, K. Nowicki and K. Senneseth (1994), 'Beyond anarchy and organization: entrepreneurs in contextual networks', *Entrepreneurship and Regional Development*, **6** (4), 329–56.

Johannisson, B., H. Kantis, R. Ascuá and N. Mahlet Quintar (2005), 'Distritos industriales en Argentina y Suecia. Una aplicación del análisis de redes para develar los secretos de la organización empresaria', in M. Casalet, M. Cimoli and G. Yoguel (eds), *Redes, jerarquías y dinámicas productivas*, Flacso, México: OIT, Madrid: Miño y Dávila Editores, pp. 233–71.

Johansson, B. (1991), 'Economic networks and self-organization', in Bergman, Maier and Tödtling (1991), pp. 17–34.

Johansson, D. (2001), 'The dynamics of firm and industry growth. The Swedish computing and communications industry', doctoral dissertation, Stockholm: Royal Institute of Technology.

Jones, R.J. (1933), *The Economics of Private Enterprise*, 2nd edition, London: Pitman & Sons.
Joshi, G. et al. (2005), *The Other India at Work: Job Quality in Micro and Small Enterprise Clusters*, New Delhi: ILO, Sub-regional Office for South Asia.
Judet, P. (2001), 'Du paysan à l'horloger. Histoire sociale d'un Faucigny pluri-actif (1850–1930)', *Ruralia*, 9.
Jun, M.S. (2005), 'Local production systems, endogenous development and industrialisation: the case of the Korean garment district, Dongdaemon', PhD dissertation, Madison, WI: University of Wisconsin-Madison.
Kahneman, D. and A. Tversky (1979), 'Prospect theory: an analysis of decisions under risk', *Econometrica*, 47, 313–27.
Kaldor, N. (1966), *Causes of the Slow Rate of Economic Growth of the United Kingdom*, Cambridge: Cambridge University Press.
Kalleberg, A. (2001), 'Organizing flexibility: the flexible firm in a new century', *British Journal of Industrial Relations*, **39** (4), 479–504.
Kaminski, B. and F. Ng (2000), 'Trade and production fragmentation: central European economies in EU networks of production and marketing', *World Bank Discussion Paper*.
Kaplan, S.N. and L. Zingales (1997), 'Do investment-cash flow sensitivities provide useful measures of financing constraints?', *The Quarterly Journal of Economics*, **112** (1), 169–215.
Kapur, D. (2001), 'Diasporas and technology transfer', *Journal of Human Development*, **2** (2), 265–86.
Kapur, D. and J. McHale (2005), 'The global migration of talent: what does it mean for developing countries?', CGD brief, October, Washington, DC: Center for Global Development.
Karlsson, C. (ed.) (2008), *Handbook of Research on Cluster Theory*, Cheltenham, UK and Northampton, MA, USA: Edward Elgar.
Kashyap, S.P. (1992), 'Recent developments in the small enterprises sector in India: economic and social aspects', *Discussion Paper*, no. 48, Geneva: IILS, ILO.
Kebir, L. (2004), 'Ressources et développement régional: une approche institutionnelle et territoriale', thèse de doctorat, Université de Neuchâtel.
Kebir, L. and O. Crevoisier (2008), 'Cultural resources and regional development: the case of the cultural legacy of watchmaking', in Cooke and Lazzeretti (2008), pp. 48–70.
Kenney, M. and R. Florida (1993), *Beyond Mass Production*, Oxford: Oxford University Press.
Kenney, M. and R. Florida (2000), 'Venture capital in Silicon Valley: fuelling new firm formation', in M. Kenney (ed.), *Understanding Silicon Valley: The Anatomy of an Entrepreneurial Region*, Stanford, CA: Stanford University Press, pp. 98–123.
Kenney, M. and W.R. Goe (2004), 'The role of social embeddedness in professorial entrepreneurship: a comparison of electrical engineering and computer science at UC Berkeley and Stanford', *Research Policy*, 33, 691–707.

Kenney, M. and D. Patton (2005), 'Entrepreneurial geographies: support networks in three high-technology industries', *Economic Geography*, **81** (2), 201–28.
Kerr, C. (1954), 'The Balkanization of labor market', in B.E. Wight (ed.), *Labour Mobility and Economic Opportunity*, Boston, MA: MIT Press, pp. 92–110.
Kerr, W. (2008), 'Ethnic scientific communities and international technology diffusion', *Review of Economics and Statistics*, **90** (3), 518–37.
Ketels, Ch. (2003), 'The development of the cluster concept. Present experiences and further developments', paper prepared for NRW Conference on Clusters, Duisburg, Germany, 5 December, www.competitiveness.org/article/articleview/484/1/54, accessed 17 December 2006.
Ketels, Ch. (2005), 'Creating the right match', in *What's Next? Strategic Views on Foreign Direct Investment*, Stockholm-Geneva: ISA-WAIPA-UNCTAD.
Ketels, Ch. (2007a), *The Role of Clusters in the Chemical Industry*, Brussels: EPCA.
Ketels, Ch. (2007b), 'Microeconomic determinants of the competitiveness of locations for multinational companies', in J.H. Dunning and Ph. Gugler (eds), *FDI, Location, and Competitiveness*, Oxford: Elsevier Publishing.
Ketels, Ch. and Ö. Sölvell (2006), *Clusters in the EU-Ten New Member Countries*, Brussels: European Commission, DG Industry.
Ketels, Ch., G. Lindqvist, S. Protsiv and Ö. Sölvell (2007), 'Geographic concentration in Europe and the United States', mimeo, Stockholm School of Economics.
Khanna, T. and Y. Yafeh (2007), 'Business groups in emerging markets: paragons or parasites', *Journal of Economic Literature*, 45, 331–72.
Kiyonari, T. (1978), *Chiiki-shugi no Jidai* ('Time of regionalism'), Tokyo: Toyokeizai-shinposha.
Kiyonari, T. and T. Hashimoto (eds) (1997), *Nihonngata Sangyo-shuseki no Mirai-zo* ('The future of the Japanese type of industrial districts'), Tokyo: Nihon-keizai-shinbunnsha.
Klepper, S. (2001), 'Employee start-ups in high-tech industries', *Industrial and Corporate Change*, **10** (3), 639–74.
Klepper, S. (2002), 'Capabilities of new firms and the evolution of the US automobile industry', *Industrial and Corporate Change*, 11, 645–66.
Knight, F. (1921), *Risk, Uncertainty and Profit*, Boston: Houghton Miffin.
Knorringa, P. (1996), *Economics of Collaboration: Indian Shoemakers Between Market and Hierarchy*, London: Sage.
Knorringa, P. (1999), 'Agra: an old cluster facing the new competition', *World Development*, **27** (9), 1587–604.
Knorringa, P. (2002), 'Cluster trajectories and the likelihood of endogenous upgrading', in M.P. van Dijk and H. Sandee (eds), *Innovation and Small Enterprises in the Third World*, Cheltenham, UK and Northampton, MA, USA: Edward Elgar.

Koepp, C.J. (1986), 'The alphabetical order: work in Diderot's *Encyclopedie*', in S.L. Kaplan and C.J. Koepp (eds), *Work in France*, Ithaca, NY: Cornell University Press, pp. 229–58.
Kokado, H. (1996), *Enjeru nettowa-ku: bencha- wo hagukumu amerika bunka* ('The American culture which cherishes an angel network of ventures'), Tokyo: Chuo-koronsha.
Kooiman, J. (2000), 'Societal governance. Levels, models, and order of social-political interaction', in J. Pierre (ed.), *Debating Governance*, Oxford: Oxford University Press, pp. 138–65.
Korolu, B.A., T. Ozelci and A. Uurlar (2007), 'The story of a jewelry cluster in Istanbul metropolitan area: Grand Bazaar', paper for the Regional Studies Association International Conference *Regions in Focus?*, Lisbon, 2–5 April.
Kreps, D. (1995), 'Corporate culture and economic theory', in O. Williamson and F. Scott (eds), *Transaction Cost Economics*, Aldershot, UK and Brookfield, US: Edward Elgar, pp. 497–552.
Kriedte, P., H. Medick and J. Schlumbohm (1984), *L'industrializzazione prima dell'industrializzazione*, Bologna: Il Mulino.
Krugman, P. (1991a), *Geography and Trade*, Cambridge, MA: MIT Press.
Krugman, P. (1991b), 'History versus expectations', *Quarterly Journal of Economics*, **106** (2), 651–67.
Krugman, P. (1991c), 'Increasing returns and economic geography', *Journal of Political Economy*, 99, 484–99.
Krugman, P. (1998), 'The role of geography in development', paper prepared for the Annual World Bank Conference on Development Economics, Washington, DC, 20–21 April.
Kuznetsov, Y. (ed.) (2006), *Diaspora Networks and the International Migration of Skills*, Washington, DC: World Bank Institute.
Kuznetsov, Y. and Ch.F. Sabel (2005), *Towards a New Open Economy Industrial Policy: Sustaining Growth without Picking Winners*, Washington, DC: World Bank Institute.
Laibson, D. (1997), 'Golden eggs and hyperbolic discounting', *Quarterly Journal of Economics*, **112** (2), 443–7.
Lajugie, J., P. Delfaud and C. Lacour (1985), *Espace régional et aménagement du territoire*, 2me édition, Paris: Dalloz.
Lamoreaux, N.R., D.M.G. Raff and P. Temin (2003), 'Beyond markets and hierarchies: toward a new synthesis of American business history', *The American Historical Review*, **108** (2), 404–33.
Landabaso, M. and A. Reid (1999), 'Developing regional innovation strategies: the European Commission as animator', in K. Morgan and C. Nauwelaers (eds), *Regional Innovation Strategies: Key Challenge for Europe's Less-favoured Regions*, London: The Stationary Office, in association with the Regional Studies Association, pp. 19–39.

Landesmann, M.A. and R. Scazzieri (eds) (1996), *Production and Economic Dynamics*, Cambridge: Cambridge University Press.

Lane, A.D. (2002), 'Complessità e interazioni locali. Verso una teoria dei distretti industriali', in A. Quadrio Curzio and M. Fortis (eds), *Complessità e distretti industriali. Dinamiche, modelli, casi reali*, Bologna: Il Mulino, pp. 111–40.

Langlois, R.N. (1998), 'Schumpeter and personal capitalism', in G. Eliasson, Ch. Green and Ch. McCann (eds), *Microfoundations of Economic Growth: A Schumpeterian Perspective*, Ann Arbor: University of Michigan Press, pp. 57–82.

Langlois, R.N. (2003), 'The vanishing hand: the changing dynamics of industrial capitalism', *Industrial and Corporate Change*, **12** (2), 351–85.

Langlois, R.N. (2007), *The Dynamics of Industrial Capitalism. Schumpeter, Chandler, and the New Economy*, London and New York: Routledge.

Langlois, R.N. and P.L. Robertson (1989), 'Explaining vertical integration: lessons from the American automobile industry', *Journal of Economic History*, **49** (2), 361–75.

Langlois, RN. and P.L. Robertson (1995), *Firms, Markets, and Economic Change: A Dynamic Theory of Business Institutions*, London: Routledge.

Lastres, H.M.M., J.E. Cassiolato and M.L. Maciel (eds) (2003), *Pequena empresa: cooperação e desenvolvimento local*, Rio de Janeiro: Relume Demará.

Lave, J. and E. Wenger (1991), *Situated Learning: Legitimate Peripheral Participation*, Cambridge, UK: Cambridge University Press.

Lavington, F. (1927), 'Technical influences on vertical integration', *Economica*, 7, 27–36.

Lavoie, D. (1989), 'Economic chaos or spontaneous order? Implications for political economy in the new view of science', *Cato Journal*, **8** (3), 613–35.

Lawton Smith, H. and K. Ho (2006), 'Measuring the performance of Oxford University, Oxford Brooks University and the government laboratories' spin-off companies', *Research Policy*, 35, 1554–68.

Lawton Smith, H., K. Dickson and S. Smith (1991), 'There are two sides to every story: innovation and collaboration within networks of large and small firms', *Research Policy*, 20, 457–68.

Lazaric, N. and E. Lorenz (1998), 'Introduction: the learning dynamics of trust, reputation, and confidence', in N. Lazaric and E. Lorenz (eds), *Trust and Economic Learning*, Cheltenham, UK and Northampton, MA, USA: Edward Elgar, pp. 1–20.

Lazerson, M.H. and G. Lorenzoni (1999a), 'Resisting organisational inertia: the evolution of industrial districts', *Journal of Management and Governance*, **3** (4), 361–77.

Lazerson, M.H. and G. Lorenzoni (1999b), 'The firms that feed industrial districts: a return to the Italian source', *Industrial and Corporate Change*, **8** (2), 235–66.

Lazonick, W., E. March and O. Tulum (2007), 'Boston's biotech boom', Working Paper, Center for Industrial Competitiveness, University of Massachusetts Lowell.

Lazzeretti, L. (2003), 'City of art as a high culture local system and cultural districtualization processes: the cluster of art restoration in Florence', *International Journal of Urban and Regional Research*, **27** (3), 635–48.

Lazzeretti, L. (ed.) (2004), *Art Cities, Cultural Districts and Museums*, Firenze: Firenze University Press.

Lazzeretti, L. (2006), 'Density dependent dynamics in Arezzo jewellery district (1947–2001): focus on foundings', *European Planning Studies*, **14** (4), 431–58.

Lazzeretti, L. (2008), 'The cultural districtualisation model', in Cooke and Lazzeretti (2008), pp. 93–120.

Lazzeretti, L. and D. Storai (2003), 'An ecology-based interpretation of district "complexification": the Prato district evolution from 1946 to 1993', in F. Belussi, G. Gottardi and E. Rullani (eds), *The Technological Evolution of Industrial Districts*, Boston and Dordrecht: Kluwer Academic Publishers, pp. 409–34.

Lazzeretti, L., R. Boix and F. Capone (2008) 'Do creative industries cluster? Mapping creative local production systems in Italy and Spain', *Industry and Innovation*, **15** (5), 549–67.

Le Galès, P. (2003), *Gouvernance des économies locales en France: à la recherche de la coordination perdue*, Paris, Communication, Forum de la Régulation, October.

Leamer, E.E. and M. Storper (2001), 'The economic geography of the internet age', co-authored with E. Leamer, *Journal of International Business Studies*, **32** (4), 641–66.

Lebeau, R. (1955), *La vie rurale dans les montagnes du Jura méridional. Etude de géographie humaine*, Lyon: Institut des études rhodaniennes.

Lee, S.Y., R. Florida and Z.J. Acs (2004), 'Creativity and entrepreneurship: a regional analysis of new firm formation', *Regional Studies*, **38** (8), 879–91.

Legge 5 ottobre 1991, n. 317, 'Interventi per l'innovazione e lo sviluppo delle piccole imprese', *Gazzetta Ufficiale della Repubblica Italiana*, Serie Generale n. 237 – Supplemento Ordinario n. 60, Roma.

Leoncini, R. and F. Lotti (2004), 'Are industrial districts more conducive to innovative production? The case of Emilia-Romagna', in G. Cainelli and R. Zoboli (eds), *The Evolution of Industrial Districts: Changing Governance, Innovation and Internationalisation of Local Capitalism in Italy*, Heidelberg and New York: Physica-Verlag, pp. 257–71.

Lescure, M. (ed.) (2006), *La mobilisation du territoire. Les districts industriels en Europe occidentale du XVIIe au XXe siècle*, Paris: Comité pour l'histoire économique et financière de la France.

Lester, R.K. and M.J. Piore (2004), *Innovation. The Missing Dimension*, Cambridge, MA: Harvard University Press.

Levi, G. (1985), 'Come Torino soffocò il Piemonte. Mobilità della popolazione e rete urbana nel '600 e '700', in *Centro e periferia di uno Stato assoluto*, Torino: Rosenberg & Sellier.

Levine, R. (1997), 'Financial development and economic growth: views and agenda', *The Journal of Economic Literature*, **35** (2), 688–726.

Li and Fung Research Centre (2006), 'Industrial clusters in the Pearl River Delta', no. 2, May, Hong Kong.

Lieberman, H. (1968), 'Technology: alchemist of Route 128', *New York Times*, 8 January, 139.

Liebovitz, J. (2004), '"Embryonic" knowledge-based clusters and cities: the case of biotechnology in Scotland', *Urban Studies*, **41** (5–6), 1133–55.

Life of Guangzhou (2007), 'Jewellery export base turns to domestic market', www.lifeofguangzhou.com, accessed 30 August 2008.

Ligabue, L. (1995) 'Creation d'un centre du service réel: l'experience italienne', www.unido.org/fileadmin/import/userfiles/russof/liga.pdf.

Lin, J.Y. (1987), 'The household responsibility system reform in china: a peasant's institutional choice', *American Journal of Agricultural Economics*, **69** (2), 410–15.

Lindqvist, G., Ö. Sölvell and Ch. Ketels (2003), *The Cluster Initiative Greenbook*, Stockholm: Ivory Tower.

Lipparini, A. and G. Lorenzoni (eds) (2000), *Imprenditori ed imprese*, Bologna: Il Mulino.

Little, J. (1993), 'Necessity and invention: trade in high-tech New England', *Federal Reserve Bank of Boston Regional Review*, **3** (1), 6–12.

Liu, W. (2003), 'Interdependent relationship between economic globalization and local development: obligated embeddedness', *World Regional Studies*, **12** (1), 1–9.

Lloyd-Jones, R. and M.J. Lewis (2003), 'Business networks, social habits and the evolution of a regional industrial cluster: Coventry, 1880s–1930s', in Wilson and Popp (2003), pp. 229–50.

Lluch, E. (2001), *La via valenciana*, Catarroja: Afers.

Loasby, B.J. (1990), 'Firms, markets, and the principle of continuity', in J.K. Whitaker (ed.), *Centenary Essays on Alfred Marshall*, Cambridge: Cambridge University Press, pp. 108–26.

Loasby, B.J. (1998), 'Industrial districts as knowledge communities', in M. Bellet and C. L'Harmet (eds), *Industry, Space and Competition. The Contribution of Economists of the Past*, Cheltenham, UK and Northampton, MA, USA: Edward Elgar, pp. 70–85.

Loasby, B.J. (2000), 'Market institutions and economic evolution', *Journal of Evolutionary Economics*, 10, 297–309.

Loasby, B.J. (2006), 'The early philosophical papers', in Raffaelli, Becattini and Dardi (2006), 16–25.

Locke, R. (1995), *Remaking the Italian Economy*, Ithaca: Cornell University Press.
Lockwood, D. (1964), 'Social integration and system integration', in G.C. Zollschan and H. Hirsh, *Exploration in Social Change*, London: Routledge, pp. 244–57.
Lorentzen, A. (2005), 'The spatial dimensions of knowledge sourcing', RSA International Conference, *Regional Growth Agendas*, Aalborg Denmark, 28–31 May.
Lorenzen, M. (1998), *Specialisation and Localised Learning. Six Studies on the European Furniture Industry*, Copenhagen: Copenhagen Business School.
Lorenzen, M. and L. Frederiksen (2008), 'Why do cultural industries cluster? Localisation, urbanization, products and projects', in Cooke and Lazzeretti (2008), pp. 155–79.
Lorenzen, M. and F.A. Taeube (2007), 'Breakout from Bollywood: globalization, institutions, and organizational transformation in Indian film industry', *DRUID Working Paper*, Copenhagen.
Lovering, J. (1999), 'Theory led by policy: the inadequacies of the "new regionalism"', *International Review of Urban and Regional Research*, **23** (2), 379–95.
Lowell, B.L. and S.G. Gerova (2004), 'Diasporas and economic development: state of knowledge', prepared for the World Bank.
Lowi, T. (1985), 'Why is there no socialism in the United States', *Society*, **22** (2), 34–42.
Lucas, R.B. (2005), *International Migration Regimes and Economic Development*, Cheltenham, UK and Northampton, USA: Edward Elgar.
Lundvall, B.-Å. (1985), *Product Innovation and User-Producer Interaction*, Aalborg: Aalborg University Press.
Lundvall, B.-Å. (1988), 'Innovation as an interactive process', in Dosi et al. (1988), pp. 349–69.
Lundvall, B.-Å. (ed.) (1992), *National Systems of Innovation: Towards a Theory of Innovation and Interactive Learning*, London: Pinter.
Lundvall, B.-A. and B. Johnson (1994), 'The learning economy', *Journal of Industry Studies*, 1, 23–42.
Luria, D. (2000), 'Good manufacturing jobs: recipe known, outlook uncertain', paper presented to conference on *What Future for Manufacturing: Trade Unions and the Challenges of Change in Manufacturing*, Harvard University.
Luzzatto, G. (1978), *Breve storia economica dell'Italia medievale*, Torino: Einaudi.
Macgregor, D.H. (1906), *Industrial Combination*, Cambridge: George Bell & Sons.
Macgregor, D.H. (1929), *The Evolution of Industry*, London: Thornton Butterworth Ltd.
MacLeod, G. (2001), 'New regionalism reconsidered: globalisation and the remaking of political economic space', *International Journal of Urban and Regional Research*, **25** (4), 804–29.

Madsen, T.K. and P. Servais (1997), 'The internationalization of born globals: an evolutionary process?', *International Business Review*, **6** (6), 561–83; reprinted in P.J. Buckley (ed.) (2003), *History of Management Thought. International Business*, Hampshire: Ashgate, pp. 421–44.

Madsen, T.K., E.S. Rasmussen and P. Servais (2000), 'Differences and similarities between born globals and other types of exporters', *Advances in International Marketing*, 10, 247–65.

Maggi, C. (2006), 'The salmon farming and processing cluster in Southern Chile', in Pietrobelli and Rabellotti (2006), pp. 109–40.

Maggi, E., I. Mariotti and F. Boscacci (2007), 'The indirect effect of manufacturing internationalisation on logistics: evidence from the Italian districts', *Economics and Statistics Discussion Paper*, no. 31, Università degli Studi del Molise.

Maitte, C. (1996), 'Le virtù del "bricolage": imprenditori e innovazioni a Prato tra '700 e '800', *Società e Storia*, 73, 553–95.

Maitte, C. (1997), 'Incertitudes et bricolages. L'industrie textile à Prato aux 18e et 19e siècles', *Annales histoire, sciences sociales*, **52** (6), 1275–303.

Maitte, C. (2001), *La trame incertaine. Le monde textile de Prato aux XVIIIe et XIXe siècles*, Villeneuve d'Ascq: Presses Universitaires du Septentrion.

Maitte, C. (2003), 'Etat, territoire et industries au Piémont, 18e siècle', *Revue du Nord*, **4** (Oct.-Dec.), 747–79.

Maitte, C. (2004), 'Adapter les produits, jouer sur les marchés. La fabrication des chéchias, XVIII–XIXe siècles', in Fontana and Gayot (2004), pp. 1115–42.

Malanima, P. (1982), *La decadenza di un'economia cittadina. L'industria di Firenze nei secoli XVI–XVIII*, Bologna: Il Mulino.

Malanima, P. (1986), 'Le attività industriali', in Fasano Guarini (1986), pp. 217–77.

Malanima, P. (1990), *Il lusso dei contadini*, Bologna: Il Mulino.

Malecki, E. (1991), *Technology and Economic Development*, London: Longman.

Malerba, F. (ed.) (2004), *Sectoral Systems of Innovation: Concepts, Issues and Analyses of Six Major Sectors in Europe*, Cambridge: Cambridge University Press.

Malerba, F. (2005), 'Sectoral systems: how and why innovation differs across sectors', in J. Fagerberg, D.C. Mowery and R.R. Nelson (eds), *The Oxford Handbook of Innovation*, Oxford: Oxford University Press, pp. 380–406.

Malinowski, B. (1939), 'The group and the individual in functional analysis', *American Journal of Sociology*, 44, 938–64.

Malmberg, A. and P. Maskell (2006), 'Localized learning revisited', *Growth and Change*, **37** (1), 1–18.

Marin-Arana, A.C. (2007), 'Full needle ahead', *IDB America Magazine*, 20 September, Washington, www.iadb.org, accessed 20 December 2008.

Mariotti I., G. Micucci and P. Montanaro (2004), 'Internationalisation strategies of Italian districts SMEs: an analysis on firm-level data', *ERSA*, no. 436; published in Italian as 'Le forme dell'internazionalizzazione nei distretti industriali: un'analisi su microdati di impresa', in C.A. Bollino and L. Diappi (eds) (2004), *Innovazioni metodologiche nelle scienze regionali*, Milano: Franco Angeli, pp. 177–99.

Mariti, P. (1980), *Sui rapporti tra imprese in una economia industriale moderna*, Milano: Franco Angeli.

Markusen, A. (1996), 'Sticky place in slippery space: A typology of industrial districts', *Economic Geography*, **72** (3), 293–313.

Markusen, A., G. Wassall, D. De Natale and R. Cohen (2008), 'Defining the creative economy: industry and occupational approaches', *Economic Development Quarterly*, **22** (1), 24–45.

Markusen, A., Y.-S. Lee and S. Digiovanna (1999), *Second Tier Cities: Rapid Growth beyond the Metropolis,* Minneapolis: University of Minnesota Press.

Marshall, A. (1919), *Industry and Trade*, London: Macmillan.

Marshall, A. (1920), *Principles of Economics*, 8th edition, London and New York: Macmillan; 1st edition 1890; 2nd edition 1891; 3rd edition 1895; 4th edition 1898.

Marshall, A. (1994), 'Ye machine', in W.J. Samuels (ed.), *Research in the History of Economic Thought and Methodology, Archival Supplement 4*, Greenwich, CT: JAI Press, pp. 116–32.

Marshall Library of Economics (1927), *Catalogue*, Cambridge: Cambridge University Press for Faculty of Economics.

Martin, R. (1993), 'Remapping regional policy: the end of the north/south divide?', *Regional Studies*, 27, 797–805.

Martin, R. (2006), 'The localization of industry', in Raffaelli, Becattini and Dardi (2006), pp. 393–400.

Martin, R. and P. Sunley (1996), 'Paul Krugman's geographical economics and its implications for regional development theory: a critical assessment', *Economic Geography*, **72** (3), 259–92.

Martin, R. and P. Sunley (2003), 'Deconstructing clusters: chaotic concept or policy panacea?', *Journal of Economic Geography*, **3** (1), 5–35.

Martin, R. and P. Sunley (2006), 'Path dependence and regional economic evolution', *Journal of Economic Geography*, **6** (4), 395–437.

Maskell, P. (2001), 'Towards a knowledge-based theory of the geographical cluster', *Industrial and Corporate Change*, **10** (4), 921–43.

Maskell, P. and M. Lorenzen (2004), 'The cluster as market organization', *Urban Studies*, **41** (5–6), 991–1009.

Maskell, P. and A. Malmberg (1999), 'Localised learning and industrial competitiveness', *Cambridge Journal of Economics*, **23** (2), 167–85.

Maskell, P., H. Barthelet and A. Malberg (2006), 'Building global knowledge pipelines: the role of temporary cluster', *European Planning Studies*, **14** (8), 997–1013.

Maskell, P., H. Eskelinen, I. Hannibalsson, A. Malmberg and E. Vatne (1998), *Competitiveness, Localised Learning and Regional Development*, London: Routledge.

Mathews, J.A. (2002), 'Competitive advantages of the latecomer firm: a resource-based account of industrial catch-up strategies', *Asia Pacific Journal of Management*, **19** (4), 467–88.

Mathews, J.A. and D.-S. Cho (1999), *Tiger Technology: The Creation of a Semiconductor Industry in East Asia*, Cambridge: Cambridge University Press.

Mathias, P. (1969), *The First Industrial Nation: An Economic History of Britain, 1700–1914*, London: Methuen.

Maturana, H. and F. Varela (1972), *De Maquinas y Seres Viventes*, Santiago, Chile: Editorial Universitaria.

McCormick, D. (1998), 'Enterprise clusters in African: on the way to industrialisation?', *IDS Discussion Paper*, no. 366, Brighton: Institute of Development Studies, University of Sussex.

McKendrick, N., J. Brewer and J.M. Plumb (eds) (1982), *The Birth of a Consumer Society: The Commercialization of Eighteenth-century England*, London: Indiana University Press.

McLoughlin, B. (1969), *Urban and Regional Planning: A Systems Approach*, London: Faber.

Medici, G. (ed.) (1956), *La distribuzione della proprietà fondiaria in Italia*, vol. 1, *Relazione generale,* Roma: Istituto Nazionale di Economia Agraria.

Mediobanca-Unioncamere (2005), *Le medie imprese industriali italiane (1996–2002)*, Milano: Mediobanca-Unioncamere.

Mediobanca-Unioncamere (2006), *Le medie imprese industriali italiane*, Milano: Mediobanca and Unioncamere.

Mehrotra, S. and M. Biggeri (eds) (2007a), *Asian Informal Workers: Global Risks, Local Protection*, London and New York: Routledge.

Mehrotra, S. and M. Biggeri (2007b), 'Upgrading informal micro- and small enterprises through clusters: towards a policy agenda', in Mehrotra and Biggeri (2007a).

Mei, L. and J. Wang (2008), 'The changing geography of chinese bicycle industry: the case of Tianjin bicycle cluster and its evolutionary trajectory', in AAG Annual Meeting, Boston.

Melitz, M.J. (2003), 'The impact of trade on intra-industry reallocations and aggregate industry productivity', *Econometrica*, **71** (6), 1695–725.

Ménard, C. (1995), 'Markets as institutions versus organizations as markets? Disentangling some fundamental concepts', *Journal of Economic Behavior and Organization*, 28, 161–82.

Mendels, F. (1972), 'Proto-industrialization: the first phase of the industrialization process', *Journal of Economic History*, **32** (March), 241–61.

Menghinello, S. (2004), 'Local engines of international trade: the case of industrial districts in Italy', in G. Cainelli and R. Zoboli (eds), *The Evolution of Local Capitalism in Italy*, Heidelberg and New York: Physica-Verlag, pp. 317–35.

Merlo, E. (1992), 'La lavorazione delle pelli a Milano fra Sei e Settecento. Conflitti, strategie, dinamiche', in C. Poni and S. Cerruti (eds), *Conflitti nel mondo del lavoro, Quaderni Storici*, special issue, **80** (2), 369–97.

Merzario, R. (1989), *Il capitalismo nelle montagne. Strategie famigliari nella prima fase di industrializzazione del Comasco*, Bologna: Il Mulino.

Metcalfe, J.S. (2007) 'Alfred Marshall's Mecca: reconciling the theories of value and development', *Economic Record*, 83, S1–22.

Meyer-Krahmer, F. (1990), *Science and Technology in the Federal Republic of Germany*, London: Longman.

Meyer-Stamer, J. (1999), 'From industrial policy to regional and local locational policy: experience from Santa Catarina, Brazil', *Bulletin of Latin American Research*, **18** (4), 451–68.

Miner, A.S., D.T. Eesley, M. Devaughn and T. Rura-Polley (2001), 'The magic beanstalk vision', in C.B. Schoonhoven and E. Romanelli (eds), *The Entrepreneurial Dynamic*, Stanford, CA: Stanford University Press.

Ministère de l'économie, des finances et de l'industrie (2006), *Les pôles de compétitivité au cœur de l'industrie*, Paris.

Ministero delle Attività Produttive and Istituto per la Promozione Industriale (2002), *L'esperienza italiana dei distretti industriali*, Roma: IPI.

Ministero dell'Industria, del Commercio e dell'Artigianato (1993a), 'Decreto Ministeriale 21 aprile 1993. Determinazione degli indirizzi e dei parametri di riferimento per l'individuazione, da parte delle regioni, dei distretti industriali', *Gazzetta Ufficiale della Repubblica Italiana*, Serie Generale n. 118 – Supplemento Ordinario n. 51, Roma.

Ministero dell'Industria, del Commercio e dell'Artigianato (1993b), 'Decreto Ministeriale 1° giugno 1993. Adeguamento alla disciplina comunitaria dei criteri di individuazione di piccola e media impresa e dei limiti di intervento previsti dalla Legge n. 317 del 5 ottobre 1991', *Gazzetta Ufficiale della Repubblica Italiana*, Serie Generale n. 151, Roma.

Mir-Artigues, P. and J. González-Calvet (2007), *Funds, Flows and Time*, Berlin: Springer Verlag.

Mistri, M. (2003), 'Procedural rationality and institutions. The production of norms by means of norms', *Constitutional Political Economy*, 14, 301–17.

Mistri, M. (2006), *Il distretto industriale marshalliano tra cognizione e istituzioni*, Roma: Carocci.

Miyashita, K. and D. Russell (1994), *Keiretsu: Inside the Hidden Japanese Conglomerates*, New York: McGraw-Hill.

Modiano, P. (1982), 'Competitività e collocazione internazionale dell'industria italiana: il problema dei prodotti tradizionali', *Economia e Politica Industriale*, 33.

Moen, O. and P. Servais (2002), 'Born global or gradual global? Examining the export behavior of small and medium-sized enterprises', *Journal of International Marketing*, **10** (3), 49–72.

Mokyr, J. (1990), *The Lever of Riches: Technological Creativity and Economic Progress*, Oxford: Oxford University Press.

Mokyr, J. (2002), *The Gifts of Athena. Historical Origins of the Knowledge Economy*, Princeton: Princeton University Press.

Molina, X. (2005), 'Estrategias de exploración y explotación en las aglomeraciones territoriales de empresas: una aproximación desde la perspectiva del capital social', *Cuadernos de Geografía. Universidad de Valencia*, 78, 215–36.

Molina, X. and M.T. Martínez (2004), 'Factors that identify industrial districts: an application in Spanish manufacturing firms', *Environment and Planning A*, 36, 111–26.

Morgan, K. (1997), 'The learning region: institutions, innovation and regional renewal', *Regional Studies*, **31** (5), 491–503.

Mori, G. (ed.) (1989), *Prato, storia di una città*, vol. 3, *Il tempo dell'industria (1815–1943)*, Firenze: Comune di Prato-Le Monnier.

Moroni, M. (2008), *Alle origini dello sviluppo locale. Le radici storiche della Terza Italia*, Bologna: Il Mulino.

Morroni, M. (1992), *Production Process and Technical Change*, Cambridge: Cambridge University Press.

Morvan, Y. (1985), 'L'économie industrielle et la filière', in ADEFI, *L'analyse de filière*, Paris: Economica.

Mottiar, Z. and D. Jacobson (2002), 'The importance of place, space and culture in the development of an industrial agglomeration in Ireland: the furniture industry in C. Monaghan', in K. Theile and C. O'Hogartaigh (eds), *International New Enterprise Developments*, Aachen: Shaker Verlag.

Moulaert, F. and F. Sekia (2003), 'Territorial innovation models: a critical survey', *Regional Studies*, **37** (3), 289–302.

Moussanet, M. and L. Paolazzi (eds) (1992), *Gioielli, bambole e coltelli. Viaggio de Il Sole-24 Ore nei distretti produttivi italiani*, Milano: Il Sole-24 Ore.

Mowery, D.C., R.R. Nelson, B.N. Sampat and A.A. Ziedonis (2004), *Ivory Tower and Industrial Innovation*, Stanford: Stanford University Press.

MTC (Massachusetts Technology Collaborative) (various years), *Index of the Massachusetts Innovation Economy*, Westborough, MA.

Musotti, F. (2001), 'Le radici mezzadrili dell'industrializzazione leggera', in Becattini et al. (2001), pp. 93–116.

Myrdal, G. (1957), *Economic Theory and Underdeveloped Regions*, London: Duckworth.

Nadvi, K. (1994), 'Industrial district experiences in developing countries', in United Nations (1994).

Nadvi, K. (1997), 'The cutting edge. Collective efficiency and international competitiveness in Pakistan', *IDS Discussion Paper*, no. 360, Brighton: Institute of Development Studies, University of Sussex.

Nadvi, K. (1999), 'Collective efficiency and collective failure: the response of the Sialkot surgical instrument cluster to global quality pressures', *World Development*, **27** (9), 1605–26.

Nadvi, K. and H. Schmitz (1994), 'Industrial clusters in less developed countries: review of experience and research agenda', *IDS Discussion Paper*, no. 339, Brighton: Institute of Development Studies, University of Sussex.

Nakamura, R. (1985), 'Agglomeration economies in urban manufacturing industries: A case of Japanese cities', *Journal of Urban Economics*, **17** (1), 108–24.

Nash, J. (1950), 'The bargaining problem', *Econometria*, 18, 153–62.

Natali, A. (2005), 'Risorse ambientali e sviluppo: i saperi e le regole', *Economia e società regionale*, **92** (4), 98–119.

Natali, A. (2007), 'Introduzione, Parte seconda: politiche per le piccole imprese e per lo sviluppo locale', in Natali, Russo and Solinas (2007).

Natali, A. and M. Russo (2006), 'Sebastiano Brusco e la scuola italiana di sviluppo locale', Summer School *Sebastiano Brusco*, Seneghe, OR, 7–9 July 2006, *Materiali di discussione*, no. 605, 2008, Dipartimento di economia politica, Unimore.

Natali, A., M. Russo and G. Solinas (eds) (2007), *Distretti industriali e sviluppo locale. Una raccolta di saggi*, Bologna: Il Mulino.

Nefussi, B. and C. Schwellnus (2007), 'Does FDI in manufacturing cause FDI in business services? Evidence from French firm-level data', *WP Cepii*, no. 21.

Nelson, A., D. Patton and M. Kenney (2007), 'Madison, Wisconsin. A university-centric high-technology cluster', report prepared under contract to the Center for Entrepreneurship and LEED Program of the Organization for Economic Cooperation and Development.

Nelson, R. and N. Rosenberg (1993), *Technological Systems and National Innovation*, New York: Oxford University Press.

NGA (National Governors Association) and Council on Competitiveness (2007), *Cluster-based Strategies for Growing State Economies*, Innovation America Initiative 2006–07, February.

Nicolis, G. and I. Prigogine (1989), *Exploring Complexity. An Introduction*, San Francisco: Freeman.

Nonaka, I. and H. Takeuchi (1995), *The Knowledge-creating Company*, Oxford: Oxford University Press.

North, D. (2005), *Understanding the Process of Economic Change*, Princeton: Princeton University Press.

Noteboom, B. (2000), *Learning and Innovation in Organizations and Economies*, Oxford: Oxford University Press.

Nunez, E.C. (ed.) (1998), *Guilds, Economy and Society*, Madrid: Fundacion Fomento de la historia economica.

Nurkse, R. (1967), *Problems of Capital Formation in Underdeveloped Countries and Patterns of Trade and Development*, New York: Oxford University Press.

Nuvolari, A. (2004), 'Collective invention during the British industrial revolution: the case of the Cornish pumping engine', *Cambridge Journal of Economics*, **28** (3), 347–63.

O'Hagan, J. and E. Kelly (2006), 'Geographic clustering of economic activity: the case of prominent western visual artists', International 2006 Conference ACEI, Vienna, July 2006.

O'Shea, R.P., T.J. Allen, A. Chevalier and F. Roche (2005), 'Entrepreneurial orientation, technology transfer and spinoff performance of US universities', *Research Policy*, 34, 994–1009.

ODI (Overseas Development Institute) (2008), 'Pro-poor growth and development. Linking economic growth and poverty reduction', *Briefing Paper*, no. 33, January.

OECD (1992), *Technology and the Economy: The Key Relationship*, Paris: OECD Publishing.

OECD (1999), *Boosting Innovation: The Cluster Approach*, Paris: OECD Proceedings.

OECD (2001a), *Innovation Clusters: Drivers of National Innovation Systems*, Paris: OECD Proceedings.

OECD (2001b), *The DAC Guidelines. Poverty Reduction*, Paris, OECD Publishing.

OECD (2002), *Redefining Territories. The Functional Regions*, Paris: OECD Publishing.

OECD (2005a), *Culture and Local Development*, Paris: OECD Publishing.

OECD (2005b), *OECD Handbook on Economic Globalisation Indicators*, Paris: OECD Publishing.

OECD (2007a), *Competitive Cities. A New Entrepreneurial Paradigm in Spatial Development*, Paris: OECD Publishing.

OECD (2007b), *Offshoring and Employment. Trends and Impacts*, Paris: OECD Publishing.

OECD (2007c), *Competitive Regional Clusters: National Policy Approaches*, Paris: OECD Publishing.

OECD (2007d), *Promoting Pro-poor Growth: Private Sector Development*, Paris: OECD Publishing.

Ogilvie, S. (2004), 'Guilds, efficiency and social capital: evidence from German proto-industry', *Economic History Review*, **57** (2), 286–333.

Ogilvie, S. (2007), 'Can we rehabilitate the guilds? A sceptical re-appraisal', *Cambridge Working Papers in Economics*, no. 0745, www.econ.cam.ac.uk/dae/repec/cam/pdf/cwpe0745.pdf, accessed 12 December 2008.

Okamoto, Y. (1994), *Italia no chusho-kigyo Senryaku* ('The strategy of small and medium-sized enterprises in Italy'), Tokyo: Mita-shuppankai.

Olivier, J.-M. (2004), *Des clous, des horloges et des lunettes. Les campagnards moréziens en industrie (1780–1914)*, Paris: Editions du CTHS.

Olson, G.M. and J.S. Olson (2000), 'Distance matters', *Human–Computer Interaction*, **15** (2), 139–78.
Olson, M. (1965), *The Logic of Collective Action*, Harvard: Harvard University Press.
Omiccioli, M. (2000), 'L'indagine sul campo: una presentazione', in Signorini (2000), pp. 289–97.
Onsager, K., A. Isaksen, M. Fraas and T. Johnstad (2007), 'Technology cities in Norway: innovation in local networks', *European Planning Studies*, **15** (4), 549–66.
Owen-Smith, J. and W.W. Powell (2004), 'Knowledge networks as channels and conduits: the effects of spillovers in the Boston biotechnology community', *Organization Science*, **15** (1), 5–21.
Owen-Smith, J. and W.W. Powell (2006), 'Accounting for emergence and novelty in Boston and Bay Area biotechnology', in Braunerhjelm and Feldman (2006), pp. 61–83.
Oyelaran-Oyeyinka B. and D. McCormick (2007), *Industrial Clusters and Innovation Systems in Africa*, Tokyo, New York and Paris: United Nations University Press.
Pagano, M. (2000), 'Banche e distretti industriali: una relazione speciale?', in Signorini (2000), 155–65.
Pagnini, M. (2000), 'I vincoli finanziari per le imprese distrettuali: un'analisi su dati bancari', in Signorini (2000), pp. 257–69.
Panciera, W. (1988), *I lanifici dell'alto Vicentino*, Vicenza: Associazione industriali della provincia di Vicenza.
Panciera, W. (1996), *L'arte matrice. I lanifici della Repubblica di Venezia nei secoli XVII e XVIII*, Treviso: Fondazione Benetton Studi Ricerche-Edizioni Canova.
Paniccia, I. (2006), 'Cutting through the chaos: towards a new typology of industrial districts and clusters', in B. Asheim, P. Cooke and R. Martin (eds), *Clusters and Regional Development: Critical Reflections and Explorations*, London: Routledge, pp. 90–114.
Papadakis, K. (ed.) (2008), *Cross-border Social Dialogue and Agreements: An Emerging Global Industrial Relations Framework?*, Geneva: IILS, ILO.
Parker, E. and J. Rogers (1999), 'Sectoral training initiatives in the US: building blocks of a new workforce preparation system?', in P.D. Culpepper and D. Finegold (eds), *The German Skills Machine: Sustaining Comparative Advantage in a Global Economy*, New York: Berghahn Books, pp. 326–62.
Parrilli, M.D. (2004), 'A stage and eclectic approach to industrial district development', *European Planning Studies*, **12** (8), 1115–31.
Parrilli, M.D. (2007), *SME Cluster Development: A Dynamic View of Survival Clusters in Developing Countries*, Basingstoke: Palgrave Macmillan.
Parrilli, M.D. (2009), 'Social embeddedness, collective efficiency and policy-inducement: drivers of ID development', *Entrepreneurship and Regional Development*, **20** (6), forthcoming.

Parrilli, M.D. and S. Sacchetti (2008), 'Linking learning and governance in clusters and networks', *Entrepreneurship and Regional Development*, **20** (4), 287–308.

Parvan, S.V. (2007), 'Community innovation statistics', *Statistics in Focus,* no. 81.

Paterson, B., S. Thorne, C. Canam and C. Jillings (2001), *Meta-study of Qualitative Health Research*, London: Sage.

Peaucelle J.L. (2007), *Adam Smith et la division du travail. La naissance d'une idée fausse*, Paris: L'Harmattan.

Pedersen, P.O., M.P. van Dijk and P. Rasmussen (1994), *Flexible Specialisation*, ITP Publications.

Peek, J. and E.S. Rosengren (1998), 'Bank consolidation and small business lending: it's not just bank size that matters', *Journal of Banking & Finance*, **22** (6–8), 799–819.

Pei, C. (2004), 'Improving China's competitiveness in the international labor division system', *China and World Economy*, **12** (2), 79–85.

Pellegrini, G. (2000), 'I fattori strutturali dello sviluppo locale nelle recenti analisi teoriche ed empiriche della crescita', in E. Cicciotti and A. Spaziante (eds), *Economia, territorio e istituzioni. I fattori delle politiche di sviluppo locale*, Milano: Franco Angeli, pp. 41–61.

Penrose, E. (1959), *The Theory of the Growth of the Firm*, 1st edition, Oxford: Basil Blackwell and New York: John Wiley and Sons; 2nd edition, Oxford: Basil Blackwell and New York: St Martins, 1980; revised edition, Oxford: Oxford University Press, 1995.

Pérez, F., V. Montesinos, L. Serrano and J. Fernández (2005), *La medición del capital social: una aproximación económica*, Bilbao: Fundación BBVA.

Perroux, F. (1961–69), 'La notion de pôle de croissance', reprinted in F. Perroux (1991), *L'économie du XXe siècle*, Grenoble: Presses Universitaires de Grenoble.

Pescarolo, A. (1989), 'Modelli di industrializzazione, ruoli sociali, immagini del lavoro (1895–1943)', in Mori (1989), vol. I, pp. 51–134.

Pesciarelli, E. (1999), 'W.E. Hearn on the industrial organisation of society', in M. Bellet and C. L'Harmet (eds), *Industry, Space and Competition*, Cheltenham, UK and Northampton, MA, USA: Edward Elgar.

Petersen, M.A. and R.G. Rajan (1994), 'The benefits of lending relationships: evidence from small business data', *Journal of Finance*, **49** (1), 3–37.

Pettersson, K. (2004) 'Masculine entrepreneurship. The Gnosjö discourse in a feminist perspective', in D. Hjorth and C. Steyaert (eds), *Narrative and Discursive Approaches in Entrepreneurship*, Cheltenham, UK and Northampton, MA, USA: Edward Elgar, pp. 177–93.

Peyrache-Gadeau, V. (2007), 'Natural resources, innovative *milieux* and the environmentally sustainable development of regions', *European Planning Studies*, **15** (7), 945–59.

Pfister, U. (1998), 'Craft guilds, the theory of the firm, and early modern Europe proto-industry', in S.R. Epstein and M. Prak (eds), *Guilds, Innovation, and the European Economy, 1400–1800*, Cambridge: Cambridge University Press.

Piedad Velasco, M. (2007), 'Casos sobre la promoción de redes horizontales de confecciones en Atuntaqui y calzado en Ambato en Ecuador', mimeo, UNIDO.
Pietrobelli, C. and R. Rabellotti (2004), 'Upgrading in clusters and value chains in Latin America: the role of policies', Sustainable Development Department, Best Practices Series, Washington, DC: Inter-American Development Bank.
Pietrobelli, C. and R. Rabellotti (2006), *Upgrading to Compete*, New York: Harvard University Press.
Pigou, A.C. (1920), *The Economics of Welfare*, London: Macmillan.
Pigou, A.C. (1922), 'Empty economic boxes: a reply', *Economic Journal*, 32, 458–65.
Pigou, A.C. (1924), 'Comment on D.H. Robertson's "Those empty boxes"', *Economic Journal*, 34, 30–33.
Pinch, S. and N. Henry (1999), 'Paul Krugman's geographical economics, industrial clustering and the British motor sport industry', *Regional Studies*, **33** (9), 815–27.
Pinch, S., N. Henry, M. Jenkins and S. Tallman (2003), 'From "industrial districts" to "knowledge clusters": a model of knowledge dissemination and competitive advantage in industrial agglomerations', *Journal of Economic Geography*, **3** (4), 373–88.
Piore, M.J. (1990), 'Responses to Amin and Robins', in Pyke, Becattini and Sengenberger (1990).
Piore, M.J. (1992), 'Work, labor, and action: work experience in a system of flexible production', in T. Kochan and M. Useem (eds), *Transforming Organizations*, New York: Oxford University Press, pp. 307–18; also published in Pyke, Becattini and Sengenberger (1990).
Piore, M.J. (1995), *Beyond Individualism*, Cambridge, MA: Harvard University Press.
Piore, M.J. (2000), *Rethinking International Labour Standards*, Geneva: IILS.
Piore M.J. and Ch.F. Sabel (1984), *The Second Industrial Divide. Possibilities for Prosperity*, New York: Basic Books.
Pirenne, H. (1937), *Economic and Social History of Medieval Europe*, New York: Harcourt and Brace.
Pitelis, C. (2006), 'Industrial policy: perspectives, experience, issues', in Bianchi and Labory (2006).
Pizzorno, A. (1977), 'Scambio politico e identità collettiva nel conflitto di classe', in C. Crouch and A. Pizzorno, *Conflitti in Europa*, Milano: ETAS, pp. 407–33.
Polanyi, K. (1944), *The Great Transformation*, Boston: Beacon Press.
Pollard, J.S. (2004), 'From industrial district to "urban village"? Manufacturing money and consumption in Birmingham's Jewellery Quarter', *Urban Studies*, **41** (1), 173–93.
Pollard, S. (1965), *The Genesis of Modern Management. A Study of the Industrial Revolution in Great Britain*, London: Arnold Ltd.

Poni, C. (1997), 'Fashion as flexible production: the strategies of the Lyon silk merchants in the eighteenth-century', in Sabel and Zeitlin (1997a), pp. 37–74.
Popp, A. (2001), *Business Structure, Business Culture and the Industrial District: The Potteries, c. 1850–1914*, Aldershot: Ashgate.
Popp, A. (2003), 'Network and industrial restructuring: the Widnes district and the formation of the United Alkali Company, 1890', in Wilson and Popp (2003), pp. 208–28.
Popp, A. (2007), 'Building the market: John Shaw of Wolverhampton and commercial travel in the early nineteenth century', *Business History*, **49** (3), 321–47.
Popp, A. and J. Wilson (2007), 'Life cycles, contingency, and agency: growth, development, and change in English industrial districts and clusters', *Environment and Planning A*, **39** (12), 2975–92.
Porter, M.E. (ed.) (1986), *Competition in Global Industries*, Boston: Harvard Business School Press.
Porter, M.E. (1990a), *The Competitive Advantage of Nations*, New York: The Free Press and London: Macmillan.
Porter, M.E. (1990b), *Ventaja competitiva*, CECAL.
Porter, M.E. (1998a), *On Competition*, Boston, MA: Harvard Business School Press.
Porter, M.E. (1998b), 'Clusters and the new economics of competition', in Porter (1998a), pp. 309–48.
Porter, M. (2000), 'Location, competition, and economic development: local clusters in a global economy', *Economic Development Quarterly*, **14** (1), 15–34.
Porter, M.E. (2003), 'The economic performance of regions', *Regional Studies*, **37** (6–7), 549–78.
Porter, M.E. and W. Emmons (2003), 'Institutions for collaboration: overview', *Harvard Business School Note*, no. 703–436.
Porter, M.E., Ch. Ketels and M. Delgado (2007), 'The microeconomic foundations of prosperity: findings from the business competitiveness index', in *Global Competitiveness Report 2007–2008*, London: Palgrave Macmillan.
Porter, M.E., Ch. Ketels, K. Miller and R. Bryden (2004), 'Competitiveness in rural US regions: learning and research agenda', prepared for the Economic Development Administration (EDA), Washington, DC: US Department of Commerce.
Posthuma, A. (2008), 'Seeking the high road to Jepara: challenges for economic and social upgrading in Indonesian wood furniture clusters', in J.A. Puppim (ed.), *Upgrading Clusters and Small Enterprises in Developing Countries*, special issue, Ashgate Economic Geography Series, Hampshire: Ashgate.
Powell, W. (1990), 'Neither market nor hierarchy: network forms of organization', in B. Staw and L.L. Cummings (eds), *Research in Organizational Behavior*, vol. 12, Greenwich, CT: JAI Press, pp. 295–336.
Powell, W., K.W. Koput and L. Smith-Doerr (1996), 'Interorganizational collaboration and the locus of innovation: networks of learning in biotechnology', *Administrative Science Quarterly*, **42** (1), 116–45.

Power, D. and A.J. Scott (2004), *Cultural Industries and Production of Culture*, London and New York: Routledge.
Pred, A.R. and T. Hagerstrand (1967), *Innovation Diffusion as a Spatial Process*, Chicago: University of Chicago Press.
Prencipe, A. (2003), 'Corporate strategy and systems integration capabilities: managing networks in complex systems industries', in A. Prencipe, A. Davies and M. Hobday, *The Business of Systems Integration*, Oxford: Oxford University Press, pp. 114–32.
Prigogine, I. (1980), *From Being to Becoming. Time and Complexity in the Physical Sciences*, San Francisco: Freeman.
Prigogine, I. and I. Stengers (1999), *La nuova alleanza. Metamorfosi nella scienza*, Torino: Einaudi.
Proexpansion (2003), *Estudio sobre cluster y asociatividad*, Lima: PROMPYME.
Proudfoot, N. (2004), 'The biopharmaceutical cluster in Oxford', in Crouch et al. (2004), pp. 237–60.
Puga, D. and A.J. Venables (1999), 'Agglomeration and economic development: import substitution versus trade liberalization', *Economic Journal*, **109** (455), 292–311.
Putnam, R.D. (1993), *Making Democracy Work: Civic Traditions in Modern Italy*, Princeton: Princeton University Press.
Pyke, F. (2007), 'Prospects for Italian Precious Jewellery Manufacturers on the UK Market', in P. Crestanello (ed.), *Competitive Positioning of Italian Jewellery on International Markets*, Veneto Region Research, Italy.
Pyke, F. and W. Sengenberger (eds) (1992), *Industrial Districts and Local Economic Regeneration*, Geneva: IILS, ILO.
Pyke, F., G. Becattini and W. Sengenberger (eds) (1990), *Industrial Districts and Inter-firm Co-operation in Italy*, Geneva: IILS, ILO.
Pyke, F., A. Nesporova and Y. Ghellab (2002), *An Employment Strategy for the Lodz Region of Poland*, Geneva: ILO.
Quazza, G. (1961), *L'industria laniera e cotoniera in Piemonte dal 1831 al 1861*, Torino: Museo nazionale del Risorgimento.
Quintar, A., R. Ascua, F. Gatto and C. Ferraro (1993), 'Un cuasi-distrito italiano a la Argentina', LC/BUE/R.179, Santiago: CEPAL.
Rabellotti, R. (1995), 'Is there an industrial district model: footwear districts in Italy and Mexico', *World Development*, **23** (1), 29–42.
Rabellotti, R. (1999), 'Recovery of a Mexican cluster: devaluation Bonanza or collective efficiency', *World Development*, **27** (9), 1571–85.
Rabelotti, R. (2001), 'The effect of globalisation on industrial districts in Italy: the case of Brenta', paper presented at the Workshop *Local Upgrading in Global Chains*, Institute of Development Studies, University of Sussex.
Rabellotti, R. (2006), 'Globalization, industrial districts and value chain', in M. Tsuji, E. Giovannetti and M. Kagami (eds), *Industrial Agglomeration and*

New Technologies: A Global Perspective, Cheltenham, UK and Northampton, MA, USA: Edward Elgar, pp. 225–45.

Rabellotti, R., A. Carabelli and G. Hirsch (2009), 'Italian industrial districts on the move: where are they going?' *European and Planning Studies*, forthcoming.

Radcliffe-Brown, A.R. (1935), 'On the concept of function in social science', *American Anthropologist*, 1, 1–12.

Raffaelli, T. (2003a), *Marshall's Evolutionary Economics*, London: Routledge.

Raffaelli, T. (2003b), 'Requirements and patterns of Marshallian evolution: their impact on the notion of industrial district', in R. Arena and M. Queré (eds), *The Economics of Alfred Marshall. Revisiting Marshall's Legacy*, New York: Palgrave Macmillan.

Raffaelli, T. (2004), 'Whatever happened to Marshall's industrial economics', in *European Journal of the History of Economic Thought*, **11** (2), 209–29.

Raffaelli, T., G. Becattini and M. Dardi (eds) (2006), *The Elgar Companion to Alfred Marshall*, Cheltenham, UK and Northampton, MA, USA: Edward Elgar.

Raffestin, C. (1980), *Géographie économique du pouvoir*, Paris: LITEC.

Ramella, F. (1984), *Terra e telai. Sistemi di parentela e manifattura nel Biellese dell'ottocento*, Torino: Einaudi.

Ramella, F. (1997), 'L'area laniera di Biella in una prospettiva comparativa', in Fontana (1997), pp. 923–36.

Ramírez-Pasillas, M. (2007), 'Global spaces for local entrepreneurship. Stretching clusters thorugh networks and international trade fairs', dissertation, Växjö: Växjö University Press.

Ravallion, M. and S. Cheng (2008), 'The developing world is poorer than we thought, but no less successful in the fight against poverty', *World Bank Research Paper*, September, Washington, DC.

Raveyre, M.-F. and J. Saglio (1984), 'Les systèmes industriels localisés: éléments pour une analyse sociologique des ensembles de PME industriels', *Sociologie du travail*, **2** (84), 157–75.

Rawski, T.G. (2005), *Chinese Industry after 25 Years of Reform*, Asia Program Special Report, Woodrow Wilson International Center for Scholars, 20–25.

Reis, J. (1992), *Os espaços da indústria. A regulação económica e o desenvolvimento local em Portugal*, Porto: Ediçoes Afrontamento.

Reynaud, J.-D. (1989), *Les règles du jeu, l'action collective et la régulation*, Paris: Armand Colin.

Richardson, G. (2001), 'A tale of two theories: monopolies and guilds in medieval England and modern imagination', *Journal of History of Economic Thought*, **23** (2), 217–42.

Richardson, G.B. (1972), 'The organization of industry', *Economic Journal*, **82** (327), 883–96.

Richardson, G.B. (2002), 'The organization of industry re-visited', *DRUID Working Paper*, no. 02(15), 1–13.

Rickert, J., J. Rogers, D. Vassina, J. Whitford and J. Zeitlin (2000), 'Common problems and collaborative solutions: OEM–supplier relationships and the Wisconsin manufacturing partnership's supplier training consortium', Madison: Center on Wisconsin Strategy.

Rifkin, J. (2000), *The Age of Access: The New Culture of Hypercapitalism. Where all of Life is a Paid-for Experience*, New York: Putnam Publishing Group.

Roback, J. (1982), 'Wages, rents, and the quality of life', *Journal of Political Economy*, **90** (6), 1257–78.

Robbins, L. (1932), *The Nature and Significance of Economic Science*, London: Macmillan.

Roberts, E. (1991), *Entrepreneurs in High Technology: Lessons from MIT and Beyond*, New York: Oxford University Press.

Robertson, D.H. (1923), *The Control of Industry*, New York: Harcourt, Brace and Co.

Robertson, D.H. (1924), 'Those empty boxes', *Economic Journal*, 34, 16–21.

Robertson, P.L. and R.N. Langlois (1994), 'Institutions, inertia, and changing industrial leadership', *Industrial and Corporate Change*, 3, 359–78.

Robertson, P.L. and P.R. Patel (2007), 'New wine in old bottles: technological diffusion in developed economies', *Research Policy*, 36, 708–21.

Robinson, E.A.G. (1958), *The Structure of Competitive Industry*, 4th edition, Cambridge: Cambridge University Press; 1st edition 1931.

Rodrik, D. (2004), 'Industrial policy for the twenty-first century', *CEPR Discussion Papers*.

Rodrik, D. (2006), 'Industrial development: stylized facts and policies', draft prepared for the UN-DESA publication *Industrial Development for the 21st Century*, pp. 1–34.

Rodrik, D. (2007), *One Economics, Many Recipes*, Princeton: Princeton University Press.

Rohlfs, J.H. (2001), *Bandwagon Effects in High-technology Industries*, Cambridge, MA: MIT Press.

Romagnoli, A. (ed.) (1996a), *Teoria dei processi produttivi*, Torino: Giappichelli.

Romagnoli, A. (1996b), 'Agricultural forms of production organisation', in Landesmann and Scazzieri (1996), pp. 229–51.

Romer, P.M. (1986), 'Increasing returns and long-run growth', *Journal of Political Economy*, **94** (5), 1002–37.

Romer, P.M. (1990), 'Endogenous technological change', *Journal of Political Economy*, **98** (5), S1071–102.

Romer, P.M. (1994), 'The origins of endogenous growth', *Journal of Economic Perspectives*, **8** (1), 3–22.

Romer, P.M. (2000), 'Thinking versus feeling', *The American Economic Review*, **90** (2), 439–43.

Rose, M. (2000), *Firms, Networks and Business Values: The British and American Cotton Industries since 1750*, Cambridge: Cambridge University Press.

Rose M., J. Rubery and R. Penn (eds) (1994), *Skill and Occupational Change*, Oxford: Oxford University Press.

Rosegrant, S. and D. Lampe (1992), *Route 128: Lessons from Boston's High-tech Community*, New York: Basic Books.

Rosenberg, N. (1963), 'Capital goods, technology and economic growth', *Oxford Economic Papers*, **15** (3), 217–27; reprinted in N. Rosenberg (1976), *Perspectives on Technology*, Cambridge, MA: Cambridge University Press.

Rosenberg, N. (1994), *Exploring the Black Box: Technology, Economics, and History*, Cambridge: Cambridge University Press.

Rosenberg, R. (1999), 'Growing with the flow: endless stream of data spawns computer-storage firms', *Boston Globe*, 14 April.

Rosenfeld, S.A. (1995), *Industrial-strength Strategies: Regional Business Clusters and Public Policy*, The Aspen Institute Rural Economic Policy Program.

Rosenfeld, S.A. (2001), *Networks and Clusters: The Yin and Yang of Rural Development*, Kansas City: Federal Reserve Bank of Kansas City.

Rosenfeld, S.A. (2002), *Creating Smart Systems: A Guide to Cluster Strategies in less Favoured Regions*, European Union, Regional Innovation Strategies, EU Commission, April.

Rosenfeld, S.A. and C. Liston (2006), 'Cluster hubs: putting learning into context', *Community College Journal*, **77** (3).

Rosenfeld, S.A., C. Liston and J. Jacobs (2003), 'Targeting clusters, achieving excellence', *Community College Journal*, **73** (6).

Rosenthal, S.S. and W.C. Strange (2003), 'Geography, industrial organization, and agglomeration', *Review of Economics and Statistics*, **85** (2), 377–93.

Rosenthal, S.S. and W.C. Strange (2004), 'Evidence on the Nature and Sources of Agglomeration Economies', in J.V. Henderson and J.-F. Thisse (eds), *Handbook of Regional and Urban Economics*, vol. 4, *Cities and Geography*, Amsterdam: Elsevier, pp. 2119–71.

Ross, L. and R. Nisbet (1991), *The Person and the Situation*, Philadelphia: Temple University Press.

Rosser, J.B. (ed.) (2004), *Complexity in Economics*, Cheltenham, UK and Northampton, MA, USA: Edward Elgar.

Rossetti, S. and R. Schiattarella (2003), 'Un approccio di sistema all'analisi della delocalizzazione internazionale. Uno studio per il settore del made in Italy', in N. Acocella and E. Sonnino (eds), *Movimenti di persone e movimenti di capitali in Europa*, Bologna: Il Mulino, pp. 385–502.

Rothaermel, F.T., S.D. Agung and L. Jiang (2007), 'University entrepreneurship: a taxonomy of the literature', *Industrial and Corporate Change*, **16** (4), 691–791.

Rothwell, R. and M. Dodgson (1991), 'Regional technology policies: the development of regional technology transfer infrastructures', in J. Brotchie (ed.), *Cities of the 21st Century*, London: Longman.

Rotondi, Z. (2005), 'Banche, finanziamento dello sviluppo e dell'innovazione e internazionalizzazione', in G. Bracchi and D. Masciandaro (eds), *Le banche*

Italiane e la finanza per lo sviluppo: territori, imprese e famiglie, X Rapporto sul Sistema finanziario italiano, Milano: Edibank-Bancaria Editrice, pp. 75–100.

Rugman, A.M. and J.R. D'Cruz (2000), 'The theory of the flagship firm', in D. Faulkner and M. de Rond (eds), *Cooperative Strategy: Economic, Business and Organizational Issues*, Oxford: Oxford University Press, pp. 58–61.

Rugman, A.M. and A. Verbeke (2005), 'Multinational enterprises and clusters: an organizing framework', in *Analysis of Multinational Strategic Management: The Selected Scientific Papers of Alan M. Rugman and Alain Verbeke*, Cheltenham, UK and Northampton, MA, USA: Edward Elgar, pp. 251–69.

Ruiz, C. (2006), 'Value chains and software clusters in Mexico', in Pietrobelli and Rabellotti (2006), pp. 191–219.

Russo, M. (1985), 'Technical change and the industrial district', *Research Policy*, 14, 329–43.

Russo, M. (1996), 'Units of investigation for local economic development policies', *Economie appliquée*, **49** (1), 85–118.

Russo, M. (2006), 'Processi di innovazione nei distretti e globalizzazione: il caso si Sassuolo', in G. Tattara, G. Corò and M. Volpe (2006), *Andarsene per continuare a crescere. La delocalizzazione internazionale come strategia competitiva*, Roma: Carocci, pp. 281–308.

Russo, M. (2008), 'L'inchiesta nell'analisi della struttura sociale e dell'organizzazione della produzione. Il contributo di Sebastiano Brusco', in E. Pugliese (ed.), *Atti del convegno 'L'inchiesta: orientamenti, contenuti e metodi nella ricerca sociale in Italia'*, CNR, 18 May 2007, Roma.

Sabbatucci Severini, P. (1999), 'Ambiente industriale e istituzioni: Vigevano e i paesi del Fermano', in Arrighetti and Seravalli (1999), pp. 93–121.

Sabel, Ch.F. (1992), 'Studied trust: building new forms of cooperation in a volatile economy', in Pyke and Sengenberger (1992), pp. 215–50.

Sabel, Ch.F. (1994), 'Turning the page in the industrial districts', paper presented at the Poiters Conference.

Sabel, Ch.F. (2004), 'The world in a bottle or window on the world? Open questions about industrial districts in the spirit of Sebastiano Brusco', *Stato e Mercato*.

Sabel, Ch.F. (2005a), 'A real-time revolution in routines', in Ch. Heckscher and P. Adler (eds), *The Corporation as a Collaborative Community*, Oxford: Oxford University Press.

Sabel, Ch.F. (2005b), 'Globalization, new public services, local democracy: what's the connection?', paper presented at the *Local Governance and Production Conference*, Trento, June, published by OECD, December.

Sabel, Ch.F. and J. Zeitlin (1982), 'Alternative storiche all'industrializzazione di massa', *Stato e Mercato*, **5** (August).

Sabel, Ch.F. and J. Zeitlin (1985), 'Historical alternative to mass production: politics, markets and technologies in nineteenth-century industrialization', *Past and Present*, **108** (1), 133–76.

Sabel, Ch.F. and J. Zeitlin (eds) (1997a), *Worlds of Possibilities. Flexibility and Mass Production in Western Industrialization*, Cambridge: Cambridge University Press.

Sabel, Ch.F. and J. Zeitlin (1997b), 'Stories, strategies, structures: rethinking historical alternatives to mass production', in Sabel and Zeitlin (1997a).

Sabel, Ch.F. and J. Zeitlin (2004), 'Neither modularity nor relational contracting: inter-firm collaboration in the new economy', *Enterprise & Society*, **5** (3), 388–403.

Sacchetti, S. and P.R. Tomlinson (2006), 'Globalisation, governance and clusters: the cases of the north Staffordshire ceramic and Prato textile industries', in C. Pitelis, R. Sugden and J.R Wilson (eds), *Clusters and Globalisation: The Development of Economies*, Cheltenham, UK and Northampton, MA, USA: Edward Elgar, pp. 232–57.

Saglio, J. (1991), 'Echange social et identité collective dans les systèmes industriels', *Sociologie du travail*, **4** (91), 529–44.

Saglio, J. (1997), 'Local industry and actors' strategies: from combs to plastics in Oyonnax', in Sabel and Zeitlin (1997a), 419–60.

Sahlins, M. (1976), *Culture and Practical Reason*, Chicago: University of Chicago Press.

Sahlins, M. (1995), *How Natives Think*, Chicago: University of Chicago Press.

Sakakibara, M. and M.E. Porter (2001), 'Competing at home to win abroad: evidence from Japanese industry', *Review of Economics and Statistics*, **83** (2), 310–22.

Salimbeni, R., R. Pini and S. Siano (2002), 'Thirty years of laser applications in conservation' in A.H. Guenther (ed.), *International Trends in Applied Optics*, Bellingham: SPIE Press, pp. 667–88.

Samuelson L. (1998), *Evolutionary Games and Equilibrium Selection*, Cambridge, MA: The MIT Press.

Sammarra, A. and F. Belussi (2006), 'Evolution and relocation in fashion-led Italian districts: evidence from two case-studies', *Entrepreneurship and Regional Development*, **18** (Nov.), 543–62.

Sandler, T. (1998), 'Global and regional public goods: a prognosis for collective action', *Fiscal Studies*, **19** (3), 221–47.

Santa María, M.J., J.M. Giner and A. Fuster (2004), 'Identificación de sistemas productivos locales en España: una aproximación desde el territorio a los fenómenos industriales', *Documento de Trabajo*, no. 01/2004, Grupo de investigación 'Economía industrial y desarrollo local', Universidad de Alicante.

Santagata, W. (2002), 'Cultural districts, property rights and sustainable economic growth', *International Journal of Urban and Regional Research*, **1** (26), 9–23.

Sapienza, P. (2002), 'The effects of banking mergers on loan contracts', *Journal of Finance*, 57, 329–67.

Sargant, W.L. (1857), *Economy and the Labouring Classes*, London: Simpkin, Marshall and Co.
Sargant Florence, P. (1948), *Investment, Location and Size of Plant*, Cambridge: Cambridge University Press.
Sargant Florence, P. (1953), *The Logic of British and American Industry*, London: Routledge.
Savage, D.A. (1994), 'The professions in theory and history: the case of pharmacy', *Business and Economic History*, **23** (2), 130–60.
Savona, M. and R. Schiattarella (2004), 'International relocation of production and the growth of services: the case of the Made in Italy industries', *Transnational Corporations*, **13** (2), 57–76.
Saxenian, A.L. (1991), 'The origins and dynamics of production networks in Silicon Valley', *Research Policy*, 20, 423–38.
Saxenian, A.L. (1992), 'Divergent patterns of business organization in Silicon Valley', in Storper and Scott (1992), pp. 316–31.
Saxenian, A.L. (1994) *Regional Advantage: Culture and Competition in Silicon Valley and Route 128*, Cambridge, MA: Harvard University Press.
Saxenian, A.L. (1999), *Silicon Valley, New Immigrant Entrepreneurs*, San Francisco: Public Policy Institute.
Saxenian, A.L. (2006), *The New Argonauts: Regional Advantage in a Global Economy*, Cambridge, MA: Harvard University Press.
Saxenian, A.L., Y. Motoyama and X. Quan (2002), *Local and Global Networks of Immigrant Professionals in Silicon Valley*, San Francisco: Public Policy Institute.
Scazzieri, R. (1993), *A Theory of Production*, Oxford: Clarendon Press.
Schmitz, H. (1989), 'Flexible specialisation: a new paradigm of small scale industrialisation', *IDS Discussion Paper*, no. 161, Brighton: Institute of Development Studies, University of Sussex.
Schmitz, H. (1995), 'Collective efficiency: growth path for small-scale industry', *Journal of Development Studies*, **31** (4), 529–66.
Schmitz, H. (1997), 'Collective efficiency and increasing returns', *IDS Working Paper*, no. 50, Brighton: Institute of Development Studies, University of Sussex.
Schmitz, H. (1998), 'Responding to global competitive pressure: local cooperation and upgrading in the Sinos Valley, Brazil', *IDS Working Paper*, no. 82, Brighton: Institute of Development Studies, University of Sussex.
Schmitz, H. (1999a), 'Global competition and local cooperation: success and failure in the Sinos Valley, Brazil', *World Development*, **27** (9), pp. 1627–50.
Schmitz, H. (1999b), 'Collective efficiency and increasing returns', *Cambridge Journal of Economics*, **23** (4), 465–83.
Schmitz, H. (2000), 'Does local co-operation matter? Evidence from industrial clusters in South Asia and Latin America', *Oxford Development Studies*, **28** (9), 323–36.

Schmitz, H. (ed.) (2004), *Local Enterprises in the Global Economy: Issues of Governance and Upgrading*, Cheltenham, UK and Northampton, MA, USA: Edward Elgar.

Schmitz, H. (2006), 'Learning and earning in global garment and footwear chains', *The European Journal of Development Research*, **18** (4), 546–71.

Schmitz, H. and P. Knorringa (2000), 'Learning from global buyers', *Journal of Development Studies*, **37** (2), 177–205.

Schmitz, H. and B. Musyck (1994), 'Industrial districts in Europe: policy lessons for developing countries', *World Development*, **22** (6), 889–910.

Schmitz H. and K. Nadvi (1999), 'Clustering and industrialization: introduction', *World Development*, **27** (9), 1503–14.

Schmitz, H. and S. Strambach (2008), 'The organizational decomposition of the innovation process: what does it mean for the global distribution of innovation activities?', *IDS Working Paper*, no. 304, Brighton: Institute of Development Studies, University of Sussex.

Scholte, J.A. (2000), *Globalization: A Critical Introduction*, New York: Basingstoke.

Schotter, A. (1981), *The Economics of Social Institutions*, Cambridge, UK: Cambridge University Press.

Schumpeter J. (1911), *Theorie der wirtschaftlichen Entwicklung*, Leipzig: Duncker and Humblot; Engl. translation J. Schumpeter (1934), *The Theory of Economic Development: An Inquiry into Profits, Capital, Credit, Interest and the Business Cycle*, Cambridge, MA: Harvard University Press.

Schumpeter, J. (1939), *Business Cycles: A Theoretical, Historical, and Statistical Analysis of the Capitalist Process*, New York: McGraw-Hill.

Scitovsky, T. (1954), 'Two concepts of external economies', *Journal of Political Economy*, **62** (April), 143–51.

Scott, A.J. (1988), *New Industrial Spaces*, London: Pion.

Scott, A.J. (1991), 'The aerospace-electronics industrial complex of Southern California: the formative years 1940–1960', *Research Policy*, 20, 439–56.

Scott, A.J. (1992), 'The role of large producers in industrial districts: a case study of high technology systems houses in Southern California', *Regional Studies*, **26** (3), 265–75.

Scott, A.J. (1994), 'Variations on the theme of agglomeration and growth: the gem and jewelry industry in Los Angeles and Bangkok', *Geoforum*, **25** (3), 249–63.

Scott, A.J. (2000), 'Economic geography: the great half-century', *Cambridge Journal of Economics*, **24** (4), 483–504.

Scott, A.J. (ed.) (2001), *Global City-regions. Trends, Theory, Policy*, Oxford: Oxford University Press.

Scott, A.J. (2005), *On Hollywood. The Place, the Industry*, Princeton: Princeton University Press.

Scott, J. (1991), *Social Network Analysis. A Handbook*, London: Sage.
Scott, P. (2007), *The Triumph of the South*, Aldershot: Ashgate.
Scranton, Ph. (1991), 'Diversity in diversity: flexible production and American industrialization, 1880–1930', *Business History Review*, **65** (1), 27–90.
Scranton, Ph. (1997), *Endless Novelty: Speciality Production and American Industrialization, 1865–1925*, Princeton, NJ: Princeton University Press.
SEBRAE (2002), *Subsídios para a Identificação de Clusters no Brasil*, São Paulo: Edição SEBRAE.
Sen, A. (1999), *Development as Freedom*, Oxford: Oxford University Press.
Sengenberger, W., G. Loveman and M. Piore (eds) (1990), *The Re-emergence of Small Enterprises: Industrial Restructuring in Industrialised Countries*, Geneva: IILS, ILO.
Sennett, J.S. (2001), 'Clusters, co-location and external sources of knowledge: the case of small instrumentation and control firms in the London region', *Planning Practice & Research*, **16** (1), 21–37.
Serpieri, A. (1946), *Istituzioni di economia agraria*, Bologna: Edizioni agricole.
Sethi, S. (2005), *The Gem and Jewellery Sectors of India and Italy: A Clusters Perspective*, Mumbai, India: Indo-Italian Chamber of Commerce and Industry.
Severin, D. (1962), *Origini e vicende del Setificio comasco: Istituto tecnico industriale Paolo Carcano*, Como: Camera di commercio.
Sewell, W.H. (1980), *Work and Revolution in France: The Language of Labour from the Old Regime to 1848*, Cambridge: Cambridge University Press.
Sforzi, F. (ed.) (1986), 'I mercati locali del lavoro in Italia', in ISTAT-IRPET, *Identificazione di sistemi territoriali. Analisi della struttura sociale e produttiva in Italia*, Proceedings of the Seminar, Roma, 3–4 December.
Sforzi, F. (1987), 'L'identificazione spaziale', in Becattini (1987a), pp. 143–167; reprinted as 'The geography of industrial districts in Italy', in Goodman and Bamford (1989), pp. 153–173.
Sforzi, F. (1990), 'The quantitative importance of Marshallian industrial districts in the Italian economy', in Pyke, Becattini and Sengenberger (1990), pp. 75–107.
Sforzi, F. (2002), 'The industrial district and the "new" Italian economic geography', *European Planning Studies*, **10** (4), 439–47.
Sforzi, F. (2004), 'Il distretto industriale e la "svolta territoriale" nell'analisi del cambiamento economico', in N. Bellanca, M. Dardi and T. Raffaelli (eds), *Economia senza gabbie. Studi in onore di Giacomo Becattini*, Bologna: Il Mulino, pp. 171–83.
Sforzi, F. (2006), 'La procedura di individuazione dei distretti industriali', in ISTAT (2006b), pp. 18–22.
Sforzi, F. (2007a), 'The industrial districts' contribution to change in the Italian economy', *Review of Economic Condition in Italy*, 1, 69–91.
Sforzi, F. (2007b), 'Presentazione', in G. Becattini, *Scritti sulla Toscana*, vol. I, *La ricerca sul campo e la 'Libera Scuola' di Artimino (1969–2007)*, edited by F. Sforzi, Firenze: Le Monnier, pp. v–xx.

Sforzi, F. (2008), 'Il distretto industriale: da Marshall a Becattini', *Il pensiero economico italiano*, **16** (2), pp. 39–48.
Sforzi, F. and F. Lorenzini (2002), 'I distretti industriali', in Istituto per la Promozione Industriale (IPI) (ed.), *L'esperienza italiana dei distretti industriali*, Roma: IPI.
Shane, S. (2004), *Academic Entrepreneurship: University Spinoffs and Wealth Creation*, Cheltenham, UK and Northampton, MA, USA: Edward Elgar.
Shapira, P. (1998), 'Manufacturing extension: performance, challenges, and policy issues', in L. Branscomb and J. Keller (eds), *Investing in Innovation: Creating a Research and Innovation Policy that Works*, Cambridge, MA: MIT Press, pp. 250–75.
Signorini, L.F. (1994a), 'Una verifica quantitativa dell'effetto distretto', *Sviluppo locale*, **1** (1), 31–70.
Signorini, L.F. (1994b), 'The price of Prato, or measuring the industrial district effect', *Papers in Regional Science*, **73** (4), 369–92.
Signorini, F. (ed.) (2000), *Lo sviluppo locale. Un'indagine della Banca d'Italia sui distretti industriali*, Corigliano Calabro, CS: Meridiana Libri and Roma: Donzelli.
Silva, M.R. (1988), 'Industrialisation et développement local: une interprétation à partir du cas portugaise', thèse de doctorat, Grenoble: Université des Sciences Sociales.
Silva, M.R. (1992), 'Development and local productive spaces: study on the Ave Valley (Portugal)', in Garofoli (1992).
Simon, H.A. (1986), 'Rationality in psychology and economics', *The Journal of Business*, **59** (4), part 2, S209–224.
Simonazzi, A. (1978), 'Domestic demand pressure and export performance: the case of selected Italian industries', *Economic Notes*, **7** (2–3), 137–58.
Simonazzi, A. (1985), 'Crediti all'esportazione e concorrenza internazionale', *Politica Economica*, **1** (2), 229–58.
Simpson, H. (2007), *An Analysis of Industrial Clustering in Great Britain*, final report, Institute for Fiscal Studies, April.
Singapore-China Economic and Trade Cooperation (2006), 'Doing business in China', www.csc.mofcom-mti.gov.cn, accessed 30 August 2008.
Singh, M. (1990), *The Political Economy of Unorganized Industry: A Study of Labor Process*, New Delhi: Sage.
Smail, J. (1992), 'Manufacturer or artisan? The relationship between economic and cultural change in the early stages of eighteenth-century industrialization', *Journal of Social History*, **25** (2), 791–814.
Small and Medium Enterprise Agency (2007), *The Survey on the General Situation of Place of Production*, Tokyo.
Smart, M.W. (1974), 'Labour market areas: uses and definitions', *Progress in Planning*, **2** (4), 239–53.

Smith, A. (1776), *An Enquiry into the Nature and Causes of the Wealth of Nations*, reprinted in R.H. Campbell, A.S. Skinner and W.B. Todd (eds) (1976), Oxford: Oxford University Press.

Sobocinski, P.Z. (1999), *Creating High-Tech Business Growth in Wisconsin*, Madison, WI: University of Wisconsin System Board of Regents.

Sodano, M. (1953), *Degli antichi lanifici biellesi e piemontesi*, Biella: Unione Biellese.

Soler, V. (2000), 'Verificación de las hipótesis del distrito industrial: Una aplicación al caso valenciano', *Economía Industrial*, 334, 13–23.

Solinas, G. (1982), 'Labour market segmentation and workers' careers: the case of Italian knitwear industry', *Cambridge Journal of Economics*, **6** (4), 331–52.

Solinas, G. (1996), *I processi di formazione, la crescita e la sopravvivenza delle piccole imprese*, Milano: Franco Angeli.

Solinas, G. and D. Baroni (2001), 'I sistemi locali manifatturieri in Italia 1991–96', in Becattini et al. (2001), pp. 395–417.

Sölvell, Ö., G. Lindqvist and C. Ketels (2003), *The Cluster Initiative Greenbook*, Stockholm: Ivory Tower.

Späth, B. (ed.) (1993), *Small Firms and Development in Latin America: The Role of the Institutional Environment, Human Resources and Industrial Relations*, Geneva: IILS, ILO.

Spencer, H. (1862), *First Principles*, 6th edition, London: William and Norgate; popular edition 1910.

Spilling, O.R. and J. Steinsli (2003) *Evolution of High-technology Clusters: Oslo and Trondheim in International Comparison*, research report no. 1, Oslo: BI.

Sraffa, P. (1926), 'The laws of returns under competitive conditions', *Economic Journal*, 36, 535–50.

Staber, U. (1998), 'Inter-firm Co-operation and Competition in industrial districts', *Organization Studies*, **19** (4), 701–24.

Staber, U. (2001), 'The structure of networks in industrial districts', *International Journal of Urban and Regional Research*, **25** (3), 537–52.

Stauffer, B. (1998), 'Etudes de la transition d'une société paysanne de l'Emilie (Italie), basée sur le métayage (*mezzadria*) et la propriété parcellaire, au capitalisme industriel à la suite de l'implantation de l'industrie des carreaux de céramique', thèse de doctorat sous la direction de M. Godelier, Paris: EHESS.

Stein, J.C. (2002), 'Information production and capital allocation: decentralized versus hierarchical firms', *Journal of Finance*, 57, 1891–921.

Steindl, J. (1945), *Small and Big Business. Economic Problems of the Size of Firms*, Oxford: Basil Blackwell.

Steiner, M. and C. Hartmann (2006), 'Organizational learning in clusters: a case study of material and immaterial dimensions of cooperation', *Regional Studies*, **40** (5), 493–506.

Stigler, G.J. (1941), *Production and Distribution Theories*, New York: Macmillan.
Stigler, G.J. (1951), 'The division of labor is limited by the extent of the market', *Journal of Political Economy*, **59** (3), 185–93.
Stigler, G.J. (1990), 'The place of Marshall's *Principles* in the development of economics', in J.K. Whitaker (ed.), *Centenary Essays on Alfred Marshall*, Cambridge: Cambridge University Press, pp. 1–13.
Stobart, J. (2004), *The First Industrial Region: North-west England, c. 1700–60*, Manchester: Manchester University Press.
Storper, M. (1995), 'The resurgence of regional economies, ten years later: the region as a nexus of untraded interdependencies', *European Urban and Regional Studies*, **2** (3), 191–221.
Storper, M. (1997), *The Regional World*, New York and London: The Guilford Press.
Storper, M. and B. Harrison (1991), 'Flexibility, hierarchy and regional development: the changing structure of industrial production systems and their forms of governance in the 1990s', *Research Policy*, 20, 407–22.
Storper, M. and R. Salais (1993), *Worlds of Production: the Action Frameworks of the Economy*, Cambridge, MA: Harvard University Press.
Storper, M. and A.J. Scott (1992), *Pathways to Industrialization and Regional Development*, London: Routledge.
Storper, M. and A.J. Venables (2004), 'Buzz: face-to-face contact and the urban economy', *Journal of Economic Geography*, 4, 351–70.
Strahan, P.E and J.P. Weston (1998), 'Small business lending and the changing structure of the banking industry', *Journal of Banking and Finance*, 22, 821–45.
Streeck, W. (1987), 'The uncertainties of management in the management of uncertainty: employers, labor relations and industrial adjustment in the 1980s', *Work, Employment & Society*, **1** (3), 281–308.
Sturgeon, T.J. (2002), 'Modular production networks: a new American model of industrial organization', *Industrial and Corporate Change*, **11** (June), 451–96.
Suzigan, W., R. Garcia and J. Furtado (2008), 'Local and global linkages of local production systems in Brazil', in M.D. Parrilli, P. Bianchi and R. Sugden, *High Technology, Productivity and Networking*, Basingstoke: Palgrave Macmillan.
Swann, G.M.P., M. Prevezer and D. Stout (eds) (1998), *The Dynamics of Industrial Clustering: International Comparisons in Computing and Biotechnology*, Oxford: Oxford University Press.
Sztompka, P. (1995), 'Trust: the missing resource in post-communist society', mimeo, Krakow: Institute of Sociology, Jagiellonian Universiy.
Tani, P. (1976), 'La rappresentazione analitica del processo di produzione: alcune premesse teoriche al problema del decentramento', *Note Economiche*,

9 (4–5); also published, with minor changes, as 'La decomponibilità del processo produttivo', in Becattini (1987a), pp. 69–72.

Tani, P. (1986), *Analisi microeconomica della produzione*, Roma: NIS.

Tani, P. (2004), 'Scomponibilità dei processi produttivi e sistemi d'imprese', in N. Bellanca, M. Dardi and T. Raffaelli (eds), *Economia senza gabbie. Studi in onore di Giacomo Becattini*, Bologna: Il Mulino.

Tappi, D. (2005), 'Clusters, adaptation and extroversion: a cognitive and entrepreneurial analysis of the Marche music cluster', *European Urban and Regional Studies*, **12** (3), 289–307.

Tattara, G. (2001), *Il piccolo che nasce dal grande. Le molteplici facce dei distretti industriali veneti*, Milano: Franco Angeli.

Taub, R. and D. Taub (1994), *Entrepreneurship in India's Small Scale Industries: An Exploration of Social Contexts*, New Delhi: Manohar Publications.

Taylor, R.W.C. (1842), *Notes of a Tour in the Manufacturing Districts of Lancashire*, 2nd edition, London: Duncan and Malcolm.

Taylor, R.W.C. (1886), *Introduction to the History of the Factory System*, London: Richard Bentley & Son.

Taylor, R.W.C. (1891), *The Modern Factory System*, London: Kegan Paul & Trübner & Co.

Taylor, R.W.C. (1894), *The Factory System and the Factory Acts*, London: Methuen and Co.

TDC (2001), 'Prospects for Hong Kong's jewellery exports', Hong Kong Trade Development Council, www.tdctrade.com/econforum/tdc/tdc010402.htm, accessed 30 August 2008.

TDC Trade (2007), 'A brand new world', Hong Kong Trade Development Council, www.tdctrade.com/prodmag/jewell/jel200702IndustryInsight.htm, accessed 30 August 2008.

Teece, D.J. (1986), 'Profiting from technological innovation: implications for integration, collaboration, licensing, and public policy', *Research Policy*, **15** (6), 285–305.

Tendler, J. (1997), *Good Government in the Tropics*, Baltimore: Johns Hopkins University Press.

Tendler, J. and M. Amorim (1996), 'Small firms and their helpers: lessons on demand', *World Development*, **24** (3), 407–26.

Terrier, D. (1996), *Les deux âges de la proto-industrie. Les tisserands du Cambrésis et du Saint-Quentinois, 1730–1880*, Paris: EHESS.

Terrier, D. (1997), 'Arrangements territoriaux et lien social dans l'industrie textile du nord de la France (fin XVIIe-début XXe siècle)', in Fontana (1997), pp. 225–40.

Terrier, D. (1998), 'La dispersion rurale du textile en France: logique d'implantation et gestion d'un espace productif, 1650–1780', in V. Giura (ed.), *Gli insediamenti economici e le loro logiche*, Napoli-Roma: Edizioni scientifiche italiane.

Tewari, M. (1996), 'Restructuring and modernization of SME clusters in India: impressions from field work in North India's diesel engine and electronics clusters', report, Vienna: UNIDO.

Tewari, M. (1998), 'Intersectoral linkages and the role of the State in shaping the conditions of industrial accumulation: a study of Ludhiana's metalworking industry', *World Development*, **26** (8), 1387–411.

Tewari, M. (1999), 'Successful adjustment in Indian industry: the case of Ludhiana's woolen knitwear cluster', *World Development*, **27** (9), 1651–71.

Thaler, R. (1985), 'Mental accounting and consumer choice', *Marketing Science*, **4** (3), 199–214.

Thaler, R. (1994), *The Winner's Curse*, Princeton, NJ: Princeton University Press.

Thiel, J., I. Pires and A. Dudleston (2000), 'Globalisaton and the Portuguese textile and clothing *filière* in the post-GATT climate', in A. Giunta, A. Langedijck and A. Pike (eds), *Restructuring Industry and Territory: The Experience of Europe's Regions*, London: The Stationary Office (TSO), pp. 109–26.

Thrupp, S. (1942), 'Medieval guilds reconsidered', *Journal of Economic History*, **2** (3), 164–73.

Todeva, E. (2006), 'Clusters in the South East of England', University of Surrey.

Tomás Carpi, J.A., J. Banyuls, E. Cano, J.L. Contreras, J.R. Gallego, J.V. Picher, J. Such and M. Torrejón (1999), *Dinámica industrial e innovación en la comunidad valenciana. Análisis de los distritos industriales del calzado, cerámica, mueble y textil*, Valencia: IMPIVA.

Toms, S. and I. Filatotchev (2003), 'Networks, corporate governance and the decline of the Lancashire textile industry', in Wilson and Popp (2003), pp. 68–90.

Tong, X. and J. Wang (2001), 'Local clustering: a case study on PC-related manufacturing in Dongguan', *Journal of Geographical Science* (in Chinese), **56** (6), 722–9.

Tönnies, F. (1965), *Community and Association*, London: Routledge & Kegan Paul; published in German in F. Tönnies (1935), *Gemeinschaft und Gesellschaft*, Darmstadt: Hans Buske.

Torrisi, S. (2002), *Imprenditorialità e distretti ad alta tecnologia*, Milano: Franco Angeli.

Townroe, P.M. and N.J. Roberts (1980), *Local–External Economies for British Manufacturing Industries*, Guildford: Gower.

Towse, R. (ed.) (2003), *A Handbook of Cultural Economics*, Cheltenham, UK and Northampton, MA, USA: Edward Elgar.

Trezzi, G.L. (1998), 'The survival of the corporation within the friendly society for artisans and workers in Milan during the first half of the nineteenth century', in Guenzi, Massa and Piola Caselli (1998).

Trigilia, C. (1986), *Grandi partiti e piccole imprese: comunisti e democristiani nelle regioni a economia diffusa*, Bologna: Il Mulino.
Trigilia, C. (1989), 'Small-firm development and political subcultures in Italy', in Goodman and Bamford (1989), pp. 174–97.
Trigilia, C. (2001), 'Social capital and local development', *European Journal of Social Theory*, **4** (4), 427–42.
Trigilia, C. (2002), *Economic Sociology. State, Market, and Society in Modern Capitalism*, Oxford: Blackwell.
Trigilia, C. (2004), 'The governance of high-tech districts', in Crouch et al. (2004), pp. 321–30.
Trigilia, C. (2005), *Sviluppo locale. Un progetto per l'Italia*, Roma-Bari: Laterza.
Trullén, J. (1990), 'Caracterización de los distritos industriales. El distrito industrial marshalliano en el debate actual sobre desarrollo regional y localización industrial', *Economía Industrial*, 273, 151–65.
Trullén, J. (2002), 'Barcelona como ciudad flexible. Economías de localización y economías de urbanización en una metrópolis polinuclear', in G. Becattini, M.T. Costa and J. Trullén (eds), *Desarrollo local: teorías y estrategias*, Madrid: Civitas.
Trullén, J. (2006), 'Distritos industriales marshallianos y sistemas locales de gran empresa en el diseño de una nueva estrategia territorial para el crecimiento de la productividad en la economía española', *Economía Industrial*, 359, 95–112.
Trullén, J. (2007), 'La nueva política industrial española: innovación, economías externas y productividad', *Economía Industrial*, 363, 17–31.
Trullén, J. and R. Boix (2008), 'Knowledge externalities and networks of cities in the creative metropolis', in Cooke and Lazzeretti (2008), pp. 211–37.
Trullén, J. and M. Callejón (2008), 'Las agrupaciones de empresas innovadoras', *Mediterráneo Económico*, 13, Fundación Cajamar.
Tsurumi, K. and T. Kawata (1989), *Naihatuteki-Hattenron* ('Theory of endogenous development'), Tokyo-Daigaku Shuppannkai, Tokyo: Tokyo University Press.
Tuomela, R. (1995), *The Importance of Us. A Philosophical Study of Basic Social Notions*, Stanford, CA: Stanford University Press.
Turkle, S. (1984), *The Second Self: Computers and the Human Spirit*, New York: Simon & Schuster.
Turner, R. (1999), 'Public policies for manufacturing revitalization: competing models in three American States', Political Science, Madison, WI: University of Wisconsin-Madison.
Tweedale, G. (1995), *Steel City: Entrepreneurship, Strategy and Technology in Sheffield, 1745–1993*, Oxford: Clarendon Press.
Udell, G.F. (2009), 'Innovation, organizations and small business lending', in P. Alessandrini, M. Fratianni and A. Zazzaro (eds), *The Changing Geography of Banking and Finance*, Berlin: Springer Verlag, forthcoming.

Ughetto, E. (2006), 'Territorial proxinity and credit constraints to innovation: evidence from Italian firms', in G. Bracchi and D. Masciandaro (eds), *Banche e geografia: nuove mappe produttive e metamorfosi del credito, XI Rapporto sul Sistema finanziario italiano*, Milano: Edibank-Bancaria Editrice, pp. 397–433.

Ughetto, E. (2006–07), 'Innovare nel distretto. Il ruolo del mercato del credito', *Sviluppo locale*, **12** (28), 33–65.

UNDP (2004), *Unleashing Entrepreneurship*, New York: UN Commission on Private Sector and Development

UNCTAD (2001), *World Investment Report: Promoting Linkages*, New York and Geneva: UNCTAD.

UNCTAD (2006), *Report on the Expert Group Meeting on Best Practices and Policy Options in the Promotion of SME-TNC Business Linkages*, Geneva, 22 December 2006.

UNCTAD (2008a), *Secretary-general's High-level Panel on the Creative Economy and Industries for Development*, Accra, Ghana, April.

UNCTAD (2008b), *Background Paper for the Secretary-General's High Level Panel on the Creative Economy and Industries for Development*, Geneva, 14–15 January.

UNESCO (2005), *Convention on Cultural Diversity*, Paris, October.

Unger, K. (2003), *Los clusters industriales en Mexico: especializaciones regionales y politica industrial*, Santiago: CEPAL.

UNIDO (2001), *Development of Clusters and Networks of SMEs: the UNIDO Programme*, Vienna: Private Sector Development Branch.

UNIDO (2004), *Industrial Clusters and Poverty Reduction: Towards a Methodology for Poverty and Social Impact Assessment of Cluster Development Initiatives*, Small and Medium Enterprises Branch, Vienna.

UNIDO (2007a), *End of Project Report. Handloom Cluster of Chanderi, Madhya Pradesh. Under the Project Thematic Cooperation between UNIDO and SDC in the Areas of SME Networking and Cluster Development.*

UNIDO (2007b), *End of Project Report. Knitwear Cluster of Ludhiana*, India.

UNIDO (2008a), *End of Project Report. MSME Cluster Development Programme in the State of Orissa 2005–07*, India.

UNIDO (2008b), *Fomento de conglomerados en Nicaragua. Estudios de caso y aprendizajes*.

UNIDO (2008c), *Report on the Merkato Cluster. Ethiopia.*

Unioncamere (2006), *Rapporto Unioncamere 2006. L'economia reale dal punto di osservazione delle Camere di Commercio*, Roma.

Unioncamere (2007), *Rapporto Unioncamere 2007*, Roma.

United Nations (1994), *Technological Dynamism in Industrial Districts: An Alternative Approach to Industrialization in Developing Countries?*, Geneva: United Nations-GATE.

Uzzi, B. (1997), 'Social structure and competition in interfirm networks: the paradox of embeddedness', *Administrative Science Quarterly*, 42, 35–67.

Valensi, L. (1969), 'Islam et capitalisme: production et commerce des chéchias en Tunisie et en France aux XVIIIe et XIXe siècles', *Revue d'histoire moderne et contemporaine*, 16, 376–400.
Van de Ven, A.H. (1993), 'The development of an infrastructure for entrepreneurship', *Journal of Business Venturing*, 8, 211–33.
Van Egeraat, C. and D. Jacobson (2005), 'Geography of production linkages in the Irish and Scottish microcomputer industry: the role of logistics', *Economic Geography*, 81, 283–303.
Van Zanden, J.L. (2004), 'Common workman, philosophers and the birth of the European knowledge economy. About the price and the production of useful knowledge in Europe, 1350–1800', paper for the GEHN conference on *Useful Knowledge*, Leiden, September 2004; revised 12 October 2004, www.iisg.nl/research/jvz-knowledge_economy.pdf, accessed 20 December 2008.
Vanberg, V. (1994), *Rules and Choices in Economics*, London: Routledge.
Varaldo, R. (ed.) (1979), *Ristrutturazioni industriali e rapporti fra imprese*, Milano: Franco Angeli.
Varaldo, R. and L. Ferrucci (1996), 'The evolutionary nature of the firm within industrial districts', *European Planning Studies*, 4, 16–23.
Vázquez Barquero, A. (1987), *Desarrollo local. Una estrategia de creación de empleo*, Madrid: Pirámide.
Vázquez Barquero, A. (2002), *Endogenous Development: Networking, Innovation, Institutions and Cities*, London: Routledge.
Veltz, P. (2000), *Le nouveau monde industriel*, Paris: Gallimard.
Verley, P. (1997), *L'échelle du monde*, Paris: Gallimard.
Vernon, R. (1971), *Sovereignty at Bay*, New York: Basic Books.
Veyrassat, B. (1997), 'Manufacturing flexibility in nineteenth century Switzerland: social and institutional foundations of decline and revival in calico-printing and watchmaking', in Sabel and Zeitlin (1997a), pp. 188–237.
Vianello, F. (2004), 'La Facoltà di Economia e commercio di Modena', in G. Garofalo and A. Graziani (eds), *La formazione degli economisti in Italia (1950–1975)*, Bologna: Il Mulino, pp. 481–534.
Vianello, F. (2008), 'Sistemi di imprese. A proposito della nuova raccolta di saggi di Sebastiano Brusco (e della precedente)', *Economia & Lavoro*, 1, 109–29.
Viesti, G. (2000), *Come nascono i distretti industriali*, Bari: Laterza.
Visser, E. (1997), 'The significance of spatial clustering', in M.P. van Dijk and R. Rabellotti, *Enterprise Clusters and Networks in Developing Countries*, EADI Book Series, London: Frank Cass, pp. 61–92.
Volpe, M. (2001), 'La mobilità del lavoro e la fedeltà al distretto', in Tattara (2001), pp. 130–89.
Von Hippel, E. (2005), *Democratizing Innovation*, Boston, MA: MIT Press.
Wall, J.W. (1973), 'External economies and localization in small-scale industry: a case of the bicycle manufacturing industry in Ludhiana district, India', Ph.D. dissertation, Durham, NC: Department of Economics, Duke University.

Wang, C. (2004), 'Basic information on China's jewellery industry', www.strategis.ic.gc.ca/epic/site/imr-ri.nsf/en/gr127569e.html, accessed 30 August 2008.

Wang, J. (2001), *The Space of Innovation: Enterprises Agglomeration and Regional Development*, Beijing: Peking University Press.

Wang, J. (2006), *The Global Impact and Local Spirit in Supply-chain Cities of China: The Case of Textile and Apparel Clusters*, Geneva: IILS, ILO.

Wang, J. (2007), 'Development of industrial districts in China and its implications', *Beijing*, 1–20.

Wang, J. and L. Mei (2008), 'Dynamics of labour-intensive clusters in China: relying exclusively on labour costs or cultivating innovation?', *Discussion Paper*, Geneva: IILS, ILO.

Wang, J. and Wang J. (1998), 'An analysis of new-tech agglomeration in Beijing: a new industrial district in the making?', *Environment and Planning A*, **30** (4), 681–701.

Wang, J. et al. (2001), *Districtization in Zhejiang Province of China*, Torino: IGU commission on the Dynamics of Economic Spaces.

Webb, D. and C. Collis (2000), 'Regional development agencies and the "new regionalism" in England', *Regional Studies*, **34** (9), 857–73.

Wei, Y.L. and C.B. Wang (2007), 'Restructuring industrial districts, scaling up regional development: a study of the Wenzhou model, China', *Economic Geography*, **83** (4), 421–44.

Weijland, H. (1999), 'Microenterprise clusters in rural Indonesia: industrial seedbed and policy target', *World Development*, **27** (9), 1515–30.

Wenger, E. (1998), *Communities of Practice: Learning, Meaning, and Identity*, Cambridge: Cambridge University Press.

Wennberg, K. and G. Lindqvist (2008), 'How do entrepreneurs in clusters contribute to economic growth?', *SSE/EFI Working Paper in Business Administration*, no. 3, Stockholm School of Economics.

Wheeler, C.H. (2001), 'Search, sorting and urban agglomeration', *Journal of Labor Economics*, **19** (4), 879–99.

Whitaker, J.K. (ed.) (1975), *The Early Economic Writings of Alfred Marshall 1967–1890)*, 2 vols, London and Basingstoke: Macmillan.

Whitaker, J.K. (ed.) (1996), *The Correspondence of Alfred Marshall Economist*, 3 vols, Cambridge: Cambridge University Press.

White, A. (1997), '"…We never knew what price we were going to have till we got to the warehouse": nineteenth-century Sheffield and the industrial district debate', *Social History*, **22** (3), 307–17.

Whitford, J. (2001), 'The decline of a model? Challenge and response in the Italian industrial districts', *Economy and Society*, **30** (1), 38–65.

Whitford, J. (2005), *The New Old Economy: Networks, Institutions, and the Organizational Transformation of American Manufacturing*, Oxford: Oxford University Press.

Whitford, J. and C. Potter (2007a), 'The state of the art: regional economies, open networks and the spatial fragmentation of production', *Socio-economic Review*, **5** (June), 497–526.
Whitford, J. and C. Potter (2007b), 'Regional economies, open networks and the spatial fragmentation of production', *Socio-economic Review*, **5** (3), 497–526.
Whitford, J. and J. Zeitlin (2004), 'Governing decentralized production: institutions, public policy, and the prospects for inter-firm collaboration in US manufacturing', *Industry and Innovation*, **11** (1–2), 11–44.
Whitford, J., J. Zeitlin and J. Rogers (2000), *Down the line: Supplier Upgrading, Evolving OEM–supplier Relations, and Directions for Future Manufacturing Modernization Policy and Research in Wisconsin*, Madison: Center on Wisconsin Strategy.
Whittam, G. and M. Danson (2001), 'Power and the spirit of clustering', *European Planning Studies*, **9** (8), 949–63.
Wigren, C. (2003), 'The spirit of Gnosjö. The grand narrative and beyond', dissertation, Jönköping: Jönköping International Business School.
Williamson, O.E. (1985), *The Economic Institutions of Capitalism, Firms, Markets and Relational Contracting*, New York: The Free Press.
Willis, R.C. (2004), 'America's biotech heartland', *Modern Drug Discovery*, June, 41–6.
Wilson, J.F. and A. Popp (eds) (2003), *Industrial Clusters and Regional Business Networks in England, 1750–1970*, Aldershot: Ashgate.
Wilson, J.F., P. Bracken and E. Kostova (2005), 'Creative cluster formation: longitudinal and contemporary perspectives on the East Midlands', final report, Nottingham: HEROBC Innovation and Regional Fellowships, Nottingham University Business School.
Winston, G.C. (1982), *The Timing of Economic Activities: Firms, Households, and Markets in Time-specific Analysis*, Cambridge: Cambridge University Press.
Wise, M.J. (1949), 'On the evolution of the jewellery and gun quarters in Birmingham', *Transaction and Papers of The Institute of British Geographers*, no. 15, 57–72.
Woldrop, M.M. (1992), *Complexity. The Emerging Science and the Edge of Order and Chaos*, New York: Simon & Schuster.
Wolek, F.W. (1999), 'The managerial principles behind guild craftsmanship', *Journal of Management History*, **5** (7), 401–13.
Wolf, M. (2004), *Why Globalization Works*, New Haven, CT: Yale University Press.
Wolfe, D. and M. Gertler (2006), 'Local antecedents and trigger events: policy implications for path dependence for cluster formation', in Braunerhjelm and Feldman (2006).
Wolfe, D., J.A. Holbrook and M. Lucas (eds) (2005), *Global Networks and Local Linkages: The Paradox of Cluster Development in an Open Economy*, Montreal: McGill-Queens University Press.

Womack, J.P., D.T Jones and D. Roos (1990), *The Machine that Changed the World: The Story of Lean Production*, New York: Macmillan.

World Bank (2008), 'China's rapid urbanization: benefits, challenges and strategies', Washington, DC.

World Commission on the Social Dimension of Globalization (2004), *A Fair Globalization: Creating Opportunities for all*, Geneva: ILO.

Yamazaki, M. (1977), *Nihon no Jiba-Sango* ('Local industry of Japan'), Tokyo: Diyamondosha.

Ybarra, J.A. (1991a), 'Determinación cuantitativa de distritos industriales: la experiencia del País Valenciano', *Estudios Territoriales*, 37, 53–67.

Ybarra, J.A. (1991b), 'Industrial districts and the Valencian community', *Discussion Papers*, no. 44, *New Industrial Organisation Programme*, Geneva: ILO.

Ybarra, J.A. (2006), 'Los distritos industriales en el desarrollo local valenciano', *Quaderns d'Innovació*, 1, 6–18.

Yeats, A.J. (1998) 'Just how big is global production sharing?', *Policy Research Working Paper*, no. 1871, January, Washington, DC: The World Bank, Development Research Group.

Young, A.A. (1913), 'Pigou's *Wealth and Welfare*', *Quarterly Journal of Economics*, 27, 672–86.

Young, A.A. (1928), 'Increasing returns and economic progress', *Economic Journal*, **38** (152), 527–42.

Young, H.P. (1998), *Individual Strategy and Social Structure: An Evolutionary Theory*, Princeton, NJ: Princeton University Press.

Zamagni, V. (1990), *Dalla periferia al centro. La seconda rinascita economica dell'Italia, 1861–1990*, Bologna: Il Mulino.

Zamagni, V. (1997), 'Una vocazione industriale diffusa', in R. Finzi (ed.), *Storia d'Italia. Le regioni dall'Unità a oggi. L'Emilia-Romagna*, Torino: Einaudi, pp. 125–61.

Zaninelli, S. (ed.) (1987–2004), *Da un sistema agricolo a un sistema industriale: il comasco dal Settecento al Novecento*, 4 vols, Como: CCIAA.

Zazzaro, A. (1997), 'Regional banking systems, credit allocation and regional economic development', *Economie appliquée*, 50, 51–74.

Zeitlin, J. (1985), 'Distretti industriali e struttura industriale in prospettiva storica', in R. Innocenti (ed.), *Piccola città & piccola impresa*, Milano: Franco Angeli.

Zeitlin, J. (1989), 'Introduction', in special issue on *Local Industrial Strategies*, *Economy and Society*, **18** (4), 367–73.

Zeitlin, J. (1992), 'Industrial districts and local economic regeneration: overview and comment', in Pyke and Sengenberger (1992), pp. 279–94.

Zeitlin, J. (1995) 'Why are there no industrial districts in the United Kingdom?', in A. Bagnasco and Ch.F. Sabel (eds), *Small and Medium-size Enterprises*, London: Pinter, pp. 123–35.

Zeitlin, J. (2007a), 'The historical alternatives approach', in G. Jones and J. Zeitlin (eds), *The Oxford Handbook of Business History*, Oxford: Oxford University Press, pp. 120–40.

Zeitlin, J. (2007b), 'Industrial districts and regional clusters?, in G. Jones and J. Zeitlin (eds), *The Oxford Handbook of Business History*, Oxford: Oxford University Press.

Zemon Davis, N. (1982), 'Women in the crafts in sixteenth-century Lyon', *Feminist Studies*, **8** (1), 45–80.

Zimmermann, E.W. (1951), *World Resources and Industries*, New York: Harper & Bros.

Zucker, L.G., M.R. Darby and J. Armstrong (1998), 'Geographically localized knowledge: spillovers or markets?', *Economic Inquiry*, **36** (1), 65–97.

Zucker, L.G., M.R. Darby and M.B. Brewer (1998), 'Intellectual human capital and the birth of US biotechnology enterprises', *The American Economic Review*, **88** (1), 290–306.

Index

All India Council for Technical Education (AICTE) 765
Association of University Technology Managers (AUTM) 556

Bolt Beranek and Newman (BB&N) 653
Brinton's Mills Kidderminster (BMK) 300, 301
Business Development Service (BDS) 761, 763, 765
Business Promotion Plan (BPP) 733

capabilities
  endogenous 596
  entrepreneurial 67, 214, 287, 395, 449, 463, 489, 529, 653, 710, 764
  formation of 587, 597, 599
  innovation 415, 458, 464–5, 489, 573, 581, 601, 608, 610, 612, 663
  latent 207
  localised 525
  technological 54, 469, 489, 577, 650, 652, 654, 661
capability maturity model 234–5
capital
  financial 247, 532
  human 5–9, 11, 30, 39, 42, 59, 61–2, 172, 174, 198, 203, 282, 285, 291–2, 389, 431, 479, 481, 510, 700, 712, 729, 758–9
  social 41, 60, 126, 189, 191, 193, 198, 203, 220–8, 292, 302, 304–5, 348, 389–90, 463, 476, 518, 578, 581, 633, 713, 739, 768
  technical 435
capitalism model 312
Centre for Industrial Technological Development (CITD) 727, 732, 735
Centres of Industrial Collaboration (CIC) 747
Chambre de Commerce et de l'Industrie (CCI) 507

cities
  urban system 52, 333
cluster
  cross-c. 583, 722–4
  governance 762
  of IDs 50
  and IDs 172–83 *see also* industrial district
Cluster Development Agent (CDA) 762
collective action 60, 72, 146, 210, 212, 214, 244–5, 251, 310, 486, 495, 497–500, 575, 596, 650, 708–11, 719, 761–2
collective invention 60
community
  epistemic 8, 42
  local 9, 15, 25, 60, 104–6, 222, 257, 319, 326–9, 332–4, 348, 376, 381, 475, 484, 487, 498, 692, 760
  of action 255, 257–8, 265
  of practice 86, 153, 234, 254, 258, 271–3, 551–3, 753
competition
  and cooperation 61, 102, 105, 114, 207–10, 212, 244, 255, 259, 264–5, 485, 613, 702
  international 180, 472, 494, 509, 579, 603, 623, 668, 670, 675, 757
competitive advantage 42, 54, 57, 60, 64, 98, 117, 182, 200, 203, 208–9, 214, 342, 362, 387–8, 392, 509, 525, 580, 633, 648, 660, 668–9, 679, 692, 713, 761
Confederation général du travail (CGT) 249
Consorcios Estratégicos Nacionales de Investigación Tecnológica (CENIT) 731
cooperation
  conscious 206
  horizontal 119, 593, 637
  inter-firm 372, 566, 568, 572, 575, 736, 756
  reciprocal 484–5
  semi-automatic 206–7

857

creativity and culture 281–94, 307–19
credit
　access to 30, 473, 498
　local c. market 383, 390–92
cross-fertilisation 256, 282, 286–8, 291–3, 382
cultural districtualisation model 434
customisation (of product) 63–4, 468, 669

decentralisation
　international 494, 496–7
　of decision making 473
　organisational 479
　productive 27, 112, 304, 411, 495, 569, 694–6, 702
Délégation à l'Aménagement du Territoire et à l'Action Régionale (DATAR) 492, 501
Délégation Interministerielle à l'Aménagement et à la Compétitivité des Territories (DIACT) 492, 508
Department of Trade and Industry (DTI) 365, 744
developing countries 175, 177, 231, 259, 283, 296, 462, 493, 498, 536, 565–640, 705, 708, 711, 754–5, 761–2, 766
differentiation
　and integration 70, 94, 270
　product 39, 41, 151, 415, 455, 464–5, 470, 673, 706
disintegration 70, 193, 362, 411, 438, 606, 699
　industrial 606
　vertical 70, 411, 699
district processes 205, 283, 484
districtualisation
　cultural d. model 282–4, 286, 290
　process of 283, 377
division of labour 70, 74–6, 79, 84, 87, 90, 93, 101, 118, 124, 141, 148–50, 154–5, 180, 205–9, 211, 213, 270, 274, 290, 297, 327, 329, 340, 438, 452, 454, 468, 470, 485, 489, 492–3, 540–41, 544, 546, 568, 572, 575, 593, 595, 597, 607, 609, 620, 622–3, 636, 639, 663, 705, 710, 712, 714, 718, 720, 756, 762

ecological methods 283
ecologies
　economic 741
　micro- 552

economies
　agglomeration 145, 182, 286, 290, 292, 327, 361–80, 384, 386, 470, 493–4, 589, 592, 608
　creative 290, 292
　external 48, 55, 69, 70, 84–6, 88, 90–102, 124–7, 168, 181, 207, 209–12, 214, 290, 324, 327, 361–2, 411, 432–3, 435, 444, 489, 496–8, 552, 558, 563, 566, 575, 584, 586, 591, 593–4, 599, 705, 710, 712–25, 726–7, 732–3, 755
　internal 85, 88, 90–91, 93, 95–6, 100, 102
　internal–external 95–7, 101
　of specialisation 207, 720
education
　and training 245, 709, 742, 748
　technical schools 32–44, 416, 431, 633
embeddedness 56, 100–101, 120, 147, 182, 254, 257–8, 269–79, 289, 303, 305, 379, 529–30, 566, 580, 586, 591, 595–6, 598, 714, 719
entrepreneurship
　agricultural 438
　collective 498, 524
　ethnic 225
　indigenous 236
　promotion of 552, 706
European Regional Development Fund Regulation (ERDF) 742
evolution
　Darwinian 90, 649–50
　economic 89, 295, 663
　social 75, 130
　Spencerian 70, 74–6, 90
external diseconomies 99, 209
externalities 96, 143–5, 155, 172–5, 181, 274–5, 468, 481, 502, 507, 652, 684, 705, 715, 718–9
　local 145
　Marshall–Arrow–Romer (MAR) 144–6
　technological 145

fairs 20, 36, 222, 267, 534, 670, 674–5, 677, 762
family
　relations 220
　structure 117, 118
female employment 28, 39, 42, 118

firm
  boundaries of 254, 361
  district/district-based 112, 114, 305, 334–5, 341, 383, 387–8, 390–92, 399, 413–15, 448, 451, 454–5, 464–5, 468, 470, 472, 475, 477–8, 493, 633, 682–8, 691, 718, 722
  external organisation 85
  family 188, 239, 266, 414, 442, 449, 454, 605, 742
  growth of 4
  high-tech 229, 484, 527, 558, 634, 649–63, 650–3, 658–60, 749–50
  joint-stock 87, 89, 91
  large 3, 25, 28, 30, 58–9, 62, 64–5, 80, 87–9, 112–14, 124–5, 151, 168, 181, 214, 243, 246–7, 254–5, 261, 266, 278, 298–99, 327, 329, 332, 341–5, 348–51, 366–9, 385, 396, 406, 418, 436, 440, 444, 446–8, 474, 489, 491–2, 494–5, 501–3, 506–8, 511, 519, 534, 536–8, 542–3, 547, 568–9, 571–2, 587–9, 591–2, 594, 596, 609, 617, 620–21, 624, 680, 694, 701, 709, 713–14, 726, 729–32, 734, 742
  multinational/transnational 64, 66, 68, 108, 139, 180, 213, 232, 238, 254, 287, 315, 398, 400–1, 449, 454–5, 459, 462, 468–70, 496, 568, 582, 599, 606, 638–9, 682, 687, 723, 729
  multi-plant 403, 406
  population of 83, 89, 105, 172, 347, 429, 757
  project 110
  representative 101, 545
  service 276, 653
  small and medium-sized 6, 62, 174, 181–2, 204–5, 207, 211, 213, 223, 239, 243, 275, 331, 346, 368, 384, 399, 411, 417, 443, 459, 471, 483, 489, 501, 514, 535, 537, 539, 558, 567, 588, 598, 631, 670, 684, 701, 726, 749
  specialised 32, 66, 167, 207, 273, 279, 286, 329, 399, 411, 515, 570, 601, 723
  teams of 520, 660, 715, 721
  venture-capital 240, 480, 557
  vertically-integrated 235, 274, 277
flexible specialisation 10, 127, 537, 573, 586, 666

Fordism 213, 303, 316, 342, 504, 567
foreign direct investment 177, 399, 400–2, 409, 411, 458, 468, 568, 600–1, 608, 636, 651–2, 683–91

goods
  club 709, 716
  collective 118, 127, 228, 715, 718, 742
  household 64, 125, 213, 334–6, 340–2, 349, 351, 355, 357, 416, 418, 425, 452
  personal 64, 334–6, 341–2, 419, 424
  public 114, 131, 208, 212, 221, 429, 431, 434, 486, 497, 550, 581, 709, 712–17, 721–4, 752, 762, 767
    local public 208, 212, 434, 715
    quasi-public 709, 716
    specific public 486, 709, 712–13
governance
  building 708, 710, 761, 768
  district 218–21
  local 189, 226–7, 431, 504, 506–7, 572, 591, 715, 719
  of international value chains 722
  process 190–91, 228, 492
Government Polytechnic for Women (GPW) 765
Groupe de Recherche Européen sur les Milieux Innovateurs (GREMI) 282, 288–9, 297, 303
guilds 4–8, 11–13, 16–17, 21, 32–42, 51, 53, 59, 60, 75, 431

Hsinchu Science-based Industrial Park (HSIP) 238–41

impannatori 26, 279, 304
Indian Standards Institute (ISI) 616–17, 619
industrial atmosphere 18
industrial districts
  and clusters 739–53 *see also* cluster
  industrial estates/parks 178, 566
  internationalisation of 323, 394, 407–8
  life cycle of 17, 44, 54, 274–77
  performance of 182, 326
  statistically defined IDs/district provinces 327–42, 446
  varieties and heterogeity of 8–9, 41, 83, 138–40, 155, 291, 415, 457, 469, 573, 644

Industrial Performance Center (IPC) 260, 265
Industrial Technology Research Institute (ITRI) 238
industry
  infant 141
  light 434, 448, 450, 452, 513, 577
  localised 86–7, 205, 325, 360–66, 372–3, 376–7, 379, 483, 617, 626, 652
innovation
  regional i. system 253, 257, 295–306, 362, 532, 740, 752
  technological 38, 141, 174, 239, 415, 485, 543, 568, 601, 610, 638, 650, 735
  research & development 143, 154, 176, 212, 214, 254, 298, 372–3, 387–8, 395, 413, 418, 426–7, 465, 469, 509–10, 522, 542, 549, 554–6, 577, 581, 588, 600–1, 608–9, 634, 636, 638, 649, 651–2, 661–2, 673, 676, 706, 709, 727, 730–32, 734–8, 740–43, 747–9, 751
Institute of Economic and Social Research (ITRES) 325
integration
  flexible 207, 209, 485
  horizontal 506–7
  vertical 5, 62, 94, 113, 165, 168–70, 190, 211, 278, 301, 363, 373, 449, 505, 663
Inter-American Development Bank (IADB) 579, 594
interdependencies
  traded 551
  untraded 526
International Institute for Labour Studies (IILS) 324, 331, 573
International Labour Organisation (ILO) 331, 573, 576
Istituto nazionale di Statistica (ISTAT) 324–5, 334, 336, 339, 343, 346–7, 353, 366, 383–5, 387, 402–4, 406, 419, 425–6, 435, 443–4, 446–7, 449, 452, 744
Istituto per la Promozione Industriale (IPI) 330
Istituto Regionale di Programmazione Economica della Toscana (IRPET) 103, 325, 329

knowledge
  codified 127, 255, 431–2, 436, 485, 533, 560, 692, 707, 741
  contextual 284, 440, 479, 485, 553, 599
  diffusion of 40–41, 72, 83, 117, 232, 254, 269, 271, 279–80, 494, 497, 596
  growth of 90–91, 724
  informal 5–6, 8–9, 30
  k. economy 253, 281, 284, 293, 362, 380, 525, 675, 679, 752
  production k. or know-how 11, 16, 53, 105, 109, 153, 192, 197, 203, 205, 209, 231, 239, 255–7, 305, 308–11, 314, 317–18, 389, 432, 454, 468, 485, 512, 514–16, 545, 687, 712, 743, 747–8
  tacit 127, 139–40, 154, 234, 272, 292, 389, 430, 551, 559–60, 591, 598, 613, 744–5

labour
  market 4, 7, 25, 42, 61–3, 82–9, 90–91, 99–102, 104, 125, 156, 173, 182, 190–92, 229, 243–52, 266, 323–4, 328, 335, 346–7, 366–80, 382–93, 401, 419, 437, 489, 515, 568–9, 577, 582–4, 599, 608, 677, 695, 700
  mobility 5, 22, 83, 105, 118, 120, 223, 243, 245, 247, 271, 315, 332, 383, 389, 489, 506, 518, 718, 741, 760
  productivity 432, 565, 635
  skilled/unskilled 32, 35, 42, 46, 62, 74, 77, 92, 245, 547, 570–71, 577, 583, 699, 756
  supply of/demand for 28, 39, 243, 489, 491, 495–6, 677–8
laissez-faire 53, 601
learning
  by-doing 144, 310, 433
  diffused 209, 464, 720
  light industrialisation (model of) 125
  local development 15, 106, 109, 111–12, 116, 120, 127, 191–2, 205, 214, 220, 227, 253, 255, 257, 285, 289, 292, 307, 331, 340, 344, 380, 415–16, 471, 475, 477–8, 480–81, 483–7, 501, 508, 516, 535–6, 573, 587, 591, 598, 601, 603, 639, 705–6, 708, 710–11, 714–15, 718, 728, 741, 756, 762, 766, 769
  paths of 253, 714
  policy for 116, 340

local labour market 104, 323, 328, 346–7, 384, 401, 419, 489, 599, 608
local government 31, 188, 226–7, 244, 246–7, 251, 300, 305, 390, 436, 440, 507, 546, 601, 762, 765
local production system 13–17, 24–31, 59–68, 102, 112–20, 302–6, 366–80, 450–6, 472–82, 492–500, 501–11, 512–20, 568–9, 577–84, 585–601, 605–12, 637–40, 644–7, 705–11, 713–25
localisation economies 382, 384, 386, 388, 392

made in Italy 213, 412–13, 417–21, 423, 425, 427, 434, 440, 468–9, 647, 668, 676, 682, 686, 688–90, 692–3
Madhya Pradesh Voluntary Health Association (MPVHA) 760
market
  community m. 197–8
  failures 96, 304, 498, 743
  imperfections 98
  niche 140, 214, 273, 275, 425, 443, 455, 462, 464, 605, 637, 684
  particular 180, 273, 275, 552
Marshallian industrial district 62, 127, 129–40, 193, 195–6, 256–8, 290, 295, 301, 303, 305–6, 343–4, 346, 350, 357, 458, 566, 568, 585–97, 602, 712, 726–31, 733, 737
milieu innovateur 289
monopoly 41, 144–6, 156, 202, 262
multi-factor productivity 635, 730

National Association of Securities Dealers Automated Quotation System (NASDAQ) 229, 241
national
  contexts/levels/markets 45, 52–3, 141, 155, 316, 533, 575, 669
  policies 486, 573, 706, 737
National Institutes of Health (NIH) 660, 662
National Programme of Reforms (NPR) 733
network
  business 66, 296, 529, 742–3
  global 155, 281, 289, 399, 409, 599
  knowledge 42, 126, 231, 697
  local 16, 62, 188, 231, 281, 396, 527, 617, 627, 687, 706–8

of firms/entrepreneurs/producers 61, 211, 235, 248, 346, 530, 615, 627, 697, 706
  social/of social relations 124, 131, 153, 189, 196, 246, 307, 659
  translocal 487, 722–3
new economic geography 97–100, 123, 172, 362, 382, 414
North American Free Trade Agreement (NAFTA) 592

Office for National Statistics (ONS) 367
Office of Corporate Relations (OCR) 557, 563
opportunism 82, 189, 206, 390, 566, 757, 761
organisation
  and knowledge 650
  as a distinct agent of production 79
  business 91, 301, 656, 662
  industrial/manufacturing 9, 41, 43, 70, 73–7, 87, 89, 90, 93–5, 97, 101–2, 111, 129, 131, 139, 197, 213, 333, 344–5, 361, 488–9, 509, 513, 515, 567, 572, 640, 645, 649, 652
  social 10, 105, 123, 218, 220, 226, 505, 567
Organisation for Economic Cooperation and Development (OECD) 287, 424–5, 573, 729
Overseas Development Aid (ODA) 634

pole
  competitiveness 486, 503, 728
  development 499
  industrial 439, 707
post-Fordism 127, 362, 537
productivity
  and innovation 108, 174
  cluster 177, 763
  collective 713
  increased 508
  individual 511
  labour 432, 565, 635
protectionism 413, 513
proto-industrialisation 14, 44, 50, 52, 463
proximity
  cognitive 86, 258, 286, 288, 292–3, 712, 714
  geographical 92, 156, 269, 271, 284, 293, 521

lateral 256, 291
local 581, 645
moral 189
physical 258, 509, 580, 647, 682
socio-cultural 756

quality of life 78, 89, 388, 435

reciprocity 131, 142, 188, 201, 235, 304, 312, 314, 531, 744, 758
region
  industrial 14, 44, 47–8, 340
  learning 362, 524–6, 529, 740–41
regional
  agencies 301
  government/State 298, 304, 328–30, 340, 345–6, 502, 516–17, 744
regulation
  market 219, 244, 250, 385, 507, 600
  political 436
return
  increasing 70, 85, 90, 95–6, 143–6, 152, 274, 302, 362, 730–31, 737, 743
  on capital 449
rivalry 173, 176, 179, 684, 715–16
routine 81, 89, 235, 266, 280, 650, 714, 747, 751
rural area 13–14, 17, 105, 416, 600, 631–2, 638, 695

saving 117, 440
Self-employed Women's Association (SEWA) 634
Self-employed Women's Union (SEWU) 634
self-organisation 189, 193–5, 296
  adaptive 296
self-reliance 53, 80
serendipity 256, 282, 286, 288, 291–3
services
  business 273, 327, 336, 342, 349, 367, 396, 660
  consumer 336–7, 349, 367
  specialised 127, 613, 617, 750–51
sharecropping 3, 13–14, 23, 105, 416
skills and competencies 706–11
social mobility 105, 118, 332, 518
spillover
  creative 256, 292
  education 389

information 100, 124, 390
knowledge 155, 173, 245, 249, 255, 273, 286, 291–2, 382, 386, 389–90, 411, 743
s. effect 434, 436, 499
technological 151, 154
standardisation (of products) 5, 63–4, 236, 317, 473, 494, 616, 619, 627, 689
State intervention 115, 364, 499, 507, 581
subcontracting relations 117, 222, 687–8, 690
  exclusive 206
  horizontal 690
  vertical 690
survival of the fittest 209
sustainable development 574
system of values 258, 347, 436, 633

talent 232, 286, 293, 741, 745, 747–8, 751
Taylorism 567
Technology Strategy Board (TSB) 675
technopole 509
territorial
  classification/data 401–4
  factors/resources 28–30, 508
  identity/specificity/vocation 126, 139, 192, 315
  levels/scales 112, 696, 714, 724
  policies/pacts 112, 118, 228
  units of analysis 323, 346–7
Third Italy 47, 50, 69, 72, 103, 125, 255, 295, 299, 339, 416, 463, 491, 537, 566, 569, 570–73, 579, 582, 598, 638, 755
trust
  and governance 761–2, 767–8
  -based relations 757, 761, 763
  mutual 198, 227–8, 566, 596, 742

UN Conference on Trade and Development (UNCTAD) 631
United Nations Industrial Development Organisation (UNIDO) 578
United Nations Industrial Development Organization (UNIDO) 754–69
United Nations International Children's Emergency Fund (UNICEF) 760
universities 173–4, 177–9, 181, 192, 226, 238, 244–5, 284, 290, 299, 345,

458, 468, 481, 487, 506, 508–9, 547, 549–64, 605, 610, 612, 649, 658–9, 661–2, 675–6, 706–7, 727–8, 732, 735, 737, 740–41, 743, 749–50
  local 248, 468, 481
University Research Park (URP) 558
urbanised countryside 433–4, 485, 714

wages
  cluster 382
  conflicts 250
  ID 388
  relations 250

Walden International Investment Group (WIIG) 240
Weinert Applied Ventures in Entrepreneurship (WAVE) Program 558
Wisconsin Alumni Research Foundation (WARF) 554, 557–9, 563
Wisconsin Regional Training Partnership (WRTP) 699–700
working class 62, 87, 249, 265–6
World Trade Organisation (WTO) 424, 608, 639–40